Programming Microsoft® SQL Server® 2012

Leonard Lobel
Andrew Brust

Published with the authorization of Microsoft Corporation by:
O'Reilly Media, Inc.
1005 Gravenstein Highway North
Sebastopol, California 95472

ISBN: 978-0-7356-5822-6

1 2 3 4 5 6 7 8 9 M 7 6 5 4 3 2

Printed and bound in the United States of America.

Microsoft Press books are available through booksellers and distributors worldwide. If you need support related to this book, email Microsoft Press Book Support at mspinput@microsoft.com. Please tell us what you think of this book at http://www.microsoft.com/learning/booksurvey.

Acquisitions Editor: Russell Jones

Developmental Editor: Russell Jones

Production Editor: Melanie Yarbrough

Editorial Production: Christian Holdener, S4Carlisle Publishing Services

Technical Reviewer: John Paul Meuller

Copyeditor: Andrew Jones

Indexer: WordCo Indexing Services

Cover Design: Twist Creative • Seattle

Cover Composition: ContentWorks, Inc.

Illustrator: Rebecca Demarest

To my partner, Mark, and our children, Adam, Jacqueline, Joshua, and Sonny. With all my love, I thank you guys, for all of yours.

— Leonard Lobel

For my three boys: Miles, Sean, and Aidan. And for my sister, Valerie Hope.

— Andrew Brust

Contents at a Glance

Contents

Introduction

—Leonard Lobel

Welcome! This is a book about Microsoft SQL Server 2012 written just for you, the developer. Whether you are programming against SQL Server directly at the database level or further up the stack using Microsoft .NET, this book shows you the way.

The latest release of Microsoft's flagship database product delivers an unprecedented, highly scalable data platform capable of handling the most demanding tasks and workloads. As with every release, SQL Server 2012 adds many new features and enhancements for developers, administrators, and (increasingly) end users alike. Collectively, these product enhancements reinforce—and advance—SQL Server's position as a prominent contender in the industry. As the product continues to evolve, its stack of offerings continues to expand. And as the complete SQL Server stack is too large for any one book to cover effectively, our emphasis in *this* book is on *programmability*. Specifically, we explore the plethora of ways in which SQL Server (and its cloud cousin, Microsoft SQL Azure) can be programmed for building custom applications and services.

How Significant Is the SQL Server 2012 Release?

SQL Server, particularly its relational database engine, matured quite some time ago. So the "significance" of every new release over recent years can be viewed—in some ways—as relatively nominal. The last watershed release of the product was actually SQL Server 2005, which was when the relational engine (that, for years, *defined* SQL Server) stopped occupying "center stage," and instead took its position alongside a set of services that today, collectively, define the product. These include the Business Intelligence (BI) components Reporting Services, Analysis Services, and Integration Services—features that began appearing as early as 1999 but, prior to SQL Server 2005, were integrated sporadically as a patchwork of loosely coupled add-ons, wizards, and management consoles. SQL Server 2005 changed all that with a complete overhaul. For the first time, the overall SQL Server product delivered a broader, richer, and more consolidated set of features and services which are built into—rather than bolted onto—the platform. None of the product versions that have been released since that time—SQL Server 2008, 2008 R2, and now 2012—have changed underlying architecture this radically.

That said, each SQL Server release continues to advance itself in vitally significant ways. SQL Server 2008 (released August 6, 2008) added a host of new features to the relational engine—T-SQL enhancements, Change Data Capture (CDC), Transparent Data Encryption (TDE), SQL Audit, FILESTREAM—plus powerful BI capabilities with Excel PivotTables, charts, and *CUBE* formulas. SQL Server 2008 R2 (released April 21, 2010), internally dubbed the "BI Refresh" while in development, added a revamped version of Reporting Services as well as PowerPivot for Excel and SharePoint, Master Data Services, and StreamInsight, but offered little more than minor tweaks and fixes to the relational engine.

The newest release—SQL Server 2012—officially launched on March 7, 2012. Like every new release, this version improves on all of the key "abilities" (availability, scalability, manageability, programmability, and so on). Among the chief reliability improvements is the new High Availability Disaster Recovery (HADR) alternative to database mirroring. HADR (also commonly known as "Always On") utilizes multiple secondary servers in an "availability group" for scale-out read-only operations (rather than forcing them to sit idle, just waiting for a failover to occur). Multisubnet failover clustering is another notable new manageability feature.

SQL Server 2012 adds many new features to the relational engine, most of which are covered in this book. There are powerful T-SQL extensions, most notably the windowing enhancements, plus 22 new T-SQL functions, improved error handling, server-side paging, sequence generators, rich metadata discovery techniques, and contained databases. There are also remarkable improvements for unstructured data, such as the FileTable abstraction over FILESTREAM and the Windows file system API, full-text property searching, and Statistical Semantic Search. Spatial support gets a big boost as well, with support for circular data, full-globe support, increased performance, and greater parity between the *geometry* and *geography* data types. And new "columnstore" technology drastically increases performance of extremely large cubes (xVelocity for PowerPivot and Analysis Services) and data warehouses (using an xVelocity-like implementation in the relational engine).

The aforementioned relational engine features are impressive, but still amount to little more than "additives" over an already established database platform. A new release needs more than just extra icing on the cake for customers to perceive an upgrade as compelling. To that end, Microsoft has invested heavily in BI with SQL Server 2012, and the effort shows. The BI portion of the stack has been expanded greatly, delivering key advances in "pervasive insight." This includes major updates to the product's analytics, data visualization (such as self-service reporting with Power View), and master data management capabilities, as well Data Quality Services (DQS), a brand new data quality engine. There is also a new Business Intelligence edition of the product that includes all of these capabilities without requiring a full Enterprise edition license. Finally, SQL Server Data Tools (SSDT) brings brand new database tooling inside Visual Studio. SSDT provides a declarative, model-based design-time experience for developing databases while connected, offline, on-premise, or in the cloud.

Who Should Read This Book

This book is intended for developers who have a basic knowledge of relational database terms and principles.

Assumptions

In tailoring the content of this book, there are a few assumptions that we make about you. First, we expect that you are a developer who is already knowledgeable about relational database concepts—whether that experience is with SQL Server or non-Microsoft platforms. As such, you already know about tables, views, primary and foreign keys (relationships), stored procedures, user-defined functions, and triggers. These essentials are assumed knowledge and are not covered in this book. Similarly, we don't explain proper relational design, rules of data normalization, strategic indexing practices, how to express basic queries, and other relational fundamentals. We also assume that you have at least basic familiarity with SQL statement syntax—again, either T-SQL in SQL Server or SQL dialects in other platforms—and have a basic working knowledge of .NET programming in C# on the client.

Having said all that, we have a fairly liberal policy regarding these prerequisites. For example, if you've only dabbled with T-SQL or you're more comfortable with Microsoft Visual Basic .NET than C#, that's okay, as long as you're willing to try and pick up on things as you read along. Most of our code samples are not that complex. However, our explanations assume some basic knowledge on your part, and you might need to do a little research if you lack the experience.

Note For the sake of consistency, all the .NET code in this book is written in C#. However, this book is in no way C#-oriented, and there is certainly nothing C#-specific in the .NET code provided. As we just stated, the code samples are not very complex, and if you are more experienced with Visual Basic .NET than you are with C#, you should have no trouble translating the C# code to Visual Basic .NET on the fly as you read it.

With that baseline established, our approach has been to add value to the SQL Server documentation by providing a developer-oriented investigation of its features, especially the new and improved features in SQL Server 2012. We start with the brand new database tooling, and the many rich extensions made to T-SQL and the relational database engine. Then we move on to wider spaces, such as native file streaming, geospatial data, and other types of unstructured data. We also have chapters on security, transactions, client data access, security, mobile/cloud development, and more.

Within these chapters, you will find detailed coverage of the latest and most important SQL Server programming features. You will attain practical knowledge and technical understanding across the product's numerous programmability points, empowering you to develop the most sophisticated database solutions for your end users. Conversely, this is not intended as a resource for system administrators, database administrators, project managers, or end users. Our general rule of thumb is that we don't discuss features that are not particularly programmable.

Who Should Not Read This Book

This book is not intended for SQL Server administrators; it is aimed squarely at developers—and only developers who have mastery of basic database concepts.

Organization of This Book

The chapters of this book are organized in three sections:

- Core SQL Server features
- Beyond relational features
- Applied SQL for building applications and services

By no means does this book need to be read in any particular order. Read it from start to finish if you want, or jump right in to just those chapters that suit your needs or pique your interests. Either way, you'll find the practical guidance you need to get your job done.

The following overview provides a summary of these sections and their chapters. After the overview, you will find information about the book's companion website, from which you can download code samples and work hands-on with all the examples in the book.

Core SQL Server Development

In Part I, we focus on core SQL Server features. These include brand new tooling (SSDT), enhancements to T-SQL, extended programmability with SQL CLR code in .NET languages such as Microsoft Visual Basic .NET and C#, transactions, and security.

- Chapter 1 Introducing SQL Server Data Tools

  Our opening chapter is all about SQL Server Data Tools (SSDT). With the release of SQL Server 2012, SSDT now serves as your primary development environment for building SQL Server applications. While SQL Server Management Studio (SSMS) continues to serve as the primary tool for database administrators, SSDT represents a brand new developer experience. SSDT plugs in to Microsoft Visual Studio for connected development of on-premise databases or SQL Azure databases running in the cloud, as well as a new database project type for offline development and deployment. Using practical, real-world scenarios, you will also learn how to leverage SSDT features such as code navigation, IntelliSense, refactoring, schema compare, and more.

- Chapter 2 T-SQL Enhancements

  In Chapter 2, we explore the significant enhancements made to Transact-SQL (T-SQL)—which still remains the best programming tool for custom SQL Server development. We cover several powerful extensions to T-SQL added in SQL Server 2008, beginning with table-valued parameters (TVPs). You learn how to pass entire sets of rows around between stored procedures and functions on the server, as well as between client and server using Microsoft ADO.NET. Date and time features are explored next, including separate date and time data types, time zone awareness, and improvements in date and time range, storage, and precision. We then show many ways to use *MERGE*, a flexible data manipulation language (DML) statement that encapsulates all the individual operations typically involved in any merge scenario. From there, you learn about INSERT OVER DML for enhanced change data capture from the *OUTPUT* clause of any DML statement. We also examine *GROUPING SETS*, an extension to the traditional *GROUP BY* clause that increases your options for slicing and dicing data in aggregation queries.

  We then dive in to the new T-SQL enhancements introduced in SQL Server 2012, starting with *windowing* features. The first windowing functions to appear in T-SQL date back to SQL Server 2005, with the introduction of several ranking functions. Windowing capabilities have been quite limited ever since, but SQL Server 2012 finally delivers some major improvements to change all that. First you will grasp windowing concepts and the principles behind the *OVER* clause, and then leverage that knowledge to calculate running and sliding aggregates and perform other analytic calculations. You will learn about every one of the 22 new T-SQL functions, including 8 analytic windowing functions, 3 conversion functions, 7 date and time related functions, 2 logical functions, and 2 string functions. We also examine improved error handling with *THROW*, server-side paging with *OFFSET/FETCH NEXT*, sequence generators, and rich metadata discovery techniques. We explain all of these new functions and features, and provide clear code samples demonstrating their use.

- Chapter 3 Exploring SQL CLR

  Chapter 3 provides thorough coverage of SQL CLR programming—which lets you run compiled .NET code on SQL Server—as well as guidance on when and where you should put it to use. We go beyond mere stored procedures, triggers, and functions to explain and demonstrate the creation of CLR types and aggregates—entities that cannot be created *at all* in T-SQL. We also cover the different methods of creating SQL CLR objects in SQL Server Database Projects in Visual Studio and how to manage their deployment, both from SSDT/Visual Studio and from T-SQL scripts in SQL Server Management Studio and elsewhere.

- Chapter 4 Working with Transactions

  No matter how you write and package your code, you must keep your data consistent to ensure its integrity. The key to consistency is transactions, which we cover in Chapter 4. Transactions can be managed from a variety of places, like many SQL Server programmability features. If you are writing T-SQL code or client code using the ADO.NET *SqlClient* provider or *System.Transactions*, you need to be aware of the various transaction isolation levels supported by SQL Server, the appropriate scope of your transactions, and best practices for writing transactional code. This chapter gets you there.

- Chapter 5 SQL Server Security

  Chapter 5 discusses SQL Server security at length and examines your choices for keeping data safe and secure from prying eyes and malicious intent. We begin with the basic security concepts concerning logins, users, roles, authentication, and authorization. You then go on to learn about key-based encryption support, which protects your data both while in transit and at rest. We then examine other powerful security features, including Transparent Data Encryption (TDE) and SQL Server Audit. TDE allows you to encrypt entire databases in the background without special coding requirements. With SQL

Server Audit, virtually any action taken by any user can be recorded for auditing in either the file system or the Windows event log. We also show how to create *contained databases*, a new feature in SQL Server 2012 that eliminates host instance dependencies by storing login credentials directly in the database. The chapter concludes by providing crucial guidance for adhering to best practices and avoiding common security pitfalls.

Going Beyond Relational

With the release of SQL Server 2012, Microsoft broadens support for semi-structured and unstructured data in the relational database. In Part II, we show how to leverage the "beyond relational" capabilities in SQL Server 2012—features that are becoming increasingly critical in today's world of binary proliferation, and the emergence of high-performance so-called "No SQL" database platforms.

- Chapter 6 XML and the Relational Database

  SQL Server 2005 introduced the *xml* data type, and a lot of rich XML support to go along with it. That innovation was an immeasurable improvement over the use of plain *varchar* or *text* columns to hold strings of XML (which was common in earlier versions of SQL Server), and thus revolutionized the storage of XML in the relational database. It empowers the development of database applications that work with hierarchical data *natively*—within the environment of the relational database system—something not possible using ordinary string columns. In Chapter 6, we take a deep dive into the *xml* data type, XQuery extensions to T-SQL, server-side XML Schema Definition (XSD) collections, XML column indexing, and many more XML features.

- Chapter 7 Hierarchical Data and the Relational Database

  But XML is not your only option for working with hierarchical data in the database. In Chapter 7, we explore the *hierarchyid* data type that enables you to cast a hierarchical structure over any relational table. This data type is implemented as a "system CLR" type, which is nothing more really than a SQL CLR user-defined type (UDT), just like the ones we show how to create on your own in Chapter 3. The value stored in a *hierarchyid* data type encodes the complete path of any given node in the tree structure, from the root down to the specific ordinal position among other sibling nodes sharing the same parent. Using methods provided by this new type, you can now efficiently build, query, and manipulate tree-structured data in your relational tables. This data type also plays an important role in SQL Server's new FileTable feature, as we explain in the next chapter on native file streaming.

- Chapter 8 Native File Streaming

  In Chapter 8, you learn all about the FILESTREAM, an innovative feature that integrates the relational database engine with the NTFS file system to provide highly efficient storage and management of large binary objects (BLOBs)—images, videos, documents, you name it. Before FILESTREAM, you had to choose between storing BLOB data in the database using *varbinary(max)* (or the now-deprecated *image*) columns, or outside the database as unstructured binary streams (typically, as files in the file system). FILESTREAM provides a powerful abstraction layer that lets you treat BLOB data logically as an integral part of the database, while SQL Server stores the BLOB data physically separate from the database in the NTFS file system behind the scenes. You will learn everything you need to program against FILESTREAM, using both T-SQL and the high-performance *SqlFileStream* .NET class. The walkthroughs in this chapter build Windows, web, and Windows Presentation Foundation (WPF) applications that use FILESTREAM for BLOB data storage.

  You will also see how FileTable, a new feature in SQL Server 2012, builds on FILESTREAM. FileTable combines FILESTREAM with the *hierarchyid* (covered in Chapter 7) and the Windows file system API, taking database BLOB management to new levels. As implied by the two words joined together in its name, one FileTable functions as two distinct things simultaneously: a table and a file system—and you will learn how to exploit this new capability from both angles.

- Chapter 9 Geospatial Support

  Chapter 9 explores the world of geospatial concepts and the rich spatial support provided by the *geometry* and *geography* data types. With these system CLR types, it is very easy to integrate location-awareness into your applications—at the database level. Respectively, *geometry* and *geography* enable spatial development against the two basic geospatial surface models: planar (flat) and geodetic (round-earth). With spatial data (represented by geometric or geographic coordinates) stored in these data types, you can determine intersections and calculate length, area, and distance measurements against that data.

  The chapter first quickly covers the basics and then provides walkthroughs in which you build several geospatial database applications, including one that integrates mapping with Microsoft Bing Maps. We also examine the significant spatial enhancements added in SQL Server 2012. Although entire books have been written on this vast and ever-expanding topic, our chapter delves into sufficient depth so you can get busy working with geospatial data right away.

Applied SQL

After we've covered so much information about what you can do on the server and in the database, we move to Part III of the book, where we explore technologies and demonstrate techniques for building client/server, n-tier, and cloud solutions on top of your databases. Whatever your scenario, these chapters show you the most effective ways to extend your data's reach. We then conclude with coverage of SQL Azure, the BI stack, and the new columnstore technology known as xVelocity.

- Chapter 10 The Microsoft Data Access Juggernaut

  Chapter 10 covers every client/server data access strategy available in the .NET Framework today. We begin with earliest Microsoft ADO.NET techniques using raw data access objects and the *DataSet* abstraction, and discuss the ongoing relevance of these .NET 1.0 technologies. We then examine later data access technologies, including the concepts and syntax of language-integrated query (LINQ). We look at LINQ to DataSet and LINQ to SQL, and then turn our focus heavily on the ADO.NET Entity Framework (EF), Microsoft's current recommended data access solution for .NET. You will learn Object Relational Mapping (ORM) concepts, and discover how EF's Entity Data Model (EDM) provides a powerful abstraction layer to dramatically streamline the application development process.

- Chapter 11 WCF Data Access Technologies

  After you have mastered the client/server techniques taught in Chapter 10, you are ready to expose your data as services to the world. Chapter 11 provides you with detailed explanations and code samples to get the job done using two technologies based on Windows Communications Foundation (WCF).

  The first part of Chapter 11 covers WCF Data Services, which leverages Representational State Transfer Protocol (REST) and Open Data Protocol (OData) to implement services over your data source. After explaining these key concepts, you will see them put to practical use with concrete examples. As you monitor background network and database activity, we zone in and lock down on the critical internals that make it all work. The second part of the chapter demonstrates data access using WCF RIA Services, a later technology that targets Silverlight clients in particular (although it can support other clients as well). We articulate the similarities and differences between these two WCF-based technologies, and arm you with the knowledge of how and when to use each one.

- Chapter 12 Moving to the Cloud with SQL Azure

  In Chapter 12, we look at the world of cloud database computing with SQL Azure. We explain what SQL Azure is all about, how it is similar to SQL Server and how it differs. We look at how SQL Azure is priced, how to sign up for it, and how to provision SQL Azure servers and databases. We examine the SQL Azure tooling and how to work with SQL Azure from SSMS and SSDT. We explain the many ways that Data-Tier Applications (DACs) can be used to migrate databases between SQL Server and SQL Azure, using SSMS, SSDT, and the native tooling of SQL Azure as well. We finish up the chapter by examining a special partitioning feature called SQL Azure Federations and we look at SQL Azure Reporting, too.

- Chapter 13 SQL Azure Data Sync and Windows Phone Development

  Chapter 13 covers the broad topic of so-called occasionally connected systems by building out a complete solution that incorporates SQL Azure Data Sync, Windows Azure, and the Windows Phone 7 development platform. On the back end, an on-premise SQL Server database is kept synchronized with a public-facing SQL Azure database in the cloud using SQL Azure Data Sync. The cloud database is exposed using WCF Data Services (also hosted in the cloud by deploying to Windows Azure), and consumed via OData by a mobile client application running on a Windows Phone 7 device. The end-to-end solution detailed in this chapter demonstrates how these technologies work to keep data in sync across on-premise SQL Server, SQL Azure databases in the cloud, and local storage on Windows Phone 7 devices.

- Chapter 14 Pervasive Insight

  In Chapter 14, we provide an overview of the entire SQL Server BI stack, including SQL Server Fast Track Data Warehouse appliances, SQL Server Parallel Data Warehouse edition, SQL Server Integration Services, Analysis Services, Master Data Services, Data Quality Services, Reporting Services, Power View, PowerPivot, and StreamInsight. In the interest of completeness, we also provide brief overviews of Excel Services and PerformancePoint Services in SharePoint and how they complement SQL Server. We explain what each BI component does, and how they work together. Perhaps most important, we show you how these technologies from the BI arena are relevant to your work with relational data, and how, in that light, they can be quite approachable. These technologies shouldn't be thought of as segregated or tangential. They are integral parts of SQL Server, and we seek to make them part of what you do with the product.

- Chapter 15 xVelocity In-Memory Technologies

  In Chapter 15, we look at Microsoft's xVelocity column store technology, and how to use it from the SQL Server relational database, as well as PowerPivot and Analysis Services. We explain how column-oriented databases work, we examine the new columnstore indexes in SQL Server 2012, and discuss its batch processing mode, too. We look at how easy it is for relational database experts to work with PowerPivot and SSAS Tabular mode, and we show how to bring all these technologies together with the SQL Server Power View data analysis, discovery, and visualization tool.

Conventions and Features in This Book

This book presents information using conventions designed to make the information readable and easy to follow.

- Boxed elements with labels such as "Note" provide additional information or alternative methods for completing a step successfully.
- Text that you type (apart from code blocks) appears in bold.
- Code elements in text (apart from code blocks) appear in italic.
- A plus sign (+) between two key names means that you must press those keys at the same time. For example, "Press Alt+Tab" means that you hold down the Alt key while you press the Tab key.
- A vertical bar between two or more menu items (for example, File | Close), means that you should select the first menu or menu item, then the next, and so on.

System Requirements

To follow along with the book's text and run its code samples successfully, we recommend that you install the Developer edition of SQL Server 2012, which is available to a great number of developers through Microsoft's MSDN Premium subscription, on your PC. You will also need Visual Studio 2010; we recommend that you use the Professional edition or one of the Team edition releases, each of which is also available with the corresponding edition of the MSDN Premium subscription product. All the code samples will also work with the upcoming Visual Studio 11, in beta at the time of this writing.

Important To cover the widest range of features, this book is based on the Developer edition of SQL Server 2012. The Developer edition possesses the same feature set as the Enterprise edition of the product, although Developer edition licensing terms preclude production use. Both editions are high-end platforms that offer a superset of the features available in other editions (Standard, Workgroup, Web, and Express). We believe that it is in the best interest of developers for us to cover the full range of developer features in SQL Server 2012, including those available only in the Enterprise and Developer editions.

To run these editions of SQL Server and Visual Studio, and thus the samples in this book, you'll need the following 32-bit hardware and software. (The 64-bit hardware and software requirements are not listed here but are very similar.)

- 1 GHz or faster (2 GHz recommended) processor.
- Operating system, any of the following:
  - Microsoft Windows Server 2008 R2 SP1
  - Windows 7 SP1 (32- or 64-bit)
  - Windows Server 2008 SP2
  - Windows Vista SP2
- For SQL Server 2012, 4 GB or more RAM recommended for all editions (except the Express edition, which requires only 1 GB).
- For SQL Server 2012, approximately 1460 MB of available hard disk space for the recommended installation. Approximately 375 MB of additional available hard disk space for SQL Server Books Online, SQL Server Mobile Everywhere Books Online, and sample databases.
- For Visual Studio 2010, maximum of 20 GB available space required on installation drive. Note that this figure includes space for installing the full set of MSDN documentation.
- A working Internet connection (required to download the code samples from the companion website). A few of the code samples also require an Internet connection to run.

- Super VGA (1024 × 768) or higher resolution video adapter and monitor recommended.
- Microsoft Mouse or compatible pointing device recommended.
- Microsoft Internet Explorer 9.0 or later recommended.

Installing SQL Server Data Tools

SSDT does not get installed with either Visual Studio or SQL Server. Instead, SSDT ships separately via the Web Platform Installer (WebPI). This enables Microsoft to distribute timely SSDT updates out-of-band with (that is, without waiting for major releases of) Visual Studio or SQL Server. Before you follow along with the procedures in Chapter 1, download and install SSDT from *http://msdn.microsoft.com/en-us/data/hh297027.*

Using the Book's Companion Website

Visit the book's companion website at the following address:

http://go.microsoft.com/FWLink/?Linkld=252994

Code Samples

All the code samples discussed in this book can be downloaded from the book's companion website.

Within the companion materials parent folder on the site is a child folder for each chapter. Each child folder, in turn, contains the sample code for the chapter. Because most of the code is explained in the text, you might prefer to create it from scratch rather than open the finished version supplied in the companion sample code. However, the finished version will still prove useful if you make a small error along the way or if you want to run the code quickly before reading through the narrative that describes it.

Sample *AdventureWorks* Databases

As of SQL Server 2005, and updated through SQL Server 2012, Microsoft provides the popular AdventureWorks family of sample databases. Several chapters in this book reference the *AdventureWorks2012* online transaction processing (OLTP) database, and Chapter 15 references the *AdventureWorksDW2012* data warehousing database.

To follow along with the procedures in these chapters, you can download these databases directly from the book's companion website. The databases posted there are the exact versions that this book was written against, originally obtained from CodePlex, which is Microsoft's open source website (in fact, all of Microsoft's official product code samples are hosted on CodePlex). To ensure you receive the same results as you follow along with certain chapters in this book, we recommend downloading the *AdventureWorks2012* OLTP and *AdventureWorksDW2012* data warehousing databases from the book's companion website rather than from CodePlex (where updated versions may cause different results than the original versions).

You can find the directions to attach (use) the sample databases on the sample database download page.

Previous Edition Chapters

In addition to all the code samples, the book's companion website also contains several chapters from the 2008 and 2005 editions of this book that were not updated for this edition in order to accommodate coverage of new SQL Server 2012 features.

You can download SQL Server 2005 chapters that cover Service Broker, native XML Web Services, SQL Server Management Studio, SQL Server Express edition, Integration Services, and debugging, as well as SQL Server 2008 chapters on data warehousing, online analytical processing (OLAP), data mining, and Reporting Services.

Errata & Book Support

We've made every effort to ensure the accuracy of this book and its companion content. Any errors that have been reported since this book was published are listed on our Microsoft Press site at *oreilly.com*:

http://go.microsoft.com/FWLink/?LinkId=252995

If you find an error that is not already listed, you can report it to us through the same page.

If you need additional support, email Microsoft Press Book Support at *mspinput@microsoft.com*.

Please note that product support for Microsoft software is not offered through the addresses above.

We Want to Hear from You

At Microsoft Press, your satisfaction is our top priority, and your feedback our most valuable asset. Please tell us what you think of this book at:

http://www.microsoft.com/learning/booksurvey

The survey is short, and we read every one of your comments and ideas. Thanks in advance for your input!

Stay in Touch

Let's keep the conversation going! We're on Twitter: *http://twitter.com/MicrosoftPress*

Acknowledgements

It's hard to believe I first began research for this book at an early Software Design Review for SQL Server "Denali" in Redmond back in October 2010. This is my second edition as lead author of this book, and although I enjoyed the work even more this time around, it was certainly no easier than the 2008 edition. My goal—upfront—was to produce the most comprehensive (yet approachable) SQL Server 2012 developer resource that I could, one that best answers, "How many ways can I program SQL Server?" I could not have even contemplated pursuing that goal without the aid of numerous other talented and caring individuals—folks who deserve special recognition. Their generous support was lent out in many different yet equally essential ways. So the order of names mentioned below is by no means an indication of degree or proportion; simply put, I couldn't have written this book without everyone's help.

With so many people to thank, Craig Branning (CEO of Tallan, Inc.) is at the top of my most wanted list. Back in mid-2010, Craig was quick to approach me about taking on this project. Next thing I knew, I was on board and we were scarfing down lunch (smooth work!). Thank you (and all the other wonderful folks at Tallan) for getting this book off the ground in the first place, and providing a continuous source of support throughout its production.

I'm also extremely fortunate to have teamed up with my colleague and friend, co-author Andrew Brust (Microsoft MVP/RD). This is actually Andrew's third time around contributing his knowledge and expertise to this resource; he not only co-authored the 2008 edition, but was lead author of the first edition for SQL Server 2005. So I thank him once again for writing four stellar chapters in this new 2012 edition. And Paul Delcogliano (who also contributed to the 2008 edition) did a superb job confronting the topic of end-to-end cloud development with SQL Azure Data Sync, Windows Azure, and Windows Phone 7—all in a single outstanding chapter. Paul, your ambition is admirable, and I thank you for your tireless work and the great job done!

Ken Jones, my pal at O'Reilly Media, gets special mention for his expert guidance, plus his steady patience through all the administrative shenanigans. Thank you Ken, and to your lovely wife, Andrea, as well, for her insightful help with the geospatial content. I was also very lucky to have worked closely with Russell Jones,Melanie Yarbrough, John Mueller, and Christian Holdener, whose superb editorial contributions, technical review, and overall guidance were vital to the successful production of this book.

The assistance provided by a number of people from various Microsoft product teams helped tackle the challenge of writing about new software as it evolved through several beta releases. Thank you to Roger Doherty, for inviting me out to Redmond for the SDR in 2010, as well as for connecting me with the right people I needed to get my job done. Gert Drapers and Adam Mahood were particularly helpful for the inside scoop on SSDT as it changed from one CTP to the next. Adam's always direct and always available lines of communication turned an entire chapter's hard work into fun work. Doug Laudenschlager also provided valuable insight, which enhanced new coverage of unstructured FILESTREAM data. And naturally, a great big thank you to the entire product team for creating the best release of SQL Server ever!

I'm also particularly proud of all the brand new .NET data access coverage in this book, and would like to give special thanks to my pal Marcel de Vries, Microsoft MVP and RD in the Netherlands. Marcel is a master of distributed architectures, and his invaluable assistance greatly helped shape coverage in the WCF data access chapter. *Ik ben heel dankbaar voor jouw inbreng!*

This book could not have been written, of course, without the love and support of my family. I have been consumed by this project for much of the past eighteen months—which has at times transformed me into an absentee. I owe an enormous debt of gratitude to my wonderful partner Mark, and our awesome kids Adam, Jacqueline, Josh, and Sonny, for being so patient and tolerant with me. And greatest thanks of all go out to my dear Mom, bless her soul, for always encouraging me to write with "expression."

—Leonard Lobel

When you're not a full-time author, there's really never a "good" time to write a book. It's always an added extra, and it typically takes significantly more time than anticipated. That creates burdens for many people, including the author's family, the book's editors, and co-authors as well. When one of the authors is starting a new business, burdens double, all around. I'd like to thank my family, the Microsoft Press team and especially this book's lead author, Lenni Lobel, for enduring these burdens, with flexibility and uncommonly infinite patience.

—Andrew Brust

PART I

Core SQL Server Development

CHAPTER 1

Introducing SQL Server Data Tools

—*Leonard Lobel*

With the release of SQL Server 2012, Microsoft delivers a powerful, new integrated development environment (IDE) for designing, testing, and deploying SQL Server databases—locally, offline, or in the cloud—all from right inside Microsoft Visual Studio (both the 2010 version and the upcoming Visual Studio 11, currently in beta at the time of this writing). This IDE is called SQL Server Data Tools (SSDT), and it represents a major step forward from previously available tooling—notably, SQL Server Management Studio (SSMS) and Visual Studio Database Professional edition (DbPro).

SSDT is not intended to be a replacement for SSMS, but instead can be viewed much more as a greatly evolved implementation of DbPro. Indeed, SSMS is alive and well in SQL Server 2012, and it continues to serve as the primary management tool for *database administrators* who need to configure and maintain healthy SQL Server installations. And although DbPro was a good first step towards offline database development, its relatively limited design-time experience has precluded its widespread adoption. So for years, programmers have been primarily using SSMS to conduct development tasks (and before SQL Server 2005, they typically used *two* database administrator [DBA] tools—SQL Enterprise Manager and Query Analyzer). It's always been necessary for programmers to use management-oriented tools (such as SSMS) rather than developer-focused tools (such as Visual Studio) as a primary database development environment when building database applications—until now.

The release of SSDT provides a single environment hosted in Visual Studio, with database tooling that specifically targets the development process. Thus, you can now design and build your databases without constantly toggling between Visual Studio and other tools. In this chapter, you'll learn how to use SSDT inside Visual Studio to significantly enhance your productivity as a SQL Server developer. We begin with an overview of key SSDT concepts and features, and then walk you through demonstrations of various connected and disconnected scenarios.

Introducing SSDT

Database Tooling Designed for Developers

The inconvenient truth is: database development is hard. Getting everything done correctly is a huge challenge—proper schema and relational design, the intricacies of Transact-SQL (T-SQL) as a language, performance tuning, and more, are all difficult tasks in and of themselves. However, with respect to the development process—the way in which you create and change a database—there are some particular scenarios that the right tooling can improve greatly. SSDT delivers that tooling.

The SSDT Umbrella of Services and Tools

SSDT encompasses more than just the new database tooling covered in this chapter; it is actually a packaging of what was formerly the Visual Studio 2008–based Business Intelligence Developer Studio (BIDS) tool. SSDT supports the traditional BIDS project types for SQL Server Analysis Services (SSAS), Reporting Services (SSRS), and Integration Services (SSIS), in addition to the new database tooling. So with SSDT, Microsoft has now brought together all of the SQL Server database development experiences inside a single version of Visual Studio.

Despite its broader definition, this chapter uses the term SSDT specifically as it pertains to the new database development tools that SSDT adds to the Visual Studio IDE.

Here are some of the challenges that developers face when designing databases.

- **Dependencies** By its very nature, the database is full of dependencies between different kinds of schema objects. This complicates development, as even the simplest changes can very quickly become very complex when dependencies are involved.
- **Late Error Detection** You can spend a lot of time building complex scripts, only to find out that there are problems when you try to deploy them to the database. Or, your script may deploy without errors, but you have an issue somewhere that doesn't manifest itself until the user encounters a run-time error.
- **"Drift" Detection** The database is a constantly moving target. After deployment, it's fairly common for a DBA to come along and tweak or patch something in the production database; for example, adding indexes to improve query performance against particular tables. When the environments fall out of sync, the database is in a different state than you and your application expect it to be—and those differences need to be identified and reconciled.
- **Versioning** Developers have grown so accustomed to working with "change scripts" that it makes you wonder, where is the *definition* of the database? Of course you can rely on it being *in* the database, but where is it from the standpoint of preserving and protecting it? How do you maintain the definition across different versions of your application? It's very difficult to revert to a point in time and recall an earlier version of the database that matches up with an

earlier version of an application. So you can't easily synchronize versions and version history between your database and application.

- **Deployment** Then there are the challenges of targeting different versions, including most recently, SQL Azure. You may need to deploy the same database out to different locations, and must account for varying compatibility levels when different locations are running different versions of SQL Server (such as SQL Server 2005, 2008, 2008 R2, 2012, and SQL Azure).

Many of these pain points are rooted in the notion that the database is "stateful." Every time you build and run a .NET application in Visual Studio, it is always initialized to the same "new" state but as soon as the application goes off to access the database, it's the same "old" database with the same schema and data in it. Thus, you are forced to think not only about the design of the database, but also about how you implement that design—how you actually get that design moved into the database given the database's current state.

If the root of these problems lies in the database being stateful, then the heart of the solution lies in working declaratively rather than imperatively. So rather than just working with change scripts, SSDT lets you work with *a declaration of what you believe (or want) the database to be*. This allows you to focus on the design, while the tool takes care of writing the appropriate change scripts that will safely apply your design to an actual target database. SSDT takes a declarative, model-based approach to database design—and as you advance through this chapter, you'll see how this approach remedies the aforementioned pain points.

Declarative, Model-Based Development

We've started explaining that SSDT uses a declarative, model-based approach. What this means is that there is always an in-memory representation of what a database looks like—an SSDT database *model*—and all the SSDT tools (designers, validations, IntelliSense, schema compare, and so on) operate on that model. This model can be populated by a live connected database (on-premise or SQL Azure), an offline database project under source control, or a point-in-time *snapshot* taken of an offline database project (you will work with snapshots in the upcoming exercises). But to reiterate, the tools are agnostic to the model's backing; they work exclusively against the model itself. Thus, you enjoy a rich, consistent experience in any scenario—regardless of whether you're working with on-premise or cloud databases, offline projects, or versioned snapshots.

The T-SQL representation of any object in an SSDT model is always expressed in the form of a *CREATE* statement. An *ALTER* statement makes no sense in a declarative context—a *CREATE* statement declares what an object should look like, and that's the only thing that you (as a developer) need to be concerned with. Depending on the state of the target database, of course, a change script containing either a *CREATE* statement (if the object doesn't exist yet) or an appropriate *ALTER* statement (if it does) will be needed to properly deploy the object's definition. Furthermore, if dependencies are involved (which they very often are), other objects need to be dropped and re-created in the deployment process. Fortunately, you can now rely on SSDT to identify any changes (the "difference") between your model definition and the actual database in order to compose the necessary change script. This keeps you focused on just the definition. Figure 1-1 depicts the SSDT model-based approach to database development.

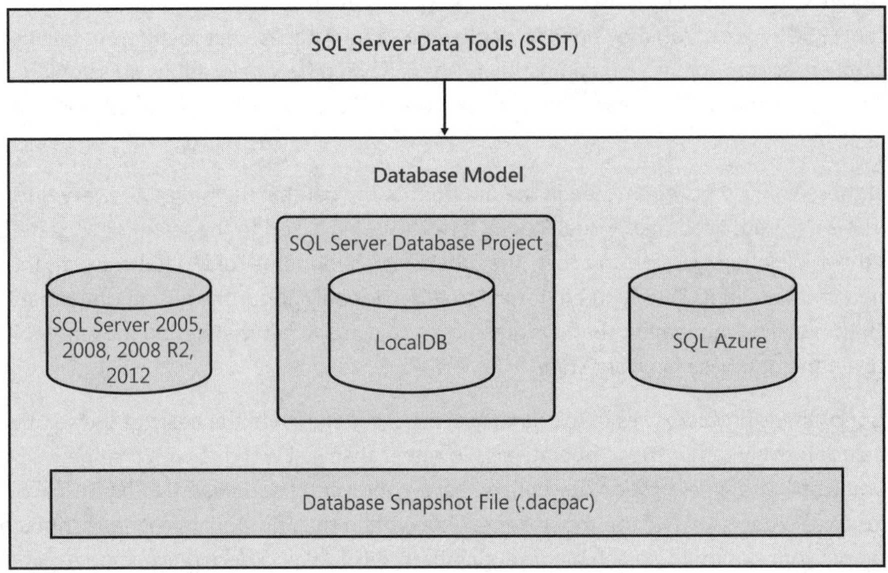

FIGURE 1-1 SSDT works with a model backed by connected databases (on-premise or in the cloud), offline database projects, or database snapshot files.

Connected Development

Although SSDT places great emphasis on the declarative model, it in no way prevents you from working imperatively against live databases when you want or need to. You can open query windows to compose and execute T-SQL statements directly against a connected database, with the assistance of a debugger if desired, just as you can in SSMS.

The connected SSDT experience is driven off the new SQL Server Object Explorer in Visual Studio. You can use this new dockable tool window to accomplish common database development tasks that formerly required SSMS. Using the new SQL Server Object Explorer is strikingly similar to working against a connected database in SSMS's Object Explorer—but remember that (and we'll risk overstating this) the SSDT tools operate only on a database *model*. So when working in connected mode, SSDT actually creates a model from the real database—on the fly—and then lets you edit that model. This "buffered" approach is a subtle, yet key, distinction from the way that SSMS operates.

When you save a schema change made with the new table designer, SSDT works out the necessary script needed to update the real database so it reflects the change(s) made to the model. Of course, the end result is the same as the connected SSMS experience, so it isn't strictly necessary to understand this buffered behavior that's occurring behind the scenes. But after you do grasp it, the tool's offline project development and snapshot versioning capabilities will immediately seem natural and intuitive to you. This is because offline projects and snapshots are simply different backings of the very same SSDT model. When you're working with the SQL Server Object Explorer, the model's backing just happens to be a live connected database.

There's an additional nuance to SSDT's buffered-while-connected approach to database development that bears mentioning. There are in fact *two* models involved in the process of applying schema changes to a database. Just before SSDT attempts to apply your schema changes, it actually creates a new model of the currently connected database. SSDT uses this model as the target for a model comparison with the model you've been editing. This dual-model approach provides the "drift detection" mechanism you need to ensure that the schema compare operation (upon which SSDT will be basing its change script) accounts for any schema changes that may have been made by another user since you began editing your version of the model. Validation checks will then catch any problems caused by the other user's changes (which would not have been present when you began making your changes).

Disconnected Development

The new SQL Server Object Explorer lets you connect to and interact with any database right from inside Visual Studio. But SSDT offers a great deal more than a mere replacement for the connected SSMS experience. It also delivers a rich offline experience with the new SQL Server Database Project type and local database runtime (LocalDB).

The T-SQL script files in a SQL Server Database Project are all declarative in nature (only *CREATE* statements; no *ALTER* statements). This is a radically different approach than you're accustomed to when "developing" databases in SSMS (where you execute far more *ALTER* statements than *CREATE* statements). Again, you get to focus on defining "this is how the database should look," and let the tool determine the appropriate T-SQL change script needed to actually update the live database to match your definition.

If you are familiar with the Database Professional (DbPro) edition of Visual Studio, you will instantly recognize the many similarities between DbPro's Database Projects and SSDT's SQL Server Database Projects. Despite major overlap however, SSDT project types are different than DbPro project types, and appear as a distinct project template in Visual Studio's Add New Project dialog. The new table designer, buffered connection mechanism, and other SSDT features covered in this chapter work only with SSDT SQL Server Database Projects. However, and as you may have guessed, it's easy to upgrade existing DbPro projects to SSDT projects. Just right-click the project in Solution Explorer and choose Convert To SQL Server Database Project. Note that this is a one-way upgrade, and that DbPro artifacts that are not yet supported by SSDT (such as data generation plans, see the following Note) will not convert.

Note There are several important features still available only in DbPro, most notably data generation, data compare, schema view, and database unit testing. Eventually, SSDT plans on providing key elements of the DbPro feature set and will completely replace the Database Professional edition of Visual Studio. For now though, you must continue to rely on DbPro for what's still missing in SSDT.

The new SQL Server Database Project type enjoys many of the same capabilities and features as other Visual Studio project types. This includes not only source control for each individual database object definition, but many of the common code navigation and refactoring paradigms that developers have grown to expect of a modern IDE (such as Rename, Goto Definition, and Find All References). The SSDT database model's rich metadata also provides for far better IntelliSense than what SSMS has been offering since SQL Server 2008, giving you much more of that "strongly-typed" confidence factor as you code. You can also set breakpoints, single step through T-SQL code, and work with the Locals window much like you can when debugging .NET project types. With SSDT, application and database development tooling has now finally been unified under one roof: Visual Studio.

A major advantage of the model-based approach is that models can be generated from many different sources. When connected directly via SQL Server Object Explorer, SSDT generates a model from the connected database, as we explained already. When you create a SQL Server Database Project (which can be imported from any existing database, script, or snapshot), you are creating an offline, source-controlled project inside Visual Studio that fully describes a real database. But it's actually a project—not a real database. Now, SSDT generates a model that's backed by your SQL Server Database Project. So the experience offline is just the same as when connected—the designers, IntelliSense, validation checks, and all the other tools work exactly the same way.

As you conduct your database development within the project, you get the same "background compilation" experience that you're used to experiencing with typical .NET development using C# or Visual Basic (VB) .NET. For example, making a change in the project that can't be submitted to the database because of dependency issues will result in design-time warnings and errors in the Error List pane. You can then click on the warnings and errors to navigate directly to the various dependencies so they can be dealt with. Once all the build errors disappear, you'll be able to submit the changes to update the database.

Versioning and Snapshots

A database project gives you an offline definition of a database. As with all Visual Studio projects, each database object (table, view, stored procedure, and every other distinct object) exists as a text file that can be placed under source code control. The project system combined with source control enables you to secure the definition of a database in Visual Studio, rather than relying on the definition being stored in the database itself.

At any point in time, and as often as you'd like, you can create a *database snapshot*. A snapshot is nothing more than a file (in the Data-tier Application Component Package, [dacpac] format) that holds the serialized state of a database model, based on the current project at the time the snapshot is taken. It is essentially a single-file representation of your entire database schema. Snapshots can later be deserialized and used with any SSDT tool (schema compare, for example). So you can develop, deploy, and synchronize database structures across local/cloud databases and differently versioned offline database projects, all with consistent tooling.

Pause for a moment to think about the powerful capabilities that snapshots provide. A snaphot encapsulates an entire database structure into a single *.dacpac* file that can be instantly deserialized back into a model at any time. Thus, they can serve as either the source or target of a schema compare operation against a live database (on-premise or SQL Azure), an offline SQL Server Database Project, or some other snapshot taken at any other point in time.

Snapshots can also be helpful when you don't have access to the target database, but are expected instead to hand a change script off to the DBA for execution. In addition to the change script, you can also send the DBA a snapshot of the database project taken just before any of your offline work was performed. That snapshot is your change script's assumption of what the live database looks like. So the DBA, in turn, can perform a schema compare between your snapshot and the live database (this can be done from SSDT's command-line tool without Visual Studio). The results of that schema compare will instantly let the DBA know if it's safe to run your change script. If the results reveal discrepancies between the live database and the database snapshot upon which your change script is based, the DBA can reject your change script and alert you to the problem.

Targeting Different Platforms

SQL Server Database Projects have a target platform switch that lets you specify the specific SQL Server version that you intend to deploy the project to. All the validation checks against the project-backed model are based on this setting, making it trivial for you to test and deploy your database to any particular version of of SQL Server (2005 and later), including SQL Azure. It's simply a matter of choosing SQL Azure as the target to ensure that your database can be deployed to the cloud without any problems. If your database project defines something that is not supported in SQL Azure (a table with no clustered index, for example), it will get flagged as an error automatically.

Working with SSDT

Our introduction to the SSDT toolset is complete, and it's now time to see it in action. The rest of this chapter presents a sample scenario that demonstrates, step-by-step, how to use many of the SSDT features that you've just learned about. Practicing along with this example will solidify your knowledge and understanding of the tool, and prepare you for using SSDT in the real world with real database projects.

Important SSDT does not get installed with either Visual Studio or SQL Server. Instead, SSDT ships separately via the Web Platform Installer (WebPI). This enables Microsoft to distribute timely SSDT updates out-of-band with (that is, without waiting for major releases of) Visual Studio or SQL Server. Before proceeding, download and install SSDT from *http://msdn.microsoft.com/en-us/data/hh297027.*

Connecting with SQL Server Object Explorer

The journey will start by creating a database. You will first use SSDT to execute a prepared script that creates the database in a query window connected to a SQL Server instance. Then you will start working with SSDT directly against the connected database. This experience is similar to using previous tools, so it's the perfect place to start. Later on, you'll switch to working disconnected using an offline database project.

Launch Visual Studio 2010, click the View menu, and choose SQL Server Object Explorer. This displays the new SQL Server Object Explorer in a Visual Studio panel (docked to the left, by default). This new tool window is the main activity hub for the connected development experience in SSDT. From the SQL Server Object Explorer, you can easily connect to any server instance for which you have credentials. In our scenario, the *localhost* instance running on the development machine is a full SQL Server 2012 Developer edition installation. This instance is assuming the role of a live production database server that you can imagine is running in an on-premise datacenter. You're now going to connect to that "production" database server.

Right-click the *SQL Server* node at the top of the SQL Server Object Explorer, choose Add SQL Server, and type in your machine name as the server to connect to. Although you can certainly, alternatively, type *localhost* instead (or even simply the single-dot shorthand syntax for *localhost*), we're directing you to use the machine name instead. This is because you'll soon learn about the new local database runtime (LocalDB) that SSDT provides for offline testing and debugging. The LocalDB instance *always* runs locally, whereas the production database on the other hand just *happens* to be running locally. Because it can be potentially confusing to see both *localhost* and *(localdb)* in the SQL Server Object Explorer, using the machine name instead of *localhost* makes it clear that one represents the production database while the other refers to the database used for local (offline) development and testing with SSDT. The screen snapshots for the figures in this chapter were taken on a Windows Server 2008 R2 machine named *SQL2012DEV*, so we'll be using that machine name throughout the chapter when referring to the production database running on *localhost*. Of course, you'll need to replace the assumed *SQL2012DEV* machine name with your own machine name wherever you see it mentioned.

If you have installed SQL Server to use mixed-mode authentication and you are not using Windows authentication, then you'll also need to choose SQL Server authentication and supply your credentials at this point, before you can connect. Once connected, SQL Server Object Explorer shows the production server and lets you drill down to show all the databases running on it, as shown in Figure 1-2.

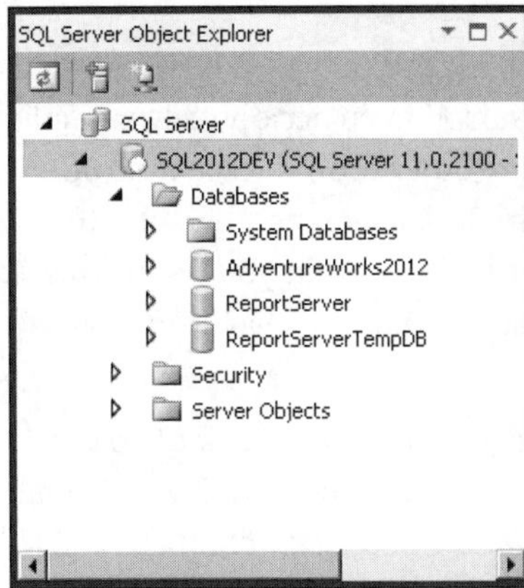

FIGURE 1-2 The new SQL Server Object Explorer in Visual Studio expanded to show several connected databases.

Once connected, right-click the server instance node *SQL2012DEV* and choose New Query. Visual Studio opens a new T-SQL code editor window, like the one shown in Figure 1-3.

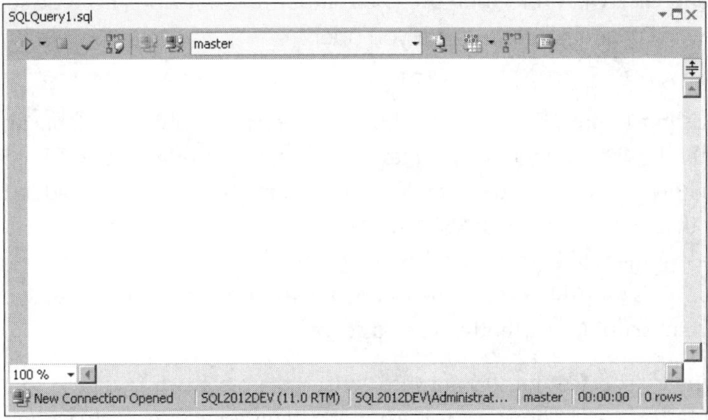

FIGURE 1-3 A connected query window.

This environment should seem very familiar to anyone experienced with SSMS or Query Analyzer. Notice the status bar at the bottom indicating that the query window is currently connected to the *SQL2012DEV* instance (again, it will actually read your machine name). The toolbar at the top includes a drop-down list indicating the current default database for the instance you're connected to. As with previous tools, this will be the *master* database (as shown at the top of Figure 1-3). You must still take care to change this setting (or issue an appropriate *USE* statement) so that you don't inadvertently access the *master* database when you really mean to access your application's database. In this exercise, you're creating a brand new database, so it's fine that the current database is set to *master* at this time.

Tip This concern stems from the fact that, by default, the *master* database is established as every login's default database. A great way to protect yourself from accidentally trampling over the *master* database when working with SSDT (or any other tool) is to change your login's default database to be your application's database, which will then become the default database (rather than *master*) for every new query window that you open. This will greatly reduce the risk of unintentional data corruption in *master*, which can have disasterous consequences.

When you navigate to your login from the Security node in SQL Server Object Explorer, you'll be able to see its default database set to *master* in the Properties window, but you won't be able to change it. This is a management task that is not supported in the SSDT tooling, although you can still use SSDT to execute the appropriate *ALTER LOGIN* statement in a query window. Alternatively, you can easily make the change in SSMS as follows. Start SSMS, connect to your server instance, and drill down to your login beneath the Security and Logins nodes in the SSMS Object Explorer. Then right-click the login and choose Properties. Click the default database drop-down list, change its value from *master* to your application's database, and click OK. From then on, your database (not *master*) will be set as the default for every new SSDT query window that you open.

Type the code shown in Listing 1-1 into the query window (or open the script file available in the downloadable code on this book's companion website; see the section "Code Samples" in the "Introduction" for details on how to download the sample code). You might next be inclined to press F5 to execute the script, but that won't work. With SSDT in Visual Studio, pressing F5 *builds and deploys* a SQL Server Database Project to a debug instance (you'll be creating such a project later on, but you don't have one yet). This is very different to the way F5 is used in SSMS or Query Analyzer to immediately execute the current script (or currently selected script).

SSDT uses a different keyboard shortcut for this purpose. In fact, there are two keyboard shortcuts (with corresponding toolbar buttons and right-click context menu items); one to execute without a debugger (Ctrl+Shift+E) and one to execute using an attached debugger (Alt+F5). You'll practice debugging later on, so for now just press **Ctrl+Shift+E** to immediately execute the script and create the database (you can also click the Execute Query button in the toolbar, or right-click anywhere within the code window and choose Execute from the context menu).

LISTING 1-1 T-SQL script for creating the *SampleDb* database

```
CREATE DATABASE SampleDb
GO

USE SampleDb
GO

-- Create the customer and order tables
CREATE TABLE Customer(
```

```
  CustomerId bigint NOT NULL PRIMARY KEY,
  FirstName varchar(50) NOT NULL,
  LastName varchar(50) NOT NULL,
  CustomerRanking varchar(50) NULL)

CREATE TABLE OrderHeader(
  OrderHeaderId bigint NOT NULL,
  CustomerId bigint NOT NULL,
  OrderTotal money NOT NULL)

-- Create the relationship
ALTER TABLE OrderHeader ADD CONSTRAINT FK_OrderHeader_Customer
 FOREIGN KEY(CustomerId) REFERENCES Customer(CustomerId)

-- Add a few customers
INSERT INTO Customer (CustomerId, FirstName, LastName, CustomerRanking) VALUES
 (1, 'Lukas', 'Keller', NULL),
 (2, 'Jeff', 'Hay', 'Good'),
 (3, 'Keith', 'Harris', 'so-so'),
 (4, 'Simon', 'Pearson', 'A+'),
 (5, 'Matt', 'Hink', 'Stellar'),
 (6, 'April', 'Reagan', '')

-- Add a few orders
INSERT INTO OrderHeader(OrderHeaderId, CustomerId, OrderTotal) VALUES
 (1, 2, 28.50), (2, 2, 169.00),  -- Jeff's orders
 (3, 3, 12.99),  -- Keith's orders
 (4, 4, 785.75), (5, 4, 250.00),  -- Simon's orders
 (6, 5, 6100.00), (7, 5, 4250.00),  -- Matt's orders
 (8, 6, 18.50), (9, 6, 10.00), (10, 6, 18.00)  -- April's orders
GO

-- Create a handy view summarizing customer orders
CREATE VIEW vwCustomerOrderSummary WITH SCHEMABINDING AS
 SELECT
   c.CustomerID, c.FirstName, c.LastName, c.CustomerRanking,
   ISNULL(SUM(oh.OrderTotal), 0) AS OrderTotal
  FROM
   dbo.Customer AS c
   LEFT OUTER JOIN dbo.OrderHeader AS oh ON c.CustomerID = oh.CustomerID
  GROUP BY
   c.CustomerID, c.FirstName, c.LastName, c.CustomerRanking
GO
```

This is a very simple script that we'll discuss in a moment. But first, notice what just happened. SSDT executed the script directly against a connected SQL Server instance, and then split the code window horizontally to display the resulting server messages in the bottom pane. The green icon labeled Query Executed Successfully in the lower-left corner offers assurance that all went well with the script execution. Because of the two multi-row *INSERT* statements used to create sample customers and order data, you can see the two "rows affected" messages in the bottom Message pane, as shown in Figure 1-4. Overall, the experience thus far is very similar to previous tools, ensuring a smooth transition to SSDT for developers already familiar with the older tooling.

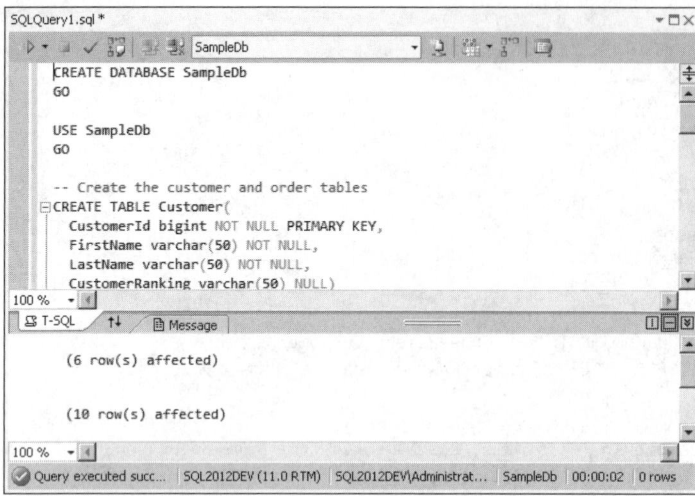

FIGURE 1-4 The query window after successfully executing a T-SQL script.

This simple script created a database named *SampleDb*, with the two tables *Customer* and *OrderHeader*. It also defined a foreign key on the *CustomerId* column in both tables, which establishes the parent-child (one-to-many) relationship between them. It then added a few customer and related order rows into their respective tables. Finally, it created a view summarizing each customer's orders by aggregating all their order totals.

Now run two queries to view some data. At the bottom of the code window, type the following two SELECT statements:

```
SELECT * FROM Customer
SELECT * FROM vwCustomerOrderSummary
```

Notice the IntelliSense as you type. After you finish typing, hover the cursor over *Customer*, and then again over *vwCustomerOrderSummary*. Visual Studio displays tooltips describing those objects respectively as a table and a view. Now hover the cursor over the star symbol in each *SELECT* statement. Visual Studio displays a tooltip listing all the fields represented by the star symbol in each query. This functionality is provided by the SSDT T-SQL language services running in the background that continuously query the database model backed by the connected *SampleDb* database.

Now select just the two *SELECT* statements (leave the entire script above them unselected) and press **Ctrl+Shift+E**. The result is similar to pressing F5 in SSMS or Query Analyzer: only the selected text is executed (which is what you'd expect). SSDT runs both queries and displays their results, as shown in Figure 1-5.

You don't need the query window any longer, so go ahead and close it now (you also don't need to save the script). Right-click the *Databases* node in SQL Server Object Explorer and choose Refresh. You'll see the new *SampleDb* database node appear. Expand it to drill down into the database. As Figure 1-6 shows, the environment is similar to the Object Explorer in SSMS, and lets you carry out most (but not all) of the developer-oriented tasks that SSMS lets you perform.

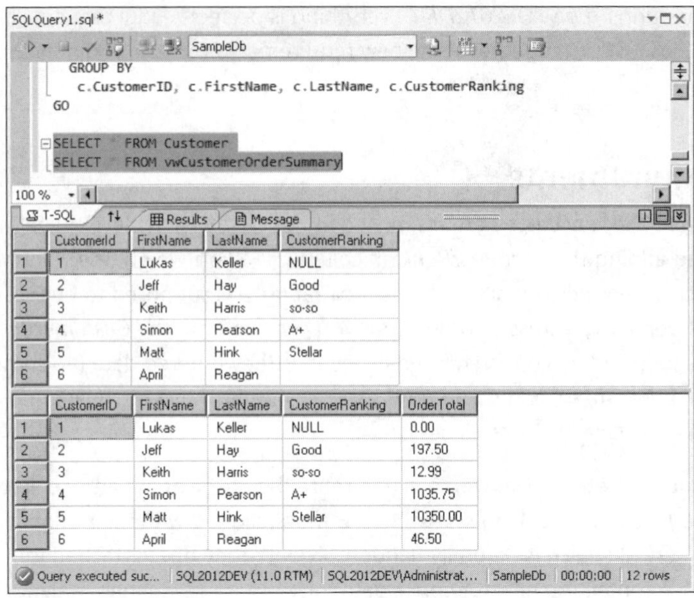

	CustomerId	FirstName	LastName	CustomerRanking
1	1	Lukas	Keller	NULL
2	2	Jeff	Hay	Good
3	3	Keith	Harris	so-so
4	4	Simon	Pearson	A+
5	5	Matt	Hink	Stellar
6	6	April	Reagan	

	CustomerID	FirstName	LastName	CustomerRanking	OrderTotal
1	1	Lukas	Keller	NULL	0.00
2	2	Jeff	Hay	Good	197.50
3	3	Keith	Harris	so-so	12.99
4	4	Simon	Pearson	A+	1035.75
5	5	Matt	Hink	Stellar	10350.00
6	6	April	Reagan		46.50

FIGURE 1-5 Viewing the results of selected statements executed in the query window.

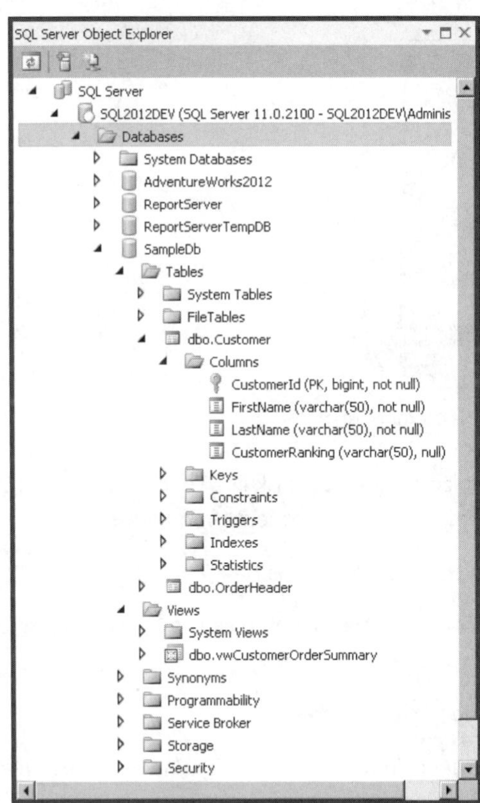

FIGURE 1-6 The *SampleDb* database in SQL Server Object Explorer expanded to show several of its objects.

The database is now up and running on *SQL2012DEV*. Everything is perfect—until that email from marketing arrives. Their team has just put together some new requirements for you, and now there's more work to be done.

Gathering New Requirements

The new requirements pertain to the way customers are ranked in the *Customer* table. Originally, the marketing team had requested adding the *CustomerRanking* column as a lightweight mechanism for data entry operators to rank customer performance. This ad-hoc rating was supposed to be loosely based on the customer's total purchases across all orders, but you can see from the *CustomerRanking* values in Figure 1-5 that users followed no consistency whatsoever as they entered data (no surprise there). They've typed things like **A+**, **so-so**, and **Good**. And some customers have no meaningful data at all, such as empty strings, whitespace, or *NULL* values.

To improve the situation, the marketing team would like to retire the ad-hoc data entry column and replace it with a formalized customer ranking system that is more aligned with their original intent. In their change request email (which is naturally flagged Urgent), they have attached the spreadsheet shown in Figure 1-7 containing new reference data for various pre-defined ranking levels. They've scribbled something about deploying to SQL Azure as well, and then they sign off with "P.S., We need it by Friday" (and no surprise there, either).

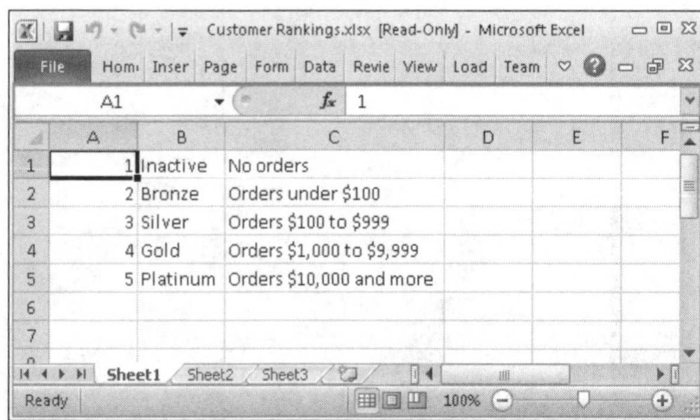

	A	B	C
1	1	Inactive	No orders
2	2	Bronze	Orders under $100
3	3	Silver	Orders $100 to $999
4	4	Gold	Orders $1,000 to $9,999
5	5	Platinum	Orders $10,000 and more

FIGURE 1-7 Reference data for the new customer ranking system.

After giving the matter some thought, you organize a high-level task list. Your list itemizes the development steps you plan on taking to fulfill the marketing department's requirements:

1. Remove the *CustomerRanking* column from the *Customer* table.

2. Create a new *CustomerRanking* table based on the spreadsheet in Figure 1-7, with a primary key column *CustomerRankingId* storing the values 1 through 5.

3. Add a new column *CustomerRankingId* to the *Customer* table.

4. Create a foreign key on the *CustomerRankingId* column to establish a relationship between the *Customer* table and the new *CustomerRanking* table.

5. Update the *vwCustomerOrderSummary* view to join on the new *CustomerRanking* table.
6. Create a new *uspRankCustomers* stored procedure to update the *Customer* table's new foreign key column, based on each customer's total order value.
7. Validate for SQL Azure, then deploy to the cloud.

The rest of this chapter walks through this procedure in detail, step by step. Along the way, you'll learn to leverage many important SSDT features and will gain insight into the way the new tooling works. It's time to get started with the first step: removing a column from a table.

Note The scenario we've presented here is admittedly somewhat artificial. We are not necessarily advocating these particular steps as the best way to solve a given problem, and certainly hope you are working with better designs than this in your own database. But for the purpose of this exercise—namely, learning how to use SSDT—we ask that you go along with it. The premise may be contrived, but the steps we've outlined for the solution are in fact quite representative of typical recurring activities in the everyday life of an average SQL Server developer.

Using the Table Designer (Connected)

In SQL Server Object Explorer, right-click the *Customer* table and choose View Designer to open the SSDT table designer, as shown in Figure 1-8.

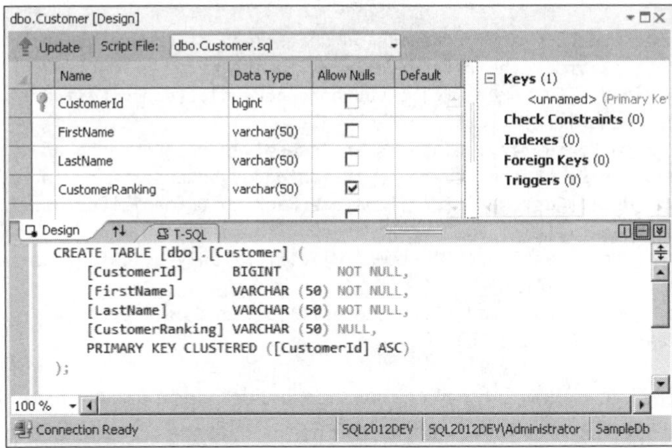

FIGURE 1-8 The new SSDT table designer.

The top-left pane of this designer window lists the defined columns in a grid just as in the SSMS table designer, but the similarity ends there. A very different mechanism is at play with the new SSDT designer, one that should be easy to understand after all the discussion we've had around declarative, model-based design. The *CREATE TABLE* statement in the bottom T-SQL pane gives it away. Knowing that the table already exists in the database, why is this a *CREATE* statement? Well, that's because this isn't actually T-SQL code that you intend to execute against the database as-is (which would fail of course, because the table exists). Rather, it's a T-SQL *declaration* of "how this table should look," whether it exists or not—and indeed, whether it exists with a *different schema* or not—in the target database.

Here's what's actually happening. The designer is operating over a memory-resident database model inside its working environment. Because you are connected at the moment, that model is backed by the live *SampleDb* database. But when you switch to working offline with a SQL Server Database Project (as you will in the next section of this chapter), you'll interact with the very same table designer over a model backed by a *project* instead of a real database. A model can also be backed by a database snapshot. Because the table designer just operates over a model, the same tool works consistently in any of these scenarios.

You want to remove the *CustomerRanking* column, and that can be done either by deleting it from the grid in the top pane or editing it out of the declarative T-SQL code in the bottom pane. Both panes are merely views into the same table, so any changes appear bidirectionally. Throughout this exercise, you'll experiment with different editing techniques in the table designer, starting with the quickest method. Just right-click *CustomerRanking* in the top grid and choose Delete. The column is removed from the grid and, as you'd expect, the T-SQL code is updated to reflect the change.

That was a pretty easy change. Applying that change to the database should be easy, too. Go ahead and click the Update button on the toolbar. Unfortunately, instead of just working as you'd like, you receive the following error message:

```
Update cannot proceed due to validation errors.
Please correct the following errors and try again.

SQL71501 :: View: [dbo].[vwCustomerOrderSummary] contains an unresolved reference to an
object. Either the object does not exist or the reference is ambiguous because it could refer
to any of the following objects: [dbo].[Customer].[c]::[CustomerRanking], [dbo].[Customer].
[CustomerRanking] or [dbo].[OrderHeader].[c]::[CustomerRanking].
SQL71501 :: View: [dbo].[vwCustomerOrderSummary] contains an unresolved reference to an
object. Either the object does not exist or the reference is ambiguous because it could refer
to any of the following objects: [dbo].[Customer].[c]::[CustomerRanking], [dbo].[Customer].
[CustomerRanking] or [dbo].[OrderHeader].[c]::[CustomerRanking].
SQL71558 :: The object reference [dbo].[Customer].[CustomerID] differs only by case from the
object definition [dbo].[Customer].[CustomerId].
SQL71558 :: The object reference [dbo].[OrderHeader].[CustomerID] differs only by case from the
object definition [dbo].[OrderHeader].[CustomerId].
```

What went wrong? Referring back to Listing 1-1, notice that the view definition for *vwCustomer-OrderSummary* specifies the *WITH SCHEMABINDING* clause. This means that the columns of the view are bound to the underlying tables exposed by the view, which protects you from "breaking" the view with schema changes—as you've done just now. The problem, as reported by the first two errors, is that the schema-bound view's *CustomerRanking* column has suddenly been removed from the *Customer* table that underlies the view. The second two errors are actually only case-sensitivity warnings that, on their own, would not prevent the update from succeeding. We will explain these case-sensitivity warnings a bit later; for now, remain focused on the dependency issue that's blocking the update.

The interesting thing worth noting at this point is that SSDT caught the condition before even *attempting* to apply your changes to the live database (which would certainly have thrown an error). In fact, you could have been aware of this issue even before clicking Update if you had previously opened the Error List pane, because SSDT constantly validates changes to the model in the background while you edit it in the designer.

Click the Cancel button to dismiss the error window. Then click the View menu and choose Error List to open the pane. Notice how the errors and warnings appear, just like compilation errors appear for C# and VB .NET projects. And just like those project types, you can double-click items in the Error List and instantly navigate to the offending code to deal with the errors. In this case, both dependency errors are in *vwCustomerOrderSummary*, so double-click either one now to open a code editor into the view, as shown in Figure 1-9.

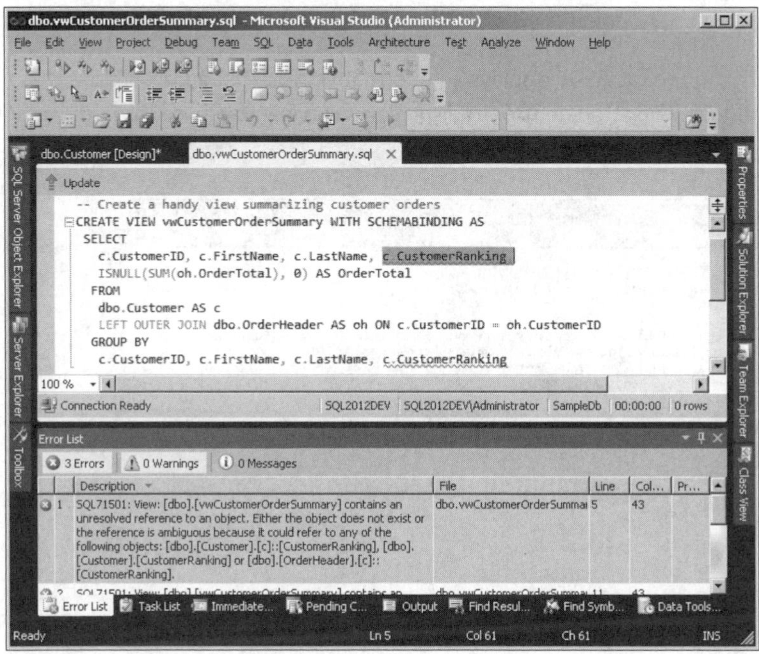

FIGURE 1-9 Detecting and navigating validation errors.

You want to revise this view to join against the new *CustomerRanking* table, but that's not coming up until step 4 in your task list. So for now, just perform the minimum edits necessary to clear the validation errors (which are identified by red squigglies like you've seen in other Visual Studio code windows) so you can update the database and move on. Delete (by commenting out) the two references to *c.CustomerRanking* column from the view (one is in the column list, the other in the *GROUP BY* clause). Notice how the errors disappear from the Error List pane as you correct the code. You're now beginning to experience the effects of model-based development with SSDT in Visual Studio.

With a clear Error List, you know that all your changes are valid. You have altered a table and a view, but those changes have been made only to the memory-resident model. The changed objects are currently open in separate Visual Studio windows, and both windows have an Update button.

Yet it makes no difference which of the two buttons you click—in either case, Update means that *all* changes that have been buffered get sent to the database. So whichever Update button you click, your edits to both the table and the view are going to get applied to the database at once.

How is that going to happen? The edits were simple enough, but the T-SQL change script needed to apply those edits is actually a bit more complex. And therein lay the beauty of this new tooling—all of that scripting complexity is handled for you by SSDT. The tool compares the edited model with a brand-new model based on the live database, and then works out the change script automatically. Creating a fresh model from the database at this time makes sure you're working with its latest state, in case it drifted because it was modeled for the current editing session. Then it runs an internal *schema compare* operation between the edited model (the source) and the latest model based on the live database (the target) to identify all their differences. Finally, SSDT generates a change script that can be executed on the live database to apply the changes. Click Update now to generate the change script.

Before running the change script, SSDT displays an informative report of all the actions that the change script is going to take. Click Update now to display the Preview Database Updates window, as shown in Figure 1-10.

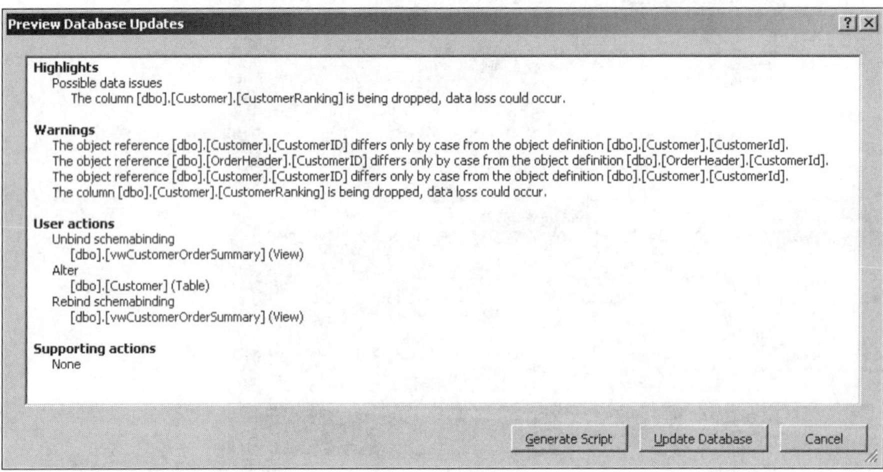

FIGURE 1-10 The Preview Database Updates window.

You should always scrutinize this preview to make sure it's consistent with the actions and results you would expect of the edits you've made. In this case, you're being warned about data loss in the *Customer* table by dropping the *CustomerRanking* column. You're also being told that the script will drop and then re-create the schema binding of the *vwCustomerOrderSummary* view, before and after the table is altered. All of this is expected. Now you can click Update Database to immediately execute the change script, or you can click Generate Script to load the change script into a code editor so you can view, possibly modify, and choose to either execute it or not.

In most cases, you'll feel comfortable just clicking Update Database, particularly if you've reviewed the warnings and actions reported by the database update preview. Doing so will immediately execute the change script to update the live database. But being that this is your very first update, click Generate Script instead so you can examine the script before you run it. The script is shown in Listing 1-2 (to conserve space, error-checking code has been commented out).

LISTING 1-2 The change script for the altered table and view automatically generated by SSDT.

```
/*
Deployment script for SampleDb
*/

// ...
:setvar DatabaseName "SampleDb"
GO
// ...
USE [$(DatabaseName)];
GO
// ...
BEGIN TRANSACTION
GO
PRINT N'Removing schema binding from [dbo].[vwCustomerOrderSummary]...';
GO
ALTER VIEW [dbo].[vwCustomerOrderSummary]
AS
SELECT   c.CustomerID,
         c.FirstName,
         c.LastName,
         c.CustomerRanking,
         ISNULL(SUM(oh.OrderTotal), 0) AS OrderTotal
FROM     dbo.Customer AS c
         LEFT OUTER JOIN
         dbo.OrderHeader AS oh
         ON c.CustomerID = oh.CustomerID
GROUP BY c.CustomerID, c.FirstName, c.LastName, c.CustomerRanking;
// ...
GO
PRINT N'Altering [dbo].[Customer]...';
GO
ALTER TABLE [dbo].[Customer] DROP COLUMN [CustomerRanking];
GO
// ...
PRINT N'Adding schema binding to [dbo].[vwCustomerOrderSummary]...';
GO

-- Create a handy view summarizing customer orders
ALTER VIEW vwCustomerOrderSummary WITH SCHEMABINDING AS
 SELECT
   c.CustomerID, c.FirstName, c.LastName,
   ISNULL(SUM(oh.OrderTotal), 0) AS OrderTotal
  FROM
   dbo.Customer AS c
   LEFT OUTER JOIN dbo.OrderHeader AS oh ON c.CustomerID = oh.CustomerID
  GROUP BY
   c.CustomerID, c.FirstName, c.LastName
```

```
GO
// ...
IF @@TRANCOUNT>0 BEGIN
PRINT N'The transacted portion of the database update succeeded.'
COMMIT TRANSACTION
END
ELSE PRINT N'The transacted portion of the database update failed.'
GO
DROP TABLE #tmpErrors
GO
PRINT N'Update complete.'
GO
```

It's great that you didn't have to *write* the change script, but it's still important that you *understand* the change script. Let's look it over quickly now.

Using variable substitution, the script first issues a *USE* statement that sets *SampleDb* as the current database and then it begins a transaction. The transaction will get committed only if the entire change script completes successfully. Then the script issues an *ALTER VIEW* statement that removes the schema binding from *vwCustomerOrderSummary* without yet changing its definition. So it still contains those two references to the *CustomerRanking* column that's about to get dropped from the *Customer* table, but that will not present a problem because *WITH SCHEMABINDING* has been removed from the view. Next, the script issues the *ALTER TABLE* statement that actually drops the column from the table. After the column is dropped, another *ALTER VIEW* statement is issued on *vwCustomerOrderSummary* with the new version that no longer references the dropped column and is once again schemabound. Finally, the transaction is committed and the update is complete.

Press **Ctrl+Shift+E**. The script is executed and output describing actions taken by the script are displayed in the Messages pane:

```
Removing schema binding from [dbo].[vwCustomerOrderSummary]...
Altering [dbo].[Customer]...
Adding schema binding to [dbo].[vwCustomerOrderSummary]...
The transacted portion of the database update succeeded.
Update complete.
```

You can close all open windows now. Visual Studio will prompt to save changes, but it's not necessary to do so because the database has just been updated. Right-click on the database and choose Refresh, and then drill down into *SampleDb* in SQL Server Object Explorer to confirm that the table and view changes have been applied. You will see that the *CustomerRanking* column has been removed from the database, and that completes step 1.

Working Offline with a SQL Server Database Project

With SQL Server Database Projects, you can develop databases with no connection whatsoever to a SQL Server instance. A SQL Server Database Project is a project that contains individual, declarative, T-SQL source code files. These source files collectively define the complete structure of a database.

Because the database definition is maintained this way inside a Visual Studio project, it can be preserved and protected with source code control (SCC) just like the artifacts in all your other Visual Studio project types. SSDT generates a model from the project structure behind the scenes, just like it generates a model from the live database when working connected. This lets you use the same SSDT tools whether working offline or connected.

You carried out your first task online while connected directly to a live database. Now you'll create a SQL Server Database Project for the database so that you can continue your work offline. Although (as you've seen) it's easy to use SSDT for connected development, you should ideally develop your databases offline with SQL Server Database Projects, and publish to live servers whenever you're ready to deploy your changes. By doing so, you will derive the benefits of source control, snapshot versioning, and integration with the rest of your application's code through the Visual Studio solution and project system.

There are several ways to create a SQL Server Database Project. You can start with an empty project, design a database structure from the ground up, and then publish the entire structure to a new database on a SQL Server instance locally or in the cloud on SQL Azure. Or, as in this scenario, you have an existing database on a local SQL Server instance from which you want to generate a SQL Server Database Project. And you want this project populated with all the declarative T-SQL source files that completely define the existing database structure.

It's easy to do this with the Import Database dialog. Right-click the *SampleDb* database under the *SQL2012DEV* instance in SQL Server Object Explorer and choose Create New Project to display the Import Database dialog, as shown in Figure 1-11.

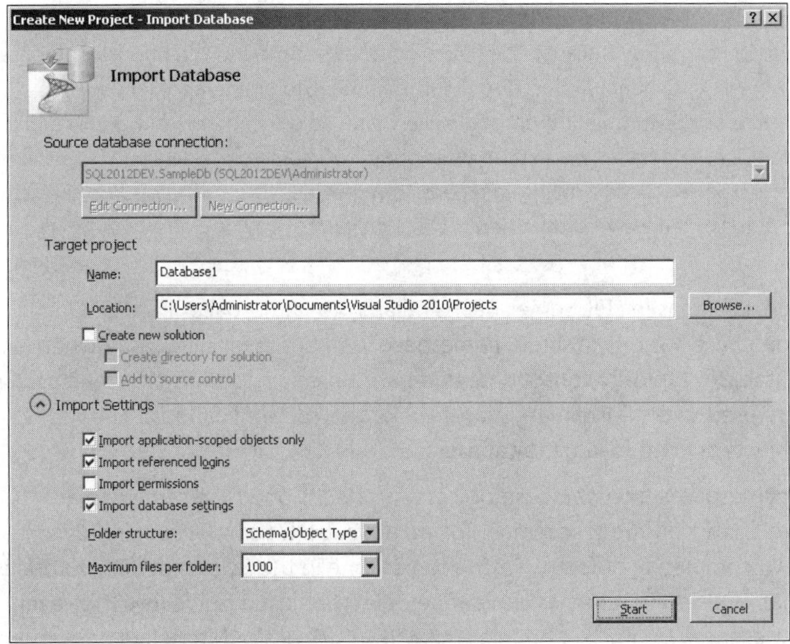

FIGURE 1-11 Creating a SQL Server Database Project from an existing database.

The source database connection confirms that your new project will be generated from the *SampleDb* database on *SQL2012DEV*. Change the target project name from Database1 to **SampleDb** (and set the location, too, if you wish). Check the Create New Solution checkbox, and if you have an SCC provider for Visual Studio, check Add To Source Control as well. Then click Start.

If you checked Add To Source Control, you will be prompted at this point to supply credentials and server information (this will depend on your default SCC provider in Visual Studio). It takes a few moments for Visual Studio to scour the database, discover its schema, and generate the declarative T-SQL source files for the new project. When done, Visual Studio displays a window with information describing all the actions it took to create the project. Click Finish to close this window. The new project is then opened in the Solution Explorer automatically (docked to the right, by default). The dbo folder represents the *dbo* schema in the database. Expand it, and then expand the Tables and Views folders, as shown in Figure 1-12.

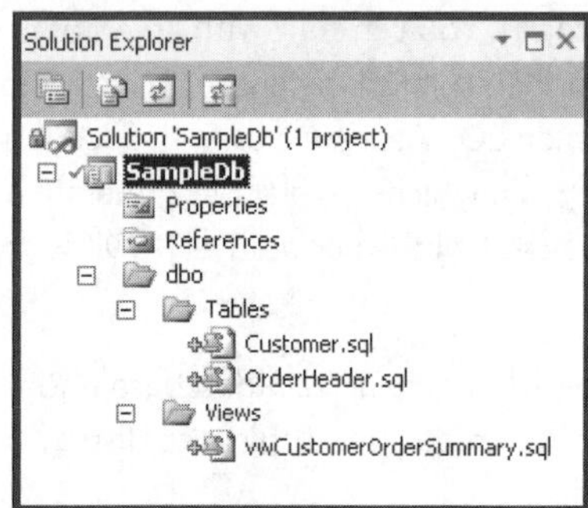

FIGURE 1-12 The source-controlled SQL Server Database Project after importing a database.

SSDT set up your project this way because the Folder Structure setting in the Import Database dialog (Figure 1-11) was set to Schema\Object Type. This tells SSDT to create a folder for each schema, and then a folder for each object type (table, view, and so on) contained in that schema. You are free to create additional folders as you extend your project. Unless you have a very specific or unique convention, it is best practice to maintain a consistent project structure based on the schema organization in the database like we've shown here.

More Information Schemas in SQL Server bear similarity to namespaces in .NET. Our simple example database has only a single namespace (*dbo*, short for database owner), but more complex databases typically consolidate database objects into multiple schemas. Just as namespaces are used to organize many classes in large .NET applications, schemas help manage many objects defined in large databases.

Like classes and namespaces, two database objects can be assigned the same name if they are contained in two different schemas. For example, both *Sales.Person* and *Billing.Person* refer to two completely different *Person* tables (one in the *Sales* schema and one in the *Billing* schema). SQL Server schemas can define objects at just a single level however, whereas .NET namespaces can be nested in as many levels as desired to define an elaborate hierarchy of classes.

Taking a Snapshot

Before you make any offline database changes, take a snapshot. This will create a single-file image of the current database schema that you can refer to or revert to at any time in the future. You'll take another snapshot when you've completed all your database changes, and thereby preserve the two points in time—just before, and just after, the changes are made. And because they are maintained as part of the project, snapshot files are also protected under source control.

Right-click the *SampleDb* project in Solution Explorer and choose Snapshot Project. After validating the project, Visual Studio creates a new Snapshots folder and, inside the Snapshots folder, it creates a new *.dacpac* file with a filename based on the current date and time. You'll usually want to give the snapshot a better name, so rename the file to **Version1Baseline.dacpac**.

Using the Table Designer (Offline Database Project)

With your "baseline" snapshot saved, you're ready to create the new *CustomerRanking* table. Recall that this is the new reference table based on the spreadsheet in Figure 1-7. In Solution Explorer, right-click the project's Tables folder (under the dbo schema folder) and choose Add | Table. Name the table **CustomerRanking** and click Add.

A new offline table designer window opens. You'll find that it looks and feels exactly the same as the one in Figure 1-8 that you used when working online. That's because it *is* the same tool, only this time it's the designer over a model backed by a source-controlled project file (*CustomerRanking.sql*) rather than a model backed by a live table. Because there's no connected database, the table designer has no Update button—instead, when working offline, schema changes are saved to the project script file for that table. This in turn updates the model, and then the same validation checks and IntelliSense you experienced when working while connected are run against the project. So you can find out right away if and when you make a breaking change, before deploying to a real database.

Earlier, when you removed the *CustomerRanking* column from the *Customer* table, we mentioned that you can design the table using either the grid in the top pane or the T-SQL code window in the bottom pane. You can also view and change parts of the schema definition from the Properties grid. We'll demonstrate all of these techniques now as you lay out the schema of the new *CustomerRanking* table.

SSDT starts you off with a new table that has one column in it: an *int* primary key named *Id*. To rename this column to *CustomerRankingId*, select the column name *Id* in the top pane's grid, replace it with **CustomerRankingId**, and press **Enter**. Beneath it, add the **RankName** column, set its data type to **varchar(20)**, and uncheck Allow Nulls. You can see that SSDT updates the T-SQL code in the bottom pane with a *CREATE TABLE* statement that reflects the changes made in the top pane.

Add the third column by editing the T-SQL code in the bottom pane. Append a comma after the second column and type **[Description] VARCHAR(200) NOT NULL**. As expected, the grid in the top pane is updated to show the new *Description* column you just added in code.

Finally, tweak the data type using the Properties grid. Click the *Description* column in the top pane and scroll to the Length property in the Properties grid (to display the Properties grid if it's not currently visible, click View and choose Properties Window). Click the drop-down list and select MAX to change the data type from *varchar(200)* to *varchar(max)*. When you're done, the table designer should look similar to Figure 1-13.

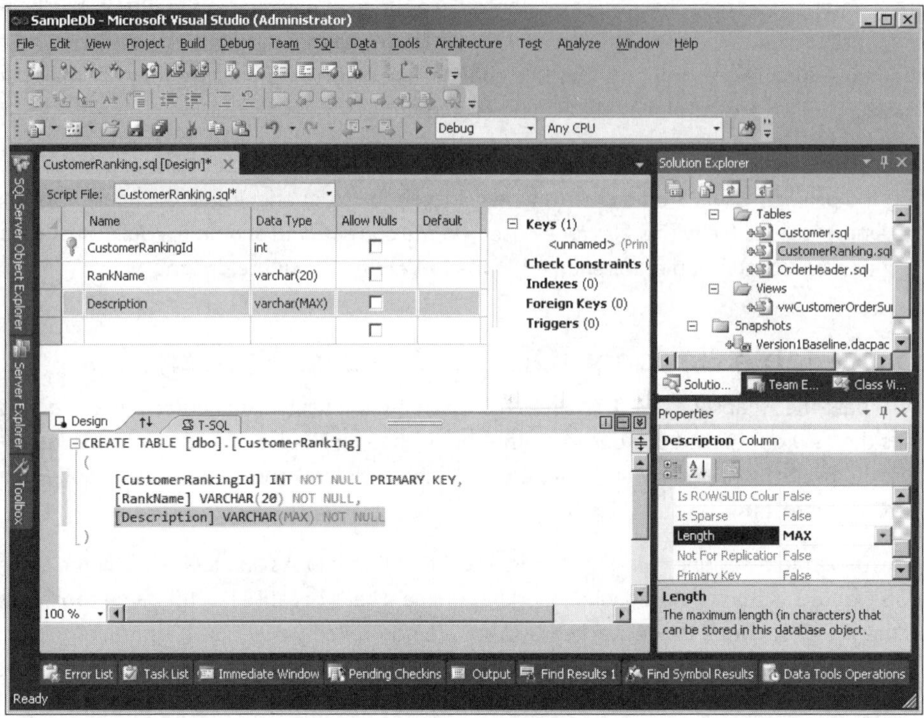

FIGURE 1-13 The table designer for the new *CustomerRanking* table in an offline SQL Server Database Project.

Save *CustomerRanking.sql* and close the table designer. This completes step 2. You are now ready to add the foreign key column to the *Customer* table (step 3) that joins to this new *CustomerRanking* table. Double-click *Customer.sql* in Solution Explorer to open the table designer for the *Customer* table. Use any technique you'd like to add a new nullable *int* column named **CustomerRankingId** (it must be nullable at this point, because it doesn't have any data yet).

Now you can establish the foreign key relationship to the *CustomerRanking* table (step 4). In the upper-righthand corner of the Table Designer is a Context View area that summarizes other pertinent objects related to the table. In the Context View, right-click Foreign Keys and choose Add New Foreign Key. Name the new foreign key **FK_Customer_CustomerRanking** (it is best practice to assign foreign key names that indicate which tables participate in the relationship). Then edit the *FOREIGN KEY* template code added to the T-SQL code window in the bottom pane to be **FOREIGN KEY (CustomerRankingID) REFERENCES CustomerRanking(CustomerRankingId)**. The table designer window should now look similar to Figure 1-14. After reviewing the table schema, save the *Customer.sql* file and close the designer.

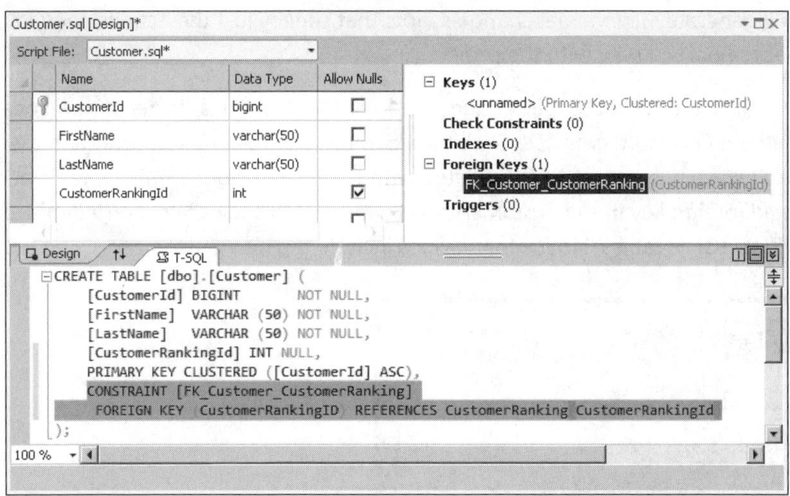

FIGURE 1-14 The table designer for the *Customer* table after creating the foreign key on *CustomerRankingId*.

Introducing LocalDB

Your next tasks involve altering a view (step 5) and creating a stored procedure (step 6). It will be very helpful to have a test SQL Server environment available as you implement these steps. You don't want to use *SQL2012DEV*, because that's the "live" server. You need another SQL Server that can be used just for testing offline.

LocalDB gives you that test environment. This is a new, lightweight, single-user instance of SQL Server that spins up on demand when you build your project. This is extremely handy when working offline and there is no other development server available to you. The official name for this new variant of SQL Server is "SQL Express LocalDB," which can be misleading because it is distinct from the Express edition of SQL Server. To avoid confusion, we refer to it simply as "LocalDB."

Note The new LocalDB does not support every SQL Server feature (for example, it can't be used with FILESTREAM). However, it does support most functionality required for typical database development.

Press **F5** to build the project. This first validates the entire database structure defined by the project and then deploys it to LocalDB. Note, however, that this is just the default behavior; you can change the project properties to target another available server for testing if you require features not supported by LocalDB (for example, FILESTREAM, which we cover in Chapter 8).

The deployment is carried out by performing a schema compare between the project and LocalDB on the target server. More precisely, and as already explained, models of the source project and target database are generated, and the schema compare actually works on the two models. Being your very first build, the database does not exist yet on the target server, so the schema compare generates a script that creates the whole database from scratch. As you modify the project, subsequent builds will generate incremental change scripts that specify just the actions needed to bring the target database back in sync with the project.

Look back over in SQL Server Object Explorer and you'll see that SSDT has started a new LocalDB instance. The host name is *(localdb)\SampleDb*, and it is a completely separate instance than the *SQL2012DEV* instance (which has not yet been updated with the new *CustomerRanking* table and the *CustomerRankingId* foreign key in the *Customer* table). Figure 1-15 shows *SampleDb* deployed to LocalDB, expanded to reveal its tables. Notice that it does include the new *CustomerRanking* table.

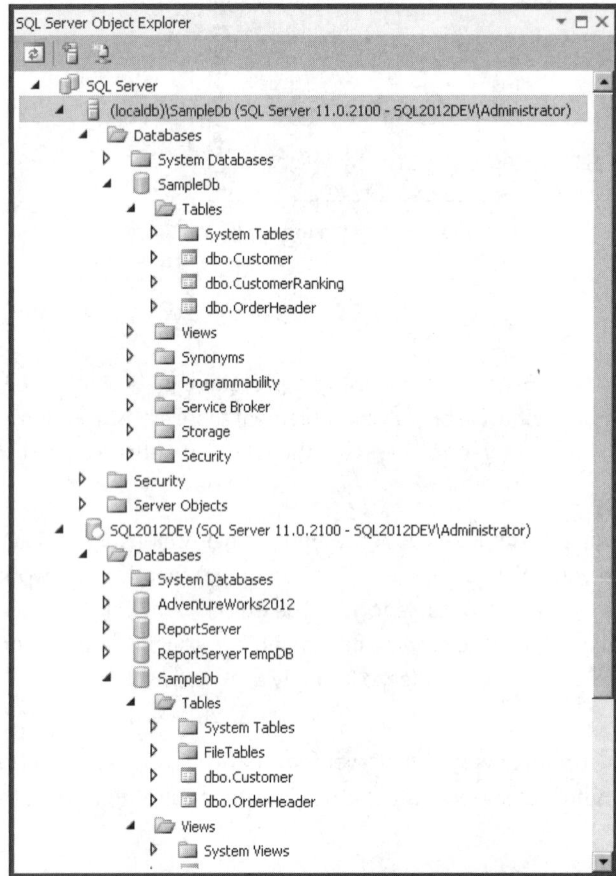

FIGURE 1-15 The local database runtime (LocalDB) after building and deploying the SQL Server Database Project.

Now you have a test database to play around with, but of course there's no data in it. You will add some now so that you can test the view you're about to alter and the stored procedure you're about to create. Using simple copy/paste, SSDT lets you import small sets of rows from any "table" source (including Microsoft Word and Excel) into a database table that has compatible columns.

First, bring in the reference data from the ranking definitions provided by the spreadsheet in Figure 1-7. You can easily grab the data straight out of the spreadsheet and dump it right into the new *CustomerRanking* table. Open the spreadsheet in Excel, select the five rows of data (complete rows, not cells or columns), then right-click the selection and choose Copy. Back in SQL Server Object Explorer, right-click the *CustomerRanking* table and choose View Data. The Editable Data Grid in SSDT opens with a template for inserting a new row. Right-click the row selector for the new row template and choose Paste (be sure to right-click the row selector in the left gray margin area, and not a cell, before pasting). As shown in Figure 1-16, SSDT faithfully copies the data from Excel into the *CustomerRanking* table.

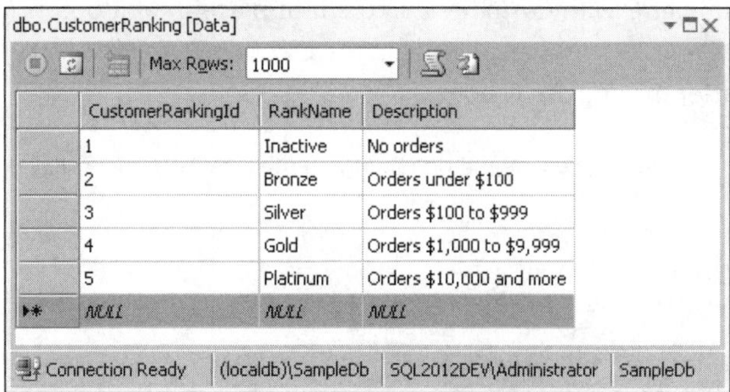

CustomerRankingId	RankName	Description
1	Inactive	No orders
2	Bronze	Orders under $100
3	Silver	Orders $100 to $999
4	Gold	Orders $1,000 to $9,999
5	Platinum	Orders $10,000 and more
NULL	NULL	NULL

FIGURE 1-16 Reference data imported into a database table from Excel via the clipboard.

You also need a few customers to work with. Using the same copy/paste technique, you will transfer rows from the *Customer* table in the production database to the test database on LocalDB (for this exercise, you won't transfer related order data in the *OrderHeader* table). There are only a handful of customers, so you'll just copy them all over. Typically though, you'd extract just the subset of data that provides a representative sampling good enough for testing purposes. Expand the production server (*SQL2012DEV*) node in SQL Server Object Explorer and drill down to the *Customer* table. Right-click the table and choose View Data. Select all the customer rows, then right-click the selection and choose Copy. Next, right-click the *Customer* table in the test database on *(localdb)\SampleDb* and choose View Data. Right-click the new row selector and choose Paste to copy in the six customer rows.

You are now at step 5, which is to update the *vwCustomerOrderSummary* view. Recall that this is the same view you edited back in step 1 (while connected), when you removed the schema-bound reference to the old *CustomerRanking* column that was being dropped from the *Customer* table. With the new reference table and foreign key relationship now in place, you will revise the view once again (offline, this time) to join with the *CustomerRanking* table on *CustomerRankingId*, so that it can expose the display name in the reference table's *RankName* column.

In Solution Explorer, double-click *vwCustomerOrderSummary.sql* in the project's Views folder (under the dbo schema folder). The view opens up in a new code window, and your attention may first be drawn to several squigglies that Visual Studio paints in the view's code. They're not red, because there is really nothing significantly wrong with the view, and so these are just warnings. Hover the cursor over one of them to view the warning text in a tooltip (you can also see all of them listed as warning items in the Error List pane). The warnings indicate that the view uses *CustomerID* (ending in a capital D) to reference a column that is actually defined as *CustomerId* (ending in a lowercase d). These are the same case-sensitivity warnings you saw earlier when attempting to update the database with dependency issues. Object names in SQL Server are normally not case-sensitive (like VB .NET), but non-default collation settings can change that behavior so that they *are* case-sensitive (like C#). This would cause a problem if you deployed the view to a SQL Server instance configured for a case-sensitive collation of object names.

Add another *LEFT OUTER JOIN* to the view to add in the *CustomerRanking* table joined on the *CustomerRankingId* of the *Customer* table, and add *RankName* to the *SELECT* and *GROUP BY* column lists. You want your code to be squeaky-clean, so now is also a good time to resolve those case-sensitivity warnings. Replace *CustomerID* with *CustomerId* in the four places that it occurs (once in the *SELECT* column list, twice in the first *JOIN*, and once more in the *GROUP BY* column list). Listing 1-3 shows the view definition after making the changes.

LISTING 1-3 The updated *vwCustomerOrderSummary* view definition joining on the new *CustomerRanking* table.

```
-- Create a handy view summarizing customer orders
CREATE VIEW vwCustomerOrderSummary WITH SCHEMABINDING AS
 SELECT
   c.CustomerId, c.FirstName, c.LastName, r.RankName,
   ISNULL(SUM(oh.OrderTotal), 0) AS OrderTotal
  FROM
   dbo.Customer AS c
   LEFT OUTER JOIN dbo.OrderHeader AS oh ON c.CustomerId = oh.CustomerId
   LEFT OUTER JOIN dbo.CustomerRanking AS r ON c.CustomerRankingId =
      r.CustomerRankingId
   GROUP BY
      c.CustomerId, c.FirstName, c.LastName, r.RankName
```

Save the *vwCustomerOrderSummary.sql* file to update the offline project. You know that pressing F5 now will deploy the changed view to the test database on LocalDB. But what if you attempt to execute the script directly by pressing **Ctrl+Shift+E**, right here in the code window? Go ahead and try. You'll receive this error message in response:

```
Msg 2714, Level 16, State 3, Procedure vwCustomerOrderSummary, Line 2
There is already an object named 'vwCustomerOrderSummary' in the database.
```

Here's what happened. First, SSDT connected the query window to the *(localdb)\SampleDb* instance. Then it attempted to execute the script imperatively against the connected database, just as you've already seen with Ctrl+Shift+E. But being part of an offline project, this script is declarative and so it's expressed as a *CREATE VIEW* statement. The view already exists in the database, so the error message makes perfect sense. Again, the proper way to update the database is to deploy it via an incremental deployment script by debugging with F5.

However, you are indeed connected to the test database on LocalDB, even though you're working inside the query window of an offline project that hasn't yet been deployed to LocalDB. This means that you can actually test the view before you deploy it. Select all the text from *SELECT* until the end of the script (that is, leave only the *CREATE VIEW* portion of the window unselected) and press **Ctrl+Shift+E** again. This time, you get a much better result. Only the chosen *SELECT* statement executes, which is perfectly valid T-SQL for the connected database. The query results show you what the view is going to return, and you got that information without having to deploy first. In this mode, you are actually working connected and offline simultaneously! You can select any T-SQL to instantly execute it, test and debug stored procedures, and even get execution plans, all while "offline."

Refactoring the Database

The view is ready to be deployed, but now you decide to change some names first. Customers are the only thing being ranked, so shortening the table name *CustomerRanking* to *Ranking* and column names *CustomerRankingId* to *RankingId* is going to make your T-SQL more readable (which is important!). Without the proper tooling, it can be very tedious to rename objects in the database. But the refactoring capabilities provided by SSDT make this remarkably easy.

In the new *LEFT OUTER JOIN* you just added, right-click on the *CustomerRanking* table reference, and then choose Refactor, Rename. Type **Ranking** for the new table name and click OK. You are presented with a preview window (Figure 1-17) that will appear very familiar if you've ever used the refactoring features in Visual Studio with ordinary .NET projects.

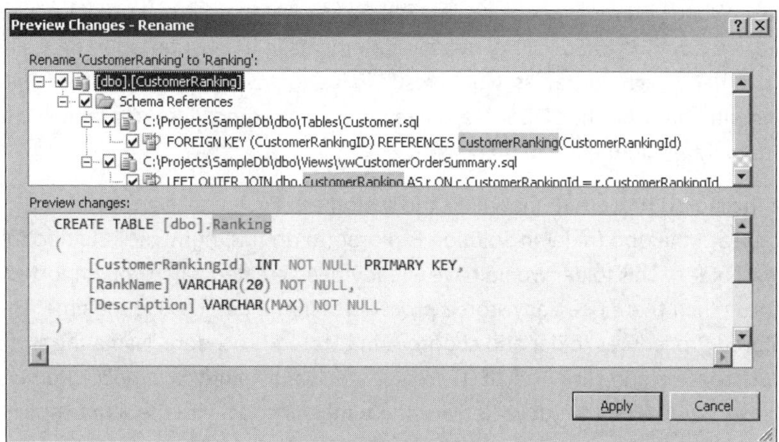

FIGURE 1-17 Previewing changes before refactoring is applied to the database.

This dialog shows all the references to the *CustomerRanking* table that will be changed to *Ranking* when you click Apply (notice that checkboxes are provided so that you can also choose which references should get updated and which should not). Scroll through the change list to preview each one, and then click Apply to immediately invoke the rename operation. Every affected project file is updated accordingly, but Visual Studio won't actually rename project files themselves. The project script file defining the newly renamed *Ranking* table is still named *CustomerRanking.sql*. Right-click the file in Solution Explorer, choose Rename, and change the filename to **Ranking.sql**.

Now rename the primary key column in the *Ranking* table along with its corresponding foreign key column in the *Customer* table, both of which are currently named *CustomerRankingId*. The two key columns are referenced on the same *LEFT OUTER JOIN* line, so this will be easy. Right-click the *r.CustomerRankingId* key column in the join and choose Refactor, Rename. Type **RankingId** for the new name, click OK, preview the changes, and click Apply to update the primary key column name in the *Ranking* table. Then repeat for the *c.CustomerRankingId* key column to update the foreign key column name in the *Customer* table (the actual order in which you refactor the column names in these tables is immaterial).

There's one more thing to rename, and that's the foreign key definition in the *Customer* table. This isn't strictly necessary of course, but the (self-imposed) convention to name foreign keys definitions after the tables they join dictates that *FK_Customer_CustomerRanking* should be renamed to *FK_Customer_Ranking*. The *Customer* table is specified first in the view's *FROM* clause, so right-click on it now and choose Go to Definition. This navigates directly to the *Customer* table definition in a new query window. In the *CONSTRAINT* clause, right-click *FK_Customer_CustomerRanking* and choose Refactor, Rename. Type **FK_Customer_Ranking** for the new name, click OK, preview the changes (just one, in this case), and click Apply.

You're all set to deploy the changes with another build, so press **F5** once again. After the build completes, click Refresh in the SQL Server Object Explorer toolbar and look at the test database running under *(localdb)\SampleDb* to confirm that the *CustomerRanking* table has been renamed to *Ranking*. Right-click the *Ranking* table and choose View Data to confirm that all the data in the renamed table is intact. When you rename objects in a SQL Server Database Project, SSDT generates a change script with corresponding *EXECUTE sp_rename* statements in it, as opposed to dropping one object and creating another (which, for tables, would result in irrevocable data loss). So the tool does the right thing, relying ultimately on the SQL Server *sp_rename* stored procedure to properly change the object's name internally within the database.

It's time to create the stored procedure that ranks the customers. First, create a **Stored Procedures** folder beneath the dbo folder in Solution Explorer (to do this, right-click the dbo folder, and choose Add | New Folder). This folder would have already been created when you imported the database into the project, had there been any stored procedures in the database at the time. Then right-click the new Stored Procedures folder and choose Add | Stored Procedure. Name the stored procedure **uspRankCustomers** and click Add. SSDT creates a new file named *uspRankCustomers.sql* and opens it in a new T-SQL editor window. Replace the template code with the script shown in Listing 1-4 and save it, but keep the window open. Now press **F5** to perform another build and push the new stored procedure out to the test database on LocalDB.

LISTING 1-4 The stored procedure to rank customers based on their total order amount.

```
CREATE PROCEDURE uspRankCustomers
AS
        DECLARE @CustomerId int
        DECLARE @OrderTotal money
        DECLARE @RankingId int

        DECLARE curCustomer CURSOR FOR
         SELECT CustomerId, OrderTotal FROM vwCustomerOrderSummary

        OPEN curCustomer
        FETCH NEXT FROM curCustomer INTO @CustomerId, @OrderTotal
```

```
WHILE @@FETCH_STATUS = 0
BEGIN
        IF @OrderTotal = 0 SET @RankingId = 1
        ELSE IF @OrderTotal < 100 SET @RankingId = 2
        ELSE IF @OrderTotal < 1000 SET @RankingId = 3
        ELSE IF @OrderTotal < 10000 SET @RankingId = 4
        ELSE SET @RankingId = 5

        UPDATE Customer
         SET RankingId = @RankingId
         WHERE CustomerId = @CustomerId

        FETCH NEXT FROM curCustomer INTO @CustomerId, @OrderTotal
END

CLOSE curCustomer
DEALLOCATE curCustomer
```

This stored procedure "ranks" the customers, examining them individually and assigning each a value based on their order total. It does this by opening a cursor against the order summary view, which returns one row per customer with their individual orders aggregated into a single order total. Based on the dollar value of the total, it then updates the customer with a ranking value between one and five. Then it advances to the next customer until it reaches the end of the cursor. As mentioned at the outset, this solution may be a bit contrived (and we're sure you can think of a better approach), but it suits our demonstration purposes here just fine.

Testing and Debugging

Are you in the habit of running new or untested code on live databases? We certainly hope not. Though you could, you should not simply push all of the changes you've made in the project (steps 2 through 6) back to the live database on *SQL2012DEV*, and then run the stored procedure there for the very first time. It's much safer to test the stored procedure offline first with LocalDB. You will now learn how to do that using the integrated debugger in Visual Studio. Then you can confidently deploy everything back to *SQL2012DEV*, and finally (step 7), to the cloud!

The *uspRankCustomers* stored procedure is still open in the code editor. Click inside the left margin on the *OPEN curCustomer* line to set a breakpoint just before the cursor is opened. The breakpoint appears as a red bullet in the margin where you clicked. This is exactly how breakpoints are set in C# or VB .NET code, and SSDT now delivers a similar debugging experience for T-SQL code as well. In SQL Server Object Explorer, expand the *Stored Procedures* node (located beneath Programmability, just as in SSMS) for *SampleDb* beneath the LocalDB instance. Right-click the *Stored Procedures* node, choose Refresh, and you will see the *uspRankCustomers* stored procedure you just deployed. Right-click on the stored procedure and choose Debug Procedure. SSDT generates an *EXEC* statement to invoke *uspRankCustomers* and opens it in a new query window. The debugger is already started, and is paused on the *USE [SampleDb]* statement above the *EXEC* statement.

More Info The debugging session began instantly in this case because the *uspRankCustomers* stored procedure being debugged has no parameters. When stored procedure parameters are expected, SSDT will first display a dialog to solicit the parameter values, and then plug those values into the EXEC statement before starting the debugger.

Press **F5** to continue execution. The debugger reaches the *EXEC* statement, enters the stored procedure, and then breaks on the *OPEN curCustomer* statement where you previously set the breakpoint. Now start single stepping through the stored procedure's execution with the debugger's F10 keystroke. Press **F10** three times to step over the next three statements. This opens the cursor, fetches the first customer from it, and you are now paused on the first *IF* statement that tests the first customer's order total for zero dollars.

Earlier, you copied six customer rows from the *SQL2012DEV* database to LocalDB, but we specifically instructed you not to copy any order data. So this loop will iterate each customer, and (based on an order total of zero dollars) assign a ranking value of 1 for every customer. Rather than interrupting your debugging session now to import some sample order data and start over, you will use the debugger's Locals window to simulate non-zero order totals for the first two customers. Click the Debug menu, and then choose Windows | Locals.

In the Locals window, you can see that *@CustomerId* is 1 (this is the first customer) and *@OrderTotal* is 0 (expected, because there's no sample order data). *@RankingId* is not yet set, but if you allow execution to continue as-is, the customer will be ranked with a 1. Double-click the 0.0000 value for *@OrderTotal* in the Locals window, type **5000** and press **Enter**. Now the stored procedure thinks that the customer actually has $5,000 in total orders. Press **F10** to single step. Because *@OrderTotal* no longer equals zero, execution advances to the next *IF* condition that tests the order total for being under $100. Press **F10** again and execution advances to the next *IF* condition that tests for under $1,000. Press **F10** once more to reach the *IF* condition testing for under $10,000. This condition yields true (there are $5,000 in total orders), so pressing **F10** to single step once more advances to the *SET* statement that assigns a ranking value of 4. This is the correct value for orders in the range of $1,000 to $10,000. Figure 1-18 shows the debugging session paused at this point.

Continue pressing **F10** to single step through the remaining *SET*, *UPDATE*, and *FETCH NEXT* statements, and then back up again to the first *IF* statement testing the second customer's order total value for zero dollars. Use the Locals window to fake another amount; this time change *@OrderTotal* to **150**. Single step a few more times to make sure that this results in the stored procedure assigning a ranking value of 3 this time, which is the correct value for orders in the range of $100 to $1,000. Now press **F5** to let the stored procedure finish processing the rest of the customers with no more intervention on your part.

When the stored procedure completes execution, right-click the *Customer* table in SQL Server Object Explorer (be sure to pick the LocalDB instance and not *SQL2012DEV*) and choose View Data. The table data confirms that the first customer's ranking was set to 4, the second customer's ranking was set to 3, and all the other customer rankings were set to 1 (if you already have a *Customer* table window open from before, the previous values will still be displayed; you need to click the Refresh button in the toolbar to update the display).

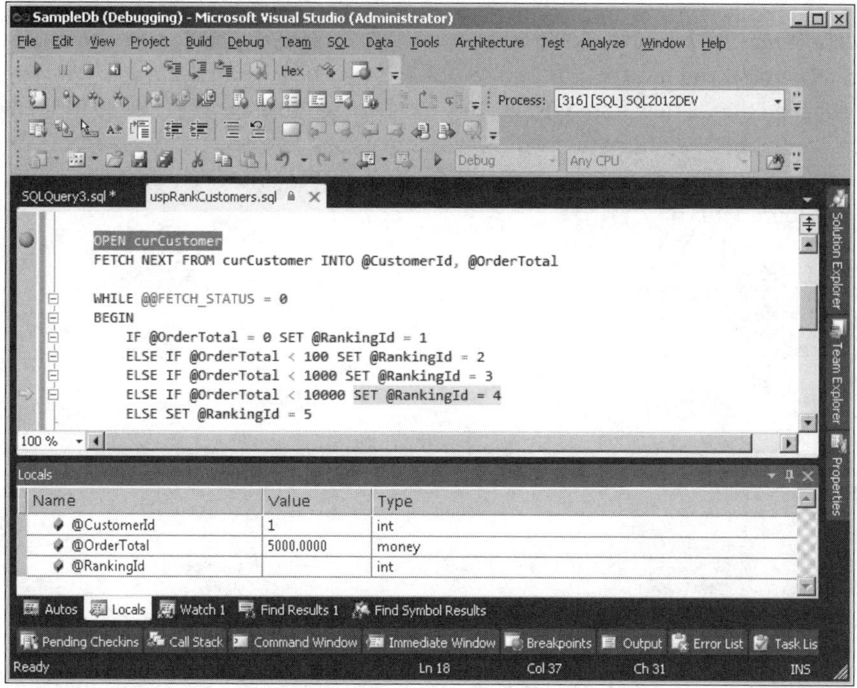

FIGURE 1-18 T-SQL debugging session of a stored procedure in Visual Studio.

This was by no means exhaustive testing, but it will suffice for demonstration purposes. The key point is that SSDT provides an environment you can use for debugging and testing as you develop your database offline, until you're ready to deploy to a live environment (as you are now).

Comparing Schemas

You are ready to deploy to the database back to the live server on *SQL2012DEV*. As you may have correctly surmised by now, the process is fundamentally the same as working offline with LocalDB each time F5 is pressed: SSDT runs a schema compare to generate a change script. The project properties (by default) specify a connection string that points to LocalDB. So building with F5 uses the test database as the target for the schema compare with the project as the source, and then executes the generated change script against the test database on LocalDB. This all happens as a completely unattended set of operations every time you press F5.

Now you will carry out those very same steps once again, only this time you'll get more involved in the process. In particular, you will specify the live *SQL2012DEV* instance as the target for the schema compare, rather than LocalDB. You will also review the results of the schema compare, and have the chance to choose to deploy or not deploy specific detected changes. Finally, you'll get the opportunity to view, edit, save, and execute the change script after it is generated, rather than having it execute automatically. So there's a bit more intervention involved in the process now, but you *want* it that way. The schema compare process itself is the same as the F5 build—you just get to exercise more control over it to support different deployment scenarios.

Right-click the *SampleDb* project in Solution Explorer and choose Schema Compare to open a new schema compare window. You need to specify a source and target for any schema compare, naturally. Because you launched the window from the SQL Server Database Project context menu in Solution Explorer, Visual Studio sets the source to the project automatically, leaving you to set just the target. To set the target, click its drop-down list and choose Select Target to display the Select Target Schema dialog, shown in Figure 1-19.

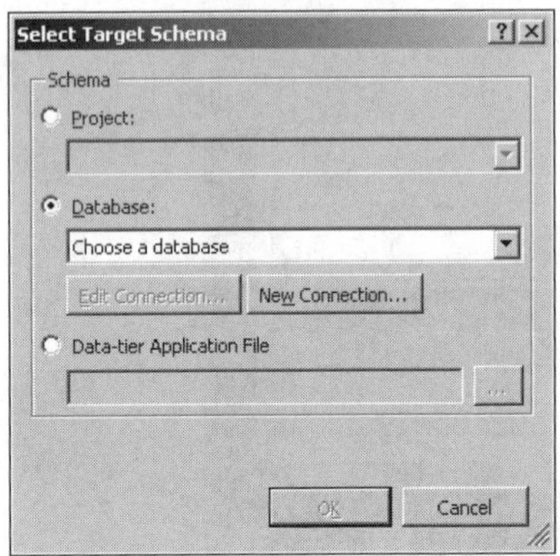

FIGURE 1-19 SSDT lets you choose between projects, databases, and snapshots for schema compare operations.

Notice how you can choose between three schemas for the target—a project, a database, or a data-tier application file (snapshot). The same choices are also supported for the source, although the SQL Server Database Project was assumed as the source automatically in this case. Any combination of source and target source schemas is supported; SSDT simply creates source and target models from your choice of backings. Then, working off the models, it shows you the differences and generates a change script for you. This flexibility is a major benefit of model-based database development with SSDT.

The Select Target Schema dialog has correctly assumed that you want to use a database as the target. All you need to do is choose the live *SampleDb* database running on *SQL2012DEV*. Click New Connection to open a Connection Properties dialog, type your actual machine name for the server name (which is *SQL2012DEV* in the current example), choose *SampleDb* from the database name drop-down list, and click OK. (Visual Studio will remember this connection for the future, and make it available for recall in the database dropdown the next time you run a schema compare.) Click OK once more, and then click the Compare button in the toolbar to start the schema compare.

It takes just a few moments for the operation to complete. When it finishes, the schema compare displays all the changes you've made offline since creating the project (steps 2 through 6). The report lets you see each added, changed, and dropped object, and it can be organized by type (table, view, and so on), schema, or action (change, add, or delete). Selecting any object in the top pane presents its T-SQL declaration in the bottom pane, side-by-side (source on the left, target on the right), with synchronized scrollbars. The T-SQL is color-coded to highlight every one of the object's differences.

If desired, you can exclude specific objects from the change script (which hasn't been generated yet) by clearing their individual checkboxes back up in the top pane.

Select the *vwCustomerOrderSummary* view in the top pane to see the source and target versions of the view in the bottom pane. As shown in Figure 1-20, the rich visual display rendered by the schema compare tool makes it easy to identify all the changes made to the view.

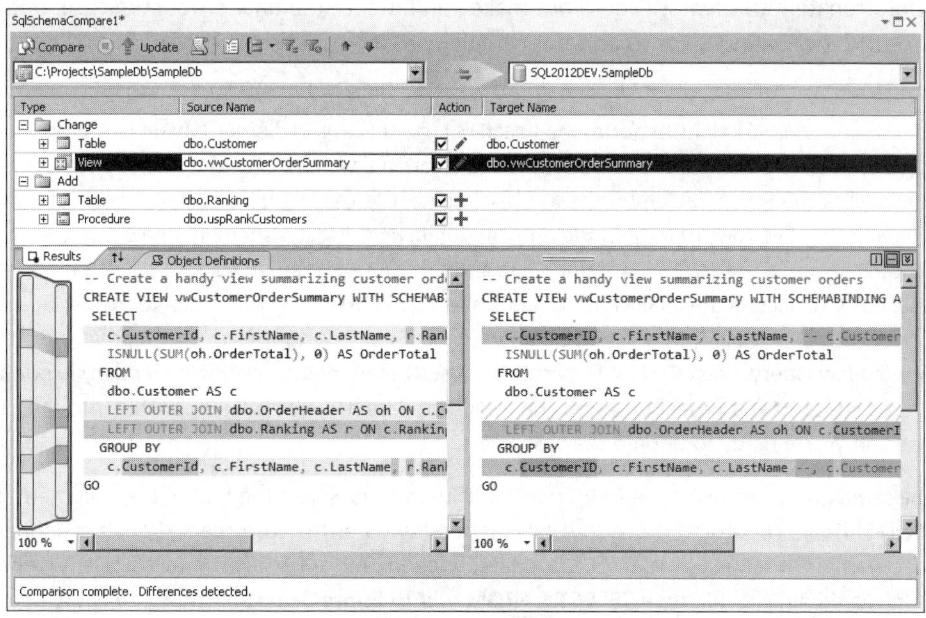

FIGURE 1-20 Viewing the schema differences between a SQL Server Database Project and a live database.

As with the table designer, you can choose to update the live database immediately by generating and running the change script without previewing it. Or you can choose to be more cautious, and just generate the change script. Then you can view, edit, and ultimately decide whether or not to execute it. Your confidence level should be very high by now, so just click the Update button in the toolbar (and then click Yes to confirm) to let it run. SSDT updates the target database and displays a completion message when it's done. Click OK to dismiss the message. The differences from before the update are still displayed in the window, now dimmed in gray (you can click Compare again to confirm that there are no longer any differences between the project and the live database on *SQL2012DEV*). In SQL Server Object Explorer, drill down on *SampleDb* under *SQL2012DEV* (or refresh already drilled down nodes) to verify that it reflects all the work performed in the project for steps 2 through 6 on your task list.

You are almost ready to run the new *uspRankCustomers* stored procedure and update the live *Customer* table, but there's one more thing to do before that. Although the deployment created the *schema* of the *Ranking* table, it didn't copy its *data*. You need to import the reference data from the spreadsheet in Figure 1-7 again, this time into the live database on *SQL2012DEV*. You can certainly use the same copy/paste trick we showed earlier when you imported the spreadsheet into the test database on LocalDB, but we'll take this opportunity now to show you how to script table data with SSDT.

Note The *Ranking* table is a typical example of reference data. Databases often rely on reference data, which are usually small sets of read-only entries, to help define their structure. Although technically not schema, it would certainly be convenient to mark the contents of the *Ranking* table as such, so that the five entries it contains become part of the SSDT database model and travel with the schema definition wherever you deploy it to. Unfortunately, this feature could not make it in time for the final product release, but Microsoft is evaluating plans to add this capability to a future version of SSDT.

Under the *(localdb)\SampleDb* node (the LocalDB instance) in SQL Server Object Explorer, right-click the *Ranking* table and choose View Data to open a window showing the five rows in the table. Next, click the Script button on the toolbar (the next to the last button). SSDT generates *INSERT* statements for the five rows of data in the *Ranking* table, and displays them in a new query window. You want to execute these *INSERT* statements in a query window connected to the live database on *SQL2012DEV*, so select all the *INSERT* statements and press **Ctrl+C** to copy them to the clipboard. Then under the *SQL2012DEV* node in SQL Server Object Explorer, right-click the *SampleDb* database and choose New Query. Press **Ctrl+V** to paste the *INSERT* statements into the new query window and then press **Ctrl+Shift+E** to execute them. The reference data has now been imported into the live database and you're ready to update the customers.

In the same query window, type **EXEC uspRankCustomers**, select the text of the statement, and press **Ctrl+Shift+E**. The stored procedure executes and updates the customers. (You can ignore the null value warning; it refers to the *SUM* aggregate function in the view, which does not affect the result.) To see the final result, type **SELECT * FROM vwCustomerOrderSummary**, select it, and press **Ctrl+Shift+E** once again. As shown in Figure 1-21, each customer's ranking is correctly assigned based on their total order amount.

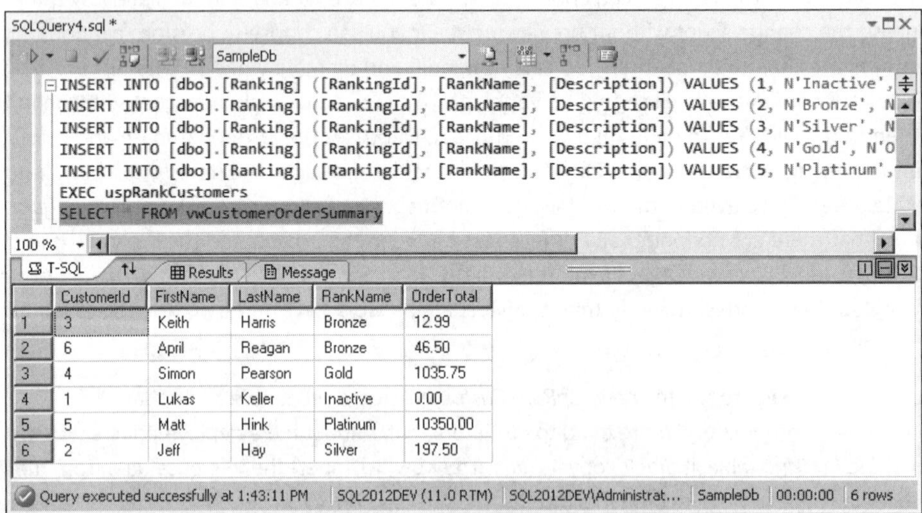

FIGURE 1-21 Viewing the final results of offline development in the live database.

Publishing to SQL Azure

The marketing team's last request was that you deploy a copy of the database to SQL Azure. To ensure that the database is cloud-ready, you just need to tell SSDT that you are targeting the SQL Azure platform by changing a property of the project. Then, if any SQL Azure compatibility issues are identified, they can be resolved before you deploy. As you might expect by now, you will use the very same techniques you've learned throughout this chapter to deploy the SQL Server Database Project to SQL Azure.

Note Our discussion in this section assumes you already have an available SQL Azure server instance that you can publish to. SQL Azure server names always begin with a unique identifier randomly assigned just to you, followed by *.database.windows.net*. Chapter 12 (which is dedicated to SQL Azure) explains how to use the Azure Management Portal to create your own cloud databases on SQL Azure, after setting up a Windows Azure account.

Right-click the *SampleDb* project in Solution Explorer and choose Properties. In the Project Settings tab, you'll notice that the Target Platform is currently set to SQL Server 2012. Change it to SQL Azure as shown in Figure 1-22, press **Ctrl+S** to save the properties, and then close the properties window.

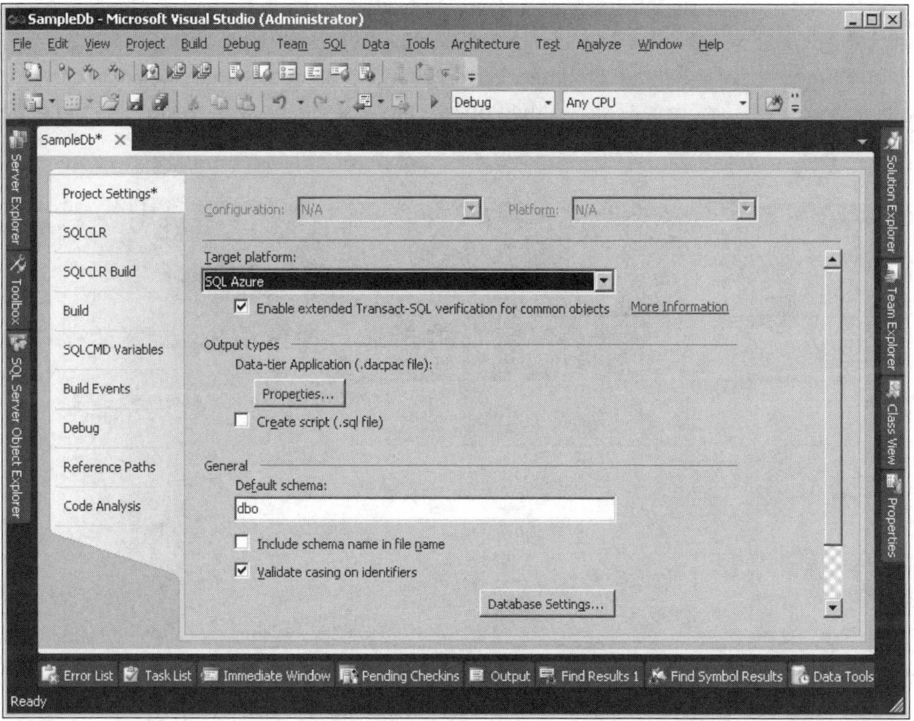

FIGURE 1-22 Changing the target platform of a SQL Server Database Project to SQL Azure.

Now press **F5** to once again build the project and deploy it to LocalDB. The build fails, and the Error List pane shows the following error:

```
SQL71560: Table [dbo].[OrderHeader] does not have a clustered index.  Clustered indexes are
required for inserting data in this version of SQL Server.
```

This error informs you that the *OrderHeader* table is missing a clustered index. The astute reader might have noticed back in Listing 1-1 that the *OrderHeaderId* column in this table does not specify *PRIMARY KEY* (like the *Customer* table does on its *CustomerId* column), and so *OrderHeader* has no clustered index. This was an oversight that might not have been caught so easily because tables in on-premise editions of SQL Server do not require a clustered index. But SQL Azure databases absolutely require a clustered index on every table, so now that you're targeting the cloud specifically, the problem is brought to your attention inside the project.

This is a quick and easy fix to make using the table designer. Back in the SQL Server Database Project (in Solution Explorer), double-click the *OrderHeader.sql* table (under the dbo and Tables folders) to open the project's definition of the table in the designer. Right-click the *OrderHeaderId* column, choose Set Primary Key, save, and then close the table designer. The primary key definition results in the creation of a clustered index on the table. This resolves the issue, and you'll see the error disappear from the Error List pane immediately.

Now that you know the database is cloud-compatible, you're ready to deploy it to SQL Azure. Right-click the SQL Server Database Project in Solution Explorer and choose Publish to display the Publish Database dialog. Click Edit, enter the server and login information for your SQL Azure database, and click OK. Figure 1-23 shows the Publish Database dialog with the target connection string pointing to a SQL Azure database.

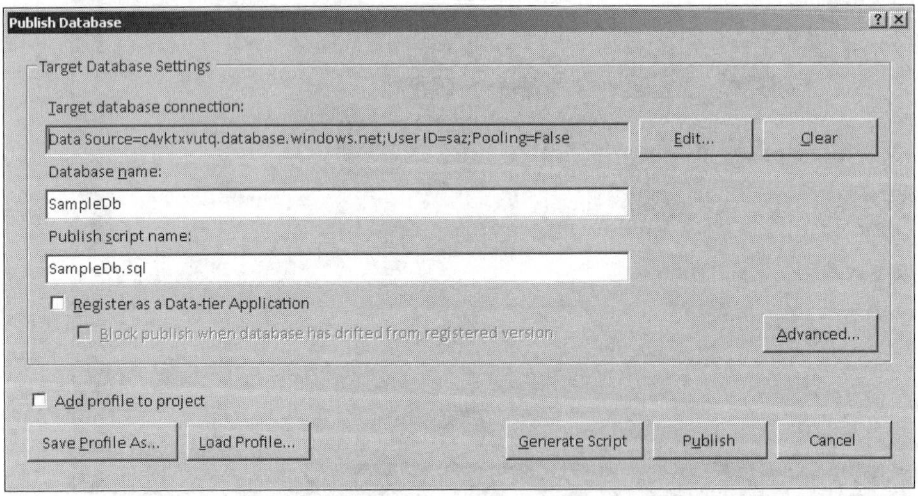

FIGURE 1-23 The Publish Database dialog set to deploy the project to a SQL Azure target instance.

As we've been noting all along, you can script the deployment without executing it by clicking Generate Script. But you're ready to deploy to SQL Azure right now. Click Publish, and Visual Studio spins up the same familiar process. It performs a schema compare between the source SQL Server Database Project and target SQL Azure instance, and then generates and executes the resulting change script on the target. As with your very first build to LocalDB, the database does not exist yet on the target, so the change script creates the whole database in the cloud from scratch. Subsequent deployments will generate incremental change scripts that specify just the actions needed to synchronize the SQL Azure database with the project.

During the deployment process, the Data Tools Operations window in Visual Studio provides a dynamic display of what's happening. Figure 1-24 shows the Data Tools Operations window after the publish process is complete.

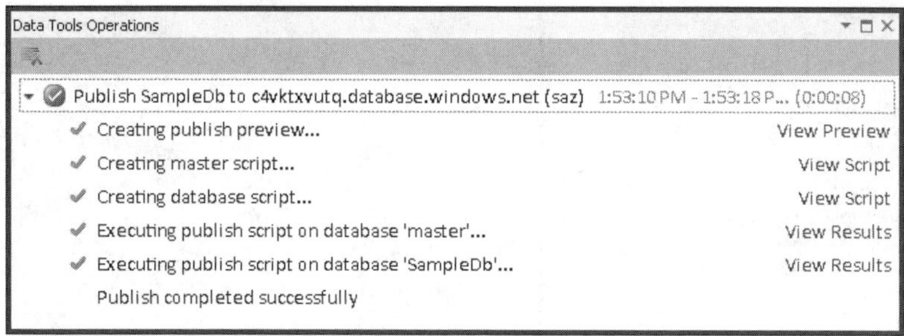

FIGURE 1-24 The Data Tools Operations pane reports all the actions taken to deploy to SQL Azure.

A really nice feature of the Data Tools Operations pane is the ability to see the scripts that were just executed inside query windows and view their execution results. Click the various links (View Preview, View Script, and View Results) to review the deployment you just ran.

After deploying, SSDT automatically adds your SQL Azure server instance to the SQL Server Object Explorer, as shown in Figure 1-25. You can drill down on SQL Azure databases in SQL Server Object Explorer and work with them using the very same development tools and techniques that we've shown throughout this chapter. It's exactly the same model-based, buffered experience you have with connected development of on-premise databases, only now it's a SQL Azure database backing the model. Thus, SQL Server Object Explorer functions as a single access point for connected development against any SQL Server database, wherever it's located.

You've used SSDT to successfully implement all the tasks to fulfill your requirements. Before concluding your work, take another snapshot. Right-click the project in Solution Explorer one last time and choose Snapshot Project. SSDT serializes the database model (based on the project's current state) into another *.dacpac* file in the Snapshots folder, which you should rename to **Version1Complete.dacpac**.

Now your project has two snapshots, *Version1Baseline.dacpac* and *Version1Complete.dacpac*, and each represents the database structure at two different points in time. The collection will grow over time as you take new snapshots during future development, and thus your project accumulates an historical account of its database structure as it changes with each new version. And because any snapshot can serve as either the source or target model of a schema compare operation, it's very easy to difference between any two points in time, or between any single point in time and either a live database (on-premise or SQL Azure) or an offline SQL Server Database Project.

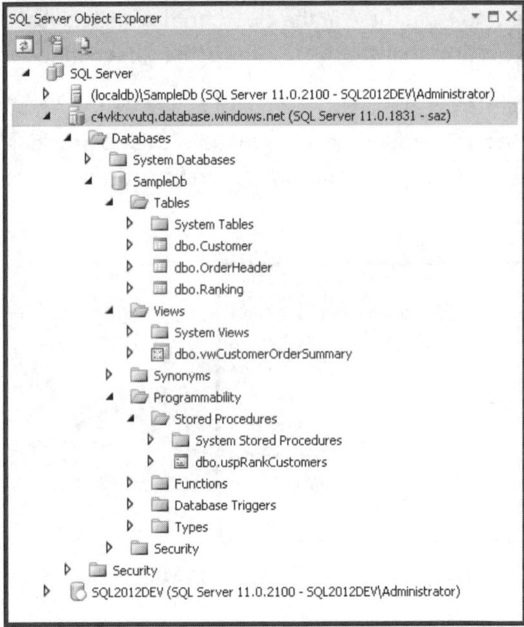

FIGURE 1-25 A SQL Azure database connected in SQL Server Object Explorer.

Adopting SSDT

No tool is perfect, and SSDT is no exception. Yet even as we call out those areas where the tool is lacking, we'll still emphasize what big believers we are in this new technology, and that we greatly encourage SSDT adoption over traditional database development methods. The SSDT team has done a fantastic job with the model-based design, and there is a lot more tooling still that can be provided by leveraging the model's rich metadata, such as database diagrams and query designers that are not yet provided. There is also no spatial viewer to graphically display spatial query results, such as the one provided in SQL Server Management Studio (we cover spatial queries and the spatial viewer in Chapter 9).

Although SSDT is intimately aware of database schema, it does not provide data-oriented functionality. So it can't generate data or compare data in the database, nor does it support database unit testing. These are important features supported by the Visual Studio Database Professional edition (DbPro) that are still missing from SSDT. This means that, although SSDT is positioned to obsolesce DbPro, that won't happen until it achieves parity with key components of the DbPro feature set.

Summary

This chapter began with a high-level overview describing the many challenges developers face working with databases during the development process. Through hands-on exercises, you then saw how the new SQL Server Data Tools (SSDT) provides features that can help you tackle those challenges.

You worked through a number of scenarios using SSDT for connected development, offline development with the local database runtime (LocalDB), source control, debugging, and testing—and then deployed to a local environment as well as the cloud—all from within Visual Studio. Along the way, you learned how to use many important SSDT features, such as schema compare, refactoring, snapshot versioning, and multi-platform targeting. Although you can always learn more about the new tools just by using them, this chapter has prepared you to use SSDT as you encounter the many challenging SQL Server development tasks that lie ahead.

CHAPTER 2

T-SQL Enhancements

—*Leonard Lobel*

As SQL Server evolves, Microsoft continues to improve and enhance Transact SQL (T-SQL)—the native procedural programming language that developers have been using since the birth of the product. Today, T-SQL maintains its role as the primary language for programming the relational database engine, even as numerous other capabilities and programmability points are added to the SQL Server stack with each new release.

It is true that SQL Server Common Language Runtime integration (SQL CLR) allows you to use C# or Visual Basic (VB) .NET as an alternative to T-SQL for writing stored procedures, triggers, and other database objects. This important capability was added in SQL Server 2005, and Chapter 3 covers SQL CLR in detail. You will see that SQL CLR is a great solution when the rich, managed environment afforded by the .NET Framework can be leveraged advantageously on the database server. Internally, SQL Server leverages SQL CLR to implement the *hierarchyid* (Chapter 7) and *geometry/geography* (Chapter 9) data types. Prior to SQL CLR, extended stored procedures were the primary means for programming functionality that could not be achieved using T-SQL alone. Thus, SQL CLR stored procedures are certainly recommended as a safe replacement for extended stored procedures (which have the potential to crash SQL Server if they encounter an error).

But in almost all other cases, you will still want to use T-SQL as your primary language for programming the most efficient set-based queries and stored procedures at the database level. In this chapter, we'll begin with in-depth coverage of these T-SQL features first introduced in SQL Server 2008:

- Table-valued parameters (TVPs)
- Date and time data types
- The *MERGE* statement
- The INSERT OVER DML syntax
- The *GROUPING SETS* operator

We'll then explore these new T-SQL features in SQL Server 2012:

- Windowing enhancements with the *OVER* clause
- New T-SQL functions

- Error handling improvements with the *THROW* statement
- Server-side result set paging with *OFFSET* and *FETCH NEXT*
- Sequential number generation with the *SEQUENCE* object
- Metadata discovery

Note You can use either SQL Server Management Studio (SSMS) or SQL Server Data Tools (SSDT), which we cover in Chapter 1, to run the code in this chapter.

Table-Valued Parameters

As the name implies, a table-valued parameter (TVP) lets you pass an entire set of rows as a single *parameter* to T-SQL stored procedures and user-defined functions (UDFs). This is extremely useful in and of itself, but arguably the most compelling facet of TVPs is their ability to marshal an entire set of rows across the network, from your .NET client to your SQL Server database, with a single stored procedure call (one roundtrip) and a single table-valued parameter.

Prior to SQL Server 2008, developers were forced to resort to clever hacks in an effort to reduce multiple roundtrips into one when inserting multiple rows—using techniques such as XML, delimited or encoded text, or even (gasp) accepting hundreds (up to 2100!) of parameters. But special logic then needs to be implemented for packaging and unpackaging the parameter values on both sides of the wire. Worse, the code to implement that logic is often gnarly and unmaintainable. None of those techniques even come close to the elegance and simplicity of using TVPs, which offer a native solution to this problem.

More Than Just Another Temporary Table Solution

A TVP is based on a *user-defined table type*, which you create to describe the schema for a set of rows that can be passed to stored procedures and UDFs. It's helpful to begin understanding TVPs by first comparing them to similar "set" constructs, such as table variables, temp tables, and Common Table Expressions (CTEs). All of these provide a source of tabular data that you can query and join against, so you can treat a TVP, table variable, temporary table, or CTE just like you would an ordinary table or view in virtually any scenario.

CTEs and table variables store their row data in memory—assuming reasonably sized sets that don't overflow the RAM cache allocated for them, in which case, they do push their data into *tempdb*. In contrast, a TVP's data is always stored in *tempdb*. When you first populate a TVP, SQL Server creates a table in *tempdb* to back that TVP as it gets passed from one stored procedure (or UDF) to another. Once the stack unwinds and the TVP falls out of scope in your T-SQL code, SQL Server cleans up *tempdb* automatically. You never interact directly with *tempdb*, because TVPs provide a total abstraction over it.

The true power of TVPs lies in the ability to pass an entire table (a set of rows) as a single parameter from client to server, and between your T-SQL stored procedures and user-defined functions. Table variables and temporary tables, on the other hand, cannot be passed as parameters. CTEs are limited in scope to the statement following their creation and are therefore inherently incapable of being passed as parameters.

Reusability is another side benefit of TVPs. The schema of a TVP is centrally maintained, which is not the case with table variables, temporary tables, and CTEs. You define the schema once by creating a new user-defined type (UDT) of type *table*, which you do by applying the *AS TABLE* clause to the *CREATE TYPE* statement, as shown in Listing 2-1.

LISTING 2-1 Defining the schema for a user-defined table type.

```
CREATE TYPE CustomerUdt AS TABLE
  (Id int,
   CustomerName nvarchar(50),
   PostalCode nvarchar(50))
```

This statement creates a new user-defined table type named *CustomerUdt* with three columns. TVP variables of type *CustomerUdt* can then be declared and populated with rows of data that fit this schema, and SQL Server will store and manage those rows in *tempdb* behind the scenes. These variables can be passed freely between stored procedures—unlike regular table variables, which are stored in RAM behind the scenes and cannot be passed as parameters. When TVP variables declared as *CustomerUdt* fall out of scope and are no longer referenced, the underlying data in *tempdb* supporting the TVP is deleted automatically by SQL Server.

You can see that, in fact, a TVP is essentially a user-defined table *type*. Populated instances of this type can be passed on as parameters to stored procedures and user-defined functions—something you still can't do with a regular table variable. Once the table type is defined, you can create stored procedures with parameters of that type to pass an entire set of rows using TVPs.

TVP types are displayed in Visual Studio's SQL Server Object Explorer in the *User-Defined Table Types* node beneath *Programmability* | *Types*, as shown in Figure 2-1 (as it does in SQL Server Management Studio's Object Explorer).

There are many practical applications for passing entire sets of data around as parameters, and we'll explore a number of them in the rest of this section.

Submitting Orders

A typical scenario in which TVPs can be applied is an order entry system. When a customer places an order, a new order row and any number of new order detail rows must be created in the database. Traditionally, this might be accomplished by creating two stored procedures—one for inserting an order row and one for inserting an order detail row. The application would invoke a stored procedure call for each individual row, so for an order with 20 details, there would be a total of 21 stored procedure calls (1 for the order and 20 for the details). There could of course be even larger orders with many more than 20 details. As a result, numerous roundtrips are made between the application and the database, each one carrying only a single row of data.

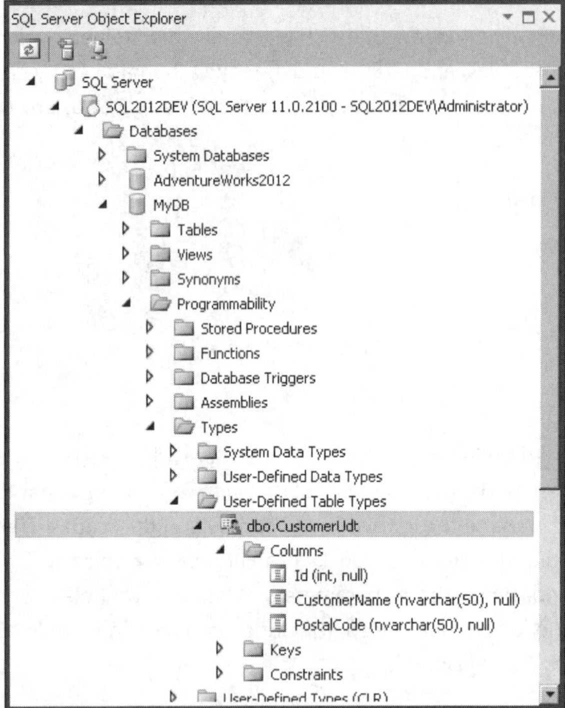

FIGURE 2-1 User-defined table types that can be used for TVPs displayed in SQL Server Object Explorer.

Enter TVPs. Now you can create a single stored procedure with just two TVPs, one for the order row and one for the order details rows. The client can now issue a single call to this stored procedure, passing to it the entire order with all its details, as shown in Listing 2-2.

Note The code in Listing 2-2 assumes that the *Order* and *OrderDetail* tables already exist, and that the *OrderUdt* and *OrderDetailUdt* table types have already been created with a column schema that matches the tables.

LISTING 2-2 Creating a stored procedure that accepts TVPs.

```
CREATE PROCEDURE uspInsertNewOrder
 (@OrderTvp AS OrderUdt READONLY,
  @OrderDetailsTvp AS OrderDetailUdt READONLY)
```

```
AS
     INSERT INTO [Order]
      SELECT * FROM @OrderTvp

     INSERT INTO [OrderDetail]
      SELECT * FROM @OrderDetailsTvp
```

As you can see, this code inserts into the *Order* and *OrderDetail* tables directly from the rows passed in through the two TVPs. You are essentially performing a bulk insert with a single call, rather than individual inserts across multiple calls wrapped in a transaction.

We'll now take look at the bulk insert possibilities for TVPs and how to create, declare, populate, and pass TVPs in T-SQL. Then we'll demonstrate how to populate TVPs and pass them across the network from .NET client application code to stored procedures using ADO.NET.

Using TVPs for Bulk Inserts and Updates

Here's an example of a stored procedure that you can create in the *AdventureWorks2012* database that accepts a TVP and inserts all of the rows that get passed in through it into the *Product.Location* table. By creating a user-defined table type named *LocationUdt* that describes the schema for each row passed to the stored procedure, any code can call the stored procedure and pass to it a set of rows for insertion into *Product.Location* using a single parameter typed as *LocationUdt*.

First, create the user-defined table data type *LocationUdt*, as shown in Listing 2-3.

LISTING 2-3 Creating the *LocationUdt* table type to be used for bulk operations with TVPs.

```
CREATE TYPE LocationUdt AS TABLE(
  LocationName varchar(50),
  CostRate int)
```

Now a TVP variable of this type can be declared to hold a set of rows with the two columns *LocationName* and *CostRate*. These rows can be fed to a stored procedure by passing the TVP variable into it. The stored procedure can then select from the TVP just like a regular table or view and thus use it as the source for an *INSERT INTO...SELECT* statement that appends each row to the *Product.Location* table.

Rows added to *Product.Location* require more than just the two fields for the location name and cost rate. The table also needs values for the availability and modified date fields, which you'll let the stored procedure handle. What you're doing here is defining a schema that can provide a *subset* of the required *Product.Location* fields (*Name* and *CostRate*), for passing multiple rows of data to a stored procedure that provides values for the remaining required fields (*Availability* and *ModifiedDate*). In the example, the stored procedure sets *Availability* to *0* and *ModifiedDate* to the

GETDATE function on each row of data inserted from the TVP (passed in as the only parameter) that provides the values for *Name* and *CostRate*, as shown in Listing 2-4.

LISTING 2-4 Creating a stored procedure to perform a bulk insert using a TVP declared as the *LocationUdt* table type.

```
CREATE PROCEDURE uspInsertProductionLocation
 (@TVP LocationUdt READONLY)
AS
     INSERT INTO [Production].[Location]
       ([Name], [CostRate], [Availability], [ModifiedDate])
      SELECT *, 0, GETDATE() FROM @TVP
```

You now have a stored procedure that can accept a TVP containing a set of rows with location names and cost rates to be inserted into the *Production.Location* table, and that sets the availability quantity and modified date on each inserted row—all achieved with a single parameter and a single *INSERT INTO...SELECT* statement! The procedure doesn't know or care *how* the caller populates the TVP before it is used as the source for the *INSERT INTO...SELECT* statement. For example, the caller could manually add one row at a time, as follows:

```
DECLARE @LocationTvp AS LocationUdt

INSERT INTO @LocationTvp VALUES('UK', 122.4)
INSERT INTO @LocationTvp VALUES('Paris', 359.73)

EXEC uspInsertProductionLocation @LocationTvp
```

Or the caller could bulk insert into the TVP from another source table using *INSERT INTO...SELECT*, as in the next example. You will fill the TVP from the existing *Person.StateProvince* table using the table's *Name* column for *LocationName* and the value *0* for *CostRate*. Passing this TVP to the stored procedure will result in a new set of rows added to *Production.Location* with their *Name* fields set according to the names in the *Person.StateProvince* table, their *CostRate* and *Availability* values set to *0*, and their *ModifiedDate* values set by *GETDATE*, as shown here:

```
DECLARE @LocationTVP AS LocationUdt

INSERT INTO @LocationTVP
 SELECT [Name], 0.00 FROM [Person].[StateProvince]

EXEC uspInsertProductionLocation @LocationTVP
```

The TVP could also be populated on the client using ADO.NET, as you'll learn in the next section.

Bulk updates (and deletes) using TVPs are possible as well. You can create an *UPDATE* statement by joining a TVP (which you must alias) to the table you want to update. The rows updated in the table are determined by the matches joined to by the TVP and can be set to new values that are also contained in the TVP. For example, you can pass a TVP populated with category IDs and names for updating a *Category* table in the database, as shown in Listing 2-5. By joining the TVP to the *Category* table on the category ID, the *uspUpdateCategories* stored procedure can update all the matching rows in the *Category* with the new category names passed in the TVP.

LISTING 2-5 Bulk updates using TVPs.

```
CREATE TABLE Category
 (Id   int PRIMARY KEY,
  Name nvarchar(max),
  CreatedAt      datetime2(0) DEFAULT SYSDATETIME())

-- Initialize with a few categories
INSERT INTO Category(Id, Name) VALUES(1, 'Housewares')
INSERT INTO Category(Id, Name) VALUES(2, 'Maternity')
INSERT INTO Category(Id, Name) VALUES(3, 'Mens Apparel')
INSERT INTO Category(Id, Name) VALUES(4, 'Womens Apparel')
INSERT INTO Category(Id, Name) VALUES(5, 'Bath')
INSERT INTO Category(Id, Name) VALUES(6, 'Automotive')

-- View the list of categories
SELECT * FROM Category

-- Will be used by uspUpdateCategories to pass in a set of category updates
CREATE TYPE EditedCategoriesUdt AS TABLE
 (Id int PRIMARY KEY,
  Name nvarchar(max))
GO

-- Receive multiple rows for the change set and update the Category table
CREATE PROCEDURE uspUpdateCategories(@EditedCategoriesTVP AS EditedCategoriesUdt
 READONLY)
AS
 BEGIN

  -- Update names in the Category table by joining on the TVP by ID
  UPDATE Category
   SET Category.Name = ec.Name
   FROM Category INNER JOIN @EditedCategoriesTVP AS ec ON Category.Id = ec.Id

 END

-- Load up a few changes into a new TVP instance (to categories 1 and 5)
DECLARE @Edits AS EditedCategoriesUdt
INSERT INTO @Edits VALUES(1, 'Gifts & Housewares')
INSERT INTO @Edits VALUES(5, 'Bath & Kitchen')

-- Call the stored procedure
EXECUTE uspUpdateCategories @Edits

-- View the updated names for categories 1 and 5 in the Category table
SELECT * FROM Category
```

Passing TVPs Using ADO.NET

We'll conclude our discussion of TVPs with the new *SqlDbType.Structured* enumeration in ADO.NET. You will learn how easy it is to marshal multiple rows of data from your client application to SQL Server, without requiring multiple roundtrips or implementing special logic on the server for processing the data.

Simply prepare an ordinary *SqlCommand* object (Chapter 10 explains the *SqlCommand* object and ADO.NET in detail), set its *CommandType* property to *CommandType.StoredProcedure*, and populate its *Parameters* collection with *SqlParameter* objects. These are the routine steps for setting up a call to any stored procedure. Then, to mark a *SqlParameter* as a TVP, set its *SqlDbType* property to *SqlDbType.Structured*. This lets you specify any *DataTable*, *DbDataReader*, or *IEnumerable<SqlDataRecord>* object as the parameter value to be passed to the stored procedure in a single call to the server.

In Listing 2-6, a new customer order is stored in separate *Order* and *OrderDetail DataTable* objects within a *DataSet*. The two tables are passed to the SQL Server stored procedure you saw earlier (Listing 2-2 in the section "Submitting Orders"), which accepts them as TVPs for insertion into the *Order* and *OrderDetail* database tables. Note that the C# code listings in this chapter are fragments of a larger solution, abbreviated to conserve space. A fully functional solution is supplied with the sample code for this chapter that you can download from the book's companion website (see the "Introduction" for details). The code for Listing 2-6 is part of the TVPsWithDataTable project in the TSqlEnhancements solution.

LISTING 2-6 Passing *DataTable* objects as TVPs to a SQL Server stored procedure from ADO.NET.

```
// Assumes conn is an open SqlConnection object and ds is
// a DataSet with an Order and OrderDetails table
using(conn)
{
    // Create the command object to call the stored procedure
    SqlCommand cmd = new SqlCommand("uspInsertNewOrder", conn);
    cmd.CommandType = CommandType.StoredProcedure;

    // Create the parameter for passing the Order TVP
    SqlParameter headerParam = cmd.Parameters.AddWithValue
     ("@OrderHeaderTvp", ds.Tables["OrderHeader"]);

    // Create the parameter for passing the OrderDetails TVP
    SqlParameter detailsParam = cmd.Parameters.AddWithValue
     ("@OrderDetailsTvp", ds.Tables["OrderDetail"]);

    // Set the SqlDbType of the parameters to Structured
    headerParam.SqlDbType = SqlDbType.Structured;
    detailsParam.SqlDbType = SqlDbType.Structured;

    // Execute the stored procedure
    cmd.ExecuteNonQuery();
}
```

This code calls a SQL Server stored procedure and passes to it an order header and the complete set of order details in a single roundtrip. Remarkably, it's just as simple as that. You just need to ensure that the schema of the *DataTable* objects match the corresponding TVP-table-type schema.

You can also send a set of rows directly to a parameterized SQL statement without creating a stored procedure. Because the SQL statement is dynamically constructed on the client, there is no stored procedure signature that specifies the name of the user-defined table type for the TVP. Therefore, you need to tell ADO.NET what the type is by setting the *TypeName* property to the name of the table type defined on the server. For example, the code in Listing 2-7 (part of the TVPAdditionalSamples project in the TSqlEnhancements solution for this chapter) passes a *DataTable* to a parameterized SQL statement.

LISTING 2-7 Passing TVPs to a parameterized SQL statement from ADO.NET.

```
// Define the INSERT INTO...SELECT statement to insert into Categories
const string TSqlStatement = @"
 INSERT INTO Categories (CategoryID, CategoryName)
  SELECT nc.CategoryID, nc.CategoryName
  FROM @NewCategoriesTvp AS nc";

// Assumes conn is an open SqlConnection object and ds is
// a DataSet with a Category table
using(conn)
{
    // Set up the command object for the statement
    SqlCommand cmd = new SqlCommand(TSqlStatement, conn);

    // Add a TVP specifying the DataTable as the parameter value
    SqlParameter catParam = cmd.Parameters.AddWithValue
     ("@NewCategoriesTvp", ds.Tables["Category"]);

    catParam.SqlDbType = SqlDbType.Structured;
    catParam.TypeName = "dbo.CategoriesUdt";

    // Execute the command
    cmd.ExecuteNonQuery();
}
```

Setting the *TypeName* property to *dbo.CategoriesUdt* in this code means that you have a user-defined table type by that name on the server, created using the *CREATE TYPE...AS TABLE* statement that defines the *CategoryID* and *CategoryName* columns.

You can also use any object derived from *DbDataReader* (that is, a connected data source) to stream rows of data to a TVP. The example shown in Listing 2-8 (part of the TVPAdditionalSamples project in the TSqlEnhancements solution for this chapter) calls an Oracle stored procedure to select data from an Oracle database into a connected *OracleDataReader*. The reader object gets passed as a single table-valued input parameter to a SQL Server stored procedure, which can then use the Oracle data in the reader as the source for adding new rows into the *Category* table in the SQL Server database (for this code to work, you must have the ADO.NET Provider for Oracle installed and a project reference set to *System.Data.OracleClient*, as well as access to an Oracle database server).

LISTING 2-8 Passing a connected *OracleDataReader* source as a TVP to SQL Server.

```
// Set up command object to select from Oracle
OracleCommand selCmd = new OracleCommand
 ("SELECT CategoryID, CategoryName FROM Categories;", oracleConn);

// Execute the command and return the results in a connected
// reader that will automatically close the connection when done
OracleDataReader rdr = selCmd.ExecuteReader(CommandBehavior.CloseConnection);

// Set up command object to insert to SQL Server
SqlCommand insCmd = new SqlCommand("uspInsertCategories", connection);

insCmd.CommandType = CommandType.StoredProcedure;

// Add a TVP specifying the reader as the parameter value
SqlParameter catParam = cmd.Parameters.AddWithValue("@NewCategoriesTvp", rdr);

catParam.SqlDbType = SqlDbType.Structured;

// Execute the stored procedure
insertCommand.ExecuteNonQuery();
```

Passing Collections to TVPs Using Custom Iterators

What if you're working with collections populated with business objects rather than *DataTable* objects populated with *DataRow* objects? You might not think at first that business objects and TVPs could work together, but the fact is that they can—and quite gracefully, too. All you need to do is implement the *IEnumerable<SqlDataRecord>* interface in your collection class. This interface requires your collection class to supply a custom iterator method named *GetEnumerator,* which ADO.NET will call for each object contained in the collection when you invoke *ExecuteNonQuery.*

Let's demonstrate with the same order entry example as Listing 2-6, only now you'll use ordinary business object collections (rather than *DataTable* and *DataRow* objects) as the source for the TVPs. You have *OrderHeader* and *OrderDetail* classes with properties to match the corresponding TVP-table-type schemas, as shown in Listing 2-9. Of course, a real implementation could include much more than this simple data transfer object, such as encapsulated business logic. The code in Listings 2-9 and 2-10 is part of the TVPsWithBizCollection project in the TSqlEnhancements solution for this chapter.

LISTING 2-9 Defining classes for passing business objects as TVPs.

```
public class OrderHeader
{
  public int OrderId { get; set; }
  public int CustomerId { get; set; }
  public DateTime OrderedAt { get; set; }
}

public class OrderDetail
{
  public int OrderId { get; set; }
  public int LineNumber { get; set; }
  public int ProductId { get; set; }
  public int Quantity { get; set; }
  public decimal Price { get; set; }
}
```

Ordinarily, working with *List<OrderHeader>* and *List<OrderDetail>* objects might be a suitable option for containing collections of *OrderHeader* and *OrderDetail* objects in your application. But in these collections they won't suffice on their own as input values for TVPs because *List<T>* does not implement *IEnumerable<SqlDataRecord>*. The solution is to create *OrderHeaderCollection* and *OrderDetailCollection* classes that inherit *List<OrderHeader>* and *List<OrderDetail>* respectively, and then implement *IEnumerable<SqlDataRecord>* in order to "TVP-enable" them as shown in Listing 2-10.

LISTING 2-10 Defining collection classes with custom iterators for passing business objects as TVPs.

```
public class OrderHeaderCollection : List<OrderHeader>, IEnumerable<SqlDataRecord>
{
  IEnumerator<SqlDataRecord> IEnumerable<SqlDataRecord>.GetEnumerator()
  {
    var sdr = new SqlDataRecord(
     new SqlMetaData("OrderId", SqlDbType.Int),
     new SqlMetaData("CustomerId", SqlDbType.Int),
     new SqlMetaData("OrderedAt", SqlDbType.Date));

    foreach (OrderHeader oh in this)
    {
      sdr.SetInt32(0, oh.OrderId);
      sdr.SetInt32(1, oh.CustomerId);
      sdr.SetDateTime(2, oh.OrderedAt);

      yield return sdr;
    }
  }
}
```

```
public class OrderDetailCollection : List<OrderDetail>, IEnumerable<SqlDataRecord>
{
  IEnumerator<SqlDataRecord> IEnumerable<SqlDataRecord>.GetEnumerator()
  {
    var sdr = new SqlDataRecord(
     new SqlMetaData("OrderId", SqlDbType.Int),
     new SqlMetaData("LineNumber", SqlDbType.Int),
     new SqlMetaData("ProductId", SqlDbType.Int),
     new SqlMetaData("Quantity", SqlDbType.Int),
     new SqlMetaData("Price", SqlDbType.Money));

    foreach (OrderDetail od in this)
    {
      sdr.SetInt32(0, od.OrderId);
      sdr.SetInt32(1, od.LineNumber);
      sdr.SetInt32(2, od.ProductId);
      sdr.SetInt32(3, od.Quantity);
      sdr.SetDecimal(4, od.Price);

      yield return sdr;
    }
  }
}
```

We'll only explain the *OrderHeaderCollection* class; you'll be able to infer how the *OrderDetailCollection* class—or any of your own collection classes—implements the custom iterator needed to support TVPs.

First, again, it inherits *List<OrderHeader>*, so an *OrderHeaderCollection* object is everything that a *List<OrderHeader>* object is. This means implicitly, by the way, that it also implements *IEnumerable<OrderHeader>*, which is what makes any sequence "*foreach*-able" or "LINQ-able." But to the heart of our discussion, it explicitly implements *IEnumerable<SqlDataRecord>*, which means it has a *custom iterator* method for ADO.NET to consume when an instance of this collection class is assigned to a *SqlDbType.Structured* parameter for piping over to SQL Server with a TVP.

Every enumera*ble* class requires a matching enumera*tor* method, so not surprisingly implementing *IEnumerable<SqlDataRecord>* requires providing a *GetEnumerator* method that returns an *IEnumerator<SqlDataRecord>*. This method first initializes a new *SqlDataRecord* object with a schema that matches the table-type schema that the TVPs are declared as. It then enters a loop that iterates all the elements in the collection (possible because *List<OrderHeader>* implicitly implements *IEnumerable<OrderHeader>*). On the first iteration, it sets the column property values of the *SqlDataRecord* object to the property values of the first *OrderHeader* element, and then issues the magic *yield return* statement. By definition, any method (like this one) which returns *IEnumerator<T>* and has a *yield return* statement in it is a custom iterator method; it is expected to return a sequence of *T* objects until the method execution path completes (in this case, when the *foreach* loop finishes).

The crux of this is that you are never calling this method directly. Instead, when you invoke *ExecuteNonQuery* to run a stored procedure with a *SqlDbType.Structured* parameter (that is, a TVP), ADO.NET expects the collection passed for the parameter value to implement *IEnumerable<SqlDataRecord>* so that *IEnumerable<SqlDataRecord>.GetEnumerator* can be called internally to fetch each new record for piping over to the server. When the first element is fetched from the collection, *GetEnumerator* is entered, the *SqlDataRecord* is initialized, and is then populated with values using the *SetInt32* and *SetDateTime* methods (there's a *SetXXX* method for each data type). That *SqlDataRecord* "row" is then pushed into the pipeline to the server by *yield return*. When the next element is fetched from the collection, the *GetEnumerator* method resumes from the point that it *yield return*ed the previous element, rather than entering *GetEnumerator* again from the top. This means the *SqlDataRecord* gets initialized with schema information only once, while its population with one element after another is orchestrated by the controlling ADO.NET code for *ExecuteNonQuery* that actually ships one *SqlDataRecord* after another to the server.

The actual code to call the stored procedure is 100 percent identical to the code in Listing 2-6 that uses a *DataTable* rather than a collection. Substituting a collection for a *DataTable* object requires no code changes and works flawlessly, provided the collection implements *IEnumerator<SqlDataRecord>*. This mean the collection has a *GetEnumerator* method that feeds each object instance to a *SqlDataRecord* and maps each object property to a column defined by the user-defined table type that the TVP is declared as.

TVP Limitations

TVPs have several noteworthy limitations. First and foremost, once TVPs are initially populated and passed, they are read-only structures. The *READONLY* keyword must be applied to TVPs in the signatures of your stored procedures, or they will not compile. Similarly, the *OUTPUT* keyword cannot be used. You cannot update the column values in the rows of a TVP, and you cannot insert or delete rows. If you must modify the data in a TVP, you need to implement a workaround, such as inserting data from the TVP into a temporary table or into a table variable to which you can then apply changes.

There is no *ALTER TABLE...AS TYPE* statement that supports changing the schema of a TVP table type. Instead, you must first drop all stored procedures and UDFs that reference the type before you can drop the type, re-create it with a new schema, and then re-create the stored procedures. Indexing is limited as well, with support only for *PRIMARY KEY* and *UNIQUE* constraints. Also, statistics on TVPs are not maintained by SQL Server.

It's also important to note that the Entity Framework (which we cover in Chapter 10) does not support TVPs. However, you can easily send any collection of Entity Framework entities to a stored procedure that accepts TVPs by coding a custom iterator just like the one you created in the section "Passing Collections to TVPs Using Custom Iterators." This technique is demonstrated in the TVPsWithEF project of the TSqlEnhancements solution that you can download from the book's companion website.

Date and Time Data Types

The *date, time, datetime2,* and *datetimeoffset* types are four date and time data types that were introduced in SQL Server 2008. These types should be used for all new database development in lieu of the traditional *datetime* and *smalldatetime* data types. The newer types are aligned with the .NET Framework, Microsoft Windows, and the SQL standard—unlike *datetime* and *smalldatetime*—and there are improvements in range, precision, and storage as well.

Separation of Dates and Times

We'll begin by looking at the separate *date* and *time* types. If you need to store only a date value (for example, a date of birth), use the *date* type. Similarly, use the *time* type for storing just a time value (for example, a daily medication time), as shown here:

```
DECLARE @DOB date
DECLARE @MedsAt time
```

The *datetime* and *smalldatetime* types, which were the only previously available options, each include both a date and a time portion. In cases where only the date or only the time is needed, the extraneous portion consumes storage needlessly, which results in wasted space in the database. In addition to saving storage, using *date* rather than *datetime* yields better performance for date-only manipulations and calculations, because there is no time portion to be handled or considered. And the *time* type is provided for those less common cases when you require a time without a date; for example, feeding time at the zoo.

More Portable Dates and Times

To store both a date and a time as a single value, use the *datetime2* data type. This data type supports the same range of values as the *DateTime* data type in the .NET Framework, so it can store dates from 1/1/0001 (*DateTime.MinValue* in .NET) to 12/31/9999 (*DateTime.MaxValue* in .NET) in the Gregorian calendar. Contrast this with the allowable date values for the old *datetime* type, which range only from 1/1/1753 to 12/31/9999. This means that dates in .NET from 1/1/0001 through 12/31/1752 can't be stored at all in SQL Server's *datetime* type, a problem solved by using either the *date, datetime2,* or *datetimeoffset* type. Because the supported range of dates is the same in both .NET and SQL Server, any date can be safely passed between these client and server platforms with no concern. You are strongly encouraged to discontinue using the older *datetime* and *smalldatetime* data types and to use only *date* and *datetime2* types for new development (or the new *datetimeoffset* type for time zone awareness, which is discussed next).

There has also been a need for greater precision of fractional seconds in time values. The *datetime* type is accurate only within roughly 3.33 milliseconds, whereas time values in Windows and .NET have a significantly greater 100-nanosecond (10-millionth of a second) accuracy. (The *smalldatetime* type doesn't even support seconds and is accurate only to the minute.) Storing times in the database therefore results in a loss of precision. Like the expanded range of supported dates, the new *time, datetime2,* and *datetimeoffset* types are now more aligned with .NET and other platforms by also providing the same 100 nanosecond accuracy. As a result, you no longer incur any data loss of fractional second accuracy between platforms when recording time values to the database. Of course, there are storage implications that come with greater time precision, and we'll discuss those momentarily.

Time Zone Awareness

The fourth and last data type in this category is *datetimeoffset*. This type defines a date and time with the same range and precision that *datetime2* provides but also includes an offset value with a range of –14:00 to +14:00 that identifies the time zone. In the past, the only practical approach for globalization of dates and times in the database has been to store them in Coordinated Universal Time (UTC) format. Doing this requires back-and-forth conversion between UTC and local time that must be handled at the application level, and that means writing code.

Using the *datetimeoffset* type, you can store values that represent the local date and time in different regions of the world and include the appropriate time zone offset for the region in each value. Because the time zone offset embedded in the date and time value is specific to a particular locale, SQL Server is able to perform date and time comparisons between different locales without any conversion efforts required on your part. Although *datetimeoffset* values appear to go in and come out as dates and times local to a particular region, they are internally converted, stored, and treated in UTC format for comparisons, sorting, and indexing, while the time zone "tags along."

Calculations and comparisons are therefore performed correctly and consistently across all dates and times in the database regardless of the different time zones in various regions. By simply appending the time zone offset to *datetimeoffset* values, SQL Server handles the conversions to and from UTC for you automatically in the background. Even better, you can obtain a *datetimeoffset* value either as UTC or local time. For those of you building databases that need to store various local times (or even just dates) in different regions of the world, this is an extremely convenient feature. The database handles all the details, so the application developer doesn't have to. Time zone functionality is simply available for free right at the database level.

For example, the database knows that 9:15 AM in New York is in fact later than 10:30 AM in Los Angeles if you store the values in a *datetimeoffset* data type with appropriate time zone offsets. Because the New York time specifies a time zone offset of –5:00 and the Los Angeles time has an offset of –8:00, SQL Server is aware of the three-hour difference between the two time zones and accounts for that difference in all date/time manipulations and calculations. This behavior is demonstrated by the code in Listing 2-11.

LISTING 2-11 Time zone calculations using *datetimeoffset*.

```
DECLARE @Time1 datetimeoffset
DECLARE @Time2 datetimeoffset
DECLARE @MinutesDiff int
```

```
SET @Time1 = '2012-02-10 09:15:00-05:00'   -- NY time is UTC -05:00
SET @Time2 = '2012-02-10 10:30:00-08:00'   -- LA time is UTC -08:00

SET @MinutesDiff = DATEDIFF(minute, @Time1, @Time2)

SELECT @MinutesDiff
```

If you run this code, you will see that the *DATEDIFF* calculation returns 255. This indicates that SQL Server is clearly able to account for the three-hour difference in the time zones. Because 10:30 AM in Los Angeles is actually 1:30 PM in New York, a difference of 255 minutes (4 hours and 15 minutes) between that time and 9:15 AM New York time was calculated correctly.

Note Time zone *names* are not supported, nor is there support for daylight savings time. Unfortunately, these features did not make it into the final release of the product, but they are on the list for the next version of SQL Server. Time zones can be expressed only by hour/minute offsets, and you must continue to handle daylight savings time considerations on your own.

Date and Time Accuracy, Storage, and Format

Date values stored in *date*, *datetime2*, and *datetimeoffset* types are compacted into a fixed storage space of 3 bytes. They use an optimized format that is 1 byte less than the 4 bytes consumed by the date portion of the older *datetime* type (supporting a greater range in a smaller space).

Time values stored in *time*, *datetime2*, and *datetimeoffset* types, by default, consume 5 bytes of storage to support the same 100-nanosecond accuracy as Windows and .NET. However, you can specify a lower degree of precision for even more compacted storage by providing an optional scale parameter when declaring *time*, *datetime2*, and *datetimeoffset* variables. The scale can range from 0 to 7, with 0 offering no fractional-second precision at all consuming 3 bytes, and 7 (the default) offering the greatest fractional-second precision (100 nanoseconds) consuming 5 bytes. The scale essentially dictates the number of digits supported after the decimal point of the seconds value, where a scale value of 7 supports a fractional precision of 100 nanoseconds (each 100 nanoseconds being 0.0000001 second).

The default scale is 7, which offers the greatest precision (to 100 nanoseconds) in the largest space (5 bytes). This means that declaring a variable as *time*, *datetime2*, or *datetimeoffset* is the same as declaring it as *time(7)*, *datetime2(7)*, or *datetimeoffset(7)*, making the following two statements equivalent.

```
DECLARE @StartDateTime datetime2
DECLARE @StartDateTime datetime2(7)
```

If you don't require any fractional precision at all, use a scale of 0, as in the following statement, which consumes only 3 bytes to store a time in *@FeedingTime*.

```
DECLARE @FeedingTime time(0)
```

Two time values with differing scales are perfectly compatible with each other for comparison. SQL Server automatically converts the value with the lower scale to match the value with the greater scale and compares the two safely.

Virtually all industry-standard string literal formats are supported for conveniently representing dates and times. For example, the date May 15, 2012, can be expressed in any of the formats shown in Table 2-1.

TABLE 2-1 Common valid date and time string literal formats

Format	Example
Numeric	5/15/2012, 15-05-2012, 05.15.2012
Alphabetical	May 15, 2012
ISO8601	2012-05-15, 201205153
ODBC	{d'2012-05-15'}
W3C XML	2012-05-15Z

You have similar flexibility for representing times. For example, the same time value can be expressed as 23:30, 23:30 :00, 23:30:00.0000, or 11:30:00 PM. Time zone offsets are expressed merely by appending a plus or minus sign followed by the UTC hours and minutes for the zone—for example, +02:00 for Jerusalem.

Note There are even more possible formatting variations than those we've indicated here, where the purpose has been to convey how accommodating SQL Server is with respect to variations in date and time syntax, rather than to duplicate content from SQL Server Books Online (which you can easily refer to on your own for a complete specification of supported string literal formats for dates and times). In addition, SQL Server 2012 provides several new T-SQL functions (covered later in the chapter in the section "New T-SQL Functions in SQL Server 2012") for parsing and creating culture-specific and culture-neutral dates.

You can use *CAST* or *CONVERT* to extract just the date or time portions of a *datetime2* column for searching. When you perform such a conversion on a *datetime2* column that is indexed, SQL Server does not need to resort to a sequential table scan and is able to perform the much faster index seek to locate the specific date or time. For example, the following code defines a table with a *datetime2* type that has a clustered index. Selecting by date or time only can be achieved using *CONVERT*, while still using the clustered index for efficient searching, as shown in Listing 2-12.

LISTING 2-12 Using *CONVERT* to extract the date and time portion from a *datetime2* column.

```
CREATE TABLE DateList(MyDate datetime2)
CREATE CLUSTERED INDEX idx1 ON DateList(MyDate)
```

```
-- Insert some rows into DateList
INSERT INTO DateList VALUES
 ('2011-10-10 12:15:00'),
 ('2012-04-07 09:00:00'),
 ('2012-04-07 10:00:00'),
 ('2011-10-10 09:00:00')

SELECT MyDate FROM DateList WHERE MyDate = '2011-10-10 12:15:00'
SELECT MyDate FROM DateList WHERE CONVERT(time(0), MyDate) = '09:00:00'
SELECT MyDate FROM DateList WHERE CONVERT(date, MyDate) = '2012-04-07'
```

If you request the estimated execution plan for this code, you will see that the clustered index is leveraged when using *CONVERT* to query either the date or time portion of the indexed *datetime2* column.

Date and Time Functions

All of the traditional date-related and time-related functions, including *DATEADD*, *DATEDIFF*, *DATEPART*, and *DATENAME*, of course fully support the newer date and time data types, and several functions have been added as well. We conclude our discussion of the SQL Server 2008 date and time data types by exploring the T-SQL extensions added to support them. A few additional handy date and time functions were added in SQL Server 2012, which we cover in the section on new SQL Server 2012 functions later in the chapter.

The *SYSDATETIME* and *SYSUTCDATETIME* functions return the date and time on the server as *datetime2* types (with full seven-scale precision accuracy within 100 nanoseconds), just as the *GETDATE* and *GETUTCDATE* functions continue to return the current date and time as *datetime* types. Another new function, *SYSDATETIMEOFFSET*, returns the date and time on the server as a *datetimeoffset* type, with a time zone offset reflecting the regional settings established on the server, which includes awareness of local daylight savings time. The code in Listing 2-13 shows the contrast between the various similar server date and time functions.

LISTING 2-13 Comparing server date and time functions.

```
SET NOCOUNT ON
SELECT GETDATE() AS 'GETDATE() datetime'
SELECT GETUTCDATE() AS 'GETUTCDATE() datetime'
SELECT SYSDATETIME() AS 'SYSDATETIME() datetime2'
SELECT SYSUTCDATETIME() AS 'SYSUTCDATETIME() datetime2'
SELECT SYSDATETIMEOFFSET() AS 'SYSDATETIMEOFFSET() datetimeoffset'
```

Running this code just after 8:20 PM on February 10, 2012 in New York results in the following output:

```
GETDATE() datetime
-----------------------
2012-02-10 20:21:19.380
```

```
GETUTCDATE() datetime
-----------------------
2012-02-11 01:21:19.380

SYSDATETIME() datetime2
---------------------------
2012-02-10 20:21:19.3807984

SYSUTCDATETIME() datetime2
---------------------------
2012-02-11 01:21:19.3807984

SYSDATETIMEOFFSET() datetimeoffset
----------------------------------
2012-02-10 20:21:19.3807984 -05:00
```

The *TODATETIMEOFFSET* and *SWITCHOFFSET* functions allow you to perform time zone offset manipulations. *TODATETIMEOFFSET* will convert any date or time type (that has no time zone offset) to a *datetimeoffset* type by applying whatever time zone offset you provide. *SWITCHOFFSET* makes it easy to find out what the same time is in two different time zones. You provide the *datetimeoffset* for a source location and a time zone offset for a target location, and *SWITCHOFFSET* returns a *datetimeoffset* representing the equivalent date and time in the target location, as shown in Listing 2-14.

LISTING 2-14 Performing time zone offset manipulations using *TODATETIMEOFFSET* and *SWITCHOFFSET*.

```
DECLARE @TheTime datetime2
DECLARE @TheTimeInNY datetimeoffset
DECLARE @TheTimeInLA datetimeoffset

-- Hold a time that doesn't specify a time zone
SET @TheTime = '2012-02-10 7:35PM'

-- Convert it into one that specifies time zone for New York
SET @TheTimeInNY = TODATETIMEOFFSET(@TheTime, '-05:00')

-- Calculate the equivalent time in Los Angeles
SET @TheTimeInLA = SWITCHOFFSET(@TheTimeInNY , '-08:00')

SELECT @TheTime AS 'Any Time'
SELECT @TheTimeInNY AS 'NY Time'
SELECT @TheTimeInLA AS 'LA Time'
```

Here is the output result:

```
Any Time
---------------------------
2012-02-10 19:35:00.0000000

NY Time
----------------------------------
2012-02-10 19:35:00.0000000 -05:00
```

```
LA Time
----------------------------------
2012-02-10 16:35:00.0000000 -08:00
```

You can use *TODATETIMEOFFSET* with *INSERT INTO...SELECT* to bulk-insert date and time values with no time zone information from a source table into a target table and to apply a time zone offset to produce *datetimeoffset* values in the target table. For example, the following code copies all the row values from the *dt2* column in table *test1* (of type *datetime2*, which has no time zone information) into the *dto* column in *test2* (of type *datetimeoffset*) and applies a time zone offset of –05:00 to each copied value:

```
INSERT INTO test2(dto)
 SELECT TODATETIMEOFFSET(dt2, '-05:00') FROM test1
```

The next example retrieves all the *datetimeoffset* values from the *dto* column in the *test2* table, which can include values across a variety of different time zones. Using a *SWITCHOFFSET* function that specifies an offset of –05:00, the values are automatically converted to New York time from whatever time zone is stored in the *test2* table:

```
SELECT SWITCHOFFSET(dto, '-05:00') FROM test2
```

Last, both the existing *DATEPART* and *DATENAME* functions have been extended to add support for microseconds (*mcs*), nanoseconds (*ns*), and time zone offsets (*tz*) in the higher-precision and time zone-aware types, as shown in Listing 2-15.

LISTING 2-15 Using the new date portions in SQL Server 2008 with *DATEPART* and *DATENAME*.

```
SET NOCOUNT ON
DECLARE @TimeInNY datetimeoffset
SET @TimeInNY = SYSDATETIMEOFFSET()

-- Show the current time in NY
SELECT @TimeInNY AS 'Time in NY'

-- DATEPART with tz gets the time zone value
SELECT DATEPART(tz, @TimeInNY) AS 'NY Time Zone Value'

-- DATENAME with tz gets the time zone string
SELECT DATENAME(tz, @TimeInNY) AS 'NY Time Zone String'

-- Both DATEPART and DATENAME with mcs gets the microseconds
SELECT DATEPART(mcs, @TimeInNY) AS 'NY Time Microseconds'

-- Both DATEPART and DATENAME with ns gets the nanoseconds
SELECT DATEPART(ns, @TimeInNY) AS 'NY Time Nanoseconds'
```

Running this code returns the following output:

```
Time in NY
----------------------------------
2012-02-10 20:50:55.7851424 -05:00
```

```
NY Time Zone Value
------------------
-300

NY Time Zone String
------------------------------
-05:00

NY Time Microseconds
--------------------
785142

NY Time Nanoseconds
-------------------
785142400
```

The *MERGE* Statement

The *MERGE* statement does just what its name says. It combines the normal insert, update, and delete operations involved in a typical merge scenario, along with the select operation that provides the source and target data for the merge. Essentially, that means it combines four statements into one. In fact, you can combine *five* statements into one using the *OUTPUT* clause, and even more than that with INSERT OVER DML (a special T-SQL feature syntax, which we cover next).

Prior to SQL Server 2008, separate, multiple statements were required to achieve what can now be accomplished with a single *MERGE* statement. This statement has a flexible syntax that allows you to exercise fine control over source and target matching, as well as the various set-based DML actions carried out on the target. The result is simpler code that's easier to write and maintain (and also runs faster) than the equivalent code using separate statements to achieve the same result.

This first example uses *MERGE* to manage stocks and trades. Begin by creating the two tables to hold stocks that you own and daily trades that you make, as shown in Listing 2-16.

LISTING 2-16 Creating the *Stock* and *Trade* tables.

```
CREATE TABLE Stock(Symbol varchar(10) PRIMARY KEY, Qty int CHECK (Qty > 0))
CREATE TABLE Trade(Symbol varchar(10) PRIMARY KEY, Delta int CHECK (Delta <> 0))
```

You start off with 10 shares of Adventure Works stock and 5 shares of Blue Yonder Airlines stock. These are stored in the *Stock* table:

```
INSERT INTO Stock VALUES ('ADVW', 10)
INSERT INTO Stock VALUES ('BYA', 5)
```

During the day, you conduct three trades. You buy 5 new shares for Adventure Works, sell 5 shares of Blue Yonder Airlines, and buy 3 shares for your new investment in Northwind Traders. These are stored in the *Trade* table, as follows:

```
INSERT INTO Trade VALUES('ADVW', 5)
```

```
INSERT INTO Trade VALUES('BYA', -5)
INSERT INTO Trade VALUES('NWT', 3)
```

Here are the contents of the two tables:

```
SELECT * FROM Stock
GO

Symbol     Qty
---------- -----------
ADVW       10
BYA        5

(2 row(s) affected)


SELECT * FROM Trade
GO

Symbol     Delta
---------- -----------
ADVW       5
BYA        -5
NWT        3

(3 row(s) affected)
```

At the closing of the day, you want to update the quantities in the *Stock* table to reflect the trades of the day you recorded in the *Trade* table. Your Adventure Works stock quantity has risen to 15, you no longer own any Blue Yonder Airlines (having sold the only 5 shares you owned), and you now own 3 new shares of Northwind Traders stock. That's going to involve joining the *Stock* and *Trade* tables to detect changes in stock quantities resulting from your trades, as well as insert, update, and delete operations to apply those changes back to the *Stock* table. All this logic and manipulation can be performed with a single statement using *MERGE*, as shown in Listing 2-17.

LISTING 2-17 Applying trades to stocks using *MERGE*.

```
MERGE Stock
 USING Trade
 ON Stock.Symbol = Trade.Symbol
 WHEN MATCHED AND (Stock.Qty + Trade.Delta = 0) THEN
   -- delete stock if entirely sold
   DELETE
 WHEN MATCHED THEN
   -- update stock quantity (delete takes precedence over update)
   UPDATE SET Stock.Qty += Trade.Delta
 WHEN NOT MATCHED BY TARGET THEN
   -- add newly purchased stock
  INSERT VALUES (Trade.Symbol, Trade.Delta);
```

Let's dissect this statement. It begins of course with the *MERGE* keyword itself, followed by *USING* and *ON* keywords that respectively identify the *target* and *source* of the merge operation, and the *joining keys* used to relate the source and target to each other for the merge. Three *merge clauses* then follow with the *WHEN...THEN* syntax, and the statement is then finally terminated with a semicolon (;).

Important The statement-terminating semicolon (part of the SQL standard) is usually unnecessary in SQL Server. However, the *MERGE* statement absolutely requires it, and you will receive an error if you omit it.

Defining the Merge Source and Target

MERGE has a very elegant implementation in SQL Server. At its core, it operates on a join between the source and target of the merge no differently than the way any standard *JOIN* predicate in the *FROM* clause of any *SELECT* statement works. As you'll see shortly when you examine SQL Server's query plan for *MERGE*, the source, the target, and the join between them are handled internally in exactly the same manner as for a regular *SELECT*. The parts of the *MERGE* syntax that express this select operation include the *MERGE* keyword itself, along with *USING* and *ON*, which respectively specify the target, source, and join predicate, as shown in this snippet from Listing 2-17:

```
MERGE Stock
 USING Trade
 ON Stock.Symbol = Trade.Symbol
```

The target can be any table or updateable view and is specified immediately following the *MERGE* keyword. It is the recipient of the changes resulting from the merge, which can include combinations of new, changed, and deleted rows. In this example, the *Stock* table is the target, and it receives changes merged into it from daily trade information (the source).

The source is the provider of the data, which is the *Trade* table in this example, and is specified with the *USING* keyword right after the target. The source can be virtually anything. This includes not only regular tables and views, but subqueries, CTEs, table variables, remote tables, table-valued functions (TVFs) and TVPs alike, and even text files accessed with *OPENROWSETBYTES*. Fundamentally, anything that is valid in the *FROM* clause of a *SELECT* statement is valid as the source of a *MERGE* statement—nothing more, nothing less.

The join predicate specified by the *ON* keyword that follows defines the column key or keys relating the source and target to each other, no differently than a standard table join. Again, anything you can put in a *SELECT* join can be specified for a *MERGE* join with *ON*. The join defines which records are considered matching or nonmatching between the source and target. In this example, source and target tables are related by the *Symbol* column. The join predicate tells SQL Server what stocks exist and don't exist in both tables so that you can insert, update, and delete data in the target table accordingly. The *type* of join (inner, left outer, right outer, or full outer) is determined by which of the various merge clauses are then applied next in the *MERGE* statement.

The *WHEN MATCHED* Clause

The previous example uses three merge clauses: two *WHEN MATCHED* clauses and one *WHEN NOT MATCHED BY TARGET* clause. Let's look at each of them closely.

The first *WHEN MATCHED* clause executes when a matching stock symbol is found in both the *Stock* and the *Trade* tables, as shown in this code snippet:

```
WHEN MATCHED AND (Stock.Qty + Trade.Delta = 0) THEN
   -- delete stock if entirely sold
   DELETE
```

A match would normally mean updating the quantity value in the *Stock* table by the delta value (amount bought or sold) in the *Trade* table. However, in this scenario, you want to physically delete the row in the *Stock* table if its updated value results in *0*, because that means you don't really own that particular stock at all anymore (as is the case with Blue Yonder Airlines). You can code for that scenario by qualifying the *WHEN MATCHED* clause with an additional predicate that tests whether the stock quantity resulting from the trade yields *0*. This gives you flexibility to provide your own criteria as predicates to your merge clauses, and apply custom business logic as filters to the various matching conditions. In this particular case, you want to remove a row from the *Stock* table using the *DELETE* statement rather than changing its value to *0*.

The next merge clause is another *WHEN MATCHED* clause, but this second one has no predicate qualifying the match condition, as shown in this code snippet:

```
WHEN MATCHED THEN
   -- update stock quantity (delete takes precedence over update)
   UPDATE SET Stock.Qty += Trade.Delta
```

This second clause handles all the other trades of preexisting stock that have not resulted in *0* and changes the stock quantity accordingly using the *UPDATE* statement (that is, the *Stock.Qty* values will go up or down depending on the positive or negative number in *Trade.Delta*). In this example, you want the Adventure Works stock quantity to go up to 15, reflecting the 5 shares purchased on top of the 10 you already owned.

Note An error would occur if you tried to sell more than you owned. In fact, an error would also occur if you tried to sell *everything* that you owned without first catching that condition by deleting the stock in the earlier merge clause. That's because a check constraint on the *Qty* column (defined when you created the *Stock* table at the beginning of the example) instructs the database not to tolerate any zero or negative *Qty* values.

SQL Server has very particular rules governing the use of multiple merge clauses. You are permitted to have one or two *WHEN MATCHED* clauses—but no more. If there are two *WHEN MATCHED* clauses, the first one must be qualified with an *AND* condition, as this example has shown.

Furthermore, one clause must specify an *UPDATE*, and the other must specify a *DELETE*. As demonstrated, *MERGE* will choose one of the two *WHEN MATCHED* clauses to execute based on whether the *AND* condition evaluates to *true* for any given row.

The *WHEN NOT MATCHED BY TARGET* Clause

The last merge clause is *WHEN NOT MATCHED BY TARGET*, as shown in this snippet:

```
WHEN NOT MATCHED BY TARGET THEN
   -- add newly owned stock
  INSERT VALUES (Trade.Symbol, Trade.Delta);
```

This clause handles rows found in the source but not in the target. This refers to stocks that are being traded for the first time, which is the new Northwind Traders stock that doesn't yet exist in the target *Stock* table. The clause has no predicate (although it could), and so there are no additional conditions for the clause. Here, you simply add the new data found in the *Trade* table to the *Stock* table using the *INSERT* statement.

Note The *BY TARGET* keywords are optional for this clause. *WHEN NOT MATCHED* is equivalent to *WHEN NOT MATCHED BY TARGET*.

Only one *WHEN NOT MATCHED BY TARGET* clause is permitted in a single *MERGE* statement. It can be qualified with an *AND* condition, as you saw earlier with *WHEN MATCHED*. (There is no purpose for an *AND* condition on the *WHEN NOT MATCHED BY TARGET* clause in this example.)

After executing the *MERGE* statement in Listing 2-17, the *Stock* table is updated to reflect all the trades of the day merged into it, as shown here:

```
SELECT * FROM Stock
GO

Symbol     Qty
---------- -----------
ADVW       15
NWT        3

(2 row(s) affected)
```

Just as desired and expected, Blue Yonder Airlines is gone, Northwind Traders has been added, and Adventure Works has been updated. This is a rather impressive result for just one statement! It took less code to write and will take less effort to maintain than the equivalent operations written as separate statements would, and it also runs faster because it is compiled and executed as a single statement. No additional overhead is incurred for the simple reason that this statement operates on the same fundamental principles as your basic *SELECT* statement's *FROM* and *JOIN* clauses.

Using *MERGE* for Table Replication

Let's move on to another example that shows how *MERGE* can be used as a tool for achieving simple replication between two tables. First, define the tables *Original* and *Replica* with identical schemas. Then create a stored procedure with a *MERGE* statement that replicates changes made in the *Original* table over to the *Replica* table, as shown in Listing 2-18.

LISTING 2-18 Creating two tables and a stored procedure that uses *MERGE* to synchronize them.

```
CREATE TABLE Original(PK int primary key, FName varchar(10), Number int)
CREATE TABLE Replica(PK int primary key, FName varchar(10), Number int)
GO

CREATE PROCEDURE uspSyncReplica AS
 MERGE Replica AS R
  USING Original AS O ON O.PK = R.PK
  WHEN MATCHED AND (O.FName != R.FName OR O.Number != R.Number) THEN
    UPDATE SET R.FName = O.FName, R.Number = O.Number
  WHEN NOT MATCHED THEN
    INSERT VALUES(O.PK, O.FName, O.Number)
  WHEN NOT MATCHED BY SOURCE THEN
    DELETE;
```

The *MERGE* statement in this stored procedure handles the replication task by joining the two tables on their primary keys (*PK*) and providing three merge clauses. The first clause processes updates, as shown here:

```
WHEN MATCHED AND (O.FName != R.FName OR O.Number != R.Number) THEN
  UPDATE SET R.FName = O.FName, R.Number = O.Number
```

Here, *WHEN MATCHED* is used to find all the records that exist in both the original and the replica, and then the *UPDATE* statement updates the matching rows on the replica side with the latest original data. Performing such an update when no data has actually changed is wasteful, so the predicate qualifies the merge clause to apply only when a row change is detected in any of the nonkey values between the original and the replica.

The second merge clause handles insertions, as follows:

```
WHEN NOT MATCHED THEN
  INSERT VALUES(O.PK, O.FName, O.Number)
```

As mentioned earlier, *WHEN NOT MATCHED* is equivalent to *WHEN NOT MATCHED BY TARGET*, which returns all the original rows not found in the replica table. These records represent new rows added to the original table since the last merge, which are now added to the replica as well using the *INSERT* statement in this clause.

The *WHEN NOT MATCHED BY SOURCE* Clause

The third, and last, merge clause handles deletions, as shown here, followed by the required semicolon terminator:

```
WHEN NOT MATCHED BY SOURCE THEN
  DELETE;
```

The *WHEN NOT MATCHED BY SOURCE* clause serves as the exact reverse of *WHEN NOT MATCHED BY TARGET* and returns target (replica) rows not found in the source (original) table. This scenario would occur as the result of removing rows from the original table after they have been replicated. Rows removed from the original table need to be removed from the replica table as well, which is accomplished by the simple *DELETE* statement in this clause.

Regarding the use of multiple clauses, *WHEN NOT MATCHED BY SOURCE* has very same rules as *WHEN MATCHED*. You are permitted up to two *WHEN NOT MATCHED BY SOURCE* clauses. If you have two, the first one must be qualified with an *AND* condition. Furthermore, one clause must specify an *UPDATE*, and the other must specify a *DELETE*. If two *WHEN NOT MATCHED BY SOURCE* clauses are specified, *MERGE* will choose one of them to execute for any given row based on whether the *AND* condition evaluates to *true*.

Let's get started with some data. Both tables are empty at this point (which does in fact mean that they are already in sync). Start by filling the original table with a few rows, as shown here:

```
INSERT Original VALUES(1, 'Sara', 10)
INSERT Original VALUES(2, 'Steven', 20)
```

Now call the *uspSyncReplica* stored procedure to bring the replica table up to date. The first time you call the stored procedure, only the *WHEN NOT MATCHED* clause will execute. It will execute twice, actually, once for each of the two rows to be added to replica table from the original table. The rows affected count displayed after running the stored procedure conveys this, as shown here:

```
EXEC uspSyncReplica
GO

(2 row(s) affected)
```

Examining both tables now verifies that the replica is synchronized with the original, as shown here:

```
SELECT * FROM Original
SELECT * FROM Replica
GO

PK          FName      Number
----------- ---------- -----------
1           Sara       10
2           Steven     20

(2 row(s) affected)
```

```
PK          FName      Number
----------- ---------- -----------
1           Sara       10
2           Steven     20

(2 row(s) affected)
```

Now perform some more changes to the original table. A mix of insert, update, and delete operations brings the two tables out of sync again:

```
INSERT INTO Original VALUES(3, 'Andrew', 100)
UPDATE Original SET FName = 'Stephen', Number += 10 WHERE PK = 2
DELETE FROM Original WHERE PK = 1
GO

SELECT * FROM Original
SELECT * FROM Replica
GO

PK          FName      Number
----------- ---------- -----------
2           Stephen    30
3           Andrew     100

(2 row(s) affected)

PK          FName      Number
----------- ---------- -----------
1           Sara       10
2           Steven     20

(2 row(s) affected)
```

Invoking the stored procedure once again brings the two tables back in sync by replicating changes from the original table to the replica, as follows:

```
EXEC uspSyncReplica
GO

(3 row(s) affected)
```

This time, you can see that three rows were affected as the result of one insert (Andrew), one update (Stephen), and one delete (Sara). Examining both tables verifies that the replica is once again synchronized with the original, as shown here:

```
SELECT * FROM Original
SELECT * FROM Replica
GO

PK          FName      Number
----------- ---------- -----------
2           Stephen    30
3           Andrew     100
```

```
(2 row(s) affected)

PK          FName      Number
----------- ---------- -----------
2           Stephen    30
3           Andrew     100

(2 row(s) affected)
```

MERGE Output

The *MERGE* statement supports the same *OUTPUT* clause introduced in SQL Server 2005 for the *INSERT*, *UPDATE*, and *DELETE* statements. This clause returns change information from each row affected by DML operations in the same *INSERTED* and *DELETED* pseudo-tables exposed by triggers. Being able to capture this information in the *OUTPUT* clause is often a better choice than capturing it in triggers, because triggers introduce nondeterministic behavior—that is, you cannot guarantee that multiple triggers on the same table will consistently fire in the same order every time. (This is often the cause of subtle bugs that can be very difficult to track down, and thus triggers should generally be avoided when possible.)

In addition to the columns of the *INSERTED* and *DELETED* pseudo-table, another virtual column named *$action* is supported when *OUTPUT* is used with the *MERGE* statement. The *$action* column will return one of the three string values—'INSERT', 'UPDATE', or 'DELETE'—depending on the action taken for each row. Listing 2-19 shows a slightly modified version of the *uspSyncReplica* stored procedure that includes an *OUTPUT* clause on the *MERGE* statement. The *OUTPUT* clause selects the virtual *$action* column and all the columns of the *INSERTED* and *DELETED* pseudo-tables so that the *MERGE* statement can provide a detailed report of every DML operation it performs. If you have been following along with the steps for the previous version, you'll need to drop everything (the tables and the stored procedure) first. Then, substitute the implementation of the stored procedure in Listing 2-18 with the code shown in Listing 2-19 and repeat the same steps.

LISTING 2-19 Using the *OUTPUT* clause and *$action* virtual column with *MERGE*.

```
CREATE PROCEDURE uspSyncReplica AS

 MERGE Replica AS R
  USING Original AS O ON O.PK = R.PK
  WHEN MATCHED AND (O.FName != R.FName OR O.Number != R.Number) THEN
    UPDATE SET R.FName = O.FName, R.Number = O.Number
  WHEN NOT MATCHED THEN
    INSERT VALUES(O.PK, O.FName, O.Number)
  WHEN NOT MATCHED BY SOURCE THEN
    DELETE
 OUTPUT $action, INSERTED.*, DELETED.*;
```

Running this modified version of the *MERGE* statement for the last set of changes in the replication example produces the following output:

```
$action PK    FName   Number PK    FName   Number
------- ----- ------- ------ ----- ------- ------
DELETE  NULL  NULL    NULL   1     Sara    10
UPDATE  2     Stephen 30     2     Steven  20
INSERT  3     Andrew  100    NULL  NULL    NULL

(3 row(s) affected)
```

This output shows all the actions taken by the merge and all the before-and-after data involved. Of course, you can use *OUTPUT...INTO* instead of just *OUTPUT* like you can with the *INSERT*, *UPDATE*, and *DELETE* statements to send this information to another table for history logging or additional processing. And concluding our treatment of *MERGE*, you'll learn about the INSERT OVER DML syntax introduced in SQL Server 2008 that provides even greater flexibility.

Choosing a Join Method

SQL Server is very smart about examining *MERGE* statements, analyzing different combinations of merge clauses, and automatically performing the appropriate type of join to return the source and target data needed on both sides of the operation. There are four types of joins, and SQL Server cleverly picks the right one for the job based on the merge clauses that it finds in the *MERGE* statement, as shown in Table 2-2.

TABLE 2-2 Source-to-target table join types chosen by SQL Server based on your merge clause(s)

Merge clause	Join type	Returns	Valid actions
WHEN MATCHED	Inner	Matching data in both source and target	Update, delete
WHEN NOT MATCHED [BY TARGET]	Left outer	Source data not found in target	Insert
WHEN NOT MATCHED BY SOURCE	Right outer	Target data not found in source	Update, delete
WHEN NOT MATCHED [BY TARGET] combined with any other clause	Full outer	Source data not found in target, and other matching or nonmatching target data	Insert, update, delete

The *WHEN MATCHED* clause returns rows that are found in both tables (that is, rows in both tables with matching values in the joining key columns defined with *ON*). The query processor treats this as an inner join, because you are retrieving only rows that exist on both sides. Either an *UPDATE* or a *DELETE* operation on matching target rows is permitted in the *WHEN MATCHED* clause.

WHEN NOT MATCHED [BY TARGET] is treated as a left outer join, because it retrieves only source rows that do not exist in the target. Therefore, only an *INSERT* can be performed in the *WHEN NOT MATCHED [BY TARGET]* clause to "fill the hole" in the target with the missing source data.

The *WHEN NOT MATCHED BY SOURCE* clause is the complement to *WHEN NOT MATCHED [BY TARGET]* and results in a right outer join to retrieve only target rows that do not exist in the source. As with *WHEN MATCHED*, you can perform an *UPDATE* or a *DELETE* operation on those target rows missing from the source.

Last, combining *WHEN NOT MATCHED [BY TARGET]* with either or both of the other two clauses retrieves source data not found in the target as well as target data found or not found in the source. In this case, a full outer join is performed between the two tables. You can perform an *INSERT* in the *WHEN NOT MATCHED [BY TARGET]* clause to add source data missing from the target and an *UPDATE* or *DELETE* in the other clause(s) to modify or remove target data.

Important The only valid statement in *WHEN MATCHED* or *WHEN NOT MATCHED BY SOURCE* is *UPDATE* or *DELETE*, and the only valid statement in *WHEN NOT MATCHED [BY TARGET]* is *INSERT*. No other T-SQL statements (including stored procedure calls) are allowed in any of these merge clauses. However, the *INSERT* and *UPDATE* statements in a merge clause are permitted to reference user-defined functions.

MERGE DML Behavior

As you've just learned, the *MERGE* statement combines the four separate DML statements (*SELECT*, *INSERT*, *UPDATE*, and *DELETE*) involved in a merge operation. The actual internal implementation of *MERGE* is the same as the distinct DML statements it encapsulates. This was a good call by Microsoft, because it means that developers can begin using *MERGE* right away to leverage its improved performance and lower maintenance benefits, without concern for breaking any existing code.

All *AFTER* and *INSTEAD OF* triggers that have already been defined in existing tables or updateable views continue to fire when those tables or updateable views are designated as the target of a *MERGE* statement. For example, the *WHEN NOT MATCHED THEN…INSERT* clause fires any insert triggers defined for the target; similarly, the *WHEN MATCHED THEN…DELETE* clause fires delete triggers. There is no concept of a "merge trigger," so it's safe for you to immediately start using *MERGE* in your T-SQL code. Triggers will fire just the same as if you used separate statements instead of *MERGE*. Existing business logic, constraints, and rules all continue to function as they did before.

The same options and features you are accustomed to using with the separate DML statements are also available with *MERGE*. For example, you can use a CTE for the source of a merge by defining it using the *WITH* clause before the *MERGE* statement and then referencing it with the *USING* clause. The *TOP* clause is similarly supported, as are traditional query hints. And of course, both source and target tables can be aliased with *AS* just like tables in regular queries can.

You can see how SQL Server internally implements the *MERGE* statement for the stored procedure that handles table replication by examining the database engine's query execution plan, shown in Figure 2-2.

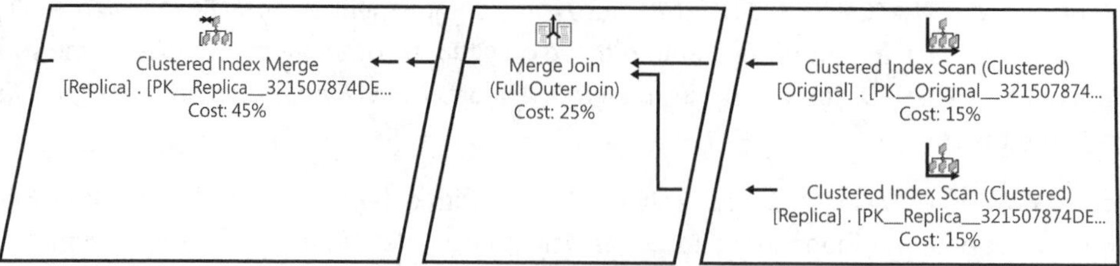

FIGURE 2-2 Query plan for a *MERGE* operation to synchronize a replica with an original (screen image has been cropped to fit the printed page).

The work begins by scanning the source and target table (query plans are read from right to left). At the right of Figure 2-2, you can see the advantage of having created indexes on the columns joining the *Original* and *Replica* tables for the merge. Because the join predicate uses the primary keys of both tables, the query optimizer uses a clustered index scan for the best possible read performance. You should therefore always create an index (possibly clustered and ideally unique) on the joined columns used for merging two tables.

The plan also reveals that a full outer join is performed between the two tables, as shown in the center of Figure 2-2. As mentioned earlier, the type of join used depends on which *WHEN...THEN* merge clauses are (or aren't) specified in the *MERGE* statement. In this case, SQL Server performs a full outer join because the *MERGE* statement uses all three of the possible merge clauses. The clustered index merge operation that follows (at the left of Figure 2-2) implements the predicate on the first merge clause that selects matching rows only if any of the nonkey columns have changed between the original and replica tables.

The clustered index merge consumes the stream delivered by the full outer join and decides on a row-by-row basis whether the row being passed to this operation should be processed as an update, an insert, or a delete, based on the syntax of the *MERGE* statement and the data in the source and target tables.

The INSERT OVER DML Syntax

As you just saw, the *MERGE* statement supports the *OUTPUT* clause to access the *INSERTED* and *DELETED* pseudo-tables, as well as a special *$action* string value that returns 'INSERT', 'UPDATE', or 'DELETE' according to the action performed for each row processed by the merge operation.

The results generated by the *OUTPUT* clause can be captured in another table or table variable using *OUTPUT...INTO*, making it possible to easily maintain historical records of changes in the database. However, because using *OUTPUT...INTO* dumps *every* row captured by the clause into the destination table or table variable, it is not possible to filter on this data.

A Filterable Alternative to *OUTPUT...INTO*

INSERT OVER DML refers to a special syntax in which you wrap an *INSERT INTO...SELECT* statement around any data manipulation language (DML) statement (*INSERT*, *UPDATE*, *DELETE*, or *MERGE*) that has an *OUTPUT* clause, rather than using *OUTPUT...INTO* on the DML statement itself. The subtle but crucial difference here is that *OUTPUT...INTO captures* the changes, while the INSERT OVER DML syntax *consumes* the changes captured by *OUTPUT*. By treating the *OUTPUT* changes as the source for a standard *INSERT INTO...SELECT* statement, you can apply any *WHERE* clause to the *INSERT INTO...SELECT* statement that you want.

Beyond that, there isn't anything more you can do with INSERT OVER DML than what you can with *OUTPUT...INTO*. But to casually overlook the significance of filtering change data is to miss the point of INSERT OVER DML entirely. By being able to filter change data with a *WHERE* clause, you can better control which data changes captured are shipped to the destination table and which aren't. The benefits of this capability are best realized with an example.

In this scenario, you are maintaining an audit of all changes that are posted from one table to another. You have a master list of book prices and shelf locations in the *Book* table where each book is identified by its ISBN number. Every week, you receive a new table named *WeeklyChanges* that contains updates to the book data, also keyed by ISBN number. In addition to price and shelf changes for existing books, the weekly update table can also include new books. You learned already that *MERGE* can handle this scenario (it was *made* to, in fact), and can effectively apply the appropriate updates and inserts from the *WeeklyChanges* table to the *Book* table by joining on *ISBN* and using the *WHEN MATCHED* and *WHEN NOT MATCHED* clauses. You also know that the *OUTPUT...INTO* clause can be used to capture and store all data changes performed by the merge into a history table. To work through the scenario, start first by using *OUTPUT...INTO* to dump these changes to the *BookHistory* table. Then you'll modify the approach to use INSERT OVER DML instead, and gain better control of the change data archival process.

Create the *Book* and *WeeklyChange* tables as shown in Listing 2-20.

LISTING 2-20 Creating the *Book* and *WeeklyChange* tables.

```
CREATE TABLE Book(
  ISBN varchar(20) PRIMARY KEY,
  Price decimal,
  Shelf int)

CREATE TABLE WeeklyChange(
  ISBN varchar(20) PRIMARY KEY,
  Price decimal,
  Shelf int)
```

Next, create the *BookHistory* table. This will be the recipient of the changes captured by the *OUTPUT INTO* clause of the *MERGE* statement, as shown in Listing 2-21.

LISTING 2-21 Creating the *BookHistory* table.

```
CREATE TABLE BookHistory(
  Action nvarchar(10),
  NewISBN varchar(20),
  NewPrice decimal,
  NewShelf int,
  OldISBN varchar(20),
  OldPrice decimal,
  OldShelf int,
  ArchivedAt datetime2)
```

Now create the *uspUpdateBooks* stored procedure to perform the weekly update merge operation. The stored procedure records all data changes to the *BookHistory* table, as shown in Listing 2-22.

LISTING 2-22 Using *OUTPUT...INTO* with *MERGE*.

```
CREATE PROCEDURE uspUpdateBooks AS
 BEGIN

  MERGE Book AS B
   USING WeeklyChange AS WC
    ON B.ISBN = WC.ISBN
   WHEN MATCHED AND (B.Price <> WC.Price OR B.Shelf <> WC.Shelf) THEN
    UPDATE SET B.Price = WC.Price, B.Shelf = WC.Shelf
   WHEN NOT MATCHED THEN
    INSERT VALUES(WC.ISBN, WC.Price, WC.Shelf)
   OUTPUT $action, inserted.*, deleted.*, SYSDATETIME()
    INTO BookHistory;

 END
```

This code should require no detailed explanation, as we just covered *MERGE* thoroughly in the previous section. What's different here, however, is the *OUTPUT...INTO* clause. This clause records the action, new values, old values, and current server date and time in the *BookHistory* table, from the *$action* virtual column, *INSERTED* pseudo-table columns, *DELETED* pseudo-table columns, and *SYSDATETIME* function. (In this particular scenario, *$action* can return only the string *'INSERT'* or *'UPDATE'*, because deletions are not being processed.)

Now populate the *Book* and *WeeklyChange* tables to set the stage for the update, as shown here:

```
INSERT INTO Book VALUES('A', 100, 1)
INSERT INTO Book VALUES('B', 200, 2)
INSERT INTO WeeklyChange VALUES('A', 101, 1)
INSERT INTO WeeklyChange VALUES('C', 300, 3)
```

The *WeeklyChange* table shows a change in price for book A from $100 to $101 and also adds a new book C priced at $300 on shelf 3. When you run the *uspUpdateBooks* stored procedure, those two operations take place as you'd expect. This is confirmed by the number of rows affected message, as shown here:

```
EXEC uspUpdateBooks
GO

(2 row(s) affected)
```

In addition, the actions and data changes made by those insert and update operations (and the dates and times that they occurred) have been saved to the *BookHistory* table as the result of the *OUTPUT...INTO* clause, as shown here:

```
SELECT * FROM BookHistory
GO

Action NewISBN NewPrice NewShelf OldISBN OldPrice OldShelf ArchivedAt
------ ------- -------- -------- ------- -------- -------- ---------------------------
UPDATE A       101      1        A       100      1        2012-02-25 14:47:23.9907552
INSERT C       300      3        NULL    NULL     NULL     2012-02-25 14:47:23.9907552
```

So far, so good, right? Until, after further consideration, you realize that most of your operations will be inserts, and there will be very few updates. Thus, an unacceptable amount of storage is going to be required for capturing the inserts that have no old values and that therefore don't provide any meaningful historical value beyond the creation date and time (which you could store in the *Book* table if you wanted to). Given that every book must be inserted but most books are not typically updated, the result will be a disproportionate amount of inserts over updates in the *BookHistory* table. That's a lot of storage to hold duplicate data that has little or no value. Unfortunately, there's simply no way to filter out the inserts and save just the updates using *OUTPUT...INTO*. In our revised scenario, you are interested in capturing only updates without inserts. This requires filtering, and INSERT OVER DML provides the solution.

You will use INSERT OVER DML in the next example, and—just to keep things interesting—the historical data will be appended to the *Book* table itself, rather than being stored to a separate history table. In the revised example, there is an *ArchivedAt* column in the *Book* table that contains the server date and time for history records added when books are updated. Thus, a *NULL* in this column identifies the rows holding the current values, whereas all other rows with non-*NULL* values in the *ArchivedAt* column represent previous values in history rows.

Start like you did the last time by creating the tables, as shown in Listing 2-23.

LISTING 2-23 Creating new versions of the *Book* and *WeeklyChange* tables for use with INSERT OVER DML.

```
-- Cleanup from previous example
DROP TABLE Book
DROP TABLE WeeklyChange
DROP TABLE BookHistory
DROP PROCEDURE uspUpdateBooks
GO
```

```
CREATE TABLE Book(
  ISBN varchar(20),
  Price decimal,
  Shelf int,
  ArchivedAt datetime2)

CREATE UNIQUE CLUSTERED INDEX UI_Book ON Book(ISBN, ArchivedAt)

CREATE TABLE WeeklyChange(
  ISBN varchar(20) PRIMARY KEY,
  Price decimal,
  Shelf int)
```

Notice this time that a unique index is created on the combined *ISBN* and *ArchivedAt* columns. A primary key cannot be created on just the *ISBN* column as before, because the *Book* table will now contain multiple records with the same ISBN number (because the table holds historical change data as well as current data). Only one row per ISBN number will have a *NULL* value in the *ArchivedAt* column, which is the row that contains the current values for a book. All other rows with the same ISBN number will have non-*NULL* values in *ArchivedAt*, which serves as the time stamp of a previous update and will contain the historical values archived for that book at that time. By ensuring uniqueness between both *ISBN* and *ArchivedAt*, you are guaranteed that only one *current* row for each book is ever stored in the *Book* table, because the table will not tolerate two rows with the same ISBN numbers and *NULL* values for *ArchivedAt*.

Consuming *CHANGES*

You will now implement a modified version of the *uspUpdateBooks* in Listing 2-24 that uses the new INSERT OVER DML syntax to capture and store historical data for updates that are appended to the *Book* table.

LISTING 2-24 Using *MERGE* with INSERT OVER DML.

```
CREATE PROCEDURE uspUpdateBooks AS
BEGIN
 INSERT INTO Book(ISBN, Price, Shelf, ArchivedAt)
  SELECT ISBN, Price, Shelf, GETDATE() FROM
  (MERGE Book AS B
    USING WeeklyChange AS WC
     ON B.ISBN = WC.ISBN AND B.ArchivedAt IS NULL
    WHEN MATCHED AND (B.Price <> WC.Price OR B.Shelf <> WC.Shelf) THEN
     UPDATE SET Price = WC.Price, Shelf = WC.Shelf
    WHEN NOT MATCHED THEN
     INSERT VALUES(WC.ISBN, WC.Price, WC.Shelf, NULL)
    OUTPUT $action, WC.ISBN, Deleted.Price, Deleted.Shelf
  ) CHANGES(RowAction, ISBN, Price, Shelf)
   WHERE RowAction = 'UPDATE';
 END
```

Because there is historical data in the *Book* table that is irrelevant for the merge operation, criteria has been added to the join predicate after the *ON* keyword that tests for *NULL* values in the *ArchivedAt* column. This tells *MERGE* to consider only *current* books as matching target rows against the source of weekly changes and to completely ignore all the archived history records.

The *CHANGES* keyword is what makes INSERT OVER DML possible. *CHANGES* exposes the columns of the *OUTPUT* clause defined on the inner *MERGE* statement to the *WHERE* clause of the outer *INSERT INTO...SELECT* statement. In Listing 2-24, this includes the virtual *$action* column, the ISBN number, and the old values for price and shelf being replaced by the update operation.

By exposing the virtual *$action* through the *CHANGES* keyword as *RowAction*, the *INSERT INTO... SELECT* statement can apply a *WHERE* clause to filter out the actions of newly inserted books and append only the actions of *changed* books back into the *Book* table. As explained, this is something that cannot be achieved using the *OUTPUT...INTO* clause on the *MERGE* statement itself, but is possible using this very specific INSERT OVER DML syntax.

The code filters out insert actions with the simple criteria *WHERE RowAction = 'UPDATE'*. You could of course apply even more sophisticated logic than that if you wanted to. For example, you may wish to save history data for certain users, regions, or any other changed data columns returned by the *OUTPUT* clause and exposed by the *CHANGES* keyword. And that's exactly the key to the power of INSERT OVER DML.

Walk through the scenario step by step. Start with two books (A and B) and one price change (book A from $100 to $110), as shown here:

```
INSERT INTO Book VALUES('A', 100, 1, NULL)
INSERT INTO Book VALUES('B', 200, 2, NULL)
INSERT INTO WeeklyChange VALUES('A', 110, 1)

SELECT * FROM Book
SELECT * FROM WeeklyChange
GO

ISBN Price Shelf ArchivedAt
---- ----- ----- -----------------------
A    100   1     NULL
B    200   2     NULL

(2 row(s) affected)

ISBN Price Shelf
---- ----- -----
A    110   1

(1 row(s) affected)
```

When you execute *uspUpdateBooks*, the inner *MERGE* statement will update the price for book A in the *Book* table and send its original values to the *OUTPUT* clause. The *OUTPUT* clause values are then consumed by the outer *INSERT INTO...SELECT* statement via the *CHANGES* keyword. The outer statement can therefore use those original book values for inserting historical data back into the

Book table with an *ArchivedAt* value set to the current server date and time (just before 5:00 PM on 2/25/2012, in this example), as follows:

```
EXEC uspUpdateBooks
SELECT * FROM Book
GO

ISBN Price Shelf ArchivedAt
---- ----- ----- ---------------------------
A    110   1     NULL
A    100   1     2012-02-25 16:57:19.8600000
B    200   2     NULL

(3 row(s) affected)
```

You can see the current data for book A (the row with an *ArchivedAt* date of *NULL*) at $110, and you also see the previous data for book A, which was changed from $100 at about 5:00 PM on 2/25/2012. Sometime later, you receive a new set of changes. This time, book A has changed from shelf 1 to shelf 6, and a new book C has been added, as shown here:

```
DELETE FROM WeeklyChange
INSERT INTO WeeklyChange VALUES('A', 110, 6)
INSERT INTO WeeklyChange VALUES('C', 300, 3)
GO
```

Just like the first time you ran the stored procedure, the current row for book A is updated, and a snapshot of the previous contents of the row is added to the table with the current server date and time, as shown here:

```
EXEC uspUpdateBooks
SELECT * FROM Book
GO

ISBN Price Shelf ArchivedAt
---- ----- ----- ---------------------------
A    110   6     NULL
A    100   1     2012-02-25 16:57:19.8600000
A    110   1     2012-02-25 16:58:36.1900000
B    200   2     NULL
C    300   3     NULL

(5 row(s) affected)
```

Now book A has two history records showing the values saved from two earlier updates identified by date and time values in the *ArchivedAt* column. There is also a new row for book C, which was inserted by the *WHEN NOT MATCHED* clause of the MERGE statement.

However, notice that there is no history row for book C, because the insert action that was actually captured by the *MERGE* statement's *OUTPUT* clause was subsequently filtered out in the *WHERE* clause of the outer *INSERT INTO...SELECT* statement. Had you not filtered out insert actions in that *WHERE* clause, another history record would have also been added to the table for book C with meaningless NULL values for both *Price* and *Shelf*. Therefore, by filtering *OUTPUT* actions by using

INSERT OVER DML, you avoid the proliferation of history rows that would get generated with each new book. You also eliminated the extra columns for the new values that were used in the previous example's *BookHistory* table, as they are stored in each updated version archived in the *Book* table itself. And you eliminated the need to store an *Action* column, because only update actions are being captured. In the end, a lot of benefit was derived by eliminating needless storage, and it was all accomplished with a single INSERT OVER DML statement.

As you can see, the combination of the *MERGE* and INSERT OVER DML features in SQL Server is a very powerful addition to T-SQL. A fully loaded *MERGE* (handling inserts, updates, and deletes) wrapped up using INSERT OVER DML delivers an enormous amount of functionality in a single, manageable statement. We recommend using these new features in lieu of the traditional multi-statement approaches in whatever future development scenarios you find it possible to do so. In addition to improved performance, you'll appreciate the greater manageability that results from consolidating multiple statements into one.

The GROUPING SETS Operator

The *GROUP BY* clause has been part of the *SELECT* statement syntax since the earliest dialects of T-SQL. You use *GROUP BY* to create queries that collapse multiple rows belonging to the same group into a single summary row and perform aggregate calculations (such as *SUM* and *AVG*) across the individual rows of each group. SQL Server 6.5 later extended the *GROUP BY* clause by adding the *WITH CUBE* and *WITH ROLLUP* operators. These operators perform additional grouping and aggregation of data in standard relational queries, similar to what is provided by online analytical processing (OLAP) queries that slice and dice your data into Analysis Services cubes, but without ever leaving the relational database world. SQL Server 2008 added the *GROUPING SETS* operator that further extends the capabilities of the *GROUP BY* clause for summarizing and analyzing your data.

In this section, you will examine *GROUP BY* in many of its variant forms. You'll start with the basic *GROUP BY* clause, and then you'll learn how the *WITH CUBE* and *WITH ROLLUP* operators can be used to enhance those summary results. Then you'll explore the *GROUPING SETS* operator added in SQL Server 2008.

Start with a simple inventory table that contains quantities for various items in diverse colors that are available at different store locations, as shown in Listing 2-25.

LISTING 2-25 Creating the *Inventory* table.

```
CREATE TABLE Inventory(
  Store varchar(2),
  Item varchar(20),
  Color varchar(10),
  Quantity decimal)
```

Next, add some inventory data. There are 13 rows that contain inventory for tables, chairs, and sofas available in blue, red, and green, at NY, NJ, and PA locations, as shown in Listing 2-26.

LISTING 2-26 Populating the *Inventory* table.

```
INSERT INTO Inventory VALUES('NY', 'Table', 'Blue', 124)
INSERT INTO Inventory VALUES('NJ', 'Table', 'Blue', 100)
INSERT INTO Inventory VALUES('NY', 'Table', 'Red', 29)
INSERT INTO Inventory VALUES('NJ', 'Table', 'Red', 56)
INSERT INTO Inventory VALUES('PA', 'Table', 'Red', 138)
INSERT INTO Inventory VALUES('NY', 'Table', 'Green', 229)
INSERT INTO Inventory VALUES('PA', 'Table', 'Green', 304)
INSERT INTO Inventory VALUES('NY', 'Chair', 'Blue', 101)
INSERT INTO Inventory VALUES('NJ', 'Chair', 'Blue', 22)
INSERT INTO Inventory VALUES('NY', 'Chair', 'Red', 21)
INSERT INTO Inventory VALUES('NJ', 'Chair', 'Red', 10)
INSERT INTO Inventory VALUES('PA', 'Chair', 'Red', 136)
INSERT INTO Inventory VALUES('NJ', 'Sofa', 'Green', 2)
```

Now use a basic *GROUP BY* clause to query on this data:

```
SELECT Item, Color, SUM(Quantity) AS TotalQty, COUNT(Store) AS Stores
 FROM Inventory
 GROUP BY Item, Color
 ORDER BY Item, Color
```

As implied by its syntax, this query groups all the inventory records by item and then by color within each item. The result set therefore includes one summary row for each unique combination of items and colors. The store location is not included in the grouping, and so the results returned by the query apply to all stores. Each summary row includes a *TotalQty* column calculated by the *SUM* aggregate function as the total quantity for all rows of the same item and color across all stores. The last column, *Stores,* is calculated by the *COUNT* aggregate function as the number of store locations at which each unique combination of items and colors is available, as shown here:

```
Item                 Color      TotalQty                       Stores
-------------------- ---------- ------------------------------ ------
Chair                Blue       123                            2
Chair                Red        167                            3
Sofa                 Green      2                              1
Table                Blue       224                            2
Table                Green      533                            2
Table                Red        223                            3

(6 row(s) affected)
```

These results show that SQL Server grouped the inventory records sharing the same item and color into a single summary row. The store location is not included in the breakdown, because you did not group by it, and so each summary row applies to all stores. For each item, the total quantity is calculated as the sum of the individual quantity values for the item and color combinations in each group, and the store count is calculated as the number of store locations at which each item and color combination is available. With *GROUP BY*, every column returned by the query must be either one of the columns actually being grouped by (such as the *Store*, *Item*, and *Color* columns) or an aggregate function that operates across all the combined member rows for the group [such as the *SUM(Quantity)* and *COUNT(Store)* functions].

Rolling Up by Level

This query demonstrates the most basic application of the *GROUP BY* clause, which simply groups and aggregates. It answers the question "How many items per color are in each store location?" by grouping items and colors. The *WITH ROLLUP* and *WITH CUBE* operators (which were introduced in SQL Server 6.5) can be used to answer more questions than that. Each of these operators supplements the results of an ordinary *GROUP BY* clause with additional summary aggregations on the underlying data. Here is the same query you ran before, only this time using *WITH ROLLUP*:

```
SELECT Item, Color, SUM(Quantity) AS TotalQty, COUNT(Store) AS Stores
 FROM Inventory
 GROUP BY Item, Color WITH ROLLUP
 ORDER BY Item, Color
GO

Item                 Color      TotalQty                       Stores
-------------------- ---------- ------------------------------ ------
NULL                 NULL       1272                           13
Chair                NULL       290                            5
Chair                Blue       123                            2
Chair                Red        167                            3
Sofa                 NULL       2                              1
Sofa                 Green      2                              1
Table                NULL       980                            7
Table                Blue       224                            2
Table                Green      533                            2
Table                Red        223                            3

(10 row(s) affected)
```

This time, you receive the same six grouped results as before, supplemented with four additional *rollup* rows (the ones with *NULL* values for *Item* or *Color*, highlighted here in bold). Rollup rows contain additional higher-level summary information that essentially "groups the groups" of the query results. Any row with *NULL* values in it is a rollup row, and the *NULL* should be thought of as "all values" in this context.

In these results, the first row is the top-level rollup, as indicated by *NULL* values for both *Item* and *Color*. This top-level rollup reports a grand total quantity of 1,272 for the entire set (all items in all colors) in all store locations (where the entire set consists of the 13 unique item/color combinations across all locations).

The next result is an item-level rollup for chairs. It reports a total quantity of 290 for chairs in all colors across 5 store locations. The two results that follow are the same summary rows for chairs returned by the first "plain" *GROUP BY* query and that were just rolled up. They show 123 blue chairs in 2 locations and 167 red chairs in 3 locations. The next result is an item-level rollup for sofas. Only one store location carries sofas, and they're available only in green. The sofa rollup therefore contains the same values as the one and only summary row for 2 green sofas available in 1 location. The last set of rows report on tables in the same way that the chair and sofa data was returned. This includes an item-level rollup showing 980 tables across 7 locations followed by the summary rows showing 224 blue tables in 2 locations, 533 green tables in 2 locations, and 223 red tables in 3 locations returned.

So by simply adding *WITH ROLLUP*, you can answer a second question that the first ordinary *GROUP BY* query couldn't: "How many chairs, tables, and sofas are in stock, *regardless* of color?"

Rolling Up All Level Combinations

Using *WITH CUBE* now instead of *WITH ROLLUP* takes this result set to the next level, as shown here:

```
SELECT Item, Color, SUM(Quantity) AS TotalQty, COUNT(Store) AS Stores
 FROM Inventory
 GROUP BY Item, Color WITH CUBE
 ORDER BY Item, Color
GO

Item                 Color      TotalQty                       Stores
-------------------- ---------- ------------------------------ ------
NULL                 NULL       1272                           13
NULL                 Blue       347                            4
NULL                 Green      535                            3
NULL                 Red        390                            6
Chair                NULL       290                            5
Chair                Blue       123                            2
Chair                Red        167                            3
Sofa                 NULL       2                              1
Sofa                 Green      2                              1
Table                NULL       980                            7
Table                Blue       224                            2
Table                Green      533                            2
Table                Red        223                            3

(13 row(s) affected)
```

You now have the same result set returned by *WITH ROLLUP*, only this time three more rollup rows have been added (again, indicated in bold here). Let's look at exactly what SQL Server did. By applying *WITH CUBE*, you instructed the database engine to create a multidimensional representation of the data on the fly, which is loosely referred to as a *cube*. The number of dimensions in the cube is based on the number of grouping columns. This inventory example has only two dimensions, but a query could have many more dimensions if it specifies more grouping columns. A cube contains rollups for all the possible permutations of dimension values, not just the combinations of one value *within* another, as per the nesting levels defined by grouping columns listed in the *GROUP BY* clause.

So *WITH CUBE* returns the same rollups returned by *WITH ROLLUP*—which includes all items regardless of color—plus additional rollups for all colors regardless of item. As a result, you can now answer a third question that the earlier *GROUP BY* queries couldn't: "How many items of *any* type in a particular color are in stock?" That means that you can now also see how many blue, green, or red items you have in inventory regardless of whether they are chairs, sofas, or tables.

Because a cube rolls up every possible combination of dimension values independent of the order of levels expressed with *GROUP BY*, each additional grouping level increases the size of the result set exponentially. For example, if you modify the query to group by store location as well, SQL Server returns 44 rows including rollups for every possible combination of values across the three grouping columns *Store*, *Item*, and *Color*, as follows:

```
SELECT Store, Item, Color, SUM(Quantity) AS TotalQty
 FROM Inventory
 GROUP BY Store, Item, Color WITH CUBE
 ORDER BY Store, Item, Color
GO

Store Item                 Color      TotalQty
----- -------------------- ---------- -----------------------------
NULL  NULL                 NULL       1272
NULL  NULL                 Blue       347
NULL  NULL                 Green      535
NULL  NULL                 Red        390
NULL  Chair                NULL       290
NULL  Chair                Blue       123
NULL  Chair                Red        167
NULL  Sofa                 NULL       2
NULL  Sofa                 Green      2
NULL  Table                NULL       980
NULL  Table                Blue       224
NULL  Table                Green      533
NULL  Table                Red        223
NJ    NULL                 NULL       190
NJ    NULL                 Blue       122
NJ    NULL                 Green      2
NJ    NULL                 Red        66
NJ    Chair                NULL       32
NJ    Chair                Blue       22
NJ    Chair                Red        10
NJ    Sofa                 NULL       2
NJ    Sofa                 Green      2
NJ    Table                NULL       156
NJ    Table                Blue       100
NJ    Table                Red        56
NY    NULL                 NULL       504
NY    NULL                 Blue       225
NY    NULL                 Green      229
NY    NULL                 Red        50
NY    Chair                NULL       122
NY    Chair                Blue       101
NY    Chair                Red        21
NY    Table                NULL       382
NY    Table                Blue       124
NY    Table                Green      229
NY    Table                Red        29
PA    NULL                 NULL       578
```

```
PA    NULL                   Green      304
PA    NULL                   Red        274
PA    Chair                  NULL       136
PA    Chair                  Red        136
PA    Table                  NULL       442
PA    Table                  Green      304
PA    Table                  Red        138

(44 row(s) affected)
```

These results can now answer inventory questions for every conceivable combination of grouping levels. For example, across all locations, there are 347 blue items (tables, chairs, and sofas), 290 chairs (all colors), and 533 green tables, whereas in NY specifically, there are 50 red items, 382 tables, and 124 blue tables, and so on. Every permutation of store location, item, and color—and their rollups—are returned by this single query.

Returning Just the Top Level

The last variation on *GROUP BY* is the *GROUPING SETS* operator introduced in SQL Server 2008. This operator returns *just* the top-level rollup rows for each grouping level and does not include the actual group level summary information that was returned by earlier versions of the query, as follows:

```
SELECT Store, Item, Color, SUM(Quantity) AS TotalQty
 FROM Inventory
 GROUP BY GROUPING SETS (Store, Item, Color)
 ORDER BY Store, Item, Color
GO

Store Item                 Color      TotalQty
----- -------------------- ---------- ------------------------------
NULL  NULL                 Blue       347
NULL  NULL                 Green      535
NULL  NULL                 Red        390
NULL  Chair                NULL       290
NULL  Sofa                 NULL       2
NULL  Table                NULL       980
NJ    NULL                 NULL       190
NY    NULL                 NULL       504
PA    NULL                 NULL       578

(9 row(s) affected)
```

GROUPING SETS is merely another variation on *GROUP BY* that you can use when you require only top-level rollups for each of your grouping levels (that is, one set of group rollups per level). In this case, you get a total quantity report for all colors, all items, and all store locations without including the summary rows for each of the combinations of grouping levels, just as earlier versions of the query did.

Mixing and Matching

But the *GROUPING SETS* story doesn't end here, of course. Unlike *WITH ROLLUP* and *WITH CUBE*—which are mutually exclusive in the same query—rollup and cube operations can be used together and with *GROUPING SETS* in any combination. This means that you can compose one query that returns only top-level rollups for certain grouping levels and also returns the lower-level rollups and summary rows for other grouping levels, just like you get using *WITH ROLLUP* or *WITH CUBE* in separate queries.

To achieve this, SQL Server provides an alternative syntax for *WITH ROLLUP* and *WITH CUBE* that makes these operators capable of being expressed with one another in the same *GROUP BY* clause. This syntax is actually quite simple: drop the *WITH* keyword, place the *ROLLUP* or *CUBE* keyword before the grouping columns rather than after, and enclose the grouping columns in parentheses.

For example, the following two *GROUP BY* clauses are interchangeable:

```
GROUP BY Item, Color WITH ROLLUP
GROUP BY ROLLUP(Item, Color)
```

Similarly, these two clauses are also equivalent:

```
GROUP BY Item, Color WITH CUBE
GROUP BY CUBE(Item, Color)
```

Although the two versions are interchangeable when used on their own, you *must* use the newer syntax if you want to combine them with one another or with *GROUPING SETS* in a single query. Here is another version of the inventory query that does just that:

```
SELECT Store, Item, Color, SUM(Quantity) AS TotalQty
 FROM Inventory
 GROUP BY GROUPING SETS(Store), CUBE(Item, Color)
 ORDER BY Store, Item, Color
```

The *GROUP BY* clause in this query includes both a *GROUPING SETS* operator on *Store* and a *CUBE* operator on *Item* and *Color*. This tells SQL Server to return top-level rollups only on the *Store* column and full summaries with multidimensional rollups on the *Item* and *Color* columns. Here are the results:

```
Store Item                 Color      TotalQty
----- -------------------- ---------- ------------------------------
NJ    NULL                 NULL       190
NJ    NULL                 Blue       122
NJ    NULL                 Green      2
NJ    NULL                 Red        66
NJ    Chair                NULL       32
NJ    Chair                Blue       22
NJ    Chair                Red        10
NJ    Sofa                 NULL       2
NJ    Sofa                 Green      2
NJ    Table                NULL       156
NJ    Table                Blue       100
```

```
NJ    Table              Red      56
NY    NULL               NULL     504
NY    NULL               Blue     225
NY    NULL               Green    229
NY    NULL               Red      50
NY    Chair              NULL     122
NY    Chair              Blue     101
NY    Chair              Red      21
NY    Table              NULL     382
NY    Table              Blue     124
NY    Table              Green    229
NY    Table              Red      29
PA    NULL               NULL     578
PA    NULL               Green    304
PA    NULL               Red      274
PA    Chair              NULL     136
PA    Chair              Red      136
PA    Table              NULL     442
PA    Table              Green    304
PA    Table              Red      138

(31 row(s) affected)
```

The rows with *NULL* values for both *Item* and *Color* (highlighted here in bold) are the top-level rollups for *Store* returned by the *GROUPING SETS(Store)* operator. These rows report just the totals for each store (all items, all colors). All of the other rows are the multidimensional rollup and summary results returned by *CUBE(Item, Color)*. These rows report aggregations for every combination of *Item* and *Color*. Because *Store* is returned by *GROUPING SETS* and not by *CUBE*, you don't see combinations that include all stores.

You can use *GROUPING SETS*, *ROLLUP*, and *CUBE* in any combination you want with the *GROUP BY* clause. As a result, you gain tremendous flexibility for grouping, aggregating, and analyzing your data just the way you need to. The only restriction in usage is the same one that applies when using *GROUP BY* on its own: columns returned by the query must be specified either in the *GROUP BY* clause (in any of the *GROUPING SETS*, *ROLLUP*, or *CUBE* operators) or in an aggregate function that operates across all the combined rows for the group (such as *SUM*, *COUNT*, *MIN*, *MAX*, and so on).

Handling *NULL* Values

We'll conclude the discussion of *GROUPING SETS* by discussing *NULL* values. As you've seen, SQL Server returns *NULL* values to represent all values in high-level rollup rows. If you're fortunate enough to be working with data that is guaranteed not to contain *NULL* values, life is good for you. But this is far more often not the case, and thus a problem arises distinguishing between "real" *NULL* values and the *NULL* values representing "all values" in rollup rows.

To demonstrate, add two more rows to the *Inventory* table for lamps that have no color association. These rows store *NULL* values in the *Color* column, as shown in Listing 2-27.

LISTING 2-27 Introducing *NULL* values into the *Inventory* table.

```
INSERT INTO Inventory VALUES('NY', 'Lamp', NULL, 36)
INSERT INTO Inventory VALUES('NJ', 'Lamp', NULL, 8)
```

Now run the exact same query you ran before:

```
SELECT Store, Item, Color, SUM(Quantity) AS TotalQty
 FROM Inventory
 GROUP BY GROUPING SETS(Store), CUBE(Item, Color)
 ORDER BY Store, Item, Color
GO

Store Item                 Color      TotalQty
----- -------------------- ---------- ------------------------------
NJ    NULL                 NULL       8
NJ    NULL                 NULL       198
NJ    NULL                 Blue       122
NJ    NULL                 Green      2
 :
NJ    Table                Blue       100
NJ    Table                Red        56
NY    NULL                 NULL       36
NY    NULL                 NULL       540
NY    NULL                 Blue       225
NY    NULL                 Green      229
 :
PA    Table                Green      304
PA    Table                Red        138

(37 row(s) affected)
```

These are very confusing results. Because both the "all colors" rollup columns and the lamp columns with "no color" have a *NULL* value for *Color*, it is impossible to distinguish between the two when analyzing the query results. For example, the first row returns the rollup for all items with *no* color in NJ (that's the 8 lamps), and the second row returns the rollup for all items in *all* colors in NJ, but there is no way to discern that difference because *NULL* is used to represent both "no color" and "all colors." The same problem occurs again further down in the results for NY, where there are also colorless lamps in stock. Once again, because "no color" and "all colors" are both represented by *NULL* values, the results are nothing short of perplexing.

The solution to this problem is to use the *GROUPING* function in your query. The *GROUPING* function returns a bit value of *1* (true) if the column passed to it represents an "all values" rollup, and it returns *0* (false) otherwise. It is therefore possible to distinguish between "all values" rollup columns (which are always *NULL*) and regular data (which *might* be *NULL*, as is the case for the lamps, which have no color values). Here is a revised version of the query that uses the *GROUPING* function in conjunction with *CASE* to produce a better result set that clears up the confusion between "all values" and "no value".

```
SELECT
  CASE WHEN GROUPING(Store) = 1 THEN '(all)' ELSE Store END AS Store,
  CASE WHEN GROUPING(Item) = 1  THEN '(all)' ELSE Item  END AS Item,
  CASE WHEN GROUPING(Color) = 1 THEN '(all)' ELSE Color END AS Color,
  SUM(Quantity) AS TotalQty
 FROM Inventory
 GROUP BY GROUPING SETS(Store), CUBE(Item, Color)
 ORDER BY Store, Item, Color
```

The *CASE* construct tests each grouping column returned by the query using the *GROUPING* function. If it returns *1* (true), that means that the column represents an "all values" rollup. In this case, the string *(all)* is returned, rather than the *NULL* value that would have otherwise been returned. If it returns *0* (false), the column contains regular data, which might or might not be *NULL*. Although there are *NULL* values only in for the *Color* column for lamps, apply the same *CASE* and *GROUPING* to the *Store* and *Item* columns as well. This is a defensive coding measure against the possibility of the *Store* or *Item* column also containing *NULL* values in the future. Taking this approach now resolves the confusion with respect to *NULL* values and rollups in the query results, as shown here:

```
Store Item                 Color      TotalQty
----- -------------------- ---------- ------------------------------
NJ    (all)                NULL       8
NJ    (all)                (all)      198
NJ    (all)                Blue       122
NJ    (all)                Green      2
  :
NJ    Table                Blue       100
NJ    Table                Red        56
NY    (all)                NULL       36
NY    (all)                (all)      540
NY    (all)                Blue       225
NY    (all)                Green      229
  :
PA    Table                Green      304
PA    Table                Red        138

(37 row(s) affected)
```

It's perfectly understandable now that the first row returns the rollup for all items with no color in NJ, whereas the second row returns the rollup for all items in all colors (including no color) in NJ. The same is true farther down in the NY results, where there are also colorless lamps in stock. Therefore, to avoid any potential confusion concerning *NULL* values in your grouping queries, you should always use the *GROUPING* function in this manner to translate the *NULL* values that mean "all values" for the user.

As long as you're modifying the query to produce more readable results, enhance it one more time. In the same way that you translated the *NULL* for "all values" to the text *(all)*, you can translate the *NULL* values for regular "missing" data to *(n/a)*. This is easy to do by adding an *ELSE* clause to the *CASE* construct that uses the *ISNULL* function on the column, as shown here:

```
SELECT
  CASE WHEN GROUPING(Store) = 1 THEN '(all)'
   ELSE ISNULL(Store, '(n/a)') END AS Store,
  CASE WHEN GROUPING(Item) = 1  THEN '(all)'
```

```
    ELSE ISNULL(Item,  '(n/a)') END AS Item,
  CASE WHEN GROUPING(Color) = 1 THEN '(all)'
    ELSE ISNULL(Color, '(n/a)') END AS Color,
  SUM(Quantity) AS TotalQty
 FROM Inventory
 GROUP BY GROUPING SETS(Store), CUBE(Item, Color)
 ORDER BY Store, Item, Color
```

The *ELSE* clause in each *CASE* construct runs if the *GROUPING* function returns *0* (false). This means that the column is not an "all values" rollup, but regular column data. You want regular column data to be returned as is, except for *NULL* values that should be returned as the string *(n/a)*. The *ISNULL* function tests for *NULL* values and performs the translation on them, as shown in the results returned by the query:

```
Store Item                 Color      TotalQty
----- -------------------- ---------- ----------------------------
NJ    (all)                (all)      198
NJ    (all)                (n/a)      8
NJ    (all)                Blue       122
NJ    (all)                Green      2
  :
NJ    Sofa                 Green      2
NJ    Stool                (all)      8
NJ    Stool                (n/a)      8
NJ    Table                (all)      156
NJ    Table                Blue       100
NJ    Table                Red        56
NY    (all)                (all)      540
NY    (all)                (n/a)      36
NY    (all)                Blue       225
  :
NY    Chair                Red        21
NY    Stool                (all)      36
NY    Stool                (n/a)      36
NY    Table                (all)      382
NY    Table                Blue       124
  :
PA    Table                Green      304
PA    Table                Red        138

(37 row(s) affected)
```

The query now returns no *NULL* values at all, which is much better for your users who don't really know or care exactly what *NULL* means anyway. By translating these values appropriately to *(all)* and *(n/a)*, you have produced a far more usable report for them.

Windowing (*OVER* Clause) Enhancements

The first *windowing* capabilities appeared in SQL Server 2005 with the introduction of the *OVER* clause and a set of four ranking functions: *ROW_NUMBER*, *RANK*, *DENSE_RANK*, and *NTILE*. In our discussion, the term "window" refers to the scope of visibility from one row in a result set relative to neighboring rows in the same result set. By default, *OVER* produces a single window over the entire result set, but its associated *PARTITION BY* clause lets you divide the result set up into multiple groups, each contained inside their own window. The row sequence within each window is determined by an associated *ORDER BY* clause, and based on this sequence, the ranking functions assign an accumulating value to the rows in the window.

In addition to the ranking functions, the *OVER* clause can be used with the traditional aggregate functions *SUM*, *COUNT*, *MIN*, *MAX*, and *AVG*. When doing so, you do not specify the *GROUP BY* clause that's normally required with the aggregate functions. Instead, each row calculates an aggregation based on the window of rows defined with *OVER*, optionally grouped using *PARTITION BY*. This is certainly useful, because it allows you to obtain aggregations without being forced to consolidate (and lose) detail rows with a *GROUP BY* clause. But unfortunately (until now), the aggregate functions could not also use *ORDER BY* in the *OVER* clause (as is required when using *OVER* with the ranking functions), making it impossible to calculate *cumulative* aggregations at the row level within each window. For example, you could use *AVG* with *OVER* (and, optionally *PARTITION BY*), but without an associated *ORDER BY*, there is no designated sequence to the rows in each window, making it impossible for SQL Server to compute a running average from one row to the next within the window. Thus, the best that *AVG* with *OVER* could do is compute the average for *all* the rows in the window (independent of row sequence), and then return that value for *every* row.

SQL Server 2012 finally addresses this shortcoming. In the following code samples, you'll see how *OVER/ORDER BY* can now be used with all the traditional aggregate functions to provide *running calculations* within ordered windows. You'll also learn how to frame windows using the *ROWS* and *RANGE* clause, which adjusts the size and scope of the window to enable *sliding calculations*. And finally, SQL Server 2012 introduces eight new analytic functions (covered in the next section) that are designed specifically to work with ordered (and optionally partitioned) windows using *OVER* with *ORDER BY* (and optionally *PARTITION BY*).

Note All remaining topics in this chapter are new features in SQL Server 2012.

The code in Listing 2-28 creates a table populated with financial transactions from several different accounts. Tangentially, note the use of the new *DATEFROMPARTS* function (also covered in the next section), which is used to construct a date value from year, month, and day parameters.

LISTING 2-28 Preparing sample transaction data for querying with window functions.

```
CREATE TABLE TxnData (AcctId int, TxnDate date, Amount decimal)
GO
INSERT INTO TxnData (AcctId, TxnDate, Amount) VALUES
  (1, DATEFROMPARTS(2012, 4, 10), 500),  -- 5 transactions for acct 1
  (1, DATEFROMPARTS(2012, 4, 22), 250),
  (1, DATEFROMPARTS(2012, 4, 24), 75),
  (1, DATEFROMPARTS(2012, 4, 26), 125),
  (1, DATEFROMPARTS(2012, 4, 28), 175),
```

```
(2, DATEFROMPARTS(2012, 4, 11), 500),  -- 8 transactions for acct 2
(2, DATEFROMPARTS(2012, 4, 15), 50),
(2, DATEFROMPARTS(2012, 4, 22), 5000),
(2, DATEFROMPARTS(2012, 4, 25), 550),
(2, DATEFROMPARTS(2012, 4, 27), 105),
(2, DATEFROMPARTS(2012, 4, 27), 95),
(2, DATEFROMPARTS(2012, 4, 29), 100),
(2, DATEFROMPARTS(2012, 4, 30), 2500),
(3, DATEFROMPARTS(2012, 4, 14), 500),  -- 4 transactions for acct 3
(3, DATEFROMPARTS(2012, 4, 15), 600),
(3, DATEFROMPARTS(2012, 4, 22), 25),
(3, DATEFROMPARTS(2012, 4, 23), 125)
```

Running Aggregations

In SQL Server 2012, an *ORDER BY* clause may be specified with *OVER* to produce running aggregations within each window, as Listing 2-29 demonstrates:

LISTING 2-29 Using *OVER* with *ORDER BY* to produce running aggregations.

```
SELECT AcctId, TxnDate, Amount,
  RAvg = AVG(Amount) OVER (PARTITION BY AcctId ORDER BY TxnDate),
  RCnt = COUNT(*)    OVER (PARTITION BY AcctId ORDER BY TxnDate),
  RMin = MIN(Amount) OVER (PARTITION BY AcctId ORDER BY TxnDate),
  RMax = MAX(Amount) OVER (PARTITION BY AcctId ORDER BY TxnDate),
  RSum = SUM(Amount) OVER (PARTITION BY AcctId ORDER BY TxnDate)
 FROM TxnData
 ORDER BY AcctId, TxnDate
```

```
AcctId TxnDate    Amount RAvg        RCnt RMin RMax RSum
------ ---------- ------ ----------- ---- ---- ---- ----
1      2012-02-10 500    500.000000  1    500  500  500
1      2012-02-22 250    375.000000  2    250  500  750
1      2012-02-24 75     275.000000  3    75   500  825
1      2012-02-26 125    237.500000  4    75   500  950
1      2012-02-28 175    225.000000  5    75   500  1125
2      2012-02-11 500    500.000000  1    500  500  500
2      2012-02-15 50     275.000000  2    50   500  550
2      2012-02-22 5000   1850.000000 3    50   5000 5550
 :
```

The results of this query are partitioned (windowed) by account. Within each window, the account's running averages, counts, minimum/maximum values, and sums are ordered by transaction date, showing the chronologically accumulated values for each account. No *ROWS* clause is specified (we'll explain how to use the *ROWS* clause next), so *ROWS BETWEEN UNBOUNDED PRECEDING AND CURRENT ROW* is assumed by default. This yields a window frame size that spans from the beginning of the partition (the first row of each account) through the current row. When the account ID changes, the previous window is "closed" and new calculations start running for a new window over the next account ID.

Sliding Aggregations

You can also narrow each account's window by framing it with a *ROWS* clause in the *OVER* clause. This enables sliding calculations, as demonstrated in Listing 2-30:

LISTING 2-30 Using *OVER* with *ORDER BY* and *PRECEDING* to produce sliding aggregations.

```
SELECT AcctId, TxnDate, Amount,
  SAvg = AVG(Amount) OVER (PARTITION BY AcctId ORDER BY TxnDate
                          ROWS BETWEEN 2 PRECEDING AND CURRENT ROW),
  SCnt = COUNT(*)    OVER (PARTITION BY AcctId ORDER BY TxnDate ROWS 2 PRECEDING),
  SMin = MIN(Amount) OVER (PARTITION BY AcctId ORDER BY TxnDate ROWS 2 PRECEDING),
  SMax = MAX(Amount) OVER (PARTITION BY AcctId ORDER BY TxnDate ROWS 2 PRECEDING),
  SSum = SUM(Amount) OVER (PARTITION BY AcctId ORDER BY TxnDate ROWS 2 PRECEDING)
 FROM TxnData
 ORDER BY AcctId, TxnDate
```

```
AcctId TxnDate    Amount SAvg        SCnt SMin SMax SSum
------ ---------- ------ ----------- ---- ---- ---- ----
1      2012-02-10 500    500.000000  1    500  500  500
1      2012-02-22 250    375.000000  2    250  500  750
1      2012-02-24 75     275.000000  3    75   500  825
1      2012-02-26 125    150.000000  3    75   250  450
1      2012-02-28 175    125.000000  3    75   175  375
2      2012-02-11 500    500.000000  1    500  500  500
2      2012-02-15 50     275.000000  2    50   500  550
2      2012-02-22 5000   1850.000000 3    50   5000 5550
  :
```

This slightly modified version of the previous query specifies *ROWS BETWEEN 2 PRECEDING AND CURRENT ROW* in the *OVER* clause for the *RAvg* column, overriding the default window size. Specifically, it frames the window within each account's partition to a maximum of three rows: the current row, the row before it, and one more row before that one. Once the window expands to three rows, it stops growing and starts sliding down the subsequent rows until a new partition (the next account) is encountered. The *BETWEEN…AND CURRENT ROW* keywords that specify the upper bound of the window are assumed default, so to reduce code clutter, the other column definitions specify just the lower bound of the window with the shorter variation *ROWS 2 PRECEDING*.

Notice how the window "slides" within each account. For example, the sliding maximum for account 1 drops from 500 to 250 in the fourth row, because 250 is the largest value in the window of three rows that begins two rows earlier—and the 500 from the very first row is no longer visible in that window. Similarly, the sliding sum for each account is based on the defined window. Thus, the sliding sum of 375 on the last row of account 1 is the total sum of that row (175) plus the two preceding rows (75 + 125) only—not the total sum for all transactions in the entire account, as the running sum had calculated.

Using *RANGE* versus *ROWS*

Finally, *RANGE* can be used instead of *ROWS* to handle "ties" within a window. Although *ROWS* treats each row in the window distinctly, *RANGE* will merge rows containing duplicate *ORDER BY* values, as demonstrated by Listing 2-31:

LISTING 2-31 Comparing *ROWS* and *RANGE* for calculating window functions.

```
SELECT AcctId, TxnDate, Amount,
  SumByRows    = SUM(Amount) OVER (ORDER BY TxnDate ROWS UNBOUNDED PRECEDING),
  SumByRange   = SUM(Amount) OVER (ORDER BY TxnDate RANGE UNBOUNDED PRECEDING)
 FROM TxnData
 WHERE AcctId = 2
 ORDER BY TxnDate
```

```
AcctId TxnDate    Amount SumByRows SumByRange
------ ---------- ------ --------- ----------
2      2012-02-11 500    500       500
2      2012-02-15 50     550       550
2      2012-02-22 5000   5550      5550
2      2012-02-25 550    6100      6100
2      2012-02-27 105    6205      6300
2      2012-02-27 95     6300      6300
2      2012-02-29 100    6400      6400
2      2012-02-30 2500   8900      8900
```

In this result set, *ROWS* and *RANGE* both return the same values, with the exception of the fifth row. Because the fifth and sixth rows are both tied for the same date (2/27/2012), *RANGE* returns the combined running sum for both rows. The seventh row (for 2/29/2012) breaks the tie, and *ROWS* "catches up" with *RANGE* to return running totals for the rest of the window.

New T-SQL Functions in SQL Server 2012

The latest version of SQL Server augments T-SQL with many new functions. In this section, we cover the 22 new functions (and 1 changed function) introduced in SQL Server 2012. We'll start by covering the new T-SQL analytic functions, because they operate using the same windowing principles we were just discussing.

New Analytic Functions

Eight new analytic functions have been added to T-SQL. All of them work in conjunction with an ordered window defined with an associated *ORDER BY* clause that can be optionally partitioned with a *PARTITION BY* clause and framed with a *BETWEEN* clause. The new functions are:

- FIRST_VALUE
- LAST_VALUE
- LAG
- LEAD
- PERCENT_RANK
- CUME_DIST
- PERCENTILE_CONT
- PERCENTILE_DISC

In Listing 2-32, the *FIRST_VALUE, LAST_VALUE, LAG,* and *LEAD* functions are used to analyze a set of orders at the product level.

LISTING 2-32 Using the *FIRST_VALUE, LAST_VALUE, LAG,* and *LEAD* functions.

```
DECLARE @Orders AS table(OrderDate date, ProductID int, Quantity int)
INSERT INTO @Orders VALUES
 ('2012-03-18', 142, 74),
 ('2012-04-11', 123, 95),
 ('2012-04-12', 101, 38),
 ('2012-05-21', 130, 12),
 ('2012-05-30', 101, 28),
 ('2012-07-25', 123, 57),
 ('2012-07-28', 101, 12)

SELECT
  OrderDate,
  ProductID,
  Quantity,
  WorstOn = FIRST_VALUE(OrderDate) OVER(PARTITION BY ProductID ORDER BY Quantity),
  BestOn = LAST_VALUE(OrderDate) OVER(PARTITION BY ProductID ORDER BY Quantity
                      ROWS BETWEEN UNBOUNDED PRECEDING AND UNBOUNDED FOLLOWING),
  PrevOn = LAG(OrderDate, 1) OVER(PARTITION BY ProductID ORDER BY OrderDate),
  NextOn = LEAD(OrderDate, 1) OVER(PARTITION BY ProductID ORDER BY OrderDate)
 FROM @Orders
 ORDER BY OrderDate
```

```
OrderDate   ProductID  Quantity  WorstOn     BestOn      PrevOn      NextOn
----------  ---------  --------  ----------  ----------  ----------  ----------
2012-03-18  142        74        2012-03-18  2012-03-18  NULL        NULL
2012-04-11  123        95        2012-07-25  2012-04-11  NULL        2012-07-25
```

```
2012-04-12  101         38          2012-07-28  2012-04-12  NULL        2012-05-30
2012-05-21  130         12          2012-05-21  2012-05-21  NULL        NULL
2012-05-30  101         28          2012-07-28  2012-04-12  2012-04-12  2012-07-28
2012-07-25  123         57          2012-07-25  2012-04-11  2012-04-11  NULL
2012-07-28  101         12          2012-07-28  2012-04-12  2012-05-30  NULL
```

In this query, four analytic functions specify an *OVER* clause that partitions the result set by *ProductID*. The product partitions defined for *FIRST_VALUE* and *LAST_VALUE* are sorted by *Quantity*, whereas the product partitions for *LAG* and *LEAD* are sorted by *OrderDate*. The full result set is sorted by *OrderDate*, so you need to visualize the sorted partition for each of the four functions to understand the output—the result set sequence is not the same as the row sequence used for the windowing functions.

The *WorstOn* and *BestOn* columns use *FIRST_VALUE* and *LAST_VALUE*, respectively, to return the "worst" and "best" dates for the product in each partition. Performance is measured by quantity, so sorting each product's partition by quantity will position the worst order at the first row in the partition and the best order at the last row in the partition. *FIRST_VALUE* and *LAST_VALUE* can return the value of any column (*OrderDate*, in this case), not just the aggregate column itself. For *LAST_VALUE*, it is also necessary to explicitly define a window over the entire partition with *ROWS BETWEEN UNBOUNDED PRECEDING AND UNBOUNDED FOLLOWING*. Otherwise, as explained in our earlier discussion about running and sliding aggregations, the default window is *ROWS BETWEEN UNBOUNDED PRECEDING AND CURRENT ROW*. This default behavior frames (constrains) the window, and does not consider the remaining rows in the partition that are needed to obtain the highest quantity for *LAST_VALUE*.

In the output, notice that *OrderDate*, *LowestOn*, and *HighestOn* for the first order (product 142) are all the same value (3/18). This is because product 142 was only ordered once, so *FIRST_VALUE* and *LAST_VALUE* operate over a partition that has only this one row in it, with an *OrderDate* value of 3/18. The second row is for product 123, quantity 95, ordered on 4/11. Four rows ahead in the result set (*not* the partition) there is another order for product 123, quantity 57, placed on 7/25. This means that, for this product, *FIRST_VALUE* and *LAST_VALUE* operate over a partition that has these two rows in it, sorted by quantity. This positions the 7/25 order (quantity 57) first and the 4/11 (quantity 95) last within the partition. As a result, rows for product 123 report 7/25 for *WorstDate* and 4/11 for *BestDate*. The next order (product 101) appears two more times in the result set, creating a partition of three rows. Again, based on the *Quantity* sort of the partition, each row in the partition reports the product's worst and best dates (which are 7/28 and 4/12, respectively).

The *PrevOn* and *NextOn* columns use *LAG* and *LEAD* to return the previous and next date that each product was ordered. They specify an *OVER* clause that partitions by *ProductId* as before, but the rows in these partitions are sorted by *OrderDate*. Thus, the *LAG* and *LEAD* functions examine each product's orders in chronological sequence, regardless of quantity. For each row in each partition, *LAG* is able to access previous (lagging) rows within the same partition. Similarly, *LEAD* can access subsequent (leading) rows within the same partition. The first parameter to *LAG* and *LEAD* specifies the column value to be returned from a lagging or leading row, respectively. The second parameter specifies the number of rows back or forward *LAG* and *LEAD* should seek within each partition, relative to the current row. Listing 2-32 passes *OrderDate* and 1 as parameters to *LAG* and *LEAD*, using product partitions that are ordered by date. Thus, the query returns the most recent past date, and nearest future date, that each product was ordered.

Because the first order's product (142) was only ordered once, its single-row partition has no lagging or leading rows, and so *LAG* and *LEAD* both return *NULL* for *PrevOn* and *NextOn* (note that both functions also optionally accept a third parameter to be used instead of *NULL* when no lagging or leading row exists). The second order (on 4/11) is for product 123, which was ordered again on 7/25, creating a partition with two rows sorted by *OrderDate*, with the 4/11 order positioned first and the 7/25 order positioned last within the partition. The first row in a multi-row window has no lagging rows, but at least one leading row. Similarly, the last order in a multi-row window has at least one lagging row, but no leading rows. As a result, the first order (4/11) reports *NULL* and 7/25 for *PrevOn* and *NextOn,* respectively, and the second order (7/25) reports 4/11 and *NULL* for *PrevOn* and *NextOn,* respectively. Product 101 was ordered three times, which creates a partition of three rows. In this partition, the second row has both a lagging row and a leading row. Thus, the three orders report *PrevOn* and *NextOn* values for product 101, respectively indicating *NULL*-5/30 for the first (4/12) order, 4/12-7/28 for the second (5/30) order, and 5/30-*NULL* for the third and last order.

The last functions to examine are *PERCENT_RANK* (rank distribution), *CUME_DIST* (cumulative distribution, or percentile), *PERCENTILE_CONT* (continuous percentile), and *PERCENTILE_DISC* (discrete percentile). The queries in Listing 2-33 demonstrate these functions, which are all closely related, by querying sales figures across each quarter of two years.

LISTING 2-33 Using the *PERCENT_RANK, CUME_DIST, PERCENTILE_CONT,* and *PERCENTILE_DISC* functions.

```
DECLARE @Sales table(Yr int, Qtr int, Amount money)
INSERT INTO @Sales VALUES
  (2010, 1, 5000), (2010, 2, 6000), (2010, 3, 7000), (2010, 4, 2000),
  (2011, 1, 1000), (2011, 2, 2000), (2011, 3, 3000), (2011, 4, 4000)

-- Distributed across all 8 quarters
SELECT
  Yr, Qtr, Amount,
  R = RANK() OVER(ORDER BY Amount),
  PR = PERCENT_RANK() OVER(ORDER BY Amount),
  CD = CUME_DIST() OVER(ORDER BY Amount)
 FROM @Sales
 ORDER BY Amount

-- Distributed (partitioned) by year with percentile lookups
SELECT
  Yr, Qtr, Amount,
  R = RANK() OVER(PARTITION BY Yr ORDER BY Amount),
  PR = PERCENT_RANK() OVER(PARTITION BY Yr ORDER BY Amount),
```

```
  CD = CUME_DIST() OVER(PARTITION BY Yr ORDER BY Amount),
  PD5 = PERCENTILE_DISC(.5) WITHIN GROUP (ORDER BY Amount) OVER(PARTITION BY Yr),
  PD6 = PERCENTILE_DISC(.6) WITHIN GROUP (ORDER BY Amount) OVER(PARTITION BY Yr),
  PC5 = PERCENTILE_CONT(.5) WITHIN GROUP (ORDER BY Amount) OVER(PARTITION BY Yr),
  PC6 = PERCENTILE_CONT(.6) WITHIN GROUP (ORDER BY Amount) OVER(PARTITION BY Yr)
 FROM @Sales
 ORDER BY Yr, Amount
```

```
Yr    Qtr  Amount   R  PR                 CD
----  ---  -------  -  -----------------  -----
2011  1    1000.00  1  0                  0.125
2011  2    2000.00  2  0.142857142857143  0.375
2010  4    2000.00  2  0.142857142857143  0.375
2011  3    3000.00  4  0.428571428571429  0.5
2011  4    4000.00  5  0.571428571428571  0.625
2010  1    5000.00  6  0.714285714285714  0.75
2010  2    6000.00  7  0.857142857142857  0.875
2010  3    7000.00  8  1                  1

Yr    Qtr  Amount   R  PR                 CD    PD5      PD6      PC5   PC6
----  ---  -------  -  -----------------  ----  -------  -------  ----  ----
2010  4    2000.00  1  0                  0.25  5000.00  6000.00  5500  5800
2010  1    5000.00  2  0.333333333333333  0.5   5000.00  6000.00  5500  5800
2010  2    6000.00  3  0.666666666666667  0.75  5000.00  6000.00  5500  5800
2010  3    7000.00  4  1                  1     5000.00  6000.00  5500  5800
2011  1    1000.00  1  0                  0.25  2000.00  3000.00  2500  2800
2011  2    2000.00  2  0.333333333333333  0.5   2000.00  3000.00  2500  2800
2011  3    3000.00  3  0.666666666666667  0.75  2000.00  3000.00  2500  2800
2011  4    4000.00  4  1                  1     2000.00  3000.00  2500  2800
```

The new functions are all based on the *RANK* function introduced in SQL Server 2005. So both these queries also report on *RANK*, which will aid both in our explanation and your understanding of each of the new functions.

In the first query, *PERCENT_RANK* and *CUME_DIST* (aliased as *PR* and *CD* respectively) rank quarterly sales across the entire two-year period. Look at the value returned by *RANK* (aliased as *R*). It ranks each row in the unpartitioned window (all eight quarters) by dollar amount. Both 2011Q2 and 2010Q4 are tied for $2,000 in sales, so *RANK* assigns them the same value (2). The next row breaks the tie, so RANK continues with 4, which accounts for the "empty slot" created by the two previous rows that were tied.

Now examine the values returned by *PERCENT_RANK* and *CUME_DIST*. Notice how they reflect the same information as *RANK*, with decimal values ranging from 0 and 1. The only difference between the two is a slight variation in the way their formulas are implemented, such that *PERCENT_RANK* always starts with 0 while *CUME_DIST* always starts with a value greater than 0. Specifically, *PERCENT_RANK* returns (*RANK* – 1) / (*N* – 1) for each row, where *N* is the total number of rows in the window. This always returns 0 for the first (or only) row in the window. *CUME_DIST* returns *RANK* / *N*, which always returns a value greater than 0 for the first row in the window (which would be 1, if there's only row). For windows with two or more rows, both functions return 1 for the last row in the window with decimal values distributed among all the other rows.

The second query examines the same sales figures, only this time the result set is partitioned by year. There are no ties within each year, so *RANK* assigns the sequential numbers 1 through 4 to each of the quarters, for 2010 and 2011, by dollar amount. You can see that *PERCENT_RANK* and *CUME_DIST* perform the same *RANK* calculations as explained for the first query (only, again, partitioned by year this time).

This query also demonstrates *PERCENTILE_DISC* and *PERCENTILE_CONT*. These very similar functions each accept a percentile parameter (the desired *CUME_DIST* value) and "reach in" to the window for the row at or near that percentile. We demonstrate by calling both functions twice, once with a percentile parameter value of .5 and once with .6, returning columns aliased as *PD5*, *PD6*, *PC5*, and *PC6*. Both functions examine the *CUME_DIST* value for each row in the window to find the one nearest to .5 and .6. The subtle difference between them is that *PERCENTILE_DISC* will return a precise (discrete) value from the row with the matching percentile (or greater), while *PERCENTILE_CONT* interpolates a value based on a continuous range. Specifically, *PERCENTILE_CONT* returns a value ranging from the row matching the specified percentile—or, if there is no exact match, a calculated value based on the specified percentile if there is no exact match—and the row with the next higher percentile in the window. This explains the values returned by these functions in this query.

For the year 2010, the .5 percentile (*CUME_DIST* value) is located exactly on quarter 1, which had $5,000 in sales. Thus *PERCENTILE_DISC*(.5) returns 5000. There is no row in the window with a percentile of .6, so *PERCENTILE_DISC*(.6) matches up against the first row with a percentile greater than or equal to .6, which is the row for quarter 2 with $6,000 in sales, and thus returns 6000. In both cases, *PERCENTILE_DISC* returns a discrete value from a row in the window at or greater than the specified percentile. The same calculations are performed for 2011, returning 2000 for *PERCENTILE_DISC*(.5) and 3000 for *PERCENTILE_DISC*(.6), corresponding to the $2,000 in sales for quarter 2 (percentile .5) and the $3,000 in sales for quarter 3 (percentile .75).

As we stated, *PERCENTILE_CONT* is very similar. It takes the same percentile parameter to find the row in the window matching that percentile. If there is no exact match, the function calculates a value based on the scale of percentiles distributed across the entire window, rather than looking ahead to the row having the next greater percentile value, as *PERCENTILE_DISC* does. Then it returns the median between that value and the value found in the row with the next greater percentile. For 2010, the .5 percentile matches up with 5000 (as before). The next percentile in the window is for .75 for 6000. The median between 5000 and 6000 is 5500 and thus, *PERCENTILE_CONT(.5)* returns 5500. There is no row in the window with a percentile of .6, so *PERCENTILE_CONT(.6)* calculates what the value for .6 would be (somewhere between 5000 and 6000, a bit closer to 5000) and then calculates the median between that value and the next percentile in the window (again, .75 for 6000). Thus, *PERCENTILE_CONT(.6)* returns 5800; slightly higher than the 5500 returned for *PERCENTILE_CONT(.5)*.

More Info The *PERCENTILE_DISC* and *PERCENTILE_CONT* functions define their window ordering using *ORDER BY* in a *WITHIN GROUP* clause rather than in the *OVER* clause. Thus, you do not (and cannot) specify *ORDER BY* in the *OVER* clause. The *OVER* clause is still required, however, so *OVER* (with empty parentheses) must be specified even if you don't want to partition using *PARTITION BY*.

New Conversion Functions

These three functions are designed to assist you with parsing and converting between different data types and culture-sensitive strings:

- TRY_CONVERT
- PARSE
- TRY_PARSE

The *TRY_CONVERT* function is the long-awaited "safe" version of the *CONVERT* function. *TRY_CONVERT* works exactly like its ubiquitous counterpart, except that it will return *NULL* rather than raise an error if the supplied data cannot be converted to the specified data type. For example, consider the code in Listing 2-34.

LISTING 2-34 Using *TRY_CONVERT* for valid and invalid conversions.

```
SELECT TRY_CONVERT(money, 'test') AS BadResult
SELECT TRY_CONVERT(money, '29.5') AS GoodResult
```

```
BadResult
-----------------
NULL

GoodResult
-----------------
29.50
```

As you can see, the *TRY_CONVERT* function has the same syntax and usage as *CONVERT*, except that it will never raise a conversion error. The first attempt to convert the string *'test'* to a *money* data type is invalid of course, but *TRY_CONVERT* simply returns *NULL* in that case and allows execution to continue. The second attempt to convert the string *'29.5'* to a *money* data type is perfectly valid, and performs just as *CONVERT* would.

The new *PARSE* function understands different date, time, and currency formats that are compatible with the various cultures supported by the .NET Framework. This function is paired with its counterpart *TRY_PARSE* that returns *NULL* if the specified string cannot be parsed as requested (rather than throwing an error as *PARSE* would). Listing 2-35 demonstrates:

LISTING 2-35 Using *PARSE* to analyze and convert culture-specific date, time, and currency strings.

```
SELECT PARSE('Monday, 13 December 2010' AS datetime2 USING 'en-US') AS USResult
SELECT PARSE('€345,98' AS money USING 'nl-NL') AS NLResult
```

```
USResult
------------------------
2010-12-13 00:00:00.000

NLResult
------------------------
345.98
```

The *USING* clause tells SQL Server how it should interpret the input string with respect to culture. You don't need to specify a culture with *PARSE*; the culture will be assumed by default based on the current language if *USING* is omitted (the current language can be set using the *SET LANGUAGE* statement).

The first statement parses an *en-US* (U.S. English) date-formatted string into the *datetime2* data type, and the second statement parses an *nl-NL* (Netherlands) Euro-formatted currency string into the *money* data type. Because both strings contain punctuation appropriate for the specified cultures, the *PARSE* function correctly interprets the input string in both cases.

However, the following statement raises an error:

```
SELECT PARSE('$345,98' AS money USING 'nl-NL') AS NLResult
```

Because the dollar sign symbol is not valid for a Netherlands-based currency string that expects and accepts the euro symbol (€), the *PARSE* function fails:

```
Msg 9819, Level 16, State 1, Line 39
Error converting string value '$345,98' into data type money using culture 'nl-NL'.
```

To handle cases where the input string hasn't been validated for the specified culture, use *TRY_PARSE* instead:

```
SELECT TRY_PARSE('$345,98' AS money USING 'nl-NL') AS NLResult
```

This statement returns *NULL* rather than raising an error. Thus, you can use *TRY_PARSE* to validate, and all you need to do is test its result for *NULL* to determine if the validation is successful.

New Date and Time Functions

A set of new functions let you construct dates and times based on discrete values you supply for the various parts of the overall value. There is a version of this function for each of the supported date and time data types in SQL Server (including the older *datetime* and *smalldatetime*, although this should not encourage their continued use).

- DATEFROMPARTS
- TIMEFROMPARTS
- DATETIME2FROMPARTS
- DATETIMEOFFSETFROMPARTS
- DATETIMEFROMPARTS
- SMALLDATETIMEFROMPARTS

There is also a new function to return the number of days in the month of a specified date:

- EOMONTH

The *xxxFROMPARTS* functions all work the same way; they each expect parameters that specify each part of the value to be generated. Using these functions, you can create explicit date and time values without the formatting and culture ambiguity concerns so common with strings. Listing 2-36 demonstrates these date and time construction functions.

LISTING 2-36 Constructing date and time values using the new *xxxFROMPARTS* functions.

```
SELECT DATEFROMPARTS(2010, 12, 31) AS ADate
SELECT TIMEFROMPARTS(23, 59, 59, 1234567, 7) AS ATime
SELECT DATETIME2FROMPARTS(2010, 12, 31, 23, 59, 59, 1234567, 7) AS ADateTime2
SELECT DATETIMEOFFSETFROMPARTS(2010, 12, 31, 14, 23, 36, 5, 12, 0, 1) ADateTimeOff
SELECT DATETIMEFROMPARTS(2010, 12, 31, 23, 59, 59, 123) AS ADateTime
SELECT SMALLDATETIMEFROMPARTS(2010, 12, 31, 23, 59) AS ASmallDateTime
```

```
ADate
-----------------------
2010-12-31

ATime
-----------------------
23:59:59.1234567

ADateTime2
---------------------------
2010-12-31 23:59:59.1234567

ADateTimeOff
----------------------------------
2010-12-31 14:23:36.5 +12:00

ADateTime
-----------------------
2010-12-31 23:59:59.123

ASmallDateTime
-----------------------
2010-12-31 23:59:00
```

The *EOMONTH* function is a handy way to determine the last day of the month of any given date. As you'd expect, leap years are accounted for as well, as Listing 2-37 demonstrates:

LISTING 2-37 Using the *EOMONTH* function to obtain the number of days in each month.

```
SELECT EOMONTH('1/1/2011') AS LastDayOfMonth UNION ALL  -- 31
SELECT EOMONTH('2/1/2011') UNION ALL  -- 28
SELECT EOMONTH('3/1/2011') UNION ALL  -- 31
SELECT EOMONTH('4/1/2011') UNION ALL  -- 30
SELECT EOMONTH('2/1/2012')            -- 29 (leap year)
```

```
LastDayOfMonth
-----------------------
2011-01-31
2011-02-28
2011-03-31
2011-04-30
2012-02-29
```

By combining *EOMONTH* with *DATEPART*, it's easy to get the day count for any given month. For example, the following query returns 29 for the number of days in February 2012 (a leap year).

```
SELECT DATEPART(day, EOMONTH('2/1/2012')) AS DaysInFeb2012
```

New Logical Functions

SQL Server 2012 also introduces these two new functions for conditional operations:

- CHOOSE
- IIF

These two functions are convenient alternatives to more verbose *CASE* statements, and work like the same-named Visual Basic for Applications (VBA) functions in Microsoft Access.

CHOOSE accepts an integer parameter (which would need to be a variable in any useful scenario), followed by any number of parameters of any data type (which can be either constants or variables). The integer acts as an index (one-based) into the list of parameters to return the item at a specific position, as demonstrated by the Listing 2-38:

LISTING 2-38 Using the *CHOOSE* function to select from a list of items.

```
DECLARE @CardTypeId int = 2  -- Master card
SELECT CHOOSE(@CardTypeId, 'Amex', 'Master', 'Visa', 'Discover') AS CardType
```

```
CardType
--------
Master
```

When deciding between one of two return values based on a Boolean (true/false) condition, the new *IIF* (Immediate IF) function offers a concise way to express your logic. The function accepts three parameters: the first is the Boolean condition to test, the second is the value to return if the condition is true, and the third is the value to return if the condition is false. Listing 2-39 demonstrates:

LISTING 2-39 Using the *IIF* function to perform conditional testing.

```
DECLARE @Num1 int = 45
DECLARE @Num2 int = 40
SELECT IIF(@Num1 > @Num2, 'larger', 'not larger' ) AS Result
```

```
Result
----------
larger
```

New String Functions

These two new string functions make it easier to build and format strings in T-SQL:

- CONCAT
- FORMAT

The *CONCAT* function concatenates strings just like the concatenation operator (+), but is tolerant of *NULL* values. When you concatenate using the + operator, the final result is always *NULL* if any of the strings being concatenated are *NULL*. This common annoyance is often dealt with by wrapping *ISNULL* conversions on all the values being concatenated. *CONCAT* offers a cleaner approach simply by treating *NULL* values as empty strings. Essentially, it implicitly converts all the specified values to strings before it concatenates them together. Consider this line of code:

```
SELECT CONCAT('Happy', ' Birthday ', 8, '/', NULL, '30') AS Greeting
```

This statement returns the string *'Happy Birthday 8/30'* by stringing together all the values supplied to *CONCAT*. The function converts the values *8* and *NULL* to the strings *'8'* and *''* (empty) respectively before concatenation.

The new *FORMAT* function brings the full power of .NET formatting to T-SQL. With it, you can easily express date, time, and currency values in virtually any desired format. Supply the value to format in the first parameter, specify the formatting code in the second parameter, and specify the culture in the third parameter (as with *PARSE* and *TRY_PARSE*, the third parameter is optional, and defaults to the culture for the currently set language). Table 2-3 shows the various supported codes to format dates, times, and currencies in any culture.

TABLE 2-3 Common date and time formatting codes.

Size	Action
d	General date format
t	General time format
D	Long date format
T	Long time format
Ddd	Abbreviated day of week
Dddd	Day of week
C	Currency (with optional decimal positions; e.g., c2)

The code in Listing 2-40 populates a table variable with a handful of different cultures, and then selects from the cultures to demonstrate various formatting capabilities of the *FORMAT* function.

LISTING 2-40 Using the *FORMAT* function to perform culture-specific date, time, and currency formatting.

```
DECLARE @Cultures table(Culture varchar(10), Lang varchar(50))
INSERT INTO @Cultures VALUES
 ('en', 'English'),
 ('nl', 'Dutch'),
 ('ja', 'Japanese'),
 ('ru', 'Russian'),
 ('no', 'Norwegian')

DECLARE @d datetime2 = DATETIME2FROMPARTS(2011, 2, 1, 16, 5, 0, 0, 7)
DECLARE @m money = 199.99

SELECT
  Lang,
  Date     = FORMAT(@d, 'd', Culture),
  TimeOnly = FORMAT(@d, 't', Culture),
  LongDate = FORMAT(@d, 'D', Culture),
  LongTime = FORMAT(@d, 'T', Culture),
  Dow      = FORMAT(@d, 'ddd', Culture),
  Currency = FORMAT(@m, 'c2', Culture)
 FROM
  @Cultures
```

```
Lang      Date       TimeOnly LongDate                   LongTime   Dow Currency
--------- ---------- -------- -------------------------- ---------- --- --------
English   2/1/2011   4:05 PM  Tuesday, February 02, 2011 4:05:00 PM Tue $199.99
Dutch     1-2-2011   16:05    dinsdag 1 februari 2011    16:05:00   di  € 199,99
Japanese  2011/02/01 16:05    2011年2月1日                16:05:00   火  ¥199.99
Russian   01.02.2011 16:05    1 февраля 2011 г.          16:05:00   вт  199,99р.
Norwegian 01.02.2011 16:05    1. februar 2011            16:05:00   ti  kr 199,99
```

You can also express custom date formats using masks (a combination of formatting codes and punctuation), as demonstrated by Listing 2-41. Exercise caution with this approach, however, as you are hardcoding formats that may not adapt properly to different cultures

LISTING 2-41 Using the *FORMAT* function with a mask to produce custom date and time formatting.

```
DECLARE @d datetime2 = DATETIME2FROMPARTS(2011, 2, 1, 16, 5, 0, 0, 7)
SELECT FORMAT(@d, 'ddd M/d/yyyy h:mm tt') AS DateAndTime
```

```
DateAndTime
---------------------------
Tue 2/1/2011 4:05 PM
```

In this example, the M/d/yyyy in the mask positions the month before the day. This is correct in the United States but reversed in European countries. Simply using D (for long date) or d (for short date) in the mask avoids this problem, as SQL Server automatically adjusts the date display for the specified culture.

Changed Mathematical Function

There is only one changed function in SQL Server 2012. It's extremely minor, but we cover it for completeness:

- LOG

This function now allows you to specify any desired base with which to compute the logarithm. Previously, you could use *LOG* only to compute the natural logarithm, or use the *LOG10* function to compute the logarithm with a base of 10. To compute the logarithm of a number using any other base, it was necessary to divide the natural logarithm of the desired number by the natural logarithm of the desired base. For example, the base 2 logarithm of 11 can be computed as follows:

```
SELECT LOG(11) / LOG(2) AS Base2LogOf11
```

In SQL Server 2012, the *LOG* function now accepts a second optional parameter to designate a specific base for the algorithm. Thus, the previous expression can now be coded as follows:

```
SELECT LOG(11, 2) AS Base2LogOf11
```

The *THROW* Statement

Error handling in T-SQL was very difficult to implement properly before SQL Server 2005 introduced the *TRY/CATCH* construct, a feature loosely based on .NET's *try/catch* structured exception handling model. The *CATCH* block gives you a single place to code error handling logic in the event that a problem occurs anywhere inside the *TRY* block above it. Before *TRY/CATCH*, it was necessary to always check for error conditions after every operation by testing the built-in system function

@@ERROR. Not only did code become cluttered with the many *@@ERROR* tests, developers (being humans) would too often forget to test *@@ERROR* in every needed place, causing many unhandled exceptions to go unnoticed.

In SQL Server 2005, *TRY/CATCH* represented a vast improvement over constantly testing *@@ERROR*, but *RAISERROR* has (until now) remained as the only mechanism for generating your own errors. In SQL Server 2012, the new *THROW* statement (again, borrowed from *throw* in the .NET model) is the recommended alternative way to raise exceptions in your T-SQL code (although *RAISERROR* does retain several capabilities that *THROW* lacks, as we'll explain shortly).

Re-Throwing Exceptions

The new *THROW* statement can be used in two ways. First, and as we just stated, it can serve as an alternative to *RAISERROR*, allowing your code to generate errors when it detects an unresolvable condition in processing. Used for this purpose, the *THROW* statement accepts parameters for the error code, description, and state, and works much like *RAISERROR*.

A more specialized use of *THROW* takes no parameters, and can appear only inside a *CATCH* block. In this scenario, an unexpected error occurs in the *TRY* block above, triggering execution of the *CATCH* block. Inside the *CATCH* block, you can perform general error handling (for example, logging the error, or rolling back a transaction), and then issue a *THROW* statement with no parameters. This will re-throw the original error that occurred—with its code, message, severity, and state intact—back up to the client, so the error can be caught and handled at the application level as well. This is an easy and elegant way for you to implement a segmented exception handling strategy between the database and application layers.

In contrast, *RAISERROR* always raises a new error. Thus, it can only simulate re-throwing the original error by capturing the *ERROR_MESSAGE*, *ERROR_SEVERITY*, and *ERROR_STATE* in the *CATCH* block and using their values to raise a new error. Using *THROW* for this purpose is much more simple and direct, as demonstrated in Listing 2-42:

LISTING 2-42 Using *THROW* in a *CATCH* block to re-throw an error.

```
CREATE TABLE ErrLog(ErrAt datetime2, Severity varchar(max), ErrMsg varchar(max))
GO

BEGIN TRY
  DECLARE @Number int = 5 / 0;
END TRY
BEGIN CATCH
  -- Log the error info, then re-throw it
  INSERT INTO ErrLog VALUES(SYSDATETIME(), ERROR_SEVERITY(), ERROR_MESSAGE());
  THROW;
END CATCH
```

In this code's *CATCH* block, error information is recorded to the *ErrLog* table and then the original error (divide by zero) is re-thrown for the client to catch:

```
Msg 8134, Level 16, State 1, Line 4
Divide by zero error encountered.
```

To confirm that the error was logged by the *CATCH* block as expected before being re-thrown, query the *ErrLog* table:

```
SELECT * FROM ErrLog
GO

ErrAt                        Severity  ErrMsg
---------------------------  --------  -------------------------------------------
2012-02-30 14:14:35.3361250  16        Divide by zero error encountered.
```

Comparing *THROW* and *RAISERROR*

The following table summarizes the notable differences that exist between *THROW* and *RAISERROR*:

TABLE 2-4 Comparing *THROW* and *RAISERROR*.

THROW	RAISERROR
Can only generate user exceptions (unless re-throwing in *CATCH* block)	Can generate user (>= 50000) and system (< 50000) exceptions
Supplies ad-hoc text; doesn't utilize *sys.messages*	Requires user messages defined in *sys.messages* (except for code 50000)
Doesn't support token substitutions	Supports token substitutions
Always uses severity level 16 (unless re-throwing in a *CATCH* block)	Can set any severity level
Can re-throw original exception caught in the *TRY* block	Always generates a new exception; the original exception is lost to the client
Error messages are buffered, and don't appear in real time	Supports *WITH NOWAIT* to immediate flush buffered output on error

A user exception is an error with a code of 50000 or higher that you define for your application's use. System exceptions are defined by SQL Server and have error codes lower than 50000. You can use the new *THROW* statement to generate and raise user exceptions, but not system exceptions. Only *RAISERROR* can be used to throw system exceptions. Note, however, that when *THROW* is used in a *CATCH* block to re-throw the exception from a *TRY* block as explained in the previous section, the actual original exception—even if it's a system exception—will get thrown (this was demonstrated in the previous "divide by zero" example).

When *RAISERROR* is used without an error code, SQL Server assigns an error code of 50000 and expects you to supply an ad-hoc message to associate with the error. The *THROW* statement always expects you to supply an ad-hoc message for the error, as well as a user error code of 50000 or higher. Thus, the following two statements are equivalent:

```
THROW 50000, 'An error occurred querying the table.', 1;
RAISERROR ('An error occurred querying the table.', 16, 1);
```

Both these statements raise an error with code 50000, severity 16, state 1, and the same message text. Compatibility between the two keywords ends there, however, as varying usages impose different rules (as summarized in Table 2-4). For example, only *RAISERROR* supports token substitution:

```
RAISERROR ('An error occurred querying the %s table.', 16, 1, 'Customer');

Msg 50000, Level 16, State 1, Line 22
An error occurred querying the Customer table.
```

THROW has no similar capability. Also, while *RAISERROR* lets you specify any severity level, *THROW* will always generate an error with a severity level of 16. This is significant, as level 11 and higher indicates more serious errors than level 10 and lower. For example:

```
RAISERROR ('An error occurred querying the table.', 10, 1);

An error occurred querying the table.
```

Because the severity is 10, this error does not echo the error code, level, state, and line number, and is displayed in black rather than the usual red that is used for severity levels higher than 10. In contrast, *THROW* cannot be used to signal a non-severe error.

The last important difference between the two keywords is the *RAISERROR* association with *sys.messages*. In particular, *RAISERROR* requires that you call *sys.sp_addmessage* to define error messages associated with user error codes higher than 50000. As explained, the *RAISERROR* syntax in our earlier examples uses an error code of 50000, and is the only supported syntax that lets you supply an ad-hoc message instead of utilizing *sys.messages*.

The following code demonstrates how to define customer user error messages for *RAISERROR*. First (and only once), a tokenized message for user error code 66666 is added to *sys.messages*. Thereafter, *RAISERROR* references the error by its code, and also supplies values for token replacements that are applied to the message's text in *sys.messages*.

```
EXEC sys.sp_addmessage 66666, 16, 'There is already a %s named %s.';
RAISERROR(66666, 16, 1, 'cat', 'morris');

Msg 66666, Level 16, State 1, Line 34
There is already a cat named morris.
```

The *THROW* statement has no such requirement. You supply any ad-hoc message text with *THROW*. You don't need to separately manage *sys.messages*, but this also means that *THROW* can't (directly) leverage centrally managed error messages in *sys.messages* like *RAISERROR* does. Fortunately, the *FORMATMESSAGE* function provides a workaround if you want to take advantage of the same capability with *THROW*. You just need to take care and make sure that the same error code is specified in the two places that you need to reference it (once for *FORMATMESSAGE* and once for *THROW*), as shown here:

```
DECLARE @Message varchar(max) = FORMATMESSAGE(66666, 'dog', 'snoopy');
THROW 66666, @Message, 1;

Msg 66666, Level 16, State 1, Line 40
There is already a dog named snoopy.
```

Server-Side Paging

Returning paged query results was difficult to achieve prior to SQL Server 2005. That release of SQL Server introduced a series of ranking functions, including the *ROW_NUMBER* function that made it possible to return one page at a time from your query. Let's first see how to use *ROW_NUMBER* added in SQL Server 2005 to implement server-side paging, and then you will learn how much easier it is to achieve the same goal using the new *OFFSET/FETCH NEXT* syntax introduced in SQL Server 2012.

Using *ROW_NUMBER*

The *ROW_NUMBER* function, as its name implies, generates a sequential number for each row in the result set returned by your query. The value returned by the *ROW_NUMBER* function can then be used in an outer query's *WHERE* clause to limit the result set to just the desired page. Listing 2-43 shows an example using the *AdventureWorks2012* database that demonstrates this technique. It returns "page 3" of the query results, which (assuming a page size of 10) are rows 21 through 30.

LISTING 2-43 Returning paged results using a nested subquery and the *ROW_NUMBER* function.

```
USE AdventureWorks2012
GO

-- Using ROW_NUMBER introduced in SQL Server 2005
DECLARE @PageNum int = 3
DECLARE @PageSize int = 10
DECLARE @FirstRow int = ((@PageNum - 1) * @PageSize) + 1
DECLARE @LastRow int = @FirstRow + @PageSize - 1

SELECT *
 FROM
   (SELECT
     RowNum = ROW_NUMBER() OVER (ORDER BY LastName, FirstName),
     Title, FirstName, LastName
    FROM
     Person.Person
    ) AS a
 WHERE RowNum BETWEEN @firstRow AND @lastRow
 ORDER BY LastName, FirstName
```

And here are the results:

```
RowNum   Title    FirstName   LastName
-------- -------- ----------- ----------
21       NULL     Bailey      Adams
22       Mr.      Ben         Adams
23       NULL     Blake       Adams
24       Ms.      Carla       Adams
25       NULL     Carlos      Adams
26       NULL     Charles     Adams
27       NULL     Chloe       Adams
28       NULL     Connor      Adams
29       NULL     Courtney    Adams
30       NULL     Dalton      Adams

(10 row(s) affected)
```

Now this certainly works, but there are two undesirables here. First, it requires you to manufacture the row number as an additional column in your result set, whether or not you want or need it. Second, the syntax is somewhat contorted; the required use of a nested *SELECT* statement and multiple *ORDER BY* clauses (as well as the required alias "*AS a*") is both awkward and unintuitive.

Using *OFFSET/FETCH NEXT*

Now take a look at how the same result can be achieved in SQL Server 2012 using the code shown in Listing 2-44.

LISTING 2-44 Returning paged results using the *OFFSET/FETCH NEXT* syntax.

```
DECLARE @PageNum int = 3
DECLARE @PageSize int = 10
DECLARE @Offset int = (@PageNum - 1) * @PageSize

SELECT Title, FirstName, LastName
 FROM Person.Person
 ORDER BY LastName, FirstName
 OFFSET @Offset ROWS FETCH NEXT @PageSize ROWS ONLY
```

The syntax couldn't be any simpler—just specify your starting row with *OFFSET* and your page size with *FETCH NEXT*. Here are the results:

```
Title    FirstName   LastName
-------- ----------- ----------
NULL     Bailey      Adams
Mr.      Ben         Adams
NULL     Blake       Adams
Ms.      Carla       Adams
NULL     Carlos      Adams
NULL     Charles     Adams
```

```
NULL    Chloe     Adams
NULL    Connor    Adams
NULL    Courtney  Adams
NULL    Dalton    Adams

(10 row(s) affected)
```

You can see that this query returns the same "page" as the previous version of the query that used the *ROW_NUMBER* function, yet it wasn't necessary to manufacture a row number column to do it, nor was it necessary to code a nested subquery. Furthermore, *OFFSET/FETCH NEXT* performs slightly faster than using *ROW_NUMBER*, and is significantly faster than the pre–SQL Server 2005 hacks involving stored procedures and temp tables. If you still want row numbers returned in your result set, you can combine *OFFSET/FETCH* with *ROW_NUMBER* if desired by replacing the SELECT statement in Listing 2-44 with:

```
SELECT RowNum = ROW_NUMBER() OVER (ORDER BY LastName, FirstName), Title, FirstName, LastName
 FROM Person.Person
 ORDER BY LastName, FirstName
 OFFSET @Offset ROWS FETCH NEXT @PageSize ROWS ONLY
```

The results of this query are identical to the results shown for Listing 2-43, but doesn't require coding the subquery seen in that listing.

Also note that *OFFSET* can be specified without *FETCH NEXT* to skip a specified number of rows and return all remaining rows.

The *SEQUENCE* Object

Historically, one notable difference between SQL Server and other database platforms (such as Oracle and DB2) has been the manner in which you implement automatically assigned integer values for primary keys when inserting new rows. SQL Server provides the *IDENTITY* attribute for the *int* and *bigint* data types, whereas other platforms require you to create an independent "sequence generator" object that feeds incrementing values to new rows in the table. These are two different ways to achieve the same thing, and SQL Server's *IDENTITY* is arguably simpler to use, but sequence generators offer their own unique advantages as well.

SQL Server 2012 now also supports sequence generators as a powerful alternative to using the *IDENTITY* attribute. Sequences can be created on integer types (both built-in and user-defined), and you can specify the minimum, maximum, start, and increment (or decrement) values for the sequence. You can also cycle back around to the minimum value when the maximum value is reached (or vice versa).

Sequences are most commonly used to assign new primary key values on *INSERT* operations as an alternative to using *IDENTITY*-attributed key columns. But because they exist as objects independent of the data tables that they feed new primary keys to, they offer more flexibility and pose fewer limitations. For example, you can obtain the next value in the sequence before you perform the *INSERT*, and you can insert any (unique) value into the primary key column without requiring *SET*

IDENTITY INSERT ON/OFF statements. The *NEXT VALUE FOR* syntax can be used in any *SELECT*, *INSERT*, or *UPDATE* statement to request and increment the next value in the sequence. Let's see how sequences work by examining the code in Listing 2-45.

LISTING 2-45 Using a sequence to generate new primary keys.

```
CREATE TABLE Customer
 (Id        int PRIMARY KEY,
  FirstName varchar(max),
  LastName  varchar(max))

-- Create the sequence with a start, increment, and min/max settings
CREATE SEQUENCE CustomerSequence AS int
 START WITH 1
 INCREMENT BY 1
 MINVALUE 0
 NO MAXVALUE

-- Use the sequence for new primary key values
INSERT INTO Customer (Id, FirstName, LastName) VALUES
 (NEXT VALUE FOR CustomerSequence, 'Bill', 'Malone'),
 (NEXT VALUE FOR CustomerSequence, 'Justin', 'Thorp'),
 (NEXT VALUE FOR CustomerSequence, 'Paul', 'Duffy')
```

The *Customer* table uses an integer primary key, but does not specify the *IDENTITY* attribute. Instead, you use the new *CREATE SEQUENCE* statement in SQL Server 2012 to create a *CustomerSequence* object that feeds new integers, starting with one and incrementing by one, with no specified upper limit (beyond the maximum size for the integer data type; a 32-bit *int* data type in this example). You then *INSERT* three new rows, each of which specifies *NEXT VALUE FOR CustomerSequence* as the new *Id* value (note the *row constructor* syntax, introduced in SQL Server 2008, that inserts the three rows with a single statement). The result, as you'd expect, appears like this:

```
SELECT * FROM Customer
GO

Id    FirstName LastName
----- --------- -------------
1     Bill      Malone
2     Justin    Thorp
3     Paul      Duffy

(3 row(s) affected)
```

Most likely, you'll want to emulate the experience of using the *IDENTITY* attribute; that is, you may wish to omit the primary key values from the *INSERT* statement and put SQL Server in charge of assigning them to new rows. This is easily done by establishing *NEXT VALUE FOR* as a *DEFAULT* constraint on the *Id* column, as shown in Listing 2-46.

LISTING 2-46 Emulating *IDENTITY*-attributed primary key columns with sequences using a *DEFAULT* constraint.

```
-- Set the default for IDENTITY-behavior
ALTER TABLE Customer
 ADD DEFAULT NEXT VALUE FOR CustomerSequence FOR Id

-- Generates customer ID 4
INSERT INTO Customer (FirstName, LastName) VALUES('Jeff', 'Smith')
```

With the DEFAULT constraint in place, the *INSERT* statement looks and works just the same as if you were using an *IDENTITY*-attributed primary key column. Customer Jeff Smith is automatically assigned an *Id* value of 4. But by using sequences, you can enjoy a few additional benefits. For example, you can peek at the current value without consuming it by querying the *sys.sequences* catalog view. Among the many parameters for each sequence object in the database exposed by this view, the *current_value* column reveals the currently assigned value:

```
SELECT current_value FROM sys.sequences WHERE name='CustomerSequence'
GO

current_value
-------------
4
```

You can also use the *ALTER SEQUENCE* statement to change the behavior of an existing sequence object, as shown in Listing 2-47.

LISTING 2-47 Changing a sequence object using *ALTER SEQUENCE.*

```
ALTER SEQUENCE CustomerSequence
  RESTART WITH 1100
  MINVALUE 1000
  MAXVALUE 9999
  CYCLE
```

Now the next value returned by *CustomerSequence* will be 1100, and it will continue to increment by one from there. When it tops 9999, it will start again from 1000 and continue incrementing normally. Naturally, given the uniqueness of primary keys, the sequence can no longer be used to populate the *Customer* table 100 rows after it recycles to 1000, because you already have customers with primary keys starting at 1100.

Sequence Limitations

Of course, sequences have some restrictions that need to be called out. Sequences cannot be used in a subquery, CTE, *TOP* clause, *CHECK CONSTRAINT* definition, or as an argument to an aggregate function. They also can't be used in views, computed columns, and user-defined functions, as those object types are not allowed to cause the side effects of sequence number generation. Finally, you cannot issue a *DROP SEQUENCE* statement to delete a sequence while you have tables with existing *DEFAULT* constraints that reference the sequence; you'll need to drop the referencing constraints before you can drop the sequence.

Metadata Discovery

Modern development tools deliver critical productivity features, such as graphical designers and code generators, and those capabilities rely heavily on database metadata discovery. Indeed, it has always been possible to interrogate SQL Server for metadata information. You can easily discover all the objects in a database (tables, views, stored procedures, and so on) and their types by directly querying system tables (not recommended, as they can change from one version of SQL Server to another) or information schema views (which are consistent in each SQL Server version). It is significantly more challenging, however, to discover the result set schema for T-SQL statements or stored procedures that contain conditional logic.

Using *SET FMTONLY ON/OFF* has been the common technique in the past for discovering the schema of a query's result set without actually executing the query itself. To demonstrate, execute the code shown in Listing 2-48.

LISTING 2-48 Using the old (now deprecated) *SET FMTONLY ON/OFF* technique for discovering a table's schema.

```
USE AdventureWorks2012
GO

SET FMTONLY ON
SELECT * FROM HumanResources.Employee;
SET FMTONLY OFF
```

This *SELECT* statement, which would normally return all the rows from the *HumanResources.Employee* table, returns no rows at all. It just reveals the columns. The *SET FMTONLY ON* statement prevents queries from returning rows of data so that their schemas can be discovered, and this behavior remains in effect until *SET FMTONLY OFF* is encountered.

SQL Server 2012 introduces several new system stored procedures and table-valued functions (TVFs) that provide significantly richer metadata discovery than what can be discerned using the relatively inelegant (and now deprecated) *SET FMTONLY ON/OFF* approach. These new procedures and functions are:

- sys.sp_describe_first_result_set
- sys.sp_describe_undeclared_parameters
- sys.dm_exec_describe_first_result_set
- sys.dm_exec_describe_first_result_set_for_object

The *sys.sp_describe_first_result_set* accepts a T-SQL statement and produces a highly detailed schema description of the first possible result set returned by that statement. The following code retrieves schema information for the same *SELECT* statement you used earlier to get information on all the columns in the *HumanResources.Employee* table:

```
EXEC sp_describe_first_result_set
 @tsql = N'SELECT * FROM HumanResources.Employee'
```

Figure 2-3 shows the wealth of information that SQL Server returns about each column in the result set returned by the T-SQL statement.

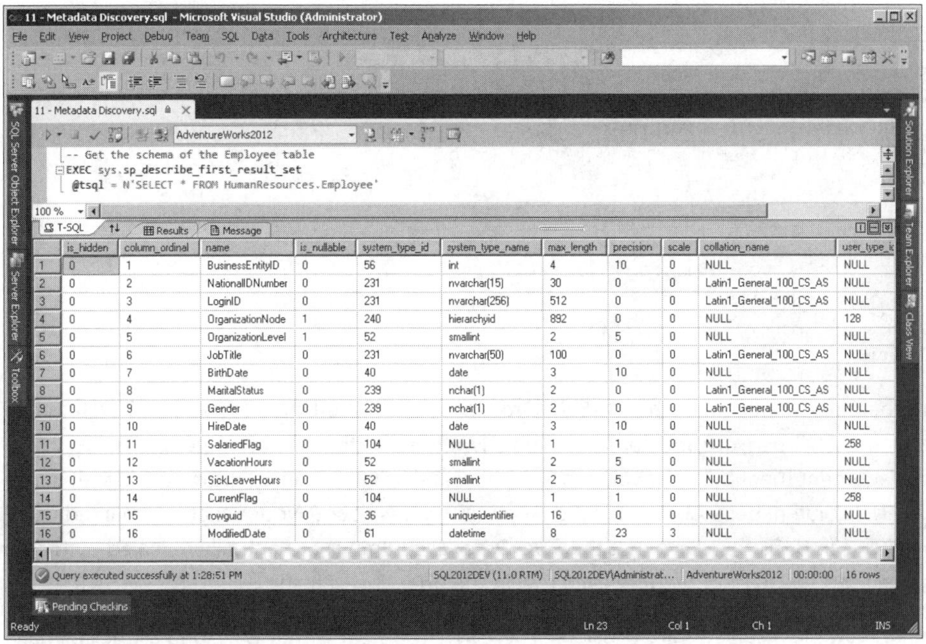

	is_hidden	column_ordinal	name	is_nullable	system_type_id	system_type_name	max_length	precision	scale	collation_name	user_type_i
1	0	1	BusinessEntityID	0	56	int	4	10	0	NULL	NULL
2	0	2	NationalIDNumber	0	231	nvarchar(15)	30	0	0	Latin1_General_100_CS_AS	NULL
3	0	3	LoginID	0	231	nvarchar(256)	512	0	0	Latin1_General_100_CS_AS	NULL
4	0	4	OrganizationNode	1	240	hierarchyid	892	0	0	NULL	128
5	0	5	OrganizationLevel	1	52	smallint	2	5	0	NULL	NULL
6	0	6	JobTitle	0	231	nvarchar(50)	100	0	0	Latin1_General_100_CS_AS	NULL
7	0	7	BirthDate	0	40	date	3	10	0	NULL	NULL
8	0	8	MaritalStatus	0	239	nchar(1)	2	0	0	Latin1_General_100_CS_AS	NULL
9	0	9	Gender	0	239	nchar(1)	2	0	0	Latin1_General_100_CS_AS	NULL
10	0	10	HireDate	0	40	date	3	10	0	NULL	NULL
11	0	11	SalariedFlag	0	104	NULL	1	1	0	NULL	258
12	0	12	VacationHours	0	52	smallint	2	5	0	NULL	NULL
13	0	13	SickLeaveHours	0	52	smallint	2	5	0	NULL	NULL
14	0	14	CurrentFlag	0	104	NULL	1	1	0	NULL	258
15	0	15	rowguid	0	36	uniqueidentifier	16	0	0	NULL	NULL
16	0	16	ModifiedDate	0	61	datetime	8	23	3	NULL	NULL

FIGURE 2-3 Detailed metadata returned by *sp_describe_first_result_set*.

A data management function named *sys.dm_exec_describe_first_result_set* works very similar to *sys.sp_describe_first_result_set*. But because it is implemented as a TVF, it is easy to query against it and limit the metadata returned. For example, the query in Listing 2-49 examines the same T-SQL statement, but returns just the name and data type of nullable columns.

LISTING 2-49 Querying the new data management function to discover nullable columns in a table.

```
SELECT name, system_type_name
 FROM sys.dm_exec_describe_first_result_set(
  'SELECT * FROM HumanResources.Employee', NULL, 1)
WHERE is_nullable = 1
```

```
name                system_type_name
------------------  ----------------
OrganizationNode    hierarchyid
OrganizationLevel   smallint
```

Parameterized queries are also supported, if you supply an appropriate parameter signature after the T-SQL. The T-SQL in the previous example had no parameters, so it passed *NULL* for the "parameters parameter." The code in the Listing 2-50 discovers the schema of a parameterized query.

LISTING 2-50 Discovering the schema returned by a parameterized query.

```
SELECT name, system_type_name, is_hidden
 FROM sys.dm_exec_describe_first_result_set('
  SELECT OrderDate, TotalDue
   FROM Sales.SalesOrderHeader
   WHERE SalesOrderID = @OrderID',
  '@OrderID int', 1)
```

```
name            system_type_name  is_hidden
--------------- ----------------  ---------
OrderDate       datetime          0
TotalDue        money             0
SalesOrderID    int               1
```

You'd be quick to question why the *SalesOrderID* column is returned for a *SELECT* statement that returns only *OrderDate* and *TotalDue*. The answer lies in the last parameter passed to the data management function. A *bit* value of 1 (for true) tells SQL Server to return the identifying *SalesOrderID* column, because it is used to "browse" the result set. Notice that it is marked true (1) for *is_hidden*. This informs the client that the *SalesOrderID* column is not actually revealed by the query, but can be used to uniquely identify each row in the query's result set.

What if multiple result sets are possible? There's no problem with this as long as they all have the same schema. In fact, SQL Server will even try to forgive cases where multiple possible schemas are not exactly identical. For example, if the same column is nullable in one result set and non-nullable in the other, schema discovery will succeed and indicate the column as nullable. It will even tolerate cases where the same column has a different name (but same type) between two possible result sets, and indicate NULL for the column name, rather than arbitrarily choosing one of the possible column names or failing altogether.

The code in Listing 2-51 demonstrates this with a T-SQL statement that has two possible result sets depending on the value passed in for the *@SortOrder* parameter. Because both result sets have compatible schemas, the data management function succeeds in returning schema information.

LISTING 2-51 Discovering the schema returned from a T-SQL statement with multiple compatible result sets.

```
SELECT name, system_type_name
 FROM sys.dm_exec_describe_first_result_set('
    IF @SortOrder = 1
      SELECT OrderDate, TotalDue
       FROM Sales.SalesOrderHeader
       ORDER BY SalesOrderID ASC
    ELSE IF @SortOrder = -1
      SELECT OrderDate, TotalDue
       FROM Sales.SalesOrderHeader
       ORDER BY SalesOrderID DESC',
   '@SortOrder AS tinyint', 0)
```

```
name          system_type_name
-----------   ----------------
OrderDate     datetime
TotalDue      money
```

Discovery won't succeed if SQL Server detects incompatible schemas. For example, in Listing 2-52, the call to the system stored procedure specifies a T-SQL statement with two possible result sets, but one returns three columns but the other returns only two columns.

LISTING 2-52 Attempting to discover schema information returned from a T-SQL statement with multiple incompatible result sets.

```
EXEC sys.sp_describe_first_result_set
  @tsql = N'
    IF @IncludeCurrencyRate = 1
      SELECT OrderDate, TotalDue, CurrencyRateID
       FROM Sales.SalesOrderHeader
    ELSE
      SELECT OrderDate, TotalDue
       FROM Sales.SalesOrderHeader'
```

In this case, the system stored procedure raises an error that clearly explains the problem:

```
Msg 11509, Level 16, State 1, Procedure sp_describe_first_result_set, Line 53
The metadata could not be determined because the statement 'SELECT OrderDate, TotalDue,
CurrencyRateID FROM Sales.SalesOrderHeader' is not compatible with the statement 'SELECT
OrderDate, TotalDue FROM Sales.SalesOrderHeader'.
```

It is noteworthy to mention that the data management function copes with this scenario much more passively. Given conflicting result set schemas, it simply returns *NULL* and does not raise an error.

The data management function *sys.dm_exec_describe_first_result_set_for_object* can be used to achieve the same discovery against any object in the database. It accepts just an object ID and the Boolean "browse" flag to specify if hidden ID columns should be returned. You can use the *OBJECT_ID* function to obtain the ID of the desired object. The example in Listing 2-53 demonstrates this by returning schema information for the stored procedure *GetOrderInfo*.

LISTING 2-53 Discovering metadata returned from a stored procedure identified by its object ID.

```
CREATE PROCEDURE GetOrderInfo(@OrderID AS int) AS
  SELECT OrderDate, TotalDue
   FROM Sales.SalesOrderHeader
   WHERE SalesOrderID = @OrderID
GO

SELECT name, system_type_name, is_hidden
 FROM sys.dm_exec_describe_first_result_set_for_object(OBJECT_ID('GetOrderInfo'), 1)
```

```
name            system_type_name   is_hidden
--------------- ------------------ ---------
OrderDate       datetime           0
TotalDue        money              0
SalesOrderID    int                1
```

Finally, the *sys.sp_describe_undeclared_parameters* stored procedure parses a T-SQL statement to discover type information about the parameters expected by the statement, as Listing 2-54 demonstrates.

LISTING 2-54 Discovering parameters (and their data types) expected by a T-SQL statement.

```
EXEC sys.sp_describe_undeclared_parameters
 N'IF @IsFlag = 1 SELECT 1 ELSE SELECT 0'
```

```
parameter_ordinal name    suggested_system_type_id suggested_system_type_name ...
----------------- ------- ------------------------ -------------------------- -------
1                 @IsFlag 56                       int                        ...
```

In this example, SQL Server detects the *@IsFlag* parameter, and suggests the *int* data type based on the usage in the T-SQL statement it was given to parse.

Summary

We covered a lot of ground in this chapter. As Microsoft continues to invest in T-SQL, developers are rewarded with many powerful enhancements to the T-SQL engine. You've learned how to use table-valued parameters (TVPs) to pass sets of rows across client, server, stored procedures, and user-defined functions (UDFs). The date and time data types were also covered, as well as the capabilities of *MERGE*, INSERT OVER DML, and *GROUPING SETS*. You also learned how to use the latest features in SQL Server 2012, including a host of new T-SQL functions, the windowing (*OVER* clause) enhancements, the *THROW* statement, server-side paging, *SEQUENCE* objects, and metadata discovery improvements.

T-SQL is still the main way you will program against your data. When your operations require you to interact with the operating system or use the .NET Framework, you can use the CLR to write your queries in Visual Basic .NET or Visual C#. In the next chapter, you'll learn how.

CHAPTER 3

Exploring SQL CLR

—Andrew Brust

The banner headline for Microsoft SQL Server 2005 was its integration of the Microsoft .NET common language runtime (CLR). This architectural enhancement gave SQL Server the ability to use certain .NET classes as basic data types, as well as accommodate the use of .NET languages for the creation of stored procedures, triggers, functions, and even user-defined aggregates.

This capability was carried forward and enhanced in SQL Server 2008 and is the underlying enabler of various "beyond relational" SQL Server data types, including *hierarchyid* (covered in Chapter 7), and *geometry* and *geography* (covered in Chapter 9). SQL CLR technology remains important in SQL Server 2012 and we will cover the technology, including its development and deployment using SQL Server Data Tools (SSDT), in this chapter.

Note Throughout this chapter, we will refer to the CLR integration in SQL Server as SQL CLR features, functionality, or integration, and we will refer to SQL CLR stored procedures, triggers, functions, aggregates, and user-defined types (UDTs) as the five basic SQL CLR entities.

In this chapter, you will learn:

- How to enable (or disable) SQL CLR integration on your SQL Server.
- How SQL Server accommodates CLR code through the loading of .NET assemblies.
- How to use SQL Server 2012, Microsoft Visual Studio 2010, and SSDT together to write SQL CLR code and deploy it, simply and quickly.
- How to deploy SQL CLR code independently of Visual Studio, using T-SQL statements, with or without the help of SQL Server Management Studio (SSMS).
- How to create simple CLR stored procedures, triggers, functions, aggregates, and UDTs, use them in your databases, and utilize them from Transact-SQL (T-SQL).
- How both the standard SQL Server client provider and the new server-side library can be combined to implement SQL CLR functionality.
- How SQL CLR security works and how to configure security permissions for your assemblies.
- When to use SQL CLR functionality, and when to opt to use T-SQL instead.

Getting Started: Enabling CLR Integration

Before you can learn how to use SQL CLR features, you need to know how to enable them. As with many new products in the Microsoft Windows Server system family, most advanced features of SQL Server are disabled by default. The reasoning behind this is sound: each additional feature that is enabled provides extra "surface area" for attacks on security or integrity of the product, and the added exposure is simply not justified if the feature goes unused.

The SQL CLR features of SQL Server 2012 are sophisticated and can be very useful, but they are also, technically, nonessential. It is possible to build high-performance databases and server-side programming logic without SQL CLR integration, so it is turned off by default.

Don't be discouraged, though; turning on the feature is easy. Microsoft provides a system stored procedure for enabling or disabling SQL CLR integration. Connect to the server you'd like to configure in SSDT or SSMS. Then, from a query window, type the following statements, and execute the script.

```
sp_configure 'clr enabled', 1
GO

RECONFIGURE
GO
```

That's all there is to it! To disable SQL CLR integration, just use a value of *0*, instead of *1*, as the second parameter value in the *sp_configure* call.

> **Tip** Don't forget that this will work from any tool that can connect to SQL Server, not just SSDT and SSMS. In fact, you could issue the previous command text from your own code using the ADO.NET *SqlCommand* object's *ExecuteNonQuery* method as long as your code can connect to your server and your server can authenticate you as a user in the *sysadmin* server role.

With SQL CLR integration enabled, you're ready to get started writing SQL CLR code. Before you dive in though, we need to discuss Visual Studio/SQL Server integration and when to use it.

Visual Studio/SQL Server Integration

SSDT and SQL Server 2012 integrate tightly in a number of ways. It's important to realize, however, that the use of SSDT is completely optional and the use of T-SQL is a sufficient substitute. With the release of SQL Server 2005, T-SQL was enhanced with new data definition language (DDL) commands for maintaining CLR assemblies, types, and aggregates, and its existing commands for stored procedures, triggers, and functions were enhanced to recognize code within deployed assemblies. Visual Studio can execute those commands on your behalf. It can also make writing individual SQL CLR classes and functions easier.

Ultimately, we think all developers should be aware of both SSDT–assisted and more manual coding and deployment methods. You might decide to use one method most of the time, but in some situations you'll probably need the other as well, so we want to prepare you. As we cover each major area of SQL CLR programming, we will discuss deployment from both points of view. We'll cover some general points about Visual Studio integration now, and then we'll move on to cover SQL CLR development.

SQL Server Database Projects in Visual Studio

The SSDT SQL Server Database Project type defines templates for the five basic SQL CLR entities. These templates inject specific code attributes and function stubs that allow you to create SQL CLR code easily. The attributes are used by SSDT to deploy your assembly and its stored procedures, triggers, and so on to your database. Some of them are also used by SQL Server to acknowledge and properly use your functions, UDTs, and aggregates.

To test out the new project type and templates, follow this procedure:

1. Start Visual Studio 2010, and then create a new project by choosing File | New | Project, clicking New Project on the toolbar, pressing **Ctrl+Shift+N**, or clicking the New Project... link on the Visual Studio Start Page.

2. In the New Project dialog box, shown in Figure 3-1, click the expand glyph to the left of the *Other Languages* node in the Installed Templates tree view on the left, click that node's *SQL Server* child node, and then click SQL Server Database Project in the middle pane. Enter your own project name if you want, and then click OK.

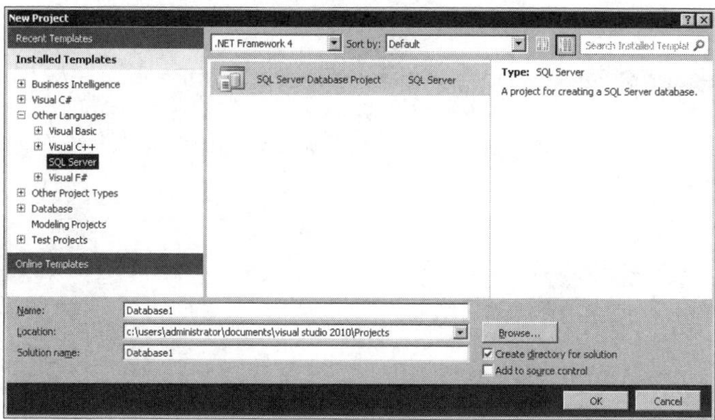

FIGURE 3-1 The Visual Studio 2010 New Project dialog box with the SQL Server Database Project type selected.

You can easily add preconfigured classes for the five basic SQL CLR entities to your project, but you must first decide whether you wish to use C# or Visual Basic .NET as the programming language for your SQL CLR Assembly.

3. Double-click the *Properties* node in the Solution Explorer, and then click the SQLCLR tab in the resulting property sheet designer. Once inside the SQLCLR tab, select C# from the Language combo box, as shown in Figure 3-2.

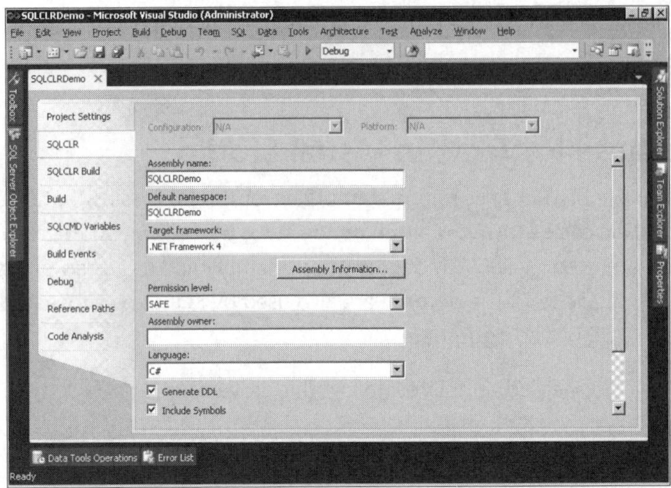

FIGURE 3-2 The SQL CLR property sheet with C# selected as the programming language.

4. Now you're ready to add a CLR entity to your project. You can do this from the Add New Item dialog box, which you display by selecting Project | Add New Item from the main menu or by choosing Add | New Item from the project node's shortcut menu in Solution Explorer. If you select the SQL CLR C# (or SQL CLR VB) template type from the "Installed Templates" list on the left of the Add New Item dialog box, it should appear as shown in Figure 3-3.

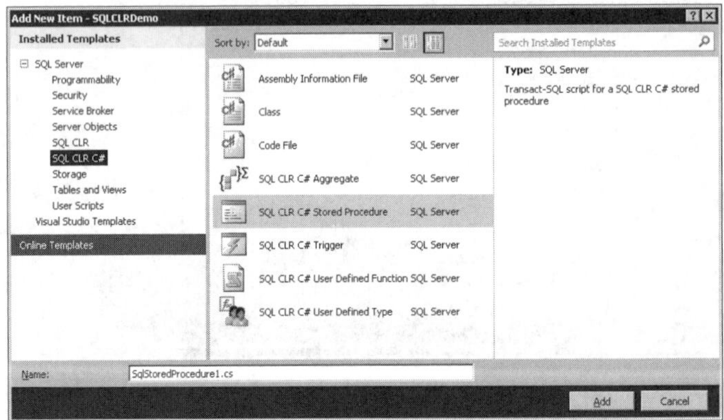

FIGURE 3-3 The Visual Studio SQL Server Database Project Add New Item dialog box, with SQL CLR C# templates displayed.

After selecting an entity type, a class template for that type will be added to your project and opened in the code editor window. Additionally, references to the *System*, *System.Data*, and *System.Xml* assemblies will be added to the project. These references are required by the stubbed code that appears in the SQL CLR class templates.

Automated Deployment

Once opened, the use of the SQL Server Database Project template adds a Publish option to the Build option of the Visual Studio main menu, which can be used to deploy the assembly and the SQL CLR entities within it.

SSDT can do a lot of deployment work for you. But as you'll learn, you can perform the same tasks on your own and, in certain circumstances, have more precise control over the deployment process when you do so.

SQL CLR Code Attributes

A number of .NET code attributes are provided for SQL CLR developers; these are contained in the *Microsoft.SqlServer.Server* namespace. Many of them are inserted in your code when you use the various templates in the SQL Server Database Project type, as is a *using* statement (or an *Imports* statement in Visual Basic) to alias the *Microsoft.SqlServer.Server* namespace itself. If you choose to develop code without these templates, you must add the appropriate attributes, and optionally the *using* (or *Imports*) statement yourself. Although all these attributes are provided in the same namespace, some are used exclusively by SSDT and others are used by both SSDT and SQL Server.

More SQL CLR attributes are available for you to use than we will be able to cover in this chapter. Specifically, we will provide coverage of the *SqlProcedure*, *SqlFunction*, *SqlTrigger*, *SqlUserDefinedAggregate*, and *SqlUserDefinedType* attributes. We will not cover the *SqlFacet* and *SqlMethod* attributes.

Just as certain attributes are not covered here, we cover only some of the parameters accepted by the attributes that we do cover. And in some cases, we cover only certain values that can be passed to these attributes of the many possible. For example, *SqlFunction* accepts several parameters, but the only ones we will cover are *Name*, *FillRowMethodName*, and *TableDefinition*. For *SqlUserDefinedAggregate* and *SqlUserDefinedType*, we will cover only a single value setting for the *Format* parameter and will not cover the several other parameters those two attributes accept.

The coverage we provide will be more than sufficient for you to implement basic, intermediate, and certain advanced functionality with all of the five basic SQL CLR entities. The attributes and parameters that we won't cover are useful mostly for optimizing your SQL CLR code, and they are well documented in SQL Server Books Online and articles on MSDN.

About the Sample Code

The sample .NET code for this chapter is provided on the book's companion website (see the "Introduction" for instructions to download the sample code) in two versions. The primary material is supplied as an SSDT SQL Server Database Project, accessible by opening the solution file *SQLCLRDemo.sln* in the SQLCLRDemo folder under the VS (Visual Studio) subfolder of the sample code folder. We also supply the code as a standard Class Library project, accessible by opening the solution file *SQLCLRDemoManual.sln* in the SQLCLRDemoManual subfolder. The code in each project is virtually identical, although the Class Library project's compiled assembly cannot be auto-deployed to a SQL Server database. As we cover each SQL CLR feature, we'll discuss how automated deployment takes place from the SSDT SQL Server Database Project and how command-driven deployment should be performed for the Class Library project.

We'll also discuss executing test scripts. As a companion to those discussions, we provide a SQL Server Management Studio project, accessible by opening *SQLCLRDemo.ssmssln* in the SQLCLRDemo folder under the sample code folder's SSMS subfolder. This project consists of a number of SQL scripts used for testing the sample SQL CLR code, and a script for cleaning up everything in the database created by the sample code and tests. The project also contains a script file named *CreateObjects.sql*, which deploys the Class Library assembly and the SQL CLR entities within it.

Your First SQL CLR Stored Procedure

Although SQL CLR programming can get quite complex and involved, in reality it offers a simple model that any .NET developer can use with high productivity in relatively short order. That's because the crux of SQL CLR functionality is nothing more than the ability of SQL Server 2012 to load .NET assemblies into your database and then allow you to use the functions and types within the assembly as you define your columns, views, stored procedures, triggers, and functions.

To gain a good understanding of SQL CLR integration, you must examine its features and techniques carefully. Before doing so, however, let's quickly walk through an end-to-end scenario for creating and executing a SQL CLR stored procedure. This will make it easier for you to understand the individual features as we describe them.

Strictly speaking, any .NET class library assembly (in certain cases, using appropriate .NET code attributes in its classes and functions) can be loaded into your database with a simple T-SQL statement. To see how easily this works, open a query window in SSDT or SSMS using a connection to the *AdventureWorks2012* sample database. In the sample code folder, confirm that the file *SQLCLRDemo.dll* is located in the VS\SQLCLRDemoManual\SQLCLRDemo\bin\Debug subfolder. If the sample code parent folder were C:\Demos, you would load the assembly into the *AdventureWorks2012* database with the following T-SQL command:

```
CREATE ASSEMBLY SQLCLRDemo
 FROM 'C:\Demos\VS\SQLCLRDemoManual\SQLCLRDemo\bin\Debug\SQLCLRDemo.dll'
```

There are other syntax options for the *CREATE ASSEMBLY* command, but for now we'll focus on the preceding limited usage.

Functions in an assembly that reside within a class and perform local computational tasks and certain types of data access can be easily exposed as SQL Server stored procedures, triggers, or functions. As with conventional T-SQL stored procedures, triggers, and functions, all it takes is a simple T-SQL *CREATE PROCEDURE*, *CREATE TRIGGER*, or *CREATE FUNCTION* statement to make this happen. We'll go through each of these options in this chapter, but for now let's create a simple CLR stored procedure.

You can view the source code for the *SQLCLRDemo* assembly by opening the solution file VS\SQLCLRDemoManual*SQLCLRDemoManual.sln* in this chapter's sample code folder. Within the project, the file *Sprocs.cs* contains the following code:

```
using System.Data.SqlClient;
using Microsoft.SqlServer.Server;

public partial class Sprocs
{
  public static void spContactsQuick()
  {
    SqlContext.Pipe.ExecuteAndSend(new SqlCommand("SELECT * FROM Person.Person"));
  }
}
```

The *spContactsQuick* method is designed to connect to the database in which its assembly has been loaded (*AdventureWorks2012*), perform a *SELECT* * against the *Person.Person* table, and then use special server-side objects to send the data back to the client application. To make this CLR code available via SQL Server as a stored procedure, also called *spContactsQuick*, you simply execute the following command from an SSMS or SSDT query window:

```
CREATE PROCEDURE spContactsQuick
 AS EXTERNAL NAME SQLCLRDemo.Sprocs.spContactsQuick
```

Important Be sure to enter the *Sprocs.spContactsQuick* portion of the command verbatim. This phrase is case sensitive.

To test the SQL CLR stored procedure, run it from an SSMS or SSDT query window as you would any conventional stored procedure, as shown here:

```
EXEC spContactsQuick
```

Or simply:

```
spContactsQuick
```

When the execution completes, you should see the contents of the *Person.Person* table in the Results tab of the query window.

As you can see from this rather trivial example, writing a CLR stored procedure can be very easy and is a lot like writing client-side or middle-tier code that performs data access using ADO.NET. The biggest differences involve the provision of a database connection and the fact that the data must be "piped" back to the client rather than merely loaded into a *SqlDataReader* and returned, manipulated, or displayed through a user interface (UI). The presence of the *SqlContext* object also differentiates SQL CLR code from conventional ADO.NET data access code. We'll cover the use of the *SqlContext* object and its *Pipe* property in the next section.

The bits of T-SQL and C# code just shown certainly don't tell the whole SQL CLR story. The use of the *ExecuteAndSend* method allowed us to skip over a number of otherwise important concepts. There are three ways to deploy assemblies, and you've seen only a simplified version of one of those ways. Security considerations must be taken into account, and we haven't even begun to look at triggers, functions, aggregates, or UDTs. So although the example showed how easy SQL CLR programming can be, we'll now take our time and show you the nooks and crannies.

CLR Stored Procedures and Server-Side Data Access

Our previous "quick and dirty" sample looked at CLR stored procedure development, but we need to cover that topic more thoroughly now. We've already covered the mechanics of writing and deploying a stored procedure, but let's back up a bit to try and understand how CLR stored procedures work from a conceptual standpoint.

SQL CLR stored procedure code runs in an instance of the .NET CLR that is hosted by SQL Server itself; it is not called as an external process, as Component Object Model (COM)–based extended stored procedures (XPs) would be. Because SQL CLR code runs in the context of the server, it treats objects in the database as native, *local* objects, more or less. As such, it must treat the client that calls it as *remote*. This contextual environment is, in effect, the opposite of that under which client and middle-tier ADO.NET code runs. There, communicating with the database requires a remote connection (even if the database is physically on the same computer) and the ADO.NET code runs locally. The SQL CLR reversal of this takes a little getting used to, but once you've mastered thinking about things this way, SQL CLR code becomes easy to write and understand.

Meanwhile, as .NET has no intrinsic way of accessing local objects on the server or transmitting data and messages to the client, you must use a special set of classes to perform these tasks. These classes are contained in the *Microsoft.SqlServer.Server* namespace.

Note As an aside, it is interesting and important to note that the *Microsoft.SqlServer.Server* namespace is actually supplied by the *System.Data.dll* .NET Framework assembly. This means that you don't need to worry about adding a reference to your project to use this namespace. The namespace's location within *System.Data.dll* also further emphasizes the tight integration between .NET and SQL Server.

If you want, you can think of *Microsoft.SqlServer.Server* as a helper library for *System.Data.SqlClient*. It supplies the SQL CLR code attributes we already mentioned, a few enumerations, an exception class, an interface, and five other classes: *SqlContext*, *SqlPipe*, *SqlTriggerContext*, *SqlMetaData*, and *SqlDataRecord*. We'll cover *SqlMetaData* and *SqlDataRecord* at the end of this section, and we'll cover *SqlTriggerContext* when we discuss CLR triggers later in this chapter. We'll cover the *SqlContext* and *SqlPipe* objects right now.

At a high level, the *SqlContext* object, which is *static*, provides a handle to the server-side context in which your code runs. It also has a channel to the client through which you can return data and text: its *Pipe* property, which in turn provides access to a properly opened and initialized *SqlPipe* object.

A *SqlPipe* object can send data and messages to the calling client though several methods: *Send*, *SendResultsStart*, *SendResultsRow*, *SendResultsEnd*, and *ExecuteAndSend*. In the preceding code sample, you used the *SqlPipe* object's *ExecuteAndSend* method to implicitly open a connection, call *ExecuteReader* on a *SqlCommand* object that uses that connection, and transmit the contents of the resulting *SqlDataReader* back to the client. Although the implicit work done by *ExecuteAndSend* might have been convenient for us to get started quickly, it's important to avoid such shortcuts in detailed discussions of SQL CLR programming.

In general, SQL CLR stored procedure code that queries tables in the database must open a connection to that database, use the *SqlCommand* object's *ExecuteReader* method to query the data, and then use one or a combination of the *Send* methods to send it back. The *Send* methods do not accept *DataSet* objects; they accept only *SqlDataReader* objects, strings, and special *SqlDataRecord* objects. Listing 3-1, which shows the implementation of the function *spContacts* from *spTest.cs* in the *SQLCLRDemo* sample project, is a representative example of how this is done.

LISTING 3-1 *spContacts* from *spTest.cs*.

```
[SqlProcedure]
public static void spContacts()
{
    SqlConnection conn = new SqlConnection("context connection=true");
    SqlCommand cm = new SqlCommand("SELECT * FROM Person.Person", conn);

    conn.Open();
    SqlDataReader dr = cm.ExecuteReader();
    SqlContext.Pipe.Send("Starting data dump");
    SqlContext.Pipe.Send(dr);
    SqlContext.Pipe.Send("Data dump complete");
    dr.Close();
    conn.Close();
}
```

Note The implementation of *spContacts* in the *SQLCLRDemoManual* project is identical to that shown in Listing 3-1, but is not decorated with the *SqlProcedure* code attribute.

Because the *Person.Person* table includes xml columns, and because such columns can cause a slowdown in SQL CLR stored procedures, the query in the sample code for *spContacts* uses a column list (which excludes the xml columns) in the *SELECT* clause rather than the * wildcard. We retained the *SELECT* * syntax in the printed code for simplicity and terseness.

For this code to work, you need to use both the *Microsoft.SqlServer.Server* and *System.Data.SqlClient* namespaces (and if you look in the chapter's sample project rather than Listing 3-1, you'll see that we have aliased both of those namespaces with *using* statements). This is because any conventional ADO.NET objects you might use, such as *SqlConnection*, *SqlCommand*, and *SqlDataReader*, are supplied from *System.Data.SqlClient*, just as they would be in a conventional client application or middle-tier assembly. And as already discussed, you need the *Microsoft.SqlServer.Server* namespace in order to use objects such as *SqlContext* and *SqlPipe*. The stored procedure template in the SSDT SQL Server Database Project template includes the *using* statement for *Microsoft.SqlServer.Server* and *System.Data.SqlClient* automatically.

Although server-side code uses *SqlClient* objects, it does so in a specialized way. For example, notice that the *context connection=true* connection string passed to the *SqlConnection* object's constructor. This essentially instructs ADO.NET to open a new connection to the database in which the CLR assembly resides. Notice also the second call to the *SqlContext.Pipe* object's *Send* method. Here, the *SqlDataReader* parameter overload of the *SqlPipe* object's *Send* method is used to push the contents of the *SqlDataReader* back to the client. You can think of this method as performing a *while (dr.Read())* loop through the *SqlDataReader* and returning the values of each column for each iteration of the loop. But instead of having to do that work yourself, the *Send* method does it for you.

Before and after the *SqlDataReader* is piped (returned to the consumer), the *String* parameter overload of the *Send* method is used to send status messages to the client. When this stored procedure is run, the piped text appears on the Results tab of the query window when you use the Results To Text option in SSMS (Results As Text in SSDT) and on the Messages tab when you use the Results To Grid (Results As Grid in SSDT) option.

The rest of the listing contains typical ADO.NET code, all of it using objects from the *SqlClient* provider. And that illustrates well the overall theme of SQL CLR programming: do what you'd normally do from the client or middle tier, and use a few special helper objects to work within the context of SQL Server as you do so.

Piping Data with *SqlDataRecord* and *SqlMetaData*

We mentioned that the *SqlPipe* object's *Send* method can accept an object of type *SqlDataRecord*, and we mentioned previously that *Microsoft.SqlServer.Server* provides this object as well as an object named *SqlMetaData*. You can use these two objects together in a CLR stored procedure to return a result set one row at a time, instead of having to supply the *SqlPipe* object's *Send* method with a

SqlDataReader. This allows (but does not require) you to inspect the data before sending it back to the client. Sending *SqlDataReader* objects prevents inspection of the data within the stored procedure because *SqlDataReader* objects are forward-only result set structures. Using the *ExecuteAndSend* method and a *SqlCommand* object has the same limitation.

The *SqlDataRecord* object permits .NET code to create an individual row to be returned to the calling client. Its constructor accepts an array of *SqlMetaData* objects, which in turn describes the metadata for each column in the row.

Listing 3-2, which shows the implementation of the *spContactCount* function from *spTest.cs* in the *SQLCLRDemo* sample project, illustrates how to use *SqlPipe.Send* together with *SqlDataRecord* and *SqlMetaData* objects to return a single-column, single-row result set from a stored procedure.

LISTING 3-2 *spContactCount* from *spTest.cs*.

```
[SqlProcedure]
public static void spContactCount()
{
  SqlConnection conn = new SqlConnection("context connection=true");
  SqlCommand cm = new SqlCommand("SELECT COUNT(*) FROM Person.Person", conn);
  SqlDataRecord drc = new SqlDataRecord(new SqlMetaData("ContactCount",
    SqlDbType.Int));

  conn.Open();
  drc.SetInt32(0, (Int32)cm.ExecuteScalar());
  SqlContext.Pipe.Send(drc);
  conn.Close();
}
```

The code declares variable *drc* as a *SqlDataRecord* object and passes its constructor a single *SqlMetaData* object. (Passing a single object rather than an array is permissible if the *SqlDataRecord* object will have only a single column.) The *SqlMetaData* object describes a column named *ContactCount* of type *SqlDbType.Int*.

Note The *SqlDbType* enumeration is contained within the *System.Data.SqlTypes* namespace. The SQL Server Stored Procedure template inserts a *using* statement for this namespace. If you are creating SQL CLR code without using this template, you will need to add the *using* statement yourself.

The rest of the code is rather straightforward. First, a context connection and command are opened and a *SELECT COUNT(*)* query is performed against the *Person.Person* table. Because the query returns a single scalar value, it is run using the *SqlCommand* object's *ExecuteScalar* method. Next, the value returned by *ExecuteScalar* is cast into a .NET *Int32* and that value is loaded into column 0 (the only returned column) of the *SqlDataRecord* object using its *SetInt32* method. The *SqlDataRecord* is then piped back to the client using the *SqlPipe* object's *Send* method.

Note If you wanted to send back multiple *SqlDataRecord* objects, you would send the first object using the *SqlContext* object's *SendResultsStart* method and then send all subsequent *SqlDataRecord* objects using the *SendResultsRow* method. You would call the *SendResultsEnd* method after all *SqlDataRecord* objects had been sent.

Once the stored procedure has been deployed (the techniques for which we will discuss shortly), you can execute it just as you would any other stored procedure. Although the result is a single value, it is presented as a column and the column name *ContactCount* is shown on the Results tab of the query window. Keep in mind that this *COUNT(*)* query result could have been returned without using the *SqlMetaData* and *SqlDataRecord* objects; the sample is provided to demonstrate the use of these objects as an alternative to piping *SqlDataReader* objects and text to the client.

CLR Stored Procedure Usage Guidelines

It's important to understand how to perform data access and retrieval in CLR stored procedures. As a .NET developer, you already know how to perform computational tasks within your code, so our samples illustrate server-side data access more than anything else. As proof-of-concept code, these samples are completely adequate.

Meanwhile, you should avoid writing CLR stored procedures that merely perform simple "CRUD" (Create, Read, Update and Delete) operations. Such tasks are better left to conventional T-SQL stored procedures, which typically perform these operations more efficiently than ADO.NET can. CLR stored procedures work well when you need to perform computations on (or using) your data, and you require the expressiveness of a .NET language or the rich functionality provided by the .NET base class libraries to do so (where such expressiveness and base class library support are missing from T-SQL).

For example, implementing a "fuzzy search" using business logic embedded in .NET assemblies to determine which data has an affinity to other data is a good use of SQL CLR stored procedures. Regular-expression-based data validation in an update or insert stored procedure is another good application of SQL CLR integration. As a general rule, straight data access should be left to T-SQL. "Higher-valued" computations are good candidates for SQL CLR integration. We'll revisit the SQL CLR usage question at various points in this chapter.

Deployment

Before you can test your SQL CLR code, you must deploy the assembly containing it and register the individual functions that you want recognized as stored procedures. A number of deployment methods are at your disposal; we will pause to cover them in this section, before discussing testing of your stored procedures and the other four basic SQL CLR entities.

Getting Ready

If you're using a SQL Server Database Project, you'll deploy your assembly using SSDT's Publish function. But before doing so, you must be able to build the project successfully. A build will not only compile the SQL CLR assembly itself, but will also check the code for various errors, including unresolved references to database objects.

Go ahead and build the project now by selecting the *SQLCLRDemo* project node in the Solution Explorer, and then selecting Build | Build SQLCLRDemo from the main menu. Equivalent UI selections (after selecting the project node) are the Build option from the project node's shortcut menu or the Shift+F6 keyboard shortcut.

If you're using the SQLCLRDemo sample code demo project, after your attempt to build the project you should see a message that the build failed, with the following error displayed in the Error List window:

```
SQL71501: Trigger: [Person].[trgUpdatePerson] has an unresolved reference to object [Person].
[Person].
```

If, in the Error List window, you double-click the error, a code editor window will open with a T-SQL deployment script generated by SSDT. In it is a *CREATE TRIGGER* command for the *trgUpdatePerson* trigger and a red squiggly under the name of the table to which the trigger is being applied, *Person. Person*. The T-SQL is actually valid, so you may wonder why SSDT might flag it with an error.

SQL Server Database projects are meant to mirror fully the databases to which their contents will be deployed. Although you can create projects that contain just a subset of a database—for example, the assets for a SQL CLR assembly—SSDT will block you as soon as any T-SQL in the project references an object in the database that is not also in your project. In the case of your project, the deployment script references the table *Person.Person* (because the *SqlTrigger* attribute applied to the *trgUpdate-Person* CLR trigger references it) and yet there is no T-SQL script in your project that defines that table. Therefore, by SSDT's criteria, the T-SQL is improper.

You could solve this by adding a script for the *Person.Person* table and then adding further scripts, in a piecemeal fashion, for any objects upon which the table is dependent. While doing so would allow the project to build, it would still be a work-around, and thus something you ought to avoid. The real solution is to import the *AdventureWorks2012* database into the project; that way your project will reflect a full definition of the database. "Importing" the database really translates into having SSDT discover the database's structure and create corresponding scripts for each object.

Let's do the import now. As a preparatory step, close Visual Studio, open Windows Explorer and navigate to the source code directory containing the project file (not the solution file) and the project's contents (e.g. *C:\Demos\VS\SQLCLRDemo\SQLCLRDemo*). Look for a file called *SQLCLRDemo.dbmdl* and delete it, then re-open the solution in Visual Studio. This preparatory step is necessary to enable the Import Database functionality that we need to use; if the step is not performed after a failed build, the Import Database option will be grayed-out.

Let's now perform the import operation. Once again, select the *SQLCLRDemo* project node in the Solution Explorer, then right-click that node and select Import | Database from the shortcut menu (you can also select Project | Import | Database from the main menu). This selection will bring up the Import Database dialog box, which is shown in Figure 3-4.

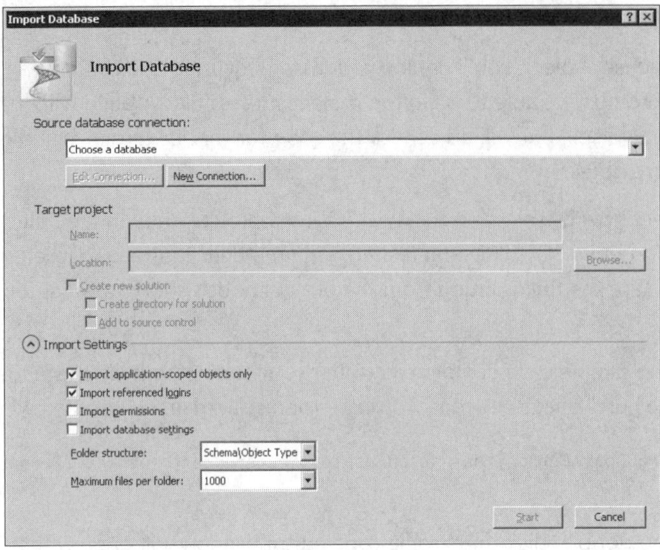

FIGURE 3-4 The Import Database dialog box.

Select the *AdventureWorks2012* database from the Source Database Connection combo box, or click the New Connection button, define a connection to the *AdventureWorks2012* database on *localhost,* and click OK. Now click Start. The Summary screen of the import database dialog box will appear and the import process will proceed. When the Finish button becomes enabled, click it to finish the import process. Now build the project once more. This time the build should succeed, in which case you are ready to deploy your assembly.

Deploying Your Assembly

Having completed a successful build, you're now ready to publish the database, and deploy the assembly in the process. Select Build | Publish SQLCLRDemo from the main menu now (or right-click the *SQLCLRDemo* project node in the Solution Explorer and select Publish from the shortcut menu); this will bring up the Publish Database dialog box, shown in Figure 3-5.

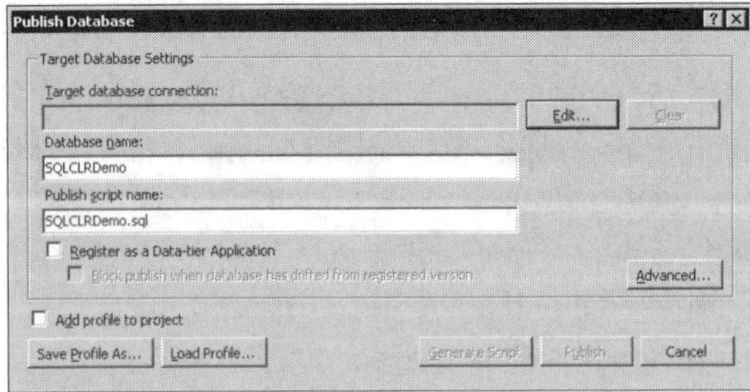

FIGURE 3-5 The Publish Database dialog box.

Click the Edit button next to the Target Database Connection read-only text box to bring up the standard Connection Properties dialog box. Configure the connection to point to your target server (e.g. *localhost*), to use Windows Authentication and to point to the *AdventureWorks2012* database (make sure *not* to accept the default database name of *SQLCLRDemo*), then click OK. Back in the Publish Database dialog box, click the Publish button to deploy your CLR assembly to the database.

Note Before clicking Publish, you can optionally click the Save Profile As button to save this publish profile. When you next publish the database, you can use the Load Profile button to retrieve the profile and avoid configuring the target database connection manually once again.

For deploying the Class Library project version, assuming C:\Demos is the sample code parent directory, you can execute the following T-SQL statement from within a query window:

```
CREATE ASSEMBLY SQLCLRDemo
 AUTHORIZATION dbo
 FROM 'C:\Demos\VS\SQLCLRDemoManual\SQLCLRDemo\bin\Debug\SQLCLRDemo.dll'
 WITH PERMISSION_SET = SAFE

GO
```

The *AUTHORIZATION* clause allows you to specify a name or role to which ownership of the assembly is assigned. The default authorization is that of the current user, and because you are most likely logged in as *dbo* for *AdventureWorks2012*, in this case the clause is unnecessary (which is why we omitted it from our previous example).

The meaning and effect of the *WITH PERMISSION_SET* clause is discussed in the "Security" section near the end of this chapter. For now, just note that this clause allows you to specify the security permissions with which your assembly runs. As with the *AUTHORIZATION* clause, in this case the *WITH PERMISSION_SET* clause is technically unnecessary because *SAFE* is the default *PERMISSION_SET* value used when a *CREATE ASSEMBLY* command is executed. Regardless, it's a good practice to include both clauses.

If your assembly has dependencies on other assemblies, SQL Server looks to see whether those assemblies have already been loaded into the database and, if so, confirms that their ownership is the same as that of the specified assembly. If the dependent assemblies have not yet been loaded into the database, SQL Server looks for them in the same folder as the specified assembly. If it finds all dependent assemblies in that location, it loads them and assigns them the same ownership as the primary assembly. If it does not find the dependent assemblies in that folder or in the global assembly cache (GAC), the *CREATE ASSEMBLY* command will fail.

You can supply a string expression instead of a literal in the *FROM* clause, allowing for some interesting data-driven possibilities. For example, you could fetch an assembly path reference from a table in your database. It is also possible to supply an assembly directly inline by providing a binary stream in the *FROM* clause instead of a file specification. You do this by specifying a *varbinary* literal value or expression (or a comma-delimited list of *varbinary* values or expressions, when dependent assemblies must be specified) that contains the actual binary content of your assembly (or assemblies). This allows the creation of a database, including any CLR assemblies it contains, to be completely scripted, without requiring distribution of actual assembly files. The binary stream can be embedded in the script itself or, using an expression, it could be fetched from a table in a database.

In addition to using Visual Studio deployment and the T-SQL *CREATE ASSEMBLY* statement, you can upload the assembly into your database interactively from SSMS. Simply right-click the *servername/Databases/AdventureWorks2012/Programmability/Assemblies* node in the Object Explorer (where *servername* is the name of your server), and then choose New Assembly from the shortcut menu. The New Assembly dialog box, shown in Figure 3-6, appears.

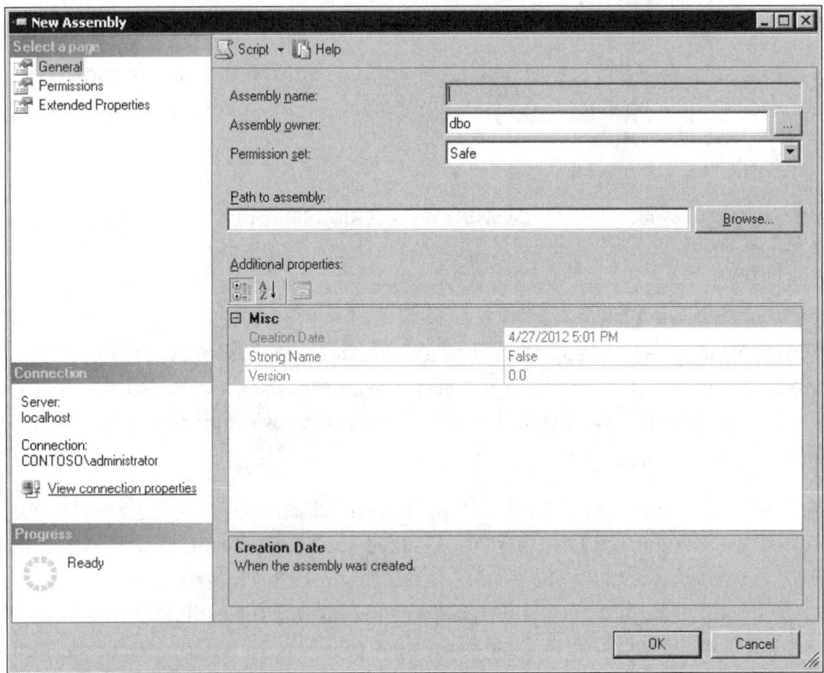

FIGURE 3-6 The SSMS New Assembly dialog box.

Type the assembly path and file name in the Path To Assembly text box, or use the Browse button to specify it interactively. You can specify *AUTHORIZATION* and *WITH PERMISSION_SET* details in the Assembly Owner text box (using the ellipsis button, if necessary) and the Permission Set combo box, respectively.

Regardless of the deployment method you use, once your assembly has been added to your database, it becomes an integral part of that database and its underlying .mdf file. This means that if your database is backed up and restored, or deployed, any assemblies within it move along with the data itself and need not be added manually as a subsequent step.

Deploying Your Stored Procedures

In the SQL Server Database Project version of the sample code, deployment of all the stored procedures is handled by Visual Studio when the assembly itself is deployed. This is due to the application of the *SqlProcedure* attribute to the methods in the *StoredProcedures* class (found in the *spTest.cs* file). The *SqlProcedure* attribute accepts an optional *Name* parameter, the value of which is the actual callable stored procedure name. If you do not supply a value for the *Name* parameter, the name of the .NET method is used as the stored procedure name.

The *SqlProcedure* attribute is used only by Visual Studio when auto-deploying SQL CLR assemblies. Therefore, it does not appear in the source code in the Class Library project. Deploying the stored procedures from that version of the source code requires issuing a *CREATE PROCEDURE* T-SQL command using the *EXTERNAL NAME* clause to specify the assembly, the fully qualified class name specifier, and the method name. For example, to load the Class Library version of *spContacts*, you would issue the following command:

```
CREATE PROCEDURE spContacts
 AS EXTERNAL NAME SQLCLRDemo.StoredProcedures.spContacts
```

The preceding command specifies that the *spContacts* method, found in the class named *Stored-Procedures*, in the loaded assembly with T-SQL name SQLCLRDemo, should be registered as a CLR stored procedure callable under the name *spContacts*.

Note All necessary *CREATE PROCEDURE* commands for the Class Library project version of the sample code are contained in the *CreateObjects.sql* script in the SSMS project supplied with the chapter's sample code on the book's companion website. You will need to run that script in order to utilize the various SQL CLR entities implemented in the Class Library project. Before running the script, you will need to edit the *CREATE ASSEMBLY* command at the top so that the assembly's file specification points to the location on your system where the assembly has been installed. By default, the script looks for the assembly in the C:\Demos\VS\SQLCLRDemoManual\SQLCLRDemo\bin\Debug folder on your PC.

Note that if the CLR stored procedure had been written in Microsoft Visual Basic .NET rather than C#, the class name specifier would change to *SQLCLRDemo.StoredProcedures*. This would necessitate a change to the deployment T-SQL code as follows:

```
CREATE PROCEDURE spContacts
 AS EXTERNAL NAME SQLCLRDemo.[SQLCLRDemo.StoredProcedures].spContacts
```

In Visual Basic projects, the default namespace for a project itself defaults to the project name, as does the assembly name. The class within the project must be referenced using the default namespace as a prefix. Because the class specifier is a multipart dot-separated name, it must be enclosed within square brackets so that SQL Server can identify it as a single indivisible name. Because C# projects handle the default namespace setting a little differently, the namespace prefix is not used in the class specifier for C# assemblies.

One last point before we discuss how to test your now-deployed SQL CLR stored procedures. It is important to realize that the class specifier and method name in the *EXTERNAL NAME* clause are *case sensitive,* and that this is true *even for assemblies developed in Visual Basic .NET.* Although this point may seem perplexing at first, it does make sense. SQL Server searches for your methods within your assemblies, not within your source code. In other words, it's looking within Microsoft Intermediate Language (MSIL) code, not Visual Basic .NET or C# source code. Because MSIL is case sensitive (it has to be to support case-sensitive languages like C#), SQL Server must be as well as it searches within an assembly for a specific class and method.

The fact that SQL Server is not case sensitive by default (even though it once was) and that Visual Basic .NET is not a case-sensitive language is of no importance! If you attempt to register a method and you receive an error that it cannot be found within the assembly, double-check that the case usage in your command matches that of your source code.

Testing Your Stored Procedures

The *TestStoredProcs.sql* script file in the SSMS project supplied with this chapter's sample code will run both CLR stored procedures (*spContactCount* and *spContacts*). Open the file in SSMS, and then click the Execute button on the SQL Editor toolbar, choose Execute from the Query menu, press **F5,** or press **Ctrl-E**. (You can also right-click anywhere inside the query window and select Execute from the shortcut menu.)

When the script runs, you should see the single-valued result of the *spContactCount* stored procedure appear first, as shown in Figure 3-7. Notice that the column name *ContactCount* appears on the Results tab and recall that this is a direct result of your using the *SqlMetaData* object in the CLR code. Below the *spContactCount* result, you will see the results from the *spContacts* stored procedure come in. Because the *Person.Person* table has almost 20,000 rows, on certain machines, these results might take some time to retrieve.

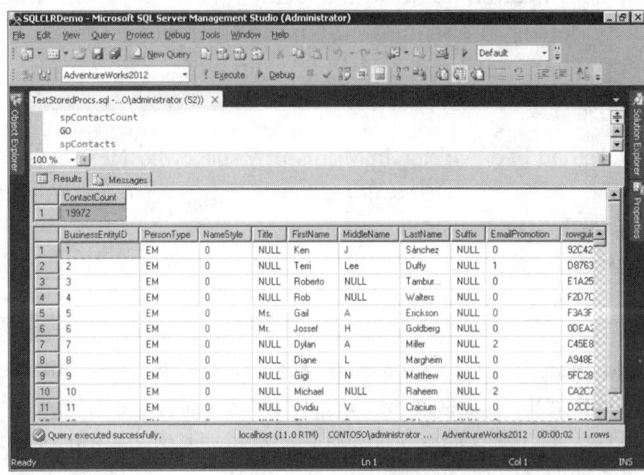

FIGURE 3-7 *TestStoredProcs.sql* script code and results.

Even while the results are coming in, the "Starting Data Dump" status message should be visible on the Messages tab (or on the Results tab if you're using the Results To Text option in SSMS). After all the rows have been fetched, you should see the "Data Dump Complete" message appear as well.

We have yet to cover CLR functions, triggers, aggregates, and UDTs, but you have already learned most of the skills you need to develop SQL CLR code. You have learned how to create a Visual Studio SQL Server Database Project and use SSDT's CLR assembly auto-deployment features. You have also learned how to develop SQL CLR code in standard Class Library projects and how to use T-SQL commands to deploy the code for you. You've learned about the subtle differences between deploying C#- and Visual Basic .NET-based SQL CLR assemblies, and we've covered the case-sensitive requirements of T-SQL–based deployment.

With all this under your belt, we can cover the remaining four basic SQL CLR entities relatively quickly.

CLR Functions

Let's take everything we've discussed about SQL CLR stored procedures and deployment and apply it to SQL CLR functions. As any programmer knows, a *function* is a procedure that returns a value (or an object). Mainstream .NET functions typically return .NET types. SQL CLR functions, on the other hand, must return a *SqlType*. So to start with, you need to make sure that your classes that implement SQL CLR functions import the *System.Data.SqlTypes* namespace with a *using* or *Imports* statement. The SQL Server Database Project C# template for user-defined functions (UDFs) contains the appropriate *using* statement by default; you will need to add the *using* statement manually to standard Class Library code.

Once the namespace is imported, you can write the functions themselves. In Visual Studio SQL Server Database Projects, they should be decorated with the *SqlFunction* attribute; this attribute accepts an optional name parameter that works identically to its *SqlProcedure* counterpart. In our sample code, a value is not supplied for this parameter. *SqlFunction* is used by Visual Studio SQL Server Database Projects for deployment of your SQL CLR functions. For scalar-valued functions in Class Library projects, the *SqlFunction* attribute is optional, so it appears in the Class Library sample code only for the table-valued function (TVF) described later in this section.

Listing 3-3, which shows the code for function *fnHelloWorld* from *fnTest.cs* in the SQLCLRDemo sample code project, implements a simple "Hello World" function that returns a value of type *SqlString*.

LISTING 3-3 *fnHelloWorld* from *fnTest.cs*.

```
[SqlFunction]
public static SqlString fnHelloWorld()
{
    return new SqlString("Hello World");
}
```

Notice that *SqlType* objects (such as *SqlString*) require explicit instantiation and constructor value passing; you cannot simply declare and assign values to them. The code in Listing 3-3 instantiates a *SqlString* object inline within the *return* statement to avoid variable declaration.

A function that accepts no parameters and returns a hard-coded value is of little practical use. Typically, functions are passed values and perform calculations with those values, and they are often used from within T-SQL statements, in effect as extensions to the functions built into the T-SQL language itself. Listing 3-4, which shows the code for function *fnToCelsius* in *fnTest.cs* in the SQLCLR-Demo sample project, implements a Fahrenheit-to-Celsius conversion function.

LISTING 3-4 *fnToCelsius* from *fnTest.cs.*

```
[SqlFunction]
public static SqlDecimal fnToCelsius(SqlInt16 fahrenheit)
{
    return new SqlDecimal((((Int16)fahrenheit) - 32) / 1.8);
}
```

The function accepts a Fahrenheit temperature (as a *SqlInt16*), converts it to Celsius, and returns it (as a *SqlDecimal*). Notice that the code casts the input parameter from a *SqlInt16* to a .NET *Int16*, applies a Fahrenheit-to-Celsius conversion formula, and then passes the result to the constructor of a new *SqlDecimal* object.

Deployment of these functions is automatic in the SSDT SQL Server Database Project version of our sample code. For the Class Library version, use the T-SQL *CREATE FUNCTION* statement in a similar fashion to how the *CREATE PROCEDURE* statement was used in the previous section, but include a data type specification for the return value. For example, to deploy the *fnHelloWorld* function, you would use this statement:

```
CREATE FUNCTION fnHelloWorld()
 RETURNS nvarchar(4000) WITH EXECUTE AS CALLER
 AS EXTERNAL NAME SQLCLRDemo.UserDefinedFunctions.fnHelloWorld
```

Notice the use of data type *nvarchar(4000)* to correspond with the *SqlString* type used in the function's implementation. The *WITH EXECUTE AS CALLER* clause specifies that the SQL CLR function should execute under the caller's identity.

Tip You can enter the *CREATE FUNCTION* command yourself, but note that all such necessary commands for the sample code SQL CLR functions are available in the *CreateObjects.sql* script file in the SSMS project supplied with this chapter's sample code.

You can test these functions in SSDT or SSMS. Use the following query to test the two functions. (You can also run the *TestScalarFunctions.sql* script file in the SSMS sample project.)

```
SELECT
 dbo.fnHelloWorld() AS HelloWorld,
 dbo.fnToCelsius(212) AS CelsiusTemp
```

T-SQL functions can return result sets as well as scalar values. Functions which return result sets are called *table-valued functions* (TVFs). Writing SQL CLR TVFs is possible, although you do so differently than you would SQL CLR scalar-valued functions or SQL CLR stored procedures. SQL CLR TVFs must return a type that implements the .NET interface *IEnumerable*, and they must also provide a "fill row" method that converts an element of that type to a collection of scalar values that comprise the corresponding table row.

Listing 3-5, which shows the code for functions *fnPortfolioTable* and *FillTickerRow* in *fnTest.cs* in the *SQLCLRDemo* sample project, implements a TVF named *fnPortfolioTable*.

LISTING 3-5 *fnPortfolioTable* and *FillTickerRow* from *fnTest.cs*.

```
[SqlFunction(
    FillRowMethodName="FillTickerRow",
    TableDefinition="TickerSymbol nvarchar(5), Value decimal")]
public static System.Collections.IEnumerable fnPortfolioTable(SqlString
tickersPacked)
{
  string[] tickerSymbols;
  object[] rowArray = new object[2];
  object[] compoundArray = new object[3];
  char[] parms = new char[1];

  parms[0] = ';';
  tickerSymbols = tickersPacked.Value.Split(parms);

  rowArray[0] = tickerSymbols[0];
  rowArray[1] = 1;
  compoundArray[0] = rowArray;

  rowArray = new object[2];
  rowArray[0] = tickerSymbols[1];
  rowArray[1] = 2;
  compoundArray[1] = rowArray;

  rowArray = new object[2];
  rowArray[0] = tickerSymbols[2];
  rowArray[1] = 3;
  compoundArray[2] = rowArray;

  return compoundArray;
}

public static void FillTickerRow(object row, ref SqlString tickerSymbol, ref
SqlDecimal value)
{
  object[] rowArray = (object[])row;
  tickerSymbol = new SqlString((string)rowArray[0]);
  value = new SqlDecimal(decimal.Parse(rowArray[1].ToString()));
}
```

Rather than implementing its own *IEnumerable*-compatible type, *fnPortfolioTable* uses an array. This is perfectly legal because arrays in .NET implement *IEnumerable*. The *fnPortfolioTable* function accepts a semicolon-delimited list of stock ticker symbols and returns a table with each ticker symbol appearing in a separate row as column *TickerSymbol* and a value for the ticker as column *Value*. The structure of the returned table is declared in the *TableDefinition* parameter of the *SqlFunction* attribute in SQL Server projects and in the *CREATE FUNCTION* T-SQL command for Class Library projects. The assigned values are hard-coded, and only three rows are returned, regardless of how many ticker symbols are passed in. As with our other samples, this one is more useful as a teaching tool than as a practical application of TVFs.

Arrays are the name of the game here. First, the *Split* method is used to crack the delimited ticker list into an array of single ticker strings. Then the TVF structures the data so that each element in the return value array (*compoundArray*) is itself a two-element array storing a single ticker symbol and its value. The function code needs only to return *compoundArray*. Next, the *FillTickerRow* function (named in the *FillRowMethodName* parameter of the *SqlFunction* attribute) takes each two-element array (passed in as the first parameter) and converts its members to individual scalars. These scalars are then returned via *ref* parameters that start in the second parameter position; the parameter names are not significant, but their positions must correspond to those of the columns in the *TableDefinition* argument of the *SqlFunction* attribute.

Because the *FillRowMethodName* parameter of the *SqlFunction* attribute is required by SQL Server, the Class Library version of the *fnPortfolioTable* function is decorated with that attribute, supplying a value for that one parameter. In the SQL Server Database Project version, a value is also supplied for the *TableDefinition* parameter to enable auto-deployment of the TVF.

As with the other functions, deployment of this function is performed by SSDT in the SQL Server Database Project sample code. For the Class Library version, you can deploy the function using the following T-SQL command (also contained in the *CreateObjects.sql* script file):

```
CREATE FUNCTION fnPortfolioTable(@TickersPacked nvarchar(4000))
 RETURNS table (
  TickerSymbol nvarchar(5),
  Value decimal
 )
 WITH EXECUTE AS CALLER
 AS EXTERNAL NAME SQLCLRDemo.UserDefinedFunctions.fnPortfolioTable
```

As with *fnHelloWorld*, the *SqlString* data type is mapped to an *nvarchar(4000)*, this time for one of the input parameters. Because *fnPortfolioTable* is a TVF, its return type is declared as *table*, with inline specifications for the table's definition.

Use the following query in SSDT or SSMS to test the TVF (or run the *TestTableValuedFunction.sql* script file in the SSMS sample project):

```
SELECT * FROM fnPortfolioTable('IBM;MSFT;ORCL')
 ORDER BY TickerSymbol
```

The following data should be returned:

```
TickerSymbol        Value
------------        ------
IBM                 1
MSFT                2
ORCL                3
```

Note that as of SQL Server 2008, it is possible to provide a "hint" to the database that your TVF returns data in a particular order. This can optimize queries or creation of indexes ordered on the same expression. To take advantage of this, you must first ensure that logic in your CLR TVF code returns data in a specific order and, second, ensure that you specify that order in an *ORDER* clause in the *CREATE FUNCTION* T-SQL command. For example, imagine that the SQL CLR TVF code ordered its results by the *TickerSymbol* column. In that case, you could modify the T-SQL code that creates the function as follows:

```
CREATE FUNCTION fnPortfolioTable(@TickersPacked nvarchar(4000))
 RETURNS table (
  TickerSymbol nvarchar(5),
  Value decimal
 )
 WITH EXECUTE AS CALLER
 ORDER (TickerSymbol)
 AS EXTERNAL NAME SQLCLRDemo.UserDefinedFunctions.fnPortfolioTable
```

Although this code does not *actually* return data in *TickerSymbol* order, you can still use the preceding T-SQL command for the Class Library version of the TVF. If you re-executed the query in the *TestTableValuedFunction.sql* script file, everything would work correctly, because the input data is coincidentally supplied in *TickerSymbol* order (*'IBM;MSFT;ORCL'*). If, however, you modified the input string to, for example, *'IBM;ORCL;MSFT'*, you would receive the following error:

```
The order of the data in the stream does not conform to the ORDER hint specified for the CLR TVF
'fnPortfolioTable'. The order of the data must match the order specified in the ORDER hint for
a CLR TVF. Update the ORDER hint to reflect the order in which the input data is ordered, or
update the CLR TVF to match the order specified by the ORDER hint.
```

We point out this error text because it is really the only outward proof (other than analysis of query execution plans) that this new ordered SQL CLR TVF feature is in fact supported, and we assume that you would prefer not to take this information merely on faith. Please note that this feature can only be taken advantage of, practically speaking, when registering a SQL CLR TVF using one's own T-SQL code. That is because there is no parameter in the *SqlFunction* attribute for specifying an *ORDER* clause, so SSDT's auto-deployment cannot emit that clause. This means that you must use the *ORDER* clause only with a Class Library project or else omit the *SqlFunction* attribute from your SQL CLR TVF code in a SQL Server Database Project and register the TVF "manually," either from an external script or by adding a script to your SQL Server Database Project that performs the deployment.

CLR Triggers

T-SQL triggers are really just stored procedures that are called by SQL Server at specific times and that can query values in the *DELETED* and *INSERTED* pseudo-tables (which expose "before and after" snapshots of data changed by the statement that fired the trigger). SQL CLR triggers are similar to SQL CLR stored procedures, and they can be created for all data manipulation language (DML) actions that modify data (that is, updates, inserts, and deletes).

SQL Server 2005 introduced the concept of data definition language (DDL) triggers, which can intercept and handle actions such as *CREATE TABLE* and *ALTER PROCEDURE*. Like DML triggers, DDL triggers can be implemented in T-SQL or SQL CLR code. We will cover both SQL CLR DML and DDL triggers in this section.

SQL CLR DML triggers, like their T-SQL counterparts, have access to the *DELETED* and *INSERTED* pseudo-tables and must be declared as handling one or more specific events for a specific table or, under certain circumstances, a specific view. Also, they can make use of the *SqlTriggerContext* object (through the *SqlContext* object's *TriggerContext* property) to determine which particular event (update, insert, or delete) caused them to fire and which columns were updated.

Once you understand these concepts, writing SQL CLR DML triggers is really quite simple. Listing 3-6, which shows the code for the *trgUpdatePerson* function from *trgTest.cs* in the *SQLCLRDemo* sample project, shows the SQL CLR code for the *trgUpdatePerson* DML trigger, which is designed to function as a *FOR UPDATE* trigger on the *Person.Person* table in the *AdventureWorks2012* database.

LISTING 3-6 *trgUpdatePerson* from *trgTest.cs*.

```
[SqlTrigger(Target="Person.Person", Event="for UPDATE")]
public static void trgUpdatePerson()
{
    SqlTriggerContext context = SqlContext.TriggerContext;
    string oldName = string.Empty;
    string newName = string.Empty;
    SqlConnection conn = new SqlConnection("context connection=true");
    SqlCommand cmOld = new SqlCommand(
                    "SELECT FirstName FROM DELETED", conn);
    SqlCommand cmNew = new SqlCommand(
                    "SELECT FirstName FROM INSERTED", conn);
    conn.Open();
    SqlDataReader drOld = cmOld.ExecuteReader();
    if (drOld.Read())
    {
        oldName = (string)drOld[0];
    }
    drOld.Close();
    SqlDataReader drNew = cmNew.ExecuteReader();
    if (drNew.Read())
    {
```

```
            newName = (string)drNew[0];
        }
        drNew.Close();
        conn.Close();
        SqlContext.Pipe.Send("Old Value of FirstName:" + oldName);
        SqlContext.Pipe.Send("New Value of FirstName:" + newName);
        for (int i = 0; i <= context.ColumnCount - 1; i++)
        {
            SqlContext.Pipe.Send("Column " + i.ToString() + ": " +
               context.IsUpdatedColumn(i).ToString());
        }
    }
```

This CLR DML trigger queries the *DELETED* and *INSERTED* pseudo-tables and echoes back the "before and after" values (respectively) for the *FirstName* column when a row is updated. It does so not by piping back *SqlDataReader* objects but by fetching values from the pseudo-tables and echoing back the values as text using the *SqlPipe* object's *Send* method. The trigger code also uses the *TriggerContext.IsUpdatedColumn* method to return a list of all columns in the *Person.Person* table and whether each was updated.

To deploy the trigger automatically, you apply a *SqlTrigger* attribute to the .NET function that implements the trigger. Because DML triggers are tied to a target object (a table or a view) and an event (for example, "for update" or "instead of insert"), the *SqlTrigger* attribute has parameters for each of these pieces of information and you must supply values for both. The *SqlTrigger* attribute deploys only a single copy of the trigger, but you can use T-SQL to deploy the same code as a separate trigger for a different event and table. Each separate deployment of the same code is assigned a unique trigger name.

Although Listing 3-6 does not demonstrate it, you can create a single piece of code that functions as both the update and the insert trigger for a given table. You can then use the *TriggerContext* object's *TriggerAction* property to determine exactly what event caused the trigger to fire, and you can execute slightly different code accordingly. Should you want to deploy such a CLR trigger using the *SqlTrigger* attribute, you would set its *Event* parameter to *FOR UPDATE, INSERT*.

The T-SQL command to register a .NET function as a SQL CLR trigger (for the update event only) is as follows:

```
CREATE TRIGGER trgUpdatePerson
 ON Person.Person
 FOR UPDATE
 AS EXTERNAL NAME SQLCLRDemo.Triggers.trgUpdatePerson
```

Note All necessary *CREATE TRIGGER* commands for the Class Library project version of the sample code are contained in the *CreateObjects.sql* script in the SSMS project supplied with the chapter's sample code available on the book's companion website.

You can use the following query to test the trigger. (This T-SQL code can be found in the *TestTriggers.sql* script file in the SSMS project.)

```
UPDATE Person.Person
 SET    FirstName = 'Gustavo'
 WHERE  BusinessEntityId = 1
```

If you place the *TriggerContext* object's *TriggerAction* property in a comparison statement, Visual Studio's IntelliSense will show you that there is a wide array of enumerated constants that the property can be equal to, and that a majority of these values correspond to DDL triggers. This demonstrates clearly that SQL CLR code can be used for DDL and DML triggers alike.

In the case of DDL triggers, a wide array of environmental information might be desirable to determine exactly what event caused the trigger to fire, what system process ID (SPID) invoked it, what time the event fired, and other information specific to the event type such as the T-SQL command that caused the event. The *SqlTriggerContext* object's *EventData* property can be queried to fetch this information. The *EventData* property is of type *SqlXml*; therefore it, in turn, has a *CreateReader* method and a *Value* property that you can use to fetch the XML-formatted event data as an *XmlReader* object or text, respectively.

The code in Listing 3-7, taken from function *trgCreateTable* in *trgTest.cs* in the *SQLCLRDemo* sample project, shows the SQL CLR code for the DDL trigger *trgCreateTable*, registered to fire for any *CREATE TABLE* statement executed on the *AdventureWorks2012* database.

LISTING 3-7 *trgCreateTable* from *trgTest.cs*.

```
[SqlTrigger(Target = "DATABASE", Event = "FOR CREATE_TABLE")]
public static void trgCreateTable()
{
  SqlTriggerContext context = SqlContext.TriggerContext;
  if (!(context.EventData == null))
  {
    SqlContext.Pipe.Send("Event Data: " + context.EventData.Value.ToString());
  }
}
```

The code interrogates the *Value* property of *SqlContext.TriggerContext.EventData*, converts it to a string, and pipes that string back to the client. To deploy this trigger, you can use attribute-based deployment in the SQL Server Database Project or the following command for the Class Library version:

```
CREATE TRIGGER trgCreateTable
 ON DATABASE
 FOR CREATE_TABLE
 AS EXTERNAL NAME SQLCLRDemo.Triggers.trgCreateTable
```

Use the following T-SQL DDL command to test the DDL trigger. (You can find this code in the *TestTriggers.sql* script file in the sample SSMS project.)

```
CREATE TABLE Test (low int, high int)
DROP TABLE Test
```

Your result should contain the message "Event Data: " followed by text similar to the following:

```
<EVENT_INSTANCE>
  <EventType>CREATE_TABLE</EventType>
  <PostTime>2012-04-27T16:16:05.150</PostTime>
  <SPID>66</SPID>
  <ServerName>KIWI</ServerName>
  <LoginName>CONTOSO\Administrator</LoginName>
  <UserName>dbo</UserName>
  <DatabaseName>AdventureWorks2012</DatabaseName>
  <SchemaName>dbo</SchemaName>
  <ObjectName>Test</ObjectName>
  <ObjectType>TABLE</ObjectType>
  <TSQLCommand>
      <SetOptions ANSI_NULLS="ON" ANSI_NULL_DEFAULT="ON" ANSI_PADDING="ON"
        QUOTED_IDENTIFIER="ON" ENCRYPTED="FALSE" />
      <CommandText>CREATE TABLE Test (low int, high int)</CommandText>
  </TSQLCommand>
</EVENT_INSTANCE>
```

Note The actual output would consist of continuous, unformatted text. Line breaks and indentation have been added here to make the *EventData* XML easier to read.

CLR Aggregates

T-SQL has a number of built-in aggregates, such as *SUM*, *AVG*, and *MAX*, but that set of built-in functions is not always sufficient. Luckily, the SQL CLR features in SQL Server 2012 allow us to implement user-defined aggregates in .NET code and use them from T-SQL. User-defined aggregates can be implemented only in SQL CLR code; they have no T-SQL equivalent. Because aggregates tend to perform computation only, they provide an excellent use case for SQL CLR code. As it turns out, they are also quite easy to build.

At first, aggregates look and feel like functions because they accept and return values. In fact, if you use an aggregate in a non-data-querying T-SQL call (for example, *SELECT SUM(8)*), you are actually treating the aggregate as if it were a function. The thing to remember is that the argument passed to an aggregate is typically a column, and so each discrete value for that column—for whichever *WHERE*, *HAVING*, *ORDER BY*, and/or *GROUP BY* scope applies—gets passed in to the aggregate. It is the aggregate's job to update a variable, which eventually will be the return value, as each discrete value is passed to it.

CLR aggregates require you to apply the *SqlUserDefinedAggregate* attribute to them. The *SqlUserDefinedAggregate* attribute accepts a number of parameters, but all of them are optional except *Format*. In our example, we will use the value *Format.Native* for the *Format* parameter. For more advanced scenarios, you might want to study SQL Server Books Online to acquaint yourself with the other parameters this attribute accepts. Sticking with *Format.Native* for the *Format* parameter is sufficient for many scenarios.

> **Note** User-defined aggregates greater than 8,000 bytes in size require use of the *Format.UserDefined* value for the *Format* parameter, rather than the *Format.Native* value used in this example.

Unlike the *SqlProcedure*, *SqlFunction*, and *SqlTrigger* attributes, the *SqlUserDefinedAggregate* attribute is required by SQL Server for your class to be eligible for use as an aggregate. Visual Studio SQL Server Database Projects do use this attribute for deployment, and the attribute is included in the aggregate template, but it also must be used in generic Class Library project code in order for T-SQL registration of the aggregate to succeed.

Aggregate classes must have four methods: *Init*, *Accumulate*, *Merge*, and *Terminate*. The *Init* method is used to clean up as necessary from previous uses of this aggregate instance, allowing it to re-start a new aggregate computation. The *Accumulate* method accepts a SQL type for processing. The *Terminate* method returns a SQL type representing the result. And finally, the *Merge* method accepts an object typed as the aggregate class itself so that it can be combined with the executing instance.

The *Accumulate* method handles the processing of a discrete value into the aggregate value, and the *Terminate* method returns the final aggregated value after all discrete values have been processed. The *Init* method provides startup code, typically initializing a class-level private variable that will be used by the *Accumulate* method. The *Merge* method is called in a specific multithreading scenario, which we will describe later in this section.

Just to be perfectly clear, your aggregate class will not implement an interface to supply these methods; you must create them to meet what we might term the "conventions" that are expected of SQL CLR aggregate classes (as opposed to a "contract" with which they must comply). When you develop your code in a Visual Studio SQL Server Database Project, the Aggregate template includes stubs for these four methods as well as the proper application of the *SqlUserDefinedAggregate* attribute.

Creating your own aggregates is fairly straightforward, but thinking through aggregation logic can be a bit confusing at first. Imagine that you want to create a special aggregate named *BakersDozen* that increments its accumulated value by 1 for every discrete value's multiple of 12 (much as a baker, in simpler times, would throw in a free 13th donut when you ordered 12). By using what you now know about CLR aggregates and combining that with integer division, you can implement a *BakersDozen* aggregate quite easily. Listing 3-8, the code from struct *BakersDozen* in *aggTest.cs* in the sample project, contains the entire implementation of the aggregate *BakersDozen*.

LISTING 3-8 *BakersDozen* struct from *aggTest.cs.*

```
[Serializable]
[Microsoft.SqlServer.Server.SqlUserDefinedAggregate(Format.Native)]
public struct BakersDozen
```

```
{
    private SqlInt32 DonutCount;

    public void Init()
    {
        DonutCount = 0;
    }

    public void Accumulate(SqlInt32 Value)
    {
        DonutCount += Value + ((Int32)Value) / 12;
    }

    public void Merge(BakersDozen Group)
    {
        DonutCount += Group.DonutCount;
    }

    public SqlInt32 Terminate()
    {
        return DonutCount;
    }
}
```

The code here is fairly straightforward. The private variable *DonutCount* is used to track the *BakersDozen*-adjusted sum of items ordered, adding the actual items ordered value and incrementing the running total by the integer quotient of the ordered value divided by 12. By this logic, bonus items are added only when an individual value equals or exceeds a multiple of 12. Twelve includes a full dozen, and so would 13. Twenty-four includes two dozen, and so would 27. Two individual orders of 6 items each would not generate any bonus items because a minimum of 12 items must be contained in a discrete value to qualify for a bonus.

To deploy the aggregate, use attribute-based deployment in the SQL Server Database Project or the following command for the Class Library version:

```
CREATE AGGREGATE BakersDozen (@input int)
 RETURNS int
 EXTERNAL NAME SQLCLRDemo.BakersDozen
```

Notice that no method name is specified because the aggregate is implemented by an entire class rather than an individual function. Notice also that the return value data type must be declared as the data type of the values this aggregate function will process. The *@input* parameter acts as a placeholder, and its name is inconsequential. Note that aggregates can be built on SQL CLR types (covered in the next section) as well as SQL scalar types.

Note The preceding *CREATE AGGREGATE* statement for the Class Library project version of the sample code is contained in the *CreateObjects.sql* script in the SSMS project supplied with the sample code on the book's companion website.

To see the aggregate work, first run the *CreateTblAggregateTest.sql* script file in the SSMS sample project to create a table named *AggregateTest* with columns *OrderItemId*, *OrderId*, and *ItemsOrdered* and several rows of data, as shown here:

```
CREATE TABLE tblAggregateTest(
    [OrderItemId] [int] IDENTITY(1,1) NOT NULL,
    [OrderId] [int] NULL,
    [ItemsOrdered] [int] NOT NULL
)
GO

INSERT INTO tblAggregateTest VALUES (1,2)
INSERT INTO tblAggregateTest VALUES (1,4)
INSERT INTO tblAggregateTest VALUES (2,1)
INSERT INTO tblAggregateTest VALUES (2,12)
INSERT INTO tblAggregateTest VALUES (3,3)
INSERT INTO tblAggregateTest VALUES (3,2)
```

With such a table built, use the following T-SQL DML statement in a query window to test the aggregate function:

```
SELECT
  OrderId,
  SUM(ItemsOrdered) AS SUM,
  dbo.BakersDozen(ItemsOrdered) AS BakersDozen
FROM tblAggregateTest
GROUP BY OrderId
```

For each distinct value in the *OrderId* column, this query effectively uses the CLR code under the following algorithm:

1. Call *Init()*.
2. Call *Accumulate* once for each row with the same *OrderId* value, passing it that row's value of the *ItemsOrdered* column.
3. Call *Terminate* to retrieve the aggregated value that the query will return to the client.

The results should be as follows:

```
OrderId              SUM                  BakersDozen
-----------          -----------          -----------
1                    6                    6
2                    13                   14
3                    5                    5
```

By including the built-in T-SQL aggregate *SUM* in the query, you can see how many bonus items were added. In this case, for *OrderId 2*, a single bonus item was added, due to one row in the table with the following values:

```
OrderItemId          OrderId              ItemsOrdered
-----------          -----------          ------------
4                    2                    12
```

All the other rows contain *ItemsOrdered* values of less than 12, so no bonus items were added for them.

Because SQL Server sometimes segments the work required to satisfy a query over multiple threads, the query processor might need to execute your aggregate function multiple times for a single query and then merge the results together. For your aggregate to work properly in this scenario, you must implement a *Merge* method.

The *Merge* method takes the result of one thread's aggregation and merges it into the current thread's aggregation. The calculation required to do this could be complicated for some aggregates; in our case, you simply added the *DonutCount* value from the secondary thread's aggregate (accessible via the *Group* input parameter) to your own. There is no need to add bonus items because they would have been added in the individual *Accumulate* calls on the other thread. Simple addition is all that's required. An aggregate that calculated some type of average, for example, would require more complex *Merge* code.

Don't forget that aggregates can be passed scalar values and can be used from T-SQL without referencing a row set. Your aggregate must accommodate this scenario, even if it seems impractical. In the case of *BakersDozen*, single scalar values are easily handled. To see for yourself, try executing the following table-less T-SQL query:

```
SELECT dbo.BakersDozen(13)
```

You will see that it returns the value *14*.

Note The *TestAggregate.sql* script file in the SSMS project contains both aggregate-testing queries.

Aggregates are an excellent use of SQL CLR programming. Because they are passed data values to be processed, they typically perform only computational tasks and no data access of their own. They consist of compiled CLR code, so they perform well, and unlike stored procedures, triggers, and functions, they cannot be implemented at all in T-SQL. That said, you must still make your aggregate code, especially in the *Accumulate* method, as "lean and mean" as possible. Injecting your own code into the query processor's stream of work is an honor, a privilege, and a significant responsibility. Take that responsibility seriously, and make sure that your code is as low-impact as possible.

More Info SQL Server 2012 provides (as did SQL Server 2008R2 and 2008 before it) support for aggregates that accept *multiple* input parameters. Implementing such aggregate functions involves accepting two or more parameters in the *Accumulate* method, processing them in your code, and then declaring them in the *CREATE AGGREGATE* T-SQL statement, if you are not using SSDT auto-deployment. Aggregates that accept multiple input parameters still must, of course, return a single value.

SQL CLR Types

The last SQL CLR feature for us to explore is user-defined types (UDTs). This feature is perhaps the most interesting facet of SQL CLR integration, yet also the most controversial. It's interesting because, technically, it allows for storage of objects in the database. It's controversial because it's prone to abuse. SQL CLR types were not implemented to allow developers to create object-oriented databases; they were created to allow multi-value or multi-behavior data types to be stored, retrieved, and easily manipulated.

SQL CLR types have certain indexing limitations, and their entire value must be updated when any of their individual property/field values is updated.

Note More information about SQL CLR UDTs is available in the MSDN article "Using CLR Integration in SQL Server 2005" by Rathakrishnan et al. You can find this article online at *http://msdn.microsoft.com/en-us/library/ms345136.aspx*. Although written for SQL Server 2005, it is nonetheless an excellent source of information that is applicable to subsequent versions of SQL Server, including SQL Server 2012.

SQL CLR type methods must be static. You cannot, therefore, call methods from T-SQL as instance methods; instead, you must use a special *TypeName::MethodName()* syntax. You can implement properties as you would in any conventional class and read from them or write to them from T-SQL using a standard *variable.property/column.property* dot-separated syntax.

Listing 3-9, the code from struct *typPoint* in *typTest.cs* in the sample project, shows the implementation of *typPoint*, a CLR type that can be used to store Cartesian coordinates in the database.

LISTING 3-9 *typPoint* struct from *typTest.cs*.

```
[Serializable]
[SqlUserDefinedType(Format.Native)]
public struct typPoint : INullable
{
    private bool m_Null;
    private double m_x;
    private double m_y;

    public override string ToString()
    {
        if (this.IsNull)
            return "NULL";
        else
            return this.m_x + ":" + this.m_y;
    }

    public bool IsNull
    {
        get
```

```
        {
            return m_Null;
        }
    }

    public static typPoint Null
    {
        get
        {
            typPoint pt = new typPoint();
            pt.m_Null = true;
            return pt;
        }
    }

    public static typPoint Parse(SqlString s)
    {
        if (s.IsNull)
            return Null;
        else
        {
            //Parse input string here to separate out points
            typPoint pt = new typPoint();
            char[] parms = new char[1];
            parms[0] = ':';
            string str = (string)s;
            string[] xy = str.Split(parms);
            pt.X = double.Parse(xy[0]);
            pt.Y = double.Parse(xy[1]);
            return pt;
        }
    }

    public static double Sum(typPoint p)
    {
        return p.X + p.Y;
    }

    public double X
    {
        get { return m_x; }
        set { m_x = value; }
    }

    public double Y
    {
        get { return m_y; }
        set { m_y = value; }
    }

}
```

Through the class's *X* and *Y* properties, you can process coordinates in a single database column or variable. You can assign coordinate values to an instance of the type as a colon-delimited string—for example, *3:4*, by using the *Parse* method (implicitly). You can then read them back in the same format by using the *ToString* method. Once a value has been assigned, you can individually read or modify its *X* or *Y* portion by using the separate *X* and *Y* properties. The class implements the *INullable* interface and its *IsNull* property. The *Sum* method demonstrates how to expose a static member and allow it to access instance properties by accepting an instance of the SQL CLR type of which it is a member.

Notice that the class is a *struct* and that the *Serializable* and *SqlUserDefinedType* attributes have been applied to it. As with the *SqlUserDefinedAggregate* attribute, *SqlUserDefinedType* is required by SQL Server and appears in the Class Library sample code as well as the SQL Server Database Project version. As with the *SqlUserDefinedAggregate*, you simply assign a value of *Format.Native* to the *Format* parameter and leave the other parameters unused.

More Info As with user-defined aggregates, CLR types greater than 8,000 bytes in size must use the *Format.UserDefined* value for the *Format* parameter of their special attribute (*SqlUserDefinedType*). You might want to study SQL Server Books Online for information about using other parameters for this attribute.

Listing 3-10, the code from struct *typBakersDozen* in *typTest.cs* in the sample project, re-implements the *BakersDozen* logic used in our aggregate example, this time in a UDT.

LISTING 3-10 *typBakersDozen* struct from *typTest.cs*.

```
[Serializable]
[SqlUserDefinedType(Format.Native)]
public struct typBakersDozen : INullable
{
    private bool m_Null;
    private double m_RealQty;

    public override string ToString()
    {
        return (m_RealQty + (long)m_RealQty / 12).ToString();
    }

    public bool IsNull
    {
        get
        {
            return m_Null;
        }
    }

    public static typBakersDozen Null
    {
        get
        {
            typBakersDozen h = new typBakersDozen();
            h.m_Null = true;
```

```
            return h;
        }
    }

    public static typBakersDozen Parse(SqlString s)
    {
        if (s.IsNull)
            return Null;
        else
        {
            typBakersDozen u = new typBakersDozen();
            u.RealQty = double.Parse((string)s);
            return u;
        }
    }

    public static typBakersDozen ParseDouble(SqlDouble d)
    {
        if (d.IsNull)
            return Null;
        else
        {
            typBakersDozen u = new typBakersDozen();
            u.RealQty = (double)d;
            return u;
        }
    }

    public double RealQty
    {
        get { return m_RealQty; }
        set { m_RealQty = value; }
    }

    public double AdjustedQty
    {
        get
        {
            return (m_RealQty + (long)m_RealQty / 12);
        }
        set
        {
            if (value % 12 == 0)
                m_RealQty = value;
            else
                m_RealQty = value - (long)value / 13;
        }
    }
}
```

The *RealQty* and *AdjustedQty* properties allow the ordered quantity to be assigned a value and the adjusted quantity to be automatically calculated, or vice versa. The real quantity is the default "input" value, the adjusted quantity is the default "output" value of the type, and the *Parse* and *ToString* methods work accordingly. If the *AdjustedQty* property is assigned a value that is an even multiple of 12 (which would be invalid), that value is assigned to the *RealQty* property, forcing the *AdjustedQty* to be set to its passed value plus its integer quotient when divided by 12.

To deploy the UDTs, you can use attribute-based deployment for the SQL Server Database Project. The script file *CreateObjects.sql* in the SSMS project supplied with the sample code contains the T-SQL code necessary to deploy the Class Library versions of the UDTs. Here's the command that deploys *typPoint*:

```
CREATE TYPE typPoint
 EXTERNAL NAME SQLCLRDemo.typPoint
```

The script file *TestTypPoint.sql* in the SSMS project contains T-SQL code that tests *typPoint*. Run it and examine the results for an intimate understanding of how to work with the type. The script file CreateTblPoint.sql creates a table with a column that is typed based on *typPoint*. Run it, and then run the script file TestTblPoint.sql to see how to manipulate tables that use SQL CLR UDTs.

The script file *TestTypBakersDozen.sql* contains T-SQL code that tests *typBakersDozen*. The *ParseDouble* method demonstrates how to implement a non-*SqlString* parse method. It is named *ParseDouble* because the *Parse* method itself cannot be overloaded. You must call *ParseDouble* explicitly as follows:

```
DECLARE @t AS dbo.typBakersDozen
SET @t = typBakersDozen::ParseDouble(12)
```

This is equivalent to using the default *Parse* method (implicitly) and assigning the string *12* as follows:

```
DECLARE @t AS dbo.typBakersDozen
SET @t = '12'
```

Notice that *typBakersDozen* essentially stores a value for the real quantity, and its properties are really just functions that accept or express that value in its native form or as an adjusted quantity. There is no backing variable for the *AdjustedQty* property; the *get* block of the *AdjustedQty* property merely applies a formula to the backing variable for *RealQty* and returns the result.

As both these examples show, you should think of CLR UDTs less as objects stored in the database and more as classes that wrap one or a set of scalar values and provide services and conversion functions for manipulating them. This is why Microsoft implemented the *geometry* and *geography* data types as SQL CLR UDTs. These types don't store complex objects, but they do manage entities that cannot be thought of as simple, single values.

More specifically, you should not think of SQL CLR UDTs as object-relational entities. Although it might seem counterintuitive, consider the use of (de)serialization and the *xml* data type as more appropriate vehicles for storing objects in the database.

We have now investigated all five SQL CLR entities. Before we finish up, we need to discuss CLR assembly security and ongoing maintenance of SQL CLR objects in your databases.

Security

Depending on the deployment method, you have numerous ways to specify what security level to grant a CLR assembly. All of them demand that you specify one of three permission sets:

- ***Safe*** Assembly can perform local data access and computational tasks only.
- ***External_Access*** Assembly can perform local data access and computational tasks and also access the network, the file system, the registry, and environment variables. Although *External_Access* is less restrictive than *Safe*, it still safeguards server stability.
- ***Unsafe*** Assembly has unrestricted permissions and can even call unmanaged code. This setting can significantly compromise SQL Server security; only members of the *sysadmin* role can create (load) unsafe assemblies. Also note the *TRUSTWORTHY* property must be set to *ON* for the database into which the unsafe assembly will be loaded, and the *dbo* must have *UNSAFE ASSEMBLY* permission (or the assembly must be specially signed). There is commented code at the top of the *CreateObjects.sql* script that sets the *TRUSTWORTHY* property to *ON* for the *AdventureWorks2012* database.

When you deploy an assembly from Visual Studio, its security level is set to *Safe* by default. To change it, double-click the *Properties* node in the Solution Explorer, click the SQLCLR tab in the resulting property sheet designer and then select SAFE, EXTERNAL_ACCESS, or UNSAFE from the Permission Level combo box, as shown in Figure 3-8.

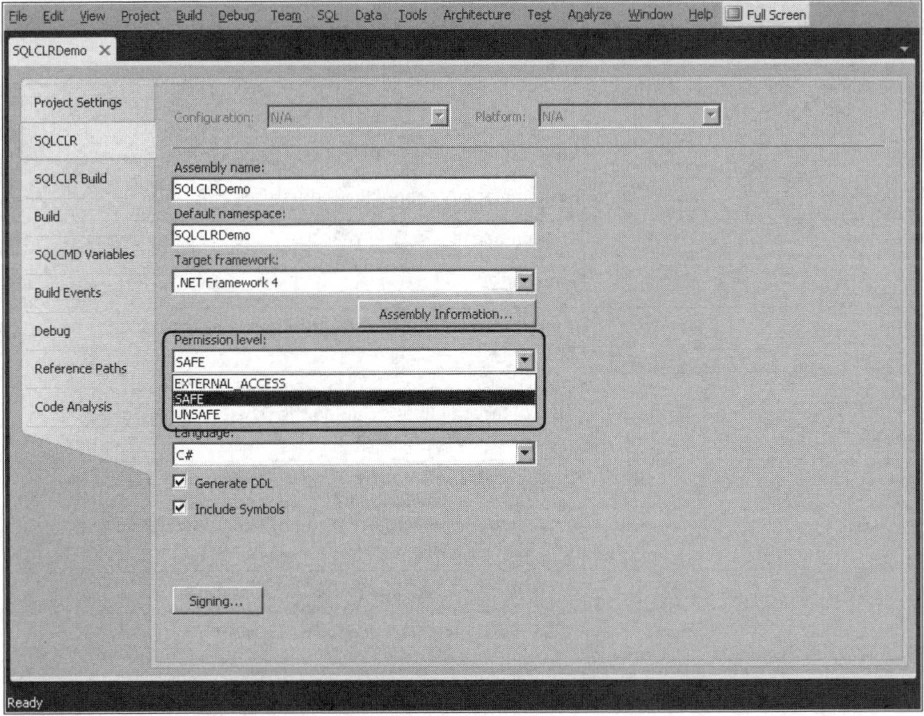

FIGURE 3-8 Selecting an assembly permission level in the SQLCLR property sheet tab.

To specify an assembly's permission set using T-SQL, simply specify *SAFE*, *EXTERNAL_ACCESS*, or *UNSAFE* within the *"WITH PERMISSION_SET"* clause of the *CREATE ASSEMBLY* statement, covered in the "Deploying Your Assembly" section, earlier in this chapter. Recall that our example used the default *SAFE* setting in this clause.

Finally, in the SSMS New Assembly dialog box (shown earlier in Figure 3-6) and the Assembly Properties dialog box, you can select Safe, External Access, or Unrestricted from the *Permission Set* combo box. The last of these three options is equivalent to selecting the UNSAFE permission set in Visual Studio or T-SQL.

Examining and Managing CLR Types in a Database

Once deployed, your SQL CLR stored procedures, functions, triggers, aggregates, and UDTs, and their dependencies, might become difficult to keep track of in your head. Luckily, you can easily perform discovery on deployed SQL CLR entities using the SSDT and SSMS UIs. All SQL CLR objects in a database can be found in the Object Explorer window in SSMS and the SQL Server Object Explorer window in Visual Studio. To find them within either window's tree view, first navigate to the *\servername\Databases\databasename* node (where *servername* and *databasename* are the names of your server and database, respectively). Refer to Table 3-1 for the subnodes of this node that contain each SQL CLR entity.

TABLE 3-1 Finding CLR Objects in the Object Explorers.

To View...	Look in...
Parent node for SQL CLR stored procedures, database-level DDL triggers, functions, aggregates, and UDTs	Programmability (see Figure 3-9)
Assemblies	Programmability\Assemblies (see Figure 3-10)
Stored procedures	Programmability\Stored Procedures (see Figure 3-11)
Functions	Programmability\Functions\Scalar-Valued Functions and Programmability\Functions\Table-Valued Functions (see Figure 3-12)
Aggregates	Programmability\Functions\Aggregate Functions (see Figure 3-12)
DML triggers	Tables*tablename*\Triggers, where *tablename* is the name of the database table, including the schema name, on which the trigger is defined (see Figure 3-13)
DDL triggers	Programmability\Database Triggers (see Figure 3-14) (also, for server-level triggers, *servername*\Server Objects\Triggers, where *servername* is the name of your server)
UDTs	Programmability\Types\User-Defined Types (see Figure 3-15 – in the SQL Server Object Explorer in Visual Studio, the node is labeled "User-Defined Types (CLR)")

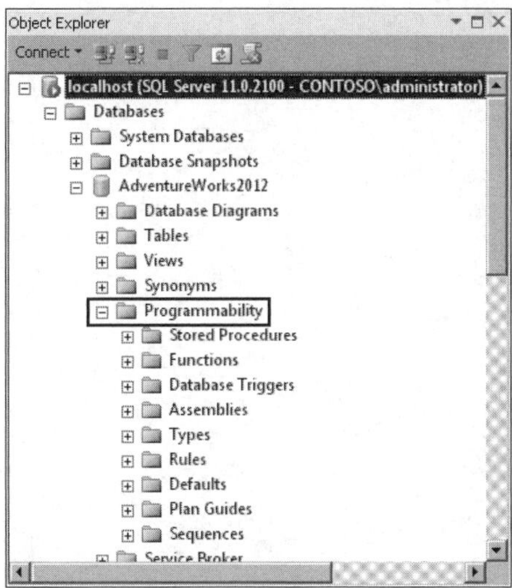

FIGURE 3-9 The SSMS Object Explorer window, with the Programmability node highlighted.

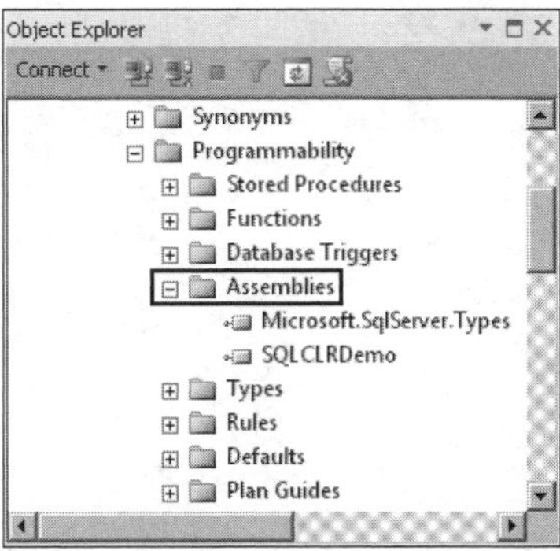

FIGURE 3-10 The Object Explorer window, with the Assemblies node highlighted (note the presence of the *Microsoft.SqlServer.Types* assembly, which is Microsoft's SQL CLR assembly for SQL Server data types such as *hierachyid*, *geometry*, and *geography*).

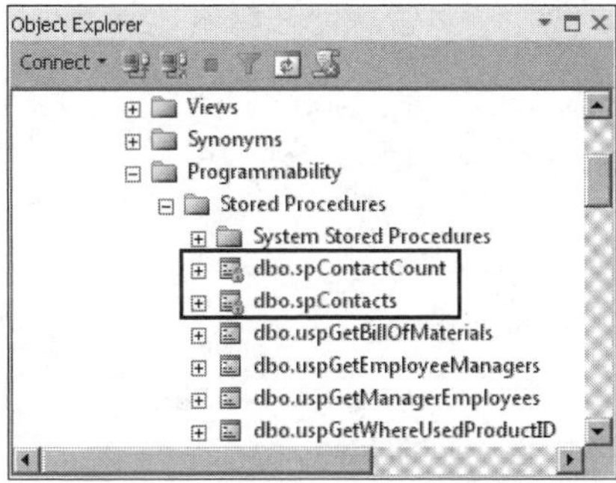

FIGURE 3-11 The Object Explorer window, with SQL CLR stored procedures highlighted.

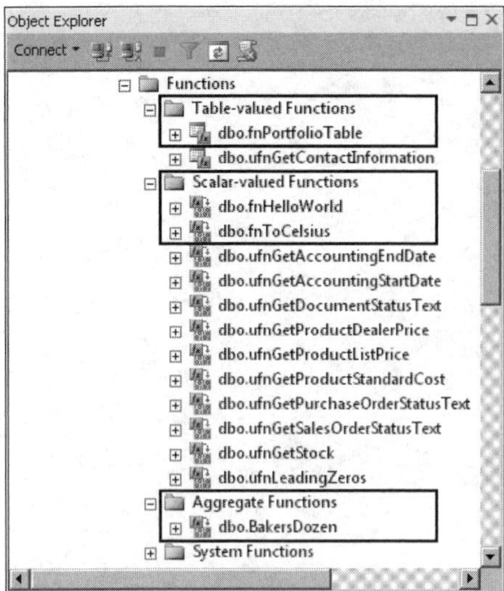

FIGURE 3-12 The Object Explorer window, with SQL CLR table-valued, scalar-valued, and aggregate functions highlighted.

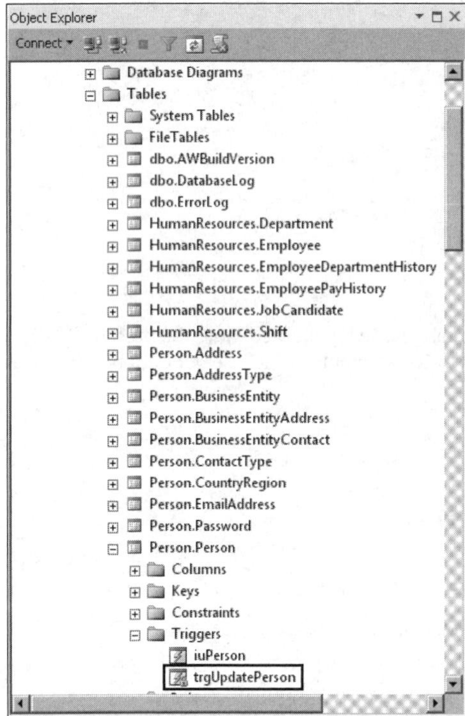

FIGURE 3-13 The Object Explorer window, with the SQL CLR DML trigger highlighted.

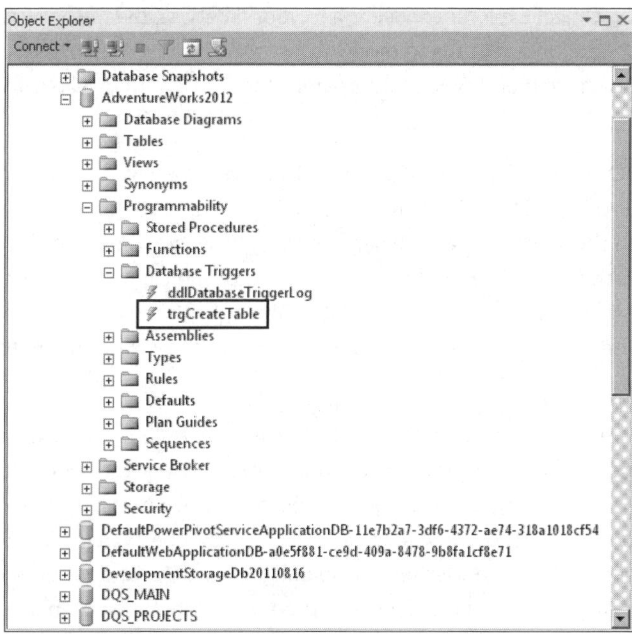

FIGURE 3-14 The Object Explorer window, with the SQL CLR DDL trigger highlighted.

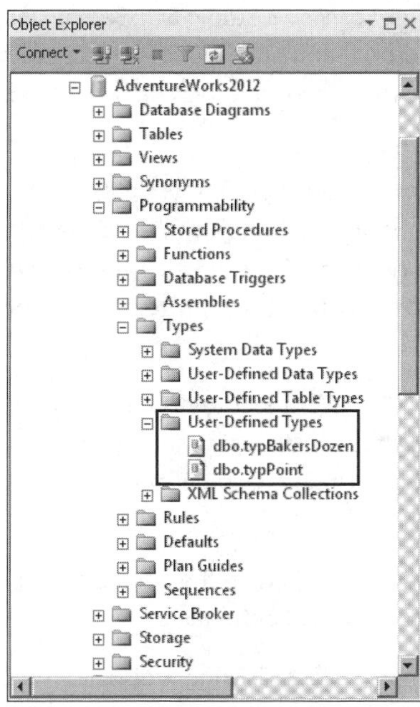

FIGURE 3-15 The Object Explorer window, with the SQL CLR UDTs highlighted.

Bear in mind that in SSMS, you might need to use the Refresh shortcut menu option on the nodes listed in the table to see your SQL CLR objects. If you've deployed or deleted any SQL CLR objects (as will be discussed shortly) since opening the Object Explorer connection to your database, the tree view will be out of date and will need to be refreshed. Notice that the tree view icons for SQL CLR stored procedures and SQL CLR DML triggers differ slightly from their T-SQL counterparts—they have a small yellow padlock on the lower-right corner.

In SSMS, once you've located a SQL CLR entity in the Object Explorer window, you can right-click its tree view node and generate *CREATE*, *DROP*, and in some cases, *ALTER* scripts for it by selecting the Script *object type* As option from the shortcut menu (where *object type* is the SQL CLR object type selected). The script text can be inserted into a new query window, a file, or the clipboard, or it can be used to create a SQL Server Agent job. In the Visual Studio SSDT Object Explorer, double-clicking a CLR assembly's or a CLR entity's tree view node opens up a T-SQL Editor window with the object's *CREATE* script code inside.

Back in SSMS, for stored procedures, you can generate *EXECUTE* scripts or, by selecting Execute Stored Procedure from the shortcut menu, execute stored procedures interactively and generate the corresponding script via the SSMS Execute Procedure dialog box. This dialog box explicitly prompts you for all input parameters defined for the stored procedure. In addition to generating scripts for your SQL CLR entities, you can view their dependencies (either objects that are dependent on them or objects on which they depend). Just right-click the object, and then choose the View Dependencies option from the shortcut menu.

To remove your SQL CLR objects, either in preparation for loading a new version of your assembly or to delete the objects permanently, you have several options. For Visual Studio SQL Server Database Project assemblies, redeploying one causes Visual Studio to drop it and any SQL CLR objects within it that had been previously deployed with it by Visual Studio. This means that new versions can be deployed from Visual Studio without any preparatory steps.

For Class Library projects, you must issue T-SQL *DROP* commands for each of your SQL CLR objects and then for the assembly itself. You must drop any dependent objects before you drop the SQL CLR entity. For example, you must drop *tblPoint* before dropping *typPoint*. You can write these *DROP* scripts by hand or generate them by using the Script *object type* As/DROP To shortcut menu options in the SSMS Object Explorer window.

You can also use the Delete shortcut menu option on any SQL CLR object to drop it. In the SSDT SQL Server Object Explorer, this option displays the Preview Database Updates window, which provides a preview of all changes along with Generate Script and Update Database buttons. This is shown in Figure 3-16.

With the SSDT delete option, all dependent objects will be deleted first, in the appropriate order. For example, deleting the assembly through SSDT would drop each CLR entity first.

In SSMS, the Delete shortcut menu option drops only a single object. Clicking it displays the Delete Object dialog box, shown in Figure 3-17.

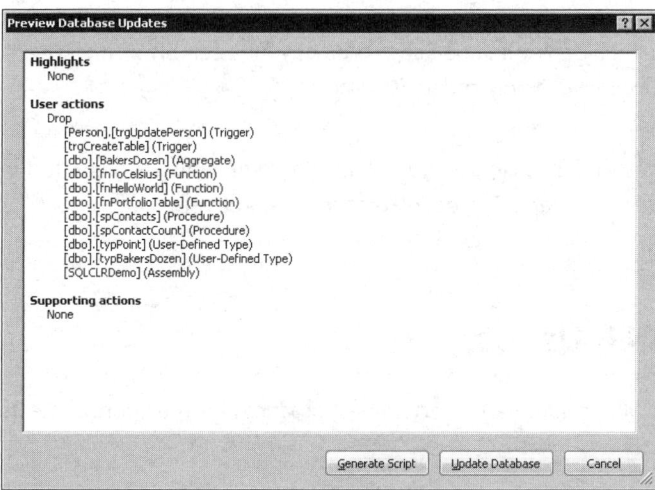

FIGURE 3-16 The Preview Database Updates window in SSDT after selecting the Delete option from the assembly's shortcut menu.

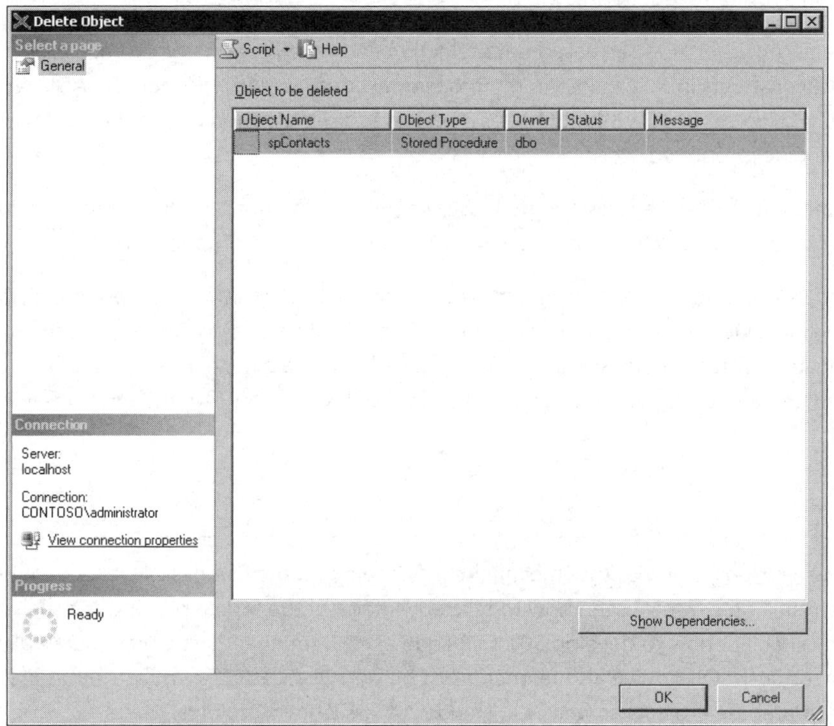

FIGURE 3-17 The SSMS Delete Object dialog box.

To compensate for the lack of a dependency object deletion feature comparable to that provided by SSDT, the script file *Cleanup.sql* in the SSMS project provided with the sample code contains all the necessary *DROP* commands, in the proper order, for removing all traces of your Visual Studio SQL Server

Database project or Class Library project assembly from the *AdventureWorks2012* database. For the Class Library project, run the script before you deploy an updated version of your assembly or, if you want to, use the script to permanently remove the assembly and its SQL CLR entities.

Note *Cleanup.sql* also removes tables *tblAggregateTest* and *tblPoint*, which are created by the scripts *CreateTblAggregateTest.sql* and *CreateTblPoint.sql*, respectively.

Best Practices for SQL CLR Usage

Before we close this chapter, we'd like to summarize certain best practices for the appropriate use of SQL CLR programming.

The CLR integration in SQL Server 2012 is a powerful technology. In some cases, it allows you to do things you can't do practically in T-SQL (such as apply complex computational logic in stored procedures or triggers), and in other cases, it allows you to do things you can't do at all in T-SQL (such as create your own aggregate functions).

The fact remains, however, that set-based data selection and modification is much better handled by the declarative constructs in T-SQL than in the procedural constructs of .NET and the ADO.NET object model. SQL CLR functionality should be reserved for specific situations when the power of .NET as a calculation engine is required.

In general, functions and aggregates are great uses of SQL CLR integration. UDTs, if used to track complex *values*, rather than objects per se, make good use of SQL CLR integration as well.

For stored procedures and triggers, we recommend that you start with the assumption that these should be written in T-SQL and write them using SQL CLR code only if a case can be made that they cannot be reasonably written otherwise. And before you make such a case, consider that SQL CLR functions, aggregates, and UDTs can be used from within T-SQL stored procedures and triggers.

Summary

In this chapter, we've exposed you to the "mechanics" of developing the five basic SQL CLR entities and using them from T-SQL. You've seen how to take advantage of the SQL Server 2012/Visual Studio 2010 integration, as well as how to develop SQL CLR code in conventional Class Library assemblies and deploy them using T-SQL. You've also learned most of the SQL CLR .NET code attributes and their use in SQL Server Database Projects as well as in standard Class Library projects.

You should now have a sense of how to use SQL Server Management Studio and the Visual Studio 2010 SQL Server Data Tools (SSDT) as management tools for your SQL CLR objects. We've discussed scenarios in which using SQL CLR integration is a good choice, as well as scenarios in which T-SQL is the better choice. You're now ready to leverage the power of SQL CLR in SQL Server.

CHAPTER 4

Working with Transactions

—*Leonard Lobel*

Have you ever intentionally written unreliable code? We assume that you haven't. Customers will not appreciate the system you wrote for them when it completely corrupts their critical data one day. Yet many professional developers treat the idea of writing reliable software all too casually. They concentrate most of their effort on getting the logic right and pay too little attention to ensuring that the logic behaves correctly under all circumstances. At the same time, more and more tasks are becoming automated, which demands increasingly complex software, which in turn is made possible by increasingly powerful hardware. Just as the desktop machine you work on today is thousands of times more powerful than the earliest microprocessors, software has grown dramatically more complex over time. This increase in complexity demands more reliability in your code, not less.

Despite this, most programmers continue to write unreliable software. Think of the last paycheck you received—the multitude of computer systems it went through and all the programmers who worked on that software. How would you feel if careless programming or inadequate testing resulted in a $100 reduction in your paycheck? Or what if a computer bug accidentally wiped out your retirement account, your Social Security number, or your identity?

Many programmers expect their careless mistakes to be caught in testing. But testing environments are often incapable of reproducing various concurrent scenarios. The reality is that most software issues manifest themselves in the production environment, not in the development or testing environment. Therefore, developers must focus on making sure that application logic is correct and behaves consistently in all scenarios. When application logic involves databases, those logical and data manipulation operations must conform to the ACID properties.

- Atomicity
- Consistency
- Isolation
- Durability

The general way to ensure these properties is to wrap your database operations in transactions. So we'll begin this chapter by exploring what a transaction is.

What Is a Transaction?

A transaction is a single operation or set of operations that succeed or fail together as a whole, thereby ensuring consistency of data should unforeseen circumstances arise. A classic scenario is the typical financial transaction. For example, let's say you buy a car. The single transaction of buying a car consists of three distinct operations:

1. You select a car.
2. You pay for it.
3. You drive the car off the lot.

Skipping any of these steps could cause major angst to one or more of the parties involved. This is a simple example of a set of steps that must always occur together in a consistent manner.

Transactions allow you to ensure consistency in your data through four basic principles. These principles provide a set of rules that must be followed for a transaction to succeed. The four principles help ensure that the state of your data is atomic, consistent, isolated, and durable, regardless of the success or failure of the transaction. Let's examine these properties now.

Note The discussion here centers around traditional two-phase commit ("XA-style") transactions. With the advent of Service-Oriented Architectures (SOAs), long-running transactions are increasingly common, so another type of transaction was created to handle those—the *compensated transaction*, which we will not be covering in this chapter.

Understanding the ACID Properties

Consider an ATM transaction where you withdraw $100 from your bank account. The data for this transaction can be represented in a database as a table with two columns, one holding your *AccountId* and the other holding your *AccountBalance*.

To begin with, your account balance is $100, so after withdrawing $100, your updated balance should be zero. Also, it makes logical sense that the system must ensure that you have the funds available in your account before the cash can be dispensed. What this means in database terms is that two database queries must be run in this transaction. The first query checks the account balance, as shown here:

```
SELECT AccountBalance FROM Account WHERE AccountId = @AccountId
```

If the query returns an *AccountBalance* value greater than or equal to the requested withdrawal, you can withdraw the cash.

After withdrawing the cash, you must update the account record with the updated balance. To do so, you run an *UPDATE* query:

```
UPDATE Account
 SET AccountBalance -= 100
 WHERE AccountId = @AccountId
```

The two distinct operations in this transaction are the two database queries that support the one operation of withdrawing cash. Both must succeed or fail together in an atomic manner, or the transaction should not be considered complete. *Atomicity* is the first ACID property.

Now let's change the nature of the transaction a bit. Let's say that the original account balance is $150 and that within the same transaction, the user requests to withdraw $100 and to transfer another $75 to a second account. The first update query will succeed, changing the account balance to $150 – $100 = $50. But the second operation will fail because there won't be enough money left in the account to transfer the $75. You therefore need a way to undo the cash withdrawal and return the database to its original state. You cannot leave the database midway through a transaction because it is in an inconsistent state. In a real-world scenario, you would not normally wrap a withdrawal and a transfer in the same transaction, but this was just a simple example to show how data can end up in an inconsistent state between multiple operations. Rolling back operations that cannot be completed in this manner demonstrates the second ACID property, *consistency*.

Let's say now that the withdrawal and transfer operations are separated into two distinct transactions instead of one, but that they happen to run simultaneously. Each transaction will have to check the current balance by attempting to execute a query like this:

```
SELECT AccountBalance FROM Account WHERE AccountId = @AccountId
```

Unless your system has explicit checks blocking concurrent reads, both transactions will get the same result: $150. Thus they will both assume that the account has enough funds for the transaction. One transaction will disburse $100, and the other will transfer $75. The result will be an overall deduction of $100 + $75 = $175, even though the account actually has only $150 available. In many systems, especially financial applications, such transactions must be isolated from each other to prevent what is known as a "dirty read." A dirty read happens when data is read at one point in a transition state and the result of the query doesn't reflect the data's true state at the end of the current operation. This leads to the third ACID property, *isolation*.

Isolation means that other transactions attempting to request a common resource will be blocked. Blocking, in turn, seriously affects the response times of your application. As it turns out, you'll often want to relax this blocking behavior to suit your application architecture. You can do that by using isolation levels, which we'll discuss later in this chapter in the section "Isolation Levels."

Lastly, when you have successfully completed all your operations within a transaction, you don't want to lose the changes made. In other words, system failures must not affect the transactional integrity of your operations. This relates to the fourth ACID property, *durability*. Durability means that the systems involved with the transaction will faithfully retain the correct transacted state even if the system sustains catastrophic failure nanoseconds after the transaction completes. Conversely, if the transaction isn't completed because of system failure, it won't be allowed to complete (or be undone) until the system is reset and the application restarted. Transacted steps are retained and the application can resume operations where it left off with no ill effects (at least from a data consistency perspective).

Let's quickly summarize the four ACID properties:

1. **Atomicity** Operations succeed or fail together. Unless all steps succeed, the transaction cannot be considered complete.
2. **Consistency** Operations leave the database in a consistent state. The transaction takes the underlying database from one stable state to another, with no rules violated before the beginning or after the end of the transaction.
3. **Isolation** Every transaction is an independent entity. One transaction will not affect any other transaction that is running at the same time.
4. **Durability** Every transaction is persisted to a reliable medium that cannot be undone by system failures. Furthermore, if a system failure does occur in the middle of a transaction, either the completed steps must be undone or the uncompleted steps must be executed to finish the transaction. This typically happens by use of a log that can be played back to return the system to a consistent state.

Important In our discussion of ACID transactional properties, we brushed over two other important concepts. The first refers to the actual process of disbursing cash as a part of the transaction. This alludes to the fact that transactions are not necessarily limited to database entities only. You will be examining more complex transactional situations later in this chapter when we discuss *System.Transactions* in detail (this is the transaction management API in the Microsoft .NET Framework that we cover in Chapter 10). The second refers to isolation levels that allow you to tweak the isolation behavior of a transaction to your specific needs, which we will also address in this chapter.

A transaction can work with a single resource, such as a database, or multiple resources, such as multiple databases or message queues. Transactions limited to a single resource are referred to as *local transactions*, and transactions that span multiple resources are called *distributed transactions*. We'll first concentrate on local transaction support in Microsoft SQL Server, and we'll talk about distributed transactions later in this chapter.

Local Transaction Support in SQL Server

SQL Server, like any industrial-strength database engine, provides built-in support that enables you to wrap one or more queries inside a transaction. Local transactions (those that deal with only one physical database) operate in one of four transaction modes:

- Autocommit
- Explicit
- Implicit
- Batch-scoped

Autocommit Transaction Mode

The *autocommit* transaction mode is the default transaction mode. Under this mode, SQL Server ensures data sanctity across the lifetime of the query execution, regardless of whether you requested a transaction. For example, if you execute a *SELECT* query, the data will not change over the execution lifetime of the query. Likewise, if you execute a data manipulation language (DML) query (*UPDATE*, *INSERT*, or *DELETE*), the changes will automatically be committed (if no errors occur) or rolled back (undone) otherwise. The execution of a single DML query will never result in a partial modification of records. The two notable exceptions to this rule are recursive common table expressions (CTEs), for which all of the returned data is not locked in advance, and situations where you explicitly request no transactional sanctity.

Explicit Transaction Mode

The autocommit transaction mode enables you to run single queries in a transactional manner, but frequently you'll want a batch of queries to operate within a single transaction. In that scenario, you use explicit transactions. Under the *explicit* transaction mode, you explicitly request the boundaries of a transaction. In other words, you specify precisely when the transaction begins and when it ends. SQL Server continues to work under the autocommit transaction mode until you request an exception to the rule, so if you want to execute a number of Transact-SQL (T-SQL) statements as a single batch, use the explicit transaction mode instead.

You specify when the transaction starts by using the *BEGIN TRANSACTION* statement. After you call *BEGIN TRANSACTION* on a database connection, the Database Engine attempts to enlist all ensuing operations within the same transaction. The *BEGIN TRANSACTION* statement uses the following syntax:

```
BEGIN { TRAN | TRANSACTION }
    [ { transaction_name | @tran_name_variable }
      [ WITH MARK [ 'description' ] ]
    ]
```

In this statement, you can specify a name for the transaction by using *transaction_name* or *@tran_name_variable*. You can also mark a transaction in the transaction log by specifying a description. This is useful if you want to restore the database to a named mark. For more information about this feature, refer to SQL Server Books Online at *http://msdn.microsoft.com/en-us/library/ms188929.aspx*.

Let's say that you call *BEGIN TRANSACTION* and then begin executing a number of DML operations. When you finish, you will want to end your transaction by saving (committing) your changes or undoing them (rolling back) in the event of an error. If you want to make the changes permanent, you execute a *COMMIT TRANSACTION* statement that uses the following syntax:

```
COMMIT { TRAN | TRANSACTION } [ transaction_name | @tran_name_variable ] ]
```

Here's an example that wraps two DML statements (an *UPDATE* and an *INSERT*) inside a single explicit transaction:

```
BEGIN TRANSACTION
  UPDATE Table1 SET Column1 = 'One'
  INSERT INTO Table2 (Column2) VALUES ('Two')
COMMIT
```

SQL Server maintains the transaction count, which returns the number of active transactions for the current connection. You can obtain the current transaction count by using the *@@TRANCOUNT* function. Every time you call *BEGIN TRANSACTION*, the *@@TRANCOUNT* value is incremented by 1. You can also have one *BEGIN TRANSACTION* statement execute after another, which also increases *@@TRANCOUNT*. Similarly, every time you call *COMMIT TRANSACTION*, SQL Server decrements *@@TRANCOUNT* by 1. Until *@@TRANCOUNT* drops back down to zero, the transaction remains active. When you call *BEGIN TRANSACTION* within a transaction block, you effectively create a *nested transaction*. But it isn't quite as simple as that. Before you can understand the nature of nested transactions in SQL Server, you must also consider the scenario in which you want the changes to be undone (not saved permanently) when an error occurs within the transaction.

If you do not want the changes to be permanent and instead want to restore the database to its previous state, you can roll back the changes with the *ROLLBACK TRANSACTION* T-SQL statement, which uses the following syntax:

```
ROLLBACK { TRAN | TRANSACTION }
     [ transaction_name | @tran_name_variable
     | savepoint_name | @savepoint_variable ]
```

ROLLBACK is the opposite of *COMMIT*. Instead of saving, it undoes all changes made in the transaction. It is important to realize that SQL Server never assumes *COMMIT*. If you disconnect from SQL Server without explicitly issuing a *COMMIT*, SQL Server assumes a *ROLLBACK*. However, as a best practice, you should never leave that decision to SQL Server. You should explicitly tell SQL Server which of the two options you want. The reason for this is connection pooling, a feature that improves performance by maintaining a pool of always available connections to any common data access application programming interface (API). Even if you close a connection, which would automatically cause the rollback if you didn't commit the transaction, it might take a while before an API such as Microsoft ADO.NET physically closes the connection. SQL Server might have to keep the transaction running and hence block valuable resources for longer than expected.

Another important difference between *COMMIT* and *ROLLBACK* is that if a severe error occurs during the execution of a transaction, SQL Server rolls back the transaction. Unfortunately, SQL Server doesn't make clear its definition of a severe error. An error with a severity level of 11 or higher stops the execution of the current batch and rolls back the transaction. Errors with a severity level of 19 or greater go as far as to terminate the connection. Which one is more severe? In both cases, batch execution stops in some indeterminate state. Because of this ambiguity, it is a good idea to explicitly call *ROLLBACK* if an error occurs.

Tip Always call *ROLLBACK* explicitly, and never rely on the API or SQL Server to issue a rollback for you.

There is another important difference between *COMMIT* and *ROLLBACK*. *COMMIT TRANSACTION* decrements *@@TRANCOUNT* by 1, but *ROLLBACK TRANSACTION* always reduces *@@TRANCOUNT* to 0. What does this mean in terms of nested transactions? We'll explore this topic next.

Nested Transactions

What does all this talk of *@@TRANCOUNT* and nested transactions mean in practical terms? Let's look at the following code snippet:

```
BEGIN TRANSACTION OUTERTRAN
  INSERT INTO TEST (TestColumn) VALUES (1)
  BEGIN TRANSACTION INNERTRAN
    INSERT INTO TEST (TestColumn) VALUES (2)
  COMMIT TRANSACTION INNERTRAN
ROLLBACK
```

When you run this code (assuming that the *TEST* table exists), no rows are inserted into the database, even though the inner transaction is committed. This is because the *ROLLBACK* statement automatically rolls back the entire transaction to the outermost *BEGIN TRANSACTION* statement, reducing *@@TRANCOUNT* to 0. So the *ROLLBACK* overrides the *COMMIT*, even though *COMMIT* was called before *ROLLBACK*. This is a subtle but important transactional processing behavior that is specific to SQL Server.

Savepoints

Another important concept related to transactions is *savepoints*. Savepoints allow you to temporarily store portions of the transaction, allowing parts of the transaction to be rolled back instead of the entire transaction. They are defined using the *SAVE TRANSACTION* statement, which uses the following syntax:

```
SAVE { TRAN | TRANSACTION } { savepoint_name | @savepoint_variable }
```

By invoking *SAVE TRANSACTION* during a transaction, you mark a point within the transaction that you can roll back to without losing everything. Consider the following code:

```
BEGIN TRANSACTION
  INSERT INTO TEST (TestColumn) VALUES (1)
  SAVE TRANSACTION SAVEPOINT1
    INSERT INTO TEST (TestColumn) VALUES (2)
  ROLLBACK TRANSACTION SAVEPOINT1
COMMIT
```

This code inserts a row and sets a savepoint with the name *SAVEPOINT1*. It then performs another insert, but because you set a savepoint prior to this insert, you can roll back to the savepoint without losing your first insert. As you might have guessed, at the end of the code block, only one row is inserted with *TestColumn = 1*.

To get a good feel for how these features of transactions work, experiment with various combinations of *BEGIN TRANSACTION*, *SAVE*, *COMMIT*, *ROLLBACK*, and *@@TRANCOUNT* on a test table in your database.

Implicit Transaction Mode

When you connect to a database using SQL Server Management Studio (SSMS) or SQL Server Data Tools (SSDT) and execute a DML query, the changes are automatically saved. This occurs because the connection is in autocommit transaction mode by default, as already mentioned. If you don't want changes committed unless you explicitly ask them to be committed, set the connection to implicit transaction mode. You can set the database connection to implicit transaction mode (or unset it) by calling the *SET IMPLICIT_TRANSACTIONS* T-SQL statement, as shown here:

```
SET IMPLICIT_TRANSACTIONS {ON | OFF}
```

When a connection is set in the implicit transaction mode and the connection is not currently in a transaction, a transaction is automatically started for you when you issue any one of the following statements: *ALTER TABLE*, *CREATE*, *DELETE*, *DROP*, *FETCH*, *GRANT*, *INSERT*, *OPEN*, *REVOKE*, *SELECT*, *TRUNCATE TABLE*, or *UPDATE*.

Note The term *implicit* refers to the fact that a transaction is implicitly started without an explicit *BEGIN TRANSACTION* statement. Thus, it is always necessary for you to explicitly commit the transaction afterward to save the changes (or roll it back to discard them).

With implicit transaction mode, the transaction that starts implicitly does not get committed or rolled back unless you explicitly request to do so. This means that if you issue an *UPDATE* statement, SQL Server will maintain a lock on the affected data until you issue a *COMMIT* or *ROLLBACK*. If you do not issue a *COMMIT* or *ROLLBACK* statement, the transaction is rolled back when the user disconnects.

In practical terms, you should avoid setting a connection to use implicit transaction mode on a highly concurrent database. For example, while administering a database through SSMS or SSDT, you will implicitly start transactions by issuing interactive queries, and might unwittingly end up locking database resources that can incapacitate the entire system. One example of the appropriate use of implicit transaction mode is on a data warehouse where the reports need just read-only access to the data and can be run under isolation levels that avoid blocking (as we'll discuss shortly) and where you want to be very careful not to inadvertently modify the data.

Batch-Scoped Transaction Mode

Since SQL Server 2005, multiple active result sets (MARS) are supported on the same connection. Note that we said multiple active results, not parallel execution of commands. The command execution is still interleaved with strict rules that govern which statements can overstep which other statements.

Connections using MARS have an associated batch execution environment. The batch execution environment contains various components—such as SET options, security context, database context, and execution state variables—that define the environment under which commands execute. When MARS is enabled, you can have multiple interleaved batches executing at the same time, so all changes made to the execution environment are scoped to the specific batch until the execution of that batch is complete. Once the execution of the batch completes, the execution settings are copied to the default environment.

Thus, a connection is said to be using batch-scoped transaction mode if it is running a transaction, has MARS enabled on it, and has multiple interleaved batches running at the same time.

MARS and Transactions

MARS lets you execute multiple interleaved batches of commands. However, MARS does not let you have multiple transactions on the same connection, only multiple active result sets. Transactions and MARS are an interesting mix, but to understand how transactions work in MARS, you must first understand the command interleaving rules.

In MARS, a command that reads results (such as *SELECT*, *FETCH*, or *READTEXT*) can, generally speaking, be interleaved freely or interrupted by a command that attempts to modify data (such as *UPDATE* or *INSERT*). Thus, a write operation can block a read operation, but a read operation cannot block a write operation. Read operations ensue once the write operation has finished. Also, if two writes show up together, they are serialized in the order of execution. Remember that command execution in SQL Server is always sequential, never parallel, even in multithreaded environments. Last, BULK INSERT statements block all other read and write operations.

So theoretically, *BULK INSERT* will block *INSERT*, *UPDATE*, and *DELETE*, which in turn will block all read operations. The problem, however, is that in most practical scenarios, you cannot accurately predict which command actually blocks which other command. This is because your read operation might have finished before the write operation interjected. You also cannot predict exactly when the read operation finished and the write operation started because the read operation depends on a number of factors—CPU speeds, network speeds, packet size, network traffic, and so on. It is thus impossible to predict whether the read data was "put on the wire" before the write operation was requested.

What this means in terms of transactions is that if you are running a transaction that inserts a row, which in turn fires a trigger, and there is a *SELECT* statement in the trigger, the MARS interleaving rules will dictate that your trigger's *SELECT* statement will be blocked by the original *INSERT* statement. Also, because of different command execution times, this behavior is impossible to predict reliably. If this ever happens, the SQL Server deadlock monitor will detect this condition and fail the *SELECT* statement. As a result, you might end up with a system that will work on a low-load developer's machine but fail in production where the load is greater. These are the most difficult types of problems to troubleshoot. Thus, when you use MARS, you must consider interleaving rules and multiple batches in your design.

MARS and Savepoints

Because you have multiple interleaved commands all working in the same transaction, the commands that issue savepoints can easily confuse each other's logic. Imagine a situation in which two interleaved batches issue a rollback to a named savepoint, and it just happens that the savepoint name is the same in both batches. You cannot predict which rollback occurred first, so which savepoint should SQL Server roll back to? In addition, because you cannot accurately predict which statement ended up interleaving which other statement, you can't really be sure if the savepoint was ever created before you issued a rollback to it.

For these reasons, if multiple serialized commands are executing, MARS allows you to set a savepoint, but as soon as commands begin to get interleaved, any request to *BEGIN TRANSACTION* will fail. Because you cannot accurately predict the exact interleaving order of commands, you cannot know for certain whether your *BEGIN TRANSACTION* statement will succeed or fail. Considering this unpredictable behavior, it is best to stay away from savepoints on a MARS connection.

Transaction Terminology

Before advancing beyond the basics of transactions, let's review some common terminology.

- **Beginning a transaction** Specifying that all subsequent operations that occur after a transaction begins are assumed to lie within the transaction.
- **Rolling back a transaction** Undoing operations that have occurred since a transaction began, thus restoring the affected data to its original state. This is done in the event of failure.
- **Committing a transaction** Making permanent all operations that have occurred since a transaction began. A transaction is committed in the event of success.
- **Dirty read** The operation of reading data that is yet to be committed. This occurs, for example, when transaction B is being blocked by transaction A, but because you have tweaked the isolation behavior to permit dirty reads, transaction B ends up reading transaction A's changes even though they have not been committed.
- **Nonrepeatable read** A condition where transaction B modifies the data that transaction A was working with, during the lifetime of transaction A. As a result, transaction A reads modified data, and the original read cannot be repeated.
- **Phantom read** Like a nonrepeatable read, except that the number of rows changes between two reads within the same transaction. The rows that differ between the two reads are referred to as *phantom rows*.

Isolation Levels

As we've started explaining, the isolation behavior of a transaction can be tweaked to your needs. This is generally done by setting the isolation level of a transaction. Put simply, isolation levels determine how concurrent transactions behave. Do they block each other? Do they let each other step over themselves? Or do they present a snapshot of a previous stable state of data in the event of an overstepped condition?

You can set isolation levels by using the *SET TRANSACTION ISOLATION LEVEL* statement, which uses the following syntax:

```
SET TRANSACTION ISOLATION LEVEL
    { READ UNCOMMITTED
    | READ COMMITTED
    | REPEATABLE READ
    | SNAPSHOT
    | SERIALIZABLE
    }
```

A sample usage of this statement with the *BEGIN TRANSACTION* statement is shown here:

```
SET TRANSACTION ISOLATION LEVEL READ UNCOMMITTED
BEGIN TRANSACTION
 SELECT TestColumn FROM TestTable
COMMIT
```

As you can see from the syntax, SQL Server supports these five isolation levels:

- Read uncommitted
- Read committed
- Repeatable read
- Snapshot
- Serializable

Read Uncommitted Isolation Level

By specifying the read uncommitted isolation level, you essentially tell the database to violate all locks and read the current immediate state of data. But by doing so, you might end up with a dirty read—reading data that is not yet committed. You should therefore avoid this isolation level if your application requires precise, committed data because transactions using this isolation level can return logically incorrect data.

Let's explore this isolation level by using an example.

LISTING 4-1 Using *SqlCommand* to execute a simple T-SQL command.

```
CREATE DATABASE MyDB
GO

USE MyDB
GO

CREATE TABLE TestTable
(
   TestID INT IDENTITY PRIMARY KEY,
   TestColumn INT
)

INSERT INTO TestTable(TestColumn) VALUES(100)
```

1. Use either SSMS or SSDT to execute the script shown in Listing 4-1 to create a simple test table.
2. Open two separate query windows, and in each instance, use the *MyDB* database that contains the *TestTable* table created in step 1. These two instances will be used to simulate two users running two concurrent transactions.
3. In instance 1, execute an *UPDATE* on the row of data by running the following code block:

   ```
   BEGIN TRANSACTION
   UPDATE TestTable SET TestColumn=200 WHERE TestId=1
   ```

4. In instance 2, execute the following query:

   ```
   SELECT TestColumn FROM TestTable WHERE TestId=1
   ```

   You will notice that your *SELECT* query is blocked. This makes sense because you are trying to read the same data that instance 1 is busy modifying. Unless instance 1 issues a *COMMIT* or a *ROLLBACK*, your query will remain blocked or will simply time out.

5. Cancel your blocked *SELECT* query by pressing **Alt+Break** or by clicking the Cancel button on the toolbar. Then execute the following statement to set the isolation level of your *SELECT* query to read uncommitted on the connection held by instance 2:

   ```
   SET TRANSACTION ISOLATION LEVEL READ UNCOMMITTED
   ```

6. Execute the *SELECT* query again, as follows:

   ```
   SELECT TestColumn FROM TestTable WHERE TestId=1
   ```

   You will find that the query isn't blocked; it produces *200* as a result.

7. Go back to instance 1, and issue a *ROLLBACK*.
8. Back in instance 2, execute the same *SELECT* query again. You should receive *100* as the result.

As you might have noticed, instance 2 returned different results for the same query at different times. As a matter of fact, the value 200 was never committed to the database, but because you explicitly requested a dirty read by specifying the *READ UNCOMMITTED* isolation level, you ended up reading data that was never meant to be final. So the downside is that you ended up reading logically incorrect data. On the upside, however, your query was not blocked.

Read Committed Isolation Level

Read committed is the default isolation level. As you will see shortly, read committed is the default because it strikes the best balance between data integrity and performance. This isolation level respects locks and prevents dirty reads from occurring. In the example you saw earlier, until you explicitly requested that the isolation level be changed to read uncommitted, the connection worked at the read committed isolation level, which caused the second transaction (the autocommit mode transaction in the *SELECT* query) to get blocked by the transaction executing the *UPDATE* query.

A read committed isolation level prevents dirty reads, but phantom reads and nonrepeatable reads are still possible when using this isolation level. This is because the read committed isolation level does not prevent one transaction from changing the same data at the same time as another transaction is reading from it.

A phantom read can occur in the following type of situation:

1. Transaction 1 begins.
2. Transaction 1 reads a row.
3. Transaction 2 begins.
4. Transaction 2 deletes the row that was read by transaction 1.
5. Transaction 2 commits. Transaction 1 can no longer repeat its initial read because the row no longer exists, resulting in a phantom row.

A nonrepeatable read can occur in the following type of situation:

1. Transaction 1 begins.
2. Transaction 1 reads a row.
3. Transaction 2 begins.
4. Transaction 2 changes the value of the same row read by transaction 1.
5. Transaction 2 commits.
6. Transaction 1 reads the row again. Transaction 1 has inconsistent data because the row now contains different values from the previous read, all within the scope of transaction 1.

Repeatable Read Isolation Level

As the name suggests, the repeatable read isolation level prevents nonrepeatable reads. It does so by placing locks on the data that was used in a query within a transaction. As you might expect, you pay a higher price in terms of concurrent transactions blocking each other, so you should use this isolation level only when necessary. The good news, however, is that a concurrent transaction can add new data that matches the *WHERE* clause of the original transaction. This is because the first transaction will place a lock only on the rows it originally read into its result set. In other words, a transaction using this isolation level acquires read locks on all retrieved data but does not acquire range locks.

If you examine this pattern closely, you'll see that although nonrepeatable reads are avoided when using this isolation level, phantom reads can still occur. They can occur under the following circumstances:

1. Transaction 1 begins.
2. Transaction 1 reads all rows with, say, *TestColumn = 100*.
3. Transaction 2 begins.
4. Transaction 2 inserts a new row with *TestID = 2, TestColumn = 100.*
5. Transaction 2 commits.
6. Transaction 1 runs an *UPDATE* query and modifies *TestColumn* for the rows where *TestColumn = 100*. This also ends up updating the row that transaction 2 inserted.
7. Transaction 1 commits.

Because shared locks are not released until the end of the transaction, concurrency is lower than when using the read committed isolation level, so care must be taken to avoid unexpected results.

Serializable Isolation Level

A transaction running at the serializable isolation level will not permit dirty reads, phantom reads, or nonrepeatable reads. This isolation level places the most restrictive locks on the data being read or modified, keeping your data perfectly clean. This might sound like an isolation level that gives you perfect isolation behavior, but there is a good reason why you should seldom use this isolation level. In a sense, this is the perfect transaction, but transactions will block other running transactions, thereby affecting concurrent performance or even creating deadlocks. Thus even if this transaction will keep your data perfectly clean, it will severely affect system performance. In most practical situations, you can get away with a lower isolation level.

Snapshot Isolation Level

In all of the isolation levels described earlier, it seems that concurrent performance is traded for logical sanctity of data. Because a transaction locks the data it is working on, other transactions that attempt to work with the same data are blocked until the first transaction commits or rolls back.

Of course, the traditional way of getting around this problem is to allow dirty reads (and hence incorrect data) or to simply reduce the duration of transactions. But neither of these solutions allows you to read logically consistent data while offering nonblocking concurrent behavior.

Application architectures frequently present circumstances in which even the smallest transactions become a problem or transactions end up modifying so much data that their duration cannot be kept small. To get around this issue, a new isolation level was introduced in SQL Server 2005: the snapshot isolation level. This isolation level gives you consistent reads without blocking.

Transactions running under the snapshot isolation level do not create shared locks on the rows being read. In addition, repeated requests for the same data within a snapshot transaction guarantee the same results, thus ensuring repeatable reads without any blocking. This sounds like the best of both worlds—the responsiveness of read uncommitted combined with the consistency of repeatable read. However, you pay a price.

This nonblocking, repeatable read behavior is made possible by storing previously committed versions of rows in the *tempdb* database. As a result, other transactions that were started before the write in the current transaction and that have already read the previous version will continue to read that version. Because the previous version is being read from *tempdb*, the write can occur in a nonblocking fashion and other transactions will see the new version. The obvious problem, of course, is the increased overhead on the *tempdb* database. For this reason, SQL Server requires you to enable the snapshot isolation level before you can use it. You shouldn't arbitrarily enable snapshot isolation on databases. But after testing, if you decide that your database needs this isolation level, you can enable it by using the following statement:

```
ALTER DATABASE MyDB
 SET ALLOW_SNAPSHOT_ISOLATION ON
```

As with all isolation levels, once you enable snapshot isolation for a database, you can use it on individual connections by using the *SET TRANSACTION ISOLATION LEVEL* statement, as follows:

```
SET TRANSACTION ISOLATION LEVEL SNAPSHOT
```

Read Committed Snapshot Isolation Level

Snapshot isolation prevents readers from being blocked by writers by providing readers with data from a previously committed version. Over the duration of the transaction, you are thus assured of repeatable reads. However, this method of ensuring a repeatable read incurs additional overhead and bookkeeping for the SQL Server Database Engine that might not be necessary in all situations. Thus, SQL Server offers a slight modification to the read committed isolation level that provides nonrepeatable reads over the duration of the transaction that are not blocked by transaction writers. This modification is called the read committed snapshot isolation level. This isolation level guarantees consistency of the data over the duration of a read query within a transaction but not over the entire transaction that holds the reader. The obvious advantage over read committed snapshot as compared to read committed is that your readers do not get blocked. When they request data, they are offered either a previous state of data (before any write operations) or the new state of data (after write operations), depending on the state of other concurrently running transactions, but they are never required to wait until other concurrent transactions release their locks on the data being requested.

To use the read committed snapshot isolation level, you must first enable it at the database level by using the following T-SQL command:

```
USE master
GO

ALTER DATABASE MyDB
 SET READ_COMMITTED_SNAPSHOT ON
```

Notice the *USE master* statement to switch away from the *MyDB* database. The *ALTER* statement waits until there are no active connections to *MyDB* (if you still have open query windows with active connections to *MyDB* from an earlier example, the *ALTER* statement will hang until you close those windows). Once you have enabled the read committed snapshot isolation level on a database, all queries using the read committed isolation level will exhibit snapshot-like behavior. Although this isolation level will give you snapshot-like behavior, you will not be able to perform repeatable reads over the duration of a transaction.

Note When FILESTREAM (covered in Chapter 8) was first introduced in SQL Server 2008, neither snapshot isolation nor read committed snapshot isolation levels could be used with FILESTREAM-enabled databases. That limitation was removed with the release of SQL Server 2008 R2, and FILESTREAM is now compatible with snapshot isolation.

Isolation Levels in ADO.NET

There is a slight mismatch between the isolation levels defined in ADO.NET (which calls SQL Server from your .NET application), compared with the isolation levels in SQL Server itself. This is because ADO.NET was not written exclusively for SQL Server, and is a generic data access technology that supports Oracle and other databases as well.

Note Chapter 10 provides detailed coverage of ADO.NET, and demonstrates how to code SQL Server transactions from the application layer using ADO.NET.

The isolation levels defined in ADO.NET 2.0 under the *System.Data.IsolationLevel* enumeration are as follows:

- *Chaos* Pending changes from more highly isolated transactions cannot be overwritten. This setting is not supported in SQL Server or Oracle.
- *ReadUncommitted* Similar to read uncommitted in SQL Server, this level means that no shared locks are placed and no exclusive locks are honored.

- *ReadCommitted* As with read committed in SQL Server, shared locks are held while the data is being read by the transaction. This avoids dirty reads, but you might still get nonrepeatable reads and phantom reads.

- *RepeatableRead* Shared locks are placed on all data that is used in the predicate (criterion) of the query. Again, as with repeatable read in SQL Server, dirty reads and nonrepeatable reads are not possible, but phantom reads are.

- *Snapshot* Similar to the snapshot isolation level in SQL Server, this isolation level provides a snapshot of earlier data while offering repeatable reads with nonblocking selects. Do not confuse this level with the read committed snapshot isolation level in SQL Server, which must be enabled at the database level.

- *Serializable* This can be considered an ideal transaction type to use, in which exclusive locks are placed on data. This prevents other users from reading or modifying the data. Keep in mind that there are always trade-offs, and exclusive locks should not be held for long periods of time.

- *Unspecified* This is a catchall isolation level for databases that support isolation levels not covered by the other choices or for scenarios in which the isolation level cannot be accurately determined.

The *System.Data.IsolationLevel* enumeration can be used with both implicit and explicit ADO.NET transactions. Chapter 10 covers ADO.NET transactions in detail, and explains why implicit ADO.NET transactions (using the *TransactionScope* object) are preferred over explicit transactions (which use the *SqlTransaction* object).

Setting the Isolation Level for Explicit ADO.NET Transactions

You can specify an isolation level for an explicit ADO.NET transaction as a parameter to the *BeginTransaction* method. For instance, the following code snippet begins a transaction with the ReadUncommitted isolation level:

```
SqlTransaction tran = conn.BeginTransaction(IsolationLevel.ReadUncommitted);
```

In this example, any *SqlCommand* with its Transaction property set to *tran* will not honor any exclusive locks and will let you perform dirty reads on data being held by other transactions.

Setting the Isolation Level for Implicit ADO.NET Transactions

Implicit ADO.NET transactions are recommended over explicit ADO.NET transactions. To set the isolation level for implicit ADO.NET transactions, create a new *TransactionOptions* object, and set its *IsolationLevel* property to the desired enumeration value. Then pass the *TransactionOptions* object to the constructor for the *TransactionScope* object. For example:

```
var tso = new TransactionOptions();
tso.IsolationLevel = IsolationLevel.ReadUncommitted;
using (var ts = new TransactionScope(tso))
```

```
{
   // ... update data
   // ... update data
   ts.Complete();
}
```

Distributed Transactions

Thus far, our discussion has been limited to transactions on a single database. What if more than one database is involved? What if more than one database server is involved? What if a nondatabase operation, such as modifying an in-memory cache, is involved? Can you use *BEGIN TRANSACTION* to bind other such operations within a single transaction? Unfortunately, you cannot. *BEGIN TRANSACTION* works only on local transactions dealing with data in a database. These transactions do not apply to an in-memory cache, because no transaction logging mechanism is available.

In this section, we'll look at a deeper theory of transactions and explore the Transaction Management API in the .NET Framework *System.Transactions* namespace. You'll also see why a transaction that is inherently expensive due to its overhead becomes even more expensive when it is being managed by an external entity—a transaction coordinator. This discussion addresses a scope broader than database-only transactions.

Distributed Transaction Terminology

You will frequently encounter the terms *resource manager, transaction manager, transaction coordinator,* and *two-phase commit* when discussing distributed transactions. Let's look at those terms more closely.

Resource Manager

Transactions (database or otherwise) manage a resource. Any operation that needs to be made transactional is managed by a logical entity—a subroutine, a function, a dynamic-link library (DLL), an executable, a machine, or anything else that is capable of supporting transactions. Any such logical entity that is eventually responsible for managing the resource in a transactional manner is called a resource manager (RM).

Thus, an RM has the ability and responsibility to enlist itself in a current running transaction and thereby supports transactional capabilities.

Transaction Manager or Transaction Coordinator

If you have an RM that manages its resources in a transactional manner by enlisting in a current running transaction, by definition you need an external entity that manages the transaction itself. This external entity is responsible for listening to and coordinating between several RMs that are all enlisted within the same transaction. It acknowledges requests for new transactions and listens for and sends notifications in the event of success and failure. This entity is referred to as a *transaction manager* (TM), *transaction coordinator* (TC), or *distributed transaction coordinator* (DTC). Two common transaction coordinators that ship with Microsoft Windows are the Lightweight Transaction Manager (LTM) and the Microsoft Distributed Transaction Coordinator (MS DTC).

Do note that a TC is not necessarily a DTC. In fact, if the RM itself has transactional capabilities built in, it might not need a TC at all. For instance, in the case of SQL Server, if a transaction is limited to a single database, SQL Server is fully capable of managing the transaction on its own. Thus, for local transactions, SQL Server chooses not to consult the MS DTC. There are good reasons for this, which will become evident once you read about the typical implementation of a distributed transaction—namely, the two-phase commit process.

Two-Phase Commit

A distributed transaction can be implemented in a number of ways. One of the most common ways is through the two-phase commit process. Here is the typical flow of a two-phase transaction involving two RMs and a DTC:

1. The transaction initiator requests a transaction from the DTC. This transaction initiator can be the application that interacts with the two RMs, or it can be one of the RMs itself.
2. The transaction initiator requests that the RMs to do their work as a part of the same transaction. The RMs register themselves with the DTC as a part of the same transaction, thus expressing an interest in receiving notifications about the success or failure of the transaction as a whole. This process is referred to as "enlisting within a transaction."
3. The RMs go ahead and do their work and notify the DTC of a success, while keeping a rollback mechanism in place. This is the first phase of a two-phase commit process, also called the *prepare phase*.
4. Once the DTC receives a success notification for the prepare phases from each of the enlisted RMs, the DTC issues a notification to go ahead and make the changes permanent. Upon receiving such a notification, all RMs make their changes permanent by committing their transient states. This is also known as the *commit phase*. The system has now gone from one stable state to another, and the distributed transaction is complete.

Rules and Methods of Enlistment

As you might have surmised, the DTC on a machine running Windows, MS DTC, engages in a lot of chatty communication with the various RMs involved in a transaction. Due to the network roundtrips involved, this chatting affects the performance of the application in general and might also be blocked by a firewall. In addition, RMs that enlist themselves in a distributed transaction often use the serializable isolation level. This architecture is the easiest to implement because when using the serializable isolation level, you have a perfect transaction—no dirty reads, no phantom reads, and no nonrepeatable reads. Of course, the downside is a serious performance impact.

But SQL Server itself is capable of managing transactions, so why should it have to escalate the isolation level to serializable in every circumstance? After all, depending on your logic, you might want to take advantage of an MS DTC–based transaction *if and only if* your transaction ends up involving more than one RM. But as long as only one database connection is involved, you shouldn't have to pay the extra cost of involving the DTC. As it turns out, the Microsoft engineers thought of this situation. And to rectify the situation, an RM can enlist within a transaction in different ways.

Volatile Enlistment

An RM that deals with resources that are volatile (not permanent) is a good candidate for volatile enlistment. Typically, in a volatile enlistment scenario, if the RM cannot perform the second (commit) phase of a distributed transaction for any reason, it doesn't explicitly need to recover the first (prepare) phase. This means that if an RM crashes in the middle of a transaction, the RM doesn't need to provide an explicit recovery contract to the TC. Volatile enlistment doesn't need the implementation of MS DTC, so it is usually managed by the LTM, which is a much lighter weight TC designed to work with volatile enlistment scenarios. An example of such an RM might be one that manages an in-memory cache. The cache data isn't meant to be permanent—it only lasts for a relatively short duration.

Durable Enlistment

Durable enlistment is necessary if the RM has permanent (durable) data that depends on the transaction for consistency. A good example is a transaction that involves disk I/O. Say you are writing to a file on disk. If the transaction fails, or if the RM crashes, the file that was written as a part of the prepare phase will need to be deleted. Thus the RM will need to prepare a transaction log and record the history of changes since the transaction was begun. In the event of a requested recovery, the RM needs sufficient information to perform a graceful rollback.

Note SQL Server's FILESTREAM feature implements a transparent coordination between database transactions and NTFS file system transactions. You will find detailed coverage of FILESTREAM in Chapter 8.

Promotable Single-Phase Enlistment

In many situations, the nature of a transaction can change as new RMs continue to enlist. For instance, a SQL Server database is perfectly capable of managing a transaction on its own, as long as the transaction is limited to one database. Or say, for instance, that an RM that manages an in-memory cache doesn't need the implementation of MS DTC because the cache by nature is temporary anyway. But if there is a transaction containing an in-memory cache RM or a SQL Server connection being managed by the LTM, and a second SQL Server connection enlists itself in the same transaction, the transaction will be promoted to MS DTC because the RMs are no longer capable of managing the transaction on their own.

It is important to note that along with the promotion comes what are sometimes considered (necessary) disadvantages of MS DTC—a higher isolation level and a more expensive and chatty transaction in general. Promotable single-phase enlistment (PSPE) offers a huge advantage in that as long as you don't really need MS DTC, you don't use it, so you don't pay the penalty for it. (However, when you truly need MS DTC, it's a godsend.)

There are well-defined rules for the promotion of a transaction from LTM to MS DTC. A transaction is escalated from LTM to MS DTC if any of the following happens:

- A durable resource that doesn't support single-phase notifications is enlisted in the transaction.
- Two durable resources that support single-phase notification enlist in the same transaction.
- The TC receives a request to marshal a transaction to a different .NET AppDomain or Windows process.

Note SQL Server 2000 connections are always promoted to MS DTC, and SQL Common Language Runtime (CLR) connections inside a *System.Transactions.TransactionScope* are promoted to MS DTC even if only one of them is enlisted in the transaction scope.

With a good theory and a common terminology in hand, we can look at the support for distributed transactions in SQL Server and the .NET Framework in general.

Distributed Transactions in SQL Server

SQL Server supports distributed transactions using the *BEGIN DISTRIBUTED TRANSACTION* statement. This statement requests the start of a T-SQL distributed transaction managed by the MS DTC. It uses the following syntax:

```
BEGIN DISTRIBUTED { TRAN | TRANSACTION }
     [ transaction_name | @tran_name_variable ]
```

The easiest way to enlist remote instances of the SQL Server Database Engine in a distributed transaction is to execute a distributed query that references a linked server. For example, you can link *ServerB* and execute a query that looks like this:

```
DELETE FROM ServerB.TestDB.TestTable Where TestID = 1
```

Enlisting the preceding query in a distributed transaction is rather simple:

```
BEGIN DISTRIBUTED TRANSACTION
  DELETE TestDB.TestTable WHERE TestID = 1
  DELETE ServerB.TestDB.TestTable WHERE TestID = 1
COMMIT
```

The obvious shortcoming of this implementation is that the second query has no way to explicitly enlist. This might seem trivial, but if the second query is a stored procedure that calls *ServerC*, which in turn calls *ServerD*, all of them will be tied up in one really expensive transaction, all managed by the one MS DTC on the initiating server.

You can get around this issue by configuring the default behavior to not promote linked server queries to MS DTC. You can do this in two ways. First, you can do it at the server level, by using the following T-SQL command:

```
sp_configure remote proc trans 0
```

Or you can do it at the connection level, by using the following syntax:

```
SET REMOTE_PROC_TRANSACTIONS OFF
```

You can then use *BEGIN TRANSACTION* and have the SQL Server Database Engine manage the transactions for you. Conversely, if you use a setting of *1* or *ON*, a *BEGIN TRANSACTION* statement involving linked servers will then involve MS DTC—but this is an all-or-nothing approach.

Distributed Transactions in the .NET Framework

The concept of distributed transactions was not introduced with the .NET Framework. Prior to the .NET Framework, you could enlist in distributed transactions using third-party transactions coordinators such as COMTI or solutions such as COM+ or Microsoft Transaction Server (MTS) to enlist in distributed transactions. Starting with the .NET Framework 1.0, you could also use the *System.EnterpriseServices* namespace to enlist within a distributed transaction. *System.EnterpriseServices* essentially wraps the COM+ infrastructure.

The problem with *EnterpriseServices*-based solutions was that you had to implement your operation as a class library, decorate it with the *TransactionOption* attribute, strongly name it, and register it in the global assembly cache (GAC). This made debugging and deployment difficult. Also, the *TransactionOption* attribute hard-coded the transactional behavior of your operation to one of the following values:

- *Disabled* Does not participate in transactions. This is the default value.
- *NotSupported* Runs outside the context of a transaction.
- *Supported* Participates in a transaction if one exists. If one doesn't exist, the operation will not request or create one.
- *Required* Requires a transaction. If no transaction exists, one is created. If one exists, the operation enlists itself in the transaction.
- *RequiresNew* Requires a transaction and creates a new transaction for itself.

You really couldn't enlist on demand in the .NET Framework 1.0, and debugging and deployment were difficult. The .NET Framework 1.1 offered a slightly better solution, which was made possible by the *ServiceConfig* class. This solution, known as "services without components," did not require you to register your assembly in the GAC or even strongly name it, but unfortunately it was at one time limited to Microsoft Windows 2003 and Windows XP with Service Pack 2, so it didn't gain a strong following. It has since been rolled out to other Windows-based operating systems but is still relatively unknown. Even so, you couldn't use concepts such as promotable enlistment. Thus, the .NET Framework 2.0 introduced a new Transaction Management API in a namespace named *System.Transactions* to address all of these issues.

Let's look at the behavior of a *System.Transactions*-based transaction by creating an example. You will set up two databases and execute one query on each.

Execute the script shown in Listing 4-2. The code creates the two databases and names them *Test1* and *Test2*. It then creates a table named *FromTable* in *Test1* and a table named *ToTable* in *Test2*, both of them with one *int* column named *Amount*. A row is then inserted into the *FromTable* table with the value *100*, and another row is inserted into the *ToTable* table with the value *0*.

LISTING 4-2 Preparing test databases for programming distributed transactions.

```
CREATE DATABASE Test1
GO
USE Test1
GO
CREATE TABLE FromTable (Amount int)
GO
INSERT INTO FromTable(Amount) VALUES (100)
GO

CREATE DATABASE Test2
GO
USE Test2
GO
CREATE TABLE ToTable (Amount int)
GO
INSERT INTO ToTable(Amount) VALUES (0)
GO
```

Now create a C# console application and name it *DistributedTrans*. Because you're using the Transaction Management API, you need to reference the *System.Transactions* assembly. Right-click the project in Solution Explorer and choose Add Reference. In the Add Reference dialog, click the .NET tab, scroll to find the *System.Transactions* component, and double-click it. Then add the code shown in Listing 4-3 to *Program.cs*.

LISTING 4-3 Programming distributed transactions in .NET.

```
using System;
using System.Data;
using System.Data.SqlClient;
using System.Transactions;

namespace DistributedTrans
{
  class Program
```

```
  {
    static void Main(string[] args)
    {
      const string ConnStr1 =
       "Data Source=(local);Initial Catalog=Test1;Integrated Security=SSPI;";
      const string ConnStr2 =
       "Data Source=(local);Initial Catalog=Test2;Integrated Security=SSPI;";

      const string CmdText1 = "UPDATE FromTable SET Amount = Amount - 50";
      const string CmdText2 = "UPDATE ToTable SET Amount = Amount + 50";

      using (var tsc = new TransactionScope())
      {
        using (var conn1 = new SqlConnection(ConnStr1))
        {
          SqlCommand cmd1 = conn1.CreateCommand();
          cmd1.CommandText = CmdText1;
          conn1.Open();
          cmd1.ExecuteNonQuery();
        }

        // Operation #1 is done, going to Operation #2

        using (var conn2 = new SqlConnection(ConnStr2))
        {
          SqlCommand cmd2 = conn2.CreateCommand();
          cmd2.CommandText = CmdText2;
          conn2.Open();
          cmd2.ExecuteNonQuery();
        }

        tsc.Complete();
      }
    }
  }
}
```

The aim of this example is to execute two queries, one on each database. One query will subtract 50 from *FromTable* in *Test1*, and the other will add 50 to *ToTable* in *Test2*. Both operations must be bound within the same transaction.

Important Before you can run this code, you need to make sure that the DTC service is started. To do so, click Start and type **services**. In the list of services, find Distributed Transaction Coordinator. If not already started, right-click on it now and choose Start.

Run the code (don't worry if you don't understand it just yet—we'll explain it in a moment). Notice that the two command objects *cmd1* and *cmd2* run in a distributed transaction. If the second query fails, the first one will automatically roll back. It's really just that simple. Of course, more complicated implementations are possible, but the basic process of implementing a distributed transaction using *System.Transaction* is really that easy. Now take a closer look at the code you just wrote.

At the beginning of the code snippet is a using block:

```
using (var tsc = new TransactionScope())
{
  // ...Do transactional operations here...
}
```

The using block ensures that the *Dispose* method is always called on the *TransactionScope* instance *tsc* when the scope of the using statement ends. The instantiation of a *TransactionScope* starts a new transaction and *Dispose* is called when the scope of the enclosing *using* block ends. By disposing *tsc*, the distributed transaction is committed. Thus, within the *using* block, any RM will attempt to enlist itself in the current running transaction and will commit the transaction, assuming the *TransactionScope's Complete* method is called prior to exiting the *using* block's scope and there is no exception within the block. The process of executing a query on the database is implemented in regular ADO.NET code, as follows:

```
using (SqlConnection conn1 = new SqlConnection(connStr1))
{
  SqlCommand cmd1 = conn1.CreateCommand();
  cmd1.CommandText = CmdText1;
  conn1.Open();
  cmd1.ExecuteNonQuery();
}
```

The magic here is that the *SqlConnection* instance conn1 knows that it is working inside a *TransactionScope*. When the transaction scope is entered, it creates an ambient transaction. Because transactional code executing within the transaction scope now has an active transaction in which to enlist, it enlists itself with the appropriate TM.

Notice that we said "appropriate TM," not MS DTC. This is because when a *SqlConnection* instance is connected with a SQL Server database, it exhibits PSPE—that is, the transaction is managed by LTM and not MS DTC until the *conn2.Open* statement is called.

Set a breakpoint on the line of code *conn2.Open* and run the application again. The breakpoint is reached just before the second connection is opened. Now examine the following value in the Immediate Window pane:

```
Transaction.Current.TransactionInformation.DistributedIdentifier.ToString()
```

While still in debug mode, execute the *conn2.Open* statement and check this value again. What do you see? You will see that right before *conn2* is opened, the value is a null globally unique identifier (GUID):

```
"00000000-0000-0000-0000-000000000000"
```

Step over the *conn2.Open* statement. Right after the second connection is opened, notice that this value changes to an actual GUID value, similar to the following:

```
"2c67c7d5-9b32-485f-9e1c-8e43174598aa"
```

If you immediately go to Administrative Tools | Component Services, and then navigate to the Transaction List, you will notice the very same GUID running there, as shown in Figure 4-1.

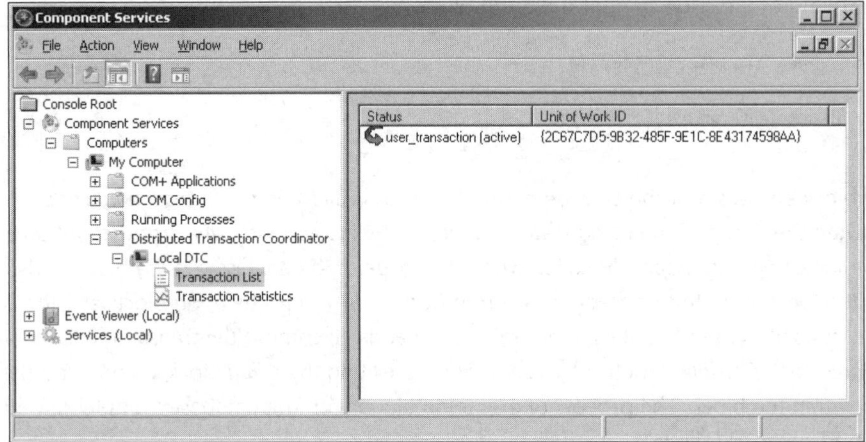

FIGURE 4-1 The current active transaction being managed by MS DTC.

What this tells you is that right before *conn2.Open* was executed, the transaction was being managed by the LTM and hence didn't have a valid *DistributedIdentifier*. But as soon as the second RM enlisted in the transaction, the transaction was bumped up to MS DTC and got a valid *DistributedIdentifier*. If you were to run this same code sample against a SQL Server 2000 database, the *DistributedIdentifier* would have a valid value right after *conn1.Open* executes, thus proving that *SqlConnection* enlists durably when connecting with a SQL Server 2000 database yet exhibits PSPE when connecting with a SQL Server 2012, 2008, or 2005 database.

It could be argued that you could easily achieve the same thing through the T-SQL statement *BEGIN DISTRIBUTED TRANSACTION*, without using the *System.Transactions* namespace. It is important to realize that *System.Transactions* provides a much more flexible architecture in which you can logically choose to enlist or not, and it deals with more than just database transactions. You can theoretically write an RM that encapsulates any operation in a transactional manner, as you'll do next.

Writing Your Own Resource Manager

It is only reasonable to expect that because databases are the most critical part of the architecture (at least to database developers and administrators!), they have had fantastic transactional support for a long time. But don't you want your other, nondatabase operations to be transactional as well if they also could benefit from transactional behavior?

Let's consider the simple operation of setting a value to an integer and wrapping that as a part of a transaction, as shown in the following code snippet. The first question is: How do you set a value for an integer?

```
int myInt;
myInt = 10;
```

Unfortunately, wrapping this code in a *TransactionScope* won't make it transactional. This is because *System.Int32* is not smart enough to understand that it is being wrapped inside a *TransactionScope* and that it should auto-enlist within a running transaction. This is probably a good thing, because in the event of a rollback, to perform a graceful recovery, *System.Int32* would have to maintain a previous version. You probably wouldn't want to pay this overhead for all your integers. So you need to write a class that lets you maintain enough history in the event of a rollback. This class should also be able to interact with a TM and listen for various two-phase commit notifications. To do so, this class, or the RM you are writing, must implement the *IEnlistmentNotification* interface. This interface requires you to implement certain methods that are called at the appropriate points in time by the TC during the two phases of a two-phase commit process.

Here are the methods that *IEnlistmentNotification* requires you to implement:

- *Commit* Notifies the RM that the transaction has been committed. The RM then makes the changes permanent.
- *Rollback* Notifies the RM that the transaction has been rolled back. The RM then reverts to the previous stable state.
- *Prepare* Called during the first (prepare) phase of a distributed transaction—when the TM asks the participants whether they are ready to commit. If the TM receives a successful notification from each participating RM, it calls the *Commit* methods.
- *InDoubt* Notifies the RMs if the TM loses contact with one or more participants in the transaction. In this situation, the status of the transaction is unknown, and the application logic must decide whether to revert to the previous consistent state or remain in an inconsistent state.

Listing 4-4 puts all of these concepts into actual code. It shows a full implementation of a volatile RM. You can also find this code in the *CreateYourOwnRM* solution on the book's companion website.

LISTING 4-4 Implementing your own resource manager.

```
public class VolatileRM : IEnlistmentNotification
{
    private string _whoAmI = "";
    public VolatileRM(string whoAmI)
    {
        this._whoAmI = whoAmI;
    }

    private int _memberValue = 0;
    private int _oldMemberValue = 0;
    public int MemberValue
    {
        get
        {
            return this._memberValue;
        }
```

```
        set
        {
            Transaction tran = Transaction.Current;
            if (tran != null)
            {
                Console.WriteLine(
                 this._whoAmI + ": MemberValue setter - EnlistVolatile");
                tran.EnlistVolatile(this, EnlistmentOptions.None);
            }
            this._oldMemberValue = this._memberValue;
            this._memberValue = value;
        }
    }

    #region IEnlistmentNotification Members

    public void Commit(Enlistment enlistment)
    {
        Console.WriteLine(this._whoAmI + ": Commit");

        // Clear out _oldMemberValue
        this._oldMemberValue = 0;
        enlistment.Done();
    }

    public void InDoubt(Enlistment enlistment)
    {
        Console.WriteLine(this._whoAmI + ": InDoubt");
        enlistment.Done();
    }

    public void Prepare(PreparingEnlistment preparingEnlistment)
    {
        Console.WriteLine(this._whoAmI + ": Prepare");
        preparingEnlistment.Prepared();
    }

    public void Rollback(Enlistment enlistment)
    {
        Console.WriteLine(this._whoAmI + ": Rollback");

        // Restore previous state
        this._memberValue = this._oldMemberValue;
        this._oldMemberValue = 0;
        enlistment.Done();
    }

    #endregion
}
```

Let's examine this code more closely. At the very top is a class that implements *IEnlistmentNotification*. This signifies that your RM will receive notifications from the current transaction manager:

```
public class VolatileRM : IEnlistmentNotification
```

The code begins with a private string variable named *_whoAmI* and a constructor. This will help you analyze the chain of events when more than one RM is involved.

```
private string _whoAmI = "";
public VolatileRM(string whoAmI)
{
    this._whoAmI = whoAmI;
}
```

Next, the code defines two class-level variables named *_memberValue* and *_oldMemberValue*, followed by a *MemberValue* property. The motivation for writing this class is the fact that *System.Int32* is unable to interact with an RM or maintain historical values to roll back integers. The *MemberValue* property's get accessor exposes *_memberValue*, and its set accessor assigns a new value to *_memberValue* and then enlists in the currently running transaction. The *_oldMemberValue* variable holds the historical value that will be used in the event of a rollback.

```
private int _memberValue = 0;
private int _oldMemberValue = 0;
public int MemberValue
{
    get { return _memberValue; }
    set
    {
        Transaction tran = Transaction.Current;
        if (tran != null)
        {
            Console.WriteLine(
             tran._whoAmI + ": MemberValue setter - EnlistVolatile");
            tran.EnlistVolatile(this, EnlistmentOptions.None);
        }
        this._oldMemberValue = this._memberValue;
        this._memberValue = value;
    }
}
```

As you can see, the code first attempts to find the current transaction in the *Transaction.Current* variable, and then uses the *EnlistVolatile* method to enlist in the current transaction in a volatile manner. Volatile enlistment is sufficient for this example. If you were working with a durable resource, you would call the *EnlistDurable* method instead. Last, the code performs the logic of assigning the new value and preserving the old value.

With the class and its data set up, the rest of the details involve hooking up implementation so that you can enlist in a current running transaction with the RM and perform the appropriate actions based on the notifications received. This functionality is implemented in the four methods that the *IEnlistmentNotification* interface requires you to implement. The TM calls the appropriate methods (*Commit*, *Rollback*, *Prepare*, and *InDoubt*) for you and passes in a *System.Transactions.Enlistment* variable as a parameter. After successfully performing each step, you should call the *enlistment.Done()* method to indicate that this step has done its work.

The only exception to this rule is the *Prepare* method, which receives a special kind of *Enlistment*, a *System.Transactions.PreparingEnlistment* variable, as a parameter, which inherits from the *System.Transactions.Enlistment* class. *PreparingEnlistment* adds a few methods to *Enlistment*:

- *ForceRollBack()* or *ForceRollBack(Exception)* Notifies the TM that an error has occurred and that the current participating RM wants to issue a rollback. You can specify your own exception if you want.
- *Prepared* Notifies the TM that this RM has successfully finished doing its part of the transaction (the prepare phase of the two-phase commit process).
- *byte[] RecoveryInformation* Used to specify information to the TM in the event of reenlistment to perform a graceful recovery (in situations such as the RM crashing). Alternatively, you can call the base class method *Done* to act as an innocent bystander and observe the transaction but not really participate in it. If you call *Done* in the prepare phase, the TM skips notifying the RM of the second (commit) phase of a two-phase notification process.

Using a Resource Manager in a Successful Transaction

Using the RM in transactional code is really simple. You just wrap it in a *TransactionScope*, as shown here:

```
var vrm = new VolatileRM("RM1");
Console.WriteLine("Member Value:" + vrm.MemberValue);

using (var tsc = new TransactionScope())
{
    vrm.MemberValue = 3;
    tsc.Complete();
}
Console.WriteLine("Member Value:" + vrm.MemberValue);
```

When you run this code, you should see the following output indicating that the resource manager participated in a successful transaction:

```
Member Value: 0
RM1: MemberValue setter - EnlistVolatile
RM1: Prepare
RM1: Commit
Member Value: 3
```

As you can see, the RM enlists in the prepare and commit phases of the two-phase commit process.

Using the Resource Manager When the Caller Issues a Rollback

Now you'll modify the code. Comment out the *tsc.Complete()* statement and run the application again. You should see the following output, indicating that the resource manager participated in a transaction that was rolled back:

```
Member Value: 0
RM1: MemberValue setter - EnlistVolatile
RM1: Rollback
Member Value: 0
```

By commenting out the *tsc.Complete()* statement, you are simulating a condition in which the application that uses the RMs enforces a rollback.

Tip It's best practice to always place the *tsc.Complete()* statement as the very last line of code within your *TransactionScope* blocks. Doing so ensures that it won't get executed if an exception occurs anywhere within the block.

Instead of managing the prepare and commit phases, the code instead reacts to the rollback phase, and the final value of the member variable is unchanged from the original value.

Using the Resource Manager When It Issues a Rollback

Now go ahead and put *tsc.Complete* back in the code and modify the *Prepare* method of the RM. Comment out the *Prepared* method call and put in a *ForceRollBack* call instead, as follows:

```
public void Prepare(PreparingEnlistment preparingEnlistment)
{
   Console.WriteLine(_whoAmI + ": Prepare");
   // preparingEnlistment.Prepared();
   preparingEnlistment.ForceRollback();
}
```

The RM now issues a rollback. When you execute the application with *tsc.Complete* in place, a *TransactionAbortedException* exception is thrown because the resource manager itself issued a rollback.

Using the Resource Manager with Another Resource Manager

Now you'll restore the *Prepare* method of the RM back to its original state so that a rollback isn't issued. Back in the host application, modify the original code to include a second RM participating in the same transaction, as shown here:

```
var vrm = new VolatileRM("RM1");
var vrm2 = new VolatileRM("RM2");
Console.WriteLine("Member Value 1:" + vrm.MemberValue);
Console.WriteLine("Member Value 2:" + vrm2.MemberValue);

using (var tsc = new TransactionScope())
{
    ...
    vrm.MemberValue = 3;
    vrm2.MemberValue = 5;
    tsc.Complete();
}

Console.WriteLine("Member Value 1:" + vrm.MemberValue);
Console.WriteLine("Member Value 2:" + vrm2.MemberValue);
```

As you can see, the code simply enlists another instance of the RM being used in the same transaction. When this code is executed, the following output indicates that two instances of the resource manager worked independently within a single transaction:

```
Member Value: 0
Member Value: 0
RM1: MemberValue setter - EnlistVolatile
RM2: MemberValue setter - EnlistVolatile
RM1: Prepare
RM2: Prepare
RM1: Commit
RM2: Commit
Member Value: 3
Member Value: 5
```

As you can see, when multiple RMs are involved in the transaction, the appropriate prepare, commit, or rollback phases are called for each RM in succession. As an exercise, you could modify the RM code to include a *ForceRollBack* and see the succession of events if one of the RMs issues a rollback to the entire transaction.

We've saved the best part for last. Remember that *SqlConnection* is also an RM, so you can retry this experiment with an instance of *SqlConnection*, a *SqlCommand*, and a database query executed within the same transaction that *VolatileRM* is enlisted in. To do so, modify the code to match this:

```
var vrm = new VolatileRM("RM1");
Console.WriteLine("Member Value:" + vrm.MemberValue);

const string connStr =
  "Data Source=(local);Initial Catalog=Test1;Integrated Security=SSPI;";

const string cmdText = "UPDATE FromTable SET Amount = Amount - 50";

using (var tsc = new TransactionScope())
{
    vrm.MemberValue = 3;

    using (SqlConnection conn1 = new SqlConnection(connStr))
    {
        SqlCommand cmd1 = conn1.CreateCommand();
        cmd1.CommandText = cmdText;
        conn1.Open();
        cmd1.ExecuteNonQuery();
    }
    tsc.Complete();
}

Console.WriteLine("Member Value:" + vrm.MemberValue);
```

By doing so, you would note that your *VolatileRM* now participates in the same transaction that a database query has enlisted itself in. This is something that *BEGIN DISTRIBUTED TRANSACTION* cannot do because by its very nature it talks to database queries, which cannot perform nondatabase operations. Unless, that is, you are using SQL CLR, which is where things can get a bit blurry. Let's clear that up now as we conclude the chapter.

Transactions in SQL CLR (CLR Integration)

No chapter on transactions is complete without a discussion of transactions in SQL CLR. Transactions behave so differently with SQL CLR that this topic warrants its own section.

So far, we have discussed local transactions in SQL Server and ADO.NET, as well as distributed transactions in ADO.NET, SQL Server, and the .NET Framework in general. We noted that in PSPE, a distributed transaction might not be distributed. Thus, the boundaries of what is distributed and what is not are already blurry. Well in SQL CLR, they are not only blurry, they are downright indistinct.

In Chapter 3, you learned about the basics of SQL CLR. Here, you will build on the same concepts and write a simple SQL CLR stored procedure to demonstrate the behavior of SQL CLR objects in a surrounding transaction. The stored procedure is simple; it accepts no parameters and inserts a row in the *TestTable* table, as shown here:

```
[Microsoft.SqlServer.Server.SqlProcedure]
public static void InsertRow()
{
    using (SqlConnection contextConn =
        new SqlConnection("context connection = true"))
    {
        SqlCommand insertCmd = contextConn.CreateCommand();
        insertCmd.CommandText =
            "INSERT INTO TestTable(TestColumn) VALUES(100)";
        contextConn.Open();
        insertCmd.ExecuteNonQuery();
        contextConn.Close();
    }
}
```

As you can see, the code uses a context connection to execute a *SqlCommand*. The *SqlCommand* inserts a row into *TestTable* using a simple *INSERT* command. This SQL CLR stored procedure, once registered with SQL Server, can be executed using the following T-SQL command:

```
EXEC InsertRow
```

As you can see, if you have a matching *TestTable* in the appropriate database, executing the stored procedure will indeed insert a row.

But what if you wrap this line of T-SQL code inside a *BEGIN TRANSACTION/ROLLBACK* block?

```
BEGIN TRANSACTION
  INSERT INTO TestTable(TestColumn) VALUES (200)
  EXEC InsertRow
ROLLBACK
```

Interestingly, the row that the *InsertRow* stored procedure would have inserted is rolled back. Thus, the *InsertRow* stored procedure can successfully enlist within a calling transaction.

Important A SQL CLR object automatically enlists within a current running transaction.

You can easily issue a rollback from T-SQL by using the *ROLLBACK* command. Can you do the same from a SQL CLR stored procedure? Luckily, due to the fantastic integration of *System.Transactions* with SQL Server transactions, the answer is "yes." You can access the current running transaction right from within SQL CLR by using the *Transaction.Current* property and using the current transaction, issue a rollback as shown here:

```
[Microsoft.SqlServer.Server.SqlProcedure]
public static void InsertRow()
{
    using (SqlConnection contextConn =
        new SqlConnection("context connection = true"))
    {
        SqlCommand insertCmd = contextConn.CreateCommand();
        insertCmd.CommandText =
            "INSERT INTO TestTable(TestColumn) VALUES(100)";
        contextConn.Open();
        insertCmd.ExecuteNonQuery();
        contextConn.Close();
    }
    Transaction.Current.Rollback();
}
```

Let's modify the T-SQL block so that it will attempt to commit, not roll back, as follows:

```
BEGIN TRANSACTION
   INSERT INTO TestTable(TestColumn) VALUES (200)
   EXEC InsertRow
COMMIT
```

Now when you attempt to execute this T-SQL code block, you'll see an ambiguous exception message resulting from the transaction that was rolled back. You may want to wrap such an error in a custom *BEGIN TRY...CATCH* or *try/catch/finally* block and display a better error message than what the framework provides.

Important A SQL CLR object is able to roll back a current running transaction with the help of *System.Transactions* integration.

So far, you have been using a context connection to insert a row in the database. Now change the connection string to the one shown here:

```
Data Source=RemoteMachine;Initial Catalog=OtherDB;Integrated Security=SSPI;
```

A subtle difference is introduced in the preceding connection string. The T-SQL code earlier connected to the local database (the Test database in the case of the chapter's sample code). In contrast, the new connection string connects to an entirely different database on an entirely different server. Now remove the *ROLLBACK* from the SQL CLR stored procedure and build and deploy it in the original database. Then execute the following T-SQL code block:

```
BEGIN TRANSACTION
   INSERT INTO TestTable(TestColumn) VALUES (200)
```

```
   EXEC InsertRow
COMMIT
```

The transaction now spans two databases. In other words, SQL CLR is smart enough not only to understand that you are calling the SQL CLR object within a transaction, but also to promote that transaction to a distributed transaction because an external resource is involved. In fact, if you tried connecting to an Oracle database, the SQL CLR function would still be enlisted within the same transaction. If you want to change this default behavior to not enlist within the same transaction, you can add *enlist=false* to the fully qualified connection string.

Important SQL CLR will attempt to enlist any external connections within the same transaction.

You have seen how to use *System.Transactions.Transaction.Current* and obtain a handle to the current transaction. The obvious next question is: What else could you use? Could you use *SqlTransaction*? Yes, you could definitely use *SqlTransaction*, and in that case, you would use *SqlConnection.BeginTransaction* in a manner identical to non–SQL CLR ADO.NET. (We therefore won't cover it in depth here.)

The other approach, of course, is to use *System.Transactions.TransactionScope*, which is preferred because you don't have to deal with the transaction. *TransactionScope* handles the details for you. In fact, in most scenarios, you probably don't want to deal with the current transaction using *Transaction.Current* directly. The only situations in which you'll want a direct handle on the transaction are the following:

- You want to roll back the external transaction by calling *Transaction.Current.Rollback*.
- You want to enlist resources that for some reason didn't auto-enlist. You can do so by using *Transaction.Current.EnlistVolatile* or *EnlistDurable*.
- You want to manually enlist in the current running transaction or modify the default behavior by explicitly listening for various callbacks in the two-phase commit process.

As mentioned, in all other cases, you probably want a more transparent method of writing transactional code, such as wrapping it in a using block so that everything is handled automatically or by using *TransactionScope*. This is easy to do by modifying your SQL CLR stored procedure code, as shown here:

```
[Microsoft.SqlServer.Server.SqlProcedure]
public static void InsertRow()
{
    using (var tsc = new TransactionScope())
    {
        using (SqlConnection contextConn =
            new SqlConnection("context connection = true"))
        {
            SqlCommand insertCmd = contextConn.CreateCommand();
            insertCmd.CommandText =
```

```
                "INSERT INTO TestTable(TestColumn) VALUES(100)";
            contextConn.Open();
            insertCmd.ExecuteNonQuery();
            contextConn.Close();
        }
        tsc.Complete();
    }
}
```

Note that you are wrapping a context connection inside a *TransactionScope*. This is usually a bad practice with SQL CLR, and we'll explain why in a moment. But if you have more than one database or RM involved in the transaction, *TransactionScope* will take care of enlisting everything in one transaction. The good part of this programming paradigm is that if there is already an active transaction, *TransactionScope* will take advantage of that transaction. If there is no active transaction, it will simply start a new transaction. This level of transparency helps you write more understandable and more manageable code.

Now comment out the *tsc.Complete()* statement from the SQL CLR stored procedure code, build and deploy the stored procedure on the SQL Server database, and try running it in the transactional T-SQL code. You'll get the following error:

```
Msg 8520, Level 16, State 1, Line 4
Internal Microsoft Distributed Transaction Coordinator (MS DTC) transaction failed to
commit: 0x8004d019(XACT_E_ABORTED).
```

This is as expected; because the *TransactionScope* did not get marked as complete, the transaction aborted. What you may find surprising here, though, is that the message is coming from MS DTC. There is only one database connection, the context connection, and yet the transaction was promoted. This raises another important point about SQL CLR transactions: when working inside SQL CLR, the *TransactionScope* object will always cause the transaction to promote to MS DTC, even if you are using only context connections. For this reason, you should avoid using *TransactionScope* and stick with *SqlTransaction* or *System.Transactions.Transaction.Current* with SQL CLR if you're only going to use context connections.

Putting It All Together

Let's end this chapter with one example that sums up the whole SQL CLR transaction story. You'll take the SQL CLR stored procedure you wrote and call it from a console application. Inside the console application, you will wrap the SQL CLR stored procedure and the RM you wrote earlier in this chapter in a single transaction, bound together with a single *TransactionScope* block.

Because you are using a context connection in the SQL CLR stored procedure, you'll follow the best practice of not using *TransactionScope* inside the SQL CLR stored procedure. This will prevent the transaction from unnecessarily being promoted to MS DTC. The SQL CLR stored procedure should look like this:

```
[Microsoft.SqlServer.Server.SqlProcedure]
public static void InsertRow()
{
    using (SqlConnection contextConn =
        new SqlConnection("context connection = true"))
    {
        SqlCommand insertCmd = contextConn.CreateCommand();
        insertCmd.CommandText =
            "INSERT INTO TestTable(TestColumn) VALUES(100)";
        contextConn.Open();
        insertCmd.ExecuteNonQuery();
        contextConn.Close();
    }
}
```

Build and deploy the stored procedure to a SQL Server database. Create a console application named *BigBang* (you can find it on the companion website), and add references to *System.Transactions* and the RM project from the *YourOwnRM* solution you wrote earlier in this chapter. Then add the code shown in Listing 4-5 to *Program.cs*.

LISTING 4-5 Combining SQL CLR and a customized resource manager within a single transaction.

```
using System;
using System.Data;
using System.Data.SqlClient;
using System.Transactions;
using TheRM;

namespace BigBang
{
  class Program
  {
    static void Main(string[] args)
    {
      const string ConnStr =
        "Data Source=(local);Initial Catalog=Test;Integrated Security=SSPI";

      const string CmdText = "InsertRow";

      var vrm = new VolatileRM("RM1");
      Console.WriteLine("Member Value:" + vrm.MemberValue);

      using (var tsc = new TransactionScope())
      {
        using (var conn1 = new SqlConnection(ConnStr))
        {
          SqlCommand cmd1 = conn1.CreateCommand();
          cmd1.CommandText = CmdText;
          cmd1.CommandType = CommandType.StoredProcedure;
          conn1.Open();
          cmd1.ExecuteNonQuery();
        }
        vrm.MemberValue = 3;
```

```
            tsc.Complete();
        }

        Console.WriteLine("Member Value:" + vrm.MemberValue);
        Console.ReadKey();
    }
  }
}
```

When you execute the application, you'll see the following output, indicating that the resource manager committed its member value (of course the SQL CLR procedure *InsertRow* was committed as well):

```
Member Value: 0
RM1: MemberValue setter - EnlistVolatile
RM1: Prepare
Member Value: 3
```

Also note that the transaction is not promoted to MS DTC. As an exercise, you should try adding more RMs (say, another *SqlConnection*) or a noncontext connection inside the SQL CLR stored procedure, try to run the procedure, and observe the behavior of the code. *System.Transactions* transparently integrates all your operations between T-SQL, ADO.NET, and SQL CLR, and it promotes your transaction to MS DTC as necessary.

Summary

In this chapter, we covered the basic theory of transactions, which is probably one of the most important topics related to application architecture. You learned about transaction support in SQL Server and the supported isolation levels and their behavior. You also saw a side-by-side comparison with ADO.NET.

We also covered implementation of distributed transactions and the support for writing transactional code that might have nothing to do with a database other than possibly enlisting in the same transaction as the database.

Last, you learned about the transaction support and implementation in SQL CLR. You saw how the *SqlConnection* object takes advantage of both local transaction implementation and distributed transaction implementation, as well as PSPE behavior when necessary.

CHAPTER 5

SQL Server Security

—Leonard Lobel

Security requirements are often dealt with far too late in the development process. This approach can have severe ramifications on your application's design and integrity. Without a clear, up-front understanding of what your security concerns are, and how Microsoft SQL Server security features can be leveraged to address those concerns, you risk wasting significant resources redesigning your architecture (or worse, exposing serious vulnerability to the system).

This chapter explains how SQL Server security works, beginning with the basic concepts of logins, users, roles, and schemas. We then explore advanced SQL Server security features, including the various ways you can implement encryption and auditing. By the time you complete the chapter, you'll have a thorough understanding of SQL Server security. Then you can implement the best security model for your database, and get it right the first time.

Back in 2003, Microsoft created the Trustworthy Computing initiative, which described the advances that needed to be made for people to feel more comfortable using devices powered by computers and software. (Information about this initiative can be found at *http://www.microsoft.com/about/twc/en/us/default.aspx*.) From this initiative, Microsoft SQL Server 2012 leverages what is known as the Security Framework, shown in Figure 5-1.

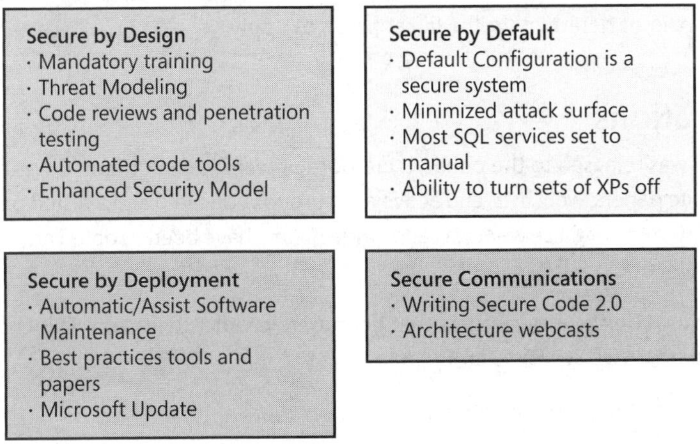

Secure by Design
- Mandatory training
- Threat Modeling
- Code reviews and penetration testing
- Automated code tools
- Enhanced Security Model

Secure by Default
- Default Configuration is a secure system
- Minimized attack surface
- Most SQL services set to manual
- Ability to turn sets of XPs off

Secure by Deployment
- Automatic/Assist Software Maintenance
- Best practices tools and papers
- Microsoft Update

Secure Communications
- Writing Secure Code 2.0
- Architecture webcasts

FIGURE 5-1 Security Framework in SQL Server 2012.

Four Themes of the Security Framework

SQL Server 2012 security is organized around four themes: Secure by Design, Secure by Default, Secure by Deployment, and Secure Communications.

Secure by Design

Security has been a design consideration in all earlier versions of SQL Server. As of SQL Server 2005, the product development group made sure that everyone was on the same page when it came to security. The entire product team went through mandatory security training, and threat models were written and reviewed for all components of all the features within the product. In addition, a massive effort was carried out to review code with respect to security for the entire product. Microsoft takes security very seriously, and designers of features within SQL Server have made security a top consideration in the final design.

Secure by Default

The Secure by Default approach is one of the most notable areas of the Security Framework that SQL Server users will experience. You can experience it by simply installing SQL Server with the default options. Users of SQL Server 2000 and earlier versions will notice that services such as SQL Server Agent are off by default. In addition, certain features such as *xp_cmdshell* and *OPENROWSET* queries are disabled. This "off by default" approach attempts to minimize the surface area for attack, and the effects of this can be seen throughout the product.

Secure by Deployment

Perhaps one of the most challenging issues with SQL Server is effective deployment in a production environment. With so many different configurations and features, it can be difficult for administrators to keep on top of the latest updates and best practices. SQL Server 2012 is now part of Microsoft Update to help alleviate the pain of determining the latest patch to apply.

Secure Communications

Even before SQL Server 2005 was released to the public, a plethora of technical information was already available in various forms. White papers, webcasts, and active newsgroups educated and assisted beta customers with the product. Today, most of these webcasts and white papers have been updated and provide rich educational content.

All editions of SQL Server include security features that help users protect their data. This chapter will cover the following aspects of SQL Server security:

- Overview of security, including authentication and authorization
- User-schema separation

- Encrypting data within the database and while in transit
- Auditing monitored server and database events
- Protecting SQL Server

Reducing the Surface Area for Attack

The more doors you have in your house, the more opportunities an intruder has to break in. Even if those doors are made of solid steel, each with a nice shiny lock, they are still considered a surface area that is vulnerable for attack. One obvious way to eliminate this vulnerability is to not have a door where you don't need one. In a computer application, the equivalent solution is that if you are not using a particular feature, you should turn it off if possible.

Out of the box, SQL Server provides a reduced surface area for attack by automatically turning off features that are optional. These features include the SQL Server Agent service, SQL Server Browser service, various server functions including *xp_cmdshell,* common language runtime (CLR) integration, and others.

In SQL Server 2005, a system stored procedure named *sp_configure* was introduced that could be used to turn many of these features on and off programmatically. SQL Server 2005 also introduced a graphical management utility named the SQL Server Surface Area Configuration Tool. This utility allowed administrators to turn these features on and off from a user interface. As of SQL Server 2008, the *sp_configure* stored procedure remains, but the Surface Area Configuration Tool has been replaced by the Surface Area Configuration *facet* in the Policy Based Management Framework (PBM).

PBM was introduced in SQL Server 2008 to declare and enforce different management policies against various target environments. Functionality formerly provided by the Surface Area Configuration Tool in SQL Server 2005 is now one of many PBM facets that can be configured in SQL Server 2012.

SQL Server Security Overview

If you are already familiar with the concepts of *users* and *roles* and SQL Server *logins*, you can probably skip ahead to the next section of this chapter. But for those who aren't, we'll provide a quick explanation. The concepts of users and roles exist both in the Microsoft Windows world and in SQL Server. In an abstract sense, they are referred to as *principals*. Principals are entities that can request resources from the application or an operating system. In the case of Windows, principals are entities such as Domain Users and Groups, and Local Users and Groups. In SQL Server, these entities are logins and server roles. Within a database, these entities are database users, database roles, and application roles, to name a few.

So what can you do with entities? Chances are you have an object such as a file or a database table that you want to allow access to. These objects, or *securables*, are the resources to which the authorization system regulates access. Some securables can be contained within other securables, creating nested hierarchies called *scopes* that can themselves be secured. The securable scopes in the SQL Server Database Engine are *server*, *database*, and *schema*. Every securable in SQL Server has an associated permission that can be granted to a principal.

Figure 5-2 shows a graphical representation of the principal-securable-permission model.

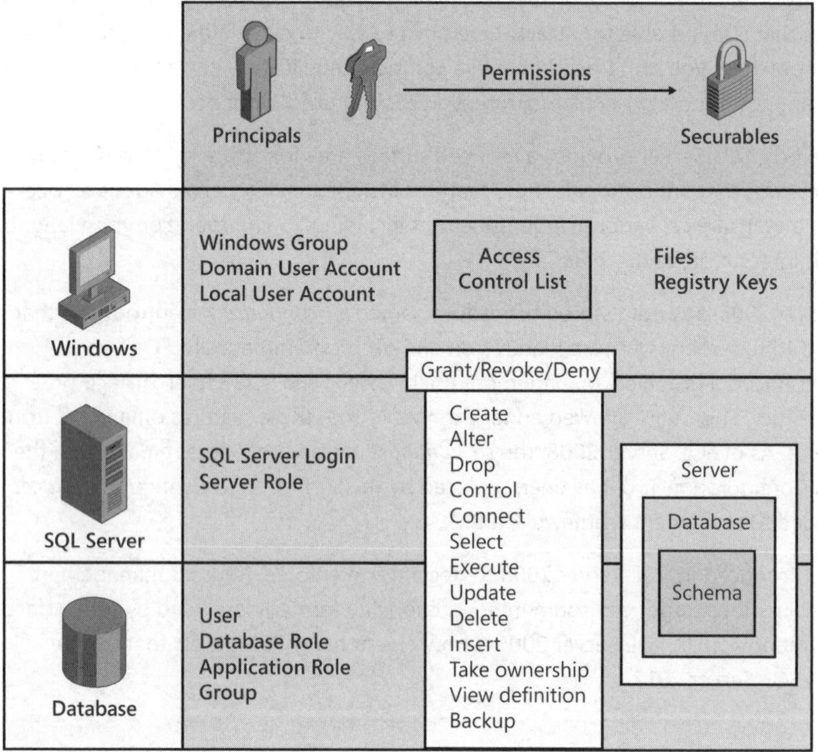

FIGURE 5-2 Principal-securable-permission model.

SQL Server Logins

Now that you have a high-level understanding of SQL Server security and how it relates to Windows security, we can get into SQL Server–specific areas. To connect to SQL Server, you need a login. This login can be a combination of a custom user name (such as *Login1*) and a complex password. Alternatively, you can add an existing Windows account as a login to SQL Server and forego the creation of a separate user name and password. Thus, SQL Server supports two types of logins: Windows logins and SQL Server logins.

Note SQL Server 2012 introduces a new feature called *contained databases* that allows users to connect to SQL Server by authenticating directly against a database, without using a server login. We cover contained database at the end of this chapter.

Logins themselves have no access to any specific database within SQL Server; they allow only for connection to a SQL Server instance. Thus, logins are entities that can be granted server-wide permissions to perform certain actions. These actions are bundled into server roles such as *sysadmin*, *diskadmin*, and *dbcreator* (to name a few). Table 5-1 shows the list of server roles and their corresponding functions. Server roles are fixed—you cannot drop them or create new ones in addition to the set of nine fixed server roles.

TABLE 5-1 Fixed server roles.

Server Role	Description
bulkadmin	Members can run the *BULK INSERT* statement. Membership in this role still requires that non-*sysadmin* users have access to the object being updated.
dbcreator	Members can create, alter, drop, and restore any database.
diskadmin	This role is used for managing disk files. Most of the capabilities relate to adding and removing backup devices.
processadmin	Members can terminate processes that are running in an instance of SQL Server. This role is useful if you want to give someone the ability to kill a long-running query or an orphaned connection.
public	All valid SQL Server logins are members of the public role.
securityadmin	Members can manage logins and their properties. They can *GRANT, DENY,* and *REVOKE* server-level permissions as well as database-level permissions. They can also reset passwords for SQL Server logins. This role has no rights to assign database permissions. If you want *securityadmin* members to be able to do this, you must make their logins part of the *db_accessadmin* fixed database role for the specific database.
serveradmin	Members can change server-wide configuration options and shut down the server.
setupadmin	Members can add and remove linked servers and also execute some system stored procedures.
sysadmin	Members can perform any activity in the server. By default, all members of the Windows *BUILTIN\Administrators* group, the local administrator's group, are members of the *sysadmin* fixed server role. The SQL Server service account is also a member of this role.

Database Users

Logins can be created using SQL Server Management Studio (SSMS) or via the Transact-SQL (T-SQL) statement *CREATE LOGIN*. After you create a login, you then grant it access to a particular database. Databases themselves have their own set of roles that define specific access and actions that users of these roles can take within a particular database. Before you can grant database access to a login, you must create a database user for the login. Again, you can create a database user by using SSMS or via the T-SQL statement *CREATE USER*.

Once you create a database user, you can optionally include it in one of the database roles. Table 5-2 lists the roles that all databases have. Like server roles, these database roles are fixed and cannot be modified. However, unlike server roles, you can define additional database roles as desired.

TABLE 5-2 Fixed database roles.

Database Role	Description
db_accessadmin	Members can add or remove access for Windows logins, Windows groups, and SQL Server logins.
db_backupoperator	Members can back up the database.
db_datareader	Members can read all data from all user tables.
db_datawriter	Members can add, delete, or change data in all user tables.
db_ddladmin	Members can run any data definition language (DDL) command in a database.
db_denydatareader	Members cannot read any data in the user tables within a database.
db_denydatawriter	Members cannot add, modify, or delete any data in the user tables within a database.
db_owner	Members can perform all configuration and maintenance activities on the database, including dropping the database.
db_securityadmin	Members can modify role membership and manage permissions.

There is a special database role that *sysadmin* users cannot explicitly give other users permissions to; it is known as the *public* role. All database users are implicitly included in the *public* role. This role captures all default permissions for users in a particular database. It cannot have users, groups, or roles assigned to it because everyone belongs to this role by default. This role cannot be dropped. Thus, to protect against unauthorized data access, you should minimize the permissions granted to the *public* role. Instead, grant permissions to other database roles and to user accounts associated with logins.

The *guest* User Account

On the topic of unauthorized data access, it is important to note a special user account available in SQL Server called *guest*. This account is created by default on new user-defined databases but does exist in *master* and *tempdb*. However, the *guest* account is disabled by default, which means that it does not have any access within the database. The *guest* account allows a login without a user account to access a database. A login assumes the identity of the *guest* account when all of the following conditions are met:

- The login has access to an instance of SQL Server but does not have access to the database through his or her own user account or via a Windows group membership.
- The database contains a *guest* account.
- The *guest* account is enabled in the database.

You can apply permissions to the *guest* account just as you can any other user account. If possible, however, you should avoid using the *guest* account entirely, because all logins without their own database permissions obtain the database permissions granted to the *guest* account. If you absolutely must use the *guest* account, be sure to grant minimum permissions to it.

Note Although we have discussed various aspects of server and database principals, a complete discussion of these topics is beyond the scope of this book. For in-depth information about user management within SQL Server, see the Identity and Access Control topics in SQL Server Books Online at *http://msdn.microsoft.com/en-us/library/bb510589(v=sql.110).aspx.*

Authentication and Authorization

Before we dive into the concepts of authentication and authorization, it is important to discuss a feature added in SQL Server 2005 called *endpoints*. In earlier versions of SQL Server, clients could connect via Transport Control Protocol (TCP), named pipes, shared memory, and Virtual Interface Architecture (VIA). As long as one of these protocols was enabled on the server and the user had a valid login, the connection was accepted. SQL Server 2005 introduced a separation of this behavior via endpoints.

Endpoints can be considered a point of entry into SQL Server. Administrators can create an endpoint not only for TCP, named pipes, shared memory, and VIA, but also for Hypertext Transfer Protocol (HTTP). Once an endpoint is created, you can restrict access so that users can connect only via a certain endpoint type. For example, you might create a login named *Login1* and grant access to the HTTP endpoint while denying access to all other endpoints. In this case, *Login1* can access SQL Server only via the HTTP endpoint; it cannot directly connect to SQL Server via TCP or any of the other protocols. To see how this endpoint verification affects authentication, let's examine the process of making a client connection.

How Clients Establish a Connection

If a TCP client wants to make a connection to SQL Server, it must first know which port to connect to. Prior to SQL Server 2005, there was always a thread waiting on User Datagram Protocol (UDP) port 1434 whose purpose was to return details on all of the running instances of SQL Server, as well as the port numbers of those instances. All a client had to do was make a UDP connection to port 1434 and then determine which port it wanted to connect to, given a specific instance of SQL Server. This process generally worked until hackers found a way to launch a Denial of Service (DoS) attack on SQL Server by continuously sending packets to this port requesting the enumeration. Because the enumeration process was part of the SQL Server service, the "SQL Slammer" worm virus created serious problems for SQL Server installations. As of SQL Server 2005, this functionality has been pulled out into a separate service named the SQL Server Browser service that can be turned on and off without touching the SQL Server service itself.

Note Of course, this means that the Browser service is now vulnerable to DoS attacks. You can mitigate this concern if you block port 1434 on your firewall. If you are concerned about intranet attacks from inside the firewall, you might want to consider not running the Browser service at all and explicitly pass port numbers on the connections strings instead.

After the network connection request and pre-login handshake have been made, SQL Server must authenticate the user to make sure that he or she has access to begin with. Figure 5-3 depicts the authentication process.

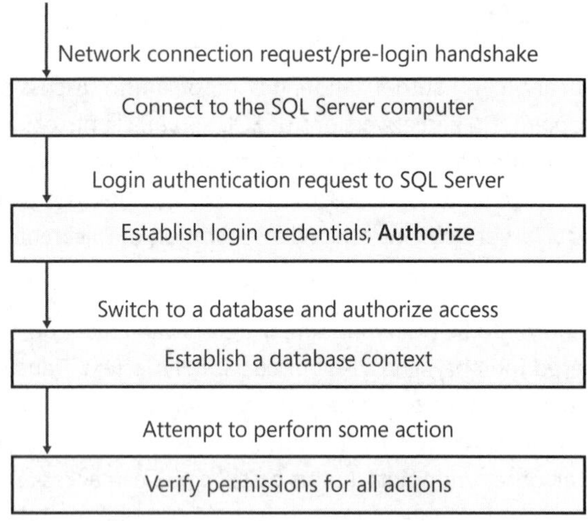

FIGURE 5-3 SQL Server authentication model.

At this point, the service accepts the login credentials supplied by the user and attempts to validate them. If successful, the login is authorized against the endpoint corresponding to the type of connection made to SQL Server. In this example, the login is checked to see whether it has been granted *CONNECT* permissions to the TCP endpoint. If this is true, the authentication process proceeds; otherwise, the connection fails at this point.

Note By default, new logins are automatically granted *CONNECT* permissions to the TCP endpoint.

Once the login has passed the endpoint check, SQL Server switches to a database context (the default database specified for the login or specified in the connection string). It then attempts to authenticate the login as a user of that database. If the login can be authenticated, the connection succeeds; otherwise, it fails. When a database context has been established and the login has been authenticated, the user can perform work against the database on the server.

Password Policies

In the Windows world, administrators can set login expirations and enforce password policies (for example, requiring passwords to be a certain length and contain a mixture of special characters). Traditionally in SQL Server, SQL logins never respected these global policy settings. Since SQL Server 2005, both Windows-authenticated and SQL logins obey the group policy settings defined in the Windows domain.

> **Note** Password policy enforcement is available only in SQL Server running on Microsoft Windows Server 2003 and later.

To help illustrate password policies, let's define a minimum password length using the Local Security Policy applet located in the Administrative Tools folder of Control Panel. This tool is shown in Figure 5-4.

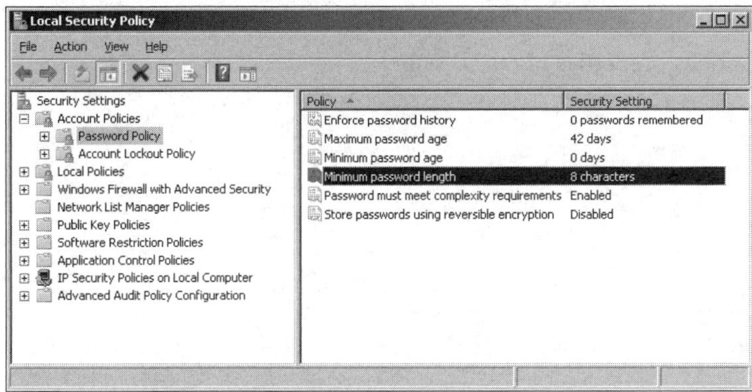

FIGURE 5-4 *Password Policy* node of Local Security Settings.

Using this tool, you can change a variety of parameters. For example, set the minimum password length to eight characters, as shown in Figure 5-4, and then attempt to create a login as shown in Listing 5-1.

LISTING 5-1 Attempting to create a login that does not satisfy the Windows password policy.

```
CREATE LOGIN SomeUser WITH PASSWORD = '2short',
 CHECK_POLICY=ON,
 CHECK_EXPIRATION=ON
```

This statement fails because the password has only seven characters and the Windows password policy requires a minimum of eight characters:

```
Msg 15116, Level 16, State 1, Line 1
Password validation failed. The password does not meet Windows policy requirements because it is
too short.
```

The system view *sys.sql_logins* returns information about logins, such as whether the policies and expirations are set. If you want additional information regarding a particular login, such as how many bad passwords were attempted, you can use the *LOGINPROPERTY* built-in function, as demonstrated in Listing 5-2.

LISTING 5-2 Querying the *LOGINPROPERTY* function.

```
SELECT 'IsLocked' AS Property,            LOGINPROPERTY('sa', 'IsLocked') AS Value
 UNION ALL SELECT 'IsExpired',            LOGINPROPERTY('sa', 'IsExpired')
 UNION ALL SELECT 'IsMustChange',         LOGINPROPERTY('sa', 'IsMustChange')
 UNION ALL SELECT 'BadPasswordCount',     LOGINPROPERTY('sa', 'BadPasswordCount')
 UNION ALL SELECT 'PasswordLastSetTime',  LOGINPROPERTY('sa', 'PasswordLastSetTime')
 UNION ALL SELECT 'BadPasswordTime',      LOGINPROPERTY('sa', 'BadPasswordTime')
 UNION ALL SELECT 'LockoutTime',          LOGINPROPERTY('sa', 'LockoutTime')
```

The query results show various properties of the sa login:

```
Property            Value
------------------- -----------------------------------
IsLocked            0
IsExpired           0
IsMustChange        0
BadPasswordCount    0
PasswordLastSetTime 2012-01-14 00:19:57.200
BadPasswordTime     1900-01-01 00:00:00.000
LockoutTime         1900-01-01 00:00:00.000
```

User-Schema Separation

Imagine that an employee in an organization who has created many tables and stored procedures leaves the company. As a database administrator, your task is to reassign ownership of all the objects that this former employee created and owned. Prior to SQL Server 2005, this was a tedious task. Since SQL Server 2005, the task is made a lot easier because of the schema feature.

SQL Server 2005 introduced a different concept of schemas than in earlier versions of SQL Server. In SQL Server 2000 (and earlier versions), database users and schemas were equivalent. Every database user was the owner of a schema that had the same name as the user. An owner of an object was effectively identical to the owner of the schema that contains the object. This one-to-one mapping behavior made it very tedious to reassign ownership.

As of SQL Server 2005, users and schemas are separate entities, and schemas are independent containers that can contain zero or more objects. Users can own one or more schemas and can be assigned a default schema. If a default schema is not specified, the user is defaulted to the *dbo* schema of the database. This default schema is used to resolve the names of securables that are referred to without using their fully qualified name. In SQL Server 2000, the location that is checked first is the schema owned by the calling database user, followed by the schema owned by *dbo*. Each user has a default schema, so when SQL Server resolves the names of securables, it checks the default schema.

You can thus transfer ownership of many securables, and a schema can contain securables owned by a database user other than the owner of the schema. This is important to note because if you leverage the old system views, such as *sysobjects*, the results returned in queries will not show up correctly. You must use a catalog view, such *sys.objects*, instead.

The *CREATE SCHEMA* statement is used to create a new schema. It can also be used to create tables and views within the new schema and to set *GRANT*, *DENY*, or *REVOKE* permissions on those objects, as shown in Listing 5-3:

LISTING 5-3 Granting and denying permissions to a table in a schema.

```
USE master
GO

-- Create three server logins
CREATE LOGIN Rob WITH PASSWORD = 'jackpot_0'
CREATE LOGIN Tammie WITH PASSWORD = 'jackpot_0'
CREATE LOGIN Vince WITH PASSWORD = 'jackpot_0'
GO

-- Create a new database
IF EXISTS(SELECT name FROM sys.databases WHERE name = 'MyDB')
 DROP DATABASE MyDB
GO
CREATE DATABASE MyDB
GO
USE MyDB
GO

-- Create three database users mapped to the logins
CREATE USER Rob FOR LOGIN Rob
CREATE USER Tammie FOR LOGIN Tammie
CREATE USER Vince FOR LOGIN Vince
GO

-- Create a schema owned by Rob
CREATE SCHEMA Sales AUTHORIZATION Rob
GO

-- Create a table in the schema owned by Rob
CREATE TABLE Sales.Leads (id int, name varchar(50), phone varchar(20))

-- Allow Tammie but not Vince to SELECT from the table in the schema owned by Rob
GRANT SELECT ON Sales.Leads TO Tammie
DENY SELECT ON Sales.Leads TO Vince
```

This example creates the *Sales* schema and assigns it to Rob. A *Leads* table is created within the *Sales* schema, and Tammie is granted select access to the table, whereas Vince is denied select access.

For Tammie to access the table in versions of SQL Server prior to SQL Server 2005, she must use Rob for the schema name, like this:

```
SELECT * FROM Production.SalesReps.Rob.Leads
```

As of SQL Server 2005, she can use the *Sales* schema name instead, like this:

```
SELECT * FROM Production.SalesReps.Sales.Leads
```

If Rob ever quits or gets fired, all the *sysadmin* user has to do is transfer ownership of the *Sales* schema to Tammie by executing the following statement:

```
ALTER AUTHORIZATION ON SCHEMA::Sales TO Tammie
```

This abstraction of database users from schemas provides many benefits to developers and administrators, including the following:

- Multiple users can own a single schema through membership in roles or Windows groups. This extends familiar functionality and allows roles and groups to own objects.
- Dropping database users is greatly simplified.
- Dropping a database user does not require renaming objects that are contained by the schema of that user. Therefore, you do not have to revise and test applications that refer explicitly to schema-contained securables after dropping the user who created them.
- Multiple users can share one default schema for uniform name resolution.
- Shared default schemas allow developers to store shared objects in a schema that was created specifically for a particular application, instead of in the *dbo* schema.
- Permissions on schemas and schema-contained securables can be managed with a greater degree of detail than in earlier releases.
- Fully qualified object names have four parts: *server.database.schema.object*.

Execution Context

Granting and managing permissions to non-*sysadmin* users has always been an interesting challenge, especially when it comes to users who own stored procedures that access tables and other objects that they do not own. The code in Listing 5-4 presents such a scenario, in which there are three logins: Login1, Login2, and Login3. Respectively, these logins are mapped to database users User1, User2, and User3 that own the schemas Schema1, Schema2, and Schema3.

LISTING 5-4 Controlling execution context with multiple database objects, owners, and permissions.

```
USE master
GO

-- Create 3 logins
CREATE LOGIN Login1 WITH PASSWORD = 'P@$$w0rd1'
CREATE LOGIN Login2 WITH PASSWORD = 'P@$$w0rd2'
CREATE LOGIN Login3 WITH PASSWORD = 'P@$$w0rd3'
GO
```

```
- Create a new database
IF EXISTS(SELECT name FROM sys.databases WHERE name = 'MyDB')
 DROP DATABASE MyDB
GO
CREATE DATABASE MyDB
GO
USE MyDB
GO

-- Create 3 users mapped to the 3 logins
CREATE USER User3 FOR LOGIN Login3
CREATE USER User2 FOR LOGIN Login2
CREATE USER User1 FOR LOGIN Login1
GO

-- Create a corresponding schema for each of the 3 users
CREATE SCHEMA Schema3 AUTHORIZATION User3
GO
CREATE SCHEMA Schema2 AUTHORIZATION User2
GO
CREATE SCHEMA Schema1 AUTHORIZATION User1
GO

-- Let User3 create tables and let User2 create stored procedures
GRANT CREATE TABLE TO User3
GRANT CREATE PROCEDURE TO User2
GO

-- Impersonate Login3 (User3)
EXECUTE AS LOGIN = 'Login3'
GO

-- Create and populate a table in Schema3
CREATE TABLE Schema3.Region(RegionName nvarchar(50))
INSERT INTO Schema3.Region VALUES('East Coast'), ('West Coast') , ('Midwest')

-- Allow User2 to SELECT from the Schema3 table
GRANT SELECT ON Schema3.Region TO User2
GO
REVERT
GO

-- Impersonate Login2 (User2)
EXECUTE AS LOGIN = 'Login2'
GO

-- Create a stored procedure in Schema2 that selects from the table in Schema3
CREATE PROCEDURE Schema2.GetRegions AS
 SELECT * FROM Schema3.Region
-GO

-- Allow User1 to EXECUTE the Schema2 stored procedure
GRANT EXECUTE ON Schema2.GetRegions TO User1
GO
```

```
REVERT
GO

-- User1 cannot access the Schema3 table, even via a Schema2 stored
-- proc that they have permission to execute
EXECUTE AS LOGIN = 'Login1'
GO
SELECT * FROM Schema3.Region  -- fails
EXEC Schema2.GetRegions       -- fails
GO
REVERT
GO

-- Modify the Schema2 stored proc so that it always run in the context
-- of the owner, not the caller
EXECUTE AS LOGIN = 'Login2'
GO
ALTER PROCEDURE Schema2.GetRegions WITH EXECUTE AS OWNER AS
 SELECT * FROM Schema3.Region
GO
REVERT
GO

-- User1 still cannot access the Schema3 table directly, but now they can
-- indirectly via the Schema2 stored procedure
EXECUTE AS LOGIN = 'Login1'
GO
SELECT * FROM Schema3.Region  -- fails
EXEC Schema2.GetRegions       -- works!
GO
REVERT
GO
```

In this example, User3 owns the *Schema3.Region* table, and User2 owns the *Schema2.GetRegions* stored procedure that retrieves data from this table. This works because User2 has been granted *SELECT* permission on the table owned by User3. Now User1 needs to execute User2's stored procedure. This is possible because User1 has been granted *EXECUTE* permission on the stored procedure, but will still fail because User1 wasn't also granted *SELECT* permission on the underlying table that the stored procedure accesses. Prior to SQL Server 2005, there was no easy solution to this problem. Now multiply this requirement across an enterprise and you can appreciate the permission management nightmare that unfolds.

Fortunately, as of SQL Server 2005, it's easy to change the *execution context* (a specialized form of impersonation) between different logins and database users, and thereby solve this issue. In our current example, User2 can simply change the execution context of the *Schema2.GetRegions* stored procedure by applying one of the various supported *WITH EXECUTE AS* clauses in an *ALTER PROCEDURE* statement:

- ***WITH EXECUTE AS CALLER*** Executes under the credentials of the caller, who requires permission to access all of the underlying objects used by the stored procedure. This is the same default behavior as in earlier versions of SQL Server.
- ***WITH EXECUTE AS SELF*** Executes under the credentials of the user who last modified the stored procedure.
- ***WITH EXECUTE AS <insert name of user>*** Executes under the credentials of the specified user. For this to work, the user creating or modifying the stored procedure must be granted the *IMPERSONATE* permission for the specified user.
- ***WITH EXECUTE AS OWNER*** Executes under the credentials of the login who owns the stored procedure. If the owner is changed after the object is created, the execution context is automatically mapped to the new owner.

As explained, without changing execution context, User1 can't access the Schema3 table owned by User3—if an attempt is made, SQL Server will issue the following error message:

```
The SELECT permission was denied on the object 'Region', database 'MyDB', schema 'Schema3'.
```

Prior to SQL Server 2005, you would have to give User1 some form of access against User3's table in order to run User2's stored procedure. But as of SQL Server 2005, User2 can simply change the execution context of the stored procedure so that User1 doesn't need to be granted access to User3's table. In Listing 5-4, User2 changes the execution context to *EXECUTE AS OWNER*, which causes the stored procedure to be executed as User2 because User2 is the owner of the stored procedure.

Now when User1 executes User2's stored procedure, the stored procedure executes under the credentials of User2 and can thus access User3's table. This access is permitted only within the context of the stored procedure. Thus, User1 is able to execute User2's stored procedure without having explicit access to the underlying table owned by User3.

Listing 5-4 also demonstrates the *EXECUTE AS* statement, which lets you change the execution context of the current connection without having to close and reopen the connection. The user must either be a *sysadmin* or have *IMPERSONATE* permission on the login for this to work. Alternatively, you can use the *EXECUTE AS* statement to switch the user context for a database user. When used for switching the context on a database, the scope of impersonation is restricted to the current database. In a context switch to a database user, the server-level permissions of that user are not inherited. In addition, a user must either be a *sysadmin* or have *IMPERSONATE* permission on the user of the database.

Executing context switching is a powerful and efficient way to reduce the number of permissions to manage. For developers and administrators, it provides an easy way to test scripts and debug without having to log out and reconnect to SQL Server.

Encryption Support

Let's face it: data that is stored in databases is interesting not only to us as users but to many others in the world whom you might not know or trust. With the increased leverage of the power of relational databases by businesses and consumers, database vendors are under increasing pressure to provide more security-related features.

Other than locking down access to SQL Server databases, administrators and developers can provide another layer of protection against the bad guys, and that is *encryption*. At a high level, encryption takes interesting information, such as your credit card number, and translates it into a binary representation that can be understood only by authorized parties. Data can be encrypted for use in transit, such as when you are passing your password back to a web server, or it can be stored in an encrypted format (on the file system or in a database, for example). In SQL Server 2008 and 2012 (Enterprise editions only), the entire database can be encrypted automatically using Transparent Data Encryption (TDE), which we describe in detail later in this chapter.

Data in SQL Server is encrypted using *encryption keys*. These keys can be either *symmetric* or *asymmetric*, and there are pros and cons to using either one. With symmetric key encryption, both the sender and the receiver of the data have the same key. The sender encrypts the data using the key and an encryption algorithm. When the data reaches the recipient, it is decrypted using the same encryption algorithm and key. The main benefit of this approach is better encryption and decryption performance compared to using asymmetric keys. The problem with symmetric key encryption comes into play when you consider what happens when someone else somehow gets hold of your symmetric key. Because you are encrypting with just one key, anyone who has that key can decrypt the data.

Asymmetric key encryption uses two keys, a public key and a private key. The sender encrypts the data using the recipient's public key, which is freely obtainable by anyone. The security comes in when the recipient receives the data; the recipient decrypts it via his or her private key. The public key in this case cannot decrypt the data. Thus, the private key is the valuable asset when using asymmetric encryption.

The other concept that arises in encryption discussions is *certificates*. Certificates are basically asymmetric keys that contain extra *metadata*. This metadata includes information such as an expiration period and the certificate authority that issued the certificate. Certificates can be created by anyone, and in some circumstances, you want to make sure that the sender or recipient of the data is actually who he or she says. This is where certificate authorities come into play. These companies act as a mediator between the sender and receiver. After you pay a nominal fee and they conduct an identity check, they provide you with a certificate that they have signed. When you use this signed certificate to send data, the recipient can validate the certificate with the certificate authority, and because both of you trust the certificate authority, it's safe to assume that the message was in fact signed by the sender.

There is another type of certificate called a *self-signed certificate*, which anyone can create. In some cases, it is acceptable to use a self-signed certificate. SQL Server automatically creates a self-signed certificate the first time it starts. This certificate is used to encrypt the connection during SQL Server authentication.

Encrypting Data on the Move

All connection login requests made to SQL Server are encrypted if the client is using the SQL Server Native Access Client application programming interfaces (APIs). This is a huge improvement, because in SQL Server 2000 and earlier versions, if a user wanted to authenticate using SQL Server Authentication, the user name and password were sent in clear text across the wire. SQL Server 2005 and higher can automatically encrypt the login packet information via the self-signed certificate it created the first time the service started.

Login packets are not all that's encrypted in the connection. The entire connection itself can optionally be encrypted for the lifetime of the connection. The request for an encrypted channel can be forced by the server (so that all connections are encrypted by default), or the request can be made by the client making the connection. It is recommended that administrators use a real certificate rather than the self-signed certification because of potential "man-in-the-middle" attacks.

To force encryption on the server, launch the SQL Server Configuration Manager tool (available in the Configuration Tools folder of the SQL Server 2012 Program Files menu item). This tool is used for managing the protocols and services of SQL Server. Expand SQL Server Network Configuration, right-click Protocols for MSSQLSERVER, and select Properties to open the Protocols for MSSQLSERVER Properties dialog box, shown in Figure 5-5.

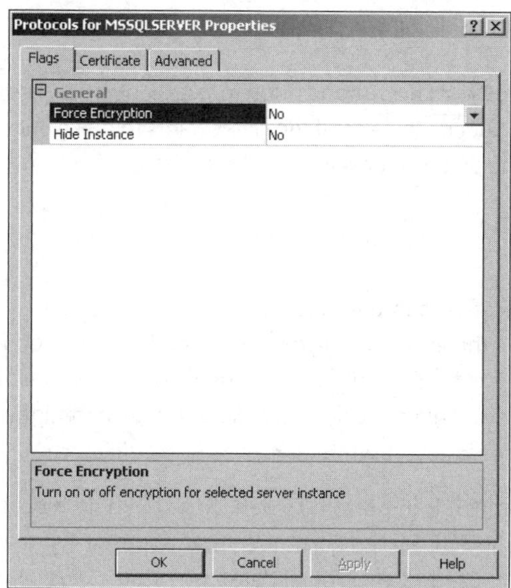

FIGURE 5-5 Protocols for MSSQLSERVER Properties dialog box.

In this dialog, the Flags tab allows you to force encryption on the server and the Certificate tab allows you to select a certificate that is already installed on the local machine to be used by SQL Server to encrypt the data. If you force encryption but do not select a certificate, SQL Server uses its self-signed certificate to encrypt the data. Remember that the SQL Server self-signed certificate is not considered trusted by the client connections. For clients to be able to use the SQL Server self-signed certificate, they must set this option in the Properties dialog box of the SQL Native Client 11.0 Configuration node in the same Configuration Manager tool. This dialog box is shown in Figure 5-6.

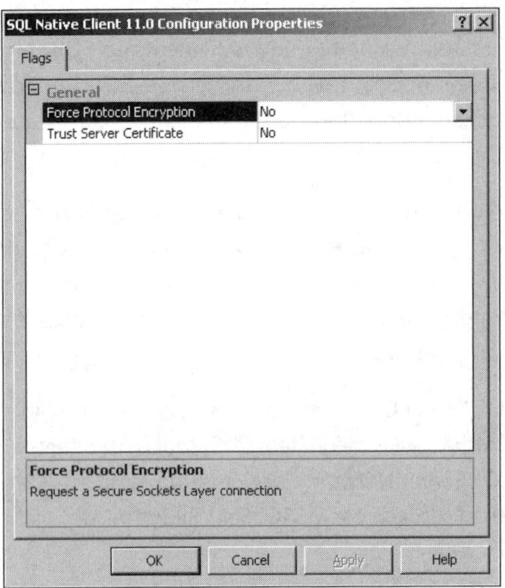

FIGURE 5-6 SQL Native Client 11.0 Configuration Properties dialog box.

This dialog box offers two options: The Force Protocol Encryption option forces clients to always make encryption connections. The second option is what needs to be set if the client wants to make encrypted connections to SQL Server and have it leverage the SQL Server self-signed certificate.

Encrypting Data at Rest

Social Security or other government-issue identification numbers, credit card numbers, salary information, driver's license numbers, passwords—the list of sensitive information just keeps going. Access to this information stored in the database has traditionally been secured by permissions. This is still the case, but another layer of protection is available natively in SQL Server 2005 and higher. Sensitive data can now be encrypted using symmetric keys, asymmetric keys, or certificates.

Before you jump in and encrypt data in a column, it is important to define the building blocks of encryption support within SQL Server. The first time SQL Server starts, it creates a special symmetric key called the Service Master Key (SMK). This key is used to encrypt all database master keys (DMKs) as well as all server-level secrets such as credential secrets or linked server login passwords. In SQL Server 2012, the key itself is an AES-encrypted key. Earlier versions of SQL Server used 3DES to encrypt the SMK and DMKs, so you should use the *ALTER SERVICE MASTER KEY STATEMENT* to regenerate the SMK and DMKs when upgrading an instance to SQL Server 2012.

Note Encryption algorithm availability depends on the cryptographic service provider of the operating system that SQL Server is running on. For example, Microsoft Windows XP Service Pack 2 (SP2) supports DES, 3DES, RC2, RC4 (deprecated in SQL Server 2012), and RSA, whereas Windows Server 2003 and 2008 support all those plus AES128, AES192, and AES256. An explanation of these algorithms is well beyond the scope of this book, but there are plenty of resources available to help you choose an appropriate encryption algorithm. For more information, see "Choosing an Encryption Algorithm" in the TechNet online documentation at *http://technet.microsoft.com/en-us/library/ms345262(v=sql.110).aspx.*

The SMK is encrypted using the Windows security API, the Data Protection API (DPAPI), and the credentials of the SQL Server service account. Because the SMK is used to encrypt all DMKs and other server-level secrets, it is very important and should be backed up regularly. You can back up and restore the SMK by using the *BACKUP SERVICE MASTER KEY* or *RESTORE SERVICE MASTER KEY* statements. In the event of a compromised SMK, or if you want to change the SMK as part of implementing a normal security best practice, you can regenerate it using the *ALTER SERVICE MASTER KEY REGENERATE* statement.

With respect to encrypting data, the SMK is used by SQL Server to decrypt the DMK so that the DMK can in turn decrypt the requested data for the client. There is only one DMK per database, and none are created by default, because a DMK is used only for data encryption.

When DMKs are created, they are encrypted by the SMK (so that SQL Server can decrypt the data for the client) and by a password. It is possible to remove the SMK encryption, but the password of the DMK would need to be specified by the user every time he or she accesses this key.

Now that we have discussed the key components of encryption, let's consider an example. This scenario will include a table named *SalaryInfo* that contains the name, department, and salary of employees at your company. A user named *HR_User* needs to be able to insert and view data into this table.

Because a lot of steps are involved in setting up this example, it is best to walk through Listing 5-5 line by line, and follow the in-line comments included throughout the listing. The comments explain exactly what each T-SQL statement does and why.

LISTING 5-5 Encryption using *ENCRYPTBYKEY* and *DECRYPTBYKEY*.

```
USE master
GO

-- Create a login
CREATE LOGIN HRLogin WITH PASSWORD = 'HRp@$$w0rd'
GO

-- Create a new database
IF EXISTS(SELECT name FROM sys.databases WHERE name = 'MyDB')
```

```
  DROP DATABASE MyDB
GO
CREATE DATABASE MyDB
GO
USE MyDB
GO

-- Create a user mapped to the login
CREATE USER HRUser FOR LOGIN HRLogin
GO

-- Create the database master key (DMK)
CREATE MASTER KEY ENCRYPTION BY PASSWORD = 'DMKp@$$w0rd'
GO

-- Create a table that will store sensitive credit card numbers. Notice
-- the varbinary data type that will store the encrypted card numbers.
CREATE TABLE CreditCardInfo
(CardType varchar(50),
 CardNumber varbinary(255))
GO

-- Give access to HRUser so they can query and add data
GRANT SELECT, INSERT TO HRUser
GO

-- Create a Symmetric Key, encrypt it with a password, and give HRUser access to it
CREATE SYMMETRIC KEY HRUserKey
 AUTHORIZATION HRUser
 WITH ALGORITHM = TRIPLE_DES
 ENCRYPTION BY PASSWORD = 'SYMp@$$w0rd'
GO

-- Impersonate HRUser and encrypt some data
EXECUTE AS LOGIN = 'HRLogin'
GO

-- Open the key that will be used to encrypt data. Notice you have to supply
-- the password for the key
OPEN SYMMETRIC KEY HRUserKey DECRYPTION BY PASSWORD = 'SYMp@$$w0rd'
GO

-- This system view shows open keys that can be used for encryption
SELECT * FROM sys.openkeys

-- Insert sensitive data into the table using ENCRYPTBYKEY, which takes the
-- GUID of the key (using KEY_GUID) and the text to be encrypted, and returns
-- the result as varbinary.
INSERT INTO CreditCardInfo VALUES
('MasterCard', ENCRYPTBYKEY(KEY_GUID('HRUserKey'), '5426-1891-5411-1369')),
 ('American Express', ENCRYPTBYKEY(KEY_GUID('HRUserKey'), '3728-847852-83004'))
```

```
-- When done, always close all keys
CLOSE ALL SYMMETRIC KEYS
GO

-- View the table as it lives in the database, notice the encrypted binary
SELECT * FROM CreditCardInfo

-- Now, decrypt and view the contents using DECRYPTBYKEY, which takes the column
-- name. You don't specify a key GUID because SQL will look at all open keys and
-- use the appropriate one automatically.
OPEN SYMMETRIC KEY HRUserKey DECRYPTION BY PASSWORD = 'SYMp@$$w0rd'
GO

SELECT *, CONVERT(varchar, DECRYPTBYKEY(CardNumber))
 FROM CreditCardInfo
GO

CLOSE ALL SYMMETRIC KEYS
GO

-- Revert back to sysadmin
REVERT
GO

-- When encrypting by password, need to know the password and pass it every time
-- you encrypt/decrypt. Alternatively you can create a certificate and give access
-- to the HR User. With this, the user doesn't have to provide a password and you
-- can easily revoke access to that encrypted data by simply removing the
-- certificate for that use.
CREATE CERTIFICATE HRCert
 AUTHORIZATION HRUser
 WITH SUBJECT = 'Certificate used by the Human Resources person'

-- Open the key so you can modify it
OPEN SYMMETRIC KEY HRUserKey DECRYPTION BY PASSWORD = 'SYMp@$$w0rd'
GO

-- You cannot remove the password because that would leave the key
-- exposed without encryption, so you need to add the certificate first
ALTER SYMMETRIC KEY HRUserKey
 ADD ENCRYPTION BY CERTIFICATE HRCert
GO

-- Now you can remove the password encryption from the key
ALTER SYMMETRIC KEY HRUserKey
 DROP ENCRYPTION BY PASSWORD = 'SYMp@$$w0rd'
GO

CLOSE ALL SYMMETRIC KEYS
GO
```

```
-- Now change context to HRLogin to test
EXECUTE AS LOGIN = 'HRLogin'
GO

-- Notice the key is opened without a password this time, because you created
-- the certificate and gave authorization on it explicitly to HRUser.
OPEN SYMMETRIC KEY HRUserKey DECRYPTION BY CERTIFICATE HRCert
GO

SELECT *, CONVERT(varchar, DECRYPTBYKEY(CardNumber))
 FROM CreditCardInfo
GO

CLOSE ALL SYMMETRIC KEYS
GO

-- Revert back to sysadmin
REVERT
GO
```

This example demonstrates the basics of encrypting and decrypting in SQL Server. The amount of data in this example is trivial to encrypt and decrypt, even for old (slow) machines. Performance for encryption depends on two factors other than how big of a server you are running on: the size of the data to encrypt and the algorithm used to encrypt the data. Using RSA2048 to encrypt a larger file might take a bit longer than encrypting a Social Security number. It is difficult to give a nice graph of size versus time because it depends on so many factors. The best thing to do is set up a test environment that simulates your production environment and run some performance tests: encrypt and decrypt various data sizes in different algorithms, or at least in the algorithm you are planning to use.

Another interesting issue with encrypted columns is indexing and searching. To SQL Server itself, these are binary columns, so there is no effective way to create an index on them because you cannot predict a random stream of bytes. The best thing to do in this case is to create or use another unencrypted column to index on. The problem with this is that you might inadvertently give information about the data that is encrypted. Imagine you want to index on salaries and create a column named *range*. Anyone who has *SELECT* permission on the table can guess what the employee makes. If you must index or search encrypted data, be creative about your unencrypted columns.

More Info Encryption is not a trivial undertaking, and a thorough discussion is outside the scope of this book. Resources are available online to help you understand more about encryption in SQL Server security. Laurentiu Cristofor, one of the Microsoft developers behind encryption in SQL Server, has a wealth of information on his blog site dedicated to encryption: *http://blogs.msdn.com/lcris*. Raul Garcia is also on the SQL Server Security team. His blog at *http://blogs.msdn.com/raulga/* has additional useful information, as does the dedicated SQL Server Security blog at *http://blogs.msdn.com/sqlsecurity/*.

Transparent Data Encryption

SQL Server can encrypt the entire database (both the data and the log files) automatically, and without requiring any programming or application changes on your part. This is achieved using a special feature in SQL Server, available only in the Enterprise edition, called Transparent Data Encryption (TDE). Data is encrypted on the fly as it is written to disk and decrypted when it is read back. Encryption is performed at the page level and does not increase the size of the database. Because the process is entirely transparent, it's extremely easy to use TDE in SQL Server. Let's see how.

Note The NTFS file system in Windows Server 2000 and later provides a feature called Encrypted File System (EFS). This feature also applies transparent encryption to any data stored on the hard drive, but it will not protect databases or backups that have been copied onto a CD or other media. TDE in SQL Server 2008 is based on a certificate that is needed to decrypt or restore any encrypted database, regardless of where the data is transferred.

Creating Keys and Certificates for TDE

To start using TDE, you need to create a certificate, and to create a TDE certificate, you need to create a DMK. Although DMKs and certificates, in general, can be created in any database, they must be created in the *master* database when you intend to use them for TDE. The code in Listing 5-6 creates a DMK and certificate in the *master* that can be used for TDE against any database and then queries the *sys.certificates* view to confirm that the certificate exists.

LISTING 5-6 Creating a database master key and certificate for transparent data encryption.

```
-- Create a DMK and Certificate in master
USE master
GO

-- Create database master key (DMK)
CREATE MASTER KEY
 ENCRYPTION BY PASSWORD = 'Hrd2GessP@sswOrd!'

-- Create TDE certificate
CREATE CERTIFICATE MyEncryptionCert
 WITH SUBJECT = 'My Encryption Certificate'

-- Verify that the certificate has been created and is protected by the DMK
SELECT name, pvt_key_encryption_type_desc FROM sys.certificates
 WHERE name = 'MyEncryptionCert'
```

The output verifies that the certificate was created and that its private key is protected by the DMK, as shown here:

```
name                             pvt_key_encryption_type_desc
-------------------------------- -----------------------------------
MyEncryptionCert                 ENCRYPTED_BY_MASTER_KEY
```

Next, create a database with sensitive information in it, and then create a *database encryption key* (DEK), as shown in Listing 5-7.

LISTING 5-7 Creating a database encryption key.

```
-- Create a new database
IF EXISTS(SELECT name FROM sys.databases WHERE name = 'MyDB')
 DROP DATABASE MyDB
GO
CREATE DATABASE MyDB
GO
USE MyDB
GO

-- Store some unencrypted sensitive data
CREATE TABLE CreditCardInfo
(CardType varchar(50),
 CardNumber varchar(20))
GO

INSERT INTO CreditCardInfo VALUES
 ('MasterCard', '1234-1234-1234-1234'),
 ('American Express', '9876-987653-98765')

-- Create the DEK
CREATE DATABASE ENCRYPTION KEY
 WITH ALGORITHM = AES_128
 ENCRYPTION BY SERVER CERTIFICATE MyEncryptionCert
```

Note Because you have not yet backed up the server certificate, SQL Server issues a warning at this time alerting you to this fact. This warning should be taken seriously, since you will not be able to access any database encrypted by the DEK without the certificate. Should the certificate be lost or damaged, your encrypted databases will be completely inaccessible. Later in this section, you will learn how to back up and restore the certificate.

This statement creates a DEK for the *MyDB* database. Based on this DEK, SQL Server will encrypt *MyDB* using the *AES_128* algorithm. The *WITH ALGORITHM* clause can also specify *AES_192*, *AES_256*, or *TRIPLE_DES_3KEY* to be used for the encryption algorithm. The DEK itself is encrypted using the *MyEncryptionCert* certificate you created in the *master* database. (A DEK can be encrypted only by a certificate; it cannot be encrypted with just a password.) The DEK will be used not only to encrypt the database, but also to protect the database backups. Without the certificate used to encrypt the DEK, an encrypted database backup cannot be restored anywhere—end of story.

Enabling TDE

Once you've created a certificate-protected DEK for the database, you can start the encryption process. Encryption occurs in the background and does not interfere with applications that are concurrently accessing the database. Use the *ALTER DATABASE* statement and specify the *SET ENCRYPTION ON* clause to start encrypting the *MyDB* database, as shown in Listing 5-8:

LISTING 5-8 Enabling transparent data encryption on a database.

```
-- Enable TDE on the database
ALTER DATABASE MyDB SET ENCRYPTION ON

-- Verify TDE is enabled on the database
SELECT name, is_encrypted
 FROM sys.databases
 WHERE is_encrypted = 1
```

The results of the query into the *sys.database* catalog view indicate that *MyDB* is the only encrypted database on the server:

```
name                           is_encrypted
------------------------------ ------------
MyDB                           1
```

Note Encrypting one or more databases results in the encryption of *tempdb* as well. This can have a performance impact for unencrypted databases on the same server instance. Because the encryption in *tempdb* is implicit, *is_encrypted* is returned as *0* (false) by *sys.databases* for *tempdb*.

From this point forward, the *MyDB* database and all of its backups will be encrypted. If an unauthorized party somehow gains access to the physical media holding any backups, the backups will be useless without the certificate protecting the DEK.

You can also query the dynamic management view *sys.dm_database_encryption_keys* to see all the DEKs and to monitor the progress of encryption (or decryption, when you disable TDE) running on background threads managed by SQL Server. This view returns the unique database ID that can be joined on *sys.databases* to see the actual database name. For example, if you run the query in Listing 5-9 after enabling TDE, you can obtain information about the DEK and background encryption process.

LISTING 5-9 Querying for DEKs and encryption progress.

```
-- Monitor encryption progress
SELECT
   sys.databases.name,
  sys.dm_database_encryption_keys.encryption_state,
```

```
    sys.dm_database_encryption_keys.percent_complete,
    sys.dm_database_encryption_keys.key_algorithm,
    sys.dm_database_encryption_keys.key_length
  FROM
    sys.dm_database_encryption_keys INNER JOIN sys.databases
    ON sys.dm_database_encryption_keys.database_id = sys.databases.database_id
  WHERE
    sys.databases.name = 'MyDB'
```

If this query is executed after you enable TDE but before SQL Server has completed encrypting the entire database in the background, you will get results similar to the following (note that the database in the current example is so small that the encryption will complete too quickly for you to ever see an in-progress result such as this):

```
name       encryption_state percent_complete key_algorithm    key_length
---------- ---------------- ---------------- ---------------- -----------
MyDB       2                78.86916         AES              128

(1 row(s) affected)
```

The value returned by *encryption_state* tells you the current status of encryption (or decryption), as follows:

- 1 = Unencrypted
- 2 = Encryption in progress
- 3 = Encrypted
- 4 = Key change in progress
- 5 = Decryption in progress (after *ALTER DATABASE...SET ENCRYPTION OFF*)

Certain database operations cannot be performed during any of the "in progress" states (2, 4, or 5). These include enabling or disabling encryption, dropping or detaching the database, dropping a file from a file group, taking the database offline, or transitioning the database (or any of its file groups) to a *READ ONLY* state.

Backing Up the Certificate

It is extremely important to back up the server certificates you use to encrypt your databases with TDE. Without the certificate, you will not be able to access the encrypted database or restore encrypted database backups (which, of course, is the point of TDE). Attempting to restore an encrypted database without the certificate will fail with an error similar to this from SQL Server:

```
Msg 33111, Level 16, State 3, Line 1
Cannot find server certificate with thumbprint '0x6B1FEEEE238847DE75D1850FA20D87CF94F71F33'.
Msg 3013, Level 16, State 1, Line 1
RESTORE DATABASE is terminating abnormally.
```

In addition to the certificate itself, the certificate's private key must also be saved to a file and protected with a password. Use the statement in Listing 5-10 to back up the server certificate to a file and its private key to a separate password-protected file.

LISTING 5-10 Backing up the TDE certificate and its private key.

```
USE master
GO

BACKUP CERTIFICATE MyEncryptionCert TO FILE='C:\Demo\Backups\MyEncryptionCert.certbak'
 WITH PRIVATE KEY (
  FILE='C:\Demo\Backups\MyEncryptionCert.pkbak',
  ENCRYPTION BY PASSWORD='Pr!vK3yP@ssw0rd')
```

This statement creates two files: *MyEncryptionCert.certbak* is a backup of the server certificate, and *MyEncryptionCert.pkbak* is a backup of the certificate's private key protected with the password *Pr!vK3yP@ssw0rd*. Password protection is absolutely required when backing up the certificate's private key. Both of these files and the password will be needed to restore an encrypted database backup onto another server or instance. At the risk of stating the obvious, these backup files and the private key password should be closely safeguarded.

Note You can—and some would say, should—add an extra layer of protection by encrypting the private key using a separate password (rather than by just the master key) at the time you create a certificate. This can be done using the *ENCRYPTION BY PASSWORD* clause in the *CREATE CERTIFICATE* statement. In such a case, you would need to provide that password with the *DECRYPTION BY PASSWORD* clause in your *BACKUP CERTIFICATE* statement, or the statement will fail. As a result, no one could then back up the certificate without knowing its private key password.

Restoring an Encrypted Database

Before an encrypted database can be restored elsewhere, the server certificate that its DEK is encrypted by must be restored first. And if the target instance does not have a DMK, one must be created for it before the server certificate can be restored, as shown in Listing 5-11:

LISTING 5-11 Creating a new database master key on the target SQL Server instance.

```
-- Simulate disaster requiring recovery to a new server
USE master
GO

-- Lose the database
DROP DATABASE MyDB
GO
```

```
-- Lose the TDE certificate
DROP CERTIFICATE MyEncryptionCert

-- Lose the DMK and create a new one
DROP MASTER KEY
CREATE MASTER KEY ENCRYPTION BY PASSWORD = 'An0thrHrd2GessP@ssw0rd!'
```

To restore the server certificate from the backup files made in Listing 5-10, use an alternative form of the *CREATE CERTIFICATE* statement, as shown in Listing 5-12:

LISTING 5-12 Restoring the TDE certificate from its backup files.

```
CREATE CERTIFICATE MyEncryptionCert
 FROM FILE='C:\Demo\Backups\MyEncryptionCert.certbak'
 WITH PRIVATE KEY(
  FILE='C:\Demo\Backups\MyEncryptionCert.pkbak',
  DECRYPTION BY PASSWORD='Pr!vK3yP@ssw0rd')
```

This statement restores the *MyEncryptionCert* server certificate from the certificate backup file *MyEncryptionCert.certbak* and the certificate's private key backup file *MyEncryptionCert.pkbak*. Naturally, the password provided in the *DECRYPTION BY PASSWORD* clause must match the one that was used when the certificate's private key was backed up or the certificate will fail to restore. With a successfully restored certificate, you can then restore backups of *MyDB*, or any other encrypted database whose DEK is based on the *MyEncryptionCert* certificate.

SQL Server Audit

SQL Server Audit is a powerful security feature that can track virtually any server or database action taken by users, and log those activities to the file system or the Windows event log. SQL Server Audit helps meet the demands of regulatory compliance standards, which typically require that enterprise installations implement highly stringent security tactics that often include some form of auditing. You can work with SQL Server Audit using either SSMS or in T-SQL (as you will in most of the upcoming examples) using a new set of DDL statements and catalog views.

Note SQL Server Audit was first introduced in SQL Server 2008, Enterprise edition only. SQL Server 2012 provides limited SQL Server Audit support in all editions of SQL Server. Specifically, *server audit specifications* can be created in all editions of SQL Server 2012, while *database audit specifications* still require Enterprise edition (or higher). We explain audit specifications shortly.

Creating an Audit Object

Our first step in using SQL Server Audit is to create an *audit object* with the *CREATE SERVER AUDIT* statement. When you create an audit object, you are essentially defining a destination to which SQL Server will record information about interesting events that occur. The specific events to be monitored are described by creating *audit specifications*, which you define after creating one or more audit objects.

An audit object can capture monitored events to either the file system or to the Application or Security event logs. The desired destination is specified after the *TO* keyword in the *CREATE SERVER AUDIT* statement. For example, the statement in Listing 5-13 creates an audit object named *MyFileAudit* that records all monitored events that will be associated with this audit object to files that SQL Server will create in the C:\Demo\SqlAudits directory (which must already exist, or the statement will fail).

LISTING 5-13 Creating an audit object targeting the file system.

```
USE master
GO

CREATE SERVER AUDIT MyFileAudit TO FILE (FILEPATH='C:\Demo\SqlAudits')
```

Notice that it is necessary to first switch to the *master* database before you can create an audit object. If you don't switch away from a user database to the master database before running this DDL statement, SQL Server will return the following error:

```
Msg 33074, Level 16, State 1, Line 1
Cannot create a server audit from a user database. This operation must be performed in the
master database.
```

When an audit object is first created, it is in a disabled state and will not audit any events until it is explicitly enabled. You cannot create and enable an audit in a single step using *CREATE SERVER AUDIT*, so the next step after creating an audit is to enable it using *ALTER SERVICE AUDIT*. The statement in Listing 5-14 enables the *MyFileAudit* audit object you just created.

LISTING 5-14 Enabling an audit object.

```
ALTER SERVER AUDIT MyFileAudit
 WITH (STATE=ON)
```

Just as when first creating an audit object, you must switch to the *master* database before you can execute an *ALTER SERVER AUDIT* statement (which is not necessary here, as you haven't yet switched away from *master* since creating the audit object).

The *ALTER SERVER AUDIT* statement can also be used with the *MODIFY NAME* clause to rename the audit object. The audit must be disabled before it can be renamed. For example, the statements in Listing 5-15 rename the audit object *MyFileAudit* to *SqlFileAudit*.

LISTING 5-15 Renaming an audit object.

```
-- Rename the audit from MyFileAudit to SqlFileAudit, then rename it back
ALTER SERVER AUDIT MyFileAudit WITH (STATE=OFF)
ALTER SERVER AUDIT MyFileAudit MODIFY NAME = SqlFileAudit
ALTER SERVER AUDIT SqlFileAudit WITH (STATE=ON)
GO
ALTER SERVER AUDIT SqlFileAudit WITH (STATE=OFF)
ALTER SERVER AUDIT SqlFileAudit MODIFY NAME = MyFileAudit
ALTER SERVER AUDIT MyFileAudit WITH (STATE=ON)
GO
```

Once an audit object is created, you can define one or more audit specifications to monitor specific events of interest and associate those specifications with the audit object. Audited events captured by all audit specifications associated with an audit object are recorded to the destination defined by that audit object. We'll talk about audit specifications shortly, but first let's discuss some more general auditing options.

Auditing Options

You can specify several important options for your audit objects. These options, declared after the *WITH* keyword in either the *CREATE SERVER AUDIT* or *ALTER SERVER AUDIT* statements (or in some cases, both), are supported independently of what the audit destination is (that is, whether you're recording to the file system or the event log).

QUEUE_DELAY

The *QUEUE_DELAY* option controls the synchronous or asynchronous behavior of audit processing. Specifying zero for this option results in synchronous auditing. Otherwise, this option specifies any integer value of 1000 or higher to implement asynchronous processing for better auditing performance. The integer value for this option specifies the longest amount of time (in milliseconds) that is allowed to elapse before audit actions are forced to be processed in the background. The default value of 1000 results in asynchronous processing in which monitored events are audited within one second from the time that they occur.

The *QUEUE_DELAY* setting can be specified when the audit object is created and then later changed as needed. To change this setting for a running audit object, you must first disable the audit object before making the change and then enable it again after.

The statements in Listing 5-16 increase the time span for asynchronous processing of our *MyFileAudit* audit object by specifying the *QUEUE_DELAY* option with a value of 60,000 milliseconds (one minute). The audit object is temporarily disabled while the change is made.

LISTING 5-16 Setting the queue delay for an audit object.

```
ALTER SERVER AUDIT MyFileAudit WITH (STATE=OFF)
ALTER SERVER AUDIT MyFileAudit WITH (QUEUE_DELAY=60000)
ALTER SERVER AUDIT MyFileAudit WITH (STATE=ON)
```

ON_FAILURE

You can use the *ON_FAILURE* option to determine what course of action SQL Server should take if an error occurs while recording audited events. The valid settings for this option are *CONTINUE* (which is the default, and simply ignores failed attempts to audit), *FAIL_OPERATION* (which fails database operations that, in turn, fail to audit their associated events), or *SHUTDOWN* (which forcibly stops SQL Server, and requires that the login be granted the *SHUTDOWN* permission). This option can be specified when the audit object is created and then later changed as desired. As with *QUEUE_DELAY*, a running audit object must be temporarily disabled while the change is made.

The statements in Listing 5-17 tell SQL Server to shut down if an error is encountered while recording audits to the *MyFileAudit* object. In that event, SQL Server will not restart until the problem that is preventing auditing is resolved.

LISTING 5-17 Setting an audit object to shut down SQL Server if it fails to audit events.

```
ALTER SERVER AUDIT MyFileAudit WITH (STATE=OFF)
ALTER SERVER AUDIT MyFileAudit WITH (ON_FAILURE=SHUTDOWN)
ALTER SERVER AUDIT MyFileAudit WITH (STATE=ON)
```

AUDIT_GUID

By default, all audits are assigned an automatically generated globally unique identifier (GUID) value. In mirroring scenarios, you need to assign a specific GUID that matches the GUID contained in the mirrored database, and the *AUDIT_GUID* option allows you to do that. Once an audit object is created, its GUID value cannot be changed.

STATE

The *STATE* option is valid only with the *ALTER SERVER AUDIT* statement. It is used to enable or disable an audit object, using the keywords *ON* and *OFF*. (As mentioned earlier, an audit object cannot be created in an enabled state.) As demonstrated earlier with the *QUEUE_DELAY* option, the *STATE* option cannot be combined with other audit options in an *ALTER SERVER AUDIT* statement.

When a running audit is disabled using *STATE=OFF*, an audit entry is created, indicating that the audit was stopped, when it was stopped, and which user stopped it.

Recording Audits to the File System

The *TO FILE* clause is used to record audits to the file system, as you've just specified for the *MyFileAudit* audit object. When you audit to the file system, you can specify several file options, as described here.

FILEPATH

Use the *FILEPATH* option to designate where in the file system SQL Server should create the files that record monitored events being audited. This can be either a local path or a remote location using a Universal Naming Convention (UNC) path to a network share. The directory specified by this path must exist, or an error will occur. Moreover, you need to make sure the appropriate permissions are granted on each directory you'll be using, especially network shares. You cannot control the file names used for the files created by SQL Server Audit. Instead, the file names are generated automatically based on the audit name and audit GUID.

MAXSIZE

The *MAXSIZE* option specifies how large an audit file is permitted to grow before it is closed and a new one is opened (known as "rolling over"). The maximum size is expressed as an integer followed by *MB*, *GB*, or *TB* for megabytes, gigabytes, or terabytes. Note that you cannot specify a value less than one megabyte.

MAXSIZE can also be specified as *UNLIMITED* (which is the default value). In this case, the audit file can grow to any size before rolling over.

MAX_ROLLOVER_FILES

The *MAX_ROLLOVER_FILES* option can be used to automatically groom the file system as auditing data accumulates over time. The default value is *UNLIMITED*, which means that no cleanup is performed as new audit files are created. (This will eventually, of course, fill the disk.) Alternatively, you can provide an integer value for this option that specifies how many audit files are retained in the file system as they roll over, whereas older audit files are deleted automatically.

MAX_FILES

The *MAX_FILES* option (new in SQL Server 2012) forces you to manually groom the file system. When the specified number of files has been created, SQL Server will begin generating errors for any action being audited. It will *not* roll over, and it will not automatically delete old files as auditing data accumulates over time. Use this option when you want to ensure that manual attention is given to maintaining audit files, and SQL Server never deletes any audit files automatically.

RESERVE_DISK_SPACE

The default setting for the *RESERVE_DISK_SPACE* option is *OFF*, which means that disk space is dynamically allocated for the audit file as it expands to record more and more events. Performance can be improved (and disk fragmentation reduced) by preallocating disk space for the audit file at the time it is created. Setting this option to *ON* will allocate the amount of space specified by the *MAXSIZE* option when the audit file is created. *MAXSIZE* must be set to some value other than its default *UNLIMITED* setting to use *RESERVE_DISK_SPACE=ON*.

Recording Audits to the Windows Event Log

You can also create audit objects that are recorded to the Windows event log. To send audit entries to either the Application or Security event logs, specify *TO APPLICATION_LOG* or *TO SECURITY_LOG*. You will see how to create an audit object that is recorded to the Application event log in an upcoming sample.

Auditing Server Events

You create a *server audit specification* to monitor events that occur at the server level, such as failed login attempts or other actions not associated with any particular database. As already described, you associate specifications to an audit object configured for recording to either the file system or the event log.

Use the *CREATE SERVER AUDIT SPECIFICATION* statement to create a specification that monitors one or more server-level events for auditing. The *FOR SERVER AUDIT* clause links the specification with an audit object that defines the destination, and *ADD* clauses list the server-level audit action groups to be monitored. Similarly, the *ALTER SERVER AUDIT SPECIFICATION* statement can be used to *ADD* additional action groups to be monitored or *DROP* existing ones that should no longer be monitored.

Unlike audit objects, audit specifications can be created and enabled at the same time using *CREATE SERVER AUDIT SPECIFICATION* with the *STATE=ON* option. The statements in Listing 5-18 create and enable a server audit specification that records all successful logins and failed login attempts to the file system (to the path C:\Demo\SqlAudits, as defined by the audit object *MyFileAudit* created earlier in the section).

LISTING 5-18 Creating a server audit specification.

```
CREATE SERVER AUDIT SPECIFICATION CaptureLoginsToFile
 FOR SERVER AUDIT MyFileAudit
  ADD (FAILED_LOGIN_GROUP),
  ADD (SUCCESSFUL_LOGIN_GROUP)
 WITH (STATE=ON)
GO
```

After executing this statement, all login attempts made against the server (whether or not they succeed) will be audited to the file system. If you later decide to also audit password changes and to stop auditing successful logins, you can alter the specification accordingly (as with audit objects, audit specifications must be disabled while they are being changed), as shown in Listing 5-19:

LISTING 5-19 Altering a server audit specification.

```
ALTER SERVER AUDIT SPECIFICATION CaptureLoginsToFile  WITH (STATE=OFF)
ALTER SERVER AUDIT SPECIFICATION CaptureLoginsToFile
 ADD (LOGIN_CHANGE_PASSWORD_GROUP),
 DROP (SUCCESSFUL_LOGIN_GROUP)
ALTER SERVER AUDIT SPECIFICATION CaptureLoginsToFile  WITH (STATE=ON)
GO
```

You'll find a complete list of server-level action groups that can be monitored for auditing in the SQL Server Audit Action Groups and Actions post at *http://technet.microsoft.com/en-us/library/cc280663(v=sql.110).aspx*. There are more than 40 action groups, including backup and restore operations, changes in database ownership, adding or removing logins from server and database roles, or creating, altering, or dropping any database object—just to name a few.

Auditing Database Events

A *database audit specification* is conceptually similar to a server audit specification. Both specify events to be monitored and directed to a designated audit object. The primary difference is that database audit specifications are associated with actions against a particular database, rather than server-level actions.

Note Database audit specifications reside in the database they are created for. You cannot audit database actions in *tempdb*.

The *CREATE DATABASE AUDIT SPECIFICATION* and *ALTER DATABASE AUDIT SPECIFICATION* statements work the same as their *CREATE* and *ALTER* counterparts for server audit specifications that you just examined. Like server audit specifications, database audit specifications can be created in an enabled state by including the clause *WITH (STATE=ON)*.

About 24 database-level action groups can be monitored for auditing, such as changes in database ownership or permissions, for example. You can find the complete list in the SQL Server Audit Action Groups and Actions post at *http://technet.microsoft.com/en-us/library/cc280663(v=sql.110).aspx*. In addition, you can monitor for specific actions directly on database objects, such as schemas, tables, views, stored procedures, and so on. The seven database-level audit actions are *SELECT, INSERT, UPDATE, DELETE, EXECUTE, RECEIVE,* and *REFERENCES*.

For example, the code in Listing 5-20 creates an event log audit object named *MyEventLogAudit*, a database named *MyDB*, and a database audit specification in the *MyDB* database named *CaptureDbActionsToEventLog*.

LISTING 5-20 Creating a database audit specification recorded to the event log.

```
-- Create an event log audit
USE master
GO

CREATE SERVER AUDIT MyEventLogAudit TO APPLICATION_LOG
ALTER SERVER AUDIT MyEventLogAudit WITH (STATE=ON)

-- Create a new database
IF EXISTS(SELECT name FROM sys.databases WHERE name = 'MyDB')
 DROP DATABASE MyDB
GO
CREATE DATABASE MyDB
GO
USE MyDB
GO

-- Monitor database for all DML actions by all users to the event log
CREATE DATABASE AUDIT SPECIFICATION CaptureDbActionsToEventLog
 FOR SERVER AUDIT MyEventLogAudit
  ADD (DATABASE_OBJECT_CHANGE_GROUP),
  ADD (SELECT, INSERT, UPDATE, DELETE
        ON SCHEMA::dbo
        BY public)
 WITH (STATE=ON)
```

The *FOR SERVER AUDIT* clause specifies that the monitored events should be directed to the server object *MyEventLogAudit*, which you created earlier to record audits to the application event log. The first *ADD* clause specifies *DATABASE_OBJECT_CHANGE_GROUP*, which watches for DDL changes made to any database object. This effectively audits any *CREATE, ALTER*, or *DROP* statement made against any object (table, view, and so on) in the database. The second *ADD* clause audits any DML action (*SELECT, INSERT, UPDATE*, or *DELETE*) made against any object in the *dbo* schema by any *public* user (which is every user).

Note DDL triggers added in SQL Server 2005 provide another mechanism for capturing DDL events. See Books Online at *http://msdn.microsoft.com/en-US/library/ms175941(v=sql.110).aspx* for more information about DDL triggers.

You get very fine-grained control with database audit specifications. The *ON* clause in the preceding statement causes every object in the *dbo* schema to be audited, but it could just as easily be written to audit DML operations on specific tables if desired. Similarly, rather than auditing all users by specifying the *public* role in the *BY* clause, individual users and roles can be listed so that only DML operations made by those particular users are audited.

Viewing Audited Events

After you enable your audit objects and audit specifications, SQL Server takes it from there. Audits for each monitored event declared in your audit specifications are recorded automatically to the destinations you've specified in your audit objects. After accumulating several audits, you'll want to view them, of course.

Audits recorded to the event log can be examined using the Event Viewer (available from Administrative Tools in Control Panel). For example, Figure 5-7 shows the properties of an event recorded by a database audit for a *DELETE* statement against the *TestTable* table displayed using the Event Viewer.

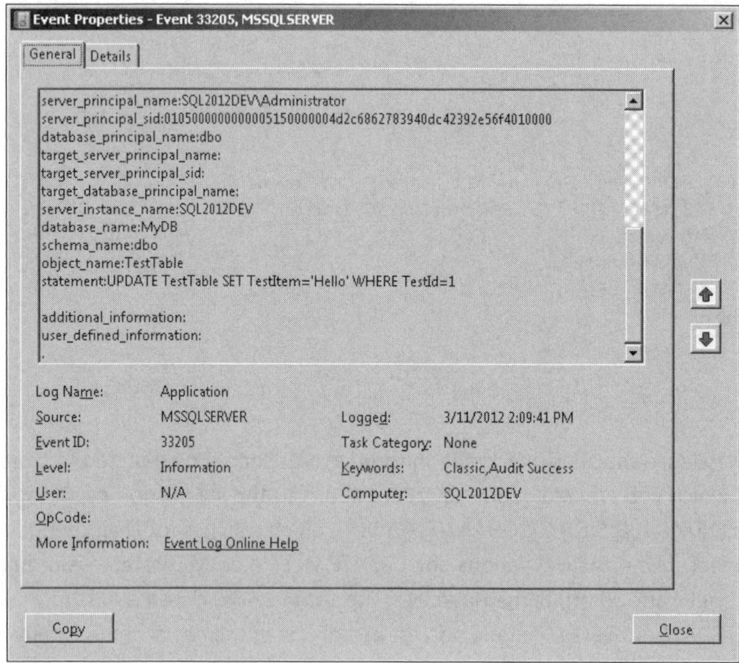

FIGURE 5-7 Displaying an audit recorded to the Application event log using Event Viewer.

Audits recorded to the file system are not stored in plain text files that can simply be viewed in Notepad. Instead, they are binary files that you can view in one of two ways. One way is from inside SQL Server Management Studio. Right-click the desired audit object beneath the *Security* node at the server instance level (not the *Security* node at the database level) in the Object Explorer, and then choose View Audit Logs. This opens the Log File Viewer window, as shown in Figure 5-8.

Each audit entry contains a wealth of detailed information about the event that was captured and recorded. This includes date and time stamp, server instance, action, object type, success or failure, permissions, principal name and ID (that is, the user that performed the audited action), database name, schema name, object name, the actual statement that was executed (or attempted), and more.

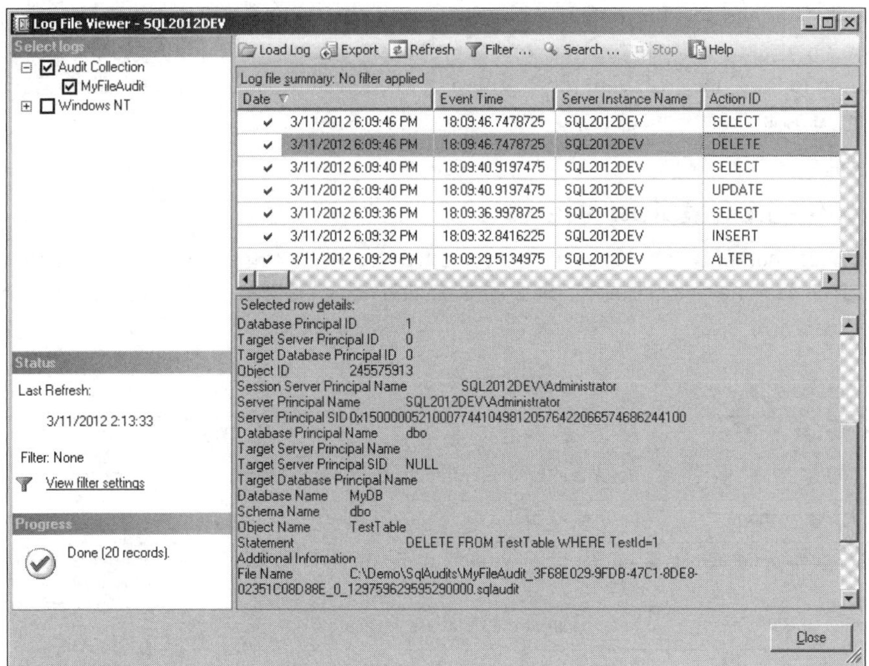

FIGURE 5-8 Displaying audits recorded to the file system using the Log File Viewer in SSMS.

Alternatively, you can use the table-valued function (TVF) named *sys.fn_get_audit_file*. This function accepts a parameter that points to one or more audit files (using wildcard pattern matching). Two additional parameters allow you to specify the initial file to process and a known offset location to start reading audit records from. (Both of these parameters are optional but must still be specified using the keyword *default*.) The function then reads the binary data from the file(s) and formats the audit entries into an ordinary table that gets returned back, as Listing 5-21 demonstrates.

LISTING 5-21 Querying audit files.

```
SELECT
  event_time, database_name, object_name, statement
 FROM
  sys.fn_get_audit_file('C:\Demo\SqlAudits\*.sqlaudit', default, default)
```

Here are some abbreviated results from this query:

```
event_time              database_name object_name statement
----------------------- ------------- ----------- ----------------------------------------
  :
2012-01-05 19:33:19.381 MyDB                      CREATE TABLE TestTable(TestId int PRIM…
2012-01-05 19:33:45.789 MyDB          TestTable   INSERT INTO TestTable VALUES(1, 'Test'…
2012-01-05 19:33:45.789 MyDB          TestTable   SELECT * FROM TestTable
2012-01-05 19:33:45.789 MyDB          TestTable   DELETE FROM TestTable WHERE TestId=1
  :
```

You can easily filter and sort this data using *WHERE* and *ORDER BY*, as well as *INSERT* the data elsewhere. The *sys.fn_get_audit_file* function represents an advantage that auditing to the file system has over auditing to the Windows event log, as there is no equivalent function provided for querying and manipulating audits in the event logs.

Querying Audit Catalog Views

SQL Server provides a number of catalog views that you can query for information about the audits and audit specifications running on any server instance. These audit catalog views are listed in Table 5-3, accompanied by a brief description of each.

TABLE 5-3 Audit catalog views.

Catalog View Name	Description
sys.server_file_audits	Returns all of the audit objects that are recorded to the file system.
sys.server_audit_specifications	Returns all of the server-level audit specifications.
sys.server_audit_specification_details	Returns detailed, monitored event information for all of the server-level audit specifications.
sys.database_audit_specifications	Returns all of the database-level audit specifications.
sys.database_audit_specification_details	Returns detailed, monitored event information for all of the database-level audit specifications.
sys.dm_server_audit_status	Returns the status of each audit object.
sys.dm_audit_actions	Returns every audit action that can be reported on and every audit action group that can be configured.
sys.dm_audit_class_type_map	Returns a table that maps the *class_type* field in the audit log to the *class_desc* field in *sys.dm_audit_actions*.

Partially Contained Databases

The dependency of database-specific users upon server-based logins poses a challenge when you need to move or restore a database to another server. Although the users move with the database, their associated logins do not, and thus the relocated database will not function properly until you also set up and map the necessary logins on the target server. To resolve these types of dependency problems and help make databases more easily portable, SQL Server 2012 introduces "partially contained" databases.

The term "*partially* contained" comes from the fact that SQL Server itself merely enables containment—it does not enforce it. It's still your job to actually implement *true* containment. From a security perspective, this means that partially contained databases allow you to create a special type of user called a *contained user*. The contained user's password is stored right inside the contained database, rather than being associated with a login defined at the server instance level and stored in the *master* database. Then, unlike the standard SQL Server authentication model (recall Figure 5-3), contained users are authenticated directly against the credentials in the contained database without ever authenticating against the server instance. Naturally, for this to work, a connection string with a contained user's credentials must include the Initial Catalog keyword that specifies the contained database name.

Creating a Partially Contained Database

To create a partially contained database, first enable the *contained database authentication* setting by calling *sp_configure* and then issue a *CREATE DATABASE* statement with the new *CONTAINMENT=PARTIAL* clause, as Listing 5-22 demonstrates.

LISTING 5-22 Creating a contained database.

```
-- Enable database containment
USE master
GO

EXEC sp_configure 'contained database authentication', 1
RECONFIGURE

-- Delete database if it already exists
IF EXISTS(SELECT name FROM sys.databases WHERE name = 'MyDB')
 DROP DATABASE MyDB
GO

-- Create a partially contained database
CREATE DATABASE MyDB CONTAINMENT=PARTIAL
GO

USE MyDB
GO
```

To reiterate, SQL Server doesn't enforce containment. You can still break containment by creating ordinary database users for server-based logins. For this reason, it's easy to convert an ordinary (uncontained) database to a partially contained database; simply issue an *ALTER DATABASE* statement and specify *SET CONTAINMENT=PARTIAL*. You'll then be able to migrate the server-based logins to contained logins and achieve server independence.

Creating a Contained User

Once you have a contained database, you can create a contained user for it by issuing a *CREATE USER* statement and specifying *WITH PASSWORD*, as shown in Listing 5-23. This syntax is valid only for contained databases; SQL Server will raise an error if you attempt to create a contained user in the context of an uncontained database.

LISTING 5-23 Creating a contained user.

```
CREATE USER UserWithPw
 WITH PASSWORD=N'password$1234'
```

That's all there is to creating partially contained databases with contained users. The only remaining point that's worth calling out is that an *Initial Catalog* clause pointing to a partially contained database must be specified explicitly in a connection string that also specifies the credentials of a contained user in that database. If just the credentials are specified without the database, SQL Server will not scan the partially contained databases hosted on the instance for one that has a user with matching credentials. Instead, it will consider the credentials to be those of an ordinary SQL Server login, and will not authenticate against the contained database.

Other Partially Contained Database Features

Our discussion of partially contained databases is motivated by the notion of contained users, a new SQL Server 2012 feature directly related to security. But aside from server-based logins, there are many other non-security-related dependencies that a database might have on its hosted instance. These include linked servers, SQL CLR, database mail, service broker objects, endpoints, replication, SQL Server Agent jobs, and *tempdb* collation. All these objects are considered to be *uncontained entities* because they all exist outside the database.

Uncontained entities threaten a database's portability. Because these objects are all defined at the server instance level, behavior can vary unpredictably when databases are shuffled around from one instance to another. We conclude our coverage of partially contained databases by examining the features they offer to help you achieve the level of containment and stability that your circumstances require.

Uncontained Entities View

SQL Server provides a new data management view (DMV) called *sys.dm_db_uncontained_entities* that you can query on to discover potential threats to database portability. This DMV not only highlights dependent objects, it will even report the exact location of all uncontained entity references inside of stored procedures, views, functions, and triggers.

Listing 5-24 joins *sys.dm_db_uncontained_entities* with *sys.objects* to report the name of all objects having uncontained entity references in them.

LISTING 5-24 Discovering threats to database portability by querying *sys.dm_db_uncontained_entities*.

```
-- Create a procedure that references a database-level object
CREATE PROCEDURE GetTables AS
BEGIN
  SELECT * FROM sys.tables
END
GO

-- Create a procedure that references an instance-level object
CREATE PROCEDURE GetEndpoints AS
BEGIN
  SELECT * FROM sys.endpoints
END
GO
```

```
-- Identify objects that break containment
SELECT
  UncType = ue.feature_type_name,
  UncName = ue.feature_name,
  RefType = o.type_desc,
  RefName = o.name,
  Stmt = ue.statement_type,
  Line = ue.statement_line_number,
  StartPos = ue.statement_offset_begin,
  EndPos = ue.statement_offset_end
 FROM
  sys.dm_db_uncontained_entities AS ue
  INNER JOIN sys.objects AS o ON o.object_id = ue.major_id
```

Here is the result of the query:

```
UncType      UncName    RefType               RefName       Stmt    Line  StartPos  EndPos
-----------  ---------  --------------------  ------------  ------  ----  --------  ---
System View  endpoints  SQL_STORED_PROCEDURE  GetEndpoints  SELECT  5     218       274
```

The DMV identifies the stored procedure *GetEndpoints* as an object with an uncontained entity reference. Specifically, the output reveals that a stored procedure references the *sys.endpoints* view in a *SELECT* statement on line 5 at position 218. This alerts you to a database dependency on endpoints configured at the server instance level that could potentially pose an issue for portability. The *GetTables* stored procedure does not have any uncontained entity references (*sys.tables* is contained), and is therefore not reported by the DMV.

Collations and *tempdb*

Ordinarily, all databases hosted on the same SQL Server instance share the same *tempdb* database for storing temporary tables, and all the databases (including *tempdb*) on the instance use the same *collation* setting (collation controls string data character set, case sensitivity, and accent sensitivity). When joining between regular database tables and temporary tables, both your user database and *tempdb* must use a compatible collation. This, again, represents an instance-level dependency with respect to the fact that the collation setting can vary from one server instance to another. Thus, problems arise when moving databases between servers that have different collation settings for *tempdb*. The code in Listing 5-25 demonstrates the problem, and how to avoid it by using a contained database.

LISTING 5-25 Achieving collation independence from *tempdb* using a partially contained database.

```
-- Create an uncontained database with custom collation
USE master
GO
IF EXISTS(SELECT name FROM sys.databases WHERE name = 'MyDB')
 DROP DATABASE MyDB
GO
```

```
CREATE DATABASE MyDB COLLATE Chinese_Simplified_Pinyin_100_CI_AS
GO

USE MyDB
GO

-- Create a table in MyDB (uses Chinese_Simplified_Pinyin_100_CI_AS collation)
CREATE TABLE TestTable (TextValue nvarchar(max))

-- Create a temp table in tempdb (uses SQL_Latin1_General_CP1_CI_AS collation)
CREATE TABLE #TempTable (TextValue nvarchar(max))

-- Fails, because MyDB and tempdb uses different collation
SELECT *
 FROM TestTable INNER JOIN #TempTable ON TestTable.TextValue = #TempTable.
TextValue

-- Convert to a partially contained database
DROP TABLE #TempTable
USE master

ALTER DATABASE MyDB SET CONTAINMENT=PARTIAL
GO

USE MyDB
GO

-- Create a temp table in MyDB (uses Chinese_Simplified_Pinyin_100_CI_AS
collation)
CREATE TABLE #TempTable (TextValue nvarchar(max))

-- Succeeds, because the table in tempdb now uses the same collation as MyDB
SELECT *
 FROM TestTable INNER JOIN #TempTable ON TestTable.TextValue = #TempTable.
TextValue

-- Cleanup
DROP TABLE #TempTable
USE master
DROP DATABASE MyDB
GO
```

This code first creates an uncontained database that uses *Chinese_Simplified_Pinyin_100_CI_AS* collation on a server instance that uses (the default) *SQL_Latin1_General_CP1_CI_AS* collation. The code then creates a temporary table and then attempts to join an ordinary database table against it. The attempt fails because the two tables have different collations (that is, they each reside in databases that use different collations), and SQL Server issues the following error message:

```
Msg 468, Level 16, State 9, Line 81
Cannot resolve the collation conflict between "SQL_Latin1_General_CP1_CI_AS" and
"Chinese_Simplified_Pinyin_100_CI_AS" in the equal to operation.
```

Then the code issues an *ALTER DATABASE...SET CONTAINMENT=PARTIAL* statement to convert the database to a partially contained database. As a result, SQL Server resolves the conflict by collating the temporary table in *tempdb* in the same collation as the contained database, and the second join attempt succeeds.

How Hackers Attack SQL Server

This final section of the chapter starts with a disclaimer: We do not cover every possible way that hackers can attempt to compromise SQL Server. Rather, we introduce the various methods of exploitation and try to get you thinking about security up front when you design database applications and configure your system. Let's start the discussion with topics related to how SQL Server is configured.

Direct Connection to the Internet

Exposing any operating system or application directly to the Internet without the use of a firewall is a bad thing—no matter whether you are using Linux, UNIX, Windows, or any other operating system. It's rather like the carnival game where someone sits on a platform above a pool of water waiting for someone else to throw a ball and hit the bull's-eye. When it happens, the person sitting on the platform is plunged into the water. Why expose your system, allowing anyone to take shots until you finally get soaked? Microsoft has done a lot of work towards protecting its operating systems and applications out of the box. When exploitation is discovered, they quickly address these problems and provide fixes.

This is only half of the battle, though. With all the switches and states of security for various products, it is not that difficult for an administrator or user to inadvertently misconfigure something and expose the systems to exploits. To mitigate these issues, it is very important that users isolate their systems from the Internet via firewalls and other isolation techniques.

Weak System Administrator Account Passwords

One of the easiest ways to give someone the keys to SQL Server is by providing a weak password for the system administrator (SA) account. In versions of SQL Server prior to SQL Server 2005, it was possible to give a blank password for the SA account without much complaint from SQL Server itself. As of SQL Server 2005, there is a lot more functionality around password policies and enforcement. Earlier in this chapter, we mentioned this topic in regard to SQL Server authentication accounts obeying the group policies of the Windows domain. Configuring a strong password length and account lockout in your domain will ensure that all users of SQL Server are supplying passwords that are more difficult to crack.

SQL Server Browser Service

SQL Server uses UDP port 1434 to return SQL Server instance names and port numbers to the requesting client. A few years back, this enumeration was the key to the "SQL Slammer" DoS virus. By consistently hitting the server with requests for enumeration, the virus left the server too busy to process other requests.

Starting with SQL Server 2005, this enumeration functionality is in a separate service called the SQL Server Browser service. The functionality no longer runs in the SQL Server process space, and it can be turned on and off without affecting SQL Server. If you do not want to use the SQL Server Browser service, you can still connect to other instances on your server, but the connection string must contain additional information (such as a specific port number in the case of TCP connections). If you want to use the Browser service in your organization, you can mitigate additional attacks by blocking UDP port 1434 on your firewall.

SQL Injection

SQL *injection* is the process by which a malicious user enters SQL statements instead of valid input. For example, suppose that a website is asking for a user name. Instead of actually typing in a user name, a malicious user could type *'blah'; DROP TABLE Sales;*. The web server will happily take the user input and pass it along to the application layer, where it is executed in code as follows:

```
SqlCommand cmd = new SqlCommand
 ("SELECT * FROM Sales WHERE Name='" + customerName + "'", conn)
```

To SQL Server, it looks like the following:

```
SELECT * FROM Sales WHERE Name='blah'; DROP TABLE Sales;
```

When this statement executes, the sales table will be erased (which is not quite what the application developer had in mind!). You can see how easy it is for malicious users to cause problems and return potentially sensitive information via simple inputs to webpages or applications that blindly accept user input to build dynamic SQL. To eliminate this potential, add the user input as a parameter to the *SqlCommand* rather than concatenating dynamic SQL strings, as shown here:

```
SqlCommand cmd = new SqlCommand("SELECT * FROM Sales WHERE Name=@CustomerName", conn));
cmd.Parameters.Add("@CustomerName", customerName);
```

By using the *Parameters* collection of the *SqlCommand* object, whatever the user types will be treated just as the value of the name part of the *WHERE* clause.

Intelligent Observation

With the advent of powerful search engines such as Google and MSN Search, finding things on the World Wide Web is relatively easy. Web crawlers from these search engines go off and fetch key words and place them into their own internal database. These key words are used within their own search algorithms so that when you type something to search on, the search engine can easily return a list of possible choices. These crawlers not only search for and store things like websites for pizza places, they also obtain various kinds of error information returned from web servers. Error information is very valuable to hackers. For example, if a hacker types *invalid password access denied* into the search string in MSN, they'll get a list of various topics that are, in general, not that interesting. However, one item might show this string: *Warning: mysql_pconnect(): Access denied for user 'root'@'localhost' (using password: YES) in /home/vhosts/<<removed for legal reasons>>/ docs/citeheader.inc.php on line 2.* Hackers know that this site is using MySQL and PHP, and they also learn some of the directory structure of the website */home/vhosts/<<removed for legal reasons>>/docs*. Now they can try to query that individual directory path using an ordinary browser to see whether they can uncover any additional goodies—a script file, perhaps. If they find a script file in this directory and the developer has hard-coded login credentials to the database, they are only one connection away from compromising the database.

The moral of the story is that search engines are very good hacker tools. Never hard-code passwords in script files, and always provide webpage redirects for errors within your web application. In addition, always pay extra attention to any web application that receives input. Make sure that these kinds of data are protected against SQL injection attacks.

Summary

Security is one of the most important considerations in any project, and the time you spend learning how to lock down SQL Server and your application is worthwhile in the long run. Microsoft has made efforts to increase the security of SQL Server 2012 out of the box by turning off features such as *xp_cmdshell*, the SQL Server Agent service, and many other optional features within the product. It has also extended the security feature set by adding the ability to easily encrypt data in transit and at rest within the database, by providing more granular permissions and allowing easy context switching, among other examples.

This chapter introduced some of the core concepts of security in SQL Server. You learned about logins, users, roles, and schemas, as well as authentication and authorization. We then went on to cover advanced security features such as encryption, auditing, partially contained databases, and contained users. Many online resources (such as SQL Server Books Online) go through these and additional security topics in more detail.

As you sit down to design your next application, never stop thinking of how someone might try to illegally gain access to your data or application. In today's world, a simple lock on the door to keep honest people honest is not enough. Everyone from IT professionals to developers needs to be diligent and must always be thinking about security.

PART II

Going Beyond Relational

CHAPTER 6

XML and the Relational Database

—Leonard Lobel

Ever since it exploded on the world scene in 1998, eXtensible Markup Language (XML) has served (and continues to serve) as *the* de facto text-based standard for exchanging information between different systems and across the Internet. XML is a markup language (derived from SGML) for documents that contain semi-structured hierarchical information. In XML, data is organized as a tree of parent and child nodes, which is quite different than the way data is structured in the tables and columns of a traditional relational database. The emerging relevance of this markup format first inspired the database to support XML in Microsoft SQL Server 2000, which was capable of reading XML into tables using the *OPENXML* function, and returning query results as XML using the *FOR XML* clause. But it was SQL Server 2005 that really positioned XML as a first-class citizen in the relational database world with the native *xml* data type, and all of the rich XML support that comes along with it, such as XML Schema Definition (XSD) validation, querying with the XML Query (XQuery) and XML Path (XPath) languages, and updating with XML DML (all of which we explore in this chapter).

Why would you want to store and work with XML in the database? Database purists would insist that you should never store XML in the database because they view XML strictly as a transfer mechanism, not a storage mechanism. They would argue that you should only use XML to transport data from one database or application to another, deconstruct the XML on import and store it in relational tables, and reconstruct it on export from the relational tables back to XML for transport. On the extreme other end of the spectrum, XML proponents view the world as just a bunch of XML files and use XML technologies (such as XSD, XQuery, XPath) to store and manipulate their data, with little interest in relational technologies and Transact SQL (T-SQL).

Both camps have good arguments and valid points. A relational database has features such as primary keys, indexes, and referential integrity that make it a far superior storage and querying mechanism for raw data. Some applications, or even databases themselves, shred XML data into relational data to store it in the database and compose XML when data is retrieved. At other times, the XML data is simply persisted as (unstructured) text in the database. When Microsoft SQL Server 2000 was introduced, it offered both of these options, yet neither is necessarily the desirable solution today. Today, the rich XML support in SQL Server 2012 makes it a compelling feature to exploit in a variety of situations.

So which do you use, a "pure" relational approach or a hybrid approach where you store XML in the database and work with it there? The answer, as with so much in SQL Server, is "it depends." When you are architecting a highly transactional application system (traditionally referred to as an online transaction processing, or OLTP, system) where many simultaneous reads and writes are performed by users, the most suitable choice is a full relational database technology that includes features such as primary keys, referential integrity, and transactions. Or, if you have a massive data warehouse and want to provide users with access to trend analysis and data mining algorithms, you will still use the traditional relational model in conjunction with the online analytical processing (OLAP) technology.

Conversely, there are certain times when you should definitely consider using XML in your database. One situation that's particularly suited to XML storage is when you are persisting objects that are being serialized and deserialized as XML in the application layer. Using the *xml* data type, as you'll learn in this chapter, provides a natural storage space for such data. It's particularly well-suited for XML-centric applications—that is, applications that work heavily with XML content storage and retrieval. XML in the database can also provide a vastly simpler solution than attribute (key/value pair) tables, when you require a flexible schema that can change without disturbing the schemas of your relational tables. And regardless of the nature or source of your XML content, you can seamlessly query against it at the database level by extending the *WHERE* clause of your ordinary relational queries with the XQuery functions that you will learn about in this chapter.

Even if you never actually store data using the *xml* data type in your underlying tables, the rich XML support in SQL Server offers powerful benefits. So conversely, you can design views, stored procedures, and table-valued functions (TVFs) that package and return complex structures (such as child entities) inside a single XML snippet as a scalar *xml* data-typed column in the query result set—while the source data is all persisted relationally in the database. For example, you can write a stored procedure that returns a single result set of orders, where each order has an *OrderDetails* column describing multiple detail rows as a single *xml* data-typed value. The stored procedure can easily manufacture the *OrderDetails* column on the fly from the related detail rows it joins on for each order. Thus you can return a set of orders with details in a single result set, rather than the more conventional approach of returning multiple result sets or making additional round-trips to the server to retrieve child entities. Similarly, you can accept hierarchical structures as an *xml* data type and shred them into rows inserted into relational tables. These are just a few of many examples where using a native *xml* data type in SQL Server can greatly simplify the processing (including storage, query, manipulation, and transport) of complex data structures.

Character Data as XML

XML, in all its dialects, is stored ultimately as string (character) data. Before the *xml* data type, XML data could only be stored in SQL Server using ordinary string data types, such as *varchar(max)* and *text*, and doing so raises several challenges. The first issue is validating the XML that is persisted (and by this we mean validating the XML against an XSD schema). SQL Server has no means of performing such a validation using ordinary strings, so the XML data can't be validated except by an outside application which can be a risky proposition (the true power of a relational database management system, or RDBMS, is applying rules at the server level).

The second issue is querying the data. Sure, you could look for data using character and pattern matching by using functions such as *CharIndex* or *PatIndex*, but these functions cannot efficiently or dependably find specific data in a structured XML document. The developer could also implement full-text search, which could also index the text data, but this solution would make things only a little better while adding the overhead of the full-text search engine. It would still be very difficult to extract data from a specific attribute in a specific child element in the XML content, and it certainly wouldn't be very efficient. You would not be able to write a query that said "Show me all data where the 'Author' attribute is set to 'Lukas Keller'."

The third issue is modifying the XML data. The developer could simply replace the entire XML contents—which is not at all efficient—or use the *UpdateText* function to do in-place changes. However, *UpdateText* requires that you know the exact locations and length of data you are going to replace, which, as we just stated, would be difficult and slow to do.

The natural evolution of persisting native XML data in the database has been realized since SQL Server 2005, with powerful T-SQL extensions that address all three of the aforementioned issues. Not only can SQL Server persist native XML data in the database, but it can index the data, query it using XPath and XQuery, and even modify it efficiently.

The *xml* Data Type

Using the *xml* data type, you can store XML in its native format, query the data within the XML, efficiently and easily modify data within the XML without having to replace the entire contents, and index the data in the XML. You can use *xml* as any of the following:

- A variable
- A parameter in a stored procedure or a user-defined function (UDF)
- A return value from a UDF
- A column in a table

There are some limitations of the *xml* data type to be aware of. Although this data type can contain and be checked for null values, unlike other native types, you cannot directly compare an instance of an *xml* data type to another instance of an *xml* data type. (You can, however, convert that instance to a *text* data type and then do a compare.) Any such equality comparisons require first casting the *xml* type to a *character* type. This limitation also means that you cannot use *ORDER BY* or *GROUP BY* with an *xml* data type. There are several other restrictions, which we will discuss in more detail later.

These might seem like fairly severe restrictions, but they don't really affect the *xml* data type when it is used appropriately. The *xml* data type also has a rich feature set that more than compensates for these limitations.

Working with the *xml* Data Type as a Variable

Let's start by writing some code that uses the *xml* data type as a variable. As with any other T-SQL variable, you simply declare it and assign data to it. Listing 6-1 shows an example that uses a generic piece of XML to represent basic order information.

LISTING 6-1 Creating XML and storing it in an *xml* variable using T-SQL.

```
DECLARE @XmlData AS xml = '
<Orders>
  <Order>
    <OrderId>5</OrderId>
    <CustomerId>60</CustomerId>
    <OrderDate>2008-10-10T14:22:27.25-05:00</OrderDate>
    <OrderAmount>25.90</OrderAmount>
  </Order>
</Orders>'

SELECT @XmlData
```

Listing 6-1 shows an *xml* variable being declared and assigned like any other native SQL Server *character* data type by using the *DECLARE* statement. The XML is then returned to the caller via a *SELECT* statement, and the results appear with the XML in a single column in a single row of data. Another benefit of having the database recognize that you are working with XML (rather than raw text that happens to be XML) is that XML results in SQL Server Developer Tools (SSDT) and SQL Server Management Studio (SSMS) are rendered as a hyperlink. Clicking the hyperlink then opens a new window displaying nicely formatted XML with color-coding and collapsible/expandable nodes.

Working with XML in Tables

Now you will define an actual column as XML in a new *AdventureWorks* database table. Execute the code shown in Listing 6-2 to create the new *OrdersXML* table.

LISTING 6-2 Creating a table to store XML in the database.

```
USE AdventureWorks2012
GO

CREATE TABLE OrdersXML(
  OrdersId int PRIMARY KEY,
  OrdersDoc xml NOT NULL DEFAULT '<Orders />')
GO
```

As we stated earlier, the *xml* data type has a few other restrictions—in this case, when it is used as a column in a table:

- It cannot be used as a primary key.
- It cannot be used as a foreign key.
- It cannot be declared with a *UNIQUE* constraint.
- It cannot be declared with the *COLLATE* keyword.

We also stated earlier that you can't compare two instances of the *xml* data type. Primary keys, foreign keys, and unique constraints all require that you must be able to compare any included data types; therefore, XML cannot be used in any of those situations. The SQL Server *COLLATE* statement is meaningless with the *xml* data type because SQL Server does not store the XML as text; rather, it uses a distinct type of encoding particular to XML. Note however that you can designate a *DEFAULT* value, as in this case, where an empty *<Orders />* element will be assigned by default if no value is supplied for *OrdersDoc* in an *INSERT* statement.

Now get some data into the column. Listing 6-3 takes some simple static XML and inserts it into the *OrdersXML* table you just created, using the xml data type as a variable.

LISTING 6-3 Storing XML in the database.

```
DECLARE @XmlData AS xml = '
<Orders>
  <Order>
    <OrderId>5</OrderId>
    <CustomerId>60</CustomerId>
    <OrderDate>2008-10-10T14:22:27.25-05:00</OrderDate>
    <OrderAmount>25.90</OrderAmount>
  </Order>
</Orders>'

INSERT INTO OrdersXML (OrdersId, OrdersDoc) VALUES (1, @XmlData)
```

You can insert data into *xml* columns in a variety of other ways: XML Bulk Load (which we will discuss later in this chapter), loading from an XML variable (as shown here), or loading from a *SELECT* statement using the *FOR XML TYPE* feature, which we will discuss shortly. Only well-formed XML (including fragments) can be inserted—any attempt to insert malformed XML will result in an exception, as shown in this fragment where there is a case-sensitivity problem in the end tag (the word *Orders* is not capitalized, as it is in the start tag):

```
INSERT INTO OrdersXML (OrdersId, OrdersDoc) VALUES (2, '<Orders></orders>')
```

The results produce the following error from SQL Server:

```
Msg 9436, Level 16, State 1, Line 1
XML parsing: line 1, character 17, end tag does not match start tag
```

XML Schema Definitions (XSDs)

One very important feature of XML is its ability to strongly type data in an XML document. The XSD language—itself composed in XML—defines the expected format for all XML documents validated against a particular XSD. You can use XSD to create an XML schema for your data, requiring that your data conform to a set of rules that you specify. This gives XML an advantage over just about all other data transfer/data description methods and is a major contributing factor to the success of the XML standard.

Without XSD, your XML data would just be another unstructured, text-delimited format. An XSD defines what your XML data should look like, what elements are required, and what data types those elements will have. Analogous to how a table definition in SQL Server provides structure and type validation for relational data, an XML schema provides structure and type validation for the XML data.

We won't fully describe all the features of the XSD language here—that would require a book of its own. You can find the XSD specifications at the World Wide Web Consortium (W3C), at *http://www.w3.org/2001/XMLSchema*. Several popular schemas are publicly available, including one for Really Simple Syndication (RSS), Atom Publishing Protocol (APP, based on RSS), which are protocols that power weblogs, blogcasts, and other forms of binary and text syndication, as well as one for SOAP, which dictates how XML Web Services exchange information.

You can choose how to structure your XSD. Your XSD can designate required elements and set limits on what data types and ranges are allowed. It can even allow document fragments.

SQL Server Schema Collections

SQL Server lets you create your own schemas and store them in the database as database objects, and to then enforce a schema on any XML instance, including columns in tables and SQL Server variables. This gives you precise control over the XML that is going into the database and lets you strongly type your XML instance.

To get started, you can create the following simple schema and add it to the *schemas* collection in *AdventureWorks2012*, as shown in Listing 6-4.

LISTING 6-4 Creating an XML Schema Definition (XSD).

```
CREATE XML SCHEMA COLLECTION OrdersXSD AS '
  <xsd:schema
    xmlns:xsd="http://www.w3.org/2001/XMLSchema"
    xmlns:sql="urn:schemas-microsoft-com:mapping-schema">
    <xsd:simpleType name="OrderAmountFloat" >
      <xsd:restriction base="xsd:float" >
        <xsd:minExclusive value="1.0" />
        <xsd:maxInclusive value="5000.0" />
      </xsd:restriction>
    </xsd:simpleType>
    <xsd:element name="Orders">
      <xsd:complexType>
        <xsd:sequence>
          <xsd:element name="Order">
            <xsd:complexType>
              <xsd:sequence>
                <xsd:element name="OrderId" type="xsd:int" />
                <xsd:element name="CustomerId" type="xsd:int" />
                <xsd:element name="OrderDate" type="xsd:dateTime" />
                <xsd:element name="OrderAmount" type="OrderAmountFloat" />
              </xsd:sequence>
            </xsd:complexType>
          </xsd:element>
```

```
        </xsd:sequence>
      </xsd:complexType>
    </xsd:element>
  </xsd:schema>'
```

This schema is named *OrdersXSD*, and you can use it on any *xml* type, including variables, parameters, return values, and especially columns in tables. This schema defines elements named *OrderId*, *CustomerId*, *OrderDate*, and *OrderAmount*. The *OrderAmount* element references the *OrderAmountFloat* type, which is defined as a *float* data type whose minimum value is anything greater than (but not including) 1 and whose maximum value is 5000.

Next, create a simple table and apply the schema to the XML column by referring to the schema name in parentheses after your *xml* data type in the *CREATE TABLE* statement, as shown in Listing 6-5.

LISTING 6-5 Creating a table with an *xml* column bound to an XML Schema Definition (XSD).

```
IF EXISTS(SELECT name FROM sys.tables WHERE name = 'OrdersXML' AND type = 'U')
 DROP TABLE OrdersXML

CREATE TABLE OrdersXML(
  OrdersId int PRIMARY KEY,
  OrdersDoc xml(OrdersXSD) NOT NULL)
```

As you can see in this example, the *OrdersDoc* column is defined not as simply *xml,* but as *xml(OrdersXSD)*. The *xml* data type has an optional parameter that allows you to specify the bound schema. This same usage also applies if you want to bind a schema to another use of an *xml* data type, such as a variable or a parameter. SQL Server now allows only a strongly typed XML document in the *OrdersDoc* column. This is much better than a *CHECK* constraint (which you can still add to this column, but only with a function). An advantage of using an XML schema is that your data is validated against it and you can enforce *xml* data types (at the XML level) and make sure that only valid XML data is allowed into the particular elements. If you were using a *CHECK* constraint, for example, you would need a separate *CHECK* constraint for each validation you wanted to perform. In this example, without an XSD, several *CHECK* constraints would be needed just to enforce the minimum and maximum ages. You would need one constraint requiring the element and then another constraint to verify the allowed low end of the range and another one to verify the high end of the allowed range.

To see the schema in action, execute the code in Listing 6-6.

LISTING 6-6 Validating XML data against an XSD.

```
-- Works because all XSD validations succeed
INSERT INTO OrdersXML VALUES(5, '
  <Orders>
    <Order>
```

```
      <OrderId>5</OrderId>
      <CustomerId>60</CustomerId>
      <OrderDate>2011-10-10T14:22:27.25-05:00</OrderDate>
      <OrderAmount>25.90</OrderAmount>
    </Order>
  </Orders>')
GO

-- Won't work because 6.0 is not a valid int for CustomerId
UPDATE OrdersXML SET OrdersDoc = '
  <Orders>
    <Order>
      <OrderId>5</OrderId>
      <CustomerId>6.0</CustomerId>
      <OrderDate>2011-10-10T14:22:27.25-05:00</OrderDate>
      <OrderAmount>25.90</OrderAmount>
    </Order>
  </Orders>'
 WHERE OrdersId = 5
GO

-- Won't work because 25.90 uses an O for a 0 in the OrderAmount
UPDATE OrdersXML SET OrdersDoc = '
  <Orders>
    <Order>
      <OrderId>5</OrderId>
      <CustomerId>60</CustomerId>
      <OrderDate>2011-10-10T14:22:27.25-05:00</OrderDate>
      <OrderAmount>25.9O</OrderAmount>
    </Order>
  </Orders>'
 WHERE OrdersId = 5
GO

-- Won't work because 5225.75 is too large a value for OrderAmount
UPDATE OrdersXML SET OrdersDoc = '
  <Orders>
    <Order>
      <OrderId>5</OrderId>
      <CustomerId>60</CustomerId>
      <OrderDate>2011-10-10T14:22:27.25-05:00</OrderDate>
      <OrderAmount>5225.75</OrderAmount>
    </Order>
  </Orders>'
 WHERE OrdersId = 5
GO
```

SQL Server enforces the schema on inserts and updates, ensuring data integrity. The data provided for the *INSERT* operation at the top of Listing 6-6 conforms to the schema, so the *INSERT* works just fine. Each of the three *UPDATE* statements that follow all attempt to violate the schema with various invalid data, and SQL Server rejects them with error messages that show the offending data (and location) that's causing the problem:

```
Msg 6926, Level 16, State 1, Line 106
XML Validation: Invalid simple type value: '6.0'. Location: /*:Orders[1]/*:Order[1]/*:Customer
Id[1]
Msg 6926, Level 16, State 1, Line 119
XML Validation: Invalid simple type value: '25.90'. Location: /*:Orders[1]/*:Order[1]/*:Order
Amount[1]
Msg 6926, Level 16, State 1, Line 132
XML Validation: Invalid simple type value: '5225.75'. Location: /*:Orders[1]/*:Order[1]/*:Order
Amount[1]
```

Lax Validation

XSD also supports *lax validation*. Say that you want to add an additional element to the XML from the preceding example, after *<OrderAmt>*, that is not part of the same schema. Schemas can use *processContents* values of *skip* and *strict* for *any* and *anyAttribute* declarations as a wildcard (if you're unfamiliar with these schema attributes and values, they're used to dictate how the XML parser should deal with XML elements not found in the schema). If *processContents* is set to *skip*, SQL Server will skip completely the validation of the additional element, even if a schema is available for it. If *processContents* is set to *strict*, SQL Server will require that it has an element or namespace defined in the current schema against which the element will be validated. Lax validation provides an additional "in-between" validation option. By setting the *processContents* attribute for this wildcard section to *lax*, you can enforce validation for any elements that have a schema associated with them but ignore any elements that are not defined in the schema.

Consider the schema you just worked with in Listing 6-4. You can modify this XSD to tolerate additional elements after *OrderAmount* that are defined in another schema, whether or not that schema is available. A schema needs to be dropped before you can re-create a modified version of it, and objects bound to the schema must be dropped before you can drop the schema. Therefore, before re-creating the schema for lax validation, you must execute the following statements:

```
DROP TABLE OrdersXML
DROP XML SCHEMA COLLECTION OrdersXSD
```

Now re-create the XSD in Listing 6-4 with one small difference—add the following additional line just after the last *xsd:element* line for *OrderAmount*:

```
<xsd:any namespace="##other" processContents="lax"/>
```

With this small change in place, arbitrary XML elements following *<OrderAmt>* will be allowed to be stored without failing validation, if the external XSD is not accessible. To see this in action, first re-create the same test table as shown in Listing 6-5. Then run the code in Listing 6-7, which inserts an order containing an additional *<Notes>* element not defined as part of the *OrdersXSD* schema.

LISTING 6-7 Using lax schema validation with XML data.

```
-- Works because all XSD validations succeed
INSERT INTO OrdersXML VALUES(6, '
  <Orders>
```

```
    <Order>
      <OrderId>6</OrderId>
      <CustomerId>60</CustomerId>
      <OrderDate>2011-10-10T14:22:27.25-05:00</OrderDate>
      <OrderAmount>25.90</OrderAmount>
      <Notes xmlns="sf">My notes for this order</Notes>
    </Order>
  </Orders>')
```

Because of the *processContents="lax"* setting in the XSD, SQL Server permits additional elements defined in another XSD (the *sf* namespace in this example, as denoted by the *xmlns* attribute). The *lax* setting in the XSD tells SQL Server to validate the *<Notes>* element in the XML using the *sf* namespace if available, but to allow the element without any validation if the *sf* namespace is not available.

Union and List Types

SQL Server also supports the union of lists with *xsd:union*, so you can combine multiple lists into one simple type. For example, in the schema shown in Listing 6-8, the *shiptypeList* accepts strings such as *FastShippers* but also allows alternative integer values.

LISTING 6-8 Using union and list types in XSD.

```
-- Cleanup previous objects
DROP TABLE OrdersXML
DROP XML SCHEMA COLLECTION OrdersXSD
GO

-- Union and List types in XSD
CREATE XML SCHEMA COLLECTION OrdersXSD AS '
  <xsd:schema
    xmlns:xsd="http://www.w3.org/2001/XMLSchema"
    xmlns:sql="urn:schemas-microsoft-com:mapping-schema">
    <xsd:simpleType name="shiptypeList">
      <xsd:union>
        <xsd:simpleType>
          <xsd:list>
            <xsd:simpleType>
              <xsd:restriction base="xsd:integer">
                <xsd:enumeration value="1" />
                <xsd:enumeration value="2" />
                <xsd:enumeration value="3" />
              </xsd:restriction>
            </xsd:simpleType>
          </xsd:list>
        </xsd:simpleType>
        <xsd:simpleType>
          <xsd:list>
            <xsd:simpleType>
              <xsd:restriction base="xsd:string">
```

```
                <xsd:enumeration value="FastShippers" />
                <xsd:enumeration value="SHL" />
                <xsd:enumeration value="PSU" />
              </xsd:restriction>
          </xsd:simpleType>
          </xsd:list>
        </xsd:simpleType>
      </xsd:union>
    </xsd:simpleType>
    <xsd:element name="Orders">
      <xsd:complexType>
        <xsd:sequence>
          <xsd:element name="Order">
            <xsd:complexType>
              <xsd:sequence>
                <xsd:element name="OrderId" type="xsd:int" />
                <xsd:element name="CustomerId" type="xsd:int" />
                <xsd:element name="OrderDate" type="xsd:dateTime" />
                <xsd:element name="OrderAmount" type="xsd:float" />
                <xsd:element name="ShipType" type="shiptypeList"/>
              </xsd:sequence>
            </xsd:complexType>
          </xsd:element>
        </xsd:sequence>
      </xsd:complexType>
    </xsd:element>
  </xsd:schema>'
```

If you use this XSD to validate an XML instance with either a numeric value or a string value in the enumerated list, it will validate successfully, as demonstrated by the code in Listing 6-9.

LISTING 6-9 Referencing an XSD list type in XML.

```
-- Works with 1 or FastShippers in ShipType
DECLARE @OrdersXML xml(OrdersXSD) = '
  <Orders>
    <Order>
      <OrderId>6</OrderId>
      <CustomerId>60</CustomerId>
      <OrderDate>2011-10-10T14:22:27.25-05:00</OrderDate>
      <OrderAmount>25.90</OrderAmount>
      <ShipType>1</ShipType>
    </Order>
  </Orders>'
```

This example is fairly basic, but it is useful if you have more than one way to describe something and need two lists to do so. One such possibility is metric and English units of measurement. This technique is useful when you need to restrict items and are writing them from a database.

We have touched only the surface of using XML schemas in SQL Server. These schemas can get quite complex, and further discussion is beyond the scope of this book. You can easily enforce sophisticated XML schemas in your database once you master the syntax. We believe that you should always use an XML schema with your XML data to guarantee consistency in your XML data.

XML Indexes

You can create an XML index on an XML column using almost the same syntax as for a standard SQL Server index. There are four types of XML indexes: a single *primary XML index* that must be created, and three types of optional *secondary XML indexes* that are created over the primary index. An XML index is a little different from a standard SQL index—it is a clustered index on an internal table used by SQL Server to store XML data. This table is called the *node table* and cannot be accessed by programmers.

To get started with an XML index, you must first create the primary index of all the nodes. The primary index is a clustered index (over the node table, not the base table) that associates each node of your XML column with the SQL Primary Key column. It does this by indexing one row in its internal representation (a B+ tree structure) for each node in your XML column, generating an index usually about three times as large as your XML data. For your XML data to work properly, your table must have an ordinary clustered primary key column defined. That primary key is used in a join of the XQuery results with the base table. (XQuery is discussed later on in the section "Querying XML Data Using XQuery.")

To create a primary XML index, you first create a table with a primary key and an XML column, as shown in Listing 6-10.

LISTING 6-10 Creating a primary XML index for XML storage in a table.

```
IF EXISTS(SELECT name FROM sys.tables WHERE name = 'OrdersXML' AND type = 'U')
 DROP TABLE OrdersXML
GO

CREATE TABLE OrdersXML(
  OrdersId int PRIMARY KEY,
  OrdersDoc xml NOT NULL)

CREATE PRIMARY XML INDEX ix_orders
 ON OrdersXML(OrdersDoc)
```

These statements create a new primary XML index named *ix_orders* on the *OrdersXML* table's *OrdersDoc* column. The primary XML index, *ix_orders*, now has the node table populated. To examine the node table's columns, run the T-SQL shown in Listing 6-11.

LISTING 6-11 Creating a primary XML index for XML storage in a table.

```
-- Display the columns in the node table (primary XML clustered index)
SELECT
  c.column_id, c.name, t.name AS data_type
```

```
FROM
 sys.columns AS c
 INNER JOIN sys.indexes AS i ON i.object_id = c.object_id
 INNER JOIN sys.types AS t ON t.user_type_id = c.user_type_id
WHERE
 i.name = 'ix_orders' AND i.type = 1
ORDER BY
 c.column_id
```

The results are shown in Table 6-1.

TABLE 6-1 Columns in a Typical Node Table.

column_id	name	data_type
1	*id*	*varbinary*
2	*nid*	*int*
3	*tagname*	*nvarchar*
4	*taguri*	*nvarchar*
5	*tid*	*int*
6	*value*	*sql_variant*
7	*lvalue*	*nvarchar*
8	*lvaluebin*	*varbinary*
9	*hid*	*varchar*
10	*xsinil*	*bit*
11	*xsitype*	*bit*
12	*pk1*	*int*

The three types of secondary XML indexes are *path*, *value*, and *property*. You can implement a secondary XML index only after you have created a primary XML index because they are both actually indexes over the node table. These indexes further optimize XQuery statements made against the XML data.

A path index creates an index on the *Path ID* (*hid* in Table 6-1) and *Value* columns of the primary XML index, using the *FOR PATH* keyword. This type of index is best when you have a fairly complex document type and want to speed up XQuery XPath expressions that reference a particular node in your XML data with an explicit value (as explained in the section "Understanding XQuery Expressions and XPath" later in this chapter). If you are more concerned about the values of the nodes queried with wildcards, you can create a value index using the *FOR VALUE XML* index. The *VALUE* index contains the same index columns as the *PATH* index, *Value*, and *Path ID (hid)*, but in the reverse order (as shown in Table 6-1). Using the property type index with the *PROPERTY* keyword optimizes hierarchies of elements or attributes that are name/value pairs. The *PROPERTY* index contains the primary key of the base table, *Path ID (hid)*, and *Value*, in that order. The syntax to create these indexes is shown here; you must specify that you are using the primary XML index by using the *USING XML INDEX* syntax as shown in Listing 6-12.

LISTING 6-12 Creating secondary XML indexes on *path*, *value*, and *property* data.

```
-- Create secondary structural (path) XML index
CREATE XML INDEX ix_orders_path ON OrdersXML(OrdersDoc)
 USING XML INDEX ix_orders FOR PATH

-- Create secondary value XML index
CREATE XML INDEX ix_orders_val ON OrdersXML(OrdersDoc)
 USING XML INDEX ix_orders FOR VALUE

-- Create secondary property XML index
CREATE XML INDEX ix_orders_prop ON OrdersXML(OrdersDoc)
 USING XML INDEX ix_orders FOR PROPERTY
```

Be aware of these additional restrictions regarding XML indexes:

- An XML index can contain only one XML column, so you cannot create a composite XML index (an index on more than one XML column).
- Using XML indexes requires that the primary key be clustered, and because you can have only one clustered index per table, you cannot create a clustered XML index.

With the proper XML indexing in place, you can write some very efficient queries using XQuery. Before we get to XQuery, however, let's take a look at some other XML features that will help you get XML data in and out of the database.

FOR XML Commands

SQL Server supports an enhancement to the T-SQL syntax that enables normal relational queries to output their result set as XML, using any of these four approaches:

- *FOR XML RAW*
- *FOR XML AUTO*
- *FOR XML EXPLICIT*
- *FOR XML PATH*

The first three of these options were introduced with the very first XML support in SQL Server 2000. We'll start with these options and then cover later XML enhancements added in SQL Server 2008, which includes the fourth option (*FOR XML PATH*).

FOR XML RAW

FOR XML RAW produces *attribute-based XML*. *FOR XML RAW* essentially creates a flat representation of the data in which each row returned becomes an element and the returned columns become the attributes of each element. *FOR XML RAW* also doesn't interpret joins in any special way. (Joins become relevant in *FOR XML AUTO*.) Listing 6-13 shows an example of a simple query that retrieves customer and order header data.

LISTING 6-13 Using *FOR XML RAW* to produce flat, attribute-based XML.

```
SELECT TOP 10
  Customer.CustomerID, OrderHeader.SalesOrderID, OrderHeader.OrderDate
 FROM
  Sales.Customer AS Customer
  INNER JOIN Sales.SalesOrderHeader AS OrderHeader
   ON OrderHeader.CustomerID = Customer.CustomerID
 ORDER BY
  Customer.CustomerID
 FOR XML RAW
```

Both SSDT in Visual Studio and SSMS render the query results as a hyperlink that you can click on to see the output rendered as properly formatted XML in a color-coded window that supports expanding and collapsing nodes.

```
<row CustomerID="11000" SalesOrderID="43793" OrderDate="2005-07-22T00:00:00" />
<row CustomerID="11000" SalesOrderID="51522" OrderDate="2007-07-22T00:00:00" />
<row CustomerID="11000" SalesOrderID="57418" OrderDate="2007-11-04T00:00:00" />
<row CustomerID="11001" SalesOrderID="43767" OrderDate="2005-07-18T00:00:00" />
<row CustomerID="11001" SalesOrderID="51493" OrderDate="2007-07-20T00:00:00" />
<row CustomerID="11001" SalesOrderID="72773" OrderDate="2008-06-12T00:00:00" />
<row CustomerID="11002" SalesOrderID="43736" OrderDate="2005-07-10T00:00:00" />
<row CustomerID="11002" SalesOrderID="51238" OrderDate="2007-07-04T00:00:00" />
<row CustomerID="11002" SalesOrderID="53237" OrderDate="2007-08-27T00:00:00" />
<row CustomerID="11003" SalesOrderID="43701" OrderDate="2005-07-01T00:00:00" />
```

As you can see, you get flat results in which each row returned from the query becomes a single element named *row* and all columns are output as attributes of that element. Odds are, however, that you will want more structured XML output, which leads us to *FOR XML AUTO*.

FOR XML AUTO

FOR XML AUTO also produces attribute-based XML (by default), but its output is hierarchical rather than flat—that is, it can create nested results based on the tables in the query's join clause. For example, using the same query just demonstrated, you can simply change the *FOR XML* clause to *FOR XML AUTO*, as shown in Listing 6-14.

LISTING 6-14 Using *FOR XML AUTO* to produce hierarchical, attribute-based XML.

```
SELECT TOP 10 -- limits the result rows for demo purposes
  Customer.CustomerID, OrderHeader.SalesOrderID, OrderHeader.OrderDate
 FROM
  Sales.Customer AS Customer
  INNER JOIN Sales.SalesOrderHeader AS OrderHeader
   ON OrderHeader.CustomerID = Customer.CustomerID
 ORDER BY
  Customer.CustomerID
 FOR XML AUTO
```

Execute this query, click the XML hyperlink in the results, and you will see the following output:

```
<Customer CustomerID="11000">
  <OrderHeader SalesOrderID="43793" OrderDate="2005-07-22T00:00:00" />
  <OrderHeader SalesOrderID="51522" OrderDate="2007-07-22T00:00:00" />
  <OrderHeader SalesOrderID="57418" OrderDate="2007-11-04T00:00:00" />
</Customer>
<Customer CustomerID="11001">
  <OrderHeader SalesOrderID="43767" OrderDate="2005-07-18T00:00:00" />
  <OrderHeader SalesOrderID="51493" OrderDate="2007-07-20T00:00:00" />
  <OrderHeader SalesOrderID="72773" OrderDate="2008-06-12T00:00:00" />
</Customer>
<Customer CustomerID="11002">
  <OrderHeader SalesOrderID="43736" OrderDate="2005-07-10T00:00:00" />
  <OrderHeader SalesOrderID="51238" OrderDate="2007-07-04T00:00:00" />
  <OrderHeader SalesOrderID="53237" OrderDate="2007-08-27T00:00:00" />
</Customer>
<Customer CustomerID="11003">
  <OrderHeader SalesOrderID="43701" OrderDate="2005-07-01T00:00:00" />
</Customer>
```

As you can see, the XML data has main elements named *Customer* (based on the alias assigned in the query) and child elements named *OrderHeader* (again from the alias). Note that *FOR XML AUTO* determines the element nesting order based on the order of the columns in the *SELECT* clause. You can rewrite the *SELECT* clause so that an *OrderHeader* column comes before a *Customer* column, by changing the order of the columns returned by the query, as shown in Listing 6-15.

LISTING 6-15 Changing the hierarchy returned by *FOR XML AUTO* by reordering query columns.

```
SELECT TOP 10
  OrderHeader.SalesOrderID, OrderHeader.OrderDate, Customer.CustomerID
 FROM
  Sales.Customer AS Customer
  INNER JOIN Sales.SalesOrderHeader AS OrderHeader
   ON OrderHeader.CustomerID = Customer.CustomerID
 ORDER BY
  Customer.CustomerID
 FOR XML AUTO
```

The output (as viewed in the XML viewer) now looks like this:

```
<OrderHeader SalesOrderID="43793" OrderDate="2005-07-22T00:00:00">
  <Customer CustomerID="11000" />
</OrderHeader>
<OrderHeader SalesOrderID="51522" OrderDate="2007-07-22T00:00:00">
  <Customer CustomerID="11000" />
</OrderHeader>
<OrderHeader SalesOrderID="57418" OrderDate="2007-11-04T00:00:00">
  <Customer CustomerID="11000" />
</OrderHeader>
<OrderHeader SalesOrderID="43767" OrderDate="2005-07-18T00:00:00">
  <Customer CustomerID="11001" />
</OrderHeader>
<OrderHeader SalesOrderID="51493" OrderDate="2007-07-20T00:00:00">
  <Customer CustomerID="11001" />
</OrderHeader>
<OrderHeader SalesOrderID="72773" OrderDate="2008-06-12T00:00:00">
  <Customer CustomerID="11001" />
</OrderHeader>
<OrderHeader SalesOrderID="43736" OrderDate="2005-07-10T00:00:00">
  <Customer CustomerID="11002" />
</OrderHeader>
<OrderHeader SalesOrderID="51238" OrderDate="2007-07-04T00:00:00">
  <Customer CustomerID="11002" />
</OrderHeader>
<OrderHeader SalesOrderID="53237" OrderDate="2007-08-27T00:00:00">
  <Customer CustomerID="11002" />
</OrderHeader>
<OrderHeader SalesOrderID="43701" OrderDate="2005-07-01T00:00:00">
  <Customer CustomerID="11003" />
</OrderHeader>
```

These results are probably not what you wanted. To keep the XML hierarchy matching the table hierarchy, you must list at least one column from the parent table before any column from a child table. If there are three levels of tables, at least one other column from the child table must come before any from the grandchild table, and so on.

FOR XML EXPLICIT

FOR XML EXPLICIT is the most complex but also the most powerful and flexible of the three original *FOR XML* options. We cover it now for completeness, but recommend using the simpler *FOR XML PATH* feature added in SQL Server 2008 (covered shortly). As you'll see, *FOR XML PATH* can shape query results into virtually any desired XML with much less effort than using *FOR XML EXPLICIT*.

With *FOR XML EXPLICIT*, SQL Server constructs XML based on a *UNION* query of the various levels of output elements. So, if again you have the *Customer* and *SalesOrderHeader* tables and you want to produce XML output, you must have two *SELECT* statements with a *UNION*. If you add the *SalesOrderDetail* table, you must add another *UNION* statement and *SELECT* statement.

As we said, *FOR XML EXPLICIT* is more complex than its predecessors. For starters, you are responsible for defining two additional columns that establish the hierarchical relationship of the

XML: a *Tag* column that acts as a row's identifier and a *Parent* column that links child records to the parent record's *Tag* value (similar to *EmployeeID* and *ManagerID*). You must also alias all columns to indicate the element, *Tag*, and display name for the XML output, as shown in Listing 6-16. Keep in mind that only the first *SELECT* statement must follow these rules; any aliases in subsequent *SELECT* statements in a *UNION* query are ignored.

LISTING 6-16 Shaping hierarchical XML using *FOR XML EXPLICIT*.

```
SELECT
  1 AS Tag, -- Tag this resultset as level 1
  NULL AS Parent,  -- Level 1 has no parent
  CustomerID AS [Customer!1!CustomerID], -- level 1 value
  NULL AS [SalesOrder!2!SalesOrderID],  -- level 2 value
  NULL AS [SalesOrder!2!OrderDate]  -- level 2 value
 FROM Sales.Customer AS Customer
 WHERE Customer.CustomerID IN(11077, 11078)
 UNION ALL
 SELECT
  2, -- Tag this resultset as level 2
  1, -- Link to parent at level 1
  Customer.CustomerID,
  OrderHeader.SalesOrderID,
  OrderHeader.OrderDate
 FROM Sales.Customer AS Customer
  INNER JOIN Sales.SalesOrderHeader AS OrderHeader
         ON OrderHeader.CustomerID = Customer.CustomerID
 WHERE Customer.CustomerID IN(11077, 11078)
 ORDER BY
  [Customer!1!CustomerID], [SalesOrder!2!SalesOrderID]
 FOR XML EXPLICIT
```

Execute this query and click the XML hyperlink to see the following output:

```
<Customer CustomerID="11077">
  <SalesOrder SalesOrderID="44407" OrderDate="2005-10-16T00:00:00" />
  <SalesOrder SalesOrderID="51651" OrderDate="2007-07-29T00:00:00" />
  <SalesOrder SalesOrderID="60042" OrderDate="2007-12-14T00:00:00" />
</Customer>
<Customer CustomerID="11078">
  <SalesOrder SalesOrderID="52789" OrderDate="2007-08-19T00:00:00" />
  <SalesOrder SalesOrderID="53993" OrderDate="2007-09-08T00:00:00" />
  <SalesOrder SalesOrderID="54214" OrderDate="2007-09-12T00:00:00" />
  <SalesOrder SalesOrderID="54268" OrderDate="2007-09-13T00:00:00" />
  <SalesOrder SalesOrderID="56449" OrderDate="2007-10-21T00:00:00" />
  <SalesOrder SalesOrderID="57281" OrderDate="2007-11-02T00:00:00" />
  <SalesOrder SalesOrderID="57969" OrderDate="2007-11-15T00:00:00" />
  <SalesOrder SalesOrderID="58429" OrderDate="2007-11-23T00:00:00" />
  <SalesOrder SalesOrderID="58490" OrderDate="2007-11-24T00:00:00" />
  <SalesOrder SalesOrderID="61443" OrderDate="2008-01-04T00:00:00" />
  <SalesOrder SalesOrderID="62245" OrderDate="2008-01-17T00:00:00" />
  <SalesOrder SalesOrderID="62413" OrderDate="2008-01-20T00:00:00" />
  <SalesOrder SalesOrderID="67668" OrderDate="2008-04-05T00:00:00" />
```

```
  <SalesOrder SalesOrderID="68285" OrderDate="2008-04-15T00:00:00" />
  <SalesOrder SalesOrderID="68288" OrderDate="2008-04-15T00:00:00" />
  <SalesOrder SalesOrderID="73869" OrderDate="2008-06-27T00:00:00" />
  <SalesOrder SalesOrderID="75084" OrderDate="2008-07-31T00:00:00" />
</Customer>
```

This result resembles the output generated by the *FOR XML AUTO* sample in Listing 6-14. So what is gained by composing a more complex query with *FOR XML EXPLICIT?* Well, *FOR XML EXPLICIT* allows for some alternative outputs that are not achievable using *FOR XML AUTO*. For example, you can specify that certain values be composed as elements instead of attributes by appending *!ELEMENT* to the end of the aliased column, as shown in Listing 6-17.

LISTING 6-17 Using *!ELEMENT* to customize the hierarchical XML generated by *FOR XML EXPLICIT*.

```
SELECT
  1 AS Tag, -- Tag this resultset as level 1
  NULL AS Parent,  -- Level 1 has no parent
  CustomerID AS [Customer!1!CustomerID], -- level 1 value
  NULL AS [SalesOrder!2!SalesOrderID],  -- level 2 value
  NULL AS [SalesOrder!2!OrderDate!ELEMENT] -- level 2 value rendered as an
element
 FROM Sales.Customer AS Customer
 WHERE Customer.CustomerID IN(11077, 11078)
 UNION ALL
 SELECT
  2, -- Tag this resultset as level 2
  1, -- Link to parent at level 1
  Customer.CustomerID,
  OrderHeader.SalesOrderID,
  OrderHeader.OrderDate
 FROM Sales.Customer AS Customer
  INNER JOIN Sales.SalesOrderHeader AS OrderHeader
         ON OrderHeader.CustomerID = Customer.CustomerID
 WHERE Customer.CustomerID IN(11077, 11078)
 ORDER BY
  [Customer!1!CustomerID], [SalesOrder!2!SalesOrderID]
 FOR XML EXPLICIT
```

Only one minor change was made (the *OrderDate* column alias has *!ELEMENT* appended to the end of it). Aliasing a column with *!ELEMENT* in a *FOR XML EXPLICIT* query results in that column being rendered as an element instead of an attribute, as shown here:

```
<Customer CustomerID="11077">
  <SalesOrder SalesOrderID="44407">
    <OrderDate>2005-10-16T00:00:00</OrderDate>
  </SalesOrder>
  <SalesOrder SalesOrderID="51651">
    <OrderDate>2007-07-29T00:00:00</OrderDate>
  </SalesOrder>
  <SalesOrder SalesOrderID="60042">
    <OrderDate>2007-12-14T00:00:00</OrderDate>
  </SalesOrder>
```

```
</Customer>
<Customer CustomerID="11078">
  <SalesOrder SalesOrderID="52789">
    <OrderDate>2007-08-19T00:00:00</OrderDate>
  </SalesOrder>
  <SalesOrder SalesOrderID="53993">
    <OrderDate>2007-09-08T00:00:00</OrderDate>
  </SalesOrder>
  <SalesOrder SalesOrderID="54214">
    <OrderDate>2007-09-12T00:00:00</OrderDate>
  </SalesOrder>
    :
```

Notice that the *OrderDate* is now being rendered as a child element of the *SalesOrder* element. Thus, *FOR XML EXPLICIT* mode enables greater customization, but it also requires creating complex queries to achieve custom results. For example, to add a few more fields from *OrderHeader* and to add some additional fields from *OrderDetail* (a third hierarchical table), you would have to write the query as shown in Listing 6-18.

LISTING 6-18 Using *FOR XML EXPLICIT* to produce three-level hierarchical XML order data.

```
SELECT
  1 AS Tag,
  NULL AS Parent,
  CustomerID AS [Customer!1!CustomerID],
  NULL AS [SalesOrder!2!SalesOrderID],
  NULL AS [SalesOrder!2!TotalDue],
  NULL AS [SalesOrder!2!OrderDate!ELEMENT],
  NULL AS [SalesOrder!2!ShipDate!ELEMENT],
  NULL AS [SalesDetail!3!ProductID],
  NULL AS [SalesDetail!3!OrderQty],
  NULL AS [SalesDetail!3!LineTotal]
 FROM Sales.Customer AS Customer
 WHERE Customer.CustomerID IN(11077, 11078)
 UNION ALL
 SELECT
  2,
  1,
  Customer.CustomerID,
  OrderHeader.SalesOrderID,
  OrderHeader.TotalDue,
  OrderHeader.OrderDate,
  OrderHeader.ShipDate,
  NULL,
  NULL,
  NULL
 FROM Sales.Customer AS Customer
  INNER JOIN Sales.SalesOrderHeader AS OrderHeader
   ON OrderHeader.CustomerID = Customer.CustomerID
 WHERE Customer.CustomerID IN(11077, 11078)
 UNION ALL
SELECT
  3,
```

```
    2,
    Customer.CustomerID,
    OrderHeader.SalesOrderID,
    OrderHeader.TotalDue,
    OrderHeader.OrderDate,
    OrderHeader.ShipDate,
    OrderDetail.ProductID,
    OrderDetail.OrderQty,
    OrderDetail.LineTotal
   FROM Sales.Customer AS Customer
    INNER JOIN Sales.SalesOrderHeader AS OrderHeader
     ON OrderHeader.CustomerID = Customer.CustomerID
    INNER JOIN Sales.SalesOrderDetail AS OrderDetail
     ON OrderDetail.SalesOrderID = OrderHeader.SalesOrderID
   WHERE Customer.CustomerID IN(11077, 11078)
   ORDER BY [Customer!1!CustomerID], [SalesOrder!2!SalesOrderID]
   FOR XML EXPLICIT
```

This query produces the following XML:

```
<Customer CustomerID="11077">
  <SalesOrder SalesOrderID="44407" TotalDue="3729.3640">
    <OrderDate>2005-10-16T00:00:00</OrderDate>
    <ShipDate>2005-10-23T00:00:00</ShipDate>
    <SalesDetail ProductID="778" OrderQty="1" LineTotal="3374.990000" />
    <SalesDetail ProductID="781" OrderQty="1" LineTotal="2319.990000" />
    <SalesDetail ProductID="880" OrderQty="1" LineTotal="54.990000" />
  </SalesOrder>
  <SalesOrder SalesOrderID="51651" TotalDue="2624.3529">
    <OrderDate>2007-07-29T00:00:00</OrderDate>
    <ShipDate>2007-08-05T00:00:00</ShipDate>
  </SalesOrder>
  <SalesOrder SalesOrderID="60042" TotalDue="2673.0613">
    <OrderDate>2007-12-14T00:00:00</OrderDate>
    <ShipDate>2007-12-21T00:00:00</ShipDate>
    <SalesDetail ProductID="969" OrderQty="1" LineTotal="2384.070000" />
    <SalesDetail ProductID="707" OrderQty="1" LineTotal="34.990000" />
  </SalesOrder>
</Customer>
<Customer CustomerID="11078">
  <SalesOrder SalesOrderID="52789" TotalDue="71.2394">
    <OrderDate>2007-08-19T00:00:00</OrderDate>
    <ShipDate>2007-08-26T00:00:00</ShipDate>
    <SalesDetail ProductID="923" OrderQty="1" LineTotal="4.990000" />
    <SalesDetail ProductID="707" OrderQty="1" LineTotal="34.990000" />
    <SalesDetail ProductID="860" OrderQty="1" LineTotal="24.490000" />
    <SalesDetail ProductID="922" OrderQty="1" LineTotal="3.990000" />
    <SalesDetail ProductID="877" OrderQty="1" LineTotal="7.950000" />
  </SalesOrder>
    :
```

As you can see, the code has become quite complex, and will become even more complex as you add additional data to the output. Although this query is perfectly valid, the same result can be achieved with far less effort using the *FOR XML PATH* statement.

Additional *FOR XML* Features

Just about all of the original XML support first introduced in SQL Server 2000 XML support revolves around *FOR XML*, a feature that is still very much underused by developers. Since then, SQL Server has enhanced *FOR XML* in the following ways:

- Using the *TYPE* option, *FOR XML* can output to an *xml* data type (as opposed to streamed results) from a *SELECT* statement, which in turn allows you to nest the results of *SELECT...FOR XML* into another *SELECT* statement.
- The *FOR XML PATH* option allows you to more easily shape data and produce element-based XML than the *FOR XML EXPLICIT* option that we just covered.
- You can explicitly specify a *ROOT* element for your output.
- You can produce element-based XML with *FOR XML AUTO*.
- *FOR XML* can produce XML with an embedded, inferred XSD schema.

The *TYPE* Option

As of SQL Server 2005, *xml* is an intrinsic data type of SQL Server. Thus, you can cast the XML output from a *FOR XML* query directly into an *xml* data type instance, as opposed to streaming XML results directly or immediately to the client. You accomplish this by using the *TYPE* keyword after your *FOR XML* statement, as shown in Listing 6-19.

LISTING 6-19 Using the *TYPE* option with *FOR XML AUTO* to cast a subquery result set as an *xml* data type.

```
SELECT
  CustomerID,
  (SELECT SalesOrderID, TotalDue, OrderDate, ShipDate
   FROM Sales.SalesOrderHeader AS OrderHeader
   WHERE CustomerID = Customer.CustomerID
   FOR XML AUTO, TYPE) AS OrderHeaders
 FROM
  Sales.Customer AS Customer
 WHERE
  CustomerID IN (11000, 11001)
```

This query returns two columns. The first is the integer *CustomerID* and the second is an *OrderHeaders* column of type *xml*. The second column is constructed by a subquery that generates

XML using *FOR XML AUTO*, and the *TYPE* option casts the generated XML from the subquery into an *xml* data type that gets returned as the *OrderHeaders* column of the main query.

FOR XML PATH

As we already mentioned, *FOR XML PATH* gives you fine control over the generated XML much like *FOR XML EXPLICIT* does, but is much simpler to use. With *FOR XML PATH*, you simply assign column aliases with XPath expressions that shape your XML output, as shown in Listing 6-20.

LISTING 6-20 Using *FOR XML PATH* to shape XML output with XPath-based column aliases.

```
SELECT
  BusinessEntityID AS [@BusinessEntityID],
  FirstName AS [ContactName/First],
  LastName AS [ContactName/Last],
  EmailAddress AS [ContactEmailAddress/EmailAddress1]
 FROM
  HumanResources.vEmployee
 FOR XML PATH('Contact')
```

The output looks like this:

```
<row BusinessEntityID="263">
  <ContactName>
    <First>Jean</First>
    <Last>Trenary</Last>
  </ContactName>
  <ContactEmailAddress>
    <EmailAddress1>jean0@adventure-works.com</EmailAddress1>
  </ContactEmailAddress>
</row>
<row BusinessEntityID="78">
  <ContactName>
    <First>Reuben</First>
    <Last>D'sa</Last>
  </ContactName>
  <ContactEmailAddress>
    <EmailAddress1>reuben0@adventure-works.com</EmailAddress1>
  </ContactEmailAddress>
</row>
 :
```

Notice that the *BusinessEntityID* column is rendered as an attribute. This is because it was aliased as *@BusinessEntityID*, and the @-symbol in XPath means "attribute." Also notice that the *FirstName* and *LastName* columns are rendered as *First* and *Last* elements nested within a *ContactName* element. This again is due to the XPath-based syntax of the column aliases, *ContactName/First* and *ContactName/Last*.

Now let's revisit the three-level hierarchical example we recently demonstrated with *FOR XML EXPLICIT* in Listing 6-18. Using the *TYPE* option in conjunction with *FOR XML PATH*, you can reproduce that awful and complex query with a much simpler version, as shown in Listing 6-21.

LISTING 6-21 Using *FOR XML PATH* to shape XML output for a three-level hierarchy.

```
SELECT
  CustomerID AS [@CustomerID],
  (SELECT
    SalesOrderID AS [@SalesOrderID],
    TotalDue AS [@TotalDue],
    OrderDate,
    ShipDate,
    (SELECT
      ProductID AS [@ProductID],
      OrderQty AS [@OrderQty],
      LineTotal AS [@LineTotal]
     FROM Sales.SalesOrderDetail
     WHERE SalesOrderID = OrderHeader.SalesOrderID
     FOR XML PATH('OrderDetail'), TYPE)
   FROM Sales.SalesOrderHeader AS OrderHeader
   WHERE CustomerID = Customer.CustomerID
   FOR XML PATH('OrderHeader'), TYPE)
 FROM Sales.Customer AS Customer
  INNER JOIN Person.Person AS Contact
   ON Contact.BusinessEntityID = Customer.PersonID
 WHERE CustomerID BETWEEN 11000 AND 11999
 FOR XML PATH ('Customer')
```

Isn't that much better than the contorted *UNION*-based approach taken by *FOR XML EXPLICIT* in Listing 6-18? In this simpler version that produces the same result, subqueries are used with the *XML PATH* statement in conjunction with *TYPE* to produce element-based XML nested inside a much larger *FOR XML PATH* statement. This returns each separate *Order* for the customer as a new child node of the *CustomerID* node. And again, XPath syntax is used in the column aliases to define element and attribute structure in the generated XML. Here are the results of the query:

```
<Customer CustomerID="11480">
  <OrderHeader SalesOrderID="51053" TotalDue="2288.9187">
    <OrderDate>2007-06-28T00:00:00</OrderDate>
    <ShipDate>2007-07-05T00:00:00</ShipDate>
    <OrderDetail ProductID="779" OrderQty="1" LineTotal="2071.419600" />
  </OrderHeader>
  <OrderHeader SalesOrderID="52329" TotalDue="2552.5169">
    <OrderDate>2007-08-10T00:00:00</OrderDate>
    <ShipDate>2007-08-17T00:00:00</ShipDate>
    <OrderDetail ProductID="782" OrderQty="1" LineTotal="2294.990000" />
    <OrderDetail ProductID="870" OrderQty="1" LineTotal="4.990000" />
    <OrderDetail ProductID="871" OrderQty="1" LineTotal="9.990000" />
  </OrderHeader>
  <OrderHeader SalesOrderID="62813" TotalDue="612.1369">
    <OrderDate>2008-01-26T00:00:00</OrderDate>
    <ShipDate>2008-02-02T00:00:00</ShipDate>
```

```
    <OrderDetail ProductID="999" OrderQty="1" LineTotal="539.990000" />
    <OrderDetail ProductID="872" OrderQty="1" LineTotal="8.990000" />
    <OrderDetail ProductID="870" OrderQty="1" LineTotal="4.990000" />
  </OrderHeader>
</Customer>
<Customer CustomerID="11197">
  <OrderHeader SalesOrderID="57340" TotalDue="46.7194">
    :
```

If you are familiar and comfortable with XPath, you will appreciate some additional *XML PATH* features. You can use the following XPath node functions to further control the shape of your XML output:

- data
- comment
- node
- text
- processing-instruction

The following example uses the *data* and *comment* methods of XPath. The *data* method takes the results of the underlying query and places them all inside one element. The *comment* method takes data and transforms it into an XML comment, as demonstrated in Listing 6-22.

LISTING 6-22 Using *FOR XML PATH* with the *comment* and *data* XPath methods.

```
SELECT
  Customer.BusinessEntityID AS [@CustomerID],
  Customer.FirstName + ' ' + Customer.LastName AS [comment()],
  (SELECT
    SalesOrderID AS [@SalesOrderID],
    TotalDue AS [@TotalDue],
    OrderDate,
    ShipDate,
    (SELECT ProductID AS [data()]
     FROM Sales.SalesOrderDetail
     WHERE SalesOrderID = OrderHeader.SalesOrderID
     FOR XML PATH('')) AS [ProductIDs]
   FROM Sales.SalesOrderHeader AS OrderHeader
   WHERE CustomerID = Customer.BusinessEntityID
   FOR XML PATH('OrderHeader'), TYPE)
 FROM Sales.vIndividualCustomer AS Customer
 WHERE BusinessEntityID IN (11000, 11001)
 FOR XML PATH ('Customer')
```

As you can see from the results, the concatenated contact name becomes an XML comment, and the subquery of *Product IDs* is transformed into one element:

```
<Customer CustomerID="11000">
  <!--Mary Young-->
  <OrderHeader SalesOrderID="43793" TotalDue="3756.9890">
```

```
    <OrderDate>2005-07-22T00:00:00</OrderDate>
    <ShipDate>2005-07-29T00:00:00</ShipDate>
    <ProductIDs>771</ProductIDs>
  </OrderHeader>
  <OrderHeader SalesOrderID="51522" TotalDue="2587.8769">
    <OrderDate>2007-07-22T00:00:00</OrderDate>
    <ShipDate>2007-07-29T00:00:00</ShipDate>
    <ProductIDs>779 878</ProductIDs>
  </OrderHeader>
  <OrderHeader SalesOrderID="57418" TotalDue="2770.2682">
    <OrderDate>2007-11-04T00:00:00</OrderDate>
    <ShipDate>2007-11-11T00:00:00</ShipDate>
    <ProductIDs>966 934 923 707 881</ProductIDs>
  </OrderHeader>
</Customer>
<Customer CustomerID="11001">
  <!--Amber Young-->
  <OrderHeader SalesOrderID="43767" TotalDue="3729.3640">
    <OrderDate>2005-07-18T00:00:00</OrderDate>
        :
```

Emitting a *ROOT* Element

Technically, an XML document must be contained inside of a single root element. You've seen many applied uses of *FOR XML* that generate all types of XML, but without a root element, the generated XML can only represent a portion of an XML document. The *ROOT* option allows you to add a main, or root, element to your *FOR XML* output so that the query results can be consumed as a complete XML document. You can combine *ROOT* with other *FOR XML* keywords. In Listing 6-23, *ROOT* is used with *FOR XML AUTO* to wrap a single *Orders* root element around the results of the query.

LISTING 6-23 Using *FOR XML* with *ROOT* to generate a root element.

```
SELECT
  Customer.CustomerID,
  OrderDetail.SalesOrderID,
  OrderDetail.OrderDate
 FROM
  Sales.Customer AS Customer
   INNER JOIN Sales.SalesOrderHeader  AS OrderDetail
    ON OrderDetail.CustomerID = Customer.CustomerID
 WHERE
  Customer.CustomerID IN (11000, 11001)
 ORDER BY
  Customer.CustomerID
 FOR XML AUTO, ROOT('Orders')
```

The output looks like this:

```
<Orders>
  <Customer CustomerID="11000">
    <OrderDetail SalesOrderID="43793" OrderDate="2005-07-22T00:00:00" />
```

```
    <OrderDetail SalesOrderID="51522" OrderDate="2007-07-22T00:00:00" />
    <OrderDetail SalesOrderID="57418" OrderDate="2007-11-04T00:00:00" />
  </Customer>
  <Customer CustomerID="11001">
    <OrderDetail SalesOrderID="43767" OrderDate="2005-07-18T00:00:00" />
    <OrderDetail SalesOrderID="51493" OrderDate="2007-07-20T00:00:00" />
    <OrderDetail SalesOrderID="72773" OrderDate="2008-06-12T00:00:00" />
  </Customer>
</Orders>
```

The code output here is the same as any *FOR XML AUTO* output for this query, except that the *XML ROOT* we specified with the *ROOT* keyword now surrounds the data. In this example, we used *ROOT ('Orders')*, so our output is surrounded with an *<Orders>* XML element.

Producing an Inline XSD Schema

As you've seen, schemas provide an enforceable structure for your XML data. When you export data using the *FOR XML* syntax, you might want to include an inline XML schema for the recipient so that the recipient can enforce the rules on their end as well. When you use the *RAW* and *AUTO* modes, you can produce an inline XSD schema as part of the output by using the *XMLSCHEMA* keyword, as shown in Listing 6-24.

LISTING 6-24 Using *FOR XML* with *XMLSCHEMA* to generate an inline XSD schema with the query results.

```
SELECT
  Customer.CustomerID,
  OrderDetail.SalesOrderID,
  OrderDetail.OrderDate
 FROM
  Sales.Customer AS Customer
   INNER JOIN Sales.SalesOrderHeader  AS OrderDetail
    ON OrderDetail.CustomerID = Customer.CustomerID
 WHERE
  Customer.CustomerID IN (11000, 11001)
 ORDER BY
  Customer.CustomerID
 FOR XML AUTO, ROOT('Orders'), XMLSCHEMA
```

The output looks like this:

```
<Orders>
  <xsd:schema targetNamespace="urn:schemas-microsoft-com:sql:SqlRowSet4"
xmlns:schema="urn:schemas-microsoft-com:sql:SqlRowSet4" xmlns:xsd="http://www.w3.org/2001/
XMLSchema" xmlns:sqltypes="http://schemas.microsoft.com/sqlserver/2004/sqltypes"
elementFormDefault="qualified">
    <xsd:import namespace="http://schemas.microsoft.com/sqlserver/2004/sqltypes"
schemaLocation="http://schemas.microsoft.com/sqlserver/2004/sqltypes/sqltypes.xsd" />
    <xsd:element name="Customer">
      <xsd:complexType>
        <xsd:sequence>
          <xsd:element ref="schema:OrderDetail" minOccurs="0" maxOccurs="unbounded" />
```

```
      </xsd:sequence>
      <xsd:attribute name="CustomerID" type="sqltypes:int" use="required" />
    </xsd:complexType>
  </xsd:element>
  <xsd:element name="OrderDetail">
    <xsd:complexType>
      <xsd:attribute name="SalesOrderID" type="sqltypes:int" use="required" />
      <xsd:attribute name="OrderDate" type="sqltypes:datetime" use="required" />
    </xsd:complexType>
  </xsd:element>
 </xsd:schema>
 <Customer xmlns="urn:schemas-microsoft-com:sql:SqlRowSet4" CustomerID="11000">
   <OrderDetail SalesOrderID="43793" OrderDate="2005-07-22T00:00:00" />
   <OrderDetail SalesOrderID="51522" OrderDate="2007-07-22T00:00:00" />
   <OrderDetail SalesOrderID="57418" OrderDate="2007-11-04T00:00:00" />
 </Customer>
 <Customer xmlns="urn:schemas-microsoft-com:sql:SqlRowSet4" CustomerID="11001">
   <OrderDetail SalesOrderID="43767" OrderDate="2005-07-18T00:00:00" />
   <OrderDetail SalesOrderID="51493" OrderDate="2007-07-20T00:00:00" />
   <OrderDetail SalesOrderID="72773" OrderDate="2008-06-12T00:00:00" />
 </Customer>
</Orders>
```

SQL Server infers the schema based on the underlying data types of the result set. For example, the *SalesOrderID* field is set to an *int* and is a required field (as per the inline schema based on the properties of the field in the underlying SQL table).

Producing Element-Based XML

Element-based XML is more verbose than attribute-based XML but is usually easier to view and work with. Initially, in SQL Server 2000, *FOR XML RAW* and *FOR XML AUTO* could only generate attribute-based XML (as shown in Listings 6-13 and 6-14). As we've demonstrated in Listings 6-17 and 6-20, you can customize the generated XML and produce element-based XML using *FOR XML EXPLICIT* and (later) *FOR XML PATH*.

Both *FOR XML RAW* and *FOR XML AUTO* were later enhanced to support the *ELEMENTS* keyword, enabling them to alternatively produce element-based XML rather than attribute-based XML. When all you need is element-based XML, and you require no other customization over the shape of generated XML, you will find it much easier to use *FOR XML RAW/AUTO* with *ELEMENT* rather than *FOR XML EXPLICIT* (and even *FOR XML PATH*). Listing 6-25 demonstrates this.

LISTING 6-25 Using *FOR XML AUTO* with *ELEMENTS* to produce element-based hierarchical XML.

```
SELECT
  Customer.CustomerID,
  OrderDetail.SalesOrderID,
  OrderDetail.OrderDate
 FROM
  Sales.Customer AS Customer
```

```
    INNER JOIN Sales.SalesOrderHeader AS OrderDetail
     ON OrderDetail.CustomerID = Customer.CustomerID
  WHERE
   Customer.CustomerID IN (11000, 11001)
  ORDER BY
   Customer.CustomerID
  FOR XML AUTO, ROOT('Orders'), ELEMENTS
```

Here are the query results:

```
<Orders>
  <Customer>
    <CustomerID>11000</CustomerID>
    <OrderDetail>
      <SalesOrderID>43793</SalesOrderID>
      <OrderDate>2005-07-22T00:00:00</OrderDate>
    </OrderDetail>
    <OrderDetail>
      <SalesOrderID>51522</SalesOrderID>
      <OrderDate>2007-07-22T00:00:00</OrderDate>
    </OrderDetail>
    <OrderDetail>
      <SalesOrderID>57418</SalesOrderID>
      <OrderDate>2007-11-04T00:00:00</OrderDate>
    </OrderDetail>
  </Customer>
  <Customer>
    <CustomerID>11001</CustomerID>
    <OrderDetail>
      <SalesOrderID>43767</SalesOrderID>
      <OrderDate>2005-07-18T00:00:00</OrderDate>
    </OrderDetail>
    <OrderDetail>
      <SalesOrderID>51493</SalesOrderID>
      <OrderDate>2007-07-20T00:00:00</OrderDate>
    </OrderDetail>
    <OrderDetail>
      <SalesOrderID>72773</SalesOrderID>
      <OrderDate>2008-06-12T00:00:00</OrderDate>
    </OrderDetail>
  </Customer>
</Orders>
```

You can see that each column of the query becomes a nested element in the resulting XML, as opposed to an attribute of one single element. The *ELEMENTS* keyword used in conjunction with *FOR XML RAW* or *FOR XML AUTO* converts each column from your result set to an individual XML element. *FOR XML AUTO* also converts each row from a joined table to a new XML element, as just demonstrated.

Shredding XML Using *OPENXML*

Up to this point, you have been using *FOR XML* to compose XML from rows of data, but what if you already have XML data and want to shred it back into relational data? SQL Server 2000 introduced a feature called *OPENXML* for this purpose. The *OPENXML* system function is designed for this purpose, and allows an XML document file to be shredded into T-SQL rows as we'll explain next. Since the introduction of the native *xml* data type in SQL Server 2005, XQuery (covered in the next section) offers even more choices for extracting data from XML input.

To shred data XML into relational rows using *OPENXML*, you first create a handle to the XML document using the system stored procedure *sp_xml_preparedocument*. This system-stored procedure takes an XML document and creates a representation that you can reference using a special handle, which it returns via an *OUTPUT* parameter. *OPENXML* uses this handle along with a specified path and behaves like a database view to the XML data, so you simply choose *SELECT* from the *OPENXML* function just as you would *SELECT* from a table or a view. The code in Listing 6-26 shows an example of *OPENXML* in action.

LISTING 6-26 Using *FOR XML AUTO* with *ELEMENTS* to produce element-based hierarchical XML.

```
DECLARE @handle int
DECLARE @OrdersXML varchar(max)
SET @OrdersXML = '
<Orders>
  <Customer CustomerID="HERBC" ContactName="Charlie Herb">
     <Order CustomerID="HERBC" EmployeeID="5" OrderDate="2011-11-04">
        <OrderDetail OrderID="10248" ProductID="16" Quantity="12"/>
        <OrderDetail OrderID="10248" ProductID="32" Quantity="10"/>
     </Order>
     <Order CustomerID="HERBC" EmployeeID="2" OrderDate="2011-11-16">
        <OrderDetail OrderID="10283" ProductID="99" Quantity="3"/>
     </Order>
  </Customer>
  <Customer CustomerID="HINKM" ContactName="Matt Hink">
     <Order CustomerID="HINKM" EmployeeID="3" OrderDate="2011-11-23">
        <OrderDetail OrderID="10283" ProductID="99" Quantity="3"/>
     </Order>
  </Customer>
</Orders>'

-- Get a handle onto the XML document
EXEC sp_xml_preparedocument @handle OUTPUT, @OrdersXML

-- Use the OPENXML rowset provider against the handle to parse/query the XML
SELECT *
 FROM OPENXML(@handle, '/Orders/Customer/Order')
 WITH (
  CustomerName varchar(max) '../@ContactName',
  OrderDate date)
```

This code allows you to query and work with the XML text as if it were relational data. The output looks like this:

```
CustomerName    OrderDate
--------------- --------------
Charlie Herb    2011-11-04
Charlie Herb    2011-11-16
Matt Hink       2011-11-23
```

This code first calls *sp_xml_preparedocument* to get a handle over the XML of customer orders. The handle is passed as the first parameter to *OPENXML*. The second parameter is an XPath expression that specifies the *row pattern*, and this identifies the nodes within the XML that are to be processed as rows. In this example, the XPath expression */Orders/Customer/Order* drills down to the order level for each customer. There are three orders in the XML, so the query produces three rows with order dates (one for each order). The customer name is not available at the order level; it must be retrieved by reaching "up" one level for the *Customer* element's *ContactName* attribute using a column pattern. This is achieved using the *WITH* clause. In this example, the *CustomerName* column is based on the column pattern *../@ContactName* to obtain the *ContactName* attribute (remember that in XPath an @-symbol means "attribute") from the parent *Customer* node (as denoted by the *../* path syntax).

Querying XML Data Using XQuery

Storing XML in the database is one thing; querying it efficiently is another. Prior to the *xml* data type in SQL Server 2005, you had to deconstruct the XML and move element and attribute data into relational columns to perform a query on the XML data residing in the text column. You could also resort to some other searching mechanism, such as character pattern matching or full-text search, neither of which provides completely reliable parsing capability. Today, XQuery provides a native and elegant way to parse and query XML data in SQL Server.

Understanding XQuery Expressions and XPath

XQuery is a language used to query and process XML data. XQuery is a W3C standard, and its specification is located at *http://www.w3.org/TR/xquery/*. The XQuery specification contains several descriptions of requirements, use cases, and data models. We encourage you to review the specification to get a full understanding of what XQuery is all about. For now, we will explain enough to cover the basics. After reading this section, you will be able to select, filter, and update XML data using XQuery.

Because XQuery is an XML language, all the rules of XML apply. XQuery uses lowercase element names ("keywords"), and because XML itself is case-sensitive, you must take this into account when writing queries. Although XQuery has some powerful formatting and processing commands, it is primarily a query language (as its name suggests), so we will focus here on writing queries. The body of a query consists of two parts: an XPath expression and a *FLWOR* (pronounced "flower") expression. (FLWOR is an acronym based on the primitive XQuery keywords *for, let, where, order by,* and *return*.)

XPath Expressions

XPath, another W3C standard (*http://www.w3.org/TR/xpath*), uses path expressions to identify specific nodes and attributes in an XML document. These path expressions are similar to the syntax you see when you work with a computer file system (for example, C:\folder\myfile.doc). Take a look at the following XML document:

```
<catalog>
  <book category="ITPro">
    <title>Windows Step By Step</title>
    <author>Jeff Hay</author>
    <price>49.99</price>
  </book>
  <book category="Developer">
    <title>Learning ADO .NET</title>
    <author>Holly Holt</author>
    <price>39.93</price>
  </book>
  <book category="ITPro">
    <title>Administering IIS</title>
    <author>Jed Brown</author>
    <price>59.99</price>
  </book>
</catalog>
```

The following XPath expression selects the root element catalog:

```
/catalog
```

This XPath expression selects all the book elements of the catalog root element:

```
/catalog/book
```

And this XPath expression selects all the author elements of all the book elements of the catalog root element:

```
/catalog/book/author
```

XPath enables you to specify a subset of data within the XML (via its location within the XML structure) that you want to work with. XQuery is more robust and allows you to perform more complex queries against the XML data using *FLWOR* expressions combined with XPath.

FLWOR Expressions

Just as *SELECT, FROM, WHERE, GROUP BY,* and *ORDER BY* form the basis of the SQL selection logic, the *for, let, where, order by,* and *return* (*FLWOR*) keywords form the basis of every XQuery query you write. You use the *for* and *let* keywords to assign variables and iterate through the data within the context of the XQuery query. The *where* keyword works as a restriction and outputs the value of the variable.

For example, the following basic XQuery query uses the XPath expression */catalog/book* to obtain a reference to all the *<book>* nodes, and the *for* keyword initiates a loop, but only of elements where the *category* attribute is equal to *"ITPro"*. This simple code snippet iterates through each */catalog/book* node using the *$b* variable with the *for* statement only where the category attribute is *"ITPro"* and then returns as output the resulting information in descending order by the author's name using the *order* keyword:

```
for $b in /catalog/book
 where $b/@category="ITPro"
 order by $b/author[1] descending
 return ($b)
```

Listing 6-27 shows a simple example that uses this XQuery expression on an *xml* data type variable. XML is assigned to the variable, and then the preceding XQuery expression is used in the *query* method (explained in the next section) of the *xml* data type.

LISTING 6-27 A simple XQuery example.

```
DECLARE @Books xml = '
<catalog>
  <book category="ITPro">
    <title>Windows Step By Step</title>
    <author>Jeff Hay</author>
    <price>49.99</price>
  </book>
  <book category="Developer">
    <title>Learning ADO .NET</title>
    <author>Holly Holt</author>
    <price>39.93</price>
  </book>
  <book category="ITPro">
    <title>Administering IIS</title>
    <author>Ted Bremer</author>
    <price>59.99</price>
  </book>
</catalog>'

SELECT @Books.query('
  <ITProBooks>
    {
      for $b in /catalog/book
      where $b/@category="ITPro"
      order by $b/author[1] descending
      return ($b)
    }
  </ITProBooks>')
```

The results are as follows:

```
<ITProBooks>
  <book category="ITPro">
    <title>Administering IIS</title>
    <author>Ted Bremer</author>
    <price>59.99</price>
```

```
  </book>
  <book category="ITPro">
    <title>Windows Step By Step</title>
    <author>Jeff Hay</author>
    <price>49.99</price>
  </book>
</ITProBooks>
```

Notice that Ted's record is first because the order is descending by the *author* element. Holly's record is not in the output because the *category* element is restricted to *"ITPro"*. There is a root element wrapped around the XQuery statement with *<ITProBooks>* and *</ITProBooks>*, so all the results for IT books extracted from source XML having a catalog root element are contained inside of an *ITProBooks* root element.

SQL Server XQuery in Action

SQL Server has a standards-based implementation of XQuery that directly supports XQuery functions on the *xml* data type by using five methods of the *xml* data type, as shown here:

- ***xml.exist*** Uses XQuery input to return 0, 1, or *NULL*, depending on the result of the query. This method returns 0 if no elements match, 1 if there is a match, and *NULL* if there is no XML data on which to query. The *xml.exist* method is often used for query predicates.
- ***xml.value*** Accepts an XQuery query that resolves to a single value as input and returns a SQL Server scalar type.
- ***xml.query*** Accepts an XQuery query that resolves to multiple values as input and returns an *xml* data type stream as output.
- ***xml.nodes*** Accepts an XQuery query as input and returns a single-column rowset from the XML document. In essence, this method shreds XML into multiple smaller XML results.
- ***xml.modify*** Allows you to insert, delete, or modify nodes or sequences of nodes in an *xml* data type instance using an XQuery data manipulation language (DML).

We will discuss all of these methods shortly. But first, you'll create some sample data in a simple table that contains speakers at a software developer conference and the corresponding classes they will teach. Traditionally, you would normalize such data and have a one-to-many relationship between a speakers table and a classes table. Taking an XML approach instead, you will model this as one table with the speakers' information and one XML column with the speakers' classes. In the real world, you might encounter this scenario when you have a speaker and his or her classes represented in a series of one-to-many tables in a back-office database. Then for the web database, you might "publish" a database on a frequent time interval (such as a reporting database) or transform normalized data and use the XML column for easy HTML display with extensible stylesheet transformation (XSLT).

First, create a schema for the XML data, as shown in Listing 6-28. The schema defines the data types and required properties for particular XML elements in the list of classes that will be maintained for each speaker.

LISTING 6-28 Creating an XML schema definition for speaker classes.

```
USE master
GO

IF EXISTS(SELECT name FROM sys.databases WHERE name = 'SampleDB')
 DROP DATABASE SampleDB
GO

CREATE DATABASE SampleDB
GO

USE SampleDB
GO

CREATE XML SCHEMA COLLECTION ClassesXSD AS '
<xs:schema xmlns:xs="http://www.w3.org/2001/XMLSchema">
  <xs:element name="class">
    <xs:complexType>
      <xs:attribute name="name" type="xs:string" use="required" />
    </xs:complexType>
  </xs:element>
  <xs:element name="classes">
    <xs:complexType>
      <xs:sequence>
        <xs:element ref="class" minOccurs="1" maxOccurs="unbounded" />
      </xs:sequence>
      <xs:attribute name="speakerBio" type="xs:string" use="required" />
    </xs:complexType>
  </xs:element>
</xs:schema>'
```

Next, create the *Speaker* table (and indexes), as shown in Listing 6-29. Notice that the *xml* column, *ClassesXML*, uses the *ClassesXSD* XSD schema we just created in Listing 6-28.

LISTING 6-29 Creating the *Speaker* table with the typed (XSD schema-based) indexed XML column *ClassesXML*.

```
CREATE TABLE Speaker(
 SpeakerId int IDENTITY PRIMARY KEY,
 SpeakerName varchar(50),
 Country varchar(25),
 ClassesXML xml(ClassesXSD) NOT NULL)

-- Create primary XML index
CREATE PRIMARY XML INDEX ix_speakers
        ON Speaker(ClassesXML)

-- Create secondary structural (path) XML index
CREATE XML INDEX ix_speakers_path ON Speaker(ClassesXML)
 USING XML INDEX ix_speakers FOR PATH
```

XQuery runs more efficiently when there is an XML index on the XML column. As you learned earlier, an XML index works only if there is a primary key constraint on the table (such as the *SpeakerId* primary key column in the *Speaker* table). The code in Listing 6-29 creates a primary and then a structural (*PATH*) index because our examples will apply a lot of *where* restrictions on the values of particular elements. It's also important to remember that XQuery works more efficiently if it is strongly typed, so you should always use a schema (XSD) on your XML column for the best performance. Without a schema, the SQL Server XQuery engine assumes that everything is untyped and simply treats it as string data.

You're now ready to get data into the table by using some *INSERT* statements, as shown in Listing 6-30. The final *INSERT* statement, *'Bad Speaker'*, will fail because it does not contain a *<classes>* element as required by the *ClassesXSD* schema. (Because XML is case sensitive, its *<CLASSES>* element is not a match for the *<classes>* element specified as required in the schema.)

LISTING 6-30 Populating the *Speaker* table with sample data.

```
INSERT INTO Speaker VALUES('Jeff Hay', 'USA', '
  <classes speakerBio="Jeff has solid security experience from years of hacking">
    <class name="Writing Secure Code for ASP .NET" />
    <class name="Using XQuery to Manipulate XML Data in SQL Server 2012" />
    <class name="SQL Server and Oracle Working Together" />
    <class name="Protecting against SQL Injection Attacks" />
  </classes>')

INSERT INTO Speaker VALUES('Holly Holt', 'Canada', '
  <classes speakerBio="Holly is a Canadian-born database professional">
    <class name="SQL Server Profiler" />
    <class name="Advanced SQL Querying Techniques" />
    <class name="SQL Server and Oracle Working Together" />
  </classes>')

INSERT INTO Speaker VALUES('Ted Bremer', 'USA', '
  <classes speakerBio="Ted specializes in client development">
    <class name="Smart Client Stuff" />
    <class name="More Smart Client Stuff" />
  </classes>')

INSERT INTO Speaker VALUES('Bad Speaker', 'France', '
  <CLASSES SPEAKERBIO="Jean has case-sensitivity issues">
          <class name="SQL Server Index" />
          <class name="SQL Precon" />
  </CLASSES>')
```

Now that you have some data, it's time to start writing some XQuery expressions in T-SQL. To do this, you will use the query-based methods of the *xml* data type inside a regular T-SQL query.

xml.exist

Having XML in the database is almost useless unless you can query the elements and attributes of the XML data natively. XQuery becomes very useful when you use it to search XML based on the values of a particular element or attribute. The *xml.exist* method accepts an XQuery query as input and returns 0, 1, or *NULL*, depending on the result of the query: 0 is returned if no elements match, 1 is returned if there is a match, and *NULL* is returned if there is no data to query on. For example, Listing 6-31 shows how to test whether a particular node exists within an XML document.

LISTING 6-31 A simple *xml.exist* example.

```
DECLARE @SomeData xml = '
<classes>
        <class name="SQL Server Index"/>
        <class name="SQL Precon"/>
</classes>'

SELECT
 @SomeData.exist('/classes') AS HasClasses,
 @SomeData.exist('/dogs') AS HasDogs
```

This query produces the following output:

```
HasClasses HasDogs
---------- -------
1          0
```

You will most likely use the return value of *xml.exist* (0, 1, or *NULL*) as part of a *WHERE* clause. This lets you run a T-SQL query and restrict the query on a value of a particular XML element. For example, here is an XQuery expression that finds every *<class>* element beneath *<classes>* with a *name* attribute containing the phrase *"SQL Server"*:

```
/classes/class/@name[contains(., "SQL Server ")]
```

Listing 6-32 shows how you put this expression to work.

LISTING 6-32 Using *xml.exist* to test for an attribute value.

```
SELECT * FROM Speaker
 WHERE
  ClassesXML.exist('/classes/class/@name[contains(., "SQL Server")]') = 1
```

The results look like this:

```
SpeakerId  SpeakerName  Country  ClassesXML
---------  -----------  -------  ----------
1          Jeff Hay     USA      <classes speakerBio="Jeff has solid security...
2          Holly Holt   Canada   <classes speakerBio="Holly is a Canadian-bor...
```

Jeff and Holly (but not Ted) each give one or more SQL Server classes. The XML returned in these results look like this for Jeff:

```
<classes speakerBio="Jeff has solid security experience based on years of hacking">
  <class name="Writing Secure Code for ASP .NET" />
  <class name="Using XQuery to Manipulate XML Data in SQL Server 2012" />
  <class name="SQL Server and Oracle Working Together" />
  <class name="Protecting against SQL Injection Attacks" />
</classes>
```

Listing 6-33 shows a query similar to the previous one. This version demonstrates how to seamlessly integrate XQuery with ordinary filtering of relational columns, by simply building out the *WHERE* clause to further restrict by *Country* for USA only.

LISTING 6-33 Combining XQuery with relational column filtering.

```
SELECT * FROM Speaker
 WHERE
  ClassesXML.exist('/classes/class/@name[contains(., "SQL Server")]') = 1
  AND Country = 'USA'
```

Executing this query returns only Jeff. SQL Server will filter out the other two rows because Ted does not have any SQL Server classes and Holly is from Canada.

xml.value

The *xml.value* method takes an XQuery expression *that resolves to a single value* and returns it, cast as the SQL Server data type you specify. You can leverage this very powerful method to completely shield the internal XML representation of your data, and expose ordinary scalar values with ordinary SQL Server data types instead. Consider the query in Listing 6-34.

LISTING 6-34 Using *xml.value* to represent XML data elements as scalar SQL Server data typed-columns

```
.SELECT
  SpeakerName,
  Country,
  ClassesXML.value('/classes[1]/@speakerBio','varchar(max)') AS SpeakerBio,
  ClassesXML.value('count(/classes/class)', 'int') AS SessionCount
 FROM
  Speaker
 ORDER BY
  ClassesXML.value('count(/classes/class)', 'int')
```

From the output generated by this query, there is no indication that—behind the scenes—the source for some of the output comes from an embedded XML document, stored in an *xml* data type column, and then shredded with XQuery:

```
SpeakerName Country SpeakerBio                                                 SessionCount
----------- ------- ---------------------------------------------------------- ------------
Ted Bremer  USA     Ted specializes in client development                      2
Holly Holt  Canada  Holly is a Canadian-born database professional             3
Jeff Hay    USA     Jeff has solid security experience from years of hacking 4
```

The *SpeakerName* and *Country* columns came right out of the *Speaker* table. However, the *SpeakerBio* and *SessionCount* columns were each extracted from the *ClassesXML* column using *xml.value* with an XQuery expression and a SQL Server data type that the expression's result was cast to. Because you are requesting a specific data type, the XQuery expression *must* resolve to a *single* value. That value can come from a node element's inner text, attribute, or XQuery function, but it must be a *single* value. For *SpeakerBio*, the XQuery drills into the *classes* element for the *speakerBio* attribute, extracts its value, and casts it as a *varchar(max)* type. The XQuery for *SessionCount* invokes the *count* function to return the number of *class* elements nested beneath the *classes* element cast as an *int*. The same XQuery is used again in the *ORDER BY* clause, so that the results of the query themselves are sorted by a value derived from data embedded in XML content.

You can build views and TVFs over queries such as this, and create an effective abstraction layer over the way XML is stored internally in your database. This means you can alter the XSD schemas and then adjust the XQuery expressions in your views and TVFs accordingly, such that consumers remain unaffected. Indeed, you could even transparently switch from XML storage to traditional column storage and back again, without disturbing any existing clients. SQL Server thus provides extremely flexible abstraction in both directions, because you've seen the myriad of ways to dynamically construct and serve XML from relational column data with the various *FOR XML* options earlier in the chapter. This flexibility means you can choose just the right degree of XML integration in your database that best suits your needs—whether that involves persisting XML data, constructing XML data, or both.

xml.query

The *xml.query* method accepts and executes an XQuery expression much like the *xml.value* method, but it always returns an *xml* data type result. So unlike *xml.value*, the XQuery expression doesn't need to resolve to a single value, and can easily return multiple values as a subset of the source XML. But furthermore, it can transform that source XML and produce entirely different XML—even injecting values from other non-*xml* columns living the in same row as the *xml* column being queried. Listing 6-35 demonstrates how this is achieved using FLWOR expressions and *sql:column* (a SQL Server XQuery extension).

LISTING 6-35 Using *xml.query* with FLWOR expressions and *sql:column* for XML transformations.

```
SELECT
  SpeakerId,
  ClassesXML.query('
    let $c := count(/classes/class)
    let $b := data(/classes[1]/@speakerBio)
    return
      <SpeakerInfo>
        <Name>{sql:column("SpeakerName")}</Name>
        <Country>{sql:column("Country")}</Country>
```

```
        <Bio>{$b}</Bio>
         <Sessions count="{$c}">
           {
             for $s in /classes/class
             let $n := data($s/@name)
             order by $n
             return
               <Session>{$n}</Session>
           }
         </Sessions>
       </SpeakerInfo>
           ') AS SpeakerInfo
  FROM
   Speaker
```

The XML returned in these results looks like this for Jeff:

```
<SpeakerInfo>
  <Name>Jeff Hay</Name>
  <Country>USA</Country>
  <Bio>Jeff has solid security experience from years of hacking</Bio>
  <Sessions count="4">
    <Session>Protecting against SQL Injection Attacks</Session>
    <Session>SQL Server and Oracle Working Together</Session>
    <Session>Using XQuery to Manipulate XML Data in SQL Server 2012</Session>
    <Session>Writing Secure Code for ASP .NET</Session>
  </Sessions>
</SpeakerInfo>
```

Let's explain the code in detail. The XQuery expression in the *xml.query* method on the *ClassesXML* column begins with a FLWOR expression. The two *let* statements use XPath expressions to capture the speaker's number of classes (using the *count* function) and bio text (using the *data* function), and stores the results into the variables *$c* and *$b* respectively. Then the *return* statement defines the shape of the XML to be constructed, starting with the root node's *<SpeakerInfo>* element. Inside the root node, the *<Name>* and *<Country>* elements are returned, with values extracted from the *SpeakerName* and *Country* columns. These are values that are not present in the XML being parsed by *xml.query*, but are available as ordinary columns elsewhere in the same row, and are exposed using the special *sql:column* SQL Server extension to XQuery.

Next, the *<Sessions>* element is returned with a *count* attribute that returns the number of class elements beneath the source XML's classes element. Within *<Sessions>*, a new (nested) FLWOR expression is used to iterate the speaker's classes and build a sequence of *<Session>* elements. The *for* statement loops through the source XML's *classes* element for each nested *class* element and stores it into the variable *$s*. The *let* statement then uses the *data* function to capture the string value inside the *name* attribute of the *class* element in *$s* and stores it into the variable *$n*. The inner FLWOR expression results (that is, the sequence of elements returned by the upcoming *return* statement) are sorted by name using the *order by* statement. Finally, the *return* statement generates a new *<Session>* element. The session name is rendered as the inner text of the *<Session>* element. This XQuery has essentially transformed the *<Classes>* and *<Class name="title">* structure of the source XML to a *<Sessions>* and *<Session>title</Session>* structure.

The *sql:variable* function is another very powerful SQL Server extension to XQuery. With it, you can easily parameterize your XQuery expressions using ordinary T-SQL parameters. This technique is demonstrated in Listing 6-36.

LISTING 6-36 Using *xml.query* with *sql:variable* for parameterized transformations.

```
DECLARE @Category varchar(max) = 'SQL Server'

SELECT
  SpeakerName,
  Country,
  ClassesXML.query('
    <classes
      category="{sql:variable("@Category")}"
      speakerBio="{data(/classes[1]/@speakerBio)}">
      {
        for $c in /classes/class
        where $c/@name[contains(., sql:variable("@Category"))]
        return $c
      }
    </classes>') AS ClassesXML
 FROM
  Speaker
 WHERE
  ClassesXML.exist
   ('/classes/class/@name[contains(., sql:variable("@Category"))]') = 1
```

The results look like this:

```
SpeakerName  Country  ClassesXML
-----------  -------  ----------
Jeff Hay     USA      <classes category="SQL Server" speakerBio="Jeff has solid e...
Holly Holt   Canada   <classes category="SQL Server" speakerBio="Holly is a Canad...
```

The XML returned in these results looks like this for Jeff:

```
<classes category="SQL Server"
   speakerBio="Jeff has solid security experience from years of hacking">
  <class name="Using XQuery to Manipulate XML Data in SQL Server 2012" />
  <class name="SQL Server and Oracle Working Together" />
</classes>
```

In this example, the T-SQL *@Category* parameter is assigned the value *SQL Server*, and the *sql:variable* is then used in several places to reference *@Category*. The first reference adds a *category* attribute to the *classes* element. The second reference applies filtering against the *name* attribute using *contains* in the inner FLWOR expression's *where* statement, and the last reference applies filtering at the resultset row level in the *SELECT* statement's *WHERE* clause. Thus, only rows having *SQL Server* in the name of at least one class are returned in the resultset, and within those rows, only classes having SQL Server in their name are returned as elements in *ClassesXML* (all other non-SQL Server classes are filtered out).

Our last *xml.query* example demonstrates how to combine child elements into a delimited string value, as shown in Listing 6-37.

LISTING 6-37 Using *xml.query* with *CONVERT* to combine child elements.

```
SELECT
  SpeakerName,
  Country,
  CONVERT(varchar(max), ClassesXML.query('
    for $s in /classes/class
    let $n := data($s/@name)
    let $p := concat($n, "|")
    return $p')) AS SessionList
 FROM
  Speaker
```

The *SessionList* column produced by this query contains a single pipe-delimited string containing the names of all the classes given by the speaker:

```
SpeakerName Country SessionList
----------- ------- -------------------------------------------------------------------
Jeff Hay    USA     Writing Secure Code for ASP .NET| Using XQuery to Manipulate XML Da...
Holly Holt  Canada  SQL Server Profiler| Advanced SQL Querying Techniques| SQL Server a...
Ted Bremer  USA     Smart Client Stuff| More Smart Client Stuff|
```

This XQuery expression in Listing 6-37 simply iterates each *class* element, extracts the *name* attribute, and concatenates it with a pipe symbol, appending each result to build a single string. Although the elements are ultimately combined to form a single value, they are still multiple values from an XPath perspective, and so *xml.value* cannot be used. Instead, *xml.query* produces the concatenated string, and *CONVERT* is used to cast the result as a *varchar(max)* data type.

XML DML

The W3C XQuery specification does not provide a way for you to modify XML data as you can modify relational table data using the *INSERT, UPDATE*, and *DELETE* keywords in T-SQL. So Microsoft has created its own XML data manipulation language, XML DML, which is included in its own XQuery implementation.

XML DML gives you three ways to manipulate the XML data of a column via the *xml.modify* method:

- ***xml.modify(insert)*** Allows you to insert a node or sequence of nodes into the *xml* data type instance you are working with.
- ***xml.modify(delete)*** Allows you to delete zero or more nodes that are the result of the output sequence of the XQuery expression you specify.
- ***xml.modify(replace)*** Modifies the value of a single node.

xml.modify(insert)

The *xml.modify(insert)* method allows you to insert a node or sequence of nodes into the *xml* data type instance you are working with. You use the *xml.modify* method in conjunction with a T-SQL *UPDATE* statement and, if necessary, a T-SQL or XQuery *where* clause (or both). For example, the code in Listing 6-38 adds another *<class>* element to Jeff's *<classes>* element in *ClassesXML*.

LISTING 6-38 Using *xml.modify* to insert a new element.

```
UPDATE Speaker
 SET ClassesXML.modify('
  insert
    <class name="Ranking and Windowing Functions in SQL Server" />
  into
    /classes[1]')
 WHERE SpeakerId = 1
```

xml.modify(delete)

The *xml.modify(delete)* method deletes zero or more nodes based on the criteria you specify. For example, the code in Listing 6-39 deletes the fourth *<class>* element from Jeff's *<classes>* element in *ClassesXML*.

LISTING 6-39 Using *xml.modify* to delete an element.

```
UPDATE Speaker
 SET ClassesXML.modify('delete /classes/class[4]')
 WHERE SpeakerId = 1
```

xml.modify(replace)

Finally, the *xml.modify(replace)* method allows you to replace XML data with new information. For example, the code in Listing 6-40 updates the *name* attribute in the third *<class>* element of Jeff's *<classes>* element in *ClassesXML*.

LISTING 6-40 Using *xml.modify* to update an element.

```
UPDATE Speaker
 SET ClassesXML.modify('
  replace value of /classes[1]/class[3]/@name[1]
        with "Getting SQL Server and Oracle to Work Together"')
 WHERE SpeakerId = 1
```

Summary

XML is ubiquitous nowadays, and in this chapter, we have taken a fairly extensive tour of the *FOR XML* clause and its various options, as well as the *xml* data type and its data manipulation mechanisms, XQuery and XML DML. As you have seen, SQL Server provides a rich feature set of XML technologies. At times, you will want to store XML in the database, other times you will want to serve XML from the database, and still other times you may want to do both. Whatever your XML needs are, the *xml* data type allows you to work with XML natively at the database level. Armed with this data type and the ability to query it using XQuery, you can fully exploit the power of XML inside your SQL Server databases and build smart, XML-aware applications.

CHAPTER 7

Hierarchical Data and the Relational Database

—*Leonard Lobel*

Hierarchical data is organized as an expandable tree structure of elements (or nodes), each one nested within another, to form parent-child relationships on multiple levels. In today's world, the most ubiquitous hierarchical data format is XML (we cover Microsoft SQL Server's rich XML support in Chapter 6). There's no doubt that XML is the right database storage choice for hierarchical data in many scenarios. It can be particularly useful when that data is consumed in XML format by client applications, in circumstances where you need to store and retrieve the entire hierarchy at a single time, or when you want to implement a loosely structured storage schema that can change dynamically without requiring you to alter a table's schema.

But XML is the *wrong* choice when you'd prefer to keep your data stored as normal rows with standard SQL Server data-typed columns, and what you really want is hierarchical *linking* capabilities between the rows. The *hierarchyid* data type is designed specifically for this purpose. In this chapter, you will learn about *hierarchyid*, and how you can use it to cast a hierarchical structure over the rows in your table. Examples include document libraries, forum threads, business organization charts, and product category assignments, just to name a few. In Chapter 8, you'll see how the new FileTable feature in SQL Server 2012 leverages *hierarchyid* to implement its logical file system behind the scenes. There are many more examples of course, but the point is that they are all hierarchical in nature, potentially growing both broad and deep, and are all typically iterated recursively.

The traditional solution for representing a tree structure in a table is to use the self-joining technique, where each row in the table holds a foreign key that references the primary key of its parent row elsewhere in the same table. One classic example is the chain-of-command hierarchy in a business organization's employee structure. A single table contains employees that have both an *EmployeeId* primary key and a *ManagerId* foreign key that points to the *EmployeeId* of each employee's manager. At the very top of the hierarchy, the CEO's *ManagerId* would be *NULL*.

The self-joining approach has certainly worked over the years, but it does require you to handle the maintenance of the tree structure yourself. SQL Server 2005 introduced common table expressions (CTEs) that support recursive queries against such a table so you can "walk" up the hierarchy all the way to the root from any given node. Although recursive CTEs do help, other types of hierarchical queries can pose a challenge to implement. Plus, it's still your job to manage the hierarchy for updates. You must maintain its structure across node manipulations involving insertions, modifications, and deletions of child, parent, and sibling rows in the table or even manipulations of entire subtrees at one time. There's also no inherent way to exercise fine control of the ordering of child entities. For example, you can't say "insert a new child node before, after, or in between other existing siblings."

The *hierarchyid* Data Type

The *hierarchyid* data type enables a robust hierarchical structure over a relational table that can relieve you from much of this maintenance burden. Like the self-joining approach, each row in the table represents a node in the tree. However, instead of storing just the parent value in a foreign key column, each row now has a unique *hierarchyid* whose encoded value describes the full path all the way from the root of the tree down to that row's node position within the tree. The *hierarchyid* value in each row therefore identifies each node's location in the tree, relative to the *hierarchyid* values of its neighboring parent, sibling, and child nodes that are stored in other rows. In this manner, the *hierarchyid* values link rows to each other as nodes that form the tree structure.

Using Transact-SQL (T-SQL) extensions for the *hierarchyid* data type, you can invoke methods to arbitrarily insert, modify, and delete nodes at any point within the structure with great efficiency. You can also reparent entire subtrees in a single update. SQL Server determines the nodes affected by the update and calculates the necessary changes to their *hierarchyid* values automatically. And with the proper indexes in place (which we discuss later on in the section "Hierarchical Table Indexing Strategies"), querying a tree-structured table based on the *hierarchyid* data type is significantly faster than running recursive queries on a traditional self-joining table using CTEs.

SQL Server employs an algorithm that encodes the path information of a *hierarchyid* value into an extremely compact variable-length format. The average number of bits that are required to represent a node in a tree with *n* nodes depends on the average number of children of a node, known as the average *fanout*. For small fanouts (0 to 7), the size is about $6^*\log_{An}$ bits, where A is the average fanout. In practical terms, this means that one node in a hierarchy of 100,000 nodes with an average fanout of 6 takes about 38 bits, which gets rounded up to 40 bits (5 bytes) for storage. The encoded value has no meaningful display representation, of course, but the *ToString* method will translate a *hierarchyid* value to a human-readable form that expresses a delimited node path, as you'll see shortly.

The *hierarchyid* type is implemented as a SQL common language runtime (CLR) user-defined type (UDT). This means that *hierarchyid* is hosted internally by the CLR, and not natively by SQL Server (this is also why functions invoked on it are called *methods*). Due to its tight integration in SQL Server, the feature is available even with SQL CLR disabled. So you don't need to enable SQL CLR to use the *hierarchyid* data type (or any of the other "system" CLR types, such as *geometry* and *geography*, which we cover in Chapter 9). The SQL CLR feature increases your exposure to security risks by allowing Microsoft .NET Framework code to run on the server, so you should enable it only if you are creating your own SQL CLR objects (stored procedures, user-defined functions, and so on).

More Info The *hierarchyid* data type is available to CLR clients as the *SqlHierarchyId* data type in the *Microsoft.SqlServer.Types* namespace. This namespace is contained in the *Microsoft.SqlServer.Types.dll* assembly, which can be found on the .NET tab in the Microsoft Visual Studio Add Reference dialog box. In the database itself, the node information represented by a *hierarchyid* value is stored as a *varbinary* data type, which can support a virtually unlimited number of child nodes per parent.

Creating a Hierarchical Table

Let's begin by implementing the classic manager-employee tree scenario using the *hierarchyid* data type. Start with the structure of the *Employee* table, as shown in Listing 7-1:

LISTING 7-1 Creating a hierarchical table.

```
USE master
GO
IF EXISTS(SELECT name FROM sys.databases WHERE name = 'MyDB')
 DROP DATABASE MyDB
GO
CREATE DATABASE MyDB
GO

USE MyDB
GO

CREATE TABLE Employee
(
   NodeId        hierarchyid PRIMARY KEY CLUSTERED,
   NodeLevel     AS NodeId.GetLevel(),
   EmployeeId    int UNIQUE NOT NULL,
   EmployeeName  varchar(20) NOT NULL,
   Title         varchar(20) NULL
)
GO
```

Notice that the *NodeId* column is declared as a *hierarchyid* type and is also defined as the table's primary key using a clustered index. The primary key is important for two reasons, the first of which is that SQL Server doesn't guarantee uniqueness of *hierarchyid* values in the table. Don't view this as a limitation—this fact actually enables advanced scenarios in which you can house multiple distinct hierarchies within a single table. With the single hierarchy in our example, defining a primary key is one way to enforce unique *NodeId* values. Defining an ordinary unique constraint instead would be another way, and you can certainly do that if some column other than the *hierarchyid* is more suitable for the table's primary key. The second reason for the primary key index is to support *depth-first indexing*, which we'll talk about shortly.

As we've started explaining, the value in the *NodeId* column identifies each row's unique node position within the structure. It can serve as the table's primary key, and you don't technically need to have any other identifying columns in the table. Practically, however, you'll most likely still want to define another unique column to serve as a more conventional identifier, because values assigned into the *hierarchyid* column as rows are added to the table based on their node positions within the tree. Those *hierarchyid* values are essentially nondeterministic and will also shift automatically as the tree's node structure is changed using the techniques that you'll start learning about just ahead. For example, if you relocate a node and all of its descendants to a new position within the tree (also known as *reparenting* a subtree), the *hierarchyid* values of those nodes are automatically updated by SQL Server to reflect their new positions within the hierarchy. You therefore define *EmployeeId* as a unique integer column assigned with values that you control and that won't change when the structure of nodes in the tree is manipulated in the future. So when you add employees, their ID values remain the same regardless of how their nodes get repositioned down the line.

Note You can also use *IDENTITY* values for the *EmployeeId* column, which puts SQL Server in control of assigning key values using incrementing integers, and which would also not change as the tree structure is altered. To stay focused on *hierarchyid*, the example here does not add the extra code for using *IDENTITY*, and you simply assign your own unique *EmployeeId* integer values explicitly.

The *GetLevel* Method

The second column defined in the *Employee* table is *NodeLevel*, which is declared as a calculated column that returns the 16-bit integer result of the *GetLevel* method applied to the *hierarchyid* value in the *NodeId* column. This is optional and provides a read-only column that returns a number indicating the level position of its row (node), extracted and decoded from the compacted *hierarchyid* value in the *NodeId* column. One and only one root row exists in any hierarchy and is positioned at level zero. Its immediate child rows are positioned at level one, grandchild rows at level two, and so on. Defining the *NodeLevel* column that calls the *GetLevel* method will allow you to later create a *breadth-first index* on the table.

The *EmployeeId* column is defined with a unique constraint and doesn't permit *NULL* values. You can therefore treat its integer value as an "alternate primary key" for your employees, because the *hierarchyid* value in the *NodeId* column has already been defined as the table's actual primary key. As we mentioned, in many practical cases, you will want to define such an alternate key to be used as an identifier with a value that you are in control of and that doesn't change unpredictably as the result of node manipulations the way a *hierarchyid* value does. You'll definitely need such identifiers if you want to establish relationships for joining with other tables, or you might want them just for your own convenience. But it's important to understand that SQL Server requires no such identifier to implement the hierarchy, and that you can certainly cast a hierarchical structure over a relational table with only the *hierarchyid* value as the primary key and no other unique columns.

Populating the Hierarchy

Let's visualize the organizational chart before you start populating the *Employee* table with hierarchical data. Figure 7-1 shows the hierarchy of employees in your fictional organization.

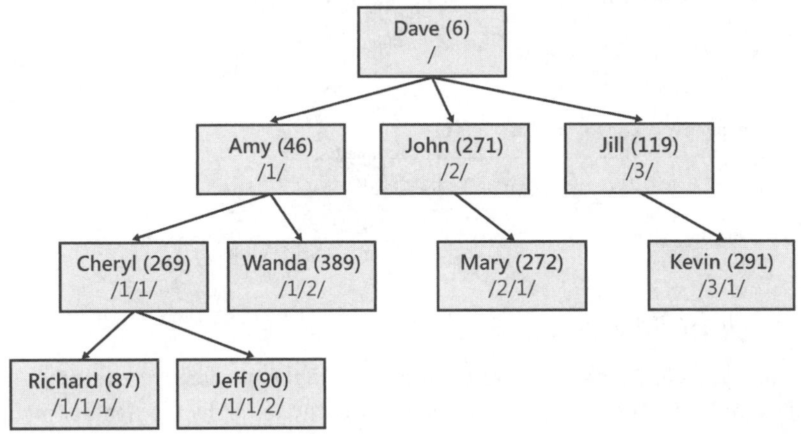

FIGURE 7-1 Hierarchical organizational chart.

The first row added to a hierarchical table is always the root node of the tree, and there can be only one root. Additional rows beneath the root are then added as child and grandchild nodes, and so on. Nodes can be rearranged as needed by invoking methods on the *hierarchyid* values. The tree can grow both *broad* (with many siblings) and *deep* (with many descendants).

The *GetRoot* Method

You begin by inserting your first row for Dave, the marketing manager, at the top of the chart with an employee ID of 6, as shown in Listing 7-2:

LISTING 7-2 Inserting the root node row in the hierarchical *Employee* table.

```
INSERT INTO Employee
  (NodeId, EmployeeId, EmployeeName, Title)
 VALUES
  (hierarchyid::GetRoot(), 6, 'Dave', 'Marketing Manager') ;
GO
```

Values can be assigned into *hierarchyid* columns by invoking methods that return *hierarchyid* values. When inserting the first row at the top of the chart, you call the *GetRoot* method on the *hierarchyid* type itself. The special double-colon (::) syntax is used when calling methods on the data type itself (akin to a static method call in object oriented languages), rather than calling methods on *values* of the data type (akin to an object instance method call), which uses the normal "dot" syntax (as you've already seen with the *GetLevel* method in Listing 7-1). Being the first row in your hierarchical table, the only meaningful *hierarchyid* value for *NodeId* is one that specifies the root, and that's exactly the value returned by *hierarchyid::GetRoot()*.

Also notice that you do not (and cannot) insert a value for *NodeLevel*, because that is a read-only calculated column that returns the level position of each row. Select the row back out from the table so that you can see what it looks like:

```
SELECT * FROM Employee
GO

NodeId    NodeLevel EmployeeId  EmployeeName   Title
--------- --------- ----------- -------------- --------------------
0x        0         6           Dave           Marketing Manager

(1 row(s) affected)
```

The *GetDescendant* Method

In the preceding output, you see Dave's record as the root node in the hierarchy at level zero. The *hierarchyid* value of *0x* for *NodeId* positions Dave as the top-level node, set by the *GetRoot* method when you inserted the row. Now it's time to add child nodes for the level-one employees who report directly to Dave. To set the *hierarchyid* values for these employees, you use the *GetDescendant* method on Dave's *hierarchyid* value. This method generates and returns a *hierarchyid* value that is a child of the *hierarchyid* it is invoked on and is a sibling positioned between the two *hierarchyid* values that get passed in as the method parameters.

Before adding the employees beneath Dave, let's take a close look at the *GetDescendant* method. Suppose that you want to construct a generic tree, organized as shown in Figure 7-2.

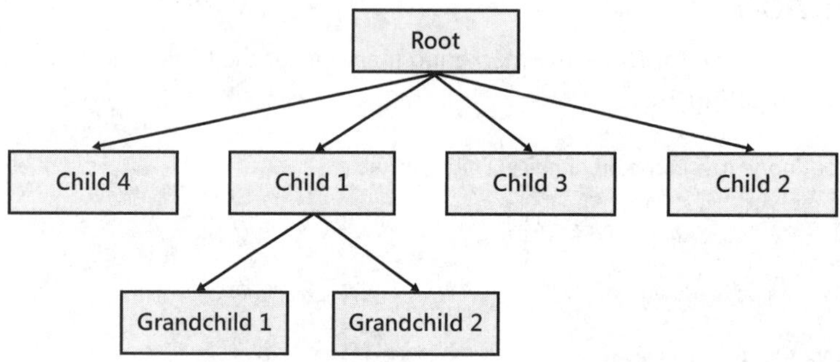

FIGURE 7-2 Sample hierarchy of nodes.

The code in Listing 7-3 shows how to use *GetDescendant* to create child and grandchild nodes of the root node created by *GetRoot*.

LISTING 7-3 Using *GetDescendant* to construct a hierarchy.

```
DECLARE @Root hierarchyid
DECLARE @Child1 hierarchyid
DECLARE @Child2 hierarchyid
DECLARE @Child3 hierarchyid
DECLARE @Child4 hierarchyid
DECLARE @Grandchild1 hierarchyid
DECLARE @Grandchild2 hierarchyid

SET @Root = hierarchyid::GetRoot()
SET @Child1 = @Root.GetDescendant(NULL, NULL)
SET @Child2 = @Root.GetDescendant(@Child1, NULL)
SET @Child3 = @Root.GetDescendant(@Child1, @Child2)
SET @Child4 = @Root.GetDescendant(NULL, @Child1)
SET @Grandchild1 = @Child1.GetDescendant(NULL, NULL)
SET @Grandchild2 = @Child1.GetDescendant(@Grandchild1, NULL)

SELECT
 @Root AS Root,
 @Child1 AS Child1,
 @Child2 AS Child2,
 @Child3 AS Child3,
 @Child4 AS Child4,
 @Grandchild1 AS Grandchild1,
 @Grandchild2 AS Grandchild2
```

The output appears as follows:

```
Root Child1 Child2 Child3 Child4 Grandchild1 Grandchild2
---- ------ ------ ------ ------ ----------- -----------
0x   0x58   0x68   0x62C0 0x48   0x5AC0      0x5B40

(1 row(s) affected)
```

The *ToString* Method

The preceding output shows the hexadecimal representation of each node's encoded *hierarchyid* value, which is hardly useful to you. To view this as human-readable text that conveys each node's path within the tree, change the *SELECT* statement in Listing 7-3 to call the *ToString* method on the *hierarchyid* values, as shown here:

```
SELECT
 @Root.ToString() AS Root,
 @Child1.ToString() AS Child1,
 @Child2.ToString() AS Child2,
 @Child3.ToString() AS Child3,
 @Child4.ToString() AS Child4,
 @Grandchild1.ToString() AS Grandchild1,
 @Grandchild2.ToString() AS Grandchild2
GO
```

```
Root Child1 Child2 Child3 Child4 Grandchild1 Grandchild2
---- ------ ------ ------ ------ ----------- -----------
/    /1/    /2/    /1.1/  /0/    /1/1/       /1/2/

(1 row(s) affected)
```

You can make several observations from this output. First, you can see that the *ToString* method decodes the *hierarchyid* value into a slash-delimited string. Each slash designates a level, so subtracting one from the number of slashes indicates what the zero-based level position of each node is (the same value that would be returned by the *GetLevel* method). *Root* is the only node with one slash, representing level zero. The *Child1*, *Child2*, *Child3*, and *Child4* nodes have two slashes, representing level one. The *Grandchild1* and *Grandchild2* nodes, naturally, have three slashes representing level two.

You can also see how the two parameters that were passed to the *GetDescendant* method influenced the assignment of *hierarchyid* values. Root of course was assigned by *hierarchyid::GetRoot()* to get the tree started, as you saw in Listing 7-2. The *hierarchyid* for each of the four child nodes beneath the root parent was assigned by invoking the *GetDescendant* method on the root. And the ordinal position of each child node among siblings of the same parent was determined by the two parameters passed to *GetDescendant*.

Child1 is the first node defined beneath the root, as follows:

```
SET @Child1 = @Root.GetDescendant(NULL, NULL)
```

Because there are not yet any other child nodes beneath the root, there is no position relative to other child nodes that can be specified. You therefore pass *NULL* as both positional values to *GetDescendant*. The result is a *hierarchyid* represented as */1/*, which refers to the one and only child node beneath the root.

Child2 is created as the second node beneath the root, which you want to be placed after *Child1*. Think of this as inserting *Child2* between *Child1* and "the end," which you pass as the two parameters *Child1* and *NULL*, respectively, when calling *GetDescendant* for *Child2*:

```
SET @Child2 = @Root.GetDescendant(@Child1, NULL)
```

The result is a *hierarchyid* represented as */2/*, which refers to the second child node beneath the root, to the right of *Child1*. You then apply the same principle to create *Child3* as a third child node beneath the root, except that you want this child to be positioned between *Child1* and *Child2* rather than being appended as *Child2* was. You explicitly request such ordering when calling *GetDescendant* for *Child3*, as shown here:

```
SET @Child3 = @Root.GetDescendant(@Child1, @Child2)
```

This code assigns a *hierarchyid* value to *Child3* between *Child1* and *Child2*. Because you specified a position between *Child1* and *Child2* with *hierarchyid* values of */1/* and */2/*, respectively, SQL Server assigns to *Child3* a *hierarchyid* value represented by *ToString* as */1.1/* (that is, after */1/* and before */2/*).

Last, you create *Child4* as another child beneath the root, this time inserted in front of all the other siblings (that is, before *Child1*). Think of this as inserting *Child4* between "the beginning" and *Child1*, which you pass as the two parameters *NULL* and *Child1*, respectively, when calling *GetDescendant* for *Child4* as follows:

```
SET @Child4 = @Root.GetDescendant(NULL, @Child1)
```

The result is a *hierarchyid* represented as */0/* assigned for *Child4*, the last child node added beneath the root, to the left of *Child1*. If you continued adding more nodes to the left of *Child4*, their *ToString* representations would begin showing negative values, such as */-1/*, */-2/*, and so on.

Adding grandchild (level-two) nodes beneath *Child1* is achieved using the very same approach:

```
SET @Grandchild1 = @Child1.GetDescendant(NULL, NULL)
```

This code assigns a *hierarchyid* value of */1/1/* to *Grandchild1*, the first child node beneath *Child1*. Once again, being the first child of a parent, there are no existing sibling nodes that you can refer to with respect to the position at which *Grandchild1* should be inserted, and so the only possible values to pass as parameters to *GetDescendant* are *NULL* and *NULL*. Last, you add *Grandchild2* as a second child beneath *Child1*, positioned after its sibling node *Grandchild1*, as shown here:

```
SET @Grandchild2 = @Child1.GetDescendant(@Grandchild1, NULL)
```

Now let's get back to the hierarchical employee table. After Dave has been added at the root, the level-one employee nodes that you will now add beneath him are assigned *hierarchyid* values returned by a call to *GetDescendant* on Dave. The first level-one employee you add is Amy, with an employee ID of 46, as shown in Listing 7-4:

LISTING 7-4 Adding the first child node beneath the root of the hierarchy.

```
DECLARE @Manager hierarchyid

SELECT @Manager = NodeId
 FROM Employee
 WHERE EmployeeId = 6

INSERT INTO Employee
  (NodeId, EmployeeId, EmployeeName, Title)
 VALUES
  (@Manager.GetDescendant(NULL, NULL), 46, 'Amy', 'Marketing Specialist')

GO
```

Let's examine this code closely. You first need to get the *hierarchyid* value of the parent (Dave, with employee ID 6), which you retrieve from the table and store in the *@Manager* variable (also declared as a *hierarchyid* data type, of course). Then you can insert Amy as the first child row by specifying a *hierarchyid* value returned by the *GetDescendant* method invoked on *@Manager*. Because there are no other child nodes yet beneath Dave, the only positional parameter values that can be passed to

GetDescendant are *NULL* and *NULL*. Let's now view both rows in the table, including a *NodeIdPath* column that translates the encoded *hierarchyid* values using the *ToString* method.

```
SELECT NodeId.ToString() AS NodeIdPath, *
 FROM Employee
GO

NodeIdPath NodeId NodeLevel EmployeeId EmployeeName Title
---------- ------ --------- ---------- ------------ --------------------
/          0x     0         6          Dave         Marketing Manager
/1/        0x58   1         46         Amy          Marketing Specialist

(2 row(s) affected)
```

Sure enough, Amy has been added as the first level-one child node beneath Dave, as indicated by the *hierarchyid* value */1/* assigned to her by *GetDescendant*.

This demonstrates that adding a child node requires a *SELECT* to first obtain the *hierarchyid* value of the desired parent before performing an *INSERT* to actually add the new row. In this manner, the new row can be assigned a *hierarchyid* value based on the result of invoking *GetDescendant* on the *hierarchyid* value of its parent. We presented the code as two separate statements to make this process clear. However, you could have just as effectively written this as a single statement without requiring the temporary *@Manager* variable to hold the parent's *hierarchyid* by embedding the *SELECT* statement as a subquery within the *VALUES* clause of the *INSERT* statement, as follows:

```
INSERT INTO Employee
  (NodeId, EmployeeId, EmployeeName, Title)
 VALUES (
  (SELECT NodeId
    FROM Employee
    WHERE EmployeeId = 6).GetDescendant(NULL, NULL),
  46,
  'Amy',
  'Marketing Specialist')

GO
```

You'll probably want to simplify the process for adding more employees. In Listing 7-5, the *uspAddEmployee* stored procedure encapsulates logic that retrieves the *hierarchyid* of any desired parent and invokes *GetDescendant* on it to obtain the appropriate *hierarchyid* for the new employee.

LISTING 7-5 Creating a stored procedure to automatically insert child nodes in a hierarchy.

```
CREATE PROC uspAddEmployee(
 @ManagerId int,
 @EmployeeId int,
 @EmployeeName varchar(20),
 @Title varchar(20))
AS
BEGIN
```

```
  DECLARE @ManagerNodeId hierarchyid
  DECLARE @LastManagerChild hierarchyid
  DECLARE @NewEmployeeNodeId hierarchyid

  -- Get the hierarchyid of the desired parent passed in to @ManagerId
  SELECT @ManagerNodeId = NodeId
   FROM  Employee
   WHERE EmployeeId = @ManagerId

  SET TRANSACTION ISOLATION LEVEL SERIALIZABLE

  BEGIN TRANSACTION

    -- Get the hierarchyid of the last existing child beneath the parent
    SELECT @LastManagerChild = MAX(NodeId)
     FROM  Employee
     WHERE NodeId.GetAncestor(1) = @ManagerNodeId

    -- Assign a new hierarchyid positioned at the end of any existing siblings
    SELECT @NewEmployeeNodeId =
     @ManagerNodeId.GetDescendant(@LastManagerChild, NULL)

    -- Add the row
    INSERT INTO Employee
      (NodeId, EmployeeId, EmployeeName, Title)
     VALUES
      (@NewEmployeeNodeId, @EmployeeId, @EmployeeName, @Title)

  COMMIT

 END

 GO
```

You can now use this stored procedure to easily insert new rows into the employee table as a child of any node within the hierarchy. The stored procedure accepts a *@ManagerId* parameter that the caller provides as the employee ID of the parent that the newly added employee should be a child of. The remaining parameters (*@EmployeeId*, *@EmployeeName*, and *@Title*) simply provide values for the new employee.

After declaring a few local *hierarchyid* variables, the procedure retrieves the *hierarchyid* of the parent specified by the *@ManagerId* input parameter, just as you did earlier for Amy, and stores the result in the local *@ManagerNodeId* variable, as shown here:

```
-- Get the hierarchyid of the desired parent passed in to @ManagerId
SELECT @ManagerNodeId = NodeId
 FROM  Employee
 WHERE EmployeeId = @ManagerId
```

This is the value on which you now want to call *GetDescendant* in order to establish an appropriate *hierarchyid* value for the new employee. You don't particularly care about the order of siblings beneath each parent, and so you can let the procedure simply append the new employee to the end of any siblings that might already exist. However, you still must provide the two positional parameters expected by *GetDescendant* that explicitly specify the point of insertion. Because you want new siblings to be appended to the end, you know that the second positional parameter should always be *NULL*. Your job therefore is to establish an appropriate value for the first positional parameter by ascertaining the *hierarchyid* value of the last existing sibling, or using *NULL* if there are no siblings. You achieve this with the following *SELECT* statement:

```
-- Get the hierarchyid of the last existing child beneath the parent
SELECT @LastManagerChild = MAX(NodeId)
 FROM  Employee
 WHERE NodeId.GetAncestor(1) = @ManagerNodeId
```

This code introduces a new *hierarchyid* method, *GetAncestor*.

The *GetAncestor* Method

The *GetAncestor* method accepts an integer parameter that specifies how many levels to traverse up from the node it is invoked on to reach one of that node's ancestors, and then returns the *hierarchyid* of the ancestor node. A value of *1*, as you are using here, returns the immediate parent of the node on which the *GetAncestor* method is invoked. By requesting all rows with *hierarchyid* values whose immediate parent is the same as the parent requested by the caller for the new employee, the preceding *WHERE* clause retrieves all the existing siblings of the employee about to be added. Because this can return multiple siblings, you apply the *MAX* aggregate function to retrieve the sibling with the highest-valued *hierarchyid* (which is the last sibling in the set) into the *@LastManagerChild* local variable. If there are no existing siblings, the *WHERE* clause will return no rows at all and *NULL* will be assigned into *@LastManagerChild*. In either case, you have established the appropriate value in *@LastManagerChild* to be used as the first positional parameter for the call to *GetDescendant*, as shown here:

```
-- Assign a new hierarchyid positioned at the end of any existing siblings
SELECT @NewEmployeeNodeId =
 @ManagerNodeId.GetDescendant(@LastManagerChild, NULL)
```

You have now assigned an appropriate *hierarchyid* value for the new employee in *@NewEmployee-NodeId* by invoking *GetDescendant* on the parent (*@ManagerNodeId*). The two parameters passed to *GetDescendant* specify that the new employee should be inserted between the last sibling that exists (*@LastManagerChild*) and the end of the sibling list (*NULL*), which effectively means that it will be appended to the end. If *NULL* was assigned into *@LastManagerChild* because there were no previously existing siblings, *GetDescendant* is called with two *NULL* values, which (as you've already seen) is the correct way to call *GetDescendant* when adding the very first child beneath a parent.

All that's needed now is a straightforward *INSERT* statement that adds the new employee to the table at the correct node position beneath the parent specified by the caller, as shown here:

```
-- Add the row
INSERT INTO Employee
  (NodeId, EmployeeId, EmployeeName, Title)
 VALUES
  (@NewEmployeeNodeId, @EmployeeId, @EmployeeName, @Title)
```

The last part of this stored procedure that bears explanation is its use of a transaction surrounding the *SELECT* and *INSERT* statements. The purpose here is to guarantee that no other sibling nodes can be added by another user between the time the *hierarchyid* value of the last sibling is obtained and the time the new row is actually inserted. Without wrapping this logic inside of a transaction, you have no such guarantee, and the *hierarchyid* value determined to be the last sibling in the set might no longer be the last sibling in the set at the time the new employee is added. A collision could therefore occur between two concurrent processes attempting to add two different new employees beneath the same parent in the same position at the same time. Such an attempt would result in a primary key constraint violation, because both inserts would be attempting to store the same *hierarchyid* value into the *NodeId* column defined as the primary key. Although the *SELECT* and *INSERT* statements could be combined into a single complex statement without using an explicit transaction (as you saw earlier when you added the employee row for Amy), the logic is much clearer (and thus more maintainable) when coding these as separate statements.

Now that you have created the *uspAddEmployee* stored procedure and understand how it works, adding the rest of the employees in your organizational chart is easy. All you need to do for each one is specify the employee ID of the new employee's parent, followed by the new employee's ID, name, and title, as shown here:

```
EXEC uspAddEmployee 6, 271, 'John', 'Marketing Specialist'
EXEC uspAddEmployee 6, 119, 'Jill', 'Marketing Specialist'
EXEC uspAddEmployee 46, 269, 'Cheryl', 'Marketing Assistant'
EXEC uspAddEmployee 46, 389, 'Wanda', 'Business Assistant'
EXEC uspAddEmployee 271, 272, 'Mary', 'Marketing Assistant'
EXEC uspAddEmployee 119, 291, 'Kevin', 'Marketing Intern'
EXEC uspAddEmployee 269, 87, 'Richard', 'Business Intern'
EXEC uspAddEmployee 269, 90, 'Jeff', 'Business Intern'
```

The *ToString* method on each row's *hierarchyid* value in *NodeId* confirms that the tree structure correctly represents your organizational chart:

```
SELECT NodeId.ToString() AS NodeIdPath, *
 FROM Employee
 ORDER BY NodeLevel, NodeId
GO

NodeIdPath NodeId NodeLevel EmployeeId  EmployeeName Title
---------- ------ --------- ----------- ------------ --------------------
/          0x     0         6           Dave         Marketing Manager
/1/        0x58   1         46          Amy          Marketing Specialist
/2/        0x68   1         271         John         Marketing Specialist
/3/        0x78   1         119         Jill         Marketing Specialist
/1/1/      0x5AC0 2         269         Cheryl       Marketing Assistant
/1/2/      0x5B40 2         389         Wanda        Business Assistant
/2/1/      0x6AC0 2         272         Mary         Marketing Assistant
/3/1/      0x7AC0 2         291         Kevin        Marketing Intern
/1/1/1/    0x5AD6 3         87          Richard      Business Intern
/1/1/2/    0x5ADA 3         90          Jeff         Business Intern

(10 row(s) affected)
```

The *ToString* method certainly displays a *hierarchyid* value in a more intelligible form than the raw internal *varbinary* value, but the string returned is still rather cryptic. With a little code, you can create a user-defined function (UDF) that will accept any *NodeId* and return a more meaningful "breadcrumb-style" representation of the path leading up to that node. Listing 7-6 shows the code for the *fnGetFullDisplayPath* UDF that uses the *GetLevel* and *GetAncestor* methods together to do just that.

LISTING 7-6 Creating a UDF that builds a breadcrumb-style display path for a given node.

```
CREATE FUNCTION dbo.fnGetFullDisplayPath(@EntityNodeId hierarchyid)
 RETURNS varchar(max)
AS
  BEGIN
    DECLARE @EntityLevelDepth smallint
    DECLARE @LevelCounter smallint
    DECLARE @DisplayPath varchar(max)
    DECLARE @ParentEmployeeName varchar(max)

    -- Start with the specified node
    SELECT @EntityLevelDepth = NodeId.GetLevel(),
           @DisplayPath = EmployeeName
     FROM  Employee
     WHERE NodeId = @EntityNodeId

    -- Loop through all its ancestors
    SET @LevelCounter = 0
    WHILE @LevelCounter < @EntityLevelDepth BEGIN

       SET @LevelCounter = @LevelCounter + 1

       SELECT @ParentEmployeeName = EmployeeName
        FROM  Employee
        WHERE NodeId = (
              SELECT NodeId.GetAncestor(@LevelCounter)
               FROM Employee
               WHERE NodeId = @EntityNodeId)

       -- Prepend the ancestor name to the display path
       SET @DisplayPath = @ParentEmployeeName + ' > ' + @DisplayPath

    END

    RETURN(@DisplayPath)
   END
```

After declaring a few local variables, the function starts by first selecting the node specified by the *@EntityNodeId* parameter (the node's *hierarchyid* value). It obtains the level of the node by calling *GetLevel* and stores it in the *@EntityLevelDepth* variable, and also retrieves the employee name into the *@DisplayPath* variable. The function will return *@DisplayPath* after it finishes prepending it with all of the employee names of the node's ancestors, all the way up to the root.

The function then establishes a *@LevelCounter* integer variable, initialized to 0, and enters a loop that increments *@LevelCounter* with each iteration. The loop is terminated when the *@LevelCounter* value reaches *@EntityLevelDepth*. Inside the loop, the incrementing *@LevelCounter* value is fed to the *GetAncestor* method to retrieve the next employee name up the chain, which is then prepended to *@DisplayPath* along with the ' > ' level-separation string. In this manner, the code obtains the parent, grandparent, great-grandparent, and so on, all the way up to the root. When the loop terminates, *@DisplayPath* is returned to the caller. Here is the output from the *fnGetFullDisplayPath* function when run against the employee table:

```
SELECT
  NodeId,
  NodeId.ToString() AS NodeIdPath,
  dbo.fnGetFullDisplayPath(NodeId) AS NodeIdDisplayPath,
  EmployeeName
 FROM
  Employee
 ORDER BY
  NodeLevel, NodeId
GO

NodeId NodeIdPath NodeIdDisplayPath             EmployeeName
------ ---------- ----------------------------- ------------
0x     /          Dave                          Dave
0x58   /1/        Dave > Amy                    Amy
0x68   /2/        Dave > John                   John
0x78   /3/        Dave > Jill                   Jill
0x5AC0 /1/1/      Dave > Amy > Cheryl           Cheryl
0x5B40 /1/2/      Dave > Amy > Wanda            Wanda
0x6AC0 /2/1/      Dave > John > Mary            Mary
0x7AC0 /3/1/      Dave > Jill > Kevin           Kevin
0x5AD6 /1/1/1/    Dave > Amy > Cheryl > Richard Richard
0x5ADA /1/1/2/    Dave > Amy > Cheryl > Jeff    Jeff

(10 row(s) affected)
```

The *NodeIdDisplayPath* in this result set shows the employee names along the hierarchical paths in each row.

Populating a hierarchical table does require some effort up front, as you've seen. However, once your data is in place, you can leverage the power of the *hierarchyid* data type by invoking its methods to easily query and reorganize the tree structure. We're almost ready to dive into that, but first let's take a moment to talk about the indexing options that you need to know about.

Hierarchical Table Indexing Strategies

You can create a *depth-first* index or a *breadth-first* index (or both) on your hierarchical tables. The two types differ in how SQL Server physically stores node references in the index. Defining depth-first and breadth-first indexes can have a significant impact on performance for accessing data in hierarchical tables.

As their names imply, depth-first indexing stores parent and child node references near each other, whereas breadth-first indexing stores references for nodes at the same hierarchical level near each other. Therefore, you will choose the appropriate type of index based on an understanding of how your hierarchical data is shaped in the table, how it will grow, and how it will be typically queried by client applications. You can create both types of indexes as well, for efficient access both vertically and horizontally across the tree.

Note Regardless of what indexing strategy you employ, comparison operations are *always* performed in depth-first order. Thus, *A* < *B* means that *A* always comes before *B* in a depth-first traversal of the tree (or *A* is to the left of *B* if they are both at the same level), even if breadth-first indexing is used.

Depth-First Indexing

Defining either a primary key index or a unique index on a *hierarchyid* column results in a depth-first index. Because the *NodeId* column (of type *hierarchyid*) is designated as the primary key in the employee table, you have already created a depth-first index.

With depth-first indexing (depicted in Figure 7-3), SQL Server tries to physically store references to nodes in a subtree as near to each other as possible. By "near each other," we mean that SQL Server records them on disk in the same page, if possible—or in the same extent, if not, and so on—in order to maximize query performance. This strategy yields high query performance if your hierarchy runs very many levels deep. Creating a depth-first index for such a hierarchy will result in very fast vertical searching on the tree (that is, querying ancestors and descendants up and down a potentially long chain).

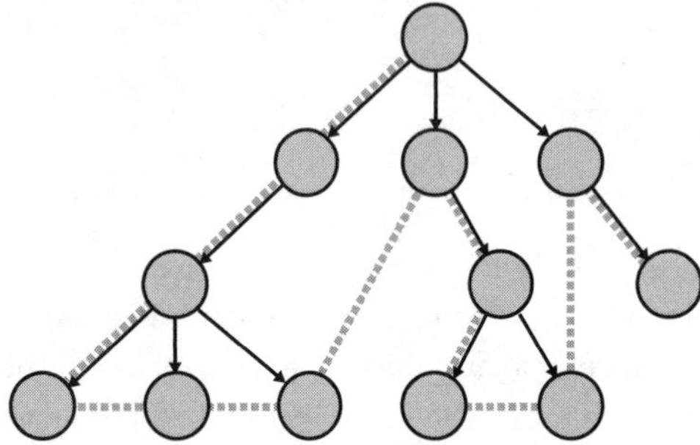

FIGURE 7-3 Physical row storage when optimized for depth-first searching.

Breadth-First Indexing

With breadth-first indexing, illustrated in Figure 7-4, reference to nodes at the same level of the hierarchy are physically stored as near to each other as possible. This type of index yields high query performance for trees that grow very broad. If there are many children beneath the parents in your hierarchy, you will want to create a breadth-first index to enable fast horizontal searching across a potentially large number of nodes at the same level.

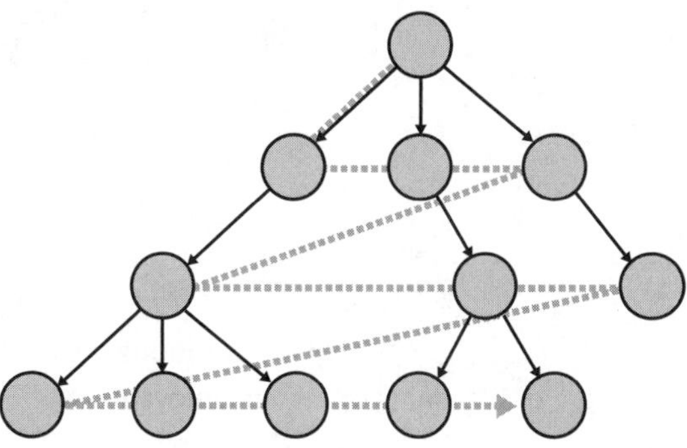

FIGURE 7-4 Physical row storage when optimized for breadth-first searching.

To define a breadth-first index, you create a composite index on your hierarchical table that includes two columns: the integer column that holds the *level* of the node within the hierarchy (such as the *NodeLevel* column defined in the employee table, based on the *GetLevel* method against the *NodeId* column) and the *hierarchyid* column itself (*NodeId*). So to create a breadth-first index, run the following code:

```
CREATE UNIQUE INDEX IX_EmployeeBreadth
 ON Employee(NodeLevel, NodeId)
```

As we mentioned already, one table can have both depth-first and breadth-first indexes by creating one primary key or unique index on the *hierarchyid* column and another composite index on the node-level column and the *hierarchyid*. This will carry slightly more overhead for data manipulation language (DML) actions, because updates will need to be performed in both indexes; however, query performance will be very fast for both horizontal and vertical searching across large hierarchies that are both very broad and very deep.

Querying Hierarchical Tables

With a hierarchical table populated and indexed, you're ready to start writing efficient queries against it using some more methods available on the *hierarchyid* type.

The *IsDescendantOf* Method

The *IsDescendantOf* method is invoked on one *hierarchyid* value and accepts another *hierarchyid* value as its parameter. It returns a *bit* (Boolean) value of *1* (true) if the *hierarchyid* that the method is invoked on is a descendant (either directly or indirectly) of the *hierarchyid* that is passed in as the parameter. Thus, this method essentially returns a subtree whose root is the node specified by the parameter. Because of its vertical traversal, it delivers very fast performance for tables that have a depth-first index.

You can easily query the employee table to return all the descendants (child rows, grandchild rows, and so on) of a particular employee using the *IsDescendantOf* method. For example, the following query lists all of Amy's descendants.

```
DECLARE @AmyNodeId hierarchyid

SELECT @AmyNodeId = NodeId
 FROM  Employee
 WHERE EmployeeId = 46

SELECT NodeId.ToString() AS NodeIdPath, *
 FROM  Employee
 WHERE NodeId.IsDescendantOf(@AmyNodeId) = 1
 ORDER BY NodeLevel, NodeId
```

This query selects all rows whose *NodeId* values are descendants of Amy (employee ID 46). Here is the result:

```
NodeIdPath NodeId NodeLevel EmployeeId EmployeeName Title
---------- ------ --------- ---------- ------------ ----------------------
/1/        0x58   1         46         Amy          Marketing Specialist
/1/1/      0x5AC0 2         269        Cheryl       Marketing Assistant
/1/2/      0x5B40 2         389        Wanda        Business Assistant
/1/1/1/    0x5AD6 3         87         Richard      Business Intern
/1/1/2/    0x5ADA 3         90         Jeff         Business Intern

(5 row(s) affected)
```

Notice that the result includes Amy in addition to all of her descendants. Amy is returned because she is considered to be her "own descendant" at the 0 level of the subtree. Thus, you have selected a subtree that includes all of Amy's descendants, no matter how many levels deep they might exist beneath her, with Amy at the root.

To select *only* Amy's immediate child rows that are just one level beneath her, you can use the *GetAncestor* method. (You used this method earlier to create the *uspAddEmployee* stored procedure.) For example:

```
SELECT NodeId.ToString() AS NodeIdPath, *
 FROM  Employee
 WHERE NodeId.GetAncestor(1) =
   (SELECT NodeId
     FROM  Employee
     WHERE EmployeeId = 46)
 ORDER BY NodeLevel, NodeId
GO

NodeIdPath NodeId NodeLevel EmployeeId EmployeeName Title
---------- ------ --------- ---------- ------------ ----------------------
/1/1/      0x5AC0 2         269        Cheryl       Marketing Assistant
/1/2/      0x5B40 2         389        Wanda        Business Assistant

(2 row(s) affected)
```

This time, the results list only Cheryl and Wanda, but not Amy nor any of Amy's deeper descendants. That's because you are requesting just the rows whose one-level-up ancestor is Amy (employee ID 46)—that is, just Amy's immediate children.

If you wanted to retrieve all the employees exactly two levels down from a particular manager, you could pass the value *2* to the *GetAncestor* method. For example, to select the employees that report to the employees beneath Dave (that is, to see all the employees two levels beneath him), you could request rows whose *grandparent* is Dave (employee ID 6; that is, just Dave's grandchildren), as shown here:

```
SELECT NodeId.ToString() AS NodeIdPath, *
 FROM  Employee
 WHERE NodeId.GetAncestor(2) =
   (SELECT NodeId
     FROM  Employee
     WHERE EmployeeId = 6)
 ORDER BY NodeLevel, NodeId
GO

NodeIdPath NodeId NodeLevel EmployeeId EmployeeName Title
---------- ------ --------- ---------- ------------ ----------------------
/1/1/      0x5AC0 2         269        Cheryl       Marketing Assistant
/1/2/      0x5B40 2         389        Wanda        Business Assistant
/2/1/      0x6AC0 2         272        Mary         Marketing Assistant
/3/1/      0x7AC0 2         291        Keven        Marketing Intern

(4 row(s) affected)
```

This query returned all employees that are two levels below Dave. The fact that some of them are cousins and not siblings (that is, some of them have different direct parents) is irrelevant. Being exactly two levels down beneath Dave qualifies them all for selection by this query. And because of its horizontal traversal, it delivers very fast performance with a breadth-first index defined on the table.

To find the root node in the hierarchy, simply invoke the *GetRoot* method on the *hierarchyid* data type itself using the double-colon syntax, as shown in the following code. This is the same method you used to create the first employee at the top of the tree (Dave, as shown in Listing 7-2).

```
SELECT NodeId.ToString() AS NodeIdPath, *
 FROM  Employee
 WHERE NodeId = hierarchyid::GetRoot()
GO

NodeIdPath NodeId NodeLevel EmployeeId EmployeeName Title
---------- ------ --------- ---------- ------------ ----------------------
/          0x     0         6          Dave         Marketing Manager

(1 row(s) affected)
```

Reordering Nodes within the Hierarchy

Reorganizing the nodes within the tree structure is a common maintenance task when working with hierarchies. You might need to alter the tree structure by adjusting the parent-child relationships within the hierarchy. The *hierarchyid* type provides a *GetReparentedValue* method that makes it easy to handle this kind of maintenance. You will start by first relocating just a single node without disturbing any other nodes in the hierarchy. Then you'll relocate an entire subtree (that is, all of a node's descendant nodes).

The *GetReparentedValue* Method

You invoke the *GetReparentedValue* method on the node you want to move, passing in two parameters. The first specifies the original parent (the source), and the second specifies the new parent (the target). Wanda formerly reported to Amy but is now reporting to Jill instead (alongside Kevin). You therefore want to move Wanda's current position as a child of Amy to be a child of Jill instead. The following code uses the *GetReparentedValue* method to perform that change.

```
DECLARE @EmployeeToMove hierarchyid
DECLARE @OldParent hierarchyid
DECLARE @NewParent hierarchyid

SELECT @EmployeeToMove = NodeId
 FROM  Employee
 WHERE EmployeeId = 389 -- Wanda

SELECT @OldParent = NodeId
 FROM  Employee
 WHERE EmployeeId = 46 -- Amy

SELECT @NewParent = NodeId
 FROM  Employee
 WHERE EmployeeId = 119 -- Jill

-- Wanda now reports to Jill and no longer to Amy
UPDATE Employee
 SET   NodeId = @EmployeeToMove.GetReparentedValue(@OldParent, @NewParent)
 WHERE NodeId = @EmployeeToMove
GO
```

The hierarchy now looks like Figure 7-5.

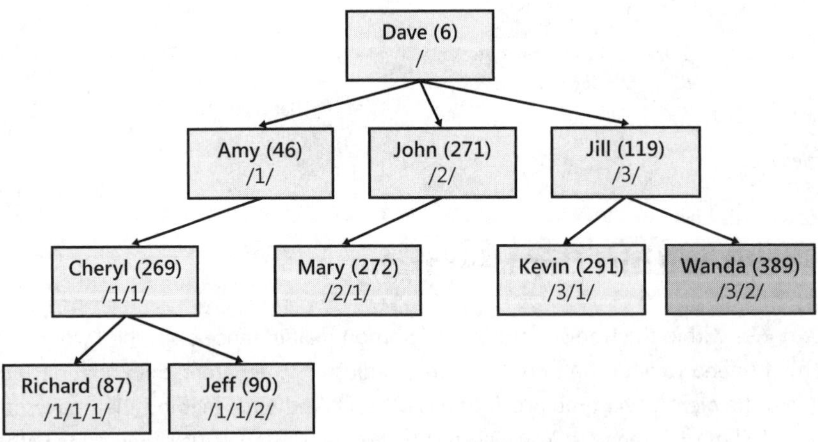

FIGURE 7-5 Reparenting a single node.

Viewing the results of the following query confirms that Wanda's *NodeIdPath* has changed from */1/2/* (child of Amy) to */3/2/* (child of Jill):

```
SELECT
  NodeId,
  NodeId.ToString() AS NodeIdPath,
  NodeLevel,
  dbo.fnGetFullDisplayPath(NodeId) AS NodeIdDisplayPath,
  EmployeeName
 FROM
  Employee
 ORDER BY
  NodeLevel, NodeId
GO

NodeId NodeIdPath NodeLevel NodeIdDisplayPath             EmployeeName
------ ---------- --------- ---------------------------- ------------
0x     /          0         Dave                          Dave
0x58   /1/        1         Dave > Amy                    Amy
0x68   /2/        1         Dave > John                   John
0x78   /3/        1         Dave > Jill                   Jill
0x5AC0 /1/1/      2         Dave > Amy > Cheryl           Cheryl
0x6AC0 /2/1/      2         Dave > John > Mary            Mary
0x7AC0 /3/1/      2         Dave > Jill > Kevin           Kevin
0x7B40 /3/2/      2         Dave > Jill > Wanda           Wanda
0x5AD6 /1/1/1/    3         Dave > Amy > Cheryl > Richard Richard
0x5ADA /1/1/2/    3         Dave > Amy > Cheryl > Jeff    Jeff

(10 row(s) affected)
```

Changing the position of a single node with the *GetReparentedValue* method as you just did does *not* affect any of that node's children (since only one row was updated). This means that if Wanda had any child nodes, they would not move along with Wanda as new descendants of Jill, now would they move up one level in the hierarchy as direct descendants of Amy to occupy the position vacated by Wanda. The same would be true if Wanda were simply deleted rather than moved. Former child nodes of Wanda would therefore end up having no parent at all, but would rather have only a *grandparent* (which in this case would be Amy, Wanda's former parent). The result is a "hole" in your hierarchy. SQL Server will not enforce integrity checks on the hierarchy to catch this condition, so it's your job to handle orphaned nodes properly. One way to ensure against orphaned nodes is to transplant an entire subtree at one time. Let's learn how to do just that.

Transplanting Subtrees

You can easily move a larger number of people at one time by reparenting an entire subtree. Because you'll be moving all of a node's descendants as a single block, no orphaned nodes can result from this operation. In the next update, you will move all of Amy's subordinates to their new manager, Kevin. This is achieved by reparenting all nodes with *hierarchyid* values that begin with */1/* (Amy) to */3/1/* (Kevin), except for Amy. You use the *IsDescendantOf* method to return all of Amy's descendants for the update. Recall from our earlier discussion of the *IsDescendantOf* method that Amy is her own descendant at the 0 level (that is, she's the root of her own subtree). You must therefore exclude her (employee ID 46) from the rows to be updated, as shown in the following code:

```
DECLARE @OldParent hierarchyid
DECLARE @NewParent hierarchyid

SELECT @OldParent = NodeId
 FROM  Employee
 WHERE EmployeeId = 46 -- Amy

SELECT @NewParent = NodeId
 FROM  Employee
 WHERE EmployeeId = 291 -- Kevin

UPDATE Employee
 SET   NodeId = NodeId.GetReparentedValue(@OldParent, @NewParent)
 WHERE NodeId.IsDescendantOf(@OldParent) = 1
       AND EmployeeId <> 46 -- This excludes Amy from the move.
GO
```

Note The employee ID values are hard-coded for Amy and Kevin in this code. This was done for demonstration purposes. In a real-world implementation, this logic should be in a stored procedure that accepts any two nodes as input parameters and wraps the *SELECT* and *UPDATE* statements in a transaction.

Running this update moves all of Amy's descendants to be descendants of Kevin, as shown in Figure 7-6. Notice that the nodes have moved not only *across* the tree, but *down* one level as well (since Kevin is one level deeper than Amy).

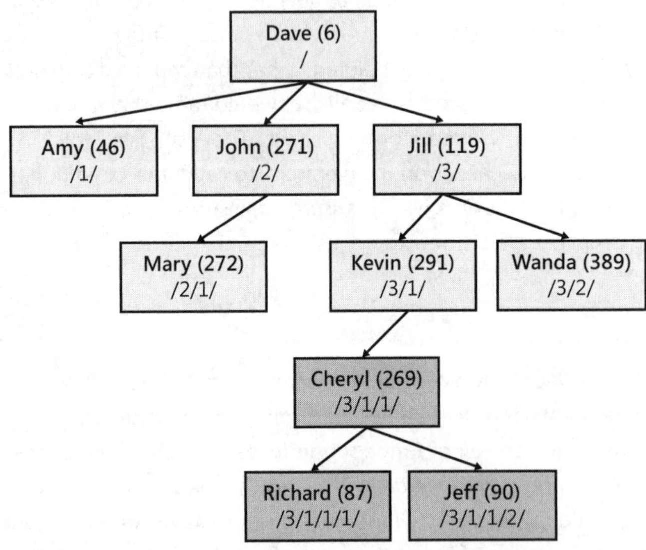

FIGURE 7-6 Reparenting an entire subtree.

Selecting all the employees one more time shows how SQL Server updated the *hierarchyid* values in *NodeId* for Cheryl, Richard, and Jeff to reflect their new positions beneath Kevin. For the first time in this scenario, the hierarchy now runs five levels deep (counting from 0 to 4), as shown here:

```
SELECT
  NodeId,
  NodeId.ToString() AS NodeIdPath,
  NodeLevel,
  dbo.fnGetFullDisplayPath(NodeId) AS NodeIdDisplayPath,
  EmployeeName
 FROM
  Employee
GO

NodeId     NodeIdPath NodeLevel NodeIdDisplayPath                        EmployeeName
---------- ---------- --------- ---------------------------------------- ------------
0x         /          0         Dave                                     Dave
0x58       /1/        1         Dave > Amy                               Amy
0x68       /2/        1         Dave > John                              John
0x78       /3/        1         Dave > Jill                              Jill
0x6AC0     /2/1/      2         Dave > John > Mary                       Mary
0x7AC0     /3/1/      2         Dave > Jill > Kevin                      Kevin
0x7B40     /3/2/      2         Dave > Jill > Wanda                      Wanda
0x7AD6     /3/1/1/    3         Dave > Jill > Kevin > Cheryl             Cheryl
0x7AD6B0   /3/1/1/1/  4         Dave > Jill > Kevin > Cheryl > Richard   Richard
0x7AD6D0   /3/1/1/2/  4         Dave > Jill > Kevin > Cheryl > Jeff      Jeff

(10 row(s) affected)
```

More *hierarchyid* Methods

Three more *hierarchyid* methods—*Parse*, *Read*, and *Write*—are provided by the *hierarchyid* data type, although they are less often used.

Parse is essentially the reverse of *ToString*. It accepts the same slash-delimited string representation that is returned by *ToString* and returns the equivalent compacted *varbinary hierarchyid* value that SQL Server uses internally to represent the nodes. This value could then be passed to *ToString*, in which case you'd get the original slash-delimited string back. It is the only other static method besides *GetRoot*, and so it uses the double-colon syntax, as follows:

```
SELECT hierarchyid::Parse('/2/1/1/') AS NodeId
GO

NodeId
----------
0x6AD6

(1 row(s) affected)
```

Together, *Parse* and *ToString* enable serialization and deserialization to and from *hierarchyid* binary values and their string representations. Although you could manage the string representations on your own and use *Parse* to convert them for storage as *hierarchyid* values, the *hierarchyid* values are best assigned by calling the *GetDescendant* method, as we've demonstrated throughout our examples.

The last two methods, *Read* and *Write*, are the only methods not available in T-SQL, and can be used only in .NET code against the *Microsoft.SqlServer.Types.SqlHierarchyId* type. These two methods are used to pass *hierarchyid* values into and out of *BinaryReader* and *BinaryWriter* objects. They are also used internally by SQL Server as necessary, such as when reading from or writing to a *hierarchyid* column or for conversions between *varbinary* and *hierarchyid*. These methods are provided to enable such internal operations, as well as for integration with your own .NET code running under SQL CLR. They don't otherwise serve any real significant function in terms of the actual implementation of a hierarchical structure.

Summary

In this chapter, we showed how to use the *hierarchyid* data type to cast a tree structure over data stored in ordinary database tables. You can now work with hierarchical structures in SQL Server, such as the new FileTable introduced in SQL Server 2012 (you'll learn all about FileTable the next chapter). The *hierarchyid* data type provides a set of methods and indexing strategies to enable efficient searching and manipulation of hierarchy nodes at the database level. This enables you to apply a hierarchical model to traditional table data rather than resorting to XML, in scenarios where it makes better sense to keep the data stored relationally than to redesign the data for XML storage.

CHAPTER 8

Native File Streaming

—*Leonard Lobel*

The ongoing proliferation of digital content in today's world is generating unstructured data at a bewildering rate. Consequently, modern applications must cope with a multitude of binary files and formats. You might have to store and process photos, videos, documents, spreadsheets, email messages, and other related unstructured artifacts with your database records. This unstructured information—which is really just a binary stream—is commonly referred to as BLOB (Binary Large Object) data.

BLOB data needs to be associated with the structured data that lives in a relational database, and it must stream efficiently into and out of your application. Traditionally, relational database management systems store all their data in *tables*, and that implies structure. Relational database systems were not originally designed to handle the massive amount of unstructured data that exists today.

To adapt, Microsoft SQL Server 2008 introduced FILESTREAM, an innovative feature that integrates the relational database engine with the NTFS file system. In this chapter, we'll start by examining traditional BLOB solutions, and then explain how FILESTREAM provides important advantages over the previous BLOB techniques. You will build some real applications and services with FILESTREAM, and then learn how the new FileTable feature in Microsoft SQL Server 2012 delivers a logical file system—implemented as a FILESTREAM-enabled table in your database—on top of your BLOBs.

Traditional BLOB Strategies

Prior to SQL Server 2008, there were two traditional solutions for combining structured table data with unstructured BLOB data: either keep BLOBs in the database (with all your structured table data), or store them outside the database (in the file system). In the former case, BLOBs are stored right inside the database. In the latter case, the database merely holds references (or, possibly, references are derived from other values in the database) that point to locations in the file system where the BLOBs actually live. Each of these strategies has pros and cons with respect to storage, manageability, performance, and programming complexity that we'll discuss—but neither of them are intrinsically native to the core database engine.

BLOBs in the Database

You can, of course, simply store BLOB data directly in the columns of your database tables. You do this by declaring a column as a *varbinary(max)* data type, which will allow it to store a single BLOB up to 2 gigabytes (GB) in size.

> **Important** You should no longer use the *image* data type that was used to store BLOBs prior to Microsoft SQL Server 2005. The *varbinary(max)* data type should be used instead of *image*, which has been deprecated and may be removed in a future version of SQL Server.

When BLOB data is stored directly inside of tables this way, it is very tightly integrated with the database. It's easy to access BLOB data, because the BLOB is right there in the table's column. Because everything is contained in a single database unit, management is also simplified. Backup, restore, detach, copy, and attach operations on the database include structured and BLOB data together. Transactional consistency is another important benefit that you enjoy with this approach. Because BLOB data is a physical part of the tables in the database, it is eligible to participate in transactions. If you begin a transaction, update some data, and then roll back the transaction, any BLOB data that was updated is also rolled back. Overall, the mixture of structured and BLOB data is handled very seamlessly with this model.

Despite all these advantages, however, physically storing BLOBs in the database is practical only for small-scale applications having very few/small BLOBs. Because BLOB content is stored in-line with structured data, you can severely impair scalability by bloating your filegroups. Query performance will degrade rapidly as a result, because the query processor must sift through much larger amounts of data in your tables that are consumed with BLOB content. The BLOBs also don't stream nearly as efficiently when backed by SQL Server *varbinary(max)* columns as they would if they were held externally in the file system or on a dedicated BLOB store. Finally, there is also a 2 GB limit on the *varbinary(max)* data type.

> **Tip** If you have modest BLOB requirements (that is, you are dealing with very few or very small BLOBs) you should store them in the database using the *varbinary(max)* data type instead of using the file system (either directly, or via FILESTREAM). Furthermore, you should consider caching small, frequently accessed BLOBs rather than repeatedly retrieving them from the database or the file system.

BLOBs in the File System

To counter these concerns, you can store BLOBs outside the database and in the file system instead. With this approach, the structured data in your relational tables merely contains path information to the unstructured BLOB data, which is held externally as ordinary files in the file system (alternatively, path information can be derived from other structured data in a row). Applications use this path information as a reference for locating and tracking the BLOB content associated with rows in the database tables. Because they are physically held in the file system, a BLOB's size is limited only by the host file system and available disk space. This approach also delivers much better streaming performance, because the file system is a native environment that's highly optimized for streaming. And because the physical database is much smaller without the BLOBs inside it, the query processor can continue to deliver optimal performance.

Although physically separating structured and unstructured content this way does address the performance concerns of BLOBs, it also raises new issues because the data is now separated not only physically, but logically as well. SQL Server has absolutely no awareness of the association between data in the database and files stored externally in the file system. Their coupling exists solely at the application level. Backup, restore, detach, copy, and attach operations on the database files therefore include only structured table data without any of the BLOB data that's in the file system. You won't get complete backups, unless you back up the file system as well, so now it's another administrative burden to separately manage the file system.

Application development against this model is also more complex because of the extra effort required for linking between the database and the file system. It's up to the developer to establish and maintain the references between structured data and external BLOBs on their own, and according to their own custom design. Last, although perhaps most significant, there is no unified transactional control across both the database and the file system. Naturally, rolling back a database transaction won't undo changes you've made in the file system.

Introducing FILESTREAM

Both of the traditional BLOB solutions present tough challenges, so what do you do? With FILESTREAM, SQL Server offers a way out of this conundrum. First, make sure you understand that FILESTREAM is technically not a SQL Server data type. Rather, it is implemented as an *attribute* that you apply to the *varbinary(max)* data type—the same data type traditionally used to store BLOBs directly inside structured tables. However, merely applying this attribute tells SQL Server to store the BLOB in the file system rather than the table's structured filegroup. With the FILESTREAM attribute applied, you continue to treat the *varbinary(max)* column *as though* its contents were stored in-line with your structured table data. Under the covers, however, SQL Server stores and maintains the data in the server's local NTFS file system, separately from the structured content of the database that remains in the normal filegroups.

With FILESTREAM, structured and unstructured data are *logically connected* while *physically separated*. The unstructured data is configured as a special filegroup in the database, so it's actually considered part of the database—it is available in all logical database operations, including queries, transactions, and backup/restore. On disk, however, the BLOBs are stored as individual physical files in the NTFS file system that are created and managed automatically behind the scenes. SQL Server establishes and maintains the link references between the structured file groups and the file system. It *knows* about the unstructured BLOB data in the file system and considers the files holding BLOB data to be an integral part of the overall database. But the unstructured data does not impede query performance because it is not physically stored in-line with table data. It's stored in the file system, which is a native BLOB environment (and where it ostensibly belongs). Logically, however, the database encompasses both the relational tables and the individual BLOB files in the file system. You therefore continue to treat BLOB data as though you were storing it in-line, from both a development and an administrative perspective.

Tip Backing up the database includes all the BLOB data from the file system in the backup automatically. However, because the BLOB data is contained in its own database filegroup, you can easily exclude it from backups if desired or as needed.

The end result is that SQL Server uses the appropriate mechanism for structured and unstructured data—storing relational (structured) data in tables and BLOB (unstructured) data in ordinary files—so it can deliver the best possible performance all around. Because it does this completely transparently, you enjoy integrated management benefits over the database. You also enjoy simplified application development as you are no longer burdened with the additional complexities of manually associating the database with the file system and keeping the two in sync. Last, by leveraging the transactional capabilities of the NTFS file system, BLOB updates participate seamlessly with database transactions. If you're starting to get excited by all this, that's the idea! You're now ready to dive in to some real code that puts FILESTREAM to work for you.

Enabling FILESTREAM

Like many other features, FILESTREAM is disabled by default in SQL Server 2012, and you must first enable it before the feature can be used. Enabling FILESTREAM is slightly more involved than enabling other SQL Server features because it requires two distinct steps. First, the feature needs to be enabled for the machine, and then it needs to be enabled for the server instance. These two independent FILESTREAM configuration layers are by design, and they draw a separation of security concerns between the role of Windows administrator and database administrator.

Enabling FILESTREAM for the Machine

The first step is to enable FILESTREAM for the machine by setting an access level. This step can actually be performed at the time that SQL Server is initially installed by choosing a FILESTREAM access level during setup. To enable FILESTREAM for the machine after SQL Server has been installed, use the SQL Server Configuration Manager to set the access level. (This tool can be launched from the Configuration Tools folder of the Microsoft SQL Server 2012 program group on the Start menu.)

The SQL Server Configuration Manager opens with a treeview on the left. In the treeview, click SQL Server Services to display the list of available services in the main panel. Right-click the SQL Server instance that you want to enable FILESTREAM for, choose Properties, and in the Properties dialog box, select the FILESTREAM tab. The three check boxes on the FILESTREAM tab allow you to select the various levels of FILESTREAM access. Figure 8-1 shows the Properties dialog box with all three check boxes selected.

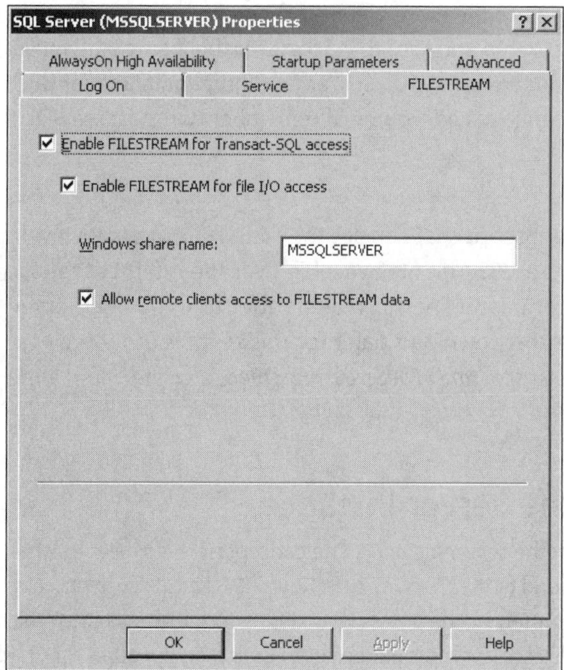

FIGURE 8-1 Enabling FILESTREAM for the machine to support file I/O streaming access by remote clients.

When all three check boxes are cleared, FILESTREAM is completely disabled. Selecting the first check box enables FILESTREAM, but only for Transact-SQL (T-SQL) access. This provides for utter transparency, where SQL Server will store BLOBs contained inside *varbinary(max) FILESTREAM* columns in the file system behind the scenes just as we've discussed. But it won't allow you to take advantage of direct file streaming between the database and your client applications using more advanced FILESTREAM features, such as *SqlFileStream* and FileTable that you'll be learning about soon.

The real power of FILESTREAM comes into play when you enable direct file I/O streaming, which delivers the best possible BLOB performance with SQL Server. You enable direct file I/O streaming access by selecting the second check box. Streamed file access also creates a Windows share name that is used to construct logical Universal Naming Convention (UNC) paths to BLOB data during FILESTREAM access, as you'll see further on when you use *SqlFileStream* and FileTable. The share name is specified in a text box after the second check box and is set by default to the same name as the server instance (*MSSQLSERVER*, in Figure 8-1).

In most cases, client applications will not be running on the same machine as SQL Server, and so you will usually also need to select the third check box to enable FILESTREAM for remote client file I/O streaming access with *SqlFileStream*. In addition, the new FileTable feature in SQL Server 2012 requires that you check this option in order to expose its data as a file system through the Windows share created by FILESTREAM (you'll examine FileTable after you finish learning about FILESTREAM). So practically, you must check all three checkboxes to get the most out of FILESTREAM (and to support all the exercises in this chapter). An exception to this general practice might be when using Microsoft SQL Server 2012 Express edition as a local data store for a client application with everything running on the same machine. In this case, you could use the more secure setting and leave the third check box cleared. Doing so would enable *SqlFileStream* and FileTable access for the local client application but deny such access to remote clients. If you are using SQL Server Configuration Manager to change this setting after SQL Server has already been installed, you must remember to restart the SQL Server instance for the setting change to take effect.

More Info There is no T-SQL equivalent script that can set the FILESTREAM access level for the machine. However, Microsoft posts a VBScript file available over the Internet that allows you to enable FILESTREAM from the command line as an alternative to using SQL Server Configuration Manager. At press time, the download page for this script is *http://www.codeplex.com/SQLSrvEngine/Wiki/View.aspx?title=FileStreamEnable&referringTitle=Home.*

Enabling FILESTREAM for the Server Instance

The second step is to enable FILESTREAM for the server instance. The concept here is similar to what we just described. Varying levels of access correspond to the checkboxes in Figure 8-1. Naturally, the access level defined for the server instance must be supported by the access level defined for the machine. Typically, therefore, the machine and server instance access levels should be set to match one another. FILESTREAM can be enabled for the server instance with a simple call to the *sp_configure* system stored procedure, as follows:

```
EXEC sp_configure filestream_access_level, n
RECONFIGURE
```

In the preceding code, replace *n* with a number from 0 to 2 to set the access level. A value of *0* disables the FILESTREAM feature completely. Setting the access level to *1* enables FILESTREAM for T-SQL access only, and setting it to *2* enables FILESTREAM for full access (which includes local or remote file I/O streaming access as enabled for the machine in the first step). To support the sample *SqlFileStream* .NET client application that you'll be building later in this chapter, you must select level 2 (full access). This corresponds to the third checkbox in Figure 8-1.

You can also set the FILESTREAM access level for the server instance in SQL Server Management Studio (SSMS) from the Advanced Server Properties dialog box. Right-click any server instance in Object Explorer, choose Properties, and then select the Advanced page. The various levels are available as choices in the Filestream Access Level drop-down list, as shown in Figure 8-2.

Note You can use either SQL Server Data Tools (SSDT) inside Visual Studio (covered in Chapter 1) or SSMS to set the access level, but only SSMS provides the ability to set it in the graphical user interface (GUI). Using SSDT, you can view the setting's property from the SQL Server Object Explorer, but you can only change it by running the *EXEC* statement in a query window.

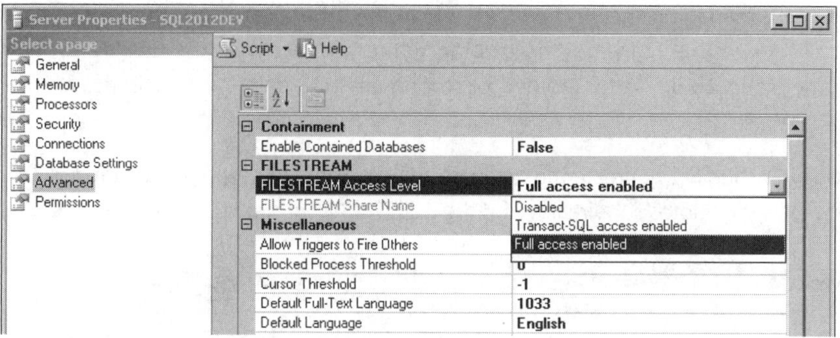

FIGURE 8-2 Selecting the FILESTREAM configuration level in SQL Server Management Studio.

Creating a FILESTREAM-Enabled Database

Once FILESTREAM is enabled for both the machine and the server instance, any database running on the server instance can support unstructured data by defining a filegroup with the special *FILEGROUP...CONTAINS FILESTREAM* clause of the *CREATE DATABASE* statement. For example, the statement in Listing 8-1 creates a *PhotoLibrary* database that can store pictures using FILESTREAM. Before you can run this code, you need to create an empty folder named C:\Demo\PhotoLibrary.

LISTING 8-1 Creating a FILESTREAM-enabled database with *FILEGROUP...CONTAINS FILESTREAM*.

```
CREATE DATABASE PhotoLibrary
 ON PRIMARY
  (NAME = PhotoLibrary_data,
   FILENAME = 'C:\Demo\PhotoLibrary\PhotoLibrary_data.mdf'),
 FILEGROUP FileStreamGroup1 CONTAINS FILESTREAM
  (NAME = PhotoLibrary_group2,
   FILENAME = 'C:\Demo\PhotoLibrary\Photos')
 LOG ON
  (NAME = PhotoLibrary_log,
   FILENAME = 'C:\Demo\PhotoLibrary\PhotoLibrary_log.ldf')
```

The *FILEGROUP...CONTAINS FILESTREAM* clause in this otherwise ordinary *CREATE DATABASE* statement enables the FILESTREAM feature for the *PhotoLibrary* database.

As when creating any database, the directory (or directories) specified for the primary and log filegroups must exist at the time the database is created. In Listing 8-1, the *CREATE DATABASE* statement will fail if the C:\Demo\PhotoLibrary directory specified by *FILENAME* in its *ON PRIMARY* and *LOG ON* clauses does not exist. For the new *FILESTREAM* group specified by the *FILEGROUP... CONTAINS FILESTREAM* clause, a *FILENAME* keyword is specified pointing to a directory (not a file) that must *not* exist at the time that the database is created (although the path leading up to the final directory must exist), or the *CREATE DATABASE* statement will fail as well. SQL Server takes control of creating and managing this directory—called the FILESTREAM data container—much as it does for creating and managing the .mdf and .ldf files in the other filegroups. In Listing 8-1, SQL Server automatically creates the C:\Demo\PhotoLibrary\Photos folder when the *CREATE DATABASE* statement is executed, and it will use that folder for storing all BLOB data (photos, in this example) in the *PhotoLibrary* database.

Execute the code in Listing 8-1 to create the database. SQL Server creates the usual .mdf and .ldf files for you, and also creates the Photos subdirectory for the FILESTREAM group, as shown in Figure 8-3.

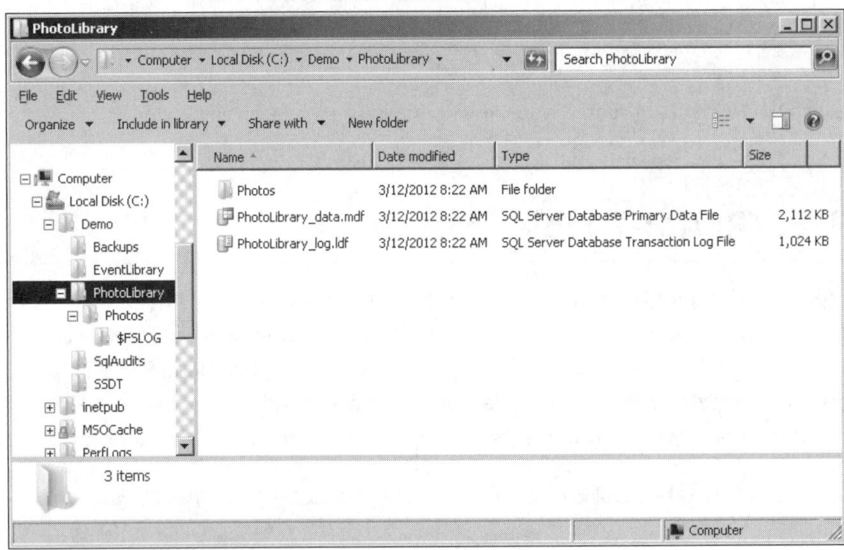

FIGURE 8-3 FILESTREAM storage in the file system.

Behind the scenes, SQL Server will store all your pictures as files in the Photos subdirectory, and will transparently associate those files and the relational tables that they logically belong to in columns defined as *varbinary(max) FILESTREAM*. Unless you explicitly exclude the *FileStreamGroup1* filegroup from a backup or restore command, all your picture files in the Photos subdirectory will be included with the relational database in the backup or restore operation.

Note You can create multiple FILESTREAM filegroups, with each one pointing to a different file system location. Doing so helps to partition BLOB data when you need to scale up, because you can designate specific filegroups for each *varbinary(max) FILESTREAM* column you define in your tables. See Microsoft Books Online for the appropriate syntax: *http://msdn.microsoft.com/en-us/library/ms176061.aspx*.

Creating a Table with FILESTREAM Columns

You're now ready to create a new *PhotoAlbum* table. SQL Server requires that any table using FILESTREAM storage has a *uniqueidentifier* column that is not nullable and specifies the *ROWGUIDCOL* attribute. You must also create a unique constraint on this column. Only one *ROWGUIDCOL* column can be defined in any given table, although you can then declare any number of *varbinary(max) FILESTREAM* columns in the table that you want for storing BLOB data. The statement in Listing 8-2 creates the *PhotoAlbum* table with a *Photo* column declared as *varbinary(max) FILESTREAM*.

LISTING 8-2 Creating a FILESTREAM-enabled table.

```
USE PhotoLibrary
GO

CREATE TABLE PhotoAlbum(
 PhotoId int PRIMARY KEY,
 RowId uniqueidentifier ROWGUIDCOL NOT NULL UNIQUE DEFAULT NEWSEQUENTIALID(),
 Description varchar(max),
 Photo varbinary(max) FILESTREAM DEFAULT(0x))
```

With this statement, you satisfy the FILESTREAM requirement for the *ROWGUIDCOL* column, yet you won't actually have to do anything to maintain that column. By declaring the *RowId* column with its *DEFAULT* value set to call the *NEWSEQUENTIALID* function, you can just ignore this column when inserting rows—simply not providing values for it will cause SQL Server to automatically generate the next available globally unique identifier (GUID) that it needs to support FILESTREAM on the table. The column is set to not accept *NULL* values and is defined with the required unique constraint.

You have also declared an integer *PhotoId* column for the table's primary key value. You'll use the *PhotoId* column to identify individual photos in the album, and SQL Server will use the *RowId* column to track and cross-reference photos in the file system with rows in the *PhotoAlbum* table. The *Photo* column holds the actual BLOB itself, being defined as a *varbinary(max)* data type with the *FILESTREAM* attribute applied. This means that it gets treated like a regular *varbinary(max)* column, but you know that its BLOB is really being stored under the covers in the file system by SQL Server. The *Photo* column is also defined with a default value of 0x, which represents a zero-length binary stream. This will come into play later when you start programming with *SqlFileStream*. We're not there yet, so you can just ignore the default assignment for now.

Storing and Retrieving FILESTREAM Data

To start, you'll use plain T-SQL to cast simple string data into and out of the *varbinary(max)* data type of the *Photo* column. This is certainly contrived, but starting small like this is the best way to learn FILESTREAM. You are going to monitor and observe effects on the NTFS file system as SQL Server utilizes it for BLOB storage. Begin with the following *INSERT* statement that adds your first row to the *PhotoAlbum* table:

```
INSERT INTO PhotoAlbum(PhotoId, Description, Photo)
 VALUES(1, 'Text pic', CAST('BLOB' As varbinary(max)))
```

This *INSERT* statement reads no differently than it would if you were using a regular *varbinary(max)* column for the *Photo* column without the *FILESTREAM* attribute. It appears to store the unstructured *Photo* column data in line with the rest of the relational columns, and it certainly appears the same way when returning the data back with a *SELECT* query, as shown here:

```
SELECT *, CAST(Photo AS varchar) AS PhotoText FROM PhotoAlbum
GO

PhotoId RowId                                Description Photo      PhotoText
------- ------------------------------------ ----------- ---------- ---------
1       FC7D28BC-E8C6-E011-9849-080027565B78 Text pic    0x424C4F42 BLOB

(1 row(s) affected)
```

However, if you peek inside the FILESTREAM data container, you can verify that SQL Server is actually storing the *Photo* column outside the database in the file system. Because SQL Server obfuscates the file system that it's managing for you behind the scenes, you can't understand the manner in which files and folders are named, organized, and referenced back to the relational database. But just by drilling down and probing the subfolders beneath the *Photos* directory, you will discover that there is in fact a new file stored in the file system. (Windows will prompt for permission before opening the *Photos* directory.) This file was created as a result of the *INSERT* statement. View it by right-clicking the file name and choosing Open, as shown in Figure 8-4:

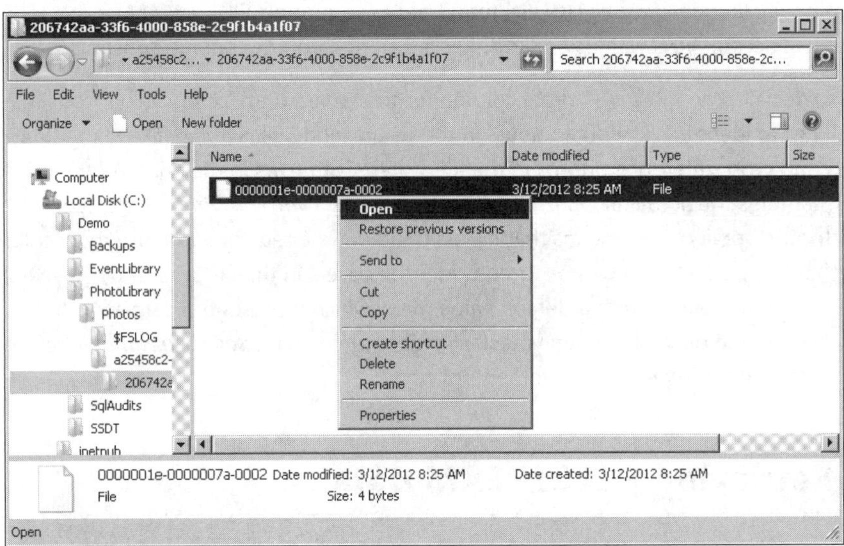

FIGURE 8-4 Exploring the FILESTREAM file system (note that the actual folder and file names will not match the ones shown in this figure).

If you select Notepad to open the file, you will see clear proof that the unstructured content of the *Photo* column is stored outside the database and in the file system. In this example, the text BLOB that was inserted into the *Photo* column is stored in the file that you've opened in Notepad, as shown in Figure 8-5:

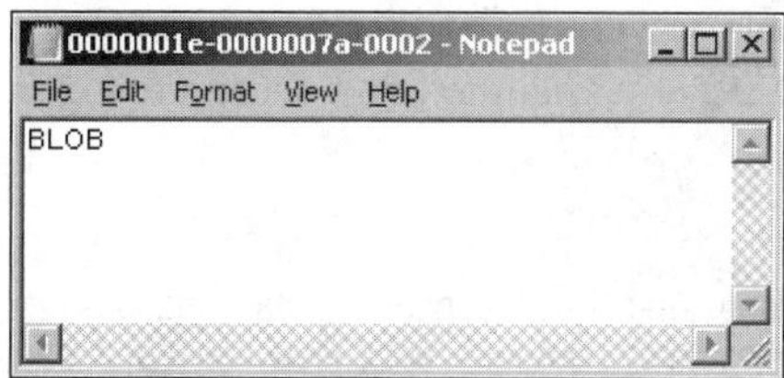

FIGURE 8-5 Examining unstructured FILESTREAM content in Notepad.

This clearly shows how FILESTREAM data is logically connected to—but physically separated from—the database. Because the unstructured data is stored entirely in the file system, you can easily alter its content by directly updating the file in Notepad without involving the database. To prove the point once again, let's change the text in the file from *BLOB* to *Cool*, and save the changes back to the file system, as displayed in Figure 8-6.

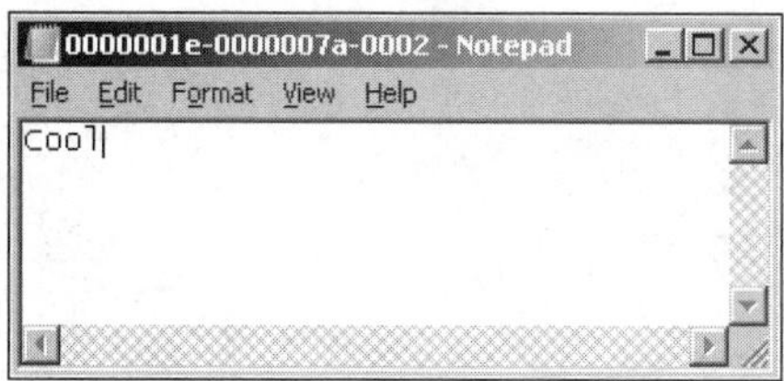

FIGURE 8-6 Changing FILESTREAM content directly in the file system.

The altered FILESTREAM data is reflected in the same *SELECT* statement you ran earlier, as shown here:

```
SELECT *, CAST(Photo AS varchar) AS PhotoText FROM PhotoAlbum
GO

PhotoId RowId                                Description Photo      PhotoText
------- ------------------------------------ ----------- ---------- ---------
1       FC7D28BC-E8C6-E011-9849-080027565B78 Text pic    0x436F6F6C Cool

(1 row(s) affected)
```

You are performing this exercise to verify that SQL Server is using the file system to store *varbinary(max) FILESTREAM* data. However, we must stress that the purpose here is purely demonstrative. Ordinarily, you must *never* tamper directly with files in the FILESTREAM data container this way. FILESTREAM provides a *total* abstraction over the *varbinary(max)* data type, and you need to consider the physical file system as part of the database (which it is, by virtue of the FILESTREAM group associated with it)—it gets managed by SQL Server exclusively. Later in the chapter, you'll learn how FileTable (new in SQL Server 2012) adds yet another layer of abstraction by exposing a network share over FILESTREAM-based BLOBs that *can* be treated and accessed just like an ordinary file system.

Note Normal SQL Server column-level security permissions apply to *varbinary(max) FILESTREAM* columns.

In-lining BLOB data in T-SQL is tedious, but it is feasible and can be done when you are working with relatively small byte streams. Run the following *INSERT* statement to add a second row, this time with a real image in the *Photo* column.

```
INSERT INTO PhotoAlbum(PhotoId, Description, Photo)
VALUES(2, 'Document icon', 0x4749463839610C000E00B30000FFFFFFC6DEC6C0C0C0000080000000D3121200000
000000000000000000000000000000000000000000000000000000021F90401000002002C000000000C000E0000042C9
0C8398525206B202F1820C80584806D1975A29AF48530870D2CEDC2B1CBB6332EDE35D9CB27DCA554484204003B)
```

Now revisit the file system and you'll find another file was just created. This new file contains the image represented by the byte stream in the *INSERT* statement you just executed. Right-click the file and choose Open, but this time select Paint to open the file with. Figure 8-7 shows the image open and magnified in Paint.

FIGURE 8-7 Examining unstructured FILESTREAM content in Paint.

More likely, the BLOB source will be an external file. In this case, you can use *OPENROWSET* with its *BULK* and *SINGLE_BLOB* options to consume the file (which can be located on a remote file share) into SQL Server as a *varbinary(max)* type. For example, if the BLOB is accessible as a file named *\\public\shared\doc.ico*, then the same result can be achieved with the following *INSERT* statement:

```
INSERT INTO PhotoAlbum(PhotoId, Description, Photo)
 VALUES(2, 'Document icon',
  (SELECT BulkColumn FROM OPENROWSET(BULK '\\public\shared\doc.ico', SINGLE_BLOB) AS x))
```

Deleting FILESTREAM Data

When a row is deleted from a FILESTREAM-enabled table, the row is removed from the table and the files associated with the row's *varbinary(max) FILESTREAM* columns are removed from the file system. The files are deleted by the FILESTREAM garbage collector running on a separate background thread, so you might notice that the physical file is not removed from the FILESTREAM data container immediately.

SQL Server triggers the FILESTREAM garbage collector thread when a *CHECKPOINT* occurs, which, for databases that are not highly transactional, might take a long time to occur. If you want to trigger the garbage collector thread yourself, you can issue an explicit *CHECKPOINT* statement to the server.

Direct Streaming in .NET with *SqlFileStream*

You just saw how to embed and extract binary streams of data in T-SQL. A similar T-SQL approach can be used with ADO.NET in your .NET applications to embed and extract byte arrays against *varbinary(max) FILESTREAM* columns. It's easy, and it works, but it is not the most efficient way to transfer BLOBs into and out of the database. Behind the scenes, SQL Server must use its own memory to stream BLOBs in and out, and it exposes BLOBs to client applications as *varbinary(max)* data types that are not optimized for streaming.

The proper (and fastest) way to get data into and out of FILESTREAM columns is to build a .NET client application (written in C# or VB .NET, for example), and use the special *SqlFileStream* class (in .NET 3.5 SP1 and higher) to access the BLOBs. *SqlFileStream* is a .NET wrapper around *OpenSqlFilestream*, a function provided by the SQL Server native client application programming interface (API) that gives your application safe, direct access to *varbinary(max) FILESTREAM* column data stored in the file system. With this approach, SQL Server does not use any of its own memory for the BLOB transfer, which reduces demand on server resources. Instead, your application, using its own resources, streams directly against the file system without the overhead of the *varbinary(max)* data type abstraction. The result is lightning fast BLOB performance—although there's a price to be paid, of course. Direct streaming with *SqlFileStream* is relatively more complex than using T-SQL, because you need to interact with the FILESTREAM data store. Overall, it's not too onerous though, and as you're about to see, it's not difficult to understand and implement the appropriate coding pattern.

Understanding *SqlFileStream*

With *SqlFileStream*, .NET applications can use the standard *FileStream* class in the *System.IO* namespace to deliver high-performance streaming of BLOB data against the SQL Server-managed file system. In the next section, you'll learn how to use *SqlFileStream* to store and retrieve pictures in the *Photo* column. But before we dig into the intricacies of coding, let's first get a high-level understanding of how *SqlFileStream* works.

Note You can also create native-code FILESTREAM applications (written in in C++, for example) by calling *OpenSqlFilestream* directly. The handle returned by this function can then use either the *ReadFile* and *WriteFile* Microsoft Win32 API functions. Our samples are .NET (managed-code) applications written in C#, but the process we describe here is fundamentally the same for native-code applications.

You begin by starting a database transaction. When working with *SqlFileStream*, you always work with transactions (even for read access). There is no way to avoid them because FILESTREAM, by design, coordinates transactional integrity across structured and unstructured data access in the database and the NTFS file system. After starting the transaction, you perform standard T-SQL operations to query or modify data. But you don't actually include *varbinary(max) FILESTREAM* columns (BLOBs) in your T-SQL statements (neither for reading nor for writing). Instead, you ask SQL Server to give you two key pieces of information that will enable you to access the BLOBs much more efficiently than using T-SQL—specifically, via direct file streaming using *SqlFileStream*.

First, you need a logical UNC path to the file holding the BLOB on the server, which you get by calling the *PathName* method on the desired *varbinary(max) FILESTREAM* value instance. Second, you need the file system transaction context, which you get by calling the *GET_FILESTREAM_TRANSACTION_CONTEXT* function (which returns *NULL* if a transaction has not yet been established). Neither of these items mean anything to your code; you just need to pass them on, along with your desired access (read or write), to the *SqlFileStream* constructor. The constructed *SqlFileStream* object inherits from *System.IO.Stream*, so you can then read or write against it using the same .NET coding patterns you use to access ordinary streams. This provides you with a streaming "tunnel" between your application and the SQL Server internally managed file system for each BLOB.

When you start the database transaction, SQL Server internally initiates an NTFS file system transaction over the BLOB data and associates it with the current database transaction. SQL Server then further ensures that both transactions will subsequently either commit or roll back together. Only when you commit the database transaction does SQL Server internally commit the NTFS file system transaction. This permanently saves changes to both the structured filegroups of the database (from the T-SQL operations) and the files in the file system (from the streaming I/O operations) at the same time. Similarly, rolling back the transaction undoes changes to both the database and file system simultaneously.

Note The UNC reference returned by the *PathName* method is not a real path to the physical file system on the server. Rather, *PathName* returns a fabricated path used by *SqlFileStream* to enable direct streaming between the file system and client applications. This UNC path always begins with the share name specified when FILESTREAM was enabled for the machine (Figure 8-1) and contains the GUID value in the corresponding row's *uniqueidentifier ROWGUIDCOL* column. The file system is secured on the server no differently than the data and transaction filegroups (.mdf and .ldf files) are secured. Users should never be granted direct access to the file system on the server (although you can grant them indirect access via a FileTable, as we'll discuss later on).

Continuing with the photo library example, you'll now create a Windows Forms application in C# that contains all the key elements that bring a FILESTREAM application together—nothing more, nothing less. Your application will allow users to create new photos in the database by streaming BLOBs into the *Photo* column. Users can also select photos, which will stream BLOBs back out from the *Photo* column and into a *PictureBox* control for display.

Building the Windows Forms Client

You'll begin with the user interface (UI), which is very simple. Start Microsoft Visual Studio 2010 and create a new C# Windows Forms application. Design a form with two separate group boxes: one at the top of the form for inserting photos and another beneath it for retrieving photos. Provide labels and text boxes for entering a photo ID, file name, and description in the top group box, along with a link label to invoke a save operation. In the bottom group box, provide a text box and label for entering a photo ID and a link label to invoke a load operation. Include a label to display the description returned from the database and a picture box to display the photo BLOB returned via FILESTREAM. After performing some aesthetic alignment and formatting, your form should appear something like the one shown in Figure 8-8.

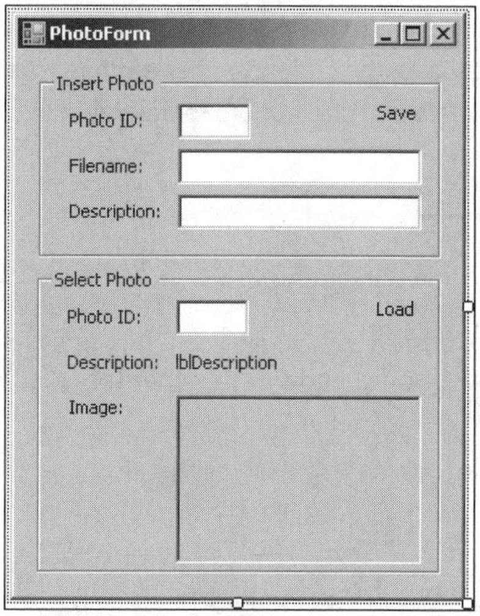

FIGURE 8-8 A simple FILESTREAM Windows UI form.

You'll write only a very small amount of code behind this Windows form, and implement the FILESTREAM logic in a separate data access class. Add the code behind the click events for the form's Save and Load link buttons, as shown in Listing 8-3.

LISTING 8-3 UI calls into FILESTREAM data access class for saving and loading image files.

```
private void lnkSave_LinkClicked(object sender, LinkLabelLinkClickedEventArgs e)
{
  int photoId = int.Parse(this.txtSavePhotoId.Text);
  string desc = this.txtDescription.Text;
  string filename = this.txtFilename.Text;

  PhotoData.InsertPhoto(photoId, desc, filename);
}
```

```
private void lnkLoad_LinkClicked(object sender, LinkLabelLinkClickedEventArgs e)
{
  int photoId = int.Parse(this.txtLoadPhotoId.Text);

  string desc;
  Image photo = PhotoData.SelectPhoto(photoId, out desc);

  this.lblDescription.Text = desc;
  this.picImage.Image = photo;
}
```

When the user supplies new photo information and clicks Save, the code retrieves the photo ID, description, and file name from the three text boxes and passes them to the *InsertPhoto* method of the *PhotoData* class. When the user specifies a photo ID and clicks Load, the code calls the *SelectPhoto* method of the *PhotoData* class to retrieve the requested image (with its textual description) for display.

Programming *SqlFileStream* Data Access

All the magic happens inside the *PhotoData* class, which is shown in Listing 8-4.

Note As with all code in this book, the full FILESTREAM demo code in this chapter is available on the book's companion website.

LISTING 8-4 Implementing a FILESTREAM data access managed client class.

```
using System;
using System.Data;
using System.Data.SqlClient;
using System.Data.SqlTypes;
using System.Drawing;
using System.IO;
using System.Transactions;

namespace PhotoLibraryApp
{
  public class PhotoData
  {
    private const string ConnStr =
      "Data Source=.;Integrated Security=True;Initial Catalog=PhotoLibrary;";

    #region "Insert Photo"

    public static void InsertPhoto(int photoId, string desc, string filename)
    {
      const string InsertTSql = @"
       INSERT INTO PhotoAlbum(PhotoId, Description)
          VALUES(@PhotoId, @Description);
```

```
    SELECT Photo.PathName(), GET_FILESTREAM_TRANSACTION_CONTEXT()
      FROM PhotoAlbum
      WHERE PhotoId = @PhotoId";

  string serverPath;
  byte[] serverTxn;

  using (TransactionScope ts = new TransactionScope())
  {
    using (SqlConnection conn = new SqlConnection(ConnStr))
    {
      conn.Open();

      using (SqlCommand cmd = new SqlCommand(InsertTSql, conn))
      {
        cmd.Parameters.Add("@PhotoId", SqlDbType.Int).Value = photoId;
        cmd.Parameters.Add("@Description", SqlDbType.VarChar).Value = desc;
        using (SqlDataReader rdr = cmd.ExecuteReader(CommandBehavior.
                                                      SingleRow))
        {
          rdr.Read();
          serverPath = rdr.GetSqlString(0).Value;
          serverTxn = rdr.GetSqlBinary(1).Value;
          rdr.Close();
        }
      }
      SavePhotoFile(filename, serverPath, serverTxn);
    }
    ts.Complete();
  }
}

private static void SavePhotoFile
  (string clientPath, string serverPath, byte[] serverTxn)
{
  const int BlockSize = 1024 * 512;

  using (FileStream source =
    new FileStream(clientPath, FileMode.Open, FileAccess.Read))
  {
    using (SqlFileStream dest =
      new SqlFileStream(serverPath, serverTxn, FileAccess.Write))
    {
      byte[] buffer = new byte[BlockSize];
      int bytesRead;
      while ((bytesRead = source.Read(buffer, 0, buffer.Length)) > 0)
      {
        dest.Write(buffer, 0, bytesRead);
        dest.Flush();
      }
     dest.Close();
    }
    source.Close();
```

```
  }
}

#endregion

#region "Select Photo"

public static Image SelectPhoto(int photoId, out string desc)
{
  const string SelectTSql = @"
    SELECT
     Description, Photo.PathName(), GET_FILESTREAM_TRANSACTION_CONTEXT()
      FROM PhotoAlbum
      WHERE PhotoId = @PhotoId";

  Image photo;
  string serverPath;
  byte[] serverTxn;

  using (TransactionScope ts = new TransactionScope())
  {
    using (SqlConnection conn = new SqlConnection(ConnStr))
    {
      conn.Open();

      using (SqlCommand cmd = new SqlCommand(SelectTSql, conn))
      {
        cmd.Parameters.Add("@PhotoId", SqlDbType.Int).Value = photoId;

        using (SqlDataReader rdr = cmd.ExecuteReader(CommandBehavior.
                                                     SingleRow))
        {
          rdr.Read();
          desc = rdr.GetSqlString(0).Value;
          serverPath = rdr.GetSqlString(1).Value;
          serverTxn = rdr.GetSqlBinary(2).Value;
          rdr.Close();
        }
      }
      photo = LoadPhotoImage(serverPath, serverTxn);
    }

    ts.Complete();
  }

  return photo;
}

private static Image LoadPhotoImage(string filePath, byte[] txnToken)
{
  Image photo;

  using (SqlFileStream sfs =
    new SqlFileStream(filePath, txnToken, FileAccess.Read))
```

```
        {
          photo = Image.FromStream(sfs);
          sfs.Close();
        }

        return photo;
      }

      #endregion
    }
  }
```

Let's explain this code in detail. We'll start at the top with some required namespace inclusions. The two *using* statements to take notice of are *System.Data.SqlTypes* and *System.Transactions*. The *System.Data.SqlTypes* namespace defines the *SqlFileStream* class that you'll be using to stream BLOBs. No special assembly reference is required to use this class, because it is provided by the *System.Data.dll* assembly that your project is already referencing (Visual Studio set this reference automatically when it created your project). The *System.Transactions* namespace defines the *TransactionScope* class that lets you code implicit transactions against the database. This class is provided by the *System.Transactions.dll* assembly, which is not referenced automatically. You'll need to add a reference to it now, or the code will not compile. Right-click the project in Solution Explorer and choose Add Reference. In the Add Reference dialog, click the .NET tab, and scroll to find the *System.Transactions* component. Then double-click it to add the reference.

More Info Chapter 10 provides detailed coverage of the conventional ADO.NET objects for SQL Server (*SqlConnection*, *SqlCommand*, *SqlDataReader*, and so on). There, we discuss explicit transactions (using the ADO.NET *SqlTransaction* object) versus implicit transactions (using *TransactionScope*). Although the former will also work with *SqlFileStream*, Chapter 10 explains why implicit transactions are preferred.

A connection string is defined at the top of the code as a hard-coded constant named *ConnStr*. This is just for demonstration purposes; a real-world application would store the connection string elsewhere (such as in a configuration file, possibly encrypted), but we're keeping the example simple.

Important We must reiterate that this code takes a minimalist approach for proof-of-concept purposes only. It is not representative of best coding practices, and has no error handling. Although the *using* constructs in this code ensure that all objects that allocate unmanaged resources (such as database connections and file handles) are disposed of properly even if an exception occurs, your production applications must implement a more robust strategy that includes the use of *try/catch/finally* blocks with a mechanism for error logging and recovery.

The first method defined in the class is *InsertPhoto*, which accepts a new photo integer ID, string description, and full path to an image file to be saved to the database, as shown here:

```
public static void InsertPhoto(int photoId, string desc, string filename)
{
  const string InsertTSql = @"
    INSERT INTO PhotoAlbum(PhotoId, Description)
      VALUES(@PhotoId, @Description);
    SELECT Photo.PathName(), GET_FILESTREAM_TRANSACTION_CONTEXT()
      FROM PhotoAlbum
      WHERE PhotoId = @PhotoId";

  string serverPath;
  byte[] serverTxn;

  using (TransactionScope ts = new TransactionScope())
  {
    using (SqlConnection conn = new SqlConnection(ConnStr))
    {
      conn.Open();

      using (SqlCommand cmd = new SqlCommand(InsertTSql, conn))
      {
        cmd.Parameters.Add("@PhotoId", SqlDbType.Int).Value = photoId;
        cmd.Parameters.Add("@Description", SqlDbType.VarChar).Value = desc;
        using (SqlDataReader rdr = cmd.ExecuteReader(CommandBehavior.SingleRow))
        {
          rdr.Read();
          serverPath = rdr.GetSqlString(0).Value;
          serverTxn = rdr.GetSqlBinary(1).Value;
          rdr.Close();
        }
      }
      SavePhotoFile(filename, serverPath, serverTxn);
    }
    ts.Complete();
  }
}
```

Notice that the *InsertTSql* string constant defined at the top of the method specifies an *INSERT* statement that includes the *PhotoId* and *Description* columns, but not the actual *Photo BLOB* column. Instead, the *INSERT* statement is followed immediately by a *SELECT* statement that retrieves two pieces of information you'll use to stream the BLOB into the *Photo* column much more efficiently than using ordinary T-SQL—namely a logical UNC pathname to the file and the transactional context token. You'll recall from the discussion earlier that those are the two values needed to use *SqlFileStream*, and you're about to see how exactly. But all you've done so far is define a constant holding two T-SQL statements. The constant is followed by two variable declarations, *serverPath* and *serverTxn*; these variables will receive the two special values when you execute those T-SQL statements later in the code.

The method then creates and enters a new *TransactionScope* block. This does not actually begin the database transaction (you've not even connected to the database yet), but rather declares that all data access within the block (and in any code called from within the block) must participate in a database transaction. Inside the *TransactionScope* block, the code creates and opens a new *SqlConnection*. Being the first data access code inside the *TransactionScope* block, this also implicitly begins the database transaction. Next, it creates a *SqlCommand* object associated with the open connection and prepares its command text to contain your T-SQL statements (the *INSERT* followed by the *SELECT*).

Invoking the *ExecuteReader* method executes the T-SQL statements and returns a reader from which you can retrieve the values returned by the *SELECT* statement. The transaction is still pending at this time. The *INSERT* statement does not provide a value for *RowId* and instead allows SQL Server to automatically generate and assign a new *uniqueidentifier ROWGUID* value by default just like before when you used T-SQL to insert the first two rows. We've also pointed out that no value is provided for the *Photo* column—and this is exactly how the default 0x value that you defined earlier for the *Photo* column comes into play (we said we'd come back to it, and here you are).

Although the row has been added by the *INSERT* statement, it will rollback (disappear) if a problem occurs before the transaction is committed. Because you didn't provide a BLOB value for the *Photo* column in the new row, SQL Server honors the default value 0x that you established for it in the *CREATE TABLE* statement for *PhotoAlbum*. This represents a zero-length binary stream, which is completely different than *NULL*. Being a *varbinary(max)* column decorated with the *FILESTREAM* attribute, an empty file gets created in the file system that SQL Server associates with the new row. At the same time, SQL Server initiates an NTFS file system transaction over this new empty file and synchronizes it with the database transaction. So just like the new row, the new file will disappear if the database transaction does not commit successfully.

Important You cannot use *SqlFileStream* to populate BLOBs against *NULL* values in a new row's *varbinary(max) FILESTREAM* column. You must always add new rows with a zero-length binary stream (0x) in the BLOB column, either by making it the default value as in this example, or by specifying it explicitly in your *INSERT* statement. This will result in the creation of a zero-length file that can be streamed to (overwritten) by calling *SqlFileStream*, as described here.

Immediately following the *INSERT* statement, the *SELECT* statement returns *Photo.PathName* and *GET_FILESTREAM_TRANSACTION_CONTEXT*. What you're essentially doing with the *WHERE* clause in this *SELECT* statement is reading back the same row you have just added (but not yet committed) to the *PhotoAlbum* table in order to reference the BLOB stored in the new file that was just created (also not yet committed) in the file system.

The value returned by *Photo.PathName* is a fabricated path to the BLOB for the selected *PhotoId*. The path is expressed in UNC format, and points to the network share name established for the server instance when you first enabled *FILESTREAM* (which is *MSSQLSERVER* in this case, as shown in Figure 8-1). It is not a path to the file's physical location on the server, but rather contains information SQL Server can use to derive the file's physical location. For example, you'll notice that it always contains the GUID value in the *uniqueidentifier ROWGUIDCOL* column of the BLOB's corresponding row. You retrieve the path value from the reader's first column and store it in the *serverPath* string variable.

Note You're able to read back the row you just added because your code is running inside the same transaction. However, with the default (and recommended) SQL Server transaction isolation mode set to Read Committed, no other users will be able to see this row because it has not yet been committed. That would be what is often referred to as a "dirty read," because the data will never actually come into existence if the code fails to commit the pending transaction. To prevent dirty reads, SQL Server imposes a lock on the page holding the uncommitted row. It's therefore very important for your transactions to be committed (or rolled back) as soon as possible after they are started. Any code that doesn't absolutely need to run inside a transaction should run outside.

We just explained how SQL Server initiated an NTFS file system transaction over the FILESTREAM data in the new row's *Photo* column when you started the database transaction. The *GET_FILESTREAM_TRANSACTION_CONTEXT* function returns a handle to that NTFS transaction (if you're not inside a transaction, this function will return *NULL* and your code won't work). You obtain the transaction context, which is returned by the reader's second column as a *SqlBinary* value, and store it in the byte array named *serverTxn*.

Armed with the BLOB path reference in *serverPath* and the transaction context in *serverTxn*, you have what you need to create a *SqlFileStream* object and perform direct file access to stream the image into the *Photo* column. You close the reader, terminate its *using* block, then terminate the enclosing *using* block for the *SqlConnection* as well. This would normally close the database connection implicitly, but that gets deferred in this case because the code is still nested inside the outer *using* block for the *TransactionScope* object. So the connection is still open at this time, and the transaction is still pending. It is precisely at this point that you call the *SavePhotoFile* method to stream the specified image file into the *Photo* column of the newly inserted *PhotoAlbum* row, overwriting the empty file just created by default. When control returns from *SavePhotoFile*, the *TransactionScope* object's *Complete* method is invoked and its *using* block is terminated, signaling the transaction management API that everything worked as expected. This implicitly commits the database transaction (which in turn commits the NTFS file system transaction) and closes the database connection.

The *SavePhotoFile* method reads from the source file and writes to the database FILESTREAM storage in 512 KB chunks at a time using ordinary .NET streaming techniques, as shown here:

```
private static void SavePhotoFile
  (string clientPath, string serverPath, byte[] serverTxn)
{
  const int BlockSize = 1024 * 512;

  using (FileStream source =
    new FileStream(clientPath, FileMode.Open, FileAccess.Read))
  {
    using (SqlFileStream dest =
      new SqlFileStream(serverPath, serverTxn, FileAccess.Write))
    {
      byte[] buffer = new byte[BlockSize];
```

```
      int bytesRead;
      while ((bytesRead = source.Read(buffer, 0, buffer.Length)) > 0)
      {
        dest.Write(buffer, 0, bytesRead);
        dest.Flush();
      }
      dest.Close();
    }
    source.Close();
  }
}
```

The method begins by defining a *BlockSize* integer constant that is set to a reasonable value of 512 KB. Picture files larger than this will be streamed to the server in 512 KB blocks at a time. The local source image file (in *clientPath*) is then opened on an ordinary read-only *FileStream* object.

Then the destination file is opened by passing the two special values (*serverPath* and *serverTxn*), along with a *FileAccess.Write* enumeration requesting write access, into the *SqlFileStream* constructor. Like the source *FileStream* object, *SqlFileStream* inherits from *System.IO.Stream*, so it can be treated just like any ordinary stream. Thus, you attain write access to the destination BLOB on the database server's NTFS file system. Remember that this output file is enlisted in an NTFS transaction and nothing you stream to it will be permanently saved until the database transaction is committed by the terminating *TransactionScope* block, after *SavePhotoFile* completes.

The rest of the *SavePhotoFile* method implements a simple loop that reads from the source *FileStream* and writes to the destination *SqlFileStream*, one 512 KB block at a time until the entire source file is processed, and then it closes both streams.

That covers inserting new photos. The rest of the code contains methods to retrieve existing photos and stream their content from the file system into an *Image* object for display. You'll find that this code follows the same pattern as the last, only now you're performing read access.

The *SelectPhoto* method accepts a photo ID and returns the string description from the database in an output parameter. The actual BLOB itself is returned as the method's return value in *a System.Drawing.Image* object. You populate the *Image* object with the BLOB by streaming into it from the database server's NTFS file system using *SqlFileStream*, as shown here:

```
public static Image SelectPhoto(int photoId, out string desc)
{
  const string SelectTSql = @"
    SELECT Description, Photo.PathName(), GET_FILESTREAM_TRANSACTION_CONTEXT()
      FROM PhotoAlbum
      WHERE PhotoId = @PhotoId";

  Image photo;
  string serverPath;
  byte[] serverTxn;

  using (TransactionScope ts = new TransactionScope())
  {
    using (SqlConnection conn = new SqlConnection(ConnStr))
    {
      conn.Open();
```

```
      using (SqlCommand cmd = new SqlCommand(SelectTSql, conn))
      {
        cmd.Parameters.Add("@PhotoId", SqlDbType.Int).Value = photoId;

        using (SqlDataReader rdr = cmd.ExecuteReader(CommandBehavior.SingleRow))
        {
          rdr.Read();
          desc = rdr.GetSqlString(0).Value;
          serverPath = rdr.GetSqlString(1).Value;
          serverTxn = rdr.GetSqlBinary(2).Value;
          rdr.Close();
        }
      }
      photo = LoadPhotoImage(serverPath, serverTxn);
    }

    ts.Complete();
  }

  return photo;
}
```

Once again, you start things off by entering a *TransactionScope* block and opening a connection. You then execute a simple *SELECT* statement that queries the *PhotoAlbum* table for the record specified by the photo ID and returns the description and full path to the image BLOB, as well as the FILESTREAM transactional context token. And once again you use the pathname and transactional context with *SqlFileStream* to tie into the server's file system in the *LoadPhotoImage* method, as shown here:

```
private static Image LoadPhotoImage(string serverPath, byte[] serverTxn)
{
  Image photo;

  using (SqlFileStream sfs = new SqlFileStream(serverPath, serverTxn, FileAccess.Read))
  {
    photo = Image.FromStream(sfs);
    sfs.Close();
  }

  return photo;
}
```

Just as when you were inserting new photos (only this time using *FileAccess.Read* instead of *FileAccess.ReadWrite*), you create a new *SqlFileStream* object from the logical pathname and transaction context. You then pull the BLOB content directly from the NTFS file system on the server into a new *System.Drawing.Image* object using the static *Image.FromStream* method against the *SqlFileStream* object. The populated image is then passed back up to the form, where it is displayed using the *Image* property of the *PictureBox* control.

It's time to see all of this in action and give the application a run! To insert a new photo, specify a unique photo ID (you've already used 1 and 2 already), an image file, and a description in the top group box in the PhotoForm window, as shown in Figure 8-9, and then click Save.

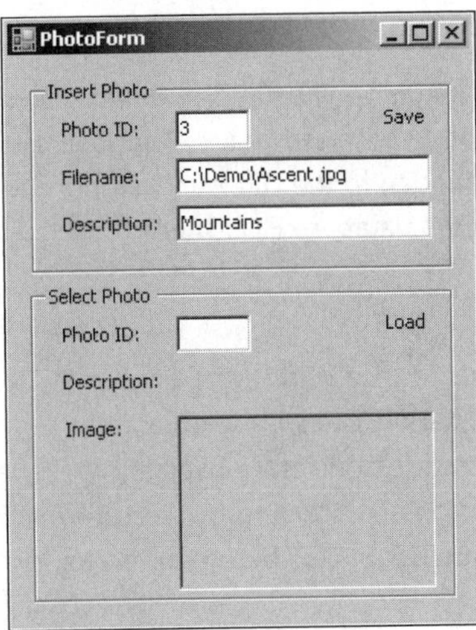

FIGURE 8-9 Inserting a new photo into FILESTREAM storage.

To select and display the photo and its description back from the database, type its photo ID in the bottom group box, and then click Load. The photo is displayed, as shown in Figure 8-10.

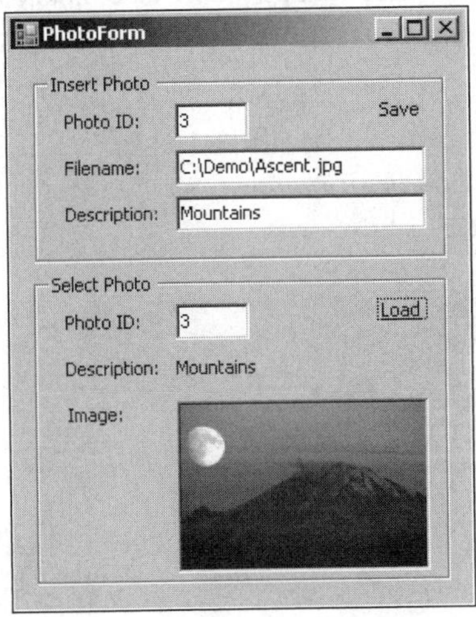

FIGURE 8-10 Retrieving a photo from FILESTREAM storage.

This application is small, but it demonstrates everything needed to leverage the power of FILESTREAM in your .NET client applications. The code that you need to write follows a fairly straightforward pattern that adapts easily to different scenarios. In the next FILESTREAM application, you'll stream content from a Hypertext Transfer Protocol (HTTP) service and consume it in a Windows Presentation Foundation (WPF) client using the very same FILESTREAM principles that you applied in this Windows Forms application.

Creating a Streaming HTTP Service

You'll now build a very simple service to deliver photos over HTTP. It will be implemented as a normal Microsoft ASP.NET Web Application project with a single PhotoService.aspx page. This page can be called by any HTTP client that passes in a photo ID value appended to the URL query string, and it will stream back the binary content for the specified photo from the database FILESTREAM storage in SQL Server to the client.

More Info We use an ordinary ASP.NET page rather than a true Windows Communications Foundation (WCF) service in this example, because the ASP.NET *Response* object has built-in streaming capabilities that are relatively easy to code against. Conversely, WCF data contracts are buffered entirely in memory before sending and receiving by design, which does not work well for potentially large byte streams (such as BLOBs being served up by FILESTREAM).

Two readily available techniques can be leveraged to create WCF services that stream BLOBs. First, the Message Transmission Optimization Mechanism (MTOM) protocol allows WCF data contracts to be streamed rather than buffered, using an approach very similar to the way SMTP transmits embedded email attachments. Your second option is to use WCF Data Services and implement a streaming provider, which returns BLOB data as a binary media resource separate from the normal text-based service response feed.

To build the service, follow these steps. Start Visual Studio and choose File | New | Project. Create a Microsoft Visual C# ASP.NET Web Application project named *PhotoLibraryHttpService* in a solution named *PhotoLibraryFileStreamDemo*, as shown in Figure 8-11.

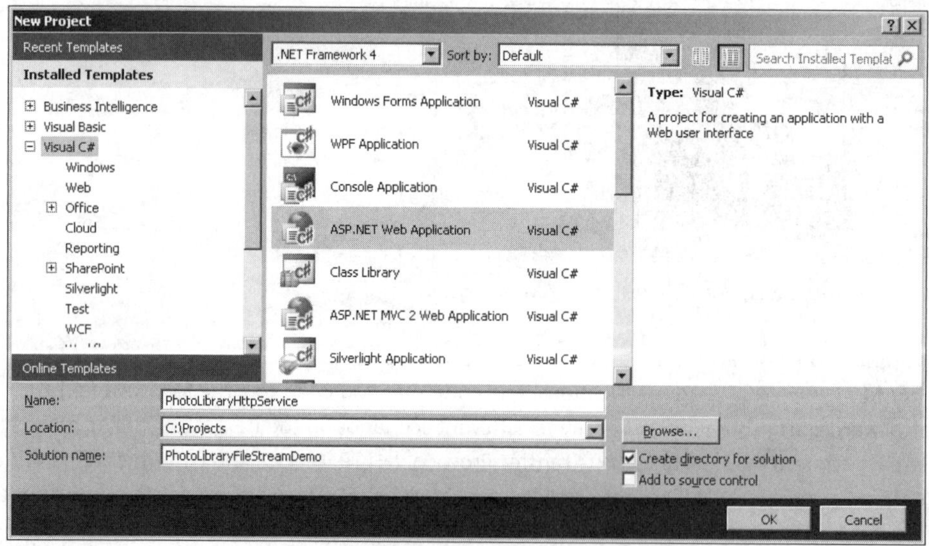

FIGURE 8-11 Creating the streaming HTTP service project.

Add a new Web Form named *PhotoService.aspx*. Unlike a typical .aspx page, this page will not return HTML content. Instead, the page's code-behind class will stream out binary content from the database directly through the *Response* object built in to ASP.NET. Therefore, delete all the HTML markup, leaving only the <@ *Page* %> directive at the very top that links the .aspx page with its code-behind class. Now make this the default startup page by right-clicking *PhotoService.aspx* in Solution Explorer and then choosing Set As Start Page. Next, switch to the code-behind class file by right-clicking again on the *PhotoService.aspx* node in Solution Explorer and then choosing View Code.

Replace the starter code provided by Visual Studio with the code shown in Listing 8-5.

LISTING 8-5 Implementing code for the streaming photo service.

```
using System;
using System.Data;
using System.Data.SqlClient;
using System.Data.SqlTypes;
using System.IO;
using System.Transactions;
using System.Web.UI;

namespace PhotoLibraryHttpService
{
  public partial class PhotoService : Page
  {
    private const string ConnStr =
      "Data Source=.;Integrated Security=True;Initial Catalog=PhotoLibrary;";

    protected void Page_Load(object sender, EventArgs e)
    {
      int photoId = Convert.ToInt32(Request.QueryString["photoId"]);
      if (photoId == 0)
      {
        return;
      }

      const string SelectTSql = @"
        SELECT Photo.PathName(), GET_FILESTREAM_TRANSACTION_CONTEXT()
         FROM PhotoAlbum
         WHERE PhotoId = @PhotoId";

      using (TransactionScope ts = new TransactionScope())
      {
        using (SqlConnection conn = new SqlConnection(ConnStr))
        {
          conn.Open();

          string serverPath;
          byte[] serverTxn;

          using (SqlCommand cmd = new SqlCommand(SelectTSql, conn))
          {
            cmd.Parameters.Add("@PhotoId", SqlDbType.Int).Value = photoId;
```

```
          using (SqlDataReader rdr = cmd.ExecuteReader(CommandBehavior.SingleRow))
          {
            rdr.Read();
            serverPath = rdr.GetSqlString(0).Value;
            serverTxn = rdr.GetSqlBinary(1).Value;
            rdr.Close();
          }
        }

        this.StreamPhotoImage(serverPath, serverTxn);
      }
      ts.Complete();
    }
  }

  private void StreamPhotoImage(string serverPath, byte[] serverTxn)
  {
    const int BlockSize = 1024 * 512;
    const string JpegContentType = "image/jpeg";

    using (SqlFileStream sfs =
      new SqlFileStream(serverPath, serverTxn, FileAccess.Read))
    {
      byte[] buffer = new byte[BlockSize];
      int bytesRead;
      Response.BufferOutput = false;
      Response.ContentType = JpegContentType;
      while ((bytesRead = sfs.Read(buffer, 0, buffer.Length)) > 0)
      {
        Response.OutputStream.Write(buffer, 0, bytesRead);
        Response.Flush();
      }
      sfs.Close();
    }
  }
 }
}
```

This code bears a strong resemblance to the photo retrieval code in the earlier Windows Forms application. This includes the use of implicit transactions with *TransactionScope*, so you'll once again need to add the appropriate project reference. Right-click the project in Solution Explorer, choose Add Reference, click the .NET tab, and then double-click the *System.Transactions* component.

The *Page_Load* method first retrieves the photo ID passed in via the *photoId* query string value. If no value is passed, the method returns without streaming anything back. (Alternatively, you could stream back an "image not found" image.) Otherwise, as before, the photo file name and transaction context is obtained after establishing a connection and transaction on the database, and invoking a *SELECT* statement calling the *PathName* method and *GET_FILESTREAM_TRANSACTION_CONTEXT* function against the photo ID specified in the *WHERE* clause.

With these two key pieces of information in hand, the *StreamPhotoImage* method is called. The method begins by defining a *BlockSize* integer constant that is set to a reasonable value of 512 KB (as before, picture files larger than this will be streamed to the client in 512 KB blocks at a time). And then once again, you use *SqlFileStream* to read the BLOB data from SQL Server.

Note Because this code is executing under the auspices of a web server, you may also need to grant access to the photo storage directory for the account executing the webpage. This might be *ASPNET* or *NETWORK SERVICE* if you're using Internet Information Services (IIS) or your user account if you're executing the page using Visual Studio's development server.

Before streaming the binary photo content, you need to change two properties of the *Response* object. In an .aspx page, by default, the *Response* object's *BufferOutput* property is set to *true* and the *ContentType* is set to *text/html*. Here, you'll change *BufferOutput* to *false* (for true streaming) and inform the client that you're sending a JPEG image by changing the *ContentType* property to *image/jpeg*.

Using the *SqlFileStream* object, the code then reads from the database FILESTREAM storage in 512 KB chunks and streams to the client using the *Reponse.OutputStream.Write* and *Response.Flush* methods. This is implemented with a simple loop that reads content from the *SqlFileStream* and sends it to the client via the *Response* object until the entire file is processed.

This completes the service application. Before moving on to build the WPF client, first test the service. Press **F5** to start the application.

When Internet Explorer launches *PhotoService.aspx*, it displays an empty page because no photo ID is present in the URL's query string. In the Address bar, append *?photoId=3* to the URL and reload the page. The code-behind class retrieves photo ID *2* from the database and streams it back for display in the browser, as shown in Figure 8-12.

FIGURE 8-12 Streaming a photo over HTTP to Internet Explorer.

You've created a functioning HTTP service application that streams pictures from the database to any HTTP client. It's now incredibly easy to build a small WPF client application that calls the service and displays photos. All that's needed is the proper URL with the desired photo ID specified in the query string, as you've just seen. You're using the ASP.NET Development Server provided by Visual Studio, which by default randomly assigns a port number on *localhost* (port 1157 was assigned this time, as indicated in Figure 8-12). You'll need to establish a fixed port number instead so that your WPF client can reliably construct a URL for calling the service. Any unused port number will suffice, and so just pick 22111 for this application. To set the port number, right-click the *PhotoLibraryHttpService* project in Solution Explorer, and then choose Properties. Select the Web tab, select the Specific Port option, and then type **22111** for the port number, as shown in Figure 8-13.

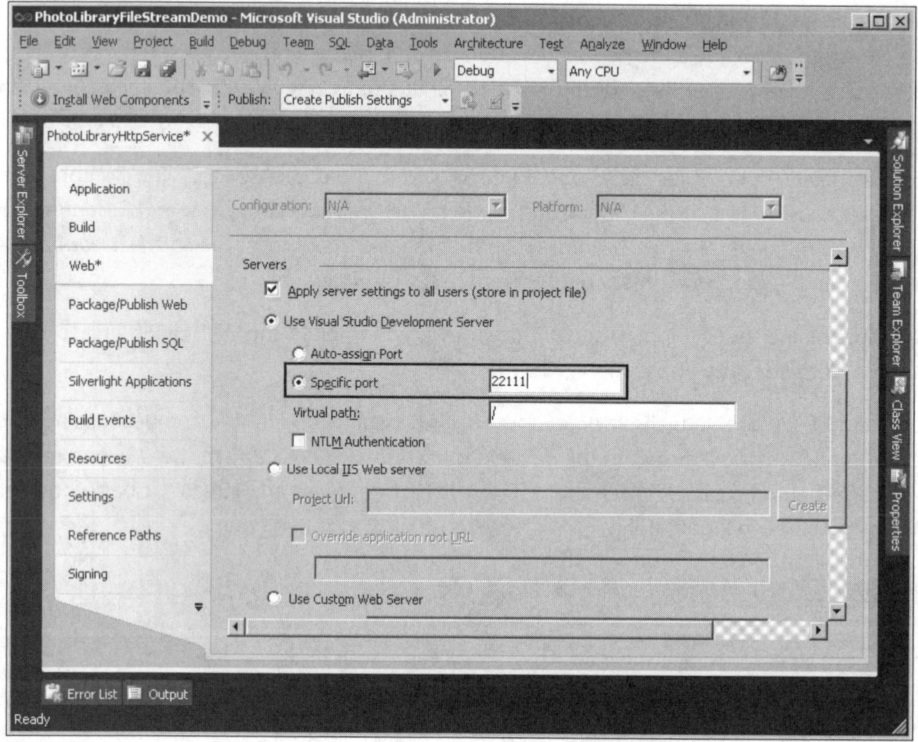

FIGURE 8-13 Setting a specific port number for the HTTP service application.

Building a WPF Client

To build the WPF client, follow these steps. In Visual Studio choose File | New | Project. Create a new Visual C# WPF Application project named *PhotoLibraryWpfClient*. Be sure to select Add To Solution in the Solution drop-down list, as shown in Figure 8-14, so that the project is added to the same *PhotoLibraryFileStreamDemo* solution that contains *PhotoLibraryHttpService*.

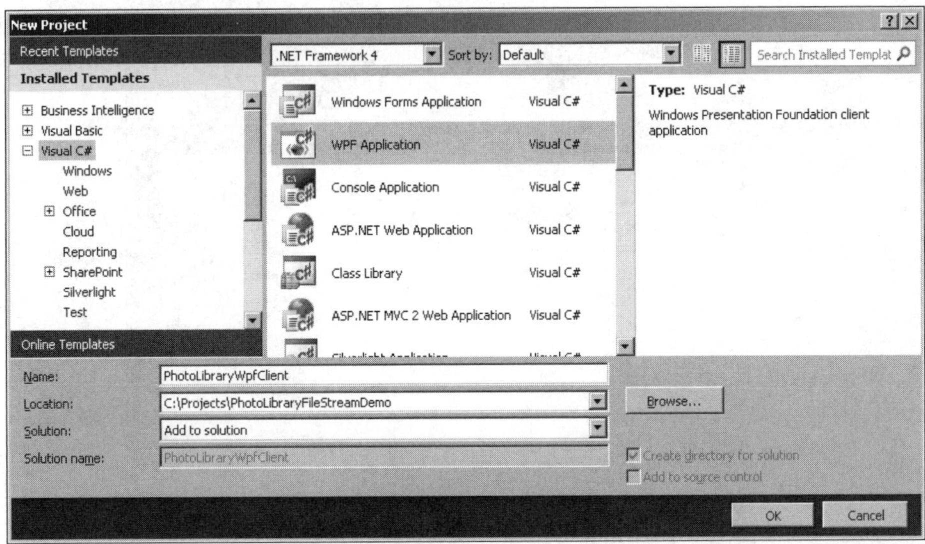

FIGURE 8-14 Creating the streaming WPF client application.

Visual Studio creates a new WPF application with a single window name MainWindow.xaml, and then opens the window designer. Replace the window's markup in the XAML window with the code shown in Listing 8-6.

LISTING 8-6 XAML markup for WPF photo client.

```
<Window x:Class="PhotoLibraryWpfClient.MainWindow"
    xmlns="http://schemas.microsoft.com/winfx/2006/xaml/presentation"
    xmlns:x="http://schemas.microsoft.com/winfx/2006/xaml"
    Title="MainWindow" Height="280" Width="300">
  <DockPanel>
    <StackPanel Orientation="Horizontal" DockPanel.Dock="Top" Margin="4">
      <Label>Photo ID</Label>
      <TextBox Name="txtPhotoId" Width="50" Margin="0,0,4,0" />
      <Button Name="btnDownload" Click="btnDownload_Click">Download Photo</Button>
    </StackPanel>
    <StackPanel Margin="4">
      <MediaElement Name="mediaElement1" />
    </StackPanel>
  </DockPanel>
</Window>
```

This is simple markup that merely defines *Label*, *TextBox*, *Button*, and *MediaElement* controls for the window, as shown in Figure 8-15.

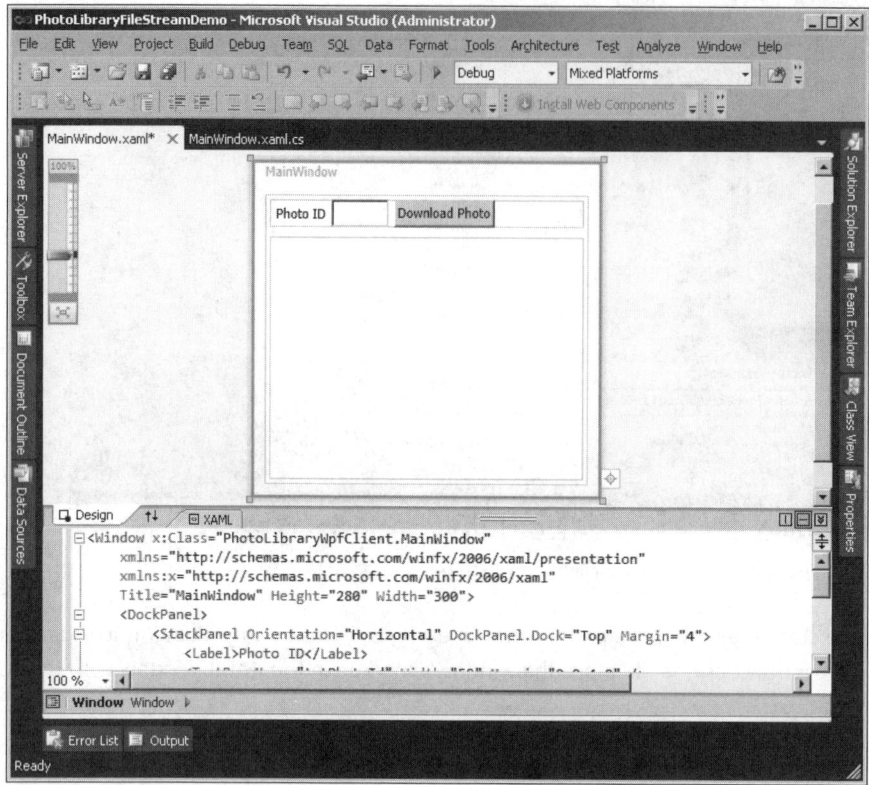

FIGURE 8-15 A simple FILESTREAM WPF UI window.

The *MediaElement* control in WPF is a scaled-down media player that is capable of rendering a variety of multimedia types, including images and video, from any source. All you need to do is set its *Source* property to a URL that it can stream its content from. Double-click the Button control, and then insert the following code in the button's event handler:

```
private void btnDownload_Click(object sender, RoutedEventArgs e)
{
    string url =
        "http://localhost:22111/PhotoService.aspx?photoId=" +
        this.txtPhotoId.Text;

    this.mediaElement1.Source = new Uri(url);
}
```

This code simply constructs a URL to the PhotoService.aspx page that is known to be running on *localhost* port 22111, passing the desired photo ID in the query string. When the *MediaElement* control's *Source* property is set to that URL, the control automatically calls the service and renders the photo that is streamed from the database to the service and then from the service to the WPF client over HTTP.

To see it work, run the application, and request photo ID *2* for display, as shown in Figure 8-16.

FIGURE 8-16 Streaming a photo from the database over HTTP to a WPF client application.

FILESTREAM Limitations and Considerations

From a programming standpoint, FILESTREAM offers a complete abstraction over the *varbinary(max)* data type. Thus, applications and frameworks (including Entity Framework) are unable to distinguish between *varbinary(max)* columns with the FILESTREAM attribute that are stored as files in the file system, and *varbinary(max)* columns without the FILESTREAM attribute that are stored inside the relational tables. This provides a high level of compatibility between FILESTREAM and existing applications that work with *varbinary(max)* data.

However, FILESTREAM's internal integration with the NTFS file system does create unique challenges that affect compatibility with several other SQL Server features. It's very important that you understand these compatibility issues before you start to use FILESTREAM, so that you can avoid unpleasant pitfalls further down the road. The essential considerations for FILESTREAM are summarized below.

- Mirroring/HADR

  FILESTREAM does not work with mirroring. Prior to SQL Server 2012, this was FILESTREAM's most egregious limitation. However, FILESTREAM *is* compatible with the new High-Availability Disaster Recovery (HADR, also known as "always on") feature in SQL Server 2012. HADR offers many improvements over the mirroring technology it replaces, and fortunately, FILESTREAM compatibility is one of them.

- Transparent Data Encryption (TDE)

  TDE (covered in Chapter 5) will not encrypt *varbinary(max) FILESTREAM* column data stored in the NTFS file system.

- Replication

  FILESTREAM can be used with both transactional replication and merge replication, with several restrictions and considerations. All subscribers must be running SQL Server 2008 or higher. For merge replication, SQL Server utilizes the same *uniqueidentifier ROWGUIDCOL* column that FILESTREAM uses (there can be only one such column in a table, and both FILESTREAM and merge replication require it). For this column to be compatible between both features, be sure to specify *NEWSEQUENTIALID* as its default value in your table. Refer to Books Online for more information about using replication with FILESTREAM.

- Log Shipping

  Log shipping fully supports FILESTREAM, as long as both the primary and secondary servers are running SQL Server 2008 or higher.

- Full-Text Search (FTS)

  The FTS engine indexes FILESTREAM columns just as ordinary *varbinary(max)* columns. It is not only 100% compatible with FILESTREAM, but actually has greater significance in SQL Server 2012 with the introduction of FileTable (see the section "Searching Documents" at the end of this chapter).

- Database Snapshots

  SQL Server 2005 introduced database snapshots, a feature that lets you create a static view of the database that can be used for reporting or rollback purposes. Database snapshots are not supported for FILESTREAM filegroups. However, you can still create a database snapshot of the standard filegroups in the database (the FILESTREAM filegroups will be marked as offline in those snapshots).

- Snapshot Isolation Level

  SQL Server 2005 also introduced snapshot isolation level for transactions (we cover snapshot isolation in Chapter 4). When FILESTREAM was first introduced with SQL Server 2008, it was incompatible with snapshot isolation. As with mirroring, this limitation prevented many people from adopting FILESTREAM. Fortunately, this limitation was removed in SQL Server 2008 R2, and FILESTREAM can now be used with snapshot isolation.

- Local NTFS File System

  FILESTREAM data can only by stored on local NTFS disk volumes. However, remote BLOB storage (RBS) solutions available from Microsoft and third-party vendors will allow you to configure a FILESTREAM-enabled SQL Server database as a dedicated BLOB store for SharePoint and other applications.

- Security

  To support *SqlFileStream*, the SQL Server instance should be configured to use mixed-mode (integrated) security.

- SQL Server Express edition

  FILESTREAM is fully supported by the free Express edition of SQL Server (though notably, it is not supported by the *LocalDB* instance of SQL Server supplied with SSDT). Furthermore, the database size limit (4 GB in SQL Server 2008, or 10 GB in SQL Server 2008 R2 and 2012) does *not* include *varbinary(max) FILESTREAM* columns stored in the file system.

Introducing FileTable

The new FileTable feature in SQL Server 2012 builds on FILESTREAM. FileTable combines FILESTREAM with *hierarchyid* and the Windows file system API to deliver exciting new BLOB capabilities in SQL Server. As implied by the two words joined together in its name, one FileTable functions as two distinct things simultaneously:

1. A FileTable is an Ordinary Table
2. A FileTable is an Ordinary File System

First and foremost, a FileTable is a regular SQL Server database table in every respect, with one exception: The schema of a FileTable is fixed. The columns of a FileTable and their data types are pre-determined by SQL Server. Specifically, every FileTable contains the columns shown in Table 8-1.

TABLE 8-1 Fixed FileTable columns.

Column Name	Data Type	Description
stream_id	*uniqueidentifier ROWGUIDCOL*	Unique row identifier
file_stream	*varbinary(max) FILESTREAM*	BLOB content (*NULL* if directory)
name	*varchar(255)*	Name of file or directory
path_locator	*hierarchyid*	Location of file or directory within the logical file system
creation_time	*datetimeoffset(7)*	Created
last_write_time	*datetimeoffset(7)*	Last modified
last_access_time	*datetimeoffset(7)*	Last accessed
is_directory	*bit*	0=file, 1=directory
is_offline *is_hidden* *is_readonly* *is_archive* *is_system* *is_temporary*	*bit*	Storage attributes

Every FileTable row represents an ordinary file or folder in a file system whose logical folder structure is implemented using the *path_locator* column. This is a *hierarchyid* value that denotes the location of each file and folder (row) within the logical file system (table). The *hierarchyid* data type was introduced in SQL Server 2008 as a binary value that, relative to other *hierarchyid* values in the same tree structure, identifies a unique node position. It is implemented as a system common language runtime (CLR) type, which means that it's a .NET framework class, and has a set of methods you can use (such as *GetAncestor*, *GetDescendant*, *GetReparentedValue*, and *IsDescendantOf*) to traverse and manipulate the hierarchy. Thus, it's perfect for casting the hierarchical structure of a file system over a relational table, which is precisely what FileTable does.

More Info A proper understanding of *hierarchyid* is required to query and manipulate a FileTable's *path_locator* column with T-SQL. Chapter 7 provides the necessary coverage.

The *path_locator* column is defined as the table's primary key (with a non-clustered index). A separate key value is also stored in the *stream_id* column (with a non-clustered unique index). This is the *uniqueidentifier ROWGUIDCOL* value required by any table with *varbinary(max) FILESTREAM* columns, so FileTable is no exception. Unlike *path_locator*, this unique value will never change once it is assigned to a new FileTable row, even if the row is later "reparented" (that is, assigned to another location in the hierarchy). You can use either *path_locator* or *stream_id* to uniquely identify each row in a FileTable. But because the *path_locator* value changes whenever the folder or file represented by the row is "moved" in the file system, you should use the *stream_id* value to store long-term (permanent) references to rows in a FileTable.

Every row in a FileTable corresponds to either a single file or folder, as determined by the *bit* value in the *is_directory* column. The file or folder name is stored in the *name* column as an *nvarchar(255)* string. All of the other column names are self-describing, and are used to store typical file system information such as various timestamps and storage attributes.

Rows representing directories have an *IsDirectory* column value of 1 (for true). Directory rows have no BLOB content, and thus always contain *NULL* in the *file_stream* column. Rows representing files have an *IsDirectory* value of 0 (for false), and the actual file content (the BLOB itself) is stored in the *file_stream* column. This is a *varbinary(max)* data type decorated with the *FILESTREAM* attribute, which means that the binary content in the *file_stream* column is stored in the NTFS file system that SQL Server is managing behind the scenes, rather than the structured filegroups where all the other table data is stored (in other words, standard FILESTREAM behavior, as explained in the first part of this chapter).

In addition to these 14 columns, each FileTable includes the three computed (read-only) columns shown in Table 8-2.

TABLE 8-2 Computed FileTable columns.

Column Name	Data Type	Description
parent_path_locator	*hierarchyid*	Parent node (derived from *path_locator*)
file_type	*nvarchar(255)*	Filename extension derived from name
cached_file_size	*bigint*	BLOB byte length derived from *file_stream*

The *parent_path_locator* column returns the result of calling *GetAncestor(1)* on *path_locator* to obtain the *path_locator* to the parent folder of any file or folder in the table. The *file_type* column returns the extension of the filename parsed from the string value in the name column. And the *cached_file_size* column returns the number of bytes stored in the *file_stream* column (that is, the size of the BLOB stored behind the scenes in the SQL Server internally managed NTFS file system).

With this fixed schema in place, every FileTable has what it needs to represent a logical file system. Thus, SQL Server is able to fabricate a Windows file share over any FileTable. This immediately exposes the FileTable to any user or application who can then view and update the table using standard file I/O semantics (for example, drag-and-drop with Windows Explorer, or programmatically with *System.IO.FileStream* and the Windows API). Thus:

- Creating a file or directory in the logical file system adds a row to the table.
- Adding a row to the table creates a file or directory in the logical file system.

Figure 8-17 shows the total FileTable picture.

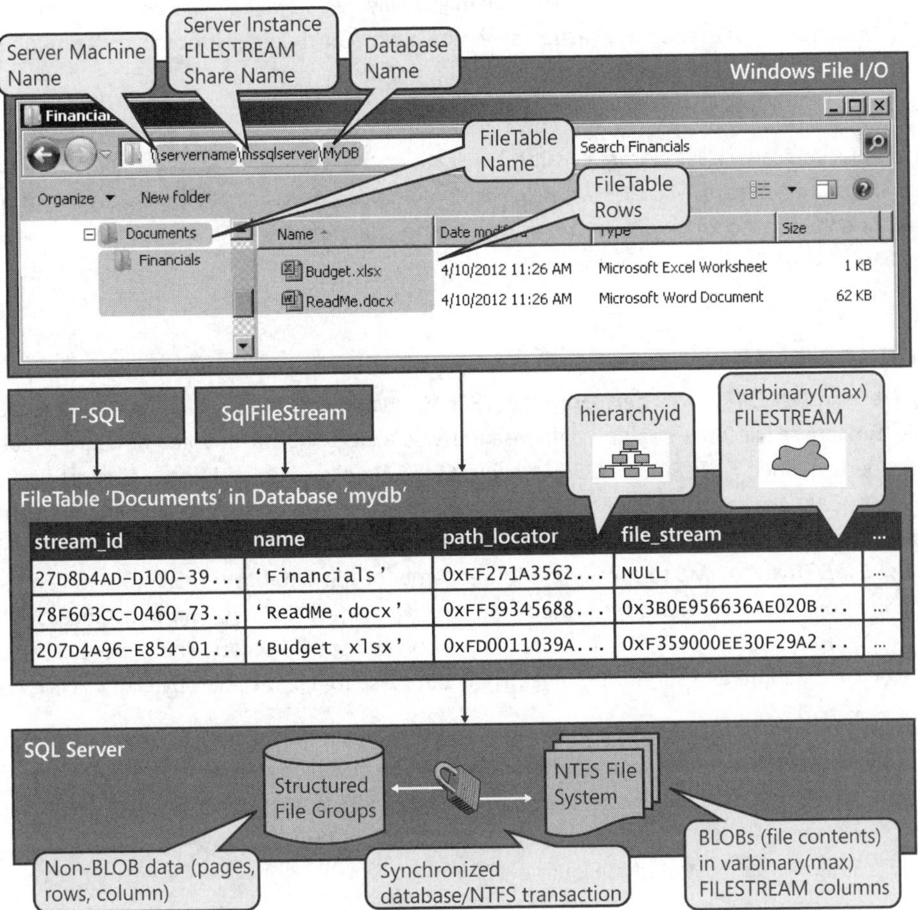

FIGURE 8-17 FileTable data can be accessed via T-SQL, *SqlFileStream*, or the Windows file system.

Take a moment to digest what's happening here. In addition to the programmatic FILESTREAM access using T-SQL or *SqlFileStream*, SQL Server 2012 now offers a third interface to FILESTREAM: a logical file system. In a sense, this fills the FILESTREAM gap in which the file system itself is completely inaccessible. This is not to say that FileTable lets you directly access SQL Server's internally managed NTFS file system; certainly not. That remains obfuscated and private, as it continues to function in standard FILESTREAM fashion against BLOB data that just happens to be in a FileTable instead of any other table. What you do get is an abstraction layer over the FileTable that functions as a standard file system. In this logical file system, everything about each file and folder—except the BLOB content of the files themselves—is stored in the FileTable's structured filegroup, whereas the BLOBs themselves are physically stored in the NTFS file system as ordinary *varbinary(max) FILESTREAM* data.

So you can see that there's really nothing new beneath the FileTable layer; as before, SQL Server synchronizes transactional access between the row in the FileTable and its corresponding BLOB content in the NTFS file system to ensure that integrity is properly maintained between them. As with T-SQL access, this synchronization occurs implicitly when manipulating the FileTable via the exposed Windows file share. And, being an ordinary table in virtually every respect, you also have the option to use *SqlFileStream* with explicit transaction synchronization for the fastest possible streaming of BLOBs into and out of a FileTable.

All of this is extremely appealing. You now have total flexibility for BLOB storage in the database. With FileTable, you can easily migrate existing applications that work against physical file systems without writing any custom T-SQL or fancy *SqlFileStream* code. Just use a FileTable, let the existing applications continue working without modification, and enjoy the benefits of your files becoming an integral part of the SQL Server database.

Creating a FileTable

FileTable relies on FILESTREAM. Therefore, FILESTREAM must be enabled before you can create a FileTable. Similarly, a FileTable-enabled database must be a FILESTREAM-enabled database created with a properly defined *FILEGROUP...CONTAINS FILESTREAM* clause. In addition, you must provide a *WITH FILESTREAM* clause in your *CREATE DATABASE* statement (or, if FileTable-enabling an existing database, you must provide a *SET FILESTREAM* clause in your *ALTER DATABASE* statement). In this clause, use *DIRECTORY_NAME* to specify the folder name for this database. This folder will appear in the root directory of the file share associated with and exposed by the SQL Server instance. Second, specify *NON_TRANSACTED_ACCESS=FULL* to enable non-transacted access. This exposes every FileTable in the database as a subfolder beneath the database folder specified by *DIRECTORY_NAME*.

Do not let the non-transacted access setting confuse you. This just allows FileTable data to be exposed via the Windows API, whose operations are non-transactional in nature. Internally, transactions are always used to synchronize *varbinary(max) FILESTREAM* data between the database and NTFS file system—either implicitly (whether using T-SQL or the Windows API) or explicitly (if using *SqlFileStream*)—as illustrated in Figure 8-17.

Listing 8-7 demonstrates creating a FileTable-enabled database with a modified version of the *CREATE DATABASE* statement you used in Listing 8-1. The *WITH FILESTREAM* clause in this statement enables FileTable for the *PhotoFileLibrary* database, and exposes a *PhotoFileLibrary* directory for the database beneath the Windows file share for the SQL Server instance (*MSSQLSERVER* in our examples).

LISTING 8-7 Creating a FileTable-enabled database.

```
CREATE DATABASE PhotoFileLibrary
 ON PRIMARY
  (NAME = PhotoFileLibrary_data,
   FILENAME = 'C:\Demo\PhotoLibrary\PhotoFileLibrary_data.mdf'),
 FILEGROUP FileStreamGroup CONTAINS FILESTREAM
  (NAME = PhotoFileLibrary_blobs,
   FILENAME = 'C:\Demo\PhotoLibrary\PhotoFiles')
 LOG ON
  (NAME = PhotoFileLibrary_log,
   FILENAME = 'C:\Demo\PhotoLibrary\PhotoFileLibrary_log.ldf')
 WITH FILESTREAM
  (DIRECTORY_NAME='PhotoFileLibrary',
   NON_TRANSACTED_ACCESS=FULL)
```

Creating the actual FileTable is the easiest part. Because SQL Server controls the schema of every FileTable, you just use a *CREATE TABLE* statement with the new *AS FileTable* clause and don't include any columns, as shown in Listing 8-8:

LISTING 8-8 Creating a FileTable.

```
USE PhotoFileLibrary
GO

CREATE TABLE PhotoFiles AS FileTable
GO
```

The *PhotoFiles* FileTable is ready to use. You will find a root *PhotoFiles* folder for the FileTable beneath the *PhotoLibrary* folder created for the database in the Windows file share for the server instance, as shown in Figure 8-18.

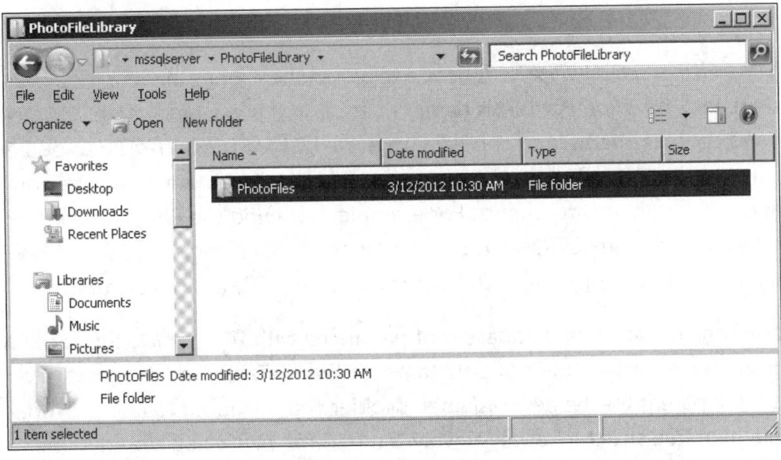

FIGURE 8-18 A Windows Explorer window open to the file share exposed by a FileTable.

Manipulating a FileTable

As with any FILESTREAM-enabled table, you can interact with the FileTable using the same T-SQL and *SqlFileStream* techniques covered earlier in this chapter. In addition, the FileTable can be accessed by users and applications via the logical file system exposed by the Windows file share. To demonstrate, run the code in Listing 8-9. This code inserts rows into the FileTable to create a folder with two files inside of it.

LISTING 8-9 Using T-SQL to create folders and files in a FileTable.

```
-- Get root pathnames for the database and FileTable
DECLARE @DbRootPath varchar(max) = FILETABLEROOTPATH()  -- \\machine\instance\db
DECLARE @TableRootPath varchar(max) = @DbRootPath + '\PhotoFiles'

-- Create folder 'Mountains' in the FileTable's root
DECLARE @TableRootNode hierarchyid = GETPATHLOCATOR(@TableRootPath)
INSERT INTO PhotoFiles(name, path_locator, is_directory) VALUES
 ('Mountains', @TableRootNode.GetDescendant(NULL, NULL), 1)

-- Get new folder's hierarchyid
DECLARE @FolderPath varchar(max) = @TableRootPath + '\Mountains'
DECLARE @FolderNode hierarchyid = GETPATHLOCATOR(@FolderPath)

-- Add a text file to the folder
DECLARE @TextFileNode hierarchyid = @FolderNode.GetDescendant(NULL, NULL)
INSERT INTO PhotoFiles(file_stream, name, path_locator) VALUES(
 CONVERT(varbinary(max), 'This folder contains pictures of mountains.'),
 'ReadMe.txt', @TextFileNode)

-- Add an image file to the folder
DECLARE @ImageFileNode hierarchyid = @FolderNode.GetDescendant(@TextFileNode,
NULL)
INSERT INTO PhotoFiles(file_stream, name, path_locator) VALUES(
 (SELECT BulkColumn FROM OPENROWSET(BULK 'C:\Demo\Ascent.jpg', SINGLE_BLOB) AS
x),
 'Ascent.jpg', @ImageFileNode)
```

This code first calls the *FILETABLEROOTPATH* function to assign the root pathname for current database's FileTable share into *@DbRootPath*. This name is based on the machine name, SQL Server instance share name, and database name. You should always use *FILETABLEROOTPATH* to obtain this information, because hard-coding the machine, instance, and database names will prevent your code from running in different environments. For example, assuming the *PhotoFileLibrary* database is running on a machine named *SQL2012DEV* under an instance named *MSSQLSERVER*, the *FILETABLEROOTPATH* function will return *\\SQL2012DEV\MSSQLSERVER\PhotoFileLibrary*.

The next line of code concatenates the database root pathname with *\PhotoFiles* (the name you assigned to the new FileTable) to obtain the root pathname for the FileTable, and assigns it into *@TableRootPath*. This is the parent for the new Mountains folder you are about to create. Node manipulation in the FileTable tree structure always involves the *hierarchyid* value stored in the *path_locator* column. To get the *hierarchyid* value of any folder or file in the FileTable, you can call the

GETPATHLOCATOR function and pass it the full pathname to the desired folder or file. In Listing 8-9, *GETPATHLOCATOR* obtains the *hierarchyid* of the FileTable's root path and assigns it into *@TableRootNode*.

In the *INSERT* statement that follows, *GetDescendant* is invoked on *@TableRootNode* to generate the appropriate *path_locator* value (a new *hierarchyid*) for the Mountains folder. As explained in Chapter 7, the *GetDescendant* method is invoked on a parent's *hierarchyid* value, and returns a new *hierarchyid* value representing a child of that parent. The method expects two other *hierarchyid* values as input parameters, which specifies two existing child nodes that the new *hierarchyid* value should be "sandwiched" in-between. Because there are no child nodes yet, *NULL* is passed for both *GetDescendant* parameters in the *INSERT* statement, which generates the proper *hierarchyid* value for the one child node in the FileTable's root: the Mountains folder. The *INSERT* statement assigns the *GetDescendant* method's result to the *path_locator* column of the new FileTable row, which identifies this row's position in the hierarchy as the first and only child beneath the FileTable root. It also assigns 'Mountains' to the *name* column and 1 (for true) to the *is_directory* column. All the other columns in the new FileTable row are assigned their default values. This means that *NULL* is stored in *file_stream*, the *varbinary(max) FILESTREAM* column that stores the BLOBs for rows in the FileTable that represent actual files. Folders have no BLOBs, so FileTable rows representing folders (that is, where *IsDirectory* is 1) will always contain *NULL* in the *file_stream* column.

Next, *GETPATHLOCATOR* is called again, this time to obtain the *hierarchyid* value of the newly created Mountains folder. This *hierarchyid* value will now be used as the parent for two more *GetDescendant* calls—one for each of the two child nodes representing the text file and image file beneath Mountains. For the first child, two *NULL* values are again passed to *GetDescendant* to generate a *hierarchyid* value for the text file, because as before, this is the first child node beneath the parent node (which is the Mountains folder this time). The *INSERT* statement assigns the *GetDescendant* result to the *path_locator* column of the new FileTable row, which identifies this row's position in the hierarchy as the first and only child beneath Mountains. It also assigns *'ReadMe.txt'* to the *name* column and the file's BLOB content to the *file_stream* column. The BLOB for this small text file is easy to in-line simply by converting an ordinary string to *varbinary(max)*. All other columns assume their default values, including *is_directory*, which defaults to 0 (false).

The image file is created in a very similar manner. The only significant difference is in the call to *GetDescendant*. Because a second child node is now being added to the Mountains folder, the *hierarchyid* of the last existing child node (currently the text file node just added) is specified as the second *GetDescendant* parameter, rather than *NULL*. It's important to understand that this technique is required to ensure uniqueness across the child nodes beneath a parent; it's not really "positioning" the child nodes in any useful way. Practically, you and your users will sort FileTable data as desired (for example, ascending by name, or descending by creation date). The third *INSERT* statement assigns the *GetDescendant* result to *path_locator* and *'Ascent.jpg'* to the *name* column. The BLOB for the image file is imported into the *file_stream* column from an external copy of *Ascent.jpg* using the *OPENROWSET* function with its *BULK* and *SINGLE_BLOB* options (this image file is supplied with the sample code for this chapter on the book's companion website, or you can just substitute one of your own images for the exercise).

After running the code in Listing 8-9, use Windows Explorer to navigate to the Mountains folder in the file system exposed by the FileTable. Almost like magic, Windows Explorer shows the folder and files created by the three *INSERT* statements, as shown in Figure 8-19.

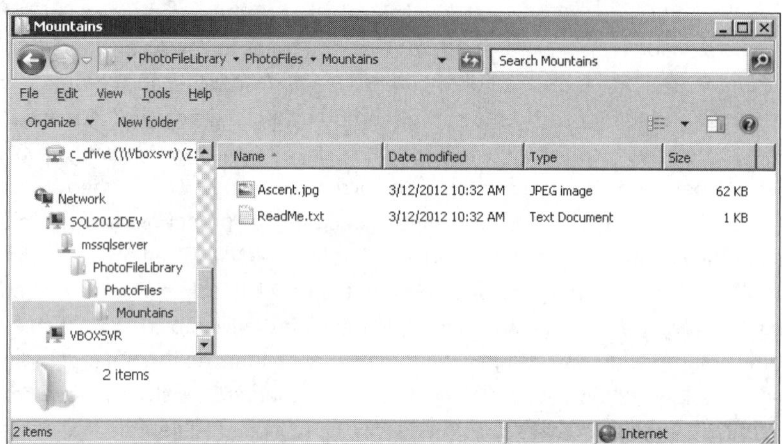

FIGURE 8-19 Windows Explorer showing folders and files inserted into a FileTable by T-SQL.

Double-click *Ascent.jpg* to view the image using Windows Photo Viewer (the default application associated with image files). Behind the scenes, SQL Server finds the FileTable row for the image file, retrieves its BLOB from the obfuscated file system where that row's *varbinary(max) FILESTREAM* column is actually stored, and streams it in to Windows Photo Viewer (which you can now close).

Now double-click the text file to open it in Notepad (the default application associated with text files). Instead of opening as expected, you may be surprised to receive the error message "The request is not supported" instead. In fact, this is not a bug, but rather a manifestation of the fact that the file system exposed by FileTable does not support *memory-mapped files*. This is a technique that some applications use to map areas of memory directly to the sectors on disk where a local file is physically stored. Thus, the application doesn't need to "load" the file into memory, which optimizes performance. Notepad uses memory mapping when editing local files, and so it can't open a file directly from a FileTable share on the local database server. This will normally not present a problem, because users and applications access the FileTable share remotely (not directly on the database server), and file memory mapping is disabled with remote file share access.

To prove that there's really nothing wrong with *ReadMe.txt*, make a copy of it from the FileTable share (you can just drag and drop it to your desktop) and then double-click the copy. You'll see that the copy opens in Notepad without a problem. You can also map a drive letter to FileTable share, and then access the files through the mapped drive letter. This fools Windows into thinking that the local FileTable share is a remote file share and, as a result, local applications will not attempt to use memory mapping for accessing FileTable files.

You created a folder and two files in the logical file system by manipulating a FileTable in T-SQL. Likewise, you can have SQL Server insert, update, and delete rows in a FileTable by manipulating files and directories in the logical file system. Similarly, organizing files and folders using drag and drop in Windows Explorer automatically adjusts the *hierarchyid* values in the *path_locator* column of all affected rows in the FileTable. It's easy to demonstrate this bidirectional capability; just use Windows Explorer to drag and drop a few of your own folders and files into the FileTable share. Then run a *SELECT* query against the FileTable. You will see that SQL Server has inserted new rows to back the folders and files you added via Windows Explorer.

More Info There are several catalog views provided to help you manage FileTables in your database. There is also a special dynamic management view and related stored procedure that lets you monitor and kill open handles on FileTable resources. Consult Books Online for detailed usage and syntax of these system-defined objects that support FileTable.

Searching Documents

You've seen how FILESTREAM and FileTable allow unstructured documents to be stored as first-class citizens inside the database with unprecedented ease and performance. So it's only natural to begin wondering how to make better use of unstructured content that lives in the database, beyond merely streaming it to client applications. This is where Full-Text Search (FTS) and the new Statistical Semantic Search in SQL Server 2012 come in.

The FTS engine was first introduced as an add-on component to SQL Server 2000, and it provides much more powerful wildcard search capabilities than the T-SQL *LIKE* operator. FTS has steadily matured with each product release, and is now a fully integrated part of the relational database engine. FTS can search *varbinary(max)* content, but prior to FILESTREAM, it wasn't feasible to store many large BLOBs in *varbinary(max)* columns. Now that doing so is not only feasible but easy, FTS is a natural tool for searching content inside many different types of documents that simply get dropped into a FileTable. FTS is able to parse many different file types, including Microsoft Word documents, Microsoft PowerPoint decks, Microsoft Excel spreadsheets, Adobe PDF files, and a host of other popular formats. It understands word-stemming and syntax rules of over 50 languages, and can also perform proximity searching with the *NEAR* keyword. In SQL Server 2012, FTS now also supports property searching and customizable distance for proximity searching with *NEAR*.

SQL Server 2012 also introduces Statistical Semantic Search, a new feature that builds on the FTS architecture, extending full-text search capabilities beyond what is offered by FTS alone. The Semantic Search engine discovers key phrases in each document, and can therefore return documents deemed similar to one another based on common key phrases. In addition to enabling FTS, you must separately install, attach, and register a special Semantic Language Statistics Database before you can start using Semantic Search. In its first release, Semantic Search supports fewer languages than FTS does (only about 15), and indexes only single-word phrases. However the ability to categorize your documents automatically, and to identify documents that are similar or related, enables powerful new features for document management applications.

Summary

For applications that work with BLOB data, FILESTREAM greatly enhances the storage and performance of unstructured content in the database by leveraging the native NTFS file system. It does this while maintaining logical integration between the database and file system that includes transactional support. As a result, you no longer need to compromise between efficiency and complexity as you did in the past when faced with the choice of storing BLOB data inside or outside the database.

You also learned how to use *SqlFileStream* to deliver high-performance streaming of BLOB content between the file system managed by SQL Server and your Windows, web, and WPF applications. Finally, you learned how FileTable in SQL Server 2012 combines FILESTREAM and *hierachyid* to furnish a database-backed file system for users and applications. You can apply the techniques you learned in this chapter to a wide range of applications that require integration between the relational database and a streaming file system.

CHAPTER 9

Geospatial Support

—Leonard Lobel

Location-aware applications are ubiquitous nowadays. You find them on phones, tablets, laptops, and desktops. Enterprise users and consumers alike rely on Geographic Information System (GIS) applications (and GIS extensions to traditional applications) in the home, car, office, and everywhere in between. GIS applications—powered by Global Positioning Satellite (GPS) technology—enhance the user experience with sophisticated mapping intelligence. In short, GIS is all about storing and processing *geospatial data* (often simply called *spatial data*), and this chapter is all about the rich support for spatial data in Microsoft SQL Server 2012.

Note We use the terms *spatial* and *geospatial* interchangeably throughout this chapter.

In SQL Server 2012, spatial data support is a powerful extension to the core relational engine that enables you to embed location awareness into the database. Using the *geometry* and *geography* data types, you can import, export, store, and process different types of spatial data. In this chapter, we will quickly cover basic spatial concepts, and then dive into more advanced examples (along with several sample applications) to get you comfortable working with spatial data.

SQL Server Spaces Out

In SQL Server 2012, the database itself is capable of understanding geospatial data (shapes—projected onto either a flat surface or the round earth) as a native data type. SQL Server can efficiently store and process instances of such data, so developers can enjoy rich spatial functionality at the database level. This feature (which was first introduced in Microsoft SQL Server 2008 and is available in all editions of SQL Server) offers an attractive alternative to performing spatial calculations at the application level, either through custom written code (which is far from trivial) or by using a third-party library (which is far from inexpensive).

The algorithms used in geospatial operations are very complex (to say the least), and a comprehensive treatment of the topic is well beyond the scope of this chapter. At the same time, abstraction of that complexity is a key aspect of the spatial data types. The geospatial support in SQL Server is based on the OpenGIS Simple Features for SQL standard. This standard enables developers to quickly program against spatial data without requiring a deep understanding of the mathematical formulae behind spatial calculations. In this chapter, we'll start by first explaining the two basic spatial models. Then we'll examine several code demonstrations that leverage the *geometry* and *geography* data types in a variety of more advanced scenarios.

Spatial Models

Let's begin our discussion with an explanation of the two spatial models. These are known as the *planar* and *geodetic* models.

Planar (Flat-Earth) Model

The planar model is a flat surface where shapes are plotted using two-dimensional *x*- and *y*-coordinates. The coordinate system semantics are entirely up to you; measurements can be anything from pixels to inches, meters, and miles. It makes sense to work with the planar model when you're dealing with relatively small areas (such as a piece of paper, building floor plan, or parking lot), or even larger areas that are either conceptually flat or still small enough where the earth's curvature does not skew the outcome of area and distance calculations.

Flattening the earth onto a two-dimensional surface results in a spatial distortion that makes it impossible to calculate measurements accurately over larger spaces on the globe's actual shape. You can see this in Figure 9-1, which shows a planar model map of the earth. The flattened projection stretches the earth more and more the farther away its parts are from the equator. For example, notice that Antarctica (way down by the South Pole) appears to be significantly larger than North America. Yet in fact, North America (at ~ 24 million sq. km) is significantly larger than Antarctica (at ~ 13 million sq. km). Now draw a straight line from New York to Amsterdam on this map. The length of that line does not really represent the accurate distance between those two cities, because the actual line would be stretched and curved against the shape of the globe. So clearly, the planar model is inappropriate for calculating spatial data over large areas of the planet.

Geodetic (Ellipsoidal Sphere) Model

If your database needs to perform spatial calculations that span significant areas of the earth, it needs to adopt the popularly held belief that the world is round. It's not perfectly round, however. Due to its rotation, the earth is wider around the equator than it is around the poles, such that it forms an *ellipsoidal sphere*. To accurately plot and compute shapes and intersections on a planetary scale, the precise curvature of the earth's unique spherical shape must be taken into consideration.

To achieve this accuracy, the geodetic model (depicted in Figure 9-2) represents locations on the planet using the earth's longitude and latitude coordinate system. Any given point on earth is represented as latitude and longitude, where latitude specifies the angle north or south of the equator, and longitude specifies the angle east or west of the Prime Meridian.

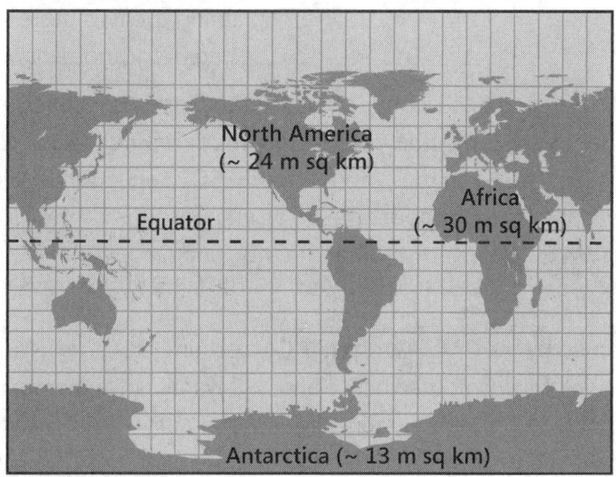

FIGURE 9-1 Planar spatial model (flat-earth projection).

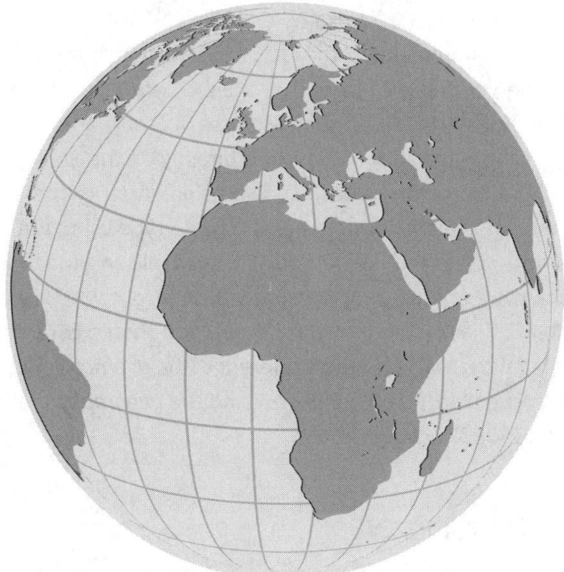

FIGURE 9-2 Geodetic spatial model (round-earth projection).

Spatial Data Standards

SQL Server provides two data types—*geometry* and *geography*—designed to work respectively with the planar and geodetic spatial models. Shapes are projected onto spatial models using *vector objects*, which are collections of points, lines, polygons (closed shapes), and—new in SQL Server 2012—curves and arcs. Both the *geometry* and *geography* data types support the three standard formats for consuming spatial data: Well-Known Text (WKT), Well-Known Binary (WKB), and Geography Markup Language (GML).

WKT, WKB, and GML are standards governed by the Open Geospatial Consortium (OGC), an international body of more than 400 companies. Microsoft is an active and highly influential member of the OGC, and SQL Server 2012 supports the OpenGIS Simple Features for SQL standard—a specification published by the OGC for the exchange of spatial data between different database platforms (you can learn more about the specification from *http://www.opengeospatial.org/standards/sfs*).

The spatial data types are .NET classes that expose more than 90 available methods. About two-thirds of those methods are named with the prefix *ST*; for example, *STArea*, *STDistance*, and *STArea*. The *ST* prefix indicates spatial methods that implement the OGC specification, but Microsoft also adds some of its own extensions to SQL Server that are not part of the OGC standard. These are distinguished with method names that do not start with *ST*; such as *Parse*, *ToString*, and *GeomFromGml*. Some are static methods (meaning that they are invoked directly on the *geometry* or *geography* data type name using the special double-colon syntax), and some are instance methods (meaning that they are invoked on an instance of a *geometry* or *geography* data type using the standard "dot" notation). Although the majority of the spatial methods are available and function identically with both data types, a few of them are unique to only *geometry* or *geography*. This chapter explains many, but certainly not all, of the available spatial methods. You should consult Microsoft Books Online for the complete spatial data type method reference (the *geometry* methods can be found at *http://msdn.microsoft.com/en-us/library/bb933973.aspx* and the *geography* methods at *http://msdn.microsoft.com/en-us/library/bb933802.aspx*).

Importing Well-Known Text (WKT)

WKT is the easiest way to work with spatial data in SQL Server. It offers a very terse syntax for defining shapes using a handful of keywords (such as *POINT*, *LINESTRING*, and *POLYGON*), and SQL Server implements a spatial data class for each of these shapes. Figure 9-3 shows all the supported spatial classes, along with their associated WKT keywords and an example instance of each shape. Note that the *CIRCULARSTRING*, *COMPOUNDCURVE*, *CURVEPOLYGON*, and *FULLGLOBE* WKT shapes are new classes in SQL Server 2012, and that we cover those and other SQL Server 2012 enhancements later in the chapter.

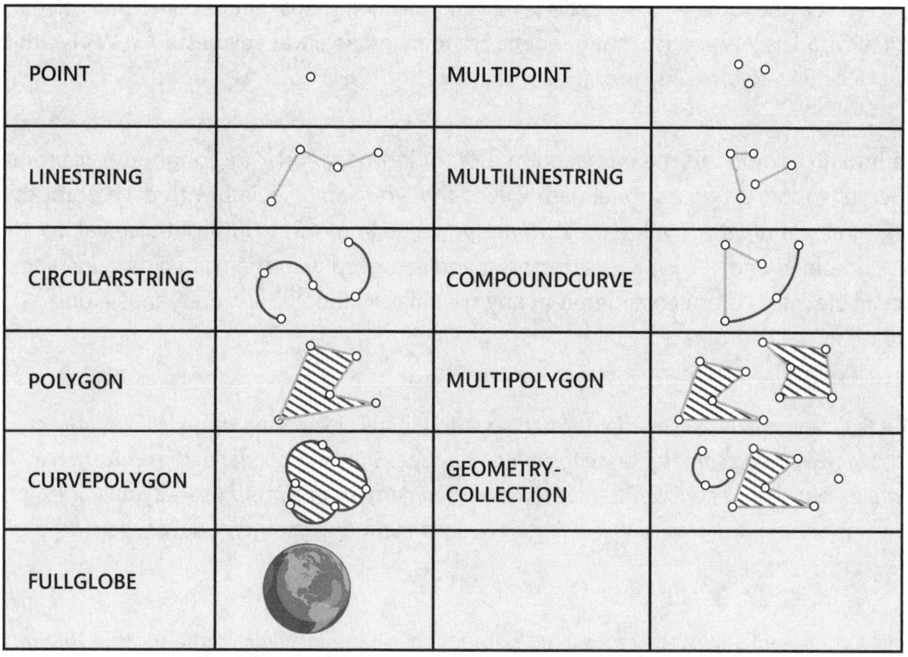

POINT		MULTIPOINT	
LINESTRING		MULTILINESTRING	
CIRCULARSTRING		COMPOUNDCURVE	
POLYGON		MULTIPOLYGON	
CURVEPOLYGON		GEOMETRY-COLLECTION	
FULLGLOBE			

FIGURE 9-3 Spatial classes and their associated WKT keywords.

Every shape from the simplest point to the most complex polygons and collections is expressed as a WKT string. The WKT string syntax combines the various shape keywords with numeric coordinates. Table 9-1 shows some examples of WKT strings.

TABLE 9-1 Examples of WKT Strings.

WKT String	Description
POINT(6 10)	A single point at *xy*-coordinates 6, 10
POINT(-111.06687 45.01188)	A single point on the earth (longitude/latitude coordinates)
LINESTRING(3 4,10 50,20 25)	A two-part line, drawn between three points specified as *xy*-coordinates
POLYGON((-75.17031 39.95601, -75.16786 39.95778, -75.17921 39.96874, -75.18441 39.96512, -75.17031 39.95601))	An enclosed shape on the earth drawn between the points specified as longitude/latitude coordinates
CIRCULARSTRING(1 5, 6 2, 7 3)	A curved line, drawn between three points specified as *xy*-coordinates
GEOMETRYCOLLECTION(POINT(6 10), CIRCULARSTRING(1 5, 6 2, 7 3), LINESTRING(3 4,10 50,20 25))	A collection with three shapes; a point, a circular string, and a line string

As you can see, the same WKT syntax is used for projecting spatial entities onto both planar and geodetic models. Also notice that geodetic coordinates are always expressed in WKT with the longitude value first, followed by the latitude value.

More Info In addition to the intersection of *X* (or latitude) and *Y* (or longitude) coordinates, SQL Server supports two optional data values that you can associate with each point to represent elevation: the *Z* value (height) and *M* value (measure). Both of these values are user-defined and, if supplied, are stored and retrieved with the spatial data instance. However, elevation is not considered in any spatial calculations; it merely tags along as metadata in the coordinates.

WKT is SQL Server's default spatial format, so string literals expressed using WKT syntax can be assigned directly into a *geometry* or *geography* data type. Similarly, spatial data is returned in WKT format when you invoke the *ToString* method on a *geometry* or *geography* data type. For example, the following statement parses a WKT string and loads it into the *geometry* data type stored in *@line*:

```
DECLARE @line geometry = 'LINESTRING(5 15, 22 10)'
```

This next statement shows the raw binary data for the shape in *@line*, and also uses *ToString* to convert it back into WKT for display.

```
SELECT @line AS AsRaw, @line.ToString() AS AsWKT
```

Here is the output:

```
AsRaw                                                            AsWKT
---------------------------------------------------------------- ------------------------
0x00000000011400000000000014400000000000002E4000000000000364... LINESTRING (5 15, 22 10)
```

The *STGeomFromText* and *STxxxFromText* Methods

The *geometry* and *geography* data types also provide a set of static methods for explicitly importing any shape—or specific shapes—expressed in WKT. The *STGeomFromText* method accepts any WKT-expressed shape and imports it as a *geometry* or *geography* type. In fact, SQL Server actually called *STGeomFromText* when you just supplied the string literal in the previous assignment. Thus, the following assignment is equivalent:

```
DECLARE @line geometry = geometry::STGeomFromText('LINESTRING(5 15, 22 10)', 0)
```

The *STxxxFromText* (for example, *STPointFromText*, *STLineFromText*, and *STPolyFromText*) methods add extra validation on the WKT string to ensure it represents the intended shape. The next statement uses the *STLineFromText* method to demonstrate yet another way of loading the same shape:

```
DECLARE @line geometry = geometry::STLineFromText('LINESTRING(5 15, 22 10)', 0)
```

This statement works just the same, but only because the WKT string is indeed a line string. For example, the following statement is invalid:

```
DECLARE @line geometry = geometry::STLineFromText('POINT(10 100)', 0)
```

This statement fails because a WKT string representing a point was passed to *STLineFromText*, which is a method that can only accept line strings.

```
Msg 6522, Level 16, State 1, Line 19
A .NET Framework error occurred during execution of user-defined routine or aggregate "geometry":
System.FormatException: 24142: Expected "LINESTRING" at position 1. The input has "POINT(10 1".
System.FormatException:
   at Microsoft.SqlServer.Types.WellKnownTextReader.RecognizeToken(String token)
   at Microsoft.SqlServer.Types.WellKnownTextReader.ParseTaggedText(OpenGisType type)
   at Microsoft.SqlServer.Types.WellKnownTextReader.Read(OpenGisType type, Int32 srid)
   at Microsoft.SqlServer.Types.SqlGeometry.GeometryFromText(OpenGisType type, SqlChars text,
Int32 srid)
```

This rather verbose error message also reveals that the spatial data types are implemented as common language runtime (CLR) types. This means that SQL Server spatial support is contained inside a .NET assembly that resides on the server, which also means that you can reference the very same assembly and utilize the same spatial types and methods in your C# and VB .NET applications. You'll see exactly how that's done in a sample application coming up later in the chapter.

Importing WKB

Well-Known Binary (WKB) is the OGC-standard binary equivalent of WKT, which is slightly different than the native binary format that SQL Server uses to store spatial data internally.

The *STGeomFromWKB* and *STxxxFromWKB* Methods

If your data source supplies spatial data in WKB, you can use *STGeomFromWKB* or one of the various *STxxxFromWKB* methods to import it. As with WKT, there is one such method for each supported shape (for example, *STPointFromWKB*, *STLineFromWKB*, and *STPolyFromWKB*).

For example, the following statement imports a WKB value and loads it into the *geometry* data type stored in *@point*:

```
DECLARE @point geometry =
 geometry::STGeomFromWKB(0x010100000000000000000059400000000000005940, 0)
```

This next statement shows the raw (SQL Server) binary data for the shape in *@point*, and uses *ToString* to convert it back into WKT for display:

```
SELECT @point AS AsRaw, @point.ToString() AS AsWKT
```

Here is the output:

```
AsRaw                                          AsWKT
---------------------------------------------- ---------------
0x00000000010C00000000000059400000000000005940 POINT (100 100)
```

Notice that the raw binary value is similar to the imported WKB value, but the two are not actually identical.

Importing Geography Markup Language (GML)

Geography Markup Language (GML) is another spatial data format, and was developed by the OGC after WKT. GML is both a language and an open interchange format for spatial information throughout the Internet. It uses an XML dialect that is significantly richer and more verbose than WKT.

The *GeomFromGml* Method

You can import spatial data from GML into SQL Server using the *GeomFromGml* method, as follows:

```
DECLARE @gml xml = '
  <LineString xmlns="http://www.opengis.net/gml">
    <posList>100 100 20 180 180 180</posList>
  </LineString>'
DECLARE @line geometry = geometry::GeomFromGml(@gml, 0)
SELECT @line AS AsRaw, @line.ToString() AS AsWKT
```

Here is the output:

```
AsRaw                                                AsWKT
---------------------------------------------------- ------------------------
0x000000000104030000000000000000005940000000000... LINESTRING (100 100, 20 180, 180 180)
```

We use WKT exclusively in the rest of this chapter's code. GML is a world unto itself (no pun intended), and detailed GML coverage is beyond the scope of this book (the GML standard is posted on the OGC website at *http://www.opengeospatial.org/standards/gml*). The key point to understand is that the *geometry* and *geography* data types (and their spatial methods) are completely agnostic to the particular OGC standard used for importing spatial data; whether it's WKT, WKB, or GML.

Spatial Data Types

The *geometry* and *geography* data types are system CLR types, which means they are implemented by the .NET CLR internally by SQL Server. The *geometry* data type is provided to store and process spatial data using the planar model, whereas its counterpart *geography* supports the geodetic model.

One nice thing about the two spatial types is that most methods are supported and work the same for both types. So if you're working with the geodetic model, you'll be using longitude and latitude coordinates with the *geography* data type. For the planar model, you'll be using *x*- and *y*-coordinates with the *geometry* data type. But in either case, you'll then use many of the same methods for dealing with your spatial entities.

Working with *geometry*

Our first example demonstrates the *geometry* data type in a very simple scenario. You will define and store shapes representing town districts and avenues, and then query that data to return interesting information, such as a list of the avenues that run through each district. This little, one-horse town has only three districts and two main avenues, and is small enough to be expressed on a planar (flat) surface using the *geometry* data type. As you progress through the example, you'll learn how to use a number of common geospatial methods.

Figure 9-4 shows a map of the town, and the *xy*-coordinates for the points of each shape on the map. The three districts are polygons (closed shapes), and the two avenues are line strings. You will store these shapes in a SQL Server database using the *geometry* data type, expressing their coordinates in WKT syntax. Then you'll query and manipulate the districts and streets using various spatial methods.

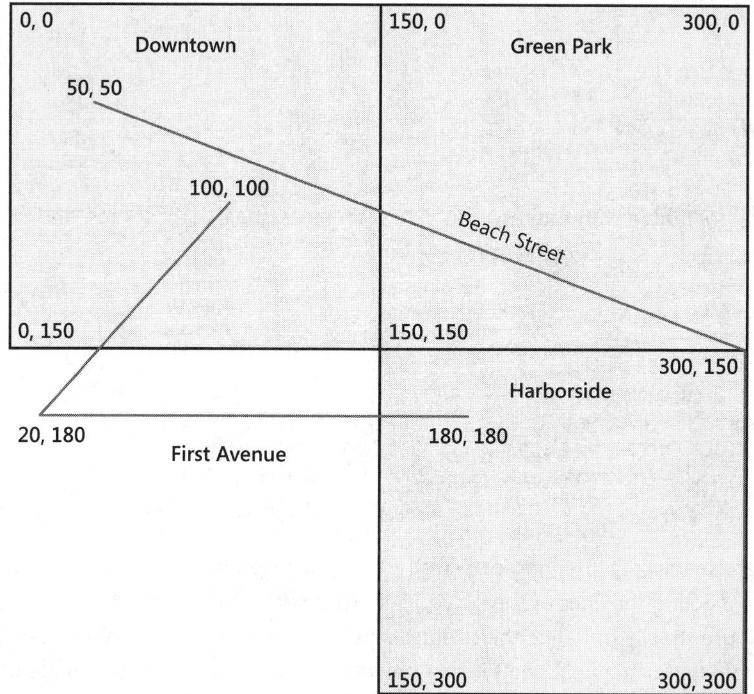

FIGURE 9-4 Small town map on a flat (planar) surface.

The first thing you need to do is create tables to hold the shapes that define the districts and streets. The *District* table will store the polygons representing Downtown, Green Park, and Harborside in a *geometry* column named *DistrictGeo*. Similarly, you'll create a *Street* table to store the line strings representing Beach Street and First Avenue in a *geometry* column named *StreetGeo*, as shown in Listing 9-1.

LISTING 9-1 Creating the *District* and *Street* tables with *geometry* columns.

```
USE master
GO
IF EXISTS(SELECT name FROM sys.databases WHERE name = 'MyDB')
 DROP DATABASE MyDB
GO
CREATE DATABASE MyDB
GO
USE MyDB
GO

CREATE TABLE District
 (DistrictId    int PRIMARY KEY,
  DistrictName  nvarchar(20),
  DistrictGeo   geometry)

CREATE TABLE Street
 (StreetId    int PRIMARY KEY,
  StreetName  nvarchar(20),
  StreetGeo   geometry)
```

Next, populate the *District* table with the three districts along with their shapes, sizes, and coordinates as polygons in WKT, as shown in Listing 9-2.

LISTING 9-2 Using WKT to insert polygons into *geometry* columns.

```
INSERT INTO District VALUES
 (1, 'Downtown', 'POLYGON ((0 0, 150 0, 150 -150, 0 -150, 0 0))'),
 (2, 'Green Park', 'POLYGON ((300 0, 150 0, 150 -150, 300 -150, 300 0))'),
 (3, 'Harborside', 'POLYGON ((150 -150, 300 -150, 300 -300, 150 -300, 150 -150))')
```

Notice how the square shapes representing each district are conveyed in WKT format as polygon elements. Each point connecting the lines of the polygon is expressed as an *xy*-coordinate. Unlike line strings (which you'll use shortly to define the streets), a polygon always represents a closed shape. In WKT, the coordinate for the final point in any polygon must be the same coordinate used for the starting point in order to close the shape. You can see how all of the district polygons in the preceding code close their shapes in this manner. If you attempt to express a polygon without closing the shape, you will receive a *FormatException*, as follows:

```
Msg 6522, Level 16, State 1, Line 81
A .NET Framework error occurred during execution of user-defined routine or aggregate "geometry":
System.FormatException: 24119: The Polygon input is not valid because the start and end points of
the exterior ring are not the same. Each ring of a polygon must have the same start and end points.
System.FormatException:
   at Microsoft.SqlServer.Types.GeometryValidator.ValidatePolygonRing(Int32 iRing, Int32
cPoints, Double firstX, Double firstY, Double lastX, Double lastY)
   at Microsoft.SqlServer.Types.Validator.Execute(Transition transition)
   at Microsoft.SqlServer.Types.ForwardingGeoDataSink.EndFigure()
```

```
   at Microsoft.SqlServer.Types.WellKnownTextReader.ParseLineStringText()
   at Microsoft.SqlServer.Types.WellKnownTextReader.ParsePolygonText()
   at Microsoft.SqlServer.Types.WellKnownTextReader.ParseTaggedText(OpenGisType type)
   at Microsoft.SqlServer.Types.WellKnownTextReader.Read(OpenGisType type, Int32 srid)
   at Microsoft.SqlServer.Types.SqlGeometry.GeometryFromText(OpenGisType type, SqlChars text,
Int32 srid)
   at Microsoft.SqlServer.Types.SqlGeometry.Parse(SqlString s)
.
The statement has been terminated.
```

This rather unfriendly error message also alludes to the fact that polygons can have multiple rings defined inside the exterior ring. This means that you can define complex polygons that have one or more "holes" inside them using WKT.

Now populate the *Street* table with line strings, as shown in Listing 9-3.

LISTING 9-3 Inserting line strings into *geometry* columns.

```
INSERT INTO Street VALUES
 (1, 'First Avenue', 'LINESTRING (100 -100, 20 -180, 180 -180)'),
 (2, 'Beach Street', 'LINESTRING (300 -300, 300 -150, 50 -50)')
```

The line string elements used to store the streets of the town specify the points that describe the paths of each street on the map. In this example, each street has three points expressing the two-part line strings for First Avenue and Beach Street.

Now execute the union query in Listing 9-4 to retrieve all the shapes from both tables combined into a single result set.

LISTING 9-4 Retrieving spatial data.

```
SELECT
  Name = StreetName, AsRaw = StreetGeo, AsWKT = StreetGeo.ToString()
 FROM Street
 UNION ALL
 SELECT
  Name = DistrictName, AsRaw = DistrictGeo, AsWKT = DistrictGeo.ToString()
 FROM District
```

Here are the results of the query:

```
Name         AsRaw              AsWKT
------------ ------------------ ------------------------------------------------------------
First Avenue 0x000000000104... LINESTRING (100 -100, 20 -180, 180 -180)
Beach Street 0x000000000104... LINESTRING (300 -300, 300 -150, 50 -50)
Downtown     0x000000000104... POLYGON ((0 0, 150 0, 150 -150, 0 -150, 0 0))
Green Park   0x000000000104... POLYGON ((300 0, 150 0, 150 -150, 300 -150, 300 0))
Harborside   0x000000000104... POLYGON ((150 -150, 300 -150, 300 -300, 150 -300, 150 -150))
```

If you execute this query in SQL Server Management Studio (SSMS), you can visualize these results using the spatial viewer (unfortunately, the spatial viewer is not available inside of Visual Studio using SQL Server Data Tools [SSDT], so we use SSMS in this chapter for spatial development). Because SSMS recognizes that the result set contains spatial data, it adds a new tab named Spatial Results in-between the Results and Messages tabs. Click the Spatial Results tab and you will be presented with a graphical rendering of the town map, as shown in Figure 9-5.

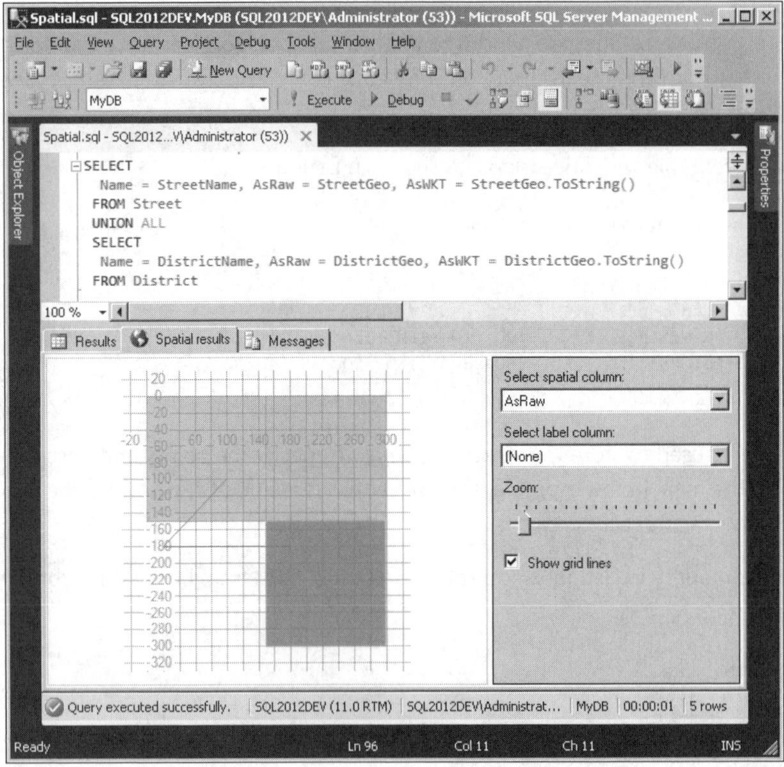

FIGURE 9-5 Displaying the town map data in SSMS using the Spatial Results viewer.

For a result set that contains multiple spatial data columns, you can graph any one of them using the first drop-down list on the right of the chart. You can also add legend labels based on another column in the result set using the second drop-down list. You can also set the chart's magnification level and toggle the display of grid lines using the slider and check box controls beneath the drop-down lists.

The *STBuffer* Method

You can invoke *STBuffer* on any spatial instance to pad a shape by any amount (distance), and return it back as a new instance. The query in Listing 9-5 demonstrates the use of *STBuffer* to widen the streets, which converts the line string into a polygon representing the padded street area.

LISTING 9-5 Padding *LINESTRING* shapes with the *STBuffer* method.

```
SELECT
  Name = StreetName,
  AsRaw = StreetGeo.STBuffer(5),
  AsWKT = StreetGeo.STBuffer(5).ToString()
 FROM Street
 UNION ALL
 SELECT
  Name = DistrictName,
  AsRaw = DistrictGeo,
  AsWKT = DistrictGeo.ToString()
 FROM District
```

The results of the query show that the line string shapes for First Avenue and Beach Street are now being returned as polygon shapes representing streets with width.

```
Name         AsRaw             AsWKT
------------ ----------------- ------------------------------------------------------------
First Avenue 0x000000000104... POLYGON ((20.000000000000881 -184.99999999999966, 180.00...
Beach Street 0x000000000104... POLYGON ((300.00000000000034 -304.9999999999992, 300.243...
Downtown     0x000000000104... POLYGON ((0 0, 150 0, 150 -150, 0 -150, 0 0))
Green Park   0x000000000104... POLYGON ((300 0, 150 0, 150 -150, 300 -150, 300 0))
Harborside   0x000000000104... POLYGON ((150 -150, 300 -150, 300 -300, 150 -300, 150 -150))
```

In SSMS, click the Spatial Results tab to view the town map with the widened streets, as shown in Figure 9-6.

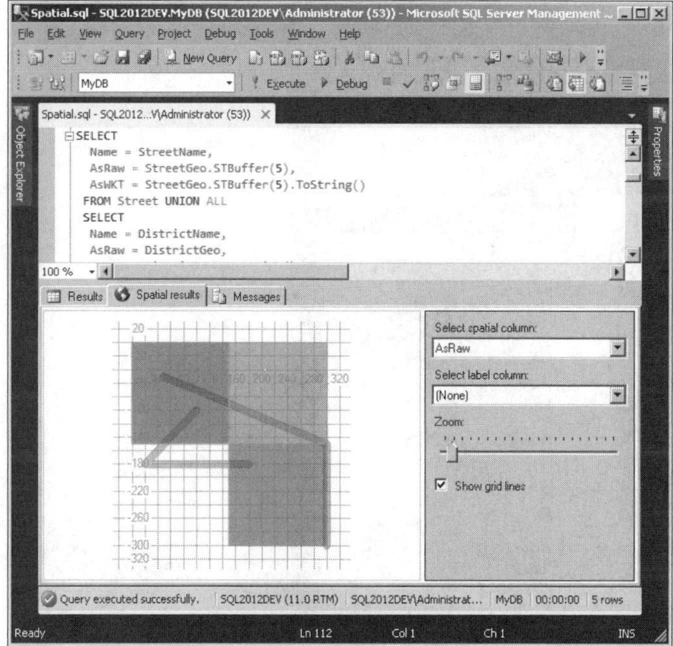

FIGURE 9-6 Viewing the result of calling *STBuffer* in the Spatial Results viewer.

The *STCentroid* and *STEnvelope* Methods

The *STCentroid* method returns the point at the center of a given shape, and the *STEnvelope* method returns a rectangle that bounds a given shape. These two methods are available only for the *geometry* data type.

The query in Listing 9-6 uses *STCentroid* to locate the center point of each district, and then uses *STBuffer* to pad the point so that it appears as a small circle that is clearly visible in the Spatial Results viewer. (Note, however, that *STBuffer* does not actually generate circular strings, but instead plots many points in a polygon very close to one another to produce the rounded padding shape.)

LISTING 9-6 Locating the center of a shape with the *STCentroid* method.

```
SELECT
  DistrictGeo,
  DistrictGeo.ToString()
 FROM District
 UNION ALL
 SELECT
  DistrictGeo.STCentroid().STBuffer(5),
  DistrictGeo.STCentroid().ToString()
 FROM District
```

The results appear as shown in Figure 9-7.

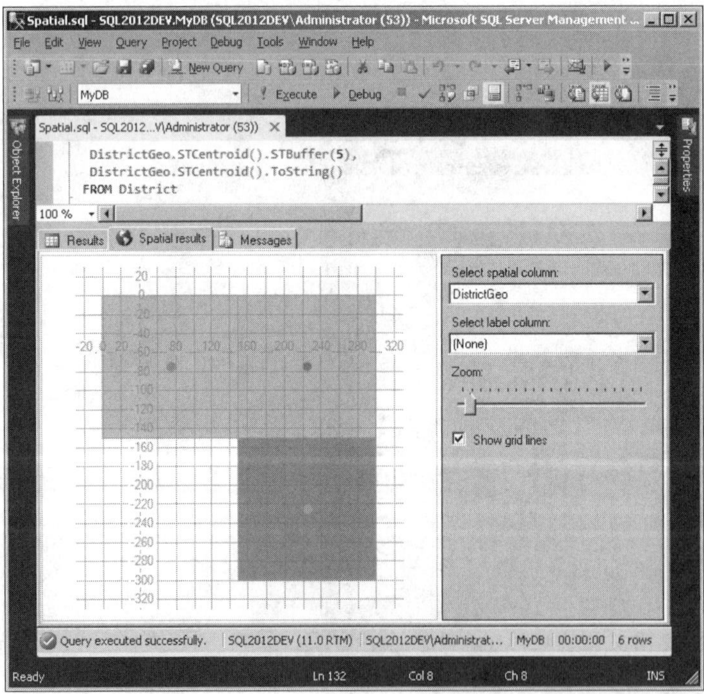

FIGURE 9-7 Using *STCentroid* to locate the center of each district.

The query in Listing 9-7 uses *STEnvelope* to identify the bounding box of each street. Each street is returned (again, padded with *STBuffer* so that streets are clearly visible in the Spatial Results viewer) along with a rectangular shape around each street generated by *STEnvelope*.

LISTING 9-7 Using the *STEnvelope* method to generate a bounding box for each street.

```
SELECT
  StreetName,
  StreetGeo.STBuffer(5),
  StreetGeo.ToString()
 FROM Street
 UNION ALL
 SELECT
  StreetName + ' Bounds',
  StreetGeo.STEnvelope(),
  StreetGeo.STEnvelope().ToString()
 FROM Street
```

The results appear as shown in Figure 9-8.

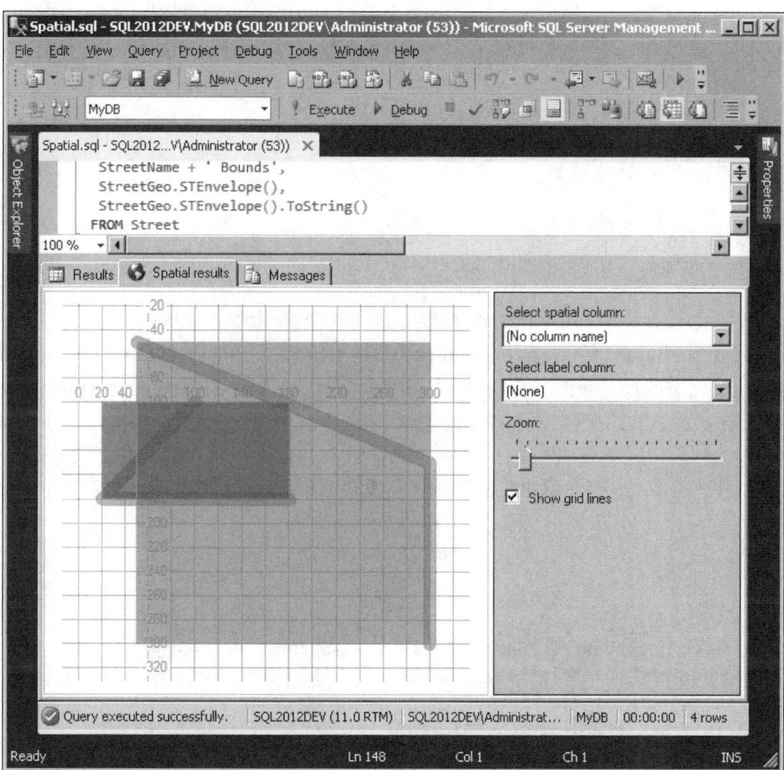

FIGURE 9-8 Result of calling *STEnvelope* for each street.

The *STIntersects* and *STIntersection* Methods

Now you're going to write a query to find out which streets intersect which districts. This query will use a *CROSS JOIN* so that it returns all possible combinations of districts and streets. You'll qualify the query with a *WHERE* clause to filter the results and report only those district and street combinations that actually intersect with one another. This is easily achieved with the *STIntersects* method. You invoke *STIntersects* on one spatial instance, passing in another spatial instance as its parameter, and SQL Server returns a *bit* (Boolean) value of *1* (true) or *0* (false) telling you whether or not the two *geometry* shapes intersect with each other. Listing 9-8 demonstrates:

LISTING 9-8 Using the *STIntersects* method to find all district and street intersections.

```
SELECT
  S.StreetName,
  D.DistrictName
 FROM District AS D CROSS JOIN Street AS S
 WHERE S.StreetGeo.STIntersects(D.DistrictGeo) = 1
 ORDER BY S.StreetName
```

When you run this query, the results indicate that Beach Street runs through all three districts, whereas First Avenue runs through Downtown and Harborside, but not Green Park.

```
StreetName           DistrictName
-------------------- --------------------
Beach Street         Downtown
Beach Street         Green Park
Beach Street         Harborside
First Avenue         Downtown
First Avenue         Harborside
```

But you can do more than just find out whether two spatial entities intersect—you can us the *STIntersection* method to actually obtain a shape that represents the overlapping area of intersection in a new spatial entity. Listing 9-9 presents a modified version of the same *STIntersects* query that also uses *STIntersection* to report which *pieces* of each road cut through each district.

LISTING 9-9 Using the *STIntersection* method to generate road fragments for each district.

```
SELECT
  S.StreetName,
  D.DistrictName,
  S.StreetGeo.STIntersection(D.DistrictGeo).STBuffer(5) AS Intersection,
  S.StreetGeo.STIntersection(D.DistrictGeo).ToString() AS IntersectionWKT
 FROM District AS D CROSS JOIN Street AS S
 WHERE S.StreetGeo.STIntersects(D.DistrictGeo) = 1
 ORDER BY S.StreetName
```

The results of the query show the line string shapes created by *STIntersection* for the portion of each street that runs through each district.

```
StreetName   DistrictName Intersection         IntersectionWKT
------------ ------------ -------------------- ------------------------------------------
Beach Street Downtown     0x0000000001047F0... LINESTRING (50 -50, 150 -89.999999999999886)
Beach Street Green Park   0x0000000001047F0... LINESTRING (150.00000000000125 -90.00000...
Beach Street Harborside   0x000000000104870... LINESTRING (300 -150, 300 -300)
First Avenue Downtown     0x000000000104870... LINESTRING (100 -100, 50.000000000000782...
First Avenue Harborside   0x000000000104870... LINESTRING (180 -180, 150.00000000000071...

(5 row(s) affected)
```

Notice that the portions of First Avenue that do not run through any of the three districts are excluded from the results. As Figure 9-9 shows, you can see a visual representation of the results by clicking the Spatial Results tab in SSMS.

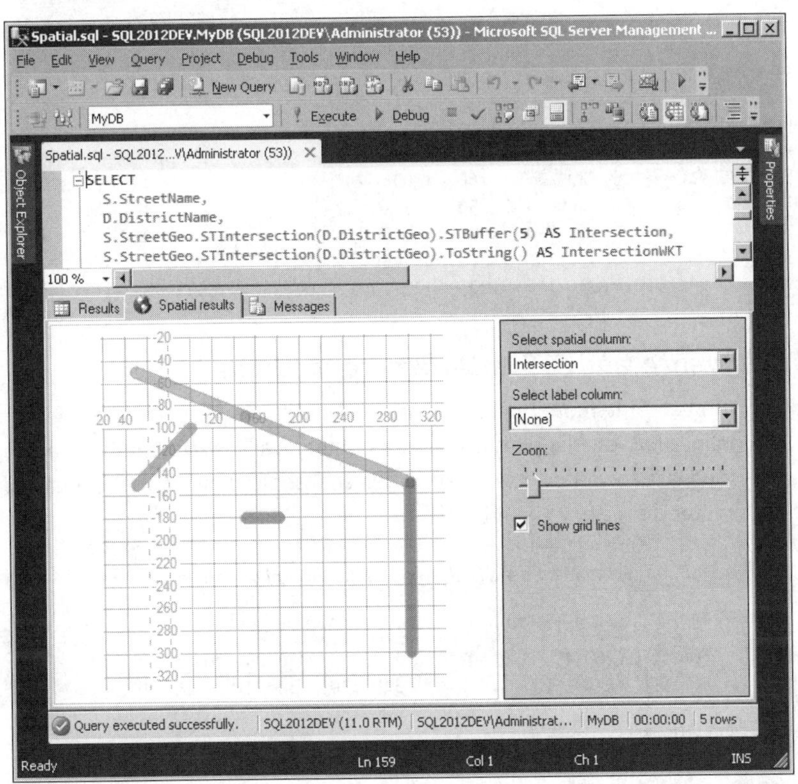

FIGURE 9-9 Viewing the road fragments of the streets in each district using *STIntersection*.

The *STDimension* Method

The *STDimension* method can be invoked on any spatial instance, and returns a number (0, 1, or 2) that indicates how many dimensions are defined by the shape in the instance. Single points have 0 dimensions; lines, circular lines, and line strings have 1 dimension; and polygons (closed shapes) have 2 dimensions. That means that all of the districts in the town are two-dimensional objects, whereas the streets are all one-dimensional objects. The code in Listing 9-10 displays the dimensions for all the spatial objects currently stored in the database.

LISTING 9-10 Using the *STDimension* method to show the number of dimensions for each shape.

```
SELECT
  StreetName AS Shape,
  StreetGeo.ToString() AS ShapeWKT,
  StreetGeo.STDimension() AS Dimensions
 FROM Street
 UNION ALL
 SELECT
  DistrictName AS Shape,
  DistrictGeo.ToString() AS ShapeWKT,
  DistrictGeo.STDimension() AS Dimensions
 FROM District
```

Here are the results:

```
Shape          ShapeWKT                                                     Dimensions
-------------  ------------------------------------------------------------ -----------
First Avenue   LINESTRING (100 -100, 20 -180, 180 -180)                     1
Beach Street   LINESTRING (300 -300, 300 -150, 50 -50)                      1
Downtown       POLYGON ((0 0, 150 0, 150 -150, 0 -150, 0 0))                2
Green Park     POLYGON ((300 0, 150 0, 150 -150, 300 -150, 300 0))          2
Harborside     POLYGON ((150 -150, 300 -150, 300 -300, 150 -300, 150 -150)) 2
```

The *STUnion*, *STDifference*, and *STSymDifference* Methods

Our next example demonstrates some more manipulations with overlapping regions between shapes. The code in Listing 9-11 defines two overlapping polygons, and then calls several methods against those shapes. The code listing is followed by a series of screen snapshots showing the Spatial Results viewer rendering of each method's result.

LISTING 9-11 Comparing the *STUnion*, *STIntersection*, *STDifference*, and *STSymDifference* methods.

```
DECLARE @S1 geometry = 'POLYGON ((60 40, 410 50, 400 270,  60 370, 60 40))'
DECLARE @S2 geometry = 'POLYGON ((300 100, 510 110,  510 330,  300 330,  300 100))'

SELECT @S1 UNION ALL SELECT @S2
SELECT S1_UNION_S2          = @S1.STUnion(@S2)
SELECT S1_INTERSECTION_S2   = @S1.STIntersection(@S2)
SELECT S1_DIFFERENCE_S2     = @S1.STDifference(@S2)
SELECT S2_DIFFERENCE_S1     = @S2.STDifference(@S1)
SELECT S1_SYMDIFFERENCE_S2 = @S1.STSymDifference(@S2)
```

The first query combines (unions) the two shapes so you can see what they look like and how they overlap, as shown in Figure 9-10.

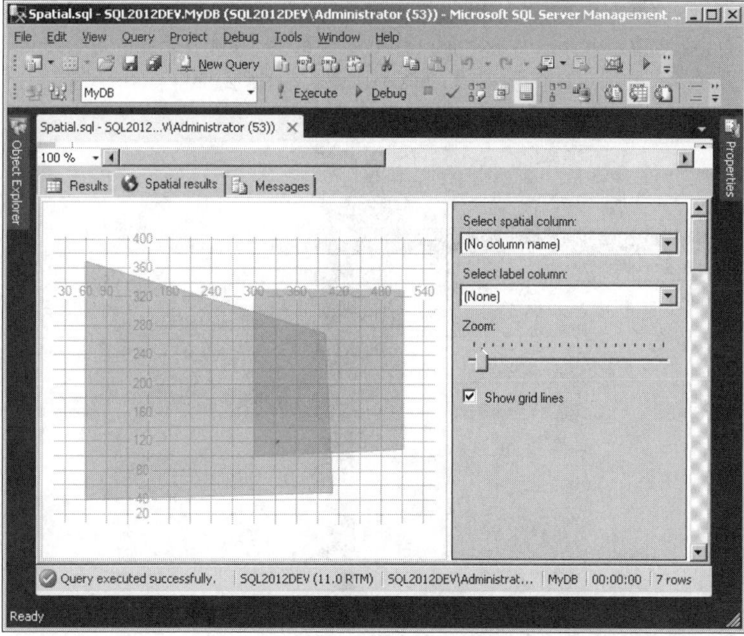

FIGURE 9-10 Two overlapping shapes.

STUnion returns a new shape based on the two source shapes (disregarding the overlapping portion), as shown in Figure 9-11.

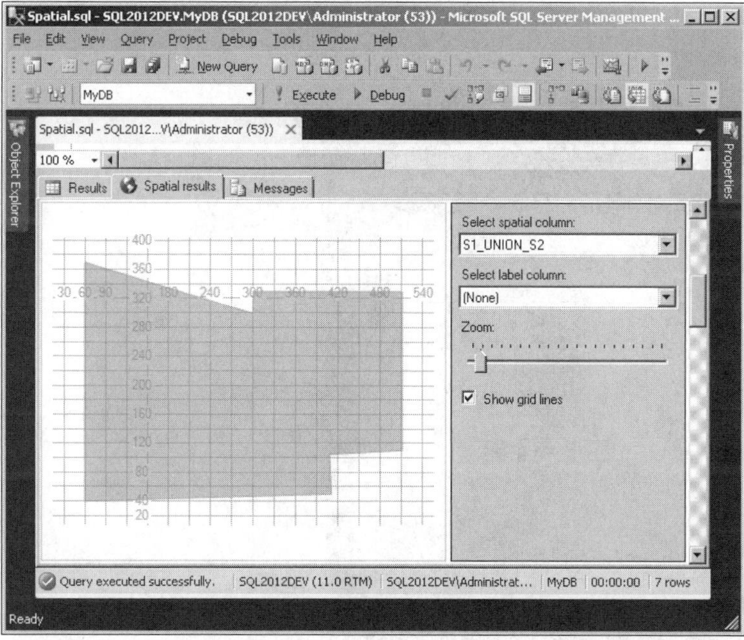

FIGURE 9-11 Combining the two overlapping shapes into one using *STUnion.*

Earlier, you used the *STIntersection* method to break down one shape (a string) into multiple shapes (by district). Once again, *STIntersection* produces a similar result by creating a new shape representing just the area of overlap (the center piece) between the two source shapes, as shown in Figure 9-12.

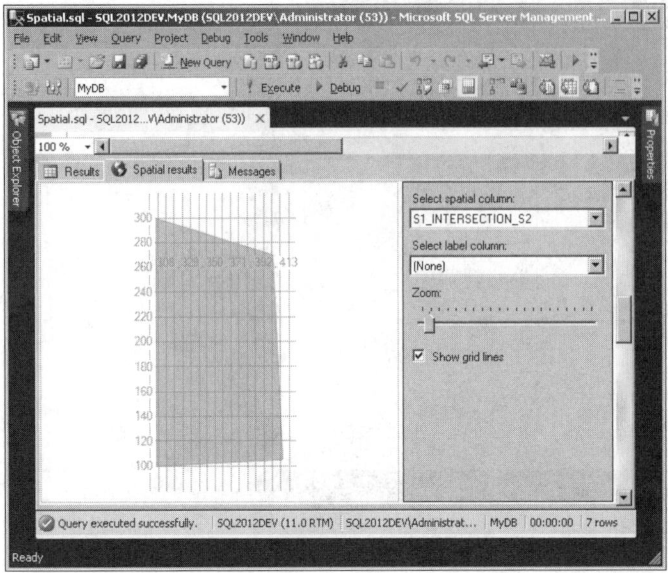

FIGURE 9-12 Identifying the area of overlap between the two shapes using *STIntersection*.

The *STDifference* method "cuts away" from one shape the overlapping area of another shape. Figure 9-13 shows the result of invoking *STDifference* to cut away the part of the first shape where the second shape overlaps.

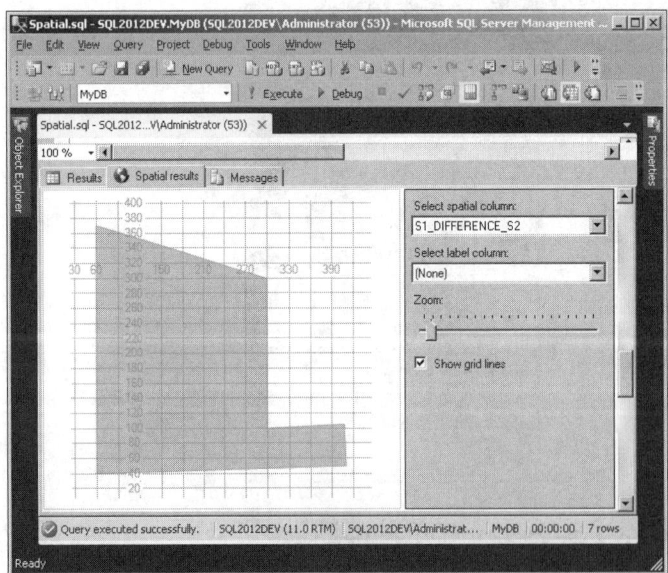

FIGURE 9-13 Differencing the second shape away from the first shape using *STDifference*.

Figure 9-14 shows the reverse, where *STDifference* is used to cut away the part of the second shape where the first shape overlaps.

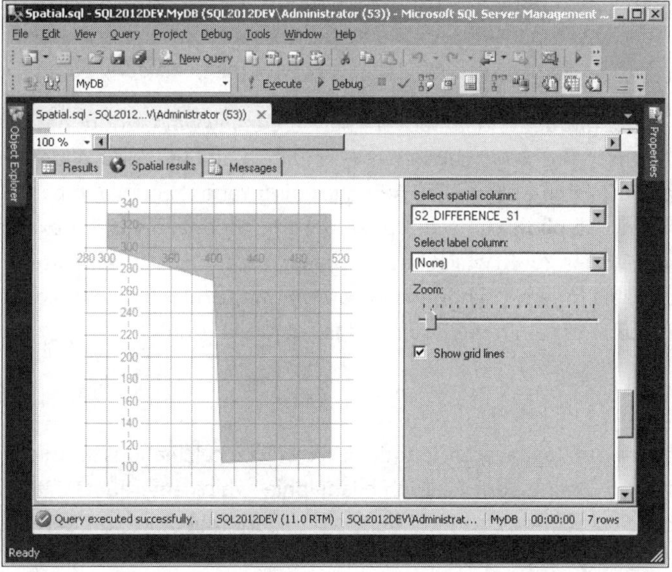

FIGURE 9-14 Differencing the first shape away from the second shape using *STDifference*.

Finally, the *STSymDifference* method returns the "symmetrical" difference between the two shapes. This is essentially the opposite of the *STIntersection* method—a new shape is generated that represents everything *except* the area of overlap between the two shapes (everything but the center piece), as shown in Figure 9-15.

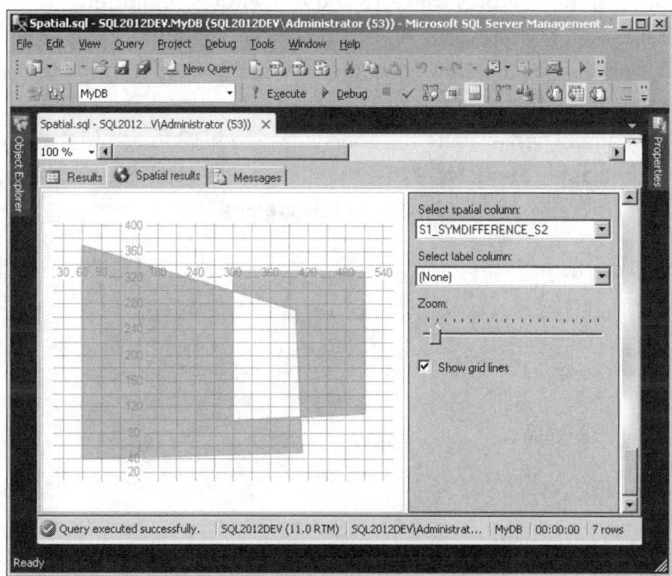

FIGURE 9-15 Obtaining the symmetric difference between two shapes using *STSymDifference*.

Working with *geography*

Most (but not all) methods of the *geometry* type are available and function similarly for the *geography* type. The primary difference is that you must use longitude and latitude values. Internally, as explained, SQL Server automatically compensates for the earth's curvature when performing calculations against our *geography* data. In this section, you'll work with the *geography* data type.

How do you get your hands on longitudes and latitudes? There are many ways. Coordinates for large cities and other major locations in the world can be easily obtained on the World Wide Web with a quick search and via readily available web service APIs, including Yahoo! and Google. The old-fashioned way still works too, so pilots can acquire them from sectional maps, for example. You can also use Microsoft Streets & Trips 2008, which has a "location sensor" tool that will tell you the longitude and latitude coordinates for any point or shape drawn on the map using the mouse. This Streets & Trips feature was used to obtain the coordinates for our next example.

On Your Mark ...

You'll use a real-life event to learn about spatial area, length, and distance calculations. In this application, you are mapping the Pro Cycling Tour held in Philadelphia (which entered its 27th year in 2011). Using longitude and latitude coordinates, you will build a database that stores different areas of the bike race. Then you'll write queries to calculate the area and length of different regions using other new spatial methods.

The map for this application is shown in Figure 9-16. The entire race area is contained in one large 14-sided polygon. Within the race area, there are two popular locations where spectators gather and take pictures. One is the Parkway Area to the south, where the race starts and finishes, and the other is the Wall Area to the north.

In this application, you'll combine spatial features with FILESTREAM. Photos submitted by spectators will be stored in the database as binary large objects (BLOBs) in the file system using the techniques you learned earlier, during our FILESTREAM coverage in Chapter 8. Refer to the section "Enabling FILESTREAM for the Machine" in that chapter, which describes how to enable FILESTREAM using SQL Server Configuration Manager. Then execute the code in Listing 9-12 to create the FILESTREAM-enabled database for the application. Note that the path to the database, C:\Demo\EventLibrary in this example, must exist before the database can be created.

LISTING 9-12 Creating the *EventLibrary* database.

```
USE master
GO

EXEC sp_configure filestream_access_level, 2
RECONFIGURE
GO

CREATE DATABASE EventLibrary
 ON PRIMARY
```

```
  (NAME = EventLibrary_data,
   FILENAME = 'C:\Demo\EventLibrary\EventLibrary_data.mdf'),
 FILEGROUP FileStreamGroup1 CONTAINS FILESTREAM
  (NAME = EventLibrary_group2,
   FILENAME = 'C:\Demo\EventLibrary\Events')
 LOG ON
  (NAME = EventLibrary_log,
   FILENAME = 'C:\Demo\EventLibrary\EventLibrary_log.ldf')
GO

USE EventLibrary
GO
```

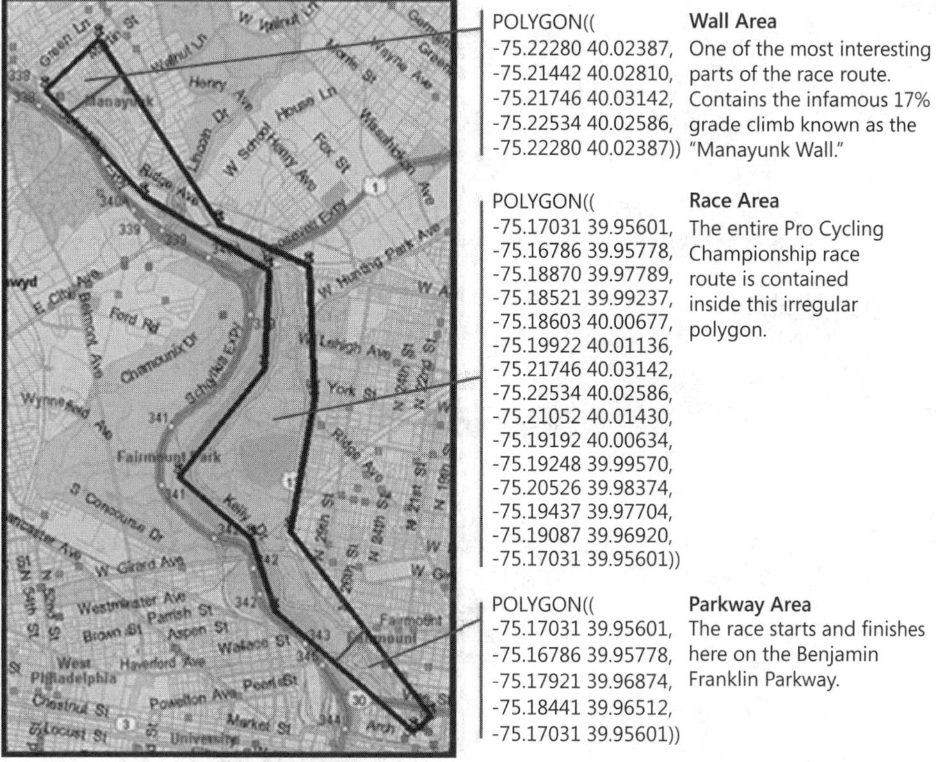

FIGURE 9-16 Pro Cycling Tour region map.

Next, create the *EventRegion* table to hold the different map regions and then populate the table with the polygons representing the three regions being mapped, as shown in Listing 9-13.

LISTING 9-13 Creating the *EventRegion* table and populating it with geographical data.

```
CREATE TABLE EventRegion
 (RegionId     int PRIMARY KEY,
  RegionName   nvarchar(32),
  MapShape     geography)

INSERT INTO EventRegion VALUES(1, 'Parkway Area', geography::Parse('POLYGON((
 -75.17031 39.95601, -75.16786 39.95778, -75.17921 39.96874,
 -75.18441 39.96512, -75.17031 39.95601 ))'))

INSERT INTO EventRegion VALUES(2, 'Wall Area', geography::Parse('POLYGON((
 -75.22280 40.02387, -75.21442 40.02810, -75.21746 40.03142,
 -75.22534 40.02586, -75.22280 40.02387))'))

INSERT INTO EventRegion VALUES(3, 'Race Area', geography::Parse('POLYGON((
 -75.17031 39.95601, -75.16786 39.95778, -75.18870 39.97789, -75.18521 39.99237,
 -75.18603 40.00677, -75.19922 40.01136, -75.21746 40.03142, -75.22534 40.02586,
 -75.21052 40.01430, -75.19192 40.00634, -75.19248 39.99570, -75.20526 39.98374,
 -75.19437 39.97704, -75.19087 39.96920, -75.17031 39.95601))'))
```

Now execute the statement *SELECT * FROM EventRegion* to query for the list of regions you just created in the *EventRegion* table. Figure 9-17 shows how the query results appear in the spatial viewer.

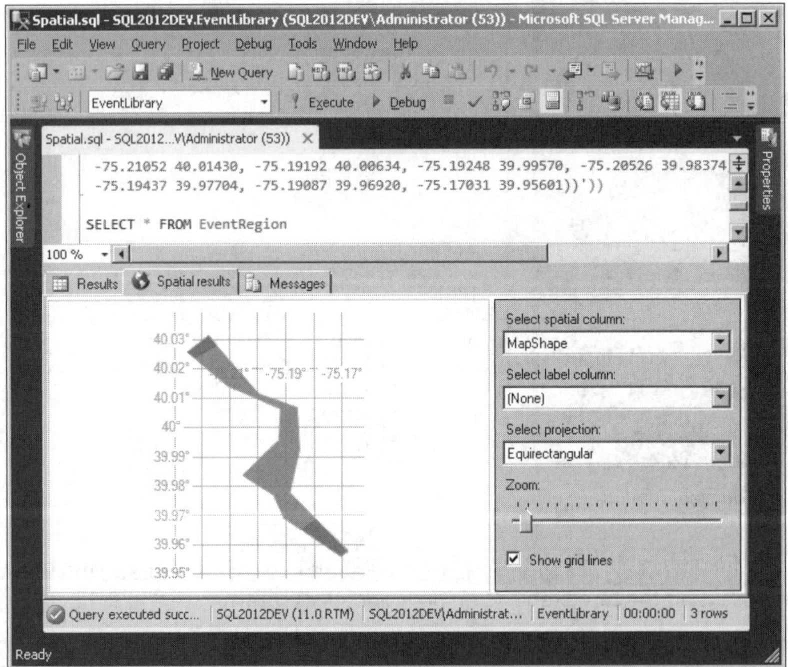

FIGURE 9-17 Viewing spatial *geography* data in SSMS.

Notice the third drop-down list labeled Select Projection. This drop-down list was not present on the spatial viewer in our earlier queries because they returned *geometry* (planar) data. This query returns *geography* (geodetic) spatial data, so the spatial viewer allows you to render the results using one of several different projections from the additional drop-down list. By default, the viewer uses the Equirectangular projection, but you can change that to observe the different ways that geodetic spatial data is skewed when flattening the globe using different flat-earth projection models. For example, change the third drop-down list to use the Mercator projection. As shown in Figure 9-18, the same geodetic data gets skewed to a slightly different shape when flattened use the Mercator projection (notice how it's narrower than the Equiractangular projection in Figure 9-17).

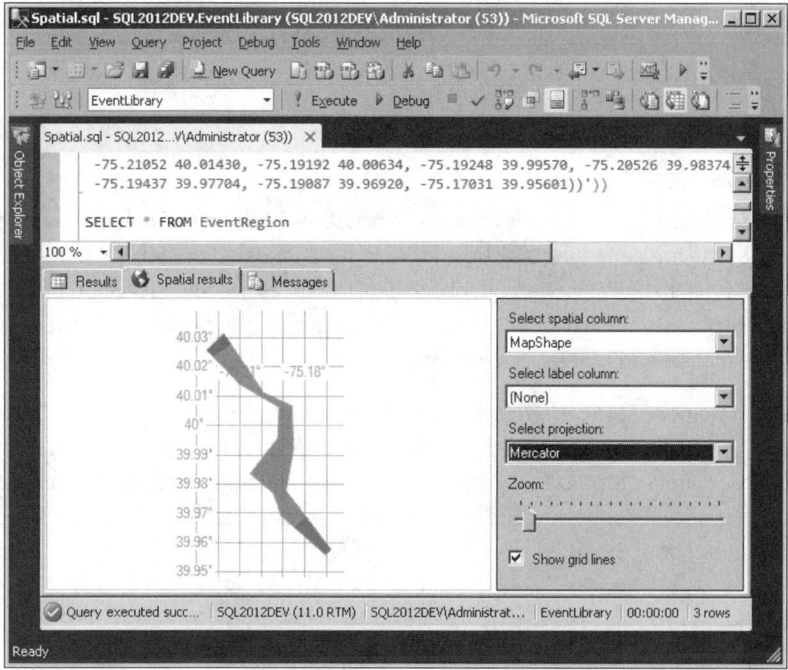

FIGURE 9-18 Viewing the same spatial data using the Mercator projection.

The *STArea* and *STLength* Methods

Area and length (perimeter) calculations are easily performed using the *STArea* and *STLength* methods. The query in Listing 9-14 displays the area and length of each region, sorted from largest to smallest.

LISTING 9-14 Calculating area and length using the *STArea* and *STLength* methods.

```
SELECT
 RegionName,
 ROUND(MapShape.STArea(), 2) AS Area,
 ROUND(MapShape.STLength(), 2) AS Length
```

```
FROM
 EventRegion
ORDER BY
 MapShape.STArea() DESC
```

Here are the results:

```
RegionName                       Area                  Length
-------------------------------- --------------------- ----------------------
Race Area                        6432902.35            22165.07
Parkway Area                     689476.79             4015.39
Wall Area                        334024.82             2529.11

(3 row(s) affected)
```

Spatial Reference IDs

The first question you're bound to ask when viewing these results is, what unit of measurement does SQL Server use to express the area and length? The answer is, it depends on the Spatial Reference ID (SRID) of the spatial data type instance. By default, *geography* instances use an SRID value of 4326, which is based on the metric system. Therefore, the area and length results shown in the preceding code are given in square meters and meters, respectively.

You can execute the statement *SELECT * FROM sys.spatial_reference_systems* to obtain a list of all the SRIDs supported by SQL Server. Some of the SRIDs support different measurement systems, including foot, Clarke's foot, Indian foot, U.S. survey foot, and German legal meter. Calculations performed between two spatial instances require both instances to use the same SRID. See Books Online for more information about SRIDs.

Building Out the *EventLibrary* Database

Now it's time to create the *EventPhoto* table, as shown in Listing 9-15. The *RowId* and *Photo* columns, respectively, provide the *ROWGUIDCOL* and *varbinary(max) FILESTREAM* columns required for FILESTREAM storage and access to binary photo files, as we explored in depth in Chapter 8. The *Location* column stores the point (longitude and latitude) where the photo was taken in a *geography* data type. This table will be populated with several photos using the very same techniques you used in the photo library FILESTREAM application from Chapter 8.

LISTING 9-15 Creating the *EventPhoto* table to hold photos and the locations where they were taken.

```
CREATE TABLE EventPhoto (
 PhotoId int PRIMARY KEY,
 RowId uniqueidentifier ROWGUIDCOL NOT NULL UNIQUE DEFAULT NEWSEQUENTIALID(),
 Description varchar(max),
 Location geography,
 Photo varbinary(max) FILESTREAM DEFAULT(0x))
```

You're about to create a Windows Forms application in C# that allows the user to select a region and retrieve all the photos taken in that region. Once again, using the same FILESTREAM techniques you've already learned for the *PhotoLibrary* application in Chapter 8, the user can then select a photo for display in a picture box control.

To support this application, you'll write several stored procedures (see Listing 9-16). *GetRegions* is called to retrieve a list of all the region IDs and names, which gets bound to a combo box for the user to make a region selection. *GetRegionPhotos* accepts the ID of the region selected by the user and returns a list of all the photo IDs and descriptions of pictures taken in the selected region, which gets bound to a list box for the user to make a photo selection. The photo list is obtained by using the *STIntersects* method you learned about earlier in this chapter with the *geometry* type. Last, *GetPhotoForFilestream* returns the *PathName* and *GET_FILESTREAM_TRANSACTION_CONTEXT* values for using *SqlFileStream* to retrieve and display the photo selected by the user.

LISTING 9-16 Creating the stored procedures for the sample event media application.

```
-- Present list of regions to user
CREATE PROCEDURE GetRegions AS
 BEGIN
    SELECT RegionId, RegionName FROM EventRegion
 END
GO

-- Get all the photos taken in the selected region
CREATE PROCEDURE GetRegionPhotos(@RegionId int) AS
 BEGIN

    DECLARE @MapShape geography

    -- Get the shape of the region
    SELECT   @MapShape = MapShape
     FROM    EventRegion
     WHERE   RegionId = @RegionId

    -- Get all photos taken in the region
    SELECT   PhotoId, Description
     FROM    EventPhoto
     WHERE   Location.STIntersects(@MapShape) = 1

 END
GO

-- Get the SqlFileStream information for retrieving the selected photo
CREATE PROCEDURE GetPhotoForFilestream(@PhotoId int) AS
 BEGIN

    -- Called by ADO.NET client during open transaction to use SqlFileStream
    SELECT   Photo.PathName(), GET_FILESTREAM_TRANSACTION_CONTEXT()
```

```
        FROM     EventPhoto
        WHERE    PhotoId = @PhotoId

    END
  GO
```

Creating the Event Media Client Application

To create the client application, start Microsoft Visual Studio 2010, and then create a new C# Windows Forms application named *EventMediaSpatialApp*. Design a form named *PhotoForm* with a combobox for selecting a region, a link label to search for photos by region, and a list box for displaying the results. Also include a picture box control for displaying the photo selected from the list box and a link label that you'll use to bulk load four photo files into the *EventPhoto* table. After performing some aesthetic alignment and formatting, your form should appear something like the one shown in Figure 9-19.

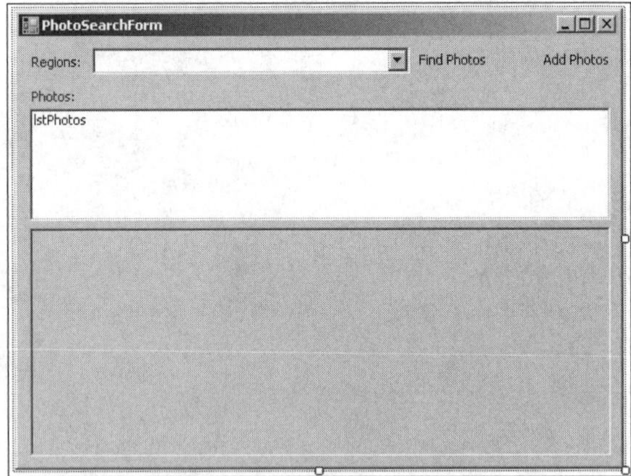

FIGURE 9-19 *EventMedia* Windows user interface (UI) form.

Listing 9-17 contains the complete code behind the form, which calls the stored procedures you created in Listing 9-16 to populate the combobox with regions, query for photos taken in any selected region, and then display any photo selected from that region. When a photo is selected, it streams the image from the *FILESTREAM* column in the database to the picture box control using *SqlFileStream*. There are also methods that use *SqlFileStream* to load geocoded images into the database. The *SqlFileStream* code requires no detailed explanation here; it follows the precise pattern we detailed in Chapter 8 to save and load the BLOB images to and from the database.

LISTING 9-17 *EventMedia* client application code.

```
using System;
using System.Data;
using System.Data.SqlClient;
using System.Data.SqlTypes;
```

```
using System.Drawing;
using System.IO;
using System.Transactions;
using System.Windows.Forms;

namespace EventMediaSpatialApp
{
  public partial class PhotoSearchForm : Form
  {
    private const string ConnStr =
     "Data Source=.;Integrated Security=True;Initial Catalog=EventLibrary;";

    public PhotoSearchForm()
    {
      InitializeComponent();
    }

    protected override void OnLoad(EventArgs e)
    {
      base.OnLoad(e);

      this.LoadRegions();
    }

    private void lnkAddPhotos_LinkClicked
     (object sender, LinkLabelLinkClickedEventArgs e)
    {
      this.AddPhotos();
    }

    private void lnkSearch_LinkClicked
     (object sender, LinkLabelLinkClickedEventArgs e)
    {
      this.FindRegionPhotos();
    }

    private void lstPhotos_SelectedIndexChanged(object sender, EventArgs e)
    {
      this.DisplayPhoto();
    }

    private void LoadRegions()
    {
      using (SqlDataAdapter adp = new SqlDataAdapter("GetRegions", ConnStr))
      {
        adp.SelectCommand.CommandType = CommandType.StoredProcedure;
        DataSet ds = new DataSet();
        adp.Fill(ds);
        this.cboRegions.DataSource = ds.Tables[0];
        this.cboRegions.ValueMember = "RegionId";
        this.cboRegions.DisplayMember = "RegionName";
      }
    }
```

```
    private void FindRegionPhotos()
    {
      this.lstPhotos.SelectedIndexChanged -=
       new System.EventHandler(this.lstPhotos_SelectedIndexChanged);

      int regionId = (int)this.cboRegions.SelectedValue;

      using (SqlDataAdapter adp = new SqlDataAdapter("GetRegionPhotos", ConnStr))
      {
        adp.SelectCommand.CommandType = CommandType.StoredProcedure;
        adp.SelectCommand.Parameters.AddWithValue("@RegionId", regionId);
        DataSet ds = new DataSet();
        adp.Fill(ds);
        this.lstPhotos.DataSource = ds.Tables[0];
        this.lstPhotos.ValueMember = "PhotoId";
        this.lstPhotos.DisplayMember = "Description";
      }
      this.lstPhotos.SelectedIndexChanged +=
       new System.EventHandler(this.lstPhotos_SelectedIndexChanged);
      this.DisplayPhoto();
    }

    private void DisplayPhoto()
    {
      int photoId = (int)this.lstPhotos.SelectedValue;
      this.picImage.Image = this.GetPhoto(photoId);
    }

    private Image GetPhoto(int photoId)
    {
      Image photo;
      using (TransactionScope ts = new TransactionScope())
      {
        using (SqlConnection conn = new SqlConnection(ConnStr))
        {
          conn.Open();

          string filePath;
          byte[] txnToken;

          using (SqlCommand cmd = new SqlCommand("GetPhotoForFilestream", conn))
          {
            cmd.CommandType = CommandType.StoredProcedure;
            cmd.Parameters.Add("@PhotoId", SqlDbType.Int).Value = photoId;

            using (SqlDataReader rdr = cmd.ExecuteReader(CommandBehavior.
SingleRow))
            {
              rdr.Read();
              filePath = rdr.GetSqlString(0).Value;
              txnToken = rdr.GetSqlBinary(1).Value;
              rdr.Close();
            }
          }
```

```
      photo = this.LoadPhotoImage(filePath, txnToken);
    }
    ts.Complete();
  }

  return photo;
}

private Image LoadPhotoImage(string filePath, byte[] txnToken)
{
  Image photo;

  using (SqlFileStream sfs =
   new SqlFileStream(filePath, txnToken, FileAccess.Read))
  {
    photo = Image.FromStream(sfs);
    sfs.Close();
  }

  return photo;
}

private void AddPhotos()
{
  this.InsertEventPhoto(1,
   "Taken from the Ben Franklin parkway near the finish line",
   -75.17396, 39.96045, "bike9_2.jpg");
  this.InsertEventPhoto(2,
   "This shot was taken from the bottom of the Manayunk Wall",
   -75.22457, 40.02593, "wall_race_2.jpg");
  this.InsertEventPhoto(3,
   "This shot was taken at the top of the Manayunk Wall.",
   -75.21986, 40.02920, "wall_race2_2.jpg");
  this.InsertEventPhoto(4,
   "This is another shot from the Benjamin Franklin Parkway.",
   -75.17052, 39.95813, "parkway_area2_2.jpg");

  MessageBox.Show("Added 4 photos to database");
}

private void InsertEventPhoto(
 int photoId,
 string desc,
 double longitude,
 double latitude,
 string photoFile)
{
  const string InsertTSql = @"
   INSERT INTO EventPhoto(PhotoId, Description, Location)
    VALUES(@PhotoId, @Description, geography::STGeomFromText(@Location, 4326))
   SELECT Photo.PathName(), GET_FILESTREAM_TRANSACTION_CONTEXT()
    FROM EventPhoto
    WHERE PhotoId = @PhotoId";
```

```
    const string PointMask = "POINT ({0} {1})";
    string location = string.Format(PointMask, longitude, latitude);

    string serverPath;
    byte[] serverTxn;

    using (TransactionScope ts = new TransactionScope())
    {
      using (SqlConnection conn = new SqlConnection(ConnStr))
      {
        conn.Open();

        using (SqlCommand cmd = new SqlCommand(InsertTSql, conn))
        {
          cmd.Parameters.Add("@PhotoId", SqlDbType.Int).Value = photoId;
          cmd.Parameters.Add("@Description", SqlDbType.NVarChar).Value = desc;
          cmd.Parameters.Add("@Location", SqlDbType.NVarChar).Value = location;
          using (SqlDataReader rdr = cmd.ExecuteReader(CommandBehavior.
SingleRow))
          {
            rdr.Read();
            serverPath = rdr.GetSqlString(0).Value;
            serverTxn = rdr.GetSqlBinary(1).Value;
            rdr.Close();
          }
        }
        this.SavePhotoFile(photoFile, serverPath, serverTxn);
      }
      ts.Complete();
    }
  }

  private void SavePhotoFile
    (string photoFile, string serverPath, byte[] serverTxn)
  {
    const string LocalPath = @"..\..\Photos\";
    const int BlockSize = 1024 * 512;

    using (FileStream source =
      new FileStream(LocalPath + photoFile, FileMode.Open, FileAccess.Read))
    {
      using (SqlFileStream dest =
        new SqlFileStream(serverPath, serverTxn, FileAccess.Write))
      {
        byte[] buffer = new byte[BlockSize];
        int bytesRead;
        while ((bytesRead = source.Read(buffer, 0, buffer.Length)) > 0)
        {
          dest.Write(buffer, 0, bytesRead);
          dest.Flush();
        }
        dest.Close();
      }
      source.Close();
```

```
            }
        }

    }
}
```

The code behind the *Add Photos* link label click event inserts four photos and their longitude and latitude coordinates into the database. Two of the photos were taken in the Wall Area, and the other two were taken in the Parkway Area. Most phone cameras and many digital cameras automatically record GPS information with each digital image file (that is, they *geocode* the image). You can use the *GetPropertyItem* method of the *Image* class to extract the geocoded information from these digital images to obtain the location where they were taken. Our example simply uses hard-coded location values in the *AddPhotos* method.

Note As with all code in this book, the full *EventMedia* demo code in this chapter is available on the book's companion website (see the "Introduction" for details). Included with the code are the four photo files named *bike9_2.jpg*, *wall_race_2.jpg*, *wall_race2_2.jpg*, and *parkway_area2_2.jpg*. If you do not have access to these images, just use any .jpg image files you have available—doing so won't change the point of the demo.

Run the application, and click *Add Photos* to populate the *EventPhoto* table. Then select different regions from the drop-down list to test out the query. Based on the *STIntersects* method in the stored procedure, the application lists two of the pictures for the Wall Area, the other two pictures for the Parkway Area, and all four pictures for the Race Area (which encompasses both of the other regions). Selecting any photo streams the image from the database into the picture box, as shown in Figure 9-20.

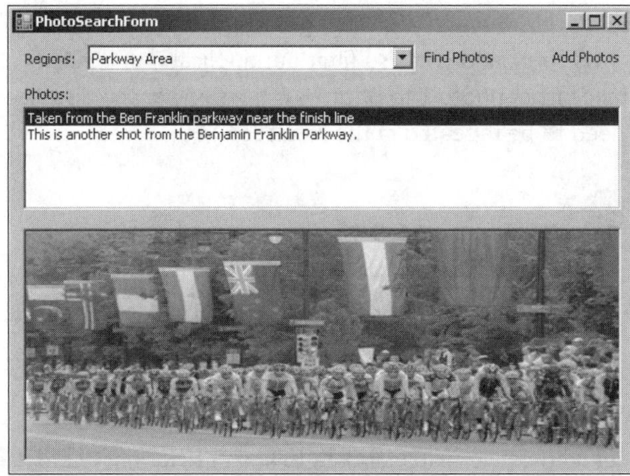

FIGURE 9-20 Performing location-based photo searching and streaming.

The *STDistance* Method

You use the *STDistance* method for distance calculations. By joining the *EventPhoto* table to itself on *PhotoId*, you can invoke this method against every combination of any two pictures, as shown in Listing 9-18. The value returned by *STDistance* is the exact distance between the two pictures expressed in meters, so dividing that value by 1000 converts the result to kilometers. (As mentioned earlier, the default SRID for the *geography* data type uses the metric system.)

LISTING 9-18 Using *STDistance* to calculate the distance between any two photos.

```
SELECT
  P1.PhotoId AS Photo1,
  P2.PhotoId AS Photo2,
  ROUND(P1.Location.STDistance(P2.location) / 1000, 2) AS Km
 FROM
  EventPhoto AS P1 JOIN EventPhoto AS P2 ON P1.PhotoId < P2.PhotoId
 ORDER BY
  P1.PhotoId
```

Here are the query results:

```
Photo1      Photo2      Km
----------- ----------- ----------------------
1           2           8.46
1           3           8.58
1           4           0.39
2           3           0.54
2           4           8.83
3           4           8.95

(6 row(s) affected)
```

Because the join is based on *P1.PhotoId* < *P2.PhotoId*, you don't get results for the distance between a photo and itself (which is always zero), and you also filter out duplicate "opposite direction" results. For example, the distance from photo 1 to photo 3 is the same as the distance from photo 3 to photo 1, so it doesn't need to be repeated in the result set.

Spatial Enhancements in SQL Server 2012

SQL Server 2012 adds many significant improvements to the spatial support that was first introduced with SQL Server 2008. In this section, we'll explore some of these latest enhancements. Particularly notable is support for curves (arcs), whereas SQL Server 2008 only supported straight lines, or polygons composed of straight lines. As you'll see, Microsoft also provides methods that test for non-2012-compatible (curved) shapes, and convert circular data to line data for backward compatibility with SQL Server 2008 (as well as other mapping platforms that don't support curves).

New Spatial Data Classes

The three new shapes in SQL Server 2012 are circular strings, compound curves, and curve polygons. All three are supported in WKT, WKB, and GML by both the *geometry* and *geography* data types, and all of the existing methods work on all of the new shapes.

Circular Strings

A circular string defines a basic curved line, similar to how a line string defines a straight line. It takes a minimum of three coordinates to define a circular string; the first and third coordinates define the end points of the line, and the second coordinate (the "anchor" point, which lies somewhere between the end points) determines the arc of the line. Figure 9-21 shows the shape represented by *CIRCULARSTRING(0 1, .25 0, 0 -1)*.

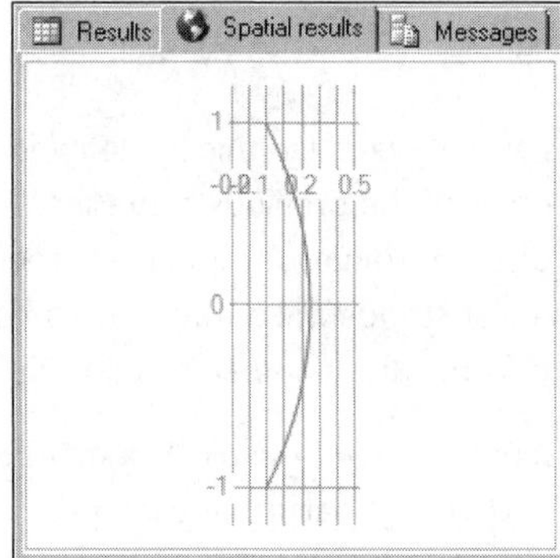

FIGURE 9-21 A simple circular string.

The code in Listing 9-19 produces four circular strings. All of them have the same start and end points, but different anchor points. The lines are buffered slightly to make them easier to see in the spatial viewer.

LISTING 9-19 Circular strings with different anchor points.

```
-- Create a "straight" circular line
SELECT geometry::Parse('CIRCULARSTRING(0 8, 4 0, 8 -8)').STBuffer(.1)
UNION ALL  -- Curve it
SELECT geometry::Parse('CIRCULARSTRING(0 8, 4 4, 8 -8)').STBuffer(.1)
UNION ALL  -- Curve it some more
SELECT geometry::Parse('CIRCULARSTRING(0 8, 4 6, 8 -8)').STBuffer(.1)
UNION ALL  -- Curve it in the other direction
SELECT geometry::Parse('CIRCULARSTRING(0 8, 4 -6, 8 -8)').STBuffer(.1)
```

Figure 9-22 shows the generated shapes from the previous code. The first shape is a "straight circular" line, because the anchor point is positioned directly between the start and end points. The next two shapes use the same end points with the anchor out to the right (4), one a bit further than the other (6). The last shape also uses the same end points, but specifies an anchor point that curves the line to the left rather than the right (-6).

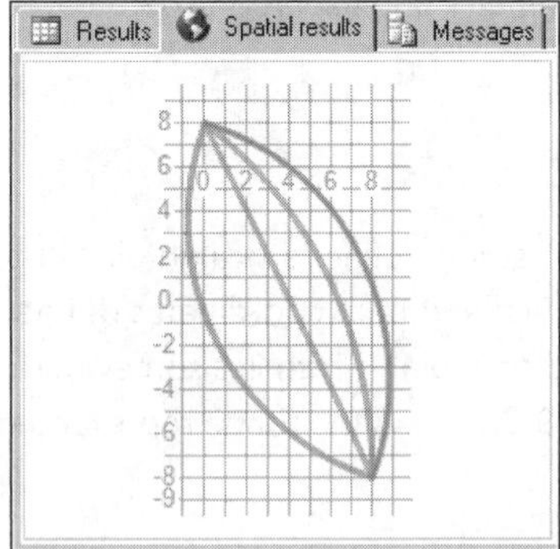

FIGURE 9-22 A set of circular strings, including one that's perfectly straight.

You can extend circular strings with as many curve segments as you want. Do this by defining another two coordinates for each additional segment. The last point of the previous curve serves as the first end point of the next curve segment, so the two additional coordinates respectively specify the next segment's anchor and second end point. Thus, valid circular strings will always have an odd number of points. You can extend a circular string indefinitely to form curves and arcs of any kind.

It's easy to form a perfect circle by connecting two semi-circle segments. For example, Figure 9-23 shows the circle produced by *CIRCULARSTRING(0 4, 4 0, 8 4, 4 8, 0 4)*. This particular example connects the end of the second segment to the beginning of the first segment to form a closed shape. Note that this is certainly not required of circular strings (or line strings), and that closing the shape by connecting the last segment to the first still does not result in a polygon, which is a two-dimensional shape that has area. Despite being closed, this circle is still considered a one-dimensional shape with no area. As you'll soon see, the curve polygon can be used to convert closed line shapes into true polygons.

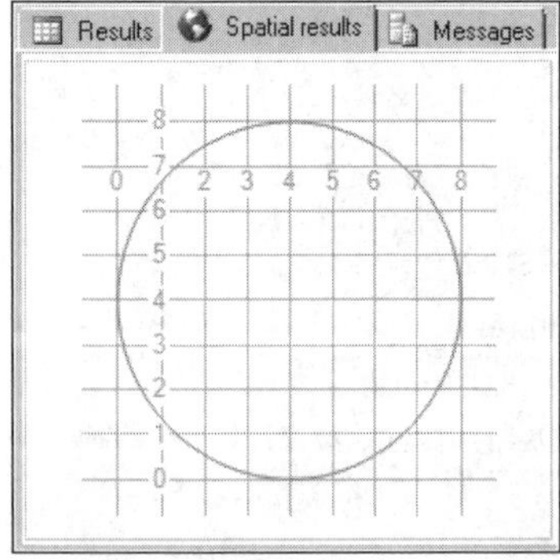

FIGURE 9-23 Two semi-circle segments linked together in one circular string.

Compound Curves

A compound curve is a set of circular strings, or circular strings combined with line strings, that form a desired curved shape. The end point of each element in the collection must match the starting point of the following element, so that compound curves are defined in a "connect-the-dots" fashion. The code in Listing 9-20 produces a compound curve and compares it with the equivalent geometry collection shape.

LISTING 9-20 Compound curve shapes.

```
-- Compound curve
DECLARE @CC geometry = '
 COMPOUNDCURVE(
  (4 4, 4 8),
  CIRCULARSTRING(4 8, 6 10, 8 8),
  (8 8, 8 4),
  CIRCULARSTRING(8 4, 2 3, 4 4)
 )'

-- Equivalent geometry collection
DECLARE @GC geometry = '
 GEOMETRYCOLLECTION(
  LINESTRING(4 4, 4 8),
  CIRCULARSTRING(4 8, 6 10, 8 8),
  LINESTRING(8 8, 8 4),
  CIRCULARSTRING(8 4, 2 3, 4 4)
 )'

-- They both render the same shape in the spatial viewer
SELECT @CC.STBuffer(.5)
UNION ALL
SELECT @GC.STBuffer(1.5)
```

This code creates a keyhole shape using a compound curve, and also creates an identical shape as a geometry collection (though notice that the *LINESTRING* keyword is not—and cannot—be specified when defining a compound curve). It then buffers both of them with different padding, so that the spatial viewer clearly shows the two identical shapes on top of one another, as shown in Figure 9-24.

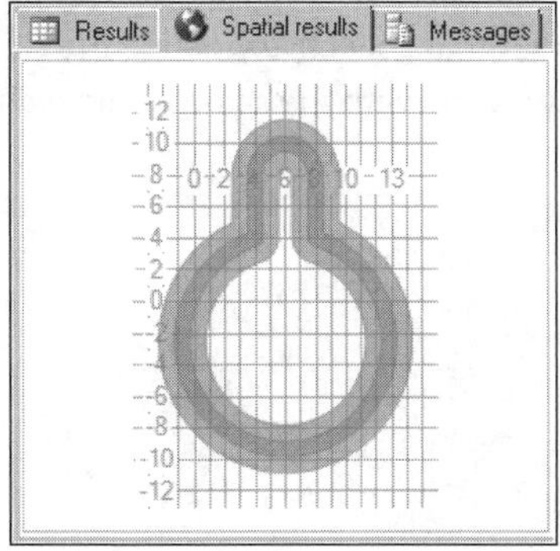

FIGURE 9-24 A compound curve over an identically shaped geometry collection.

Both the compound curve and the geometry collection yield identical shapes. In fact, the expression *@CC.STEquals(@GC)*, which compares the two instances for equality, returns *1* (for true). The *STEquals* method tests for "spatial equality," meaning it returns true if two instances produce the same shape even if they are being rendered using different spatial data classes. Furthermore, recall from Listing 9-19 and Figure 9-22 that segments of a circular string can be made perfectly straight by positioning the anchor directly between the end points, meaning that the circular string offers yet a third option for producing the very same shape. So which one should you use? Comparing these spatial data classes will help you determine which one is best to use in different scenarios.

A geometry collection (which was already supported in SQL Server 2008) is the most accommodating, but carries the most storage overhead. Geometry collections can hold instances of any spatial data class, and the instances don't need to be connected to (or intersected with) each other in any way. The collection simply holds a bunch of different shapes as a set, which in this example just happens to be several line strings and circular strings connected at their start and end points.

In contrast, the new compound curve class in SQL Server 2012 has the most constraints but is the most lightweight in terms of storage. It can *only* contain line strings or circular strings, and each segment's start point must be connected to the previous segment's end point (although it is most certainly not necessary to connect the first and last segments to form a closed shape as in this example). The *DATALENGTH* function shows the difference in storage requirements; *DATALENGTH(@CC)* returns 152 and *DATALENGTH(@GC)* returns 243. This means that the same shape requires 38% less storage space by using a compound curve instead of a geometry collection. A compound curve is also more storage-efficient than a multi-segment circular line string when straight lines are involved. This is because there is overhead for the mere potential of a curve, because the anchor point requires storage even when its position produces straight lines, whereas compound curves are optimized specifically to connect circular strings and (always straight) line strings.

Curve Polygons

A curve polygon is very similar to an ordinary polygon; like an ordinary polygon, a curve polygon specifies a "ring" that defines a closed shape, and can also specify additional inner rings to define "holes" inside the shape. The only fundamental difference between a polygon and a curve polygon is that the rings of a curve polygon can include circular shapes, whereas an ordinary polygon is composed exclusively with straight lines. Specifically, each ring in a curve polygon can consist of any combination of line strings, circular strings, and compound curves that collectively define the closed shape. For example, the code in Listing 9-21 produces a curve polygon with the same keyhole outline that we just demonstrated for the compound curve.

LISTING 9-21 A curve polygon.

```
-- Curve polygon
SELECT geometry::Parse('
  CURVEPOLYGON(
   COMPOUNDCURVE(
    (4 4, 4 8),
```

```
    CIRCULARSTRING(4 8, 6 10, 8 8),
    (8 8, 8 4),
    CIRCULARSTRING(8 4, 2 3, 4 4)
  )
 )')
```

This code has simply specified the same compound curve as the closed shape of a curve polygon. Although the shape is the same, the curve polygon is a two-dimensional object, whereas the compound curve version of the same shape is a one-dimensional object. This can be seen visually by the spatial viewer results, which shades the interior of the curve polygon as shown in Figure 9-25.

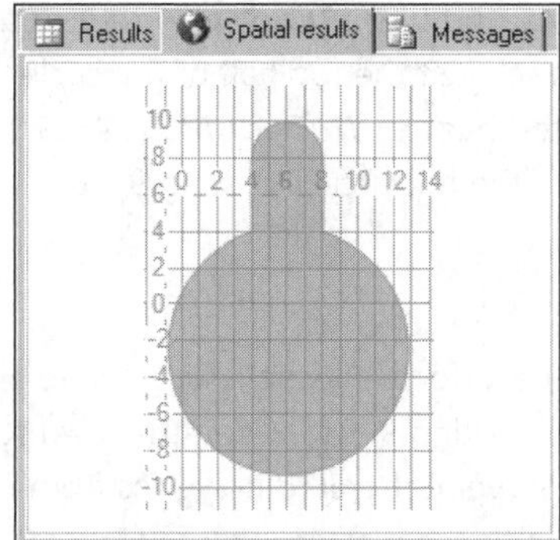

FIGURE 9-25 A curve polygon.

New Spatial Methods

Let's now explore some of the new spatial methods in SQL Server 2012. Some of these new methods complement the new curved shapes, whereas others add new spatial features that work with all shapes.

The *STNumCurves* and *STCurveN* Methods

These two methods can be invoked on any *geometry* or *geography* instance. They can be used together to discover information about the curves contained within the spatial instance. The *STNumCurves* method returns the total number of curves in the instance. You can then pass any number between 1 and what *STNumCurves* returns to extract each individual curve, and thus iterate all the curves in the instance. Listing 9-22 demonstrates these two methods with the same circle that you saw in Figure 9-23. Recall that this is a circular string with two connected segments. The circle is defined by the two halves, each of which is a curved line defining a semi-circle.

LISTING 9-22 Using *STNumCurves* and *STCurveN* to obtain curve information from a circular string.

```
-- Create a full circle shape (two connected semi-circles)
DECLARE @C geometry = 'CIRCULARSTRING(0 4, 4 0, 8 4, 4 8, 0 4)'
```

```
-- Get the curve count (2) and the 1st curve (bottom semi-circle)
SELECT
  CurveCount = @C.STNumCurves(),
  SecondCurve = @C.STCurveN(2),
  SecondCurveWKT = @C.STCurveN(2).ToString()
```

This query produces the following output:

```
CurveCount SecondCurve                                        SecondCurveWKT
---------- -------------------------------------------------- -------------------------------
2          0x00000000020403000000000000000000002040000000... CIRCULARSTRING (8 4, 4 8, 0 4)
```

You can see that *STNumCurves* indicates there are two curves, and that *STCurveN(2)* returns the second curve. If you view the results in the spatial viewer, you'll see just the top half of the circle. This is the semi-circle defined by the second curve, which is converted back to WKT as *CIRCULARSTRING (8 4, 4 8, 0 4)*. Notice that this represents the second segment of the full circle in Listing 9-21.

The *BufferWithCurves* Method

You've already learned how the *STBuffer* method can "pad" a line, effectively converting it into a polygon. To reprise our "small town" demo, *STBuffer* was used in Listing 9-5 to widen the town streets, and the output from that code listing clearly showed that SQL Server generated polygons from the line strings. If you look closely at the resulting polygon shapes in the spatial viewer (see Figure 9-6), it appears that points of each line string (including the midpoints) are transformed into rounded edges in the polygon. However, the rounded edge look is actually produced by plotting many short straight lines that are clustered very closely together, presenting the illusion of a curve. This approach is because curves were not previously supported before SQL Server 2012 (but the *STBuffer* method was).

Clearly, using native curve definitions in a curve polygon is more efficient than clustering a multitude of straight lines in an ordinary polygon. For backward compatibility, *STBuffer* continues to return the (inefficient) polygon as before. So SQL Server 2012 introduces a new method, *BufferWithCurves*, for this purpose. The code in Listing 9-23 uses *BufferWithCurves* to pad the street lines as before, and compares the result with its straight-line cousin, *STBuffer*.

LISTING 9-23 Comparing *BufferWithCurves* and *STBuffer*.

```
DECLARE @streets geometry = '
 GEOMETRYCOLLECTION(
  LINESTRING (100 -100, 20 -180, 180 -180),
  LINESTRING (300 -300, 300 -150, 50 -50)
 )'
SELECT @streets.BufferWithCurves(10)

SELECT
  AsWKT = @streets.ToString(),
```

```
  Bytes = DATALENGTH(@streets),
  Points = @streets.STNumPoints()
 UNION ALL
 SELECT
  @streets.STBuffer(10).ToString(),
  DATALENGTH(@streets.STBuffer(10)),
  @streets.STBuffer(10).STNumPoints()
 UNION ALL
 SELECT
  @streets.BufferWithCurves(10).ToString(),
  DATALENGTH(@streets.BufferWithCurves(10)),
  @streets.BufferWithCurves(10).STNumPoints()
```

Figure 9-26 shows the resulting shape (the collection of padded street shapes) returned by the first *SELECT* statement in the spatial viewer.

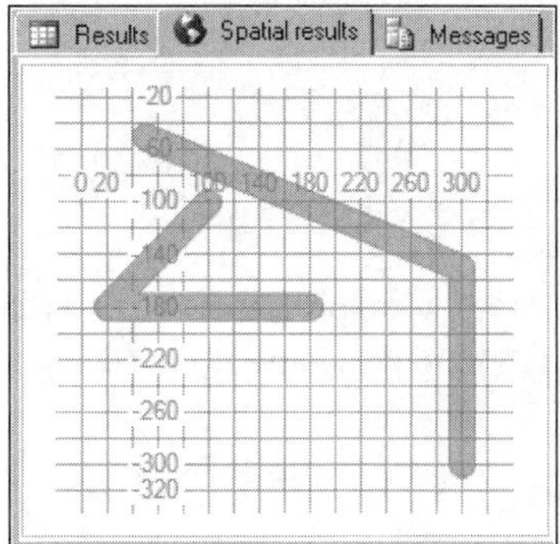

FIGURE 9-26 Using *BufferWithCurves* to pad a line string with true rounded edges.

As with *STBuffer* back in Figure 9-6, the new shapes have rounded edges around the points of the original line strings. However, *BufferWithCurves* generates actual curves and, thus, produces a significantly smaller and simpler polygon. The second *SELECT* statement in Listing 9-23 demonstrates this by comparing the three shapes—the original line string collection, the polygon returned by *STBuffer*, and the curve polygon returned by *BufferWithCurves*. Here are the results:

```
AsWKT                                                                     Bytes  Points
------------------------------------------------------------------------- -----  ------
GEOMETRYCOLLECTION (LINESTRING (100 -100, 20 -180, 180 -180), LINESTRIN...  151    6
MULTIPOLYGON (((20.000000000000796 -189.99999999999858, 179.99999999999...  5207   322
GEOMETRYCOLLECTION (CURVEPOLYGON (COMPOUNDCURVE ((20.000000000000796 -1...  693    38
```

The first shape is the original geometry collection of streets (line strings) used for input, which requires only 151 bytes of storage, and has only 6 points. For the second shape, *STBuffer* pads the line strings to produce a multi-polygon (a set of polygons) that consumes 5,207 bytes and has a total of 322 points—a whopping 3,448 percent increase from the original line strings. In the third shape, *BufferWithCurves* is used to produce the equivalent padding using a collection of curve polygons composed of compound curves, so it consumes only 693 bytes and has only 38 points—a (relatively) mere 458 percent increase from the original line strings.

The *ShortestLineTo* Method

This new method examines any two shapes and figures out the shortest line between them. Listing 9-24 demonstrates this.

LISTING 9-24 Finding the shortest distance between two shapes using *ShortestLineTo*.

```
DECLARE @Shape1 geometry = '
 POLYGON ((-20 -30, -3 -26, 14 -28, 20 -40, -20 -30))'

DECLARE @Shape2 geometry = '
 POLYGON ((-18 -20, 0 -10, 4 -12, 10 -20, 2 -22, -18 -20))'

SELECT @Shape1
UNION ALL
SELECT @Shape2
UNION ALL
SELECT @Shape1.ShortestLineTo(@Shape2).STBuffer(.25)
```

This code defines two polygons and then uses *ShortestLineTo* to determine, generate, and return the shortest straight line that connects them. *STBuffer* is also used to pad the line string so that it is more clearly visible in the spatial viewer, as shown in Figure 9-27.

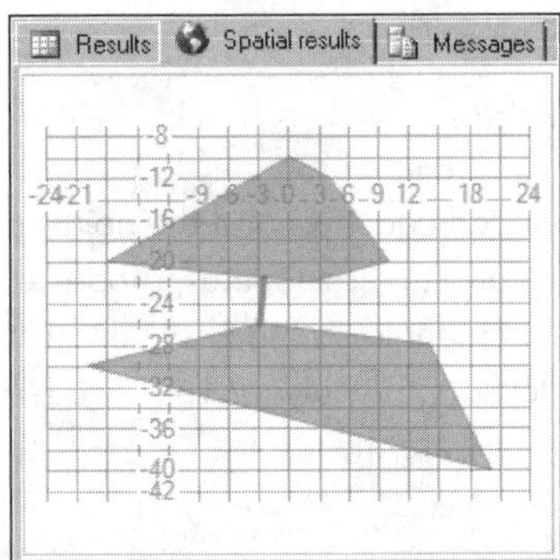

FIGURE 9-27 Using the *ShortestLineTo* method to calculate the shortest straight line between two shapes.

The *MinDbCompatibilityLevel* Method

With the added support for curves in SQL Server 2012 comes support for backward compatibility with previous versions of SQL Server (2008 and 2008 R2) that don't support curves. The new *MinDbCompatibilityLevel* method accepts any WKT string and returns the minimum version of SQL Server required to support the shape defined by that string. For example, consider the code in Listing 9-25.

LISTING 9-25 Testing for version compatibility with the *MinDbCompatibilityLevel* method.

```
DECLARE @Shape1 geometry = 'CIRCULARSTRING(0 50, 90 50, 180 50)'
DECLARE @Shape2 geometry = 'LINESTRING (0 50, 90 50, 180 50)'

SELECT
 Shape1MinVersion = @Shape1.MinDbCompatibilityLevel(),
 Shape2MinVersion = @Shape2.MinDbCompatibilityLevel()
```

The *MinDbCompatibilityLevel* method returns 110 (referring to version 11.0) for the first WKT string and 100 (version 10.0) for the second one. This is because the first WKT string contains a circular string, which requires SQL Server 2012 (version 11.0), whereas the line string in the second WKT string is supported by SQL Server 2008 (version 10.0) and higher.

The *STCurveToLine* and *CurveToLineWithTolerance* Methods

These are two methods you can use to convert curves to roughly equivalent straight line shapes. Again, this is to provide compatibility with previous versions of SQL Server and other mapping platforms that don't support curves.

The *STCurveToLine* method converts a single curve to a line string with a multitude of segments and points that best approximate the original curve. The technique is similar to what we just discussed for *STBuffer*, where many short straight lines are connected in a cluster of points to simulate a curve. And, as explained in that discussion, the resulting line string requires significantly more storage than the original curve. To offer a compromise between fidelity and storage, the *CurveToLineWithTolerance* method accepts "tolerance" parameters to produce line strings that consume less storage space than those produced by *STCurveToLine*. The code in Listing 9-26 demonstrates this by using both methods to convert the same circle from Figure 9-23 into line strings.

LISTING 9-26 Converting curves to lines with *STCurveToLine* and *CurveToLineWithTolerance*.

```
-- Create a full circle shape (two connected semi-circles)
DECLARE @C geometry = 'CIRCULARSTRING(0 4, 4 0, 8 4, 4 8, 0 4)'

-- Render as curved shape
SELECT
  Shape = @C,
  ShapeWKT = @C.ToString(),
  ShapeLen = DATALENGTH(@C),
  Points = @C.STNumPoints()

-- Convert to lines (much larger, many more points)
SELECT
  Shape = @C.STCurveToLine(),
  ShapeWKT = @C.STCurveToLine().ToString(),
  ShapeLen = DATALENGTH(@C.STCurveToLine()),
  Points = @C.STCurveToLine().STNumPoints()
```

```
-- Convert to lines with tolerance (not as much larger, not as many more points)
SELECT
  Shape = @C.CurveToLineWithTolerance(0.1, 0),
  ShapeWKT = @C.CurveToLineWithTolerance(0.1, 0).ToString(),
  ShapeLen = DATALENGTH(@C.CurveToLineWithTolerance(0.1, 0)),
  Points = @C.CurveToLineWithTolerance(0.1, 0).STNumPoints()
```

The query results show that the original circle consumes only 112 bytes and has 5 points. Invoking *STCurveToLine* on the circle converts it into a line string that consumes 1,072 bytes and has 65 points. That's a big increase, but the resulting line string represents the original circle in high fidelity; you will not see a perceptible difference in the two when viewing them using the spatial viewer. However, the line string produced by *CurveToLineWithTolerance* consumes only 304 bytes and has only 17 points; a significantly smaller footprint, paid for with a noticeable loss in fidelity. As shown by the spatial viewer results in Figure 9-28, using *CurveToLineWithTolerance* produces a circle made up of visibly straight line segments.

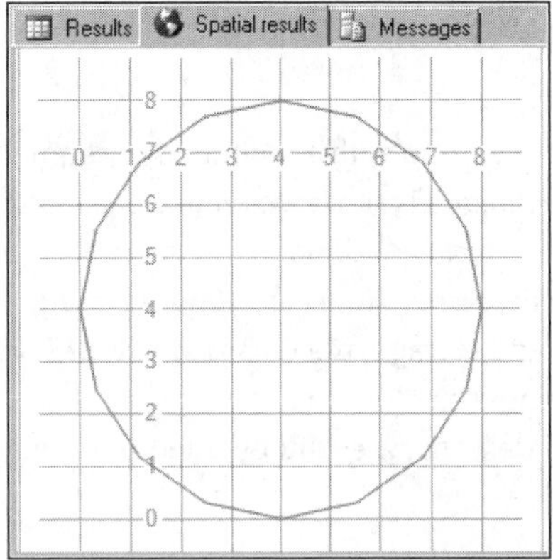

FIGURE 9-28 Fidelity loss converting a curve to a line using *CurveToLineWithTolerance*.

The *STIsValid, IsValidDetailed,* and *MakeValid* Methods

Spatial instance validation has improved greatly in SQL Server 2012. The *STIsValid* method evaluates a spatial instance and returns a *1* (for true) or *0* (for false), indicating if the instance represents a valid shape (or shapes). As Listing 9-27 demonstrates, if the instance is invalid, the new *IsValidDetailed* method will return a string explaining the reason why.

LISTING 9-27 Using *IsValidDetailed* to determine why a *geometry* instance is invalid.

```
DECLARE @line geometry = 'LINESTRING(1 1, 2 2, 3 2, 2 2)'

SELECT
 IsValid = @line.STIsValid(),
 Details = @line.IsValidDetailed()
```

This line string is invalid because the same point (2 2) is repeated, which results in "overlapping edges," as revealed by the output from *IsValidDetailed*:

```
IsValid  Details
-------  ------------------------------------------------------------
0        24413: Not valid because of two overlapping edges in curve (1).
```

SQL Server 2012 is more tolerant of invalid spatial instances than previous versions. For example, you can now perform metric operations (such as *STLength*) on invalid instances, although you still won't be able to perform other operations (such as *STBuffer*) on them.

The new *MakeValid* method can "fix" an invalid spatial instance and make it valid. Of course, the shape will shift slightly, and there are no guarantees on the accuracy or precision of the changes made. The code in Listing 9-28 uses *MakeValid* to remove overlapping parts (which can be caused by anomalies such as inaccurate GPS traces), effectively converting the invalid line string from Listing 9-27 into a valid spatial instance.

LISTING 9-28 Using *MakeValid* to convert an invalid line string to a valid spatial instance.

```
DECLARE @line geometry = 'LINESTRING(1 1, 2 2, 3 2, 2 2)'
SELECT @line.MakeValid().ToString() AS Fixed
```

The WKT string returned by the *SELECT* statement shows the "fixed" line string:

```
Fixed
-------------------------------------------------------------
LINESTRING (3 2, 2 2, 1.0000000000000071 1.0000000000000036)
```

Other Enhancements

The remainder of this section gives brief mention to several other noteworthy spatial enhancements added in SQL Server 2012. These include better *geography* support, and precision and optimization improvements.

Note Full coverage of these enhancements (and others, such as aggregates, histograms, the nearest neighbor query plan, spatial indexes, hints, and performance improvements) is beyond the scope of this chapter. Consult SQL Server Books Online for the complete spatial reference.

Support for *geography* Instances Exceeding a Logical Hemisphere

Previous versions of SQL Server supported *geography* objects as large as (slightly less than) a logical hemisphere (half the globe). This limitation has been removed in SQL Server 2012, which now supports *geography* instances of any size (even the entire planet).

When you define a *geography* polygon, the order in which you specify the ring's latitude and longitude coordinates (known as *vertex order*) is significant (unlike *geometry*, where vertex order is insignificant). The coordinate points are always defined according to the *left-foot inside* rule; when you "walk" the boundary of the polygon, your left foot is on the inside. Thus, vertex order determines whether you are defining a small piece of the globe, relative to the larger piece defined by the entire globe except for the small piece (that is, the rest of the globe).

Because previous versions of SQL Server were limited to half the globe, it was impossible to specify the points of a polygon in the "wrong order," simply because doing so resulted in too large a shape (and thus, raised an error). That error potential no longer exists in SQL Server 2012, so it's even more critical to make sure your vertex order is correct, or you'll be unwittingly working with the exact "opposite" shape.

If you have a *geography* instance that is known to have the wrong vertex order, you can repair it using the new *ReorientObject* method. This method operates only on polygons (it has no effect on points, line strings, or curves), and can be used to correct the ring orientation (vertex order) of the polygon, as Listing 9-29 demonstrates.

LISTING 9-29 Using *ReorientObject* to change the vertex order.

```
-- Small (less than a logical hemisphere) polygon
SELECT geography::Parse('POLYGON((-10 -10, 10 -10, 10 10, -10 10, -10 -10))')

-- Reorder in the opposite direction for "rest of the globe"
SELECT geography::Parse('POLYGON((-10 -10, -10 10, 10 10, 10 -10, -10 -10))')

-- Reorient back to the small polygon
SELECT geography::Parse('POLYGON((-10 -10, -10 10, 10 10, 10 -10, -10 -10))')
 .ReorientObject()
```

Three *geography* polygon instances are defined in this code. The first *geography* instance defines a very small polygon. The second instance uses the exact same coordinates, but because the vertex order is reversed, it defines an enormous polygon whose area represents the entire globe *except* for the small polygon. As explained, such a definition would cause an error in previous versions of SQL Server, but is now accommodated without a problem by SQL Server 2012. The third instance reverses the vertex order on the same shape as the second instance, thereby producing the same small polygon as the first instance.

Full Globe Support

Along with the aforementioned support for *geography* instances to exceed a single logical hemisphere comes a new spatial data class called *FULLGLOBE*. As you may have guessed, this is a shape that represents the entire planet. If you've ever wondered how many square meters there are in the entire world, the query in Listing 9-30 gives you the answer (which is 510,065,621,710,996 square meters, so you can stop wondering).

LISTING 9-30 Using *FULLGLOBE* to calculate the area of the entire earth.

```
-- Construct a new FullGlobe object (a WGS84 ellipsoid)
DECLARE @Earth geography = 'FULLGLOBE'

-- Calculate the area of the earth
SELECT PlanetArea = @Earth.STArea()
```

All of the common spatial methods work as expected on a full globe object. So you could, for example, "cut away" at the globe by invoking the *STDifference* and *STSymDifference* method against it using other polygons as cookie-cutter shapes.

New "Unit Sphere" Spatial Reference ID

Earlier we noted that the default SRID is 4326, which uses the metric system as its unit of measurement. This SRID also represents the true ellipsoidal sphere shape of the earth. Although this representation is most accurate, it's also more complex to calculate precise ellipsoidal mathematics. SQL Server 2012 offers a compromise in speed and accuracy, by adding a new spatial reference id (SRID), 104001, which uses a sphere of radius 1 to represent a *perfectly* round earth.

You can create *geography* instances with SRID 104001 when you don't require the greatest accuracy. The *STDistance*, *STLength*, and *ShortestLineTo* methods are optimized to run faster on the unit sphere, because it takes a relatively simple formula to compute measures against a perfectly round sphere (compared to an ellipsoidal sphere).

Better Precision

Internal spatial calculations in SQL Server 2012 are now performed with 48 bits of precision, compared to 27 bits used in SQL Server 2008 and SQL Server 2008 R2. This can reduce the error caused by rounding of floating point coordinates for original vertex points by the internal computation.

Integrating with Microsoft Bing Maps

We'll end this chapter with one final (and fun) geospatial application, in which you will construct a Microsoft Bing Maps *mash-up*. The term "mash-up" is used to describe a unified presentation combining one set of data with another. For this mash-up, you will create a web application that layers customer coordinates over Bing Maps imagery to show the location of customers in the database as pushpin icons on a map.

Start with a new database. Create the *Customer* table with a *geography* column to hold customer locations and populate it with some sample data, as shown in Listing 9-31.

LISTING 9-31 Creating the *Customer* table and populating it with geographical data.

```
USE master
GO
IF EXISTS(SELECT name FROM sys.databases WHERE name = 'MyDB')
 DROP DATABASE MyDB
GO
CREATE DATABASE MyDB
GO
USE MyDB
GO

CREATE TABLE Customer
 (CustomerId  int PRIMARY KEY,
  Name        varchar(50),
  Company     varchar(50),
  CustomerGeo geography)
GO

INSERT INTO Customer VALUES
 (1, 'Adam', 'Coho Vineyard & Winery', 'POINT(-111.06687 45.01188)'),
 (2, 'John', 'ACME Corp.', 'POINT(-104.06 41.01929)'),
 (3, 'Paul', 'Litware, Inc.', 'POINT(-111.05878 41.003)'),
 (4, 'Joel', 'Tailspin Toys', 'POINT(-121.05878 41.003)'),
 (5, 'Martin', 'ABC Travel', 'POINT(-110.05878 43.003)'),
 (6, 'Remon', 'Wingtip Toys', 'POINT(-113.05878 35.003)'),
 (7, 'Jason', 'School of Fine Art', 'POINT(-116.05878 34.003)'),
 (8, 'Fred', 'Fourth Coffee', 'POINT(-114.05878 43.003)')
```

Now create a stored procedure to retrieve all the customers and their locations, as shown in Listing 9-32.

LISTING 9-32 Creating a stored procedure to retrieve customers and their locations.

```
CREATE PROCEDURE GetCustomers
AS
 BEGIN
    SELECT  Name, Company, CustomerGeo
      FROM   Customer
 END
GO
```

With the database set up, you're ready to create your Bing Maps mash-up. Start Visual Studio, and then choose File | New | Project. From the templates listed under Visual C#, Web, create an ASP.NET Empty Web Application project named *BingMapsSpatialApp*, as shown in Figure 9-29.

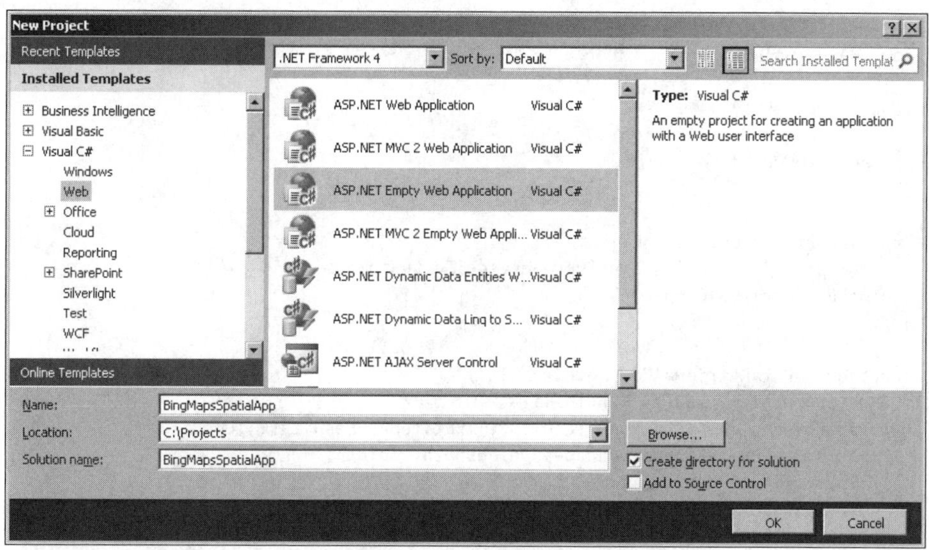

FIGURE 9-29 Creating the *BingMapsSpatialApp* project.

In *Default.aspx*, replace the starter markup provided by Visual Studio with the code shown in Listing 9-33.

LISTING 9-33 Creating a Virtual Earth mash-up with geography data.

```
<%@ Page Language="C#" AutoEventWireup="true" CodeBehind="Default.aspx.cs"
Inherits="BingMapsSpatialApp.Default" %>
<!DOCTYPE html PUBLIC "-//W3C//DTD XHTML 1.0 Transitional//EN" "http://www.
w3.org/TR/xhtml1/DTD/xhtml1-transitional.dtd">
<html xmlns="http://www.w3.org/1999/xhtml">
<head runat="server">
  <title></title>
</head>
<body>
  <form id="form1" runat="server">
  <asp:ScriptManager ID="ScriptManager1" runat="server">
    <Services>
      <asp:ServiceReference Path="CustomerQueryService.asmx" />
    </Services>
    <Scripts>
      <asp:ScriptReference
        Path="http://dev.virtualearth.net/mapcontrol/mapcontrol.ashx?v=6" />
    </Scripts>
  </asp:ScriptManager>
  <div>
    <div id='divBingMap' style="position: relative; width: 640px; height: 400px;" />
  </div>
  <input id="btnGetCustomers" type="button" value="Get Customers"
    onclick="btnGetCustomers_Click()" />
  <script type="text/javascript">
```

```
    var _map = null;

    function pageLoad() {
      _map = new VEMap('divBingMap');
      _map.LoadMap();
    }

    function btnGetCustomers_Click() {
      BingMapsSpatialApp.CustomerQueryService.GetCustomers
       (OnDataRetrievalComplete);
    }

    function OnDataRetrievalComplete(results) {
      for (i = 0; i < results.length; i++) {
        var point = new VELatLong(results[i].Latitude, results[i].Longitude);
        var pin = new VEShape(VEShapeType.Pushpin, point);
        pin.SetTitle(results[i].Company);
        pin.SetDescription(results[i].Name);
        _map.AddShape(pin);
      }
    }
  </script>
  </form>
</body>
</html>
```

This webpage uses Asynchronous JavaScript and XML (AJAX) to render a map using Microsoft Bing Maps, upon which it draws pushpin icons for each customer. There are absolutely no page postbacks to the server; all the service calls are made directly from the client browser. Let's dissect this page carefully.

Every AJAX-enabled webpage requires a *ScriptManager* element, which you've placed at the top of the form. Nested within the *ScriptManager* element, two service references are declared. The first reference points to *CustomerQueryService.asmx*, which is a Windows Communications Foundation (WCF) Service that you will create momentarily to call the stored procedure that retrieves customers and their locations. The second reference is to the Microsoft Bing Maps web services application programming interface (API) at *dev.virtualearth.net*. This API provides the Bing Maps Ajax Control that can be used to render and manipulate a map on any webpage. The map renders with a UI that provides zoom and pan controls simply by clicking and dragging the mouse.

Note The script reference indicates the name Virtual Earth, which is the original name for Bing Maps. Currently, the Bing Maps Ajax Control API still reflects the old name by using objects prefixed with *VE*. Thus, we interchange the terms "Bing Maps" and "Virtual Earth" throughout our discussion of the code.

After the *ScriptManager*, the page declares a *<div>* section that defines the rectangular area of the page (640 by 400 pixels in this example) in which the map should be displayed. The element is assigned an ID named *divBingMap* that will be referenced later by a call into the Bing Maps API when the map is created. Beneath the map, the page displays a button named *btnGetCustomers* that is wired to a client-side event handler named *btnGetCustomers_click()*. The rest of the page contains the JavaScript that interacts with the two services from the user's browser.

At the top of the script, a page-level variable named *_map* is declared. This variable will hold a reference to the *VEMap* (Virtual Earth map) object created in the *pageLoad* function, which fires on the client when the browser loads the page. The *pageLoad* function instantiates the *_map* variable by declaring it as a new *VEMap* object. This results in a call to the Bing Maps web service that returns a *VEMap* object that is stored in the *_map* variable. The object is bound to the *<div>* tag named *divBingMap* (declared earlier in the markup) that was passed in as a parameter into the *VEMap* constructor. As a result, the map loads and displays itself in the *divBingMap* section of the page when the page loads.

Next, the button's click event handler is defined in the *btnGetCustomers_click()* function. The single line of code in this function calls your own *CustomerQueryService.asmx* web service (which you're about to create), declared in the preceding *ScriptManager* section. This results in an asynchronous call to the service, which runs in the background to call your stored procedure and retrieve customers and their locations from the database. When the call is made, the page specifies the name of the callback function *OnDataRetrievalComplete* to be invoked when the results are returned by the service.

Finally, the *OnDataRetrievalComplete* function is defined to receive and process the results of the customer query, which is a list of customers and their locations that is passed to the function as a parameter named *results*. The list is processed as an array of objects iterated with *a for* loop. Each element in the array is an object with properties defined for the *Customer* class (which is a WCF data contract that you're about to create with the service). For each customer, the *Latitude* and *Longitude* properties are used to construct a *VELatLong* (Virtual Earth latitude/longitude) object stored in a variable named *point*. (Note that the *VELatLong* constructor requires the latitude value for the first parameter and the longitude value for the second parameter, unlike WKT, which uses the reverse order of longitude followed by latitude.) A new *VEShape* (Virtual Earth shape) object is then created for the point as a *VEShapeType.Pushpin* shape stored in the variable *pin*. The *Company* and *Name* properties are then used to set the pushpin's title and description using the *SetTitle* and *SetDescription* methods. The pushpin is then added to the map by invoking the *AddShape* method on the *_map* variable, which represents the map displayed in the *<div>* tag named *divVirtualEarthMap* on the page.

That completes the webpage. Your next step is to create the WCF Service called by the page to retrieve your customers and their locations from the database. In Solution Explorer, right-click the *VirtualEarthSpatialApp* project, and select Add | New Item. In the installed templates listed under Web, WCF Service, name the service *CustomerGeoService.svc*, as shown in Figure 9-30.

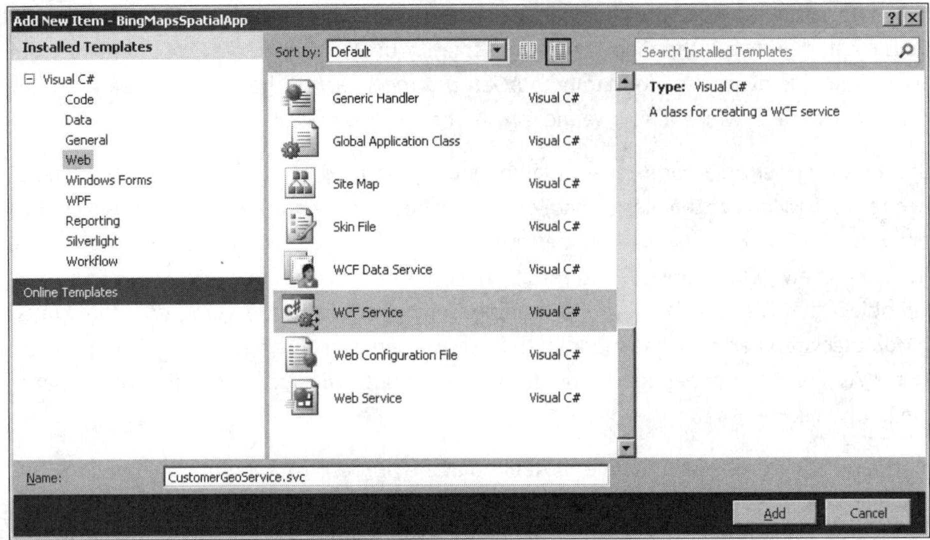

FIGURE 9-30 Creating the customer query web service.

To keep the example simple, you won't separate interface from implementation. Therefore, you can delete the *ICustomerGeoService.cs* file that Visual Studio created for you to define the interface. Then, open the service's *CustomerGeoService.svc.cs* code-behind file and replace the starter code that Visual Studio provided with the code shown in Listing 9-34.

LISTING 9-34 Implementing a WCF Service to retrieve customer spatial data.

```
using System;
using System.Collections.Generic;
using System.Data;
using System.Data.SqlClient;
using System.Runtime.Serialization;
using System.ServiceModel;
using System.ServiceModel.Activation;

using Microsoft.SqlServer.Types;

namespace BingMapsSpatialApp
{
  [DataContract]
  public class Customer
  {
    [DataMember]
    public string Name { get; set; }

    [DataMember]
    public string Company { get; set; }

    [DataMember]
    public double Latitude { get; set; }

    [DataMember]
```

```
    public double Longitude { get; set; }
  }

  [ServiceContract(Namespace = "BingMapsSpatialApp")]
  [AspNetCompatibilityRequirements
    (RequirementsMode = AspNetCompatibilityRequirementsMode.Allowed)]
  public class CustomerGeoService
  {
    private const string ConnStr =
      "Data Source=.;Initial Catalog=MyDb;Integrated Security=True;";

    [OperationContract]
    public List<Customer> GetCustomers()
    {
      var customers = new List<Customer>();

      using (var conn = new SqlConnection())
      {
        conn.ConnectionString = ConnStr;
        conn.Open();

        using (var cmd = new SqlCommand())
        {
          cmd.Connection = conn;
          cmd.CommandText = "GetCustomers";
          cmd.CommandType = CommandType.StoredProcedure;

          using (var rdr = cmd.ExecuteReader())
          {
            while (rdr.Read())
            {
              var customer = new Customer();
              customer.Name = rdr["Name"].ToString();
              customer.Company = rdr["Company"].ToString();

              // Get the CustomerGeo column bytes into a geography instance
              var geo = SqlGeography.Deserialize(rdr.GetSqlBytes(2));
              customer.Latitude = (double)geo.Lat;
              customer.Longitude = (double)geo.Long;

              customers.Add(customer);
            }
            rdr.Close();
          }
        }

        conn.Close();

        return customers;
      }

    }
  }
}
```

The *Customer* data contract class is defined first, and simply exposes properties to define the object that gets returned to the webpage. Then the *CustomerGeoService* service contract class is defined, which in turn defines the *GetCustomers* operation contract called by the webpage. The *GetCustomers* method extracts the latitude and longitude values from the *geography* typed *Location* column returned by the *GetCustomers* stored procedure that you created in Listing 9-32. In Microsoft .NET, you can work with the SQL Server system CLR types (such as *geography*) by using classes defined in the *Microsoft.SqlServer.Types* namespace. This namespace is declared by a *using* statement at the top of the code (highlighted in bold). The *SqlGeography* class in this namespace corresponds to the *geography* data type in SQL Server. The *Lat* and *Long* properties of a *SqlGeography* object expose the latitude and longitude values contained in the *geography* instance it encapsulates (as *double* data types).

Before using any types in this namespace, you must first establish a reference to its assembly. To do so, right-click the *BingMapsSpatialApp* project in Solution Explorer, and then select *Add Reference*. On the .NET tab, scroll down and select *Microsoft.SqlServer.Types*, as shown in Figure 9-31, and then click OK.

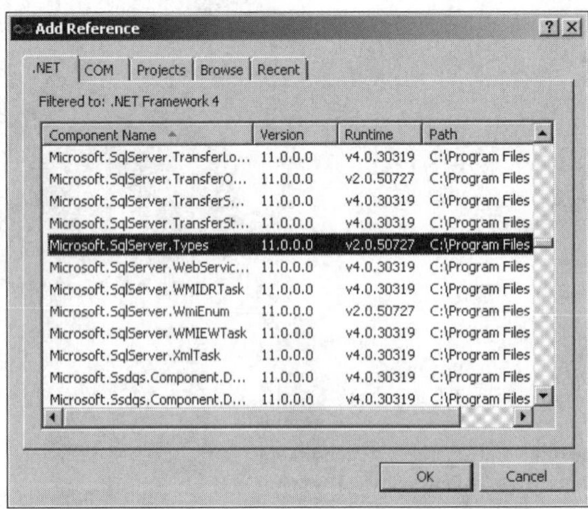

FIGURE 9-31 Adding a reference to the *Microsoft.SqlServer.Types* assembly.

After opening a connection to the database, the *GetCustomers* method prepares a *SqlCommand* object to call the *GetCustomers* stored procedure in the database and then invokes the *ExecuteReader* method to obtain a *SqlDataReader* object that returns the results. The method loops through all the rows in the reader returned by the stored procedure and populates a generic *List<Customer>* object with the results. For each row, a *Customer* object is created and populated with the *Name* and *Company* columns, as well as location information extracted from the *CustomerGeo* column. The location value is obtained by calling the static *Deserialize* method on the *SqlGeography* class, passing in the bytes from the *CustomerGeo* column of the reader, and receiving back a *geography* instance. The bytes are retrieved by calling the reader's *GetSqlBytes* method, passing in the zero-based index of the desired column (in this case *2* refers to the third column, *CustomerGeo*). Then the customer's *Latitude* and *Longitude* properties (*double* values) are populated from the geography instance's *Lat* and *Long* properties, respectively. The *Customer* object is then added to the generic *List<Customer>* object that is returned to the caller after all the customers have been processed.

Your next and final step is to configure the service for asynchronous calls, which is required to support Ajax client applications like the one you are building. Specifically, you need to edit *Web.config* and define a custom behavior for the service endpoint to enable web scripting calls, as shown in Listing 9-35.

LISTING 9-35 Configuring the WCF Service for Ajax clients.

```
<?xml version="1.0"?>
<configuration>
  <system.web>
    <compilation debug="true" targetFramework="4.0" />
  </system.web>
  <system.serviceModel>
    <services>
      <service name="BingMapsSpatialApp.CustomerGeoService">
        <endpoint
          behaviorConfiguration="AspNetAjaxBehavior"
          binding="webHttpBinding"
          contract="BingMapsSpatialApp.CustomerGeoService" />
      </service>
    </services>
    <behaviors>
      <endpointBehaviors>
        <behavior name="AspNetAjaxBehavior">
          <enableWebScript />
        </behavior>
      </endpointBehaviors>
    </behaviors>
  </system.serviceModel>
</configuration>
```

After modifying *Web.config*, you can give the application a run. To view the webpage, right-click *Default.aspx* in Solution Explorer, and choose Set as Start Page. Then press **F5** to run the application. When the page loads, it runs the client-side JavaScript you wrote in the *pageLoad* function and displays the map in the browser. Click the Get Customers button to invoke the database query and display the pushpins corresponding to the locations of the customers returned by the query, as shown in Figure 9-32.

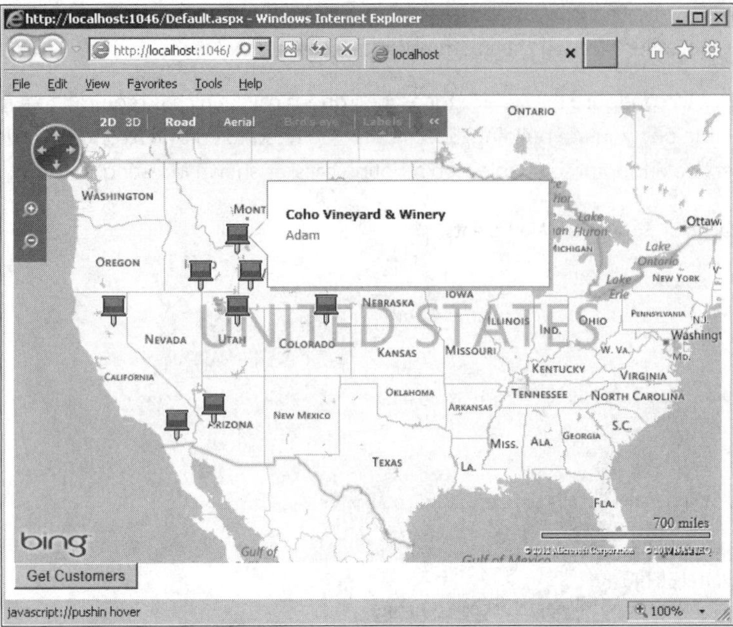

FIGURE 9-32 Running the Bing Maps mash-up against *geography* data in SQL Server.

This page delivers full Bing Maps capability. Users can zoom, pan, and render aerial views of the map while the pushpins remain bound to your geographic data, as shown in Figure 9-33.

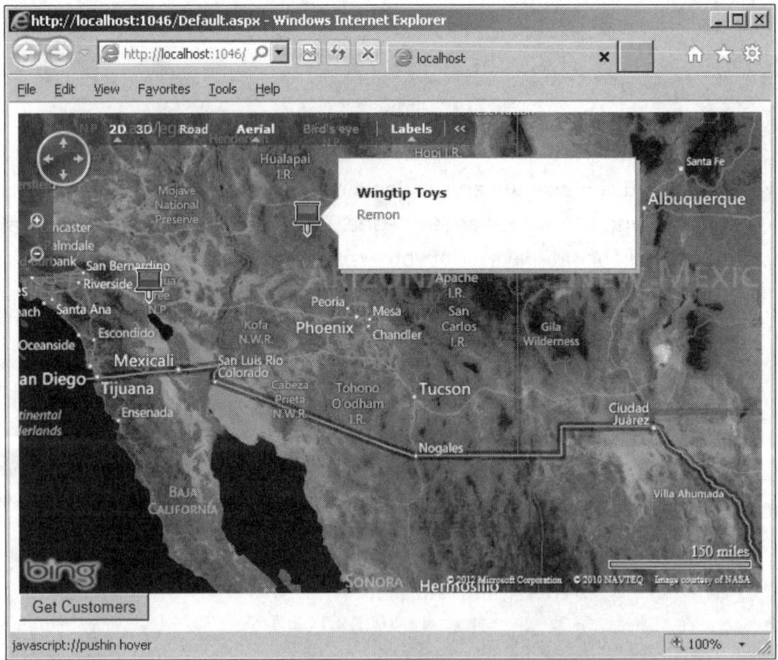

FIGURE 9-33 Zoom, pan, and aerial view capabilities of the Bing Maps Ajax Control.

Summary

The power of spatial processing is now readily available to all developers using the *geometry* and *geography* data types built into SQL Server 2012, enabling the rapid development of sophisticated GIS applications.

In this chapter, you saw how easy it is to express and project coordinates against either the planar (flat-earth) or geodetic (ellipsoidal sphere) spatial models using the Well-Known Text (WKT), Well-Known Binary (WKB), and Geography Markup Language (GML) formats. We walked you through numerous samples and demos, and, along the way, examined the many methods available for manipulating spatial data. You also created several geospatial applications that integrate location intelligence and mapping capabilities for end users.

Although this chapter has only scratched the surface of spatial data and spatial programming, it does provide the foundation you need to work with the powerful spatial support available in SQL Server 2012.

PART III

Applied SQL

CHAPTER 10

The Microsoft Data Access Juggernaut

–Leonard Lobel

At some point, and in some way, you need to expose your SQL Server data so that client applications can consume it. From the perspective of the database, every consumer is a "client application"—whether you are building an application to communicate directly with Microsoft SQL Server (traditional client/server architecture), or you are building a middle-tier service layer that, in turn, is consumed by other types of client applications (n-tier architecture). Regardless of the nature of the consuming application, it is your responsibility as a professional developer to architect a data access layer that exchanges information between SQL Server and your application (or the tiers of your application) in a reliable, scalable, and maintainable manner.

In the next series of chapters, you will learn how to do just that using all of the techniques available with the Microsoft .NET Framework—and there are many. Although the number of choices might seem daunting, don't feel intimidated. We will take things step by step so that you gain a clear understanding of what all the pieces are, and how the entire stack fits (or doesn't fit) together.

This chapter covers all your client/server options, including raw ADO.NET objects, the *DataSet*, Language-Integrated Query (LINQ), and the ADO.NET Entity Framework. In the next chapter, you will learn how to extend your data's reach by using two special Windows Communication Foundation (WCF) technologies. WCF Data Services, which exposes your data using Open Data Protocol (OData), and WCF RIA Services, a richer framework that targets Microsoft Silverlight in particular. The two chapters that follow then carry the discussion up to the cloud, where you will learn how to create solutions using SQL Azure, SQL Azure Data Sync, Windows Azure, and Windows Phone 7. This comprehensive coverage will help you choose the right .NET data access strategy for your SQL Server applications.

.NET Data Access Evolution

ADO.NET was released with the very first version of the .NET Framework in early 2002, and it offers you two ways to access the database programmatically: using raw objects or *DataSets* (or combinations of the two). You can use the raw ADO.NET objects to interact directly with the database by explicitly connecting to it, executing direct T-SQL or stored procedures, and pulling data back with streaming readers. Alternatively, you can work at a higher level of abstraction with *DataSets*, using *DataAdapters* as wrappers around the raw objects to fill and update the *DataSet*. Because *DataAdapters* are merely wrappers around the very same raw objects, you can use a combination of raw objects and *DataSets* as desired. In our discussion, we define both of these methods collectively as "conventional ADO.NET," to distinguish them from data access technologies added to later versions of the .NET Framework.

Conventional ADO.NET was the only data access option for .NET programmers from the time the framework was first released in 2002 until .NET 3.5 was released in late 2007, followed shortly thereafter by .NET 3.5 SP1 in 2008. Since .NET 3.5 (and especially SP1), things have been accelerating quite rapidly. The advent of Language-Integrated Query (LINQ), in .NET 3.5, radically changed the way developers write code against many different types of back-end data stores. For SQL Server in particular, programmability options have increased greatly with the release of LINQ to SQL in .NET 3.5 and the ADO.NET Entity Framework—first released as part of .NET 3.5 SP1, and greatly enhanced in .NET 4.0 as of 2010. New application programming interfaces (APIs) and tools have also emerged, such as WCF Data Services and WCF RIA Services (covered in Chapter 11). These tools promote rapid development of n-tier database applications by providing even richer abstractions at the WCF layer.

When technology churns this fast, it is only natural to feel overwhelmed. Keeping pace is certainly challenging, but this chapter will help you meet the challenge with minimal pain. You will learn the necessary coding techniques for working with all of the .NET data access options as you study each with practical, hands-on use cases. This comparative approach will help bring the similarities and differences between each option to light, so that you effectively gain a solid understanding across the spectrum.

Anyone who has worked with .NET for any length of time is already quite familiar with conventional ADO.NET, but may now question its relevance in the wake of all the technologies that have emerged since. In fact, conventional ADO.NET—the raw data access objects in particular, but the *DataSet* as well—is not only still relevant, but remains core to the .NET framework. The newer APIs complement conventional ADO.NET—they do not replace it. This is a vast quality-of-life improvement over standard Microsoft practice in the days of the Component Object Model (COM) platform that preceded the .NET Framework.

In the days of COM, each new data access API would typically render previous APIs obsolete. Data access objects (DAO) provided an object model around the Open Database Connectivity (ODBC) API that was very powerful, until it was made obsolete by Remote Data Objects (RDO). Yet it was not long after RDO that ActiveX Data Objects (ADO) completely obsolesced RDO. And of course, all of these COM-based APIs were rendered obsolete by the .NET Framework, and the notion of managed code providers with ADO.NET. One simply accepted obsolescence with the release of each new API, as part of the inevitable price to be paid if one wanted to leverage the latest technologies. As a result of this painful cycle, production code became stigmatized as "legacy code" very quickly in those days.

Since .NET, the situation has improved greatly. There is nothing "classic" or "legacy" (more polite terms for "obsolete") about conventional ADO.NET. The newer APIs layer and extend, but most certainly do *not* obsolesce conventional ADO.NET. And while they each have different use cases and provide different levels of abstraction, they also typically do not obsolesce one another (though depending on one's subjective definition of the term "obsolete," LINQ to SQL might be considered an exception to this statement, as it has been essentially eclipsed by the latest version of the ADO.NET Entity Framework). Like *DataAdapters* with *DataSets*, the latest APIs provide varying degrees of abstraction beneath which lie the very same managed code providers that .NET developers have been working with since the birth of the framework (SqlClient, in the case of SQL Server). This new and improved style of evolution serves as a testament to the stability and maturity of the .NET Framework, and significantly extends the shelf-life of your applications. Although keeping pace still continues to pose a challenge, the fact is that the newer APIs broaden rather than narrow your choices, and we believe that's a good thing.

So regardless of which API you choose, the same ADO.NET data provider (SqlClient) is used to send commands to SQL Server and stream data back to your application. This is true no matter which API you are using. *DataSets* are filled and updated using *DataAdapters*, which wrap the raw connection, command, and reader objects. With LINQ to SQL, there is a *DataContext* object that will also utilize SqlClient to retrieve and update data in SQL Server. If you are using ADO.NET Entity Framework, the storage layer similarly does the same. WCF Data Services and WCF RIA Services (which we cover in the next chapter) provide abstractions at the communications transport layer further up in the stack, so client requests handled by those service-oriented APIs will also ultimately boil down to raw ADO.NET data access when the time comes to hit the database. This technology stack is depicted in Figure 10-1.

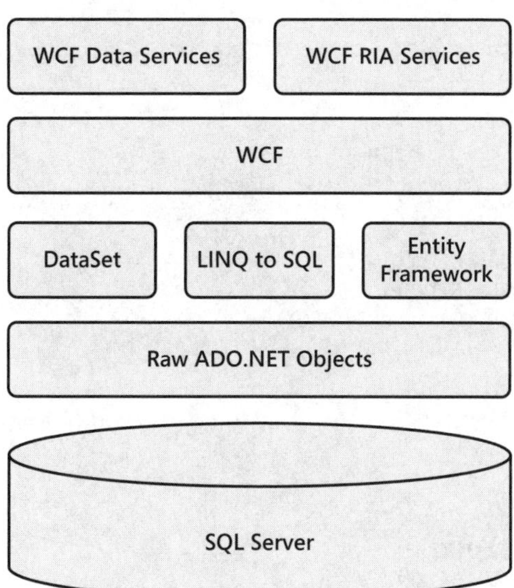

FIGURE 10-1 The .NET data access technology stack over SQL Server.

> **Note** In our discussions, we will refer to the ADO.NET Entity Framework frequently as Entity Framework, or abbreviate it simply as EF.

Conventional ADO.NET today still remains a perfectly viable option for data access in many scenarios. It is not only helpful but prudent for even experienced developers to refresh their understanding of it. Therefore, our coverage of conventional ADO.NET is recommended reading even if you're a seasoned developer who may be tempted to skip ahead to the newer technologies further on in the chapter.

Preparing the Sample Database

Start by creating a basic order entry database in SQL Server. Then you'll build application code over the database that queries and updates using each of the available data access APIs. Use either SQL Server Data Tools (SSDT) in Visual Studio (covered in Chapter 1) or SQL Server Management Studio (SSMS) to execute the script shown in Listing 10-1 and create the sample database.

LISTING 10-1 T-SQL script for creating the *SampleDb* database.

```
USE master
GO
IF EXISTS(SELECT name FROM sys.databases WHERE name = 'SampleDb')
 DROP DATABASE SampleDb
GO
CREATE DATABASE SampleDb
GO
USE SampleDb
GO

CREATE TABLE Customer(
  CustomerId bigint IDENTITY(1,1) NOT NULL,
  FirstName varchar(50) NOT NULL,
  LastName varchar(50) NOT NULL,
  Balance money NOT NULL DEFAULT 0,
  CreatedAt datetime2(7) NOT NULL DEFAULT SYSDATETIME(),
  UpdatedAt datetime2(7) NOT NULL DEFAULT SYSDATETIME(),
  CONSTRAINT PK_Customer PRIMARY KEY CLUSTERED (CustomerId ASC))

CREATE TABLE OrderHeader(
  OrderHeaderId bigint IDENTITY(1,1) NOT NULL,
  CustomerId bigint NOT NULL,
  ShipVia varchar(20) NOT NULL,
  OrderStatus varchar(20) NULL,
  Notes varchar(max) NULL,
  CreatedAt datetime2(7) NOT NULL DEFAULT SYSDATETIME(),
  UpdatedAt datetime2(7) NOT NULL DEFAULT SYSDATETIME(),
  CONSTRAINT PK_OrderHeader PRIMARY KEY CLUSTERED (OrderHeaderId ASC))

ALTER TABLE OrderHeader WITH CHECK ADD CONSTRAINT FK_OrderHeader_Customer
 FOREIGN KEY(CustomerId) REFERENCES Customer(CustomerId)

CREATE TABLE Employee(
  EmployeeId bigint IDENTITY(1,1) NOT NULL,
  FirstName varchar(50) NOT NULL,
  LastName varchar(50) NOT NULL,
```

```
  Salary decimal(18, 9) NOT NULL,
  CreatedAt datetime2(7) NOT NULL,
  UpdatedAt datetime2(7) NOT NULL,
  CONSTRAINT PK_Employee PRIMARY KEY CLUSTERED (EmployeeId ASC))

CREATE TABLE CustomerEmployee(
  CustomerId bigint NOT NULL,
  EmployeeId bigint NOT NULL,
  CONSTRAINT
   PK_CustomerEmployee PRIMARY KEY CLUSTERED (CustomerId ASC, EmployeeId ASC))

ALTER TABLE CustomerEmployee
 WITH CHECK ADD CONSTRAINT FK_CustomerEmployee_Customer
 FOREIGN KEY(CustomerId) REFERENCES Customer(CustomerId)

ALTER TABLE CustomerEmployee
 WITH CHECK ADD CONSTRAINT FK_CustomerEmployee_Employee
 FOREIGN KEY(EmployeeId) REFERENCES Employee(EmployeeId)

GO

CREATE PROCEDURE SelectCustomer(@CustomerId bigint)
AS
  SELECT    CustomerId, FirstName, LastName, Balance, CreatedAt, UpdatedAt
   FROM     Customer
   WHERE    CustomerId = @CustomerId
GO

CREATE PROCEDURE SelectCustomers
AS
  SELECT    CustomerId, FirstName, LastName, Balance, CreatedAt, UpdatedAt
   FROM     Customer
   ORDER BY CustomerId
GO

CREATE PROCEDURE InsertCustomer(
  @FirstName varchar(20),
  @LastName varchar(20),
  @Balance money = 0)
AS
  DECLARE @CreatedAt datetime2 = SYSDATETIME()

  INSERT INTO Customer (FirstName, LastName, Balance, CreatedAt, UpdatedAt)
   VALUES (@FirstName, @LastName, @Balance, @CreatedAt, @CreatedAt)

  SELECT
    CustomerId = CAST(SCOPE_IDENTITY() AS bigint),
    CreatedAt = @CreatedAt,
    UpdatedAt = @CreatedAt
GO

CREATE PROCEDURE UpdateCustomer(
  @CustomerId bigint,
  @FirstName varchar(20),
```

```
  @LastName varchar(20),
  @Balance money,
  @OriginalUpdatedAt datetime2)
AS
  DECLARE @NewUpdatedAt datetime2 = SYSDATETIME()

  UPDATE Customer
   SET
    FirstName = @FirstName,
    LastName = @LastName,
    Balance = @Balance,
    UpdatedAt = @NewUpdatedAt
   WHERE
    CustomerId = @CustomerId AND UpdatedAt = @OriginalUpdatedAt

  IF @@ROWCOUNT = 0
    THROW 50000, 'The customer does not exist, or has been updated/deleted', 1;
  ELSE
    SELECT UpdatedAt = @NewUpdatedAt
GO

CREATE PROCEDURE DeleteCustomer(@CustomerId bigint)
AS
  DELETE  Customer
   WHERE  CustomerId = @CustomerId
GO

CREATE PROCEDURE GetCustomerBalance(
  @CustomerId bigint,
  @Balance money OUTPUT)
AS
  SELECT  @Balance = Balance
   FROM   Customer
   WHERE  CustomerId = @CustomerId
GO
```

We've kept the database design small, while still demonstrating key concepts, such as the use of stored procedures for create, retrieve, update, and delete (CRUD) operations; optimistic concurrency checks; identity-based primary keys; and many-to-many relationships.

The script first creates the *Customer* and *OrderHeader* tables, along with a foreign key constraint that establishes a one-to-many relationship between them. Then it creates the *Employee* table. There is a many-to-many relationship between customers and employees, which is implemented by the *CustomerEmployee* junction table—the fourth and last table created in the script. The junction table contains just the two keys relating customers with employees and has foreign key constraints to both tables, which is how you implement a many-to-many relationship in SQL Server.

The three tables *Customer*, *OrderHeader*, and *Employee* each follow a similar pattern. Their primary keys are *long* values (64-bit integers), and they each have an *IDENTITY* specification that instructs SQL Server to automatically assign the next available integer when inserting new rows. Each of them also has a pair of *datetime2* columns named *CreatedAt* and *UpdatedAt* that are used for auditing and concurrency checks in the CRUD stored procedures, created next.

Your first exercise will work directly against tables. But in real production environments, client applications are often denied permission to execute direct *SELECT, INSERT, UPDATE*, and *DELETE* operations against tables in the database. Instead, typically, each table is "wrapped" by a set of stored procedures that expose CRUD operations in a controlled manner. In later examples, you'll work with stored procedures instead of direct SQL to access the *Customer* table. (For brevity, the code only creates CRUD stored procedures for the *Customer* table; you can extrapolate from that how a similar set of procedures would be implemented for the *OrderHeader* and *Employee* tables.)

Two stored procedures retrieve customers. *SelectCustomer* accepts a *@CustomerID* parameter and returns a single row for the specified customer. *SelectCustomers* takes no parameters, and returns every customer in the table sorted by last name, first name. Both stored procedures return every column from the *Customer* table. Of course, your typical application would have many more parameterized stored procedures for retrieval (such as *SelectCustomersByThis* and *SelectCustomersByThat*), but these two will suffice for this exercise.

Next, the script defines the *InsertCustomer* stored procedure that creates a new customer. The stored procedure accepts one parameter for each customer column, except for *CustomerId, CreatedAt*, and *UpdatedAt*. The client cannot supply a *CustomerId* because SQL Server will automatically assign the next identity value for the primary key and then return it back to the client. Values are also not accepted for *CreatedAt* and *UpdatedAt* because the stored procedure will ensure that both of these values get set to the current time on the *database server* clock, and then return them back to the client along with *CustomerId* after the *INSERT*.

InsertCustomer first declares *@CreatedAt* as a *datetime2* variable, assigns it the current date and time using the *SYSDATETIME* function, and then executes the *INSERT* statement that creates the new row. The *INSERT* statement supplies the *SYSDATETIME* value captured in *@CreatedAt* for both the *CreatedAt* and *UpdatedAt* columns, and supplies the incoming parameter values for all the other columns. The only column missing from the *INSERT* statement is the *CustomerId* primary key (this can't be specified because you've put SQL Server in charge of assigning the next available *IDENTITY* value to new primary keys). The stored procedure returns all the column values assigned by the server (*CustomerId, CreatedAt*, and *UpdatedAt*) to the client as a single-row result set in the *SELECT* statement immediately following the *INSERT*. This *SELECT* statement returns the *SCOPE_IDENTITY* function that gives you the new primary key value assigned to *CustomerId*, and returns the *@CreatedAt* value assigned to both *CreatedAt* and *UpdatedAt*. A client application can use this return information to refresh its local view of the newly added customer, rather than being forced to retrieve the entire customer again from the database.

The *UpdateCustomer* stored procedure is defined next. This stored procedure modifies an existing customer, and enforces an optimistic concurrency check ensuring that users do not overwrite each other's changes. It accepts a *@CustomerId* parameter specifying the customer row to be updated, followed by one parameter for each customer column to be updated, except for *CreatedAt* and *UpdatedAt*. This design prevents the *CreatedAt* column from being changed once it has been assigned by *InsertCustomer*, and thus provides you with a reliable audit of each customer's original creation time. The last parameter taken by *UpdateCustomer* is *@OriginalUpdatedAt*, which is used for the multiuser concurrency check. This parameter must be passed the original *UpdatedAt* value of the row to be changed, which implies that you must first retrieve a customer before you can change it.

UpdateCustomer first declares *@NewUpdatedAt* as a *datetime2* variable and assigns it the current date and time on the server using the *SYSDATETIME* function. This value overwrites the current value in the *UpdatedAt* column, and then gets returned to the client, assuming that the optimistic concurrency check doesn't fail. The *UPDATE* statement executes with a *WHERE* clause that finds the desired row to be updated by *@CustomerId*, but also checks that the *UpdatedAt* column still contains the value passed in to *@OriginalUpdatedAt*. Because *UpdatedAt* gets overwritten with each modification, the WHERE clause will no longer find the row if another user selected and updated the same customer since the time you originally retrieved it. This prevents you from overwriting changes already committed by the other user. After the *UPDATE* statement, *@@ROWCOUNT* is tested to see if the specified customer was actually found and updated. A value of 0 indicates that either a multiuser conflict occurred, or the specified *CustomerId* never existed in the first place. The stored procedure treats either of those conditions as an error, and issues a *THROW* statement that will raise an exception on the .NET side. Otherwise, the *UPDATE* has succeeded, and the stored procedure returns the new *UpdatedAt* value as a single-row, single-column result set with the *SELECT* statement following the *UPDATE*. As with *InsertCustomer*, this return information enables client applications to refresh their local view of updated customers.

DeleteCustomer is the last—and simplest—of the CRUD stored procedures for the *Customer* table. It takes just an *@CustomerId* parameter and issues a *DELETE* statement that deletes that customer's row from the table.

Note Although this delete operation does not check for multiuser conflicts, business requirements will ultimately dictate how you implement a concurrency strategy in your application. You might need to be more stringent and put checks on deletions as well as updates, by requiring an *@OriginalUpdatedAt* parameter and then testing it in the *WHERE* clause like you did for *UpdateCustomer*.

You may also need to devise a more sophisticated conflict resolution strategy than merely throwing an error. For example, you can provide a merge facility that lets the user select which version of each column should "win" for the update. Conversely, if the probability of a multiuser collision is very low in your particular application, you may be able to do away with concurrency checks altogether (that is, if a conflict does occur, just blindly let the "last user win," and don't worry about the few cases where they overwrite another user's earlier changes).

There is one more stored procedure in the database that is not used for CRUD operations. The *GetCustomerBalance* stored procedure demonstrates how to return a scalar value using an output parameter (as opposed to a result set with one row and one column). This stored procedure returns the balance for the specified *@CustomerId* in the *@Balance* output parameter.

That completes the explanation of the database. You are ready to access it from .NET (and you will start to in a moment using conventional ADO.NET). But first, fire up a SQL Profiler trace.

Monitoring Database Activity with SQL Server Profiler

SQL Server Profiler (or SQL Profiler for short) is an indispensable tool that lets you see the direct commands as they are sent to the server by ADO.NET on behalf of your running application. You will use it throughout this chapter to observe database activity behind the scenes, so now is a good time to start tracing.

Launch SQL Server Profiler from the Performance Tools folder in the Microsoft SQL Server 2012 group on the Start menu. Press **CTRL+N** to create a new trace, and click Connect to connect to the server. SQL Profiler displays the Trace Properties dialog. Clicking Run will start the trace, but don't click it just yet. You'll want to tailor the trace first.

By default, SQL Profiler hides transactional events from the trace, so you won't get to see the transactional statements being sent to SQL Server by ADO.NET unless you change the default settings. These include the *BEGIN TRANSACTION* and *COMMIT TRANSACTION* statements issued implicitly by the *TransactionScope* object that you will use in an upcoming example to batch updates to SQL Server. To monitor these events, click the Events Selection tab, check the Show All Events checkbox, scroll the Events list down, and expand the Transactions category. Then check all the "complete" events beginning with TM: (which stands for Transaction Manager), such as TM: Begin Tran complete, TM: Commit Tran complete, and so on, as shown in Figure 10-2.

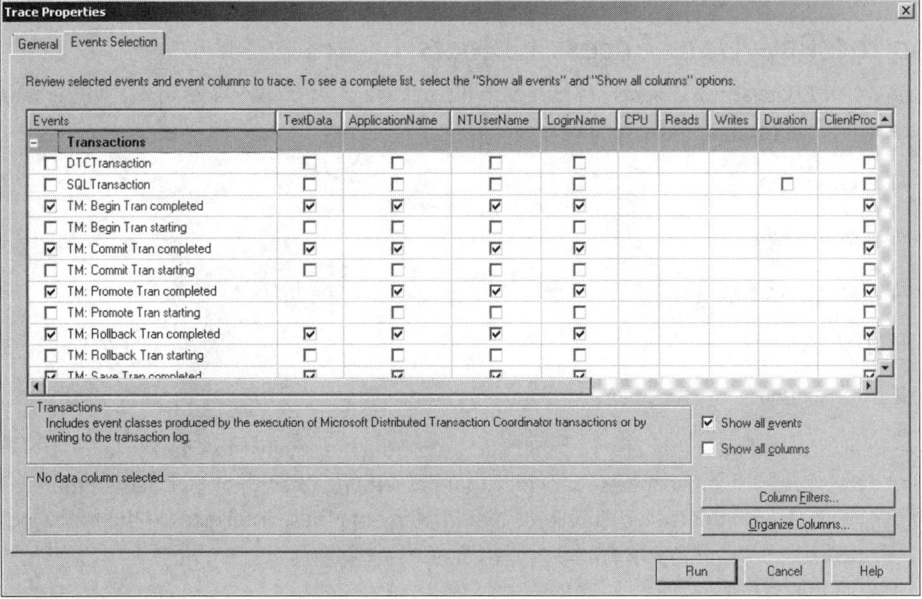

FIGURE 10-2 Configuring a SQL Profiler trace.

You also want to limit the trace to show commands sent only from your application, because it will show commands sent to SQL Server from any client by default. Click the Column Filters button to display the Edit Filter dialog. Choose ApplicationName from the list on the left, expand the *Like* node in the treeview on the right to create a new Like filter, and type **.Net SqlClient Data Provider**. Then click OK to close the dialog. Now the trace will only display commands issued by the ADO.NET SqlClient provider (which come from your application), and filter out "noise" generated by other running applications and services that talk to SQL Server (such as SQL Server Reporting Services, for example). With transactional events enabled and the ApplicationName filter now set, click *Run* to start the trace.

Tip You can save these settings in a template and have them loaded by default whenever you start a new trace. Click the File menu, choose Templates, and select New Template. Give the template a name, and check the "Use as a default template" checkbox. Then set the transactional events and column filter in the Events Selection tab and save the template.

Conventional ADO.NET

We've already defined conventional ADO.NET as the two available data access options that were introduced with .NET 1.0; namely, the raw data access objects and the *DataSet/DataAdapter* abstraction over those objects. You'll now explore both of these approaches, beginning with the raw objects.

Using the Raw Data Access Objects

The raw ADO.NET data access objects are based on the following set of interfaces in the .NET Framework, which are defined in the *System.Data* namespace:

- *IDbConnection*
- *IDbCommand*
- *IDbParameter*
- *IDbDataReader*
- *IDbTransaction*

These interfaces define the operations that can be conducted against the database (or other back-end data source) by any concrete provider that implements them. For SQL Server, there is a managed ADO.NET provider (called SqlClient) that implements these interfaces in the following set of classes, which are defined in the *System.Data.SqlClient* namespace:

- *SqlConnection*
- *SqlCommand*

- *SqlParameter*
- *SqlDataReader*
- *SqlTransaction*

As the interface and class names convey, an ADO.NET provider gives you a connection object so you can talk to the database, a command object with parameters so you can express your queries and update data, a reader object to stream query results into your application, and a transaction object to batch your updates atomically.

Arguably, these raw objects are all you need to perform any SQL Server data access in .NET. Any conceivable command can be sent to the database, any conceivable result set can be retrieved back, and multiple updates can be transactionalized. Those really are all the pieces you need to build a data access layer in .NET. And that is why they continue to serve as the underlying objects used by all the various .NET data access abstractions available today. But that is also precisely why you need to still consider using them in situations that call for it, as opposed to using something "later and greater," misguided by the notion that you must conform to a more fashionable way of doing things in order to maintain your credibility as a developer. Our guidance here is to not fall into that trap, but rather stick to the old adage of using the right tool for the right job (and hold your head up high).

It isn't always necessary to pile layers and layers of abstractions over each other; in many cases, it hinders more than helps. When your needs are simple and lightweight, you can and should continue to use the raw objects to get the job done quickly and efficiently, without the overhead of a *DataSet*, LINQ to SQL model, or Entity Data Model (EDM) added to the mix. There's absolutely nothing wrong with hooking up a simple connection object to a command object configured with parameters for calling a stored procedure, and streaming back the results with a reader, when that's more or less all you need to do.

And so there really are no hard and fast rules either for or against using raw objects directly versus any of the available abstractions offered by the more advanced alternative technologies. It all comes down to your understanding of each (which you'll get from this chapter), combined with the proper judgment on your part (which you can gain only from experience). You must deem when it is appropriate to leverage the benefit of (and create a dependency on) more robust frameworks, commensurate with the level of complexity that your application calls for, and the degree of abstraction you wish to layer over that complexity. With this understanding in mind, let's start at the very beginning: connections and commands.

Creating Connections and Commands

You can't do anything without a connection object. That is obvious. At the same time, you can't do anything with *just* a connection object. You're going to need to wrap a command object around that connection. With those minimal requirements met, you have what you need to execute any direct T-SQL or stored procedure on the server. Add a few parameter objects to the command, and you can pass input parameters to the server and even retrieve scalar values back via output parameters. Invoking the *ExecuteNonQuery* method on the command object causes the T-SQL or stored procedure to execute on the server. Figure 10-3 depicts the process.

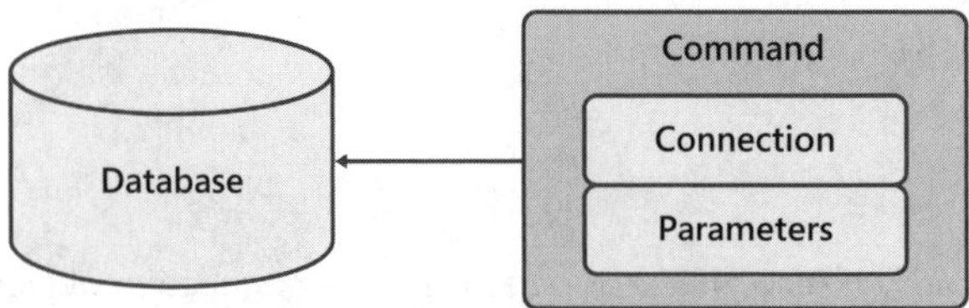

FIGURE 10-3 The raw ADO.NET objects used to execute a basic command in SQL Server.

You'll write your first bit of .NET code with just these objects. Start with a simple command to add a new customer to the database. Launch Visual Studio, create a new Visual C# Windows Forms application, and name it **DemoRawDataAccess**. Drag a button control from the Toolbox and drop it onto the form *Form1* created automatically by Visual Studio. In the Properties window, name the button **btnDirectSql**, and set the Text property to **Direct SQL**. Then double-click the button. Visual Studio will automatically create a click event handler for the button, and then open the code editor so that you can implement the handler. Add the code shown in Listing 10-2.

LISTING 10-2 Performing a simple *INSERT* operation using *ExecuteNonQuery*.

```
private void btnDirectSql_Click(object sender, EventArgs e)
{
  const string ConnStr =
    "Data Source=localhost;Initial Catalog=SampleDb;Integrated Security=true;";

  const string TSql =
    "INSERT INTO Customer (FirstName, LastName) VALUES ('Lukas', 'Keller')";

  using (var conn = new SqlConnection())
  {
    conn.ConnectionString = ConnStr;
    conn.Open();
    using (var cmd = new SqlCommand())
    {
      cmd.Connection = conn;
      cmd.CommandText = TSql;
      cmd.ExecuteNonQuery();
    }
    conn.Close();
  }
}
```

The compiler is unaware that the *SqlConnection* and *SqlCommand* class names referred to in your code can be found in the *System.Data.SqlClient* namespace, unless you direct it to look there. Do so by adding the following *using* directive at the very top of the source code:

```
using System.Data.SqlClient;
```

The code begins by defining the *ConnStr* constant, and points it to the sample database running on the local SQL Server instance (you must change the *Data Source* accordingly if you have created the database on another server or instance). Hardcoding the connection string in this manner is unacceptable in production applications. But in order to best lock down concepts as you progress, you're starting with absolutely minimal code. Later on, you'll store the connection string in a configuration file so that it can be altered without recompiling the application.

Next, the *TSql* constant is defined. This string contains the *INSERT* statement to be executed by SQL Server (note that you can also batch multiple T-SQL statements to be executed in a single call, by separating them with semicolons). Hardcoding the first and last name values Lukas and Keller is even more unrealistic than using a hardcoded connection string, but again, you'll soon graduate to more practical coding techniques in upcoming examples. With the connection string and T-SQL statement defined, you're ready to start working with the raw ADO.NET data objects for SQL Server.

A new *SqlConnection* object is then created and assigned to the variable *conn* at the top of a *using* block. The *using* statement ensures that the *SqlConnection* object disposes its resources when the object is no longer needed (see sidebar). You will see the *using* statement applied frequently in our code samples, and we encourage you to follow this best practice whenever you are working with disposable objects.

Disposable Objects and the *using* Statement

Disposable objects are objects that, internally, allocate unmanaged resources (meaning resources not managed by the .NET Framework, such as database connections). Because of the nondeterministic nature of .NET garbage collection, there's no way to know for certain when these objects will actually be "finalized" (destroyed). This is true even after no more object references remain. Thus, there's no inherent mechanism in the .NET Framework for automatically releasing unmanaged resources (like database connections) when they are no longer needed. A disposable object therefore implements the *IDisposable* interface, which exposes a *Dispose* method that can be called explicitly as soon as you know that you no longer need it. Calling *Dispose* instructs the object to release its unmanaged resources at that point in time, regardless of the fact that the object itself won't get destroyed by .NET garbage collection until some (possibly distant) future time.

The *using* statement (which is valid only with an *IDisposable* object) makes it very easy to work with disposable objects. (This is not to be confused with the completely unrelated *using* directive that imports a namespace, like you did a moment ago.) The statement declares a variable assigned to an *IDisposable* object that gets scoped to a code block following the *using* statement. With this pattern, you never actually write the line of code that calls *Dispose*; instead, the framework guarantees that *Dispose* gets called on the object once it falls out of scope (that is, at the end of the code block). This guarantee is absolutely reliable, even if an unhandled exception occurs at any point within the *using* code block which would cause the block to terminate prematurely.

After creating the *SqlConnection* object, the *ConnectionString* property is set to the previously defined constant and the *Open* method is invoked on it to establish the database connection.

A second *using* statement then creates a new *SqlCommand* object and assigns it to the variable *cmd*. It is perfectly okay to nest *using* blocks like this; once the second one is entered, the framework guarantees that *Dispose* will get called on both the *SqlConnection* and the *SqlCommand* objects regardless of if, when, or where an exception occurs. The *SqlCommand* object's *Connection* property is then associated with the open connection in *conn*, and its *CommandText* property is set to the *TSql* constant (the T-SQL you want to execute) defined earlier. Then the *ExecuteNonQuery* method is invoked on it, which passes the command along to SQL Server.

The command, in this case, is a single *INSERT* statement that adds a new row to the *Customer* table. Because values for only two columns (*FirstName* and *LastName*) are specified, all other columns in the new *Customer* row (besides *CustomerId*) will be assigned the default values designated for them when the *Customer* table was defined at the beginning of the chapter. The *CustomerId* column will be assigned automatically to the next available identity value, because *IDENTITY* was specified on that primary key column in the *Customer* table definition.

After the command executes on the server, the inner *using* block closes, which implicitly disposes the *SqlCommand* object and dereferences the *cmd* variable. Finally, you invoke the *Close* method on the connection and the outer *using* block closes, which implicitly disposes the *SqlConnection* object and dereferences the *conn* variable.

Run the code and click the button. Then select the new row to view it:

```
SELECT * FROM Customer
```

The output confirms that the *Customer* table now has one row in it, the one you just added for Lukas Keller:

```
CustomerId  FirstName  LastName  Balance  CreatedAt                UpdatedAt
----------  ---------  --------  -------  -----------------------  ----------------------
1           Lukas      Keller    0.00     2012-04-06 12:34:16.50   2012-04-06 12:34:16.50
```

As expected, the *CustomerId* column was assigned a value of *1*, and the *Balance*, *CreatedAt*, and *UpdatedAt* columns were assigned the default values of *0*, *SYSDATETIME*, and *SYSDATETIME*, respectively. These values were assigned automatically based on the *IDENTITY* specification and default values for the *Customer* table definition in Listing 10-1.

Using Parameters

In practice, you would never hardcode values for a new customer like you just did. The values would come from elsewhere, and then get passed into your application's data access layer. You can certainly use string concatenation to embed the input values into a dynamically composed T-SQL statement, but doing so exposes your application to potential SQL injection attacks (a security risk that we explain in Chapter 5). Furthermore, your code would need to sanitize the input values (for example, by doubling up literal single quotation characters in strings), or you further risk runtime exceptions resulting from strings that contain T-SQL syntax errors. So the proper way to handle variable values in T-SQL is to use parameters, as demonstrated by a modified version of the previous code.

Drag two text box controls from the Toolbox and drop them onto the form. In the Properties window, name the text boxes **txtFirstName** and **txtLastName**. Now drag a button control from the Toolbox and drop it onto the form, name it **btnParameterizedDirectSql**, and set the Text property to **Parameterized Direct SQL**. Then double-click the button and add the code in Listing 10-3.

LISTING 10-3 Using parameters with a command object.

```
private void btnParameterizedDirectSql_Click(object sender, EventArgs e)
{
  const string ConnStr =
    "Data Source=localhost;Initial Catalog=SampleDb;Integrated Security=true;";

  const string TSql =
    "INSERT INTO Customer (FirstName, LastName) VALUES (@FirstName, @LastName)";

  using (var conn = new SqlConnection())
  {
    conn.ConnectionString = ConnStr;
    conn.Open();
    using (var cmd = new SqlCommand())
    {
      cmd.Connection = conn;
      cmd.CommandText = TSql;
      cmd.Parameters.AddWithValue("@FirstName", this.txtFirstName.Text);
      cmd.Parameters.AddWithValue("@LastName", this.txtLastName.Text);
      cmd.ExecuteNonQuery();
    }
    conn.Close();
  }
}
```

This version of the code is almost identical to the previous version, but has some important differences. You'll notice that the hardcoded first and last name values in the *INSERT* statement defined by the *TSql* constant have been replaced with parameter placeholders. The parameter names, along with their values which you get from the text boxes on the form, are added to the *Parameters* collection of the *SqlCommand* object with the *AddWithValue* method.

More Info *AddWithValue* is a very convenient method. In one line of code, it creates a new *SqlParameter* object with its *ParameterName* and *Value* properties set, and adds the *SqlParameter* object to the *Parameters* collection. More elaborate ways of configuring the *Parameters* collection give you fine control over the data type, length, precision, direction (input or output), and source column mapping of each parameter. You shall see an example of this shortly, when you learn how to return scalar values using output parameters. But for simple input parameters such as the ones in this example, calling the *AddWithValue* method is sufficient.

By using parameters (rather than string concatenation), your code is not vulnerable to SQL injection attacks, nor do you need to concern yourself with sanitizing the first and last name values. ADO.NET will automatically parse the command text and parameter values to produce a T-SQL statement that is both safe and valid for execution (for example, it will double-up literal single quotation marks entered in either the first or last name text box).

Now go ahead and run the application. Type values in the first and last name text boxes, and click the button to create a new customer row. Then, to confirm, select and view the new customer as you did after creating the first customer.

Calling Stored Procedures

So far, you've used the *SqlCommand* object to execute a direct T-SQL statement on the server and insert a new customer row. However, it's a better practice to use stored procedures rather than direct SQL to perform such updates. Using stored procedures draws a clear separation between .NET code and T-SQL code. Primary benefits to this approach include maintainability, reusability, and security. Direct SQL can quickly lead to code duplication and escalate into a maintenance nightmare, with .NET and T-SQL logic intertwined and tightly coupled in your application. Good arguments can be made on both sides of the great "direct SQL versus stored procedure debate" (read the sidebar in the upcoming ADO.NET Entity Framework coverage), but the fact is that sometimes you just don't have the choice. It is very common practice for database administrators in the enterprise to lock down tables and deny direct access to them by client applications. The database instead exposes a "service layer" of stored procedures that indirectly provide controlled access to the underlying tables. This is unquestionably far more secure than just allowing clients to execute any SQL that they want directly against your tables. Arguing the merits and disadvantages between direct SQL and stored procedures is pointless in such environments—you're stuck with using stored procedures and that's all there is to it.

Now revise the code to call the *InsertCustomer* stored procedure instead of using direct SQL. Drag another button control from the Toolbox and drop it onto the form, name it **btnStoredProcedureInsert**, and set its Text property to **Stored Procedure INSERT**. Then double-click the button and add the code in Listing 10-4.

LISTING 10-4 Calling a stored procedure with parameters.

```
private void btnStoredProcedureInsert_Click(object sender, EventArgs e)
{
  const string ConnStr =
    "Data Source=localhost;Initial Catalog=SampleDb;Integrated Security=true;";

  const string StoredProcName = "InsertCustomer";

  using (var conn = new SqlConnection())
  {
    conn.ConnectionString = ConnStr;
    conn.Open();
    using (var cmd = new SqlCommand())
```

```
    {
      cmd.Connection = conn;
      cmd.CommandText = StoredProcName;
      cmd.CommandType = CommandType.StoredProcedure;
      cmd.Parameters.AddWithValue("@FirstName", this.txtFirstName.Text);
      cmd.Parameters.AddWithValue("@LastName", this.txtLastName.Text);
      cmd.ExecuteNonQuery();
    }
    conn.Close();
  }
}
```

Again, notice the two differences from the previous example. First, rather than coding the actual T-SQL *INSERT* statement right inside the C# method, you refer only to the name of the stored procedure in the database, *InsertCustomer*. The logic for adding the new customer row, including the actual *INSERT* statement, is contained in the stored procedure. Second, you inform the *SqlCommand* object that the string you have set in its *CommandText* property is the name of a stored procedure and not a direct T-SQL statement. You do this by setting its *CommandType* property to *CommandType.StoredProcedure* (overriding the default value of *CommandType.Text* for direct T-SQL). The rest looks and works the same. Give the code a run to add a third customer, and then view the new customer row as before.

But the *InsertCustomer* stored procedure does more than just execute the *INSERT* statement to add the new customer row. Referring back to Listing 10-1, recall that it also executes a *SELECT* statement right after the *INSERT* to return columns values assigned to the new row by the stored procedure. In particular, the *SELECT* statement returns a single-row result set to the client that contains the unique primary key value assigned to *CustomerId* (by virtue of its *IDENTITY* specification), and the current server date and time values assigned to *CreatedAt* and *UpdatedAt* (by virtue of their default values of *SYSDATETIME*, the built-in function that returns the server clock's current date and time as a *datetime2* data type). In this manner, the client can obtain values assigned to a new customer by SQL Server when control is returned from the stored procedure that creates the new customer, rather than issuing another command (and incurring another server round trip) to retrieve them.

You can obtain a data reader to retrieve these values from the stored procedure by invoking *ExecuteReader* rather than *ExecuteNonQuery* on the *SqlCommand* object. Although data readers are most commonly used to retrieve multiple rows of data from SQL Server, they are also used to retrieve a single-row result set in cases like this. In the next section, you'll experiment with both use cases.

Iterating Data Readers

If your T-SQL statement or stored procedure call returns a result set (or multiple result sets), you retrieve it (or them) using a data reader (also called a connected data reader, and sometimes referred to as a "firehose cursor"). Data is streamed from SQL Server directly into your application as quickly as possible via a data reader in a read-only, forward-only fashion. Figure 10-4 depicts the process.

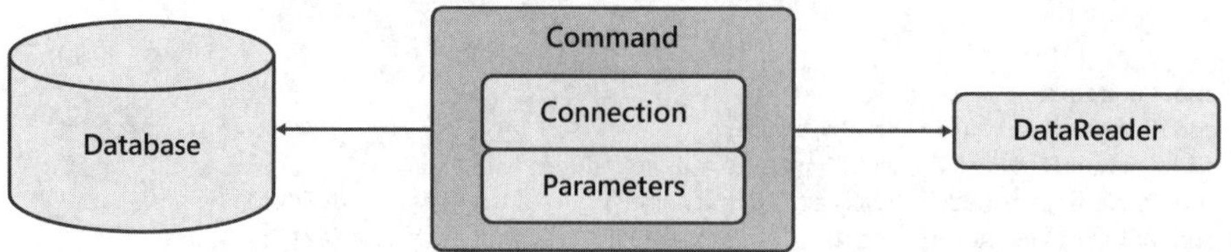

FIGURE 10-4 The raw ADO.NET objects used to execute a command in SQL Server that returns results in a data reader.

The *SqlDataReader* advances through the result set one row at a time, giving your code the opportunity to extract the column values of each row. What you do with the row data is entirely up to you; you can instantiate and populate objects, or you can process one row at a time without ever caching the data (but do remain cognizant of the fact that the database connection remains open while you iterate the reader; you should generally strive to keep connections open for the shortest duration of time possible).

The connection, command, and parameter objects get configured just as you've been doing all along, only now you invoke the *ExecuteReader* method rather than *ExecuteNonQuery* against the *SqlCommand* object to execute the command. Internally, the *ExecuteReader* method invokes the command on the server just like *ExectuteNonQuery* does, but then also creates a new *SqlDataReader* object positioned at the very beginning of the result set to be streamed back, and returns the *SqlDataReader* for your code to iterate one row at a time. This is the only way to create a reader object. The *SqlDataReader* class has no constructor, so you cannot instantiate one with the *new* keyword; you can only obtain a new reader by calling *ExecuteReader*.

You will now use a data reader to retrieve the *CustomerId*, *CreatedAt*, and *UpdatedAt* values assigned to the newly inserted row (for a new customer, the same value is expected to returned for *CreatedAt* and *UpdatedAt*). Drag another button control from the Toolbox and drop it onto the form, name it **btnStoredProcedureInsertWithReader**, and set the Text property to **Stored Procedure INSERT with Reader**. Then double-click the button and add the code in Listing 10-5.

LISTING 10-5 Using a data reader to retrieve values assigned to a new row added by the *InsertCustomer* stored procedure.

```
private void btnStoredProcedureInsertWithReader_Click(object sender, EventArgs e)
{
  const string ConnStr =
    "Data Source=localhost;Initial Catalog=SampleDb;Integrated Security=true;";

  const string StoredProcName = "InsertCustomer";

  using (var conn = new SqlConnection())
  {
    conn.ConnectionString = ConnStr;
    conn.Open();
    using (var cmd = new SqlCommand())
    {
```

```
        cmd.Connection = conn;
        cmd.CommandText = StoredProcName;
        cmd.CommandType = CommandType.StoredProcedure;
        cmd.Parameters.AddWithValue("@FirstName", this.txtFirstName.Text);
        cmd.Parameters.AddWithValue("@LastName", this.txtLastName.Text);
        using (var rdr = cmd.ExecuteReader(CommandBehavior.CloseConnection))
        {
          rdr.Read();
          var customerId = rdr.GetInt64(0);
          var createdAt = rdr.GetDateTime(1);
          var updatedAt = rdr.GetDateTime(2);
          rdr.Close();
          MessageBox.Show(
            string.Format("Customer ID {0}; Created at {1}; Updated at {2}",
              customerId, createdAt, updatedAt));
        }
      }
    }
  }
```

Everything is the same until it comes time to execute the command, at which point you invoke *ExecuteReader* to obtain a *SqlDataReader* object assigned to the variable *rdr*. Because *SqlDataReader* is a disposable object, you call *ExecuteReader* with a *using* statement block to ensure that the reader will always be disposed properly. You should close a data reader when you are done working with it, after which time you should also close the underlying database connection. The *CommandBehavior.CloseConnection* enumeration passed to *ExecuteReader* offers a convenience here, by instructing ADO.NET to close the *SqlConnection* automatically when you close the *SqlDataReader*. Therefore, you'll notice that the line *conn.Close()* has been removed from this version of the code, because the connection will be closed automatically when the reader is closed on the line *rdr.Close()*.

When you receive the reader, it is positioned *before* the first row (which in this case is the only row) in the result set. Invoking the *Read* method advances the reader to the row so you can retrieve its values. The reader exposes a set of *GetXxx* methods for all available data types, each of which accepts an integer parameter that specifies the ordinal position of the column from which to retrieve the value. Because the row is expected to return one long (64-bit) integer for the new *CustomerId* and two date/time values for *CreatedAt* and *UpdatedAt*—in that order—you call the *GetInt64* and *GetDateTime* methods passing in the values 0, 1, and 2 respectively.

You can also extract column values by accessing the *SqlDataReader* object using indexed notation. In this example, you could have obtained the three values by coding *rdr[0]*, *rdr[1]*, and *rdr[2]*, rather than using the *GetXxx* methods. With this approach, column values are returned as the type *object*, so you must cast or convert to the desired type. If you know the column names, you can use a string index rather than a numeric index, such as *rdr["CustomerId"]*, *rdr["CreatedAt"]*, and *rdr["UpdatedAt"]* (though be aware that doing so is slightly slower than using a numeric index, because ADO.NET needs to find the desired column matched by name). You will use string indexes in the next data reader example.

> **More Info** All techniques for extracting data reader values require that you know the data type of the column you are accessing. In this case, as in most, you will have that knowledge at design time. However, there are some scenarios in which you may not know what a column's data type is, or indeed, what the actual columns being returned are altogether. You can call the reader's *GetDataTypeName* method and pass it a column index to discover the data type of any particular column. If you need to dynamically discover all the columns in the result set being returned, you can call the *GetSchemaTable* method on the reader to obtain a *DataTable* populated with schema information. You can then glean the result set schema (before streaming in from the reader) by examining the *DataTable*. It will contain one *DataRow* per result set column, populated with descriptive information about each column (name, data type, scale, precision, and so on).

Run the example now to add a fourth row to the *Customer* table. The *MessageBox* dialog will display the *CustomerId* (which should be 4, if you ran the three previous examples), *CreatedAt*, and *UpdatedAt* values returned by the stored procedure.

Because the *InsertCustomer* stored procedure returns a result set that is known to always contain one and only one row, the code is based on that as being a reliable assumption. That is, the *Read* method is called on the *SqlDataReader* unconditionally, and exactly once. In many other scenarios, you will not know if you are getting back zero, one, or more rows in the reader, and so you can't make any assumptions. Your code will need to test the reader for an end-of-stream condition, because an exception will occur when you attempt to retrieve data if there are no rows in the result set, or if you have already advanced beyond the last row in the result set. The next example demonstrates how to implement this pattern. You will call the *SelectCustomers* stored procedure to return the entire set of customers, and then build a list of display strings formatted as "last name, first name."

Drag a list box control from the Toolbox and drop it onto the form. In the Properties window, name the list box **lstNames**. Now drag a button control from the Toolbox and drop it onto the form, name it **btnStoredProcedureWithReader**, and set the Text property to **Stored Procedure with Reader**. Then double-click the button and add the code in Listing 10-6.

LISTING 10-6 Processing a data reader.

```
private void btnStoredProcedureWithReader_Click(object sender, EventArgs e)
{
  const string ConnStr =
    "Data Source=localhost;Initial Catalog=SampleDb;Integrated Security=true;";

  const string StoredProcName = "SelectCustomers";

  var names = new List<string>();
  using (var conn = new SqlConnection())
  {
    conn.ConnectionString = ConnStr;
```

```
      conn.Open();
      using (var cmd = new SqlCommand())
      {
        cmd.Connection = conn;
        cmd.CommandText = StoredProcName;
        cmd.CommandType = CommandType.StoredProcedure;
        using (var rdr = cmd.ExecuteReader(CommandBehavior.CloseConnection))
        {
          while (rdr.Read())
          {
            var name = string.Format("{0}, {1}",
             rdr["LastName"], rdr["FirstName"]);
            names.Add(name);
          }
          rdr.Close();
        }
      }
    }
    this.lstNames.DataSource = names;
  }
```

This time, the *SqlCommand* object's *CommandText* property is set to point to the *SelectCustomers* stored procedure. Then *ExecuteReader* is invoked to obtain a *SqlDataReader* object that returns the results as before. This time, however, there is no way to know how many rows will come back. So the code implements a *while* block, and tests for an end-of-stream condition before each call to the reader's *Read* method as it loops through the result set. If there are no customers, *Read* will return true the very first time it is called, and the *while* block will never execute. Otherwise, the block will execute once for each customer row returned by the stored procedure.

For each row, a string index is used against the *SqlDataReader* to extract the *LastName* and *FirstName* values so the customer name can be formatted (this is a more convenient, albeit slightly slower alternative to calling *GetString* on the reader and passing in the ordinal column positions of the name fields). Each formatted name is added to the *List<string>* collection that is initialized before creating the *SqlConnection*. After closing the reader (which, because *CommandBehavior.CloseConnection* was specified, also closes the connection), the *DataSource* property of the list box binds it to the string collection.

Give the application a run, and confirm that the list box displays the names of all the customers you added in the earlier exercises.

Returning Scalar Values

In the first data reader example, you retrieved three scalar values back from calling the *InsertCustomer* stored procedure. If you only need to return a single scalar value, ADO.NET offers a shortcut that eliminates the need to work with a data reader altogether. By invoking the *ExecuteScalar* method (rather than *ExecuteReader*) on the *SqlCommand* object, ADO.NET simply returns the value in the first column of the first row of whatever result set gets returned by SQL Server. If there are more columns (or rows), they are ignored, and if no result set at all gets returned, an exception is thrown. The scalar value is returned as the type *object*, which you then cast or convert as necessary to the expected data type.

The *UpdateCustomer* stored procedure is a good example. It returns the one and only value affected by an update operation, namely the *UpdatedAt* column value assigned by the *SYSDATETIME* function (in Listing 10-1, this is the line of code that reads *SELECT UpdatedAt = @NewUpdatedAt*). Although you can use the same data reader approach you used when calling *InsertCustomer* (where you needed to retrieve three values), you can retrieve the new *UpdatedAt* value returned by *UpdateCustomer* with less code by using *ExecuteScalar* instead of *ExecuteReader*, as shown in the following code snippet:

```
// This code...
using (var rdr = cmd.ExecuteReader())
{
  rdr.Read();
  var updatedAt = rdr.GetDateTime(0);
  rdr.Close();
}

// ...is equivalent to this code
var updatedAt = Convert.ToDateTime(cmd.ExecuteScalar());
```

The *ExecuteScalar* method is clearly a coding convenience, but don't think that it works any faster than using *ExecuteReader*. All the work still goes on behind the scenes to build and return a result set that *could* potentially contain multiple columns and rows, and then you're saying that you only want the first column of the first row. That can amount to needless server overhead and network transport, considering that you can return output parameters to send scalar values back from SQL Server. With output parameters, you don't use a single-row result set to return scalar values (although you can effectively combine the use of output parameters with multi-row result sets to return both scalar and tabular data). Instead, you add a *Parameter* object corresponding to each output parameter expected by the stored procedure and set its *Direction* property to *ParameterDirection.Output*. Then you call *ExecuteNonQuery* to run the stored procedure. After the stored procedure executes, you can extract the value(s) set by the server from the *Value* property of the *Parameter* object(s).

The *GetCustomerBalance* stored procedure returns the balance of any specified customer using an output parameter. Let's see how you write the ADO.NET code to call *GetCustomerBalance* and retrieve its return value. Drag another text box control from the Toolbox and drop it onto the form. In the Properties window, name the text box **txtCustomerId**. Now drag a button control from the Toolbox and drop it onto the form, name it **btnOutputParameter**, and set the Text property to **Output Parameter**. Then double-click the button and add the code in Listing 10-7.

LISTING 10-7 Retrieving an output parameter value returned by a stored procedure.

```
private void btnOutputParameter_Click(object sender, EventArgs e)
{
  const string ConnStr =
    "Data Source=localhost;Initial Catalog=SampleDb;Integrated Security=true;";

  const string StoredProcName = "GetCustomerBalance";

  var customerId = Convert.ToInt64(this.txtCustomerId.Text);
  decimal balance;
```

```
  using (var conn = new SqlConnection())
  {
    conn.ConnectionString = ConnStr;
    conn.Open();
    using (var cmd = new SqlCommand())
    {
      cmd.Connection = conn;
      cmd.CommandText = StoredProcName;
      cmd.CommandType = CommandType.StoredProcedure;
      cmd.Parameters.AddWithValue("@CustomerId", customerId);
      var outputParam = new SqlParameter()
      {
        ParameterName = "@Balance",
        SqlDbType = SqlDbType.Money,
        Direction = ParameterDirection.Output
      };
      cmd.Parameters.Add(outputParam);
      cmd.ExecuteNonQuery();
      balance = (decimal)outputParam.Value;
    }
    conn.Close();
  }
  MessageBox.Show(string.Format("Customer ID {0} balance is {1:c}",
    customerId, balance));
}
```

The stored procedure accepts two parameters. The first one is the *@CustomerId* input parameter (a 64-bit integer; *bigint* in SQL Server, corresponding to *long* in .NET), and the second one is the *@Balance* output parameter (a *money* value in SQL Server, corresponding to *decimal* in .NET). The customer ID is obtained from the value entered in the text box and converted into a 64-bit integer in *customerId* that will be passed for the *@CustomerId* input parameter. Then the *balance* variable is declared as a *decimal* that will get assigned the value returned by the *@Balance* output parameter returned by the stored procedure, after it executes a few lines further down in the code.

After the connection and command objects are configured, you add the parameters. The *@CustomerId* input parameter is added by calling *AddWithValue,* as you've been doing thus far. The *@Balance* output parameter, however, cannot be added in just a single line of code. Instead, you need to explicitly instantiate the new *SqlParameter* instance yourself, set the appropriate properties, and add it to the *Parameters* collection. Specifically, you set the *ParameterName*, *SqlDbType*, and *Direction* properties to *@Balance*, *SqlDbType.Money*, and *ParameterDirection.Output*, respectively. With the *Parameters* collection properly configured, *ExecuteNonQuery* runs the stored procedure. When control returns to the application, you extract the output parameter value set by the stored procedure into the *balance* variable.

Run the application now and give it a try. Enter any existing customer ID (you should have four customers with IDs 1 through 4) and click the button to run the stored procedure and confirm that the balance is being returned via the output parameter. All the customers entered to this point have zero balances (because you've not yet explicitly provided a value for the *Balance* column, which has a default value of 0.00). In the next section, you'll perform some updates that change customer balances, after which you can run this code again to verify that the stored procedure is returning balance data as expected.

Batching Updates with Transactions

The last raw ADO.NET object left to cover is also, interestingly, the only one which you should no longer use, and that is *SqlTransaction* object. ADO.NET 2.0 introduced the *TransactionScope* object, which is now the recommended way to manage transactions at the application level with ADO.NET.

The *SqlConnection* object has a *BeginTransaction* method that, at the time you invoke it, issues a *BEGIN TRANSACTION* command to SQL Server over the open connection. A *SqlTransaction* object is returned back for you to hold as a handle onto the pending transaction. You then perform the necessary updates, setting the *Transaction* property of each *SqlCommand* object involved in the updates to the *SqlTransaction* object. Finally, you invoke either the *CommitTransaction* or *Rollback-Transaction* method on the *SqlTransaction* object, depending on the success or failure of all the updates. These methods issue, respectively, a *COMMIT TRANSACTION* or *ROLLBACK TRANSACTION* command to the server. Because your .NET code explicitly issues methods that translate directly to T-SQL statements controlling transactions, it is said to be managing *explicit* transactions.

There are a number of pain points with explicit transactions. The first difficulty lies in the requirement that every *SqlCommand* object used to perform updates inside the transaction must have its *Transaction* property set to the *SqlTransaction* object returned by *BeginTransaction*. This means that you must take care to pass along the *SqlTransaction* object to any place in your code that performs an update, because failing to assign it to the *Transaction* property of every *SqlCommand* object in the transaction results in a runtime exception. The issue is compounded when you need to track the *SqlTransaction* object across multiple method calls that perform updates. It becomes even harder to manage things when these methods need to be flexible enough to work whether or not a transaction is involved or required.

The problem is worse when working with any of the other technologies we'll be covering later that provide abstraction layers over the raw objects. For example, because a *SqlDataAdapter* actually wraps three distinct *SqlCommand* objects (for insert, update, and delete), you must dig beneath the data adapter and hook into its three underlying command objects so that you can set their *Transaction* properties. (We don't generally recommend that you mix and match different data access APIs within your application, but if you must transactionalize updates across a combination of technologies, implicit transactions make it easy.)

The *TransactionScope* object, introduced as part of a dedicated transaction management API with .NET 2.0 in 2005, lets you code transactions implicitly. This is a superior approach that relieves you from all of the aforementioned burdens associated with explicit transactions. So the guidance here is to always work with implicit transactions whenever possible. You will write less code that is more flexible when you allow the framework to handle transaction management for you. However, it is still also important to understand explicit transactions with the *SqlTransaction* object, as you might need to integrate with and extend existing code that already uses explicit transactions. Therefore, we will cover both transaction management styles to prepare you for all situations.

More Info The transaction management API offers many more benefits besides implicit transactions. For example, *TransactionScope* is capable of promoting a lightweight transaction (one associated with a single database) to a distributed transaction automatically, if and when your updates involve changes across multiple databases. Furthermore, you can enlist updates other than database changes to participate in the transaction. Chapter 4 covers these concepts in more detail.

The next example demonstrates how to code explicit transactons. It performs a balance transfer between customers, allowing a portion of one customer's balance to be subtracted, and then added to another customer's balance. Both update operations obviously need to succeed or fail as a whole, and so they must be transactionalized.

Drag three text box controls from the Toolbox and drop them onto the form. In the Properties window, name the text boxes **txtTransferFromCustomerId**, **txtTransferToCustomerId**, and **txtTransferAmount**. Now drag a button control from the Toolbox and drop it onto the form, name it **btnUpdateWithExplicitTransaction**, and set the Text property to **Update with Explicit Transaction**. Then double-click the button and add the code in Listing 10-8.

LISTING 10-8 Updating data using explicit transactions.

```
private void btnUpdateWithExplicitTransaction_Click(object sender, EventArgs e)
{
  const string ConnStr =
    "Data Source=localhost;Initial Catalog=SampleDb;Integrated Security=true;";

  const string TSql =
    "UPDATE Customer SET Balance += @Transfer WHERE CustomerId = @CustomerId";

  var fromCustomerId = Convert.ToInt64(this.txtTransferFromCustomerId.Text);
  var toCustomerId = Convert.ToInt64(this.txtTransferToCustomerId.Text);
  var transferAmount = Convert.ToDecimal(this.txtTransferAmount.Text);

  using (var conn = new SqlConnection())
  {
    conn.ConnectionString = ConnStr;
    conn.Open();
    using (var txn = conn.BeginTransaction())
    {
      try
      {
        using (var cmd1 = new SqlCommand())
        {
          cmd1.Connection = conn;
          cmd1.CommandText = TSql;
          cmd1.Transaction = txn;
          cmd1.Parameters.AddWithValue("@CustomerId", fromCustomerId);
          cmd1.Parameters.AddWithValue("@Transfer",
           decimal. Negate(transferAmount));
```

```
                cmd1.ExecuteNonQuery();
            }
            using (var cmd2 = new SqlCommand())
            {
                cmd2.Connection = conn;
                cmd2.CommandText = TSql;
                cmd2.Transaction = txn;
                cmd2.Parameters.AddWithValue("@CustomerId", toCustomerId);
                cmd2.Parameters.AddWithValue("@Transfer", transferAmount);
                cmd2.ExecuteNonQuery();
            }
            txn.Commit();
        }
        catch
        {
            txn.Rollback();
            throw;
        }
    }
    conn.Close();
  }
}
```

Make sure that your SQL Server Profiler trace is properly configured and running, as we explained earlier (see Figure 10-2). Then set a breakpoint at the top of the method in Listing 10-8 and run the code. Enter two existing customer IDs and an amount to transfer, click the *Update with Explicit Transaction* button, and hit the breakpoint. Then step through the code one line at a time as you monitor database activity in the SQL Profiler trace.

Two *SqlCommand* objects are involved in the balance transfer, both of which execute the *UPDATE* statement defined by the *TSql* constant. The *UPDATE* statement accepts the two parameters @ *CustomerId* and *@TransferAmount* and adjusts the *Balance* of the specified customer by the specified amount. The statement is executed first for the source customer, passing in the negated transfer amount (this subtracts from the first customer's balance), and is then executed again for the target customer, passing in the actual transfer amount (this adds to the second customer's balance). Clearly, you must use a transaction to ensure that both operations succeed or fail together.

To transactionalize these updates explicitly, you invoke *BeginTransaction* on the *SqlConnection* to start the transaction (the SQL Profiler trace shows that this method sends a *BEGIN TRANSACTION* statement to SQL Server) and obtain a *SqlTransaction* object assigned to the variable *txn*. Because *SqlTransaction* is a disposable object, you call *BeginTransaction* with a *using* statement block to ensure that the transaction gets disposed of properly at the end of the block. The two updates are then executed using the standard *ExecuteNonQuery* pattern, with the additional step of setting the *Transaction* property of both *SqlCommand* objects to the *SqlTransaction*.

After the second update, you call *txn.CommitTransaction*. Only then are both updates permanently applied to the database (the SQL Profiler trace shows that this method sends a *COMMIT TRANSACTION* statement to SQL Server). The two updates are wrapped in a *try/catch* block so that you can call *txn.RollbackTransaction* in the event of an error (this would send a *ROLLBACK TRANSACTION* statement to SQL Server). Of course, SQL Server will never commit the transaction if *txn.CommitTransaction* doesn't execute, and will eventually roll it back anyway, so the *try/catch* block isn't strictly necessary. But it's a bad idea to keep transactions pending any longer than necessary; you should instead handle exceptions that occur inside transactions so you can roll back immediately. In this case, you're not really handling the exception in the *catch* block; you just want to ensure an explicit rollback on error. So the exception is then simply rethrown (and now needs to be handled further up the stack) after calling *txn.RollbackTransaction*.

Now consider a more realistic scenario with multiple updates implemented in separate methods. It then becomes a greater burden to manage the transaction, because you need to pass the *SqlTransaction* object around and make sure it gets assigned to the *Transaction* property of every *SqlCommand* object executing within the transaction. Things are much easier using implicit transactions, as you'll see now.

Tip Although our coverage of implicit transactions is provided here in the section on raw data access objects, it pertains to all the layered technologies as well. You should implicitly transactionalize your updates using a *TransactionScope* block (as demonstrated here) whether you are working with raw objects, *DataAdapters* with *DataSets*, LINQ to SQL, or Entity Framework.

Drag another button control from the Toolbox and drop it onto the form, name it **btnUpdateWithImplicitTransaction**, and set the Text property to **Update with Implicit Transaction**. Then double-click the button and add the code in Listing 10-9.

LISTING 10-9 Updating data using implicit transactions.

```
private void btnUpdateWithImplicitTransaction_Click(object sender, EventArgs e)
{
  const string ConnStr =
    "Data Source=localhost;Initial Catalog=SampleDb;Integrated Security=true;";

  const string TSql =
    "UPDATE Customer SET Balance += @Transfer WHERE CustomerId = @CustomerId";

  var fromCustomerId = Convert.ToInt64(this.txtTransferFromCustomerId.Text);
  var toCustomerId = Convert.ToInt64(this.txtTransferToCustomerId.Text);
  var transferAmount = Convert.ToDecimal(this.txtTransferAmount.Text);

  using (var ts = new TransactionScope())
  {
    using (var conn = new SqlConnection())
    {
      conn.ConnectionString = ConnStr;
      conn.Open();
      using (var cmd1 = new SqlCommand())
      {
        cmd1.Connection = conn;
```

```
        cmd1.CommandText = TSql;
        cmd1.Parameters.AddWithValue("@CustomerId", fromCustomerId);
        cmd1.Parameters.AddWithValue("@Transfer",
         decimal.Negate(transferAmount));
        cmd1.ExecuteNonQuery();
      }
      using (var cmd2 = new SqlCommand())
      {
        cmd2.Connection = conn;
        cmd2.CommandText = TSql;
        cmd2.Parameters.AddWithValue("@CustomerId", toCustomerId);
        cmd2.Parameters.AddWithValue("@Transfer", transferAmount);
        cmd2.ExecuteNonQuery();
      }
      conn.Close();
    }
    ts.Complete();
  }
}
```

The key object here is *TransactionScope*, which is not technically part of ADO.NET. *TransactionScope* is provided by the transaction management API introduced with .NET 2.0, and is contained in the *System.Transactions* assembly (detailed coverage of this API is provided in Chapter 4, which is dedicated to transactions). So before this code will compile, you need to reference that assembly and import its namespace with a *using* directive. Right-click the project in Solution Explorer and choose Add Reference. In the Add Reference dialog, click the .NET tab, scroll to find the *System.Transactions* component, and double-click it. Then add the following *using* directive at the very top of the source code:

```
using System.Transactions;
```

The project should now build successfully. Once again, start a SQL Profiler trace and single-step through the code. You'll now see how explicit transactions behave differently than implicit transactions.

Rather than explicitly beginning, committing, and rolling back transactions, you instead wrap your updates inside of a *TransactionScope* block. Then you signal success by invoking the *Complete* method on the *TransactionScope* object before the end of the block, such that an exception occurring within the block means that *Complete* won't get called. SQL Profiler reveals that the transaction does *not* start when you instantiate the *TransactionScope*, nor does it commit when you invoke its *Complete* method. Rather, the *TransactionScope* block merely *declares* that all updates inside the block need to be transactionalized. This includes calls inside the block that you make to other methods which may themselves declare additional *TransactionScope* blocks that are nested inside the caller's block.

You can nest *TransactionScope* blocks as many levels as you need to. As long as each block invokes the *Complete* method before it ends (and no unhandled exceptions occur within any of the blocks), the transaction will commit when the outermost block terminates. Nesting blocks provides you with great flexibility, because the transaction is always created and committed at the outermost block level. Nested blocks simply piggyback off that transaction. The outermost block creates and maintains a single transaction associated with the database connection, even if the database connection is opened and closed multiple times inside of nested blocks. This is because ADO.NET is smart enough not to actually close and reopen the connection while inside of a pending implicit transaction. With this scheme, transactions get started and committed automatically as needed at runtime.

So the actual database transaction begins implicitly, *some time after* the outermost *TransactionScope* block is entered. The SQL Profiler trace shows that ADO.NET issues the *BEGIN TRANSACTION* statement to SQL Server when the connection is opened, several lines into the *TransactionScope* block. Similarly, the database transaction commits implicitly, just after the outermost *TransactionScope* block is exited (again, under the condition that *Complete* has been called within the block and all nested blocks). The trace shows a *COMMIT TRANSACTION* statement sent to SQL Server just after the *TransactionScope* block ends, even though that occurs after you close the connection (which, being inside a pending implicit transaction, won't actually close the connection) and call the *Complete* method. Unlike with explicit transactions, there is no transaction object for you to pass around and keep track of, nor do you need to worry about setting the *Transaction* property of every *SqlCommand* object that is participating in the update. Your only concern is to call *Complete* before the *TransactionScope* block ends, and this dramatically simplifies the task of writing transactional code.

More Info Chapter 4 is dedicated to the subject of atomic database transactions, and includes detailed discussion on the various transaction *isolation levels* supported by SQL Server. In that chapter, we show how you can control these isolation levels from the application layer using ADO.NET as well.

Now that you know to use the raw data access objects, you can advance to the second component of conventional ADO.NET, the *DataSet*.

Working with *DataSets*

Technically, one can create a data access layer entirely on just the raw objects—indeed, many successful applications have been built that way. Still, Microsoft could not realistically have released the .NET Framework initially without also providing the *DataSet*. Doing so would have been an unacceptable step backward for COM-based developers already accustomed to the convenience of the *RecordSet* object. In classic ADO, the *RecordSet* provides a scrollable cursor that can randomly navigate a result set returned by SQL Server. And so, the *DataSet* was introduced in ADO.NET 1.0 as a disconnected, multi-table cache to replace the (usually) connected single-table *RecordSet* cursor in classic ADO.

There is by now a great deal of existing *DataSet*-based .NET code in production that still won't be phased out for 5 years or more (some companies are still running code today that is easily 10 or more years old). Plus, there may still be times when it is appropriate to use *DataSets*. So developers will need to keep their *DataSet* skills sharp for a long time to come.

To Use or Not to Use *DataSets*

Should you work with *DataSets*? That has been the subject of much debate since the dawn of .NET, and is even more debatable with the advent of Silverlight, ADO.NET Entity Framework, and the newest WinRT runtime in Windows 8. Some developers dismiss *DataSets* out of hand, primarily because—despite their ability to be strongly typed and to encapsulate business logic—they are not true business objects. For example, you need to navigate through relationship objects in the *DataSet* to connect between parent and child rows. This is not intuitive to object-oriented programmers, who think of parent–child relationships in simpler terms; each parent has as a child collection property and each child has a parent property. Furthermore, the *DataSet* paradigm does not allow for inheritance, which is also extremely important to object-oriented developers. Special handling is also required for null values in a *DataSet*.

Notwithstanding these concerns, we don't generally advocate dismissing *any* technology out of hand. Every application is different, and you are doing yourself a disservice if you don't examine the facets of all available choices on a case-by-case basis. Like anything else, *DataSets* can be used or they can be abused, and it's true that they do present limitations if you try to utilize them as business objects. But if what you need is a generic in-memory database model, then that's what a *DataSet* is, and that's what a *DataSet* gives you. Although the aforementioned concerns are all valid, the fact remains that *DataSets* are very powerful and can serve extremely well as data transfer objects. Furthermore, they have the unique ability to dynamically adapt their shape according to the schema of whatever data is streamed into them, which is something that none of the newer APIs can do.

So to reiterate, *DataSets* are *not* obsolete. The *DataSet* is a cornerstone of the .NET Framework, and it continues to be supported by the newest .NET Framework 4.5 in the Windows 8 Win32 compatibility runtime. Even when LINQ to SQL and Entity Framework were first released, Microsoft was enhancing the *DataSet*. For example, the *TableAdapterManager* was added in .NET 3.5 to greatly simplify hierarchical updates, as you'll see in an example shortly. The fact is that *DataSets* do still have their place, and you will continue to encounter them for a long time to come as you maintain existing applications.

Having said that, we must also stress that Microsoft has clearly positioned ADO.NET Entity Framework as the preferred data access technology today and in the future, eclipsing both *DataSets* and LINQ to SQL. Furthermore, neither Silverlight nor the .NET Framework 4.5 in the Windows 8 native WinRT runtime supports the *DataSet*.

A *DataSet* contains one or more *DataTable* objects, each of which in turn contains rows and columns. The *DataSet* has all of the basic characteristics of a relational database, such as primary keys, default values, relationships and constraints, but has no awareness of any particular underlying data store. In fact, it's possible to use a *DataSet* with multiple data stores, or even none at all (that is, an entirely in-memory scenario). It is the job of a *DataAdapter* to shuttle data back and forth between a *DataSet* and a specific back-end data store. The *DataAdapter*—not the *DataSet*—works as an abstraction over the raw ADO.NET command objects that are used to get data into and out of the *DataSet*.

Many ADO.NET data providers are available today that offer a *DataAdapter* to bridge the *DataSet* with different platforms. With the SQL Server provider (SqlClient), the *DataSet* is paired with the *SqlDataAdapter*. Figure 10-5 depicts these objects and shows the interaction between the database, *DataAdapter*, and *DataSet*.

Note This chapter covers just the SQL Server provider, though we often refer to the *SqlDataAdapter* object using the more generic term *DataAdapter*. Similarly, we refer to data readers as *SqlDataReader* and *DataReader* interchangeably.

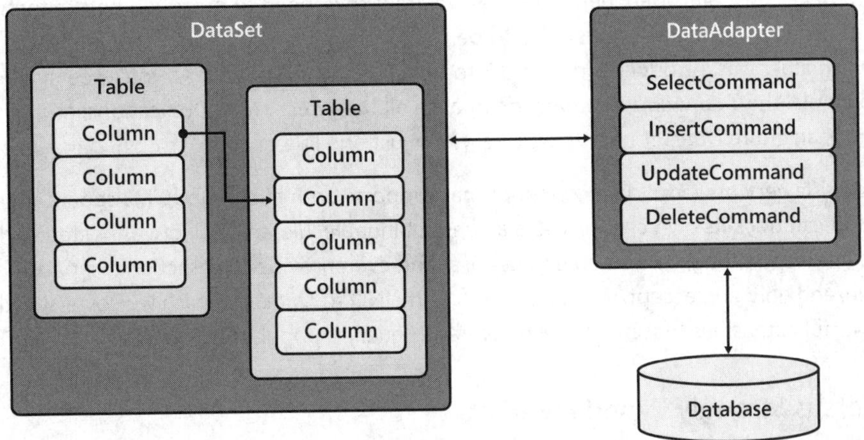

FIGURE 10-5 The *DataSet* and *DataAdapter* work together to retrieve and update data in SQL Server.

The *SqlDataAdapter* facilitates filling and updating (via its aptly named *Fill* and *Update* methods) data in the *DataSet*. It holds four distinct *SqlCommand* objects, exposed by the *SelectCommand* property (used when you call *Fill*), and the *InsertCommand*, *UpdateCommand*, and *DeleteCommand* properties (used when you call *Update*).

It is a common misconception that *DataSets* are slower than *DataReaders*, when in fact *DataReaders* are used internally when you call *Fill* on a *DataAdapter*. What it really comes down to is whether you are caching the data versus processing it as you stream it. Behind the scenes, the *Fill* method works just like what you'd code by hand to populate a collection of objects in memory using the *DataReader* techniques we just covered.

Specifically, calling *Fill* invokes *ExecuteReader* on the *SqlCommand* object referenced by the *SelectCommand* of the *DataAdapter*, and thus obtains a *SqlDataReader*. The adapter is smart enough to open the *SqlConnection* (referenced by the *Connection* property of the *SqlCommand* object) first, if it isn't already opened. It then calls *Read* to iterate the results one row at a time. For each row, it instantiates and populates a *DataRow* object, and adds the *DataRow* to a *DataTable* in the *DataSet*. If multiple result sets are returned by the server, then multiple *DataTables* are automatically instantiated to accommodate them. After the last row of data in the last result set is processed, it closes the reader when done. Finally, if the connection wasn't opened before the *Fill*, the connection is closed as well. At this stage, the connection with the server has been severed, and the *DataAdapter* can be discarded if desired.

Calling *Update* on the *DataAdapter* provides a similar abstraction to push changes made in the *DataSet* (inserts, updates, and deletes) back to the database. Specifically, ADO.NET examines the *RowState* property of each row in a *DataTable* to determine whether *ExecuteNonQuery* should be called, and on which *SqlCommand* object (*InsertCommand*, *UpdateCommand*, or *DeleteCommand*) it should be called. Each *DataRow* holds current and original values, making it easy to map both versions of any column to the three update commands. Because *Update* works only on one table at a time, it can be tricky to handle hierarchical updates when the database is enforcing referential integrity constraints between tables. New parent rows need to be added before their child rows get added, whereas deletions need to be coded in the reverse order. Fortunately, the *TableAdapterManager* was introduced in .NET 3.5 to do all that work for you. As you'll see in an upcoming example, the *TableAdapterManager* can push all the insertions, modifications, and deletions across an entire *DataSet* back to SQL Server in just one line of code.

The *DataSet* is a very powerful data container that supports both binary and XML serialization across tiers and can track its own changes. It is an easily bindable, hierarchical, disconnected cache that features filtering, sorting, computed expressions, and even provides transactional capabilities (such as begin/end edit, and accept/reject changes). And LINQ to *DataSet* (which we cover shortly) provides powerful extensions that make it even easier to query a populated *DataSet*.

Generic Versus Strongly Typed *DataSets*

The term *generic* can be somewhat ambiguous when used with *DataSets*. In one sense, and as already explained, *DataSets* are always generic with respect to their back-end data store. But more commonly, generic *DataSets* refer to *DataSets* that have no schema definition, as opposed to *strongly typed DataSets* that do. Generic *DataSets* are useful in (the very small minority of) cases when you are not aware of the schema of the data that you're working with at design time. In those situations, it's actually quite powerful and convenient to have a *DataSet* object that starts out schema-less (no defined tables or columns) and just dynamically adapts to whatever data you stream into it (even Entity Framework can't do that!). When you call *Fill* on the *SqlDataAdapter*, one *DataTable* gets created for each result set returned by the *SelectCommand* and one *DataColumn* within each *DataTable* gets created for each column of each result set (the column data types get inferred from the result set). Then the rows get populated with the actual data.

However, in the vast majority of cases, you *are* aware of the schema of the data that you're working with at design time, and so you want to work with strongly typed *DataSets* (also called typed *DataSets*). You'll start now with examples using a generic *DataSet*, and then move on to create an XML Schema Definition (XSD) for examples using a typed *DataSet*. As you progress, you will see many benefits of working with typed *DataSets*.

Filling and Updating a Generic *DataSet*

Let's get busy with *DataSets*. Launch Visual Studio, create a new Visual C# Windows Forms application, and name it **DemoDataSets**. Drag a button control from the Toolbox and drop it onto the form *Form1* created automatically by Visual Studio. In the Properties window, name the button **btnGenericDataSet**, and set the Text property to **Generic DataSet**. Then double-click the button. Visual Studio will automatically create a click event handler for the button, and then open the code editor so that you can implement the handler. Add the code as shown in Listing 10-10.

LISTING 10-10 Filling and updating with a generic *DataSet*.

```
private void btnGenericDataSet_Click(object sender, EventArgs e)
{
  const string ConnStr =
    "Data Source=localhost;Initial Catalog=SampleDb;Integrated Security=true;";

  const string SelectTSql = "SELECT * FROM Customer";

  const string UpdateTSql = @"
    UPDATE Customer
      SET FirstName = @FirstName, LastName = @LastName, UpdatedAt = SYSDATETIME()
      WHERE CustomerId = @CustomerId";

  var ds = new DataSet();

  using (var cn = new SqlConnection())
  {
    cn.ConnectionString = ConnStr;
    using (var cm = new SqlCommand())
    {
      cm.Connection = cn;
      cm.CommandText = SelectTSql;

      using (var da = new SqlDataAdapter())
      {
        da.SelectCommand = cm;
        da.Fill(ds);
      }
    }
  }

  // The self-tracking DataSet can now be serialized across the tiers

  var customerTable = ds.Tables[0];
  if (customerTable.Rows.Count == 0)
  {
    MessageBox.Show("There are no customers");
    return;
  }

  var firstCustomerRow = customerTable.Rows[0];
```

```
    // Type casting required
    var customerId = (long)firstCustomerRow["CustomerId"];
    var updatedAt = (DateTime)firstCustomerRow["UpdatedAt"];

    MessageBox.Show(string.Format("Customer {0} was updated at {1}",
      customerId, updatedAt));

    firstCustomerRow["FirstName"] = "Brian";
    firstCustomerRow["LastName"] = "Perry";

    using (var cn = new SqlConnection())
    {
      cn.ConnectionString = ConnStr;
      using (var cm = new SqlCommand())
      {
        cm.Connection = cn;
        cm.CommandText = UpdateTSql;
        cm.Parameters.Add("@FirstName", SqlDbType.VarChar, 50, "FirstName");
        cm.Parameters.Add("@LastName", SqlDbType.VarChar, 50, "LastName");
        cm.Parameters.Add("@CustomerId", SqlDbType.BigInt, -1, "CustomerId");

        using (var da = new SqlDataAdapter())
        {
          da.UpdateCommand = cm;
          da.Update(customerTable);
        }
      }
    }
  }
```

As with the previous project, you must import the namespace so that the compiler can recognize classes in the *System.Data.SqlClient* namespace. So also add the following *using* directive at the very top of the source code:

```
using System.Data.SqlClient;
```

Listing 10-10 demonstrates the fundamental principles of data access using *DataSets* and *DataAdapters*. With generic *DataSets*, there are no XSDs, designers, or other visual tools involved; it's a pure coding experience in ADO.NET.

The code begins with a hard-coded connection string constant, as before. This is the last time that you will follow this anti-practice; the remaining examples in the chapter store the connection string in a configuration file so that it can be altered without recompiling the application. Two string constants, *SelectTSql* and *UpdateTSql,* are then defined as direct T-SQL statements against the *Customer* table that, respectively, retrieve all the customers from the database and update a single customer's *FirstName* and *LastName* fields. For now, you aren't supporting deletions and insertions, nor are you dealing with any other *Customer* columns or the related *OrderHeader* table. A new generic *DataSet* is then instantiated and assigned to the variable *ds*. The code is now going to fill *ds* with customers, change one of the customer's information, and then save those changes back to the database. Let's start with the fill operation.

The *SqlConnection* and *SqlCommand* are instantiated with *using* blocks, just as we've demonstrated in all the previous examples. Notice, however, that the code does not actually open the *SqlConnection*. This signals the fill operation to automatically open the connection before it loads the result set and closes it afterwards (conversely, if you did open the connection, the fill operation would not try to open it again, nor would it close the connection afterwards). Now the *SqlDataAdapter* object is created, and its *SelectCommand* property is pointed to the *SqlCommand* object configured to *SELECT* the entire customer table. All the pieces are now in place to call the *Fill* method.

When you call the *Fill* method on the *SqlDataAdapter*, the *SqlCommand* object of the adapter's *SelectCommand* property is executed to fill the *DataSet*. As explained, this happens by calling *ExecuteReader* and iterating a *SqlDataReader* behind the scenes to populate a *DataTable* inside the *DataSet* with *DataRows*. Because this is purely a retrieval operation, the *SqlDataAdapter* doesn't care that you haven't set the other three *SqlCommand* properties. After the *Fill*, the *DataSet* (which had been devoid of both schema and data) now has a single populated *DataTable* in it with a schema derived from the results. Specifically, the *Columns* collection of the *DataTable* is populated with *DataColumn* objects whose data types are inferred by the result set returned from the server. At this time, every *DataRow* in the *DataTable* has a *RowState* property whose value is set to *Unchanged*.

The server connection is severed at this point, and the data access objects are disposed. Only the populated *DataSet* remains. The code now makes some changes in the *DataSet* and updates those changes with another *DataAdapter*. Although everything is coded in a single method, this demonstrates that a *DataSet* exists entirely independently of the *DataAdapter*, and the *DataAdapter's* underlying connections and commands used to shuttle data into and out of the *DataSet*. Between the time that one *SqlDataAdapter* is used to call *Fill* and the time that another *SqlDataAdapter* is used to call *Update*, the *DataSet* could potentially be serialized across multiple tiers up to the presentation layer, bound to controls in the user interface, and then transported back down to the data access layer to be updated.

Note We stress this point because it highlights a key difference between *DataSets* and the much newer and more advanced Entity Framework that is coming up later in the chapter. The independence of the *DataSet* as a self-tracking container makes it extremely easy to develop for n-tier scenarios. With EF, conversely, stateful entity objects rely on the *ObjectContext* for change tracking, posing much greater challenges in n-tier architectures. We will elaborate more on this point when discussing EF.

Next the code gets a handle onto the *DataTable* holding the results, which is the first (and currently only) member in the *DataSet's Tables* collection. If there are no customers it simply displays a message and exits the method. Otherwise, it gets a handle onto the *DataRow* holding the first customer, which is the first member in the *DataTable's Rows* collection. It then uses string indexes into the *DataRow* to extract the *CustomerId* and *UpdatedAt* values of the first customer and displays them in a *MessageBox*.

After the *MessageBox*, the customer's name is changed to Brian Perry. The code that directly changes the value of the *FirstName* and *LastName* columns automatically alters the *RowState* property of the customer *DataRow* from *Unchanged* to *Modified*. This is exactly the way the *DataSet* would be affected if a user typed the changes into a grid on a form that was bound to the *DataTable*. Furthermore, the previous first and last name values just overwritten are still available, so you can always access original values in a modified *DataSet* (across all tiers) for any purpose that your application requires.

Now the changes are ready to be saved. In a real n-tier application, you can imagine this would be the point where the user clicks Save and the *DataSet* gets serialized back down across the tiers to the data access layer so that it can be updated with another *SqlDataAdapter*—this one configured for calling *Update* rather than *Fill*.

Once again, the code instantiates *SqlConnection* and *SqlCommand* objects. And again, by not opening the connection, the adapter internally opens and closes the connection on its own. The *SqlCommand* will be used to update every row in the *DataTable* whose *RowState* property is set to *Modified*, and the *Parameters* collection of the *SqlCommand* object is populated using an overload of the *Add* method that maps parameter names in the T-SQL statement to corresponding column names in the *DataTable*. Finally, the *SqlDataAdapter* object is created, its *UpdateCommand* property is pointed to the *SqlCommand* object, and its *Update* method is invoked. As explained, this causes *ExecuteNonQuery* to be invoked on each *DataRow* in the *DataTable* passed to the *Update* method that has a *RowState* of *Modified*.

Start a SQL Profiler trace and give the code a run. Watch the trace as you single-step over the *Fill* and *Update* methods to see the action as it happens behind the scenes. (The *Update* method will update all rows with a *RowState* of *Modified*, but because your code only modifies one customer row, you will only see a one *UPDATE* in the trace.)

This code works because it knows that the only *RowState* value that the adapter's *Update* method is going to encounter (other than *Unchanged*) will be *Modified*. If a *RowState* of *Added* or *Deleted* would be encountered, this code will fail, because the *Update* method would look respectively to the *InsertCommand* and *DeleteCommand* properties for the appropriate *SqlCommand* to execute, and those properties haven't been set. To support insertions and deletions, you'd need to add the correct parameterized T-SQL statements to the code, as demonsrated for updates. And to support the *OrderHeader* table as well would require even more code to deal with another table's *Fill* and *Update* operations, as well as the extra logic to properly handle the order of deletions and insertions across the hierarchical composition of parent and child relationships. This quickly adds up to a lot of code that you need to write and maintain for typical applications that work with many related tables. Strongly typed *DataSets* (along with the *TableAdapterManager*) come to the rescue here. In the next section you will learn how to write less code and get more done using typed *DataSets* instead of generic *DataSets*.

Building Strongly Typed *DataSets*

A typed *DataSet* (short for strongly typed *DataSet*) offers numerous benefits over the generic *DataSet*. When creating your application, you use a graphical designer in Visual Studio to visually build the schema of your typed *DataSet*. You lay out the *DataSet* by dragging and dropping tables and relationships from the Server Explorer, and then further customize its properties (occasionally with the assistance of a wizard). When you perform these actions, you are actually editing an XML Schema Definition (XSD) file in the background that describes all the tables, columns, data types, and relationships you've laid out for the *DataSet*.

Visual Studio provides a custom code-generation tool that then reads the XSD file and produces .NET source code from it. The process is triggered when any change is made to the XSD file, which is any time you make a change with the graphical designer. The generated code defines a class that inherits from *DataSet*—so that a typed *DataSet* is everything that a generic *DataSet* is—but it also provides strongly typed members for all of the elements (tables, columns, relationships) defined by the XSD.

In addition to strongly typed *DataTable* schemas, .NET 2.0 enhanced the combined visual-designer/code-generation experience by introducing *TableAdapters*. These are simply strongly typed wrappers around *DataAdapters* that are pre-configured (as you'll see in the next example) with the four *SqlCommand* objects—complete with parameters, connection string, and just about any other properties you can think of setting. The result is a drastic reduction in the amount of code you need to write, because the designer-generated code is now doing the work to hook up all four command objects and their parameters to an adapter, for *each* table.

Now that we've explained some of the benefits, let's tap into the power of typed *DataSets*. In Solution Explorer, right-click the project and choose Add | New Item. In the Add New Item dialog, scroll down to find and click on *DataSet*. Name the new *DataSet* **SampleDS.xsd** and click Add. Visual Studio creates the file and opens it in the typed *DataSet* designer. In the center of the empty design surface, click the Server Explorer link. The Server Explorer will help you get started quickly with building your typed *DataSet*, but you'll first need to give it a connection to the database.

In the Server Explorer, right-click Data Connections and choose Add Connection. Select Microsoft SQL Server as the data source and click Continue. In the Add Connection dialog, type **localhost** for the Server name, select *SampleDB* from the database drop-down list, and click OK (you must choose different settings if you have created the database on another server or instance). Visual Studio creates the connection beneath the *Data Connections* node in the Server Explorer. Expand the new connection node in Server Explorer, and then expand the *Tables* node beneath that, as shown in Figure 10-6.

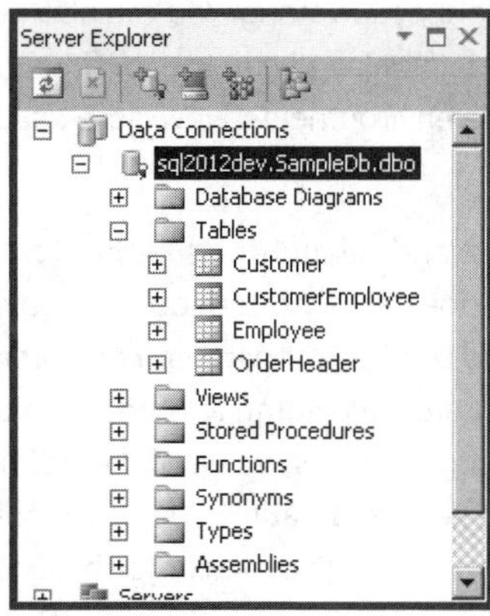

FIGURE 10-6 Viewing data connections in Visual Studio's Server Explorer.

Click the first table (*Customer*), hold down the Shift key, and then click on the last table (*OrderHeader*) to select all four tables. Then drag the four tables from the Server Explorer and drop them onto the *DataSet* design surface. After rearranging the tables to get a better view of how they relate, your *DataSet* should look similar to Figure 10-7.

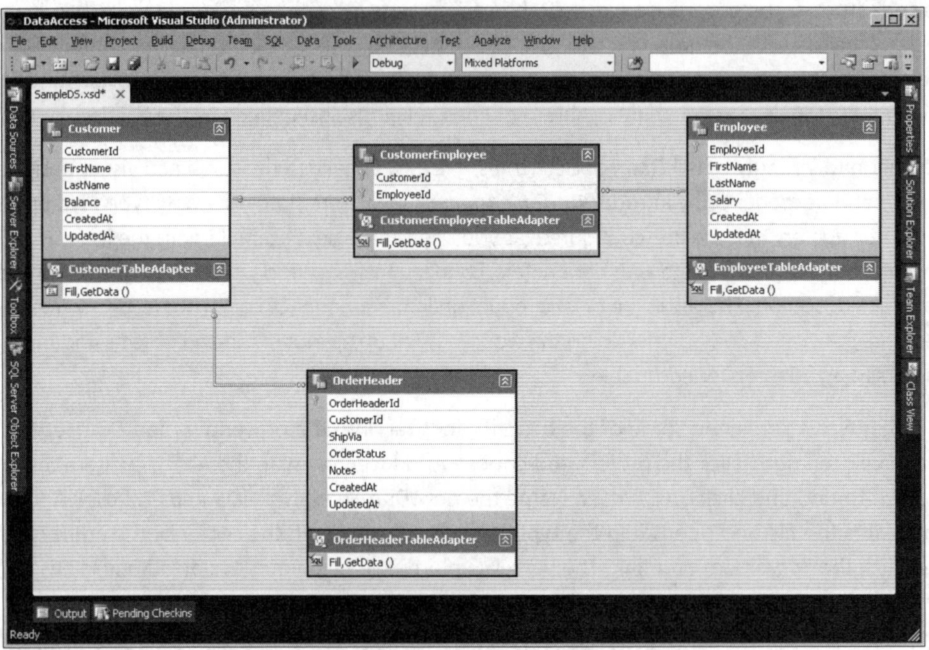

FIGURE 10-7 The typed *DataSet* design surface in Visual Studio.

Several very important things have happened automatically at this point. First, notice that an application configuration file (named *app.config*) has been added to the project. Open *app.config* and you'll see a *<connectionStrings>* element with an *<add>* element nested inside of it. The *<add>* element defines a name for the connection, and also contains the complete connection string to the database. If and when you need to change the connection string, you'll be able to edit the configuration file and won't need to recompile the application as you would with a hard-coded connection string. You can also deploy the application to different environments (development, testing, production), and edit the configuration file accordingly to adjust the connection string appropriately for those environments. Now close *app.config* and return to the typed *DataSet* designer.

Next, you can see that the designer has created tables, columns, and relationships in the *DataSet* that essentially mimic the database structure. The Server Explorer does a very good job at discovering and replicating schema from the database to the *DataSet* designer, but it's not perfect. For example, it won't pick up on default values. In the *Customer* table, click the *Balance* column and notice in the Properties window that it does not have a default value, even though a default value of 0 is defined for *Balance* in the database. You can use the Properties window to set the default value and make other tweaks as necessary after dragging and dropping tables from Server Explorer onto the *DataSet*.

Finally, the designer displays *TableAdapters* attached at the bottom of each table. Being that there is one *TableAdapter* for filling and updating each *DataTable*, this is a reasonably convenient display. However, it can also be quite misleading. Remember that *TableAdapters* are really just *DataAdapters*, and that *DataTables* contained inside of *DataSets* exist entirely independently of *DataAdapters*. So while you use the designer to easily configure each table together with its adapters, the code generator actually produces distinct *DataSet* and *TableAdapter* classes. An instance of a typed *DataSet* includes only typed *DataTables*; it does not include the corresponding *TableAdapters*. This makes sense, because when the *DataSet* is serialized up to the client across the network, the adapter information is meaningless. *TableAdapters* are instantiated independently of *DataSets* only on the application server connected to the database inside the firewall, in order to fill and update them just as you've been doing all along.

By default, the designer has generated a *TableAdapter* for each table, with each one already configured with the four command objects needed to fill and update the table. It also generated appropriate direct T-SQL statements for each command in each table, and configured their parameter collections. Compared with the amount of code in the previous generic *DataSet* example, it is obvious that typed *TableAdapters* offer a huge savings in time and effort.

Mapping Stored Procedures to the Typed *DataSet*

Now you will use the CRUD stored procedures defined for the *Customer* table instead of the direct SQL generated by the designer for each of the four command objects in its *TableAdapter*. Click the *CustomerTableAdapter* heading in the designer. The Properties window shows the four command properties: *SelectCommand*, *InsertCommand*, *UpdateCommand*, and *DeleteCommand*. Examine each of them and you will see lengthy direct T-SQL statements assigned to the *CommandText* property and corresponding parameters populated in the *Parameters* collection property. You'll use the TableAdapter Configuration Wizard to change this so that the CRUD stored procedures are used instead.

Right-click the *CustomerTableAdapter* heading and choose Configure. It may seem odd, but this drops you off in the *middle* of the wizard, so click the Previous button to go back to the Choose a Command Type page. The Use SQL Statements radio button is selected by default, which means that the *Customer* table should use the direct SQL statements generated automatically when you dragged and dropped from Server Explorer. The second radio button will actually create new stored procedures, which would contain the same automatically generated SQL statements. Select the third radio button to tell the wizard that you want to use existing stored procedures, as shown in Figure 10-8.

Click Next. For the Select, Insert, Update, and Delete drop-down lists, choose *SelectCustomers*, *InsertCustomer*, *UpdateCustomer*, and *DeleteCustomer*, respectively. When you map the Select, the wizard discovers the columns returned by the stored procedure and displays them in the panel on the right, as shown in Figure 10-9 (the caption "Set Select procedure parameters" above the column list is actually incorrect; it should really state "Select procedure columns"). When you map the Insert, Update, and Delete, the wizard discovers the parameters required by the stored procedure and displays them in the right-hand panel.

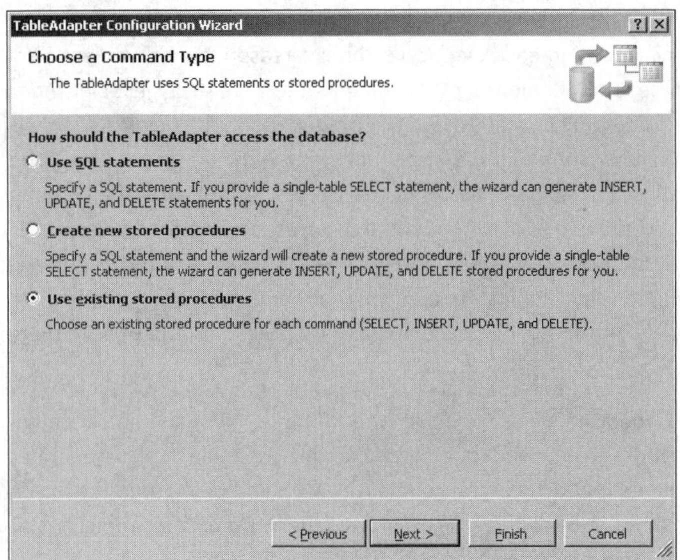

FIGURE 10-8 Telling the wizard to use existing stored procedures for a table adapter.

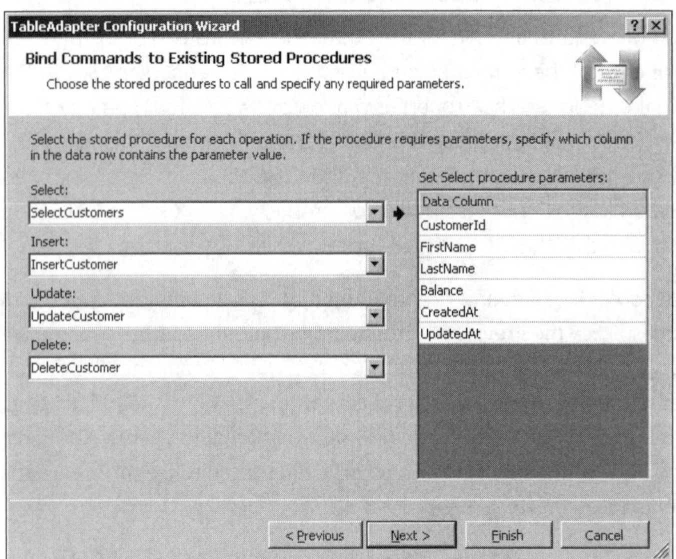

FIGURE 10-9 Mapping stored procedures to a table adapter.

Now click Finish. Revisit the Properties window for the *CustomerTableAdapter* and you'll see something very different than before. Rather than a lengthy T-SQL statement, the four *CommandText* properties merely contain the stored procedure name, as shown in Figure 10-10.

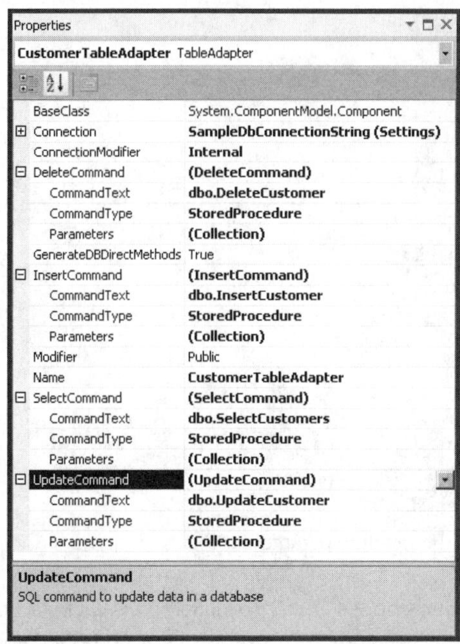

FIGURE 10-10 Table adapter properties showing mapped stored procedures.

Because stored procedures parameters are consistently named with the table columns, the wizard correctly mapped all the parameters to columns. It even guessed to map the parameter *@OriginalUpdatedAt* to the *UpdatedAt* column for the *UpdateCustomer* stored procedure. But you still need to tweak that mapping. In the Properties window, expand the *UpdateCommand* property and click the ellipses next to *Parameters* to open the Parameters Collection Editor. Then click the *@OriginalUpdatedAt* parameter. The designer correctly set the *SourceColumn* to *UpdatedAt* column even though the parameter name is prefixed with the word *Original*, but the *SourceVersion* is still set to *Current*. This will work fine as long as the client never changes the *UpdatedAt* value after they retrieve it, but you can never trust what the client might do. So instead, you want to specify the original *UpdatedAt* column that was retrieved from the database and not worry about the client possibly overwriting it (accidentally or deliberately). Because each *DataRow* retains every column's original value, it is easy for you to map the original value of any column to any stored procedure parameter that needs it. (Tangentially, it is also very convenient that the validations rule and calculations in your business logic can access original values in a *DataSet*.) Change the *SourceVersion* for *@OriginalUpdatedAt* from *Current* to *Original*, as shown in Figure 10-11, and click OK. Then save and build the project to make sure that it compiles successfully.

Although the whole point of the designer is to shield you from the details of the XSD and the typed *DataSet* class that gets generated from it, familiarizing yourself with both of these files is very enlightening, and will go a long way in helping you understand the technology. So before writing the code for this final *DataSet* example, go have a quick look at the files behind the designer.

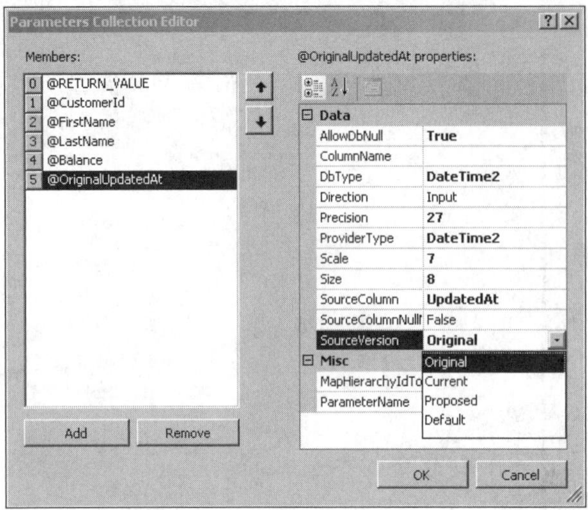

FIGURE 10-11 Mapping a column's original value to a stored procedure parameter.

Right-click *SampleDS.xsd* in the Solution Explorer and choose Open With. Select XML (Text) Editor and click OK to view the XSD file as XML. This *is* the XML that you are composing as you build your typed *DataSet* in the designer with Server Explorer drag-and-drop, the Table Adapter Configuration Wizard, and the Properties window. Scroll through the XSD, and you will find an XML representation of everything you added to the *DataSet* using the designer. Next, expand the *SampleDS.xsd* file in the Solution Explorer to reveal the *SampleDS.Designer.cs* file nested beneath it. Double-click it to open the C# code, which is generated automatically whenever the XSD is updated. In this code, you will see the *SampleDS* class that inherits from *DataSet*, as well as table classes that inherit from *DataTable* with fully described columns. Scroll a bit more and you will find the generated *TableAdapter* code, which uses code similar to what you wrote by hand earlier to set up the four command objects and their parameters with an adapter for each table.

With all of this functionality now baked into your typed *DataSet*, you're going get a lot more done with a lot less code, compared to working with generic *DataSets*. Drag another button control from the Toolbox and drop it onto the form. In the Properties window, name the button **btnTypedDataSet**, and set the Text property to **Strongly Typed DataSet**. Then double-click the button and add the code in Listing 10-11.

LISTING 10-11 Filling and updating with a strongly typed *DataSet*.

```
private void btnTypedDataSet_Click(object sender, EventArgs e)
{
  var ds = new SampleDS();
  using (var da = new SampleDSTableAdapters.CustomerTableAdapter())
  {
    da.Fill(ds.Customer);
  }
```

```
using (var da = new SampleDSTableAdapters.OrderHeaderTableAdapter())
{
  da.Fill(ds.OrderHeader);
}

// The self-tracking DataSet can now be serialized across the tiers

if (ds.Customer.Count == 0)
{
  MessageBox.Show("There are no customers");
  return;
}

var firstCustomerRow = ds.Customer[0];

// No type casting required
var customerId = firstCustomerRow.CustomerId;
var updatedAt = firstCustomerRow.UpdatedAt;

var orderRows = firstCustomerRow.GetOrderHeaderRows();

MessageBox.Show(
  string.Format("Customer {0} was updated at {1} and has {2} order(s)",
    customerId, updatedAt, orderRows.Length));

// Change the customer's name
firstCustomerRow.FirstName = "David";
firstCustomerRow.LastName = "Jones";

// Add a customer order
ds.OrderHeader.AddOrderHeaderRow(firstCustomerRow,
  "Regular Mail", "Open", string.Empty, DateTime.Now, DateTime.Now);

using (var tam = new SampleDSTableAdapters.TableAdapterManager())
{
  tam.CustomerTableAdapter =
    new SampleDSTableAdapters.CustomerTableAdapter();

  tam.OrderHeaderTableAdapter =
    new SampleDSTableAdapters.OrderHeaderTableAdapter();

  tam.UpdateAll(ds);
}
}
```

First, a new instance of *SampleDS* (your typed *DataSet*) is created. Unlike a newly instantiated generic *DataSet*, this *DataSet* is fully loaded with schema information, and has *DataTable*, *DataColumn*, and *DataRelation* objects for everything defined in the XSD already created inside of it the moment it is instantiated. The only thing missing are the rows of data themselves.

Next, all the customers and orders are retrieved from the database. Each table is filled using the *TableAdapter* you configured in the designer. For the *CustomerTableAdapter*, you know that means the *SelectCustomers* stored procedure will be called. For the *OrderHeadersTableAdapter*, the default designer-generated T-SQL *SELECT* statement will be called. When you run the application, single step over both *Fill* method calls as you examine the running trace in SQL Profiler to verify that these are indeed the statements being sent by ADO.NET to SQL Server.

Note Realistically, your fill operations will be parameterized to filter just a subset of the data from the database. In the designer, you can create multiple data retrieval queries in addition to the one associated with the *SelectCommand* property. These queries can be tied to parameterized stored procedures, and the designer will generate *FillByXxx* methods (for example *FillByNameSearch*, *FillByState*, *FillByCategory*, and so on) with .NET parameters that match the T-SQL parameters of the stored procedure. This way, through its associated *TableAdapter*, each *DataTable* can be filled using any number of queries with varying parameters for controlling the subsets of data that will get retrieved from the database.

Once again, the server connection is now severed, the data adapters are disposed, and only the populated *DataSet* remains. In an n-tier scenario, it would be serialized across multiple tiers up to the presentation layer at this point.

Now you start to enjoy the benefits of strong typing. You don't need to refer to the customer *DataTable* by index, as in *ds.Tables[0]* or *ds.Tables["Customer"]*, because the typed *DataSet* has a property called *Customer* (that the compiler won't let you misspell), and it has a *Count* property that tells you how many customer rows were retrieved. If there are no customers, the code displays a message and exits the method. Otherwise, it gets a handle onto the *DataRow* holding the first customer, which is the first member in the typed *DataRow* collection exposed by the *Customer* property. It then extracts the *CustomerId* and *UpdatedAt* values of the first customer as in the last example. Only this time, it uses genuine *long* and *DateTime* properties exposed by the strongly typed *DataRow*. You don't need to cast from a *generic* object type or use string indexes—both of which are undesirable, inconvenient, and error-prone practices. The Intellisense feature in Visual Studio makes it very easy to find the right property, and if you still manage to misspell a property name, your project won't build.

Because of the relationship defined in the typed *DataSet* between *Customer* and *OrderHeader*, the typed customer *DataRow* is also equipped with a *GetOrderHeaderRows* method. This method returns an array of *DataRow* objects for the orders belonging to this customer (which is a subset of the complete list of orders belonging to all customers that you filled from the database). You call *GetOrderHeaderRows* and then show a *MessageBox* that displays the customer's ID, updated date, and order count.

After the *MessageBox*, the customer's name is changed to David Jones. Again, strongly typed properties for *FirstName* and *LastName* are vastly superior to the generic approach in the previous example, where you were constantly casting back and forth between *object* and specific data types. You won't be able to assign incorrect data types or misspell column names with typed *DataSets*. Making these (extremely common) mistakes with generic *DataSets* do not get caught by the compiler, and it will be the poor unsuspecting user that discovers the problem with an ugly error message displayed by an unhandled exception. You should be getting the idea that our very strong recommendation is to always use typed *DataSets* over generic *DataSets*, except for cases where you need to discover schema dynamically at runtime. Generic *DataSets* are the perfect tool for the job in such scenarios (they're also great for "throw-away" apps, like quick demos or proof-of-concepts).

In addition to changing the customer name, the code adds a new customer order. Again, due to the relationship between *Customer* and *OrderHeader*, the *OrderHeader* table property of the typed *DataSet* is equipped with an *AddOrderHeaderRow* method that was created automatically by the typed *DataSet* code generator. This method accepts appropriately typed parameters for each column of a new order. The first parameter identifies the new *OrderHeader*'s parent *Customer*. Interestingly, this passed as the parent *Customer* row, rather than the *CustomerId* foreign *long* value. The remaining parameters supply values for the new order's *ShipVia*, *OrderStatus*, *Notes*, *CreatedAt*, and *UpdatedAt* columns. The typed *DataRow* requires values for *CreatedAt* and *UpdatedAt*, which are supplied as *DateTime.Now* (based on the application's clock). If there were CRUD stored procedures for *OrderHeader* as there are for *Customer*, the insert and update stored procedures would be using *SYSDATETIME* (based on SQL Server's clock) for these columns, ignoring and then replacing the values set in the *DataRow*.

Now imagine that the user clicks Save and the *DataSet* gets serialized back down across the tiers to the data access layer so that its changes can be pushed back to the database. This time, the *TableAdapterManager* is used, and this handles all the concerns of hierarchical updates when dealing with compositional object graphs of related entities. If you have referential integrity constraints on the relationships in the database tables (and we strongly recommend that you do) that aren't enabled for cascading deletes (and we strongly recommend that they aren't), a two-phase approach needs to be taken when persisting insertions and deletions from the *DataSet* back to the database. In particular, new parent rows need to be *INSERT*ed before new child rows are, whereas removed child rows need to be *DELETE*ed before removed parent rows. Prior to .NET 3.5, you needed to code this logic yourself using individual *DataAdapters* (or *TableAdapters*). But the *TableAdapterManager* removes all that pain. As the code demonstrates, you simply create an instance of a new *TableAdapterManager* and provide it with a new *TableAdapter* instance for each table involved in the update. With a single call to the *UpdateAll* method, the *TableAdapterManager* updates both tables inside a transaction, automatically reversing the order of insertions and deletions between parent and child tables as necessary. Run the code and watch the SQL Profiler trace as it executes.

You've now learned the most important techniques for using conventional ADO.NET with SQL Server. Despite how old conventional ADO.NET is compared with LINQ to SQL or Entity Framework, these newer technologies (which are very different than *DataSets*) are based on many of the same principles that have proven so successful with typed *DataSets*—namely the use of a designer to author an XML document representing your data model, combined with a code generator to produce typed entities for your applications to work with programmatically. So the firm grasp you now have on these concepts will make learning the newer technologies much easier. You'll start by entering the world of LINQ.

Language-Integrated Query (LINQ)

The expressiveness and flexibility of language-integrated query (LINQ), first introduced with .NET 3.5, brought radical change to the way developers program in C# and Visual Basic (VB) .NET. That's a bold statement, but don't misinterpret it to mean that LINQ is always the answer. There are many implementations of LINQ, and we will soon be examining many factors that you need to consider before determining which ones are the right (or wrong) choices for your application. But all LINQ implementations ultimately rest on top of LINQ to Objects, and LINQ to Objects is *always* the right choice when working with objects. This means that—at the very least—you should be using LINQ instead of writing loops wherever possible to query lists, collections, and arrays in your .NET application. You will enjoy producing tighter, more elegant code that expresses what you want to do, not how to do it.

> **Note** LINQ is a huge topic, and this is a book on SQL Server, not LINQ. We demonstrate only a fraction of the real power of LINQ in our examples, and focus instead on how different LINQ implementations can be made to work with data in SQL Server. For a detailed and concise treatment of LINQ, we recommend the *LINQ Pocket Reference* (O'Reilly) by Joseph Albahari and Ben Albahari.

In T-SQL, you work with set-based operations. It would be absurd to implement a query in T-SQL by coding a cursor that scans a table, loops through it one row at a time, and examines each row for some criteria. That's what *SELECT/WHERE* is for! Yet before LINQ, that's exactly what developers had been doing with object arrays and collections. How many times have you coded a loop that scans some enumerable sequence of objects? You could be filtering for a subset, calculating an aggregation, or perhaps you just need to determine if a particular item is present in a collection. LINQ was designed to eliminate all such looping constructs from your code. You might still code a *foreach* loop to process the results of a LINQ query, but the LINQ query itself is coded as a single statement rather than a procedural loop, just like set-based operations in the database world.

So although you should always use LINQ to Objects to query in-memory object sequences, other LINQ implementations need to be evaluated individually. When making your determination, the first thing to consider is whether you are querying directly over memory-resident data structures or external data stores. Besides "ordinary" objects queried with LINQ to Objects, memory-resident data structures include cached XML documents (the *XDocument* object, which can be queried with LINQ to XML) or—more relevant to this chapter—populated *DataSets* (queried with LINQ to DataSet). To work with in-memory data structures such as these, again, you'll always want to use a specialized LINQ implementation (if available) over the more traditional, procedural approaches. Because the source data resides locally in memory, your LINQ query will be able to call into any .NET method in the framework or your application.

Then there are the other LINQ implementations designed to query external data stores. These LINQ providers dynamically, at runtime, form an expression tree from your LINQ query to generate a query in *another* language (such as T-SQL) that will then execute against an external data store (such as SQL Server).

This is the case with both LINQ to SQL and Entity Framework. So now you seriously need to question the wisdom of writing a query in one language (LINQ) only to have it translated into another language (T-SQL). If you are already well versed in T-SQL, you may feel that you can produce better T-SQL code than the LINQ runtime. Conversely, this is a very appealing approach when T-SQL skills are lacking. Regardless, it's important to understand that such LINQ queries can only call methods in the .NET Framework that have a compatible equivalent in T-SQL (for example, the way *StartsWith* can be implemented using *LIKE*), and that you obviously won't be calling methods in your own application because they don't exist in SQL Server. We'll be examining LINQ to SQL and Entity Framework a bit further on, but you'll start your first LINQ exercise by extending the previous examples to work with LINQ to DataSet.

LINQ to DataSet

To reiterate, LINQ to DataSet operates on a memory-resident *DataSet* that is already populated. This means that you continue to use conventional ADO.NET to fill the *DataSet*. Then once you've filled the *DataSet*, you use LINQ to DataSet to further query over the data retrieved from the database.

Here is an example of a LINQ to DataSet query:

```
var list =
 (from cust in ds.Customer
  where !cust.LastName.StartsWith("A")
  select cust).ToList();
```

Now how do you *know* this is a LINQ to DataSet query, and not LINQ to something else? Well, that's part of the idea behind LINQ. What you're LINQ-ing to is not supposed to be immediately obvious, the advantage being that all LINQ queries kind of look the same regardless of the underlying data source. So you want to zone in on what follows the *in* clause; that's what tells you which LINQ implementation is being used. In this example, the *in* clause is followed by a *DataTable* in a typed *DataSet*, so this is LINQ to DataSet. This query builds a list of customers whose last names don't begin with the letter A, and is equivalent to the following code that you might have written before LINQ to achieve the same thing:

```
var list = new List<Customer>();
foreach (SampleDS.CustomerRow cust in ds.Currency)
{
  if (!cust.LastName.StartsWith("A"))
  {
    list.Add(currencyCode);
  }
}
```

If you're already familiar with *DataSets*, you probably know that even before LINQ, the *RowFilter* property of the *DataView* object could have been used to achieve the very same thing, like so:

```
var dv = new DataView(ds.Customer);
dv.RowFilter = "Customer NOT LIKE 'A*'";
```

True, the query is expressed in a single statement. But there are two problems with this approach. First, the *RowFilter* property is a *string* property. Even though it is being used to filter the strongly typed *Customer* table, misspelling *Customer* in the query (or any other typo) will not get caught by the compiler. Second, ask yourself what query language is being used here, because it is most certainly *not* T-SQL. Remember that you've already hit the database to fill the *Customer* table from SQL Server. Indeed, this couldn't be T-SQL because the *LIKE* operator in T-SQL uses the percent symbol (%) and not the asterisk (*) symbol to denote a wildcard match. So what syntax is this? As it turns out, it's a mini-query language understood only by the *RowFilter* property of the *DataView* object, and a prime example of why LINQ was invented. With LINQ, you don't need to start learning different query languages (some more obscure than others) for different data sources. If you use LINQ to DataSet, then you don't need to learn this *RowFilter* language to query *DataSets*; if you use LINQ to XML, then you don't need to learn XPath to query XML documents; that's the idea. And yes, with LINQ to SQL and Entity Framework, you don't have to (necessarily) learn T-SQL to query SQL Server! You just query everything with LINQ.

Querying a Generic *DataSet*

LINQ to DataSet is easy to use, and works both with generic *DataSets* and typed *DataSets*. This first example will use a generic *DataSet*. So drag another button control from the Toolbox and drop it onto the form. In the Properties window, name the button **btnLinqToGenericDataSet**, and set the Text property to **LINQ to Generic DataSet**. Then double-click the button and add the code in Listing 10-12.

LISTING 10-12 Querying a generic *DataSet* with LINQ to DataSet.

```
private void btnLinqToGenericDataSet_Click(object sender, EventArgs e)
{
  const string ConnStr =
    "Data Source=localhost;Initial Catalog=SampleDb;Integrated Security=true;";

  const string SelectTSql = "SELECT * FROM Customer";

  var ds = new DataSet();

  using (var cn = new SqlConnection())
  {
    cn.ConnectionString = ConnStr;
    using (var cm = new SqlCommand())
    {
      cm.Connection = cn;
      cm.CommandText = SelectTSql;

      using (var da = new SqlDataAdapter())
      {
        da.SelectCommand = cm;
        da.Fill(ds);
      }
    }
  }

  var query =
    from cust in ds.Tables[0].AsEnumerable()
```

```
    where !cust.Field<string>("LastName").StartsWith("A")
    orderby cust.Field<string>("LastName") descending
    select cust;

  var dv = query.AsDataView();

  MessageBox.Show(string.Format(
    "Filtered {0} of {1} customers", dv.Count, ds.Tables[0].Rows.Count));
}
```

None of the code in this listing before the LINQ query requires any explanation. That's because, as we've said, you're still hitting the database using conventional ADO.NET just like you did in Listing 10-10. In this example, you've retrieved all the customers into a generic *DataSet*, and now you're using LINQ to DataSet to query the result set by filtering out all customers whose last name starts with A. Let's examine this LINQ to DataSet query up close.

Although the *DataTable* does have a *Rows* collection property that could theoretically be queried using LINQ to Objects, there is a special .NET assembly for LINQ to DataSet that supplies a few extension methods designed specifically for using LINQ against cached *DataSets*.

More Info Visual Studio automatically set a reference to this assembly when you created the project. The assembly is named *System.Data.DataSetExtensions.dll*, and you will see it listed under the *References* node in Solution Explorer. Because the extension methods in this assembly are all defined in the *System.Data* namespace, you don't need to add any special *using* directive to the top of the source file to make them recognizable.

The key extension method in LINQ to DataSet is *AsEnumerable*, which you invoke on the *DataTable*. LINQ operates over any object that implements *IEnumerable*, but the *DataTable* object does not implement *IEnumerable* (the table itself is not a collection). With LINQ to DataSet, you query the *DataTable* itself, not its *Rows* collection, and so you call *AsEnumerable* on the *DataTable* to LINQ-enable it. The rest is an ordinary LINQ query that scans the *DataTable*, filtering and sorting on *LastName*.

Note This is the first of several examples that filter customers by last names not beginning with the letter A. To get conclusive results as you walk through these examples, you should have at least one customer in the database with a last name that starts with the letter A. If you've not given any of the customers from earlier examples a last name that starts with A, go ahead and add another customer now with a last name beginning with A so you can test that the filtering logic works as expected.

You're also using the *Field<T>* extension method to extract the *LastName* value from each *DataRow* being scanned by the query. This method makes working with generic *DataSets* a little bit easier by saving you the need to cast between *object* and specific data types when referencing columns in a generic *DataRow*. Because the *LastName* column is a *string* type, you use *Field<string>* to obtain its value as a *string* in the *where* and *orderby* clauses without having to directly cast it.

So now you've defined the LINQ query and assigned it to the query variable, which is declared using *var*. Just like the input sequences they consume, LINQ queries always return an *IEnumerable* of *something*; and with LINQ to DataSet in particular, that will be some specialized class that implements *IEnumerable<DataRow>* defined in the extensions assembly. But you will typically not need to know or care exactly which class that is, and so *var* is a convenient way of telling the compiler to infer the actual return type from the context of the LINQ query. All you really care about is the fact that it returns an *IEnumerable<DataRow>* object, meaning that the results can be retrieved as a sequence of *DataRows*.

Finally, there are two more extension methods that are unique to LINQ to DataSet, and those are *AsDataView* and *CopyToDataTable*. In this example, you are using *AsDataView* to execute the query and return the results in an ordinary *DataView* (just as if you used an old-fashioned *RowFilter*). The *DataView* contains the filtered results, and holds live *DataRow* instances tied to the underlying *DataTable*. Changes made to the *DataView* are reflected in the *DataSet* and will get pushed back to the database when you update the *DataSet* with a *DataAdapter*. The *CopyToDataTable* method is similar to *AsDataView*, but it makes a copy of the results in a new *DataTable* instead of returning live references in a *DataView*. This is useful when you need to clone the results so that they exist independently of the source *DataTable* in the *DataSet*.

Querying a Strongly Typed *DataSet*

LINQ to DataSet is even easier to use with typed *DataSets*. The next example will perform the same function as the last one, only this time using a typed *DataSet*. Drag another button control from the Toolbox and drop it onto the form. In the Properties window, name the button **btnLinqToTypedDataSet**, and set the Text property to **LINQ to Strongly Typed DataSet**. Then double-click the button and add the code in Listing 10-13.

LISTING 10-13 Querying a strongly typed *DataSet* with LINQ to DataSet.

```
private void btnLinqToTypedDataSet_Click(object sender, EventArgs e)
{
  var ds = new SampleDS();
  using (var da = new SampleDSTableAdapters.CustomerTableAdapter())
  {
    da.Fill(ds.Customer);
  }

  var query =
    from cust in ds.Customer
    where !cust.LastName.StartsWith("A")
    orderby cust.LastName descending
    select cust;

  var dv = query.AsDataView();
```

```
    MessageBox.Show(string.Format(
      "Filtered {0} of {1} customers", dv.Count, ds.Customer.Count));
  }
```

Again, the code to fill the *Customer* table works the same as the earlier typed *DataSet* example in Listing 10-11. And the LINQ query that follows also works the same as the previous LINQ to generic DataSet example in Listing 10-12. But this version of the LINQ query is even neater and tighter. Notice that there are no string literals at all (other than the parameter passed to *StartsWith*); column names are strongly typed and there's no need for any casting to and from *object*, either explicitly or using the *Field<T>* method. Also, because one of the base classes (called *TypedTableBase<T>*) between the strongly typed *Customer* table and the underlying *DataTable* implements *IEnumerable<T>*, you don't need to use the *AsEnumerable* method either. Once again, you see that typed *DataSets* offer numerous advantages over generic *DataSets*.

Let's venture forward now into the next generation of .NET data access APIs. Armed with the techniques and concepts we've covered thus far, grasping them all will be easier than you imagine.

Object Relational Modeling (ORM) Comes to .NET

There is no doubt that *DataSets* have served programmers well over the years. And if what you need is an in-memory database object model, or a generic data container, they still remain useful today. The *DataSet* also has many features to make it "work" like a business object. You've seen how a typed *DataSet* supplies properties for the *Customer* table similar to how you'd code the properties a *Customer* entity class yourself. And because you can embed your own business logic and validations directly into a typed *DataSet* by leveraging partial classes, *DataSets* can deliver many of the same encapsulation benefits that object-oriented designs offer when working with pure business entities.

But close is not close enough. Though the *DataSet* functions as an excellent data transfer object, the fact is that *DataSets* are not true business objects. The *DataSet* paradigm of tables, columns, and relationships does not always translate well to the object-oriented ideas of classes, properties, and collections. A row in the typed *DataSet's Customer* table is just that—a *DataRow*, with columns—and not really a conventional business entity object with its own ordinary properties, methods, and events. Because it inherits from *DataRow*, it can't also inherit from a base class of your own, nor is it possible to have one table type inherit from another. Furthermore, the manner in which parent-child hierarchies of a *DataSet* are navigated via relationships and specialized code-generated methods is unintuitive to object-oriented programmers in .NET who think of "regular" objects in simpler terms. A parent entity has a property that holds a collection of child entities, and each child entity has a property that refers back to its parent. Manipulating hierarchies in a *DataSet* is quite different, and somewhat more cumbersome.

Serious object-oriented programmers demand that their business entity classes leverage inheritance, polymorphism, and design patterns. Furthermore, they insist that the middle tier remains free of dependencies on any particular technology. The philosophy is that data access and presentation layer technologies will come and go, but business logic in the middle tier—written in entity classes (such as the quintessential *public class Customer*)—is built to last. The term "plain old CLR object" (POCO) is used to refer to such business classes that are designed to be insulated from orbiting platform changes. Investments in middle-tier development are thus better protected, and business logic code survives even as new technologies replace old ones in other layers of the application. These concerns (among other factors) have driven the development of Object Relational Mapping (ORM) technologies, such as LINQ to SQL and Entity Framework, which enable you to build data access layers much more aligned with object-oriented principles than *DataSets*.

Defining ORM

Business entities are represented as *objects* at the application level and as *relational* data in the database, and—one way or another—you need to *map* the two in your application. The key words italicized in that sentence define Object Relational Mapping, or ORM. Take the simplest cases where you write the code yourself to shuttle values, one at a time, between a *SqlDataReader* or a *DataRow* and the properties of an object. Such code is mapping relational data to objects, and so there's your ORM.

Typically though, the term *ORM* refers to robust frameworks designed specifically to eliminate this manual labor by automating the process in some way. Less time and effort expended on the mundane intricacies of CRUD operations between SQL Server and your objects means more time and resources available to focus on more important and creative things, like core business logic, application features, and user interface design. Both LINQ to SQL and Entity Framework (as well as other non-Microsoft ORM technologies, such as the open-source NHibernate library) completely abstract the persistence details between business entities and the database away from you. But ORM abstraction can be raised much higher than this.

One generally associates tables, columns, and relationships in the database with classes, properties, and collections in the application, and this simplistic view might be adequate for some basic applications. But in most real-world scenarios, you encounter the so-called *impedance mismatch* problem, where there isn't always a one-to-one correspondence between relational tables in the database and business objects in the application. Beyond merely handling persistence details, more advanced ORMs (such as Entity Framework, but notably not LINQ to SQL) provide rich abstractions over the data model itself that can automatically resolve many impedance mismatch scenarios.

A common example is the many-to-many relationship between two tables, implemented in the database with a third junction table. The junction table holds foreign keys that relate entities in the other two tables to one another, supporting the many-to-many relationship. The sample database does this with the *CustomerEmployee* junction table between *Customer* and *Employee*. That's three tables in the database physically, but only two objects conceptually. In the application, you only work with *Customer* and *Employee* objects. Each of those objects has a collection property that holds multiple object instances of the other type, which establishes the many-to-many relationship at the application level. Entity Framework automatically manages the *CustomerEmployee* junction table behind the scenes, so that your application is concerned only with the two logical entities *Customer* and *Employee*. You'll see this in action a bit further on with an example, and we will also talk about other impedance mismatch scenarios that Entity Framework can handle.

Multiple ORM Offerings from Redmond

Both LINQ to SQL and Entity Framework were designed to give developers something better than conventional ADO.NET, where you can build a data access layer based on much more ordinary objects than a *DataSet*. These ORM technologies raise the level of abstraction above the raw ADO.NET classes even more than *DataSets* and *DataAdapters*. As the examples will show, you no longer interact with *SqlConnection* and *SqlCommand* objects at all. Instead, you will use a special *context* object that acts as a controller for querying and updating data between SQL Server and objects (true ordinary objects; not "row" objects) in your application.

Despite these (and other) important differences with conventional ADO.NET, the two ORM technologies deliver a Visual Studio developer experience that is strikingly similar to that of typed *DataSets*. LINQ to SQL and Entity Framework each sport a graphical designer that's used as a front-end to author XML markup (in dialects other than XSD), which in turn drives .NET code generation of strongly typed objects. With the knowledge you already have of building typed *DataSets* in Visual Studio, the LINQ to SQL and Entity Framework modeling tools will seem very familiar and intuitive. That's the good news. The availability of two technologies so overlapping in purpose is the bad news, and requires some explaining.

LINQ to SQL: Then and Now

LINQ to SQL was released in 2007 as part of .NET 3.5. With LINQ to SQL, you write LINQ queries in your .NET application that get translated into T-SQL queries dynamically at runtime. LINQ to SQL provides a *DataContext* object that you use as the source of your LINQ queries, providing functionality similar to the way a *DataAdapter* fills a *DataSet*. The *DataContext* also tracks any changes made to all objects returned from the query results. You can then instruct the *DataContext* to send the appropriate insert, update, and delete commands back to SQL Server, much like the way a *DataAdapter* updates a *DataSet*. Here's a simple example of a LINQ to SQL query:

```
using (var ctx = new SampleL2SDataContext())
{
  var q =
    from customer in ctx.Customers
    where !customer.LastName.StartsWith("A")
    orderby customer.LastName descending
    select customer;

  var list = q.ToList();
```

```
  MessageBox.Show(string.Format("Non-A customer count: {0}", list.Count));
}
```

At runtime, LINQ to SQL will parse this query into an expression tree and generate a T-SQL query for SQL Server to execute. The LINQ to SQL runtime implements the functionality of the .NET *StartsWith* method in T-SQL by appending the percent sign (%) wildcard symbol to a parameterized value for the *LIKE* operator:

```
exec sp_executesql N'SELECT [t0].[CustomerId], [t0].[FirstName], [t0].[LastName], [t0].
[Balance], [t0].[CreatedAt], [t0].[UpdatedAt]
FROM [dbo].[Customer] AS [t0]
WHERE NOT ([t0].[LastName] LIKE @p0)
ORDER BY [t0].[LastName] DESC',N'@p0 varchar(8000)',@p0='A%'
```

LINQ to SQL evolved from the original LINQ project, and was created by the language development team at Microsoft as an abstraction layer that provides a simple, one-to-one mapping between objects in your application and database tables in SQL Server. The Entity Framework, first released in 2008 as part of .NET 3.5 SP1, was a project of the data programmability team not related to LINQ. It is substantially more advanced and provides many more capabilities than LINQ to SQL. The EF team focused on the Entity Data Model (EDM) and created Entity SQL as the native language for querying the EDM (you'll soon work hands-on with the EDM and Entity SQL). With the advent of LINQ, however, it was natural (almost compulsory) for the team to also provide LINQ to Entities as a strongly typed way of querying the EDM, so that learning Entity Framework doesn't (necessarily) require learning Entity SQL.

Like typed *DataSets*, both LINQ to SQL and EF deliver a design-time experience in Visual Studio for building an object model around the database and auto-generating typed classes based on the model. In code, EF also provides an *ObjectContext* object that works similarly to the LINQ to SQL's *DataContext*. And with LINQ to Entities available as an alternative to Entity SQL, both technologies can use LINQ to query the database mapped to the object model. It was becoming obvious that Microsoft had two competing .NET data access methodologies that targeted the same scenarios, yet they were offering little or no guidance over which one to use. Developers became more confused, and eventually one of these technologies had to emerge as the victor.

Not surprisingly, Entity Framework won and LINQ to SQL lost. Microsoft has finally made its vision clear, and (as of the second version of EF released with .NET 4 in 2010) recommends the Entity Framework over LINQ to SQL as the data access solution for LINQ to relational scenarios.

More Info A post on the ADO.NET team blog explains Microsoft's position on the future of Entity Framework and LINQ to SQL. You can read it at *http://blogs.msdn.com/b/adonet/archive/2008/10/29/update-on-linq-to-sql-and-linq-to-entities-roadmap.aspx.*

So what does this mean for LINQ to SQL?

As far is this book is concerned, it means that our LINQ to SQL coverage is limited to the guidance in this section. You should not consider LINQ to SQL for any new development, and it wasn't around long enough before being eclipsed by EF for it to have gained very much of a stronghold (though it has definitely won quite a number of fans). For a long time still, you will encounter mostly *DataSet* code and relatively little LINQ to SQL in maintaining existing production applications. Our earlier coverage on conventional ADO.NET prepares you for that. But because EF is recommended over LINQ to SQL for new applications, we have made the decision not to dig into LINQ to SQL and to focus instead on Entity Framework development.

For Microsoft, getting their message out has not been easy. It was a tough sell to recommend the first version of Entity Framework (EF1) over LINQ to SQL, because the former lacked many important capabilities offered by the latter. This resulted in an opposition group that banded together and posted a "vote of no confidence" in the new technology, dismissing it as incomplete and citing a litany of complaints against it. At the top of the list was the lack of support for lazy loading (also known as on-demand loading, where child entities are loaded automatically as needed) and POCOs (where it isn't necessary for entities to inherit from, and thus be tied to, any base class). EF1 did not support lazy loading, and although it did support inheritance, entity classes were still forced to derive from *EntityObject*. LINQ to SQL supported lazy loading and POCO support from the beginning. EF1 was also sharply criticized for doing a poor job of dynamically generating T-SQL queries translated from your LINQ queries at runtime. It was painfully obvious that Entity Framework was released before it was ready, and that it definitely needed to catch up with LINQ to SQL. In its initial form, there was no way for Microsoft to even hope for widespread adoption of Entity Framework.

Fortunately, the second version of the ADO.NET Entity Framework (which was released with the .NET Framework 4.0 in 2010, and is actually referred to as EF4) represents a major improvement over the first release. EF4 supports lazy loading, and there are now several ways to use POCOs so that it is no longer necessary to inherit from *EntityObject*. Improvements were made in dynamic T-SQL code generation as well, and EF4 will usually generate T-SQL that's as good as (if not better than) what you might code by hand. Many other criticisms were addressed, and new features were added as well. Microsoft really listened this time, and they deserve a lot of credit for the work they did with its vastly matured second release, so we will overlook the fact that, officially, there was no EF2 or EF3.

LINQ to SQL is relatively far more impaired when you compare it with EF4. LINQ to SQL can only be used with SQL Server, but EF4 works with any database platform that has a compatible ADO.NET provider. LINQ is the only way to query with LINQ to SQL (limiting its use to C# and VB .NET), whereas while EF offers LINQ as a strongly typed alternative to the more powerful Entity SQL (which can be used with any .NET language). LINQ to SQL supports only a one-to-one correspondence between the relational table structure and your object model, and thus will not resolve many of the impedance mismatch scenarios that EF can with its EDM. You can also detach and attach entities to the *ObjectContext* in EF4, enabling practical n-tier development that was impossible with EF1 (as well as LINQ to SQL).

Although it's been a rough road (and there is still more room for improvement), the turning point has definitely been reached where you can accept Entity Framework seriously as Microsoft's data access strategy of choice. Although LINQ to SQL will not evolve, it is not deprecated either. LINQ to SQL remains part of the .NET Framework. It is relatively straightforward to migrate from LINQ to SQL to Entity Framework if you have good reasons to do so, but it isn't necessary otherwise. Migration makes more sense if the application is being extended with functionality that could benefit from features available only in EF. Fortunately, the migration path is fairly straightforward, as you are moving toward a wider feature set where pretty much every LINQ to SQL concept has an EF equivalent.

Note In Chapter 13, you build a Windows Phone 7 application that accesses local device storage in SQL Server Compact edition (CE) using LINQ to SQL. This represents an exception to the general rule of avoidance that we just advocated, and is the one scenario in which LINQ to SQL is not only appropriate but preferred. Specifically, LINQ to SQL can and should be used *client-side* to access against the (single-user) local SQL Server CE database running on a Windows Phone 7 device—which is very different than accessing a full SQL Server 2012 or SQL Azure instance running in a data center. As you will see in Chapter 13, the phone application also includes a service component that synchronizes local data on the phone with a SQL Azure database running in the cloud, and this service component uses WCF Data Services with the Entity Framework—not LINQ to SQL—to access the SQL Azure database.

Entity Framework: Now and in the Future

With all of the earlier technologies and guidance discussed to this point, you are now primed and ready to dive into Entity Framework, Microsoft's recommended data access solution now and for the future. The very first thing you need to learn about is the Entity Data Model (EDM), which lies at the heart of Entity Framework.

Building an Entity Data Model (EDM)

There are three parts to the EDM. First there is the *storage schema*, which is a thorough description of how tables, columns, and relationships are physically arranged in the database. Then there is the *conceptual schema*, which describes the classes, properties, and navigation paths of business entities in the application. Finally, you have the *mapping schema*, which defines how the storage and conceptual schemas relate to one another. These three pieces (collectively called the model's *metadata*) are self-contained in a single *.edmx* file inside your project. You author the *.edmx* file in Visual Studio using a graphical designer similar to the one used to build an XSD-based typed *DataSet* earlier in the chapter—with one critical difference: *the EDM design surface only displays the conceptual schema.*

And therein is the crux of programming against the Entity Framework. Your application works only with objects defined in the conceptual schema as it appears in the designer, and has no awareness of the underlying database structure defined in the storage schema. You'll soon use the Model Browser and various other panels in Visual Studio to view and configure the storage schema and mappings at design time. Then at runtime, it is the Entity Framework's job to retrieve and persist data between your application and SQL Server, and to resolve the differences between storage and conceptual models automatically and dynamically using the mapping schema. Thus, all three schemas need to be present and available to the application while it's running.

By default, Visual Studio embeds the three schemas as resources within the application to guarantee that they are always available. You can also keep the schema definitions *outside* your application's assembly, so they can be edited independently without requiring you to recompile and redeploy. Because the mapping layer effectively serves as a buffer between SQL Server and your application, it serves as insulation from database changes that are made in the future. For example, if a column name is changed, you can keep the old name in the conceptual schema by making the change only in the storage schema of the EDM, and then adjust the mapping schema accordingly. Your application can continue running unaffected with the unaltered conceptual schema.

If you have a one-to-one correspondence between every table in the database and every class in the business object model, then both the storage and conceptual schemas will match exactly, and the mapping schema simply connects them up one-to-one. That is nothing different than what you get with LINQ to SQL or typed *DataSets*, and the true power of the EDM isn't really being tapped. But real-world applications rarely have storage and conceptual schemas that match exactly. There is usually some form of *impedance mismatch* that needs to be resolved (see the sidebar "Defining ORM" earlier in the chapter), and the EDM is a powerful tool that can help to resolve it.

Many-to-many relationships are a good example. In the sample database, the *CustomerEmployee* table serves as a junction table for the many-to-many relationship between the *Customer* and *Employee* tables. But this join table is really only an implementation detail of the underlying physical database structure. SQL Server does not inherently support many-to-many relationships, and so you require *CustomerEmployee* to serve as an intermediary table between the *Customer* and *Employee* tables, both of which it has a one-to-many relationship with. In the world of objects, you care only about *Customer* and *Employee*, whose many-to-many relationships are implemented with child collections on each side of each entity instance. Through the EDM, the Entity Framework understands the physical table layout in the storage schema and shields you from it. This makes it easier to code your application, because you stay focused on logical entities and don't get entangled with the physical database details. As you're about to see, EF will automatically join on the junction table for queries, and update the junction table for relationship changes without a *CustomerEmployee* entity in the conceptual schema.

Now that you understand the EDM, you're ready to create one. Launch Visual Studio, create a new Visual C# Windows Forms application, and name it **DemoEntityFramework**. In Solution Explorer, right-click the project and choose Add | New Item. In the Add New Item dialog, scroll down to find and click on *ADO.NET Entity Data Model*. Name the new model **SampleEF.edmx** and click Add. Visual Studio launches the Entity Data Model Wizard so that you can begin building the model. This wizard is your primary tool for creating or updating models from an existing database, which is notably different than the Server Explorer drag-and-drop approach taken by the typed *DataSet* and LINQ to SQL designers. The database is already in place, so choose Generate From Database on the first page of the wizard and click Next.

More Info There will often be an existing database that you can base a new model on using the wizard, as in this scenario. But other design strategies are possible as well. EF also supports *model-first* development, where you start by first building the conceptual model in the Visual Studio designer. This generates Data Definition Language (DDL) statements in a T-SQL script that will create the database from the model. *Code-first* design is another possible strategy introduced with Entity Framework 4.2, where you start out with neither a database nor a model, and just write your entities in plain code. Both the model and database are then derived and generated from your code.

First you set up the connection. If you walked through the earlier typed *DataSet* examples, then the database connection *SampleDb* will still be available in the Server Explorer and the EDM Wizard will select it by default. Other previously used connections will also be available in the drop-down list for you to recall easily, or you can click New Connection to create a new one on the fly from within the wizard.

Tip If you didn't follow along with the typed *DataSet* examples earlier, you'll need to create the connection now. Click New Connection, select Microsoft SQL Server as the data source, and click Continue. In the Add Connection dialog, type **localhost** for the Server name, select *SampleDB* from the database drop-down list, and click OK (you must choose different settings if you have created the database on another server or instance).

The wizard displays the entity connection string, which it bases on the *SampleDb* connection, as shown in Figure 10-12.

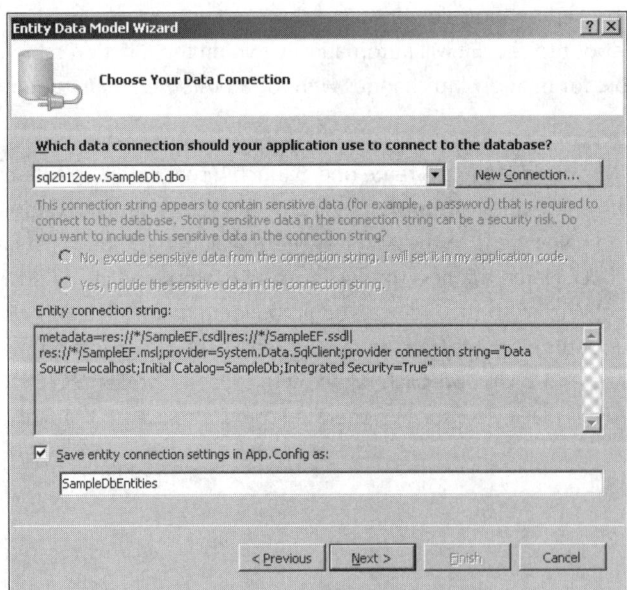

FIGURE 10-12 Setting the connection for an EDM.

Let's explain this connection string:

```
metadata=res://*/SampleEF.csdl|res://*/SampleEF.ssdl|res://*/SampleEF.msl;
provider=System.Data.SqlClient;
provider connection string="Data Source=localhost;Initial Catalog=SampleDb;Integrated
Security=True;"
```

This might look scary at first, but you can easily decipher what it all means from what you've already learned of the Entity Framework. Remember that with the EDM, you code only against the conceptual schema, while Entity Framework figures out how to do all the database work at runtime using the information in the storage and mapping schemas. Therefore, all three distinct schemas must be available at runtime, and so it makes sense that a connection string in EF must point to where they can be found. The *metadata* keyword in the connection string specifies a pipe-delimited list of the three schema files: *SampleEF.csdl* (conceptual schema definition language), *SampleEF.ssdl* (storage schema definition language), and *SampleEF.msl* (mapping schema language). Recall from our earlier discussion that these three files are housed in the single *.edmx* file inside your project at design time, and that they (by default) get embedded as resources in the assembly when you build the solution. The *res://*/* designation tells the EF runtime that the files can be located in the resources of the running assembly (or any referenced assemblies).

The rest of the connection string specifies which particular ADO.NET provider is being used. The *provider* keyword specifies SqlClient, which indicates SQL Server. Remember that EF can be made to work with any database platform that has a compatible ADO.NET Entity Framework provider. The *provider connection string* keyword points to the provider-specific connection string, which for SqlClient is the familiar *SampleDb* database connection string. Thus, an entity connection string always contains references to the three schemas that define the model, plus a "nested" connection string in the syntax of the particular back-end provider being used with the Entity Framework.

Beneath the connection string, the wizard displays an already checked checkbox telling you that the connection string will be saved in the application's configuration file as *SampleDbEntities*. This is just what you want, so click Next.

The wizard now scours the database to discover all the tables, views, and stored procedures that it can pull into the model. There are four tables and a handful more stored procedures, and you will import them all. Click the checkbox next to Tables and the one next to Stored Procedures, as shown in Figure 10-13 on the next page, and then click Finish.

The wizard builds the model, and automatically adds the required reference to *System.Data.Entity* (the Entity Framework assembly) to your project. The model then opens up in the designer, as shown in Figure 10-14.

Are you wondering why you see only three entities when you selected four tables? That's already been answered. The designer shows only the conceptual entities, and the *CustomerEmployee* junction table is not a part of the conceptual model. The wizard detected the role of this table as the physical connection between two logical entities and excluded it from the conceptual schema. *CustomerEmployee* has a presence only in the EDM's mapping and storage schemas.

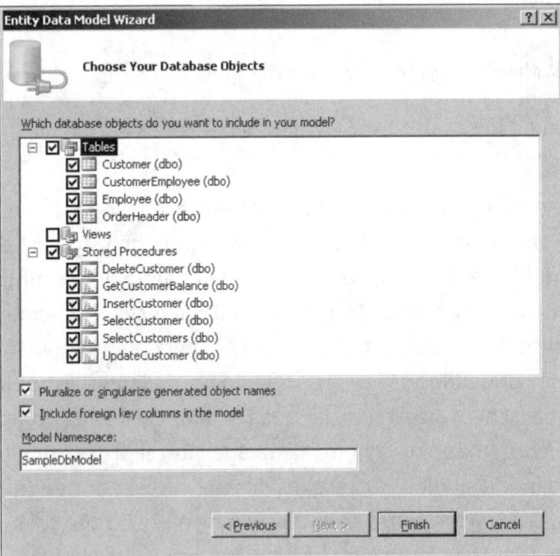

FIGURE 10-13 Selecting database objects to be imported into an EDM.

The Model Browser is one of several windows and panes in Visual Studio that you use to view and configure the storage and mapping schemas. To open it, right-click on an empty area of the design surface and choose Model Browser. In the Model Browser, find and expand the *Entity Types and Tables / Views* nodes. Figure 10-14 shows the Model Browser on the right.

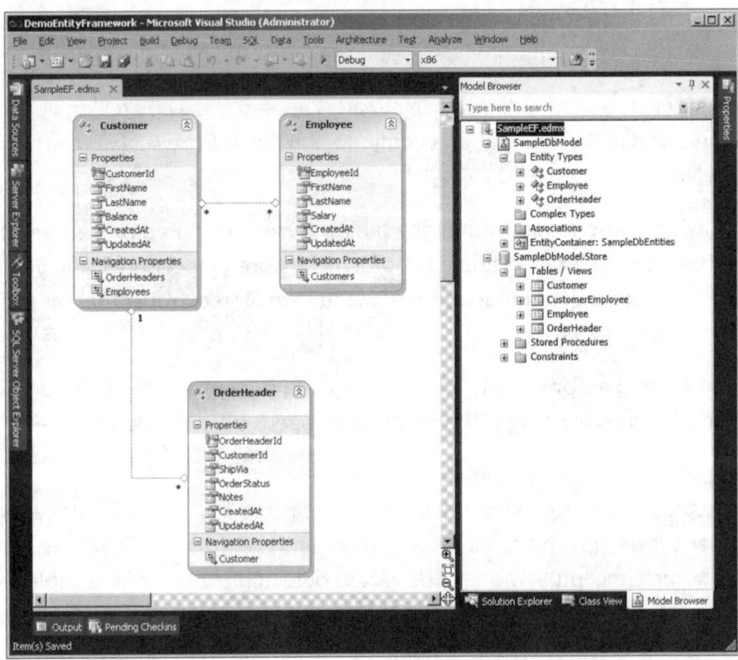

FIGURE 10-14 The entity data model design surface in Visual Studio.

The Model Browser lists *CustomerEmployee* among the four tables in the storage schema, which is denoted by the suffix in *SampleEFModel.Store*. You are going to become fast friends with the Model Browser as you use it to dig into the EDM—much deeper than we will be demonstrating here. Take the time to browse around and get comfortable with all of the elements of the model structure.

More Info Our coverage of Entity Framework in this chapter merely scratches the surface of this powerful API. If you really want to become an EF expert, we recommend reading Julia Lerman's *Programming Entity Framework*, Second Edition (O'Reilly), for an excellent and thorough treatment of the technology.

Notice how the wizard created *associations* between the entities, which it based on table relationships detected in the storage schema. The many-to-many association between *Customer* and *Employee* has an asterisk (*) symbol (indicating multiplicity) on both ends, whereas the association between *Customer* and *OrderHeader* indicates the one-to-many relationship between those two tables. In addition to scalar properties, each entity also has one or more *navigation properties* that are based on its association(s) with other entities. These navigation properties surface as child collection and parent reference properties that your application can use to access related entities in code.

The wizard also singularized or pluralized each navigation property appropriately. For example, look at the one-to-many relationship between *Customer* and *OrderHeader*. Each *Customer* entity has an *OrderHeaders* property (plural) that holds a collection of *OrderHeader* (singular) entities. Conversely, each *OrderHeader* entity has a *Customer* property (singular) that points back to its parent entity. Similarly, *Customer* and *Employee* each have pluralized navigation collection properties of each other (*Customer* has *Employees*, and *Employee* has *Customers*), because those entities are joined in a many-to-many relationship. This is just the way an object-oriented programmer expects the world to be, and is a great deal easier to work with in code than the *DataSet* when navigating between related entities.

As with typed *DataSets*, the EDM designer acts as a front end that you use to author an XML document transparently in the background. But instead of using the XSD format, this dialect of XML represents the metadata for the three schemas of the EDM. And rather than triggering the generation of typed *DataSet* and *TableAdapter* classes from the XML, typed entity and *ObjectContext* classes are generated instead. Most of the time, the designer will shield you from the details of the underlying XML and the code that it generates, but it definitely pays to become familiar with them if you really want to gain a solid understand of EF. So before writing the code for your first Entity Framework example, let's quickly look over the two files.

Right-click *SampleEF.edmx* in the Solution Explorer and choose Open With. Select XML (Text) Editor and click OK to view the file as raw XML. Visual Studio will prompt you first to close the model open in the designer before opening the raw XML (which *is* the very XML that you are composing as you build your entity model in the designer). Scroll through the file, and you will find an XML representation of everything you've done using the designer. If you collapse the nodes beneath <edmx:Runtime>, you will see the high-level view of the three sections for the conceptual, storage, and mapping schemas. As explained, this is the metadata that is required at runtime and gets embedded as a resource in the project's assembly when you build the solution. After the metadata, you will see the <Designer> section, which is used only by Visual Studio at design time. This is where the designer saves information about the layout of shapes (size, position, and so on) in the model diagram. Layout information is ignored by the runtime, and you can ignore it now as well. When you build your application, the <Designer> section is not included with the metadata that gets embedded as an assembly resource.

Next, expand the *SampleEF.edmx* file in the Solution Explorer to reveal the *SampleEF.Designer.cs* file nested beneath it. Double-click it to open the C# code, which is generated automatically whenever the *.edmx* file is updated. The code is organized in regions, so start by expanding the Entities region. You will find three classes for the three entities: *Customer*, *Employee*, and *OrderHeader*; and you'll see that they all inherit from *EntityObject*. This is based on the default code generation strategy which was the only choice available with EF1. With EF4, you can use an alternative code generator based on T4 template technology to produce POCO entities—classes that don't inherit from anything (besides perhaps other classes in the model, if your model defines inheritance). Expand the nested regions further, and you'll find the definitions for each property with change notification logic built into the property setters.

In addition to the entities themselves, the generated code includes a context class for programming queries and updates against the model. Expand the Contexts region (at the top of the source file, just beneath the *namespace* declaration) and you'll see the *SampleDbEntities* class that inherits from *ObjectContext* and functions as the primary access point to your model at runtime. This becomes clearer when you expand the ObjectSet Properties region inside the context class. There you will find all of the *entity sets* exposed by the context (one set for each entity), named in the plural (*Customers*, *Employees*, and *OrderHeaders*). You will conduct LINQ queries against the entity sets exposed by the *SampleDbEntities* context and materialize the results from the database into live object instances. The context will also track any changes you make to the live objects so that the changes can be saved back to the database later.

That's enough exploring behind the scenes. Close the XML document and let's move on to the first EF example using LINQ to Entities.

Using LINQ to Entities

Entity SQL is the native language in Entity Framework for querying the EDM, and later on, we will discuss when or why you'd choose to use it. But for now, start with the easiest way to query entities, which is to use LINQ to Entities.

Drag a button control from the Toolbox and drop it onto the form *Form1* created automatically by Visual Studio. In the Properties window, name the button **btnLinqWithDirectSql**, and set the Text property to **LINQ to Entities Query (Direct SQL)**. Then double-click the button and add the code in Listing 10-14.

LISTING 10-14 Querying an EDM with LINQ to Entities using direct SQL.

```
private void btnLinqWithDirectSql_Click(object sender, EventArgs e)
{
  // Retrieve via direct SQL:
  using (var ctx = new SampleDbEntities())
  {
    // Define, but do not execute, the query (deferred execution)
    //  'q' is of type System.Data.Objects.ObjectQuery<Customer>
    var q =
      from customer in ctx.Customers
      where !customer.LastName.StartsWith("A")
      orderby customer.LastName descending
      select customer;

    // Implicitly execute query on the server, returning List<Customer>
    var list = q.ToList();

    MessageBox.Show(string.Format("Non-A customer count: {0}", list.Count));
  }
}
```

Before running the application, set a breakpoint on the line that declares the *q* variable and assigns it to the LINQ query. Also start a new SQL Profiler trace, if one isn't still running from the earlier examples. Now start the application and click the button. You will hit the breakpoint right before the LINQ query is assigned to *q*. Single-step over the line and switch immediately over to the SQL Profiler trace. You may be surprised to see that no query was sent to SQL Server. This highlights a key principle of LINQ known as *deferred execution*. All you've done is *define* your query and assign it to *q*. There is no magical method that you call to actually *execute* the query; execution is implied, and will automatically kick off anytime you try to access a result from the query. This could happen simply by trying to *foreach* your way through *q*, by binding it to a control in the user interface, or by calling a method like *ToList* on it as you're doing here. Go back to Visual Studio, single-step over the next line, and then switch right back to the trace. Sure enough, you can see the *SELECT* statement that was just sent to SQL Server, transformed from a LINQ to Entities query into native T-SQL:

```
SELECT
[Extent1].[CustomerId] AS [CustomerId],
[Extent1].[FirstName] AS [FirstName],
[Extent1].[LastName] AS [LastName],
[Extent1].[Balance] AS [Balance],
[Extent1].[CreatedAt] AS [CreatedAt],
[Extent1].[UpdatedAt] AS [UpdatedAt]
FROM [dbo].[Customer] AS [Extent1]
WHERE NOT ([Extent1].[LastName] LIKE 'A%')
ORDER BY [Extent1].[LastName] DESC
```

It's critical to realize that executing another *q.ToList*, or any other attempt to "tap" at *q*—for example, even just getting a count with *q.Count*—fires another query execution in SQL Server. Needless round-tripping is obviously something to avoid, so it is imperative for you to remain cognizant of deferred execution in your code. You'll typically want to query the database just once, and then hold onto the results in some cached form such as an array, collection, or dictionary. The *IEnumerable* extension methods *ToArray*, *ToList*, and *ToDictionary* are provided so you can do just that.

The generated SQL may not be pretty, but you can see that the .NET *StartsWith* method in the LINQ query's *where* clause was correctly expressed using the *LIKE* operator in the T-SQL query's *WHERE* clause. Thus, the filtering and sorting occurs in SQL Server, and only the results of interest get returned to your application. EF is quite capable of producing queries that perform at least as well as what you'd code by hand—*most* of the time. You'd never alias the *Customer* table as *Extent1* because *Extent1* is a meaningless word to you, but the alias in no way negatively impacts the query performance. The runtime must be flexible enough to compose queries far more complex than this simple example, and so it will sometimes generate strange syntax that doesn't resemble anything you'd write by hand, but still doesn't *necessarily* represent a performance hit.

Of course there are exceptions, so you definitely need to keep an eye on SQL Profiler to make sure that the EF's dynamically generated queries are reasonable. Enjoying the convenience offered by an abstraction layer does not mean you can be totally ignorant of what's going on beneath the surface. This is true even more as you raise the level of abstraction. With the great power that EF hands you comes the great responsibility of understanding how it operates and being aware of the consequences of your actions, such as how you use deferred execution or lazy loading. In some cases, you might need to refactor a LINQ query to encourage the rutime to generate a better T-SQL query. In other cases, you may determine that it's better to write the T-SQL query yourself inside a parameterized stored procedure, and then use a simple LINQ query that merely calls the stored procedure. That's perfectly fine, because EF doesn't impose an all-or-nothing choice. You can allow EF to generate direct T-SQL from fully expressed LINQ queries, and also maintain total control over T-SQL query syntax when necessary by using stored procedures.

Note If you have strong feelings on the subject of direct SQL and stored procedures, you are not alone. Read the sidebar "Rethinking the Great Direct SQL vs. Stored Procedure Debate" a bit further on in the chapter for a brief discussion on major factors to consider.

Mapping Stored Procedures to the EDM

Even though you imported the set of CRUD stored procedures for the *Customer* table into the model, EF still generated a direct T-SQL dynamically. Importing stored procedures merely defines them in the *storage* schema, but they aren't actually mapped to anything yet. Entity Framework won't know to use imported stored procedures unless you map them to the conceptual schema using the designer, which you'll do next. Stored procedures that retrieve data are mapped as *function imports* using the Model Browser. You will now import a function to map the *SelectCustomers* stored procedure.

Double-click *SampleEF.edmx* in the Solution Explorer to open the model in the designer. If the Model Browser is not already visible, right-click on an empty area of the design surface and choose Model Browser. Beneath *SampleDbModel* in the Model Browser, expand the *EntityContainer: SampleDbEntities* node. Right-click the *Function Imports* node and select Add Function Import, as shown in Figure 10-15.

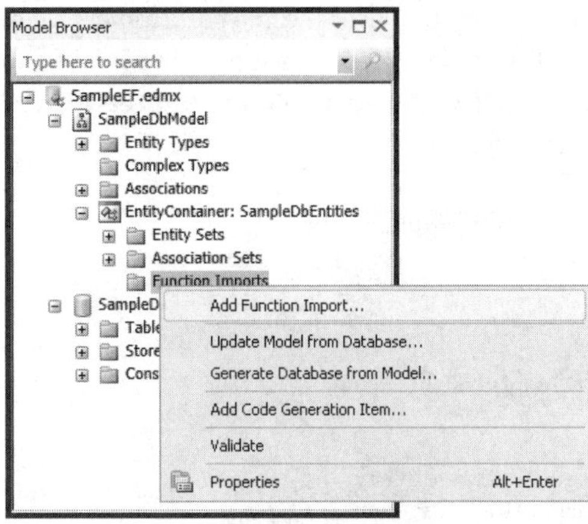

FIGURE 10-15 Importing a function into the conceptual model.

Name the function *SelectCustomers*, after the stored procedure you're mapping the function to (though it certainly doesn't need to match). This is the name that you'll refer to in your next LINQ query so that the stored procedure gets called instead of direct SQL.

Next, choose *SelectCustomers* from the drop-down list of available stored procedures in the storage schema. Finally, because you know that this stored procedure returns the columns for a *Customer* entity, click the Entities radio button beneath Returns A Collection Of, and then select *Customer* from the drop-down list. This tells EF that it can and should return a collection of *Customer* entities when you use the *SelectCustomers* function import in a LINQ query. Figure 10-16 shows the Add Function Import dialog box configured to import *SelectCustomers*.

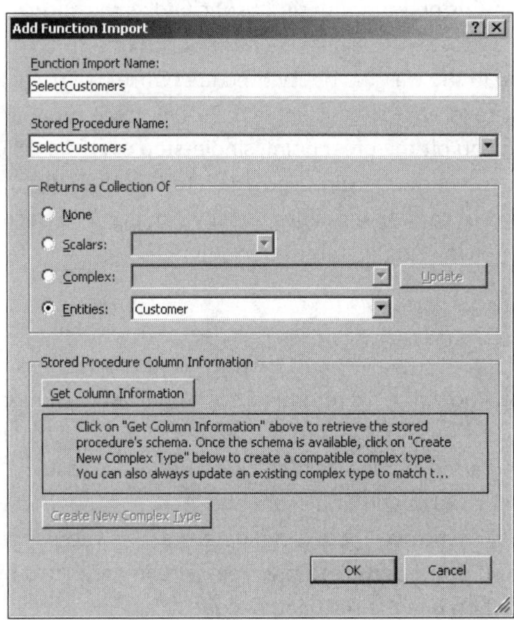

FIGURE 10-16 Mapping a stored procedure that returns a result set to a function that returns an entity collection.

Now write a modified version of the previous LINQ query that uses the *SelectCustomers* function you just mapped. Drag another button control from the Toolbox and drop it onto the form, name it **btnLinqWithStoredProc**, and set the Text property to **LINQ to Entities Query (Stored Procedure)**. Then double-click the button and add the code in Listing 10-15.

LISTING 10-15 Querying an EDM with LINQ to Entities using a stored procedure.

```
private void btnLinqWithStoredProc_Click(object sender, EventArgs e)
{
  // Retrieve via a function import mapped to a stored procedure:
  using (var ctx = new SampleDbEntities())
  {
    // Execute the stored procedure on the server immediately
    //  'q' is of type System.Linq.OrderedEnumerable<Customer>
    var q =
      from customer in ctx.SelectCustomers()
      where !customer.LastName.StartsWith("A")
      orderby customer.LastName descending
      select customer;

    // Filter & sort stored proc results on the client, returning List<Customer>
    var list = q.ToList();

    MessageBox.Show(string.Format("Non-A customer count: {0}", list.Count));
  }
}
```

This LINQ query is virtually identical to the previous one (see Listing 10-14), except that the *SelectCustomers* function import, rather than the *Customers* entity set, is specified as the source of the query after the *in* keyword. Everything else is exactly the same. As you're about to see, however, this small change makes an enormous difference in the way the query executes. Once again, set a breakpoint on the line declaring *q* and make sure you've got a current SQL Profiler trace running. Start the application and click the button. When you hit the breakpoint, single-step over the LINQ query and switch back to the SQL Profiler trace. You might be surprised again to find that, this time, EF calls out to SQL Server immediately on the line of code that defines the LINQ query. The trace shows the stored procedure call being made when you single-step over that line:

```
exec [dbo].[SelectCustomers]
```

But wait. The *SelectCustomers* stored procedure returns *every* customer in the database. You know this—you *wrote* the stored procedure! You know that it's returning everything, so that means that—unlike the previous version—the filtering and sorting operations specified in the LINQ query are being executed on the *client*. This is occurring after sending all the *Customer* rows across the network from SQL Server to your application—even rows you don't care about, even rows that will get thrown away because they don't pass the *where* criteria. There is still deferred execution at play, but it's merely the in-memory filtering and sorting of the complete result set (already returned by SQL Server) that gets deferred until you call *ToList* on *q* in the next line of code.

So it comes down to this: If you LINQ against any of the entity sets in the model, then it will always be deferred execution of direct SQL against the table(s)/view(s) mapped to the entity, and results will be filtered on the server by a dynamically generated *WHERE* clause that's based on the LINQ query's *where* clause. This is a true LINQ to Entities query. But if you LINQ against a function import mapped to a stored procedure instead, then the stored procedure will execute immediately, all of its results will get sent back to the client, where the results will subsequently get filtered by the LINQ query's *where* clause just like an ordinary LINQ to Objects query.

More Info This behavior stems from the fact that tables and views are composable (they can be combined with a parameterized *WHERE* clause in T-SQL) while stored procedures are not. Table-valued functions (TVFs) offer the best of both worlds; they provide the encapsulation benefits of stored procedures yet they are composable like tables and views. Unfortunately, TVFs are not currently supported in EF, though Microsoft has confirmed TVF support for the next major release of the Entity Framework.

This highlights the importance of understanding what goes on under the covers with EF. Once you know what's really happening, you learn how to use (and not misuse) the technology. Thus, if you're pulling in a moderately sized result set from the database with your stored procedure, and then extracting a reasonable subset of that data on the client in the *where* clause, then that's a perfectly acceptable use case. On the other hand, if the stored procedure returns a massive amount of data and the *where* clause in your LINQ query filters the result set on the client down to just a handful of rows, then you know you are doing something wrong.

The *SelectCustomers* stored procedure in this example has no parameters, but you can certainly map parameterized stored procedures to function imports as well. In that case, a *WHERE* clause in the stored procedure can first filter the result set on the server (using parameters passed to it through the function import), and then the *where* clause in the LINQ query can filter the results further on the client. This is quite the same thing as filling a *DataSet* from the database via a parameterized stored procedure and then further filtering on that result set in memory using LINQ to DataSet.

Ultimately, this begs the question "where's the *where*?," and the answer is that it's really up to your own judgement of how to best distribute filtering logic between client and server in a way that makes the most sense for your application.

Rethinking the Great Direct SQL vs. Stored Procedure Debate

Entity Framework (and LINQ to SQL) has good stored procedure support, but is really designed to query the database with direct SQL. Yet many database professionals reject and forbid the use direct SQL, insisting exclusively on the use of stored procedures. So now is a good time to re-visit this heated debate, in which security, performance, and maintainability are the most often cited points of argument.

Security—Direct SQL is vulnerable to SQL injection attacks. But this is true only if you are building T-SQL statements dynamically using string concatenation. Don't forget that even stored procedures are vulnerable in this respect, if they generate direct SQL by concatenating strings and embed content of an unknown and unparsed origin. The primary line of defense against SQL injection attacks it to parameterize the query, which is easily done with direct SQL. As evidenced by observing a SQL Profiler trace, EF generated a parameterized database command that protects against SQL injection.

Performance—This is actually an outdated concern, based on the notion that direct SQL doesn't get compiled like stored procedures do, and so stored procedures therefore run faster. It's true that stored procedures would get partially compiled to speed multiple executions in SQL Server versions 6.5 (released in 1996) and earlier. But as of SQL Server 7.0 (released in 1999), that is no longer the case. Instead, SQL Server 7.0 (and later) compiles and caches the query execution plan to speed multiple executions of the same query (where only parameter values vary), and that's true whether executing a stored procedure or a direct T-SQL statement.

Maintainability—In production applications, it is very poor practice to embed T-SQL directly in .NET code. Doing so tightly couples client and server logic in a way that quickly snowballs into a maintenance nightmare. But this is not the case with LINQ to Entities (or with LINQ to SQL). You are only composing and maintaining the LINQ query in .NET code; the translation to direct T-SQL occurs on the fly at runtime when you execute your application, so this concern simply doesn't apply.

These considerations should change your perspective somewhat. If you're fortunate enough to be in total control over your application's architecture, you can enjoy a good compromise with a hybrid approach. You can allow direct SQL against tables and views for *SELECT* queries only, but continue using stored procedures for *INSERT*, *UPDATE*, and *DELETE* operations. With this strategy, updates at the application level rest on top of a stored procedure layer that can perform critical validations at the database level. You can also consider creating views to expose a limited or altered subset of table data, and then granting *SELECT* access only to the views and not the tables. Then you can map the entities in your data model to the views rather than tables for querying, while updates get persisted back using stored procedures.

So we recommend that you stick to using stored procedures for *INSERT*, *UPDATE*, and *DELETE* operations, while denying direct access to the underlying tables (except for *SELECT*). Doing so allows you to perform additional validation that cannot be bypassed by circumventing the application layer and communicating directly with the database server. At the same time, your LINQ queries will translate "naturally" to direct SQL because *SELECT* permissions are still granted against the table (or view) being queried.

If you're still paused at the breakpoint in the previous example, continue execution now and close the application. It's time to start updating some data with Entity Framework.

Saving Entity Changes

When it comes to update operations, things are much more straightforward. EF will either dynamically generate a direct SQL statement (which is its default behavior) or call a stored procedure (if you've mapped one) for each changed row. Either way, entities get updated one at a time.

Revisit the model and wire up the three stored procedures for saving *Customer* entity changes to the database (they were created at the beginning of the chapter; refer to Listing 10-1 if you need to review them). You will instruct EF *not* to generate direct SQL statements for saving *Customer* entities in the database, but to call these stored procedures instead. Double-click *SampleEF.edmx* in the Solution Explorer to open it in the designer. Then right-click anywhere on the *Customer* entity and choose Stored Procedure Mapping to display the Mapping Details pane (pin it down to keep it in view). Initially, there are no mappings defined, which means that EF dynamically generates direct SQL statements for *INSERT*, *UPDATE*, and *DELETE*. You're now going to change that behavior and map all three stored procedures along with their parameters and return values.

Click <Select Insert Function> and choose the *InsertCustomer* stored procedure from the drop-down list. You need to map each stored procedure parameter to the corresponding entity property, but the designer helps out where it can. Because parameters and columns are consistently named, all of the input parameters required by the stored procedure were correctly mapped. The only additional thing you need to do is map the three values returned by the stored procedure back into the entity in the Result Column Bindings.

Recall (from Listing 10-1) that the *InsertCustomer* stored procedure returns the *CustomerId*, *CreatedAt*, and *UpdatedAt* values—assigned to the new customer row in the database—as scalar values in a single-row result set. With the Result Column Bindings, you can shove those values right back into the client instance and refresh its view of the new entity after the stored procedure executes. Thus, the client doesn't need to retrieve the entire entity after adding it only to obtain these three values. You just need to type the name of each column in the single-row result set and map it to the appropriate property. Click <Add Result Binding> and type **CustomerId**. Add the other two return values the same way, typing their respective names **CreatedAt** and **UpdatedAt**. Unfortunately, the designer offers no help mapping the result bindings, and all three are mapped to the *CustomerId* property by default. This happens to be a correct assumption for the first binding, but the other two bindings need to be changed. Click the Property drop-down list for each of them and select *CreatedAt* and *ModifiedAt*, respectively. You're done with the *Insert* function and can move on to the *Update* function.

Important The ADO.NET Entity Framework 4 supports stored procedures that return scalar values either as output parameters or as a single-row result set, with one glaring exception. The new primary key value assigned by SQL Server can only be sent back to a newly created entity's key using a single-row result set; an output parameter cannot be used. Thus, if the *InsertCustomer* stored procedure was written to return its three server-assigned values (one of them being the newly assigned *CustomerId* primary key value) using output parameters rather than a single-row result set, you could not use Entity Framework to call *InsertCustomer*.

Click <Select Update Function> and choose the *UpdateCustomer* stored procedure from the drop-down list. Once again, all of the same-named parameters and properties get mapped automatically by the designer. The only parameter that doesn't have a matching property is *@OriginalUpdatedAt*. Click the Property drop-down list and select *UpdatedAt* to set the mapping, but *also* check the Use Original Value checkbox. This is an important guarantee that the *UpdatedAt* value originally retrieved from the database is what gets sent back to *UpdateCustomer* in this parameter. Because the context preserves the original values of every property, the designer allows you to map them to any stored procedure parameters you desire.

The *UpdateCustomer* stored procedure raises a concurrency error if another user changes the *UpdatedAt* value between the time that you originally retrieve the customer and the time you attempt to save it back. Passing in the original *UpdatedAt* value in the *@OriginalUpdatedAt* parameter you just mapped allows the stored procedure to perform the check. If the update succeeds normally, *UpdateCustomer* returns the new *UpdatedAt* value that got assigned to the changed customer row in the database as a scalar value in a single-row result set. As with the *Insert* function, you want to bring the updated scalar value for *UpdatedAt* back into the client instance to refresh its view of the modified entity after the stored procedure executes. Click <Add Result Binding> and type **UpdatedAt**. Then click the Property drop-down list to the right and select *UpdatedAt* to map the return value back into the entity. That does it for the *Update* function; the *Delete* function is next and last (and easiest).

Click <Select Delete Function> and choose the *DeleteCustomer* stored procedure from the drop-down list. The one and only *@CustomerId parameter* is automatically mapped to the *CustomerId* property and you're done! Figure 10-17 shows the Mapping Details pane with all three functions mapped to stored procedures.

Mapping Details - Customer

Parameter / Column	Operator	Property	Use Original Value	Rows Affected Parameter
Functions				
Insert Using InsertCustomer				
Parameters				
FirstName : varchar	←	FirstName : String		☐
LastName : varchar	←	LastName : String		☐
Balance : money	←	Balance : Decimal		☐
Result Column Bindings				
CustomerId	→	CustomerId : Int64		
CreatedAt	→	CreatedAt : DateTime		
UpdatedAt	→	UpdatedAt : DateTime		
<Add Result Binding>				
Update Using UpdateCustomer				
Parameters				
CustomerId : bigint	←	CustomerId : Int64	☐	☐
FirstName : varchar	←	FirstName : String	☐	☐
LastName : varchar	←	LastName : String	☐	☐
Balance : money	←	Balance : Decimal	☐	☐
OriginalUpdatedAt : datetime2	←	UpdatedAt : DateTime	☑	☐
Result Column Bindings				
UpdatedAt	→	UpdatedAt : DateTime		
<Add Result Binding>				
Delete Using DeleteCustomer				
Parameters				
CustomerId : bigint	←	CustomerId : Int64		☐

FIGURE 10-17 Mapping three stored procedures for an entity's insert, update, and delete operations.

With all the CRUD stored procedures mapped, you're ready to write some more code. Drag another button control from the Toolbox and drop it onto the form, name it **btnUpdatingData**, and set the Text property to **Updating Data**. Then double-click the button and add the code in Listing 10-16.

LISTING 10-16 Updating an EDM object graph.

```
private void btnUpdatingData_Click(object sender, EventArgs e)
{
  using (var ctx = new SampleDbEntities())
  {
    var customers =
      (from cust in ctx.Customers
       where !cust.LastName.StartsWith("A")
       orderby cust.LastName descending
       select cust).ToList();

    if (customers.Count == 0)
    {
      MessageBox.Show("There are no customers");
      return;
    }

    var firstCustomer = customers[0];
    var orderCount = firstCustomer.OrderHeaders.Count;
    MessageBox.Show(string.Format(
      "Customer {0} has {1} order(s)", firstCustomer.CustomerId, orderCount));

    // Change the customer's name
    firstCustomer.FirstName = "Keith";
    firstCustomer.LastName = "Harris";

    // Add a customer order
    firstCustomer.OrderHeaders.Add(new OrderHeader()
    {
      ShipVia = "Regular Mail",
      OrderStatus = "Open",
    });

    ctx.SaveChanges();
  }
}
```

Set a breakpoint at the top of the method (on the *using* statement that instantiates the new *SampleDbEntities* object). Make sure you've got a SQL Profiler trace running, and then run the application. Click the button and you'll hit the breakpoint. Step over the line to create the context and advance to the next line of code. This time, the LINQ to Entities query is wrapped inside parentheses and *ToList* is called on it all in one line of code. This effectively short-circuits deferred execution, and forces the query to run immediately (and only once). The *ToList* method materializes the query results into *Customer* objects, and returns a populated *List<Customer>* collection in *customers*. When you single-step over the line, the SQL Profiler trace shows that EF generates and executes the same *SELECT* statement you saw used with Listing 10-14. Again, direct SQL is being used because you're querying against the *Customers* entity set, and not the *SelectCustomers* function mapped to the *SelectCustomers* stored procedure. So this is a real LINQ to Entities query that executes in SQL Server and returns only filtered *Customer* rows to your application.

Step over the test that checks for no customers. You've already added several customers in earlier examples, so the code should jump right to the line that gets the first customer from the list. Step over that line, and also over the next line that gets the customer's order count. Although you are performing similar operations as you did with *DataSets* earlier (see Listing 10-11), this code is significantly more flexible and object-oriented than that example. Let's explain further to see how.

The *Customer* object in *firstCustomer* has an *OrderHeaders* collection which, like any ordinary collection, has a *Count* property that tells you how many orders the customer has. This is much more intuitive than needing to call the *GetOrderHeaderRows* method to get an array of child rows so that you can get the order count with the array's *Length* property, as you did with the typed *DataSet*.

Object Context Lazy Loading and Change Tracking

But wait—your LINQ to Entities query retrieves only customers from the database, but none of their orders. The earlier *DataSet* example selected both customers and orders, so *GetOrderHeaderRows* simply returned an array of in-memory order rows already retrieved from the database. So how is EF able to get the count of orders that you haven't yet retrieved? The answer is lazy loading, which is on by default. If you single-step some more and switch back to SQL Profiler trace, you will see that EF issues a second T-SQL query to retrieve the orders belonging to just the first customer. This was triggered by your request to obtain the count through the customer's *OrderHeader* collection's *Count* property. Now the context is tracking all customers retrieved by the original query, plus the orders for this one customer just retrieved by lazy loading. At this time, all of the objects being tracked by the context have an *EntityState* property whose value is set to *EntityState.Unchanged*.

Compare the flexibility afforded by EF lazy loading with the typed *DataSet* approach taken in Listing 10-11. In that example, you loaded every child entity, not knowing which ones will really be needed and which won't. With EF, it's much easier to strike the optimum balance of what gets loaded and when, which often varies in different situations. You can eager-load some related entities up front (by using the *Include* method in your initial LINQ query to generate the appropriate T-SQL join), and allow lazy loading to automatically fetch other related entities when you reference them. Or you can disable lazy loading by setting the *LazyLoadingEnabled* property on the context object to *false* and control everything yourself. Then you could eager-load some related entities up front, and defer the loading of other related entities until you need them (by explicitly invoking the *Load* method on a child collection or parent reference property).

Step over the next line and dismiss the *MessageBox* that displays the customer ID and order count. Now the customer's name is changed by setting its *FirstName* and *LastName* properties. This in turn automatically changes the *EntityState* of the customer to *EntityState.Modified*. A new order is then created for the customer. Again the code is cleaner than Listing 10-11. Rather than being forced to call a special method like *AddOrderHeaderRow* to add a new *DataRow* to a *DataTable*, you treat your entities as plain objects and collections. The customer object has an *OrderHeaders* property, which is an ordinary collection with an ordinary *Add* method. The new order is created inline directly inside the *Add* method, using *object initializers* to set values for all its properties. Now the context starts tracking the new order, and EF sets its *EntityState* property to *EntityState.Added*.

It's now time to push all your data changes back to SQL Server. Persistence is simple; just invoke the single *SaveChanges* method on the context. EF does all the work of issuing transactionalized, properly-ordered updates to the database for all the objects being tracked for changes by the context. Step over the *SaveChanges* method call and then switch over to SQL Profiler to examine the trace. You will see that EF sent two commands to SQL Server. First it generated and issued a direct *INSERT* statement to add the new order to the *OrderHeader* table. Then, because of the stored procedure mappings you established for the *Customer* entity, EF called the *UpdateCustomer* stored procedure to save the changes made to the customer name. You can also see that EF wrapped those two operations up inside *BEGIN TRANSACTION* and *COMMIT TRANSACTION* statements automatically.

Note If you did not enable transactional events for the SQL Profiler trace as we explained earlier, you will not see the *BEGIN TRANSACTION* and *COMMIT TRANSACTION* statements in the SQL Profiler trace. Stop the trace, and start a new one with transactional events enabled, as shown in Figure 10-4. When you rerun the code, you will see these statements appear in the trace surrounding the insert and update operations.

The EF n-Tier Challenge

We've critiqued the *DataSet* quite sharply as we compared it with EF. But *DataSets* are still easier than EF in n-tier scenarios. Recall how the earlier *DataSet* example (back in Listing 10-10) used *two* adapters (and thus, two separate connections)—one with a command to do the fill and another with three commands to do the update. You didn't *need* to use two adapters; you could just have easily used one adapter configured with all four commands. We directed you to do so only to simulate the disconnected state that the *DataSet* experiences in an n-tier architecture, in which it traverses the tiers between the fill and the update. While disconnected, the *DataSet* tracked all changes in each row's *RowState* property so they could be saved back to the database. It is entirely self-reliant for tracking its own changes, and you aren't required to hold on to the same adapter that filled it in order to update it after the round-trip.

The Entity Framework is very different. You must perform the fill and update using one and the same context, or you'll be faced with serious problems. Although each entity does indeed have an *EntityState* property that functions like the *RowState* property does with *DataSets*, that property value is merely a reflection of the entity state stored internally in the *context* object that's actually tracking the entity. Entity instances are not self-tracking as *DataSets* are; they depend on the context for change tracking. Yet the context is not serializable, and does not travel along with the entity instances it is tracking as they traverse the tiers. The context therefore does not survive the round trip.

When you retrieve objects from the database and then destroy the context, those objects are no longer able to track changes on their own as you pass them through the tiers. Without the context, the *EntityState* property is always set to *EntityState.Detached*, and will no longer update automatically as you apply changes to the objects. That means it becomes someone else's job to track their changes while disconnected from a context, if you want to be able to persist those changes back to the database later. When the time does come to save the changes, you will also need to re-attach the objects to a new context with the change information, so that the context can carry out the correct commands to update the database.

These concerns must be addressed if you want to implement an n-tier architecture built on the Entity Framework. Fortunately, there are a number of readily available solutions that you can leverage to aid you in the task. As of EF4, you can hook up detached objects received from the client to a new context and explicitly set change information for the update. You can also override Visual Studio's default code generation strategy in the EDM designer and produce real self-tracking POCO entities from the model.

WCF Data Services and WCF RIA Services are two other technologies that can help you build n-tier applications with the Entity Framework. Each in their own unique way, these two APIs streamline CRUD operations in disconnected n-tier scenarios, and they both work seamlessly with the entity classes produced by the default EDM code generator in Visual Studio. We cover WCF Data Services and WCF RIA Services in the next chapter.

Resolving Impedance Mismatch

The mapping layer in the EDM is a very powerful aspect of Entity Framework. With it, you can design many different types of abstractions over a physical database structure. For example, you can define a single conceptual entity based on two tables in the database that have a one-to-one relationship with each other. You can also derive multiple conceptual entities from a single table. In the sample database, there is a many-to-many relationship junction table that is completely abstracted away from you by the mapping layer. These are examples are what's commonly referred to as *impedance mismatch*—where you don't have an exact one-to-one correspondence between tables in the database and entities in the application (see the sidebar "Defining ORM" earlier in the chapter).

Revisit the Mapping Details pane to see how it can be used to customize the model and reduce impedance mismatch. Double-click *SampleEF.edmx* in the Solution Explorer to open it in the designer. Then right-click anywhere on the *Customer* entity and choose Table Mapping to display the Mapping Details pane, as shown in Figure 10-18.

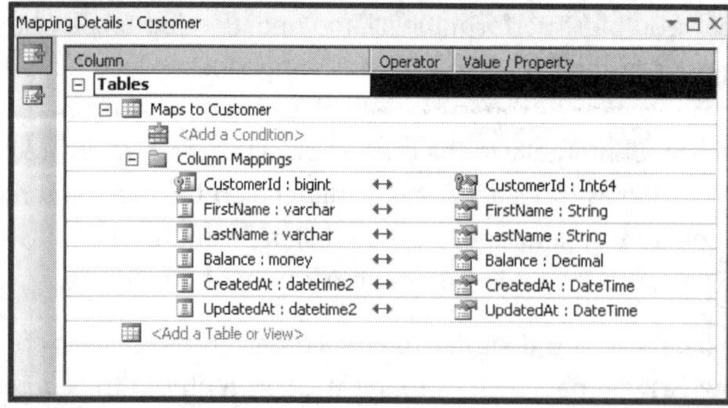

FIGURE 10-18 Mapping an entity and its properties with tables or views and their columns.

You used the Mapping Details pane earlier to map three update stored procedures to the *Customer* entity, but stored procedure mapping is only one of two purposes that this pane serves. Its other purpose is to let you map tables and columns with entities and properties. You get dropped into the appropriate mode based on whether you choose Stored Procedure Mapping or Table Mapping from the right-click context menu in the designer, and you can also toggle between the two modes by clicking the two buttons in the left margin of the Mapping Details pane.

The mapping shows that the *Customer* entity is mapped to the single *Customer* table, and that there is a one-to-one mapping between same-named properties and columns. This is how the wizard set things up originally by default. The Mapping Details pane lets you take things further than this, by allowing you to map additional tables or views from the storage schema to the logical *Customer* entity. For example, if you had another table in the database that had a one-to-one relationship with *Customer*, you could click the <Add a Table or View> drop-down list to bring the second table and its columns into the entity mapping. You would then remove the second table from the conceptual schema, and the single *Customer* entity would have a collective set of properties whose values are backed by two separate tables in the database. EF would automatically join the two tables together when querying for a single *Customer*, and also split a *Customer* update operation into separate commands to update each of the tables individually.

Also notice the <Add a Condition> drop-down list, which lets you embed a row filter into the model for the mapping. For example, imagine that instead of having two separate tables, both *Customer* and *Employee* entities in the model were based on a single underlying *Person* table in the database. This *Person* table would have a *PersonType* column to distinguish between customers and employees. The *PersonType* column (called the *discriminator*) could be specified accordingly in the table mapping conditions for the *Customer* and *Employee* entities. As a result, you could continue working conceptually with customers and employees as distinct entity types (or, if you wish to leverage inheritance, as distinct entity types that derive from the same base *Person* type), and allow EF to manage the mapping to the *Person* table automatically behind the scenes. If you were to query for a *Customer* or an *Employee*, EF would test *PersonType* in the database query accordingly to return rows of the correct type. Similarly, EF would automatically store the correct value in the *PersonType* column depending on whether you were saving a customer or an employee to the database. At no time would your code be aware of the actual *Person* table or the *PersonType* column. In fact, you could change the database design in the back-end from using two tables to one (and back again) without impacting your application's code whatsoever.

Working with Many-to-Many Relationships

Let's demonstrate this abstraction concept with the many-to-many relationship between *Customer* and *Employee* in the sample database. Drag two list box controls from the Toolbox and drop them onto the form. Name one of them **lstCustomers** and the other **lstEmployees**. Next, drag and drop another button control, name it **btnManyToMany**, and set its Text property to **Many To Many Relationships**. Now double-click the button and add the code in Listing 10-17.

LISTING 10-17 Working with many-to-many relationships.

```
private void btnManyToMany_Click(object sender, EventArgs e)
{
  using (var ctx = new SampleDbEntities())
  {
    // Create 3 customers and 3 employees

    var custClaus = new Customer() { FirstName = "Claus", LastName = "Hansen" };
    var custTerry = new Customer() { FirstName = "Terry", LastName = "Adams" };
    var custDan = new Customer() { FirstName = "Dan", LastName = "Park" };

    ctx.Customers.AddObject(custClaus);
    ctx.Customers.AddObject(custTerry);
    ctx.Customers.AddObject(custDan);

    var empDavid = new Employee() { FirstName = "David", LastName = "Alexander" };
    var empAndy = new Employee() { FirstName = "Andy", LastName = "Jacobs" };
    var empErik = new Employee() { FirstName = "Erik", LastName = "Ryan" };

    ctx.Employees.AddObject(empDavid);
    ctx.Employees.AddObject(empAndy);
    ctx.Employees.AddObject(empErik);

    // Create these many-to-many relationships:
    //  Customer : Employees          | Employee : Customers
    //    Claus   :  Andy, Erik        |  Andy     :  Claus, Terry
    //    Terry   :  Andy, David       |  David    :  Terry, Dan
    //    Dan     :  David, Erik       |  Erik     :  Claus, Dan

    // Can either add employees to customers...

    custClaus.Employees.Add(empAndy);
    custClaus.Employees.Add(empErik);

    custTerry.Employees.Add(empAndy);
    custTerry.Employees.Add(empDavid);

    // ...or add customers to employees

    empErik.Customers.Add(custDan);
    empDavid.Customers.Add(custDan);

    // Save new customers, employees, and their relationships to the database
    ctx.SaveChanges();

    // Get customers belonging to employee David (Terry and Dan)
    this.lstCustomers.Items.Clear();
    foreach (var cust in empDavid.Customers)
    {
      this.lstCustomers.Items.Add(
        string.Format("{0} {1}", cust.FirstName, cust.LastName));
    }
```

```
      // Get employees belonging to customer Terry (Andy and David)
      this.lstEmployees.Items.Clear();
      foreach (var emp in custTerry.Employees)
      {
        this.lstEmployees.Items.Add(
          string.Format("{0} {1}", emp.FirstName, emp.LastName));
      }
    }
  }
```

This is really simple code. All it does is create three customers and three employees, and then establishes many-to-many relationships between them by adding into each other's collections. Notice how it doesn't matter which direction you work in; you can add customers to an employee's *Customers* collection, or you can add employees to a customer's *Employees* collection. Single-step through the code while running a SQL Profiler trace to watch it work.

When the *SaveChanges* method is called on the context, the trace shows all the commands sent to the database. As expected, the customers are created with individual calls to the *InsertCustomer* stored procedure, and the employees are created with individually generated *INSERT* statements into the *Employee* table. But you'll also notice that additional *INSERT* statements into the *Customer-Employee* junction table were generated to create the many-to-many relationships in the database. This is more EF magic at work. Similarly, if you were to break relationships by removing objects from collections in the application, EF would automatically issue the appropriate *DELETE* statements against the *CustomerEmployee* table in the database.

Next, the code starts a *foreach* loop to iterate all of the customers associated with employee David. If you single-step the code's entry into the loop, you will see in the trace that EF automatically issues a query to SQL Server to retrieve the related customers from the *Customer* table by joining on the *CustomerEmployee* junction table. Then there is another *foreach* loop that is similar, but works in the opposite direction. This one iterates all of the employees associated with customer Terry, and the trace shows that EF runs a query in SQL Server to retrieve the related employees from the *Employee* table by again joining on *CustomerEmployee*.

Exploring the Entity SQL Alternative

You will now learn about the Entity SQL language, which offers a way to query the EDM without using LINQ to Entities.

Why two ways to query the EDM? Well, first understand that Entity SQL is actually the native language of EF designed specifically for querying an EDM. It was created as a core part of Entity Framework before the LINQ revolution, and exists independently of LINQ. Most of the time, you'll still use LINQ to Entities and enjoy the benefits of strong-typing and object materialization that it provides. However, there may be times when you'll need to use Entity SQL to write a query that can't be expressed as well (or at all) in LINQ. Entity SQL also offers a way to stream query results into a data reader when you don't need to materialize them into objects, as we'll demonstrate shortly.

Entity SQL bears a strong resemblance to the T-SQL language upon which it is based. The key difference between them is that Entity SQL expressions refer to conceptual entities and properties in the model, rather than physical tables and columns in the database. Let's write a simple query to demonstrate. Drag another button control from the Toolbox and drop it onto the form. Name the button **btnEntitySql** and set its Text property to **Entity SQL**. Then double-click the button and add the code in Listing 10-18.

LISTING 10-18 Using Entity SQL instead of LINQ to return entity objects.

```
private void btnEntitySql_Click(object sender, EventArgs e)
{
  const string EntitySql = @"
    SELECT VALUE cust
      FROM SampleDbEntities.Customers AS cust
      WHERE cust.LastName NOT LIKE 'A%'
      ORDER BY cust.LastName";

  using (var ctx = new SampleDbEntities())
  {
    // Define, but do not execute, the Entity SQL query (deferred execution)
    var q = ctx.CreateQuery<Customer>(EntitySql);

    // Implicitly execute query on the server, returning List<Customer>
    var list = q.ToList();

    MessageBox.Show(string.Format("Non-A customer count: {0}", list.Count));
  }
}
```

This code is functionally equivalent to what you wrote in Listing 10-14. The only difference is that you're using Entity SQL instead of LINQ to Entities to query the database for the desired customers. The EDM still continues to function as a mapping layer between conceptual and physical models, and the context is still used to invoke the query and track any changes made to the results.

Observe how the code runs by single-stepping through it with a running SQL Profiler trace as usual. The *CreateQuery<Customer>* method is invoked on the context, rather than a LINQ to Entities query as in Listing 10-14. This method accepts a string parameter that contains an Entity SQL expression expected to return a sequence of *Customer* entities. As with LINQ, this method merely defines the query but does not execute it. Execution is deferred until the next line of code that calls *ToList*. The *ToList* method call kicks off the query in SQL Server as before. You can see this by watching the SQL Profiler trace as a step over the method call with the debugger. Take a closer look at the syntax of this Entity SQL query:

```
SELECT VALUE cust
  FROM SampleDbEntities.Customers AS cust
  WHERE cust.LastName NOT LIKE 'A%'
  ORDER BY cust.LastName
```

As mentioned, Entity SQL queries look very similar to T-SQL queries. They can even be parameterized just like T-SQL queries are. But remember that you're dealing with the conceptual model here, not tables. In this query, *Customers* refers to the entity set of *Customer* entities exposed by the SampleDbEntities model, not the *Customer* table in the database (even though they currently happen to be mapped one-to-one). Similarly, *LastName* refers to a property of the *Customer* entity, not the *LastName* column of the *Customer* database table. The *VALUE* keyword specifies that the query returns a single strongly typed object, which is a *Customer* entity in this case. Also note that you must alias entity set names specified in the *FROM* clause, unlike T-SQL where table aliases are optional. In this example, *Customer* entities in the *Customers* entity set are aliased as *cust*.

Working with EntityClient

We conclude our Entity Framework coverage (and this chapter) with *EntityClient*, which is yet another way to query the EDM. EntityClient only understands Entity SQL; it doesn't know anything about LINQ. Using EntityClient, you will query the model with Entity SQL and stream the results back using just a reader object.

Drag another button control from the Toolbox and drop it onto the form. Name the button **btnEntityClient** and set its Text property to **EntityClient**. Then double-click the button and add the code in Listing 10-19.

LISTING 10-19 Using Entity SQL with EntityClient to return a streaming reader.

```
private void btnEntityClient_Click(object sender, EventArgs e)
{
  const string ConnStr = "name=SampleDbEntities";

  const string EntitySql = @"
    SELECT VALUE cust
      FROM SampleDbEntities.Customers AS cust
      WHERE cust.LastName NOT LIKE @Pattern
      ORDER BY cust.LastName";

  var names = new List<string>();
  using (var conn = new EntityConnection())
  {
    conn.ConnectionString = ConnStr;
    conn.Open();
    using (var cmd = new EntityCommand())
    {
      cmd.Connection = conn;
      cmd.CommandText = EntitySql;
      cmd.Parameters.AddWithValue("Pattern", "A%");
      using (var rdr = cmd.ExecuteReader(CommandBehavior.CloseConnection |
       CommandBehavior.SequentialAccess))
      {
        while (rdr.Read())
        {
          var firstName = rdr.GetString(1);
```

```
                var lastName = rdr.GetString(2);
                var name = string.Format("{0}, {1}", lastName, firstName);
                names.Add(name);
            }
            rdr.Close();
        }
    }
    this.lstCustomers.DataSource = names;
  }
}
```

Look familiar? It should! Compare this code with Listing 10-6 way back at the beginning of the chapter. You're using *raw* ADO.NET objects to query the EDM with the EntityClient provider, just like raw objects have been used to query SQL Server directly with the SqlClient for years. It's the *exact* same pattern developers have been following since .NET 1.0, though there are a few subtle differences that we'll point out as we explain the code.

EntityClient is supplied by the *System.Data.Entity* assembly that your project is already referencing (recall that the EDM designer automatically added that reference for you when you created the model). Just as with SqlClient at the beginning of the chapter, you need to inform the compiler where it can find the *EntityConnection* and *EntityCommand* classes referred to in your code by adding the following *using* directive at the top of the source file:

```
using System.Data.EntityClient;
```

The *ConnStr* constant defined at the top of the method simply points to the named connection *SampleDbEntities*. This named connection refers to the actual entity connection string (stored and maintained in the application configuration file) that fully describes the metadata location and provider-specific connection information for the model.

Next, the *EntitySql* constant is defined, and is set to the same Entity SQL expression as the last example, except that you are parameterizing the value for *LIKE* with *@Pattern* rather than hard-coding it as *'A%'*. After initializing an empty list of strings in *names*, you create a new *EntityConnection* in *conn*, set its *ConnectionString* property to the *ConnsStr* constant you defined earlier, and invoke the *Open* method on it to establish a connection to the model.

Next, you create an *EntityCommand* object in *cmd* and set its *Connection* property to associate the command with the open connection. The *CommandText* property gets set to the Entity SQL statement defined earlier in the *EntitySql* constant. Because the Entity SQL has a parameter called *@Pattern*, you supply the parameter name and value to the command's *Parameters* collection using the *AddWithValue* method just as you did in Listing 10-3 with T-SQL. Note, however, that you do not prefix parameter names with the at-sign (@) symbol in the *Parameters* collection as you do with the SqlClient, and so the parameter name is specified as *Pattern* rather than *@Pattern*.

Now you invoke *ExecuteReader* to invoke the query and obtain an *EntityDataReader* object that returns the query results. The *EntityDataReader* works just like the *SqlDataReader*, with several additional constraints. First, notice the *CommandBehavior.SequentialAccess* setting that you're combining with the *CommandBehavior.CloseConnection* setting that you were using earlier when creating a *SqlDataReader* by calling *ExecuteReader* on a *SqlCommand.* This additional setting is required with EntityClient, and forces strict sequential consumption of the data stream.

Although a data reader is an inherently sequential mechanism, the *SqlDataReader* will still let you access column values randomly within each row delivered sequentially by the result set. The same is not true with an *EntityDataReader* because the data returned by an Entity SQL query can include hierarchical results, in which case child entities get unpacked during the reader's streaming process. This imposes the requirement for you to retrieve individual column values sequentially—once you extract a column value from the current entity being returned by the reader, you will not be able to extract the value of any previous column for the same entity because the reader has already advanced past it.

Not knowing how many entities you'll get back, you test for an end-of-stream condition with each call to the reader's *Read* method at the top of a *while* block. If there are no entities, *Read* will return true the very first time it is called, and the *while* block will never execute. Otherwise, the block will execute once for each customer entity returned by the query.

For each entity, the reader's *GetString* method is used to extract the first and last name values so you can format the customer name. This points out another important difference with the *SqlDataReader*—column values can only be extracted from an *EntityDataReader* by ordinal position using the *GetXxx* methods supplied for each data type (such as *GetString*, *GetDateTime*, *GetInt64*, and so on). You cannot use indexed notation like you can with a *SqlDataReader* to access columns by name (such as *rdr["FirstName"]*). Also notice that you extract the first name before the last name, because they are returned by the query in that order as columns 1 and 2. Even though you're displaying last name first, you must extract them in the order they are returned because of the *CommandBehavior.SequentialAccess* setting (as just explained).

Each formatted name is added to the *List<string>* collection that got initialized at the top of the method before you created the *EntityConnection.* After closing the reader (which also closes the connection because of the *CommandBehavior.CloseConnection* setting), you set the *DataSource* property on the *lstCustomers* list box to bind the string collection to it.

Now run the application and single-step through it with a SQL Profiler trace as usual. This is a good demonstration of how EF can be used to execute queries and process their results without involving objects or LINQ.

By now you've learned a great deal about the Entity Framework—more than enough to get started building real applications with it. You built a functional Entity Data Model, and in the next chapter you will learn how to use WCF Data Services and WCF RIA Services to extend the reach of your EDMs to client applications across the Internet.

Summary

This chapter has delivered a fairly critical analysis across the gamut of .NET data access APIs and tools that Microsoft has released over more than the past decade, with guidance to help you intelligently distinguish between them. We walked through numerous examples and demonstrated coding techniques for working with each of them, and also provided important guidelines to keep in mind as you do.

We started by explaining the continued relevance of conventional ADO.NET—both raw data access obects and *DataSets*—alongside newer technologies. You started with raw connections, commands, readers, adapters, and *DataSets* to run direct SQL statements and execute stored procedures in SQL Server. You also learned about explicit and implicit transactions and SQL Server Profiler. Then we introduced the concept of LINQ, and its various implementations, and you saw how LINQ to DataSet extends conventional ADO.NET for querying both generic and strongly typed *DataSets*.

We then advanced the discussion to Object Relational Mapping, what ORM technologies are, and the types of problems they are designed to solve. We also clarified Microsoft's position on their two ORM offerings LINQ to SQL and ADO.NET Entity Framework: although LINQ to SQL will continue being supported in future versions of .NET, the Entity Framework is positioned as the current and future recommended data access solution for developing applications.

Then we dug into the extensive capabilities of the Entity Framework, starting by examining the Entity Data Model and its underlying conceptual, storage, and mapping schemas. From there, you built functional .NET applications using LINQ to Entities to query and update data in SQL Server, demonstrating powerful key EF features such as lazy loading, entity mappings, change tracking, many-to-many relationships, Entity SQL, and EntityClient.

But the .NET data access story does not end here. In the next chapter, you will learn about WCF Data Services and WCF RIA Services—two frameworks you can use to build data access services and n-tier applications for clients over the World Wide Web.

CHAPTER 11

WCF Data Access Technologies

–Leonard Lobel

Windows Communication Foundation (WCF) is a communications platform that provides all the support you need to build distributed, service-oriented solutions in the .NET Framework. Microsoft first introduced WCF in late 2006 as part of the .NET Framework 3.0 release. Since then, WCF has established itself as a cornerstone of the framework, and is regarded today as the de facto solution for building any kind of service in .NET.

Defining Services

There are many types of services. Some are intended for use only within an organization's private intranet, where communication occurs only behind the corporate firewall (with remote access enabled via Virtual Private Network [VPN] connections). These services can be tightly coupled with .NET clients via sockets and efficient binary remoting protocols. Other services may be exposed publicly over the Internet. Public services must be able to penetrate firewalls and support any type of client, which typically requires them to use eXtensible Markup Language (XML) or the relatively terser JavaScript Object Notation (JSON) message format over a standard transport (usually HTTP). These text-based serialization formats are bulkier and less efficient than binary serialization, but they do support a much wider range of clients—Microsoft and non-Microsoft alike.

And there are many more variables. Some services require authentication, whereas many do not—and those that do use some authentication methods but not others. Some services operate synchronously, others asynchronously. Services are usually stateless, but some support client sessions. Messaging protocols vary as well; some services use Simple Object Access Protocol (SOAP), whereas others are based on the Representational State Transfer (REST) protocol and return data as an Atom Publishing Protocol (AtomPub) response (an XML dialect very similar to the Really Simply Syndication [RSS] feed format).

Before WCF, such particulars were typically hard-coded into an application. If you built a private service using binary remoting and then decided to open up the service to the public Internet, you needed to modify significant code in your application to support that change. This is not normally the case with WCF. Typically, you build your application to communicate using WCF proxy classes, and configure WCF separately to meet the requirements of your particular networking environment.

Although WCF configuration can be coded using C# or Visual Basic (VB) .NET (which essentially embeds it into an assembly), it is usually (and best) managed declaratively in the application's external configuration file (this is either *Web.config* or *App.config* in your Microsoft Visual Studio project). So, for instance, to enable public access to services that were formerly private, you can simply open a text file in Notepad and add SOAP with HTTP in addition to the binary serialization with sockets configuration that is already in place. Or, you could just as easily tweak the WCF configuration to enable asynchronous behavior for service methods that formerly supported only synchronous behavior. These are just a few examples of the advantages offered by WCF's configuration-based approach.

WCF Data Access Options

You can certainly work with WCF directly to create custom services and expose data from an Entity Data Model (EDM) with the ADO.NET Entity Framework, or any other data access layer (DAL) of your choosing. To take this "raw" approach, you need to start with the basics, or what is commonly referred to as the ABC's of WCF: Addresses, Bindings, and Contracts. You must create service, operation, and data *contracts*, and then configure your service model with appropriate endpoint *addresses* and compatible *bindings* to be reachable by clients. Services are usually stateless, so you must also handle client-side change tracking and multi-user conflict resolution entirely on your own. The learning curve can be quite steep, after which you will still need to expend a great deal of effort to make it work.

Alternatively, you can turn to one of the two later technologies that Microsoft has built on top of WCF, which are the focus of this chapter. These are WCF Data Services and WCF RIA Services, and they represent two very different approaches for building data-oriented services. Both provide abstractions that shield you from many underlying WCF particulars, so you get to spend more time focusing on your application and less time on plumbing. For one thing, you don't need to code WCF contracts or manage change tracking on the client; all that gets done for you. With WCF RIA Services (and Microsoft Silverlight), you don't even need to create and update service references; Visual Studio generates code automatically via a special link that keeps your client and WCF RIA Services projects in sync at all times.

In this chapter, you will learn how to use WCF Data Services and WCF RIA Services by exposing the *SampleDb* database's EDM that you created in the previous chapter as services, and then building clients over those services. By detailed comparison, you will learn how to choose intelligently between these two frameworks for any given scenario.

Monitoring Network Activity with Fiddler

In Chapter 10, you used SQL Profiler to monitor the database activity that Entity Framework was conducting behind the scenes. Now that you are extending the client-server model to an n-tier service-oriented architecture, you will similarly want to monitor the network activity further up the stack (HTTP traffic) as you build separate client and server components. A number of tools are available that will let you do this (so-called "packet sniffers"). In our walkthrough, we use Fiddler (which is small, free, and easy to use) to watch and see exactly how client requests and service responses are being transmitted to and from WCF services on the other end of the wire. This is an invaluable tool for learning the technology as you experiment with the examples in this chapter. And once you start building production systems with the technology, it will also prove to be an indispensable tool for routine debugging—whether you are programming raw WCF, WCF Data Services, or WCF RIA Services.

Go to *http://www.fiddler2.com* to download and install Fiddler. When you start the tool, it displays a split screen with requests on top and responses on bottom, and then immediately begins to monitor HTTP traffic (see Figure 11-8). You will refer to Fiddler output routinely to observe client/server communication as you test and debug the code in this chapter. You should also begin a SQL Profiler trace so that you can monitor the database activity of your WCF services as well (instructions for starting a trace can be found in Chapter 10 under the section "Monitoring Database Activity with SQL Server Profiler").

WCF Data Services

Microsoft designed WCF Data Services as a thin layer over Entity Framework that exposes data-centric services to client applications across the Internet. You can think of WCF Data Services as universal Web Services built *just* for data. The platform is based on open industry standards and protocols, which means that these services are consumable by virtually every type of client in the world. And you can quickly build a WCF Data Services over an EDM with almost no effort whatsoever. Before building your very first service (and a corresponding client piece), let's first explain the industry standards that WCF Data Services is based upon—which are REST and the Open Data Protocol (OData).

REST provides a uniform interface for querying and updating data. It is based on HTTP, meaning that client requests are issued in the form of *GET*, *POST*, *MERGE*, and *DELETE* actions—standard verbs understood by all HTTP clients. Any REST query can be invoked with an HTTP *GET* request by expressing all the elements of the query in a properly formed Uniform Resource Identifier (a URI, which is a more general term than Uniform Resource Locator [URL]). You can even test the service with an ordinary browser by typing the URI directly into the address bar. The *POST*, *MERGE*, and *DELETE* verbs correspond respectively to insert, update, and delete operations supported by the service. Unlike *GET*, the payload (parameters, data, and other metadata) for these operations is passed in HTTP headers; it is not embedded in the URI. So you cannot use the browser's address bar to insert, update, or delete data. However, it is easy to view HTTP headers using Fiddler, and you will be doing that shortly to inspect the complete payload for each client request issued to the service.

Just as REST enables universal data access via HTTP, OData establishes universal data structure via standard serialization formats (see *http://www.odata.org*). All clients can handle plain-text formats such as JSON and XML, and so OData defines standard response formats based on both formats. JSON provides a compact structure suitable for many basic types of services, whereas XML forms the basis for the more verbose AtomPub feed format. AtomPub is the default serialization format in WCF Data Services, because it effectively leverages the hierarchical nature of XML to describe the rich structure of data and metadata in an EDM.

WCF Data Services without Entity Framework

Microsoft designed WCF Data Services with a data source provider tailored especially for the Entity Framework, making it virtually effortless to create services over any Entity Data Model. This is rational, given that Entity Framework is Microsoft's preferred .NET data access solution. Nonetheless, there are alternative data source providers available to make WCF Data Services work with other data access layers as well. This approach requires substantial additional effort, details of which are beyond the scope of this chapter. Here is a brief mention of the alternatives to guide you in the right direction if you need to learn more.

Microsoft supplies two data source providers that you can use to expose data sources other than Entity Framework with WCF Data Services. These are the Reflection and Streaming providers. To use the Reflection provider, your data classes implement *IQueryable* to support querying, and optionally implement *IUpdateable* to support updates as well. You can map these classes to memory-resident objects or any back-end data store that you want—even LINQ to SQL or typed DataSets. The Streaming provider gives you a special *IDataServiceStreamProvider* interface that you can implement to expose large binary objects (BLOBs), such as FILESTREAM data in SQL Server (which we cover in Chapter 8). Finally, custom service providers let you dynamically define data models of any type. This approach requires the most effort to implement, and should be used only if the other available providers are inadequate. For more information about providers for WCF Data Services, visit *http://msdn.microsoft.com/en-us/library/dd672591.aspx*.

Building a WCF Data Service

To build the service, follow these steps. Start Visual Studio and choose File | New | Project. From the list of template categories on the left, beneath Visual C#, choose Web. Then select the ASP.NET Empty Web Application template to create a project named **DemoRestService** in a solution named **DemoWcfDataServices**, as shown in Figure 11-1.

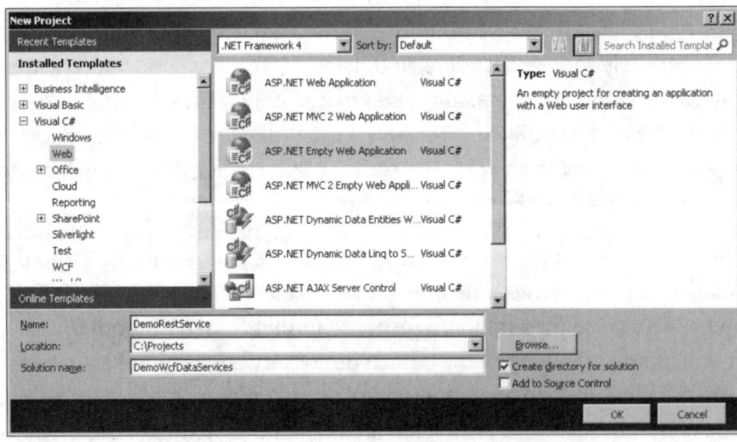

FIGURE 11-1 Creating an ASP.NET Web Application project for the WCF Data Service.

Every ASP.NET application is hosted on a web server, typically Internet Information Services (IIS) in production environments, or the more lightweight Visual Studio Development Web Server (also known as "Cassini") on development desktops and laptops. But rather than serving up ordinary webpages, this project will expose a special .svc file that exposes an EDM using WCF Data Services, using the same *SampleDb* EDM (and underlying database) from the previous chapter.

Creating the Entity Data Model

The next step is to create the EDM. (If you skipped the previous chapter, you first need to create the database by running the T-SQL script in Listing 10-1 of that chapter.) Then, you can repeat the same steps in the previous chapter (see the section "Building an Entity Data Model") to create the same EDM in this project, or—if you have already built the EDM in the previous chapter—it is much easier to simply copy it (and its connection string) from the previous chapter's project. To do so, open Windows Explorer to the previous chapter's project, drag the *SampleEF.edmx* file, and drop it on the *DemoRestService* project in Solution Explorer. Then copy the *connectionStrings* section in the *App.config* file from previous chapter's project and paste it into this *DemoRestService* project's *Web.config* file (just after the opening *<Configuration>* tag toward the top):

```
<connectionStrings>
  <add
    name="SampleDbEntities"
    connectionString="
     metadata=res://*/SampleEF.csdl|res://*/SampleEF.ssdl|res://*/SampleEF.msl;
     provider=System.Data.SqlClient;
     provider connection string=&quot;Data Source=localhost;Initial Catalog=SampleDb;
      Integrated Security=True;MultipleActiveResultSets=True&quot;"
    providerName="System.Data.EntityClient" />
</connectionStrings>
```

Note The complete code—including the T-SQL script and a Visual Studio solution with the EDM already built—is available for download from the book's companion website (see the "Introduction" for details).

Your EDM is now in place. If you have been following along with the previous chapter, the EDM's underlying database now contains random sample data from earlier exercises; if you have just created the database now, then it is empty. In either case, refresh the database now with new sample data by running the script in Listing 11-1.

LISTING 11-1 Populating the database with sample data.

```
USE SampleDb
GO

DELETE FROM OrderHeader
DELETE FROM CustomerEmployee
DELETE FROM Customer
```

```
SET IDENTITY_INSERT Customer ON
INSERT INTO Customer (CustomerId, FirstName, LastName, Balance) VALUES
 (1, 'Lukas', 'Keller', 35),
 (2, 'Andy', 'Jacobs', 10),
 (3, 'Mike', 'Ray', 40),
 (4, 'Josh', 'Barnhill', 5)
SET IDENTITY_INSERT Customer OFF

SET IDENTITY_INSERT OrderHeader ON
INSERT INTO OrderHeader (OrderHeaderId, CustomerId, ShipVia, OrderStatus) VALUES
 (1, 1, 'Regular Mail', 'Shipped'),
 (2, 1, 'Express Mail', 'Pending'),
 (3, 2, 'Priority Mail', 'Shipped'),
 (4, 3, 'Priority Mail', 'Shipped'),
 (5, 3, 'Regular Mail', 'Cancelled'),
 (6, 3, 'Priority Mail', 'Shipped'),
 (7, 3, 'Express Mail', 'Pending'),
 (8, 4, 'Regular Mail', 'Shipped'),
 (9, 4, 'Express Mail', 'Shipped')
SET IDENTITY_INSERT OrderHeader OFF
```

All that's left to implement the service is to create an associated .svc file, which will instantly expose your EDM to any REST client. Right-click the *DemoRestService* project, choose Add | New Item, and select Web from the list of template categories on the left. Then scroll down the list of installed templates and choose WCF Data Service. Name the file **CustomerDataService.svc** and then click Add, as shown in Figure 11-2.

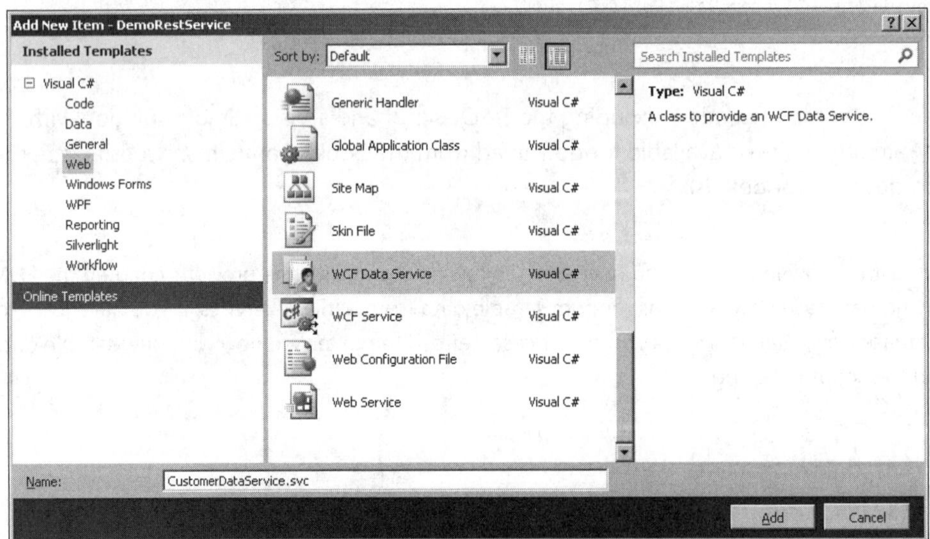

FIGURE 11-2 Creating an ASP.NET Web Application project for the WCF Data Service.

Now replace the starter code that Visual Studio creates by default with the code shown in Listing 11-2.

LISTING 11-2 A simple WCF Data Service.

```
using System;
using System.Data.Services;
using System.Data.Services.Common;
using System.Linq;
using System.ServiceModel.Web;

namespace DemoRestService
{
  public class CustomerDataService : DataService<SampleDbEntities>
  {
    public static void InitializeService(DataServiceConfiguration config)
    {
      config.SetEntitySetAccessRule("Customers", EntitySetRights.All);
      config.SetEntitySetAccessRule("OrderHeaders", EntitySetRights.All);
      config.SetEntitySetAccessRule("Employees", EntitySetRights.AllRead);

      config.DataServiceBehavior.MaxProtocolVersion = DataServiceProtocolVersion.V2;
    }
  }
}
```

This is all the code you need for create a fully functional service. Any client can call this service to query and update your EDM using REST and OData. It is still WCF under the covers, but you did not have to write any server-side logic, create a single WCF contract, or tweak a single WCF configuration setting—which is quite remarkable.

As the code demonstrates, you need to do only two simple things. First, inherit from *DataService<T>*, where *T* is your Entity Data Model's object context class (*SampleDbEntities*, in our current example). Second, implement the *InitializeService* method to control which parts of the EDM (that is, which entity sets) are to be exposed by the service, and what access levels are permitted (read-only versus updateable). In our example, all three entity sets in the EDM can be queried, but only *Customers* and *OrderHeaders* are updateable.

Testing WCF Data Services with Internet Explorer

Even a plain web browser can supply a properly formatted URI to query this service and display the XML content of the AtomPub feed that gets returned in response. This is a quick and easy way to test that your WCF Data Services are working properly before writing even one line of client code. Try it out now by using Internet Explorer 9 to issue a few URI queries to the service.

Important These instructions work specifically with Internet Explorer; other browsers may exhibit different or undesirable behavior. If you have another browser set as your default, open up Internet Explorer explicitly and copy the URL into its address bar after your default browser opens. We also recommend 32-bit Internet Explorer over the 64-bit version, as the 64-bit Internet Explorer apparently crashes consistently in our test environment when displaying RSS feeds.

Right-click the *CustomerDataService.svc* file in Solution Explorer and choose View In Browser. This immediately starts the ASP.NET Development Web Server that hosts the service on a randomly assigned port (1055 in this example, but yours will be different) and then launches Internet Explorer. The browser navigates to the .svc file, and the service responds with the list of available entity sets. As shown in Figure 11-3, these are the *Customers*, *Employees*, and *OrderHeaders* entity sets specified in the *InitializeService* method (Listing 11-2).

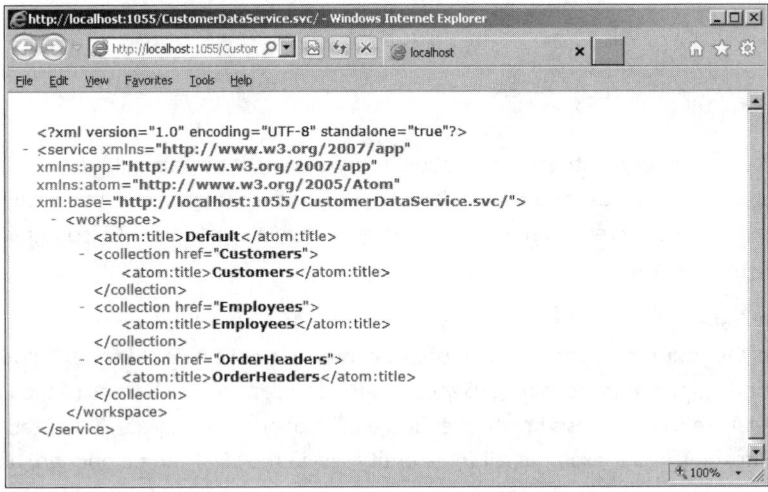

FIGURE 11-3 Navigate to the service's .svc file to discover the available entity sets.

Based on the "discovery" of available entity sets, you can append any entity set name to the URI to request all data in that entity set to be returned. For example, to view all the customers simply append **Customers** to the URL in the browser's address bar. The complete URI (again, with a different randomly assigned port number than 1055) is:

```
http://localhost:1055/CustomerDataService.svc/Customers
```

Go ahead and browse to this URL. Instead of displaying the raw AtomPub response feed, the feed reading view (which is on by default) in Internet Explorer attempts unsuccessfully to format the feed for display. To view the AtomPub feed in its raw XML form instead, you need to turn off feed reading view. Open the Internet Options dialog in Internet Explorer, click the Content tab, and then click the Settings button under Feeds and Web Slices to display the Feeds and Web Slice Settings dialog. Then uncheck Turn On Feed Reading View, as shown in Figure 11-4, and click OK twice to dismiss both dialogs.

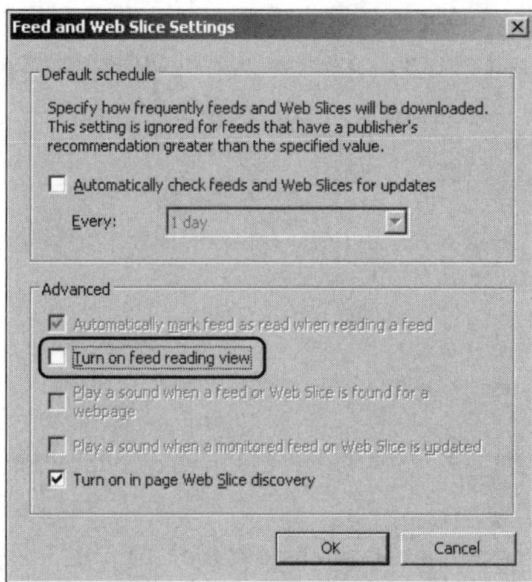

FIGURE 11-4 Turn off feed reading view in Internet Explorer to view the raw XML content of AtomPub responses.

This particular change may not take effect until Internet Explorer is restarted. So close the browser now and then once again right-click the *CustomerDataService.svc* file in Solution Explorer, choose View In Browser, and append **Customers** to the URL. This time Internet Explorer displays the AtomPub feed in readable XML, and you can see that the URI query returns all customers in the database, as shown in Figure 11-5.

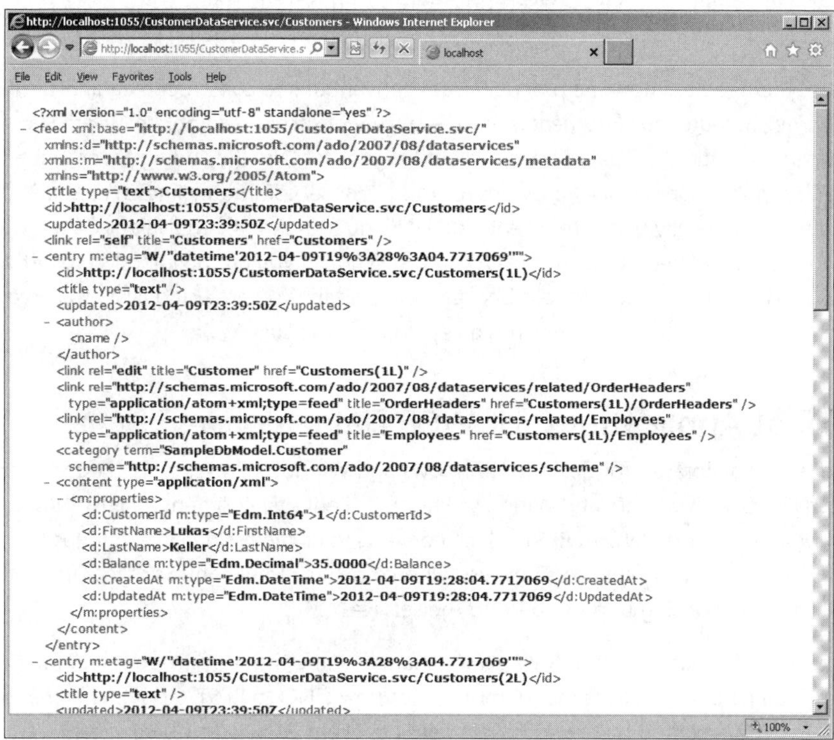

FIGURE 11-5 Customer data returned as an AtomPub feed by WCF Data Services.

To return a single entity by primary key, append its unique ID in parentheses after the entity set name. For example, modify the URL as follows to return the single customer with a *CustomerId* value of 3 (Mike Ray).

```
http://localhost:1055/CustomerDataService.svc/Customers(3L)
```

Notice that the terminating L is required to convey the data type (long integer, corresponding to SQL Server's 64-bit *bigint* type) of the primary key value.

The syntax can quickly grow contorted, as ad-hoc filtering, sorting, and a host of other directives are supported as well. For example, consider the following URI:

```
http://localhost:1055/CustomerDataService.svc/Customers?$filter=Balance gt 10&$expand=OrderHeade
rs&$orderby=LastName
```

The *$filter* option in this URI queries for all customers with a balance higher than 10. The *$expand* option tells WCF Data Services to return all the related *OrderHeader* entities with each *Customer* entity in the response feed, and *$orderby* requests that the results in the response should be sorted by *LastName*. If you enter this URI into the browser's address bar, the service returns the two customers that meet the filter criteria: Lukas Keller and Mike Ray (having balances of 35 and 40, respectively).

Note An OData URI always resolves to a specific resource or set of resources. Taking this approach is often known as implementing *resource-based* services, in contrast with more traditional domain-oriented services based on operation methods.

As you can see, you need to know the precise OData conventions to construct meaningful URI queries (visit *http://www.odata.org/documentation/uri-conventions* for the complete OData URI specification). Fortunately, the WCF Data Services client libraries for .NET (including Silverlight and Windows Phone 7) supply a special LINQ provider for this purpose, commonly known as LINQ to REST. This provider automatically translates client-side LINQ queries into an equivalent OData URI, meaning that you really *don't* need to learn the OData URI syntax if you are building Microsoft clients over WCF Data Services. This is a huge benefit because, once again, you are using LINQ to avoid learning yet another querying language (which is a key objective of LINQ).

Building Client Applications for WCF Data Services

Microsoft provides special libraries for desktop (Windows and Windows Presentation Foundation [WPF]), web (ASP.NET and Silverlight), and Windows Phone 7 client development against WCF Data Services. These libraries support LINQ to REST, which converts your client-side LINQ queries into the OData URI syntax expected by the service. They also all provide a stateful context object for tracking changes on the client and pushing updates back to the service.

In this section, you will create two Windows clients that consume the service you built in the previous section. The first is a test client that demonstrates how LINQ to REST, OData, and change tracking features are implemented by the WCF Data Services client library. This bare sample has no user interface (in fact, we may just as well have implemented it as a console application), and is designed to teach you how to code against the WCF Data Services client libraries. You will then apply that knowledge to build a more robust, interactive data entry client that supports hierarchical CRUD (create, retrieve, update, and delete) operations.

Building a Test Client

Let's get started with the test client. Right-click the *DemoWcfDataServices* solution in Solution Explorer and choose Add | New Project. From the list of template categories on the left, beneath Visual C#, choose Windows. Then select the Windows Forms Application template to create a new project named *DemoRestClientTest*, as shown in Figure 11-6.

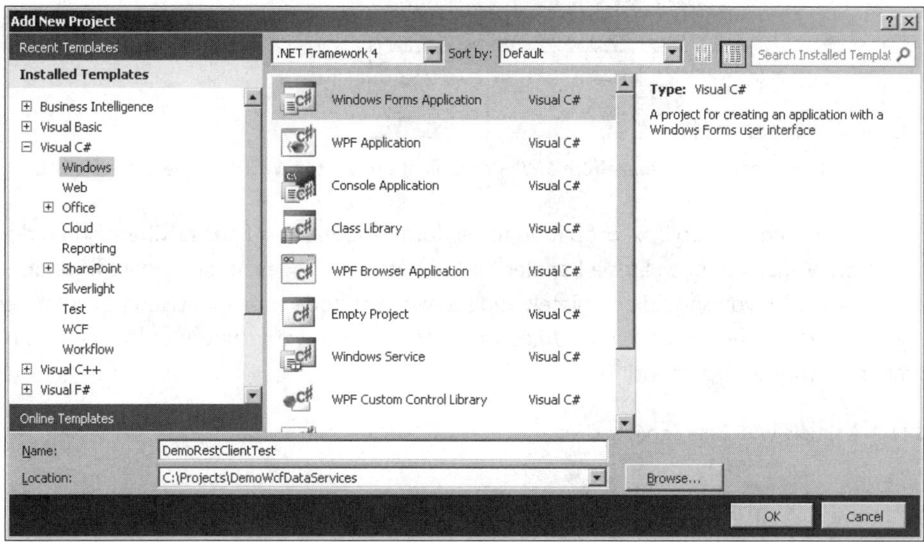

FIGURE 11-6 Adding a new Windows Forms client application to the WCF Data Services demo solution.

The *DemoWcfDataServices* solution now has two projects in it: an ASP.NET project (the service) and a Windows Forms project (the new *DemoRestClientTest* project with an empty form). Your next step is to set a reference from the client project to the service project. To do this, right-click the *DemoRestClientTest* project in Solution Explorer and choose Add Service Reference. In the Add Service Reference dialog, click the Discover button. Visual Studio locates the WCF Data Services file *CustomerDataServices.svc* in the ASP.NET project. Expand the treeview on the left to reveal the entities exposed by the service. Then type **CustomerDataService** for the Namespace at the bottom of the dialog, as shown in Figure 11-7.

Click OK to establish the WCF Data Services reference. These are the same steps you would perform for setting a reference to an ordinary WCF service. And as with an ordinary WCF service, Visual Studio creates a client-side proxy with strongly typed data classes that correspond to data contracts (entity types) exposed by the service, along with the plumbing that serializes and deserializes entities as they are sent and received across the wire. But a WCF Data Services client proxy goes even further—it also supports LINQ to REST, OData, and change tracking, as this client application will demonstrate.

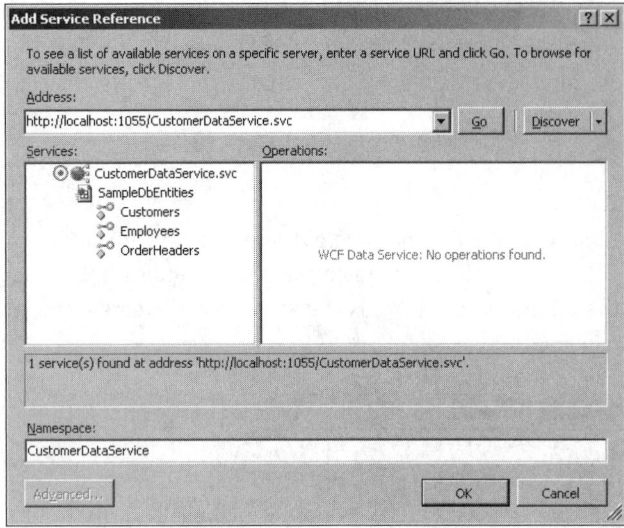

FIGURE 11-7 Creating a service reference from a Windows client project to a WCF Data Services project.

Drag a button from the Toolbox, drop it on to the form, and name it **btnTestClient**. Then double-click the button. Visual Studio creates a handler for the button's *Click* event and opens a window to the form's code, which you should completely replace with the code shown in Listing 11-3 (remember to change the port number in the *ServiceUri* constant definition toward the top of the code with the port number for your environment).

LISTING 11-3 A simple WCF Data Services client.

```
using System;
using System.Linq;
using System.Windows.Forms;

using DemoRestClientTest.CustomerDataService;

namespace DemoRestClientTest
{
  public partial class Form1 : Form
  {
    public Form1()
    {
      InitializeComponent();
    }

    // - The "." after "localhost" is a hack to enable Fiddler packet-sniffing
    // - Change the port number accordingly for your dev machine
    public const string ServiceUri =
     "http://localhost.:1055/CustomerDataService.svc";

    private void btnTestClient_Click(object sender, EventArgs e)
    {
```

```
    // Create the client context
    var ctx = new SampleDbEntities(new Uri(ServiceUri));

    // Construct an OData URI query
    var q =
      from cust in ctx.Customers.Expand("OrderHeaders")
      where !cust.FirstName.StartsWith("A")
      orderby cust.LastName descending
      select cust;

    // Call the service (issues an HTTP GET)
    var customers = q.ToList();

    if (customers.Count == 0)
    {
      MessageBox.Show("There are no matching customers");
      return;
    }

    var firstCustomer = customers[0];
    var orderCount = firstCustomer.OrderHeaders.Count;
    MessageBox.Show(string.Format(
      "Customer {0} has {1} order(s)", firstCustomer.CustomerId, orderCount));

    // Change the customer's name
    firstCustomer.FirstName = "Cassie";
    firstCustomer.LastName = "Hicks";

    // Add a customer order
    var newOrder = new OrderHeader()
    {
      ShipVia = "Regular Mail",
      OrderStatus = "Open",
    };
    firstCustomer.OrderHeaders.Add(newOrder);

    ctx.UpdateObject(firstCustomer);
    ctx.AddRelatedObject(firstCustomer, "OrderHeaders", newOrder);

    // Issues an HTTP MERGE to update the customer's name,
    //  and an HTTP POST to INSERT the customer's new order
    ctx.SaveChanges();
  }
 }
}
```

You will learn exactly how this client code works by single-stepping through it with the debugger, as you keep an eye on background HTTP conversation with Fiddler (and back-end database activity with SQL Profiler). Set a breakpoint at the very top of the button's click event handler by clicking in the left margin area on the line *private void btnTestClient_Click(object sender, EventArgs e)*. Visual Studio displays a red bullet in the margin, indicating that the breakpoint is set.

You are now ready to run the solution. Right-click *DemoRestClientTest* in Solution Explorer, choose Set As Startup Project, and press **F5**. Visual Studio builds the solution and launches the client Windows form. Click the button on the form and you will hit the breakpoint you just set in the event handler. Before proceeding from this point, make sure you have both Fiddler and SQL Profiler running (instructions for starting Fiddler are given in the "Monitoring Network Activity with Fiddler" sidebar earlier in this chapter; steps for running a SQL Profiler trace are provided in Chapter 10).

Use the debugger to single-step over the first line of code (F10 is the default keystroke in Visual Studio for single-stepping). This line creates the client-side context and stores it in the variable ctx:

```
var ctx = new SampleDbEntities(new Uri(ServiceUri));
```

The context class is named *SampleDbEntities*, and was generated automatically when you created the service reference. Visual Studio generated this class in a namespace derived by appending the name *CustomerDataService* that you specified in Figure 11-7 (when creating the service reference) to the project name *DemoRestClientTest*. By including a *using DemoRestClientTest.CustomerDataService* statement at the very top of the listing, the compiler is able to recognize *SampleDbEntities* as the client context class generated by the service reference.

The name of the context class, *SampleDbEntities*, is based on the EDM exposed by the service. But the class has nothing to do with Entity Framework—it runs entirely on the client. Specifically, *SampleDbEntities* on the client is a stateful context object that derives from *DataServiceContext*, and it provides strongly typed properties based on the *SampleDbEntities* EDM discovered when the service reference is created (or updated). This context is capable of querying entities from the service, tracking client-side changes, and pushing updates back to the service.

Notice the *ServiceUri* passed in to the *SampleDbEntities* constructor. This is a string constant that points to the service, and is defined a bit further up in the code (just before the event handler) as follows:

```
// - Change the port number accordingly for your dev machine
// - The "." after "localhost" is a hack to enable Fiddler packet-sniffing
public const string ServiceUri =
 "http://localhost.:1055/CustomerDataService.svc";
```

As we've already mentioned, and as indicated in the comments, you need to change the port number from 1055 to whatever port number is randomly assigned by the Visual Studio Development Web Server on your machine. Alternatively, you could leave the code as-is and explicitly set port 1055 in the Web tab of the service project's properties page. In either case, make sure to include the "dot" after *localhost* or Fiddler will not monitor HTTP traffic as the code executes.

Now step over the next line. This is a strongly typed LINQ query that filters by first name, sorts by last name, and returns matching customers along with their related orders:

```
var q =
  from cust in ctx.Customers.Expand("OrderHeaders")
  where !cust.FirstName.StartsWith("A")
  orderby cust.LastName descending
  select cust;
```

The query source *ctx* is a *DataServiceContext* (that is, a WCF Data Services client context). It provides strongly typed properties based on the *SampleDbEntities* EDM exposed by the service, such as the *Customers* entity set and the *FirstName* and *LastName* properties of the *Customer* entity in this example (unfortunately, the *Expand* method uses a string literal rather than strong typing to reference the *OrderHeaders* navigation property). This is a LINQ to REST query, which may not be immediately obvious, but is clearly evident the moment you hover over the *q*. The tooltip that appears shows that the LINQ query has just been transformed dynamically at runtime into the following equivalent OData URI query string:

```
http://localhost.:1055/CustomerDataService.svc/Customers()?$filter=not startswith(FirstName,'A')
&$orderby=LastName desc&$expand=OrderHeaders
```

At this point, the query has been defined, but it has not been invoked (the HTTP *GET* operation has not yet been issued). Both Fiddler and SQL Profiler show that no activity has yet occurred behind the scenes. Stepping over the next line of code actually executes the query:

```
var customers = q.ToList();
```

In general LINQ terms, this line of code simply means: "execute the query and return a list of objects." For the LINQ to REST provider in this particular example, it means "issue a *GET* request to a REST service with an OData URI query based on the LINQ query, and deserialize the AtomPub feed returned by the service into a list of strongly typed *Customer* entities." That's quite a lot to accomplish with just a single line of code, yet the output from Fiddler and SQL Profiler confirms that this is exactly what occurs.

First look at Fiddler. Select the last HTTP request in the list on the left (the one made to *CustomerDataService.svc*). Then click the Inspectors tab to view the request and response in a split panel display. Click the Raw button at the top of the request and response panels to read them in plain text, as shown in Figure 11-8.

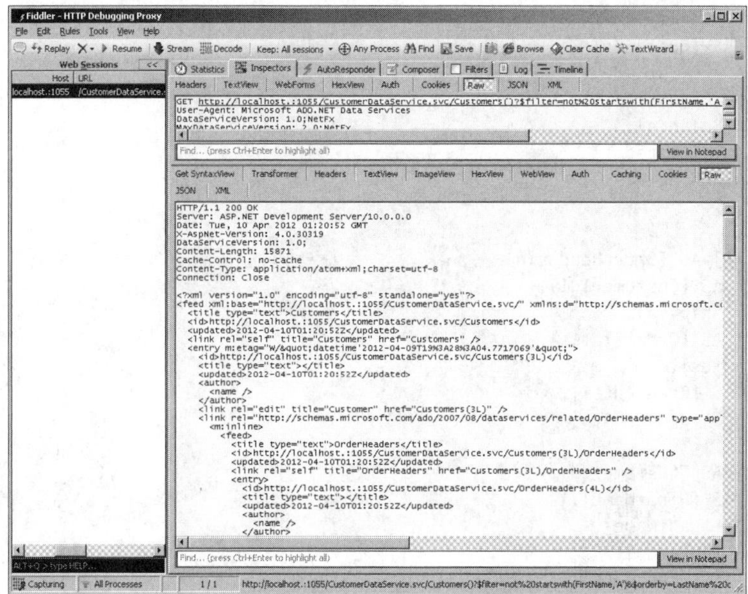

FIGURE 11-8 Using Fiddler to view the WCF Data Services conversation over HTTP.

The request panel at the top shows the *GET* request issued by the client, with the OData URI query string generated from the LINQ query. Beneath, the response panel shows the AtomPub feed result with all of the entities returned by the query (notice the *application/atom+xml* value returned by *Content-Type* in the HTTP response header). The WCF Data Services client library automatically deserializes this response into a list of *Customer* entities (each of which includes *OrderHeader* entities populated in the *OrderHeaders* collection). So the very next line of client code is able to work immediately with objects returned by the service.

Of course, the service sits in front of an EDM managed by Entity Framework, which in turn communicates with SQL Server (see Chapter 10 for detailed coverage of EF and the EDM). When the service receives the URI query, it runs an equivalent query against the EDM, which generates the actual T-SQL statements that ultimately hit the database. That's a lot of layers, so let's spell it out clearly once more. For the request:

- The client defines a LINQ query
- The WCF Data Services client library converts the LINQ query into OData URI syntax
- An HTTP *GET* is issued to WCF Data Services with an OData URI query string
- WCF Data Services generates an equivalent query against the EDM
- Entity Framework generates the required T-SQL statement to query the database
- The T-SQL statement is executed in SQL Server

Now switch over to SQL Profiler. As shown in the SQL Profiler trace, EF generates and executes a direct T-SQL statement that satisfies the EDM query.

```
SELECT
[Project1].[C1] AS [C1],
[Project1].[CustomerId] AS [CustomerId],
[Project1].[FirstName] AS [FirstName],
[Project1].[LastName] AS [LastName],
[Project1].[Balance] AS [Balance],
[Project1].[CreatedAt] AS [CreatedAt],
[Project1].[UpdatedAt] AS [UpdatedAt],
[Project1].[C2] AS [C2],
[Project1].[C3] AS [C3],
[Project1].[OrderHeaderId] AS [OrderHeaderId],
[Project1].[CustomerId1] AS [CustomerId1],
[Project1].[ShipVia] AS [ShipVia],
[Project1].[OrderStatus] AS [OrderStatus],
[Project1].[Notes] AS [Notes],
[Project1].[CreatedAt1] AS [CreatedAt1],
[Project1].[UpdatedAt1] AS [UpdatedAt1]
FROM ( SELECT
  [Extent1].[CustomerId] AS [CustomerId],
  [Extent1].[FirstName] AS [FirstName],
  [Extent1].[LastName] AS [LastName],
  [Extent1].[Balance] AS [Balance],
  [Extent1].[CreatedAt] AS [CreatedAt],
  [Extent1].[UpdatedAt] AS [UpdatedAt],
```

```
  1 AS [C1],
  N'OrderHeaders' AS [C2],
  [Extent2].[OrderHeaderId] AS [OrderHeaderId],
  [Extent2].[CustomerId] AS [CustomerId1],
  [Extent2].[ShipVia] AS [ShipVia],
  [Extent2].[OrderStatus] AS [OrderStatus],
  [Extent2].[Notes] AS [Notes],
  [Extent2].[CreatedAt] AS [CreatedAt1],
  [Extent2].[UpdatedAt] AS [UpdatedAt1],
  CASE WHEN ([Extent2].[OrderHeaderId] IS NULL) THEN CAST(NULL AS int) ELSE 1 END AS [C3]
  FROM  [dbo].[Customer] AS [Extent1]
  LEFT OUTER JOIN [dbo].[OrderHeader] AS [Extent2]
   ON [Extent1].[CustomerId] = [Extent2].[CustomerId]
  WHERE  NOT ([Extent1].[FirstName] LIKE 'A%')
)  AS [Project1]
ORDER BY [Project1].[LastName] DESC, [Project1].[CustomerId] ASC, [Project1].[C3] ASC
```

Notice how this query joins *Customer* with *OrderHeader*, which returns related order data with each selected customer. This is because of the client-side LINQ query specified the *Expand* method. When calling the service, the LINQ to REST provider translated *Expand("OrderHeaders")* into the equivalent OData URI syntax *$expand=OrderHeaders*, which EF then translated into the appropriate T-SQL join.

After this T-SQL query executes in SQL Server:

- The results are returned to Entity Framework
- EF materializes the result set into conceptual entities
- WCF Data Services serializes the conceptual entities into AtomPub format
- The AtomPub response feed is sent back to the client
- The WCF Data Services client library deserializes the AtomPub response feed into objects

Based on the sample data that you populated the database with (in Listing 11-1), this query returns the three customers whose first names do not begin with the letter A (along with their orders) to the client. At this time, the client-side context is aware of three *Customer* entities and their related *OrderHeader* entities.

Note WCF Data Services can be called either synchronously (blocking the client from executing while waiting for a response to each request) or asynchronously (without blocking). Some clients, notably Silverlight and Windows Phone 7, support only asynchronous service calls. This Windows desktop application is working synchronously, which is a bit simpler to code (and delivers a less responsive user experience) than asynchronous communication. Later in this chapter, you will create a Silverlight client with WCF RIA Services that works asynchronously, and in Chapter 13, you will build a Windows Phone 7 OData client that makes asynchronous calls to WCF Data Services hosted in the cloud on Windows Azure.

Continue single-stepping. After first ensuring that there is at least one customer in the list returned by the service, the code extracts the first customer from the list and displays the customer ID and the number of orders for that customer.

```
var firstCustomer = customers[0];
var orderCount = firstCustomer.OrderHeaders.Count;
MessageBox.Show(string.Format(
  "Customer {0} has {1} order(s)", firstCustomer.CustomerId, orderCount));
```

Next, the code modifies the customer's name and adds another order for them. Single-step through it now:

```
// Change the customer's name
firstCustomer.FirstName = "Cassie";
firstCustomer.LastName = "Hicks";

// Add a customer order
var newOrder = new OrderHeader()
{
  ShipVia = "Regular Mail",
  OrderStatus = "Open",
};
firstCustomer.OrderHeaders.Add(newOrder);
```

Notice how this is the same coding experience as server-side Entity Framework, because there is a virtually identical data model defined on the client. Of course these client-side entities may look and feel like EF entities, but they most certainly *are not*. The client has no awareness of EF's *ObjectContext* (or any other data source that may sit behind the service); it just works blissfully with local objects that are automatically sent back and forth between itself and the WCF Data Services.

The next two lines of code inform the client context of the changes made to the customer.

```
ctx.UpdateObject(firstCustomer);
ctx.AddRelatedObject(firstCustomer, "OrderHeaders", newOrder);
```

The *UpdateObject* method marks the *Customer* entity (with updated *FirstName* and *LastName* properties) as "modified," and the *AddRelatedObject* method marks the new *OrderHeader* entity added to the customer's *OrderHeaders* collection as "new." This step is essential—you must use these context methods to explicitly mark entities as changed, or the WCF Data Services client library will not track them as such. Single-step through this code, stopping just before the last line in the method that calls *SaveChanges*:

```
ctx.SaveChanges();
```

Before executing the *SaveChanges* method, take a quick look over at Fiddler and SQL Profiler. They show that no activity (from this application) has transpired since the query that initially retrieved the three customers. This is expected—all changes made thus far have occurred entirely on the client, where those changes are being and tracked by the WCF Data Services client context. The *SaveChanges* method issues the appropriate HTTP requests to push all the buffered up changes on the client back to the service and update the database. Step over the *SaveChanges* method call now, and then switch right back to Fiddler and Profiler to see the result.

In Fiddler, you can see that two requests were sent to the service: The first is an HTTP *MERGE* that updates the customer with the name change, and the second is an HTTP *POST* that adds the new order. Let's examine these requests (and their responses) in detail, starting with the *MERGE* request for the update shown in Listing 11-4.

LISTING 11-4 An HTTP *MERGE* request that updates a *Customer* entity.

```
MERGE http://localhost.:1055/CustomerDataService.svc/Customers(3L) HTTP/1.1
User-Agent: Microsoft ADO.NET Data Services
DataServiceVersion: 1.0;NetFx
MaxDataServiceVersion: 2.0;NetFx
Accept: application/atom+xml,application/xml
Accept-Charset: UTF-8
Content-Type: application/atom+xml
If-Match: W/"datetime'2012-02-01T12%3A32%3A18.2991875'"
Host: localhost.:1055
Content-Length: 991
Expect: 100-continue

<?xml version="1.0" encoding="utf-8" standalone="yes"?>
<entry xmlns:d="http://schemas.microsoft.com/ado/2007/08/dataservices"
xmlns:m="http://schemas.microsoft.com/ado/2007/08/dataservices/metadata"
xmlns="http://www.w3.org/2005/Atom">
  <category scheme="http://schemas.microsoft.com/ado/2007/08/dataservices/scheme"
term="SampleDbModel.Customer" />
  <title />
  <author>
    <name />
  </author>
  <updated>2012-02-01T19:51:38.2358239Z</updated>
  <id>http://localhost.:1055/CustomerDataService.svc/Customers(3L)</id>
  <content type="application/xml">
    <m:properties>
      <d:Balance m:type="Edm.Decimal">40.0000</d:Balance>
      <d:CreatedAt m:type="Edm.DateTime">2012-02-01T12:32:18.2991875</
d:CreatedAt>
      <d:CustomerId m:type="Edm.Int64">3</d:CustomerId>
      <d:FirstName>Cassie</d:FirstName>
      <d:LastName>Hicks</d:LastName>
      <d:UpdatedAt m:type="Edm.DateTime">2012-02-01T12:32:18.2991875</
d:UpdatedAt>
    </m:properties>
  </content>
</entry>
```

The *MERGE* (update) request is made with an OData URI that specifies the customer to be updated as *Customers(3L)*, followed by several HTTP headers and the updated data itself. Interestingly, the User-Agent header (which identifies the HTTP client making the request) still reads *Microsoft ADO.NET Data Services* (the old name for WCF Data Services). Fortunately, the service does not mind the client identifying itself with the outdated brand name and accepts the request anyway. The *If-Match* header (a few lines down) is far more noteworthy and significant. Recall from Chapter 10 that the *Customer* entity in the EDM is mapped to an *UpdateCustomer* stored procedure, and that *UpdateCustomer* expects the original value of the *UpdatedAt* column to implement a concurrency check against multi-user conflicts. The WCF Data Services client library detected this original value mapping in the EDM when the service reference was established, so it is aware that the original value of every *Customer* entity's *UpdatedAt* property needs to be preserved. It is thus able to return that original value in the *If-Match* header in the *MERGE* request, so that the service can pass it on to EF, and EF can pass it on to the *UpdateCustomer* stored procedure.

SQL Profiler shows the actual stored procedure call executed in SQL Server:

```
exec [dbo].[UpdateCustomer] @CustomerId=3,@FirstName='Cassie',@LastName='Hicks',@
Balance=40.0000,@OriginalUpdatedAt='2012-02-01 14:51:38.6967614'
```

After the update, the service response is returned to the client. It contains several HTTP headers, as shown in Listing 11-5.

LISTING 11-5 The new *UpdatedAt* concurrency value returned to the client as an *ETag* response header.

```
HTTP/1.1 204 No Content
Server: ASP.NET Development Server/10.0.0.0
Date: Wed, 01 Feb 2012 19:51:38 GMT
X-AspNet-Version: 4.0.30319
DataServiceVersion: 1.0;
Cache-Control: no-cache
ETag: W/"datetime'2012-02-01T14%3A51%3A38.6967614'"
Content-Length: 0
Connection: Close
```

Again, because of the original *UpdatedAt* value mapping, the service retrieves the newly assigned value (set by the stored procedure after a successful update) and returns it to the client in the *ETag* header. The WCF Data Services client library then automatically refreshes the client-side instance of the entity with this updated value, thereby synchronizing it with the entity updated in the database.

Now look at the how the new order was inserted. In Fiddler, click the second request to view the HTTP traffic for the *POST* that inserted the order. The request data appears in the top panel, as shown in Listing 11-6.

LISTING 11-6 An HTTP *POST* request that inserts a new *OrderHeader* entity.

```
POST http://localhost.:1055/CustomerDataService.svc/Customers(3L)/OrderHeaders
HTTP/1.1
User-Agent: Microsoft ADO.NET Data Services
DataServiceVersion: 1.0;NetFx
MaxDataServiceVersion: 2.0;NetFx
Accept: application/atom+xml,application/xml
Accept-Charset: UTF-8
```

```
Content-Type: application/atom+xml
Host: localhost.:1055
Content-Length: 961
Expect: 100-continue

<?xml version="1.0" encoding="utf-8" standalone="yes"?>
<entry xmlns:d="http://schemas.microsoft.com/ado/2007/08/dataservices"
xmlns:m="http://schemas.microsoft.com/ado/2007/08/dataservices/metadata"
xmlns="http://www.w3.org/2005/Atom">
  <category scheme="http://schemas.microsoft.com/ado/2007/08/dataservices/scheme"
term="SampleDbModel.OrderHeader" />
  <title />
  <author>
    <name />
  </author>
  <updated>2012-02-01T19:51:38.8188317Z</updated>
  <id />
  <content type="application/xml">
    <m:properties>
      <d:CreatedAt m:type="Edm.DateTime">0001-01-01T00:00:00</d:CreatedAt>
      <d:CustomerId m:type="Edm.Int64">0</d:CustomerId>
      <d:Notes m:null="true" />
      <d:OrderHeaderId m:type="Edm.Int64">0</d:OrderHeaderId>
      <d:OrderStatus>Open</d:OrderStatus>
      <d:ShipVia>Regular Mail</d:ShipVia>
      <d:UpdatedAt m:type="Edm.DateTime">0001-01-01T00:00:00</d:UpdatedAt>
    </m:properties>
  </content>
</entry>
```

As with the *MERGE* request, the *POST* (insert) request is made with an OData URI that specifies the customer orders collection to be inserted into as *Customers(3L)/OrderHeaders*, followed by several HTTP headers and the new order data. And as before, the request is forwarded by WCF Data Services to Entity Framework. The *OrderHeader* entity is not mapped to stored procedure mappings in the EDM like the *Customers* entity is, so this time EF dynamically generates and executes a direct parameterized *INSERT* statement for the new order, as shown in the SQL Profiler trace:

```
exec sp_executesql N'insert [dbo].[OrderHeader]([CustomerId], [ShipVia], [OrderStatus], [Notes],
[CreatedAt], [UpdatedAt])
values (@0, @1, @2, null, @3, @4)
select [OrderHeaderId]
from [dbo].[OrderHeader]
where @@ROWCOUNT > 0 and [OrderHeaderId] = scope_identity()',N'@0 bigint,@1 varchar(20),@2
varchar(20),@3 datetime2(7),@4 datetime2(7)',@0=3,@1='Regular Mail',@2='Open',@3='0001-01-01
00:00:00',@4='0001-01-01 00:00:00'
```

After the insert, the service response is returned to the client. The response indicates that the entity was created, and returns the entire new entity to the client, as shown in Listing 11-7.

LISTING 11-7 The HTTP response for a newly inserted entity.

```
HTTP/1.1 201 Created
Server: ASP.NET Development Server/10.0.0.0
Date: Wed, 01 Feb 2012 19:51:39 GMT
X-AspNet-Version: 4.0.30319
DataServiceVersion: 1.0;
Content-Length: 1345
Location: http://localhost.:1055/CustomerDataService.svc/OrderHeaders(10L)
Cache-Control: no-cache
Content-Type: application/atom+xml;charset=utf-8
Connection: Close

<?xml version="1.0" encoding="utf-8" standalone="yes"?>
<entry xml:base="http://localhost.:1055/CustomerDataService.svc/"
xmlns:d="http://schemas.microsoft.com/ado/2007/08/dataservices" xmlns:m="http://
schemas.microsoft.com/ado/2007/08/dataservices/metadata" xmlns="http://www.
w3.org/2005/Atom">
  <id>http://localhost.:1055/CustomerDataService.svc/OrderHeaders(10L)</id>
  <title type="text"></title>
  <updated>2012-02-01T19:51:39Z</updated>
  <author>
    <name />
  </author>
  <link rel="edit" title="OrderHeader" href="OrderHeaders(10L)" />
  <link rel="http://schemas.microsoft.com/ado/2007/08/dataservices/
related/Customer" type="application/atom+xml;type=entry" title="Customer"
href="OrderHeaders(10L)/Customer" />
  <category term="SampleDbModel.OrderHeader" scheme="http://schemas.microsoft.
com/ado/2007/08/dataservices/scheme" />
  <content type="application/xml">
    <m:properties>
      <d:OrderHeaderId m:type="Edm.Int64">10</d:OrderHeaderId>
      <d:CustomerId m:type="Edm.Int64">3</d:CustomerId>
      <d:ShipVia>Regular Mail</d:ShipVia>
      <d:OrderStatus>Open</d:OrderStatus>
      <d:Notes m:null="true" />
      <d:CreatedAt m:type="Edm.DateTime">0001-01-01T00:00:00</d:CreatedAt>
      <d:UpdatedAt m:type="Edm.DateTime">0001-01-01T00:00:00</d:UpdatedAt>
    </m:properties>
  </content>
</entry>
```

Building a Data Entry Client

Now that you have a firm understanding of the core WCF Data Services concepts (REST, OData, and the client libraries), you are ready to build a more useful application. This next WCF Data Services client combines the techniques you just learned with a Windows Forms user interface and some data binding to let the user edit customers and orders.

Note Data binding is a vast topic, and Windows Forms, ASP.NET, and WPF/Silverlight each support very different data binding architectures that are beyond the scope of this book. The minimal data binding code in our examples is provided to demonstrate client/server data access techniques with WCF Data Services (and, in the next section, WCF RIA Services).

Right-click the *DemoWcfDataServices* solution in Solution Explorer and choose Add | New Project. From the list of template categories on the left, beneath Visual C#, choose Windows. Then select the Windows Forms Application template to create a new project named *DemoRestClientDataEntry*.

The *DemoWcfDataServices* solution now has three projects in it: an ASP.NET project (the service) and two Windows Forms projects (the previous *DemoRestClientTest* project and the new *DemoRestClientDataEntry* project with an empty form). Set a reference from the *DemoRestClientDataEntry* project to the service project as you did for the test client: Right-click the *DemoRestClientDataEntry* project, choose Add Service Reference, and click Discover. Then type **CustomerDataService** for the Namespace and click OK.

Now drag several controls onto the empty form. For viewing and editing customers, create two buttons named **btnNewCustomer** and **btnDeleteCustomer** along with a *DataGridView* named **grdCustomers**. Create two more buttons named **btnNewOrder** and **btnDeleteOrder** along with another *DataGridView* named **grdOrders** for viewing and editing orders. Then add two buttons named **btnLoad** and **btnSave** to querying from the service and send changes back to it. Finally, set the *AllowUserToAddRows* and *AllowUserToDeleteRows* properties of both *DataGridView* controls False (this is because adding and deleting entities will be handled by code behind the respective New and Delete buttons). After performing some aesthetic alignment and formatting, your form should appear something like the one shown in Figure 11-9.

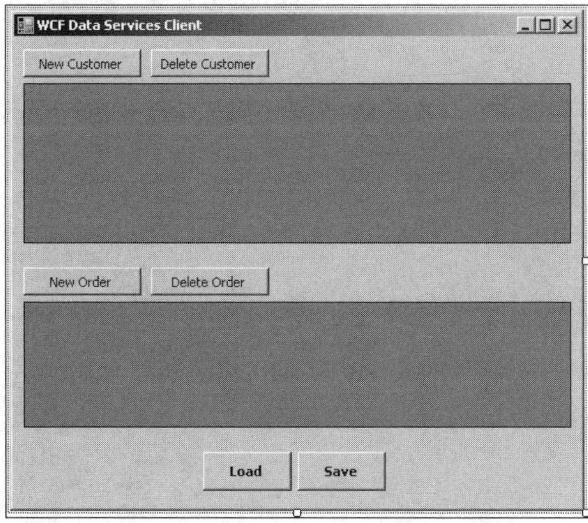

FIGURE 11-9 The WCF Data Services data entry client user interface.

Next, right-click on the form's design surface and choose View Code to open a window to the form's code. Replace it entirely with the code shown in Listing 11-8 (once again, remember to change the port number in the *serviceUri* constant—this time defined in the *CreateNewContext* method—with the port number for your environment).

LISTING 11-8 Code for the WCF Data Services data entry client form.

```
using System;
using System.Collections.Generic;
using System.Data.Services.Client;
using System.Linq;
using System.Windows.Forms;

using DemoRestClientDataEntry.CustomerDataService;

namespace DemoRestClientDataEntry
{
  public partial class Form1 : Form
  {
    private SampleDbEntities _context;

    private List<Customer> _customers;
    private Customer _currentCustomer;

    private BindingSource _customersBindingSource;
    private BindingSource _ordersBindingSource;

    public Form1()
    {
      InitializeComponent();
    }

    private void btnLoad_Click(object sender, EventArgs e)
    {
      this.CreateNewContext();

      var query =
        from customer in this._context.Customers.Expand("OrderHeaders")
        select customer;

      this._customers = query.ToList();

      this._customersBindingSource = new BindingSource(this._customers, null);
      this.BindGrid(this.grdCustomers, this._customersBindingSource);

      this.grdOrders.DataSource = null;

      this.ShowCustomerOrders();
    }

    private void CreateNewContext()
    {
      // - The "." after "localhost" is a hack to enable Fiddler packet-sniffing
```

```
    // - Change the port number accordingly for your dev machine
    var serviceUri = new Uri("http://localhost.:1055/CustomerDataService.svc");
    this._context = new SampleDbEntities(serviceUri);
}

private void grdCustomers_SelectionChanged(object sender, EventArgs e)
{
    this.ShowCustomerOrders();
}

private void ShowCustomerOrders()
{
    if (this.grdCustomers.SelectedRows.Count == 1)
    {
        this._currentCustomer =
         (Customer)this.grdCustomers.SelectedRows[0].DataBoundItem;

        this._ordersBindingSource =
         new BindingSource(this._currentCustomer.OrderHeaders, null);

        this.BindGrid(this.grdOrders, this._ordersBindingSource);
    }
}

private void btnNewCustomer_Click(object sender, EventArgs e)
{
    this._customersBindingSource.AddNew();
}

private void grdCustomers_CellValueChanged
 (object sender, DataGridViewCellEventArgs e)
{
    var customer = (Customer)this.grdCustomers.SelectedRows[0].DataBoundItem;

    var changeInfo =
     this._context.Entities.SingleOrDefault(ed => ed.Entity == customer);

    if (changeInfo == null)
    {
        this._context.AddToCustomers(customer);
    }
    else if (changeInfo.State == EntityStates.Unchanged)
    {
        this._context.UpdateObject(customer);
    }
}

private void btnDeleteCustomer_Click(object sender, EventArgs e)
{
    var customer = (Customer)this.grdCustomers.SelectedRows[0].DataBoundItem;
    this._customersBindingSource.RemoveCurrent();
    this.grdOrders.DataSource = null;
```

```
      var changeInfo =
       this._context.Entities.SingleOrDefault(ed => ed.Entity == customer);

      if (changeInfo != null)
      {
        foreach (var orderHeader in customer.OrderHeaders)
        {
          this._context.DeleteObject(orderHeader);
        }

        this._context.DeleteObject(customer);
      }
    }

    private void btnNewOrder_Click(object sender, EventArgs e)
    {
      if (this.grdOrders.Columns.Count == 0)
      {
        this.ShowCustomerOrders();
        this.grdCustomers.EndEdit();
      }

      var orderHeader = (OrderHeader)this._ordersBindingSource.AddNew();

      orderHeader.CustomerId = this._currentCustomer.CustomerId;
      orderHeader.Customer = this._currentCustomer;
    }

    private void grdOrders_CellValueChanged
     (object sender, DataGridViewCellEventArgs e)
    {
      var orderHeader = (OrderHeader)this.grdOrders.SelectedRows[0].
DataBoundItem;

      var changeInfo =
       this._context.Entities.SingleOrDefault(ci => ci.Entity == orderHeader);

      if (changeInfo == null)
      {
        this._context.AddToOrderHeaders(orderHeader);
      }
      else if (changeInfo.State == EntityStates.Unchanged)
      {
        this._context.UpdateObject(orderHeader);
      }
    }

    private void btnDeleteOrder_Click(object sender, EventArgs e)
    {
      var orderHeader = (OrderHeader)this.grdOrders.SelectedRows[0].
DataBoundItem;

      this._ordersBindingSource.RemoveCurrent();
      this.grdOrders.DataSource = null;
```

```
    var changeInfo =
     this._context.Entities.SingleOrDefault(ed => ed.Entity == orderHeader);

    if (changeInfo != null)
    {
      this._context.DeleteObject(orderHeader);
    }
  }

  private void btnSave_Click(object sender, EventArgs e)
  {
    this.grdCustomers.EndEdit();
    this.grdOrders.EndEdit();

    try
    {
      this._context.SaveChanges(SaveChangesOptions.Batch);
    }
    catch (Exception ex)
    {
      MessageBox.Show
       (ex.Message, "Error", MessageBoxButtons.OK, MessageBoxIcon.Error);
    }

    this.grdCustomers.Refresh();
    this.grdOrders.Refresh();
  }

  private void BindGrid(DataGridView grd, BindingSource bs)
  {
    var readOnlyColumns = new string[]
     { "CustomerId", "OrderHeaderId", "CreatedAt", "UpdatedAt" };

    var hiddenColumns = new string[] { "Customer" };

    grd.DataSource = bs;
    foreach (DataGridViewColumn col in grd.Columns)
    {
      col.ReadOnly = readOnlyColumns.Contains(col.HeaderText);
      col.Visible = !hiddenColumns.Contains(col.HeaderText);
    }
    grd.AutoResizeColumns();
  }

 }
}
```

Your last step is to wire up the event handlers. Return to the form designer and click the Events button in the toolbar at the top of the Properties grid. Then, one at a time, select individual controls and assign them to event handlers in the code, as follows:

- Assign the *btnNewCustomer* button's *Click* event to *btnNewCustomer_Click*

- Assign the *btnDeleteCustomer* button's *Click* event to *btnDeleteCustomer_Click*
- Assign the *grdCustomers* grid's *SelectionChanged* event to *grdCustomers_SelectionChanged*
- Assign the *grdCustomers* grid's *CellValueChanged* event to *grdCustomers_CellValueChanged*
- Assign the *btnNewOrder* button's *Click* event to *btnNewOrder_Click*
- Assign the *btnDeleteOrder* button's *Click* event to *btnDeleteOrder_Click*
- Assign the *grdOrders* grid's *CellValueChanged* event to *grdOrders_CellValueChanged*
- Assign the *btnLoad* button's *Click* event to *btnLoad_Click*
- Assign the *btnSave* button's *Click* event to *btnSave_Click*

This client code adds some basic data binding to the concepts you learned with the test client. Before you run the solution, let us explain the important aspects of the code in Listing 11-8.

First, notice the private *SampleDbEntities* form variable named *_context*. This means that the client context maintains its state during the lifetime of the form, tracking the user's changes made from the time they click Load to retrieve data and the time they click Save to update it back. Clicking Load fires *btnLoad_Click* which instantiates the client context by calling *CreateNewContext*. As with the test client, you must adjust the service URL's port number 1055 in the *CreateNewContext* method accordingly, and ensure that there is a "dot" after *localhost* so that Fiddler can monitor HTTP requests. After creating the context, the *btnLoad_Click* method executes a LINQ to REST query that retrieves all customers and their orders into a list, stores the list in the private form variable *_customers*, and binds the list to the top grid (*grdCustomers*) using a *BindingSource* object.

As soon as the list is bound to the top grid, the first customer row gets selected automatically, so *btnLoad* calls the *ShowCustomerOrders* method to bind the first customer's orders to the bottom grid (*grdOrders*). When the user selects any other customer in the top grid, the *grdCustomers_Selection* event handler responds with another *ShowCustomerOrders* call to update the bottom grid for the selected customer. The *ShowCustomerOrders* method uses the *DataBoundItem* property to obtain the object bound to the currently selected row in the top grid, which it casts to the expected *Customer* entity type. With the selected *Customer* entity in hand, the method binds its *OrderHeaders* collection to *grdOrders* using a second *BindingSource* object.

The next three methods handle *Customer* inserts, updates, and deletes actions made by the user in the top grid. In particular, these methods respond to events that fire as the user edits data, and inform the client context to track changes as the user makes them.

When the user clicks New Customer, the *btnNewCustomer* method calls *AddNew* on the customer binding source. This internally creates a new *Customer* object and adds it to the list bound to *grdCustomers*, which in turn appends a new row to the bottom of the grid for the user to enter the new customer's data. The context is not yet aware of the new entity; it will be informed about the new customer as soon as the user edits the first cell in the new grid row.

In *grdCustomers_CellValueChanged*, the code responds to edits made by the user on any customer row. This method determines whether the user is editing a new or existing customer by querying the client context's *Entities* collection for the current customer. This collection holds change information for all of the entities being tracked on the client, and the *SingleOrDefault* method searches the collection for the particular customer that the user is editing. If it is not found, that means that the context is not yet tracking the object, which must mean that this is a new customer (added when the user clicked New Customer). In this case, *AddToCustomers* is called on the context, instructing it to track this customer as new. If the context is already tracking the object, *and* the change information's *State* property equals *EntityStates.Unchanged*, it means that this is an existing customer that has not yet been modified. In this case, *UpdateObject* is called on the context, instructing it to track this customer as modified.

It is important to remember that the *grdCustomers_CellValueChanged* method fires for each cell changed in a grid's row, but the context needs to be instructed to track that row's entity state once and only once. That is why it's critical to check the *State* property. For example, consider the new customer scenario. The *AddToCustomers* method is called the first time a cell is edited in a new customer row. When another cell is edited in the same row, the event handler fires again, only this time the new *Customer* entity is found in the *Entities* collection because of the previous *AddToCustomers* call. Therefore, the *State* property is checked to prevent the action from being interpreted incorrectly as an update to be tracked rather than an insert that's already being tracked. The *State* property for the new customer is *EntityStates.Added*, not *EntityStates.Unchanged*, which prevents the event handler from erroneously tracking the same customer again as modified. Similarly, the first time the user edits the cell or an existing customer's row, the *State* property is changed from *EntityStates.Unchanged* to *EntityStates.Modified* by the call to *UpdateObject*, which prevents existing customer entities from being tracked as modified multiple times. Once a customer is being tracked as either new or changed, it will have an entry in the context's *Entities* collection with a *State* other than *EntityStates.Unchanged*, in which case the *grdCustomers_CellValueChanged* event handler does nothing.

When the user clicks Delete Customer, the *btnDeleteCustomer* method first obtains the customer being deleted and then calls *RemoveCurrent* on the customer binding source. This internally deletes the *Customer* object from the list bound to the current grid row, which in turn removes the row from the grid on the form. It is important to perform these steps in this order, because you will not be able to reference the deleted customer entity once it has been removed from the binding source. The code then attempts to locate the change tracking entry for the deleted customer by querying the context's *Entities* collection as before. If the user clicked Delete Customer immediately after clicking New Customer, then the context has no change tracking information for this customer, and so no action needs to be taken. Otherwise, the method enters a loop that calls *DeleteObject* on the customer's related *OrderHeader* entities, and then calls *DeleteObject* for the parent *Customer* entity. This informs the client context to track the customer and its orders as deleted.

The next three methods that follow handle *OrderHeader* inserts, updates, and deletes actions made by the user in the bottom grid. These methods monitor for changes using the very same techniques we just explained, and keep the client context informed of data that the user edits in the bottom grid.

Finally, the *btnSave_Click* event handler fires when the user clicks Save. This method first calls *EndEdit* on both grids to apply any pending changes (which is important if the user clicks Save while in the middle of editing a cell; calling *EndEdit* forces the grid's *CellValueChanged* event to fire, whereas otherwise it would not). Then, *SaveChanges* is invoked on the context to push all the client updates to the service, just as we demonstrated with the test client. But notice that this code specifies *SaveChangesOptions.Batch*, which is *required* to support hierarchical updates (that is, updates involving both parent and child entities). The *SaveChangesOptions.Batch* setting instructs the WCF Data Services client library to batch up all the entity changes into a single request, rather than individual requests as you saw with the test client. This means that only one HTTP request will be issued to WCF Data Services no matter how many entities are inserted, updated, or deleted on the client.

To see everything work, monitor the HTTP traffic with Fiddler as you run the solution. First, make sure that both Fiddler and SQL Profiler are running. Then right-click *DemoRestClientDataEntry* in Solution Explorer, choose Set As Startup Project, and press **F5**. Visual Studio builds the solution and launches the form.

Click the Load button. This queries the service and then binds the customer and order data returned by the service to the user interface, as shown in Figure 11-10.

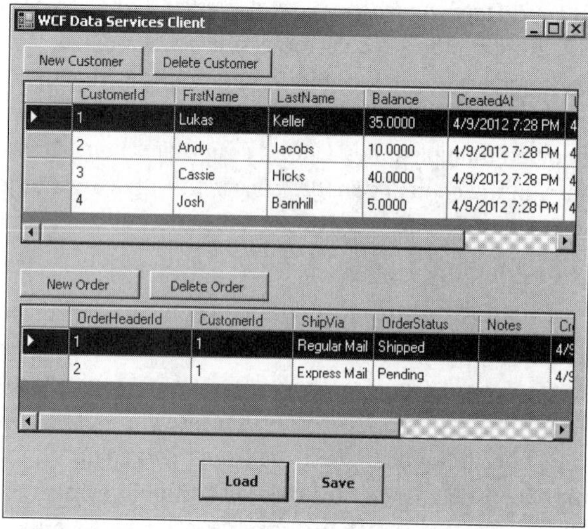

FIGURE 11-10 The client form populated with data returned by WCF Data Services.

Now edit the data as follows:

- Insert a new order for Andy Jacobs by selecting Andy's row in the top grid and clicking New Order. Then enter any random text into the *ShipVia* and *OrderStatus* columns for the new order.
- Update the balance for Cassie Hicks by changing the value from 40 to 50 in the top grid.
- Delete customer Josh Barnhill by selecting Josh's row in the top grid and clicking Delete Customer. Recall from our explanation of the code that this not only marks Josh's customer entity as deleted, but all the child orders as well.

You have just performed a mix of insert, update, and delete operations on the client. Now click Save to push all those changes to the service.

Switch over to Fiddler to examine the HTTP conversation that just took place. You will see that two HTTP requests were made; the first one is the *GET* issued by the LINQ to REST query when you first clicked the Load button. The second one is a *POST* issued by *SaveChanges*, and it contains all of the individual entity changes batched up inside a single HTTP request, as shown in Listing 11-9.

LISTING 11-9 A batch of client updates posted to WCF Data Services as a single request.

```
POST http://localhost.:1055/CustomerDataService.svc/$batch HTTP/1.1
User-Agent: Microsoft ADO.NET Data Services
DataServiceVersion: 1.0;NetFx
MaxDataServiceVersion: 2.0;NetFx
Accept: application/atom+xml,application/xml
Accept-Charset: UTF-8
Content-Type: multipart/mixed; boundary=batch_74726ae1-e572-4e88-a53f-
beb080591cdd
Host: localhost.:1055
Content-Length: 3509
Expect: 100-continue
Connection: Keep-Alive

--batch_74726ae1-e572-4e88-a53f-beb080591cdd
Content-Type: multipart/mixed; boundary=changeset_d7d5bcea-d717-4c2e-8134-
80e730c80738

--changeset_d7d5bcea-d717-4c2e-8134-80e730c80738
Content-Type: application/http
Content-Transfer-Encoding: binary

POST http://localhost.:1055/CustomerDataService.svc/OrderHeaders HTTP/1.1
Content-ID: 25
Content-Type: application/atom+xml;type=entry
Content-Length: 965

<?xml version="1.0" encoding="utf-8" standalone="yes"?>
<entry xmlns:d="http://schemas.microsoft.com/ado/2007/08/dataservices"
xmlns:m="http://schemas.microsoft.com/ado/2007/08/dataservices/metadata"
xmlns="http://www.w3.org/2005/Atom">
  <category scheme="http://schemas.microsoft.com/ado/2007/08/dataservices/scheme"
term="SampleDbModel.OrderHeader" />
  <title />
  <author>
    <name />
  </author>
  <updated>2012-02-02T19:43:04.539875Z</updated>
  <id />
  <content type="application/xml">
    <m:properties>
      <d:CreatedAt m:type="Edm.DateTime">0001-01-01T00:00:00</d:CreatedAt>
      <d:CustomerId m:type="Edm.Int64">2</d:CustomerId>
      <d:Notes m:null="true" />
```

```
      <d:OrderHeaderId m:type="Edm.Int64">0</d:OrderHeaderId>
      <d:OrderStatus>Pending</d:OrderStatus>
      <d:ShipVia>Regular Mail</d:ShipVia>
      <d:UpdatedAt m:type="Edm.DateTime">0001-01-01T00:00:00</d:UpdatedAt>
    </m:properties>
  </content>
</entry>
--changeset_d7d5bcea-d717-4c2e-8134-80e730c80738
Content-Type: application/http
Content-Transfer-Encoding: binary

MERGE http://localhost.:1055/CustomerDataService.svc/Customers(3L) HTTP/1.1
Content-ID: 26
Content-Type: application/atom+xml;type=entry
If-Match: W/"datetime'2012-02-02T14%3A21%3A07.89925'"
Content-Length: 991

<?xml version="1.0" encoding="utf-8" standalone="yes"?>
<entry xmlns:d="http://schemas.microsoft.com/ado/2007/08/dataservices"
xmlns:m="http://schemas.microsoft.com/ado/2007/08/dataservices/metadata"
xmlns="http://www.w3.org/2005/Atom">
  <category scheme="http://schemas.microsoft.com/ado/2007/08/dataservices/scheme"
term="SampleDbModel.Customer" />
  <title />
  <author>
    <name />
  </author>
  <updated>2012-02-02T19:43:04.539875Z</updated>
  <id>http://localhost.:1055/CustomerDataService.svc/Customers(3L)</id>
  <content type="application/xml">
    <m:properties>
      <d:Balance m:type="Edm.Decimal">50.0000</d:Balance>
      <d:CreatedAt m:type="Edm.DateTime">2012-02-02T14:20:55.696125</d:CreatedAt>
      <d:CustomerId m:type="Edm.Int64">3</d:CustomerId>
      <d:FirstName>Cassie</d:FirstName>
      <d:LastName>Hicks</d:LastName>
      <d:UpdatedAt m:type="Edm.DateTime">2012-02-02T14:21:07.89925</d:UpdatedAt>
    </m:properties>
  </content>
</entry>
--changeset_d7d5bcea-d717-4c2e-8134-80e730c80738
Content-Type: application/http
Content-Transfer-Encoding: binary

DELETE http://localhost.:1055/CustomerDataService.svc/OrderHeaders(8L) HTTP/1.1
Content-ID: 27

--changeset_d7d5bcea-d717-4c2e-8134-80e730c80738
Content-Type: application/http
Content-Transfer-Encoding: binary

DELETE http://localhost.:1055/CustomerDataService.svc/OrderHeaders(9L) HTTP/1.1
Content-ID: 28
```

```
--changeset_d7d5bcea-d717-4c2e-8134-80e730c80738
Content-Type: application/http
Content-Transfer-Encoding: binary

DELETE http://localhost.:1055/CustomerDataService.svc/Customers(4L) HTTP/1.1
Content-ID: 29
If-Match: W/"datetime'2012-01-01T00%3A00%3A00'"

--changeset_d7d5bcea-d717-4c2e-8134-80e730c80738--
--batch_74726ae1-e572-4e88-a53f-beb080591cdd--
```

If you break down this request, you can see that it contains multiple parts, each of which represents a single entity change request. The service URI for the main request is terminated with *$batch*, which informs the service that it is actually receiving a batch of requests, all packaged up inside the main HTTP request. Also notice that the *Content-Type* header reads *multipart/mixed* with a string defining the boundaries of the batch (this string appears before the first request in the batch and again after the last request in the batch).

Each of the requests in the batch is identified with a unique *Content-ID* header, and they are all handled the same as the individual requests you saw in the test client. The first is a *POST* to insert the new order for Andy Jacobs. That is then followed by the *MERGE* to update the balance for Cassie Hicks. Finally, three *DELETE* operation requests are issued to delete Josh Barnhill; the first two delete the customer's related orders, and the third deletes the customer itself.

Switch over now to SQL Profiler to see the database activity generated by these requests. As shown in Figure 11-11, EF automatically generated *INSERT* and *DELETE* statements to update the *OrderHeader* table and stored procedure calls to *UpdateCustomer* and *DeleteCustomer* that update the *Customer* table. This is expected, again, because there are stored procedure mappings in the EDM for the *Customers* entity set but not *OrderHeaders*. Also notice that all the updates are batched inside a transaction, which ensures that they all succeed or fail together.

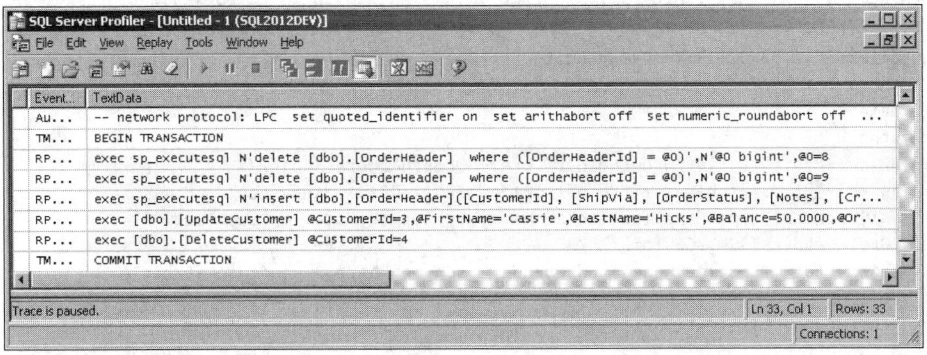

SQL Server Profiler - [Untitled - 1 (SQL2012DEV)]

File Edit View Replay Tools Window Help

Event...	TextData
Au...	-- network protocol: LPC set quoted_identifier on set arithabort off set numeric_roundabort off ...
TM...	BEGIN TRANSACTION
RP...	exec sp_executesql N'delete [dbo].[OrderHeader] where ([OrderHeaderId] = @0)',N'@0 bigint',@0=8
RP...	exec sp_executesql N'delete [dbo].[OrderHeader] where ([OrderHeaderId] = @0)',N'@0 bigint',@0=9
RP...	exec sp_executesql N'insert [dbo].[OrderHeader]([CustomerId], [ShipVia], [OrderStatus], [Notes], [Cr...
RP...	exec [dbo].[UpdateCustomer] @CustomerId=3,@FirstName='Cassie',@LastName='Hicks',@Balance=50.0000,@Or...
RP...	exec [dbo].[DeleteCustomer] @CustomerId=4
TM...	COMMIT TRANSACTION

Trace is paused. Ln 33, Col 1 Rows: 33

Connections: 1

FIGURE 11-11 SQL Server Profiler output showing the T-SQL statements executed by the batched WCF Data Services request.

Now switch back to Fiddler and examine the HTTP response returned to the client, as shown in Listing 11-10.

LISTING 11-10 A batch of WCF Data Services results returned as a single response.

```
HTTP/1.1 202 Accepted
Server: ASP.NET Development Server/10.0.0.0
Date: Thu, 02 Feb 2012 19:43:04 GMT
X-AspNet-Version: 4.0.30319
DataServiceVersion: 1.0;
Content-Length: 2898
Cache-Control: no-cache
Content-Type: multipart/mixed; boundary=batchresponse_f525ef65-e8fb-4cd6-8108-
40e1212fe166
Connection: Close

--batchresponse_f525ef65-e8fb-4cd6-8108-40e1212fe166
Content-Type: multipart/mixed; boundary=changesetresponse_0eb669ef-4471-4777-
85a6-8c0ed3993cd4

--changesetresponse_0eb669ef-4471-4777-85a6-8c0ed3993cd4
Content-Type: application/http
Content-Transfer-Encoding: binary

HTTP/1.1 201 Created
Content-ID: 25
Cache-Control: no-cache
DataServiceVersion: 1.0;
Content-Type: application/atom+xml;charset=utf-8
Location: http://localhost.:1055/CustomerDataService.svc/OrderHeaders(33L)

<?xml version="1.0" encoding="utf-8" standalone="yes"?>
<entry xml:base="http://localhost.:1055/CustomerDataService.svc/"
xmlns:d="http://schemas.microsoft.com/ado/2007/08/dataservices" xmlns:m="http://
schemas.microsoft.com/ado/2007/08/dataservices/metadata" xmlns="http://www.
w3.org/2005/Atom">
  <id>http://localhost.:1055/CustomerDataService.svc/OrderHeaders(33L)</id>
  <title type="text"></title>
  <updated>2012-02-02T19:43:04Z</updated>
  <author>
    <name />
  </author>
  <link rel="edit" title="OrderHeader" href="OrderHeaders(33L)" />
  <link rel="http://schemas.microsoft.com/ado/2007/08/dataservices/
related/Customer" type="application/atom+xml;type=entry" title="Customer"
href="OrderHeaders(33L)/Customer" />
  <category term="SampleDbModel.OrderHeader" scheme="http://schemas.microsoft.
com/ado/2007/08/dataservices/scheme" />
  <content type="application/xml">
    <m:properties>
      <d:OrderHeaderId m:type="Edm.Int64">33</d:OrderHeaderId>
      <d:CustomerId m:type="Edm.Int64">2</d:CustomerId>
      <d:ShipVia>Regular Mail</d:ShipVia>
      <d:OrderStatus>Pending</d:OrderStatus>
```

```
      <d:Notes m:null="true" />
      <d:CreatedAt m:type="Edm.DateTime">0001-01-01T00:00:00</d:CreatedAt>
      <d:UpdatedAt m:type="Edm.DateTime">0001-01-01T00:00:00</d:UpdatedAt>
    </m:properties>
  </content>
</entry>
--changesetresponse_0eb669ef-4471-4777-85a6-8c0ed3993cd4
Content-Type: application/http
Content-Transfer-Encoding: binary

HTTP/1.1 204 No Content
Content-ID: 26
Cache-Control: no-cache
DataServiceVersion: 1.0;
ETag: W/"datetime'2012-02-02T14%3A43%3A04.9305'"

--changesetresponse_0eb669ef-4471-4777-85a6-8c0ed3993cd4
Content-Type: application/http
Content-Transfer-Encoding: binary

HTTP/1.1 204 No Content
Content-ID: 27
Cache-Control: no-cache
DataServiceVersion: 1.0;

--changesetresponse_0eb669ef-4471-4777-85a6-8c0ed3993cd4
Content-Type: application/http
Content-Transfer-Encoding: binary

HTTP/1.1 204 No Content
Content-ID: 28
Cache-Control: no-cache
DataServiceVersion: 1.0;

--changesetresponse_0eb669ef-4471-4777-85a6-8c0ed3993cd4
Content-Type: application/http
Content-Transfer-Encoding: binary

HTTP/1.1 204 No Content
Content-ID: 29
Cache-Control: no-cache
DataServiceVersion: 1.0;

--changesetresponse_0eb669ef-4471-4777-85a6-8c0ed3993cd4--
--batchresponse_f525ef65-e8fb-4cd6-8108-40e1212fe166--
```

You can see that the response is also batched. Notice that individual responses inside the batch are each tagged with *Content-ID* values so that the WCF Data Services client library can correlate each response that comes back with the original request that went out. As explained for the test client, each individual response's content is used to refresh the client-side instances of each updated entity.

Extending WCF Data Services

We have conducted a fairly detailed study of WCF Data Services. Still, the examples thus far have been based on very simple client-side queries and straightforward updates. Although OData URI queries can be quite flexible, they do not support the more advanced LINQ query operations. Therefore, some LINQ to REST queries simply cannot be converted into an equivalent OData URI string. Furthermore, you may need to supplement the default query/update functionality provided by the service with your own custom business logic that filters or validates data.

Fortunately, WCF Data Services has several extensibility features available that allow your services to overcome the limitations of OData URI queries and provide much more functionality than straightforward CRUD operations. We conclude our WCF Data Services coverage by discussing custom service operations, service method overrides, and query interceptors.

Creating Custom Service Operations

It is very easy to expose your own custom methods as additional service operations. Simply define any public method that returns *IQueryable<T>* (where *T* is any entity type in your EDM), and decorate the method with the *WebGet* attribute. Then add one line of code to the *InitializeService* method to expose the method as a service operation. You can use this technique to implement queries on the service that are difficult or impossible to express on the client using LINQ to REST and an OData URI. It is also a great way to extend the service with custom business logic.

To demonstrate, return to the *CustomerDataService.cs* file in the *DemoRestService* project (Listing 11-2). Double-click the file in Solution Explorer and add the code shown in Listing 11-11, just beneath the *InitializeService* method.

LISTING 11-11 Adding a custom operation to WCF Data Services.

```
[WebGet]
public IQueryable<Customer> GetCustomersByBalance(decimal minBalance)
{
  return
    from customer in base.CurrentDataSource.Customers
    where customer.Balance > minBalance
    select customer;
}
```

Then add this one line to the *InitializeService* method (you can add it anywhere inside the method):

```
config.SetServiceOperationAccessRule("GetCustomersByBalance", ServiceOperationRights.All);
```

Now rebuild the solution and WCF Data Services will immediately expose the method as a custom service operation.

This simple example may not do much, but it does illustrate all the essentials points. The *WebGet* attribute exposes the public method *GetCustomersByLastName* as a service operation. The service operation accepts a decimal parameter, which it uses in the *where* clause of a LINQ query—only this is a *true* LINQ to Entities query, using Entity Framework on the server. The LINQ query obtains access to the *ObjectContext* via the *CurrentDataSource* property defined in the service's base class, *DataService<SampleDbEntities>*.

Here is the OData URI syntax for calling this service operation that returns those customers whose balance exceeds 15 (the M suffix in 15M represents the *money* data type in SQL Server, corresponding to *decimal* in .NET):

```
http://localhost.:1055/CustomerDataService.svc/GetCustomersByBalance()?minBalance=15M
```

Any time you modify your service, you need to update the service reference on the client to regenerate the proxy classes. So you would be correct to assume that your next step is to do just that, but unfortunately updating the service reference will not expose *GetCustomersByBalance* on the client side (as it should). This is due to a limitation in Visual Studio's WCF Data Services client proxy generator tool that fails to detect custom service operations (it only recognizes entity sets exposed by the *InitializeService* method).

The workaround is to manually extend the automatically generated client-side context class *SampleDbEntities* with a public method that wraps the service operation. Essentially, this means adding the code that the proxy generator should have added for you. The generated *SampleDbEntities* context class is marked *partial*, making it very easy for you to fill in the missing functionality by adding the wrapper method.

Try this out with the earlier *DemoRestClientTest* project by adding the code shown in Listing 11-12 anywhere to the project. You can simply append the code to the bottom of the form's code you added from Listing 11-3. Alternatively, you can create a new class file for custom proxy wrapper extensions and add the code there; it really doesn't matter. Just be sure you don't add it directly to the generated proxy code, as that code gets overwritten whenever you update the service reference.

LISTING 11-12 Extending the client context class with a custom service operation wrapper method.

```
namespace DemoRestClientTest.CustomerDataService
{
  using System.Data.Services.Client;
  using System.Collections.Generic;

  public partial class SampleDbEntities
  {
    public DataServiceQuery<Customer> GetCustomersByBalance(decimal minBalance)
    {
      return base
        .CreateQuery<Customer>("GetCustomersByBalance")
        .AddQueryOption("minBalance", string.Format("{0}M", minBalance));
    }

  }
}
```

This code extends the client context class by giving it a *GetCustomersByBalance* method. The method accepts a minimum balance parameter, and internally calls the base class *CreateQuery<T>* and *AddQueryOption* methods to produce a *DataServiceQuery<T>* object. Embedding this code into the context itself makes it completely reusable, so this plumbing logic does not need to be duplicated anywhere else. The context class now makes the *GetCustomersByBalance* method as easy to invoke as LINQ to REST queries against ordinary entity sets. For example, this line of code calls the service operation to get the customers with a balance exceeding 15 and populates a list with the results:

```
var list = ctx.GetCustomersByBalance(15).ToList();
```

You can easily test this out as follows. Create another button on the form and add this line of code to the button's *Click* event handler. Set a breakpoint on the line, right-click *DemoRestClientTest* in Solution Explorer, choose Set As Startup Project, and press **F5**. Then click the button to hit the breakpoint, and single-step over the line of code so you can monitor the activity with Fiddler and SQL Profiler to confirm the results returned in *list*.

Overriding Service Methods

The service's base class, *DataService<SampleDbEntities>*, has two virtual protected methods that you can override (akin to, but not exactly the same as, an event) to inject custom logic that executes on each request or whenever an exception occurs. Respectively, these are named *OnStartProcessingRequest* and *HandleException*, and each of them accepts an arguments parameter with information you can use in handling these "events." Both of them should invoke the base class implementation before adding extended functionality. Listing 11-13 below demonstrates how to implement these method overrides.

LISTING 11-13 Overriding the *OnStartProcessingRequest* and *HandleException* base class methods.

```
protected override void OnStartProcessingRequest(ProcessRequestArgs args)
{
  base.OnStartProcessingRequest(args);

  // add code here...
}

protected override void HandleException(HandleExceptionArgs args)
{
  base.HandleException(args);

  // add code here...
}
```

The *OnStartProcessingRequest* override executes with each incoming client request. In this method, you can examine the *ProcessRequestArgs* parameter to discover and act upon a host of information, such as the request URI, method, and headers, as well as the response headers, and an *IsBatchRequest* flag indicating that this is a batch (multi-part) request.

The *HandleException* override effectively serves as a global "catch block" for the service. The *HandleExceptionArgs* parameter has an *Exception* property that hands you the unhandled exception object. The arguments parameter also exposes a *UseVerboseErrors* property that controls whether detailed information about the exception is returned to the client, plus several useful read-only response-related properties (*ResponseContentType*, *ResponseStatusCode*, and *ResponseWritten*).

Writing Interceptors

Finally, you can write special methods to intercept each query or change request at the entity set level. This provides you with a great deal of control over service behavior.

There are two types of interceptors. Query interceptors allow you to filter data being returned out of an entity set that is satisfying *any* query in the service. Change interceptors allow you to examine each entity change just before it occurs, so you can take special action if desired.

Both types of interceptors operate at the entity set level. At runtime, the framework uses Reflection to discover interceptors in the service by locating methods decorated with the *QueryInterceptor* or *ChangeInterceptor* attribute. The entity set name is specified as a string parameter to the method attribute, whereas the method name itself is insignificant. Interceptor methods must be coded with the correct signatures; query interceptors are expected to return a lambda that filters the entity set, while change interceptors are expected to accept two parameters containing information about the entity being changed, as Listing 11-14 demonstrates.

LISTING 11-14 Implementing a query interceptor and change interceptor for the *Customers* entity set.

```
[QueryInterceptor("Customers")]
public Expression<Func<Customer, bool>> OnQueryCustomers()
{
  return c => c.Balance > 15;
}

[ChangeInterceptor("Customers")]
public void OnChangeCustomers(Customer customer, UpdateOperations op)
{
  if (op == UpdateOperations.Delete)
  {
    throw new DataServiceException("Customers cannot be deleted");
  }
}
```

The first method declares a query interceptor for the *Customers* entity. As such, it returns a lambda expression that will be used to filter customer data returned for all queries. Think of it as a global "where clause" for the *Customers* entity set. A lambda expression is merely a method pointer, which in the case of *Func<Customer, bool>* refers to a method that accepts a *Customer* object and returns a *bool* result. In this example, the lambda returns true if the customer balance is greater than 15, effectively hardcoding a filter that excludes all customers with a balance of 15 and lower from every query that gets serviced. Note that to use the actual return data type *Expression<T>*, you must add the following *using* statement at the top of the code:

```
using System.Linq.Expressions;
```

The second method implements a change interceptor, also for the *Customers* entity. Change interceptors return no data, and must accept two parameters. The first is an object of the entity set type (which is *Customer* in this example), and the second is an *UpdateOperations* enumeration. You can inspect the entity being updated as well as the type of update being attempted, and take any custom action required by your service. This provides you with a much finer degree of control over security than the global read-only versus writable control provided by the *InitializeService* method. In this example, the service simply does not permit customers to be deleted.

WCF Data Services supports authentication, although it does not implement authentication on its own. Instead, it relies on authentication options supported by the host (typically IIS), including anonymous, basic, digest, Windows, ASP.NET forms, and claims-based authentication. With authentication enabled, you can perform user-based security checks in your change interceptors, as well as user-based filtering in your query interceptors. For example, if your WCF Data Services are hosted as an ASP.NET Web Application (like those in this chapter are), you can retrieve the principal (security information) of the request by examining the *HttpContext.Current.User* property. Then you can leverage that information (for example, user name, or user ID) to implement user-specific interceptors in your WCF Data Services.

WCF RIA Services

WCF RIA Services is, well, *richer* than WCF Data Services (and also newer). Indeed, the R in RIA means rich, although the full TLA (Three-Letter Acronym) can stand for Rich *Internet* Application or Rich *Interactive* Application—depending on who you're talking to. Since its earliest days, WCF RIA Services was designed to work best with Silverlight, although it now also supports OData, SOAP, and JSON to reach a wider range of clients. You can build WCF RIA Services over any data access layer, including Entity Framework, LINQ to SQL, or Plain Old CLR Objects (POCOs), in which case you handle the persistence yourself using any data access technique you want, including conventional ADO.NET.

Both WCF Data Services and WCF RIA Services solve many of the same problems, so it is only natural to question which one to use. The answer extends a bit beyond the standard "it depends on your scenario" response, since WCF RIA Services offers a lot more than just data access functionality. It also features client-side self-tracking entities, client-side validation, automatic server-to-client code generation, and more. A full treatment of WCF RIA Services is well beyond the scope of this section, where our objective is to demonstrate how WCF RIA Services facilitates data access for functionality similar to the WCF Data Services solution in the previous section. After working through a WCF RIA Services version of the same solution, the chapter concludes with a side-by-side comparison of the two frameworks. This approach will give you a clear understanding of when it is better to use one over the other (or perhaps, when it might be best to use neither).

Establishing a WCF RIA Services Link

When WCF RIA Services is used with Silverlight, Visual Studio provides a special link between your client and service projects. Like a service reference, this link binds the two projects together, only a WCF RIA Services link couples them much more tightly than an ordinary service reference does. Public changes on the service side are reflected automatically in corresponding classes on the client side every time you perform a build—you never need to worry about working against an outdated proxy in the client project simply because you forgot to manually update a service reference. You can create a Visual Studio solution with a Silverlight client project and a WCF RIA Services project already linked to each other in a single step. You will do that right now to build the demo.

Important The complete WCF RIA Services framework is distributed as two separate downloads that you must install on top of Visual Studio 2010. Before you can follow along with the sample application, download and install WCF RIA Services SP2 for Silverlight 4 and 5 from *http://www.microsoft.com/download/en/details.aspx?id=28357*, and then go to *http://www.microsoft.com/download/en/details.aspx?id=26939* for the WCF RIA Services Toolkit.

You may also need the latest Silverlight Developer Runtime, which you can download from *http://go.microsoft.com/fwlink/?LinkId=146060*. If you have a non-developer version of Silverlight installed, be sure to uninstall it before attempting these installations.

Start Visual Studio and choose File | New | Project. From the list of template categories on the left, beneath Visual C#, choose Silverlight. Then select the Silverlight Application template to create a project named **DemoSL** in a solution named **DemoWcfRiaServices**, as shown in Figure 11-12.

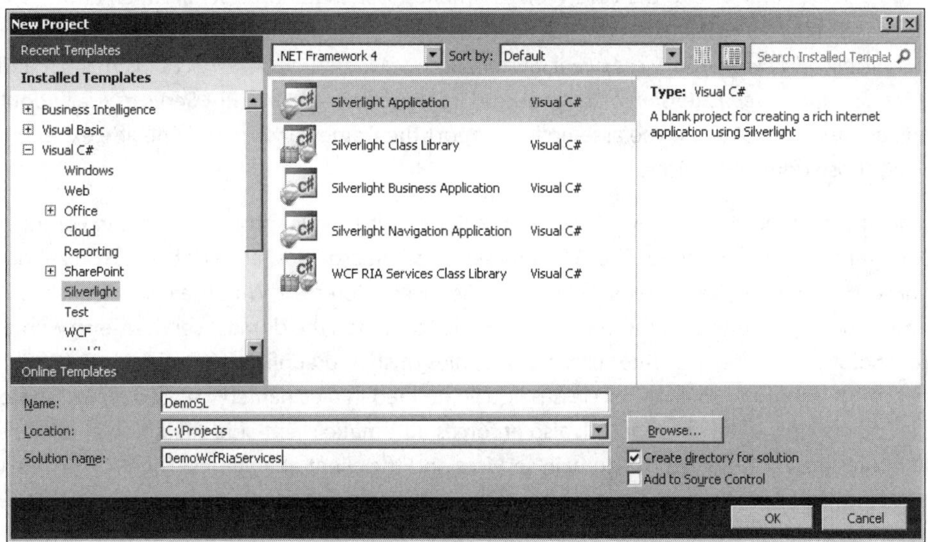

FIGURE 11-12 Creating a Silverlight Application project.

After you click OK, Visual Studio displays the New Silverlight Application dialog. Check the Enable WCF RIA Services option at the bottom of the dialog as shown in Figure 11-13, and click OK.

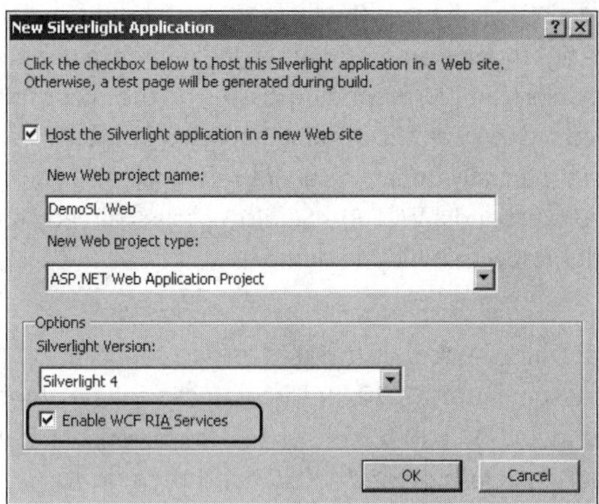

FIGURE 11-13 Checking the Enable WCF RIA Services option to link the client and service projects.

When you click OK, Visual Studio creates a solution with two projects. One is the Silverlight client project, and is named *DemoSL* just as you specified in the New Project dialog. The other is the service counterpart, which is an ASP.NET Web Application Project named *DemoSL.Web*, as specified in the New Silverlight Application dialog. Ordinary Silverlight solutions also begin at this starting point, but because you enabled Enable WCF RIA Services, Visual Studio also performs two important additional steps.

First, it adds a number of special references to the Silverlight client project. In addition to the lightweight *WebRequest* and *WebResponse* classes provided by *System.Net* in ordinary Silverlight projects, Visual Studio sets a reference to the core WCF assemblies *System.Runtime.Serialization* and *System.ServiceModel*, as well as the WCF RIA Services client-side runtime assemblies *System.ServiceModel.DomainServices.Client*, *System.ServiceModel.DomainServices.Client.Web*, and *System.ServiceModel.Web.Extensions*. As suggested by these names, WCF RIA Services is all about building *domain services*, and these assemblies support the framework's rich client-side experience by consuming those domain services.

Second, it establishes the WCF RIA Services link that binds the two projects together. Forget service references; there are none. The WCF RIA Services link provides far better synchronization than an ordinary WCF service reference (or a WCF Data Services reference). With the link established, Visual Studio continuously regenerates the client-side proxies to match the domain services, every time you build your solution. It auto-generates client-side copies of shared application logic you define in the services project, simply by looking for classes you've defined in files named *.shared.cs, or *.shared.vb (rather than simply .cs or .vb). The link also enforces automatic client-side validation and keeps validation rules in sync between the domain services and the client at all times. The WCF RIA Services link greatly simplifies the n-tier pattern, and makes traditional n-tier development feel more like the client/server experience.

After Visual Studio creates the solution, right-click *DemoSL* (the client project) in Solution Explorer and choose Properties. The WCF RIA Services link is shown in the drop-down list on the bottom of the client project's Silverlight properties page, and the additional referenced assemblies are visible in the *References* node in Solution Explorer, as shown in Figure 11-14.

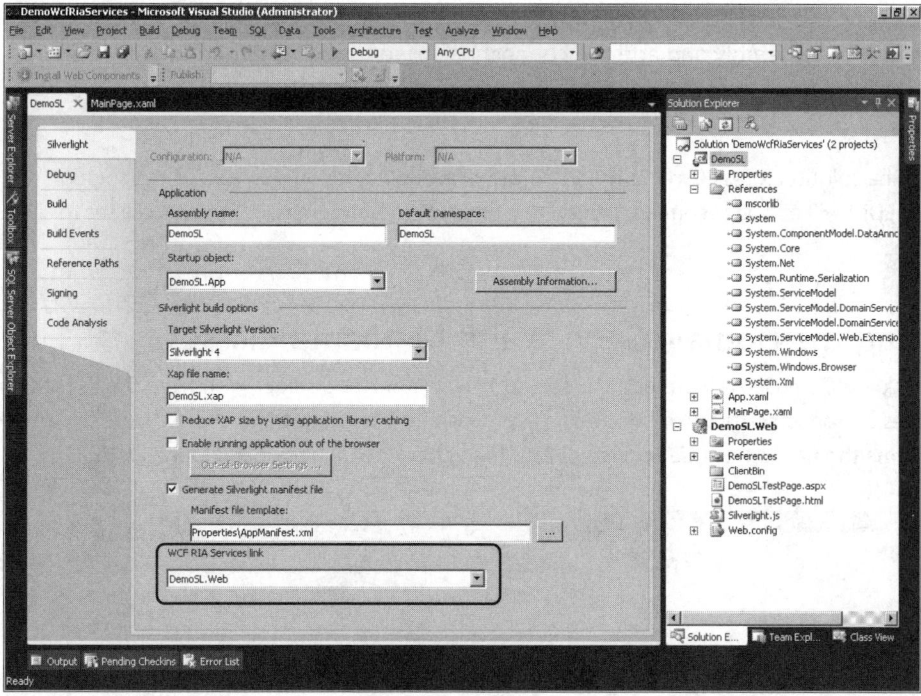

FIGURE 11-14 A Silverlight solution with a WCF RIA Services link.

Creating the Entity Data Model

The next step is to create the EDM, just as you did for the WCF Data Services project in the previous section. You can either repeat the same steps to build the EDM from scratch as explained in Chapter 10, or copy the *SampleEF.edmx* file (and the *connectionStrings* section in *Web.config*) from the WCF Data Services project as follows. Open Windows Explorer to the WCF Data Services project, drag the *SampleEF.edmx* file, and drop it on the *DemoSL.Web* project in Solution Explorer. Then copy the *connectionStrings* section in the *Web.config* file from WCF Data Services project and paste it into this *DemoSL.Web* project's *Web.config* file (just after the opening <*Configuration*> tag toward the top):

```
<connectionStrings>
  <add
    name="SampleDbEntities"
    connectionString="
     metadata=res://*/SampleEF.csdl|res://*/SampleEF.ssdl|res://*/SampleEF.msl;
     provider=System.Data.SqlClient;
     provider connection string=&quot;Data Source=localhost;Initial Catalog=SampleDb;
      Integrated Security=True;MultipleActiveResultSets=True&quot;"
    providerName="System.Data.EntityClient" />
</connectionStrings>
```

Tip This is the second time that we have instructed you to copy the EDM from one project to another. For your production applications, it is best practice to maintain a single version of the EDM in a class library and compile it into an assembly. Then all you need to do is reference the assembly and add the connection string to the configuration file in all the projects that need to share the EDM.

Build the solution (press **Ctrl+Shift+B**) before proceeding. If you don't build the solution now, then the EDM will not be recognized when you attempt to build domain services classes for it in the next step.

Building the Domain Service and Metadata Classes

Right-click the *DemoSL.Web* project, choose Add | New Item, and select Web from the list of template categories on the left. Then scroll down the list of installed templates and choose Domain Service Class. Name the file **SampleRiaService.cs** and then click Add, as shown in Figure 11-15.

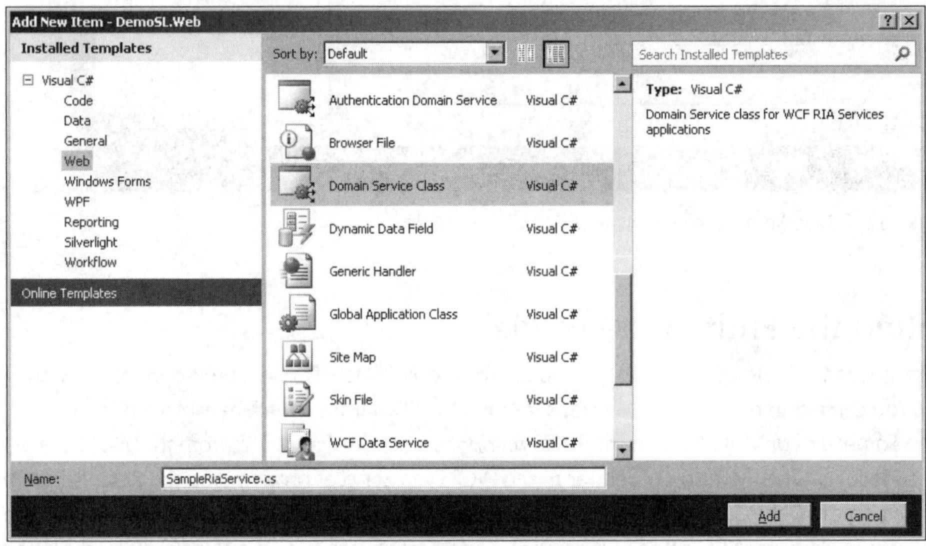

FIGURE 11-15 Creating a WCF RIA Services domain service class.

When you click Add, Visual Studio displays the Add New Domain Service Class dialog, shown in Figure 11-16.

The purpose of this dialog is to generate template code that helps you get started writing the domain service class and associated *metadata* classes for entities in your EDM. But we will take a slightly different approach, and have you write the code for these classes from scratch instead. This method will help you better understand what these classes are all about. So don't check off any entities in this dialog, and just click OK.

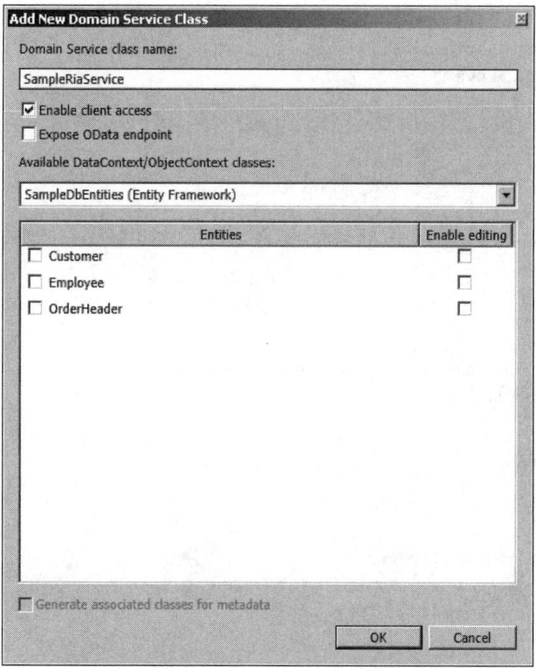

FIGURE 11-16 The Add New Domain Service Class dialog.

Because you did not select any entities, Visual Studio generates an empty class file. So why go through this process instead of simply adding an empty class file? The answer is that the required WCF RIA Services assembly references were not automatically added to the service project when the solution was created, as they were for the client project. Visual Studio (for some reason) defers automatically setting the references in the service project until the very first time you use this dialog—and it will set those references at that time even if you don't select any entities. Now that the references are set, you can create domain service classes and associated metadata classes simply by adding ordinary classes to your service project (or you could have also manually added the references, but getting Visual Studio to add them for you is a neat little time-saving trick). The only reason to use this dialog again in the future is if you want to get a head start on writing the CRUD code in your domain services.

You will now plug in the code for the both the domain service class and the metadata classes. Then we will explain the meaning of these classes, and walk through the code in detail. Replace the generated empty *SampleRiaService* class with the code shown in Listing 11-15.

LISTING 11-15 The WCF RIA Services domain service.

```
using System;
using System.Data;
using System.Linq;
using System.ServiceModel.DomainServices.EntityFramework;
```

```
using System.ServiceModel.DomainServices.Hosting;
using System.ServiceModel.DomainServices.Server;
using System.Transactions;

namespace DemoSL.Web
{
  [EnableClientAccess()]
  public class SampleRiaService : LinqToEntitiesDomainService<SampleDbEntities>
  {
    public IQueryable<Customer> GetCustomers()
    {
      var q =
        from cust in base.ObjectContext.Customers.Include("OrderHeaders")
        orderby cust.LastName, cust.FirstName
        select cust;

      return q;
    }

    public void InsertCustomer(Customer addedCustomer)
    {
      base.ObjectContext.Customers.AddObject(addedCustomer);
    }

    public void UpdateCustomer(Customer customer)
    {
      var originalCustomer = base.ChangeSet.GetOriginal(customer);

      if (originalCustomer == null)
      {
        base.ObjectContext.Customers.Attach(customer);
      }
      else
      {
        base.ObjectContext.Customers.AttachAsModified(customer,
originalCustomer);
      }

      var orderChanges = this.ChangeSet.GetAssociatedChanges
        (customer, o => o.OrderHeaders);

      foreach (OrderHeader order in orderChanges)
      {
        var changeOperation = this.ChangeSet.GetChangeOperation(order);
        switch (changeOperation)
        {
          case ChangeOperation.Insert:
            base.ObjectContext.ObjectStateManager.ChangeObjectState
             (order, EntityState.Added);
            break;

          case ChangeOperation.Update:
            base.ObjectContext.OrderHeaders.AttachAsModified
```

```
           (order, base.ChangeSet.GetOriginal(order));
          break;

        case ChangeOperation.Delete:
          base.ObjectContext.OrderHeaders.Attach(order);
          base.ObjectContext.DeleteObject(order);
          break;
      }
    }
  }

  public void DeleteCustomer(Customer removedCustomer)
  {
    base.ObjectContext.Customers.Attach(removedCustomer);
    base.ObjectContext.DeleteObject(removedCustomer);

    var orderChanges = this.ChangeSet.GetAssociatedChanges
     (removedCustomer, o => o.OrderHeaders);

    foreach (OrderHeader order in orderChanges)
    {
      base.ObjectContext.OrderHeaders.Attach(order);
      base.ObjectContext.DeleteObject(order);
    }
  }

  public override bool Submit(ChangeSet changeSet)
  {
    var result = false;
    using (var ts = new TransactionScope())
    {
      var commit = true;

      result = base.Submit(changeSet);
      if (this.ChangeSet.HasError)
      {
        commit = false;
      }

      // Other out-of-band updates run in the same transaction scope

      if (commit)
      {
        ts.Complete();
      }
    }

    return result;
  }
 }
}
```

Notice the *TransactionScope* object used in the *Submit* method. Using *TransactionScope* enables your service to have other (non-domain service) updates participate in the domain service update. The *TransactionScope* object is provided by the transaction management API in the *System.Transactions* assembly, which you need to reference in order for this code to compile. Right-click the *DemoSL.Web* project in Solution Explorer and choose Add Reference. In the Add Reference dialog, click the .NET tab, scroll to find the *System.Transactions* component, and double-click it.

Next, right-click the *DemoSL.Web* project again, and choose Add | Class. Name the new class file **SampleRiaService.metadata.cs** and click Add. Then replace the empty class with the code shown in Listing 11-16.

LISTING 11-16 The WCF RIA Services metadata classes.

```
using System;
using System.ComponentModel.DataAnnotations;
using System.Data.Objects.DataClasses;
using System.ServiceModel.DomainServices.Server;

namespace DemoSL.Web
{
  [MetadataType(typeof(Customer.CustomerMetadata))]
  public partial class Customer
  {
    internal sealed class CustomerMetadata
    {
      private CustomerMetadata() { }

      [Composition]
      [Include]
      public EntityCollection<OrderHeader> OrderHeaders { get; set; }

      [RoundtripOriginal]
      public DateTime UpdatedAt { get; set; }
    }
  }

  [MetadataType(typeof(OrderHeader.OrderHeaderMetadata))]
  public partial class OrderHeader
  {
    internal sealed class OrderHeaderMetadata
    {
      private OrderHeaderMetadata() { }

      [RoundtripOriginal]
      public DateTime UpdatedAt { get; set; }
    }
  }
}
```

Let's explain what this domain service class does and the purpose of these metadata classes. We will start with the metadata classes first, and then circle back around to the domain service class.

The Metadata Classes

Metadata is "data about data," meaning that metadata classes contain specific instructions and hints for the WCF RIA Services framework to recognize about your data source. You don't actually code any logic in metadata classes. Instead, the framework looks for metadata by examining your assembly (using Reflection) for types with special attributes that you are expected to supply to better describe your data source.

The framework searches first for a *MetadataType* attribute on each public entity class exposed by the data source—which is the EDM in your current *DemoSL.Web* project. The public entity classes are generated automatically by a custom tool in Visual Studio whenever the EDM changes, so adding the *MetadataType* attribute directly to those classes is not a viable option (the attribute would get lost the next time the classes are overwritten by the EDM designer). Instead, you create a separate code file and leverage the partial class feature to add the *MetadataType* attribute. The auto-generated entity classes are all defined with the *partial* keyword by design, so that you can easily and safely extend them in this manner. Listing 11-16 demonstrates the technique. This code extends the designer-generated *Customer* and *OrderHeader* entity classes by defining partial classes with the same names and in the same namespace as those in the EDM, and decorating the classes with the *MetadataType* attribute. At build time, the compiler merges this code with the auto-generated code to produce a single logical entity class.

The *MetadataType* attribute takes a single type parameter that specifies the metadata class for the entity. That is, the *MetadataType* attribute itself is merely a pointer that tells the framework which class contains the actual metadata. These classes can be defined anywhere, but to keep code neatly organized, they are defined as nested classes right inside of the entity classes themselves. For example, the *Customer* class has a *MetadataType* attribute that points to the metadata class *Customer.CustomerMetadata*, which is nested inside the *Customer* class. In Listing 11-16, notice how both metadata classes *Customer.CustomerMetadata* and *OrderHeader.OrderHeaderMetadata* implement a private constructor that does nothing. This suppresses the default public constructor, which prevents the metadata classes from ever being instantiated. Again, no logic goes into these classes, so there is never a reason to instantiate them. They just need to be defined, so that they can be reflected.

Once it finds the actual metadata class, the class is examined for attributes that attach special meaning and behaviors to individual properties of the entity. That is, for each public property defined in the data source's entity class, the framework looks for corresponding properties with the same name and type in the metadata class. The properties have no logic in their get and set blocks—instead, they are declared only so that they can be declared with attributes. These attributes are very often related to validation. For example, there is a *Required* attribute that designates a property as mandatory, and there is a *StringLength* attribute to constrain a string property with a maximum length. Validation rules bubble up to the client auto-magically, and are enforced by databound controls in the Silverlight application without any coding effort on your part.

Although WCF RIA Services supports data sources other than Entity Framework, there are definite advantages to using an EDM as the data source. One of them is that you don't need to declare validation attributes in metadata classes for every single entity property—they surface automatically from the metadata in the EDM itself. Meaning for example, properties designated as required or having a maximum length in the EDM will be recognized as such by the Silverlight client automatically, without defining *Required* and *StringLength* attributes in the metadata classes. This avoids duplicating validation rules between the EDM and the metadata classes, which is why you see so few properties in the *Customer.CustomerMetadata* and *OrderHeader.OrderHeaderMetadata* classes. The only properties that you need to define are those you want to decorate with attributes that attach special meaning to them (beyond validation). The metadata classes in Listing 11-16 demonstrate the *Composition*, *Include*, and *RoundtripOriginal* attributes.

The *Composition* attribute is applied to the *OrderHeaders* property in the *Customer.CustomerMetadata* class. *OrderHeaders* is a navigation property; it "navigates" from a parent *Customer* object to its related collection of *OrderHeader* objects. When the WCF RIA Services framework sees *Composition* on a navigation property, it treats the parent and child objects as part of the same "composition"—two parts of a larger entity to be treated as a whole. Compositions can include additional related entities simply by marking navigation properties with the *Composition* attribute in each parent's metadata class. Even with this attribute, however, child entities will not be retrieved automatically with parent entities unless you also specify the *Include* attribute. You will therefore typically always specify *Include* with *Composition*, as shown for the *OrderHeader* property in Listing 11-16.

On the client, a composition is considered changed whenever any of its participating entities are changed, and the composition as a whole is then transmitted back to the service for updating. In the current demo, this means that the "customer" is considered changed if any order data changes—even if the *Customer* entity itself was not modified—and that the entire composition (including the unmodified customer) is sent to the service for updating. A single domain service method is then responsible for updating the parent entity and all of its related child entities. There are obvious advantages and disadvantageous to compositions, so be judicious with their use. There is certainly a convenience factor in passing all the entities one at a time, but you also incur larger data transfers by passing individual entities that have no changes.

Next, notice the *RoundtripOriginal* attribute on the *UpdatedAt* properties in both the *Customer.CustomerMetadata* and *OrderHeader.OrderHeaderMetadata* classes. This attribute facilitates the optimistic concurrency checks that rely on the original *UpdatedAt* value to detect multi-user conflicts. Recall from Chapter 10 that this functionality is implemented for the *Customer* entity in the EDM by the *UpdateCustomer* stored procedure.

Note Although we did not walk you through the same process for the *OrderHeader* entity, you would similarly implement an *UpdateOrderHeader* stored procedure and map it in the EDM if this were a production application. The EDM, as it is currently configured, generates direct DML statements to update the *OrderHeader* table rather than using stored procedures, and makes no use of the original *UpdatedAt* value.

You can preserve and return the original value of any property simply by marking it with *RoundtripOriginal*, which is helpful for more than just concurrency checks. This capability can eliminate the need for business rules to reload data before applying an update. Imagine that the *Balance* property was also marked with *RoundtripOriginal*. Upon update, the domain service class would have access to the original value so that it could ensure, just for example, that the new balance does not exceed the previous balance by 10 percent. Without the original value round-tripped, the update method in the domain service class would be forced to go back to the database for the original balance in order to test for the same condition.

The Domain Service Class

Now we can shift focus to the domain service class in Listing 11-15, *SampleRiaService.* This class has all the public methods for querying and updating the data source, and can be extended with any other custom operations you may wish to expose to the client. The class is decorated with the *EnableClientAccess* attribute, which is what causes the client-side code for the class to be generated automatically by the WCF RIA Services link each time you build the solution.

The *SampleRiaService* class inherits from *LinqToEntitiesDomainService<T>*, meaning that it uses Entity Framework as the data source. The *T* specifies the EDM's object context class, *SampleDbEntities*. A WCF RIA Services domain service class can also inherit from *LinqToSqlDomainService<T>* to expose LINQ to SQL models, or inherit from *DomainService* to expose POCOs (ordinary business objects based on any data access layer).

The first method simply retrieves all customers and their orders. Notice that no attribute is required on the method; simply defining public methods that return *IQueryable<T>* exposes those methods as query operations that can be called by the client. The other three methods work to insert, update, and delete *Customer* entities received back from the client, and because of the *Composition* attribute in the *Customer.CustomerMetadata* class, they handle child *OrderHeader* entities as well. Without the *Composition* attribute in the metadata class, another three methods would be needed in the domain service class to separately insert, update, and delete *OrderHeader* entities.

When the client submits changes back to the service, a new EF object context for the EDM is instantiated behind the scenes on the server. This context is maintained across calls that the WCF RIA Services runtime makes to the set of insert, update, and delete methods that you must supply in the domain service class. These methods are responsible for attaching incoming objects to the context, which the base class exposes through its *ObjectContext* property. These methods also set the proper state information (inserted, updated, or deleted) for the objects it attaches to the context, so EF behaves as though this context originally retrieved the data and has been tracking its changes all along.

The *InsertCustomer* method is simplest. It has only one line of code in it that calls the *AddObject* method on the new *Customers* entity. With composition, a new "customer" is straightforward: it's always going to involve a new parent *Customer* entity and a collection of new child *OrderHeader* entities. So adding the parent entity automatically adds the child entities and the object context tracks the entire composition as new.

The *UpdateCustomer* method is a bit more involved. This one method must account for both *Customer* and *OrderHeader* entities separately, and instruct the object context to track their changes accordingly. The *Customer* entity must be attached first, but remember that it may or may not actually be modified as part of the overall composition. If only order data changed, then the

Customer entity needs to be attached by calling *Attach*; otherwise, it needs to be attached by calling *AttachAsModified*. The *GetOriginal* method is called on the *ChangeSet* property exposed by the base class to make this determination. This method returns *null* if there is no original version of the entity in the changeset, which means that the *Customer* was not modified, and *Attach* is called. Otherwise, *AttachAsModified* is called to inform the context that the *Customer* was modified, and what its original values were. The *Customer* object returned by *GetOriginal* contains original values only for those properties marked with *RoundtripOriginal* in the metadata class (such as *UpdatedAt*); all other properties of the "original" customer are initialized to default values (nulls and zeros).

Next, *GetAssociatedChanges* is called on the *ChangeSet* to return the collection of *OrderHeader* changes. For each element in the collection, *GetChangeOperation* is called to obtain a *Change-Operation* enumeration value that tells you if the *OrderHeader* was inserted, updated, or deleted. For an insert, the *ChangeObjectState* method is invoked on the context's *ObjectStateManager* to attach the child entity as added. For an update, *AttachAsModified* is called to attach the child entity with its original values, just as *AttachAsModified* was called to attach the parent *Customer* entity when it was detected as modified. Finally, child deletions work by first calling *Attach* on the *OrderHeaders* entity set, and then calling *DeleteObject* on the *ObjectContext*.

The *DeleteCustomer* method performs a straightforward delete of the entire composition—parent entity, and all related child entities. As you saw with deleted child entities in *UpdateCustomer*, entities are deleted by first calling *Attach* and then calling *DeleteObject*. After deleting the parent *Customer* entity, *GetAssociatedChanges* is called to return the collection of child *OrderHeader* entities. There is no need to evaluate the *ChangeOperation* of each entity; it is always going to indicate a deletion. Therefore, each *OrderHeader* entity is simply deleted by calling *Attach* and then *DeleteObject*.

Finally, the domain service base class also exposes a *Submit* method that you can override to intercept that point in time just before all the changes are written back to the database. Inside this method, you can add any custom processing logic. Think of the *Submit* method as the domain service's "global update trigger" that you can leverage to inspect, adjust, or reject pending data changes, or take any other desired action before committing changes to the database.

As shown in the *Submit* method override in Listing 11-15, you can also start a *TransactionScope* block and then call other methods to perform separate, out-of-band updates. Within the *TransactionScope* block, calling the base *Submit* method saves the changes from the domain service update request as part of a broader database transaction that the other updates contribute to. In this manner, all of the updates either succeed or fail as a whole.

More Info Chapter 10 explains how to use *TransactionScope* in detail, and Chapter 4 is dedicated to the topic of database transactions.

Building the Silverlight Client

With the domain service class and metadata classes in place in the *DemoSL.Web* service project, you are ready to create the Silverlight user interface in the *DemoSL* client project. This user interface shall support similar ad-hoc data entry capabilities as the Windows Forms client you created with WCF Data Services in the previous section. As with the Windows Forms client, this user interface (UI) will include grid controls for customer and order data. But Visual Studio does not automatically bring in all of the supported Silverlight controls (including the DataGrid control) when you create your project. So before you can use the DataGrid to build the UI, you must add a reference to *System.Windows.Controls.Data*. Right-click the *DemoSL* project in Solution Explorer and choose Add Reference. In the Add Reference dialog, click the .NET tab, and scroll to find and select the *System.Windows.Controls.Data* component, as shown in Figure 11-17. Then click OK.

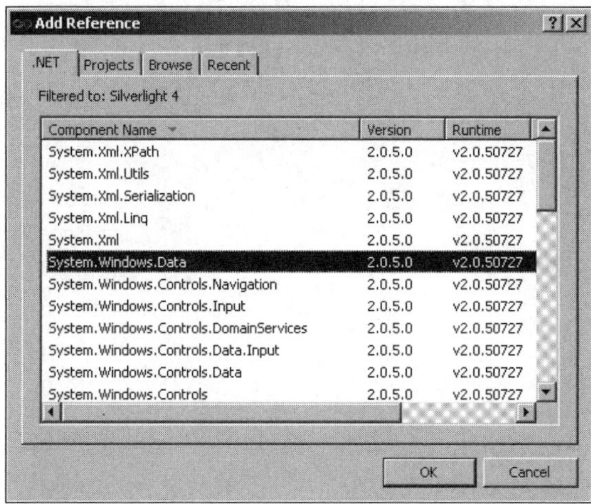

FIGURE 11-17 Setting a reference to *System.Windows.Controls.Data* provides a DataGrid control for Silverlight.

Now open *MainPage.xaml*, and replace the markup with the code shown in Listing 11-17.

LISTING 11-17 The Silverlight client XAML.

```
<UserControl x:Class="DemoSL.MainPage"
    xmlns="http://schemas.microsoft.com/winfx/2006/xaml/presentation"
    xmlns:x="http://schemas.microsoft.com/winfx/2006/xaml"
    xmlns:d="http://schemas.microsoft.com/expression/blend/2008"
    xmlns:mc="http://schemas.openxmlformats.org/markup-compatibility/2006"
    xmlns:dc=
     "clr-namespace:System.Windows.Controls;assembly=System.Windows.Controls.Data"
    mc:Ignorable="d"
    d:DesignHeight="400" d:DesignWidth="400">
  <StackPanel x:Name="LayoutRoot" Margin="8">
    <StackPanel Orientation="Horizontal">
      <Button x:Name="btnNewCustomer" Margin="4" Width="100"
        Content="New Customer" Click="btnNewCustomer_Click" />
```

```
      <Button x:Name="btnDeleteCustomer" Margin="4" Width="100"
        Content="Delete Customer" Click="btnDeleteCustomer_Click" />
    </StackPanel>
    <dc:DataGrid x:Name="grdCustomers" Height="120"
      SelectionChanged="grdCustomers_SelectionChanged" />
    <StackPanel Orientation="Horizontal" Margin="0,8,0,0">
      <Button x:Name="btnNewOrder" Margin="4" Width="100"
        Content="New Order" Click="btnNewOrder_Click" />
      <Button x:Name="btnDeleteOrder" Margin="4" Width="100"
        Content="Delete Order" Click="btnDeleteOrder_Click" />
    </StackPanel>
    <dc:DataGrid x:Name="grdOrders" Height="160" />
    <StackPanel Orientation="Horizontal"
      Margin="0,8,0,0" HorizontalAlignment="Center">
      <Button Margin="4" x:Name="btnLoad" Content="Load" FontWeight="Bold"
        Click="btnLoad_Click" />
      <Button Margin="4" x:Name="btnSave" Content="Save" FontWeight="Bold"
        Click="btnSave_Click" />
    </StackPanel>
  </StackPanel>
</UserControl>
```

The design view of your Silverlight user control should look similar to Figure 11-18.

FIGURE 11-18 The WCF RIA Services data entry client user interface.

Your last step is to add the code-behind for the user control. Right-click anywhere on the design surface and choose View Code. Then replace the empty *MainPage* class with the code shown in Listing 11-18.

LISTING 11-18 Code for the WCF RIA Services data entry client Silverlight form.

```
using System;
using System.ServiceModel.DomainServices.Client;
using System.Text;
using System.Windows;
using System.Windows.Controls;

using DemoSL.Web;

namespace DemoSL
{
  public partial class MainPage : UserControl
  {
    private SampleRiaContext _ctx = new SampleRiaContext();

    public MainPage()
    {
      InitializeComponent();
    }

    private void btnLoad_Click(object sender, RoutedEventArgs e)
    {
      this.btnLoad.IsEnabled = false;

      var lo = this._ctx.Load(
        this._ctx.GetCustomersQuery(),
        this.LoadOperationComplete,
        null);

      this.grdCustomers.ItemsSource = lo.Entities;
    }

    private void LoadOperationComplete(LoadOperation<Customer> lo)
    {
      if (lo.HasError)
      {
        MessageBox.Show(lo.Error.Message, "Load failed", MessageBoxButton.OK);
        lo.MarkErrorAsHandled();
      }
      this.btnLoad.IsEnabled = true;
    }

    private void btnSave_Click(object sender, RoutedEventArgs e)
    {
      this.btnSave.IsEnabled = false;

      this._ctx.SubmitChanges(this.SaveOperationCompleted, null);
    }

    private void SaveOperationCompleted(SubmitOperation so)
    {
      this.btnSave.IsEnabled = true;
      if (!so.HasError)
```

```
    {
      return;
    }

    var sb = new StringBuilder();
    sb.AppendLine(so.Error.Message);

    foreach (var badEntity in so.EntitiesInError)
    {
      sb.AppendFormat(string.Format("Entity {0} Error", badEntity.
GetIdentity()));
      sb.AppendLine();
      foreach (var ve in badEntity.ValidationErrors)
      {
        sb.AppendLine(" " + ve.ErrorMessage);
      }
    }

    MessageBox.Show(sb.ToString(), "Submit failed", MessageBoxButton.OK);

    so.MarkErrorAsHandled();
  }

  private void grdCustomers_SelectionChanged
   (object sender, SelectionChangedEventArgs e)
  {
    var cust = this.grdCustomers.SelectedItem as Customer;
    if (cust != null)
    {
      this.grdOrders.ItemsSource = cust.OrderHeaders;
    }
  }

  private void btnNewCustomer_Click(object sender, RoutedEventArgs e)
  {
    var cust = new Customer();
    this._ctx.Customers.Add(cust);
    this.grdCustomers.ItemsSource = this._ctx.Customers;
  }

  private void btnDeleteCustomer_Click(object sender, RoutedEventArgs e)
  {
    var cust = this.grdCustomers.SelectedItem as Customer;
    if (cust != null)
    {
      this._ctx.Customers.Remove(cust);
      this.grdCustomers.ItemsSource = this._ctx.Customers;
    }
  }

  private void btnNewOrder_Click(object sender, RoutedEventArgs e)
  {
    var cust = this.grdCustomers.SelectedItem as Customer;
```

```
        if (cust != null)
        {
          var order = new OrderHeader();
          cust.OrderHeaders.Add(order);
          this.grdOrders.ItemsSource = cust.OrderHeaders;
        }
      }

      private void btnDeleteOrder_Click(object sender, RoutedEventArgs e)
      {
        var cust = this.grdCustomers.SelectedItem as Customer;
        if (cust != null)
        {
          var order = new OrderHeader();
          cust.OrderHeaders.Remove(order);
          this.grdOrders.ItemsSource = cust.OrderHeaders;
        }
      }

    }
  }
```

This completes the entire solution. Go ahead and build it, but don't run it just yet. We'll first explain the client code you just added, and then you can run the application to give it a test-drive.

The client Silverlight project knows all about the public services and entities defined in the service project. Without establishing a service reference, how does it obtain this knowledge? The answer is that Visual Studio automatically generates client proxies every time you build the solution. This is triggered by the WCF RIA Services link that exists between the two projects. The code is written to a source file and added to the Generated_Code folder in your Silverlight project. These items are hidden by default, but you can view them by selecting the *DemoSL* project and then clicking Show All Files (the second toolbar button at the top of Solution Explorer), as shown in Figure 11-19.

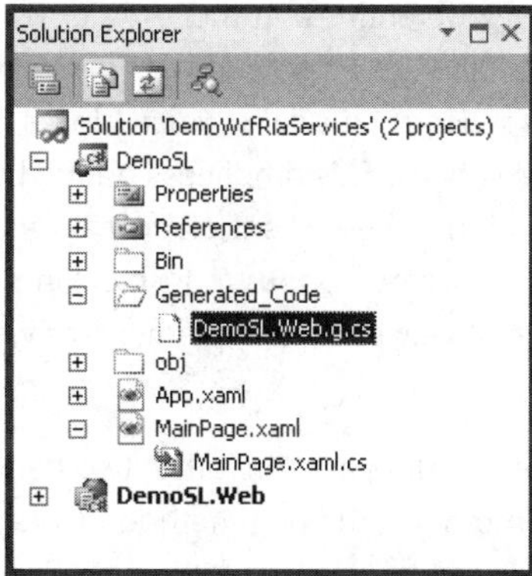

FIGURE 11-19 The hidden generated code file containing WCF RIA Services client proxies.

In addition to the generated proxy code in *DemoSL.Web.g.cs*, the WCF RIA Services link automatically copies any code file in the service project with a name ending in .shared.cs (or .shared.vb) into the Generated_Code folder. For example, you could define a service project class in a file named *CommonHelpers.shared.cs*, and that code file would be instantly copied and updated to the client project for use there as well. This automated sharing of metadata and logic between the client and service projects is what the WCF RIA Services link is all about.

Examining the proxy code in *DemoSL.Web.g.cs* is very enlightening. It will help you better understand the WCF RIA Services framework and the client code in Listing 11-18. Take some time now to explore it, and you will find several interesting classes in there. As you probably expect, there are *Customer* and *OrderHeader* classes that correspond to the same-named entities exposed by the service's data source. These client-side classes were generated because of the *MetadataType* attribute added to the entity metadata classes in the service project.

The most important generated class is *SampleRiaContext*, which inherits from *DomainContext*. This is a stateful client context object that facilitates data access (queries and updates) with the service, much the way the *SampleDbEntities* client context was used in the WCF Data Services version of this solution earlier in the chapter. However, there is an important difference here that makes client development much easier with WCF RIA Services than WCF Data Services. You do not need to manually notify the *SampleRiaContext* object of every change to every entity, as you are required to do with the WCF Data Services client library. These *Customer* and *OrderHeader* classes are completely self-tracking entities. Because these entities track their own changes, your client code does not need to be concerned at all with change tracking—you just query the context, and then issue an update to it whenever you want to save changes back to the service.

At the top of the *MainPage* class in Listing 11-18, a new *SampleRiaContext* object is declared and instantiated in *_ctx*. This creates the stateful *DomainContext* for the UI when the *MainPage* class is constructed, which is accessible by all the code in the class via the *_ctx* variable.

If you compare Listing 11-18 with the equivalent client code for the WCF Data Services version of this solution in Listing 11-8, you can see there is significantly less code and complexity required, thanks to the self-tracking capabilities of WCF RIA Services client-side entities. At the same time, this Silverlight code works asynchronously, which introduces a new challenge. The Windows Forms clients you built for the WCF Data Services earlier in the chapter made synchronous calls, which blocks client execution (and the UI) while awaiting a response from the service. This simplifies coding, but is expressly prohibited in Silverlight and Windows Phone 7 applications. These client platforms require the UI to remain responsive at all times, and thus, they only permit asynchronous (non-blocking) service calls. Fortunately, the necessary callback mechanism is relatively easy to implement, as we explain next.

Four methods implement the data access; the first two handle loading and the other two handle saving. Every asynchronous operation always involves a pair of methods; the first method invokes the operation and the second method (the callback) handles the response. Code that follows the invocation in the first method continues to execute immediately after issuing the service call, before the response has come back for it. This keeps the UI responsive, but also means that you cannot know if or when the service call completes successfully. The second method gets called automatically when the service completes, and receives information that you use to determine the success or failure of the operation.

The *btnLoad_Click* event handler fires when the user clicks Load, and immediately disables the Load button. This prevents the user from clicking Load again, because the UI will let them do so while the first request is still processing. It then invokes the *Load* method on the context to invoke the query request asynchronously:

```
var lo = this._ctx.Load(
  this._ctx.GetCustomersQuery(),
  this.LoadOperationComplete,
  null);
```

The first parameter passed to *Load* specifies the method to be called in the domain service class. Every query method available in the service has a corresponding context method that identifies it on the client. This client-side method is named the same as the method in the domain service class, followed by *Query*. Thus, the first parameter to *Load* calls the context's *GetCustomersQuery* method, which references the *GetCustomers* method in the domain service.

The next *Load* parameter specifies the callback; that is, the method to be called when the service method completes. This method is expected to match a particular signature; specifically, it can be any method that returns *void* and accepts a *LoadOperation<T>* object, where *T* is the entity type returned by the service (*Customer*, in this case). The *LoadOperationComplete* method uses this exact signature, which allows it to be used as the callback to receive control when the service operation completes.

The line of code following the *Load* method call is most interesting:

```
this.grdCustomers.ItemsSource = lo.Entities;
```

This code binds the *ItemsSource* property of the customer's grid to the *Entities* property of the *LoadOperation<Customer>* object returned by the *Load* method. In traditional asynchronous programming, data binding does not occur until the callback method receives the service response. But this line of code executes right after invoking the asynchronous call, which is *before* the results have been returned to the client. At the time the *ItemsSource* property is set on the customer's grid, the client is aware of the schema of the data that it expects to receive, but it hasn't actually received the data itself yet. Instead, the grid will auto-magically display the data as soon as it arrives. This behavior is illustrated when you run the application; you will notice that the column headers of the grid appear the instant *Load* is clicked, whereas the rows are populated with data a moment later.

The *LoadOperationComplete* method has the required signature expected for the callback; it returns *void* and accepts a *LoadOperation<Customer>*. Binding is already taken care of by the framework as just explained, so the primary purpose of the callback is to re-enable the Load button and check if an error occurred during the load operation. The *HasError* property returns *true* if there was an error, and the *Error* property exposes the *Exception* object that was thrown on the service. Because the UI handles the error, it also calls *MarkErrorAsHandled* on the *LoadOperation* object. If this method is not called, the framework re-throws the exception at runtime to make sure the problem does not slip by unnoticed.

The asynchronous pattern of the two save methods works exactly the same. The *btnSave_Click* event handler fires when the user clicks Save. It disables the Save button (preventing the user from clicking Save again while a previous request is processing), and then invokes the *SubmitChanges* method on the context to kick off the asynchronous save request:

```
this._ctx.SubmitChanges(this.SaveOperationCompleted, null);
```

The client does not call the individual public methods for insert, update, and delete defined in domain service directly. As explained when discussing the domain service class implementation, the WCF RIA Services framework manages a server-side EF object context and orchestrates the calls to the domain service methods internally as appropriate. All you need to do is call *SubmitChanges*.

The *SubmitChanges* method takes a parameter that specifies the callback, which is expected to be any method that returns *void* and accepts a *SubmitOperation* object. The *SaveOperationComplete* method uses this exact signature, and is specified as the callback to receive control when the service operation completes.

The *SaveOperationComplete* callback method re-enables the Save button and checks for errors that might have occurred during the save operation. Just like the *LoadOperation* object, there is a *HasError* property to tell you if there was an error, and an *Error* property holding the *Exception* thrown on the service. The *SubmitOperation* object's *EntitiesInError* property exposes a collection that reports the specific details of each entity that has validation problems. If an error is detected, these details are combined using a *StringBuilder* and displayed to the user. Finally, *MarkErrorAsHandled* signals that the error was handled, which prevents an exception from being thrown.

More Info We presented each operation as two distinct methods to help you grasp the idea of asynchronous programming. In practice, you will find it common instead to embed the callback as an anonymous method inside of the calling method using a *Lambda*. You will learn the Lambda technique in Chapter 13, when you build a Windows Phone 7 application that calls WCF Data Services hosted in Windows Azure. The same asynchronous programming concepts apply whether you are "inlining" the callback method using a Lambda or coding a separate callback method, as shown in Listing 11-18.

The rest of the client code is relatively simple. In *grdCustomers_SelectionChanged*, the bottom grid is bound to the *OrderHeaders* property to show the orders for customers selected in the top grid. The four remaining event handlers respond to New Customer, Delete Customer, New Order, and Delete Order button clicks. The *btnNewCustomer_Click* and *btnDeleteCustomer_Click* methods respectively add and remove *Customer* entities to and from the context's *Customers* collection. And the *btnNewOrder_Click* and *btnDeleteOrder_Click* methods respectively add and remove *OrderHeader* entities to and from their parent *Customer* object's *OrderHeaders* collection.

None of the elaborate change tracking code (see Listing 11-8) that was needed with the WCF Data Services client library is required here, because all of the entities track their own changes. When the user edits data in the UI, the self-tracking entities bound to the UI automatically inform the context about the change, so you don't have to.

Inspecting the .NET Framing Protocol with Fiddler

The solution is ready to run, and as before, you will want to monitor background activity with Fiddler and SQL Profiler. But unless you first install a special Fiddler "inspector," you won't be able to read the raw HTTP requests in clear text as you did with the REST/OData packets in the earlier WCF Data Services solution. This is because, by default, WCF RIA Services uses the .NET Framing protocol which combines XML and binary elements. Using Fiddler's "raw" inspector, the binary elements are unreadable. Fortunately, Joe Zhou of the WCF RIA Services team at Microsoft has written a special inspector that deciphers the binary elements so that you can view the traffic as raw (readable) XML text.

Installing the inspector is a simple matter of copying *BinaryMessageFiddlerExtension.dll* into the *Inspectors* folder beneath Fiddler's program directory. This is typically *C:\Program Files (x86)\Fiddler2\Inspectors*, on 64-bit machines. You can get the .dll file by downloading *BinaryMessageFiddlerExtension.zip* from *http://archive.msdn.microsoft.com/Project/Download/FileDownload.aspx?ProjectName=silverlightws&DownloadId=12007*. The .zip file includes a complete Visual Studio solution, but you only need to copy the *BinaryMessageFiddlerExtension.dll* file from the bin\debug folder. We also supply the .dll file in the Lib folder of the solution for this chapter's code, which you can download from the book's companion website (see the "Introduction" for details).

Once the .dll file is copied into its *Inspectors* folder, Fiddler displays a new WCF Silverlight option in the request and response panels of the Inspectors tab. You will use this option to monitor .NET Framing requests and responses that are passed over HTTP by this WCF RIA Services solution.

Testing the Complete WCF RIA Services Solution

Make sure you have installed the .NET Framing inspector for Fiddler, and that both Fiddler and SQL Profiler are running before running the solution. Then press **F5** to build and run the solution. The browser launches to the URL for the main page, which is running off of localhost. However, Fiddler won't monitor traffic as you use the application because there is no "dot" in the URL. So use the same trick explained earlier, and add a . (dot) immediately after *localhost* in the browser's address bar and press **Enter** to reload the page. Now Fiddler will recognize the HTTP traffic in the application, and display it for your inspection.

Click the Load button. If you watch very closely as you do, you will notice that column headers appear instantly on the customer grid, and then rows of data appear a brief moment later. This is because of the asynchronous databinding behavior in Listing 11-18 that we explained earlier. Click on the first customer (Cassie Hicks) in the top grid to display the customer orders in the bottom grid, as shown in Listing 11-20.

Now edit the data to exercise the application as you did with the Windows Forms client in the WCF Data Services solution. First insert a new order for Andy Jacobs by selecting Andy's row in the top grid and clicking New Order. Then enter any random text into the *ShipVia* and *OrderStatus* columns for the new order. As you enter the new order row, you immediately experience the auto-magical validation features of the WCF RIA Services framework. Without writing any code, the grid is aware of required fields. As shown in Figure 11-21, the grid displays error messages as the user enters data, and then clears those messages as the user satisfies the validation rules. Where did the rules come from? They bubbled up from the metadata in the service project and surfaced automatically in the client project. And as explained earlier, the metadata derives validation rules from the conceptual model in the underlying EDM automatically as well.

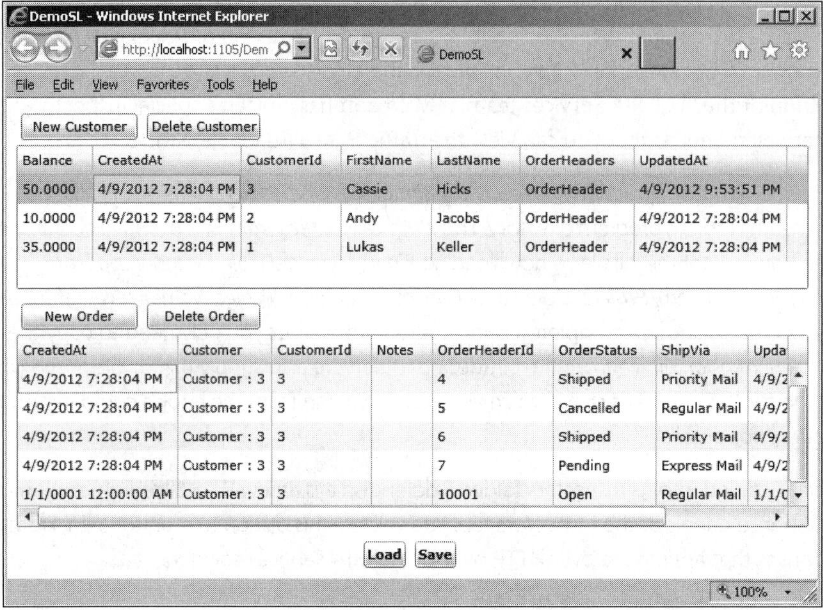

FIGURE 11-20 The client form populated with data returned by WCF RIA Services.

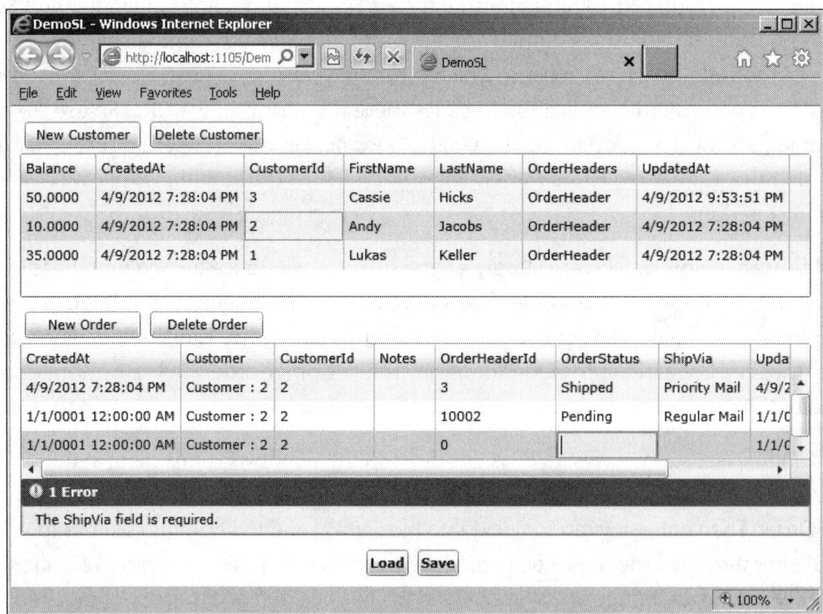

FIGURE 11-21 The client form populated with data returned by WCF RIA Services.

After supplying values for *OrderStatus* and *ShipVia*, the error messages disappear from the grid and the new order for Andy is accepted. Now update the balance for Cassie Hicks by changing the value from 50 to 60 in the top grid. Finally, delete customer Lukas Keller (and all his orders) by selecting his row in the top grid and clicking Delete Customer. Now click Save to push all the changes back to the service, and switch over to Fiddler to view the HTTP traffic that just transpired.

On the left, click the last HTTP request. The raw view in the Inspectors tab shows that a *POST* was issued to a *SubmitChanges* operation, but the content is not readable. Notice the *Content-Type* header that reads *application/msbin1*, which refers to the .NET Framing protocol. Now switch away from raw view by clicking on the WCF Silverlight options at the top of the request and response panels. The .NET Framing protocol inspector you added to Fiddler now presents the content in a perfectly readable format. Listing 11-19 shows the *SubmitChanges* request (irrelevant portions of the request are omitted to conserve space).

LISTING 11-19 The WCF RIA Services *SubmitChanges* request.

```
<SubmitChanges xmlns="http://tempuri.org/">
  <changeSet xmlns:a="DomainServices" xmlns:i="http://www.w3.org/2001/XMLSchema-
instance">
    <a:ChangeSetEntry>
      <a:Entity i:type="c:OrderHeader" xmlns:b="http://schemas.datacontract.
org/2004/07/System.ServiceModel.DomainServices.Client" xmlns:c="http://schemas.
datacontract.org/2004/07/DemoSL.Web">
        <c:CreatedAt>0001-01-01T00:00:00</c:CreatedAt>
        <c:CustomerId>2</c:CustomerId>
        <c:Notes i:nil="true"></c:Notes>
        <c:OrderHeaderId>0</c:OrderHeaderId>
        <c:OrderStatus>Pending</c:OrderStatus>
        <c:ShipVia>Priority Mail</c:ShipVia>
        <c:UpdatedAt>0001-01-01T00:00:00</c:UpdatedAt>
      </a:Entity>
      <a:EntityActions i:nil="true" xmlns:b="http://schemas.microsoft.
com/2003/10/Serialization/Arrays"></a:EntityActions>
      <a:HasMemberChanges>false</a:HasMemberChanges>
      <a:Id>0</a:Id>
      <a:Operation>Insert</a:Operation>
    </a:ChangeSetEntry>
      :
    <a:ChangeSetEntry>
      <a:Associations xmlns:b="http://schemas.microsoft.com/2003/10/
Serialization/Arrays">
        <b:KeyValueOfstringArrayOfintty7Ep6D1>
          <b:Key>OrderHeaders</b:Key>
          <b:Value>
            <b:int>8</b:int>
            <b:int>9</b:int>
            <b:int>10</b:int>
            <b:int>11</b:int>
            <b:int>12</b:int>
          </b:Value>
```

```
        </b:KeyValueOfstringArrayOfintty7Ep6D1>
      </a:Associations>
      <a:Entity i:type="c:Customer" xmlns:b="http://schemas.datacontract.
org/2004/07/System.ServiceModel.DomainServices.Client" xmlns:c="http://schemas.
datacontract.org/2004/07/DemoSL.Web">
        <c:Balance>60</c:Balance>
        <c:CreatedAt>2012-02-10T11:55:39.667375</c:CreatedAt>
        <c:CustomerId>3</c:CustomerId>
        <c:FirstName>Cassie</c:FirstName>
        <c:LastName>Hicks</c:LastName>
        <c:UpdatedAt>2012-02-10T12:00:23.261125</c:UpdatedAt>
      </a:Entity>
      <a:EntityActions i:nil="true" xmlns:b="http://schemas.microsoft.com/2003/10/
Serialization/Arrays"></a:EntityActions>
      <a:HasMemberChanges>true</a:HasMemberChanges>
      <a:Id>2</a:Id>
      <a:Operation>Update</a:Operation>
      <a:OriginalAssociations xmlns:b="http://schemas.microsoft.com/2003/10/
Serialization/Arrays">
        <b:KeyValueOfstringArrayOfintty7Ep6D1>
          <b:Key>OrderHeaders</b:Key>
          <b:Value>
            <b:int>8</b:int>
            <b:int>9</b:int>
            <b:int>10</b:int>
            <b:int>11</b:int>
            <b:int>12</b:int>
          </b:Value>
        </b:KeyValueOfstringArrayOfintty7Ep6D1>
      </a:OriginalAssociations>
      <a:OriginalEntity i:type="c:Customer" xmlns:b="http://schemas.datacontract.
org/2004/07/System.ServiceModel.DomainServices.Client" xmlns:c="http://schemas.
datacontract.org/2004/07/DemoSL.Web">
        <c:Balance>0</c:Balance>
        <c:CreatedAt>0001-01-01T00:00:00</c:CreatedAt>
        <c:CustomerId>3</c:CustomerId>
        <c:FirstName i:nil="true"></c:FirstName>
        <c:LastName i:nil="true"></c:LastName>
        <c:UpdatedAt>2012-02-10T12:00:23.261125</c:UpdatedAt>
      </a:OriginalEntity>
    </a:ChangeSetEntry>
    <a:ChangeSetEntry>
      <a:Entity i:type="c:Customer" xmlns:b="http://schemas.datacontract.
org/2004/07/System.ServiceModel.DomainServices.Client" xmlns:c="http://schemas.
datacontract.org/2004/07/DemoSL.Web">
        <c:Balance>35.0000</c:Balance>
        <c:CreatedAt>2012-02-10T11:55:39.667375</c:CreatedAt>
        <c:CustomerId>1</c:CustomerId>
        <c:FirstName>Lukas</c:FirstName>
        <c:LastName>Keller</c:LastName>
        <c:UpdatedAt>2012-02-10T11:55:39.667375</c:UpdatedAt>
      </a:Entity>
      <a:EntityActions i:nil="true" xmlns:b="http://schemas.microsoft.
com/2003/10/Serialization/Arrays"></a:EntityActions>
```

```
      <a:HasMemberChanges>false</a:HasMemberChanges>
      <a:Id>3</a:Id>
      <a:Operation>Delete</a:Operation>
      <a:OriginalAssociations xmlns:b="http://schemas.microsoft.com/2003/10/
Serialization/Arrays">
        <b:KeyValueOfstringArrayOfintty7Ep6D1>
          <b:Key>OrderHeaders</b:Key>
          <b:Value>
            <b:int>4</b:int>
            <b:int>5</b:int>
          </b:Value>
        </b:KeyValueOfstringArrayOfintty7Ep6D1>
      </a:OriginalAssociations>
    </a:ChangeSetEntry>
    <a:ChangeSetEntry>
      <a:Entity i:type="c:OrderHeader" xmlns:b="http://schemas.datacontract.
org/2004/07/System.ServiceModel.DomainServices.Client" xmlns:c="http://schemas.
datacontract.org/2004/07/DemoSL.Web">
        <c:CreatedAt>2012-02-10T11:55:39.667375</c:CreatedAt>
        <c:CustomerId>0</c:CustomerId>
        <c:Notes i:nil="true"></c:Notes>
        <c:OrderHeaderId>1</c:OrderHeaderId>
        <c:OrderStatus>Shipped</c:OrderStatus>
        <c:ShipVia>Regular Mail</c:ShipVia>
        <c:UpdatedAt>2012-02-10T11:55:39.667375</c:UpdatedAt>
      </a:Entity>
      <a:EntityActions i:nil="true" xmlns:b="http://schemas.microsoft.
com/2003/10/Serialization/Arrays"></a:EntityActions>
      <a:HasMemberChanges>true</a:HasMemberChanges>
      <a:Id>4</a:Id>
      <a:Operation>Delete</a:Operation>
      <a:OriginalEntity i:type="c:OrderHeader" xmlns:b="http://schemas.
datacontract.org/2004/07/System.ServiceModel.DomainServices.Client"
xmlns:c="http://schemas.datacontract.org/2004/07/DemoSL.Web">
        <c:CreatedAt>0001-01-01T00:00:00</c:CreatedAt>
        <c:CustomerId>1</c:CustomerId>
        <c:Notes i:nil="true"></c:Notes>
        <c:OrderHeaderId>1</c:OrderHeaderId>
        <c:OrderStatus i:nil="true"></c:OrderStatus>
        <c:ShipVia i:nil="true"></c:ShipVia>
        <c:UpdatedAt>2012-02-10T11:55:39.667375</c:UpdatedAt>
      </a:OriginalEntity>
    </a:ChangeSetEntry>
    <a:ChangeSetEntry>
      <a:Entity i:type="c:OrderHeader" xmlns:b="http://schemas.datacontract.
org/2004/07/System.ServiceModel.DomainServices.Client" xmlns:c="http://schemas.
datacontract.org/2004/07/DemoSL.Web">
        <c:CreatedAt>2012-02-10T11:55:39.667375</c:CreatedAt>
        <c:CustomerId>0</c:CustomerId>
        <c:Notes i:nil="true"></c:Notes>
        <c:OrderHeaderId>2</c:OrderHeaderId>
        <c:OrderStatus>Pending</c:OrderStatus>
        <c:ShipVia>Express Mail</c:ShipVia>
```

```
        <c:UpdatedAt>2012-02-10T11:55:39.667375</c:UpdatedAt>
      </a:Entity>
      <a:EntityActions i:nil="true" xmlns:b="http://schemas.microsoft.
com/2003/10/Serialization/Arrays"></a:EntityActions>
      <a:HasMemberChanges>true</a:HasMemberChanges>
      <a:Id>5</a:Id>
      <a:Operation>Delete</a:Operation>
      <a:OriginalEntity i:type="c:OrderHeader" xmlns:b="http://schemas.
datacontract.org/2004/07/System.ServiceModel.DomainServices.Client"
xmlns:c="http://schemas.datacontract.org/2004/07/DemoSL.Web">
        <c:CreatedAt>0001-01-01T00:00:00</c:CreatedAt>
        <c:CustomerId>1</c:CustomerId>
        <c:Notes i:nil="true"></c:Notes>
        <c:OrderHeaderId>2</c:OrderHeaderId>
        <c:OrderStatus i:nil="true"></c:OrderStatus>
        <c:ShipVia i:nil="true"></c:ShipVia>
        <c:UpdatedAt>2012-02-10T11:55:39.667375</c:UpdatedAt>
      </a:OriginalEntity>
    </a:ChangeSetEntry>
        :
  </changeSet>
</SubmitChanges>
```

You can see that each modified *Customer* and *OrderHeader* entity in the composition is represent in the request with an *<a:Operation>* element that indicates *Insert*, *Update*, or *Delete*. In the case of the *Update*, notice that the request includes an *<a:OriginalEntity>* element that supplies the original values of the customer entity being updated. If you look at the original customer entity, you will notice that it only contains the original value for the *UpdatedAt* property. This is because that is the only property designated with the *RoundtripOriginal* attribute in the metadata; all the other (non-key) properties are initialized to the default values of their respective data types.

Now switch over to Profiler to see the database activity, as shown in Figure 11-22.

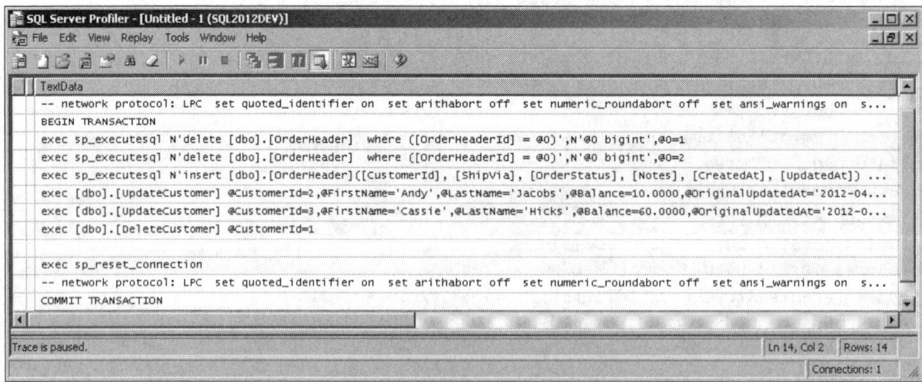

FIGURE 11-22 SQL Server Profiler output showing the T-SQL statements executed by the WCF RIA Services update request.

The appropriate T-SQL commands were generated by EF based on the entities in the changeset received from the client that were attached to the *ObjectContext* by the domain service class methods. The updates are wrapped up inside of a database transaction because of the *Transaction-Scope* block in the *Submit* method override added to the domain service class (see Listing 11-15).

Now switch back to Fiddler and examine the response returned to the client, shown in Listing 11-20. You can see that WCF RIA Services returns updated views of each entity back to the client. In the case of the *Insert* operation for Andy's new order, the *OrderHeaderId* value 13 indicates the primary key value assigned by the SQL Server *IDENITY* column in the underlying *OrderHeader* table.

LISTING 11-20 The WCF RIA Services *SubmitChangesResponse*.

```
<SubmitChangesResponse xmlns="http://tempuri.org/">
  <SubmitChangesResult xmlns:a="DomainServices" xmlns:i="http://www.w3.org/2001/
XMLSchema-instance">
      :
    <a:ChangeSetEntry>
      <a:Entity i:type="b:OrderHeader" xmlns:b="http://schemas.datacontract.
org/2004/07/DemoSL.Web">
        <b:CreatedAt>0001-01-01T00:00:00</b:CreatedAt>
        <b:CustomerId>2</b:CustomerId>
        <b:Notes i:nil="true"></b:Notes>
        <b:OrderHeaderId>13</b:OrderHeaderId>
        <b:OrderStatus>Pending</b:OrderStatus>
        <b:ShipVia>Priority Mail</b:ShipVia>
        <b:UpdatedAt>0001-01-01T00:00:00</b:UpdatedAt>
      </a:Entity>
      <a:EntityActions i:nil="true" xmlns:b="http://schemas.microsoft.com/2003/10/
Serialization/Arrays"></a:EntityActions>
      <a:HasMemberChanges>false</a:HasMemberChanges>
      <a:Id>0</a:Id>
      <a:Operation>Insert</a:Operation>
    </a:ChangeSetEntry>
    <a:ChangeSetEntry>
      <a:Entity i:type="b:Customer" xmlns:b="http://schemas.datacontract.
org/2004/07/DemoSL.Web">
        <b:Balance>60</b:Balance>
        <b:CreatedAt>2012-02-10T11:55:39.667375</b:CreatedAt>
        <b:CustomerId>3</b:CustomerId>
        <b:FirstName>Cassie</b:FirstName>
        <b:LastName>Hicks</b:LastName>
        <b:UpdatedAt>2012-02-10T18:18:39.2757928</b:UpdatedAt>
      </a:Entity>
      <a:EntityActions i:nil="true" xmlns:b="http://schemas.microsoft.com/2003/10/
Serialization/Arrays"></a:EntityActions>
      <a:HasMemberChanges>true</a:HasMemberChanges>
      <a:Id>2</a:Id>
      <a:Operation>Update</a:Operation>
    </a:ChangeSetEntry>
      :
    <a:ChangeSetEntry>
```

```
      <a:Entity i:type="b:Customer" xmlns:b="http://schemas.datacontract.
org/2004/07/DemoSL.Web">
        <b:Balance>35.0000</b:Balance>
        <b:CreatedAt>2012-02-10T11:55:39.667375</b:CreatedAt>
        <b:CustomerId>1</b:CustomerId>
        <b:FirstName>Lukas</b:FirstName>
        <b:LastName>Keller</b:LastName>
        <b:UpdatedAt>2012-02-10T11:55:39.667375</b:UpdatedAt>
      </a:Entity>
      <a:EntityActions i:nil="true" xmlns:b="http://schemas.microsoft.com/2003/10/
Serialization/Arrays"></a:EntityActions>
      <a:HasMemberChanges>false</a:HasMemberChanges>
      <a:Id>3</a:Id>
      <a:Operation>Delete</a:Operation>
    </a:ChangeSetEntry>
    <a:ChangeSetEntry>
      <a:Entity i:type="b:OrderHeader" xmlns:b="http://schemas.datacontract.
org/2004/07/DemoSL.Web">
        <b:CreatedAt>0001-01-01T00:00:00</b:CreatedAt>
        <b:CustomerId>1</b:CustomerId>
        <b:Notes i:nil="true"></b:Notes>
        <b:OrderHeaderId>1</b:OrderHeaderId>
        <b:OrderStatus i:nil="true"></b:OrderStatus>
        <b:ShipVia i:nil="true"></b:ShipVia>
        <b:UpdatedAt>2012-02-10T11:55:39.667375</b:UpdatedAt>
      </a:Entity>
      <a:EntityActions i:nil="true" xmlns:b="http://schemas.microsoft.com/2003/10/
Serialization/Arrays"></a:EntityActions>
      <a:HasMemberChanges>true</a:HasMemberChanges>
      <a:Id>4</a:Id>
      <a:Operation>Delete</a:Operation>
    </a:ChangeSetEntry>
    <a:ChangeSetEntry>
      <a:Entity i:type="b:OrderHeader" xmlns:b="http://schemas.datacontract.
org/2004/07/DemoSL.Web">
        <b:CreatedAt>0001-01-01T00:00:00</b:CreatedAt>
        <b:CustomerId>1</b:CustomerId>
        <b:Notes i:nil="true"></b:Notes>
        <b:OrderHeaderId>2</b:OrderHeaderId>
        <b:OrderStatus i:nil="true"></b:OrderStatus>
        <b:ShipVia i:nil="true"></b:ShipVia>
        <b:UpdatedAt>2012-02-10T11:55:39.667375</b:UpdatedAt>
      </a:Entity>
      <a:EntityActions i:nil="true" xmlns:b="http://schemas.microsoft.com/2003/10/
Serialization/Arrays"></a:EntityActions>
      <a:HasMemberChanges>true</a:HasMemberChanges>
      <a:Id>5</a:Id>
      <a:Operation>Delete</a:Operation>
    </a:ChangeSetEntry>
  </SubmitChangesResult>
</SubmitChangesResponse>
```

Congratulations! You have learned how to build n-tier applications using the latest and most important data technologies available in the .NET stack: Entity Framework, WCF Data Services, and WCF RIA Services.

Making the Right WCF Data Access Choice

Our coverage in this chapter has highlighted several key differences between WCF Data Services and WCF RIA Services, and you have probably already made some educated guesses about when to select one over the other. To better guide you in the decision-making process, we conclude the chapter with a more focused comparison of these two frameworks.

TABLE 11-1 Comparing WCF Data Services and WCF RIA Services.

	WCF Data Services	**WCF RIA Services**
Supported Clients	Resource-based API, supports all clients via deep REST and OData support.	Domain-based API, most tailored for use with Silverlight, but supports other clients via SOAP, JSON, and OData support.
Supported Data Access Layers	Targets EF. Other DALs are supported, but greater effort is required.	Supports EF, LINQ to SQL, and POCO (custom persistence layer).
Client Development	Requires you to notify the context for change tracking.	Supports self-tracking entities, synchronized client/server logic, and much more (particularly with Silverlight).
Service Development	Instant, code-less, extensible REST services out of the box (with EF); "free CRUD."	Requires you to code CRUD operations manually in domain service classes.

Several casual observations can be made from the comparison in Table 11-1. WCF RIA Services is more attractive for Silverlight clients than non-Silverlight clients—regardless of which data access layer is used. And WCF Data Services is more appropriate for use with Entity Framework than it is with other data access layers—regardless of which client is used.

If your scenario uses EF on the back end and targets Silverlight on the front end, then you are in the best position. Both WCF frameworks pack a huge win over writing traditional WCF services "by hand." Your decision at this point is based on whether you simply require services to provide data access (that is, you primarily need CRUD support), or if you are seeking to leverage additional benefits. Another consideration is whether you are targeting Silverlight as the client *exclusively* or not.

WCF Data Services is relatively lightweight, and requires almost no effort to get up and running with it. So it's the better choice if you only need data access functionality in your services, particularly if you want to keep your service open to non-Silverlight clients as well. WCF RIA Services is more robust, and offers numerous additional features. This makes it a very compelling choice for the development of rich client applications. Although it began as a platform almost exclusively designed for Silverlight, support is steadily emerging for other client platforms via OData, SOAP, and JSON, as well as self-tracking entity libraries now available for JavaScript and jQuery. Conversely, it still requires the additional effort to create domain service classes.

Finally, both frameworks are extensible, and both can be secured by traditional authentication and authorization techniques. They are also both capable of integrating with the ASP.NET Membership provider for role management and personalization.

What if you are using neither Silverlight nor Entity Framework? Well, then your work will be cut out for you whatever choice you make. With WCF Data Services, you will need to implement either the Reflection or Streaming provider, or write your own custom provider. And with WCF RIA Services, you will not get to fully enjoy all the benefits of the framework, plus you will still need to write domain services and metadata classes. After careful consideration, you may well conclude that neither choice is appropriate, and decide instead to stick with tried and true WCF services, coding your own service contracts, data contracts, binding configurations, change tracking, validations, and so on.

Summary

This chapter built on the Entity Framework coverage of our previous chapter, and taught you how to expose your Entity Data Model (EDM) as services using two flexible Windows Communication Foundation technologies: WCF Data Services and WCF RIA Services.

We began by exploring the protocols underlying WCF Data Services, including Representational State Transfer (REST) and Open Data Protocol (OData). You learned about the OData URI query syntax, and how they expose resource-based services over your EDM. We also described many WCF Data Services extensibility features, such as custom service operations, base class overrides, and interceptors. Then you learned how to use the WCF Data Services client library to build front-end applications. After writing a simple test client, you built a complete Windows Forms data entry client to consume the service. You got an up-close look at the action behind the scenes by monitoring HTTP traffic with Fiddler and observing database activity with SQL Profiler.

Then you built a similar solution using WCF RIA Services and Silverlight. You saw how the special link between client and server projects in your Visual Studio solution enables rich client development against domain services. Then you learned how to create a domain service class to support queries and updates, as well as metadata classes for your entities to customize service behavior. After completing the service, you built the Silverlight front end using the client-side context and self-tracking entities automatically generated by the WCF RIA Services link. Finally, we concluded by focusing on the similarities and differences between WCF Data Services and WCF RIA Services, with a comparison to help you make the right choices in any given scenario.

These past two chapters have covered all of the data access techniques available in .NET for client/server and n-tier development. Today, n-tier development extends into the cloud, and the next chapter is all about Microsoft's cloud database, SQL Azure. The chapter that follows combines technologies in all three preceding chapters, and adds synchronization and mobile development. In that chapter, you will build an end-to-end solution with SQL Azure, SQL Azure Data Sync, WCF Data Services hosted on Windows Azure, and Windows Phone 7 development tools.

CHAPTER 12

Moving to the Cloud with SQL Azure

—*Andrew Brust*

In technology, things typically start out as exclusive, expensive, and complex, before eventually becoming mainstream, affordable, and simple. As computing advances, barriers to entry are lowered, and that's good for everyone. This has happened with most technologies, including Microsoft SQL Server.

How so? Although it's pretty easy to get SQL Server up and running these days, it wasn't always that way. When SQL Server first came out for the Windows operating system, it ran only on Windows NT—and only on a server. The very determined could use NT Server as a workstation OS and thus have SQL Server running on their development machine. But for all intents and purposes, using SQL Server required setting up a real server, which inhibited the product's adoption by developers.

Today though, SQL Server runs fine on client operating systems, so developing for SQL Server has far fewer obstacles than it once did. But what about *production*? What if you want to deploy and maintain a SQL Server database for a substantial number of users? If you have an IT department supporting you, then you're all set. Ask to have a server provisioned and managed, and away you go.

But if you don't have an IT department, or you have one, but it's overburdened or unable to assist you, then you're on your own. You can certainly buy and set up a beefy PC, or even a server, install SQL Server on it and administer it yourself, and you could make that workable for a while. But are you ready to properly manage network traffic, backups, warm spares, and the like? Probably not, which means the do-it-yourself approach is risky, leaving you and your users vulnerable. For example, if more users come online, you will have a big problem making your one-person operation scale.

The "cloud" can help. As a database developer, what would probably suit you well would be a hosted database service, where network operations, server management and configuration, database mirroring/replication, backups, and other infrastructure-related tasks are taken care of for you. Actually, what would probably work even better is an arrangement whereby you have to manage just the database (or a collection of databases). Everything else—even all the administrative tasks associated with the database, other than design-level optimizations—would ideally be handled for you, just as if you had an IT department supporting you and even a part-time database administrator (DBA).

This service would be different than a simple SQL Server offering from a hosting provider. And it would be different from infrastructure as a service (IaaS) offerings, where a virtualized server is provided, but the installation, care, and feeding of SQL Server would still be your responsibility. The ideal service we have described would be a cloud-based database platform as a service (PaaS) offering, where you would need only to provision and operate a database; the rest would be taken care of by the service.

SQL Azure *is* that ideal database PaaS offering. Even better, in functional terms, it is largely equivalent to the on-premises version of SQL Server. For readers of this book, that means the learning curve for setting up a public-facing relational database with A-list Internet peering and infrastructure management is very shallow. So shallow, in fact, that we can cover what you need to know to get up and running with SQL Azure in this one chapter alone!

In this chapter, you will learn:

- How to sign up for a SQL Azure subscription, then provision a SQL Azure server and database.
- How to manage, design, and maintain your database using the Windows Azure Management Portal, the SQL Azure Management Portal, SQL Server Management Studio (SSMS), and SQL Server Developer Tools (SSDT) in Visual Studio.
- How to deploy and migrate databases to, and between, SQL Server and SQL Azure using Data-Tier Applications (DACPAC and BACPAC files).
- What SQL Azure Federations are, when to use them, and how to do so in the SQL Azure Management Portal and SSMS.
- How to get up and running with SQL Azure Reporting, using the Windows Azure Management Portal, Reporting Services projects in Visual Studio, and Report Builder.

In short, you'll learn the procedures and approaches unique to SQL Azure for getting up and running with the product, and you will then see how you can keep going with things you already know.

Important One big difference between on-premises software and cloud services is that the latter can be updated and enhanced much more frequently than the former, given that no installation on customer infrastructure is required in the cloud case. Cloud services are subject to frequent changes in pricing as well. As such, costs, limitations, features, the tooling user interface or even the branding of SQL Azure and/or SQL Azure Reporting, as described in this chapter, may have evolved by the time you read it. (For example, while this chapter was being written, SQL Azure's pricing was reduced—by as much as 75% for certain configurations—and this chapter was updated to reflect the change.) Regardless of the potential for such changes, the principles and techniques covered here should help you achieve comfort with and mastery of SQL Azure. Just make sure to review online what features may have been added or limitations removed from SQL Azure and SQL Azure Reporting since the timeframe of SQL Server 2012's release, so you can read this chapter in the proper context.

History

When we wrote the last edition of this book, we provided brief coverage of a cloud service from Microsoft called SQL Server Data Services (SSDS), which was in beta. Although that service used SQL Server as its infrastructure, it presented an interface to the developer that was completely different from the relational structure of SQL Server. SSDS used a model called "ACE," which stood for Authority-Container-Entity, and was essentially a key-value store NoSQL database (although we didn't have the vocabulary at the time to call it that).

Subsequent to the beta release of SSDS, two things happened: (1) Microsoft launched Azure Table Storage (among other services), which had a model very similar to ACE, and (2) feedback came in from SQL Server customers that they wanted a true SQL Server relational database service, and weren't satisfied with the ACE model.

Microsoft listened, discontinued SSDS, and offered in its place SQL Azure Database, in which it offered a PaaS flavor of SQL Server that used T-SQL, worked with SQL Server's Tabular Data Stream (TDS) protocol, and was compatible with existing SQL Server database drivers and APIs. That meant that .NET developers, and especially Azure developers using .NET, could access SQL Azure in the same way they did on-premises SQL Server, from on-premises applications, changing only their connection string and avoiding certain SQL Server features that SQL Azure did not support. The public beta period for SQL Azure Database began in 2009 and SQL Azure was released as a commercial service in 2010.

SQL Azure started out with a number of limitations, primitive tooling, and a maximum database size of 10 GB, which limited its use to only certain application scenarios. But the service is now robust and feature-rich, has much richer tooling, offers a maximum database size of 150 GB, and supports Federations, a scale-out model which allows developers to transcend even that physical limitation.

But What *Is* SQL Azure?

The best way to think of SQL Azure is as a bank of SQL Server boxes that someone else is managing, and because someone else is managing those boxes, you have to abide by some important restrictions and requirements. For example:

- Every table must have a clustered index.
- The absolute largest database you can have is 150 GB (but Federations offer a work-around for bigger databases).
- There is no full-text search.
- While the XML data type is supported, there is no support for XML indexes, XML schemas, or schema collections.
- Only the SQL Server security authentication model is supported.
- There is no support for conventional SQL Server partitioning.

Note More comprehensive inventories of SQL Azure restrictions, relative to the feature set of the full SQL Server product, can be found at *http://msdn.microsoft.com/en-us/library/windowsazure/ff394115.aspx* and *http://msdn.microsoft.com/en-us/library/windowsazure/ee336241.aspx*.

SQL Azure features only the relational database component of SQL Server. There is a separate, limited implementation of SQL Server Reporting Services (which we cover later in this chapter), but there is currently no cloud implementation of Integration Services, Analysis Services, Master Data Services, Data Quality Services, StreamInsight, or any other discrete component of the "greater" SQL Server family.

Keeping the above restrictions and limitations in mind summons an important paradox: You can consider SQL Azure to be just like SQL Server, except that it's sometimes different. Is that a little obtuse of us to say? Perhaps. But the more you work with SQL Azure, the more you will come to appreciate this observation's accuracy. Meanwhile, here are a few things the two Microsoft databases have in common:

- Both can be managed from SSMS and SSDT.
- Both can serve as data sources for Reporting Services, Integration Services, PowerPivot, or Analysis Services.
- The SQL Server Native Client driver and the *SqlClient* ADO.NET provider can connect to, query, and perform data manipulation language (DML) operations on both.
- And, although the two code bases differ somewhat, SQL Azure *is* SQL Server.

Why the Limitations?

Let's talk about that last point. If SQL Azure is really just SQL Server, then why doesn't it support its full feature set? The thing to keep in mind is that SQL Azure databases run on shared servers and yet are automatically replicated and transparently fault-tolerant. As such, they can responsibly only offer features that keep the service scalable and the databases "fit and trim" enough to be duplicated and maintained very quickly. That's why the databases have size limitations, and that's why less scalable features, like full-text search, are not supported.

Other features are unsupported less for reasons of scalability and more because the service is still evolving. Not all SQL Server features have yet been fully implemented and/or tested in SQL Azure's multi-tenant environment. But SQL Azure is being improved all the time, and by the time you read this, some of the restrictions enumerated here may no longer exist.

Pricing

Cloud services' feature sets and pricing schemes tend to be refreshed at a greater frequency than are printed books. That's a long-winded way of saying that any discussion of SQL Azure pricing in this book is subject to falling out-of-date. However, it's hard to judge the efficacy of a cloud-based version of SQL Server without some understanding of its costs and billing tenets.

So let's proceed with a discussion of SQL Azure's pricing as it stands at press time, and let's treat this discussion as a contextual tool for understanding when and where implementation of SQL Azure might make sense. Make sure to check online for up-to-date pricing information and combine that with the concepts provided in this section to sketch out for yourself the full business case for SQL Azure.

SQL Azure is available in two "editions": the Web edition includes databases of up to 1 GB or up to 5 GB. The Business edition includes databases which can be any of the following maximum sizes: 10 GB, 20 GB, 30 GB, 40 GB, 50 GB, 100 GB, or 150 GB. Rates range from $10/GB/month for a 1 GB database to as little as $1.51/GB/month for a 150 GB database. If absolute cost is more important to you than per-GB rates, there is also a 100 MB database option for $4.995/month.

Inbound data—including data sent for *INSERT, UPDATE,* or submitted via Bulk Copy Program (BCP) operations—is not charged for. Outbound data (including data queried or requested via BCP operations) however, is billable, currently at $0.12/GB from North American and European data centers, and $0.19/GB from Asian data centers. Data qualifies for egress (i.e., outbound) charges not when it leaves SQL Azure per se, but when it leaves the data center and goes over the Internet. Therefore, data queried by a Windows Azure application running in the same data center as the SQL Azure server is not billed (although outbound data transfer charges from the Windows Azure application will apply).

These rates are for "pay-as-you-go" service, and are based on actual metered usage. This is especially efficient in cases where you are uncertain of how much or little capacity you will really need. However, in cases where you have an awareness of certain minimum usage needs, and can commit to those service levels for six months, you can pay a subscription rate for the service as follows: you purchase "units," each one of which covers $100 worth of monthly SQL Azure services (based on pay-as-you go rates) but costs only $79.99/month. This is a little bit like buying minutes on a mobile calling plan without a rollover mechanism: just as you might lose unused minutes, you will lose any unused SQL Azure services. Therefore the units you purchase should be based on your minimal needs. Service over and above what your subscription covers will be billed at the regular pay-as-you-go rates.

The First One's Free

Unlike running SQL Server on your development machine, working with SQL Azure requires setting up an account, and paying for it. That creates a barrier to entry that could dissuade some developers from trying the product. Microsoft is aware of this and, at press time, is offering a solution: free trial subscriptions to Windows Azure and SQL Azure.

As long as you feel comfortable providing a credit card number, and you don't need to exceed the allowances provided in the trial, you'll be able to sign up for SQL Azure immediately and work with it extensively, free-of-charge, for three months. To give this chapter some real-world context, we'll discuss how to sign up for the trial subscription.

Note Even if the trial offer is withdrawn at some point, the end-to-end coverage in this chapter should make things more concrete and make you more comfortable with the rather small investment necessary to work with SQL Azure at the regular rates (as little as $4.995/month for a 100 MB database) already discussed.

If you are a Visual Studio Professional, Premium, or Ultimate with MSDN subscriber, you are already entitled to a monthly allowance of Azure services, including SQL Azure, at no additional charge. Although the free trial subscription is available to you as well, you may prefer simply to activate the Azure subscription that is included with your MSDN subscription. Although the sign-up process will differ somewhat from what trial offer users will experience, everything from provisioning of a server and beyond (i.e., the vast majority of what we cover in this chapter) will align perfectly.

Getting Set Up

Now that we have a good overview of what SQL Azure is, what it includes, and what it omits, and we have established that you can work with it for little or no money up-front, let's look at how to sign up for a free trial account.

To sign up, you will need a Windows Live ID. Most readers of this book will already have one but if you don't, or if you'd like to create a special Live ID for use with the Azure trial subscription, then go to *http://signup.live.com* and create one. For the purposes of this chapter, we set up a special Live ID under the email address programmingmssql2012@live.com. The account was deactivated before this book went to press, but we mention this so that you will recognize this address as a Live ID in some of the screenshots in this chapter.

Note If you have an Xbox Live account, a Zune account, a Hotmail account, a Windows Live Messenger account, or an activated Windows Phone, your login credentials for those services are in fact Live IDs and can be used to provision a Windows Azure trial account.

Tip You will have separate accounts/login credentials for your Live ID, your SQL Azure server, and your SQL Azure Reporting account. Make sure to record each set of credentials carefully, in a place that is secure yet accessible.

Beyond the Prerequisites

Once you have your Live ID credentials, perform the following steps to provision your trial account:

1. Point your browser to *http://www.windowsazure.com*.
2. Click the Free Trial link on the upper-right hand of the page. This will take you to a page with, among other content, a description of the usage allowances provided with the trial.

   > **Info** As of this writing, the relevant allowance information for SQL Azure is that the trial includes a 1 GB Web edition SQL Azure database, unlimited inbound data transfer, and 20 GB of outbound data transfer, per month.

3. Click the "Try It Free" button in the middle of the new page.
4. Log in with your Live ID credentials and then click Next (the right-arrow button) on the first pop-up page.
5. Enter a mobile phone number at which to receive an activation code via text message, and click Send Text Message.
6. Once you receive the text message, enter the activation code it contains and then click Verify Code.
7. Once the code is validated, click Next (the right-arrow button).
8. Enter the requested credit card, account, and billing information. Check or uncheck the acknowledgment and opt-in checkboxes at the bottom of the form and then click Next.
9. After a brief pause, your account will be provisioned and your browser will be redirected to a welcome page.

   > **Info** Although sign-up for the trial subscription requires entry of a valid credit card number, you can still rest easy about unintended and unwanted charges. Trial accounts are configured by default to disable automatically for the remainder of any month where and if a monthly usage limit is reached, and to expire automatically at the end of the three-month trial period. Should you reach your usage limit during month 1 or 2, although your account will be disabled, your database will not be deleted, and your account will automatically re-enable at the beginning of month 2 or 3, respectively. If you wish to remove this mechanism and keep your account active, you can disable the spending limit. If you do so, all usage beyond the monthly allowance in months 1–3 and any usage at all after month 3 will be billed to your credit card at the SQL Azure standard pay-as-you-go rates already described.

Provisioning Your Server

Once your account is set up, click the Portal link toward the upper-right of the new page. Doing so will bring you into the Windows Azure Management Portal (if you don't have the latest version of Silverlight on your machine, you'll need to install it first). Click the Database button in the lower-left-hand Outlook-style navigation menu and you'll be taken to a screen where you can create SQL Azure servers and databases. Click the 3 Month Free Trial node under the Subscriptions folder, above the Outlook-style navigation bar. This will enable the Create button in the ribbon's Server group, as shown in Figure 12-1.

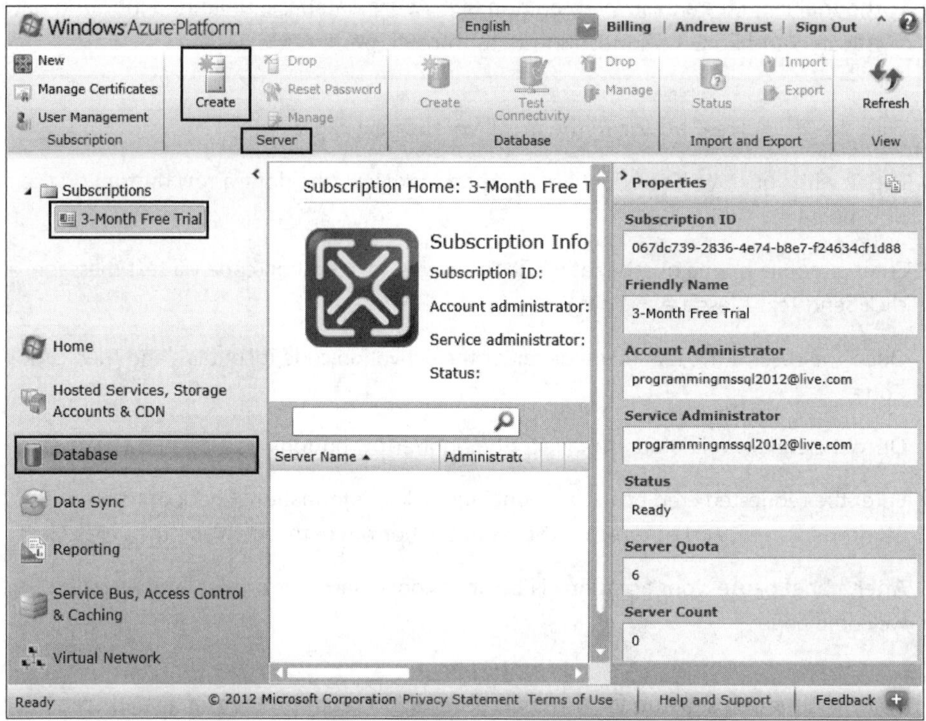

FIGURE 12-1 The Database page in Windows Azure Management Portal.

Click the Create button in the Server group of the ribbon (highlighted in Figure 12-1), and you'll launch the Create Server wizard. The wizard will first ask you to select a geographic region. This region—which can be set to South Central US, West US, East US, North Central US, North Europe, West Europe, East Asia, or Southeast Asia—corresponds to the physical location of the data center on whose infrastructure your database will be located. This choice should be made carefully; there are a few reasons why (a couple of which we've already alluded to):

- As a rule, performance will be better if you pick a data center that is physically close to your customers.
- There may be certain regulatory considerations important to you that impact your selection.
- Data transfer fees for certain data centers are slightly higher than for others.

- If you will be pairing your SQL Azure database with a Windows Azure application, or SQL Azure Reporting, you will want to locate them in the same region/data center to avoid outgoing data transfer fees from the database to the app or report. You can only assure that your Windows Azure hosted service and/or your SQL Azure Reporting server will be in the same region as your SQL Azure server if you keep track of what region you selected for SQL Azure in the first place!

Note At press time, SQL Azure Reporting services were not offered in the East US or West US data centers. Therefore, users wishing to locate both SQL Azure and SQL Azure Reporting services in a single US data center would be required to select South Central US or North Central U.S. as the location for their SQL Azure server.

Configuring the Administrative User and Firewall

After selecting a region, click Next and you'll be asked to provide a user name and password for the server-wide administrative user (similar to the *sa* user in SQL Server). Enter that information and click Next. Your next step will be to specify initial firewall rules. By default, your SQL Azure server will block all network traffic. If you want to use the server from your own development machine, you'll need to unblock its IP address. You'll probably want to allow access by Windows Azure services as well. The Create Server wizard lets you take care of this. It provides a checkbox that, when selected, will open up SQL Azure's firewall to Windows Azure services; it also provides an Add button which allows you to configure individual IP addresses, or IP address ranges, that will be allowed through.

Click the Add button and the Add Firewall Rule dialog box will appear. At the bottom, the IP address from which you're connecting will be shown. You can copy that address (by highlighting it with the mouse and pressing **Ctrl+C**) and paste it (with **Ctrl+V**) into the IP Range Start and IP Range End edit controls, and then enter a name in the Rule Name textbox, as shown in Figure 12-2.

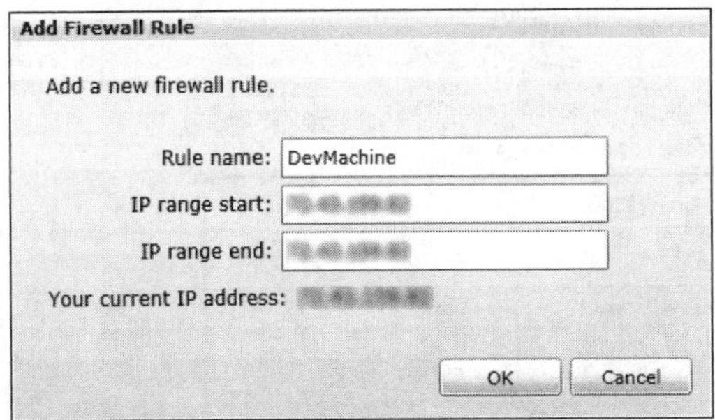

FIGURE 12-2 Adding a SQL Azure firewall rule.

> **Tip** You don't need to use the SQL Azure Management Portal to set firewall rules; you can use T-SQL instead. With the *master* database selected, simply use the *sp_set_firewall_rule* system stored procedure supplying the rule name, IP range start address, and IP range end address as parameters (each as quoted strings). To do this, you will need to connect to your SQL Azure server from SSMS, SSDT, or another client—this will be covered later in this chapter.

When you're done, click OK. Back in the Create Server wizard, enter additional firewall rules if you'd like, and then click the Finish button to return to the Windows Azure Management Portal. When you get there, you'll see that your server has been created and given a randomly assigned 10-character alphanumeric unique name. This name will be displayed in the tree view at the upper-left hand corner of the screen, under the node for your subscription, once you expand the latter.

If you click your new server's node in the tree view, the name will also be displayed at the top-center of the screen, along with a summary of your firewall rules. The server name, combined with the *database.windows.net* domain name, constitutes an accessible host name that you can use when creating connections or connection strings for your SQL Azure database. If you expand the server's tree view node, you will see that a *master* database for your server has been created for you. There's also a button in the middle of the ribbon that will allow you to create a new database. All of this is shown and highlighted in Figure 12-3.

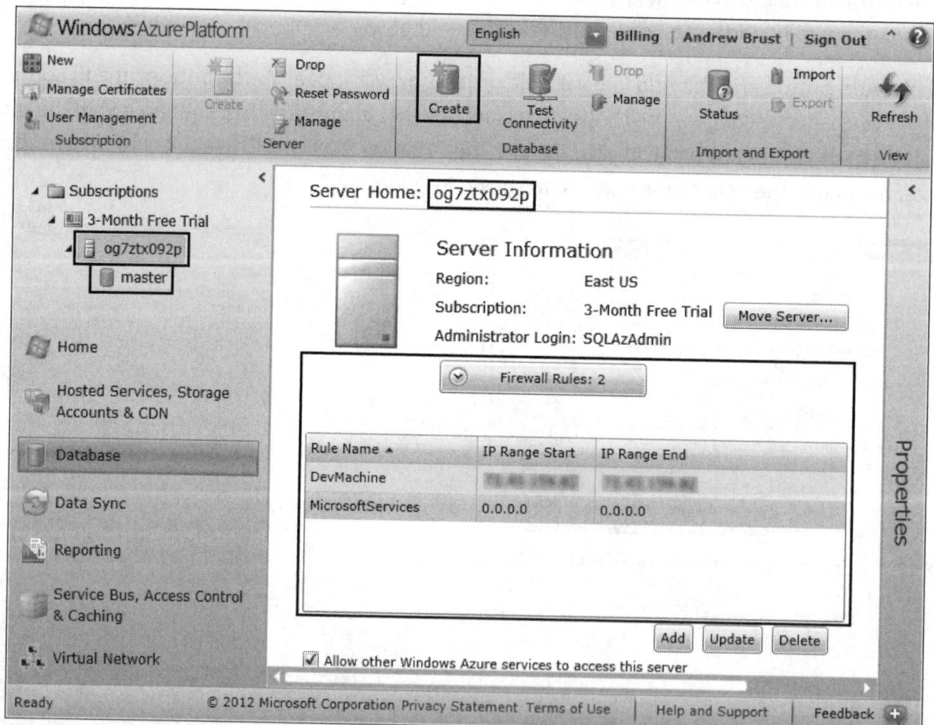

FIGURE 12-3 Viewing the information page for a new SQL Azure server.

Provisioning Your Database

Click the Create button in the Database group at the center of the ribbon to bring up the Create Database dialog. Enter a database name, and make sure Web is selected for Edition, and 1 GB for Maximum Size. Now click OK to return to the Windows Azure Management Portal.

Your database should appear in the tree view at the upper left of the screen. Select it and you should see a summary of your database displayed. A button in the ribbon will appear that allows you to test connectivity to the database. You'll also see Manage buttons that let you manage the server or the database in a separate tool called the SQL Azure Management Portal. At the bottom-right of the screen you will also see an *https* URL that can be used to navigate to the SQL Azure Management Portal directly. All of this is shown and highlighted in Figure 12-4.

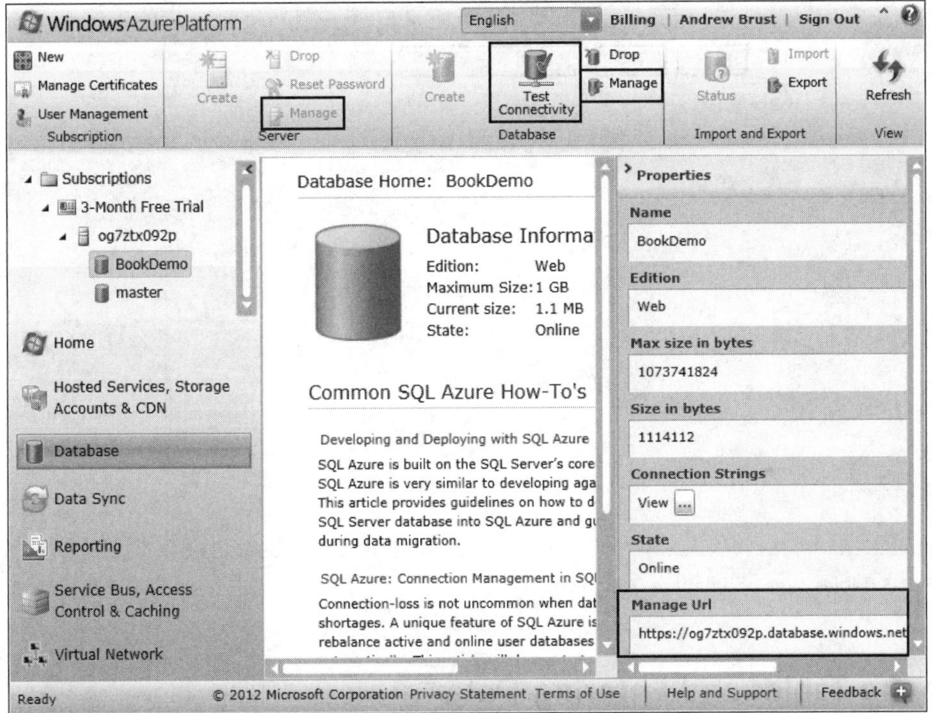

FIGURE 12-4 SQL Azure Management Portal server page after provisioning a database.

Managing Your Database

At this point, you're done with the Windows Azure Management Portal and can use the SQL Azure Management Portal instead. Click the Manage button in the ribbon's Database group to bring up the SQL Azure Management Portal. Use your SQL Azure server-wide administrative user credentials (not your Live ID and its password) to log in, and then allow the portal a few moments to load up.

The SQL Azure Management Portal, which is relatively new as of this writing, is a separate management tool for administering your SQL Azure server and databases, as well as designing, maintaining data in, and querying your databases. The tool features a Metro-style UI using the same elements of Live Tiles, semantic zoom, uncluttered design, and emphasis on typography as is used in the Windows Phone, Windows 8, and Xbox dashboard environments.

Click the Design tab (at the bottom left of the screen) and the Design screen will come up. It has pages for maintenance of Tables, Views, and Stored Procedures. The Tables page is selected by default and shown in Figure 12-5.

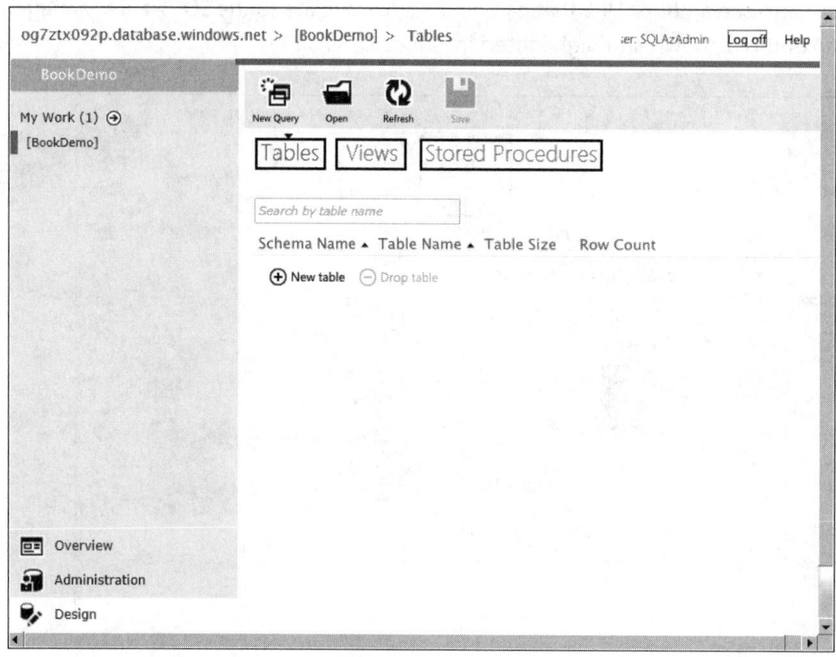

FIGURE 12-5 Tables page of database Design screen.

Creating Tables and Entering Data

Notice the "breadcrumb bar" at the top of the screen and the screen tab well at the upper left. The elements in each are all clickable to allow you to easily navigate to a prior screen, or to a different maintenance screen in the server > database > object collection hierarchy.

Click the New Table link (near the center of the screen) to bring up the table designer, and then enter a table name and details for its columns. Your screen should appear somewhat like the one shown in Figure 12-6.

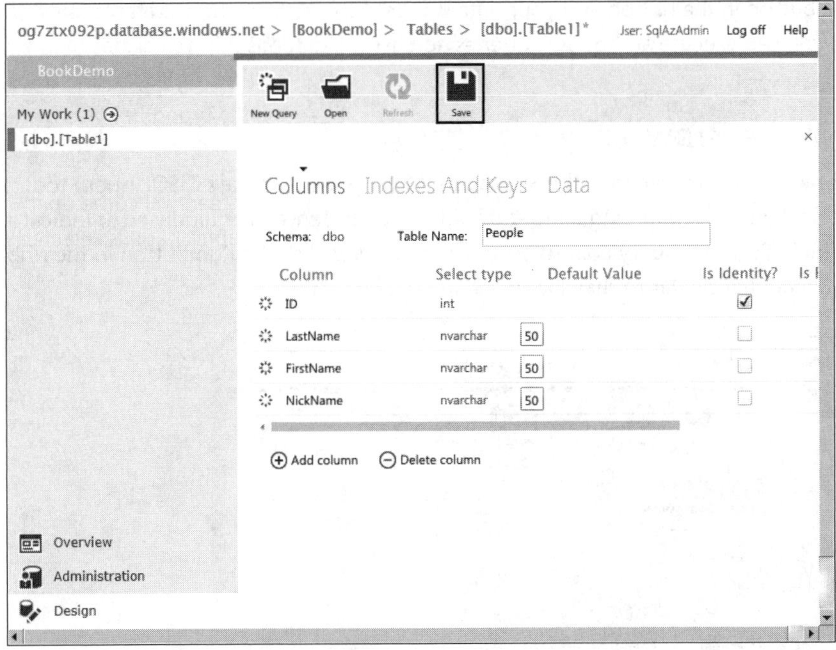

FIGURE 12-6 Columns page of the table Design screen.

When you're done, click the Save button in the ribbon (highlighted in Figure 12-6), then select the Data screen and enter a few rows of data, as shown in Figure 12-7.

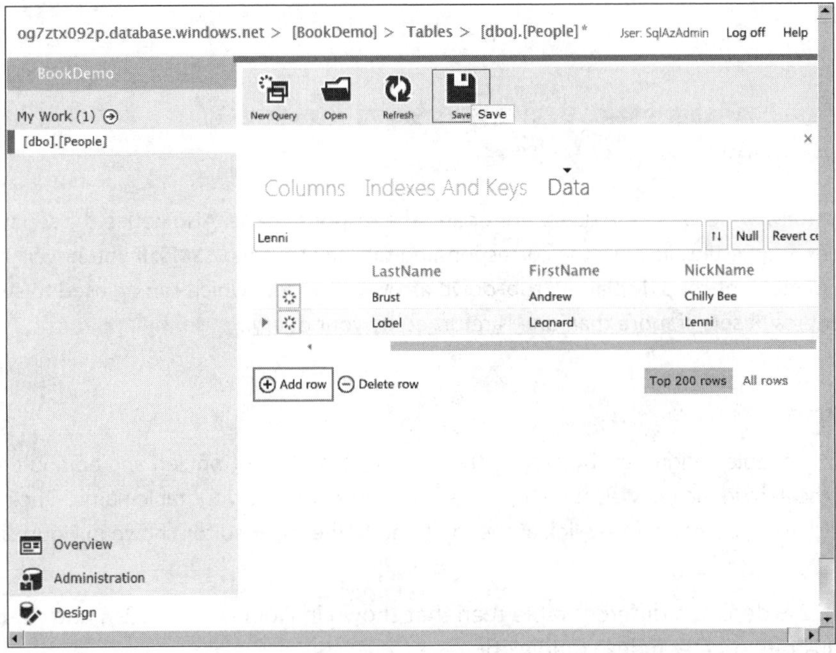

FIGURE 12-7 Data page of the table Design screen with two new rows pending.

Click the Save button in the ribbon and your data will be displayed, in a non-editable state, in a grid. From here, you can execute ad hoc SQL queries against the database.

Querying in the Browser

Click New Query and you'll be placed in the SQL Azure Management Portal's T-SQL query tool, complete with color syntax highlighting (although without IntelliSense or squiggly error indicators). Try entering a simple *SELECT* * query against your new table and click the Run button in the ribbon. Your screen should appear similar to that shown in Figure 12-8.

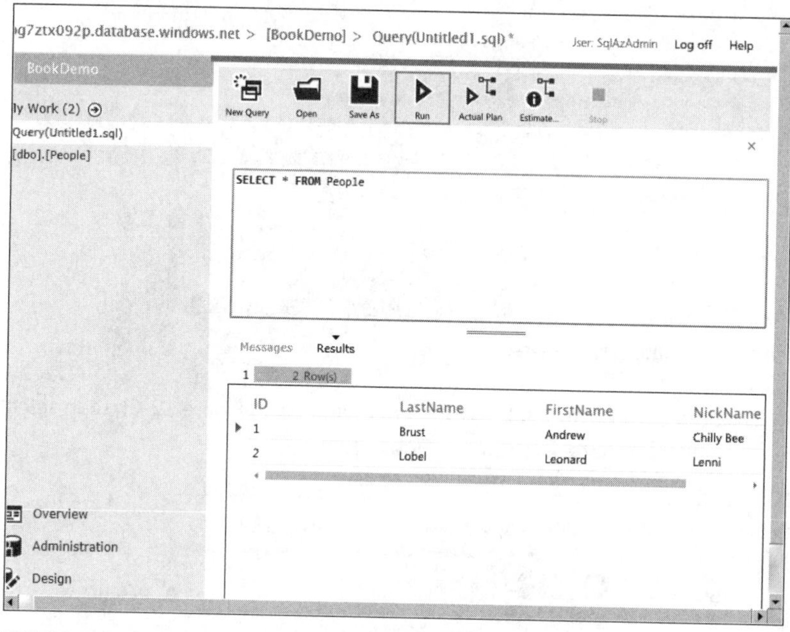

FIGURE 12-8 Query screen with results.

Notice the splitter bar between the query editor and the response pane. Also notice the separate links for Messages and Results, just like the corresponding tabs in SSDT and SSMS. If you hover your mouse over the number-of-rows display, a drop-down arrow will appear which can be used to switch between different result sets, if more than one is returned by your query.

Index Design

You can return to the table design view by clicking the Design tab at the bottom left and editing the table or clicking the item in the tab well at the upper left, corresponding to your table name. Once there, you can click the Indexes And Keys link at the top to go to the index editor, shown in Figure 12-9.

Note Figure 12-9 depicts a different table than that shown in Figures 12-6, 12-7, and 12-8, in order to illustrate greater index complexity.

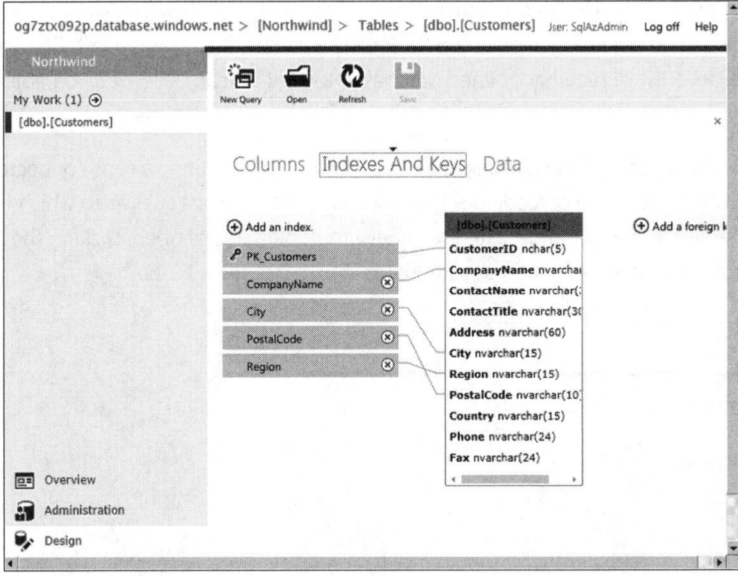

FIGURE 12-9 Indexes And Keys page of the table Design screen.

Management and Visualizations

The SQL Azure Management Portal also provides a great server-level dashboard. To see it, click the Log Off link at the top right of the screen and then log in again, this time leaving the Database edit control blank. Your screen should appear similar to the one shown in Figure 12-10.

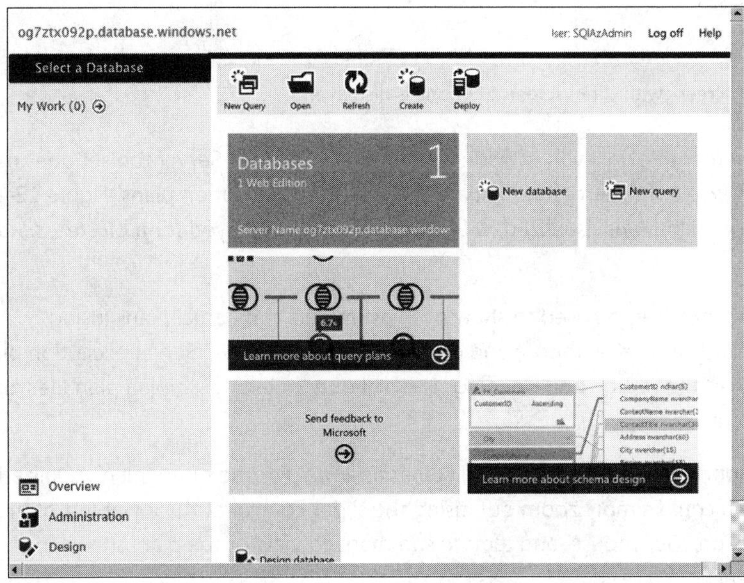

FIGURE 12-10 The Overview page in SQL Azure Management Portal.

With only one database, there's not a lot to see here yet, but once you have a few, you'll appreciate the server-level control that this screen gives you. Notice the Select a Database link at the top left. Clicking this would allow you to select from a list of recently opened databases, as well as from a list of all databases on the server.

The tab well right below the Select a Database link allows you to switch between screens connected to different databases on your server. A color-coding scheme would provide visual cues as to which tabs were linked with which database. In the situation where you have multiple screens open, clicking the My Work link will bring you to a thumbnail view of those screens, as shown in Figure 12-11.

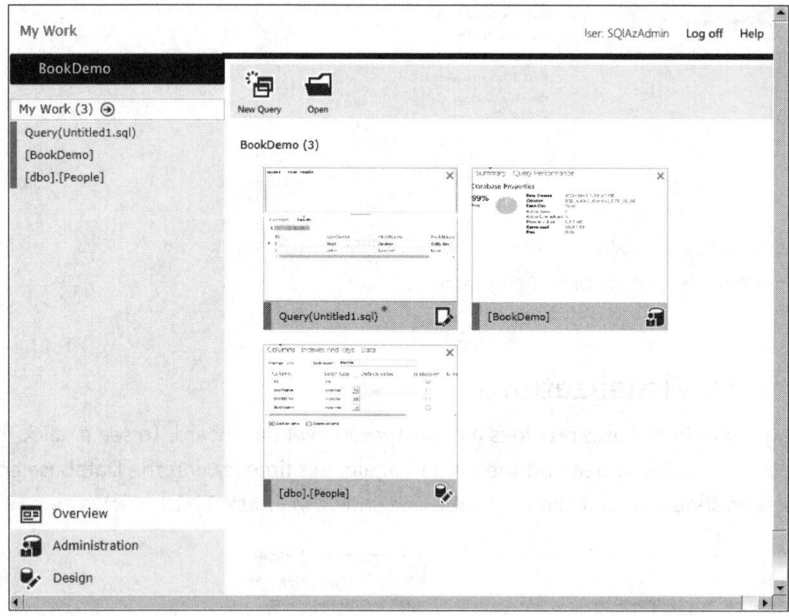

FIGURE 12-11 The My Work screen, with three screen thumbnails displayed.

The SQL Azure Management Portal even provides features that the SQL Server toolset does not. One example of this is an excellent Metro-style visualization of query execution plans. Figure 12-12 shows a partial view of one such plan, visualized, with a details panel displayed for a *Clustered Index Seek* node in the plan.

The execution plan visualizer can be used to show both estimated and actual plans (using correspondingly labeled buttons in the ribbon) and can even be used on SQL Server execution plans, by using the Open button in the ribbon and opening up a .sql query file or a .sqlplan plan file from a local drive or network share.

The visualizer also supports the Metro concept of semantic zoon. For the query plan visualization shown in Figure 12-12, you could simply zoom out, using the slider control at the lower left of the visualization, or the wheel on your mouse, and a more summarized view of the plan, shown in Figure 12-13, would appear.

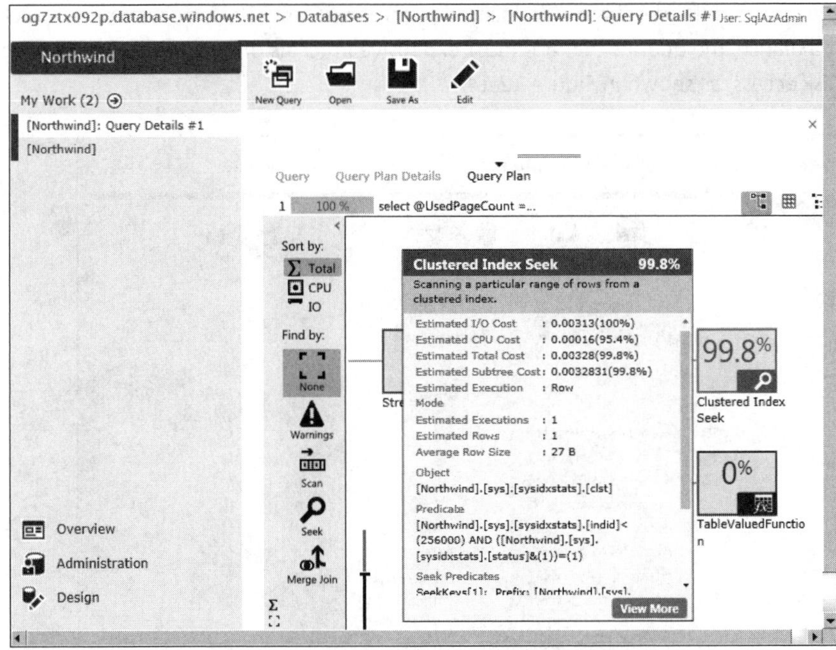

FIGURE 12-12 Query Plan page of Query screen, with details panel displayed.

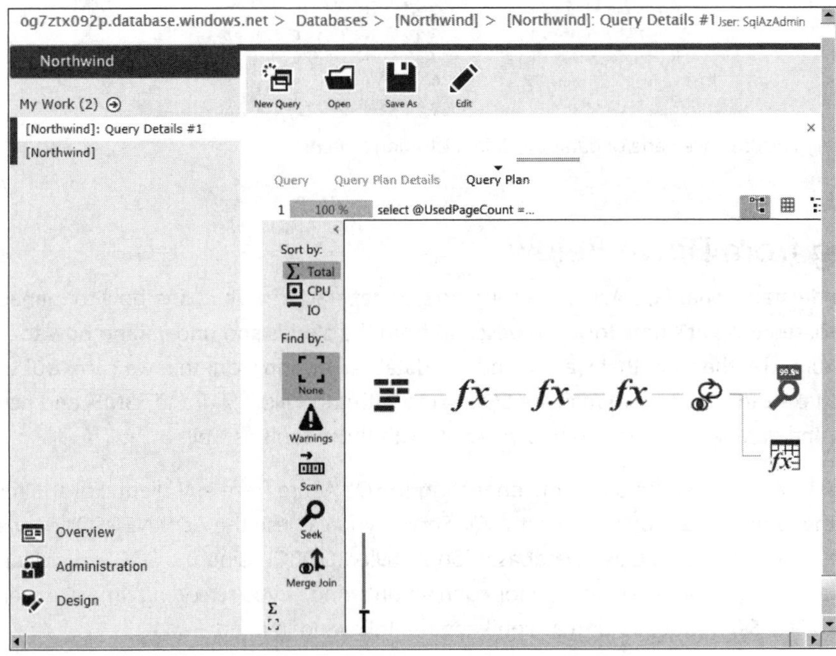

FIGURE 12-13 Query Plan page, zoomed out to summary view.

Another handy feature is the database Administration screen's Query Performance page which can show you, at a glance, the queries that are most expensive in terms of CPU utilization, duration of execution, and disk access, as shown in Figure 12-14.

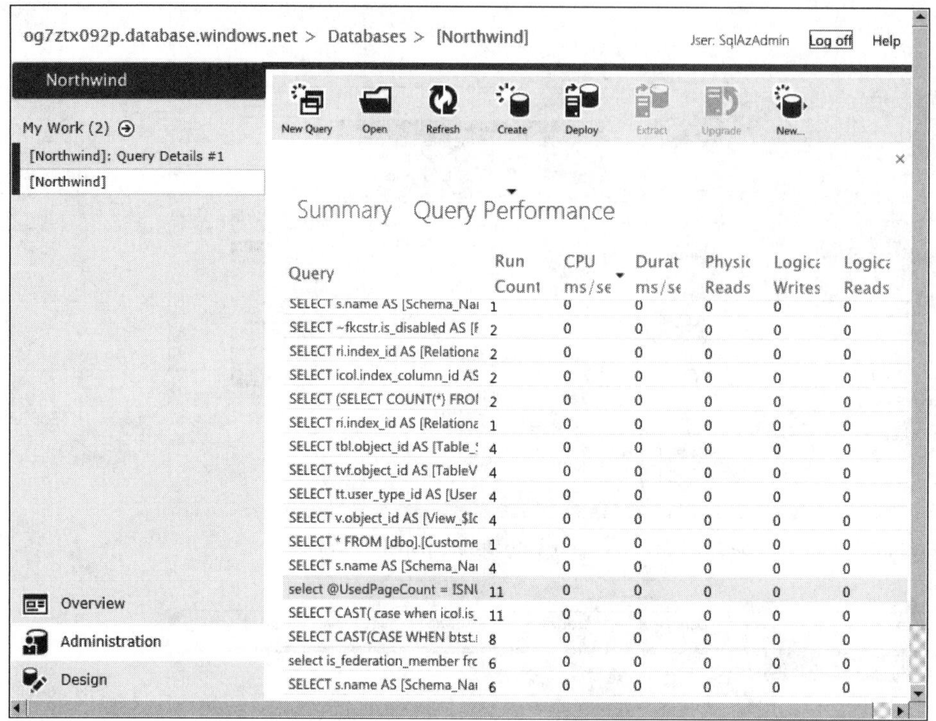

FIGURE 12-14 Query Performance page of database Administration screen.

Connecting from Down Below

Now that you understand what SQL Azure is about, how to get started with it, and how to manage it from browser-based tools, it's time for us to descend from the clouds and understand how to integrate SQL Azure with the tools that we use and the database design work that we carry out with SQL Server. Let's take a look at how to manage SQL Azure with tools like SSDT and SSMS, and how to move databases and database designs up to SQL Azure with those tools as well.

First things first: Let's discuss the basics of connecting to SQL Azure from any client. For the most part, you do so the same way as you would with SQL Server: you can use the ADO.NET SQL Server provider (*SqlClient*) or connect via Open Database Connectivity (ODBC) using the SQL Server Native Client driver. You'll configure your connection (or connection string, if you're coding) in a like manner as you would with SQL Server too, as long as you keep the following in mind:

- Set the server name to the full host name for your server, in the form servername.*database.windows.net*. In the examples we've been using, the server name would be set to *og7ztx092p.database.windows.net*.

- Set authentication to SQL Server Authentication (or set *Integrated Security=False* in your connection string, if you're coding). Then set the login and password credentials to those for a valid SQL Azure login in your database (not your Live ID credentials).
- Some clients will require you to add an @ sign and the server name after the user name (e.g., *sqlazadmin@og7ztx092p*).
- Keep in mind that SQL Azure always operates over TCP port 1433. SQL Server uses the same port by default, but it allows it to be configured to a different port, whereas SQL Azure does not. As such, any local or network firewalls must allow outbound traffic on TCP port 1433.
- You need to set firewall rules on your SQL Azure server in the Windows Azure Management Portal for all IP addresses from which a client may connect. If you don't do this, you may find yourself unable to connect to your SQL Azure database, and you may incorrectly assume that one of the above settings is in error, when it's simply a matter of needing to authorize the client's IP address.

In addition to the connection tips shared so far, there really is one other we should discuss: You should set *Encrypt=True* and *TrustServerCertificate=False*, whether in your connection string if you're coding, or in the advanced properties of a connection dialog if you're not. This will prevent "man-in-the-middle" attacks on your SSL connection to SQL Azure.

Tip If your client application allows you to select SQL Azure specifically (rather than SQL Server generically) as your data source, then the *Encrypt* and *TrustServerCertificate* settings may be configured correctly by default. But you should check to make sure, and set them yourself if necessary.

From SSMS and SSDT, setting these connection string parameters can be a little tricky. Although an encrypted connection can be turned on by clicking the Connect to Server dialog's Options button and then checking the Encrypt Connection check box in the Connection Properties tab, there is no such GUI option to set *TrustServerCertificate=False*. Therefore, the easiest way to set both of these is to enter **TrustServerCertificate=False;Encrypt=True** in the Additional Connection Parameters tab. Figure 12-15 shows the properly configured Login and Additional Connection Parameters tabs of the Connect to Server dialog box.

Note A sample ASP.NET application, *SARASPNETTest*, is included with this chapter. The code connects to a SQL Azure database, performs a generic *SELECT* * query on it, and binds the result set to an ASP.NET GridView control. The code uses a generic SQL Azure connection string in the *web.config* file. Just edit the connection string's server name, user id, and password in *web.config*, and the SQL query in *default.aspx.cs*, to be appropriate for your own SQL Azure database, and run the application for a complete practical demo.

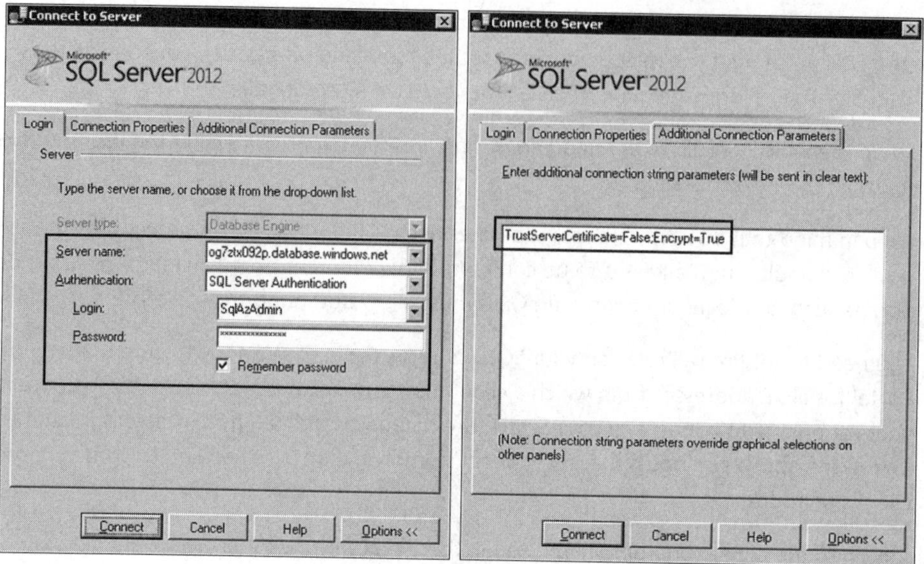

FIGURE 12-15 Connecting to SQL Azure from SSMS and SSDT.

Note You may very well prefer not to use the server-wide administrative login to connect to your SQL Azure database from the SQL Server tools. If that's the case, you'll need to connect as the server-wide administrative user once and then, either in SSMS or SSDT, create a new login and database user with the T-SQL templates both tools provide for these tasks. You may wish to make this user a member of the *db_owner* role.

Once you have entered the correct connection information, click the Connect button. Figure 12-16 shows the resulting appearance of the Object Explorer in SSMS (top) and the SQL Server Object Explorer in Visual Studio/SSDT (bottom). (The server and *Databases* nodes are collapsed by default and were manually expanded to reveal the underlying database).

Tip After creating a database-level user, you can disconnect and then reconnect using that user's credentials. However, your login will fail unless you set Default Database in the Connection Properties tab of the Connect To Server dialog box to a database that user has permissions on.

Although our database has already been created, you could instead connect to the server and create a database via T-SQL. For example, to create a 40 GB Business edition database, you'd connect to your SQL Azure server and issue the following command:

```
CREATE DATABASE MyNewDB (EDITION='BUSINESS', MAXSIZE=40GB)
```

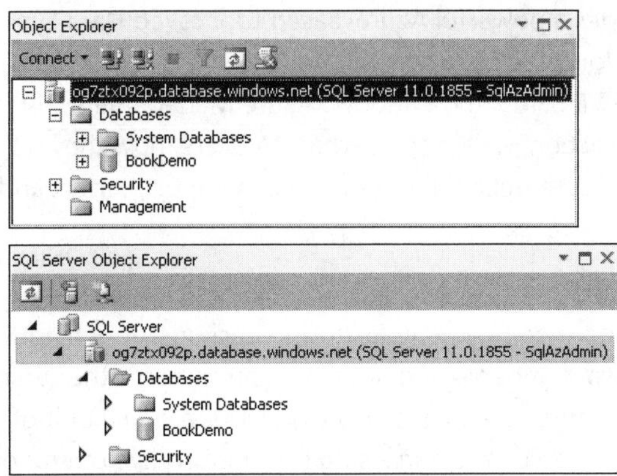

FIGURE 12-16 SQL Azure connection displayed in SSMS Object Explorer and Visual Studio/SSDT SQL Server Object Explorer.

The *EDITION* and *MAXSIZE* parameters also apply to the *ALTER DATABASE* command, thereby allowing you to change the maximum size of your SQL Azure database (to be either bigger or smaller), should the need arise.

Note the server glyph in both tools depicts a light-blue (azure, in fact) database drum icon as a visual queue that the server connection is to SQL Azure. Other differences will manifest themselves based on the delta in functionality between SQL Server and SQL Azure. For example, there are no *Server Objects* or *Replication* child nodes for a SQL Azure connection as there would be for a SQL Server connection.

Although things differ, there is also a lot of parity. If you drill down on a database's node in the SSDT SQL Server Object Explorer, you can see, design, and query its tables, views, stored procedures, functions, and triggers. The Object Explorer in SSMS provides less designer support for these objects and requires you to work more at the T-SQL level, but because SSDT constructs the same in-memory database model for SQL Azure databases that it does for SQL Server databases, virtually all the tooling support for the latter is available for the former.

Migrating and Syncing Between Earth and Cloud

The danger in writing a discrete chapter on SQL Azure in a vast book on SQL Server is that we will prepare you to use both products, but in a rather segregated fashion. If that happened it would be a huge failing though, because the intersection between the two products is rather large. Not only can you take an agnostic approach to tools, query, and development that works with SQL Azure and SQL Server relatively interchangeably, but you can also move databases and database designs from one to the other very elegantly.

In practical terms, what does this mean? You can move a database from SQL Server to SQL Azure, and vice versa; you can also export database schemas from one platform to the other, interchangeably; you can compare and sync schemas; and sync and replicate data.

For the task of syncing data, Microsoft provides a powerful Azure-based tool called Data Sync, which is covered in depth in the next chapter. Alongside Data Sync, though, lies SQL Server Data-Tier Applications (DACs), and support for them in SSDT, SSMS, the Windows Azure Management Portal, and the SQL Azure Management Portal. In this section, we'll discuss what DACs are, how they're used by various SQL Server tools, and how SQL Azure utilizes them for various import/export and migration tasks.

Data-Tier Applications were introduced in SQL Server 2008 R2 as both a tooling approach for database design and a package format for database deployment. Restoring backups, attaching MDF files, or just running T-SQL scripts also provide ways of deploying databases on servers other than where they were designed. But none of the latter three techniques truly provides a single unit of database deployment, nor the ability to create or deploy them in a single administrative operation.

DACPACs to the Rescue

The files that store the contents of a Data-Tier Application do supply such a deployment unit though. They have a .DACPAC extension but are actually zip file archives containing a number of constituent xml files.

SSMS has the ability to extract or deploy DACPAC files each through a menu option. The SQL Server Database Projects in SSDT generate DACPACs as a matter of course, and SSDT can create a project from a DACPAC as well. Given all this DACPACing in the SQL Server toolset, it should come as no surprise that SQL Azure uses the DACPAC format for its own deployment-related features, too.

Data-Tier Applications and SQL Azure also support a BACPAC format, which is used as a container for both schema and data (DACPACs contain schema only), and can thus be used for import/export functions to migrate a database, rather than merely deploy a new (and initially empty) database instance.

Let's take a look now at the mechanics of moving and updating database schemas and data, with Data-Tier Applications, between SQL Server and SQL Azure using SSMS, SSDT, and the Windows Azure and SQL Azure Management Portals.

Extract, Deploy, Export, and Import DAC files

Let's begin by documenting the mechanics of how and where we can create and open DACPAC and BACPAC files. Afterwards we'll discuss how and where we can use them. Providing this inventory of menu and ribbon UI techniques is, honestly, a rather dry documenting process, so we will cover it in table form, rather than in our narrative.

SQL Server Management Studio

SSMS is the most logical tool to start with as it can work bidirectionally with both DACPAC and BACPAC files. SSMS contains a number of wizards that assist in the generation and use of Data-Tier Applications. All of these are launched from context menus on the Object Explorer. Table 12-1 summarizes your options.

TABLE 12-1 Working with DACPAC and BACPAC files in SSMS.

Action	Result
Right-click a server's *Databases* child node, and then select Deploy Data-Tier Application from the context menu	Creates a database from a DACPAC file selected in the Deploy Data-Tier Application Wizard
Right-click a database node, and then click Tasks | Deploy Database to SQL Azure	Creates a BACPAC file from the selected database and deploys it directly to SQL Azure
Right-click a database node, and then click Tasks | Export Data-Tier Application	Creates a BACPAC file from the selected database which can be manually imported, subsequently
Right-click a database node, and then click Tasks | Extract Data-Tier Application	Creates a DACPAC file from the selected database
Right-click a database node, and then click Tasks | Register As Data-Tier Application	Creates a DACPAC from, and embeds it in, the selected database
Right-click a server's *Databases* child node, and then select Import Data-Tier Application from the context menu	Creates a database, and imports its data, from a BACPAC file on local disk or in Windows Azure Blob Storage.
Right-click a BACPAC file from an Azure Storage connection, and then click Import Data-Tier Application	Creates a database, and imports its data, from a BACPAC file in Windows Azure Blob Storage. All Windows Azure Storage details in the Import Settings screen of the resulting Import Data-Tier Wizard will be pre-populated.

SQL Server Data Tools

SQL Server Database Projects in Visual Studio are themselves premised on the generation of DACPAC files. There are several other integration points for Data-Tier Application files in SSDT as well, including, but not limited to, its Snapshot functionality. A summary of these appears in Table 12-2.

TABLE 12-2 Working with DACPAC files in SSDT.

Action	Result
Right-click the project node in Solution Explorer and select Import | Data-Tier Application (*.dacpac) from the context menu	Creates SQL Server Database Project from a DACPAC file
Right-click the project node in Solution Explorer and select Snapshot Project from the context menu	Generates DACPAC file (in Snapshots folder), reflecting current state of SQL Server Database Project
Build | Build Solution or Build | Build *project*	Generates DACPAC file in bin\debug or bin\release folder (depending on build configuration)

Windows Azure Management Portal

The Windows Azure Management Portal hosts a special SQL Azure Import/Export service that reads and writes BACPAC files from and to Windows Azure Blob Storage, requiring credentials for both SQL Azure and Windows Azure Storage as it does so. Table 12-3 documents the options.

TABLE 12-3 Working with the BACPAC files in the Windows Azure Management Portal.

Action	Result
Click the Import button in the ribbon's Import And Export group	Creates a database, and imports its data, from specified BACPAC file in Windows Azure Blob Storage
Click the Export button in the ribbon's Import And Export group	Exports a database, including its data, to specified BACPAC file in Windows Azure Blob Storage

SQL Azure Management Portal

Unlike the Windows Azure Management Portal, which imports and exports using BACPAC files in Blob Storage, the SQL Azure Management Portal, much like SSMS, features Deploy, Extract, and Upgrade buttons in its ribbon that work with DACPAC files on a local disk or network share. Table 12-4 details all the options.

TABLE 12-4 Working with DACPAC files in the SQL Azure Management Portal.

Action	Result
In Overview tab, click Deploy button in ribbon or click the Deploy A Data-Tier Application tile	Creates a database from a DACPAC file on local disk or network share
In Administration tab, in the Databases or Tasks page, or in the Design tab, click Deploy button in ribbon	Creates a database from a DACPAC file on local disk or network share
In Administration tab, in the Databases page, click the Extract button	Creates a DACPAC file from the currently open database and saves it to a local disk or network share
In Administration tab, in the Databases page, click the Upgrade button	Updates schema of currently open database from a DACPAC file on a local disk or network share

Scenarios

Now you know *what* to click to work with DACPAC and BACPAC files, but do you know *when*? It's one thing to list out all the places where DACPACs and BACPACs can be created and consumed, but now let's discuss some SQL Azure–related scenarios where these capabilities would be most helpful.

New Deployment to SQL Azure

If you've been designing a database specifically for SQL Azure, be it in SSMS or SSDT, then at some point you will need to deploy it. There are several ways to do this. Let's look at a few.

From SSDT

For readers of this book, the ideal deployment situation would involve designing the database in SSDT, specifically for SQL Azure, and "publishing" the (empty) database from there. Designing your database in this way ensures that you will not inadvertently use a SQL Server feature that SQL Azure does not support, because SSDT wouldn't allow it. Just make sure that you select SQL Azure as the target platform in the Project Settings tab of the Properties sheets.

To deploy the database to SQL Azure, you'll then need to select the Build | Publish *projectname* main menu option or right-click the project node in Solution Explorer and select the Publish option from the resulting context menu. This will bring up the Publish Database dialog box. In that dialog box, click the Edit button next to the Target Database Connection (read-only) text box and in the resulting Connection Properties dialog box, supply connection information similar to that shown in the Login tab in Figure 12-15. Make sure to click the Advanced button and set the *Encrypt* and *TrustServerCertificate* properties, as shown in Figure 12-17.

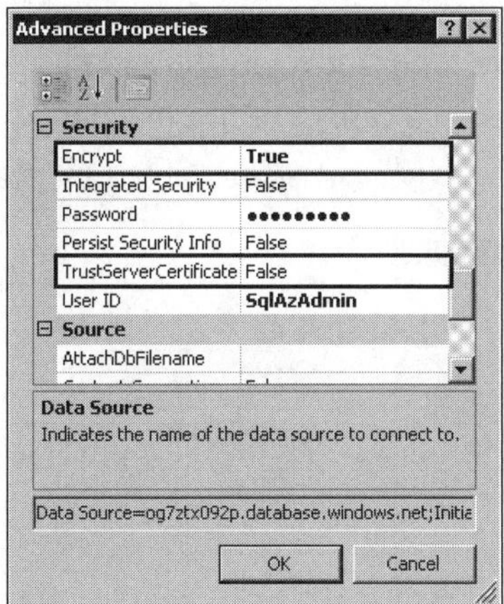

FIGURE 12-17 Advanced Properties dialog box for SSDT database connection to SQL Azure.

When you're done, just click OK through the Advanced Properties and Connection Properties dialog boxes. From there, you may wish to click the Save Profile As button to save out these settings for easy retrieval during a subsequent publish operation (you would re-load those settings by clicking the Load Profile button). When you're done, click Publish, and SSDT will generate and execute the appropriate T-SQL script on your SQL Azure server.

From SSMS

You could also design the database on SQL Server with SSMS and then use that tool's Deploy to SQL Azure feature, or use its Export Data-Tier Application function coupled with the Import feature in the Windows Azure Management Portal. For the latter technique, you would need to upload the BACPAC file generated by SSMS into Blob Storage in a Windows Azure Storage account. Although there are a number of ways to do this, one option is using Neudesic's free Azure Storage Explorer, a desktop application available at *http://azurestorageexplorer.codeplex.com/*.

Keep in mind that the SSMS Export Data-Tier Application feature allows you to export selected objects from your database, rather than requiring you to export all of them. The key here is to click the Advanced tab in the Export Settings screen of the Export Data-Tier Application wizard. This will reveal a collapsed tree view. Drill down on the *Select All* and schema name nodes to reveal a list of database objects, all of which will be selected by default. You'll need to uncheck the objects you wish to omit from the BACPAC file. Figure 12-18 shows the *EmployeeTerritories* table omitted from an export of the *Northwind* database.

Note To upload your BACPAC with the Azure Storage Explorer (or using any Azure Storage upload technique) you'll need to create a new storage account in the Windows Azure Management Portal. Do this by clicking on the Hosted Services, Storage Accounts & CDN tab in the Outlook-style left-hand navigation bar. Use the New Storage Account and View Access Keys buttons in the ribbon to create the account and fetch the keys needed to access it. Supply the name of the storage account and an access key to the Azure Storage Explorer, and then use that application to create a "Container" (a folder, essentially) into which you can upload your BACPAC file. From there you can use the Import facility in the Windows Azure Management Portal to import the BACPAC into SQL Azure. Be careful during this process because the file name must be entered in a case-sensitive manner.

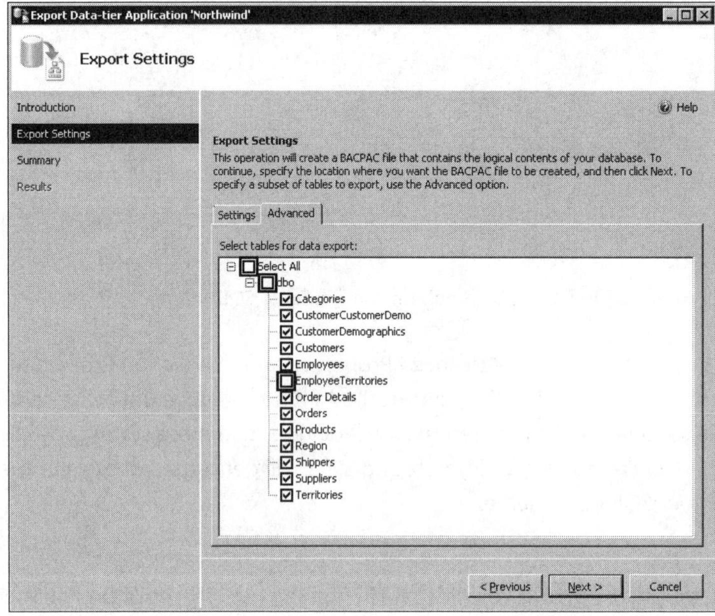

FIGURE 12-18 Excluding a table from a BACPAC file with the SSMS Export Data-Tier Application wizard.

From the SQL Azure Management Portal

Finally, you could use the Deploy feature in the SQL Azure Management Portal to create a new SQL Azure database based on a DACPAC. The file could be sourced from a DACPAC file created in SSDT through the Build or Snapshot processes, or a DACPAC created in SSMS with the Extract Data-Tier Application feature.

Deploy Update to SQL Azure

DACPACs and the SSDT Publish operations are not just for initial database deployments; they're for interim schema update deployments too. For this scenario, you could perform a subsequent Publish operation from SSDT. You could also use the Upgrade feature in SQL Azure Management Portal along with a DACPAC file created in SSDT, or one created in SSMS with the Extract Data-Tier Application feature.

Migration from SQL Server to SQL Azure

One common scenario with the cloud is a developer or corporate decision to migrate a database from an on-premises environment to the cloud environment. As such, the scenario in which an on-premises SQL Server database is migrated to SQL Azure will be a common one.

SSDT One way to accommodate this scenario is to use SSDT as follows:

1. Create a SQL Server Database Project with the target platform set to SQL Azure.
2. Import an existing SQL Server database by right-clicking on the *project* node in Solution Explorer and then clicking Import | From Database in the resulting context menu.
3. Publish the database to SQL Azure following the steps described previously.

After importing the database, SSDT will warn you of anything in the database's design that is not compatible with SQL Azure. One such issue that can be common is the lack of clustering indexes on specific tables. Figure 12-19 depicts some other errors for a SQL Server Database Project targeting SQL Azure into which the *AdventureWorksLT* sample database has been imported.

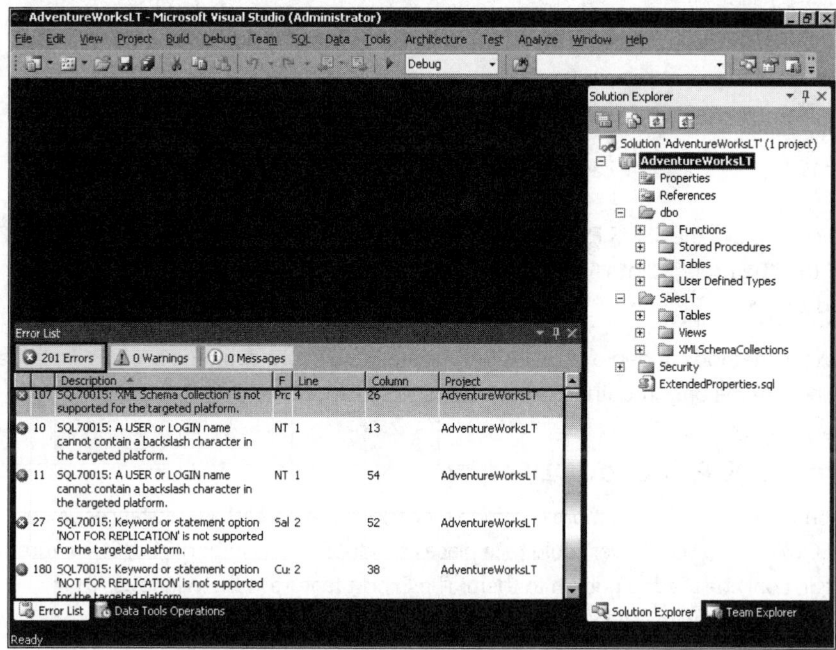

FIGURE 12-19 SSDT flagging SQL Azure compatibility errors.

SSMS

The on-premises-to-cloud migration scenario can also be accommodated in various ways with SSMS. For example, the SSMS Deploy Database to SQL Azure feature could be used to migrate the database in one step. In this case, the Results page of the Deploy Database wizard will ensure compatibility of the candidate SQL Server database with SQL Azure. In case of incompatibilities, it will report errors and prevent the deployment, as shown in Figure 12-20.

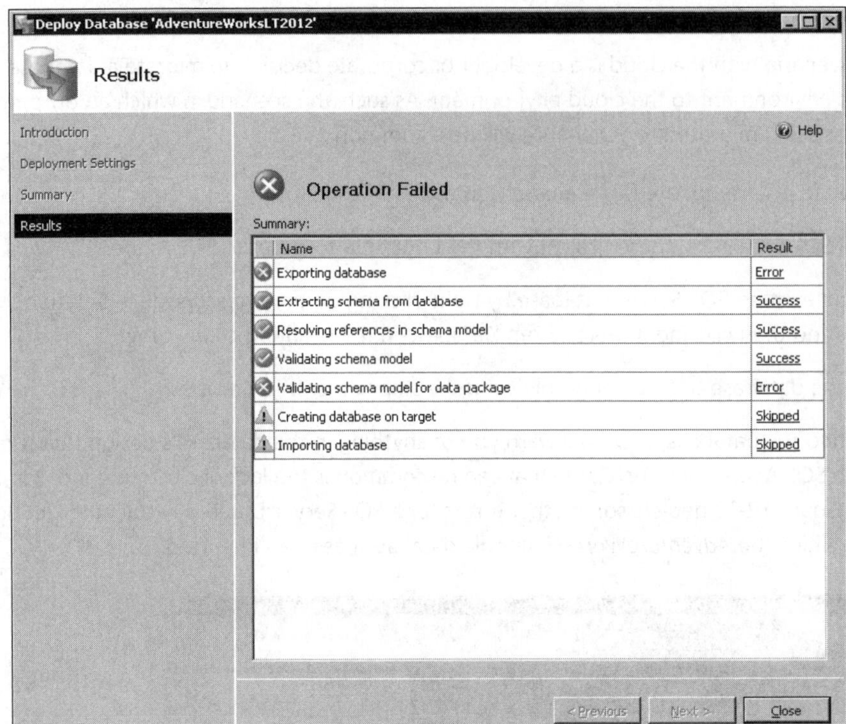

FIGURE 12-20 SSMS flagging SQL Azure compatibility errors.

Another choice is to use the SSMS Export Data-Tier Application feature to generate a BACPAC file which could then be brought into SQL Azure using the Import feature in Windows Azure Management Portal.

Although various methods of deploying DACPAC files to SQL Azure could be used as well, these would migrate the schema only, requiring other means to transport the data.

Migration from SQL Azure to SQL Server

Although migrating to the cloud is the more common scenario, there are certainly instances when migrating *from* SQL Azure to SQL Server could take place as well. SSDT can import from SQL Azure databases; it needn't only be used to publish to them. The Export feature in the Windows Azure Management Portal coupled with the SSMS Import Data-Tier Application feature could be used as well.

Again, various methods of deploying DACPAC files to SQL Server that were extracted from SQL Azure could be used as well, but these would migrate the schema only, requiring other means to transport the data.

We have now covered scenarios of working exclusively with SQL Azure and its tools, as well as situations where SQL Server tools and databases are added to the mix. With these basics established, let's take a look at an advanced feature of SQL Azure.

SQL Azure Federations

We've spent a lot of time so far discussing certain features in SQL Azure that are not supported in SQL Server. But as it turns out, one converse case exists as well: SQL Azure offers a very interesting feature called Federations, which is not offered by SQL Server. And because the Federations feature is extremely useful in the kind of multi-tenancy scenarios (i.e., coexistence of multiple customers' data) that cloud products are extremely suitable for, it's important that we cover Federations here in this chapter.

Federations are the SQL Azure implementation of a partitioning pattern called *sharding*. Sharding is a very common feature in NoSQL (non-relational) databases, but is not often seen in the relational world. In a sharding scheme, each partition is in fact a separate physical database and/or resident on a separate physical server.

When SQL Azure was first introduced, it had the restriction of a 10 GB maximum database size. Many customers expressed surprise and skepticism towards this limitation, and Microsoft responded by saying customers could implement a sharding scheme to combat it. In effect, Microsoft was saying that if you needed a database of *x* GB, then divide x by 10 and create that number of 10 GB databases. From there, the guidance suggested you implement your own programming logic for splitting up the data amongst these multiple databases when writing data, or for gathering data from each appropriate database when querying.

Quite frankly, many customers found that prescriptive guidance to be a bit glib, and so did we. Perhaps in response to this, Microsoft implemented the Federations feature, which keeps customers from having to implement a sharding infrastructure of their own. Microsoft also implemented very strong tooling support for Federations in the SQL Azure Management Portal, and the SQL Server 2012 version of SSMS provides good support as well.

To understand how Federations work, we'll discuss Federations concepts and vocabulary, as well as the corresponding T-SQL syntax and the SQL Azure Management Portal techniques needed to create and use the objects discussed.

A SQL Azure Federations Lexicon

In SQL Azure, a Federation is the collection of physical databases that together comprise a single, logical, federated database. The first database to join the Federation is called the Federation Root; it stores the *Federation* object itself, and it can be thought of as the "home base" or directory node for the Federation. The other physical databases that comprise the Federation are called Federation Members, and they store the federated data. The Federation Key, also known as the Distribution, defines a data key which is used to determine how different data is mapped to specific Federation members.

All data for a given Federation Key value is contained within a single Atomic Unit, so named because it is never to be split across Federation Members. That said, no other specific correspondence between Atomic Units and Federation Members exists. One Federation Member may, and likely will, contain multiple Atomic Units, although it could, theoretically, contain just one. But any Atomic Unit contained by a Federation Member will be contained in its entirety in that Federation Member. This supports multi-tenancy scenarios nicely, as we will cover at the end of this section.

Creating a Federation

Federations are created with the *CREATE FEDERATION* T-SQL command, and require that the database to be used as the Federation Root is currently selected. Here's an example:

```
CREATE FEDERATION MyFed (MyDist BIGINT RANGE)
```

The above example assumes *MyFed* is the Federation being created and *MyDist* is the Distribution name. It further assumes that the Distribution Key will be of type *bigint* (the other choices are *int*, *uniqueidentifier*, and *varbinary*) and that the Distribution will be defined such that each Federation Member maps to a *RANGE* of values (which, as of this writing, is the only choice).

In the SQL Azure Management Portal, you create a Federation by selecting an existing database and clicking the New button on the far right of the ribbon. A form then pops up which essentially provides a UI for the *CREATE FEDERATION* command, asking you to supply the Federation name, Distribution name, Distribution Key data type, and Distribution type (where, again, *RANGE* is the only choice).

Clicking Save on this form, and then waiting for the UI to update itself, will result in the Federation being listed in the database's summary screen. Clicking the Federation's right-arrow glyph then brings you to a Federation Members map screen, as shown in Figure 12-21.

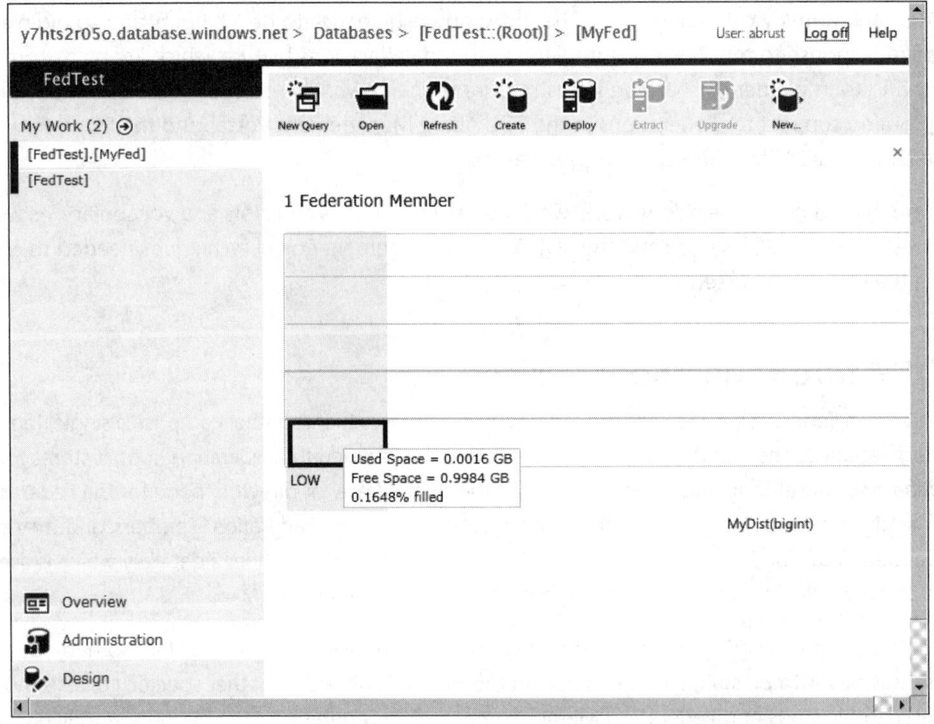

FIGURE 12-21 Federation Member map in SQL Azure Management Portal.

Federated Tables

A Distribution defines how things are split, and Federation Members house specific constituent data for each so-called Federated Table (i.e., each table that you decide ought to be split). Federated Tables must have a column that stores the Federation Key values, which cannot be *NULL*.

Imagine a distribution where one Federation Member is designated to contain data for the range of Federation Key values between 1 and 99 and another will contain data for Federation Key column values of 100 and above. In this hypothetical, any data for any Federated Table whose Federation Key column's value is 99 or less will go in that table in the first Federation Member and data for Federation Key column values of 100 and higher will go in that table in the other Federation Member.

Creating a Federated Table is done using almost the same T-SQL that is used for a conventional table, but a Federation Member must be selected first and a *FEDERATED ON* clause, specifying the Distribution name and the name of the column in the table containing the Federation Key, must be supplied in the *CREATE TABLE* command. For example:

```
USE FEDERATION [MyFed] ([MyDist] = -9223372036854775808) WITH FILTERING = OFF, RESET
GO

CREATE TABLE MyFederatedTable(
  ID bigint NOT NULL,
  lastname varchar(50),
  firstname varchar(50),
  CONSTRAINT PKFederated PRIMARY KEY CLUSTERED (ID ASC)
  )
FEDERATED ON (MyDist=ID)
```

The above T-SQL code selects the first Federation Member (identified with a maximal negative number as the Federation Key value) and assumes that *MyFed* is the Federation, *MyDist* is the Distribution, *MyFederatedTable* is the Federated Table, and *ID* is the column which will contain the Federation Key values. The table is given a clustered primary key because all SQL Azure tables must have a clustered index and the column *ID* is configured as *NOT NULL* because that is a requirement for the Federation Key column. Executing the above T-SQL code assures that the specified Federation Member would have its own instance of *MyFederatedTable*, containing rows with values of *ID* corresponding to the range of values defined for that Federation Member.

If your federated database has multiple Federation Members when this table is created, then the data definition language (DDL) query must be executed against each such Federation Member to have that table represented in each. If you create the table when the federated database has only one Federation Member, then the query need only be executed once, of course. If you later split the Federation Member, the table will automatically be present in the new Federation Members that result.

Using a Federation Member

When it comes time to insert, update, delete, or query data, the appropriate Federation Member(s) must be selected with the T-SQL *USE* command. While that may seem inconvenient, the good news is that rather than needing to know what data lies where and selecting the corresponding Federation Member by name, you instead specify a key value in the *USE* command to select the corresponding Federation Member (as was shown in the previous T-SQL snippet). For example, to select the Federation Member containing data with a Federation Key value of 100, you would issue the following T-SQL *USE* command:

```
USE FEDERATION [MyFed] ([MyDist] = 100) WITH RESET
```

In the SQL Azure Management Portal, you can bring up a query window containing the necessary T-SQL in a template to create or query a Federated Table, preceded by the appropriate *USE FEDERATION* query. To do so, click a Federation Member in the Federation Members map screen shown in Figure 12-21, select Query from the resulting pop-up menu, and then click Create Federated Table or New Query, respectively.

Splitting and Dropping Federation Members

The pop-up menu also contains options for splitting or dropping a Federation Member. These options provide UIs for the *ALTER FEDERATION* T-SQL command, using the *SPLIT* or *DROP* clause, respectively. These commands let you add or remove a Federation Member by adding or removing a split, defined by a specific key value.

For example, your federated database will start off having only a single Federation Member, containing all values for the Federation Key. Using our earlier example, you could use the *ALTER FEDERATION…SPLIT* command (or the Split menu option on the Federation Member in the SQL Azure Management Portal) to split the Federation Member at a boundary value of 100, which would create a second Federation Member and transfer all data with key values of 100 and higher to it. You also could later decide to remove one of those two Federation Members using the *ALTER FEDERATION…DROP* command (or the Drop Federation Member menu option in the SQL Azure Management Portal).

Regardless of whether you split or drop, and whether you do so with a T-SQL command or the SQL Azure Management Portal tooling, your federated database will remain online and query-able while the operation takes place. This is an excellent capability and one which is unprecedented among other databases that support sharding.

Central Tables and Reference Tables

Not all tables need to be federated (i.e., split). Those which are not federated and exist solely in the Federation Root are called Central Tables. Other tables, which are neither federated nor central, and instead are *duplicated* across Federation Members, are called Reference Tables. Typically, Reference Tables contain lookup data which can be used to optimize queries on any Federation Member.

Fan-Out Queries and Multi-Tenancy

SQL Azure Federations require explicit use of Federation Members in order to query their data. For queries that span multiple Federation Members, multiple queries must be performed, one for each Federation Member whose data is in scope. The SQL Azure Federations feature does not support the concept of fan-out queries, where a single SQL query spanning multiple Federation Members is issued and all data is returned in a single operation.

Although this may seem inconvenient, keep in mind that the most appropriate use of Federations involves architecting your database so that many, or even most, queries can be satisfied entirely from a single Federation Member. That may seem far-fetched until you consider that the Federations feature is present mostly to support multi-tenancy, where data corresponding to *various* workloads is comingled in one *database*. But, if the Federation splits are designed correctly, data for any *given* workload will be completely contained in a single Federation Member.

For example, imagine a software as a service (SaaS) system for outsourced web-based invoice lookups. Although such a service could maintain separate databases for each customer's records, it would be far more efficient to keep them in a single database, and manage the data in a way where each customer's records were virtually segregated. This could be easily achieved using Federations, using the customer ID as the Federation Key.

In such a scenario, most queries would be within the scope of a single Federation Key value (i.e., a specific customer ID), and therefore a single Atomic Unit. Since Atomic Units are never split over Federation Members, support for fan-out queries would become moot. Queries could be carried out as if against a conventional database as long as they were preceded by a *USE FEDERATION* command referencing the customer's ID as the Federation Key value.

Federations Support in SSMS and SSDT

SSMS also provides tooling support for Federations. The SSMS Object Explorer will show the Federation Root, and allows you to view one or many Federation Members by specifying a Federation Key value. There are also context menu operations for creating Federations and Federated Tables, as well as splitting and dropping Federation Members. These commands open query windows containing T-SQL templates for the corresponding task. If you prefer a UI to a command-driven approach, then you'll be more comfortable in the SQL Azure Management Portal.

The SSDT SQL Server Object Explorer in Visual Studio (VS) does not explicitly support SQL Azure Federations. The Federation Root will appear under the federated database's name. The Federation Members, however, appear under their system-generated physical database names. Figure 12-22 shows both Object Explorers, each displaying the Federation Root, Federation Members, and Federated Tables of the same SQL Azure database, all of which are highlighted.

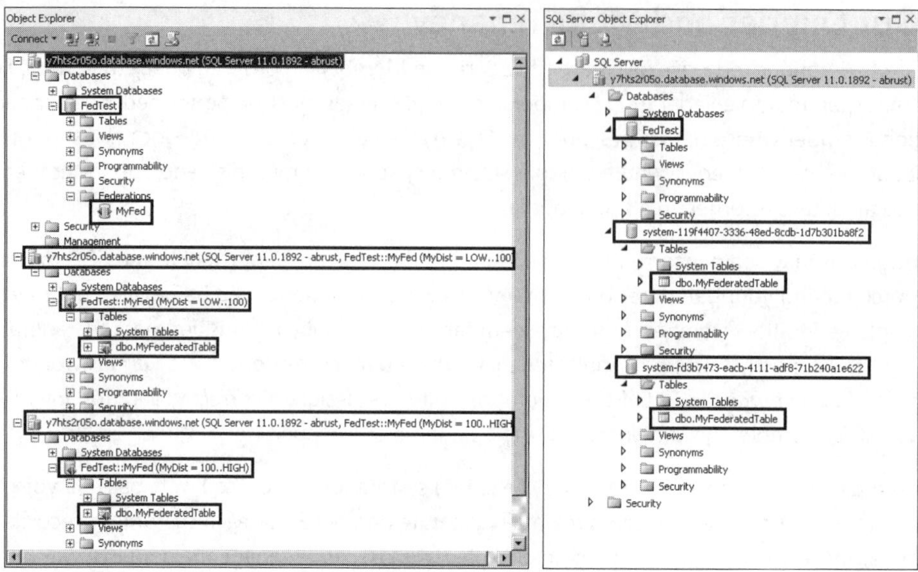

FIGURE 12-22 Federated databases in SSMS Object Explorer and SSDT SQL Server Object Explorer in VS.

Federations Make Sense in the Cloud

SQL Azure Federations both mitigate the SQL Azure maximum database size (which, at press time, was 150 GB) and provide a horizontal scale-out strategy that works well in many cloud scenarios. The T-SQL and tooling support is strong, and the feature is relatively intuitive. Support for fan-out queries would be a welcome addition, but if the splits and Distribution for a federated database are well designed, the lack of fan-out query should be less impactful.

Federations are a powerful SQL Azure feature that SQL Azure customers should become familiar with.

SQL Azure Reporting

We thought it sensible and useful, before we close this chapter, to cover SQL Azure Reporting (SAR), a cloud-hosted version of SQL Server Reporting Services (SSRS). Just as SQL Azure can be thought of as a limited version SQL Server, SAR can be thought of as a limited version of SSRS. In this section, we'll cover how to provision a SQL Azure Reporting server, how to create reports for it, and what the limitations are around doing so.

In reality, SAR is more easily presented in terms of its on-premises counterpart than is SQL Azure, because SAR is a true subset of SSRS. It doesn't even offer its own tooling; instead, you'll use Reporting Services projects in Visual Studio or the stand-alone Report Builder application to design your reports, and then deploy them to SAR.

As we did with SQL Azure, let's enumerate important restrictions of SAR, compared to its full-fledged, on-premises counterpart:

- The *only* valid data source for SAR reports is SQL Azure. No other data source, not even a public-facing SQL Server instance, is supported.
- SAR has its own (forms-based) authentication scheme. It does not support Windows integrated security, nor does it support SQL Server authentication. Therefore, users (or applications) must authenticate separately into both SAR and the SQL Azure database(s) which serve as the data source(s) for reports.
- SAR runs only in its own stand-alone mode; it does not offer a SharePoint-integrated mode, be it with SharePoint Server or SharePoint Online/Office 365.
- SAR supports the SOAP Web Services interface of SSRS, but does not offer the standard in-browser Report Manager UI. Windows Azure Management Portal offers a SAR UI, but navigation to the SAR server URL in a browser provides only a directory browsing-style interface.
- SAR does not support OData rendering of reports and therefore is not a valid data source for PowerPivot or SQL Server Analysis Services Tabular mode.

As long as you are mindful of the above restrictions, you can develop SAR reports and integrate them into applications (whether those applications are cloud-based or run on-premises). Of course, you can't do that until you provision a SAR server, so let's quickly cover how to do so.

Provisioning

The process for setting yourself up in SAR is similar to that for SQL Azure. Once you are logged into the Windows Azure Management Portal, click the Reporting button in the lower left-hand Outlook-style navigation menu, and then click the Create button in the Server group on the ribbon to bring up the Create Server wizard, shown in Figure 12-23.

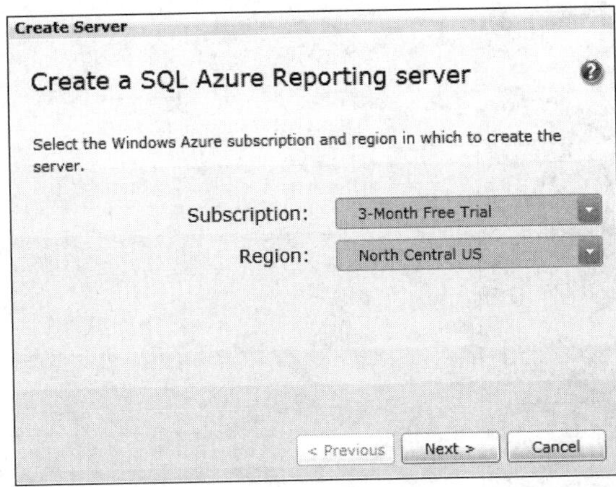

FIGURE 12-23 Subscription and Region specification for a SQL Azure Reporting server.

Select the appropriate subscription and region and, as with other region selections, consider configuring your SAR server to be in the same Azure data center as your SQL Azure server, in order to minimize data egress charges. Click Next and then supply credentials to be used in the creation of an administrative user on the server. After you click Finish, allow the provisioning process to take place, and then drill down through the tree view nodes on the upper left to reveal the node for your server. Select that node and the Reporting page should display the web service URL, name, and region of your SAR server.

You can consider the Reporting page to be equivalent to the Reporting Manager interface offered by SSRS in stand-alone mode (you can skip ahead to Figure 12-26 to see what it looks like). The lower half of the screen displays a list of reports, data sources, and folders (which is initially empty, of course) and the ribbon features a button for uploading RDL files from a local disk or network share.

There are also buttons for creating folders and shared data sources, as well as setting permissions on the former. The Manage button allows you to create and maintain SAR user accounts (recall that this must be tended to separately from SQL Azure account management).

Once you are done with these administrative tasks, you should highlight the web service URL and copy it into the clipboard, using the **Ctrl+C** keyboard shortcut. Now paste it somewhere safe, as you will need it to configure the deployment server's address when you publish your authored reports. This will enable you to deploy your reports directly to SAR from the SSRS authoring tools, rather than manually uploading your RDL files in the Windows Azure Management Portal.

Report Authoring

Now all you have to do is create your report! But remember, in order for your report to be SAR-compatible, all of its data sources must be SQL Azure databases. As such, when you define your data source, make sure to select SQL Azure, rather than SQL Server. If you're using the Report Wizard to create your report, then in the Select The Data Source page, select SQL Azure from the Type drop-down list, as shown in Figure 12-24.

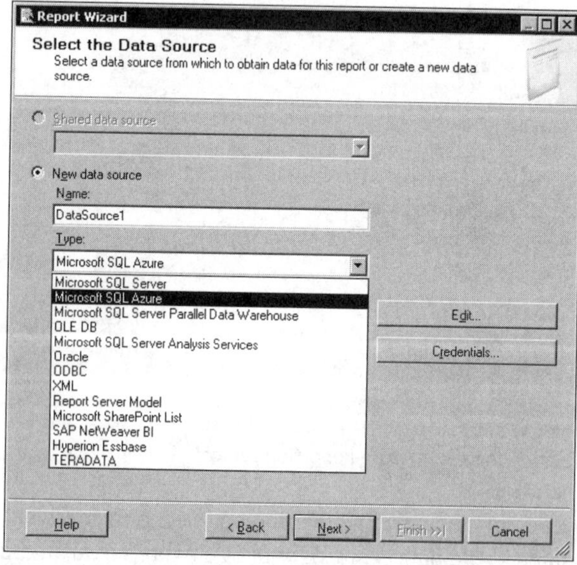

FIGURE 12-24 Selecting SQL Azure as a report's data source type.

After selecting SQL Azure as your data source type, click the Edit button (or the Build button in Report Builder) and configure the data source as shown previously Figure 12-15 (on the left-hand side) and Figure 12-17. Make sure to specify a database, in addition to the server details. After your data source is defined, build out your Dataset as you would normally. Next, in the Choose the Deployment Location page of the Report Wizard, select SQL Server 2008 R2 Or Later in the Report Server Version drop-down list and paste the web service URL you copied earlier from the Windows Azure Management Portal into the Report Server edit control. Finally, specify a deployment folder that has been created, or will be created prior to deployment (recall that you can create a folder using the Create button in the Folder group of the ribbon in Windows Azure Management Portal). All of this is shown and highlighted in Figure 12-25.

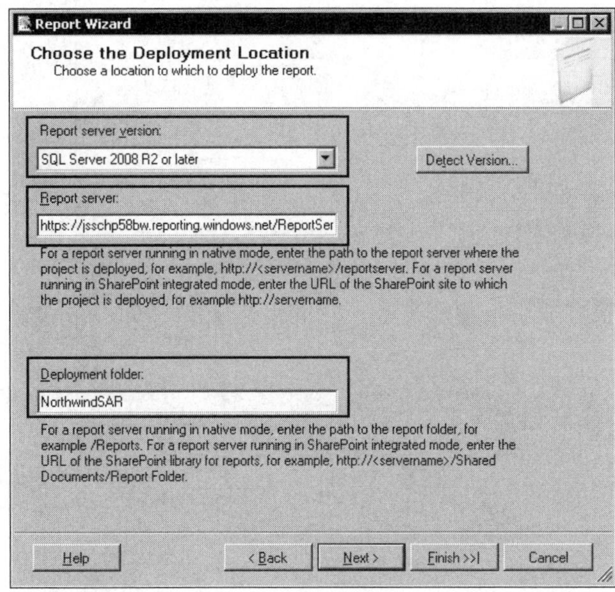

FIGURE 12-25 Deployment details for SQL Azure Reporting.

Note that, unlike in the typical SSRS case, the SAR server web service works over an SSL connection, using a URL beginning with *https://*.

When you're finished using the Report Wizard, design your report as you normally would for SSRS.

Deploying Reports

When it comes time for deployment, things are logically simple, but the mechanical steps may not be obvious at first. If you're using the Reporting Services project tooling in Visual Studio, right-click the *project* node in Solution Explorer and select Properties from the context menu. Confirm the *TargetServerURL* and *TargetReportFolder* properties are set as they were configured in the Report Wizard (if you didn't use the wizard, then set them manually now), and that all other *TargetxxxFolder* properties are either blank or set to appropriate, existing SAR folders. Now deploy the report(s).

If you're using Report Builder, the deployment procedure is a bit more simple. In the Save As Report dialog box, just paste the web service URL in the Name text box, click Save, navigate to the desired deployment folder, enter a report name in the Name text box, and then click Save again.

Regardless of which tool you use, you will be required to supply a user name and password, in a pop-up login dialog box, to connect to the SAR server. Login with your SAR credentials (not your SQL Azure or Live ID credentials) and click OK. When finished, visit the Reporting screen in the Windows Azure Management Portal (if it's already open, then refresh your browser). You should see your report(s) listed in the folder(s) to which it was (they were) deployed, as shown in Figure 12-26.

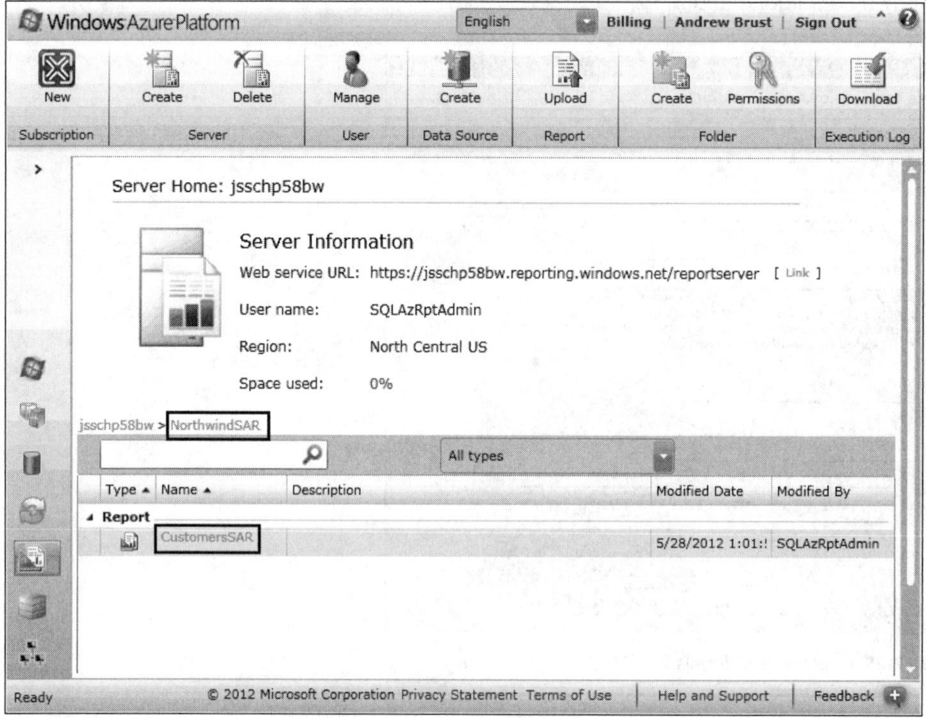

FIGURE 12-26 Browsing SQL Azure Reporting reports in the Windows Azure Management Portal.

Click the link for your report, and it will be displayed in the browser.

For a .NET application, you can use standard reporting controls, but you will need special code to provide the authentication credentials necessary to login to the SAR server.

Note The sample ASP.NET project provided with this chapter demonstrates this technique using the ASP.NET Report Viewer control. The code fetches the SQL Azure Reporting server URL, report path, user id, and password from the *appSettings* section of *web.config*. Just edit these to be appropriate for your own SQL Azure Reporting server and report, then run the application, and click the SQL Azure Reporting link at the top of the page for a complete practical demo. The code of interest is in *Report.aspx.cs* and *ReportServerCredentials.cs*.

Getting Your Bearings

The use of SSRS tools to author SAR reports can be a bit disorienting, in terms of what needs to be cloud-based, and what does not. To make this a bit more clear, here are some things to keep in mind:

- Conventional SSRS reports can be built for SQL Azure databases. You don't have to use SAR. (Just make sure to configure your SQL Azure firewall rules to permit your SSRS server access to the database.)
- Such conventional reports can be converted to SAR reports simply by deploying them to your SAR server or using the Upload feature in Windows Azure Management Portal. Just make certain that any shared data sources used by the reports are deployed as well.
- SAR reports can be integrated into any application, be it on-premises or in the cloud, as long as the SAR URL and credentials are properly applied and the proper SQL Azure authorization settings are configured.

With this coverage of SQL Azure Reporting, you now have a comprehensive set of information for building applications whose database features and, optionally, reporting features are cloud-based.

Summary

Cloud computing, in general, is gaining significant traction in the IT marketplace, but even as it does so, hybrid approaches that combine cloud services with on-premises technology, are emerging as the most common pattern in cloud technology adoption. And because SQL Azure is at once a cloud-centric service and a product featuring significant commonality with on-premises SQL Server, it is very well suited for this market environment.

We've seen in this chapter that SQL Azure can be used completely on its own, using browser-based tooling for provisioning, managing, designing, and querying. We have discussed how the Federations feature helps SQL Azure databases scale and accommodates the kind of multi-tenancy scenarios that occur frequently in the cloud. We even learned how SQL Azure Reporting provides a companion cloud-based reporting service for data in SQL Azure databases.

But we also saw how on-premises SQL Server tooling, including SSMS and SSDT, can be used with SQL Azure and how databases can rather easily be migrated from on-premises environments to the cloud, and vice versa. Reports against SQL Azure data are designed with on-premises tools and can be deployed to on-premises SQL Server Reporting Services installations or to SQL Azure Reporting. Applications that work with SQL Azure, and even SQL Azure Reporting, can also run on-premises, in the cloud, or both.

SQL Azure lets you take your SQL Server skill set and move it to the cloud. The product employs availability and partitioning strategies that are sensitive to the cloud, but makes them easy for SQL Server developers to use or, in some cases, implements them behind the scenes, presenting developers with zero additional learning requirements. In general, SQL Azure provides an approachable, economical, and flexible on-ramp to cloud computing for SQL Server professionals. The goal of this chapter has been to convey that with clarity and inspire you to try the service or even adopt it for production use.

CHAPTER 13

SQL Azure Data Sync and Windows Phone 7 Development

—Paul Delcogliano

One major reason for the rise of mobile applications in recent years is their ability to provide users ubiquitous access to data. Applications for smartphones and tablets deliver a seemingly endless stream of data to consumers. The one requirement for "data everywhere" is a reliable connection to either a corporate network or the Internet.

There are several downsides to needing an ever-present connection. For one, the Wi-Fi (wireless networks) and 3 and 4G (cell phone networks) radios on smartphones and tablets quickly drain the device's battery. Second, although we are gradually getting closer to global network coverage, we simply aren't there yet. Reliable network connections are still hard to come by in certain parts of the world. Third, data plans from mobile providers today generally have a monthly cap to the amount of data consumed. Applications that constantly transmit data eat away at the monthly allowance like a contestant at a hot dog eating contest. Finally, performance suffers due to the increased latency of the network connection.

An occasionally connected system is a solution architected to operate without depending on a constant network connection. The client application stores data locally and transmits it to a server whenever a connection is obtainable, which addresses nearly all of the aforementioned downsides of a constantly connected application.

By eliminating the need for a connection, the remote user can turn off the Wi-Fi and 3G radios on their devices, which increases battery life. The lack of a connection is irrelevant to the client component of an occasionally connected system; the application works whether a connection is present or not. Reducing the frequency of transmissions helps to keep data rates under the allowance, leading to lower costs. It also leads to reduced latency, which increases performance as well.

Occasionally connected systems provide benefits for consumer applications and line-of-business applications alike. Enterprises are extending traditional desktop applications beyond the workstation by building mobile counterparts. Mobilizing an application untethers employees from their desks and allows them to work at remote locations while away from the office.

Characteristics of an Occasionally Connected System

Building an application that operates whether connected or not requires a different architecture than a "traditional" application. An application designed to work without a continuous network connection has several characteristics that are not present in a typical desktop application. An occasionally connected system must be able to manage changes made while disconnected, resolve data conflicts that arise during synchronization, and update the local data store appropriately. Collectively, these processes are known as *data synchronization*. The system's ability to synchronize data is its primary characteristic.

A secondary characteristic stems from the limitations of the devices the system runs on. The devices are typically smartphones, tablets, and laptops with significantly less storage, memory, battery life, and processing power, than their big cousin, the desktop PC. Their smaller display area translates to less screen real estate available for viewing the application. An occasionally connected system must be capable not only of managing device resources, but also displaying information efficiently given the constrained screen space.

Data Management

The very nature of working while disconnected means the data on the device is a copy of data from some central database. In an occasionally connected scenario, users receive copies of the data they need for the application to function while they are disconnected from the network. When a connection becomes available, data synchronization occurs during which the client uploads any changes made on the device to the server, and downloads any updated data from the server back to the device. When the network connection is severed, all data needed to run the application productively must be available on the device.

Data synchronization can transpire in one of two modes, one-way and two-way. One-way synchronization sends data from server to client or from client to server. It is typically used for lookup or read-only data, like a list of products or movie names. One-way synchronization is also a great solution for creating data cache scenarios where data is co-locating around the globe. Putting data closer to your users leads to better application responsiveness.

A two-way synchronization (often referred to as bidirectional synchronization) is one in which the data changes on the server are sent to the client, and data changes on the client are sent to the server. Two-way synchronization requires the client application to store changes on the device until they can be uploaded to the server. For example, a mobile worker might download a customer list to their Windows Phone and then update customer phone numbers throughout the day. All of the changed customer information is stored in the phone's local database. When an Internet connection is established at the end of the day, all changed customer data is uploaded to the central server, and any new customer information is downloaded to the device.

In a two-way scenario, there is a higher chance for data conflicts to occur, because data on the device has a tendency to turn stale. Changes made to a particular customer contact record may be made by two different users on two different devices. When these changes are uploaded to the server a conflict may occur between the different changes. Any conflicts can be handled and resolved by the synchronizing protocol.

Typically, the synchronization provider is responsible for coordinating changes to data between the client and the server. In the next section, we'll introduce a new cloud-based synchronization provider Microsoft is making available to developers called SQL Azure Data Sync.

Getting to Know SQL Azure Data Sync

SQL Azure Data Sync (Data Sync) is a new synchronization service built on top of the Microsoft Sync Services Framework. Data Sync is part of the Azure family of services and is available to Windows Azure subscribers. It is capable of performing synchronizations in a variety of scenarios including SQL Azure to SQL Azure, SQL Azure to SQL Server, or SQL Server to SQL Azure.

Important Microsoft frequently updates its cloud services. As such, costs, limitations, features, the tooling user interface, or even the branding of SQL Azure and/or SQL Azure Data Sync, as described in this chapter, may have evolved by the time you read it.

You manage and configure Data Sync via the Windows Azure Management Portal. The portal's wizards and graphical dialogs facilitate creating, scheduling, and monitoring synchronizations. The portal also provides tools for grouping the data to be synchronized, and establishing the servers participating in a synchronization job.

Data Sync is capable of bidirectional synchronization of data between two or more geographically distributed SQL Azure and SQL Server databases. The SQL Azure databases could be hosted in any of the Windows Azure data centers around the globe. The SQL Server databases may also be geographically distributed. Data Sync must have at least one SQL Azure database which acts as the *hub* for synchronizations (we discuss Data Sync hubs and Data Sync requirements later in the chapter).

As of this writing, Data Sync is provided as a "preview" release available to all SQL Azure subscribers, and so information in this chapter is subject to change. Although it is a preview release, Data Sync should not be used for production applications. In its current incarnation, Data Sync cannot perform mobile to cloud data synchronization directly—so this chapter demonstrates the use of Data Sync to synchronize between SQL Server (on-premise) and SQL Azure (cloud), combined with the Open Data Protocol (OData) and WCF Data Services to communicate between the client component running on the mobile device and SQL Azure.

Capabilities and Features

Data Sync supports three different sync direction options: Bi-Directional, Sync From The Hub, and Sync To The Hub. A sync direction determines the flow of data between databases during synchronization. The Bi-Directional option permits the changes to be synchronized between the selected database and the hub database in both directions. The Sync From The Hub option permits the changes to be synced from the hub database to the selected database only. Changes in the selected database are not uploaded to the hub. And the Sync To The Hub option permits the changes to be synced from the selected database to the hub database only. Changes on the hub database are not downloaded to the selected database.

Each sync direction option is appropriate for a different set of scenarios. The Sync From The Hub scenario is appropriate for replicating data for failover or scaling, or to improve application response time by co-locating data around the globe. The Sync To The Hub option can be used to gather data from remote locations and aggregate that data as a store for a data warehouse or online analytical processing (OLAP). The Bi-Directional option is appropriate for scenarios where data conflicts can occur and need to be resolved. In these scenarios, Data Sync can be configured to manage the data conflicts using a conflict resolution policy.

In bi-directional synchronization scenarios, conflict resolution can detect and resolve conflicts between multiple locations attempting to modify the same records. Conflict resolution policies are configured to determine what actions to take when a conflict is detected.

Data Sync's optional row filtering feature allows smaller sets of data to be transmitted during synchronization. A row filter works essentially as a T-SQL *WHERE* clause; it selects a sub-set of rows from a table. Filters improve performance and help to keep costs down by synchronizing only relevant data, not an entire table.

Data Sync Terminology

Before diving in, let's establish some basic Data Sync terms that we use in this chapter's Data Sync coverage. Some of these terms will be described in greater detail throughout the chapter. Table 13-1 defines the terminology.

TABLE 13-1 Common Data Sync terms.

Term	Definition
Sync Group	A Sync Group is a group of SQL Azure and SQL Server databases configured for synchronization with each other.
Hub Database	The hub database is the central database in a Sync Group. It must be a SQL Azure database.
Member Database	A member database is any SQL Azure database, excluding the hub, or on-premise SQL Server that is part of the Sync Group.
Client Sync Agent	The SQL Azure Client Sync Agent is a Windows service installed on the on- premise database server. It enables communication between the on-premis SQL Server database and the SQL Azure hub database.
Sync Schedule	A Sync Schedule can be created to execute a data synchronization at defined intervals. The scheduled synchronization task is called a Sync Job.
Sync Loop	A Sync Loop is a condition that occurs when one Sync Group's synchronization triggers the synchronization of another Sync Group.
Synchronization Conflict	A synchronization conflict occurs when changes take place on the same piece of data in two or more databases in the Sync Group; for example, when two users update the same customer record at the same time.

Sync Groups

A Sync Group is a collection of databases grouped together for the purpose of synchronizing shared data. A Sync Group is comprised of several elements. Collectively, the elements define:

- the databases in the group
- the data to be synchronized
- the conflict resolution policy
- an optional synchronization schedule

The databases in a Sync Group are arranged in a hub-spoke topology. Data Sync mandates that a SQL Azure database serves as the hub. Once the hub is selected, it cannot be changed to a different database or removed. Any combination of SQL Azure and SQL Server databases make up the spokes, which are called *members,* in the group. A member database can be added to or removed from a Sync Group at any time as long as data synchronization is not actively taking place.

The hub/spoke arrangement allows SQL Azure Data Sync to support different synchronization scenarios, including cloud-to-cloud synchronizations and synchronizations involving both cloud and on-premise SQL Server databases.

Synchronization

The data to be synchronized in a Sync Group is called a *dataset.* Datasets are composed of tables, columns, and any filtered rows. When a synchronization job runs, only the selected tables, columns, and rows are synchronized. For example, you can select the *Movies* table along with its *Name* and *Genre* columns, and apply the filter *Theater = 'Roxy'* so only movies from the Roxy theater get synchronized. Once the Sync Group is deployed, the tables in a dataset cannot be added or removed. The Sync Group must be re-created to change a dataset.

Data Sync supports most common SQL Server data types, including all the string, date/time, and numeric types, as well as *sql_variant*, *table*, *uniqueidentifier*, and *xml*. However, some of the more specialized types are not supported. For a complete list, see *http://msdn.microsoft.com/library/hh667319.aspx*).

Data in a Sync Group can be synchronized manually or according to a schedule. Performing a manual synchronization is a simple matter of clicking a button on the Windows Azure Management Portal. The Sync Group is capable of setting up a schedule for a recurring synchronization; this is known as configuring a Sync Schedule. A Sync Schedule creates a Sync Job which is executed at a specified interval. The interval is set in units of minutes, hours, days, or months and specifies the elapsed time between synchronization jobs. The interval value must fall between 5 minutes and 1 month. The interval does not specify the local or international time that the Sync Job executes. You can always invoke a manual synchronization, even if you have configured a Sync Schedule.

Synchronization occurs only among the databases in the associated Sync Group. During synchronization, the rows in each of the tables participating in the Sync Group are updated according to a particular workflow. First, the changes in the member databases are synchronized with the hub database. Then, the changes in the hub database are synchronized with the member databases.

Data conflicts can occur in any synchronization scenario in which changes occur in two or more databases. Imagine someone updating a row in a table in the hub database, and another user updating that same row in a member database. Under this condition, Data Sync must determine the appropriate version of the record to retain. A Sync Group makes this decision using a conflict resolution policy.

Conflict Resolution

The Sync Group's conflict resolution policy determines the rows to be retained and the rows to be discarded whenever the same record is changed in different databases. The conflict resolution policy cannot be changed once the first synchronization has taken place. If you need to change the policy, you have to re-create the Sync Group. Data Sync provides two options for resolving conflicts: Hub Wins and Client Wins.

If the policy is set to Hub Wins, changes in the hub record always overwrite changes in the member database(s). Under this setting, the first row change written to the hub is kept. Subsequent attempts to write to the same row in the hub are ignored. Because all other changes to the row are ignored, the first change written to the hub is the change that is distributed to all members in the group.

If the policy is set to Client Wins, changes to a record in the member database are written to the hub. If multiple members have changed the record, the last member's change is written to the hub, and this version of the record is the one that gets synchronized to all member databases.

The Client Sync Agent

The SQL Azure Client Sync Agent is a lightweight Windows service that is responsible for communicating with the Data Sync service. The agent is installed to a server on your network and provides the Data Sync server direct access to your on-premise SQL Server databases. The agent is responsible for communication between the on-premise database and the SQL Azure hub database. It grants access to your SQL Server database without the need to open the firewall. Each Data Sync server requires its own agent, and an agent can connect to multiple SQL Server databases from different servers in your enterprise.

Through the agent, Data Sync can access the tables in your SQL Server database. The Client Sync Agent supports encrypted, bidirectional communication between the on-premise SQL Server database and the SQL Azure hub database.

A small Windows application is included with the agent installation which you can use to manage the agent. The application's user interface (UI) lets you maintain registered databases and test connectivity to the Data Sync service. We discuss setting up the agent in the "Creating the Sync Group" section later in the chapter.

SQL Azure Data Sync Considerations

Whenever evaluating a new piece of software or platform, you need information on certain aspects such as security, performance, and costs. This section touches on these topics as they pertain to Data Sync. This information will help you decide whether or not Data Sync is an appropriate solution for your unique scenario.

Data Sync Security

Data Sync provides security in two ways, using encryption and authentication. Data is encrypted whenever it is stored in the cloud or transmitted between components. Stored data includes items such as login credentials for SQL Azure connections, configuration data for the client agent, and service credentials for both SQL Azure system databases and Windows Azure system storage. Data Sync also enforces authentication whenever connections are made.

In the Data Sync model, data is transmitted between several components; for instance, between SQL Azure and SQL Server. Whenever a connection is made between two components, the connection is encrypted. Encrypted connections are established between the Data Sync service and the following components:

- the SQL Azure system database
- the Windows Azure system storage
- the client agent
- the Windows Azure Management Portal

Data Sync employs authentication across all connection points to prevent unauthorized users and services from accessing the system and data. The Windows Azure Management Portal authenticates users using Windows Live IDs and the Windows Azure subscription database. Connections made between components are authenticated using certificates. The client agent responsible for synchronizing data between the hub and member database performs authentication using a unique token generated when the agent is installed. Only a user with Administrator privileges can manage the agent.

Performance and Costs

Synchronization performance is affected by many factors. When using Data Sync, there are several things you can do to ensure you gain the best possible performance, starting with the location of your SQL Azure databases. The geographic location where your SQL Azure databases are hosted can impact both the efficiency and cost of your synchronizations. To minimize latency, locate your SQL Azure databases in data centers as close to your SQL Server databases as possible.

Next, limit your datasets to include just the items you need to sync. Data Sync doesn't require the entire database to participate in a Sync Group, so you should always select the fewest tables and columns possible and apply an applicable row filter when you configure your dataset. This practice improves performance by reducing the overall payload of a Sync Job.

Another consideration to bear in mind is the frequency with which a Sync Job occurs. If a Sync Job attempts to synchronize a Sync Group that has not yet completed a prior synchronization, the attempt fails. When planning a Sync Schedule, take care that you set the interval sufficiently large enough to ensure that synchronization completes before the next Sync Job is started.

The Sync Schedule can affect your SQL Azure costs as well. Although Microsoft currently offers Data Sync as a free service, SQL Azure fees are charged according to the amount of data moved into and out of a data center. To minimize costs, you should consider dividing data into separate Sync Groups according to the frequency with which the data changes. Volatile data should be synchronized at a higher frequency than static or lookup data. Partitioning Sync Groups in this way allows you to configure an optimal schedule that helps reduce costs by sending data less frequently.

One pitfall to avoid when setting up multiple Sync Groups is a condition known as a Sync Loop. A Sync Loop occurs when a change in a record in one Sync Group is re-written to the same record by a second Sync Group, similar to a circular reference. This highly undesirable condition can potentially enter an infinite loop and consume enough resources to significantly degrade performance. Furthermore, you will pay fees for moving data into and out of SQL Azure unnecessarily. You can avoid Sync Loops in a few ways:

- Design your Sync Groups such that a loop cannot exist; that is, don't let the same table be synchronized by two different Sync Groups. Also, avoid adding the same database more than once to the same Sync Group, even if the database is registered with a different Client Sync Agent.
- If multiple Sync Groups synchronize the same table, use row filtering to prevent the same rows from being updated by all of the Sync Groups.
- Specify a sync direction such that a loop condition cannot exist.

Creating an Occasionally Connected System

At the time of this writing, Data Sync does not support direct synchronization between mobile devices and SQL Server or SQL Azure. Although this functionality may be added to a future version of Data Sync, for now, you simply cannot build synchronization capabilities directly into the phone application using Data Sync. But consider as well that you may not *want* to expose your SQL Server database via the Internet directly to the mobile application. Adding a SQL Azure database to the design to act as a buffer between mobile clients and the on-premise "back office" database introduces an extra layer of security to the solution. With this architecture, you protect SQL Server behind the corporate firewall and install the agent on a public facing server or perimeter network (also known as DMZ, or demilitarized zone). Such a configuration allows the agent to communicate with the database for syncing with SQL Azure, and restricts all other access to your SQL Server.

This chapter demonstrates how to build such a solution by taking a deep dive into SQL Azure Data Sync, Windows Azure, and the Windows Phone SDK. The solution also incorporates two additional technologies, SQL Azure and WCF Data Services, each of which we have dedicated entire chapters to in this book.

The FlixPoll Application

FlixPoll is the fictitious survey application that demonstrates how all these various technologies work together in an occasionally connected system. A FlixPoll user interviews patrons as they exit a movie theater and records their responses on a Windows Phone 7 device. The client application on the phone requires no network connection to store data locally. Once a connection is available, the client uploads data to, and downloads data from, SQL Azure. This is achieved by calling the FlixPoll service, implemented with WCF Data Services and hosted in Windows Azure. The service, in turn, obtains data from the SQL Azure hub database. At that point, Data Sync is responsible for synchronizing changes between SQL Azure and the on-premise SQL Server database. Data Sync updates the on-premise database and resolves any conflicts between data uploaded from the phone and data entered by users in the back office.

Note This application is merely a learning tool that demonstrates how to build an occasionally connected system with WCF Data Services and SQL Azure Data Sync. FlixPoll uses basic WCF Data Services that do not handle conflict resolution between the phone client and SQL Azure. Changes uploaded by FlixPoll users are propagated out to the member database, and these changes overwrite any changes made to the on-premise SQL Server. Conflict resolution between SQL Azure and on-premise SQL Server is handled by policies defined in SQL Azure Data Sync, as we explain later in the chapter.

When the FlixPoll client application starts, it checks the local device for previously downloaded movie data that is required to run the application. If the data is available, it is retrieved and displayed; otherwise, a connection is made to the service and the data is downloaded. The user then interviews movie-goers, storing the gathered polling information locally on the device. The user can also update movie information locally. Then the user initiates a connection with the service to upload their changes to SQL Azure.

Microsoft Sync Framework Toolkit

The previous edition of this book showed how to create an occasionally connected system for SQL Server 2008 using the Microsoft Sync Service Framework. Since then, the Microsoft Sync Service Framework has gone through several transformations, and Microsoft has deferred new development of that framework in favor of SQL Azure Data Sync. The last release of the framework was version 4.0, which remains in beta.

The Sync Service Framework can still be used to add synchronization support to your applications. In fact, Microsoft has released the Microsoft Sync Framework Toolkit, based on Sync Framework version 4.0, to support that notion. However, given Microsoft's decision to suspend development of the framework, we have written this brand new chapter that guides you in Microsoft's current direction for data synchronization, SQL Azure Data Sync. To find out more about the Microsoft Sync Framework Toolkit, visit *http://go.microsoft.com/fwlink/p/?LinkId=235330*).

The remainder of this chapter is divided into three major sections, and each section dives into the details of one major component of the application. This first section walks you through setting up the application database and configuring SQL Azure Data Sync. In the second section, you will use WCF Data Services to create a service (itself hosted in Windows Azure) that exposes the SQL Azure data. In the final section, you will build the Windows Phone application that consumes the data service.

Creating the FlixPoll Databases

Your first objective is to build the databases. There are two databases in the FlixPoll application, one on-premise SQL Server database and a second one hosted in SQL Azure. The on-premise database is named *FlixPollOnPrem*. This is the application's member database. The SQL Azure database is the hub, and is named *FlixPollOnCloud*.

For demonstration purposes, we kept both databases very simple. Still, we represent tables like those you see in a typical database: there are lookup tables as well as tables for storing transactional data.

To create the *FlixPollOnPrem* database, open SQL Server Data Tools (SSDT) in Visual Studio or SQL Server Management Studio (SSMS) to connect to your local SQL Server 2012 instance. Then open a new query window and run the script in Listing 13-1 to create the database and populate its tables with sample data.

LISTING 13-1 Creating the *FlixPollOnPrem* database and tables, and inserting data.

```
CREATE DATABASE FlixPollOnPrem
GO

USE FlixPollOnPrem
GO

CREATE TABLE Movie(
 MovieId int IDENTITY(1,1) NOT NULL CONSTRAINT PK_Movie PRIMARY KEY,
 Name varchar(100) NOT NULL,
 YearReleased smallint NOT NULL)
GO

CREATE TABLE Inquiry(
 InquiryId int IDENTITY(1,1) NOT NULL CONSTRAINT PK_Inquiry PRIMARY KEY,
 Question varchar(100) NOT NULL)
GO

CREATE TABLE Response(
  ResponseId int IDENTITY(1,1) NOT NULL CONSTRAINT PK_Response PRIMARY KEY,
  MovieId int NOT NULL,
  InquiryId int NOT NULL,
  Answer bit NOT NULL CONSTRAINT DF_Answer DEFAULT(0)
)
GO

INSERT INTO Movie (Name, YearReleased) VALUES
 ('SQL Wars', 2011),
 ('Like Water for SQL', 2011),
```

```
  ('SQL Mission Impossible', 2011),
  ('Amazing SQL-man', 2012),
  ('Chipmonks, The SQL', 2012),
  ('The SQL Avengers', 2012)
GO

INSERT INTO Inquiry (Question) VALUES
  ('Did you like the movie?'),
  ('Is the movie a potential award nominee?'),
  ('Did you pay a fair ticket price?')
GO
```

Now create an empty *FlixPollOnCloud* database. The tables will be created and populated later as part of the first synchronization job. Open a connection to your SQL Azure server and execute the following statement:

```
CREATE DATABASE FlixPollOnCloud
```

SQL Azure is covered in Chapter 12. Refer to that chapter for a detailed discussion explaining how to use the Azure Management Portal to create your own cloud databases on SQL Azure. The "Getting Set Up" section in that chapter describes how to provision your server and create the firewall rule necessary to access a SQL Azure server. When creating your SQL Azure server for use with the sample application, be sure you check the option Allow Other Windows Azure Services To Access This Server. Doing so sets up the firewall rule that allows access to your SQL Azure server. You will need this access later when running your WCF Data Services. If you do not create this firewall rule, neither Data Sync nor WCF Data Services will have access to the SQL Azure server.

Note MSDN subscribers receive free access to Windows Azure. The level of access you receive is dependent upon your subscription level. See *https://www.windowsazure.com/en-us/pricing/member-offers/msdn-benefits* for details.

Prerequisites

To build this solution, you will need the additional software and subscriptions listed below:

- A Windows Live ID
- A Windows Azure subscription, with Windows Azure and SQL Azure accounts
- Windows Azure SDK for .NET
- Windows Azure Tools For Microsoft Visual Studio
- Windows Phone 7.1 SDK
- Silverlight Toolkit for Windows Phone

Configuring SQL Azure Data Sync

Setting up SQL Azure Data Sync is a two-step process that you accomplish using the Windows Azure Management Portal. The first step is to provision the SQL Azure Data Sync server. Then you create a Sync Group. These steps are further divided into many smaller steps, as we explain ahead.

Provisioning the SQL Azure Data Sync Server

Your first step to complete in setting up SQL Azure Data Sync is to provision a SQL Azure server. The provisioned server is referred to as the Data Sync server. A Data Sync server can host multiple Sync Groups, but you can only provision one SQL Azure server as the Data Sync server per Windows Azure subscription.

Provisioning a server requires two items, an active Windows Azure platform account and a SQL Azure server. To provision a server now, log in to the Windows Azure portal at *http://windows.azure.com* using your Windows Live ID. On the left vertical menu, click Data Sync. Then start the provisioning wizard by either clicking on the Provision button in the toolbar or the large Provision Data Sync Preview Server button shown in Figure 13-1.

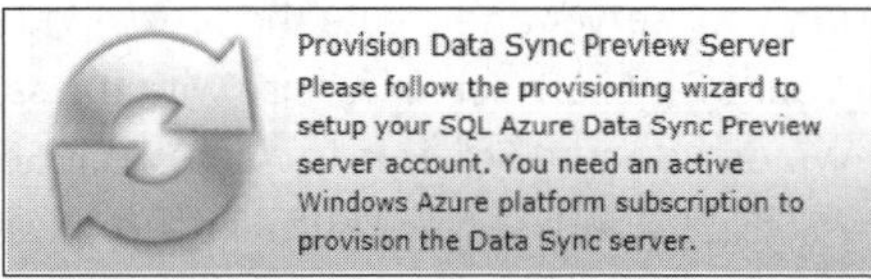

Provision Data Sync Preview Server
Please follow the provisioning wizard to setup your SQL Azure Data Sync Preview server account. You need an active Windows Azure platform subscription to provision the Data Sync server.

FIGURE 13-1 The Provision Data Sync Preview Server button in the Windows Azure portal.

Provisioning a server is a straightforward, three-step process. Step one is to accept the terms of use agreement. Read through the agreement, check the I Agree To The Terms Of Use Statement Above check box, and then click Next to continue to step two.

Step two asks you to select the SQL Azure subscription you want to provision. Expand the Subscription drop-down list and select a subscription from the list. Click Next to move on to the final step.

In the final step, you select a region where the Data Sync server will be hosted. Azure uses regions to manage the physical location of your application and data. A region represents a Microsoft data center where your application or database can be deployed. Expand the Region drop-down list and select an appropriate region. Since you are building a sample application, the region you select doesn't matter much. For production applications however, you should consider selecting a region where most of your application's users are located, or in close proximity to your data center. As we mentioned, the main benefit in doing so is reduced network latency. Provisioning a server closest to your users increases your application's response time by decreasing the distance the data must travel to its destination. Click the Finish button after selecting the region.

Creating the Sync Group

With the Data Sync server provisioned, you are ready to create the Sync Group. A Sync Group is created in six, high-level steps:

1. Supply a name for the Sync Group
2. Add the SQL Server database to the group
3. Add the SQL Azure hub database
4. Set the Sync Schedule and conflict resolution policy
5. Define the tables, columns, and rows that make up the dataset
6. Deploy the Sync Group to the Data Sync server

FlixPoll uses a Sync Group composed of one SQL Azure database named *FlixPollOnCloud* (the hub) and one SQL Server database named *FlixPollOnPrem* (the member). From within the Windows Azure Management Portal click on the Data Sync button on the left-hand side of the portal. Select the subscription under which you want to create the Sync Group from the tree view in the portal's left pane (if you don't select the subscription now, you will be prompted to select one as the first step in the wizard). Then click the large Sync between On-Premise And SQL Azure Databases button shown in Figure 13-2.

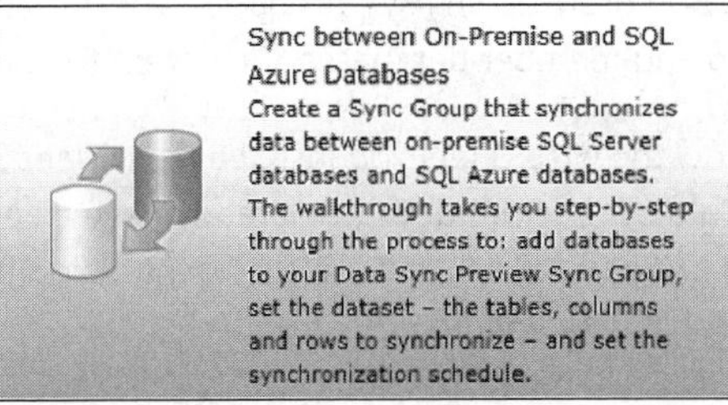

Sync between On-Premise and SQL Azure Databases
Create a Sync Group that synchronizes data between on-premise SQL Server databases and SQL Azure databases. The walkthrough takes you step-by-step through the process to: add databases to your Data Sync Preview Sync Group, set the dataset - the tables, columns and rows to synchronize - and set the synchronization schedule.

FIGURE 13-2 This button in the portal's center pane starts the Sync Group wizard to create a Sync Group composed of SQL Azure and SQL Server databases.

More Info The portal actually provides three different ways to create a Sync Group. The Sync Between On-Premise And SQL Azure Databases button starts a wizard with steps for creating a SQL Azure to SQL Server Sync Group, as in our FlixPoll solution. The Sync Between SQL Azure Databases starts a different wizard for creating a Sync Group consisting only of SQL Azure databases. Clicking the Create button on the toolbar allows you to add any combination of SQL Azure and SQL Server databases to a Sync Group, in any order.

Step 1: Name the Sync Group

A good rule of thumb is to provide a name that is meaningful and describes the purpose of the Sync Group, while also being unique. Go ahead and name the Sync Group **FlixPollSyncGroup**. After entering the Sync Group name, move on to the next step by clicking the arrow above and to the right of the Sync Group Name textbox or by pressing the **Enter** key.

Step 2: Add the On-Premise Database

A wizard now guides you through the process of adding a SQL Server member database to the group. As you advance through the wizard, you will:

- Add a new SQL Server database to the group.
- Install and configure a new Client Sync Agent.
- Register your SQL Server database with the agent.
- Select the SQL Server database for inclusion in the group.

Add a new SQL Server database to the group Start the process of adding the member database by clicking on the "Add SQL Server database" icon (it's the image of the database with a plus sign embedded inside). This opens the Add Database To Sync Group dialog box. This is the first Sync Group you are creating, so select the Add A New SQL Server Database To The Sync Group option, and then select the Bi-Directional option in the Sync Direction drop-down list. This option specifies that data changes flow in both directions between the hub and member databases. Click Next to continue.

Install and configure a new Client Sync Agent Now the wizard lets you install a new Client Sync Agent, which you must do because the provisioned Data Sync server does not already have an agent installed. Choose the Install a New Agent option. This brings up the Install A New Agent dialog box, as shown in Figure 13-3. Click the Download button to begin downloading the installer.

Note Be sure to review the prerequisites for using the agent on the Client Sync Agent download page.

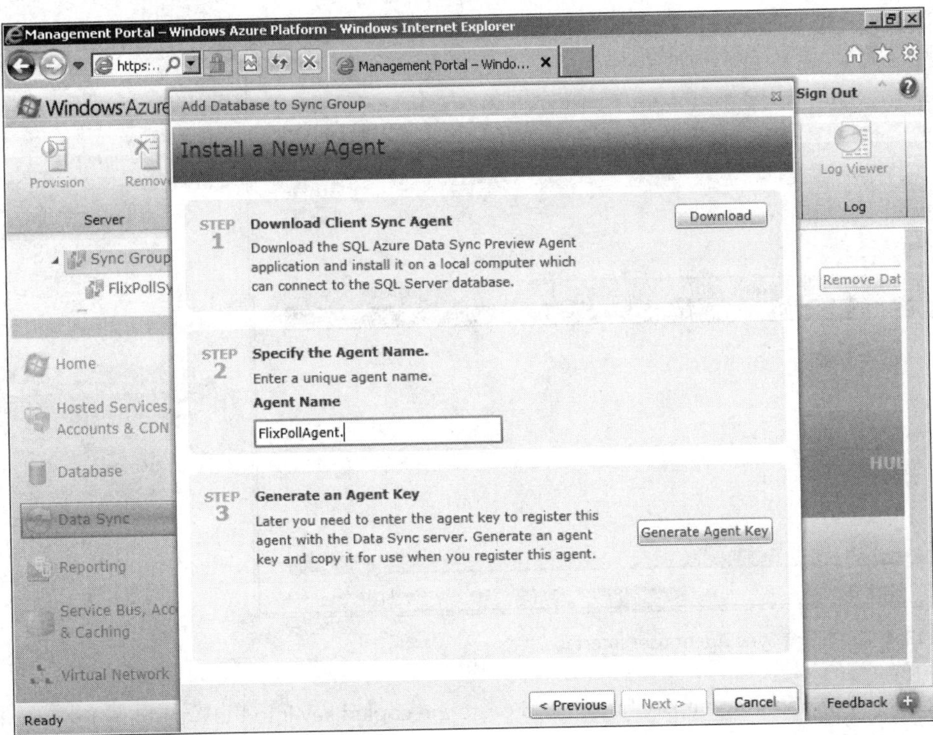

FIGURE 13-3 Installing a new Client Sync Agent.

Run the installer when it finishes downloading. Accept the license agreement and default location for the installation folder. You will then be prompted for a user account with Administrator privileges. Be sure to use a Windows Service account that has permissions to connect to all of the SQL Server databases you want to register.

Register your SQL Server database with the agent After the agent software is installed, return to the Windows Azure Management Portal and enter **FlixPollAgent** for the agent name. Next, click the Generate Agent Key button. This generates and displays an encrypted string that is required by the Client Sync Agent. Click the Copy button to copy the key to the clipboard and then click Next to advance the wizard to the next step.

With the agent key copied, you'll temporarily leave the portal to configure the agent. Don't close the portal, as you will return to it momentarily. Click Start | All Programs | Microsoft SQL Azure Data Sync | and Microsoft SQL Azure Data Sync Agent Preview to start the agent UI, as shown in Figure 13-4.

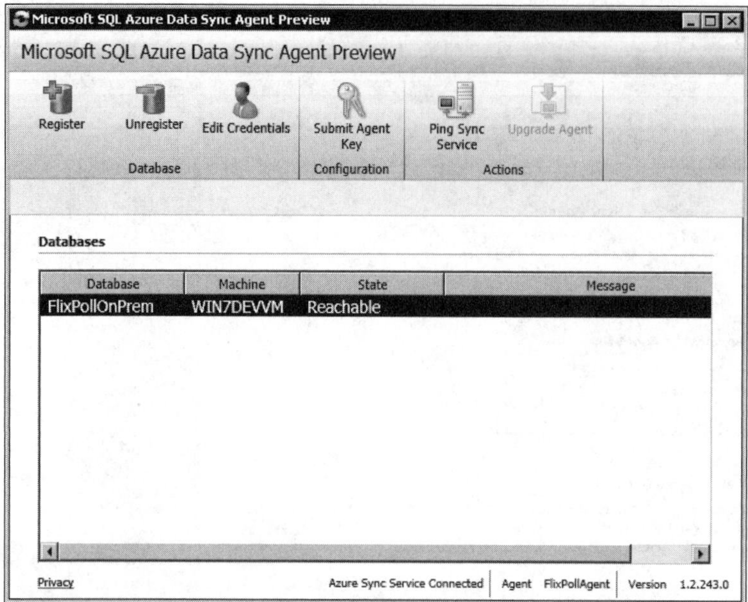

FIGURE 13-4 The Client Sync Agent user interface.

First, click the Submit Agent Key button and paste the copied key into the Agent Key textbox. Then click OK. You are now ready to register the *FlixPollOnPrem* database with the agent.

Click the Register button to open the SQL Server Configuration dialog box. When the dialog box opens, supply the necessary login credentials. Next, enter the name of your local database server and enter **FlixPollOnPrem** for the database name. Do not select the option of using SSL with this connection, but consider enabling it in a production environment. Now click the Test Connection button to verify your credentials are entered properly and can access the database server. Then click the Save button to continue.

You can confirm that the *FlixPollOnPrem* database is registered when you see it appear in the agent UI form's Status pane. The last thing to do before closing the application is to click on the Ping Sync Service button to test your connection to the Data Sync service. When you receive a message stating your ping was successful, close the agent UI application.

Note If you cannot ping the sync service and your enterprise uses a network proxy, you may need to set the appropriate firewall rules to allow outbound connections to the sync service. In some cases you can resolve the problem by simply toggling the proxy server setting in Internet Explorer.

Select the SQL Server database for inclusion in the group Return back to the Windows Azure portal. You should see the form shown in Figure 13-5.

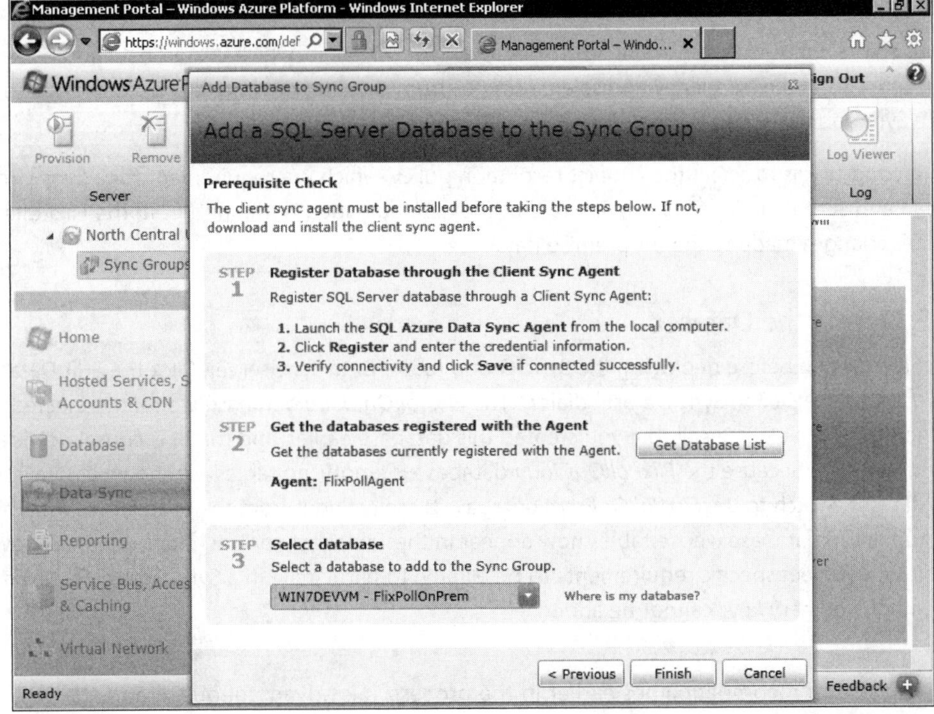

FIGURE 13-5 The final form in the wizard adds a SQL Server database to a Sync Group.

Visually verify that the agent name shown in the second section reads *FlixPollAgent*, then click the Get Database List button. Expand the Select Database drop-down list in the third section, and you should see the *FlixPollOnPrem* database in the list. Select it and click the Finish button.

Step 3: Select the SQL Azure Hub Database

To complete this step, you will need your SQL Azure server's administrator login credentials and its fully qualified DNS Name (which always begin with a unique identifier randomly assigned just to you, followed by *.database.windows.net*). You can get the SQL Azure server's DNS name from the portal by clicking on the Database tab.

Once you have the DNS name and login credentials, click on the "Add A SQL Azure Database" icon (it's the image of the database with the crisscrossing lines embedded inside). You will be prompted to supply your SQL Azure server name (this is the DNS name), user ID, and password. After entering your server and login credentials, click on the Database Name drop-down list, select the *FlixPollOnCloud* database, and then click Add. If you don't see the *FlixPollOnCloud* database in the drop-down list, type it manually.

Step 4: Configuring Sync Schedule and Conflict Resolution

Step four consists of two tasks. The first is to create a Sync Schedule, which is optional and enabled by default. Enter **10** as the frequency and select Minutes from the interval drop-down list to have FlixPoll invoke a Sync Job every 10 minutes.

The second task is to select the conflict resolution policy, which is a requirement for a Sync Group. Go ahead and set the policy to Hub Wins so that the data uploaded to the hub from the FlixPoll UI overwrites changes made to the on-premise database.

Step 5: Define the Dataset

This is the final step before deploying the Sync Group to the Data Sync server. Click the Edit Dataset button to open the Define Sync Dataset dialog. The *FlixPollOnCloud* database is already selected when the dialog appears. Recall that you created this database earlier, and that it is completely devoid of schema or data. Because the *FlixPollOnCloud* database is empty, no tables are shown as available for the dataset. Switch to the *FlixPollOnPrem* database by selecting it from the drop-down list. This is a fully populated database whose tables now appear in the Tables list control under the drop-down list. Tables must meet specific requirements to be eligible to participate in a Sync Group. For example, tables without primary keys cannot be added.

Tip To discover incompatibilities earlier in the process, it is advantageous to add the source database to the Agent prior to provisioning. You can then resolve issues such as unsupported data types or missing primary key constraints by modifying the offending table's schema. Then just click the Refresh Schema button to reload and revalidate the schema.

Select the *Movie, Inquiry,* and *Response* tables from the list. After selecting each table, notice that the list control to the right of the tables shows all of the columns available for synchronization. Each table should have all columns selected.

Now set up a filter on the *Movie* table so that only the movies from the year 2012 will be included in the dataset. This excludes rows for years other than 2012 from being synchronized. Select the *Movie* table. In the list of fields, place a check in the *Filter* column next to the *YearReleased* field. At the bottom section of the form, you will see a series of controls for building a filter clause. The *YearReleased* field should be pre-selected; if it isn't, select it now from the drop-down list. Set the Operator to Equals (=) and enter **2012** in the Value textbox. The Define Sync Dataset dialog should look like Figure 13-6.

Click OK to complete step five. The portal displays a message instructing you to deploy the FlixPoll Sync Group. Before you deploy, quickly review the details displayed in the portal and shown in Figure 13-7. Verify that the values for the sync schedule and conflict resolution policy are correct. Confirm the tables you included in the dataset are found in the Synced Tables drop-down list along with each table's associated columns and the filter on the *YearReleased* column. In the main pane, you'll notice that neither the *FlixPollOnCloud* nor the *FlixPollOnPrem* databases are deployed.

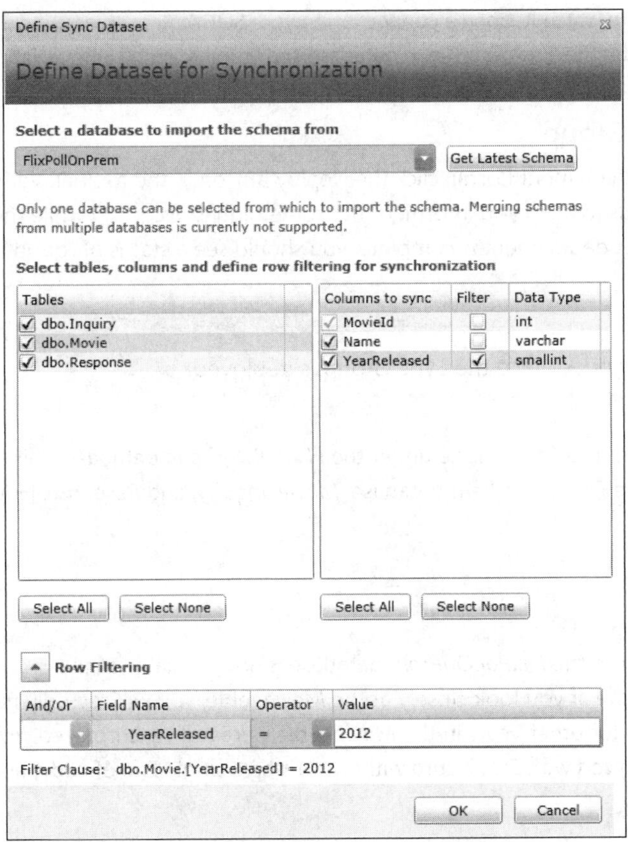

FIGURE 13-6 The completed Define Sync Dataset dialog box.

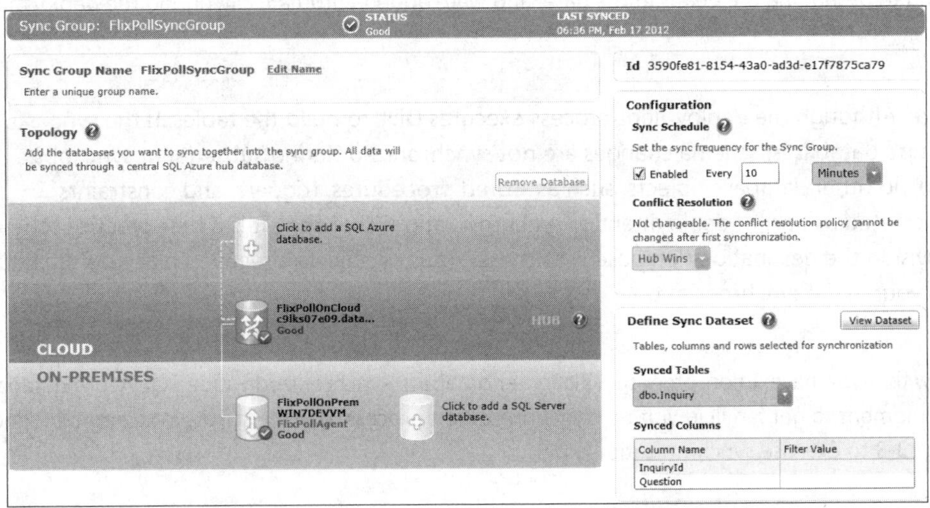

FIGURE 13-7 The Windows Azure Management Portal main pane after creating the Sync Group.

A little magic is about to happen. To watch it, open a connection to your SQL Azure server using SSDT or SSMS. Expand the *Tables* node under the *FlixPollOnCloud* database and verify that no tables exist.

Step 6: Deploying the Sync Group

From within the Windows Azure Management Portal, click the Deploy button in the toolbar. Various icons will begin to update their status to keep you informed that something is occurring while the deployment process is running. After deployment is complete, you should see a status of "good" next to each database in the group.

Note The dataset cannot be changed once the Sync Group is deployed.

Go back to SSDT/SSMS and refresh the *Tables* node under the *FlixPollOnCloud* database. This time you will see the three tables from the *FlixPollOnPrem* database: *Movie*, *Inquiry*, and *Response*. Now issue these simple queries:

```
SELECT * FROM Inquiry
SELECT * FROM Movie
```

The results reveal that the data from the *FlixPollOnPrem* database is now available in the *FlixPollOnCloud* database. Furthermore, if you look closely at the *Movie* table, you will see only rows with the *YearReleased* of 2012. Rows for other years in the *Movie* table were not synchronized. Your enterprise database can be synchronized with SQL Azure without writing a single line of code, and we call that magical!

Upon further review of the tables in both databases, you will see new tables added that were not part of the script to create the databases. These tables provide change tracking capabilities and are used to determine the deltas in the data, and were added automatically during the deployment process.

Note Although the deployment process executes DDL to build the tables in the sync group's databases, schema changes are not synchronized during subsequent sync jobs. Also, no other database objects, such as stored procedures, triggers, and constraints are created as part of deployment or synchronization. Therefore it is a best practice to provision the destination database with these types of objects already in place before you run your initial synchronization.

Now that you have an on-premise SQL Server database synchronized with a SQL Azure database, take a moment to get familiar with the synchronization process. Use the scripts in Listing 13-2 and Listing 13-3 to exercise synchronization a bit.

LISTING 13-2 Modifying *Movie* records in the *FlixPollOnPrem* database.

```
-- Issue these queries in the FlixPollOnPrem database
INSERT INTO Movie (Name, YearReleased) VALUES
  ('OnPrem New Movie One', 2012),
  ('OnPrem New Movie Two', 2012),
  ('OnPrem New Movie Three', 2011)  -- this insert will not be sync'd
                                    -- since it isn't for year 2012
UPDATE Movie
 SET Name = 'Chipmonks, The Three-quel'
 WHERE Name = 'Chipmonks, The SQL'

-- this is a conflict w/ the hub and will be over written during sync
UPDATE Movie
 SET Name = 'Amazing SQL-man 2'
 WHERE Name = 'Amazing SQL-man'
```

LISTING 13-3 Modifying *Movie* records in the *FlixPollOnCloud* database.

```
-- Issue these queries in the FlixPollOnCloud database
INSERT INTO Movie (Name, YearReleased) VALUES
  ('OnCloud New Movie One', 2012),
  ('OnCloud New Movie Two', 2012),
  ('OnCloud New Movie Three', 2011)  -- this insert will not be sync'd
                                     -- since it isn't for year 2012

-- this update over writes the members update to the same record
UPDATE Movie
 SET Name = 'Revenge of the Amazing SQL-man'
 WHERE Name = 'Amazing SQL-man'
```

The *FlixPollSyncGroup* is configured to propagate changes out to the databases in the group every 10 minutes, but you don't have to wait to see the results of executing these scripts. You can force a sync job by clicking the Sync Now button in the Windows Azure Management Portal. The portal also provides facilities to check the health and status of the Sync Group. You can see the status of the last Sync Job by selecting the agent from the portal. Status information is shown in the portal's main pane. You can also view details by clicking the link provided to examine the log.

After running the scripts above and completing a synchronization job, issue the following *SELECT* query against the *Movie* table in both the *FlixPollOnPrem* and *FlixPollOnCloud* databases:

```
SELECT * FROM Movie
```

The combined results of both queries are shown in Table 13-2. The results show the records from the *FlixPollOnPrem* have been synchronized with the *Movie* table in the *FlixPollOnCloud* database.

TABLE 13-2 Database contents after synchronization.

Records from the *FlixPollOnCloud* Movie Table		
MovieId	Name	YearReleased
4	Revenge of the Amazing SQL-man	2012
5	Chipmonks, The Three-quel	2012
6	The SQL Avengers	2012
7	OnCloud New Movie One	2012
8	OnCloud New Movie Two	2012
9	OnCloud New Movie Three	2011
17	OnPrem New Movie One	2012
18	OnPrem New Movie Two	2012

Records from the *FlixPollOnCloud* Movie Table		
MovieId	Name	YearReleased
1	Squid Wars	2011
2	Like Water for SQL	2011
3	SQL Mission Impossible	2011
4	Revenge of the Amazing SQL-man	2012
5	Chipmonks, The Three-quel	2012
6	The SQL Avengers	2012
7	OnCloud New Movie One	2012
8	OnCloud New Movie Two	2012
17	OnPrem New Movie One	2012
18	OnPrem New Movie Two	2012
19	OnPrem New Movie Three	2011

Note Because the *MovieId* column is defined as an Identity, the values in the column on your system will probably differ from those shown in Table 13-2.

Notice how the change made to the "Amazing SQL-man" record (Movie ID 4) in the member database was overwritten by the change made to the same record in the hub database. The record is now "Revenge of the Amazing SQL-man" in both databases, because you set the conflict resolution strategy to Hub Wins earlier in step 4.

A few scenarios will cause synchronization to fail. To ensure that everything runs smoothly, keep the following points in mind:

- A primary key is required on every table being synchronized.

- Changes to a primary key value will prevent the record from being synchronized. This is not considered a best practice in general, but with regards to Data Sync, after changing the primary key value the keys no longer match and therefore the row cannot be synchronized.
- Applying a filter to a non-nullable column with no default value will also present a problem. In this scenario, clients that have the filtered version will never be able to sync up their changes, and will always get sync failures.
- Visit *http://msdn.microsoft.com/library/hh667303.aspx* for more information on known Data Sync issues.

Other authors may have stopped here, but not us. In the next section we are going to forge onward to build a WCF Data Service for the *FlixPollOnCloud* database hosted in Windows Azure. The service will be consumed by the FlixPoll UI. Ultimately, the UI will update data in *FlixPollOnCloud* via the WCF Data Service where the data will be synchronized with the *FlixPollOnPrem* database.

Hosting WCF Data Services in Windows Azure

In Chapters 10 and 11, you were introduced to the Entity Framework (EF) and WCF Data Services, respectively. Those chapters describe how to create an Entity Data Model (EDM) over a SQL Server database, and how to query and update the EDM with any HTTP client using Representational State Transfer Protocol (REST) and OData. In this section, you are going to build on the knowledge you obtained from those chapters to create WCF Data Services deployed to Windows Azure—Microsoft's cloud-based server operating system. Then, in the final section, you will consume these services from a FlixPoll client application built for Windows Phone 7.

About Windows Azure

Windows Azure (or simply, Azure) is the core of Microsoft's cloud platform. Azure facilitates the creation, deployment, and management of applications across Microsoft-managed datacenters around the globe. Windows Azure provides the ability to quickly scale your applications up or down to meet demand. This capability is referred to as "Compute capacity," which is determined using "Compute resources." Compute resources are assigned to your application and are added to, or removed from, your application dynamically to adjust for increasing or decreasing demand.

Compute resources are utilized through one or more Compute containers called "roles." There are three different types of roles available: Web, Worker, and Virtual Machine (VM). A role is essentially a virtual machine pre-configured for a specific purpose. For example, the Web role is a VM configured with Internet Information Services (IIS) 7 enabled. For the *FlixPoll* application you are only concerned with the Web role type. You will assign the role in a moment when you create the WCF Data Service.

More Info Visit *http://www.windowsazure.com/en-us/home/tour/overview* to learn more about Windows Azure.

Windows Azure Best Practices

Windows Azure is a great cloud platform, but hosting an application in the cloud produces new concerns that you need to be aware of. Here are a few guidelines to help you minimize cost and consume services securely on Windows Azure.

Windows Azure fees are based on the amount of outgoing data. There are a couple of benefits to minimizing that data:

- Less data equals lower costs,
- Less data equals reduced latency and increased application performance.

To help reduce the amount of outgoing data, you should consider using compression with XML formats. If your client application is not a Windows Phone client, another option is to use JSON. Unfortunately the Windows Phone WCF Data Service Library currently does not support serializing to JSON format. However, the *DataContractJsonSerializer* class is available on the device to serialize a JSON response into objects on the client. If you go this route, you are trading off ease of development for operating lower costs.

As a developer, it is your responsibility to mitigate security risks when implementing a cloud service in your applications. To make your hosted applications more secure, use an authentication mechanism such as Access Control Services (ACS) or ASP.NET Forms-Based Authentication. Both are supported on Windows Phone clients. ACS is a cloud-based service that enables clients to offload the task of authentication to a trusted provider, like Windows Live ID. ASP.NET Web roles also support ASP.NET Forms-Based Authentication. Both of these authentication mechanisms are available with the Windows Azure Toolkit for Windows Phone. In all cases, always use SSL when exchanging login credentials with an Azure service.

Creating the FlixPoll Solution

Azure development in Visual Studio 2010 requires elevated privileges, so you need to start Visual Studio as an Administrator. Right-click the Microsoft Visual Studio 2010 shortcut, choose Run As Administrator from the context menu, and then click Yes in the User Account Control dialog when prompted.

Now create a new blank solution. Expand the *Other Project Types* node in the template list and select Visual Studio Solution. From the list of project types select Blank Solution and name it **FlixPoll_Walkthru**.

Add a new project to the solution. From the list of template categories on the left, beneath Visual C#, choose Cloud. If this is your first time creating a project using the Cloud template, you may be surprised to see a project type option called Enable Windows Azure Tools. This is an indication that you first need to install the Windows Azure Tools for Visual Studio. Figure 13-8 shows Visual Studio's New Project dialog box prompting you to install the tools.

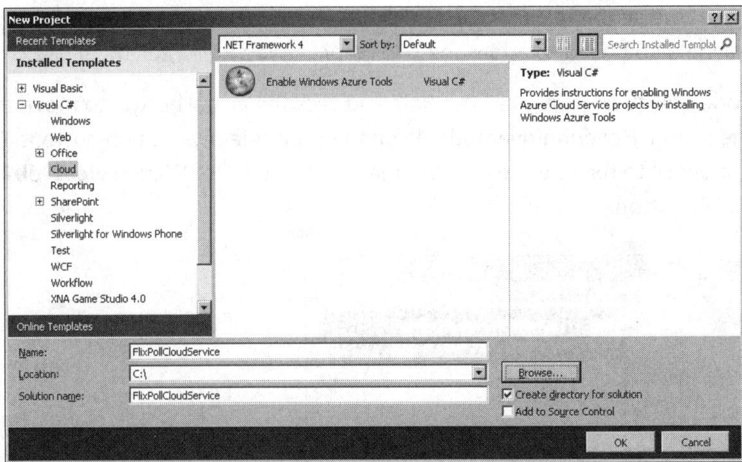

FIGURE 13-8 Installing Windows Azure Tools.

Choose Enable Windows Azure Tools to start the installation. Depending on your Visual Studio configuration, this may start the Web Platform Installer (WPI). If it does, click through the dialogs to install WPI. Once installed, WPI prompts you with a dialog displaying all of the software and configuration changes installing Windows Azure Tools makes to your computer. Click I Accept to accept the licensing terms for the software being installed. Then follow the prompts to complete the installation.

Adding the FlixPoll Data Service

You will now create a Windows Azure project to host the service, although you won't actually deploy the service to Windows Azure until a bit later. Once the tools are installed, navigate back to the Installed Templates project templates and select the Cloud template under Visual C#. This time you should see the Windows Azure Project type, shown in Figure 13-9. Type **FlixPollWindowsAzure** in the Name textbox and click OK.

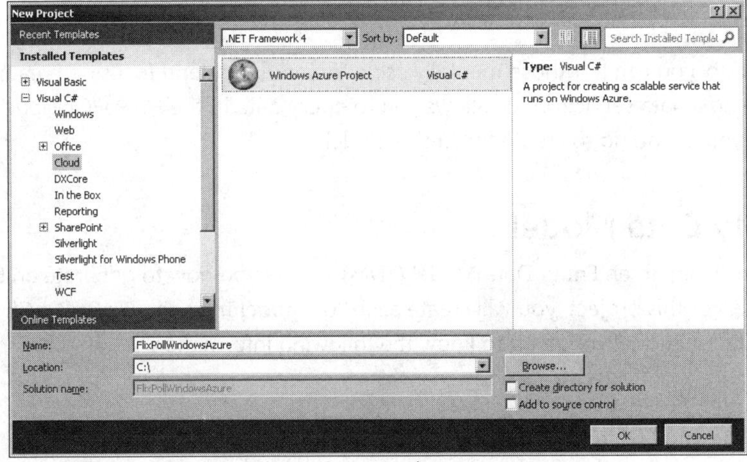

FIGURE 13-9 Visual Studio's Windows Azure Project project type.

Next, you will be asked to choose the roles for the FlixPoll service as shown in Figure 13-10. To host the FlixPoll service, the only role you need to add is the WCF Service Web Role.

Under the *Visual C#* node, select WCF Service Web Role and click the arrow button to move the role to the right side of the dialog. Hovering over the role on the right side reveals two buttons. Click the button that looks like a pencil to rename the role. Set the name to **FlixPollWcfServiceWebRole** and then click the dialog's OK button.

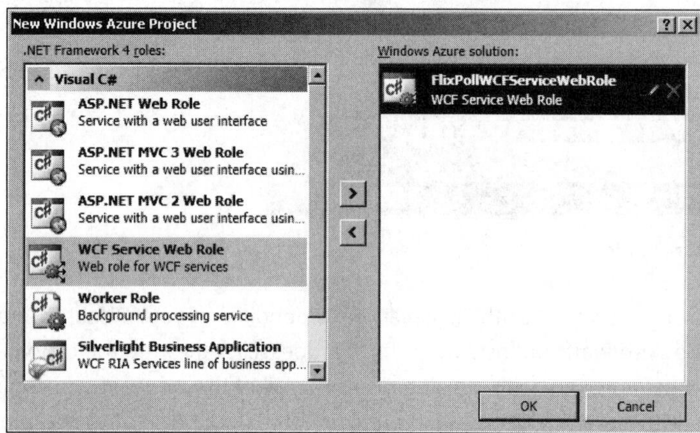

FIGURE 13-10 Selecting the appropriate Windows Azure role for the FlixPoll WCF Data Service.

Visual Studio creates a Windows Azure solution with two projects, one named *FlixPollWindowsAzure* and a second named *FlixPollWCFServiceWebRole*. The *FlixPollWindowsAzure* project is just for Azure server configuration files and the application's web roles. You will use this project later to package the service for deployment to the cloud. The *FlixPollWCFServiceWebRole* project is an ASP.NET application that you can program against as you would any ordinary ASP.NET application.

Note Windows Azure, or any other cloud platform, is not a requirement for an occasionally connected system. You could host the FlixPoll service on your own IIS servers.

With both projects set up, you can put those mentally aside for a moment and focus on creating the service. You are creating a data service which allows you to query data in the *FlixPollOnCloud* database. To begin with, you are going to create the entity model.

Adding the Entity Data Model

In Chapter 10, the section "Building an Entity Data Model (EDM)" shows you how to generate an EDM from an existing database. For this project, you will create a FlixPoll model from the *FlixPollOnCloud* database. Before you build the model you need to know the following information:

- Fully qualified DNS name
- Login credentials for your SQL Azure database
- Your computer's IP address

All of these items can be viewed on the Windows Azure Management Portal.

The server's DNS name and login credentials are required to make a connection both to build the model and for executing queries. Before deploying the service to Windows Azure, you will be running the service locally on your development machine. Running the service on your computer means your computer needs direct access to the SQL Azure server. Therefore, you also need to know your IP address so you can create a firewall rule in Azure to allow your computer access to SQL Azure.

Log into the portal, navigate to the Database, and select the Azure server hosting your *FlixPollOnCloud* database. Then copy the fully qualified DNS name to the clipboard. Next, review the firewall rules, looking for a rule granting access to your IP address. If it is not in the firewall rule list, click the Add button to open the Add Firewall Rule dialog box, as shown in Figure 13-11.

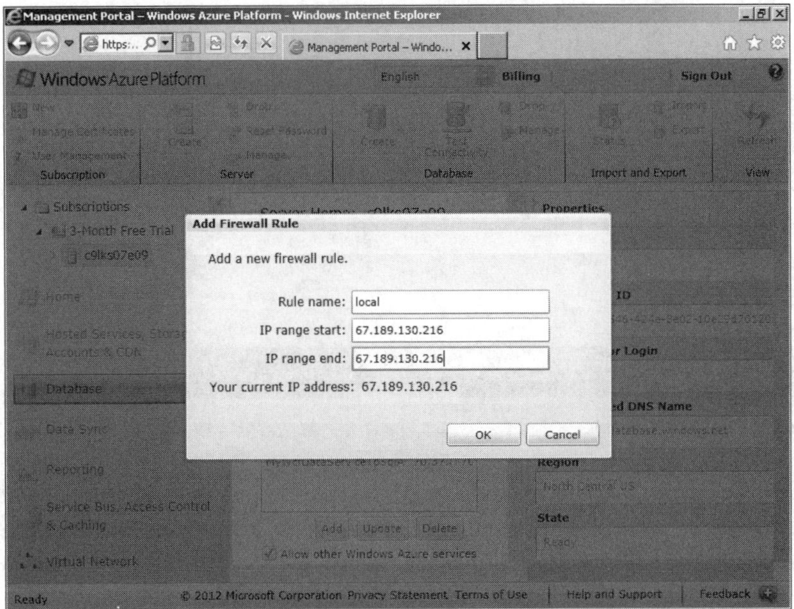

FIGURE 13-11 The Add Firewall Rule dialog box.

Your IP address is displayed toward the bottom of the dialog box. Enter a value for the rule name and type your IP address into both the IP Range Start and IP Range End textboxes. Then click OK to create the rule.

Now go back to Visual Studio and expand the *FlixPollWCFServiceWebRole* project in Solution Explorer. Delete the *IService.cs* and *Service.cs* files from the project and then add a new entity model to the project (see the section "Building an Entity Data Model" in Chapter 10 for detailed information about this process). Name the model **FlixPollModel** and, when prompted, select the Generate From Database option. Create a new connection to your SQL Azure server by supplying the server's fully qualified DNS name and your login credentials. Then select the *FlixPollOnCloud* database from the drop-down list, enable the Save My Password option, then click *Next*. Acknowledge that you want to save sensitive information in the connection string. Since this is a demo application, it is okay to forgo the best practice of saving the connection string without user credentials. Select the *Inquiry, Movie,* and *Response* tables for the model. Be sure *not* to include any of the change tracking tables added by Data Sync, such as *Movie_dss_tracking*. Enter **FlixPollModel** into the Model Namespace textbox, and then click Finish. The completed model should look similar to Figure 13-12.

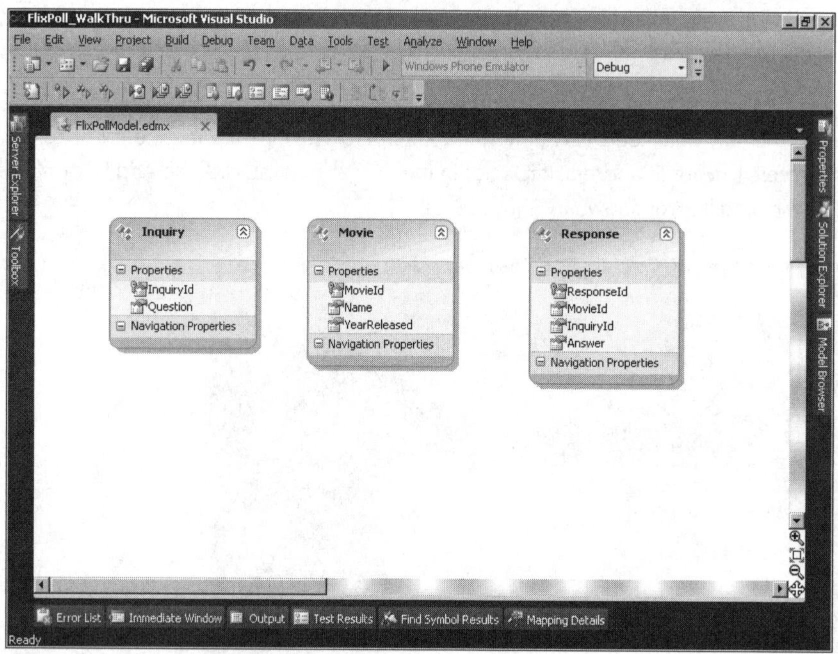

FIGURE 13-12 The *FlixPollModel* entity model.

Now you are ready to add a new service to the project. Under Installed Templates, expand the *Visual C#* node and choose the Web template. Then select the WCF Data Service item and name the service **FlixPollDataService.svc**. Change the service's class definition so that it inherits from *DataService<FlixPoll OnCloudEntities>* and replace the service's *InitializeService* method as shown in Listing 13-4.

LISTING 13-4 Implementing the WCF Data Service.

```
public class FlixPollDataService : DataService<FlixPollOnCloudEntities>
{
  public static void InitializeService(DataServiceConfiguration config)
  {
    config.UseVerboseErrors = true;

    config.SetEntitySetAccessRule("Movies", EntitySetRights.All);
    config.SetEntitySetAccessRule("Inquiries", EntitySetRights.AllRead);
    config.SetEntitySetAccessRule("Responses", EntitySetRights.AllWrite);

    config.DataServiceBehavior.MaxProtocolVersion = DataServiceProtocolVersion.V2;
  }
}
```

This code exposes service endpoints for the *Movies*, *Inquiries*, and *Responses* entity sets. It also sets the class's *UseVerboseErrors* property to true. Enabling this property in the development environment is crucial for debugging, especially after you deploy the service to Windows Azure. If it is not set, errors will return generic messages, making it near impossible to debug problems. At the same time, the extra details returned by verbose error messages often include sensitive internal information that should remain hidden from clients. Therefore, *UserVerboseErrors* should be set to false once your code is running in production environments.

That's all you need to do to create the service. You can now turn your attention to the FlixPoll UI.

Creating the FlixPoll Client

The FlixPoll client is a Windows Phone 7 application with a single page named MainPage. This page has controls that let users select and edit movies, and enter responses to interview questions.

Note You need to install the Windows Phone 7.1 SDK to create the FlixPoll client. You can download the SDK from *http://msdn.microsoft.com/en-us/library/ff637516.aspx*.

Open Visual Studio and add a new project to your solution. Under the project templates select the Silverlight For Windows Phone template and then the Windows Phone Databound Application project type. Name the project **FlixPoll** and click OK, and you will be prompted to select the target Windows Phone Operating System (OS) version. Select Windows Phone OS 7.1 from the drop-down list and click OK.

Creating the View

This project template creates pages and classes for building a phone application using data binding. FlixPoll builds on this template. You will not use the *DetailsPage.xaml* file so go ahead and delete it from the project.

Note Space constraints prevent us from walking you through the complete FlixPoll client code. Instead, the *Movie* entity serves as the canonical example for building FlixPoll. All of the walkthroughs for *Movies* related to data binding, consuming OData with LINQ to REST, and accessing the local SQL Server Compact edition (SQL CE) database storage using LINQ to SQL can be applied to the remaining entities in the application. The complete source code can be downloaded from the book's companion website (see the book's "Introduction" for details).

Open the *MainPage.xaml* page in the designer. Then add the following attribute to the *PhoneApplicationPage* element at the top of the XAML to gain access to the Windows Phone controls:

```
xmlns:toolkit="clr-namespace:Microsoft.Phone.Controls;assembly=Microsoft.Phone.Controls.Toolkit"
```

Locate the *StackPanel* named *TitlePanel*. Change the *Text* property of the *ApplicationTitle TextBlock* to **FlixPoll** and then change the *Text* property of the *PageTitle TextBlock* to **Movies**. Next, replace the markup inside of the *Grid* control named *ContentPanel* with the XAML shown in Listing 13-5. This XAML adds *ListPicker*, *ListBox*, and *TextBox* controls to the page and sets up the data binding template for displaying movies and inquiries on the page.

Note The *MainPage.xaml* file uses controls from the SilverLight Toolkit for Windows Phone. You will need to install that library to compile this code. Download the toolkit from CodePlex at *http://silverlight.codeplex.com*.

LISTING 13-5 The XAML markup for the FlixPoll user interface.

```
<ListBox x:Name="Questions" Margin="6,243,-6,6" ItemsSource="{Binding
FlixPollQuiz}">
  <ListBox.ItemTemplate>
    <DataTemplate>
      <StackPanel>
        <toolkit:ToggleSwitch Content="No" IsChecked="{Binding Answer,
Mode=TwoWay}" Header="{Binding Question}" Name="toggleSwitch1">
        </toolkit:ToggleSwitch>
      </StackPanel>
    </DataTemplate>
  </ListBox.ItemTemplate>
</ListBox>

<toolkit:ListPicker x:Name="movieListPicker" ItemsSource="{Binding Movies}"
      FullModeHeader="Movies" CacheMode="BitmapCache" Header="Movies"
Margin="12,6,12,451" SelectionChanged="MovieListPicker_SelectionChanged">
  <toolkit:ListPicker.FullModeItemTemplate>
    <DataTemplate x:Name="PickerFullModeItemTemplate">
      <StackPanel Orientation="Horizontal" Margin="16 21 0 20" Background="Blue"
Width="300" Height="110" HorizontalAlignment="Center" VerticalAlignment="Center">
        <TextBlock Text="{Binding Name, Mode=TwoWay}"
HorizontalAlignment="Center" VerticalAlignment="Center" Margin="5"/>
      </StackPanel>
    </DataTemplate>
  </toolkit:ListPicker.FullModeItemTemplate>
  <toolkit:ListPicker.ItemTemplate>
    <DataTemplate x:Name="PickerItemTemplate">
      <StackPanel Orientation="Horizontal" Background="Transparent">
        <TextBlock Text="{Binding Name, Mode=TwoWay}" Margin="12 0 0 0"  />
      </StackPanel>
    </DataTemplate>
  </toolkit:ListPicker.ItemTemplate>
</toolkit:ListPicker>

<TextBox Name="MovieNameTextBox" Text="{Binding Name, Mode=TwoWay}"
Margin="0,100,5,350"></TextBox>
```

Towards the bottom of the XAML, you will see design time code for the ApplicationBar control. By default it is commented out. FlixPoll uses the ApplicationBar control on the Main page. Replace the commented out ApplicationBar control with the following XAML:

```
<phone:PhoneApplicationPage.ApplicationBar>
  <shell:ApplicationBar IsVisible="True" IsMenuEnabled="True">
    <shell:ApplicationBarIconButton IconUri="appbar.sync.rest.png" Text="Sync"
      Click="ApplicationBarIconButton_SyncClick" />
    <shell:ApplicationBarIconButton IconUri="appbar.add.rest.png" Text="New"
      Click="ApplicationBarIconButton_NewClick" />
    <shell:ApplicationBarIconButton IconUri="appbar.save.rest.png" Text="Save"
      Click="ApplicationBarIconButton_SaveClick" />
    </shell:ApplicationBar>
</phone:PhoneApplicationPage.ApplicationBar>
```

This XAML produces a result similar to Figure 13-13.

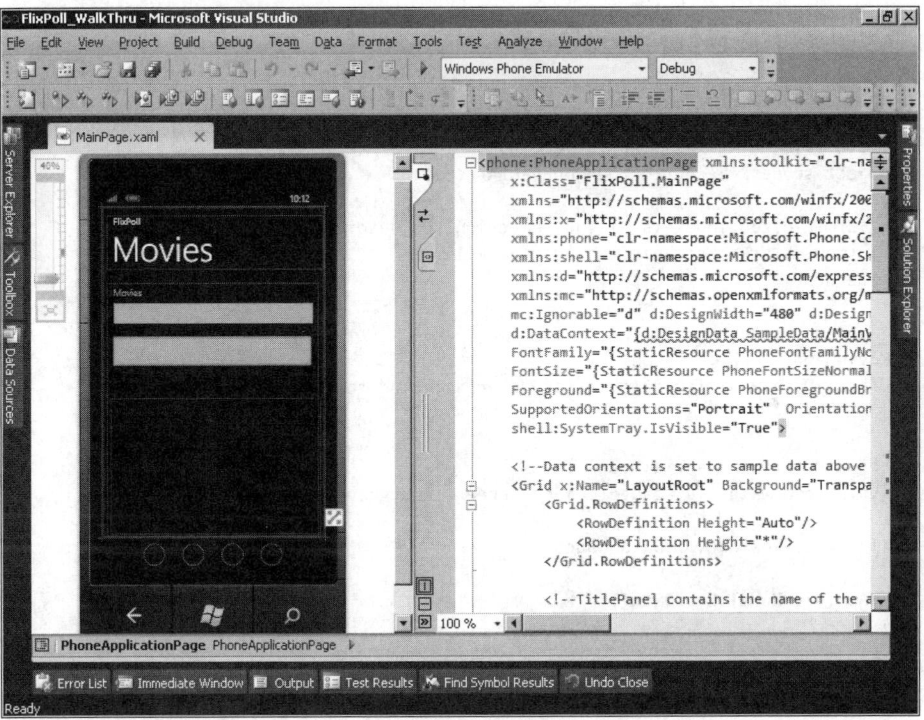

FIGURE 13-13 Design time look at the completed Main page.

Now open the page's code-behind file *MainPage.xaml.cs* and replace its contents with the code shown in Listing 13-6.

LISTING 13-6 Code-behind logic for the FlixPoll UI page.

```
using System;
using System.Windows;
using System.Windows.Controls;

using Microsoft.Phone.Controls;

namespace FlixPoll
{
  public partial class MainPage : PhoneApplicationPage
  {
    // Constructor
    public MainPage()
    {
      InitializeComponent();

      DataContext = App.ViewModel;
      this.Loaded += new RoutedEventHandler(MainPage_Loaded);
    }

    // Handle selection changed on ListBox
    private void MovieListPicker_SelectionChanged
     (object sender, SelectionChangedEventArgs e)
    {
      // If selected index is -1 (no selection) do nothing
      if (movieListPicker.SelectedIndex == -1)
        return;

      // bind the textbox to the movie
      MovieNameTextBox.DataContext =
       (LocalData.MovieTable)movieListPicker.SelectedItem;
    }

    // Load data for the ViewModel Items
    private void MainPage_Loaded(object sender, RoutedEventArgs e)
    {
      if (!App.ViewModel.IsDataLoaded)
      {
        App.ViewModel.LoadData();
      }
    }

    private void ApplicationBarIconButton_SaveClick(object sender, EventArgs e)
    {
      // save changes to the movie's name
      App.ViewModel.SaveMovieToLocalDb();
    }

    private void ApplicationBarIconButton_SyncClick(object sender, EventArgs e)
    {
      App.ViewModel.SyncDone +=
       new EventHandler<SyncDoneEventArgs>(Cloud_UpdateDone);
      App.ViewModel.UpdateToCloud();
    }
```

```
    private void ApplicationBarIconButton_NewClick(object sender, EventArgs e)
    {
      // save the answers and reset the quiz for the next person
      App.ViewModel.NewQuiz
       ((movieListPicker.SelectedItem as LocalData.MovieTable).MovieId);
    }

    // called after upload to cloud has taken place to refresh local db
    private void Cloud_UpdateDone(object sender, SyncDoneEventArgs e)
    {
      // reset the data stored locally.
      App.ViewModel.DeleteResponsesAfterSync();
      App.ViewModel.ResetMoviesAfterSync();

      // show the message box on the UI thread
      Deployment.Current.Dispatcher.BeginInvoke(() =>
      {
        MessageBox.Show("sync is complete");
      });
    }
  }
}
```

This code is relatively minimal and uninteresting, because the main data access code is actually implemented separately (we will get to that code in a moment). In this code-behind file, the constructor sets the *DataContext* property to the *App* class's *ViewModel* property to facilitate data binding. After the constructor, the *MovieListPicker_SelectionChanged* event handler fires when the user taps on a movie in the list, and copies the movie name into the *TextBox* where it can be edited. Next, the *MainPage_Loaded* event handler fires when the page loads (this occurs after the constructor code executes). The code in this method calls the ViewModel's *LoadData* method. Finally, there are three event handers for handling button clicks on the ApplicationBar.

Understanding the Model-View-ViewModel (MVVM) Pattern

The page code is only concerned with navigation and presentation of data; it contains no other logic. Data access and business logic are abstracted away and encapsulated in separate classes as per the popular Model-View-ViewModel (MVVM) pattern implemented by the Windows Phone DataBound Application project template. MVVM is a user interface design pattern that separates concerns among code and relies on data binding as a mechanism for displaying data. In a Windows Phone application, the Model is the data or business logic, the View is the collection of UI pages and visual elements (controls), and the ViewModel is a special class sitting between the View and the Model. The ViewModel exposes properties that the View uses for data binding and also interacts with the Model to process data.

In FlixPoll, *MainPage.xaml* is the View. The entities available via WCF Data Services define the Model. The ViewModels are classes with properties corresponding to fields from the Models; for example, *MovieId* and *Name*. The FlixPoll ViewModels are responsible for converting between entity model types and custom types stored in the local database. The conversion process is discussed a bit later when we talk about querying the local database.

The FlixPoll ViewModels can connect to the service to retrieve and save data. The Windows Phone 7.1 SDK includes a WCF Data Services client library you can use to create a service reference to the *FlixPollDataService* you created earlier. To use the client library you must add a reference to the *System.Data.Services.Client* assembly. The assembly is located under the *Extensions* node of the Assemblies tab in the Add Reference dialog box. The process of creating the service reference for a Windows Phone 7 application is exactly the same as for a Windows desktop application. In Solution Explorer, right-click the *FlixPoll* project and choose Add Service Reference. Then click Discover to find the WCF services in your solution. The *FlixPollDataService* should appear in the Address drop-down list. Take note of the URL as you will use it later when setting up the *App* class. In the Namespace textbox, enter **FlixPollODataService**. This will be the namespace you use in client code to reference the proxy classes that Visual Studio generates for the service. Click OK to create the service reference.

FlixPoll has one ViewModel named *MovieViewModel*, which is the ViewModel used by the Main page. To create the ViewModel class, add a new class to the ViewModels folder named **MovieViewModel**, and supply the code shown in Listing 13-7.

LISTING 13-7 The complete *MovieViewModel* class.

```
using System;
using System.Collections.Generic;
using System.Collections.ObjectModel;
using System.ComponentModel;
using System.Data.Services.Client;
using System.Linq;

namespace FlixPoll
{
  public class MovieViewModel : INotifyPropertyChanged
  {
    private List<LocalData.MovieTable> _movies;
    private List<LocalData.Quiz> _flixPollQuiz;

    public EventHandler<SyncDoneEventArgs> SyncDone;

    public List<LocalData.MovieTable> Movies
    {
      get
      {
        if (this._movies == null)
          this._movies = new List<LocalData.MovieTable>();

        return this._movies;
      }
      set
      {
        if (this._movies != value)
        {
          this._movies = value;
          RaisePropertyChanged("Movies");
        }
```

```
  }
}

public List<LocalData.Quiz> FlixPollQuiz
{
  get
  {
    if (this._flixPollQuiz == null)
      this._flixPollQuiz = new List<LocalData.Quiz>();

    return this._flixPollQuiz;
  }
  set
  {
    if (this._flixPollQuiz != value)
    {
      this._flixPollQuiz = value;
      RaisePropertyChanged("FlixPollQuiz");
    }
  }
}

private void RaisePropertyChanged(string propertyName)
{
  PropertyChangedEventHandler temp = this.PropertyChanged;

  if (temp != null)
    temp(this, new PropertyChangedEventArgs(propertyName));
}

public event PropertyChangedEventHandler PropertyChanged;

public bool IsDataLoaded
{
  get;
  private set;
}

// Get data and display on the page
public void LoadData()
{
  if (MoviesInLocalDb())
  {
    GetMoviesFromLocalDb();
  }
  else
  {
    GetMoviesFromService();
  }

  if (InquiriesInLocalDb())
  {
    GetInquiriesFromLocalDb();
  }
```

```
    else
    {
      GetInquiriesFromService();
    }
    this.IsDataLoaded = true;
  }

  private bool MoviesInLocalDb()
  {
    // see if there are any movies in the local CE db
    using (var flixPollDc =
            new LocalData.FlixPollDataContext(App.DBConnectionString))
    {
      var movies =
          from m in flixPollDc.Movies
          select m.MovieId;

      return (movies.Count() > 0);
    }
  }

  private bool InquiriesInLocalDb()
  {
    // see if there are any questions in the local CE db
    using (var flixPollDc =
            new LocalData.FlixPollDataContext(App.DBConnectionString))
    {
      var inquiries = from i in flixPollDc.Inquiries
              select i.InquiryId;

      return (inquiries.Count() > 0);
    }
  }

  private void GetMoviesFromLocalDb()
  {
    using (var flixPollDc =
            new LocalData.FlixPollDataContext(App.DBConnectionString))
    {
      // populate the movie list
      var movies =
          from m in flixPollDc.Movies
          select m;

      this.Movies = movies.ToList();
    }
  }

  private void GetInquiriesFromLocalDb()
  {
    // create a new quiz. When saved later, we'll add the movie id.
    // this model is bound to the form.
    using (var flixPollDB =
            new LocalData.FlixPollDataContext(App.DBConnectionString))
```

```
    {
      var q =
        from i in flixPollDB.Inquiries
        select new LocalData.Quiz
        { Answer = false,
          InquiryId = i.InquiryId,
          Question = i.Question
        };

      this.FlixPollQuiz = q.ToList();
    }
  }

  public void GetMoviesFromService()
  {
    // create a client context for the service
    var ctx = new FlixPollODataService.FlixPollOnCloudEntities(
                new Uri(App.FlixPollServiceUrl));

    // define the query (deferred execution)
    var q =
        from m in ctx.Movies
        select m;

    // load the movies asynchronously
    var movies = new DataServiceCollection<FlixPollODataService.Movie>();
    movies.LoadCompleted += (o, e) =>
    {
      // Executes when the query completes
      if (e.Error != null)
        throw e.Error;

      // once the data is retrieved, save it to local db
      CacheInLocalDb(movies);

      // once we have it locally, populate the list
      GetMoviesFromLocalDb();
    };

    // begin the async query
    movies.LoadAsync(q);
  }

  private void GetInquiriesFromService()
  {
    // create a client context for the service
    var ctx = new FlixPollODataService.FlixPollOnCloudEntities(
                new Uri(App.FlixPollServiceUrl));

    // deferred execution
    var q =
        from i in ctx.Inquiries
        select i;
```

```
    var inquiry = new DataServiceCollection<FlixPollODataService.Inquiry>(ctx);
    inquiry.LoadCompleted += (o, e) =>
    {
      if (e.Error != null)
        throw e.Error;

      // once the data is retrieved, save it to local db
      CacheInLocalDb(inquiry);

      // once we have it locally, populate the list
      GetInquiriesFromLocalDb();
    };

    // begin the async query
    inquiry.LoadAsync(q);
  }

  private void CacheInLocalDb(IEnumerable<FlixPollODataService.Movie> movies)
  {
    using (var flixPollDc =
            new LocalData.FlixPollDataContext(App.DBConnectionString))
    {
      // first remove old movies from local db
      flixPollDc.Movies.DeleteAllOnSubmit(flixPollDc.Movies);

      // next, cache the movies in local db
      foreach (FlixPollODataService.Movie m in movies)
      {
        LocalData.MovieTable newMovie = new LocalData.MovieTable();
        newMovie.MovieId = m.MovieId;
        newMovie.Name = m.Name;

        flixPollDc.Movies.InsertOnSubmit(newMovie);
      }
      flixPollDc.SubmitChanges();
    }
  }

  private void CacheInLocalDb(IEnumerable<FlixPollODataService.Inquiry>
inquiries)
  {
    using (var flixPollDc =
            new LocalData.FlixPollDataContext(App.DBConnectionString))
    {
      // first remove old questions from local db
      flixPollDc.Inquiries.DeleteAllOnSubmit(flixPollDc.Inquiries);

      // next, cache the questions in local db
      foreach (FlixPollODataService.Inquiry q in inquiries)
      {
        LocalData.InquiryTable newQuestion = new LocalData.InquiryTable();
        newQuestion.InquiryId = q.InquiryId;
        newQuestion.Question = q.Question;
```

```
        flixPollDc.Inquiries.InsertOnSubmit(newQuestion);
      }
      flixPollDc.SubmitChanges();
    }
  }

  public void NewQuiz(int movieId)
  {
    using (var flixPollDc =
            new LocalData.FlixPollDataContext(App.DBConnectionString))
    {
      // determine the next new response id. start from -1 and work backwards
      int newId = (flixPollDc.Responses.Count() > 0 ?
                   flixPollDc.Responses.Min(r => r.ResponseId) :
                   0);

      // insert each response into the SQL CE db
      foreach (LocalData.Quiz quiz in this.FlixPollQuiz)
      {
        newId--;
        LocalData.ResponseTable response = new LocalData.ResponseTable();
        response.Answer = quiz.Answer;
        response.InquiryId = quiz.InquiryId;
        response.MovieId = movieId;
        response.ResponseId = newId;

        flixPollDc.Responses.InsertOnSubmit(response);

        // reset the questions to be asked again
        quiz.Answer = false;
      }
      flixPollDc.SubmitChanges();
    }
  }

  public void SaveMovieToLocalDb()
  {
    using (var flixPollDc =
            new LocalData.FlixPollDataContext(App.DBConnectionString))
    {
      // save any movie name changes
      List<LocalData.MovieTable> changes =
       this.Movies.Where(m => m.MovieChanged == true).ToList();

      if (changes != null && changes.Count > 0)
      {
        foreach (LocalData.MovieTable c in changes)
        {
          var localMovieRecord =
             (from m in flixPollDc.Movies
              where m.MovieId == c.MovieId
              select m).Single();
```

```
        localMovieRecord.Name = c.Name;
        localMovieRecord.UpdateToCloud = true;  // flag the record as changed.
                                    // (will be updated to SQL Azure during sync)

        // reset the ischanged flag so record is not constantly updated
        c.MovieChanged = false;
      }
    }
    // save the changes to local db.
    // changes will be uploaded to SQL Azure during sync process
    flixPollDc.SubmitChanges();
  }
}

private void RaiseSyncDone(SyncDoneEventArgs e)
{
  EventHandler<SyncDoneEventArgs> temp = this.SyncDone;

  if (temp != null)
  {
    temp(this, e);
  }
}

public void UpdateToCloud()
{
  using (var flixPollDc =
          new LocalData.FlixPollDataContext(App.DBConnectionString))
  {
    // Any changed movies stored locally need to be updated to SQL Azure
    var q =
        from m in flixPollDc.Movies
        where m.UpdateToCloud == true
        select m;

    foreach (LocalData.MovieTable localMovieRecord in q.ToArray())
    {
      UpdateMovieInCloud(localMovieRecord);
    }
  }
  SendResponsesToCloud();
}

private void UpdateMovieInCloud(LocalData.MovieTable localMovieRecord)
{
  // create a client context for the service
  var ctx = new FlixPollODataService.FlixPollOnCloudEntities(
          new Uri(App.FlixPollServiceUrl));

  // get the movie from the service
  var q = from m in ctx.Movies
      where m.MovieId == localMovieRecord.MovieId
      select m;
```

```
    var dsq = q as DataServiceQuery<FlixPollODataService.Movie>;

    dsq.BeginExecute(r =>
    {
      var result = r.AsyncState as DataServiceQuery<FlixPollODataService.Movie>;
      var cloudMovieRecord = result.EndExecute(r).Single();

      if (cloudMovieRecord != null)
      {
        if (localMovieRecord.MovieId == cloudMovieRecord.MovieId)
        {
          // Update the movie w/ the new name
          cloudMovieRecord.Name = localMovieRecord.Name;

          ctx.UpdateObject(cloudMovieRecord);

          // push the changes back up to the service
          ctx.BeginSaveChanges(CloudSync_Completed, ctx);
        }
      }
    }, dsq);
  }

  private void SendResponsesToCloud()
  {
    using (var flixPollDc =
            new LocalData.FlixPollDataContext(App.DBConnectionString))
    {
      // We are only storing NEW responses; just insert into the db
      var q =
          from r in flixPollDc.Responses
          select r;

      InsertToCloud(q.ToList());
    }
  }

  private void InsertToCloud(List<LocalData.ResponseTable> responses)
  {
    // create a client context for the service
    var ctx = new FlixPollODataService.FlixPollOnCloudEntities(
              new Uri(App.FlixPollServiceUrl));

    bool hasChanges = (responses.Count() > 0);

    foreach (LocalData.ResponseTable localResponse in responses)
    {
      FlixPollODataService.Response newResponse =
       new FlixPollODataService.Response()
      {
        Answer = localResponse.Answer,
        InquiryId = localResponse.InquiryId,
```

```
          MovieId = localResponse.MovieId
        };
        ctx.AddToResponses(newResponse);
      }

      if (hasChanges == true)
      {
        // async call to insert the new responses. perform insert as a batch
        ctx.BeginSaveChanges(SaveChangesOptions.Batch, CloudSync_Completed, ctx);
      }
    }

    private void CloudSync_Completed(IAsyncResult result)
    {
      var ctx =
        result.AsyncState as FlixPollODataService.FlixPollOnCloudEntities;

      DataServiceResponse response = ctx.EndSaveChanges(result);

      // TODO: a better idea is to use a progress bar and check result for errors
      this.RaiseSyncDone(new SyncDoneEventArgs { Success = true });
    }

    public void ResetMoviesAfterSync()
    {
      using (var flixPollDc =
              new LocalData.FlixPollDataContext(App.DBConnectionString))
      {
        // reset UpdateToCloud flag in local db after updating cloud
        foreach (LocalData.MovieTable m in flixPollDc.Movies)
        {
          m.UpdateToCloud = false;
        }
        flixPollDc.SubmitChanges();
      }
    }

    public void DeleteResponsesAfterSync()
    {
      using (var flixPollDc =
              new LocalData.FlixPollDataContext(App.DBConnectionString))
      {
        // remove responses from local db after updating cloud
        flixPollDc.Responses.DeleteAllOnSubmit(flixPollDc.Responses);
        flixPollDc.SubmitChanges();
      }
    }
  }
}
```

At the top of the code, you can see that the *MovieViewModel* class implements the *INotifyPropertyChanged* interface. This interface is crucial to data binding, as it is responsible for notifying bound UI elements to a change in property values. Alerting bound clients that a value has changed is done in the property's setter method. For example, the *MainPage* binds the *movieListPicker's ItemsSource* property to the *MovieViewModel's* Movies collection. After the *MovieViewModel* loads data, several events occur. First, setting the *Movies* property calls the *RaisePropertyChanged("Movies")* method to raise the *PropertyChanged* event. Then the *movieListPicker* receives a notification that the list of items it is displaying has changed. Finally, the control refreshes the items in its list and displays the updated movies data to the user.

Modifying the *App* Class

Earlier, you saw that the Main page's code-behind sets the *App* class's *ViewModel* property. The *App* class is derived from the *Application* class, which in turn encapsulates a Silverlight application, and provides application-level services such as unhandled exception handling and lifecycle management. The *App* class extends *Application* to provide the starting point for a Windows Phone application.

The *ViewModel* property is a static property on the *App* class, and is provided by the project template so you can implement the MVVM pattern. By default, the *ViewModel* property is specified as *MainViewModel*, which is a class that Visual Studio created automatically as a starting point for MVVM development. FlixPoll uses its own *MovieViewModel* instead of building out *MainViewModel*, so you will now tweak code in the *App* class to change its *ViewModel* property declaration from *MainViewModel* to *MovieViewModel*. In Solution Explorer, find and open the *App.xaml.cs* file, and then look for the following code toward the top of the file:

```
private static MainViewModel viewModel = null;

/// <summary>
/// A static ViewModel used by the views to bind against.
/// </summary>
/// <returns>The MainViewModel object.</returns>
public static MainViewModel ViewModel
{
  get
  {
    // Delay creation of the view model until necessary
    if (viewModel == null)
      viewModel = new MainViewModel();

    return viewModel;
  }
}
```

Replace all instances of *MainViewModel* in this code with *MovieViewModel*, and then save your changes. Then you can delete the unneeded *MainViewModel* class from the project's ViewModels folder.

While you have the *app.xaml.cs* file open, go ahead and make a few more code edits, as shown in Listing 13-8. This defines constants for the service URL and local SQL Server Compact edition (SQL CE) database connection string. Add these constants just after the class declaration.

LISTING 13-8 Constants added to the *App* class for the service URL and local database connection strings.

```
// Define a string constant pointing to FlixPoll WCF Data Services
public static string FlixPollServiceUrl =
 "<Local hosted or Azure Service URL/FlixPollDataService.svc>";

// example when running the app against local hosted WCF Data Service
// http://localhost:49448/FlixPollDataService.svc/

// example when running the app against Windows Azure hosted WCF Data Service
// http://e26a38c22af74bdc825e4306ffeb91dd.cloudapp.net/FlixPollDataService.svc/

// Define a string constant pointing to the phone's local SQL Server CE database
public static string DBConnectionString = "Data Source=isostore:/FlixPoll.sdf";
```

When adding this code, replace the *FlixPollServiceUrl* string with the URL of your locally hosted WCF Data Service (the second example URL above, with the port number replaced by the port number assigned in your development environment). This is the same one you specified when you set the service reference earlier.

Lastly, add the code shown in Listing 13-9 to the end of the constructor method to create the local SQL CE database on the phone when the user runs FlixPoll for the very first time.

LISTING 13-9 Code added to the *App* class constructor initializes the local SQL CE database.

```
// Create the local database if it does not exist.
using (var flixPollDc = new
 LocalData.FlixPollDataContext(App.DBConnectionString))
{
  if (flixPollDc.DatabaseExists() == false)
  {
    flixPollDc.CreateDatabase();
  }
}
```

FlixPoll leverages SQL CE to persist relational data retrieved by the service on the local device. This code, SQL CE, and the role of local device storage are discussed in greater detail shortly. But first, we shift focus back to the *MovieViewModel* class.

Consuming OData on Windows Phone

The *MovieViewModel* class uses virtually the same pattern for calling WCF Data Services that the Windows desktop clients use in Chapter 11. In particular, it uses the Windows Phone 7 version of the WCF Data Services client library to convert LINQ to REST queries into OData URI strings, and materializes the AtomPub response feed returned by the service into client-side entities exposed by the *ViewModel*. The primary difference from the Windows clients in Chapter 11 is that FlixPoll issues asynchronous calls to the service rather than synchronous calls. As we explained in Chapter 11, WCF Data Services supports both synchronous and asynchronous operation, but Windows Phone 7 clients support only asynchronous calls. If you try to execute a synchronous query like the ones in Chapter 11, your code will compile but you will receive an exception with the following message at runtime:

```
Silverlight does not enable you to directly enumerate over a data service query. This is because
enumeration automatically sends a synchronous request to the data service. Because Silverlight
only supports asynchronous operations, you must instead call the BeginExecute and EndExecute
methods to obtain a query result that supports enumeration.
```

In Chapter 11, you learned how to code asynchronous calls between a Silverlight client and WCF RIA Services. Although the code syntax is different with WCF Data Services, you will see that the concept is exactly the same: issue a service request and wait for the response in a callback method. Take a closer look at the *GetMoviesFromService* method in the *MovieViewModel* to see how the FlixPoll client makes asynchronous calls to its WCF Data Services counterpart:

```
public void GetMoviesFromService()
{
  // create a client context for the service
  var ctx = new FlixPollODataService.FlixPollOnCloudEntities(
             new Uri(App.FlixPollServiceUrl));

  // define the query (deferred execution)
  var q =
      from m in ctx.Movies
      select m;

  // load the movies asynchronously
  var movies = new DataServiceCollection<FlixPollODataService.Movie>();
  movies.LoadCompleted += (o, e) =>
  {
    // Executes when the query completes
    if (e.Error != null)
      throw e.Error;

    // once the data is retrieved, save it to local db
    CacheInLocalDb(movies);

    // once we have it locally, populate the list
    GetMoviesFromLocalDb();

  };

  // begin the async query
  movies.LoadAsync(q);
}
```

At the top of the method, the client context is instantiated and stored in the variable *ctx* (notice that the URL pointing to the service is passed into the constructor as a *Uri* object). Then a LINQ to REST query is defined in *q*. This defines the query to retrieve movies from the service, but does not invoke it.

Next, the *movies* collection is defined as a *DataServiceCollection<T>*, where *T* specifies *FlixPollODataService.Movie* as the type of object that will be contained in collection. This type is exposed on the client, and reflects the actual *Movie* entity type defined by the EDM on the service side. Recall that you designated *FlixPollODataService* as the namespace for generated client proxy classes when you established the service reference.

The *DataServiceCollection<T>* class has a *LoadAsync* method that you invoke to kick off the query on the server. With asynchronous behavior, your application does not wait for service operations to complete. Instead, client code can continue executing and the UI remains responsive while service operations run in the background. To allow the client to respond once the service operation is complete, this special collection class also provides a *LoadCompleted* event. This event accepts a function pointer to another method on the client, known as the *callback method.* The callback executes as soon as the service has completed the request. In FlixPoll, this callback function pointer is expressed as a lambda using the => (goes to) syntax, which essentially embeds the event handler inline. Methods defined this way have no name, and are hence often called *anonymous* methods. The (*o, e*) syntax refers to the standard .NET event handler signature, where *o* (object) is the sender (the object raising the event) and *e* contains event arguments that the client can inspect to determine the success or failure of the service call. These arguments are passed into the anonymous callback method when it receives control upon completion of the service operation.

With the context, query, and callback in place, the client calls the service by invoking the *LoadAsync* method on the *movies* collection and passing in the query to execute (defined in *q*). As you learned in Chapter 11, the WCF Data Services client library automatically converts the LINQ to REST query into an OData URI string, and then invokes an *HTTP GET* against the service to run the query. When the service returns the results, the callback method on the client is invoked automatically. The first thing the callback does is raise an exception if the service indicates that an error occurred. Otherwise, the data retrieved from the service is available in the *movies* collection variable, which the callback then stores in the local SQL Server CE database by calling *CacheInLocalDb*. Finally, movie records are retrieved from the local database and displayed on the page by calling *GetMoviesFromLocalDb.* We will explain the innards of that method in a moment, but let's first have a look at some more asynchronous programming techniques in FlixPoll.

When the user taps the Sync button on the Main page, changes stored in the local database are uploaded to the SQL Azure database. The *UpdateMovieInCloud* method is called for each changed movie, and it sends the changes to the data service asynchronously:

```
private void UpdateMovieInCloud(LocalData.MovieTable localMovieRecord)
{
  // create a client context for the service
  var ctx = new FlixPollODataService.FlixPollOnCloudEntities(
              new Uri(App.FlixPollServiceUrl));

  // get the movie from the service
  var q = from m in ctx.Movies
      where m.MovieId == localMovieRecord.MovieId
      select m;

  var dsq = q as DataServiceQuery<FlixPollODataService.Movie>;
```

```
    dsq.BeginExecute(r =>
    {
      var result = r.AsyncState as DataServiceQuery<FlixPollODataService.Movie>;
      var cloudMovieRecord = result.EndExecute(r).Single();

      if (cloudMovieRecord != null)
      {
        if (localMovieRecord.MovieId == cloudMovieRecord.MovieId)
        {
          // Update the movie w/ the new name
          cloudMovieRecord.Name = localMovieRecord.Name;

          ctx.UpdateObject(cloudMovieRecord);

          // push the changes back up to the service
          ctx.BeginSaveChanges(CloudSync_Completed, ctx);
        }
      }
    }, dsq);
  }
```

The first few lines of code set up the context and LINQ query that looks for a movie record in the cloud matching the movie ID of the local changed movie. This is similar to the code in *GetMoviesFromService*, but *UpdateMovieInCloud* now takes a different approach to invoke the query. The *GetMoviesFromService* method used *LoadAsync* and *LoadComplete* with *DataServiceCollection<T>* to load an entire collection asynchronously. This method needs to retrieve just a single entity, so it instead uses *BeginExecute* and *EndExecute* with *DataServiceQuery<T>*. Specifically, it casts the LINQ query to a *DataServiceQuery<FlixPollODataService.Movie>* object in *dsq* and invokes the *BeginExecute* method to start the asynchronous service operation. This method takes two parameters; the first is the callback method (which is coded inline using the lambda syntax as before) and the second is an object that gets passed into the callback method. This is the query object itself (*dsq* in this example), that gets passed along to the callback as the variable *r* (for result). To complete the query, the callback obtains the *AsyncState* property from *r* and passes it in to the *EndExecute* method. The *Single* method is then invoked to obtain the single *Movie* entity. The *Single* method is used to retrieve the one and only one entity returned by the query, and will fail if the query returns multiple (or zero) entities.

Once the callback has obtained the movie from the service, the code simply updates it by setting its *Name* property to the new value in the *Name* property of the local version of this movie record passed in to *UpdateMovieInCloud*. The modified *Movie* entity is then passed to *UpdateObject*, which informs the context to track this entity as changed. Finally, the *BeginSaveChanges* issues an asynchronous service call to update the database in the cloud.

As with *BeginExecute*, the *BeginSaveChanges* method accepts two parameters: one for the callback and one for the context object itself so that it gets passed to the callback. This time, the callback is implemented in a "normal" method called *CloudSync_Completed*, instead of using the lambda approach that implements an anonymous method. We did this merely to help illustrate how lambdas work to define anonymous methods just like ordinary methods. Certainly, the callback could instead have been embedded inline as an anonymous method using a lambda, as you've seen done several times by now. Whether you implement the callback as an anonymous method or not, it is expected to receive the single *IAsyncResult* parameter that is used to "end" the operation. As with *BeginExecute/EndExecute*, the *CloudSync_Completed* callback specified in *BeginSaveChanges* completes the save operation by calling *EndSaveChanges*:

```
private void CloudSync_Completed(IAsyncResult result)
{
  var ctx =
   result.AsyncState as FlixPollODataService.FlixPollOnCloudEntities;

  DataServiceResponse response = ctx.EndSaveChanges(result);

  // TODO: a better idea is to use a progress bar and check result for errors
  this.RaiseSyncDone(new SyncDoneEventArgs { Success = true });
}
```

You are now ready to start developing the part of FlixPoll that stores data locally on the phone.

SQL Server on the Phone

The original Windows 7 Phone OS allows you to store data locally on the device using either Isolated Storage or local resource files. Both of these methods are designed for a specific, non-relational storage scenario. Isolated Storage is appropriate for key/value pair data like application settings, whereas local resource files are useful for embedding images or localized strings into your application. But neither approach is suitable for storing relational data.

Note Phone resources have limited physical storage capacity. Your applications should minimize the amount of data stored on a phone to help conserve resources.

Fortunately, the Windows Phone 7.1 release (codenamed "Mango") introduces a new way for storing data locally on the phone: Microsoft SQL Server Compact edition (SQL CE). With SQL CE, you can create a relational database directly on the device. There are three ways to use SQL CE. The first way is to create the database separately from the phone using the SQL Server Compact Toolbox. The second way is to use the command line utility *ExportSqlCe* to export the database to a file. Using either of these approaches, you can then embed the SQL CE database as a resource into your phone application.

Important If you choose to develop an application by embedding your own SQL CE database as a resource file, you must use SQL Server CE version 3.5 Service Pack 2.

The third way is to programmatically create the database and tables from code executed inside your application. When you create a database this way, it exists as a file stored in isolated storage. FlixPoll creates the database using this "pure code" approach.

LINQ to SQL Strikes Back

Regardless of how you create the SQL CE database, you use LINQ to SQL to access its data. Recall from Chapter 10 that Entity Framework is the preferred .NET data access API, and that the use of LINQ to SQL is discouraged for new development. This remains true for client/server or n-tier multi-user applications that are built over SQL Server. However, for single-user scenarios on a local device (such as a Windows Phone), LINQ to SQL lives on as the preferred data access method for accessing SQL CE.

The LINQ to SQL implementation on Windows Phone does have a few limitations. For one thing, only SQL CE data types are supported. For a complete list of LINQ to SQL features not supported on Windows Phone, visit *http://msdn.microsoft.com/library/hh202872.aspx*.

Leveraging SQL CE as the offline storage mechanism enables FlixPoll to operate while disconnected from a network or the Internet. This is the primary characteristic of any occasionally connected system.

Securing Local Data

By the very nature of their use, mobile client devices typically contain sensitive data. Here are some steps you can take to ensure that information does not fall into the wrong hands if a user's device is lost or stolen:

- Do not hard code connection user names and passwords in the application or config files. This technique is only appropriate for demos and sample code. In practice, *always* prompt the user for connection information upon first use, and be sure to encrypt credentials before storing them on the device.

- SQL Server Compact 3.5 supports data encryption in the device's local database. Use this encryption whenever possible to protect private data from unwanted exposure.

Create the SQL CE Database

Creating a SQL CE database is very straightforward. First add a reference *SQL.Data.Linq*, which is the assembly for LINQ to SQL. The assembly is located under the Assemblies | Framework tab in the Add Reference dialog. You use a LINQ to SQL *DataContext* class to connect to and interact with a SQL CE instance. *DataContext* is responsible for bridging the application's object model with the data in the database. You create a context class for your own entities by inheriting from *DataContext* and exposing tables and columns as properties.

Create a new folder in the *FlixPoll* project named LocalData, and add a new class to the folder named *FlixPollDataContext*. Then implement the class with the code shown in Listing 13-10.

LISTING 13-10 The *FlixPollDataContext* class exposes the SQL CE database for LINQ to SQL.

```
using System;
using System.Data.Linq;

namespace FlixPoll.LocalData
```

```
{
  public class FlixPollDataContext : DataContext
  {
    // Pass the connection string to the base class.
    public FlixPollDataContext(string connectionString)
      : base(connectionString)
    { }

    public Table<MovieTable> Movies;
    public Table<InquiryTable> Inquiries;
    public Table<ResponseTable> Responses;

  }
}
```

The *FlixPollDataContext* class exposes three fields: *Movies*, *Inquiries*, and *Responses*. Each field is of type *Table<T>* type where *T* is a separate class that you will create for each table—*MovieTable*, *InquiryTable*, and *ResponseTable*. These table classes, in turn, are marked with special attributes that define schema information you would typically find in a database table, such as columns, data types, and primary key constraints.

Add a new class named **MovieTable** to the LocalData folder. Then implement the class with the code shown in Listing 13-11.

LISTING 13-11 The *MovieTable* class defines the schema for the *Movie* table in the SQL CE database.

```
using System;
using System.ComponentModel;
using System.Data.Linq;
using System.Data.Linq.Mapping;

namespace FlixPoll.LocalData
{
  // Define the table as a class marked with the [Table] attribute

  [Table]
  public class MovieTable : INotifyPropertyChanged, INotifyPropertyChanging
  {
    public bool MovieChanged { get; set; }

    // Define columns as properties marked with the [Column] attribute

    private int _movieId;

    [Column(IsPrimaryKey = true, IsDbGenerated = false, DbType = "INT NOT NULL",
          CanBeNull = false)]
    public int MovieId
    {
      get
```

```
    {
      return _movieId;
    }
    set
    {
      if (_movieId != value)
      {
        NotifyPropertyChanging("MovieId");
        _movieId = value;
        NotifyPropertyChanged("MovieId");
      }
    }
  }

  private string _name;

  [Column]
  public string Name
  {
    get
    {
      return _name;
    }
    set
    {
      if (_name != value)
      {
        // used to track if update has taken place
        if (this._name != null)
          this.MovieChanged = true;

        NotifyPropertyChanging("Name");
        this._name = value;
        NotifyPropertyChanged("Name");
      }
    }
  }

  private bool _updateToCloud;

  [Column]
  public bool UpdateToCloud
  {
    get
    {
      return _updateToCloud;
    }
    set
    {
      if (_updateToCloud != value)
      {
        NotifyPropertyChanging("IsChanged");
        _updateToCloud = value;
```

```
                NotifyPropertyChanged("IsChanged");
            }
        }
    }

    // Notify the page that a data context property changed
    public event PropertyChangedEventHandler PropertyChanged;

    private void NotifyPropertyChanged(string propertyName)
    {
        if (PropertyChanged != null)
        {
            PropertyChanged(this, new PropertyChangedEventArgs(propertyName));
        }
    }

    // Notify the data context that a data context property is about to change
    public event PropertyChangingEventHandler PropertyChanging;

    private void NotifyPropertyChanging(string propertyName)
    {
        if (PropertyChanging != null)
        {
            PropertyChanging(this, new PropertyChangingEventArgs(propertyName));
        }
    }
  }
}
```

The SQL CE tables are designed to store data downloaded from the service, and so their schema closely matches that of the tables in the *FlixPollOnCloud* database. As you can see, *MovieTable* is an ordinary class decorated with the *[Table]* attribute. This tells LINQ to SQL that the *MovieTable* class represents the schema for creating a table in the database. Within the class, the table's columns are defined as properties marked with the *[Column]* attribute. Notice that the *[Column]* attribute for the *MovieId* property has extra information that identifies it as the primary key.

The code you added earlier to the *App* class (Listing 13-9) creates the database once, the very first time the user launches FlixPoll on their Windows Phone. That code calls the *CreateDatabase* method on the *DataContext* to build the database file and save it in Isolated Storage. The file location is determined from the connection string parameter passed to the *DataContext*'s constructor. The connection string was also added earlier to the *App* class (Listing 13-8), and points to the database file in Isolated Storage:

```
Data Source=isostore:/FlixPoll.sdf
```

SQL CE uses the LINQ to SQL classes you created earlier to create the database. Using Reflection, it looks for the *[Table]* and *[Column]* attributes to determine the database schema. After the call to *CreateDatabase* completes, you will have a new database populated with just schema information—no data.

Note A word about using connection strings on the Windows Phone. The local folder on the phone where the SQL CE database is stored determines the type of the access permitted to the database. SQL CE databases stored in the special *app_data* folder are read-only, whereas those stored in Isolated Storage are read-write. For more information about connection strings for SQL CE on Windows Phone, see *http://msdn.microsoft.com/library/hh202861.aspx.*

Issuing LINQ to SQL Queries Against SQL CE

Retrieving data from SQL CE is accomplished using LINQ to SQL queries. You first create a new instance of *FlixPollDataContext* to issue queries against. Then you issue LINQ queries that get converted dynamically at runtime into the T-SQL statements that execute against SQL CE. The *GetMoviesFromLocalDb* method in the *MovieViewModel* class (Listing 13-7) demonstrates this process. It uses LINQ to SQL to get movie records from the local SQL CE database:

```
private void GetMoviesFromLocalDb()
{
  using (var flixPollDc =
          new LocalData.FlixPollDataContext(App.DBConnectionString))
  {
    // populate the movie list
    var movies =
        from m in flixPollDc.Movies
        select m;

    this.Movies = movies.ToList();
  }
}
```

Running Against a Local WCF Data Service

To enforce this chapter's concepts, the walkthrough thus far has focused just on the *Movie* entity, and you have a partially completed client application at this point. Download the code located at the book's companion website to complete the code for FlixPoll (see the book's "Introduction" for the URL). You need to add the *InquiryTable*, *Quiz*, and *ResponseTable* classes in the LocalData folder and the *SyncDoneEventArgs* class in the project's main folder. Once you have added the remaining code, you can run FlixPoll against your local WCF Data Service. Figure 13-14 shows you what FlixPoll looks like running in the Windows Phone Emulator.

The service is still running locally at this point. Before deploying it to Windows Azure, test the client application for a bit. To select a new movie, tap on the movie name in the *movieListPicker* on the top of the page. Once you select a movie, you can change the movie's title by tapping the movie name in the TextBox. This brings up the keyboard. After you modify a movie name, move off of the *TextBox* control and you will see the name change in the *movieListPicker*. Tap the Save button to save the change to the movie title.

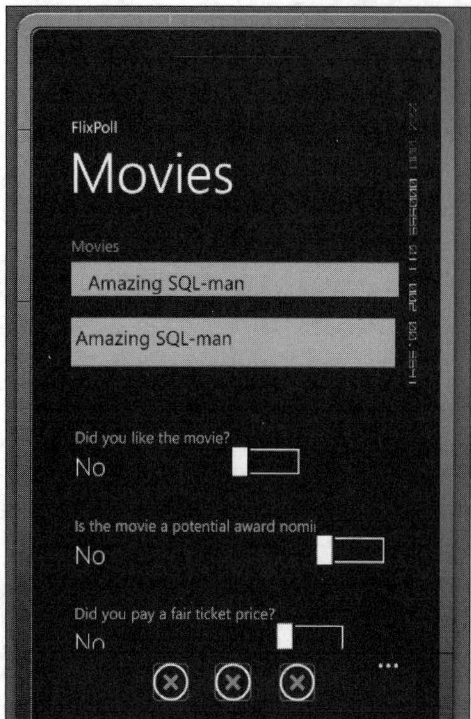

FIGURE 13-14 FlixPoll running in the Windows Phone emulator.

To add responses, you tap each slider control to the right or left, right for "yes," left for "no." After answering all questions, tap the New button to save the responses and refresh the quiz so you can enter new responses. Then click the Sync button to send the data to the SQL Azure database.

The Sync Schedule you set up toward the beginning of this chapter is still in effect. After modifying a few movies and entering some responses, log in to the Windows Azure Management Portal and perform a manual sync job. Then (using either SSMS or SSDT) issue *SELECT* statements against the *Movie* and *Response* tables in both the *FlixPollOnPrem* and *FlixPollOnCloud* databases. The results returned reflect changes to the data as a result of the update from phone to cloud, and the subsequent Sync Job to update the on-premise database.

Deploying to Windows Azure

When satisfied with the locally running service, you are ready to deploy it to Windows Azure. We conclude this chapter by walking you through the steps to set up and host the FlixPoll WCF Data Services in Windows Azure.

In Solution Explorer, right-click on the *FlixPollWindowsAzure* project and choose Package to begin the deployment process. A dialog appears with several options. Accept the default settings and click the Package button. At some point during the deployment process, a Windows Explorer window will open, showing two files in a folder on your local computer. Make a copy of the path to the folder as you will need it in a subsequent step. Close the window after you have copied the folder path.

Log into the Windows Azure Management Portal and click on the New Hosted Service button in the toolbar. The Create A New Hosted Service dialog box appears, shown in Figure 13-15.

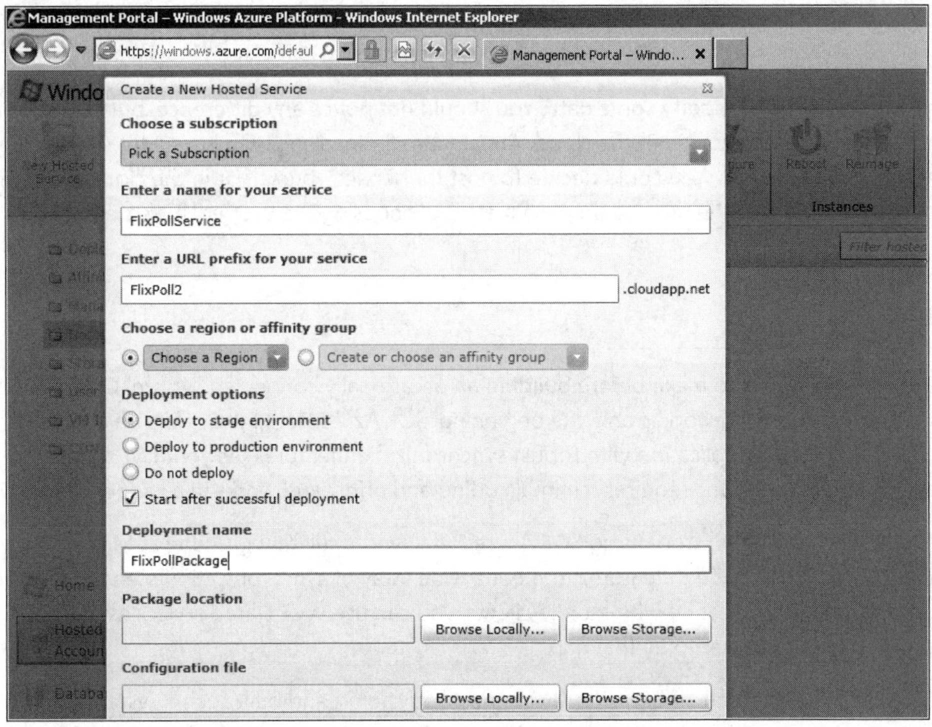

FIGURE 13-15 Creating a hosted service in Windows Azure.

Name your service **FlixPollService**. When entering a URL prefix for the service, remember that the prefix name must be unique. If you enter a value that has already been used by anyone, you will be prompted to enter a different prefix. Select a region from the drop-down list and then select the Deploy To Stage Environment radio button. Ensure that the Start After Successful Deployment checkbox is checked. Then enter the name **FlixPollPackage** for the Deployment Name.

Specify the Package Location file by clicking the Browse Locally button. In the Windows Explorer window that opens, paste the path you copied earlier from Visual Studio when you created the package into the Windows Explorer address bar and press **Enter**. Select the Service Package file and click the Open button. Repeat the same steps to specify the Cloud Service Configuration file. Then click OK to start the deployment.

Now Windows Azure begins to validate the package (if you receive a warning regarding "... a role with only one instance..." you can ignore the warning and continue the deployment). When the deployment successfully completes, the *FlixPollService* will be shown in the management portal with a status of Ready.

That's all it takes is to deploy WCF Data Services for FlixPoll to Windows Azure. Your last step is to configure FlixPoll to run against the hosted service. Copy the DNS name from the portal and then open the *App.xaml.cs* file in the FlixPoll Windows Phone project. Edit the line of code that defines the *FlixPollServiceUrl* constant by pasting in the URL value with the DNS value you copied from the portal. For example:

```
public static string FlixPollServiceUrl =
 "http://e26a38c22af74bdc825e4306ffeb91dd.cloudapp.net/FlixPollDataService.svc/";
```

Run FlixPoll again and modify some data. You should not notice any difference, but FlixPoll is now running against a service hosted in the cloud. Architecturally speaking, you have a lot of flexibility with an application like this. You could decide to host the service yourself or in the cloud. Switching from one environment to the other is simply a matter of choosing the proper URL string.

Summary

You have many decisions to make before building an occasionally connected system. Choosing the right synchronization framework is only the beginning. SQL Azure Data Sync offers an attractive solution for building an application with robust synchronization features. As you have learned in this chapter, SQL Azure Data Sync requires minimal coding and effort and works in a variety of scenarios.

The data synchronization story using SQL Azure Data Sync is still taking shape at Microsoft. Even at this early stage, it packs enough features to meet a wide array of synchronization scenarios. However, until it supports synchronization with mobile clients, you can use WCF Data Services as we've demonstrated in this chapter to fill that gap.

We explored the concepts of occasionally connected systems, and built such a system using SQL Azure Data Sync services coupled with a Windows Phone client and WCF Data Service hosted in Windows Azure. You saw how to build applications for Windows Phone 7 devices that consume REST services and work in both offline and online modes. You also learned how to synchronize data between the cloud and your on-premise databases. With the fundamentals covered in this chapter, you can now extend your business systems with all sorts of new and exciting "occasionally connected" capabilities.

CHAPTER 14

Pervasive Insight

—Andrew Brust

Despite this book's detailed focus on the relational database engine, and transactional use, of Microsoft SQL Server, it's imperative to realize and discuss the product's wide range of business intelligence (BI) capabilities, some of which are arguably the best in the industry. Depending on the edition of SQL Server you purchase, you will have access to some or all of the following services:

- Data Warehousing
- Reporting and data visualization
- Online analytical processing (OLAP)
- Column store, in-memory analytics
- Data Mining
- Extract, Transform and Load (ETL)
- Complex event processing (CEP)
- Master Data Management (MDM)
- Data Quality.

Note We'll cover SQL Server editions, and their included BI feature sets, at the end of this chapter.

Covering these technologies in depth would require a separate book. But even if you are primarily focused on the relational capabilities of SQL Server, it is important to have an understanding of the BI components included with SQL Server and, at a high-level, what each BI component does. In this chapter, therefore, we will give you that information. We will describe each component, provide screenshots that will help make the concepts more concrete, and present those concepts from the context of relational database technology so that you won't feel you need to shift gears too much.

Note Microsoft Press has an excellent book — *Smart Business Intelligence Solutions with Microsoft® SQL Server®* 2008 by Langit, Goff, et al. — that covers much of the SQL Server BI stack in great detail.

Each of the BI components in SQL Server covers part of a larger data strategy, and participates in a full life cycle around the treatment and analysis of data, after that data has been captured by transactional systems. We will present the BI components of SQL Server in a sequence that follows that workflow; that way you can understand each component in the context of the others, as well as in the context of the relational engine. We'll also briefly discuss elements of Microsoft Excel and SharePoint that complement these capabilities and interface with SQL Server BI technologies.

In this chapter, you will learn:

- How SQL Server manages, cleans, and migrates data with Master Data Services, Data Quality Services, and Integration Services.
- The constituent parts of the SQL Server data warehouse platform, including SQL Server Enterprise edition, Fast Track Data Warehouse, and Parallel Data Warehouse edition.
- Data Warehouse terminology.
- The capabilities of SQL Server Analysis Services (SSAS), including its multidimensional, Tabular, and data mining capabilities.
- OLAP, column store, and in-memory database terminology and capabilities.
- Why Data Visualization and Analysis are important and how Power View establishes a new precedent in making these easy and fun.
- How and why SQL Server Reporting Services (SSRS) is a true BI component and not merely an operational reporting tool.
- How Microsoft Office and SharePoint fit into the picture with the BI capabilities of Excel, PowerPivot, Excel Services, and PerformancePoint Services.
- What StreamInsight is, how it fits in with SQL Server, and how it functions as a stand-alone developer tool.
- The range of SQL Server editions, and the BI features of each.

The Microsoft BI Stack: What's It All About?

The point of BI is to move beyond the tactical and operational aspects of databases, which involve the fast collection, updating, and retrieval of data. BI aims to take the "raw material" that is the data collected from such activities and refine it into the "finished goods" of information about the data:

summaries, trends, patterns, visualizations, and even predictions. These artifacts can help drive business decisions, and in fact, BI used to be called "Decision Support."

Doing this kind of work requires making sure the data is clean and consistent; transforming its schema to be more optimized for querying; having tools that visualize summarized views of the data; and using specialized database engines that make analytical queries fast and painless. The Microsoft BI stack, which is anchored by SQL Server, aims to provide you with all of these. Let's discuss how, by looking at each component in the stack.

Master Data Services

It's a bit unorthodox to begin our discussion of SQL Server BI with the Master Data Services (MDS) component, because it was only added to SQL Server in the 2008 R2 release. Often it's easier to talk about older components first and then sketch out the nuances that make the newer components useful and necessary. Nonetheless, since we're covering the BI stack in logical workflow order, MDS is the right place to start. MDS is Microsoft's entry into the area of BI known as Master Data Management (MDM), which concerns itself with the maintenance of authoritative reference data like lists of customers, store locations, product categories, personnel titles, and even more generic entities like countries, states, and provinces, or honorifics like Mr., Mrs., and Ms.

If you think about it from an application database perspective, master data tends to be re-created for each application, resulting in various tables appearing in numerous databases that contain identical, or nearly identical, data. And it's the *nearly* identical part that is the problem, because when it comes time to look at data from more than one of these databases in a consolidated way, slight misalignments in master data can make the consolidation process difficult.

For example, how could users drill down revenue numbers and sales projections by store location if the forecasting system and the order system don't work form the same list of stores, or if they do but use different key values for the same location? MDM aims to solve this problem by providing tools and a repository for authoring, refining, and storing the authoritative set of master data needed in an organization. In the SQL Server arena, Master Data Services is the MDM tool supplied for this job.

MDS allows you to define *Models*, which contain related sets of master data, and can accommodate multiple versions of each model in the repository. It allows you to define *Entities*, representing classes of master data (like customers or countries), the *Attributes* of those entities (essentially the entity's columns, if you think of an entity as a table), and *Attribute Groups*, which are subdivisions of the attributes used to make the latter easier to manage and secure.

Once your Entities are defined, you can go about defining their *Members*, the actual Entity data. Members can be arranged in *Hierarchies*, which may be *Derived*, where a Member of an Entity is the parent (via an assigned attribute value) of one or more members of another Entity (e.g., specific product categories might be parents of specific products); *Explicit*, where parents are manually entered because they are not members of a defined entity; or *Recursive*, where one member of an entity is the parent of one or more other members of that same entity (e.g., employees have other employees who are direct reports, and those employees have direct reports of their own). Entities may also belong to *Collections*, which are arbitrarily named sets of members that may often be reported on together.

In most organizations, there is governance around MDM work; not just anyone can add and modify master data. As such, MDS offers its own role-based security mechanism that manages *Users*, *Groups*, and *Permissions*. It also allows for the definition of *Business Rules* that can be used to validate master data entries, supply default attribute values, send email notifications, and more. MDS also has *Workflow* facilities to ensure master data tasks are properly vetted and approved.

SQL Server MDS came to Microsoft through the acquisition of a company called Stratature, which was an independent software vendor selling a stand-alone ASP.NET application for MDM. Stratature's application, after some rebranding and tweaks, became MDS in SQL Server 2008 R2 and remained an ASP.NET web application. For SQL Server 2012, the application was rewritten in Silverlight, though it still bears a strong resemblance to its ASP.NET predecessor. It is shown in Figure 14-1.

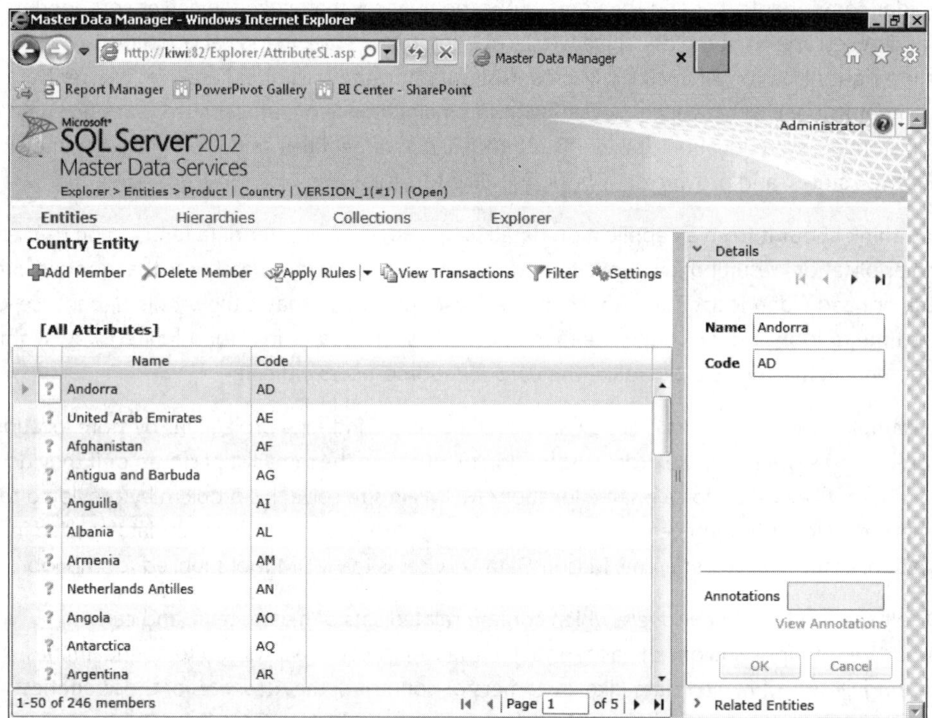

FIGURE 14-1 Editing members of the *Country* entity in the Master Data Services Silverlight client.

Also new in SQL Server 2012 is an Excel add-in for MDS that, while not as fully featured as the stand-alone Silverlight application, provides a lot of functionality and allows master data to be entered and edited right in Excel worksheets. To be frank, the Excel interface is much easier to use than the stand-alone Silverlight application, and we would recommend it. That said, there are certain tasks that can only be carried out in the Silverlight client.

The Excel add-in is shown in Figure 14-2. The add-in's Master Data ribbon tab is highlighted, as are the model and connection information, the member data area, the Master Data Explorer task pane, and the ribbon group for the integrated Data Quality Services functionality.

Note Data Quality Services, and its integration with MDS, will be discussed next.

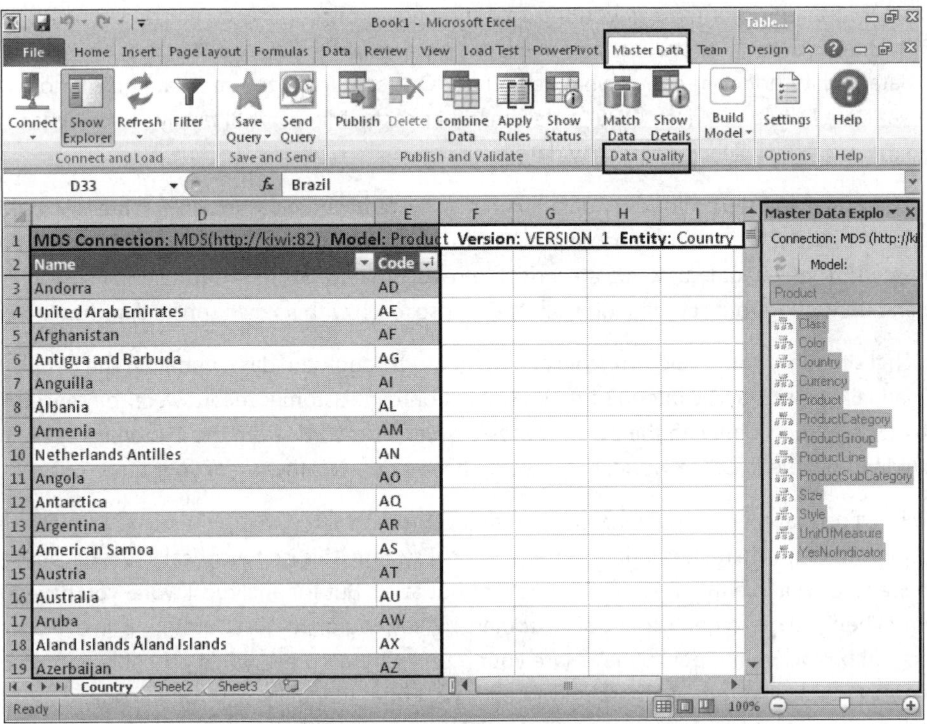

FIGURE 14-2 Editing members of the *Country* entity in the Master Data Services add-in for Excel.

Another way to access MDS is through its Web Services interface. Although not widely implemented this way, the Web API allows individual line-of-business applications to communicate with MDS in order to retrieve, and update, master data. The API also allows third-party applications to present alternate user interfaces on top of the MDS engine. One product that does this is MiDaS from VisionWare (*http://www.visionwareplc.com*).

In addition to entering member data in the stand-alone MDS application and in Excel via the add-in, member data can also be imported into MDS, and it can be exported as well. These are crucial functions. Most master data is not established via manual entry into an MDM system, but rather by importing that data from existing transactional systems. Likewise, although the Web Services are convenient, many transactional systems will most easily be fed authoritative master data by having that data exported into the application's own database tables which store data for those same entities.

MDS has not been widely adopted by Microsoft customers. That may start to change with SQL Server 2012, given the Excel add-in as an alternate user interface and the integration of MDS with a brand-new Microsoft BI component: Data Quality Services.

Data Quality Services

MDM and MDS are all about preventing the problem of inconsistent, inaccurate, or erroneous master data. But what if you're in a situation (and many people are) where you already have a bunch of master data and it's not clean? Then what do you do? One solution is to use a data quality tool like SQL Server Data Quality Services (DQS), a new member of the Microsoft BI family, which aims to manage the process of cleaning up "dirty data."

There can be many causes for dirty data. Imagine a system where a *Customers* table is littered with variants of the same company name like "Contoso," "Contoso Inc.," Contoso, Inc," and "Contoso Incorporated." Then imagine that you are writing a report that needs to group sales by customer, and so you end up getting four separate groups for Contoso, each with its own subtotal, rather than one.

In such a situation, you would probably end up going through the data, updating the *Orders* table (manually or with a SQL query) so that a single Contoso customer record were referenced consistently, and then eliminate the other Contoso customer records from the *Customers* table. Doing this wouldn't be the end of the world, but it would hardly be a worthy use of your time.

Now imagine that there are other records in that *Customers* table where the company name is blank, or has random characters in it. In a transactional system, this isn't a critical issue, because those customer entries would either be selected rarely or not at all. But for analytical work, you have a problem: When you go to get a count of customers by, say, region, or just determine an average, your numbers will be off. So in order to make sure your reports are accurate, you'd probably go through the *Customers* table and remove these unwanted rows, either manually or through code, if the number and type of bad rows warranted. Again, this is tedious work that drains productivity.

Data Quality software is designed to automate these data cleansing tasks, and DQS is Microsoft's new BI component in this category. It de-dupes and cleanses based on a combination of supplied information and artificial intelligence functionality, and it lets you review the changes it suggests before they are committed.

In DQS, you define *Knowledge Bases* and then create data quality *Projects* that use them. Knowledge Bases contain *Domains*, which in turn have *Rules* (which specify patterns and formats that the data must adhere to) and *Term-Based Relations* (which handle corrections/replacements of names or terms, for example replacing all occurrences of "Corp." to "Corporation"). Domains also have *Domain Values* (valid domain data) and have their own Reference Data which can be sourced from a number of outlets, including Microsoft's Azure DataMarket. Knowledge Bases also contain *Matching Policies* which in turn consist of *Matching Rules*: criteria for how well various domain values should match inspected data in order for the latter to be considered matches.

Data Quality Projects split into two types: *Cleansing* and *Matching*. Cleansing projects evaluate new data based on the logic in a Knowledge Base. The cleansing process then judges each row of data and will mark many rows as *correct* or *invalid* or *new*. Other rows may be changed and marked as *suggested* or *corrected* depending on the confidence level assigned to the change by DQS. Matching projects perform de-duplication, using the matching policy of a Knowledge Base to identify (and eliminate) exact and approximate matches.

DQS has both a server component and a (desktop) client application. The client application, shown in Figure 14-3, allows you to create Knowledge Bases, as well as Projects.

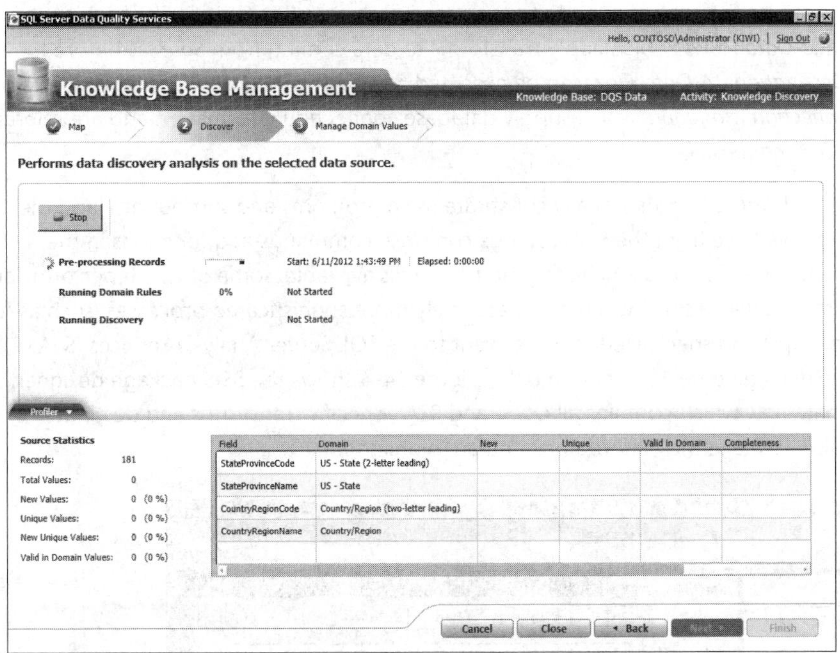

FIGURE 14-3 The Data Quality Service client, during a data discovery analysis operation in a Knowledge Base.

DQS can be used on its own to perform its data quality duties as a discrete process. But it can also be integrated with MDS and with SQL Server Integration Services (SSIS—which we will discuss in the next section). In other words, instead of creating discrete Cleansing and Matching projects in the DQS client, DQS can be called upon in an embedded fashion to perform cleansing and matching against MDS Entity Member data or a dataset passed to it in an SSIS package.

Integration Services

SSIS is Microsoft's Extract, Transform, and Load (ETL) tool. It offers a rich development environment for taking source datasets and running them through various processes of sorting, filtering, reshaping, and testing, followed by deployment of the modified data to a destination.

ETL becomes useful in a number of scenarios. For example, automated, unattended processing of flat files into a database, or periodic replication of data from one transactional system to another. You can also use SSIS to run administrative tasks, for example database backups, processing of Analysis Services cubes, or even data quality checks, as discussed in the previous section.

But in the realm of BI, the primary use for ETL is the transfer of data from a transactional system into a data mart or data warehouse. This requires not just copying the data, but also changing its structure from a normalized design to one conformed to a star schema, something that we'll discuss in the next section.

SSIS packages can be thought of as coded programs. They consist of *Control Flows* which perform *Tasks*, and *Data Flows*, which apply transforms to data coming from *Sources* before they are dispatched to *Destinations*. A *Data Flow* can be executed as a *Task*, within the *Control Flow*. Packages also contain *Connection Managers* which supply database connection information and are referenced by *Sources* and *Destinations*.

Control Flows and *Data Flows* essentially constitute main programs and subroutines, and the various transforms available from the SSIS Toolbox comprise commands and functions in the programming "language." There is a rich array of transforms available, some of which perform very mechanical operations (like a sort), whereas others apply more sophisticated processes (such as fuzzy grouping and lookups) and specialized tasks relevant to the SQL Server Analysis Services (SSAS) components (like managing new dimension data). Figure 14-4 shows the SSIS package designer while editing a data flow which contains all DQS- and SSAS-specific transforms and destinations. The transforms are also visible in the SSIS Toolbox and are highlighted.

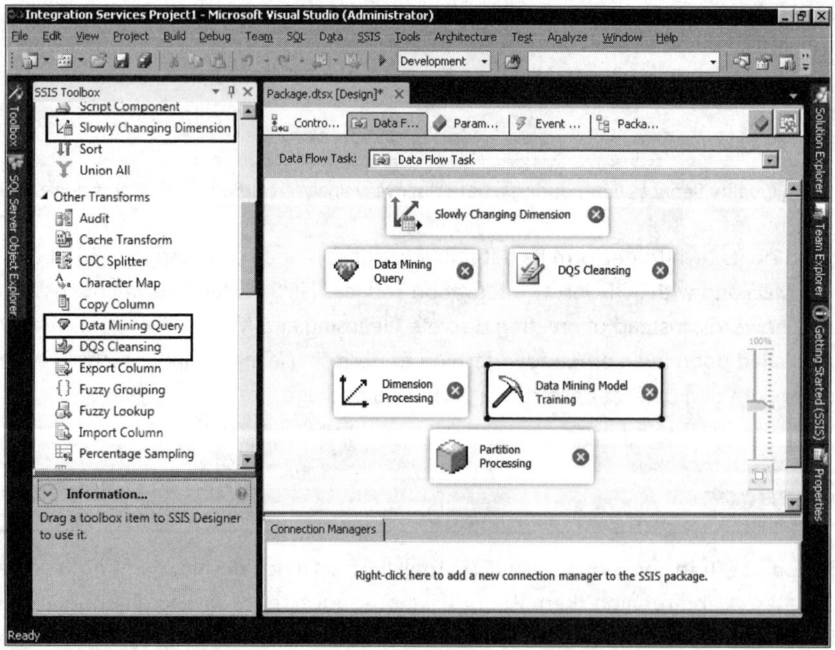

FIGURE 14-4 The SSIS designer, while editing a Data Flow task with various BI-specific transforms and destinations.

SSIS is a specialty in and of itself. It is a rich tool, with many optimization points, and it competes directly (and favorably) with expensive stand-alone ETL products. Each transform offers an array of configurable options, through elaborate tabbed dialogs. As if that weren't enough, the notion of SSIS as a programming language can be taken beyond its metaphorical sense: a Script component (which can serve as a Source, a Destination, or a Transform), allows you to write code in Visual Basic .NET or C# to produce data, consume data, or perform transform tasks, based on advanced computations, executed through imperative code.

In the BI workflow, SSIS plays a crucial role in moving data out of transactional databases and into analytical ones. It serves this function during the initial build-out of the latter, but SSIS is not relegated to that one-off role. Analytical databases need to be kept in sync with their transactional source systems, with as little latency as possible, and SSIS can be indispensable in keeping those operational ETL tasks running smoothly. It is a very important component in the Microsoft BI stack.

SQL Server RDBMS, Fast Track DW, and SQL Server PDW

It may strike you as odd that, as we're well into our coverage of the Microsoft BI stack, we mention the SQL Server Relational Database Management System (RDBMS) itself. We do so because while the primary application of the SQL Server RDBMS is as a transactional database, it is also an excellent data mart and data warehouse solution. Before we explain why, let's define what these terms actually mean.

Data Marts and Data Warehouses

The purpose of both data marts and data warehouses is to provide consolidation points for disparate systems, reconcile their data structures, unify their data, and allow queries across the universe of transactions. There's no hard and fast definition that distinguishes a data mart from a data warehouse, other than the relative criterion that the latter is bigger than the former. A good rule of thumb, however, is that data marts tend to be more departmental in scope and more ad hoc in construction and design. Data warehouses tend to be enterprise-wide and all-encompassing and should be very carefully and formally designed, in order to be properly factored and fully accommodating (insofar as possible) of all data that is enterprise-wide in relevance.

Data marts and data warehouses differ from transactional databases not just in their purpose, but in their structure. The highly normalized schemas that are the basis of transactional databases work very well for operations oriented around retrieving and writing single rows of data, or small sets of rows. The almost obsessive imperative of avoiding repeated information and factoring related information out into separate tables makes for efficiency in storage, and it's both logical and elegant. But when it comes time to query and aggregate data across numerous related tables, the number of joins that may be required in a single query quickly becomes impractical. So too does the need to scan through so many rows where the granular detail is at the level of a transaction.

The Star Schema

It is for this reason that data marts and data warehouses are typically structured using a so-called *star schema*. In this configuration, designers determine the numerical columns that need to be analyzed (known as the *measures*, e.g., sales), and the categories these will need to be analyzed across (known as *dimensions*, e.g., time, geography, account manager, distributor, etc.). Designers also need to determine the "grain" at which measures should be stored. For example, rather than storing sales numbers down to the level of an individual transaction or line item, you may only care to know the total sales per day, zip code, account manager, and distributor. In other words, even before your queries aggregate anything, your mart or warehouse already stores the data at a grain that involves some small amount of aggregation.

Once these design decisions are made, the mart or warehouse schema is designed in such a way that all measure data is placed in a single table (called the *fact table*) and each dimension is placed in its own table. The fact table contains foreign keys to link to the dimension tables at the level of the grain, and these serve as the primary keys for the dimension tables. Dimension tables will contain a denormalized view of each of the hierarchical levels in a dimension. So, for example, a geography dimension table's primary key would be at the level of postal code, but each row might contain the corresponding city, state/province, and country. Therefore the same city, state/province, and country names would appear repeatedly. Dimensions can be defined over a set of normalized tables instead (one table per hierarchical level), but typically the single denormalized table approach is used instead. When the normalized approach is used, the dimension is said to follow a *snowflake schema*, rather than a star schema.

This approach to building an analytical database using relational technology is effective, clever, and popular. It is also problematic in certain ways. When performing queries with multiple dimensions at aggregated levels (e.g., sales by account manager, country, fiscal quarter, and some distributor grouping), SQL Server must perform a sometimes complex *star join* (so named because it joins tables in a star schema formation), and must use a *GROUP BY* clause in order to do it. These can be expensive queries on their own, but having to perform a number of them iteratively can really become taxing on the RDBMS engine.

SQL Server Data Warehouse Appliances

Microsoft has several special-purpose architectures and technologies, both within and beyond the relational database realm, to optimize dimensional query workloads. One approach prescribes building out SQL Server infrastructure using optimized processing, network and storage architectures, and packaging up all the hardware and software, pre-tuned and configured, as an appliance. Some of Microsoft's OEMs, like Dell and HP, sell such turnkey SQL Server-based data warehouse appliances under the Fast Track Data Warehouse moniker. Customers can acquire these appliances through Microsoft Fast Track partners who may further tune them. The architectures are published, allowing partners and customers to build them out on their own, but the labor and expertise involved in their configuration can be significant, so the appliances may offer compelling value.

Another appliance-based approach involves a relatively new addition to the SQL Server product family: SQL Server Parallel Data Warehouse (PDW) edition. SQL PDW is based on a data warehousing approach called Massively Parallel Processing (MPP). The MPP approach involves aggregating a number of SQL Server instances together in a cluster and distributing the query processing workloads amongst them.

When queries are sent to PDW, it dispatches subqueries to nodes in the cluster with each subquery scoped to a subset of the overall data to be queried. The node-level result sets are then merged into a single result set that is returned to the client. The subqueries are carried out in parallel, allowing the overall query to execute much more quickly than if a conventional SQL Server instance were to execute it. The architecture of SQL Server PDW is illustrated in Figure 14-5.

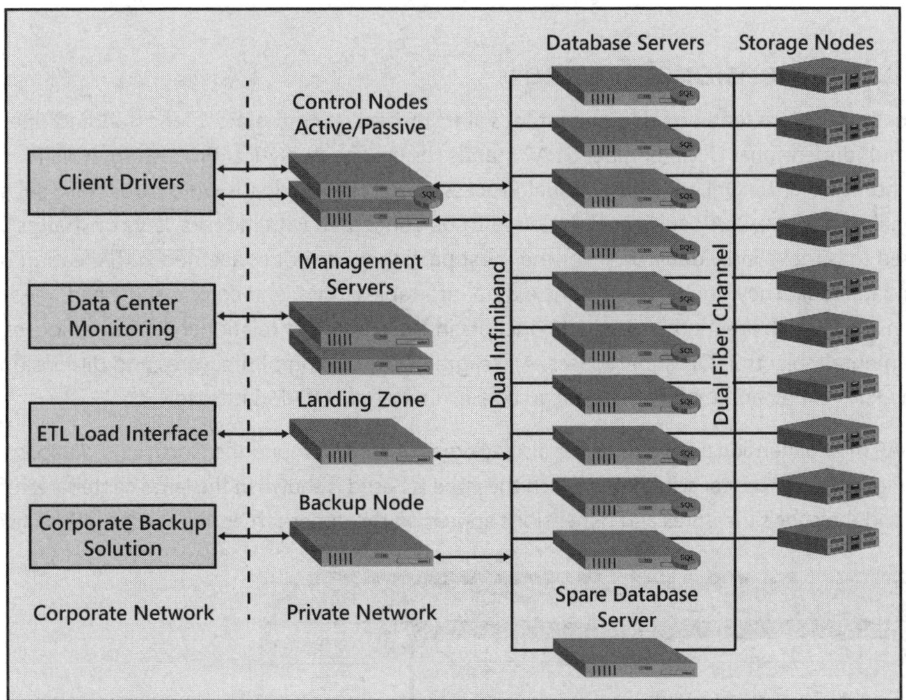

FIGURE 14-5 Architecture diagram for SQL Server Parallel Data Warehouse edition.

In addition, the same sorts of CPU-, networking-, and storage-optimized architectures used by Fast Track are employed by PDW and the product is sold as an appliance, assuring well-executed configuration and installation.

PDW is not cheap, and it's not the only MPP product out there. But it is highly competitive with the other MPP products on the market, both in performance and price. For data warehouses in the hundreds-of-terabytes scale, PDW offers a hugely powerful and effective SQL Server–based data warehouse solution.

Analysis Services

As innovative and well performing as the Fast Track and PDW approaches are, they are still nonetheless based on the idea of using star schemas to repurpose relational databases to perform dimensional queries and take on analytical workloads. Aggregations still need to be performed with T-SQL's limited aggregation functions and *GROUP BY* construct, performing often very complex joins. Although it's impressive that optimized CPU/networking/storage strategies make such queries feasible, the fact remains that relational databases really were not designed with these workloads in mind. So what if SQL Server offered *another* database engine that were? Enter OLAP and SSAS.

The Multidimensional Engine

SSAS actually has more than one engine, but let's start by discussing the most longstanding one: its basic multidimensional OLAP engine. OLAP stands for OnLine Analytical Processing, which distinguishes it from the OnLine Transactional Processing (OLTP) workloads which are the sweet spot of relational databases. OLAP engines don't need to be concerned with indexes, key constraints, or the need to retrieve individual rows. For the most part, they are not concerned with creating or updating data at all. They don't even organize data into tables, rows, and columns! Instead, measures and dimensions, which are merely abstract concepts in the context of relational data warehouses, are the fundamental objects in OLAP databases. A like-grained grouping of measures and dimensions coexist in OLAP *cubes*, and multiple cubes can coexist in a single OLAP database.

The SSAS multidimensional cube designer displaying a cube built around the Northwind database is shown in Figure 14-6. The star schema on which the cube is based is shown in the large center area of the designer, and the cube's measures and dimensions appear on the upper-left and lower-left, respectively.

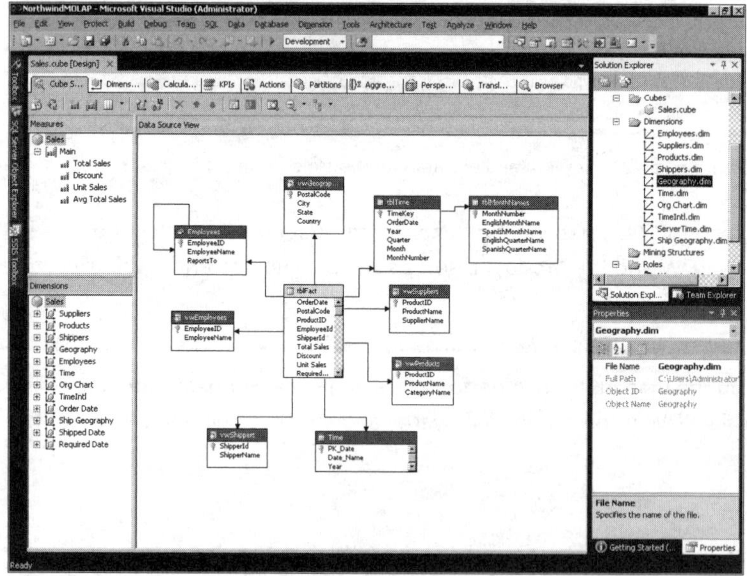

FIGURE 14-6 The SSAS multidimensional cube designer.

With such a structure in place, the whole notion of joining across tables and grouping rows is gone, as that work takes place only when the cube is built or updated, not when it is queried. Instead, SSAS queries simply specify the necessary measures and the dimensional levels across which the measures should be aggregated. Queries can also be expressed across more than two axes. So, conceptually, instead of returning data in a structure representing an individual spreadsheet, SSAS can return a structure representing a workbook (that is, a collection of spreadsheets each in its own tab), a folder (with a collection of such workbooks), a drive (with a collection of such folders), and so forth.

SSAS has its own query language called MDX (which stands for MultiDimensional eXpressions). MDX is optimized for dimensional queries, and offers an almost dizzying array of functions that are far superior to the relatively limited set of aggregating and analytic functions in SQL. Analysis Services is optimized for aggregating during query time, but it also can pre-calculate certain aggregations before queries even take place. This is achieved through the creation of aggregations in, and knowledge of the hierarchical relationships within, the cube. For example, imagine a cube had a geography dimension with postal code as the grain, but that:

- The cube was configured to recognize the natural, hierarchical relationships between postal code, city, state/province, and country.
- The cube also stored aggregations of sales by state/province.

These settings and aggregations would allow the cube to return sales at the state/province level without having to aggregate the sales for all postal codes in each city and all cities in each state. Beyond that, if sales at the country level were needed, SSAS would know that it could derive these values by summing the sales for all states/provinces in each country and since these would be pre-aggregated, it would not need to aggregate anything at the lower levels of city or postal code.

These sorts of optimizations make analytical queries run very quickly on SSAS. Aggregations can be built algorithmically, or built based on the degree to which they would benefit logged queries. Aggregations can also be created manually, although that is a feature geared to very advanced SSAS users.

SSAS cubes must be periodically processed, in order to be updated with any data in the data warehouse that is new or changed since the cube was last processed (or first built). Cubes are usually partitioned so that processing, which can be time-consuming, need be applied only to a physically small partition of the cube.

PowerPivot and SSAS Tabular Mode

The release of SQL Server 2008 R2 brought with it a product called PowerPivot, which runs on desktop PCs in the form of an Excel add-in, and runs as a shared server within SharePoint. This may sound immaterial to Analysis Services, but that's actually not the case at all. Although PowerPivot executes separately from standard Analysis Services, it is nonetheless based on SSAS technology, and the SharePoint version of PowerPivot must actually be installed from the SQL Server installation media. That technology uses a different storage technology than do "conventional" SSAS cubes, but with the release of SQL Server 2012, that same storage model becomes available (as an option) on SSAS itself.

The new storage engine, called VertiPaq, is part of SQL Server's family of xVelocity in-memory technologies, and is a *column store*–type database engine (Chapter 15 covers xVelocity in-memory technologies in detail). Column stores organize their data such that values of a given column are stored together rather than all the values in a row being stored together. For BI, this works well, since most analytical queries end up aggregating over one or, at most, a few columns, and adding their values is faster when the values for other columns don't have to be skipped over during aggregation. In addition, storing column values in proximity makes for high compression rates, since values of a column are often close, at least in order of magnitude. High compression rates, in turn, allow databases of a reasonable size to be placed in memory, and xVelocity in-memory technologies exploit that strategy. Querying an in-memory database is extremely fast, and avoids the need to create aggregations, as must be done with conventional cubes.

The PowerPivot Excel add-in supplies its own client window, which is shown in Figure 14-7. Three explicit measures and one key performance indicator (KPI) are highlighted at the bottom, as are the small buttons available to switch between the Data View mode (pictured) and the Diagram View mode (more similar to what's displayed in Figure 14-6).

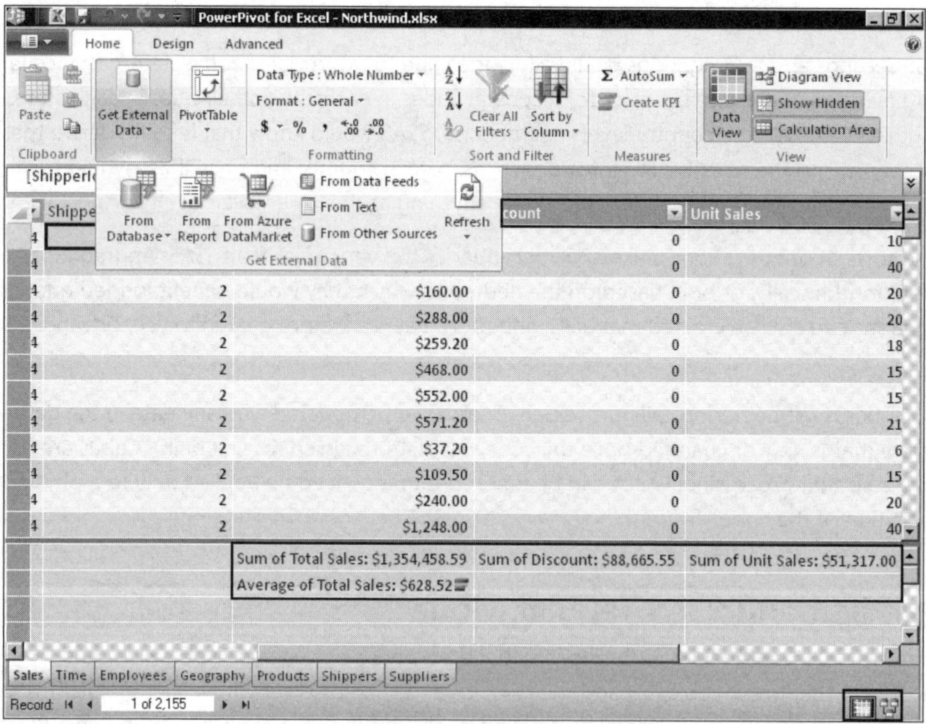

FIGURE 14-7 The PowerPivot client window, in Data View mode.

In the 2008 R2 timeframe, the conventional multidimensional (OLAP) mode was the only one available in the standard SSAS product. Databases of the "BI Semantic Model" (BISM) type—that is, VertiPaq/xVelocity column store–based models—were only available through PowerPivot. In SQL Server 2012, BI Semantic Models can be created in SSAS as well. When SSAS maintains BI Semantic Models, it is said to be operating in "Tabular" mode, so-named because the BI Semantic Model explicitly references its constituent relational tables, rather than measures and dimensions per se.

Figure 14-8 shows the SSAS Tabular mode designer; note that although it is hosted in Visual Studio, it bears a strong resemblance to the PowerPivot client. The Formula bar and Data View/Diagram View controls (highlighted) are essentially the same in both environments. A special extra toolbar and menus (also highlighted) replace the PowerPivot client window's ribbon. Unlike with PowerPivot, SSAS BI Semantic Models feature a DirectQuery mode, which allows their source databases, instead of the column store model itself, to be queried directly. This mode can be turned on or off (it is off by default) using a Properties window setting which is highlighted as well.

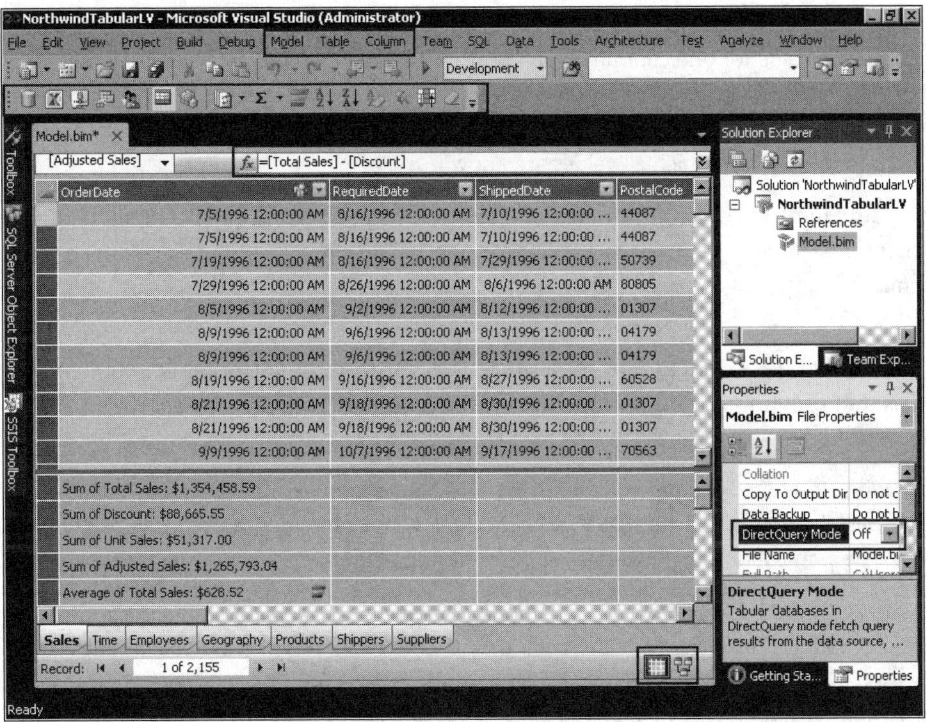

FIGURE 14-8 The SSAS Tabular designer.

When an SSAS instance is installed, it must be configured in either multidimensional mode *or* Tabular mode. If you wish to have both multidimensional and Tabular mode SSAS databases on the same machine, you will need to install two instances of SSAS (for example, the default instance and a named instance) with one instance configured in multidimensional mode and the other in Tabular mode.

Like PowerPivot, SSAS Tabular mode supports the use of a new expression syntax called DAX (Data Analysis eXpressions), which uses an Excel-like set of functions for analytical query. PowerPivot and SSAS Tabular models also support MDX, allowing existing SSAS client applications to query PowerPivot models on SharePoint and Tabular models in SSAS (PowerPivot models on local machines can only be queried by Excel).

In the Enterprise edition of SQL Server 2012, an implementation of xVelocity in-memory technologies for the *relational* engine also exists. Although the full BISM architecture is not involved, creating a special "Columnstore" index on a SQL Server table does in fact create an xVelocity column store in the background. Chapter 15 discusses this and other aspects of xVelocity technologies in more detail.

Data Mining

In addition to its OLAP/BISM capabilities, SSAS has its own elaborate data mining engine. This engine can examine a body of data and create statistical models (using various algorithms) that can be used to predict a value for one column given known values for the others. These predictions can be delivered within result sets generated from specially formulated SQL queries. The predictions and models are based on linear regression and other analytical methods that generalize the observed correlations in the data for which all values are known.

Mining structures, which in turn contain one or more mining models, can be added to SSAS multidimensional models. Typically each mining model within a mining structure will use a different algorithm.

Tip Sometimes it's advantageous for a single mining structure to contain multiple mining models that use the same algorithm, but with different parameter settings.

The mining structure designer is shown in Figure 14-9, with an existing Decision Trees algorithm-based model displayed. The viewer shows how the various data used to train the model splits into data populations, then splits again into subpopulations, and so on.

Also known by the names *predictive analytics* and *machine learning,* data mining can be used to optimize promotional mailings, or as the engine for e-commerce upsell/cross-sell facilities, and can even be used in medical applications, based on examined data around treatment efficacy, and so forth. SSAS data mining is very neat technology and is relatively easy to use, especially with the Data Mining add-in for Excel. Unfortunately, SSAS data mining has had very little investment since the SQL Server 2005 version of the engine was released. A company called Predixion Software, founded by a former leading member of the SSAS Data Mining team, has products which build on top of SSAS data mining and extend its capabilities.

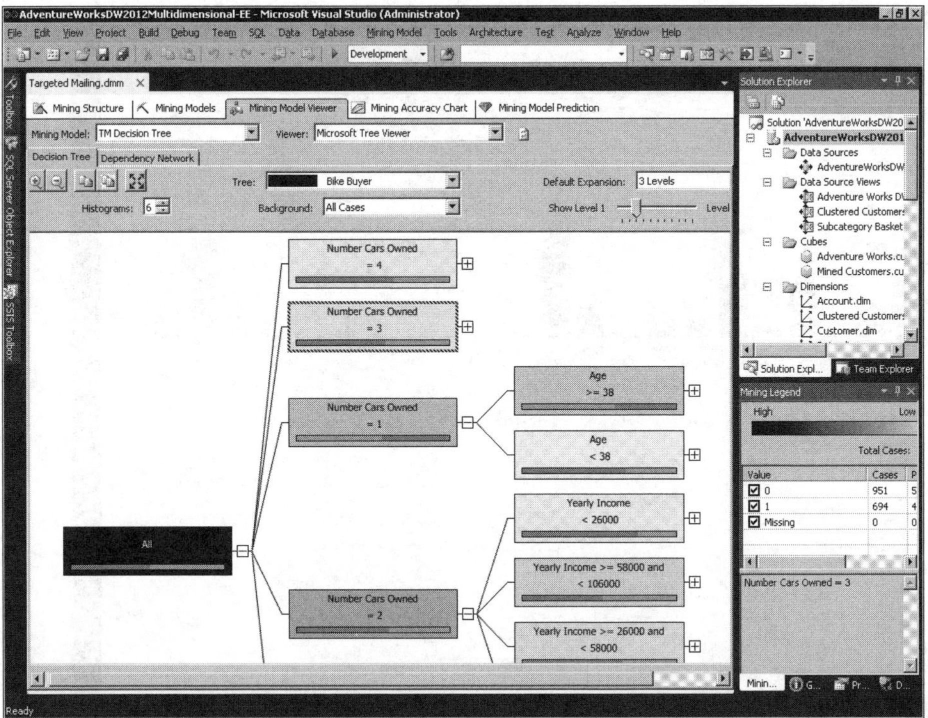

FIGURE 14-9 The SSAS mining structure editor, shown viewing an existing model built with the Decision Trees algorithm.

Power View

Just as the server version of PowerPivot runs within SharePoint but is actually shipped with SQL Server, so too is a new BI component called Power View. Power View is an ad hoc reporting, analysis, and data visualization tool for BISM data sources. Power View uses Silverlight to render compelling, animated visualizations, and runs within SharePoint, utilizing its document-based security model. Many advanced properties that can be configured in BISM data sources are directly recognized by Power View.

A Power View report, in full screen mode, is shown in Figure 14-10. The report contains a single page, with a column chart at the top and a bubble chart at the bottom. Notice the selections in the bubble chart are filtering the data shown in the column chart. The filtered values appear in a dark color and the values for the totals appear in the lighter color at the top of each column.

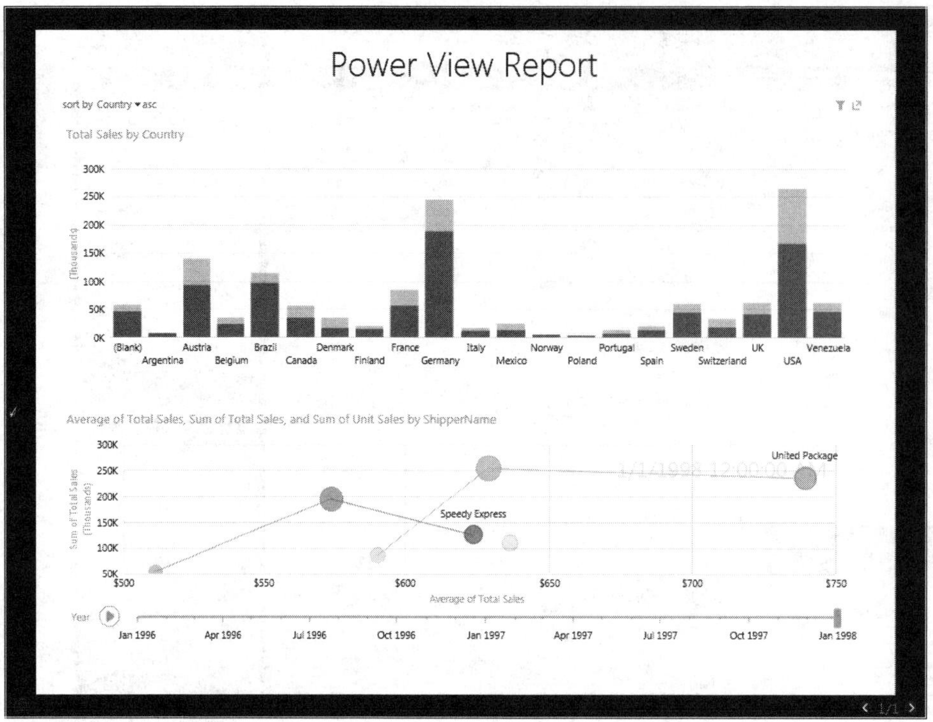

FIGURE 14-10 A Power View report with column chart and bubble chart visualizations. Selections in the latter are filtering values in the former.

Reporting Services

It may seem counterintuitive to mention SSRS in a BI context, given how prevalent use of SSRS is for operational reporting against transactional, relational databases. But SSRS is a bona fide BI tool, too, due to several lesser known features that it supports.

First among those features is the native ability in SSRS to issue MDX queries against SSAS cubes, bringing back the multidimensional results in the form of "flattened" tabular result sets. The MDX queries can be supplied by the report developer, but they can also be defined visually. This means SSRS can be used as an SSAS client, and one which requires no MDX knowledge, but still allows that knowledge to be applied, if desired. Furthermore, this functionality works against SSAS multidimensional cubes, PowerPivot workbooks (if they have been uploaded to SharePoint), and SSAS Tabular models.

SSRS also features some of the best visualization technology in the Microsoft BI stack, including numerous types of charts, gauges, maps, data bars, sparklines, and indicators. Although these work just fine against relational data, they work especially well for SSAS aggregated data, in the context of a dashboard.

Report Parts

With SQL Server 2008 R2, SSRS gained the ability (using the stand-alone Report Builder 3.0 application) to publish out the individual tables, matrices, and visualizations from any report to a gallery—where they can be selected later, through drag-and-drop, for inclusion in new reports. Publishing these so-called Report Parts enables a self-service usage scenario and allows end-users to construct SSRS reports more easily, especially since all underlying data sources and datasets are implicitly imported with the selected gallery elements.

Report Builder, with its Publish Report Parts dialog box displayed, is shown in Figure 14-11.

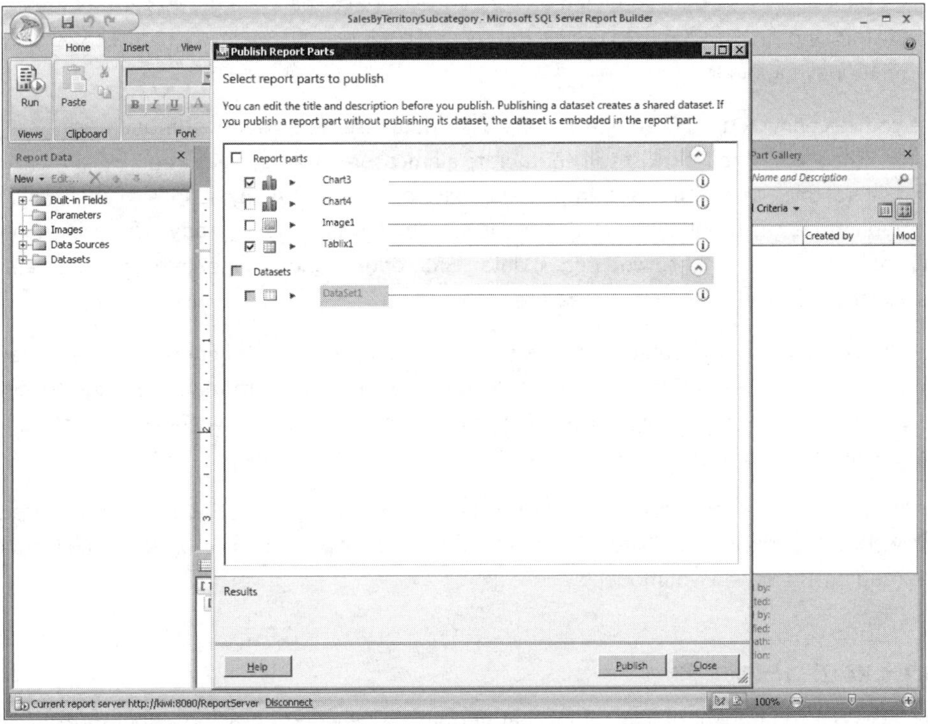

FIGURE 14-11 The Publish Report Parts dialog box, with a table and chart selected for publication.

Alerting

New to SSRS in SQL Server 2012 is an Alerting feature. Alerting automatically emails specified recipients when a value in a report exceeds or falls below a defined threshold, or meets some other formulaic condition. To some extent, SSRS Alerting restores functionality that was lost with the deprecation of SQL Server Notification Services (which was removed in SQL Server 2008). The alerting administrative interface is SharePoint-based, but only requires SharePoint Foundation, which is the free element of SharePoint included with Windows Server. On the SQL Server side, Alerting functionality is only available in the BI and Enterprise editions of the product.

Dashboard Components

Finally, as we will detail shortly, SSRS reports can be included in PerformancePoint dashboards, making SSRS a full-fledged BI tool.

Excel and Excel Services

Excel may seem well outside the SQL Server universe, until you realize that it includes a number of features specifically geared towards Analysis Services. Excel can connect to Analysis Services natively. In the Data tab of Excel's ribbon, you need only click the Get External Data group's From Other Sources button, and Analysis Services will be the second option in the menu, right after SQL Server (i.e., the relational engine) itself.

Once you've connected, you can easily query SSAS databases or PowerPivot models using PivotTables. The PivotTable Field List will enumerate all measure groups, measures, KPIs, dimensions, attributes, hierarchies, and named sets in your database or model, and any actions will be available in the PivotTable through a right-click shortcut menu selection. (Actions are an advanced SSAS feature creating context sensitive links to web pages, data, SSRS reports, and other external content relevant to a particular dimension, member, or measure.)

Excel charts can be easily created from PivotTables, making Excel a full-fledged data visualization tool for SSAS and PowerPivot. Excel also features several functions in its formula language specifically for querying cubes, so even regular spreadsheet cells (as opposed to just PivotTable regions) can be SSAS- and PowerPivot-connected.

As with Reporting Services, Excel (and thus Excel Services, discussed next) can query multidimensional cubes, PowerPivot workbooks on SharePoint, and SSAS Tabular models. Figure 14-12 shows an Excel chart built against data in a PowerPivot model.

Using Excel Services

Excel Services is a component of SharePoint that permits entire workbooks, individual spreadsheets, or specific PivotTables, charts, and cell regions to be exported to SharePoint and viewed *interactively* from a web browser. This means that workbooks containing SSAS-or PowerPivot-querying PivotTables, charts, and cell ranges can be shared with anyone with a web browser and permissions to a properly outfitted SharePoint server. PivotTables can be drilled down upon, and filters and parameter values can be applied interactively, in the browser, without any version of Excel required on the client machine. Figure 14-13 shows an Excel Services display of a PowerPivot-connected chart with a "slicer" control allowing the data to be filtered by product color.

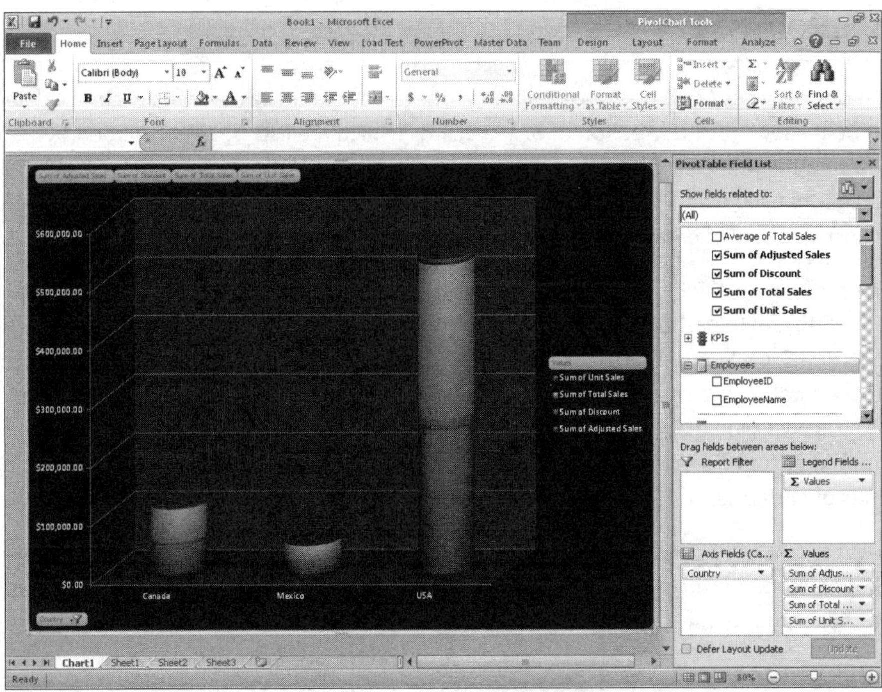
FIGURE 14-12 An Excel chart data-driven from a PowerPivot model.

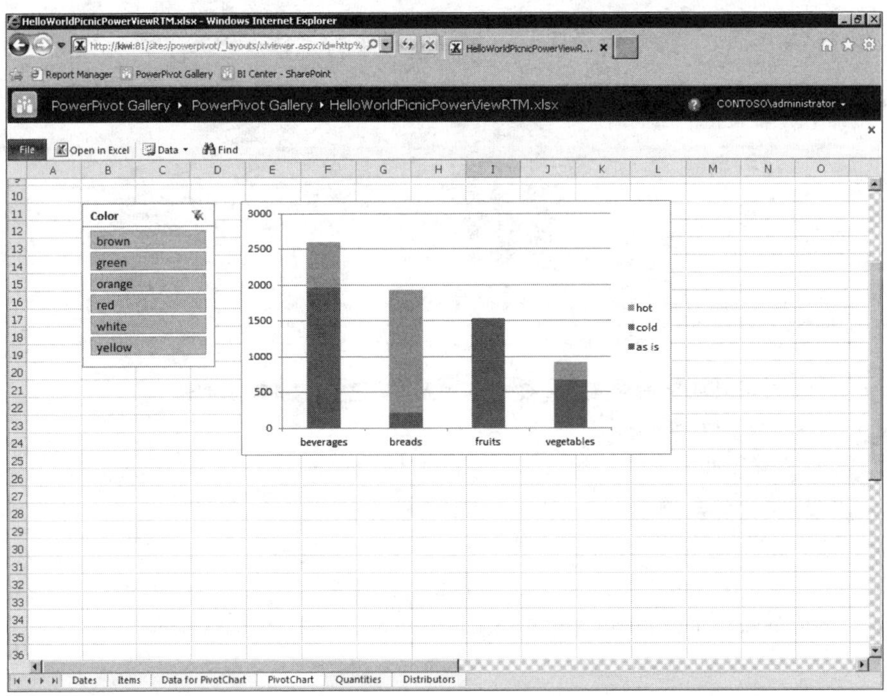
FIGURE 14-13 Excel Services view of a worksheet with PowerPivot-driven chart and slicer.

PerformancePoint Services

PerformancePoint Services (PPS) was once a stand-alone product but was eventually consolidated into SharePoint. It allows for the creation of BI scorecards (which are lists of KPIs, grouped by objective, showing the KPI values, and their status assessments), analytic grids, and analytic charts (grids and charts that allow drill-down operations, as well as drilling across dimensions, right from the browser) against a variety of data sources, with SSAS foremost among them.

These features alone make PPS relevant to this chapter's discussion. But what makes it a lock is the ability of PPS to create dashboards that integrate its own assets described above with content built with SSRS and Excel Services. Not only can these disparate BI dashboard components appear side-by-side, but filters can be added that will alter the content of all or some of them simultaneously. In this way, PPS acts as glue that bonds together different elements of the Microsoft BI stack and in turn simplifies things for end users, who don't have to use multiple tools separately to benefit from the capabilities of each one.

Figure 14-14 shows a PPS dashboard containing a PPS scorecard and analytic chart, as well as both a map and gauges created with Reporting Services. The PPS and SSRS components coexist in the dashboard rather seamlessly.

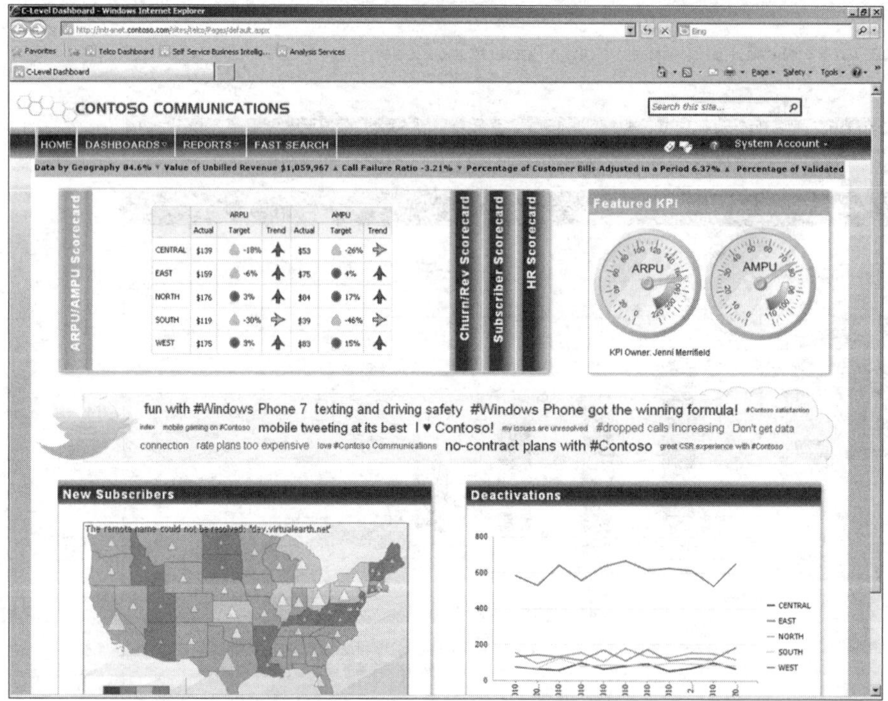

FIGURE 14-14 A PerformancePoint Services (PPS) dashboard with native PPS and SSRS elements.

StreamInsight

The last BI stack component to discuss is StreamInsight, Microsoft's complex event processing (CEP) engine that premiered with SQL Server 2008 R2. CEP engines process data streams where the magnitude and frequency of data is extremely high. Think about sensor data or financial market data as examples; in both cases, you can imagine the immense volume of data and the speed with which it streams in. Ordinarily, keeping up with this kind of data feed is very difficult; CEP seeks to make it manageable.

In the case of StreamInsight, its code, written in C++, runs very "close to the metal," allowing for low latency in processing. An adapter architecture is used to abstract away interfaces with specific source and destination data systems. Once collected, the data is held in abeyance until processing code, which can be written in .NET and can use LINQ to query StreamInsight, comes around to digest the data, or until an output adapter pushes the data somewhere.

Figure 14-15 depicts an architectural summary of StreamInsight.

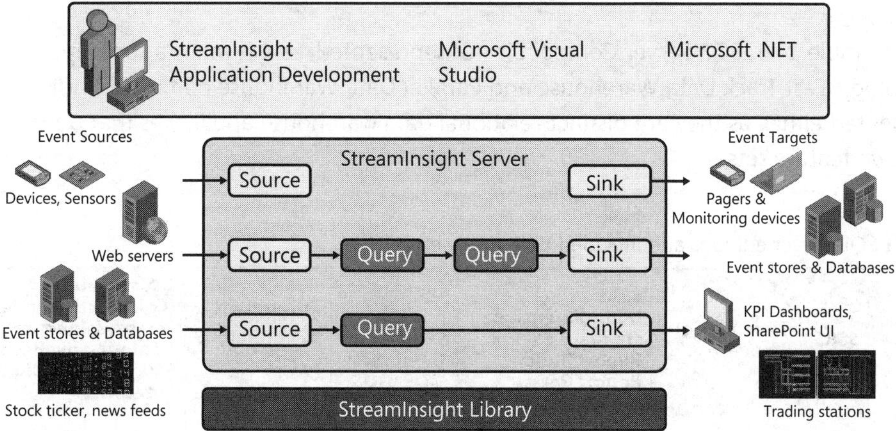

FIGURE 14-15 An architectural summary of StreamInsight.

StreamInsight neither uses SQL Server as a repository, nor does it integrate directly with SSAS or other Microsoft BI stack components. But it does ship with SQL Server and one can certainly imagine a data warehouse and/or cube being built on top of its streaming data, especially for operational BI applications.

SQL Server Editions and SharePoint Version Requirements

Prior to SQL Server 2012, customers who were interested in the BI capabilities of SQL Server really had to purchase the Enterprise edition of the product. Although SQL Server Standard edition includes SSAS, several of its features are unavailable in that edition. This had meant top-of-the-line licenses were needed for BI work, even for customers who were still getting their toes wet with it. But SQL

Server 2012 introduces a new BI edition, with prices and features that fall between Standard and Enterprise. The BI edition does not include advanced data warehouse features in the SQL Server *relational* engine, like partitioning and xVelocity in-memory technology-based columnstore indexes, but it does include MDS, DQS, SSIS, SSAS, SSRS, PowerPivot for SharePoint, Power View, and StreamInsight. This significantly lowers barriers to entry for sophisticated BI work on the Microsoft platform and makes the latter compare even more favorably on economic terms with its competitors.

Power View requires the SharePoint Enterprise Client Access License (eCAL), as do Excel Services, PPS, and the SharePoint implementation of PowerPivot. So an enterprise license on the SharePoint side is still required for the most sophisticated web-based analysis work, but the reduction in license burden on the SQL Server side is a welcome development.

Note that while Excel 2007 and SharePoint Server 2007 support some of what has been discussed in this chapter, the 2010 versions are needed for the full suite of functionality. In particular, PowerPivot and Power View will not work at all with the 2007 editions of those products.

Table 14-1 provides a summary of SQL Server 2012 editions and the SQL Server BI features each includes.

Note In Table 14-1, SQL Server Compact is not represented, as it is really a separate technology. Fast Track Data Warehouse and Parallel Data Warehouse edition are not represented either, as they are distinct relational data warehouse appliances that define their own feature sets.

TABLE 14-1 SQL Server editions and included BI feature sets.

Edition	SSRS	StreamInsight Standard	SSAS Multidimensional, standard SSIS, Report Builder, Report Parts,	SSRS Alerting, SSAS Tabular, MDS, DQS	PowerPivot for SharePoint, Power View	DW features (Columnstore indexes, compression, partitioning), advanced SSIS, StreamInsight Enterprise
Express	A					
Web	•	•				
Standard	•	•	B			
Business Intelligence	•	•	•	•	S	
Enterprise, Developer	•		•	•	S	•

Legend: A= Advanced Services (free download) required; B = basic feature set for SSAS;
S = SharePoint Enterprise Client Access License (eCAL) required.

Summary

Many SQL Server practitioners work exclusively with the product's relational engine, and many users in the BI market continue to pay significant sums to license stand-alone BI products and suites from other vendors. Meanwhile, Microsoft includes with SQL Server one of the most capable and complete BI stacks in the industry.

The 2008 R2 stack was already impressive, as it included Master Data Management, reporting, ETL, multidimensional OLAP, complex event processing, and in-memory column store analytics embedded into Office and SharePoint. But SQL Server 2012 makes the stack significantly more capable by adding Alerting, Data Quality, stand-alone column store analytics, relational Columnstore indexes, and advanced self-service analysis and data visualization.

Whether or not you wish to get heavily into BI, it's crucial to understand what SQL Server's BI capabilities are, and to know how easy some of them (like PowerPivot and Power View) are to use. This chapter has taken you past that hurdle and maybe even piqued your interest in exploring these technologies further.

CHAPTER 15

xVelocity In-Memory Technologies

—*Andrew Brust*

With the release of SQL Server 2008 R2, Microsoft delivered massive new Business Intelligence (BI) value in the form of PowerPivot, which brought column store technology to the Microsoft BI stack. Column stores organize data in a column-oriented fashion and use advanced algorithms to compress their data. The column store and compression technologies combine to allow even very large data models to fit entirely in memory, thus allowing for lightning-fast response times for analytical queries.

PowerPivot runs on the client PC as a Microsoft Excel add-In, and that's great. But it also runs on Microsoft SharePoint as a true server, allowing for shared analysis of data models and, by way of a few cool tricks, allowing any Analysis Services client, including Reporting Services, to connect to and query the model with MDX. So PowerPivot was a great start for column store technology in the Microsoft world.

But now there's more. SQL Server 2012 ups the ante with enhancements to PowerPivot and the introduction of column store technologies into SQL Server. These features and capabilities are together branded "xVelocity in-memory technologies." They include a new "Tabular" mode in SQL Server Analysis Services (SSAS) which hosts PowerPivot-style models, adding enterprise features like partitioning and security, all without any dependency on Excel or SharePoint.

Such an advance was expected, as PowerPivot is and was a manifestation of SSAS. The other way SQL Server 2012 has improved its column store game is quite unexpected, however: the technology behind PowerPivot has now been implemented in the SQL Server Enterprise edition *relational* engine as a special type of index called a *columnstore* index. With it, Microsoft has also devised a new query processing mode called Batch mode.

> **Info** Don't get hung up on the word "batch" as it relates to the "batch jobs" of old or a Transact SQL (T-SQL) statement batch. SQL Server Batch mode isn't about punch cards, submitting queries to run overnight, or combining several T-SQL queries before a *GO* command. Instead, it refers to processing batches of rows together, rather than one at a time. The latter, conventional processing mode is now called Row mode.

When SQL Server uses a columnstore index and Batch mode together, it can process queries with vastly improved speed—sometimes an order of magnitude faster than what would be possible with conventional indexes. In fact, it makes frequent, iterative, analytical queries highly feasible right inside a relational data warehouse. For some scenarios, it can even eliminate the need to use SSAS. Arguably, then, xVelocity in-memory technology in the SQL Server relational engine gives you BI without the cubes.

But wait; not so fast. As much as xVelocity may seem to "liberate" relational practitioners from SSAS, it also provides a bunch of incentives for them to check it out. That's because the SSAS models that use xVelocity technologies also implement something called the Business Intelligence Semantic Model (BISM), which provides a relational-friendly facility and a new expression language called Data Analysis eXpressions (DAX; also used in PowerPivot) that makes reporting and analysis against your data easier for your users and also easier for you.

Have "xVelocity whiplash" yet? Confused about whether columnstore indexes or BISMs are where it's at? Well, don't be torn because, as it happens, you can use the two together, and then tie in visualization tools like Power View to provide self-service analytics, high-performance query capabilities, and relational storage together, all in one. We'll cover all of that in this chapter.

In this chapter, you will learn:

- What column store databases are and their role in today's BI marketplace.
- How xVelocity compression works, in "short strokes."
- Which queries are most suitable for columnstore index optimization.
- How to create a SQL Server columnstore index and how to make sure it's being used.
- All about the BI Semantic Model and what it does.
- How to use DAX for measures, Key Performance Indicators (KPIs), and calculated columns.
- How to enable the DirectQuery mode for Tabular models in SSAS.
- The basics of Power View, how it integrates with the BI Semantic Model, and by extension, relational databases.

Column Store Databases

Column store databases have become very hot commodities in the data warehousing and BI markets. For those used to thinking of BI products as "dimensional," the notion of a "column" simply sounds like relational technology being used in place of online-analytical processing (OLAP) technology. And while in a sense that is true, it's not really the point. Column store databases are so-named because they store values for a *column* together rather than segregating data by row. At first, that may sound absurd. But when you look at the reasoning behind a column store and the ramifications of using one, you see that it greatly benefits the analytical query process.

Figure 15-1 displays the transformation from a row store structure to a column store for a table (simplified for conceptual clarity).

Row Store

EmpID	Age	Income
1	43	90000
2	38	100000
3	35	100000
...	...	...

Column Store

EmpID	1	2	3	...
Age	43	38	35	...
Income	90000	100000	100000	...

FIGURE 15-1 Mapping row stores to column stores.

This table contains employee data and a more realistically complex version of it could be the basis for a fact table in a data warehouse. If you look at the Income column's data in its column-oriented format, two things become clear:

- Aggregating the data over a large number of rows becomes very easy, since this involves scanning *adjacent* data.
- Some of the values repeat, and all of them are close in value.

What are the ramifications of these two observations? First, aggregation queries can be performed very efficiently. Second, the Income column (which might serve as measure data) is a great candidate for high-ratio compression. When values repeat, they can be represented as one value with a number of occurrences, and when data is close in value, it can be represented by a base value that is expressed once, along with the deltas from that base value for each individual data point (where the deltas will require less storage than the full values).

Merely storing column values together aids the performance of analytical queries, but compression lowers storage costs and accelerates performance even more. Less I/O is involved in reading the data, and large parts, or all, of query working sets — even entire databases — can be loaded into memory, eliminating disk access and the latency that accompanies it.

Column Store Tech in the BI Industry

Numerous column store products exist in the market, many of which have been acquired by the larger IT vendors. A number of data warehouse appliance products employ column store technology, as do the in-built BI engines in various dashboard and data visualization products. So Microsoft is not the only vendor using the technology, nor is it the first to do so. But with the release of SQL Server 2012 and the advent of xVelocity in-memory technologies, Microsoft has integrated column store technology in its technology stack in a widespread way, both in specialized products like PowerPivot and SSAS Tabular mode, as well as in the mainstream SQL Server relational database. That is unique, unprecedented, and, most important, an extremely powerful tool for SQL Server professionals.

xVelocity in the RDBMS: Columnstore Indexes

We believe BI technology should not be viewed as separate from relational technology, but rather as something adjacent to it on the data spectrum. The addition of columnstore indexes to the SQL Server relational engine supports this view of data technology in a very concrete way. Many queries which before would have had reasonable elapsed timings only in SSAS can now be accommodated inside relational databases, too.

Columnstore indexes are indexes in every sense of the word. They reside in the relational database, are backed up and restored along with it, and are based on the columns you desire. The cost-based query optimizer in SQL Server will do a good job of using columnstore indexes when they are useful and will instead use conventional row store indexes at other times.

But columnstore indexes can also be thought of, in effect, as data stores in their own right. That's actually true of all indexes, as they contain the data for the columns on which they're built. But you will typically build columnstore indexes on *all* the columns in the indexed table. As such, any queries where the columnstore index would be useful can get most or all of their data, rather than just some of it, from the index itself.

Building a Columnstore Index

Building a columnstore index requires use of the standard T-SQL *CREATE INDEX* syntax, with the addition of the *COLUMNSTORE* keyword. For our simplified table in Figures 15-1 and 15-2, we might create a columnstore index on all columns in the table like this:

```
CREATE NONCLUSTERED COLUMNSTORE INDEX
ColStoreEmployee ON Employee (EmpID, Age, Income)
```

Once a columnstore index is built, your aggregating queries stand to be highly accelerated.

We've cut to the chase to show you how easy columnstore indexes are to create, and how completely integrated they are into the normal T-SQL workflow. But in reality, there are several things you need to understand before you can productively put columnstore indexes to work. So let's take a look at them.

What You Can't Do

In order to take full advantage of columnstore indexes, you have to know where they help and how to ensure they are being used. But before you learn any of that, it's important to know what the limitations are for columnstore indexes. Microsoft Books Online provides a comprehensive reference on these limitations, but we'll list some of the highlights here:

- Columnstore indexes (and thus the tables on which they're built) are read-only
- Columnstore indexes cannot be clustered or unique
- Columnstore indexes are not compatible with *Filestream* data

- Columnstore indexes cannot include sparse columns or columns of the following data types: *binary, varbinary, ntext, text, image, varchar(max), nvarchar(max), uniqueidentifier, rowversion, timestamp, sql_variant,* CLR types (including *hierarchyid* and spatial types), and *xml*
- Columnstore indexes cannot accommodate *decimal* (or *numeric*) columns with precision greater than 18 digits or *datetimeoffset* columns with scale greater than 2
- Columnstore indexes cannot be created on views or indexed views, and cannot contain more than 1,024 columns
- Columnstore indexes are incompatible with replication, change tracking, and change data capture

At first blush, this seems like a long list of restrictions. But read over them carefully and you will realize that very few of the things that a columnstore index *can't* do are things you *would* do in a data warehouse. Most data warehouses have fact tables with numeric measures and keys, and dimension tables with corresponding keys and string/character data. The disallowed binary, large text, versioning, variant, CLR, and XML data types are not things that you would aggregate, or use as key values. And while you might use a *uniqueidentifier* as a key value in your transactional database, a numeric key can be easily substituted for it in a data warehouse.

The read-only restriction on columnstore indexes is perhaps the most limiting of them all. But since many data warehouses operate on a nightly data load, in many cases it will be acceptable to drop the columnstore index before the load and rebuild it as soon as the load is complete. This assures a minimal maintenance window once per night. In cases where loads occur more frequently, new data can be loaded in a staging table, which can periodically be columnstore-indexed and then swapped in as a new partition in the read-only table.

Does all of this mean that columnstore indexes work only with data warehouses? Technically, no, columnstore indexes can be used with any database, including transactional ones. Nonetheless columnstore indexes improve performance the most in analytical queries typically performed in data warehouse scenarios. Specifically, columnstore indexes work with queries that:

- Group, and aggregate large row sets
- Use star joins (preferably) and inner joins (exclusively)

The ideal use case for a columnstore index is when it is built on a data warehouse fact table and includes all columns in that table. That said, transactional tables that contain measure data and keys can be treated as if they were fact tables, and building columnstore indexes on the fact table-like columns can greatly aid performance on analytical queries against those tables. So think of indexes on fact tables as the ideal pedagogical columnstore example and then realize that columnstore indexes can help you in scenarios that are comparable, even if less than perfectly compliant, with that optimal case.

Actually, the very notion that data warehouse- and dimensional-style BI work can be done on databases that do not feature a formal star schema is exactly the idea that the BI Semantic Model, especially in PowerPivot, is based upon.

How Columnstore Indexes Work

Now you have an overview understanding of creating columnstore indexes, and a sense of when and where you should do so. But you are still taking on authority how and why they help with certain types of queries. Not only can that be intellectually dissatisfying, but in practical terms it prevents you from troubleshooting when the query optimizer in SQL Server ends up not using your columnstore indexes, and you think it should have.

The diagram in Figure 15-2 represents the page structure of a columnstore index, and points out that only the columns of interest are fetched and scanned.

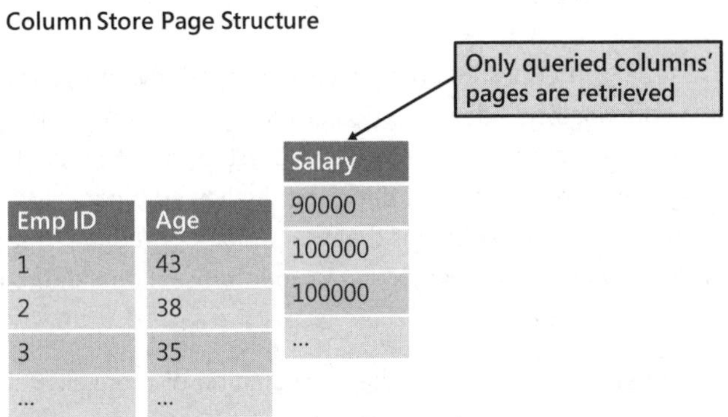

FIGURE 15-2 Only pages from queried columns are retrieved from a columnstore index.

Each column's data is stored in its own series of special pages. A group of such pages makes up a "segment," each of which holds approximately 1 million rows' worth of a single column's compressed data. Each segment is, in fact, nothing more than a SQL Server binary large object (BLOB) stored in the database along with all conventional table data.

Column data can be compressed in a number of ways. Run-length encoding can be used to compress consecutive appearances of the same value as a single expression of that value and the number of times it occurs. If a relatively small set of distinct values exist in the column, then each one can be assigned a small key value and the keys can be stored instead of the values they represent. Also, since columnstore index segments store metadata identifying their smallest and largest values, whole segments can be skipped if a condition in the query rules out the range of values in the segment. This technique is called "segment elimination."

Columnstore indexes involve multiple layers of efficiency allowing, in many cases, the entire working set to fit in memory. But it gets better: the query processor (QP) can process column values in batches of approximately 1,000 rows, rather than one at a time. So not only are scans made faster due to removal of extraneous columns from the data, but whole batches of data can be processed together as the scan takes place.

This gives rise to the new Batch execution mode in SQL Server, which is where the really huge performance gains come from. In other words, columnstore indexes do accelerate certain queries, but their indirect contribution—of facilitating Batch execution mode—provides the real boost. This does add a little complexity though, because it's possible for the QP to use a columnstore index but still work in Row mode. And while that may still be beneficial, it forfeits much of the speed-up.

To make certain the QP is entering Batch mode, you'll need to look at your query execution plan. And because Batch mode is invoked only in parallel processing scenarios, you'll need to make sure that the server's max degree of parallelism (MDOP) configuration option is set either to zero or a value greater than one. You must, of course, also ensure that SQL Server has multiple processor cores at its disposal. The latter requirement is especially important to check if you're working with a virtualized instance of SQL Server since, by default, Hyper-V allocates only a single logical processor to its virtual machines (VMs). To use Batch mode, you must make sure to allocate at least two.

To do this with Hyper-V, you'll need to shut down your VM fully, as the number of logical processors setting is not editable while the VM is running or saved. Once you've shut down the VM, right-click it and choose Settings from the context menu. In the Settings dialog box, click the Processor option in the left-hand sidebar (fourth from the top), then click the drop-down arrow for the Number Of Logical Processors setting and select a value greater than one. This task is shown in Figure 15-3.

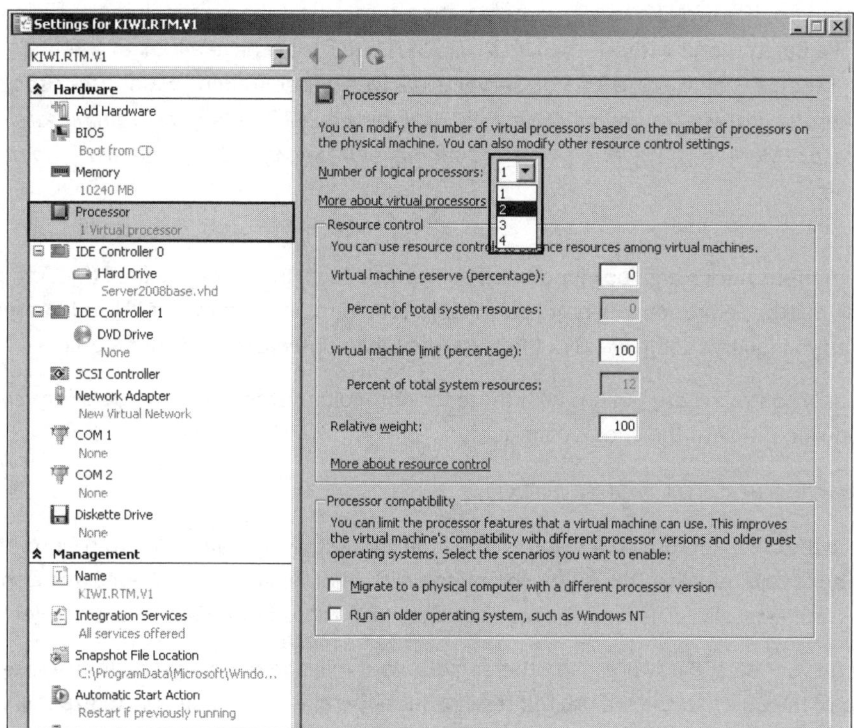

FIGURE 15-3 Assigning the number of logical processors to a VM.

Once this change is made, click the OK button (not shown in Figure 15-3) and start the VM again.

Once your multicore environment is ready, go ahead and open SQL Server Management Studio (SSMS), connect to your database, enter a query suited to columnstore index optimization as described above, and click the Show Estimated Plan toolbar button. Look in the plan for usage of your columnstore index (for example, in a Columnstore Index Scan), scrolling to the right if necessary. Point to that node in the plan to reveal the details tooltip. The processing mode for the estimated plan will be displayed on the third line of the tooltip. Make certain that third line says "Batch" for Estimated Execution Mode, and that the fourth line indicates "ColumnStore" for Storage, as shown in Figure 15-4.

Tip If the table you are querying has a relatively small number of rows, the query processor may not invoke Batch mode, even if multiple processor cores are available. You can simulate the presence of a greater number of rows using the *ROWCOUNT* and *PAGECOUNT* options of the *UPDATE STATISTICS* T-SQL command, as described in a blog post from the SQL Server query optimization team at *http://blogs.msdn.com/b/queryoptteam/archive/2006/07/21/674350.aspx*. The *UPDATE STATISTICS* command with the *ROWCOUNT* and *PAGECOUNT* options should never be used on a production database. Even in a development database, it's best to run the command on a *copy* of your table with the relevant columnstore index created. Once you are done profiling the columnstore index, you can drop the copy of the table permanently, thus removing any bogus statistics from the database. If you'd like to experiment with a sample database containing sufficient data to invoke Batch mode without the *UPDATE STATISTICS* trick, have a look at the first two units in Module 3 of Microsoft's SQL Server 2012 Developer Training Kit at *http://social.technet.microsoft.com/wiki/contents/articles/6982.sql-server-2012-developer-training-kit-bom-en-us.aspx#Module_3_Exploring_and_Managing_SQL_Server_2012_Database_Engine_Improvements.*

Beyond columnstore index scans, look for other shapes where Batch mode may be used (for example, in a related Hash Match). Before your query, if you'd like, you can turn on statistics for CPU and elapsed times. Then when your query's complete, click the Messages tab to observe the timings for each.

You could easily contrast these timings with those for non-columnstore-assisted operations by adding the following clause at the end of your query:

```
OPTION (IGNORE_NONCLUSTERED_COLUMNSTORE_INDEX)
```

This will force the QP *not* to use your columnstore index. View the estimated plan to confirm this, and then execute the query. When the query completes, click the Messages tab to reveal the non-columnstore-assisted statistics. They may be much greater than those from the previous query.

Depending on your data, hardware, and other factors, your mileage may vary, and it may take some tweaking of the query to see the desired results. But hopefully you will be able to experience first-hand just how revolutionary columnstore index technology is.

Tip Improved results from columnstore indexes tend to be more prominent when queries are run against data sets of 2 to 3 million rows.

Columnstore Index Scan (NonClustered)
Scan a columnstore index, entirely or only a range.

Physical Operation	Columnstore Index Scan
Logical Operation	Index Scan
Estimated Execution Mode	Batch
Storage	ColumnStore
Estimated I/O Cost	0.0090509
Estimated Operator Cost	0.559059 (12%)
Estimated Subtree Cost	0.559059
Estimated CPU Cost	0.550008
Estimated Number of Executions	1
Estimated Number of Rows	10000000
Estimated Row Size	19 B
Ordered	False
Node ID	6

Object
[AdventureWorksDW2012].[dbo].[FactResellerSalesCS].[NonClusteredColumnStoreIndex]
Output List
[AdventureWorksDW2012].[dbo].[FactResellerSalesCS].ResellerKey, [AdventureWorksDW2012].[dbo].[FactResellerSalesCS].SalesAmount

FIGURE 15-4 Checking execution and storage modes in a query plan.

At this point, you should have a good appreciation for the power of xVelocity column store and compression technology, and of how it can be applied in the relational database realm. We will now move to examining its application in the analytical realm. But have no fear. We will come full circle and bring this discussion back to the relational context by the end of the chapter.

xVelocity for Analysis: PowerPivot and SSAS Tabular Models

In the last section we focused pretty heavily on the inner workings of xVelocity column store and compression technology. In this section, we will move away from that level of discussion, and discuss the specially purposed analytical database technology that xVelocity also supports. Rest assured that the same clever technology is there, under the covers, but the specifics of it are less important. Instead, the extra capabilities and features that result are important.

As we mentioned earlier, PowerPivot is based on SSAS. But instead of using the conventional SSAS multidimensional storage and execution engine, PowerPivot uses xVelocity in-memory technologies to enable a new column store and in-memory BI (IMBI) execution engine, called VertiPaq. The in-memory operations are, of course, made possible by the column store and compression in VertiPaq.

Note With the introduction of the xVelocity brand, Microsoft has officially renamed VertiPaq to the "xVelocity in-memory analytics engine." We continue to use the older name here, though we identify VertiPaq as being part of the family of xVelocity in-memory technologies.

Clearing Up the Analysis Services Vocabulary

With SQL Server 2012, Analysis Services now runs in two different modes—the mode it had worked in exclusively in all SQL Server versions from 7 through 2008 R2, and a new mode that is based on the same VertiPaq engine that is in PowerPivot. The vocabulary used to refer to each mode can be rather inconsistent and confusing. Before we go any further, let's establish what's what, and our own convention for how we will consistently refer to each mode.

The original mode in SSAS didn't need a name before, because it was the only mode the engine worked in. It was, and is, based on OLAP technology and offers three storage options: MOLAP (Multidimensional OLAP), wherein it uses its own storage technology; ROLAP (Relational OLAP), wherein it uses and stores data in the relational database; and HOLAP (Hybrid OLAP), a combination of the two techniques. Because MOLAP was the only fully native storage mode, this is the name sometimes assigned to the entire original non-VertiPaq mode of SSAS.

You might think one name would be good enough, but in fact a few interchangeable terms have arisen. For example, since the "M" in "MOLAP" stands for multidimensional, that term is sometimes used as the original mode's name. As a variant of the multidimensional moniker, the acronym UDM, which stands for Unified Dimensional Model, and was used heavily when Analysis Services 2005 was introduced, is sometimes used as well. So the original Analysis Services mode has three names: MOLAP, multidimensional, and UDM. In this chapter, we will consistently use the term "multidimensional" to avoid confusion, but be aware that the other two names are used interchangeably elsewhere.

Now, what about the new mode based on PowerPivot's technology? Well, one thing it does not get called is "PowerPivot mode," which is probably for the best. But several other names, including VertiPaq mode, BISM, IMBI, Columnar, and Tabular mode, are bandied about. In this chapter we'll use the last of these terms ("Tabular mode") to refer to the new mode. The name "Tabular" is used by Microsoft because models that use it explicitly recognize tables (and columns), rather than measures and dimensions, as first-class members of the model.

And speaking of the word "model," it's important to note that this term is typically applied only when the Tabular mode is in use, whereas the word "cube" is applied when the multidimensional mode is in force. That makes sense, to a point, but it also can get very confusing, since Tabular mode does support MDX queries, and thus MDX clients, which will view a Tabular *model* as if it were a multidimensional *cube*. It's unfortunate that the vocabulary has evolved without much rigor, but it's understandable, given that one mode can emulate the other. By using the terms "multidimensional" and "Tabular" in this chapter, we hope to mitigate the confusion, since these terms refer to the unique storage technology used in each mode.

When we speak of the technology that PowerPivot and Analysis Services Tabular mode have *in common*, though, we will use the term *BISM,* since both products do in fact implement BI Semantic Models. So, *BISM* will reference the technology, and Tabular will reference the Analysis Services configuration mode that uses it, and the databases that SSAS manages in that mode.

The Lowdown on BISM

What BISM enables is Analysis Services–like functionality (including support for MDX queries, essentially for backward compatibility) but with far simpler modeling. Instead of requiring precise design of measures, dimensions, attributes, aggregations, and the like, BISM allows the mashing up of tables from various data sources, and then requires specifying the relationships between them.

In the case of PowerPivot, BISM allows users to build their own queries, selecting numeric fields that act as measures, and grouping them by other columns that will act as dimensions. But users don't need to be aware of that distinction, nor do they need to understand that their data is in a special database that can be queried with the new DAX language or the old MDX language. Users just think they're working with data. Tech-savvy users will recognize the environment as relational; other users won't really worry about it. BISM can treat any table as a fact table, a dimension table, or *both*. So while a database organized along a star schema will work really well, it's not truly necessary.

If this sounds familiar, it should. In the previous section, we saw how columnstore indexes enable analytical queries in a relational database, and can do so against normalized transactional tables, even if they work best with star schema fact and dimension tables. To us, that's the real xVelocity story: it brings analytical query power to you, rather than making you travel to where that power exists.

But if you are willing to travel a bit, xVelocity and BISM reward you, especially in the new Tabular mode of Analysis Services, and the corresponding new version of PowerPivot. In this new version, a number of classic Analysis Services features—including formally defined measures, hierarchies, and KPIs—have been added. Also, a number of advanced properties have been added to make the data more discoverable in analysis clients like Power View. Let's take a look at these modeling features on the PowerPivot and SSAS side, and then see how they can be combined with the immediacy of columnstore indexes on the relational side.

Friends, Countrymen, Bring Me Your Data

First, let's cover the basics of BISM data source compatibility. BISM lets you import data from a wide array of data sources. Here they are, broken down by category:

- Client/Server: SQL Server (and SQL Azure), Oracle, DB2, Sybase, and Informix
- Data warehouse appliances: SQL Server Parallel Data Warehouse edition (PDW) and Teradata
- BI data sources: Analysis Services
- Data Feeds/OData: Including Azure DataMarket, Reporting Services reports, and SharePoint lists

- Small databases and flat files: Access, CSV, and other text files
- Excel: cell ranges and tables
- General: OLE DB and ODBC data sources

The reason that so many disparate data sources can feed a single model is that the model is a separate database, so once the data is in the model it can be mashed up with data from other sources as long as relationships can be set.

If you've worked with Analysis Services in its multidimensional mode, then you'll recognize a similar process in creating multiple data sources and marrying them in a unified data source view. However, with an Analysis Services multidimensional mode database, you would then have to design a cube. With BISM, you can start querying the model right away. And, in some cases, you can even postpone the specification of relationships and allow them to be automatically detected (subject to your review) later on.

Building the BISM

Let's see how all of this works. We'll start from PowerPivot and we'll then move to Analysis Services Tabular mode. That will be easy, since upsizing from one to the other is explicitly supported, as you will see. From here on, we'll cover various features and capabilities by building out a sample, and querying it in various tools. We'll document our steps in the form of step-by-step instructions, which will enable you to follow along. If you prefer just to read the steps and follow the screen shots, that's okay too. But consider the hands-on approach, as it tends to be a great way to learn.

To start, you'll need to be running Excel 2010 and to download and install its PowerPivot add-in from *www.powerpivot.com.* The add-in is free. Just make sure to download the appropriate version (32- or 64-bit) to match the version of Excel 2010 that you are running. Once the add-in is downloaded and installed, start Excel, and click on the PowerPivot tab in the ribbon, then click on the PowerPivot Window button at the far left, as shown in Figure 15-5.

Doing this will bring up the PowerPivot window, where you can import and model your data. The window has its own ribbon, whose Home tab's entire Get External Data group contains buttons for importing different types of data. This is shown and highlighted in Figure 15-6.

Note The Get External Data group is shown as a drop-down menu in Figure 15-6 due to the resolution of the screen capture. On your PC, the entire group will likely display within the ribbon itself.

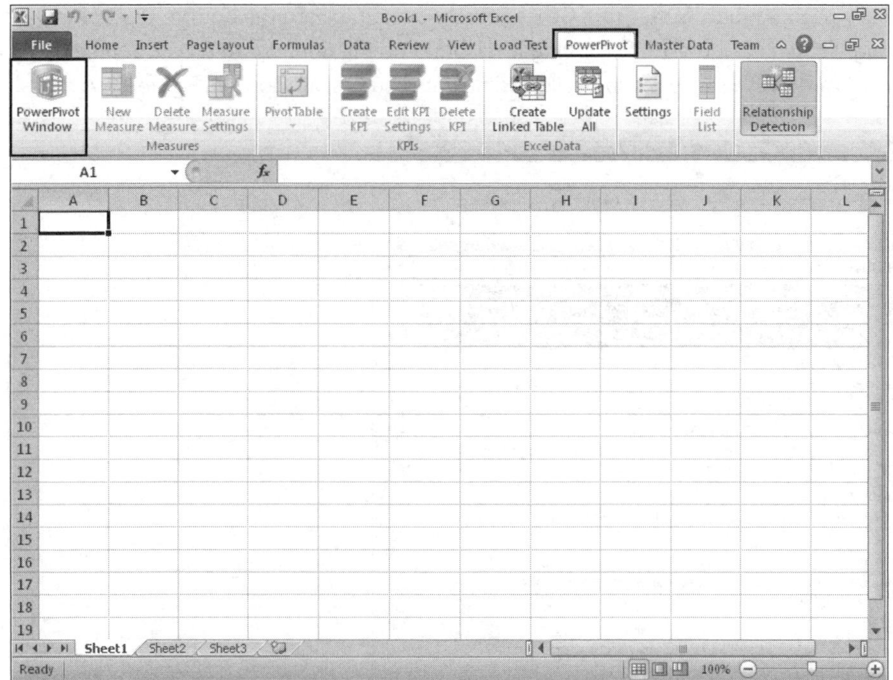

FIGURE 15-5 The PowerPivot ribbon tab and its PowerPivot Window button.

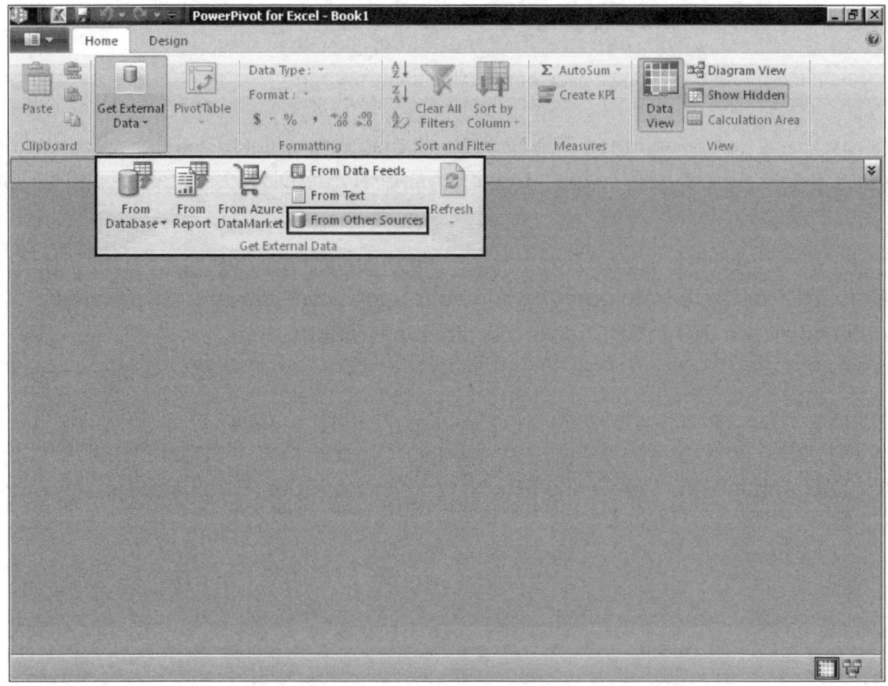

FIGURE 15-6 The Get External Data ribbon group in the PowerPivot window.

All you really need, though, is the From Other Sources button toward the bottom-right of that ribbon group (also highlighted in Figure 15-6). Clicking it will bring up the Connect To A Data Source page of the Table Import Wizard with a single menu of all possible data sources, as shown in Figure 15-7.

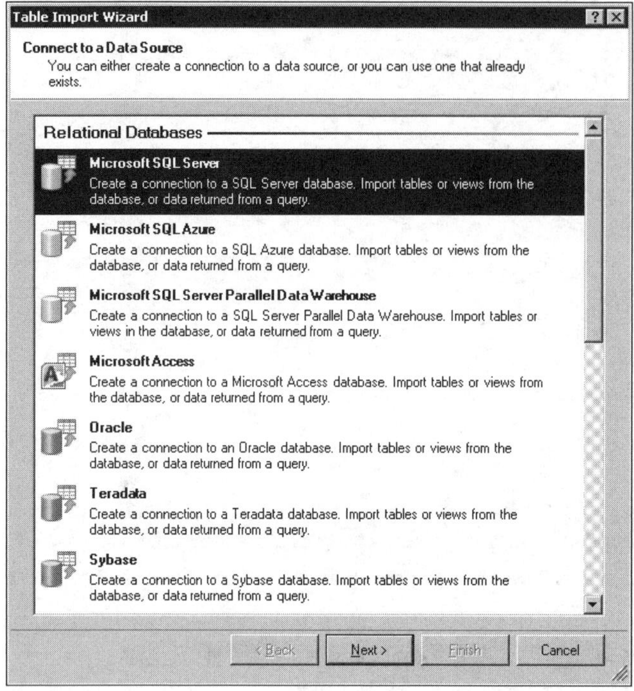

FIGURE 15-7 The Connect To A Data Source page of the Table Import Wizard.

Select Microsoft SQL Server, and then click Next. You'll then be presented with a data connection dialog. Fill in the details necessary to connect to the *AdventureWorksDW2012* database and click Next.

Note If the *AdventureWorksDW2012* database is not installed on your SQL Server instance, download its MDF data file from *http://msftdbprodsamples.codeplex.com/downloads/get/165405* and attach to it in SQL Server Management Studio.

Once you have connected to the *AdventureWorksDW2012* database, click Next. In the Select Tables And Views page, you'll be asked if you want to select your data from a list of tables or supply your own SQL query; choose the former and click Next. Once the list of tables comes up, select the following eight:

- *DimDate*
- *DimEmployee*
- *DimProduct*
- *DimProductCategory*

- *DimProductSubcategory*
- *DimPromotion*
- *DimSalesTerritory*
- *FactResellerSales*

Notice that for each table, you can select it, then click the Preview And Filter button to browse the data and, optionally, enter filter conditions. This is merely a convenience feature, as you'll be able to filter the data after importing it as well. You can also set a model-friendly alias for each table in the Friendly Name grid column. Go ahead and do that now: remove the "Dim" prefix from the first seven table names, set the friendly name for *FactResellerSales* to, simply, **Sales,** and add spaces for any tables that have intercapped friendly names (e.g., change *SalesTerritory* to **Sales Territory**). Now click Finish; once you do, the Importing page will appear and your data will import. When the import is complete, click Close and your screen should look something like the one shown in Figure 15-8.

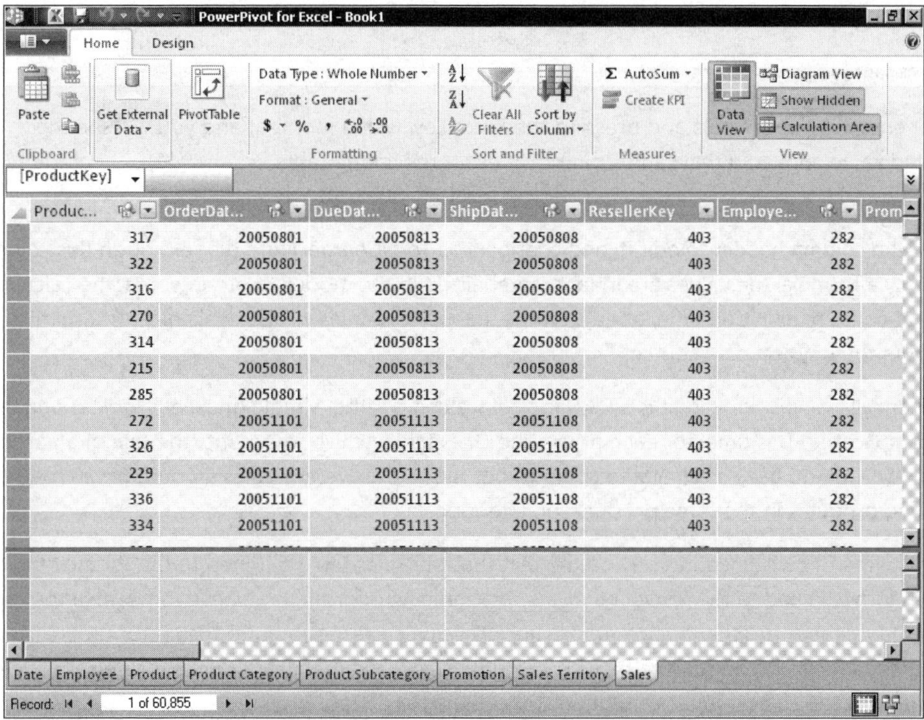

FIGURE 15-8 The PowerPivot window, with imported data.

Dial M for Modeling

As you can see, PowerPivot provides a spreadsheet-like look and feel, with each table having its own tab (although, remember, it uses its own window, separate from the actual Excel client). Each column can be hidden, unhidden, deleted, or renamed, by right-clicking the column header and selecting the appropriate option from the context menu. You can click on the ribbon's Design tab and use the Add or Delete buttons for performing those functions on columns, or double-click the column header to rename the column. You can also click the column header drop-down button and enter filter conditions in the resulting pop-up window.

Tables can likewise be deleted or renamed by right-clicking the corresponding tab and selecting the corresponding function from the context menu, or by double-clicking the tab to rename. Tables can also be moved within the tab order, either through the tab's Move context menu option and the resulting Move Table dialog box, or by dragging the tab of the table to be moved to the desired location. In this way you can model your data, and you can do so in a manner that smoothes out the differences between naming conventions in different databases.

Calculated Columns

PowerPivot also lets you define calculated columns. And it's pretty easy, too: just click a cell in a table's first empty column, then click in the formula bar, enter a formula there, and press the **Enter** key. You can try this on the *Sales* table, rather easily, with the following formula:

```
=[SalesAmount]+[TaxAmt]+[Freight]
```

After entering this formula and pressing the Enter key, wait a moment and you will see the calculated value appear in that same column, in every row in the table.

You might also notice that the name of your new column is *CalculatedColumn1*. Double-click that name in the column header to edit it, and change it to *TotalCharge*. Note that although this column is defined by a formula, the values are in fact materialized in the model. In other words, the calculation is done at column definition time; at query-time, the actual values will be available, just as if they had come from the physical data source.

The formula we just looked at is a DAX formula, albeit a rather simple one. Let's look at one that's more complicated. This time, for each row in the *Sales* table, which represents the sale of a particular product, we want to have a calculated column that shows the average sales amount for all rows containing products in the same product subcategory.

To calculate this we'll need to rely on the fact that the *Sales* table is joined to the *Product* table which, in turn is joined to the *Product Subcategory* table. Our formula will have to traverse the "hop" to the *Product* table, get the *ProductSubcategoryID* value corresponding to the current row's product, then look at all rows in the *Sales* table whose products are also in that product subcategory and get the average of the *SalesAmount* column for that whole set of data.

To make things a bit easier on ourselves, we can create an intermediate calculated column called *ProductSubcat*, and define it as

```
=RELATED('Product Subcategory'[EnglishProductSubcategoryName])
```

Tip In DAX, table names are always surrounded by single quotes and column names are surrounded by square brackets. There is no space or period between the two.

This DAX formula tells PowerPivot to use the value of the *EnglishProductSubcategoryName* column in the related row in the *Product Subcategory* table and make it the value of *ProductSubcat*. Implicitly, the formula must traverse the *Product* table to get to the corresponding row in the *Product Subcategory* table.

With *ProductSubcat* defined, we can get the average sales number we need with one more calculated column, called *AvgSalesForSubcat*. Here is its formula:

```
=AVERAGEX(FILTER('Sales',[ProductSubcat]=EARLIER([ProductSubcat])),'Sales'[SalesAmount])
```

Because this formula nests three different DAX functions, it requires some explanation. The *FILTER* function supplies the table *Sales* as its first parameter, indicating that we want to take all rows in that table and supply a filter condition to them. The filter condition we want is one that says select all rows whose *ProductSubCat* value is equal to that for this particular row. The expression *[ProductSubcat]= EARLIER([ProductSubcat])* gives us just that (think of "earlier" as meaning "this one"). We then apply the *AVERAGEX* function over all those rows for the *SalesAmount* column, giving us the average sales amount for all products in that subcategory.

We could now create one more calculated column, called *SalesAboveAverage*, using this formula:

```
=[SalesAmount]-[AvgSalesForSubcat]
```

This would give us the amount above or below the product subcategory average that a particular row's sale represents. Aggregating that over various categories can provide a useful benchmark of how good sales are, in relative terms.

Notice we never had to specify the relationships between *Sales*, *Product*, and *Product Subcategory*, but we rather could just assume they were in place. That's because the relationships were built for us automatically when PowerPivot encountered the corresponding constraints in the database. Typically you'll only need to specify relationships between tables imported from different data sources. Let's take a look at how this works by importing data from Excel.

Analysis in Excel, Using Data from Excel

To connect to an Excel workbook, use the From Other Sources button in the PowerPivot window again. In the Connect To Data Source page of the Table Import Wizard, select Excel File from the list (it's the second-to-last entry), and then click Next. In the Connect to Microsoft Excel page, click the Browse button, and then navigate to and select the *Resellers.xlsx* workbook from this chapter's sample code. Check the Use First Row As Column Headers checkbox, and then click Next. In the Select Tables and Views page, you should see the *DimReseller$* sheet listed and selected; change its friendly name from *DimReseller* to **Reseller** and click Finish. The data will then import. When the import is done, click Close and the new reseller data will be displayed in its own new tab.

It's All about Relationships

Now let's take a look at the relationships that already exist in the model. Click the ribbon's Design tab and then the Manage Relationships button. You should see a list of relationships, all involving tables from the *AdventureWorksDW2012* SQL Server database. Note that the relationship from the *Sales* table to the *Sales Territory* table is not active; we will need to fix this later, but we need to create a relationship between the *Sales* table and newly imported *Reseller* table now. Close out of the Maintain Relationships dialog box, and then click the ribbon's Create Relationship button. In the Create Relationship dialog box, select *Sales* from the Table drop-down list and *ResellerKey* from the Column drop-down list. The other two drop-down lists in the dialog box should now be enabled, so select *Reseller* from the Related Lookup Table drop-down list. *ResellerKey* should have been automatically selected for you in the Related Lookup Column drop-down list; if not, then select it manually now. Now just click OK, and the relationship will be added.

Modeling, Part Deux

So far, the modeling techniques we've looked at were all available in the first version of PowerPivot, which was released with SQL Server 2008 R2. But since the second version accompanies SQL Server 2012, which also features BISM-based databases in SSAS Tabular mode, a number of new features have been added to both BISM hosts to support common SSAS features. Let's take a look.

Although we haven't yet looked at Excel queries against PowerPivot models (we will soon), we'll explain now that merely using a PowerPivot model's column in the Values section of an Excel PivotTable or PivotChart makes that column into a measure in the eyes of the VertiPaq engine. But while that's convenient for end users who don't want to spend too much time with data modeling, it would be nice if we could create explicit measures in the model, and then hide the raw columns behind them. It would also be nice if we could construct explicit hierarchies rather than forcing users to, for example, select individual fields like *EnglishPromotionCategory, EnglishPromotionType,* and *EnglishPromotionName* into a PivotTable and arrange them in nested fashion. The good news is that the SQL Server 2012 version of PowerPivot lets you construct such hierarchies as well.

Creating Measures

The easiest way to create an explicit measure is to select one row of a column's data, and click on the AutoSum button toward the top-right of the ribbon's Home tab. This will create a sum-based measure on that column. Try it with the *SalesAmount* column in the *Sales* table and you will get a measure called *Sum Of Sales Amount*. It will be represented by a single entry beneath the *SalesAmount* column data in the PowerPivot window's calculation area (which can be hidden or shown by clicking the Calculation Area button at the far right of the ribbon's Home tab). Click that entry and you will see that the measure is backed by another DAX formula, displayed in the formula bar. Edit the formula so that the name on the left side of the := assignment operator is **Sales Amount** (with a space), rather than *Sum of SalesAmount,* and press the Enter key. This is all shown in Figure 15-9.

Now create four more measures in the same manner. Base one on the *UnitPrice* column (and name it **Unit Price**, with a space), and the others on the *TotalCharge*, *AvgSalesForSubcat*, and *SalesAbove-Average* calculated columns you created earlier (naming them **Total Charge**, **Average Sales For Subcat**, and **Sales Above Average**, respectively). Now create one more measure on *SalesAmount*, but make this one average-based instead of sum-based, by clicking the drop-down arrow on the AutoSum ribbon button and choosing Average, as shown in Figure 15-10.

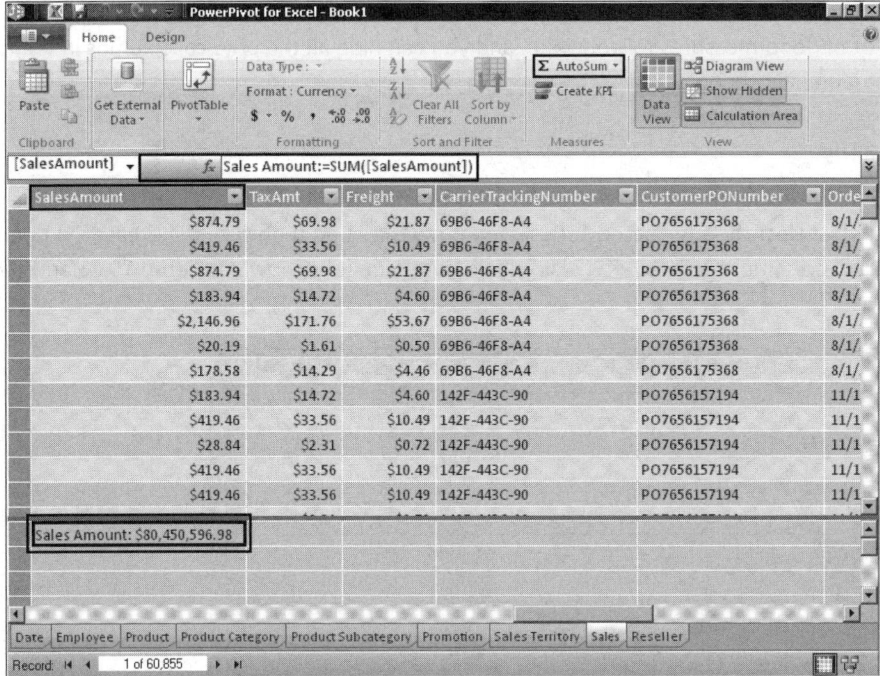

FIGURE 15-9 A newly created measure.

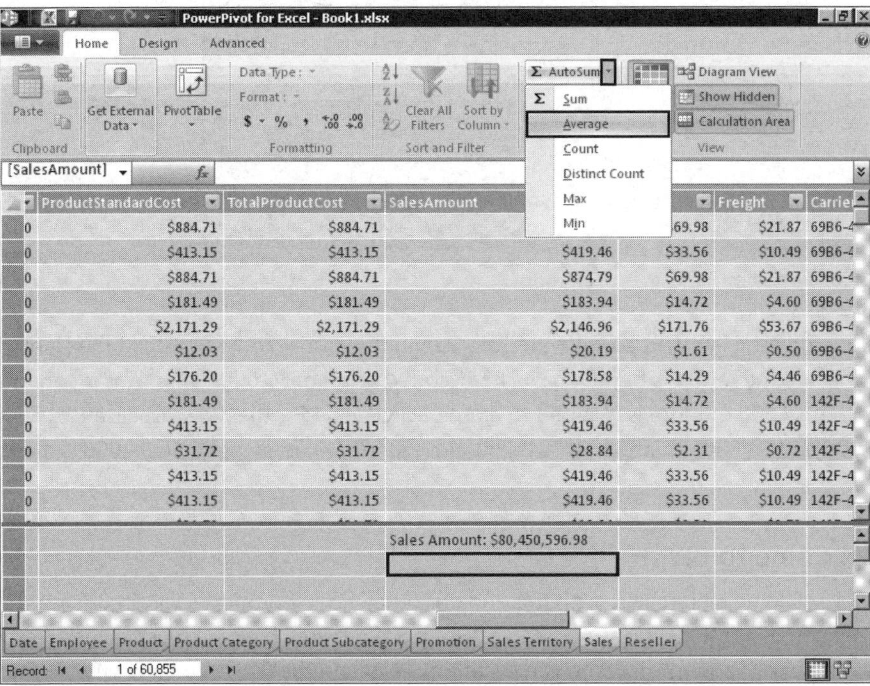

FIGURE 15-10 Building an average-based measure.

Edit the formula of the new measure so that it's named **Average Sales Amount**. With this done, you have a lot of good measures to work with, and you can hide all the physical columns in the table. We'll do that a bit later though.

Building KPIs

KPIs allow you to create scorecards. As a final modeling adjustment before we look at hierarchies, let's create a KPI. Select the sum-based *Sales Amount* measure and then click the Create KPI ribbon button. This will bring up the Create KPI dialog box. Configure it as shown in Figure 15-11 and then click OK.

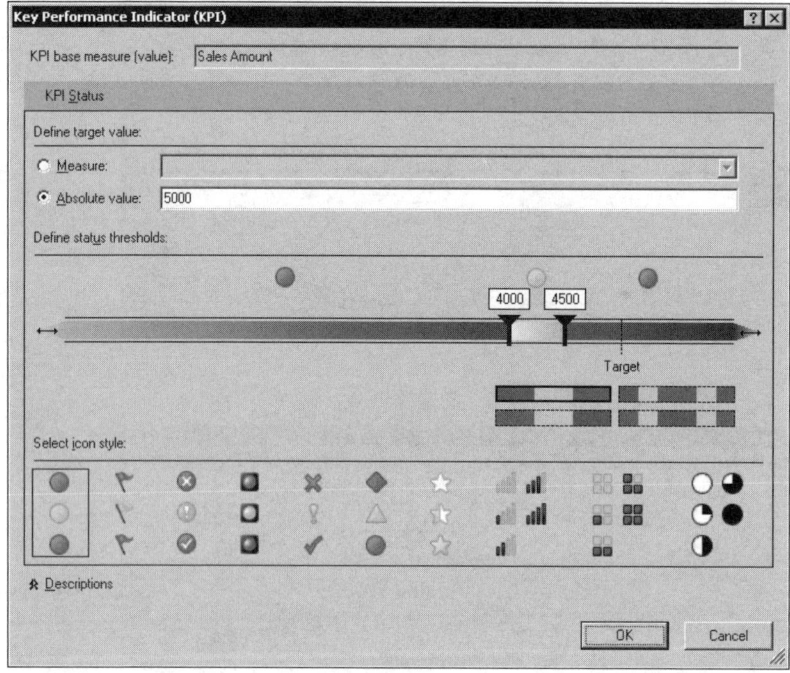

FIGURE 15-11 Building a Key Performance Indicator.

This configuration will in effect convert the *Sales Amount* measure to a KPI. The KPI's value is the measure's value and the target is based on the hard-coded value of $5,000. The status is configured so that a value of $4,500 or more is mapped to a green circle icon for the KPI's visualization, a value between $4,000 and $4,500 is mapped to a yellow circle, and a value of less than $4,000 is mapped to a red circle.

Hierarchies Come to BISM

Now let's build out some hierarchies. With this and our other work, our model will, in BI-speak, expose pre-defined dimensions, measures, and a KPI. To build hierarchies, we must change from the Excel-like Grid view to Diagram view. You can do this by selecting the Diagram View button (third from right, at higher resolutions) in the ribbon's Home tab or the Diagram button at the far-lower right of the data grid. Both are highlighted in Figure 15-12.

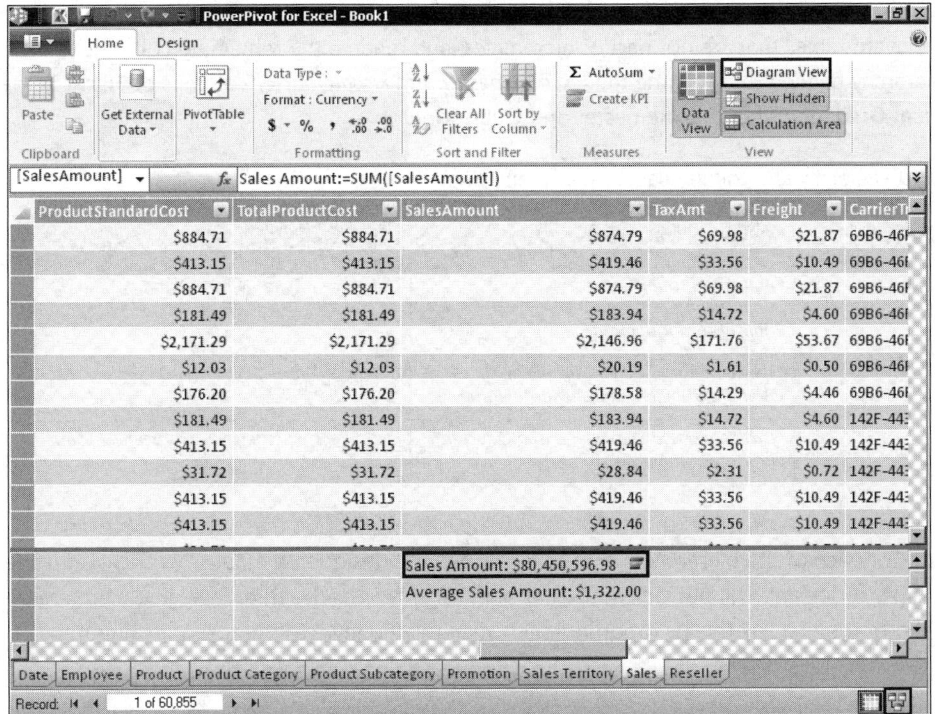

FIGURE 15-12 Switching to Diagram view.

Once in the Diagram view, you should see a layout of the tables in our model, along with a depiction of the relationships between them. BI pros will recognize this as a star schema, but that actually doesn't matter so much. The table in the middle (essentially, our fact table) has the numbers we'll be querying and the other tables (essentially, our dimension tables) have the category data we'll be aggregating by.

If we look at the *Sales Territory* table, we can see that the columns for *SalesTerritoryCountry* and *SalesTerritoryRegion* could form a hierarchy. Click the *Sales Territory* table's Maximize button (at the upper-right), then rename the aforementioned to columns to just **Country** and **Region** (bring the column name into edit mode by double-clicking the name or right-clicking it and choosing Rename from the context menu). Now hold down the **Ctrl** key and click both fields, in any order. When they are selected, right-click one of them and choose Create Hierarchy from the context menu. The Hierarchy will be created for you, but with the name *Hierarchy1*; rename it to **Country – Region** instead. Finally, select all four remaining columns, then right-click one of them and choose Hide From Client Tools from the context menu.

Tip We could actually hide the *Country* and *Region* columns too, since in Excel they will still be exposed through the hierarchy. However, BISM hierarchies are not visible in Power View, so hiding the columns would leave nothing selectable for the *Sales Territory* table in that tool.

Table 15-1 lists three other hierarchies that you can build. In each case, you should hide all columns in the relevant tables that are not part of hierarchies, and rename the remaining columns to match their hierarchy naming (but rename the *FiscalSemester* and *FiscalQuarter* columns to **Fiscal Semester** and **Fiscal Quarter**, rather than Semester and Quarter).

TABLE 15-1 Hierarchy and column name assignments.

Table	Columns	New Hierarchy (and Implied New Column Names)
Promotion	*EnglishPromotionCategory, EnglishPromotionType, EnglishPromotionName*	*Category – Type – Promotion*
Date	*CalendarYear, CalendarSemester, CalendarQuarter, EnglishMonthName*	*Calendar Year – Semester – Quarter – Month*
Date	*FiscalYear, FiscalSemester, FiscalQuarter, EnglishMonthName*	*Fiscal Year – Semester – Quarter – Month*

Note For each of the hierarchies in the *Date* table, the designer will guess wrong about the hierarchy order, and will put *Calendar Year* and *Fiscal Year* as the third level in each hierarchy, instead of the first. Fix this by dragging each year-related level to the top of its hierarchy.

Finishing Touches

To finish up, there's a little more work to do. First, right-click on the relationship between the *Employee* and *Sales Territory* tables, select Delete from the context menu, and confirm the deletion in the resulting message box. Next, double-click the relationship between *Sales* and *Sales Territory* (represented as a dotted line). In the resulting Edit Relationship dialog box, check the Active checkbox and click OK.

Now maximize the *Sales* table, select all the columns, but not the five measures or the KPI (the icons at the left edge indicate if an item is a measure or KPI), then right-click one of the columns and choose Hide From Client Tools from the context menu. When you're done, click the *Sales* table's Restore button, at the upper-right.

Now, do these final few cleanup steps:

- Hide all columns in the *Product*, *Product Subcategory,* and *Product Category* tables except *EnglishProductName*, *EnglishProductSubcategoryName,* and *EnglishProductCategoryName,* respectively. Rename those three columns to **Product**, **Product Subcategory**, and **Product Category**, respectively.
- In the *Employee* table, rename the *FirstName* and *LastName* columns to have spaces before their intercapped letters, and hide all other columns.
- In the *Reseller* table, rename *BusinessType*, *ResellerName*, *AnnualSales*, and *AnnualRevenue* to have spaces before their intercapped letters, and hide all the other columns.

- In order to remove error messages on some of the calculated columns that resulted from one of our column name changes, switch back to Data View mode and edit the formula for the *Product-Subcat* column to reference *Product Subcategory* rather than *EnglishProductSubcategoryName*. The new formula should appear as follows:

```
=RELATED('Product Subcategory'[Product Subcategory])
```

  Press Enter once you're done editing and any exclamation point warnings should disappear.

Exploring Advanced Mode

You're almost ready to query your model in Excel now, but before you do, click the ribbon's File tab and then the Switch To Advanced Mode option. This will add the Advanced tab to the ribbon. Click that tab; it should appear as shown in Figure 15-13.

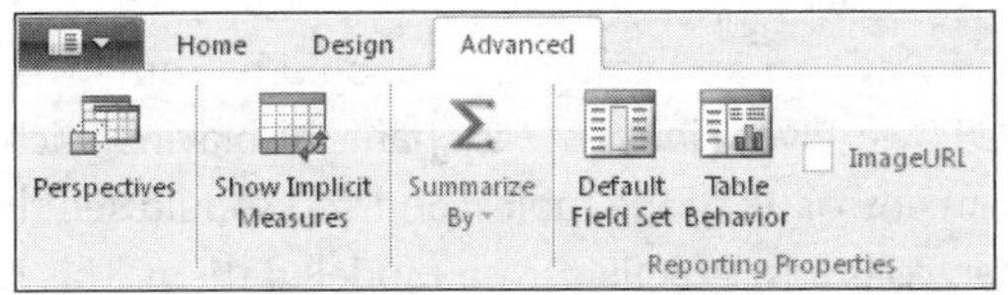

FIGURE 15-13 The PowerPivot window ribbon's Advanced tab.

The advanced options allow you to add more semantic information to your model. That information is then exposed to analysis and reporting clients which can take advantage of it. At the time of this writing, the only such client application is Microsoft's Power View, which we looked at briefly in the last chapter and will look at again a bit later in this one. Here is a summary of the advanced functions, including explanations of what they do:

- The Perspectives button lets you define limited views of your model that include only certain tables, or even certain fields within them. Perspectives can then be queried by client tools as if the former were models in their own right. This is great when you have complex models and groups of users who will only be interested in part of what's in them.
- The Show Implicit Members button will display in the Measures grid any columns that were added to the Values section of an Excel PivotTable or PivotChart, and which are thus treated by the VertiPaq engine as measures.
- The Summarize By button, which becomes enabled when a numeric column is selected, lets you define the default aggregation that a client application (including Excel and Power View) will apply to the column when it's selected.
- The Default Field Set button invokes a dialog box of the same name, and lets you indicate which columns should show by default when the whole table, rather than specific columns, is selected.
- The Table Behavior button invokes a like-named dialog box that lets you define the table's primary key and configure upon which column or columns aggregation grouping should be based. It also lets you define the column that will supply a row's default image and default label, both of which are important with specific visualizations, like the Card, in Power View.

- The Image URL checkbox, which becomes enabled when a text column is selected, lets you specify that the data in that column contains URLs to images, rather than text that should itself be treated as data.

Querying in Excel

That's about all the modeling we need to do, so let's move on to querying the model with Excel. This is pretty straightforward. Just click the drop-down arrow on the PivotTable button (in the middle of the ribbon's Home tab), and then select the Chart And Table (Horizontal) option (the third one down).

The Create PivotChart and PivotTable (Horizontal) dialog box will pop up with options to place the content in a new worksheet or in the existing one. The default selection is New Worksheet and it's fine, but we usually find Existing Worksheet to make more sense. If you do select the latter, then make sure that the Location text box displays the cell *'Sheet1'!A1*. Edit it if necessary, so that it does, and then click OK.

You should then see an empty PivotTable and PivotChart and your cursor should be somewhere inside the former. At the right of the screen is the PowerPivot Field List task pane, displaying each table from your model in its top half. Drill down on any or all of the tables, and you should see their measures, KPIs, and hierarchies, plus any unhidden columns, exactly as you modeled them. This is shown in Figure 15-14.

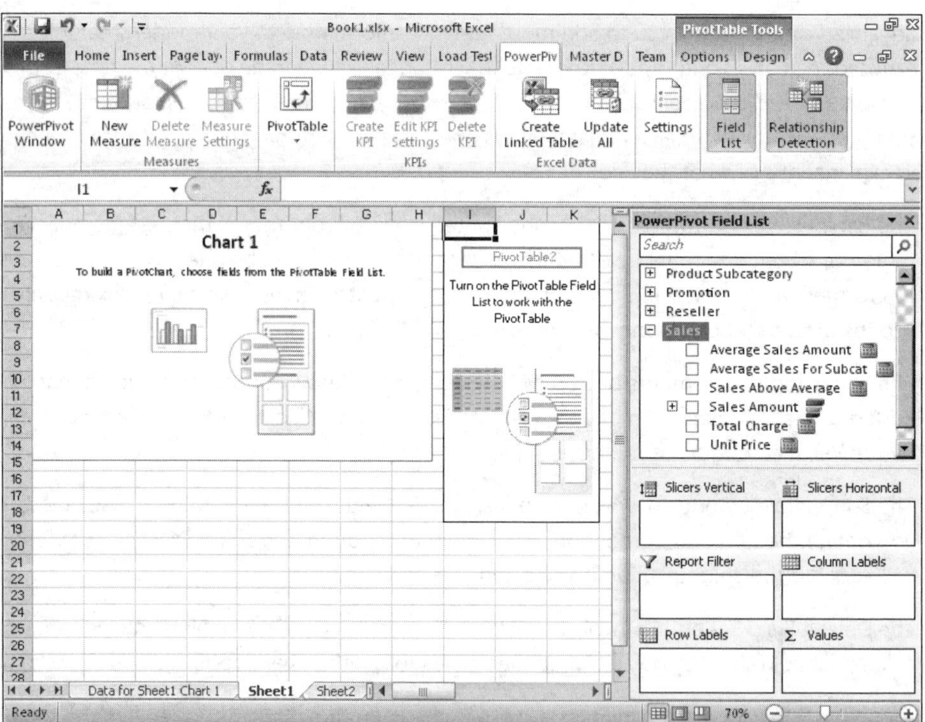

FIGURE 15-14 Empty PivotChart and PivotTable inserted from PowerPivot window, and the PowerPivot Field List.

Below the list of tables, you should see six panes, one each for Slicers Vertical, Slicers Horizontal, Report Filter, Column Labels, Row Labels, and Values. Drag and drop fields and one hierarchy into certain sections, as specified in Table 15-2.

TABLE 15-2 PivotTable field and hierarchy assignments.

Field List Area	Table	Fields (or Hierarchy)
Values	*Sales*	*Sales Amount Value, Sales Amount Status, Average Sales Amount, Sales Above Average*
Row Labels	*Date*	*Calendar Year – Semester – Quarter – Month*
Slicers Vertical	*Reseller*	*Reseller Name, Annual Sales*
Slicers Horizontal	*Sales Territory*	*Country, Region*

Next, click somewhere inside the PivotChart. The Column Labels and Row Labels sections of the PowerPivot Field List should change to the Legend Fields and Axis Fields sections, respectively, and all areas except Slicers Vertical and Slicers Horizontal will once again be empty. Drag and drop fields into certain sections, as specified in Table 15-3.

TABLE 15-3 PivotChart field assignments.

Field List Area	Table	Fields
Values	*Sales*	*Total Charge, Sales Amount Value, Unit Price*
Axis Fields	*Promotion*	*Category*

When you're done, your workbook should appear as shown in Figure 15-15.

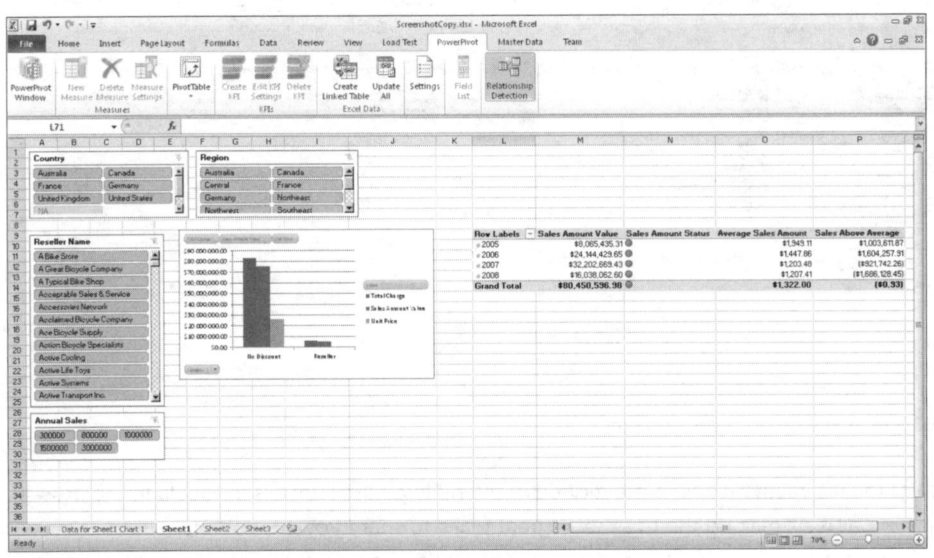

FIGURE 15-15 PivotChart, PivotTable, and Slicers in PowerPivot workbook.

A few things bear mentioning before we continue, with regard to the interactivity of the visualization we have created:

- Each year in the PivotTable can be drilled down to reveal its constituent semesters, quarters, and months.
- Each rectangle in the "Slicers" that appear above and to the left of the PivotChart can be clicked upon for interactive simultaneous filtering of the PivotChart and the PivotTable.
- If you hold down the Ctrl key, you can select multiple Slicer members. You can also click on the Clear Filter glyph at the top-right of the Slicer to clear your selections.

PowerPivot for SharePoint

If you have SharePoint Enterprise 2010 at your disposal, and PowerPivot for SharePoint has been installed on the SharePoint server farm, you can save your Excel workbook to SharePoint and then view your analysis work in the browser. To do this, simply click on the Excel ribbon's File tab, select the Save & Send option, and then click Save To SharePoint. When the Save As dialog box comes up, enter the URL to your PowerPivot Gallery click Save to navigate there, and then click Save once more to save the workbook. Your workbook should then appear in the browser and look similar to Figure 15-16.

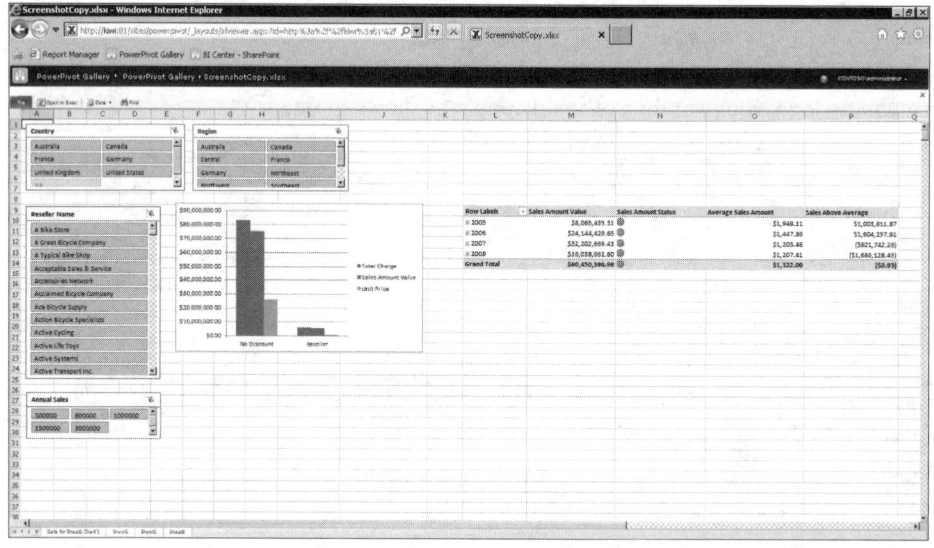

FIGURE 15-16 A PowerPivot for SharePoint workbook.

Each of the interactivity points mentioned in the bulleted list above is available in the browser environment as well, making the browser a great place to share PowerPivot analyses built in Excel. Of course, what you can't do in the browser is change the makeup (i.e., add and/or remove columns, measures, KPIs, hierarchies, and the like) of the PivotTable and PivotChart, but you can perform drill downs and make selections in the Slicers.

Notice the PowerPivot Gallery breadcrumb at the top of the page in Figure 15-16. If you click it, you'll be able to view your documents in Gallery view. Each workbook in the gallery will be listed, and you should notice that next to each one, at the far right-hand side, are buttons to open a new Excel workbook that uses the model in the current workbook as its data source, and to open a new Power View report against the model. We'll cover that option soon, but instead of using Power View against the workbook, we'll use it against a full-fledged SSAS Tabular model.

Moving to SSAS Tabular

How do we construct that model? While we could start from scratch, a far easier method is to import the workbook model into a new SSAS Tabular mode project. To do this, close Excel, save your changes, and then fire up Microsoft Visual Studio 2010 and select New Project from within the menu or on the Start Page. In the New Project dialog, select the Business Intelligence\Analysis Services node from the Installed Templates tree view on the left, and then select Import From PowerPivot from the list in the center, as shown in Figure 15-17.

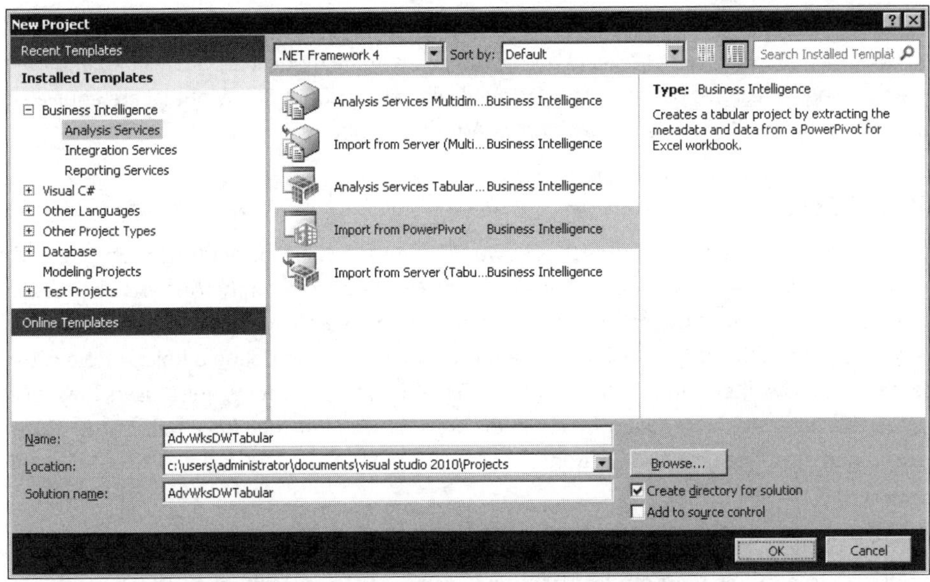

FIGURE 15-17 Creating an SSAS Tabular project by importing from PowerPivot.

Click OK. A standard file open dialog box will appear, in which you should navigate to and select the workbook you just created in Excel. Double-click the file, or select it and click Open. The PowerPivot model will then be imported into the SSAS Tabular project.

Tip Because of security restrictions on the workbook file, you may see a warning message box explaining that the data from your PowerPivot model cannot be imported, but that the metadata can. Should this happen, click Yes. Then, once your project has opened, click the Existing Connections button (third from left) on the Analysis Services toolbar, and then select the SQL Server–based connection and click Process. This will restore your SQL Server data (the Excel-based data will not be needed).

As we pointed out in Chapter 14, and showed in Figure 14-8, all of the settings and options that were available in the PowerPivot for Excel window are available inside Visual Studio as well. However, since Visual Studio has no ribbon, these options are hosted in a combination of Visual Studio menus, the Analysis Services toolbar, and the Properties window. For example, the equivalent of the From Other Sources button in the Get External Data group of the ribbon's Home tab in the PowerPivot window is the Import From Data Source button on the Analysis Services toolbar or the Model | Import From Data Source menu option.

Many of the features in the PowerPivot window's Advanced ribbon tab are available in the Properties window in Visual Studio. For example, select one of the tables in the model (i.e., click its tab) and note that the Properties window features properties for Default Field Set and Table Behavior that are equivalent to their namesake buttons in the PowerPivot window's Advanced ribbon tab.

Role-Based Security

SSAS Tabular mode offers a few features that PowerPivot does not. Security is one example, and it's rather powerful. To add security to your model, click the Roles button on the Analysis Services toolbar or choose Model | Roles from the main menu. This brings up the Role Manager dialog box, and if you click the New button within it, you will go into a mode where you can define a Role. A Role is defined by its permissions, row filters, and members (users). Together, these specify which users have access to which data, whether they can read it, process it, do both, or whether they have full control. Row filters can be expressed as per-table DAX functions.

Partitions

It's also possible to partition your model. Partitions are created within tables, and each partition is defined by a subset of that table's data. To create partitions, select a table by clicking on its tab, then take one of these three actions: click the Partitions button on the Analysis Services toolbar, choose Table | Partitions from the main menu, or edit the Partitions property in the Properties window.

The Partition Manager dialog box will come up on-screen. At the top is a list of partitions. Initially there will be only one, named the same as its parent table, but you can click the New button to create additional partitions. A text box and a drop-down list in the middle of the dialog box let you set the name and processing option for the selected partition, and you can define the partition's data membership at the bottom. For the last of these, the Table Preview mode is displayed by default, and allows you to create filter conditions on the columns in the table; however, to the upper-right of the grid is a Query Editor button that shifts you to a view where you can enter a SQL query instead.

The idea is that each partition should be defined in such a way that when put together, the partitions return all required data from the underlying table. If your model is configured to run in DirectQuery mode (which we discuss next), then keep in mind only one partition in a table may be configured for DirectQuery. By default, the first partition in the table is the DirectQuery partition, but you can transfer that status to any partition by selecting it from the list at the top of the Partition Manager dialog, and then clicking the Set As DirectQuery button (that button will not appear unless the model is configured for DirectQuery mode). Figure 15-18 shows the Partition Manager dialog box, with the Set As DirectQuery button, Query Editor button, and one filter drop-down button highlighted.

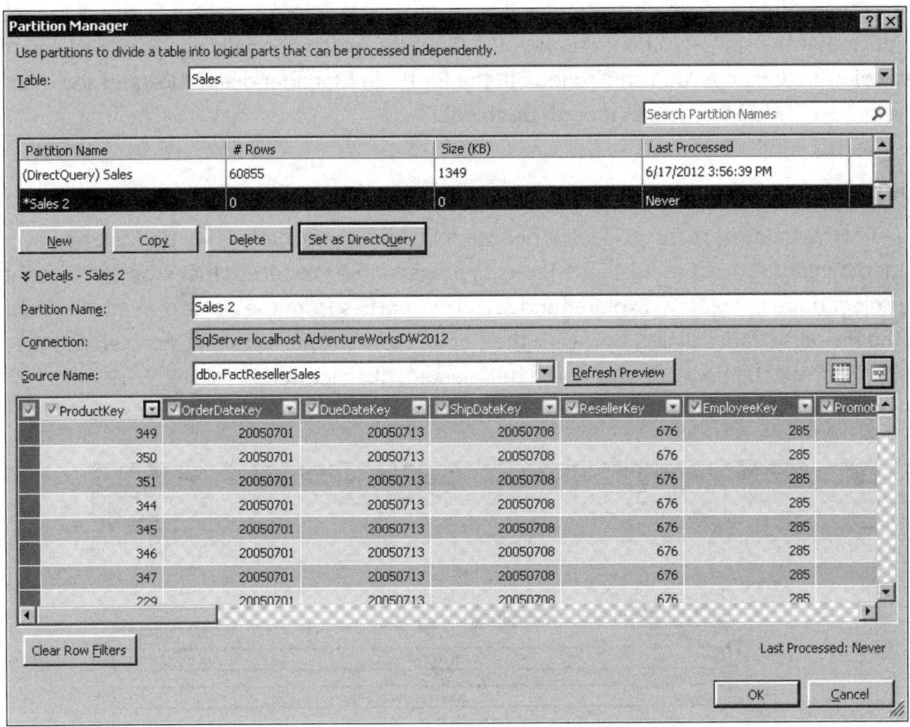

FIGURE 15-18 The Partition Manager dialog for a DirectQuery model.

Moving to DirectQuery

DirectQuery is an SSAS Tabular feature that causes queries on your model to be sent to the SQL Server relational database on which it is built. Enabling DirectQuery on an SSAS Tabular model configures it to serve as a semantic layer for reporting and analysis, rather than a data store in and of itself.

As we also pointed out in Chapter 14, it's possible to set the *DirectQuery Mode* property to *On* inside the Visual Studio environment. Before we can do so, however, we need to ready the model to work in DirectQuery mode. This means we must remove all calculated columns (since their values are normally materialized in the model, they are not compatible with DirectQuery), and we must also remove the *Reseller* table, since it was sourced from Excel (DirectQuery works only for models with a single, SQL Server data source). In addition to the *Reseller* table itself, the Excel data source pointing to *Resellers.xlsx* must be removed. To do this, delete the calculated columns from the *Sales* table, click the Existing Connections button on the Analysis Service toolbar (third from the left) and then, in the Existing Connections dialog box, select the Excel connection, click Delete, and then click OK. If any security roles were created with row filters, those filters must be removed (the roles can stay, however).

Once the above criteria are met, we can switch to DirectQuery mode: just select the *Model.bim* node in Solution Explorer, then set the *DirectQuery Mode* property to *On* in the Properties window. If you look at the status bar you should see a message saying "Switching the model to DirectQuery mode…" and then, after a pause, the setting will be applied. If you look carefully at any of the tables, you will notice that the special blank column at the far-right, which normally allows you to create calculated columns, is gone. You can also look in the Partition Manager dialog box and see that the Set As DirectQuery button is visible (though disabled).

SSAS Deployment

At this point, we are almost ready to deploy our model to the server. Before we do that, however, let's set a few deployment properties. Click the Project | *projectname* Properties menu option or right-click the project node in Solution Explorer and select Properties from the context menu. This will bring up the Property Pages dialog box, with the Deployment properties sheet selected (it's the only sheet available, so it's the only one that could be selected). It's pictured in Figure 15-19, with a few properties of interest highlighted.

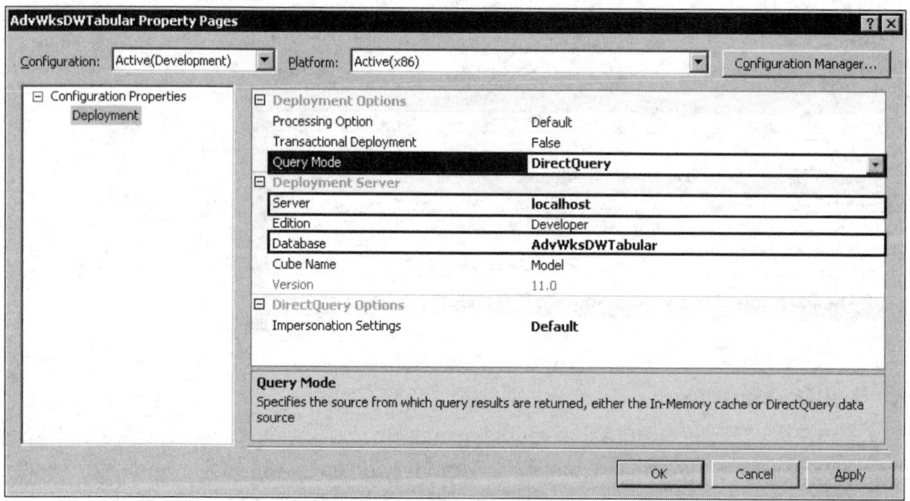

FIGURE 15-19 The Property Pages dialog box.

The Query Mode setting will be set to In-Memory by default. Set it to DirectQuery instead, as it is shown in Figure 15-19. Here is an explanation of that setting and the others:

- In-Memory: all queries will be sent to the Tabular model
- DirectQuery: all queries will be sent to the relational engine/database

- DirectQuery with In-Memory: all queries will be sent to the relational engine/database by default, but can instead be sent to the SSAS Tabular model if the connection string in use so specifies
- In-Memory with DirectQuery: all queries will be sent to the SSAS Tabular model by default, but can instead be sent to the relational engine/database if the connection string in use so specifies

Note Regardless of the Query Mode setting selected at deployment time, you can change the setting post-deployment in SSMS.

Once the Query Mode property is set, there are two other properties that merit attention. Make sure the Server setting is set correctly and remember to add a backslash and an instance name, if necessary, to target an SSAS Tabular mode server instance. The Database setting, by default, is set to be the project name, but you can change it (and thus change the database name) if you'd like.

Once you're done, click OK, and then select Build | Deploy Solution or Build | Deploy *projectname* from the main menu or right-click the project node in Solution Explorer and select Deploy from the context menu. The Deploy dialog will then pop up. This is the same dialog box PowerPivot displays when data is imported into the model. However, when you deploy a DirectQuery model, only the metadata is deployed and a message to that effect will be displayed when deployment is complete. In either case, click the Close button once deployment has concluded.

Making the Connection

Our next, and almost last, step is to query this model with Power View. Unlike with PowerPivot workbooks, where a Power View button is displayed next to the workbook's thumbnail images in the PowerPivot Gallery, Power View can't query an Analysis Services Tabular model unless we create a BI Semantic Model Connection file for it. To do this, point your browser to the PowerPivot Gallery, then click on the Documents tab (under Library Tools) in the ribbon. Click on the drop-down arrow on the ribbon's New Document button (at the far left) and select BI Semantic Model Connection from the drop-down menu, as shown in Figure 15-20:

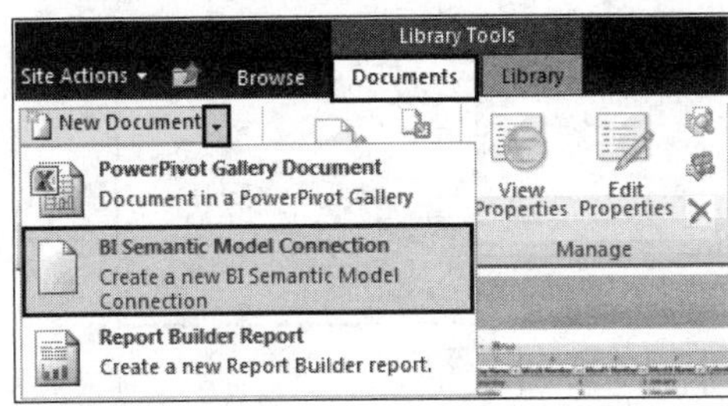

FIGURE 15-20 Creating a BI Semantic Model Connection file in the SharePoint PowerPivot Gallery.

Note In order to create BI Semantic Model Connection files, the content type of the same name must be enabled in the Library Settings of your PowerPivot Gallery. If the content type is not enabled, the option for such a file will not appear when you click the New Document drop-down button.

The New BI Semantic Model Connection page will come up in the browser. Enter a name for the file (in the File Name text box), the name of your server, including a backslash and instance name if necessary (in the Workbook URL or Server Name text box), and the name of your database (in the Database (If Connecting To A Server) text box). Since there's no drop-down list of databases, double-check to make sure you've typed in the database name correctly; better yet, copy the name from the Property Pages dialog box in Visual Studio and paste it in. Click OK when you're done.

Power View Here We Come

Your connection file should be created and your browser should automatically return to the PowerPivot Gallery. Now look for the connection file, scrolling down through the alphabetically ordered list of documents, as necessary. When you get there, you should see it has its own Create Power View Report button toward the far-right. Click it to enter Power View. A blank Power View report should be displayed with the tables from your model (and their columns, measures, and KPIs if you expand the table nodes) displayed on the right, as shown in Figure 15-21.

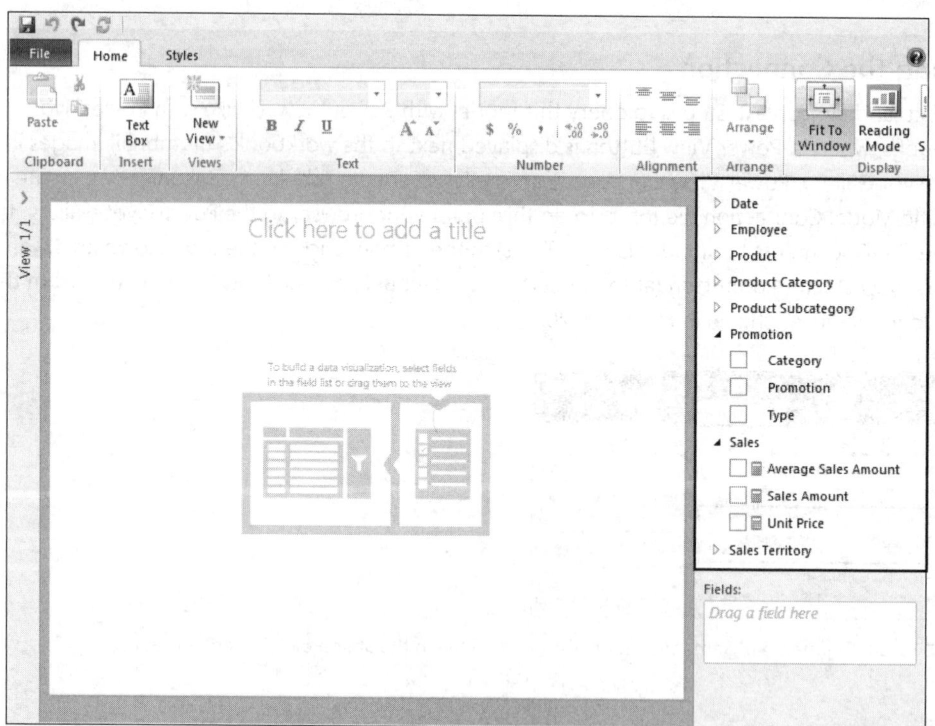

FIGURE 15-21 A blank Power View report with our model's tables, columns, measures, and KPI displayed.

Building the Report

You can build a nice analysis of the DirectQuery model in Power View by combining a few visualizations in one page. If you'd like, you can follow the steps below to create such a report. The resulting report should look like the one shown in Figure 15-22.

1st visualization:

1. Check Sales\Sales Amount
2. Check Sales\Unit Price
3. Change visualization type to Line
4. Add Promotion\Promotion to Axis section
5. Size and position to upper half, left 2/3 of page

2nd visualization:

1. Click on a blank area of the report
2. Check Sales\Average Sales Amount
3. Change visualization type to Scatter
4. Size and position to entire bottom half of page
5. Drag Sales\Sales Amount into the Y Value section
6. Drag Sales\Unit Price into the Size section
7. Drag Sales Territory\Region into Details

3rd visualization:

1. Click on a blank area of the report
2. Check Date\Year
3. Size and position to upper right (i.e., remaining area) of page
4. Click the Slicer button in the ribbon

When you're done, click on different years in the slicer to see the line and scatter charts animate and update.

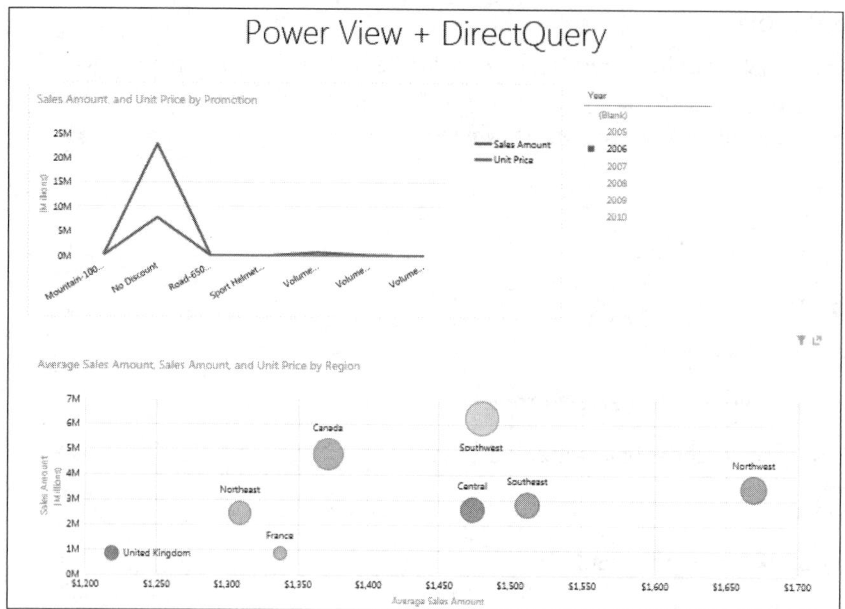

FIGURE 15-22 A completed Power View report.

Welcome Back to VertiPaq

To bring this conversation full circle, let's create a columnstore index on the *FactResellerSales* table in *AdventureWorksDW2012* (which corresponds to the *Sales* table in our model). Here are the necessary steps:

- Connect to your SQL Server relational server in SSMS.
- Drill down on the *Datab`ases* node.
- Drill down on the child *AdventureWorksDW2012* node.
- Drill down on the child *Tables* node.
- Drill down on the child *dbo.FactResellerSales* node.
- Right-click the child *Indexes* node and select New Index | Non-Clustered Columnstore Index from the context menu.
- In the New Index dialog, click the Add button.

The Select Columns dialog box will then come up. Click the select-all checkbox at the far left of the gray-backgrounded column headers bar, and then click OK. The Select Columns dialog box is shown in Figure 15-23, with the select-all checkbox and OK button highlighted.

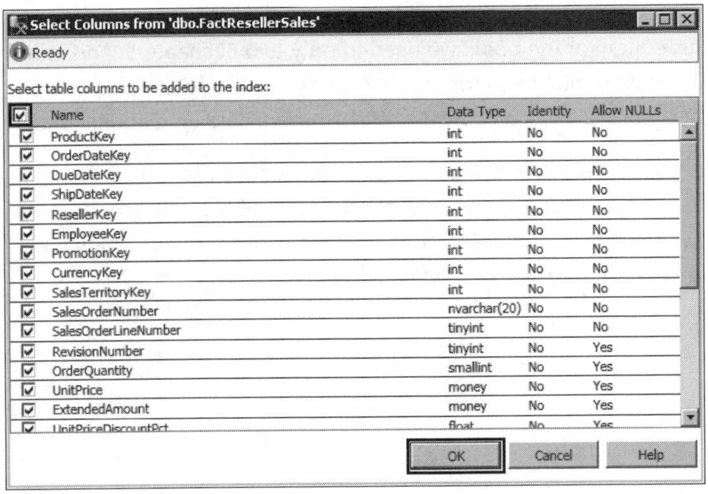

Select Columns from 'dbo.FactResellerSales'

Ready

Select table columns to be added to the index:

☑	Name	Data Type	Identity	Allow NULLs
☑	ProductKey	int	No	No
☑	OrderDateKey	int	No	No
☑	DueDateKey	int	No	No
☑	ShipDateKey	int	No	No
☑	ResellerKey	int	No	No
☑	EmployeeKey	int	No	No
☑	PromotionKey	int	No	No
☑	CurrencyKey	int	No	No
☑	SalesTerritoryKey	int	No	No
☑	SalesOrderNumber	nvarchar(20)	No	No
☑	SalesOrderLineNumber	tinyint	No	No
☑	RevisionNumber	tinyint	No	Yes
☑	OrderQuantity	smallint	No	Yes
☑	UnitPrice	money	No	Yes
☑	ExtendedAmount	money	No	Yes
☑	UnitPriceDiscountPct	float	No	Yes

OK Cancel Help

FIGURE 15-23 The Select Columns dialog box in SSMS, with all columns selected for a columnstore index.

Click OK again, this time in the New Index dialog box.

Now go back to Power View and try some more queries. You may or may not notice a difference in speed. Since the *FactResellerSales* table has only 60,855 rows, it is, frankly, hard to realize a benefit from the columnstore index. But with a large production data warehouse, you should be able to gain real benefit from a columnstore index, and now you know how to create one.

You have now seen how the various xVelocity in-memory technologies (i.e. the BISM model in PowerPivot and SSAS Tabular mode and columnstore indexes in the SQL Server relational engine) can work together to allow fast analytical queries against a semantic model layer that then forwards the queries to the up-to-date relational database, allowing for real-time BI with excellent performance.

Summary

Since the first edition of this book, we have argued that BI should not be considered a niche area, separate from relational database work. We believed then, as now, that relational technology and BI existed along a continuum, and that it is important to know both. We've proven that point in this chapter by starting with the relational capability of columnstore indexes then moving to PowerPivot and the Tabular mode of Analysis Services, which then gave us the capability to make the round-trip back to a relational database using DirectQuery. We then went to Power View, a BI tool if ever there was one, and used it to report from a BI Semantic Model acting as a thin layer around our relational data. The *pièce de rèsistance* was adding a columnstore index to that relational database to aid in the performance of the report's interactive capabilities.

Whether you're using a relational database, a multidimensional OLAP cube, or a BI Semantic Model, data is data. The question is whether you want to limit yourself to the operational collection and maintenance of that data, or if you want to branch out and facilitate business users' analysis of that data, to understand their business better. We think you should branch out in that manner.

In the previous two editions of this book we had several BI chapters, including three focused mostly on building OLAP cubes. In this edition of the book, we needed only two BI chapters. And in this chapter alone, we've shown you how to build and report on BI Semantic Models that can serve as data sources in their own right or as analytical abstractions over the live data in relational databases.

We've shown the versatility of SQL Server, in bringing you an entire data platform, and not just a relational database. And in SQL Server 2012, even the BI components of the platform become relational database-friendly. We think this chapter has conveyed the value of this diversity and usability, and we think that's a very fitting place to end this book.

Index

Symbols

A

B

C

D

E

F

G

H

I

M

N

O

P

Q

R

S

T

U

V

W

X

Z

About the Authors

Leonard Lobel is a Microsoft MVP in SQL Server and a Principal Consultant at Tallan, Inc., a Microsoft National Systems Integrator and Gold Competency Partner. With over 30 years of experience, Lenni is one of the industry's leading .NET and SQL Server experts, having consulted for Tallan's clients in a variety of domains, including publishing, financial services, retail, health care, and e-commerce. Lenni has served as chief architect and lead developer on large scale projects, as well as advisor to many high-profile clients.

About Tallan

Tallan (*http://www.tallan.com*) is a, national technology consulting firm that provides web development, business intelligence, customer relationship management, custom development, and integration services to customers in the financial services, health care, government, retail, education, and manufacturing industries.

Tallan is one of 40 Microsoft National Systems Integrators (NSI) in the United States, and a member of Microsoft's Business Intelligence Partner Advisory Council. For more than 25 years, Tallan's hands-on, collaborative approach has enabled its clients to obtain real cost and time savings, increase revenues, and generate competitive advantage.

Lenni is also chief technology officer (CTO) and cofounder of Sleek Technologies, Inc., a New York-based development shop with an early adopter philosophy toward new technologies. He is a sought after and highly rated speaker at industry conferences such as Visual Studio Live!, SQL PASS, SQL Bits, and local technology user group meetings. He is also lead author of this book's previous edition, *Programming Microsoft SQL Server 2008*. Lenni can be reached at *lenni.lobel@tallan.com* or *lenni.lobel@sleektech.com*.

Andrew J. Brust is Founder and CEO of Blue Badge Insights (*http://www.bluebadgeinsights.com*), an analysis, strategy and advisory firm serving Microsoft customers and partners. Brust pens ZDNet's "Big on Data" blog (*http://bit.ly/bigondata*); is a Microsoft Regional Director and MVP; an advisor to the New York Technology Council; Co-Chair of Visual Studio Live!;

a frequent speaker at industry events and a columnist for Visual Studio Magazine. He has been a participant in the Microsoft ecosystem for 20 years; worked closely with both Microsoft's Redmond-based corporate team and its field organization for the last 10; has served on Microsoft's Business Intelligence Partner Advisory Council; and is a member of several Microsoft "insiders" groups that supply him with insight around important technologies out of Redmond.

Paul Delcogliano is a technology director at Broadridge Financial Services, Inc. Paul has been working with the Microsoft .NET Framework since its first public introduction and has been developing Microsoft SQL Server applications even longer. He builds systems for a diverse range of platforms including Microsoft Windows, the Internet, and mobile devices. Paul has authored many articles and columns for various trade publications on a variety of topics. He can be reached by email at *pdelco@hotmail.com*.

Paul would like to thank his family for their patience and understanding while he was frantically trying to meet his deadlines. He would also like to thank Lenni for offering him another opportunity to contribute to the book. The second time around was better than the first.

What do you think of this book?

We want to hear from you!

To participate in a brief online survey, please visit:

microsoft.com/learning/booksurvey

Tell us how well this book meets your needs—what works effectively, and what we can do better. Your feedback will help us continually improve our books and learning resources for you.

Thank you in advance for your input!